BIRTH COUNTS
statistics of pregnancy and childbirth

Volume 2, tables

Alison Macfarlane

Miranda Mugford

Jane Henderson

Ann Furtado

Joanne Stevens

Alistair Dunn

with assistance from the

Office for National Statistics

Department of Health

National Assembly for Wales, formerly the Welsh Office

Communicable Disease Surveillance Centre

Information and Statistics Division of the Common Services
Agency of the National Health Service in Scotland

General Register Office, Scotland

Northern Ireland Statistics and Research Agency

Department of Health, Social Services and Public Safety,
Northern Ireland

States of Jersey, Health and Social Services

States of Guernsey, Board of Health

Civil Registry of the Isle of Man

Central Statistics Office, Republic of Ireland

London: The Stationery Office

First published 1984

Second edition 2000

Volume 2: ISBN 0 11 620917 8

also available, Volume 1:ISBN 0 11 621049 4

Published by The Stationery Office and available from:

The Stationery Office
(mail, telephone and fax orders only)
PO Box 29, Norwich NR3 1GN
General enquiries/Telephone orders 0870 600 5522
Fax orders 0870 600 5533

www.the-stationery-office.co.uk

The Stationery Office Bookshops
123 Kingsway, London WC2B 6PQ
020 7242 6393 Fax 020 7242 6412
68–69 Bull Street, Birmingham B4 6AD
0121 236 9696 Fax 0121 236 9699
33 Wine Street, Bristol BS1 2BQ
0117 926 4306 Fax 0117 929 4515
9–21 Princess Street, Manchester M60 8AS
0161 834 7201 Fax 0161 833 0634
16 Arthur Street, Belfast BT1 4GD
028 9023 8451 Fax 028 9023 5401
The Stationery Office Oriel Bookshop
18–19 High Street, Cardiff CF1 2BZ
029 2039 5548 Fax 029 2038 4347
71 Lothian Road, Edinburgh EH3 9AZ
0870 606 5566 Fax 0870 606 5588

The Stationery Office's Accredited Agents
(*see* Yellow Pages)

and through good booksellers

Printed in the United Kingdom for The Stationery Office by Albert Gait Ltd, Grimsby, N.E. Lincs

TJ000110 C10 5/00 9385 12678

Foreword to tables

This book brings together statistics collected by government departments and the National Health Service about pregnancy, childbirth and newborn babies, the care provided and the social, economic and environmental factors which can have an impact on the outcome of pregnancy. It is intended that this book should be used alongside the first edition of *Birth counts*. This offers a critical appraisal of data, showing how their strengths and limitations arise from the context in which they are collected. It also contains an index to both volumes.

These tables were compiled during 1997 and 1998 and revised during the latter half of 1999. This was a time of change, when moves toward national statistics for the United Kingdom coincided with changes in administrative structures as a consequence of devolution. The current names of the government offices are listed on the title page, but the names cited in the source lines of the tables are those used prior to July 1999. On July 1 1999, the functions of the Welsh Office were transferred to the National Assembly for Wales and the Scottish Office Department of Health became the Scottish Executive Health Department. On December 2 1999, the functions of the Department of Health and Social Services, Northern Ireland were transferred to the Department of Health, Social Services and Public Safety and the Department for Social Development of the Northern Ireland Executive. These departments retained their names and functions when the Executive was suspended on February 12 2000.

Alison Macfarlane
Miranda Mugford

March 2000

Tables in Volume 2

Birthweight and gestational age

A3.4 Incidence of low birthweight and preterm birth

A3.5 Mortality by birthweight and gestational age

A3.6 Age at death

Trends in certified causes of stillbirths and deaths

Births by day of the week

A3.11 Births, birthweight and mortality by day of the week of birth

Regional and national differences in birth and infant death rates

**A3.12 Live births, stillbirths and infant deaths by old and new
NHS region and country of residence of mother**

**A3.13 Time trends in births and perinatal and infant mortality
by region and country of residence of mother**

**A3.14 Fertility and conception rates by regional office and
country of residence of mother**

**A3.15 Incidence of low birthweight by region and country of
residence of mother**

**A3.16 Mortality by birthweight and region and country of residence of
mother**

4. Fertility control and fetal loss in early pregnancy

Birth control

A4.1–4.3 Use of clinics and services

A4.4–4.5 Prescriptions and sales of contraceptives

A4.6 Use of contraception

Sterilisation

A4.7–4.11 Sterilisations and gynaecological operations leading to sterility

5. Inequalities in the social background of parents and the circumstances in which they live

A5.4–5.7 Stillbirth and infant mortality rates by social class of father

A5.8 Deaths of one, two and three year olds by social class of father and marital status of parents

A5.9 Stillbirth and infant mortality rates by social class of mother

A5.10–5.15 Marriage, divorce and family composition

A5.16–5.19 Ethnic origin and country of birth

Mother's age

A5.20–5.23 Stillbirth and mortality rates by social class and age of mother

A5.24 Teenage pregnancies

6. Characteristics of babies

Birthweight and gestational age

A6.1 Birthweight and multiplicity

A6.2 Birthweight and cause of death

A6.3–6.5 Gestational age

Gender

Multiple births

Ethnic group of children

7. Care of mothers and babies

Facilities for maternity care, neonatal care and child care

A7.6–7.7 Nurses and health visitors

A7.8–7.10 Doctors

Care provided

A7.11–7.12 Medical management of sub-fertility

A7.13–7.14 Use of maternity services

A7.15–7.18 Place of birth

A7.28 Feeding of babies

A7.30–7.31 Visits by health visitors, clinic attendances and immunisation

A7.32–7.33 Child protection and children in care

8. Measuring disability and impairment in childhood

9. Illness in babies

10. Maternal mortality and reproductive health

11. Costs of having a baby

12. Statistics from international organisations

Notes on tables

Symbols and conventions used:

Numbers		Rates	
0	zero	0.0	<0.5
		0.00	<0.05
–	empty cell	–	empty cell
..	not available	..	not available

A3.1.1

Live births, infant mortality and childhood mortality by age, England and Wales, 1838–1998

| Year | Live births | | | Infant and childhood deaths | | | | | |
| | Number | Rate per 1,000 women aged 15–44 | Sex ratio of live births male/female | Numbers | | | Rates | | |
				Under 1 year	1–4 years	5–9 years	Under 1 year*	1–4 years+	5–9 years+
1838	463,787	126.9	1.045	..	..	..	..	..	..
1839	492,574	132.8	1.048	..	..	..	..	..	..
1840	502,303	133.1	1.051	..	..	..	..	..	..
1841	512,158	134.5	1.053	..	..	..	..	..	..
1842	517,739	134.4	1.050	..	..	..	..	..	..
1843	527,325	135.4	1.054	..	..	..	..	..	..
1844	540,763	137.4	1.054	..	..	..	..	..	..
1845	543,521	136.6	1.050	..	..	..	..	..	..
1846	572,625	142.4	1.049	93,644	66,976	16,190	163.5	40.4	8.1
1847	539,965	132.9	1.043	88,508	69,863	19,120	163.9	40.7	9.5
1848	563,059	137.1	1.050	86,407	70,098	20,586	153.5	40.6	10.1
1849	578,159	139.3	1.043	92,171	68,929	22,794	159.4	39.9	11.1
1850	593,422	141.6	1.042	86,302	58,359	16,832	145.4	33.6	8.1
1851	615,865	145.4	1.047	94,753	65,192	18,122	153.9	37.4	8.6
1852	624,012	145.7	1.046	98,660	67,454	18,932	158.1	38.0	8.9
1853	612,391	141.4	1.051	97,931	67,147	17,807	159.9	37.0	8.3
1854	634,405	144.8	1.044	99,299	78,886	20,202	156.5	43.2	9.3
1855	635,043	143.4	1.041	97,503	68,240	17,832	153.5	36.7	8.1
1856	657,453	146.8	1.042	94,407	64,660	16,165	143.6	34.4	7.2
1857	663,071	146.5	1.052	103,227	70,777	17,441	155.7	37.2	7.8
1858	655,481	143.3	1.045	103,837	83,092	23,813	158.4	42.7	10.5
1859	689,881	149.2	1.046	105,629	78,635	21,417	153.1	40.4	9.3
1860	684,048	146.4	1.047	100,984	65,800	15,967	147.6	33.0	6.8
1861	696,406	147.5	1.046	106,428	74,701	15,890	152.8	37.1	6.8
1862	712,684	149.3	1.041	101,373	77,140	17,992	142.2	38.0	7.5
1863	727,417	150.8	1.047	108,089	93,921	24,380	148.6	45.8	10.1
1864	740,275	151.8	1.042	112,935	86,868	23,635	152.6	41.7	9.6
1865	748,069	151.8	1.040	119,810	80,033	19,733	160.2	38.0	7.9
1866	753,870	151.4	1.043	120,299	82,720	19,029	159.6	38.7	7.5
1867	768,349	152.7	1.043	117,261	71,337	16,177	152.6	33.1	6.3
1868	786,858	154.8	1.036	122,075	81,054	19,750	155.1	37.1	7.6
1869	773,381	150.6	1.042	120,274	83,288	21,183	155.5	37.4	8.0
1870	792,787	152.8	1.041	126,638	85,056	23,051	159.7	37.8	8.6
1871	797,428	152.2	1.035	125,868	80,745	21,445	157.8	35.3	7.9
1872	825,907	155.4	1.041	123,596	73,843	18,658	149.6	32.0	6.7
1873	829,778	154.0	1.039	123,768	70,611	16,195	149.2	30.2	5.8
1874	854,956	156.5	1.037	128,858	84,941	20,636	150.7	36.1	7.3
1875	850,607	153.5	1.043	134,614	81,936	19,119	158.3	34.1	6.6
1876	887,968	158.2	1.038	129,940	76,613	17,917	146.3	31.6	6.1
1877	888,200	156.1	1.036	120,817	75,757	17,310	136.0	30.8	5.8
1878	891,906	154.7	1.042	135,927	88,408	19,177	152.4	35.4	6.4
1879	880,389	150.8	1.036	119,252	80,423	18,527	135.5	31.4	6.0
1880	881,643	149.1	1.036	134,686	89,755	19,352	152.8	34.5	6.2
1881	883,642	147.5	1.039	114,976	69,206	18,084	130.1	26.2	5.7
1882	889,014	146.2	1.038	125,020	82,729	19,540	140.6	31.4	6.1

1

Live births, infant mortality and childhood mortality by age, England and Wales, 1838–1998

Year	Live births			Infant and childhood deaths					
	Number	Rate per 1,000 women aged 15–44	Sex ratio of live births male/female	Numbers			Rates		
				Under 1 year	1–4 years	5–9 years	Under 1 year*	1–4 years+	5–9 years+
1883	890,722	144.4	1.035	122,226	75,654	19,225	137.2	28.7	6.0
1884	906,750	144.8	1.041	133,128	79,167	18,888	146.8	30.0	5.8
1885	894,270	140.8	1.040	123,130	74,219	16,609	137.7	28.1	5.1
1886	903,760	140.3	1.038	134,870	75,193	15,707	149.2	28.5	4.8
1887	886,331	135.7	1.039	128,277	75,930	16,845	144.7	28.6	5.1
1888	879,868	132.9	1.033	120,079	67,985	15,665	136.5	25.4	4.7
1889	885,944	132.0	1.038	127,198	74,604	15,802	143.6	28.0	4.7
1890	869,937	127.9	1.033	130,955	75,437	16,773	150.5	28.1	5.0
1891	914,157	132.7	1.038	135,801	74,477	16,000	148.6	28.2	4.7
1892	897,957	128.0	1.035	132,463	73,401	15,865	147.5	27.3	4.6
1893	914,572	128.1	1.038	145,061	71,772	17,330	158.6	26.8	5.1
1894	890,289	122.5	1.036	121,799	64,777	14,607	136.8	23.8	4.3
1895	922,291	124.8	1.034	148,093	71,546	14,144	160.6	26.5	4.1
1896	915,331	121.8	1.036	135,013	72,140	15,423	147.5	26.4	4.5
1897	921,683	120.6	1.037	143,589	66,483	13,716	155.8	24.3	4.0
1898	923,165	118.9	1.032	148,013	66,752	13,202	160.3	24.3	3.8
1899	928,646	117.7	1.039	150,975	64,797	14,400	162.6	23.5	4.1
1900	927,062	115.6	1.033	142,912	67,048	14,644	154.2	24.1	4.2
1901	929,807	114.2	1.040	140,648	61,099	14,162	151.3	20.8	4.1
1902	940,509	114.4	1.039	124,996	60,028	14,225	132.9	20.5	4.1
1903	948,271	114.1	1.035	124,718	55,622	12,424	131.5	19.0	3.5
1904	945,389	112.3	1.037	137,392	62,286	12,780	145.3	21.1	3.6
1905	929,293	109.6	1.036	119,091	55,167	12,431	128.2	18.6	3.5
1906	935,081	109.2	1.041	123,895	54,786	12,904	132.5	18.4	3.6
1907	918,042	106.1	1.039	107,978	55,275	12,609	117.6	18.5	3.5
1908	940,383	107.3	1.036	113,254	51,065	12,255	120.4	17.0	3.4
1909	914,472	103.6	1.041	99,430	50,834	12,555	108.7	16.9	3.4
1910	896,962	100.6	1.040	94,579	45,267	11,216	105.4	14.9	3.0
1911	881,138	98.3	1.039	114,600	54,470	12,668	130.1	17.6	3.4
1912	872,737	97.0	1.040	82,779	44,295	11,486	94.8	14.5	3.1
1913	881,890	97.6	1.038	95,608	45,349	11,822	108.4	15.0	3.2
1914	879,096	96.3	1.035	91,971	46,006	12,763	104.6	15.4	3.4
1915	814,614	88.3	1.040	89,380	55,607	14,388	109.7	18.6	3.8
1916	785,520	84.4	1.049	71,646	38,320	12,101	91.2	12.8	3.3
1917	668,346	71.3	1.044	64,483	40,511	12,009	96.5	13.8	3.3
1918	662,661	70.3	1.048	64,386	59,767	20,866	97.2	21.3	5.7
1919	692,438	73.5	1.060	61,715	31,924	12,876	89.1	12.4	3.5
1920	957,782	101.7	1.052	76,552	29,186	11,799	79.9	12.2	3.3
1921	848,814	89.7	1.051	70,250	26,391	9,707	82.8	10.4	2.8
1922	780,124	82.0	1.049	60,121	33,641	8,730	77.1	12.5	2.6
1923	758,131	79.3	1.044	52,582	25,992	7,228	69.4	9.0	2.3
1924	729,933	75.8	1.047	54,813	28,919	6,971	75.1	9.5	2.3
1925	710,582	73.6	1.045	53,316	27,764	7,687	75.0	9.6	2.5
1926	694,563	71.9	1.041	48,757	23,001	7,755	70.2	8.4	2.4
1927	654,172	67.5	1.042	45,610	24,306	7,846	69.7	9.2	2.3

Live births, infant mortality and childhood mortality by age, England and Wales, 1838–1998

Year	Live births			Infant and childhood deaths					
	Number	Rate per 1,000 women aged 15–44	Sex ratio of live births male/ female	Numbers			Rates		
				Under 1 year	1–4 years	5–9 years	Under 1 year*	1–4 years+	5–9 years+
1928	660,267	67.9	1.044	42,960	19,822	8,174	65.1	7.7	2.3
1929	643,673	65.9	1.043	47,868	26,629	8,923	74.4	10.7	2.5
1930	648,811	66.2	1.044	38,908	16,756	7,871	60.0	6.9	2.3
1931	632,081	64.4	1.049	41,939	18,038	7,073	66.4	7.5	2.1
1932	613,972	62.6	1.050	39,933	16,542	6,601	65.0	6.9	2.1
1933	580,413	59.4	1.046	36,960	15,507	6,827	63.7	6.6	2.2
1934	597,642	61.4	1.055	35,017	15,278	7,402	58.6	6.6	2.4
1935	598,756	60.9	1.056	34,092	11,509	6,105	56.9	5.1	2.0
1936	605,292	61.0	1.054	35,425	12,254	5,877	58.5	5.5	2.0
1937	610,557	61.2	1.056	35,175	11,311	5,459	57.6	5.1	1.9
1938	621,204	62.2	1.051	32,724	10,215	5,379	52.7	4.6	1.9
1939	614,479	61.3	1.056	31,190	7,924	4,197	50.8	3.5	1.5
1940	590,120	58.7	1.053	33,892	11,104	5,491	57.4	4.8	2.0
1941	579,091	58.4	1.053	34,550	12,149	5,677	59.7	5.3	2.1
1942	651,503	67.0	1.063	32,258	7,772	4,129	49.5	3.4	1.5
1943	684,334	71.3	1.064	33,431	7,583	3,904	48.9	3.3	1.4
1944	751,478	78.6	1.065	33,455	6,612	3,895	44.5	2.8	1.4
1945	679,937	71.5	1.061	31,959	6,441	3,360	47.0	2.6	1.2
1946	820,719	84.3	1.060	33,541	5,334	2,427	40.9	2.1	0.9
1947	881,026	91.1	1.061	36,849	5,765	2,549	41.8	2.2	0.9
1948	775,306	80.4	1.061	26,766	5,019	2,174	34.5	1.8	0.8
1949	730,518	76.2	1.061	23,882	4,641	2,045	32.7	1.6	0.7
1950	697,097	73.0	1.060	20,817	4,087	1,971	29.9	1.4	0.6
1951	677,529	71.6	1.060	20,223	4,133	1,771	29.8	1.4	0.6
1952	673,735	71.8	1.055	18,555	3,356	1,715	27.5	1.2	0.5
1953	684,372	73.5	1.059	18,324	3,204	1,763	26.8	1.2	0.5
1954	673,651	72.9	1.059	17,160	2,501	1,503	25.5	0.9	0.4
1955	667,811	72.8	1.060	16,613	2,638	1,579	24.9	1.0	0.4
1956	700,335	77.0	1.057	16,554	2,376	1,456	23.6	0.9	0.4
1957	723,381	80.0	1.060	16,720	2,554	1,426	23.1	1.0	0.4
1958	740,715	82.2	1.059	16,685	2,348	1,351	22.5	0.9	0.4
1959	748,501	83.0	1.063	16,629	2,461	1,351	22.2	0.9	0.4
1960	785,005	86.8	1.061	17,118	2,431	1,426	21.8	0.9	0.4
1961	811,281	89.2	1.062	17,393	2,662	1,320	21.4	0.9	0.4
1962	838,736	90.8	1.060	18,187	2,550	1,271	21.7	0.9	0.4
1963	854,055	91.2	1.055	18,042	2,780	1,365	21.1	0.9	0.4
1964	875,972	92.9	1.062	17,445	2,552	1,345	19.9	0.8	0.4
1965	862,725	91.9	1.056	16,395	2,665	1,396	19.0	0.8	0.4
1966	849,823	90.5	1.060	16,417	2,783	1,341	19.3	0.8	0.4
1967	832,164	88.9	1.058	15,266	2,574	1,386	18.3	0.8	0.4
1968	819,272	87.6	1.058	14,982	2,687	1,441	18.3	0.8	0.4
1969	797,538	85.3	1.058	14,391	2,559	1,337	18.0	0.8	0.3
1970	784,486	83.9	1.058	14,267	2,326	1,354	18.2	0.7	0.3
1971	783,155	83.5	1.061	13,720	2,204	1,484	17.5	0.7	0.4
1972	725,440	77.0	1.064	12,498	2,308	1,426	17.2	0.7	0.3

A3.1.1 *continued*

Live births, infant mortality and childhood mortality by age, England and Wales, 1838–1998

Year	Live births			Infant and childhood deaths					
	Number	Rate per 1,000 women aged 15–44	Sex ratio of live births male/female	Numbers			Rates		
				Under 1 year	1–4 years	5–9 years	Under 1 year*	1–4 years+	5–9 years+
1973	675,953	71.3	1.065	11,407	2,099	1,327	16.9	0.7	0.3
1974	639,885	67.2	1.061	10,459	1,922	1,225	16.3	0.7	0.3
1975	603,445	63.0	1.062	9,488	1,699	1,140	15.7	0.6	0.3
1976	584,270	60.4	1.058	8,334	1,469	1,127	14.3	0.6	0.3
1977	569,259	58.1	1.060	7,841	1,383	1,008	13.8	0.6	0.3
1978	596,418	60.1	1.061	7,881	1,346	1,045	13.2	0.6	0.3
1979	638,028	63.3	1.060	8,178	1,168	970	12.8	0.5	0.3
1980	656,234	64.2	1.049	7,899	1,186	866	12.0	0.5	0.3
1981	634,492	61.3	1.055	7,021	1,180	749	11.1	0.5	0.2
1982	625,931	59.9	1.055	6,775	1,137	644	10.8	0.5	0.2
1983	629,134	59.7	1.056	6,381	1,093	660	10.1	0.4	0.2
1984	636,818	59.8	1.049	6,037	1,064	608	9.5	0.4	0.2
1985	656,417	61.0	1.054	6,141	1,135	588	9.4	0.5	0.2
1986	661,018	60.6	1.052	6,313	1,064	573	9.6	0.4	0.2
1987	681,511	62.0	1.053	6,272	1,067	546	9.2	0.4	0.2
1988	693,577	63.0	1.048	6,270	1,085	606	9.0	0.4	0.2
1989	687,725	62.5	1.051	5,808	1,078	612	8.4	0.4	0.2
1990	706,140	64.2	1.048	5,564	1,027	553	7.9	0.4	0.2
1991	699,217	63.6	1.052	5,158	993	589	7.4	0.4	0.2
1992	689,656	63.5	1.053	4,539	874	516	6.6	0.3	0.2
1993	671,224	62.6	1.056	4,242	884	470	6.3	0.3	0.1
1994	664,256	61.9	1.055	4,120	796	465	6.2	0.3	0.1
1995	648,001	60.4	1.051	3,982	724	465	6.1	0.3	0.1
1996	649,489	60.5	1.055	3,959	761	411	6.1	0.3	0.1
1997	643,095	59.8	1.051	3,799	710	444	5.9	0.3	0.1
1998	635,901	59.1	1.051	3,605	722	417	5.7	0.2	0.1

* Rates per 1,000 live births
+ Rates per 1,000 population

Rates are based on the female home population aged 15–44 years except for the years 1939–1947 when they are based on the female total population aged 15–44 years.

Source: GRO. *Annual reports of the Registrar General*

  GRO. *Statistical reviews of the Registrar General*

  OPCS and ONS *Birth statistics*, Series FM1 and *Mortality statistics*, Series DH1 and DH3

This was Table 3.1 in the first edition of *Birth counts*

A3.1.2

Live births, infant and childhood mortality by age, Scotland, 1855–1998

Year	Live births			Infant and childhood deaths					
	Number	Rate per 1,000 women aged 15–44	Sex ratio of live births male/female	Numbers			Rates		
				Under 1 year	1–4 years	5–9 years	Under 1 year*	1–4 years+	5–9 years+
1855	93,349	..	1.050	11,691	10,980	2,838	125.2	37.4#	8.0
1856	101,821	..	1.054	12,058	11,314	2,995	118.4	40.3#	8.6
1857	103,415	..	1.058	12,191	11,652	2,954	117.9	41.4#	8.4
1858	104,018	..	1.067	12,622	12,223	3,217	121.3	38.0	9.0
1859	106,543	..	1.052	11,523	11,972	3,493	108.2	37.0	9.7
1860	105,629	..	1.062	13,413	12,780	3,405	127.0	39.3	9.4
1861	107,009	..	1.042	11,869	11,232	3,059	110.9	34.3	8.4
1862	107,069	..	1.066	12,556	12,641	3,293	117.3	38.4	9.0
1863	109,341	..	1.059	13,125	15,926	4,185	120.0	48.1	11.4
1864	112,333	..	1.044	14,180	14,195	4,118	126.2	42.7	11.1
1865	113,070	..	1.061	14,099	12,238	3,345	124.7	36.6	8.8
1866	113,667	..	1.055	13,915	12,027	3,437	122.4	35.8	9.2
1867	114,044	..	1.054	13,521	11,598	3,209	118.6	34.3	8.5
1868	115,514	..	1.052	13,600	12,755	3,431	117.7	37.5	9.1
1869	113,354	..	1.060	14,654	14,387	4,105	129.3	..	..
1870	115,390	..	1.045	14,166	12,497	4,076	122.8	..	..
1871	116,128	..	1.070	15,134	12,801	3,779	130.3	..	..
1872	118,765	..	1.066	14,720	12,242	3,772	123.9	..	..
1873	119,700	..	1.056	14,950	12,391	3,618	124.9	..	..
1874	123,711	..	1.058	15,447	14,376	4,911	124.9	..	..
1875	123,578	..	1.055	16,320	14,007	4,202	132.1	..	..
1876	126,534	..	1.050	15,340	12,125	3,382	121.2	..	..
1877	126,822	..	1.054	14,571	11,233	3,042	114.9	..	..
1878	126,773	..	1.059	15,599	13,342	3,446	123.0	..	..
1879	125,730	..	1.048	13,571	11,299	3,191	107.9	..	..
1880	124,570	..	1.049	15,523	13,011	3,667	124.6	..	..
1881	126,171	..	1.053	14,198	10,382	3,142	112.5	..	..
1882	126,158	..	1.046	14,883	11,665	3,339	118.0	..	..
1883	124,458	..	1.054	14,812	11,813	3,296	119.0	..	..
1884	129,157	..	1.057	15,228	11,490	3,335	117.9	..	..
1885	126,100	..	1.049	15,200	10,891	2,968	120.5	..	..
1886	127,890	..	1.063	14,797	10,185	2,901	115.7	..	..
1887	124,418	..	1.054	15,202	11,537	3,111	122.2	..	..
1888	123,269	..	1.050	13,945	9,649	2,734	113.1	..	..
1889	122,783	..	1.064	14,895	10,807	2,693	121.3	..	..
1890	121,526	..	1.048	15,877	11,847	2,886	130.6	..	..
1891	125,986	..	1.058	16,110	10,409	2,862	127.9	..	..
1892	125,043	..	1.060	14,693	10,095	2,651	117.5	..	..
1893	127,110	..	1.047	17,286	11,922	2,836	136.0	..	..
1894	124,367	..	1.055	14,516	9,041	2,401	116.7	..	..
1895	126,494	..	1.050	16,874	10,868	2,515	133.4	..	..
1896	129,172	..	1.052	14,924	8,965	2,270	115.5	..	..
1897	128,877	..	1.044	17,773	10,354	2,331	137.9	..	..
1898	130,861	..	1.043	17,566	10,412	2,296	134.2	..	..

Live births, infant and childhood mortality by age, Scotland, 1855–1998

Year	Live births			Infant and childhood deaths					
	Number	Rate per 1,000 women aged 15–44	Sex ratio of live births male/ female	Numbers			Rates		
				Under 1 year	1–4 years	5–9 years	Under 1 year*	1–4 years+	5–9 years+
1899	130,733	..	1.044	17,132	9,354	2,202	131.0	..	..
1900	131,401	..	1.045	16,888	9,509	2,252	128.5	..	..
1901	132,192	..	1.051	17,104	9,880	2,334	129.4	..	..
1902	132,267	120.6	1.040	15,004	8,433	2,148	113.4	..	..
1903	133,525	120.6	1.040	15,693	8,139	2,058	117.5	..	..
1904	132,603	118.6	1.046	16,329	9,199	2,086	123.1	..	..
1905	131,410	116.4	1.032	15,275	8,677	1,968	116.2	..	..
1906	132,005	115.8	1.045	15,174	8,075	2,113	115.0	..	..
1907	128,840	111.9	1.047	14,140	9,002	2,225	109.7	..	..
1908	131,362	113.0	1.035	15,900	9,543	2,073	121.0	..	..
1909	128,669	112.7	1.044	13,856	7,992	2,146	107.7	..	..
1910	124,059	108.0	1.037	13,436	8,124	2,066	108.3	..	..
1911	121,850	106.6	1.045	13,707	7,333	1,934	112.5	13.8	3.8
1912	122,790	108.1	1.051	12,949	7,368	1,828	105.5	14.1	3.6
1913	120,516	106.8	1.041	13,214	7,133	1,833	109.6	13.8	3.6
1914	123,934	109.5	1.033	13,710	7,148	1,887	110.6	13.9	3.8
1915	114,181	99.9	1.047	14,441	9,120	2,060	126.5	17.8	4.1
1916	109,942	95.1	1.056	10,674	6,650	1,846	97.1	13.2	3.7
1917	97,441	83.4	1.054	10,473	7,245	1,704	107.5	14.8	3.4
1918	98,554	83.4	1.045	9,836	8,015	2,407	99.8	17.1	4.8
1919	106,268	89.3	1.064	10,795	6,506	1,928	101.6	14.7	3.9
1920	136,546	114.6	1.043	12,565	4,361	1,530	92.0	9.5	3.1
1921	123,201	103.7	1.049	11,130	4,461	1,377	90.3	9.4	2.9
1922	115,085	97.1	1.046	11,664	7,524	1,282	101.4	15.3	2.8
1923	111,902	94.7	1.051	8,825	4,926	1,178	78.9	9.7	2.7
1924	106,900	91.1	1.057	10,446	6,570	1,190	97.7	12.5	2.9
1925	104,137	88.6	1.054	9,430	4,819	1,182	90.6	9.6	2.8
1926	102,449	87.5	1.045	8,514	4,228	1,143	83.1	8.7	2.6
1927	96,672	83.0	1.041	8,576	4,103	1,212	88.7	8.7	2.7
1928	96,822	83.5	1.050	8,299	4,247	1,240	85.7	9.3	2.6
1929	92,880	80.0	1.059	8,061	4,140	1,160	86.8	9.5	2.4
1930	94,549	81.7	1.034	7,852	3,426	1,195	83.0	8.0	2.6
1931	92,220	79.8	1.038	7,544	3,306	1,107	81.8	7.8	2.4
1932	91,000	78.4	1.049	7,840	3,386	1,108	86.2	8.1	2.5
1933	86,546	74.5	1.072	7,019	2,638	995	81.1	6.4	2.3
1934	88,836	76.5	1.046	6,901	2,961	1,137	77.7	7.2	2.7
1935	87,928	74.9	1.047	6,754	2,202	918	76.8	5.4	2.2
1936	88,928	75.1	1.039	7,315	2,437	877	82.3	6.0	2.1
1937	87,810	73.7	1.053	7,050	2,195	851	80.3	5.5	2.1
1938	88,627	74.0	1.053	6,163	2,098	769	69.5	5.2	1.2
1939	86,913	72.3	1.058	5,955	1,422	699	68.5	3.5	1.8
1940	86,392	71.4	1.049	6,766	2,182	897	78.3	5.3	2.2
1941	89,748	73.5	1.056	7,426	2,186	929	82.7	5.2	2.3
1942	90,703	76.4	1.048	6,283	1,429	639	69.3	3.5	1.6
1943	94,669	83.1	1.049	6,174	1,360	718	65.2	3.3	1.7

A3.1.2 *continued*

Live births, infant and childhood mortality by age, Scotland, 1855–1998

Year	Live births			Infant and childhood deaths					
	Number	Rate per 1,000 women aged 15–44	Sex ratio of live births male/female	Numbers			Rates		
				Under 1 year	1–4 years	5–9 years	Under 1 year*	1–4 years+	5–9 years+
1944	95,920	84.7	1.067	6,237	1,191	652	65.0	2.8	1.6
1945	86,924	77.2	1.062	4,889	1,092	534	56.2	2.6	1.3
1946	104,413	92.2	1.065	5,621	1,052	499	53.8	2.5	1.2
1947	113,147	97.3	1.052	6,309	995	480	55.8	2.3	1.2
1948	100,344	86.8	1.070	4,486	805	388	44.7	1.8	1.0
1949	95,674	83.6	1.058	3,961	751	357	41.4	1.6	0.9
1950	92,530	81.2	1.070	3,569	694	279	38.6	1.5	0.7
1951	90,639	80.0	1.063	3,391	664	309	37.4	1.4	0.8
1952	90,422	80.5	1.048	3,181	539	282	35.2	1.2	0.7
1953	90,913	81.8	1.063	2,800	499	286	30.8	1.1	0.7
1954	92,315	83.8	1.056	2,861	435	229	31.0	1.0	0.5
1955	92,539	84.7	1.056	2,811	411	252	30.4	1.0	0.6
1956	95,313	88.2	1.056	2,727	371	189	28.6	0.9	0.4
1957	97,977	91.6	1.057	2,802	364	236	28.6	0.8	0.5
1958	99,481	93.7	1.053	2,758	338	190	27.7	0.8	0.4
1959	99,251	93.9	1.062	2,816	432	161	28.4	0.9	0.4
1960	101,292	96.7	1.052	2,673	379	218	26.4	0.8	0.5
1961	101,169	97.2	1.056	2,615	406	189	25.8	0.9	0.4
1962	104,334	99.5	1.070	2,768	391	196	26.5	0.8	0.5
1963	102,691	97.5	1.053	2,624	408	199	25.6	0.8	0.5
1964	104,355	99.2	1.060	2,508	347	173	24.0	0.7	0.4
1965	100,660	96.9	1.070	2,327	350	205	23.1	0.7	0.5
1966	96,536	94.1	1.064	2,239	354	199	23.2	0.7	0.4
1967	96,221	94.9	1.065	2,024	323	192	21.0	0.7	0.4
1968	94,786	94.0	1.065	1,970	356	202	20.8	0.8	0.4
1969	90,290	89.7	1.069	1,902	330	177	21.1	0.7	0.4
1970	87,335	86.8	1.065	1,714	315	207	19.6	0.7	0.4
1971	86,728	85.8	1.052	1,722	262	164	19.9	0.6	0.3
1972	78,550	77.7	1.053	1,477	279	195	18.8	0.7	0.4
1973	74,392	73.1	1.079	1,412	276	194	19.0	0.7	0.4
1974	70,093	68.2	1.045	1,326	257	156	18.9	0.7	0.3
1975	67,943	65.8	1.064	1,168	217	168	17.2	0.6	0.4
1976	64,895	62.2	1.067	959	196	132	14.8	0.5	0.3
1977	62,342	59.1	1.054	1,004	176	126	16.1	0.5	0.3
1978	64,295	60.3	1.058	830	160	100	12.9	0.5	0.2
1979	68,366	63.4	1.071	878	148	116	12.8	0.5	0.3
1980	68,892	63.3	1.057	831	144	106	12.1	0.5	0.3
1981	69,054	63.1	1.045	780	117	85	11.3	0.4	0.2
1982	66,196	60.1	1.050	753	127	88	11.4	0.4	0.3
1983	65,078	58.7	1.071	646	118	86	9.9	0.4	0.3
1984	65,106	58.3	1.037	672	149	85	10.3	0.5	0.3
1985	66,676	59.5	1.048	624	112	86	9.4	0.3	0.3
1986	65,812	58.5	1.061	581	116	60	8.8	0.4	0.2
1987	66,241	58.8	1.053	563	98	67	8.5	0.3	0.2
1988	66,212	59.1	1.059	543	97	61	8.2	0.3	0.2

7

A3.1.2 *continued*

Live births, infant and childhood mortality by age, Scotland, 1855–1998

| Year | Live births | | | Infant and childhood deaths | | | | | |
| | Number | Rate per 1,000 women aged 15–44 | Sex ratio of live births male/ female | Numbers | | | Rates | | |
				Under 1 year	1–4 years	5–9 years	Under 1 year*	1–4 years+	5–9 years+
1989	63,480	56.7	1.049	554	118	47	8.7	0.4	0.1
1990	65,973	58.8	1.057	510	94	47	7.7	0.3	0.1
1991	67,024	59.8	1.056	473	113	64	7.1	0.3	0.2
1992	65,789	59.3	1.044	449	101	51	6.8	0.3	0.2
1993	63,337	57.4	1.046	412	95	73	6.5	0.3	0.2
1994	61,656	56.0	1.038	382	71	38	6.2	0.2	0.1
1995	60,051	54.5	1.043	375	63	46	6.2	0.2	0.1
1996	59,296	54.0	1.061	365	65	54	6.2	0.3	0.2
1997	59,440	54.3	1.055	316	55	50	5.3	0.2	0.2
1998	57,319	52.6	1,160	320	63	62	5.6	0.3	0.2

* Rates per 1,000 live births
+ Rates per 1,000 population
# Denominators derived by subtracting numbers of live births from population aged 0–4 years

Rates are based on the female home population aged 15–44 years except for the years 1939–1947 when they are based on the female total population aged 15–44 years

Source: GRO Scotland. *Annual report of the Registrar General for Scotland*

This was Table A3.2 in the first edition of *Birth counts*

A3.1.3

Live births, infant and childhood mortality by age, Ireland, 1864–1921

Year	Live births			Infant and childhood deaths					
	Number	Rate per 1,000 women aged 15–44	Sex ratio of live births male/female	Numbers			Rates		
				Under 1 year	1–4 years	5–9 years	Under 1 year*	1–4 years+	5–9 years+
1864	136,414	..	1.056	13,425	11,608	3,954	98.4	..	..
1865	144,970	..	1.054	14,170	11,393	4,246	97.7	..	..
1866	146,090	..	1.058	13,725	10,464	4,366	93.9	..	..
1867	144,388	..	1.061	13,959	10,155	3,469	96.7	..	..
1868	146,051	..	1.061	13,883	10,364	3,489	95.1	..	..
1869	145,659	..	1.059	13,594	9,719	3,596	93.3	..	..
1870	149,846	..	1.051	14,175	9,217	3,382	94.6	..	..
1871	151,355	127.2	1.044	13,773	8,783	3,111	91.0	16.9	4.9
1872	149,278	..	1.063	14,475	10,344	3,773	97.0	..	..
1873	144,377	..	1.058	13,896	10,462	3,568	96.2	..	..
1874	141,288	..	1.054	13,220	11,021	4,206	93.6	..	..
1875	138,320	..	1.058	13,128	10,240	4,156	94.9	..	..
1876	140,469	..	1.056	13,252	9,076	3,227	94.3	..	..
1877	139,659	..	1.055	12,850	9,195	3,173	92.0	..	..
1878	134,117	..	1.045	12,993	10,513	3,537	96.9	..	..
1879	135,328	..	1.067	13,646	9,994	3,583	100.8	..	..
1880	128,086	..	1.063	14,386	11,934	4,118	112.3	..	..
1881	125,847	108.1	1.061	11,481	8,009	3,072	91.2	17.0	4.9
1882	122,648	..	1.058	11,603	8,375	3,120	94.6	..	..
1883	118,163	..	1.056	11,598	8,523	3,492	98.2	..	..
1884	118,875	..	1.059	10,885	7,851	3,072	91.6	..	..
1885	115,951	..	1.053	11,053	8,277	3,089	95.3	..	..
1886	113,927	..	1.070	10,760	7,281	2,661	94.4	..	..
1887	112,400	..	1.059	10,732	8,636	3,021	95.5	..	..
1888	109,557	..	1.053	10,619	8,476	2,979	96.9	..	..
1889	107,841	..	1.048	10,149	7,004	2,327	94.1	..	..
1890	105,254	..	1.064	9,975	7,045	2,271	94.8	..	..
1891	108,116	101.3	1.054	10,252	6,078	2,154	94.8	16.0	4.2
1892	104,234	..	1.057	10,938	7,153	2,282	104.9	..	..
1893	106,082	..	1.050	10,830	6,666	2,223	102.1	..	..
1894	105,354	..	1.048	10,703	6,405	2,292	101.6	..	..
1895	106,113	..	1.062	11,041	5,847	2,119	104.0	..	..
1896	107,641	..	1.058	10,200	5,865	2,166	94.8	..	..
1897	106,664	..	1.052	11,648	7,262	2,190	109.2	..	..
1898	105,457	..	1.060	11,611	6,312	1,970	110.1	..	..
1899	103,900	..	1.055	11,200	6,822	1,985	107.8	..	..
1900	101,459	..	1.061	11,088	6,073	2,064	109.3	..	..
1901	100,976	96.2	1.061	10,161	5,769	1,942	100.6	16.2	4.3
1902	101,863	..	1.066	10,161	6,182	1,883	99.8	..	..
1903	101,831	..	1.051	9,772	5,550	1,836	96.0	..	..
1904	103,811	..	1.049	10,381	5,814	1,865	100.0	..	..
1905	102,832	..	1.043	9,792	5,331	1,803	95.2	..	..
1906	103,536	..	1.065	9,644	5,003	1,631	93.1	..	..
1907	101,742	..	1.052	9,334	5,236	1,681	91.7	..	..
1908	102,039	..	1.055	9,895	5,636	1,645	97.0	..	..

A3.1.3 *continued*

Live births, infant and childhood mortality by age, Ireland, 1864–1921

Year	Live births			Infant and childhood deaths					
	Number	Rate per 1,000 women aged 15–44	Sex ratio of live births male/female	Numbers			Rates		
				Under 1 year	1–4 years	5–9 years	Under 1 year*	1–4 years+	5–9 years+
1909	102,759	..	1.054	9,405	4,991	1,677	91.5	..	..
1910	101,963	..	1.045	9,648	4,972	1,543	94.6	..	..
1911	101,758	103.8	1.064	9,555	4,579	1,487	93.9	13.0	3.4
1912	101,035	..	1.048	8,727	4,946	1,356	86.4	..	..
1913	100,094	..	1.045	9,721	4,972	1,558	97.1	..	..
1914	98,806	..	1.052	8,622	4,784	1,585	87.3	..	..
1915	95,583	..	1.064	8,753	4,724	1,500	91.6	..	..
1916	91,437	..	1.065	7,627	4,246	1,473	83.4	..	..
1917	86,370	..	1.052	7,583	3,911	1,300	87.8	..	..
1918	87,304	..	1.047	7,540	5,858	2,060	86.4	..	..
1919	89,325	..	1.071	7,841	4,479	1,841	87.8	..	..
1920	99,536	..	1.062	8,262	3,975	1,484	83.0	..	..
1921	90,720	..	..	7,005	3,241	1,263	77.2	..	..

* Rate per 1,000 live births
+ Rate per 1,000 population

Source: GRO Ireland. *Annual reports of the Registrar General for Ireland*

This is a new table for this edition of *Birth counts*

A3.1.4

Live births, infant and childhood mortality by age, Northern Ireland, 1922–98

Year	Live births			Infant and childhood deaths					
	Number	Rate per 1,000 women aged 15–44	Sex ratio of live births male/ female	Numbers			Rates		
				Under 1 year	1–4 years	5–9 years	Under 1 year*	1–4 years+	5–9 years+
1922	29,531	..	1.046	2,280	1,050	308	77.2	..	..
1923	30,097	..	1.038	2,302	1,077	269	76.5	..	..
1924	28,496	..	1.081	2,411	1,348	281	84.6	..	..
1925	27,686	..	1.051	2,391	1,344	322	86.4	..	..
1926	28,162	..	1.073	2,390	1,191	326	84.9	..	..
1927	26,676	..	1.055	2,074	927	266	77.7	9.0	2.3
1928	25,963	..	1.073	2,022	1,042	284	77.9	..	..
1929	25,410	..	1.055	2,174	1,244	304	85.6	..	..
1930	25,879	..	1.038	1,754	699	257	67.8	..	..
1931	25,673	..	1.052	1,885	875	255	73.4	..	..
1932	25,107	..	1.052	2,084	786	242	83.0	..	..
1933	24,601	..	1.058	1,960	892	285	79.7	..	..
1934	25,365	..	1.079	1,767	654	265	69.7	..	..
1935	24,742	..	1.068	2,136	1,026	311	86.3	..	..
1936	25,909	..	1.051	1,992	585	256	76.9	..	..
1937	25,412	85.3	1.049	1,969	614	207	77.5	6.9	1.8
1938	25,742	..	1.052	1,933	773	233	75.1	..	..
1939	25,240	..	1.044	1,779	434	165	70.5	..	..
1940	25,363	..	1.082	2,179	765	215	85.9	..	..
1941	26,887	..	1.096	2,059	617	260	76.6	..	..
1942	29,645	..	1.060	2,265	509	190	76.4	..	..
1943	31,521	..	1.076	2,464	474	186	78.2	..	..
1944	30,900	..	1.052	2,083	377	170	67.4	..	..
1945	29,007	..	1.063	1,975	366	150	68.1	..	..
1946	30,134	..	1.056	1,626	340	125	54.0	..	..
1947	31,254	..	1.050	1,658	384	125	53.0	..	..
1948	29,532	..	1.070	1,347	297	86	45.6	..	..
1949	29,106	..	1.067	1,317	240	78	45.2	..	..
1950	28,794	..	1.073	1,166	207	91	40.5	..	..
1951	28,477	95.5	1.058	1,173	206	94	41.2	1.9	0.7
1952	28,760	..	1.067	1,117	163	78	38.8	..	..
1953	28,984	98.3	1.078	1,090	152	73	37.6	1.4	0.5
1954	28,803	98.1	1.059	951	131	59	33.0	..	0.4
1955	28,965	98.7	1.087	938	128	63	32.4	..	0.5
1956	29,489	101.7	1.049	850	92	48	28.8	..	0.4
1957	30,108	104.8	1.060	869	119	66	28.9	..	0.5
1958	30,301	105.9	1.075	850	113	44	28.1	..	0.3
1959	30,809	107.3	1.063	875	107	46	28.4	..	0.3
1960	31,989	110.8	1.080	870	134	67	27.2	..	0.5
1961	31,915	111.7	1.058	877	119	52	27.5	1.0	0.4
1962	32,565	112.6	1.067	864	132	55	26.5	..	..
1963	33,414	116.9	1.077	902	107	59	27.0	0.9	0.4
1964	34,345	116.5	1.053	904	84	55	26.3	..	0.4
1965	33,890	114.5	1.094	849	111	51	25.1	..	0.4
1966	33,228	113.6	1.090	849	139	59	25.6	1.1	0.4

Live births, infant and childhood mortality by age, Northern Ireland, 1922–98

Year	Live births			Infant and childhood deaths					
	Number	Rate per 1,000 women aged 15–44	Sex ratio of live births male/ female	Numbers			Rates		
				Under 1 year	1–4 years	5–9 years	Under 1 year*	1–4 years+	5–9 years+
1967	33,415	114.4	1.057	785	110	51	23.5	..	0.3
1968	33,173	113.3	1.070	796	89	56	24.0	..	0.4
1969	32,428	110.4	1.049	790	104	63	24.4	..	0.4
1970	32,086	108.7	1.064	734	96	65	22.9	..	0.4
1971	31,765	107.4	1.081	722	102	56	22.7	0.8	0.4
1972	29,994	101.3	1.078	616	111	68	20.5	..	..
1973	29,200	98.4	1.079	610	123	67	20.9	..	0.4
1974	27,160	91.1	1.062	567	109	58	20.9	..	0.4
1975	26,130	87.8	1.065	534	83	61	20.4	..	0.4
1976	26,361	88.5	1.056	534	83	61	20.3	..	0.4
1977	25,437	83.8	1.071	438	79	41	17.2	..	0.3
1978	26,239	77.8	1.007	417	75	61	15.9	..	
1979	28,178	90.4	1.058	417	49	50	14.8	..	0.4
1980	28,582	90.2	1.057	382	58	46	13.4	..	0.3
1981	27,166	85.8	1.040	360	73	35	13.3	0.7	0.3
1982	26,872	84.0	1.045	369	57	28	13.7	0.5	0.2
1983	27,026	83.2	1.070	329	51	41	12.2	0.5	0.3
1984	27,477	83.4	1.069	291	49	34	10.6	0.5	0.3
1985	27,427	82.1	1.054	265	55	33	9.7	0.5	0.3
1986	27,975	82.7	1.076	286	34	29	10.2	0.3	0.2
1987	27,653	81.2	1.055	242	42	29	8.8	0.4	0.2
1988	27,514	80.6	1.056	248	50	30	9.0	0.5	0.2
1989	25,831	75.5	1.063	180	54	26	7.0	0.5	0.2
1990	26,251	76.5	1.049	198	42	25	7.5	0.4	0.2
1991	26,028	75.1	1.066	194	42	22	7.5	0.4	0.2
1992	25,354	72.7	1.040	153	39	28	6.0	0.4	0.2
1993	24,722	70.3	1.025	176	39	21	7.1	0.4	0.2
1994	24,098	68.0	1.053	147	40	21	6.1	0.4	0.2
1995	23,693	66.4	1.078	169	30	27	7.1	0.3	0.2
1996	24,382	67.6	1.032	142	18	16	5.8	0.2	0.1
1997	24,087	66.3	1.048	137	25	21	5.7	0.3	0.2
1998	23,668	64.9	1.039	134	25	17	5.7	0.3	0.1

* Rates per 1,000 live births
+ Rates per 1,000 population
Numbers of live and stillbirths for 1981 onwards were revised in 1999 to exclude all births to non-residents.

Source: GRO Northern Ireland. *Annual reports of the Registrar General, Northern Ireland.*

This is a new table for this edition of *Birth counts*

A3.1.5

Live births, infant and childhood mortality by age, Irish Republic, 1922–96

Year	Live births			Infant and childhood deaths					
	Number	Rate per 1,000 women aged 15–44	Sex ratio of live births male/female	Numbers			Rates		
				Under 1 year	1–4 years	5–9 years	Under 1 year*	1–4 years+	5–9 years+
1922	58,849	..	1.065	4,054	2,483	867	68.9	..	..
1923	61,690	..	1.064	4,098	1,973	768	66.4	..	..
1924	63,402	..	1.066	4,543	2,320	662	71.7	..	..
1925	62,069	..	1.052	4,216	2,140	689	67.9	..	..
1926	61,176	97.6	1.053	4,552	2,230	784	74.4	9.6	2.8
1927	60,054	..	1.039	4,254	2,142	739	70.8	..	..
1928	59,176	..	1.051	4,016	1,947	698	67.9	..	..
1929	58,280	..	1.303	4,102	1,890	714	70.4	..	..
1930	58,353	..	1.052	3,965	1,774	730	67.9	..	..
1931	57,086	..	1.063	3,935	1,892	644	68.9	..	..
1932	56,240	..	1.053	4,060	1,828	732	72.2	..	..
1933	57,364	..	1.050	3,742	1,643	730	65.2	..	..
1934	57,897	..	1.062	3,664	1,295	657	63.3	..	..
1935	58,266	..	1.054	3,988	1,572	630	68.4	..	..
1936	58,115	94.1	1.038	4,309	1,527	606	80.4	7.1	2.2
1937	56,488	..	1.047	4,121	1,627	577	73.0	..	..
1938	56,925	..	1.046	3,794	1,352	541	66.6	..	..
1939	56,070	..	1.056	3,691	1,139	491	65.8	..	..
1940	56,594	. ..	1.053	3,759	1,067	469	66.4	..	..
1941	56,780	88.0	1.059	4,175	1,153	461	73.5	..	..
1942	66,117	..	1.059	4,591	1,235	530	69.4	..	..
1943	64,375	..	1.068	5,319	1,322	536	82.6	..	..
1944	65,425	..	1.058	5,198	1,286	527	79.4	..	..
1945	66,861	..	1.056	4,739	1,103	395	70.9	..	..
1946	67,922	110.0	1.071	4,390	860	326	64.6	..	1.2
1947	68,978	..	1.071	4,687	1,055	344	67.9	..	..
1948	65,930	..	1.064	3,313	781	282	50.3	..	..
1949	64,153	..	1.051	3,415	723	248	53.2	..	..
1950	63,565	107.4	1.071	2,922	580	242	47.8	2.3	0.9
1951	62,878	107.6	1.057	2,876	644	228	45.3	2.6	0.8
1952	64,631	107.5	1.045	2,674	521	221	43.2	2.1	0.8
1953	62,558	111.0	1.063	2,463	478	203	41.0	1.9	0.7
1954	62,534	109.3	1.054	2,364	443	159	39.3	1.8	0.5
1955	61,622	110.7	1.045	2,264	366	174	38.2	1.5	0.6
1956	60,740	110.6	1.060	2,162	382	163	36.7	1.6	0.6
1957	61,242	110.8	1.048	2,027	327	159	34.1	1.4	0.5
1958	59,510	114.3	1.051	2,109	298	120	36.6	1.2	0.4
1959	60,188	112.6	1.040	1,927	308	135	32.9	1.3	0.5
1960	60,735	115.7	1.052	1,777	308	145	30.0	1.3	0.5
1961	59,825	118.5	1.053	1,827	314	133	29.1	1.3	0.5
1962	61,782	116.3	1.050	1,800	261	144	29.8	1.1	0.5
1963	63,246	119.3	1.056	1,682	230	120	27.1	0.9	0.4
1964	64,072	121.6	1.046	1,712	247	124	27.2	1.0	0.4
1965	63,525	122.6	1.043	1,604	229	134	25.7	0.9	0.5
1966	62,215	121.3	1.071	1,552	238	119	24.4	0.9	0.4

13

Live births, infant and childhood mortality by age, Irish Republic, 1922–96

Year	Live births			Infant and childhood deaths					
	Number	Rate per 1,000 women aged 15–44	Sex ratio of live births male/ female	Numbers			Rates		
				Under 1 year	1–4 years	5–9 years	Under 1 year*	1–4 years+	5–9 years+
1967	61,307	117.9	1.067	1,498	202	118	24.9	0.8	0.4
1968	61,004	115.5	1.065	1,280	200	130	21.3	0.8	0.4
1969	62,912	114.2	1.045	1,293	214	111	20.9	0.8	0.4
1970	64,284	116.6	1.061	1,180	192	110	18.6	0.8	0.4
1971	67,551	117.8	1.059	1,214	202	123	18.7	0.8	0.4
1972	68,527	120.4	1.067	1,236	206	159	18.3	0.8	0.5
1973	68,713	119.2	1.057	1,234	218	90	18.0	0.9	0.3
1974	68,907	116.2	1.058	1,227	207	112	18.3	0.8	0.3
1975	67,178	110.2	1.058	1,176	221	105	17.3	0.8	0.3
1976	67,718	107.3	1.060	1,052	177	111	15.6	0.7	0.3
1977	68,892	107.3	1.064	1,069	186	141	15.9	0.7	0.4
1978	70,299	106.9	1.036	1,046	194	107	15.2	0.7	0.3
1979	72,539	107.4	1.062	927	190	110	13.0	0.7	0.3
1980	74,064	107.4	1.069	821	185	115	11.3	0.7	0.3
1981	72,158	102.2	1.057	746	170	105	10.2	0.6	0.3
1982	70,843	98.3	1.048	745	175	103	10.5	0.6	0.3
1983	67,117	91.7	1.067	677	161	85	9.7	0.6	0.2
1984	64,062	86.0	1.077	617	110	88	9.3	0.4	0.2
1985	62,388	82.8	1.058	552	122	82	8.7	0.5	0.2
1986	61,620	81.0	1.072	546	102	84	8.9	0.4	0.2
1987	58,433	76.1	1.050	464	99	68	7.7	0.4	0.2
1988	54,600	71.0	1.059	484	114	66	8.4	0.5	0.2
1989	52,018	67.8	1.059	423	109	71	7.9	0.5	0.2
1990	53,044	69.0	1.081	434	88	57	8.4	0.4	0.2
1991	52,718	67.9	1.060	401	76	58	7.6	0.3	0.2
1992	51,089	65.1	1.062	331	70	51	6.3	0.3	0.2
1993	49,304	62.6	1.059	302	66	53	6.1	0.3	0.2
1994	48,255	60.2	1.071	277	66	41	5.7	0.3	0.1
1995	48,787	60.3	1.064	311	62	43	6.4	0.3	0.1
1996	50,390	61.3	..	..	..	..	..	..	..

* Rate per 1,000 live births
+ Rate per 1,000 population

Source: Central Statistics Office, Republic of Ireland

This is a new table for this edition of *Birth counts*

A3.1.6

Live births, infant and childhood mortality by age, Jersey, 1915–98

Year	Live births			Infant and childhood deaths					
	Number	Rate per 1,000 women aged 15–44	Sex ratio of live births male/female	Numbers			Rates		
				Under 1 year	1–4 years	5–9 years	Under 1 year*	1–4 years+	5–9 years+
1915	..	..	..	..	..	..	118.9	..	..
1921	..	..	..	..	..	..	..	..	..
1925	..	..	..	..	..	..	73.1	..	..
1931	..	..	..	..	..	..	..	..	..
1935	..	..	..	..	..	..	40.5	..	..
1939	862	..	..	30	11	..	34.8	..	..
1940	..	..	..	..	..	..	..	..	..
1941	..	..	..	..	..	..	..	..	..
1942	..	..	..	..	..	..	..	..	..
1943	..	..	..	..	..	..	..	..	..
1944	..	..	..	..	..	..	..	..	..
1945	..	..	..	..	..	..	27.4	..	..
1946	876	..	..	30	10	..	34.2	..	..
1947	1,018	..	..	30	15	..	29.5	..	..
1948	965	..	..	25	11	..	25.9	..	..
1949	936	..	..	27	2	..	28.8	..	..
1950	865	..	..	26	3	0	30.1	..	..
1951	844	..	..	27	7	3	32.0	..	..
1952	852	..	..	20	3	1	23.5	..	..
1953	774	..	..	18	3	1	23.3	..	..
1954	840	..	..	22	3	2	26.2	..	..
1955	736	..	..	25	1	6	34.0	..	..
1956	820	..	..	15	2	2	18.3	..	..
1957	833	..	..	20	5	2	24.0	..	..
1958	942	..	..	17	0	3	18.0	..	..
1959	950	..	..	18	2	1	18.9	..	..
1960	1,032	..	..	31	3	2	30.0	..	..
1961	1,086	85.1	..	29	4	3	26.7	..	..
1962	1,186	..	0.96	27	3	2	22.8	..	..
1963	1,282	..	1.06	22	4	2	17.2	..	..
1964	1,235	..	1.02	29	3	2	23.5	..	..
1965	1,213	..	1.02	20	2	1	16.5	..	..
1966	1,158	..	0.98	19	6	0	16.4	..	..
1967	1,124	..	1.05	25	4	0	22.2	..	..
1968	1,079	..	..	18	3	4	16.7	..	..
1969	1,031	..	1.06	12	2	0	11.6	..	..
1970	986	..	1.16	20	1	0	20.3	..	..
1971	984	68.1	1.13	18	1	0	18.3	0.3	–
1972	862	..	1.09	10	0	1	11.6	..	..
1973	847	..	1.07	6	1	1	7.1	..	..
1974	818	..	0.98	14	0	1	17.1	..	..
1975	828	..	0.99	5	2	0	6.0	..	..
1976	786	..	1.03	11	3	0	14.0	..	..
1977	857	..	0.95	14	0	0	16.3	..	..

A3.1.6 *continued*

Live births, infant and childhood mortality by age, Jersey, 1915–98

Year	Live births			Infant and childhood deaths					
	Number	Rate per 1,000 women aged 15–44	Sex ratio of live births male/ female	Numbers			Rates		
				Under 1 year	1–4 years	5–9 years	Under 1 year*	1–4 years+	5–9 years+
1978	852	..	1.10	18	4	0	21.1	..	..
1979	884	53.0	1.02	12	3	2	13.6	0.9	0.5
1980	867	51.8	0.95	9	3	0	10.4	0.9	–
1981	857	48.0	0.91	7	2	1	8.2	0.6	0.2
1982	865	48.1	1.09	6	0	0	6.9	–	–
1983	884	49.5	1.04	7	0	0	7.9	–	–
1984	931	52.3	1.04	8	0	1	8.6	–	0.3
1985	907	51.0	1.17	9	3	1	9.9	0.8	0.3
1986	948	48.2	1.06	5	0	1	5.3	–	0.2
1987	1,009	51.4	1.18	14	1	0	13.9	0.3	–
1988	1,071	54.5	1.10	11	0	1	10.3	–	0.2
1989	1,074	52.6	1.04	4	1	0	3.7	0.3	–
1990	1,112	54.5	1.03	7	0	0	6.3	–	–
1991	1,057	51.1	1.05	5	1	0	4.7	0.3	–
1992	1,137	55.0	1.11	3	0	0	2.6	–	–
1993	1,057	51.1	1.08	7	3	1	6.6	0.8	0.2
1994	1,142	55.2	1.07	2	0	3	1.8	–	0.7
1995	1,112	53.8	1.17	7	0	0	6.3	–	–
1996	1,108	55.5	1.01	6	0	0	5.4	–	–
1997	1,100	55.1	1.08	3	0	0	2.7	–	–
1998	1,126	56.4	1.01	4	2	0	3.6	0.5	–

* Rate per 1,000 live births
+ Rate per 1,000 population

Populations for 1981, 1991 and 1996 were derived from censuses taken in those years. Populations for 1979 and 1982–90 are age band estimates based on previous censuses. Populations for 1992–95 and 1997 are derived from global estimates, with age bands as in the previous census.

Source: States of Jersey. *Reports of the Medical Officer of Health*

This is a new table for this edition of *Birth counts*

A3.1.7

Live births and infant mortality, Guernsey, 1891–1998

Year	Live births			Infant deaths	
	Number	Rate per 1,000 women aged 15–45	Sex ratio male/female live births	Number	Rate per 1,000 live births
1891	1,065	127.4	1.0	..	..
1899	1,121	..	1.0	..	..
1901	1,096	114.6	1.1	..	..
1906	1,112	..	1.1	..	..
1911	946	90.9	1.0	..	..
1916	698	..	1.1	..	..
1921	768	80.5	1.2	..	..
1926	787	..	0.9	..	..
1931	764	80.5	1.1	..	..
1935	777	..	..	..	59.2
1936	708	..	..	..	59.3
1937	827	..	..	..	53.2
1938	851	..	..	..	43.4
1939	744	81.4	..	..	44.3
1940	568	..	..	..	46.4
1941	243	86.3	..	..	20.5
1942	262	..	..	..	38.1
1943	337	75.2	..	..	47.5
1944	395	..	..	..	43.0
1945	391	..	1.1	..	28.1
1946	872	..	..	35	40.1
1947	900	..	..	30	33.3
1948	870	..	..	17	19.5
1949	795	..	..	20	25.1
1950	746	..	1.1	22	29.5
1951	775	81.4	..	11	14.2
1952	736	..	..	24	32.6
1953	727	..	..	23	31.6
1954	689	..	..	9	13.1
1955	667	..	1.2	18	26.9
1956	701	..	..	14	19.9
1957	725	..	..	24	33.0
1958	717	..	..	16	22.3
1959	709	..	0.9	14	19.7
1960	769	..	1.1	12	14.3
1961	757	86.3	1.0	16	21.1
1962	797	..	1.2	15	18.8
1963	842	..	1.0	24	28.5
1964	891	..	0.5	19	21.3
1965	816	..	1.0	16	19.6
1966	780	..	1.0	13	16.7
1967	741	..	1.1	24	32.4
1968	752	..	1.0	16	21.3
1969	830	..	1.0	14	16.9
1970	794	..	1.0	13	16.4

A3.1.7 *continued*

Live births and infant mortality, Guernsey, 1891–1998

Year	Live births			Infant deaths	
	Number	Rate per 1,000 women aged 15–45	Sex ratio male/female live births	Number	Rate per 1,000 live births
1971	766	75.2	1.1	10	13.1
1972	790	..	1.2	14	17.7
1973	652	..	1.0	11	16.9
1974	679	..	1.0	9	13.3
1975	611	..	1.1	9	14.7
1976	623	58.0	1.2	9	14.5
1977	587	..	1.0	5	8.5
1978	582	..	1.0	9	15.5
1979	646	..	1.2	8	12.4
1980	622	..	1.2	8	12.9
1981	619	55.0	1.1	11	17.8
1982	589	..	1.0	6	10.2
1983	660	..	1.0	5	7.6
1984	596	..	1.1	6	10.1
1985	642	..	0.9	4	6.2
1986	671	55.1	1.0	2	3.0
1987	644	..	1.1	4	6.2
1988	680	..	1.1	5	7.4
1989	688	..	1.0	4	5.8
1990	728	..	1.1	1	1.4
1991	737	53.5	0.9	5	6.8
1992	701	52.1	1.0	8	11.4
1993	681	50.5	1.0	7	10.3
1994	676	50.6	1.0	3	4.6
1995	624	48.6	1.1	2	3.2
1996	660	51.3	1.0	5	7.6
1997	672	..	1.0	3	4.5
1998	678	..	1.2	2	3.0

Between 1990 and 1994, there was no Medical Officer of Health in post in Guernsey and discrepancies appeared in published data. Recent data are for Guernsey only. Earlier data may include events in Alderney and Sark.

Source: States of Guernsey, *Reports of the Medical Officer of Health*

This is a new table for this edition of Birth counts

A3.1.8

Live births, infant and childhood mortality by age, Isle of Man, 1879–1998

Year	Live births		Infant and childhood deaths					
	Numbers	Rate per 1,000 women aged 15–44	Numbers			Rates		
			Under 1 year	1–4 years	5–9 years	Under 1 year*	1–4 years+	5–9 years+
1879	1,569	..	164	94	33	104.5	..	..
1880	1,539	..	236	174	59	153.3	..	..
1881	1,398	..	139	91	41	99.4	..	..
1882	1,474	..	153	87	32	103.8	..	..
1883	1,392	..	157	103	37	112.8	..	..
1884	1,448	..	173	126	38	119.5	..	..
1885	1,439	..	166	77	45	115.4	..	..
1886	1,575	..	176	79	45	111.7	..	..
1887	1,515	..	209	118	54	138.0	..	..
1888	1,564	..	203	142	49	129.8	..	..
1889	1,578	..	187	80	38	118.5	..	..
1890	1,458	..	199	115	38	136.5	..	..
1891	1,493	..	166	83	39	111.2	..	..
1892	1,331	..	168	92	33	126.2	..	..
1893	1,415	..	181	85	32	127.9	..	..
1894	1,336	..	190	110	46	142.2	..	..
1895	1,515	..	161	104	27	106.3	..	..
1896	1,437	..	197	112	32	137.1	..	..
1897	1,445	..	173	83	34	119.7	..	..
1898	1,400	..	195	70	27	139.3	..	..
1899	1,473	..	221	95	32	150.0	..	..
1900	1,376	..	163	101	29	118.5	..	..
1901	1,204	..	157	93	29	130.4	..	..
1902	1,256	..	119	58	26	94.7	..	..
1903	1,910	..	144	47	29	75.4	..	..
1904	1,227	..	154	65	21	125.5	..	..
1905	1,139	..	139	84	45	122.0	..	..
1906	1,123	..	111	67	28	98.8	..	..
1907	1,073	..	107	43	22	99.7	..	..
1908	1,044	..	126	56	19	120.7	..	..
1909	1,036	..	109	79	30	105.2	..	..
1910	1,023	..	90	69	16	88.0	..	..
1911	979	..	114	52	21	116.4	..	..
1912	921	..	81	31	21	87.9	..	..
1913	899	..	101	35	14	112.3	..	..
1914	899	..	91	35	7	101.2	..	..
1915	805	..	77	38	14	95.7	..	..
1916	728	..	52	23	9	71.4	..	..
1917	647	..	54	20	6	83.5	..	..
1918	535	..	52	28	13	97.2	..	..
1919	679	..	50	34	15	73.6	..	..
1920	900	..	78	29	16	86.7	..	..
1921	847	..	71	27	11	83.8	..	..

Live births, infant and childhood mortality by age, Isle of Man, 1879–1998

Year	Live births		Infant and childhood deaths					
	Numbers	Rate per 1,000 women aged 15–44	Numbers			Rates		
			Under 1 year	1–4 years	5–9 years	Under 1 year*	1–4 years+	5–9 years+
1922	822	..	61	30	10	74.2	..	..
1923	808	..	53	26	9	65.6	..	..
1924	812	..	69	44	5	85.0	..	..
1925	761	..	57	27	9	74.9	..	..
1926	750	..	53	17	5	70.7	..	..
1927	700	..	43	18	9	61.4	..	..
1928	698	..	38	21	9	54.4	..	..
1929	678	..	36	29	5	53.1	..	..
1930	667	..	47	22	14	70.5	..	..
1931	679	..	27	9	6	39.8	..	..
1932	631	..	42	10	4	66.6	..	..
1933	644	..	34	11	16	52.8	..	..
1934	664	..	28	13	12	42.2	..	..
1935	666	..	29	14	5	43.5	..	..
1936	668	..	36	12	4	53.9	..	..
1937	644	..	47	8	4	73.0	..	..
1938	639	..	33	8	5	51.6	..	..
1939	649	..	41	5	5	63.2	..	..
1940	740	..	32	7	4	43.2	..	..
1941	886	..	44	11	8	49.7	..	..
1942	883	..	27	7	5	30.6	..	..
1943	788	..	24	14	6	30.5	..	..
1944	823	..	32	11	1	38.9	..	..
1945	752	..	32	5	6	42.6	..	..
1946	866	..	31	4	3	35.8	..	..
1947	969	..	29	4	2	29.9	..	..
1948	821	..	33	4	2	40.2	..	..
1949	840	..	25	4	3	29.8	..	..
1950	849	..	25	10	2	29.4	..	..
1951	837	63.0	26	6	1	31.1	1.8	0.3
1952	806	..	28	2	2	34.7	..	..
1953	719	..	24	3	2	33.4	..	..
1954	625	..	10	3	3	16.0	..	..
1955	615	..	16	2	2	26.0	..	..
1956	632	..	13	2	0	20.6	..	..
1957	632	..	5	1	1	7.9	..	..
1958	662	..	11	0	0	16.6	..	..
1959	641	..	15	1	0	23.4	..	..
1960	683	..	23	2	2	33.7	..	..
1961	663	66.2	16	4	1	24.1	1.7	0.3
1962	675	..	16	2	0	23.7	..	..
1963	708	..	12	1	1	16.9	..	..
1964	687	..	12	0	0	17.5	..	..
1965	712	..	14	0	0	19.7	..	..

A3.1.8 *continued*

Live births, infant and childhood mortality by age, Isle of Man, 1879–1998

Year	Live births		Infant and childhood deaths					
	Numbers	Rate per 1,000 women aged 15–44	Numbers			Rates		
			Under 1 year	1–4 years	5–9 years	Under 1 year*	1–4 years+	5–9 years+
1966	642	75.6	10	2	0	15.6	0.7	0.0
1967	702	..	14	0	2	19.9	..	..
1968	686	..	22	4	2	32.1	..	..
1969	760	..	11	1	1	14.5	..	..
1970	840	..	22	3	2	26.2	..	..
1971	804	70.7	20	2	1	24.9	0.7	0.3
1972	843	..	11	1	1	13.0	..	..
1973	807	..	12	2	2	14.9	..	..
1974	748	..	18	1	2	24.1	..	..
1975	692	..	11	1	1	15.9	..	..
1976	721	69.1	5	2	0	6.9	0.6	0.0
1977	672	..	7	3	1	10.4	..	..
1978	694	..	7	1	2	10.1	..	..
1979	758	..	5	2	2	6.6	..	..
1980	741	..	6	2	0	8.1	..	..
1981	752	61.7	12	1	1	16.0	0.4	0.2
1982	724	..	7	0	1	9.7	..	..
1983	680	..	12	3	0	17.6	..	..
1984	666	..	7	0	3	10.5	..	..
1985	703	..	4	1	1	5.7	..	..
1986	709	..	11	0	0	15.5	..	..
1987	729	..	4	2	0	5.5	..	..
1988	781	..	5	1	0	6.4	..	..
1989	817	..	5	2	1	6.1	..	..
1990	888	..	10	1	1	11.3	..	..
1991	892	62.5	3	0	0	3.4	0.0	0.0
1992	858	..	2	1	0	2.3	..	..
1993	853	..	5	0	0	5.9	..	..
1994	883	..	8	0	1	9.1	..	..
1995	847	..	1	3	1	1.2	..	..
1996	835	59.0	2	0	0	2.4	0.0	0.0
1997	870	..	3	2	0	3.4	..	..
1998	936	..	1	1	0	1.1	..	..

* Rate per 1,000 live births
+ Rate per 1,000 population

Source: Isle of Man. *Chief Registrar's annual report and statistical review of births, deaths and marriages in the Isle of Man.*

This is a new table for this edition of *Birth counts*

A3.2.1

Age-specific fertility, England and Wales, 1939–98

Year	Live births, per 1,000 women in each age group								Total period fertility rate
	Under 20*	20–24	25–29	30–34	35–39	40–44	45 and over~	All+	
1939	16.0	92.7	113.3	81.3	46.5	15.2	1.5	61.3	1.82
1940	15.3	90.7	108.4	75.2	43.0	14.8	1.4	58.7	1.75
1941	15.2	93.8	105.9	72.3	43.2	15.5	1.3	58.4	1.73
1942	15.8	107.9	122.8	85.8	48.7	16.7	1.4	67.0	1.94
1943	16.5	116.3	127.1	94.3	54.1	17.8	1.4	71.3	2.02
1944	16.9	124.1	140.3	108.1	63.6	19.5	1.4	78.6	2.24
1945	17.6	117.9	123.6	95.0	58.0	18.6	1.4	71.5	2.04
1946	17.0	125.1	155.8	118.4	66.3	19.1	1.4	84.3	2.47
1947	19.5	148.7	170.3	117.7	65.7	19.5	1.4	91.1	2.68
1948	21.6	138.1	145.5	99.3	56.2	17.4	1.3	80.4	2.38
1949	22.8	133.3	138.6	92.5	50.7	15.2	1.2	76.2	2.27
1950	22.2	126.3	136.2	89.4	48.3	14.2	1.1	73.0	2.18
1951	21.2	126.1	133.6	88.8	45.9	13.4	1.0	71.6	2.14
1952	21.3	128.8	134.8	88.7	44.4	13.1	1.0	71.8	2.16
1953	22.0	134.7	139.5	89.0	44.2	13.0	0.9	73.5	2.22
1954	22.7	136.3	139.2	84.9	44.3	12.9	0.8	72.9	2.21
1955	23.6	137.0	141.7	84.3	44.2	12.4	0.8	72.8	2.22
1956	27.3	146.8	150.6	88.2	45.5	12.4	0.8	77.0	2.35
1957	29.7	152.7	157.4	91.4	46.5	12.2	0.8	80.0	2.45
1958	31.0	158.3	161.5	93.6	45.8	12.0	0.8	82.2	2.52
1959	31.6	160.3	163.8	94.7	44.1	12.3	0.8	83.0	2.56
1960	34.0	165.6	171.9	100.8	46.4	13.8	0.8	86.8	2.68
1961	37.3	172.6	176.9	103.1	48.1	14.1	0.9	89.2	2.77
1962	39.2	178.8	181.6	104.5	48.6	14.1	0.8	90.8	2.85
1963	40.1	180.1	184.5	105.6	50.3	13.4	0.8	91.2	2.88
1964	42.5	181.6	187.3	107.7	49.8	13.0	0.9	92.9	2.93
1965	45.1	178.8	180.2	102.7	48.1	12.6	0.9	91.9	2.85
1966	47.7	176.0	174.0	97.3	45.3	11.7	0.9	90.5	2.75
1967	48.9	166.5	166.8	93.0	43.2	11.2	0.8	88.9	2.65
1968	49.0	162.3	162.5	89.0	40.3	10.4	0.7	87.6	2.57
1969	49.6	156.2	157.5	84.6	37.3	9.5	0.6	85.3	2.47
1970	49.6	155.0	153.7	79.8	34.7	8.6	0.6	83.9	2.40
1971	50.6	152.9	153.2	77.1	32.8	8.1	0.5	83.5	2.37
1972	48.0	140.4	141.8	69.3	28.9	7.1	0.5	77.0	2.17
1973	43.9	130.2	134.0	63.1	24.5	6.1	0.4	71.3	2.00
1974	40.5	123.2	128.0	59.9	21.5	5.4	0.4	67.2	1.89
1975	36.4	114.1	121.9	58.0	19.9	4.8	0.4	63.0	1.78
1976	32.2	109.3	118.7	57.2	18.6	4.4	0.3	60.4	1.71
1977	29.4	103.7	117.5	58.6	18.2	4.1	0.3	58.1	1.66
1978	29.4	106.9	122.6	63.1	19.5	4.2	0.4	60.1	1.73
1979	30.3	111.3	131.2	69.0	21.3	4.3	0.4	63.3	1.84
1980	30.4	112.7	133.6	70.5	22.3	4.3	0.5	64.2	1.88
1981	28.1	105.3	129.1	68.6	21.7	4.4	0.5	61.3	1.80

A3.2.1 *continued*

Age-specific fertility, England and Wales, 1939–98

Year	Live births, per 1,000 women in each age group								Total period fertility rate
	Under 20*	20–24	25–29	30–34	35–39	40–44	45 and over~	All+	
1982	27.4	101.6	126.3	69.1	22.8	4.2	0.5	59.9	1.76
1983	26.9	98.6	126.3	71.5	23.1	4.4	0.5	59.7	1.76
1984	27.4	95.6	126.0	73.6	23.6	4.5	0.4	59.8	1.75
1985	29.4	94.6	127.4	76.4	24.1	4.6	0.4	61.0	1.78
1986	30.1	92.7	123.8	78.0	24.6	4.5	0.4	60.6	1.77
1987	30.9	93.3	125.1	81.2	26.5	4.8	0.4	62.0	1.81
1988	32.5	94.6	124.0	82.4	27.9	4.8	0.4	63.0	1.82
1989	32.0	91.7	120.4	83.2	29.4	4.9	0.3	62.5	1.80
1990	33.3	91.4	122.6	86.9	31.1	5.0	0.3	64.2	1.84
1991	33.0	88.9	118.5	85.7	31.6	5.0	0.3	63.6	1.82
1992	31.7	86.2	117.3	87.2	33.4	5.5	0.3	63.5	1.80
1993	31.0	82.7	114.1	87.0	34.1	5.9	0.3	62.6	1.76
1994	29.0	79.4	112.1	88.7	35.8	6.1	0.3	61.9	1.75
1995	28.5	76.8	108.6	87.3	36.2	6.5	0.3	60.4	1.72
1996	29.8	77.5	106.9	88.6	37.2	6.9	0.3	60.5	1.73
1997	30.2	76.6	104.8	88.8	38.9	7.3	0.3	59.8	1.73
1998	30.7	75.4	102.6	89.9	39.9	7.5	0.3	59.1	1.73

* Rate per 1,000 women aged 15–19

~ Rate per 1,000 women aged 45–49

+ Rate per 1,000 women aged 15–44

Source:GRO. *Statistical reviews of the Registrar General*.

ONS and OPCS. *Birth statistics*, Series FM1.

ONS. *Health Statistics quarterly 3*.

This was Table A3.3 in the first edition of *Birth counts*

A3.2.2

Age-specific fertility, Scotland, 1939–98

Year	Live births, per 1,000 women in each age group								Total period fertility rate
	Under 20*	20–24	25–29	30–34	35–39	40–44	45 and over	All+	
1939	20.8	104.4	127.9	98.1	60.4	19.3	1.5	72.0	..
1940	19.3	107.2	129.0	93.8	56.6	18.8	1.5	71.0	..
1941	18.0	109.8	130.0	97.7	60.0	20.0	1.4	72.9	..
1942	18.5	121.9	137.8	98.8	61.2	19.7	1.7	75.8	..
1943	19.2	144.1	147.6	110.4	68.9	22.1	1.7	82.6	..
1944	17.4	144.0	156.6	116.6	71.0	22.7	1.4	84.0	..
1945	17.2	125.5	147.3	107.3	65.4	20.6	1.6	76.6	..
1946	17.6	131.9	189.4	134.2	76.3	21.3	1.5	91.6	..
1947	19.9	143.5	181.8	134.1	78.3	23.0	1.6	96.8	..
1948	20.5	133.8	157.6	116.3	68.4	21.1	1.4	86.5	..
1949	22.0	131.6	151.5	109.3	64.4	18.8	1.3	83.2	..
1950	20.9	128.6	147.3	108.3	61.2	18.2	1.3	80.8	..
1951	19.6	128.6	147.3	105.9	59.4	17.0	1.2	79.7	..
1952	19.8	131.1	149.1	105.2	58.6	16.5	0.9	80.2	..
1953	20.6	136.6	152.3	104.8	57.2	16.0	1.2	81.5	2.45
1954	21.9	146.1	154.0	103.8	57.8	16.3	1.0	83.6	2.51
1955	23.1	149.2	161.0	103.0	56.0	15.5	0.9	84.5	2.54
1956	26.6	157.9	166.4	106.3	57.6	15.1	0.8	88.0	2.65
1957	28.1	168.1	173.5	108.4	58.0	15.1	0.9	91.4	2.76
1958	29.4	174.4	178.7	109.5	56.3	15.0	0.9	93.5	2.83
1959	30.5	174.1	180.6	109.9	54.4	14.5	0.8	93.7	2.84
1960	32.1	179.1	187.0	113.5	55.5	15.3	0.9	96.5	2.93
1961	33.7	179.4	188.9	115.2	56.7	16.1	0.8	97.1	2.95
1962	35.6	189.0	195.7	115.6	57.2	16.2	1.1	99.2	3.06
1963	36.7	183.7	193.9	116.1	54.8	14.8	0.9	97.3	3.03
1964	40.1	187.2	195.1	117.4	57.1	15.0	0.9	99.0	3.09
1965	42.5	184.5	188.8	110.5	55.2	13.8	1.0	96.7	3.00
1966	46.1	181.7	180.5	103.8	50.8	13.8	0.8	93.9	2.88
1967	49.0	179.1	180.1	101.7	49.5	13.4	0.9	94.7	2.87
1968	48.0	179.8	177.6	98.3	46.8	11.8	0.7	93.8	2.82
1969	47.3	169.4	170.6	92.6	42.8	10.8	0.7	89.5	2.68
1970	47.6	166.2	164.5	87.0	37.9	9.6	0.6	86.7	2.57
1971	47.5	162.9	163.8	84.5	36.4	9.2	0.4	85.7	2.53
1972	47.0	147.4	146.6	74.6	30.8	7.8	0.4	77.6	2.27
1973	44.5	138.7	141.1	68.2	27.1	6.2	0.3	73.0	2.13
1974	42.7	129.9	131.3	61.6	22.5	5.8	0.4	68.0	1.97
1975	39.6	124.9	128.2	59.3	21.3	5.0	0.4	65.6	1.90
1976	35.3	115.6	124.3	57.3	19.2	4.4	0.2	62.0	1.80
1977	32.1	108.9	119.8	57.4	18.0	4.2	0.3	58.9	1.70
1978	32.2	109.0	124.6	61.3	18.2	3.5	0.2	60.1	1.74
1979	32.0	111.6	134.7	65.9	20.5	3.9	0.2	63.3	1.84
1980	32.0	112.3	132.5	66.7	20.3	3.7	0.2	63.2	1.84
1981	30.5	112.3	131.3	66.2	20.8	3.7	0.2	63.0	1.84
1982	30.7	104.8	123.2	64.6	20.5	3.7	0.2	60.0	1.74
1983	28.6	100.7	120.8	65.4	20.6	3.5	0.1	58.7	1.70
1984	28.7	96.2	121.6	65.9	20.1	3.6	0.2	58.2	1.68
1985	30.8	95.4	122.4	67.9	20.7	3.4	0.2	59.4	1.70
1986	30.7	91.6	119.0	69.8	20.2	3.4	0.2	58.4	1.67
1987	31.6	90.7	118.1	71.7	21.1	3.3	0.1	58.7	1.67
1988	31.9	88.7	119.5	71.9	22.9	3.2	0.1	59.0	1.68
1989	31.1	82.5	112.6	71.5	22.9	3.6	0.1	56.6	1.61
1990	31.9	82.7	116.8	76.1	24.5	3.4	0.2	58.7	1.66
1991	33.3	82.3	116.5	78.3	26.8	3.8	0.2	59.6	1.69

A3.2.2 *continued*

Age-specific fertility, Scotland, 1939–98

Year	Live births, per 1,000 women in each age group								Total period fertility rate
	Under 20*	20–24	25–29	30–34	35–39	40–44	45 and over	All+	
1992	33.1	77.6	113.6	80.7	27.8	3.9	0.1	59.3	1.68
1993	31.2	72.4	109.7	79.7	28.0	4.1	0.1	57.4	1.61
1994	28.4	68.2	106.1	81.2	28.9	4.4	0.2	55.9	1.58
1995	28.1	66.7	100.8	80.5	30.5	4.8	0.1	54.5	1.55
1996	29.6	64.6	97.9	81.6	31.4	5.5	0.2	53.9	1.55
1997	30.9	65.5	97.0	83.5	33.9	5.3	0.1	54.3	1.58
1998	30.4	62.7	94.2	82.6	34.1	5.7	0.2	52.6	1.55

* Rate per 1,000 women aged 15–19
+ Rate per 1,000 women aged 15–44

Source: GRO Scotland. *Annual report of the Registrar General for Scotland*

This is a new table for this edition of *Birth counts*

A3.2.3

Age-specific fertility, Northern Ireland, 1974–98

Year	Live births per 1,000 women in each age group								Total period fertility rate
	15–19	20–24	25–29	30–34	35–39	40–44	45–49	All+	
1974	37.0	154.3	178.4	112.3	54.1	17.1	1.0	93.8	2.78
1975	36.5	149.3	173.5	105.1	52.9	15.7	1.0	90.0	2.68
1976	32.7	152.0	176.8	109.1	50.5	15.8	1.3	90.1	2.70
1977	30.9	141.9	173.6	105.8	48.7	14.7	0.8	86.0	2.59
1978	31.0	142.2	177.4	112.8	51.4	12.9	1.0	87.6	2.66
1979	30.9	145.4	188.6	123.2	57.0	14.7	0.7	92.2	2.82
1980	29.2	143.2	191.6	122.1	56.6	12.9	1.0	91.6	2.79
1981	27.2	134.5	171.9	116.8	51.9	12.5	0.7	85.8	2.59
1982	26.8	131.7	167.2	115.5	52.0	11.9	0.5	84.0	2.53
1983	26.9	127.1	167.6	115.2	50.8	13.3	0.7	83.2	2.51
1984	28.0	127.4	164.9	114.3	51.3	12.8	0.6	83.4	2.50
1985	27.6	122.3	162.9	114.0	50.7	10.8	0.5	82.1	2.45
1986	29.6	121.0	162.9	113.4	50.3	11.2	0.5	82.7	2.44
1987	29.2	116.8	158.8	112.7	49.1	10.7	0.4	81.2	2.39
1988	30.6	113.9	156.7	112.2	46.7	10.9	0.4	80.6	2.35
1989	29.0	101.4	148.5	104.3	45.0	10.2	0.6	75.5	2.19
1990	29.2	100.4	148.0	107.6	47.4	9.6	0.6	76.5	2.21
1991	28.7	97.2	146.4	105.3	45.8	9.0	0.6	75.1	2.16
1992	30.2	90.1	141.3	103.1	43.0	8.8	0.6	72.7	2.08
1993	26.1	83.1	136.0	104.2	44.0	8.9	0.4	70.3	2.01
1994	25.4	74.8	130.8	104.9	44.4	9.2	0.4	68.0	1.94
1995	23.4	73.3	128.2	102.8	45.6	8.4	0.4	66.4	1.91
1996	25.6	73.5	128.3	108.2	45.4	8.4	0.4	67.6	1.95
1997	26.5	70.8	123.3	109.2	46.5	8.8	0.3	66.3	1.92
1998	27.9	69.5	117.9	108.2	47.1	8.2	0.4	64.9	1.89

+ Rate per 1,000 women aged 15–44

Numbers of live births from 1981 onwards were revised in 1999 to exclude births to non-residents

Source: GRO Northern Ireland. *Annual report of the Registrar General, Northern Ireland*

This is a new table for this edition of *Birth counts*

A3.2.4

Age-specific fertility, Irish Republic, 1956–96

Year	Live births per 1,000 women in each age group								Total period fertility rate
	15–19	20–24	25–29	30–34	35–39	40–44	45 and over	All+	
1956	9.5	92.1	183.1	195.8	139.1	53.9	3.8	109.1	..
1961	9.4	107.4	215.3	208.0	151.1	57.3	2.2	116.8	..
1966	13.4	127.1	230.6	211.3	143.2	54.5	2.2	118.7	..
1971	19.0	149.6	242.6	199.5	131.1	46.4	1.7	123.7	..
1980	22.7	124.1	200.4	164.1	96.4	29.3	2.3	107.4	3.23
1981	21.9	116.4	188.7	160.2	92.8	26.3	2.4	102.2	3.07
1982	20.3	109.0	183.0	155.2	90.6	24.6	2.1	98.3	2.96
1983	18.4	101.3	170.0	145.0	83.5	24.7	1.6	91.7	2.76
1984	17.8	94.3	161.4	136.8	78.0	21.5	1.9	86.0	2.59
1985	16.3	85.9	156.2	136.3	74.1	21.3	1.5	82.8	2.50
1986	16.2	81.5	152.5	137.3	72.5	20.9	1.5	80.9	2.45
1987	15.9	74.5	146.3	130.8	67.8	19.6	1.3	76.1	2.31
1988	15.1	68.8	139.4	124.2	62.5	17.6	1.1	71.0	2.17
1989	14.7	63.4	133.2	121.0	61.8	16.9	1.1	67.8	2.08
1990	16.5	62.7	136.3	125.0	62.5	15.3	1.1	69.0	2.12
1991	16.9	63.4	130.6	123.2	62.9	15.1	1.0	67.9	2.08
1992	16.6	58.4	123.2	121.7	60.8	14.3	0.8	65.1	1.99
1993	16.0	53.4	116.7	121.4	58.5	14.0	0.9	62.4	1.91
1994	14.8	50.4	113.6	120.4	58.7	12.7	0.7	60.6	1.85
1995	14.8	50.3	109.1	125.4	60.8	13.1	0.8	60.6	1.84
1996	16.3	51.6	104.8	126.1	63.9	11.9	0.6	61.3	1.89

+ Rate per 1,000 women aged 15–44. Includes births where the mother's age was not stated

Source: Central Statistics Office, Republic of Ireland

This is a new table for this edition of *Birth counts*

A3.2.5

Births by age of mother, Jersey, 1966–98

Year	Number of live births to women in each age group							
	Under 15	15–19	20–24	25–29	30–34	35–39	40 and over	All ages
1966	..	103	381	371	181	94	28	1,158
1967	..	110	368	348	203	77	18	1,124
1968	1	106	379	326	160	80	27	1,078
1969	..	70	375	313	178	69	26	1,031
1970	..	84	359	297	163	62	21	986
1971	..	87	311	324	173	68	21	984
1972	..	91	265	278	146	65	17	862
1973	..	60	232	310	162	67	16	847
1974	..	66	205	331	155	50	11	818
1975	..	48	220	325	168	51	16	828
1976	..	39	192	315	185	41	14	786
1977	..	52	213	333	192	57	10	857
1978	..	31	192	322	218	72	17	852
1979	..	42	208	341	237	41	15	884
1980	..	30	222	318	219	63	15	867
1981	..	27	183	314	246	67	20	857
1982	..	35	169	324	237	90	10	865
1983	..	39	180	315	238	102	10	884
1984	..	34	195	324	276	89	13	931
1985	..	31	177	334	271	85	9	907
1986	..	35	180	345	267	102	19	948
1987	..	39	169	393	305	90	13	1,009
1988	..	35	187	399	312	121	17	1,071
1989	..	31	181	369	356	116	21	1,074
1990	..	48	202	389	319	130	24	1,112
1991	..	36	158	353	336	148	26	1,057
1992	0	37	173	401	364	135	27	1,137
1993	1	49	170	334	337	142	24	1,057
1994	1	31	161	390	398	140	21	1,142
1995	..	32+	156	334	397	193*		1,112
1996	..	41+	136	336	395	196*		1,108
1997	..	56+	116	312	415	199*		1,100
1998	..	38+	141	303	392	248*		1,126

* 35 and over   4 births of unknown maternal age added to 1996 total
+ All under 20

Source: States of Jersey. *Report of the Medical Officer of Health*.

This is a new table for this edition of *Birth counts*

A3.3.1

Live births, stillbirths and infant mortality, England and Wales, 1905–98

Year	Sex ratio of total births male/female	Stillbirth*	Perinatal*	Early neonatal+	Late neonatal+	Neonatal+	Postneonatal+	Infant+
	Ratio	**Rates**						
1905	..	..	..	25.2	16.6	41.8	86.4	128.1
1906	..	..	..	25.0	16.9	41.9	90.6	132.5
1907	..	..	..	24.4	16.3	40.7	76.9	117.6
1908	..	..	..	24.3	16.0	40.3	80.1	120.4
1909	..	..	..	24.7	15.1	39.8	68.9	108.7
1910	..	..	..	24.1	14.4	38.5	66.9	105.4
1911	..	..	..	24.3	16.3	40.6	88.6	129.2
1912	..	..	..	24.2	14.2	38.4	56.3	94.7
1913	..	..	..	24.5	15.0	39.5	69.4	108.9
1914	..	..	..	24.1	14.4	38.5	65.9	104.4
1915	..	..	..	23.4	14.3	37.7	68.1	105.8
1916	..	..	..	23.2	13.7	36.9	54.2	91.1
1917	..	..	..	23.4	13.7	37.1	54.0	91.1
1918	..	..	..	23.2	13.4	36.6	61.3	97.9
1919	..	..	..	25.9	14.5	40.4	52.8	93.2
1920	..	..	..	21.9	13.1	35.0	49.5	84.5
1921	..	..	..	22.4	12.8	35.2	46.0	81.2
1922	..	..	..	22.0	11.9	33.9	40.8	74.7
1923	..	..	..	21.1	10.8	31.9	37.3	69.2
1924	..	..	..	21.8	11.2	33.0	41.2	74.2
1925	..	..	..	21.2	11.1	32.3	42.2	74.5
1926				21.3	10.6	31.9	38.3	70.2
1927	1.049	38.3	59.6	22.2	10.1	32.3	37.4	69.7
1928	1.050	40.1	60.8	21.6	9.5	31.1	34.0	65.1
1929	1.051	40.0	61.4	22.3	10.6	32.8	41.5	74.4
1930	1.051	40.8	61.9	22.0	8.9	30.9	29.1	60.0
1931	1.056	40.9	62.1	22.1	9.5	31.6	34.8	66.4
1932	1.056	41.3	62.8	22.4	9.1	31.6	33.5	65.0
1933	1.051	41.4	63.4	22.9	9.3	32.2	31.5	63.7
1934	1.060	40.5	62.2	22.6	8.7	31.3	27.3	58.6
1935	1.061	40.7	61.9	22.0	8.4	30.4	26.6	56.9
1936	1.059	39.7	60.8	21.9	8.3	30.2	28.4	58.5
1937	1.061	39.0	60.2	22.0	7.7	29.8	27.9	57.6
1938	1.056	38.3	58.6	21.1	7.2	28.3	24.4	52.7
1939	1.060	38.1	58.5	21.3	7.0	28.3	22.4	50.8
1940	1.057	37.2	57.7	21.4	8.3	29.7	27.8	57.4
1941	1.057	34.8	54.7	20.6	8.3	28.9	30.7	59.7
1942	1.066	33.2	52.1	19.5	7.6	27.1	22.4	49.5
1943	1.067	30.1	47.9	18.3	6.9	25.2	23.6	48.9
1944	1.068	27.6	44.5	17.4	6.8	24.2	20.3	44.5
1945	1.064	27.6	45.2	18.1	6.8	24.9	22.1	47.0
1946	1.063	27.2	44.3	17.6	6.6	24.2	16.7	40.9
1947	1.064	24.1	40.3	16.6	6.2	22.8	19.0	41.8
1948	1.063	23.2	38.5	15.7	4.1	19.8	14.8	34.5
1949	1.063	22.7	38.0	15.6	3.7	19.3	13.4	32.7
1950	1.063	22.6	37.4	15.2	3.3	18.5	11.3	29.9
1951	1.063	23.0	38.2	15.5	3.4	18.9	11.0	29.8
1952	1.057	22.7	37.5	15.1	3.2	18.3	9.2	27.5
1953	1.061	22.4	36.9	14.8	2.9	17.7	9.1	26.8
1954	1.060	23.5	38.0	14.9	2.8	17.7	7.7	25.5
1955	1.061	23.2	37.4	14.6	2.6	17.2	7.6	24.9

Live births, stillbirths and infant mortality, England and Wales, 1905–98

Year	Sex ratio of total births male/female	Stillbirth*	Perinatal*	Early neonatal+	Late neonatal+	Neonatal+	Postneonatal+	Infant+
	Ratio	**Rates**						
1956	1.058	22.9	36.7	14.2	2.6	16.8	6.8	23.6
1957	1.061	22.5	36.2	14.1	2.4	16.5	6.7	23.1
1958	1.059	21.5	35.0	13.8	2.4	16.2	6.4	22.5
1959	1.063	20.8	34.1	13.6	2.3	15.9	6.3	22.2
1960	1.061	19.8	32.8	13.3	2.2	15.5	6.3	21.8
1961	1.062	19.0	32.0	13.3	2.1	15.3	6.1	21.4
1962	1.060	18.1	30.8	13.0	2.1	15.1	6.6	21.7
1963	1.056	17.2	29.3	12.3	2.0	14.3	6.9	21.1
1964	1.062	16.3	28.2	12.0	1.8	13.8	6.1	19.9
1965	1.057	15.8	26.9	11.3	1.7	13.0	6.0	19.0
1966	1.060	15.3	26.3	11.1	1.7	12.9	6.1	19.0
1967	1.059	14.8	25.4	10.7	1.8	12.5	5.8	18.3
1968	1.058	14.3	24.7	10.6	1.8	12.4	5.9	18.3
1969	1.059	13.2	23.4	10.3	1.7	12.0	6.0	18.0
1970	1.058	13.0	23.5	10.6	1.7	12.3	5.9	18.2
1971	1.061	12.5	22.3	9.9	1.7	11.6	5.9	17.5
1972	1.063	12.0	21.7	9.8	1.7	11.5	5.7	17.2
1973	1.065	11.6	21.0	9.5	1.6	11.1	5.7	16.9
1974	1.061	11.1	20.4	9.4	1.7	11.0	5.3	16.3
1975	1.061	10.3	19.3	9.1	1.7	10.7	5.0	15.7
1976	1.058	9.7	17.7	8.2	1.5	9.7	4.6	14.3
1977	1.061	9.4	17.0	7.6	1.6	9.3	4.5	13.8
1978	1.061	8.5	15.5	7.1	1.6	8.7	4.5	13.2
1979	1.060	8.0	14.7	6.8	1.5	8.2	4.6	12.8
1980	1.049	7.2	13.3	6.2	1.5	7.7	4.4	12.0
1981	1.055	6.6	11.8	5.3	1.4	6.7	4.4	11.1
1982	1.056	6.3	11.3	5.0	1.2	6.3	4.6	10.8
1983	1.057	5.7	10.4	4.7	1.2	5.9	4.3	10.1
1984	1.050	5.7	10.1	4.4	1.1	5.6	3.9	9.5
1985	1.055	5.5	9.8	4.3	1.0	5.4	4.0	9.4
1986	1.052	5.3	9.6	4.3	1.0	5.3	4.3	9.6
1987	1.054	5.0	8.9	3.9	1.1	5.1	4.1	9.2
1988	1.049	4.9	8.7	3.9	1.0	4.9	4.1	9.0
1989	1.051	4.7	8.3	3.7	1.1	4.8	3.7	8.4
1990	1.048	4.6	8.1	3.5	1.0	4.6	3.3	7.9
1991	1.052	4.6	8.0	3.4	0.9	4.4	3.0	7.4
1992	1.053	4.3	7.6	3.3	1.0	4.3	2.3	6.6
1993	1.056	4.4	7.6	3.2	0.9	4.2	2.2	6.3
1994	1.056	4.4	7.6	3.2	0.9	4.1	2.1	6.2
1995	1.052	4.2	7.4	3.2	0.9	4.2	2.0	6.1
1996	1.055	4.0	7.2	3.2	0.9	4.1	2.0	6.1
1997	1.052	3.9	6.9	3.0	0.9	3.9	2.0	5.9
1998	1.052	3.9	6.8	2.9	0.9	3.8	1.9	5.7
	Including stillbirths at 24–27 weeks of gestational age							
1993	1.056	5.7	9.0	3.2	0.9	4.2	2.2	6.3
1994	1.056	5.7	8.9	3.2	0.9	4.1	2.1	6.2
1995	1.052	5.5	8.7	3.2	0.9	4.2	2.0	6.1
1996	1.055	5.4	8.6	3.2	0.9	4.1	2.0	6.1
1997	1.051	5.3	8.3	3.0	0.9	3.9	2.0	5.9
1998	1.052	5.3	8.2	2.9	0.9	3.8	1.9	5.7

A3.3.1 *continued*

Live births, stillbirths and infant mortality, England and Wales, 1905–98

Year	Live births	Stillbirths	Perinatal deaths	Early neonatal	Late neonatal	Neonatal deaths	Postneonatal	Infant deaths
	Numbers							
1921	848,814	..	..	19,023	10,909	29,932	40,318	70,250
1922	780,124	..	..	17,160	9,422	26,582	33,539	60,121
1923	758,131	..	..	16,005	8,156	24,161	28,421	52,582
1924	729,933	..	..	15,916	8,224	24,140	30,673	54,813
1925	710,582	..	..	15,080	7,891	22,971	30,345	53,316
1926	694,563	..	..	14,771	7,354	22,125	26,632	48,757
1927	654,172	26,021#	40,527#	14,506	6,635	21,141	24,469	45,610
1928	660,267	27,580	41,826	14,246	6,267	20,513	22,447	42,960
1929	643,673	26,847	41,178	14,331	6,805	21,136	26,732	47,868
1930	648,811	27,577	41,844	14,267	5,793	20,060	18,848	38,908
1931	632,081	26,933	40,914	13,981	5,985	19,966	21,973	41,939
1932	613,972	26,471	40,244	13,773	5,615	19,388	20,545	39,933
1933	580,413	25,084	38,388	13,304	5,384	18,688	18,272	36,960
1934	597,642	25,209	38,733	13,524	5,187	18,711	16,306	35,017
1935	598,756	25,435	38,618	13,183	5,009	18,192	15,900	34,092
1936	605,292	25,045	38,300	13,255	4,999	18,254	17,171	35,425
1937	610,557	24,806	38,252	13,446	4,722	18,168	17,007	35,175
1938	621,204	24,729	37,835	13,106	4,466	17,572	15,152	32,724
1939	614,479	24,320	37,390	13,070	4,331	17,401	13,789	31,190
1940	590,120	22,779	35,390	12,611	4,892	17,503	16,389	33,892
1941	579,091	20,876	32,829	11,953	4,793	16,746	17,804	34,550
1942	651,503	22,383	35,081	12,698	4,978	17,676	14,582	32,258
1943	684,334	21,262	33,785	12,523	4,728	17,251	16,180	33,431
1944	751,478	21,306	34,404	13,098	5,120	18,218	15,237	33,455
1945	679,937	19,333	31,639	12,306	4,604	16,910	15,049	31,959
1946	820,719	22,915	37,369	14,454	5,403	19,857	13,684	33,541
1947	881,026	21,795	36,428	14,633	5,469	20,102	16,747	36,849
1948	775,306	18,399	30,546	12,147	3,179	15,326	11,440	26,766
1949	730,518	16,947	28,369	11,422	2,684	14,106	9,776	23,882
1950	697,097	16,084	26,690	10,606	2,311	12,917	7,900	20,817
1951	677,529	15,985	26,487	10,502	2,286	12,788	7,435	20,223
1952	673,735	15,636	25,834	10,198	2,133	12,331	6,224	18,555
1953	684,372	15,681	25,808	10,127	1,961	12,088	6,236	18,324
1954	673,651	16,200	26,248	10,048	1,898	11,946	5,214	17,160
1955	667,811	15,829	25,579	9,750	1,766	11,516	5,097	16,613
1956	700,335	16,405	26,334	9,929	1,850	11,779	4,775	16,554
1957	723,381	16,615	26,792	10,177	1,727	11,904	4,816	16,720
1958	740,715	16,288	26,502	10,214	1,756	11,970	4,715	16,685
1959	748,501	15,901	26,070	10,169	1,712	11,881	4,748	16,629
1960	785,005	15,819	26,294	10,475	1,716	12,191	4,927	17,118
1961	811,281	15,727	26,495	10,768	1,675	12,443	4,950	17,393
1962	838,736	15,464	26,352	10,888	1,768	12,656	5,531	18,187
1963	854,055	14,989	25,487	10,498	1,675	12,173	5,869	18,042
1964	875,972	14,546	25,083	10,537	1,569	12,106	5,339	17,445
1965	862,725	13,841	23,573	9,732	1,468	11,200	5,195	16,395
1966	849,823	13,243	22,689	9,446	1,487	10,933	5,214	16,147
1967	832,164	12,528	21,473	8,945	1,489	10,434	4,832	15,266
1968	819,272	11,848	20,530	8,682	1,443	10,125	4,857	14,982

A3.3.1 *continued*

Live births, stillbirths and infant mortality, England and Wales, 1905–98

Year	Live births	Stillbirths	Perinatal deaths	Early neonatal	Late neonatal	Neonatal deaths	Postneonatal	Infant deaths
	Numbers							
1969	797,538	10,654	18,883	8,229	1,370	9,599	4,792	14,391
1970	784,486	10,345	18,671	8,326	1,335	9,661	4,606	14,267
1971	783,155	9,899	17,649	7,750	1,363	9,113	4,607	13,720
1972	725,440	8,799	15,943	7,144	1,231	8,375	4,123	12,498
1973	675,953	7,936	14,374	6,438	1,090	7,528	3,879	11,407
1974	639,885	7,175	13,169	5,994	1,073	7,067	3,392	10,459
1975	603,445	6,295	11,769	5,474	998	6,472	3,016	9,488
1976	584,270	5,709	10,472	4,763	900	5,663	2,671	8,334
1977	569,259	5,405	9,757	4,352	926	5,278	2,563	7,841
1978	596,418	5,108	9,350	4,242	945	5,187	2,694	7,881
1979	638,028	5,125	9,432	4,307	949	5,256	2,922	8,178
1980	656,234	4,773	8,815	4,042	981	5,023	2,876	7,899
1981	634,492	4,207	7,563	3,356	870	4,226	2,795	7,021
1982	625,931	3,939	7,087	3,148	777	3,925	2,850	6,775
1983	629,134	3,631	6,582	2,951	731	3,682	2,699	6,381
1984	636,818	3,643	6,464	2,821	723	3,544	2,493	6,037
1985	656,417	3,645	6,498	2,853	678	3,531	2,610	6,141
1986	661,018	3,549	6,372	2,823	666	3,489	2,824	6,313
1987	681,511	3,423	6,107	2,684	764	3,448	2,824	6,272
1988	693,577	3,382	6,083	2,701	720	3,421	2,849	6,270
1989	687,725	3,236	5,751	2,515	757	3,272	2,536	5,808
1990	706,140	3,256	5,754	2,498	723	3,221	2,343	5,564
1991	699,217	3,254	5,650	2,396	656	3,052	2,106	5,158
1992	689,656	2,944	5,238	2,294	661	2,955	1,584	4,539
1993	671,224	2,960	5,138	2,178	618	2,796	1,446	4,242
1994	664,256	2,925	5,067	2,142	607	2,749	1,371	4,120
1995	648,001	2,704	4,808	2,104	594	2,698	1,284	3,982
1996	649,489	2,598	4,664	2,066	579	2,645	1,314	3,959
1997	643,095	2,546	4,487	1,941	576	2,517	1,282	3,799
1998	635,901	2,475	4,310	1,835	575	2,410	1,195	3,605
	Including stillbirths at 24–27 weeks of gestational age							
1993	671,224	3,866	6,044	2,178	618	2,796	1,446	4,242
1994	664,256	3,816	5,958	2,142	607	2,749	1,371	4,120
1995	648,001	3,597	5,701	2,104	594	2,698	1,284	3,982
1996	649,489	3,539	5,605	2,066	579	2,645	1,314	3,959
1997	643,095	3,439	5,380	1,941	576	2,517	1,282	3,799
1998	635,901	3,417	5,252	1,835	575	2,410	1,195	3,605

* Rate per 1,000 total births
+ Rate per 1,000 live births
# Stillbirth registration began on July 1 1927, so the figures for 1927 are estimates

Source: GRO, *Annual reports of the Registrar General.*

GRO, *Statistical reviews of the Registrar General.*

OPCS and ONS *Birth statistics*, Series FM1 and *Mortality statistics*, Series DH1, DH3 and DH6

This was Table A3.4 in the first edition of *Birth counts*

A3.3.2

Live births, stillbirths and infant mortality, Scotland, 1922–98

Year	Sex ratio of total births male/female	Stillbirth*	Perinatal*	Early neonatal+	Late neonatal+	Neonatal+	Postneonatal+	Infant+
	Ratio	**Rates**						
1922	..	..	..	24.2	15.1	39.4	62.0	101.4
1923	..	..	..	23.0	13.3	36.3	42.6	78.9
1924	..	..	..	23.6	14.9	38.4	59.3	97.7
1925	..	..	..	23.6	13.3	36.9	53.7	90.6
1926	..	..	..	24.0	12.4	36.4	46.7	83.1
1927	..	..	..	24.5	12.6	37.2	51.6	88.7
1928	..	..	..	23.5	13.2	36.7	49.0	85.7
1929	..	..	..	24.6	12.7	37.3	49.5	86.8
1930	..	..	..	23.6	11.6	35.2	47.8	83.0
1931	..	..	..	24.7	11.1	35.8	46.0	81.8
1932	..	..	..	23.8	12.3	36.1	50.1	86.2
1933	..	..	..	26.1	11.5	37.6	43.5	81.1
1934	..	..	..	24.7	11.5	36.2	41.5	77.7
1935	..	..	..	24.8	13.7	38.5	38.3	76.8
1936	..	..	..	24.9	12.7	37.6	44.7	82.3
1937	..	..	..	25.2	13.1	38.3	42.0	80.3
1938	..	..	..	24.3	10.7	35.0	34.5	69.5
1939	1.06	42.2	67.5	26.3	10.2	36.6	31.9	68.5
1940	1.06	42.1	66.5	25.5	11.8	37.3	41.1	78.3
1941	1.06	39.6	64.4	25.8	14.1	39.9	42.8	82.7
1942	1.05	38.2	60.7	23.5	11.6	35.0	34.2	69.3
1943	1.05	35.6	56.9	22.1	10.8	32.9	32.3	65.2
1944	1.07	32.5	53.2	21.4	11.4	32.8	32.2	65.0
1945	1.06	32.8	52.8	20.7	7.8	28.5	27.7	56.2
1946	1.07	32.3	53.9	22.3	7.5	29.9	24.0	53.8
1947	1.06	30.5	49.9	20.0	8.5	28.5	27.2	55.8
1948	1.07	28.7	46.8	18.7	6.4	25.1	19.6	44.7
1949	1.06	27.1	44.9	18.3	4.9	23.2	18.2	41.4
1950	1.07	26.9	45.1	18.7	4.3	23.0	15.5	38.6
1951	1.06	26.6	44.2	18.0	4.2	22.3	15.1	37.4
1952	1.05	26.2	43.7	18.0	3.7	21.7	13.5	35.2
1953	1.06	24.8	40.6	16.3	3.0	19.3	11.5	30.8
1954	1.06	25.3	42.7	17.8	2.8	20.6	10.4	31.0
1955	1.06	24.6	41.1	16.9	2.8	19.7	10.6	30.4
1956	1.05	23.9	39.8	16.3	2.8	19.1	9.5	28.6
1957	1.06	23.7	40.0	16.7	2.9	19.6	9.0	28.6
1958	1.05	22.8	38.6	16.2	2.5	18.7	9.0	27.7
1959	1.06	22.2	38.4	16.6	2.8	19.4	9.0	28.4
1960	1.05	21.7	37.2	15.8	2.4	18.2	8.1	26.4
1961	1.06	20.8	36.0	15.6	2.4	17.9	7.9	25.8
1962	1.07	19.9	34.8	15.2	2.7	17.9	8.6	26.5
1963	1.05	19.1	33.4	14.6	2.3	16.8	8.7	25.6
1964	1.06	17.9	32.1	14.5	1.9	16.4	7.6	24.0
1965	1.07	17.9	31.5	13.8	2.1	15.9	7.2	23.1
1966	1.06	16.2	29.3	13.3	1.9	15.2	8.0	23.2
1967	1.06	15.8	27.5	11.9	2.0	13.8	7.2	21.0
1968	1.06	14.8	25.9	11.2	2.1	13.3	7.5	20.8
1969	1.07	14.0	25.2	11.4	2.1	13.5	7.5	21.1

A3.3.2 *continued*

Live births, stillbirths and infant mortality, Scotland, 1922–98

Year	Sex ratio of total births male/female	Stillbirth*	Perinatal*	Early neonatal[+]	Late neonatal[+]	Neonatal[+]	Postneonatal[+]	Infant[+]
	Ratio	**Rates**						
1970	1.06	13.9	24.8	11.1	1.7	12.8	6.9	19.6
1971	1.05	13.1	24.5	11.5	2.0	13.5	6.4	19.9
1972	1.05	13.2	23.7	10.6	1.8	12.4	6.4	18.8
1973	1.08	11.6	22.5	11.0	1.7	12.7	6.3	19.0
1974	1.04	12.0	22.8	10.9	1.9	12.8	6.1	18.9
1975	1.06	11.1	21.1	10.1	1.7	11.8	5.4	17.2
1976	1.07	9.6	18.3	8.8	1.5	10.3	4.5	14.8
1977	1.05	8.8	18.3	9.6	1.7	11.3	4.8	16.1
1978	1.06	8.1	15.4	7.4	1.4	8.8	4.1	12.9
1979	1.07	6.9	14.1	7.3	1.4	8.7	4.2	12.8
1980	1.06	6.7	13.1	6.5	1.3	7.8	4.3	12.1
1981	1.05	6.3	11.6	5.4	1.5	6.9	4.4	11.3
1982	1.05	5.8	11.5	5.7	1.4	7.1	4.2	11.4
1983	1.07	5.8	10.6	4.9	1.0	5.8	4.1	9.9
1984	1.04	5.8	11.0	5.2	1.2	6.4	3.9	10.3
1985	1.05	5.5	9.8	4.3	1.1	5.5	3.9	9.4
1986	1.06	5.8	10.2	4.4	0.8	5.2	3.6	8.8
1987	1.05	5.1	8.9	3.8	0.9	4.7	3.8	8.5
1988	1.06	5.4	8.9	3.6	1.0	4.5	3.7	8.2
1989	1.05	5.0	8.7	3.7	1.0	4.7	4.0	8.7
1990	1.06	5.3	8.7	3.4	1.0	4.4	3.3	7.7
1991	1.06	5.5	8.6	3.2	1.2	4.4	2.7	7.1
1992	1.05	4.9	8.5	3.7	1.0	4.6	2.2	6.8
1993	1.06	4.8	8.0	3.2	0.8	4.0	2.5	6.5
1994	1.05	4.5	7.4	2.9	1.1	4.0	2.2	6.2
1995	1.06	4.9	7.9	3.1	0.9	4.0	2.2	6.2
1996	1.05	5.0	7.9	2.9	1.0	3.9	2.2	6.2
1997	1.06	4.1	6.6	2.5	0.7	3.2	2.1	5.3
1998	1.06	4.5	7.2	2.7	0.9	3.6	2.0	5.6
	Including stillbirths at 24–27 weeks of gestational age							
1992	1.05	5.4	9.0	3.7	1.0	4.6	2.2	6.8
1993	1.05	6.4	9.6	3.2	0.8	4.0	2.5	6.5
1994	1.04	6.1	9.0	2.9	1.1	4.0	2.2	6.2
1995	1.04	6.6	9.6	3.1	0.9	4.0	2.2	6.2
1996	1.06	6.4	9.2	2.9	1.0	3.9	2.2	6.2
1997	1.05	5.3	7.8	2.5	0.7	3.2	2.1	5.3
1998	1.06	6.1	8.7	2.7	0.9	3.6	2.0	5.6

	Live births	Stillbirths	Perinatal deaths	Early neonatal	Late neonatal	Neonatal deaths	Postneonatal	Infant deaths
	Numbers							
1922	115,085	..	..	2,788	1,743	4,531	7,133	11,664
1923	111,902	..	..	2,577	1,483	4,060	4,765	8,825
1924	106,900	..	..	2,519	1,590	4,109	6,337	10,446
1925	104,137	..	..	2,456	1,383	3,839	5,591	9,430

A3.3.2 *continued*

Live births, stillbirths and infant mortality, Scotland, 1922–98

	Live births	Stillbirths	Perinatal deaths	Early neonatal	Late neonatal	Neonatal deaths	Postneonatal	Infant deaths
	Numbers							
1926	102,449	..	..	2,458	1,272	3,730	4,784	8,514
1927	96,672	..	..	2,370	1,222	3,592	4,984	8,576
1928	96,822	..	..	2,273	1,277	3,550	4,749	8,299
1929	92,880	..	..	2,286	1,177	3,463	4,598	8,061
1930	94,549	..	..	2,234	1,098	3,332	4,520	7,852
1931	92,220	..	..	2,274	1,026	3,300	4,244	7,544
1932	91,000	..	..	2,166	1,119	3,285	4,555	7,840
1933	86,546	..	..	2,263	993	3,256	3,763	7,019
1934	88,836	..	..	2,193	1,024	3,217	3,684	6,901
1935	87,928	..	..	2,183	1,206	3,389	3,365	6,754
1936	88,928	..	..	2,216	1,127	3,343	3,972	7,315
1937	87,810	..	..	2,209	1,152	3,361	3,689	7,050
1938	88,627	..	..	2,155	949	3,104	3,059	6,163
1939	86,913	3,832	6,121	2,289	890	3,179	2,776	5,955
1940	86,392	3,799	5,999	2,200	1,019	3,219	3,547	6,766
1941	89,748	3,698	6,014	2,316	1,268	3,584	3,842	7,426
1942	90,703	3,602	5,729	2,127	1,052	3,179	3,104	6,283
1943	94,669	3,494	5,586	2,092	1,024	3,116	3,058	6,174
1944	95,920	3,221	5,274	2,053	1,093	3,146	3,091	6,237
1945	86,924	2,949	4,746	1,797	681	2,478	2,411	4,889
1946	104,413	3,483	5,816	2,333	786	3,119	2,502	5,621
1947	113,147	3,563	5,827	2,264	965	3,229	3,080	6,309
1948	100,344	2,966	4,840	1,874	647	2,521	1,965	4,486
1949	95,674	2,666	4,415	1,749	468	2,217	1,744	3,961
1950	92,530	2,557	4,288	1,731	400	2,131	1,438	3,569
1951	90,639	2,479	4,113	1,634	385	2,019	1,372	3,391
1952	90,422	2,430	4,054	1,624	334	1,958	1,223	3,181
1953	90,913	2,308	3,789	1,481	275	1,756	1,044	2,800
1954	92,315	2,401	4,042	1,641	263	1,904	957	2,861
1955	92,539	2,330	3,898	1,568	258	1,826	985	2,811
1956	95,313	2,329	3,884	1,555	264	1,819	908	2,727
1957	97,977	2,378	4,012	1,634	286	1,920	882	2,802
1958	99,481	2,324	3,934	1,610	252	1,862	896	2,758
1959	99,251	2,252	3,900	1,648	274	1,922	894	2,816
1960	101,292	2,252	3,855	1,603	245	1,848	825	2,673
1961	101,169	2,147	3,721	1,574	239	1,813	802	2,615
1962	104,334	2,122	3,709	1,587	280	1,867	901	2,768
1963	102,691	1,997	3,494	1,497	232	1,729	895	2,624
1964	104,355	1,900	3,414	1,514	201	1,715	793	2,508
1965	100,660	1,835	3,224	1,389	212	1,601	726	2,327
1966	96,536	1,589	2,874	1,285	185	1,470	769	2,239
1967	96,221	1,544	2,685	1,141	190	1,331	693	2,024
1968	94,786	1,425	2,491	1,066	195	1,261	709	1,970
1969	90,290	1,283	2,312	1,029	193	1,222	680	1,902
1970	87,335	1,234	2,200	966	149	1,115	599	1,714
1971	86,728	1,155	2,151	996	172	1,168	554	1,722
1972	78,550	1,053	1,888	835	139	974	503	1,477
1973	74,392	873	1,690	817	125	942	470	1,412

A3.3.2 continued

Live births, stillbirths and infant mortality, Scotland, 1922–98

	Live births	Stillbirths	Perinatal deaths	Early neonatal	Late neonatal	Neonatal deaths	Postneonatal	Infant deaths
	Numbers							
1974	70,093	850	1,617	767	130	897	429	1,326
1975	67,943	765	1,448	683	116	799	369	1,168
1976	64,895	629	1,199	570	96	666	293	959
1977	62,342	553	1,150	597	109	706	298	1,004
1978	64,295	524	999	475	89	564	266	830
1979	68,366	475	973	498	96	594	284	878
1980	68,892	463	909	446	89	535	296	831
1981	69,054	436	808	372	102	474	306	780
1982	66,196	386	766	380	92	472	281	753
1983	65,078	379	696	317	62	379	267	646
1984	65,106	379	718	339	77	416	256	672
1985	66,676	366	656	290	74	364	260	624
1986	65,812	385	673	288	55	343	238	581
1987	66,241	339	594	255	57	312	251	563
1988	66,212	357	594	237	63	300	243	543
1989	63,480	319	553	235	65	300	254	554
1990	65,973	349	574	225	64	289	221	510
1991	67,024	369	582	213	79	292	181	473
1992	65,789	321	562	241	63	304	145	449
1993	63,337	306	508	202	52	254	158	412
1994	61,656	281	458	177	69	246	136	382
1995	60,051	294	479	185	56	241	132	375
1996	59,296	300	471	171	62	233	132	365
1997	59,440	245	392	147	42	189	127	316
1998	57,319	259	412	153	53	206	114	320
	Including stillbirths at 24–27 weeks of gestational age							
1992	65,789	356	597	241	63	304	145	449
1993	63,337	409	611	202	52	254	158	412
1994	61,656	381	558	177	69	246	136	382
1995	60,051	397	582	185	56	241	132	375
1996	59,296	381	552	171	62	233	132	365
1997	59,440	319	466	147	42	189	127	316
1998	57,319	351	504	153	53	206	114	320

* Rate per 1,000 total births
+ Rate per 1,000 live births

Source: GRO Scotland. *Annual report of the Registrar General for Scotland*

This was Table A3.5 in the first edition of *Birth counts*

A3.3.3

Live births, stillbirths and infant mortality, Northern Ireland, 1922–98

Year	Sex ratio of total births male/female	Stillbirth*	Perinatal*	Early neonatal+	Late neonatal+	Neonatal+	Postneonatal+	Infant+
	Ratio	**Rates**						
1922	..	..	..	..	..	30.1	47.1	77.2
1923	..	..	..	..	..	31.4	45.1	76.5
1924	..	..	..	..	..	30.9	53.7	84.6
1925	..	..	..	..	..	32.3	54.0	86.4
1926	..	..	..	..	..	34.1	50.8	84.9
1927	..	..	..	..	..	30.2	47.5	77.7
1928	..	..	..	..	..	29.3	48.6	77.9
1929	..	..	..	20.2	11.6	31.8	53.8	85.6
1930	..	..	..	20.3	11.2	31.5	36.3	67.8
1931	..	..	..	21.4	10.8	32.2	41.2	73.4
1932	..	..	..	22.8	13.4	36.2	46.8	83.0
1933	..	..	..	22.3	10.7	33.0	46.7	79.7
1934	..	..	..	23.9	10.4	34.3	35.4	69.7
1935	..	..	..	22.8	11.4	34.3	52.1	86.3
1936	..	..	..	24.6	11.6	36.2	40.6	76.9
1937	..	..	..	23.1	12.7	35.8	41.7	77.5
1938	..	..	..	25.0	9.8	34.8	40.2	75.1
1939	..	..	..	22.3	9.4	31.7	38.8	70.5
1940	..	..	..	23.3	11.5	34.8	51.1	85.9
1941	..	..	..	21.7	12.1	33.8	42.8	76.6
1942	..	..	..	21.7	13.3	35.0	41.4	76.4
1943	..	..	..	21.6	17.5	39.2	39.0	78.2
1944	..	..	..	21.9	13.6	35.5	31.9	67.4
1945	..	..	..	21.1	11.2	32.4	35.7	68.1
1946	..	..	..	20.4	5.5	26.0	28.0	54.0
1947	..	..	..	18.2	6.1	24.3	28.7	53.0
1948	..	..	..	15.4	4.9	20.3	25.3	45.6
1949	..	..	..	19.5	4.2	23.7	21.6	45.2
1950	..	..	..	18.5	4.9	23.4	17.1	40.5
1951	..	..	..	20.4	4.2	24.6	16.6	41.2
1952	..	..	..	19.7	3.7	23.4	15.5	38.8
1953	..	..	..	17.2	4.2	21.5	16.1	37.6
1954	..	..	..	18.5	3.1	21.6	11.4	33.0
1955	..	..	..	17.5	3.7	21.1	11.3	32.4
1956	..	..	..	17.3	3.3	20.6	8.2	28.8
1957	..	..	..	16.8	2.7	19.6	9.3	28.9
1958	..	..	..	16.2	2.9	19.1	8.9	28.1
1959	..	..	..	17.0	2.7	19.7	8.7	28.4
1960	..	..	..	17.8	2.2	20.0	7.2	27.2
1961	..	22.3	38.3	16.4	3.1	19.5	8.0	27.5
1962	..	22.4	38.0	16.0	2.2	18.1	8.4	26.5
1963	..	19.5	35.8	16.6	2.1	18.7	8.3	27.0
1964	..	19.4	35.1	16.0	2.3	18.3	8.0	26.3
1965	..	19.1	34.5	15.7	2.1	17.8	7.3	25.1
1966	..	16.3	30.8	14.7	2.3	17.0	8.5	25.6
1967	..	17.5	31.3	14.1	2.2	16.3	7.2	23.5
1968	..	16.0	29.4	13.6	2.1	15.7	8.3	24.0

Live births, stillbirths and infant mortality, Northern Ireland, 1922–98

Year	Sex ratio of total births male/female	Stillbirth*	Perinatal*	Early neonatal+	Late neonatal+	Neonatal+	Postneonatal+	Infant+
	Ratio	**Rates**						
1969	..	15.2	28.8	13.7	2.1	15.9	8.5	24.4
1970	..	14.3	27.6	13.6	2.2	15.8	7.1	22.9
1971	..	14.3	27.2	13.1	2.8	15.9	6.8	22.7
1972	..	14.3	26.0	11.9	2.1	8.2	6.6	11.7
1973	..	13.1	25.6	12.6	2.0	14.6	6.3	20.9
1974	..	13.6	25.3	11.9	2.0	13.8	7.1	20.9
1975	..	14.1	25.5	11.6	1.6	13.2	7.3	20.4
1976	..	10.4	22.3	11.9	1.3	13.3	5.0	18.3
1977	..	12.0	21.1	9.2	1.5	10.7	6.6	17.2
1978	..	9.2	18.1	9.0	1.8	10.5	5.4	15.9
1979	..	8.7	16.6	8.0	1.4	9.4	5.4	14.8
1980	..	9.2	15.6	6.4	1.6	8.0	5.4	13.4
1981	1.04	8.8	15.4	6.6	1.7	8.3	4.9	13.2
1982	1.04	6.9	13.4	6.5	1.3	7.8	5.9	13.7
1983	1.07	7.5	13.2	5.7	1.6	7.3	4.8	12.1
1984	1.07	5.8	10.8	4.9	1.8	6.7	3.8	10.5
1985	1.05	6.4	11.1	4.7	0.9	5.6	4.0	9.6
1986	1.08	4.4	9.5	5.1	0.9	6.0	4.2	10.2
1987	1.06	6.1	9.8	3.8	1.1	4.8	3.8	8.7
1988	1.06	5.0	9.3	4.3	1.0	5.4	3.6	8.9
1989	1.06	5.1	8.2	3.1	0.9	4.0	2.9	6.9
1990	1.05	4.4	7.6	3.2	0.8	4.0	3.5	7.5
1991	1.06	4.7	8.4	3.7	0.9	4.6	2.8	7.4
1992	1.04	4.6	8.0	3.3	0.7	4.1	1.9	6.0
1993	1.03	4.1	7.7	3.6	1.3	4.9	2.1	7.1
1994	1.05	5.2	8.6	3.4	0.8	4.2	1.9	6.1
1995	1.08	4.5	8.9	4.3	1.2	5.5	1.6	7.1
1996	1.03	4.7	7.8	3.1	0.6	3.7	2.0	5.8
1997	1.05	4.1	7.3	3.3	0.9	4.2	1.4	5.6
1998	1.04	3.7	6.8	3.0	0.9	3.9	1.7	5.7
	Including stillbirths at 24–27 weeks of gestational age							
1993	1.03	5.2	8.8	3.6	1.3	4.9	2.1	7.1
1994	1.05	6.3	9.7	3.4	0.8	4.2	1.9	6.1
1995	1.08	6.1	10.4	4.3	1.2	5.5	1.6	7.1
1996	1.03	6.2	9.4	3.1	0.6	3.7	2.0	5.8
1997	1.05	5.4	8.6	3.3	0.9	4.2	1.4	5.6
1998	1.04	5.1	8.1	3.0	0.9	3.9	1.7	5.7

Year	Live births	Stillbirths	Perinatal deaths	Early neonatal	Late neonatal	Neonatal deaths	Postneonatal	Infant deaths
	Numbers							
1922	29,531	..	..	..	..	889	1,391	2,280
1923	30,097	..	..	..	..	946	1,356	2,302
1924	28,496	..	..	..	..	880	1,531	2,411
1925	27,686	..	..	..	..	895	1,496	2,391
1926	28,162	..	..	..	..	960	1,430	2,390

A3.3.3 *continued*

Live births, stillbirths and infant mortality, Northern Ireland, 1922–98

Year	Live births	Stillbirths	Perinatal deaths	Early neonatal	Late neonatal	Neonatal deaths	Postneonatal	Infant deaths
	Numbers							
1927	26,676	..	..	..	..	806	1,268	2,074
1928	25,963	..	..	..	..	760	1,262	2,022
1929	25,410	..	..	514	294	808	1,366	2,174
1930	25,879	..	..	525	290	815	939	1,754
1931	25,673	..	..	549	277	826	1,059	1,885
1932	25,107	..	..	572	337	909	1,175	2,084
1933	24,601	..	..	548	264	812	1,148	1,960
1934	25,365	..	..	606	263	869	898	1,767
1935	24,742	..	..	565	283	848	1,288	2,136
1936	25,909	..	..	638	301	939	1,053	1,992
1937	25,412	..	..	588	322	910	1,059	1,969
1938	25,742	..	..	644	253	897	1,036	1,933
1939	25,240	..	..	562	237	799	980	1,779
1940	25,363	..	..	590	292	882	1,297	2,179
1941	26,887	..	..	583	326	909	1,150	2,059
1942	29,645	..	..	642	395	1037	1,228	2,265
1943	31,521	..	..	682	553	1235	1,229	2,464
1944	30,900	..	..	676	420	1096	987	2,083
1945	29,007	..	..	613	326	939	1,036	1,975
1946	30,134	..	..	616	167	783	843	1,626
1947	31,254	..	..	569	191	760	898	1,658
1948	29,532	..	..	454	145	599	748	1,347
1949	29,106	..	..	568	121	689	628	1,317
1950	28,794	..	..	533	142	675	491	1,166
1951	28,477	..	..	580	120	700	473	1,173
1952	28,760	..	..	567	105	672	445	1,117
1953	28,984	..	..	499	123	622	468	1,090
1954	28,803	..	..	533	89	622	329	951
1955	28,965	..	..	506	106	612	326	938
1956	29,489	..	..	510	97	607	243	850
1957	30,108	..	..	507	82	589	280	869
1958	30,301	..	..	491	88	579	271	850
1959	30,809	..	..	524	82	606	269	875
1960	31,989	..	..	571	69	640	230	870
1961	31,915	727	1,250	523	98	621	256	877
1962	32,565	745	1,265	520	71	591	273	864
1963	33,414	663	1,219	556	70	626	276	902
1964	34,345	680	1,230	550	79	629	275	904
1965	33,890	660	1,192	532	70	602	247	849
1966	33,228	550	1,039	489	77	566	283	849
1967	33,415	594	1,066	472	73	545	240	785
1968	33,173	541	992	451	71	522	274	796
1969	32,428	502	947	445	69	514	276	790
1970	32,086	465	900	435	72	507	227	734
1971	31,765	462	877	415	90	505	217	722
1972	29,994	434	790	356	62	247	198	350

A3.3.3 *continued*

Live births, stillbirths and infant mortality, Northern Ireland, 1922–98

Year	Live births	Stillbirths	Perinatal deaths	Early neonatal	Late neonatal	Neonatal deaths	Postneonatal	Infant deaths
	Numbers							
1973	29,200	389	757	368	57	425	185	610
1974	27,160	374	696	322	53	375	192	567
1975	26,130	375	677	302	42	344	190	534
1976	26,361	278	593	315	35	350	133	483
1977	25,437	310	544	234	37	271	167	438
1978	26,239	243	480	237	48	275	142	417
1979	28,178	246	472	226	39	265	152	417
1980	28,582	266	450	184	45	229	153	382
1981	27,166	240	421	181	46	227	133	360
1982	26,872	187	363	176	34	210	159	369
1983	27,026	204	359	155	44	199	130	329
1984	27,477	161	301	137	49	186	105	291
1985	27,427	178	308	130	25	155	110	265
1986	27,975	125	268	143	26	169	117	286
1987	27,653	170	276	105	30	135	107	242
1988	27,514	137	259	120	29	149	99	248
1989	25,831	133	214	81	23	104	76	180
1990	26,251	115	202	86	20	106	92	198
1991	26,028	123	222	98	23	121	73	194
1992	25,354	117	205	85	19	104	49	153
1993	24,722	101	193	90	33	123	53	176
1994	24,098	126	209	82	19	101	46	147
1995	23,693	108	213	103	28	131	38	169
1996	24,382	114	193	77	15	92	50	142
1997	24,087	99	179	79	23	102	35	137
1998	23,668	89	162	72	21	93	41	134
	Including stillbirths at 24–27 weeks of gestation							
1993	24,722	128	220	90	33	123	53	176
1994	24,098	153	236	82	19	101	46	147
1995	23,693	145	250	103	28	131	38	169
1996	24,382	153	232	77	15	92	50	142
1997	24,087	131	211	79	23	102	35	137
1998	23,668	122	195	72	21	93	41	134

∗ Rate per 1,000 total births

+ Rate per 1,000 live births

Numbers of live and still births were revised in 1999 to exclude all births to non-residents from 1981 onwards.
Babies born to non-residents are still included in denominators for perinatal and infant deaths.

Source: GRO Northern Ireland. *Annual report of the Registrar General, Northern Ireland*

This is a new table for this edition of *Birth counts*

A3.3.4

Live births, late fetal deaths and infant mortality, Irish Republic, 1922–95

Year	Sex ratio of total births male/female	Late fetal*	Perinatal*	Early neonatal+	Late neonatal+	Neonatal+	Postneonatal+	Infant+
	Ratio	**Rates**						
1922	..	..	..	..	..	26.6	42.2	68.9
1923	..	..	..	14.1	10.9	25.0	41.4	66.4
1924	..	..	..	15.7	10.5	26.2	45.4	71.7
1925	..	..	..	14.3	10.4	24.7	43.2	67.9
1926	..	..	..	15.8	10.9	26.7	47.7	74.4
1927	..	..	..	16.0	10.2	26.2	44.7	70.8
1928	..	..	..	15.0	10.7	25.7	42.2	67.9
1929	..	..	..	16.4	12.0	28.3	50.1	78.5
1930	..	..	..	16.7	10.1	26.8	41.2	67.9
1931	..	..	..	16.0	10.5	26.5	42.4	68.9
1932	..	..	..	15.1	10.9	25.9	46.2	72.2
1933	..	..	..	15.5	10.4	25.9	39.3	65.2
1934	..	..	..	14.9	9.6	24.5	38.8	63.3
1935	..	..	..	16.6	10.7	27.3	41.1	68.4
1936	..	..	..	16.7	13.4	30.1	44.1	74.1
1937	..	..	..	16.5	14.0	30.5	42.5	73.0
1938	..	..	..	14.9	9.6	24.5	38.4	66.6
1939	..	..	..	18.7	12.8	31.5	36.8	65.8
1940	..	..	..	16.9	11.0	27.9	38.5	66.4
1941	..	..	..	17.0	13.3	30.3	43.3	73.5
1942	..	..	..	14.5	9.9	24.4	45.0	69.4
1943	..	..	..	16.7	16.5	33.2	49.4	82.6
1944	..	..	..	16.2	17.0	33.2	46.2	79.4
1945	..	..	..	15.9	15.7	31.6	39.3	70.9
1946	..	..	..	15.7	12.7	28.4	36.2	64.6
1947	..	..	..	15.7	13.1	28.8	39.1	67.9
1948	..	..	..	14.6	8.5	23.2	27.1	50.3
1949	..	..	..	15.2	9.4	24.6	28.6	53.2
1950	..	..	..	15.6	7.5	23.1	22.9	46.0
1951	..	..	..	17.3	7.6	24.9	20.8	45.7
1952	..	..	..	16.4	6.5	23.0	18.4	41.4
1953	..	..	..	16.2	5.9	22.1	17.3	39.4
1954	..	..	..	16.8	5.5	22.3	15.5	37.8
1955	..	..	..	16.6	6.3	22.9	13.9	36.7
1956	..	..	..	15.7	7.1	22.7	12.9	35.6
1957	1.05	22.2	38.0	16.1	5.9	22.0	11.1	33.1
1958	1.05	20.8	37.8	17.4	6.3	23.6	11.8	35.4
1959	1.04	20.6	36.7	16.4	4.8	21.2	10.8	32.0
1960	1.05	21.9	37.7	16.1	4.3	20.4	8.9	29.3
1961	1.05	20.7	36.1	15.7	5.0	20.7	9.9	30.5
1962	1.05	19.7	34.4	15.0	4.0	19.0	10.1	29.1
1963	1.06	18.1	32.0	14.1	3.7	17.8	8.8	26.6
1964	1.05	17.3	31.8	14.8	3.4	18.2	8.5	26.7
1965	1.04	16.6	30.0	13.6	3.6	17.2	8.1	25.2
1966	1.07	15.8	28.6	13.0	3.3	16.3	8.6	24.9
1967	1.07	16.0	28.5	12.6	3.4	16.0	8.5	24.4
1968	1.07	15.1	26.6	11.7	2.3	13.9	7.0	21.0
1969	1.04	14.0	25.8	12.0	2.4	14.3	6.2	20.6

Live births, late fetal deaths and infant mortality, Irish Republic, 1922–95

Year	Sex ratio of total births male/female	Late fetal*	Perinatal*	Early neonatal+	Late neonatal+	Neonatal+	Postneonatal+	Infant+
	Ratio	**Rates**						
1970	1.06	13.9	24.3	10.6	2.2	12.8	6.8	18.4
1971	1.06	12.9	22.8	10.0	2.2	12.2	5.8	18.0
1972	1.07	13.0	23.2	10.3	1.8	12.1	6.0	18.0
1973	1.06	11.9	22.9	11.1	1.6	12.7	5.3	18.0
1974	1.06	12.4	22.0	9.7	2.0	11.6	6.2	17.8
1975	1.06	11.4	21.5	10.3	1.7	12.0	5.6	17.5
1976	1.06	11.3	19.9	8.7	1.7	10.5	5.2	15.7
1977	1.06	10.9	19.2	8.4	1.5	9.9	5.6	15.5
1978	1.04	9.3	17.6	8.4	1.5	9.8	5.0	14.9
1979	1.06	9.3	16.2	6.9	1.5	8.4	4.4	12.8
1980	1.07	9.1	14.8	5.8	1.0	6.7	4.4	11.1
1981	1.06	8.2	13.4	5.2	1.3	6.5	3.8	10.3
1982	1.05	8.0	13.5	5.6	1.0	6.6	3.9	10.5
1983	1.07	8.6	13.7	5.1	1.0	6.1	4.0	10.1
1984	1.08	8.4	13.6	5.3	0.7	6.0	3.7	9.6
1985	1.06	8.2	12.3	4.2	1.1	5.3	3.6	8.8
1986	1.07	7.7	11.8	4.1	0.9	5.0	3.9	8.9
1987	1.05	7.1	10.4	3.3	1.0	4.3	3.6	7.9
1988	1.06	7.0	11.3	4.4	1.0	5.3	3.5	8.9
1989	1.06	6.3	10.4	4.1	0.7	4.8	3.3	8.1
1990	1.08	6.1	10.2	4.1	0.7	4.8	3.4	8.2
1991	1.06	5.7	9.5	3.8	1.2	5.0	2.6	7.6
1992	1.06	5.5	9.3	3.7	0.5	4.3	2.2	6.5
1993	1.06	5.9	9.1	3.2	0.8	4.0	2.1	6.1
1994	1.07	6.1	9.3	3.2	0.8	4.0	1.7	5.7
1995	1.06	..	..	3.9	0.9	4.8	1.6	6.4

Year	Live births	Late fetal deaths	Perinatal deaths	Early neonatal	Late neonatal	Neonatal deaths	Postneonatal	Infant deaths
	Numbers							
1922	58,849	..	..	..	..	1,568	2,486	4,054
1923	61,690	..	..	868	674	1,542	2,556	4,098
1924	63,402	..	..	996	668	1,664	2,879	4,543
1925	62,069	..	..	886	647	1,533	2,683	4,216
1926	61,176	..	..	967	666	1,633	2,919	4,552
1927	60,054	..	..	960	612	1,572	2,682	4,254
1928	59,176	..	..	888	631	1,519	2,497	4,016
1929	52,280	..	..	856	626	1,482	2,620	4,102
1930	58,353	..	..	972	590	1,562	2,403	3,965
1931	57,086	..	..	912	600	1,512	2,423	3,935
1932	56,240	..	..	848	611	1,459	2,601	4,060
1933	57,364	..	..	890	595	1,485	2,257	3,742
1934	57,897	..	..	..	..	1,419	2,245	3,664
1935	58,266	..	..	..	..	1,591	2,397	3,988
1936	58,115	..	..	..	..	1,747	2,562	4,309

Live births, late fetal deaths and infant mortality, Irish Republic, 1922–95

Year	Live births	Late fetal deaths	Perinatal deaths	Early neonatal	Late neonatal	Neonatal deaths	Postneonatal	Infant deaths
	Numbers							
1937	56,488	..	..	..	..	1,720	2,401	4,121
1938	56,925	..	..	..	..	1,608	2,186	3,794
1939	56,070	..	..	..	..	1,626	2,065	3,691
1940	56,594	..	..	956	622	1,578	2,181	3,759
1941	56,780	..	..	964	755	1,719	2,456	4,175
1942	66,117	..	..	958	657	1,615	2,976	4,591
1943	64,375	..	..	1,072	1,065	2,137	3,182	5,319
1944	65,425	..	..	1,061	1,113	2,174	3,024	5,198
1945	66,861	..	..	1,063	1,047	2,110	2,629	4,739
1946	67,922	..	..	1,065	866	1,931	2,459	4,390
1947	68,978	..	..	1,086	901	1,987	2,700	4,687
1948	65,930	..	..	965	563	1,528	1,785	3,313
1949	64,153	..	..	975	605	1,580	1,835	3,415
1950	63,565	..	..	994	474	1,468	1,454	2,922
1951	62,878	..	..	1,089	479	1,568	1,308	2,876
1952	64,631	..	..	1,063	422	1,485	1,189	2,674
1953	62,558	..	..	1,015	367	1,382	1,081	2,463
1954	62,534	..	..	1,052	344	1,396	968	2,364
1955	61,622	..	..	1,023	386	1,409	855	2,264
1956	60,740	..	..	951	429	1,380	782	2,162
1957	61,242	1,391	2,377	986	362	1,348	679	2,027
1958	59,510	1,264	2,297	1,033	372	1,405	704	2,109
1959	60,188	1,267	2,253	986	290	1,276	651	1,927
1960	60,735	1,361	2,338	977	259	1,236	541	1,777
1961	59,825	1,264	2,204	940	297	1,237	590	1,827
1962	61,782	1,241	2,167	926	247	1,173	627	1,800
1963	63,246	1,169	2,061	892	232	1,124	558	1,682
1964	64,072	1,126	2,076	950	219	1,169	543	1,712
1965	63,525	1,072	1,936	864	228	1,092	512	1,604
1966	62,215	996	1,807	811	205	1,016	536	1,552
1967	61,307	1,000	1,773	773	206	979	519	1,498
1968	61,004	934	1,645	711	139	850	430	1,280
1969	62,912	893	1,645	752	148	900	393	1,293
1970	64,284	904	1,584	680	141	821	434	1,180
1971	67,551	881	1,558	677	148	825	389	1,214
1972	68,527	901	1,608	707	120	827	409	1,236
1973	68,713	829	1,590	761	112	873	361	1,234
1974	68,907	867	1,532	665	135	800	427	1,227
1975	67,178	774	1,463	689	114	803	373	1,176
1976	67,178	765	1,352	587	117	704	348	1,052
1977	68,892	757	1,334	577	104	681	388	1,069
1978	70,299	659	1,246	587	105	692	354	1,046
1979	72,539	684	1,186	502	108	610	317	927
1980	74,064	681	1,107	426	72	498	323	821
1981	72,158	600	978	378	93	471	275	746
1982	70,843	571	967	396	70	466	279	745
1983	67,117	581	926	345	64	409	268	677
1984	64,062	542	879	337	45	382	235	617
1985	62,388	516	776	260	68	328	224	552

A3.3.4 *continued*

Live births, late fetal deaths and infant mortality, Irish Republic, 1922–95

Year	Live births	Late fetal deaths	Perinatal deaths	Early neonatal	Late neonatal	Neonatal deaths	Postneonatal	Infant deaths
	Numbers							
1986	61,620	479	732	253	55	308	238	546
1987	58,433	416	610	194	58	252	212	464
1988	54,600	386	624	238	53	291	193	484
1989	52,018	330	542	212	37	249	174	423
1990	53,044	327	543	216	39	255	179	434
1991	52,718	301	502	201	63	264	137	401
1992	51,089	285	476	191	28	219	112	331
1993	49,304	291	450	159	39	198	104	302
1994	48,255	297	451	154	39	193	84	277
1995	48,787	..	..	190	42	232	79	311

* Rate per 1,000 total births
+ Rate per 1,000 live births

Stillbirth registration began in Ireland in 1995
Data in this table are from notification of late fetal deaths

Source: Central Statistics Office, Republic of Ireland

This is a new table for this edition of *Birth counts*

A3.3.5

Live births, stillbirths and infant mortality, Jersey, 1950–98

Year	Live births	Stillbirths	Early neonatal	Late neonatal	Neonatal deaths	Postneonatal	Stillbirth*	Perinatal*	Infant+
	Numbers						**Rates**		
1950	865	6	14	1	15	11	6.9	23.0	30.1
1951	844	12	20	2	22	5	14.0	37.4	32.0
1952	852	12	10	4	14	6	13.9	25.5	23.5
1953	774	18	8	3	11	7	22.7	32.8	23.3
1954	840	12	14	4	18	4	14.1	30.5	26.2
1955	736	14	15	3	18	7	18.7	38.7	34.0
1956	820	16	9	1	10	5	19.1	29.9	18.3
1957	833	11	15	3	18	2	13.0	30.8	24.0
1958	942	22	10	2	12	5	22.8	33.2	18.0
1959	950	15	12	1	13	5	15.5	28.0	18.9
1960	1,032	14	20	2	22	9	13.4	32.5	30.0
1961	1,086	20	14	3	17	12	18.1	30.7	26.7
1962	1,186	27	13	7	20	7	22.3	33.0	22.8
1963	1,282	18	12	2	14	8	13.8	23.1	17.2
1964	1,235	23	19	3	22	7	18.3	33.4	23.5
1965	1,213	20	8	3	11	9	16.2	22.7	16.5
1966	1,158	23	14	1	15	4	19.5	31.3	16.4
1967	1,124	14	19	1	20	5	12.3	29.0	22.2
1968	1,079	13	10	3	13	5	11.9	21.1	16.7
1969	1,031	21	8	0	8	4	20.0	27.6	11.6
1970	986	13	17	1	18	2	13.0	30.0	20.3
1971	984	11	12	1	13	5	11.1	23.1	18.3
1972	862	12	8	0	8	2	13.7	22.9	11.6
1973	847	12	5	0	5	1	14.0	19.8	7.1
1974	818	15	10	1	11	3	18.0	30.0	17.1
1975	828	13	1	2	3	2	15.5	16.6	6.0
1976	786	7	7	1	8	3	8.8	17.7	14.0
1977	857	7	11	1	12	2	8.1	20.8	16.3
1978	852	10	13	0	13	5	11.6	26.7	21.1
1979	884	11	9	1	10	2	12.3	22.3	13.6
1980	867	6	7	0	7	2	6.9	14.9	10.4
1981	857	1	4	1	5	2	1.2	5.8	8.2
1982	865	5	2	0	2	4	5.7	8.0	6.9
1983	884	2	1	0	1	6	2.3	3.4	7.9
1984	931	5	3	1	4	4	5.3	8.5	8.6
1985	907	5	6	0	6	3	5.5	12.1	9.9
1986	948	1	4	0	4	1	1.1	5.3	5.3
1987	1,009	5	6	2	8	6	4.9	10.8	13.9
1988	1,071	4	7	1	8	3	3.7	10.2	10.3
1989	1,074	2	3	0	3	1	1.9	4.6	3.7
1990	1,112	6	4	1	5	2	5.4	8.9	6.3
1991	1,057	3	3	0	3	2	2.8	5.7	4.7
1992	1,137	6	1	0	1	2	5.2	6.1	2.6
1993	1,057	5	4	0	4	3	4.7	8.5	6.6
1994	1,142	4	1	0	1	2	3.5	4.4	2.6
1995	1,112	6	6	1	7	0	5.4	10.7	6.3
1996	1,108	3	2	1	3	3	2.7	4.5	5.4
1997	1,100	2	3	0	3	2	1.8	4.5	4.5
1998	1,126	1	5	0	5	1	0.9	5.3	5.3

* Rate per 1,000 total births
+ Rate per 1,000 live births

Source: States of Jersey. *Report of the Medical Officer of Health.*

This is a new table for this edition of *Birth counts*

A3.3.6

Live births, stillbirths and infant mortality, Guernsey, 1911–98

Year	Live births	Stillbirths	Early neonatal	Late neonatal	Neonatal deaths	Postneonatal	Stillbirth*	Perinatal*	Infant+
	Numbers						**Rates**		
1911	946	53	..	..	..	..	53.1	..	..
1916	698	36	..	..	..	..	49.0	..	..
1921	768	46	..	..	..	..	56.5	..	..
1926	787	35	..	..	..	..	42.6	..	..
1931	764	27	..	..	..	..	34.1	..	..
1935	777	..	..	..	..	..	..	..	59.2
1936	708	..	..	..	..	..	..	..	59.3
1937	827	..	..	..	..	..	37.8	..	53.2
1938	851	..	..	..	..	..	37.6	..	43.4
1939	744	..	..	..	..	..	43.2	..	44.3
1940	568	..	..	..	..	..	28.5	..	47.5
1941	243	21	..	..	..	..	20.8	..	20.5
1942	262	..	..	..	..	..	30.7	..	38.1
1943	337	..	..	..	..	..	15.1	..	47.5
1944	395	..	..	..	..	..	20.2	..	43.0
1945	391	..	..	..	..	..	23.0	..	28.1
1946	872	..	..	..	..	..	21.7	..	40.1
1947	900	..	..	..	..	..	18.9	..	33.3
1948	870	..	..	..	..	..	24.2	..	19.5
1949	795	..	..	..	..	..	23.9	..	25.1
1950	746	..	..	..	..	..	20.1	..	29.5
1951	775	..	..	..	..	..	14.2	..	14.2
1952	736	..	..	..	..	..	21.7	..	32.6
1953	727	..	..	..	..	..	20.6	..	31.6
1954	689	..	..	..	..	..	13.1	..	13.1
1955	667	..	..	..	..	..	8.9	..	26.9
1956	701	..	..	..	..	..	24.2	..	19.9
1957	725	..	..	..	..	..	18.0	..	33.0
1958	717	..	..	..	..	..	22.3	..	22.3
1959	709	..	..	..	..	..	19.7	..	19.7
1960	769	17	..	..	10	2	21.6	..	14.3
1961	757	19	..	..	13	3	24.5	..	21.1
1962	797	15	..	..	9	6	18.5	..	18.8
1963	842	13	..	..	21	3	15.2	..	28.5
1964	891	7	11	3	14	5	7.8	20.1	21.3
1965	816	11	8	3	11	5	13.3	23.0	19.6
1966	780	12	10	2	12	1	15.2	27.8	16.7
1967	741	16	10	6	16	8	21.1	42.3	32.4
1968	752	10	9	0	9	7	13.1	24.9	21.3
1969	830	8	10	0	10	4	9.5	21.5	16.9
1970	794	7	10	0	10	3	8.7	21.2	16.4
1971	766	12	7	1	8	2	15.4	24.4	13.1
1972	790	7	7	2	9	5	8.8	17.6	17.7
1973	652	8	8	0	8	3	12.1	24.2	16.9

A3.3.6 continued

Live births, stillbirths and infant mortality, Guernsey, 1911–98

Year	Live births	Stillbirths~	Early neonatal	Late neonatal	Neonatal deaths	Postneonatal	Stillbirth*	Perinatal*	Infant+
	Numbers						**Rates**		
1974	679	10	5	1	6	3	14.5	21.8	13.3
1975	611	10	6	2	8	1	16.1	25.8	14.7
1976	623	7	8	0	8	1	11.1	23.8	14.5
1977	587	3	1	0	1	4	5.1	6.8	8.5
1978	582	6	4	0	4	5	10.2	17.0	15.5
1979	646	3	5	0	5	3	4.6	12.3	12.4
1980	622	5	4	2	6	2	7.9	14.4	12.9
1981	619	5	4	3	7	4	8.0	14.4	17.8
1982	589	3	2	3	5	1	5.1	8.5	10.2
1983	660	4	2	2	4	1	6.1	9.0	7.6
1984	596	3	4	0	4	2	5.0	11.7	10.1
1985	642	7	3	0	3	1	10.8	15.4	6.2
1986	671	4	1	0	1	1	5.9	7.4	3.0
1987	644	4	2	1	3	1	6.2	9.3	6.2
1988	680	3	3	0	3	2	4.4	8.8	7.4
1989	688	3	2	0	2	2	4.3	7.2	5.8
1990	728	4	0	0	0	1	5.3	5.3	1.4
1991	737	3	2	2	4	1	4.1	6.5	6.8
1992	701	6	4	2	6	2	8.5	13.5	11.4
1993	681	4	3	0	3	4	5.9	10.2	10.3
1994	676	4	2	0	2	2	5.9	5.9	4.6
1995	624	4	1	0	1	1	6.4	7.9	3.2
1996	660	3	2	2	4	1	4.5	7.5	7.6
1997	672	3	3	0	3	0	2.2	8.9	4.5
1998	678	7	2	0	2	0	10.2	13.1	3.0

* Rate per 1,000 total births

~ Up to 1996, fetal deaths at 28 or more weeks of gestation were registrable as stillbirths. The limit was lowered to 24 weeks in 1997

+ Rate per 1,000 live births

Between 1990 and 1994, there was no Medical Officer of Health in post in Guernsey and discrepancies appeared in published data. Recent data are for Guernsey only. Earlier data may include events in Alderney and Sark. In some years, no distinction was made between early and late neonatal deaths in published tables.

Source: States of Guernsey, *Reports of the Medical Officer of Health*

This is a new table for this edition of *Birth counts*

A3.3.7

Live births, stillbirths and infant mortality, Isle of Man, 1992–98

Year	Live births	Stillbirths	Neonatal	Postneonatal	Infant	Stillbirth*	Infant+
	Numbers					**Rates**	
1992	858	2	2	0	2	2.3	2.3
1993	853	2	3	2	5	2.3	5.9
1994	883	5	2	6	8	5.6	9.1
1995	847	4	1	0	1	4.7	1.2
1996	835	3	2	0	2	3.6	2.4
1997	870	5	3	0 .	3	5.7	3.4
1998	936	4	1	0	1	4.3	1.1

* Rate per 1,000 total births
+ Rate per 1,000 live births

Source: Isle of Man. *Chief Registrar's annual report and statistical review of births, deaths and marriages in the Isle of Man.*

This is a new table for this edition of *Birth counts*

A3.4.1

Incidence of low birthweight, England and Wales, 1953–86

Year	All births notified	Number of births with birthweight, g						
		1,000 and under	1,001– 1,500	1,500 and under	1,501– 2,000	2,001– 2,250	2,251– 2,500	2,500 and under*
	Live births							
1953	688,999	..	..	5,358	8,584	8,948	22,575	45,465
1954	671,063	..	..	5,193	8,451	9,074	23,300	46,018
1955	665,414	..	..	5,368	8,477	9,204	23,083	46,132
1956	697,141	..	..	5,455	8,711	9,705	23,641	47,512
1957	721,511	..	..	5,782	9,112	10,007	25,267	50,168
1958	741,364	..	..	5,661	9,228	10,160	25,693	50,742
1959	747,891	..	..	5,789	8,783	10,197	25,541	50,310
1960	784,268	..	..	5,970	9,503	10,599	26,561	52,633
1961	810,595	..	..	6,387	9,815	11,008	27,422	54,632
1962	837,852	..	..	6,249	9,797	11,550	28,403	55,999
1963	852,708	2,319	4,031	6,350	10,160	11,917	27,745	56,172
1964	875,800	2,358	4,037	6,395	9,958	11,545	27,954	55,852
1965	860,716	2,202	3,785	5,987	9,756	11,209	27,791	54,743
1966	848,408	2,211	3,682	5,893	9,759	11,746	27,807	55,205
1967	827,762	2,004	3,743	5,747	9,492	11,300	27,265	53,804
1968	814,609	2,211	3,776	5,987	9,687	11,519	26,987	54,180
1969	795,842	2,058	3,570	5,628	9,484	11,707	26,587	53,406
1970	782,357	2,013	3,818	5,831	9,460	11,759	26,464	53,514
1971	782,396	1,889	3,437	5,326	8,826	11,071	24,663	49,886
1972	726,959	1,667	3,285	4,952	8,415	10,779	23,795	47,941
1973	675,927	1,519	2,988	4,507	7,689	9,924	21,479	43,599
1974	639,113	1,615	2,865	4,480	7,309	9,294	20,247	41,330
1975	603,726	1,394	2,866	4,260	6,902	8,840	18,610	38,612
1976	584,512	1,326	2,773	4,099	6,840	8,564	17,932	37,435
1977	569,368	1,332	2,622	3,954	6,865	8,411	17,685	36,915
1978	597,003	1,366	3,042	4,408	7,200	8,650	18,762	39,020
1979	638,124	1,582	3,174	4,756	7,924	9,672	20,536	42,888
1980	656,812	1,604	3,478	5,082	8,362	9,944	21,241	44,629
1981	635,942	1,568	3,403	4,971	8,128	9,609	20,224	42,932
1982	625,066	1,533	3,398	4,931	7,853	9,509	19,801	42,094
1983	628,467	1,737	3,496	5,233	8,007	9,260	19,824	42,568
1984	636,441	1,880	3,564	5,444	8,207	9,427	19,876	43,132
1985	655,868	1,887	3,839	5,726	8,476	9,709	20,480	44,531
1986	662,637	1,982	3,802	5,784	8,919	10,067	20,599	45,473
	Stillbirths							
1953	15,434	..	..	..	..	..	..	..
1954	15,771	..	..	..	..	..	..	..
1955	15,427	..	..	3,551	2,227	946	1,337	8,061
1956	16,133	..	..	3,697	2,273	961	1,374	8,305
1957	16,193	..	..	3,955	2,378	999	1,391	8,723
1958	16,026	..	..	3,928	2,326	1,039	1,372	8,665
1959	15,403	..	..	3,756	2,314	976	1,292	8,338
1960	15,442	..	..	3,828	2,259	963	1,377	8,427
1961	15,278	..	..	3,913	2,363	981	1,322	8,579
1962	15,162	..	..	3,985	2,279	1,021	1,251	8,536

A3.4.1 *continued*

Incidence of low birthweight, England and Wales, 1953–86

Year	All births notified	Number of births with birthweight, g						
		1,000 and under	1,001– 1,500	1,500 and under	1,501– 2,000	2,001– 2,250	2,251– 2,500	2,500 and under*
1963	14,654	1,549	2,358	3,907	2,343	949	1,287	8,486
1964	14,434	1,615	2,289	3,904	2,185	942	1,171	8,202
1965	13,644	1,463	2,174	3,637	2,089	910	1,132	7,768
1966	13,088	1,499	2,036	3,535	2,110	940	1,109	7,694
1967	12,295	1,417	1,994	3,411	1,956	901	1,100	7,368
1968	11,758	1,332	1,904	3,236	1,801	805	967	6,809
1969	10,489	1,277	1,744	3,021	1,598	752	822	6,193
1970	10,094	1,250	1,731	2,981	1,580	767	843	6,171
1971	9,795	1,248	1,612	2,860	1,501	678	742	5,781
1972	8,638	1,097	1,435	2,532	1,346	625	658	5,161
1973	7,696	1,029	1,362	2,391	1,251	628	622	4,892
1974	6,891	894	1,236	2,130	1,109	510	500	4,249
1975	6,196	814	1,049	1,863	925	449	455	3,692
1976	5,640	734	1,065	1,799	904	391	429	3,523
1977	5,324	721	1,014	1,735	916	379	429	3,459
1978	5,039	690	996	1,686	841	362	392	3,281
1979	5,039	708	986	1,694	811	387	403	3,295
1980	4,737	667	917	1,584	804	352	381	3,121
1981	4,161	635	746	1,381	707	297	333	2,718
1982	3,892	515	669	1,184	613	269	310	2,418
1983	3,589	504	615	1,119	574	292	263	2,282
1984	3,604	511	625	1,136	512	292	312	2,291
1985	3,595	513	555	1,068	598	289	304	2,282
1986	3,548	510	599	1,109	511	296	286	2,225

Year	All births notified	Percentage of births with birthweight g						
		1,000 and under	1,001– 1,500	1,500 and under	1,501– 2,000	2,001– 2,250	2,251– 2,500	2,500 and under*
	Live births							
1953	688,999	..	..	0.78	1.25	1.30	3.28	6.60
1954	671,063	..	..	0.77	1.26	1.35	3.47	6.86
1955	665,414	..	..	0.81	1.27	1.38	3.47	6.93
1956	697,141	..	..	0.78	1.25	1.39	3.39	6.82
1957	721,511	..	..	0.80	1.26	1.39	3.50	6.95
1958	741,364	..	..	0.76	1.24	1.37	3.47	6.84
1959	747,891	..	..	0.77	1.17	1.36	3.42	6.73
1960	784,268	..	..	0.76	1.21	1.35	3.39	6.71
1961	810,595	..	..	0.79	1.21	1.36	3.38	6.74
1962	837,852	..	..	0.75	1.17	1.38	3.39	6.68
1963	852,708	0.27	0.47	0.74	1.19	1.40	3.25	6.59
1964	875,800	0.27	0.46	0.73	1.14	1.32	3.19	6.38
1965	860,716	0.26	0.44	0.70	1.13	1.30	3.23	6.36
1966	848,408	0.26	0.43	0.69	1.15	1.38	3.28	6.51
1967	827,762	0.24	0.45	0.69	1.15	1.37	3.29	6.50

A3.4.1 *continued*

Incidence of low birthweight, England and Wales, 1953–86

Year	All births notified	Percentage of births with birthweight, g						
		1,000 and under	1,001– 1,500	1,500 and under	1,501– 2,000	2,001– 2,250	2,251– 2,500	2,500 and under*
	Live births							
1968	814,609	0.27	0.46	0.73	1.19	1.41	3.31	6.65
1969	795,842	0.26	0.45	0.71	1.19	1.47	3.34	6.71
1970	782,357	0.26	0.49	0.75	1.21	1.50	3.38	6.84
1971	782,396	0.24	0.44	0.68	1.13	1.42	3.15	6.38
1972	726,959	0.23	0.45	0.68	1.16	1.48	3.27	6.59
1973	675,927	0.22	0.44	0.67	1.14	1.47	3.18	6.45
1974	639,113	0.25	0.45	0.70	1.14	1.45	3.17	6.47
1975	603,726	0.23	0.47	0.71	1.14	1.46	3.08	6.40
1976	584,512	0.23	0.47	0.70	1.17	1.47	3.07	6.40
1977	569,368	0.23	0.46	0.69	1.21	1.48	3.11	6.48
1978	597,003	0.23	0.51	0.74	1.21	1.45	3.14	6.54
1979	638,124	0.25	0.50	0.75	1.24	1.52	3.22	6.72
1980	656,812	0.24	0.53	0.77	1.27	1.51	3.23	6.79
1981	635,942	0.25	0.54	0.78	1.28	1.51	3.18	6.75
1982	625,066	0.26	0.56	0.82	1.29	1.52	3.17	6.84
1983	628,467	0.28	0.56	0.83	1.27	1.47	3.15	6.77
1984	636,441	0.30	0.56	0.86	1.29	1.48	3.12	6.78
1985	655,868	0.29	0.59	0.87	1.29	1.48	3.12	6.79
1986	662,637	0.30	0.57	0.87	1.35	1.52	3.11	6.86
	Total births							
1955	665,414	..	..	1.31	1.57	1.49	3.59	7.96
1956	697,141	..	..	1.28	1.54	1.50	3.51	7.83
1957	721,511	..	..	1.32	1.56	1.49	3.61	7.98
1958	741,364	..	..	1.27	1.53	1.48	3.57	7.84
1959	747,891	..	..	1.25	1.45	1.46	3.52	7.68
1960	784,268	..	..	1.23	1.47	1.45	3.49	7.64
1961	810,595	..	..	1.25	1.47	1.45	3.48	7.65
1962	837,852	..	..	1.20	1.42	1.47	3.48	7.57
1963	852,708	0.45	0.74	1.18	1.44	1.48	3.35	7.45
1964	875,800	0.45	0.71	1.16	1.36	1.40	3.27	7.20
1965	860,716	0.42	0.68	1.10	1.35	1.39	3.31	7.15
1966	848,408	0.43	0.66	1.09	1.38	1.47	3.36	7.30
1967	827,762	0.41	0.68	1.09	1.36	1.45	3.38	7.28
1968	814,609	0.43	0.69	1.12	1.39	1.49	3.38	7.38
1969	795,842	0.41	0.66	1.07	1.37	1.55	3.40	7.39
1970	782,357	0.41	0.70	1.11	1.39	1.58	3.45	7.53
1971	782,396	0.40	0.64	1.03	1.30	1.48	3.21	7.03
1972	726,959	0.38	0.64	1.02	1.33	1.55	3.32	7.22
1973	675,927	0.37	0.64	1.01	1.31	1.54	3.23	7.09
1974	639,113	0.39	0.63	1.02	1.30	1.52	3.21	7.06
1975	603,726	0.36	0.64	1.00	1.28	1.52	3.13	6.94
1976	584,512	0.35	0.65	1.00	1.31	1.52	3.11	6.94
1977	569,368	0.36	0.63	0.99	1.35	1.53	3.15	7.03
1978	597,003	0.34	0.67	1.01	1.34	1.50	3.18	7.03
1979	638,124	0.36	0.65	1.00	1.36	1.56	3.26	7.18

A3.4.1 *continued*

Incidence of low birthweight, England and Wales, 1953–86

Year	All births notified	Percentage of births with birthweight, g						
		1,000 and under	1,001– 1,500	1,500 and under	1,501– 2,000	2,001– 2,250	2,251– 2,500	2,500 and under*
	Total births							
1980	656,812	0.34	0.66	1.01	1.39	1.56	3.27	7.22
1981	635,942	0.34	0.65	0.99	1.38	1.55	3.21	7.13
1982	625,066	0.34	0.66	1.00	1.38	1.55	3.20	7.18
1983	628,467	0.35	0.65	1.00	1.36	1.51	3.18	7.10
1984	636,441	0.37	0.65	1.03	1.36	1.52	3.15	7.10
1985	655,868	0.36	0.67	1.03	1.38	1.52	3.15	7.10
1986	662,637	0.37	0.66	1.03	1.42	1.56	3.14	7.16

* Including a small number of low birthweight babies whose actual birthweight was not stated.

Source: DHSS annual summaries of LHS 27/1 low birthweight returns

Data for more recent years are in table A3.4.2

This was Table A3.6 in the first edition of *Birth counts*

A3.4.2

Incidence of low birthweight, England and Wales, 1982–98

Year	All births	All with stated birthweight	Number of births with birthweight, g											Not stated
			Under 500	500–999	Under 1,000	1,000–1,499	1,500–1,999	2,000–2,499	2,500–2,999	3,000–3,499	3,500–3,999	4,000–4,499	4,500 and over	
Live births														
1982	625,931	598,579	108	1,334	1,442	3,330	7,529	27,632	112,628	231,590	163,335	44,553	6,540	27,352
1983	629,134	628,269	121	1,595	1,716	3,590	7,917	28,866	116,936	242,998	171,972	47,424	6,850	865
1984	636,818	636,006	143	1,731	1,874	3,680	8,145	28,932	117,201	245,018	175,909	47,992	7,255	812
1985	656,417	655,549	141	2,171	1,922	3,978	8,556	30,208	120,463	251,653	180,646	50,527	7,596	868
1986	661,018	660,394	148	1,917	2,065	4,016	8,894	30,753	119,810	252,035	183,114	51,842	7,865	624
1987	681,511	681,009	150	1,993	2,143	4,362	9,066	30,958	120,696	258,658	191,057	55,482	8,587	502
1988	693,577	692,746	173	2,036	2,209	4,302	8,989	30,181	118,808	260,932	198,593	59,299	9,433	831
1989	687,725	666,612	479	1,959	2,438	4,109	8,785	29,646	115,065	249,378	190,572	57,226	9,393	21,113
1990	706,140	678,374	255	2,059	2,314	4,186	8,924	30,631	116,754	252,688	193,742	59,439	9,696	27,766
1991	699,217	673,299	130	2,173	2,303	4,171	9,131	30,764	113,813	249,729	193,530	59,864	9,994	25,918
1992	689,656	663,719	128	2,282	2,410	4,232	8,693	29,496	110,594	242,400	193,393	61,951	10,550	25,937
1993	671,224	649,328	313	2,224	2,537	4,176	9,036	28,712	106,941	235,562	190,054	61,532	10,778	21,896
1994	664,256	647,380	428	2,427	2,855	4,429	9,145	28,752	107,109	234,250	188,920	61,199	10,721	16,876
1995	648,001	645,784	260	2,619	2,879	4,704	9,679	30,062	109,436	234,752	185,122	59,095	10,055	2,217
1996	649,489	647,951	317	2,833	3,150	4,770	9,405	29,862	109,053	234,310	187,009	59,852	10,540	1,538
1997	643,095	641,979	342	2,684	3,026	4,850	9,846	30,090	108,577	231,804	184,244	59,120	10,422	1,116
1998	635,901	635,116	285	2,763	3,048	4,692	9,505	30,265	106,887	227,978	182,504	59,863	10,374	785
Stillbirths at 28 or more completed weeks of gestation														
1982	3,943	3,501	48	392	440	618	568	558	558	455	198	67	39	442
1983	3,632	3,580	56	416	472	642	587	565	577	425	217	74	21	52
1984	3,650	3,581	65	424	490	612	533	615	563	427	237	72	32	69
1985	3,650	3,589	71	427	499	580	584	575	576	472	189	84	30	61
1986	3,548	3,521	72	426	497	621	500	589	530	466	213	69	36	27
1987	3,421	3,388	75	385	461	566	579	495	553	407	218	70	39	33
1988	3,385	3,365	74	340	413	545	541	525	525	460	241	84	31	20
1989	3,231	3,110	66	325	391	449	502	521	506	423	217	66	35	121
1990	3,259	3,107	60	326	386	511	544	465	455	442	215	61	28	152
1991	3,255	3,091	46	321	367	492	509	476	500	420	219	68	40	164
1992	3,156	2,992	67	287	522	417	426	435	438	429	221	69	35	164
1993	2,960	2,744	106	278	384	398	413	426	438	387	204	64	30	216
1994	2,925	2,796	125	288	413	402	386	414	443	403	213	88	34	129

A3.4.2 continued

Incidence of low birthweight, England and Wales, 1982–98

Year	All births	All with stated birthweight	Number of births with birthweight, g											Not stated
			Under 500	500–999	Under 1,000	1,000–1,499	1,500–1,999	2,000–2,499	2,500–2,999	3,000–3,499	3,500–3,999	4,000–4,499	4,500 and over	
1995	2,704	2,654	90	263	353	419	391	400	426	375	198	65	27	50
1996	2,598	2,555	113	257	370	367	370	373	441	365	185	60	24	43
1997	2,546	2,501	..	..	344	348	366	397	416	348	202	80*		45

Stillbirths at 24 or more completed weeks of gestation

Year	All births	All with stated birthweight	Under 500	500–999	Under 1,000	1,000–1,499	1,500–1,999	2,000–2,499	2,500–2,999	3,000–3,499	3,500–3,999	4,000–4,499	4,500 and over	Not stated
1993	3,866	3,586	293	843	1,136	472	420	430	440	388	204	64	32	280
1994	3,816	3,666	339	856	1,195	473	396	416	444	403	214	90	35	150
1995	3,597	3,522	304	815	1,119	506	399	402	429	376	198	65	28	75
1996	3,539	3,477	354	860	1,214	435	376	374	443	365	185	60	25	62
1997	3,439	3,362	..	..	1,122	410	380	400	417	351	202	80*		77
1998	3,417	3,358	..	..	1,128	458	374	391	393	343	..	..	..	59

Percentage of births with stated birthweight, g

Year	Under 1,000	1,000–1,499	Under 1,500	1,500–1,999	2,000–2,499	Under 2,500	2,500–2,999	3,000–3,499	3,500–3,999	4,000–4,499	4,500 and over	Percentage of births having birthweight unstated
Live births												
1982	0.24	0.56	0.80	1.26	4.62	6.67	18.82	38.69	27.29	7.44	1.09	4.37
1983	0.27	0.57	0.84	1.26	4.59	6.70	18.61	38.68	27.37	7.55	1.09	0.14
1984	0.29	0.58	0.87	1.28	4.55	6.70	18.43	38.52	27.66	7.55	1.14	0.13
1985	0.29	0.61	0.90	1.31	4.61	6.81	18.38	38.39	27.56	7.71	1.16	0.13
1986	0.31	0.61	0.92	1.35	4.66	6.92	18.14	38.16	27.73	7.85	1.19	0.09
1987	0.31	0.64	0.96	1.33	4.55	6.83	17.72	37.98	28.05	8.15	1.26	0.07
1988	0.32	0.62	0.94	1.30	4.36	6.59	17.15	37.67	28.67	8.56	1.36	0.12
1989	0.37	0.62	0.98	1.32	4.45	6.75	17.26	37.41	28.59	8.58	1.41	3.07
1990	0.34	0.62	0.96	1.32	4.52	6.79	17.21	37.25	28.56	8.76	1.43	3.93
1991	0.34	0.62	0.96	1.36	4.57	6.89	16.90	37.09	28.74	8.89	1.48	3.71
1992	0.36	0.64	1.00	1.31	4.44	6.75	16.66	36.52	29.14	9.33	1.59	3.76

A3.4.2 *continued*

Incidence of low birthweight, England and Wales, 1982–98

	Percentage of births with stated birthweight, g											Percentage of births having birthweight unstated
	Under 1,000	1,000–1,499	Under 1,500	1,500–1,999	2,000–2,499	Under 2,500	2,500–2,999	3,000–3,499	3,500–3,999	4,000–4,499	4,500 and over	
1993	0.39	0.64	1.03	1.39	4.42	6.85	16.47	36.28	29.27	9.48	1.66	3.26
1994	0.44	0.68	1.13	1.41	4.44	6.98	16.54	36.18	29.18	9.45	1.66	2.54
1995	0.45	0.73	1.17	1.50	4.66	7.33	16.95	36.35	28.67	9.15	1.56	0.34
1996	0.49	0.74	1.22	1.45	4.61	7.28	16.83	36.16	28.86	9.24	1.63	0.24
1997	0.47	0.76	1.23	1.53	4.69	7.45	16.91	36.10	28.70	9.21	1.62	0.17
1998	0.48	0.74	1.22	1.50	4.76	7.48	16.83	35.90	28.74	9.43	1.63	0.12
Total births excluding stillbirths at 24–27 weeks of gestation												
1982	0.31	0.66	0.97	1.34	4.68	7.00	18.80	38.54	27.16	7.41	1.09	4.41
1983	0.35	0.67	1.02	1.35	4.66	7.02	18.60	38.53	27.25	7.52	1.09	0.14
1984	0.37	0.67	1.04	1.36	4.62	7.02	18.41	38.38	27.54	7.51	1.14	0.14
1985	0.37	0.69	1.06	1.39	4.67	7.12	18.36	38.25	27.44	7.68	1.16	0.14
1986	0.39	0.70	1.08	1.41	4.72	7.22	18.13	38.03	27.61	7.82	1.19	0.10
1987	0.38	0.72	1.10	1.41	4.60	7.11	17.72	37.85	27.95	8.12	1.26	0.08
1988	0.38	0.70	1.07	1.37	4.41	6.85	17.14	37.55	28.56	8.53	1.36	0.12
1989	0.42	0.68	1.10	1.39	4.50	6.99	17.26	37.30	28.49	8.55	1.41	3.07
1990	0.40	0.69	1.09	1.39	4.56	7.04	17.20	37.14	28.46	8.73	1.43	3.94
1991	0.39	0.69	1.08	1.43	4.62	7.13	16.90	36.98	28.64	8.86	1.48	3.71
1992	0.44	0.70	1.14	1.37	4.49	6.99	16.65	36.42	29.04	9.30	1.59	3.77
1993	0.45	0.70	1.15	1.45	4.47	7.07	16.47	36.18	29.18	9.45	1.66	3.28
1994	0.50	0.74	1.25	1.47	4.49	7.20	16.54	36.09	29.09	9.43	1.65	2.55
1995	0.50	0.79	1.29	1.55	4.70	7.54	16.94	36.26	28.58	9.12	1.55	0.35
1996	0.54	0.79	1.33	1.50	4.65	7.48	16.83	36.08	28.78	9.21	1.62	0.24
1997	0.52	0.81	1.33	1.58	4.73	7.64	16.91	36.02	28.62	10.80*		0.18

A3.4.2 continued

Incidence of low birthweight, England and Wales, 1982–98

	Percentage of births with stated birthweight, g										Percentage of births having birthweight unstated
	Under 1,000	1,000–1,499	Under 1,500	1,500–1,999	2,000–2,499	Under 2,500	2,500–2,999	3,000–3,499	3,500–3,999	4,000–4,499	4,500 and over	
Total births including stillbirths at 24–27 weeks of gestation												
1993	0.56	0.71	1.27	1.45	4.46	7.19	16.45	36.14	29.14	9.43	1.66	3.28
1994	0.62	0.75	1.38	1.47	4.48	7.32	16.52	36.04	29.05	9.41	1.65	2.55
1995	0.62	0.80	1.42	1.55	4.69	7.66	16.92	36.21	28.54	9.11	1.55	0.35
1996	0.67	0.80	1.47	1.50	4.64	7.61	16.81	36.02	28.74	9.20	1.62	0.25
1997	0.64	0.82	1.46	1.58	4.72	7.77	16.89	35.97	28.58	10.79*		0.18
1998	0.65	0.81	1.46	1.55	4.80	7.81	16.80	35.76	..	..	..	0.13

* 4,000g and over

Source: Authors' analysis of ONS data up to 1996
1997 data from *Mortality statistics, Series DH3, no 30*
1998 data from VS 5 tabulations.

Data for earlier years are in Table A3.4.1

Data extract: live births 1993 (7/94), 1994 (7/95), 1995 (3/7/96), 1996 (8/4/97)
linked 1993 (3/4/96), 1994 (18/9/96), 1995 (3/11/97)

This is similar to Table A3.6 in the first edition of *Birth counts*

A3.4.3

Stillbirths by gestational age, England and Wales, 1974–98

Year	Gestational age, weeks										Total
	28–29	30–31	32–33	34–35	36–37	38–39	40	41–42	43 and over	Not stated	
1974	496	688	911	893	1,174	1,104	955	434	40	480	7,175
1975	458	618	759	826	1,001	993	800	397	42	401	6,295
1976	393	618	726	763	856	891	752	344	20	346	5,709
1977	439	571	720	720	882	836	613	307	25	292	5,405
1978	408	569	683	669	832	744	615	270	19	299	5,108
1979	447	533	678	682	814	798	558	259	10	346	5,125
1980	413	530	648	659	742	729	483	228	12	329	4,773
1981	207	216	262	243	282	308	209	117	6	171	2,021
1982	339	432	508	463	622	604	417	213	8	332	3,938
1983	333	405	435	452	574	603	363	185	9	272	3,631
1984	386	415	469	467	580	563	368	182	10	203	3,643
1985	372	404	473	444	552	626	345	171	10	248	3,645
1986	395	416	444	452	556	567	335	202	13	169	3,549
1987	370	391	443	446	544	534	327	197	9	162	3,423
1988	401	405	379	411	555	542	344	209	12	124	3,382
1989	379	322	407	403	526	553	347	168	7	124	3,236
1990	377	404	418	394	473	553	302	210	9	116	3,256
1991	381	381	397	410	490	556	294	209	11	125	3,254
1992	336	294	359	358	456	501	305	207	5	23	2,944

Year	Gestational age, weeks						Total
	24–27	28–31	32–35	36–39	40 and over	Not stated	
1993	906	665	695	956	455	189	3,866
1994	891	692	676	936	509	112	3,816
1995	893	668	661	926	424	25	3,597
1996	941	620	652	919	392	15	3,539
1997	894	605	628	889	421	4	3,441
1998	942	578	632	829	425	11	3,417

Source: ONS and OPCS. Mortality statistics, perinatal and infant, Series DH3.

This is a new table for this edition of *Birth counts*

A3.4.4

Singleton low birthweight and pre-term births, Scotland, 1976–98

Year	Total singleton births	Birthweight under 2,500 g		Born before 37 weeks of gestation	
		Number	Percentage of all singleton births	Number	Percentage of all singleton births
1976	63,051	4,123	6.5	4,632	7.3
1977	60,726	3,966	6.5	4,470	7.4
1978	62,948	3,989	6.3	4,380	7.0
1979	66,001	4,214	6.4	4,754	7.2
1980	66,419	4,068	6.1	3,675	5.5
1981	67,288	4,075	6.1	3,492	5.2
1982	64,351	3,807	5.9	3,407	5.3
1983	63,294	3,795	6.0	3,540	5.6
1984	63,530	3,746	5.9	3,686	5.8
1985	64,280	3,889	6.1	3,557	5.5
1986	63,968	3,808	6.0	3,557	5.6
1987	64,206	3,760	5.9	3,511	5.5
1988	64,722	3,824	5.9	3,769	5.8
1989	62,290	3,601	5.8	3,505	5.6
1990	63,819	3,750	5.9	3,763	5.9
1991	65,280	3,857	5.9	3,689	5.7
1992	63,433	3,690	5.8	3,756	5.9
1993	61,728	3,492	5.7	3,502	5.7
1994	59,929	3,565	5.9	3,582	6.0
1995+	58,377	3,479	6.0	3,486	6.0
1996+	56,231	3,289	5.8	3,448	6.1
1997*	57,449	3,346	5.8	3,436	6.0
1998*	53,180	3,146	5.9	3,237	6.1

Source: ISD. SMR2 returns

* provisional
+ revised

This is a new table for this edition of Birth counts

A3.5.1

Stillbirth and neonatal mortality rates by birthweight, England and Wales, 1953–86

Year	1,000g and under	1,001–1,500g	1,500g and under	1,501–2,000g	2,001–2,250g	2,251–2,500g	2,500 and under	2,501 and over, estimated

Stillbirth rates at 28 or more weeks gestation per 1,000 total births

Year	1,000g and under	1,001–1,500g	1,500g and under	1,501–2,000g	2,001–2,250g	2,251–2,500g	2,500 and under	2,501 and over, estimated
1953	..	..	..	..	..	..	140.1	..
1954	..	..	..	..	..	..	150.4	..
1955	..	..	398.1	208.1	93.2	54.8	148.7	12.3
1956	..	..	404.0	206.9	90.1	54.9	148.8	12.3
1957	..	..	406.2	207.0	90.8	52.2	148.1	11.6
1958	..	..	409.6	201.3	92.8	50.7	145.9	10.9
1959	..	..	393.5	208.5	87.4	48.1	142.2	10.7
1960	..	..	390.7	192.1	83.3	49.3	138.0	10.0
1961	..	..	379.9	194.0	81.8	46.0	135.7	9.4
1962	..	..	389.4	188.7	81.2	42.2	132.3	8.8
1963	400.5	369.1	380.9	187.4	73.8	44.3	131.2	7.7
1964	406.6	361.8	379.1	179.9	75.4	40.2	128.0	7.5
1965	399.2	364.8	377.9	176.4	75.1	39.1	124.3	7.2
1966	404.0	356.1	374.9	177.8	74.1	38.4	122.3	6.7
1967	414.2	347.5	372.5	170.9	73.8	38.8	120.4	6.3
1968	376.0	335.2	350.9	156.8	65.3	34.6	111.6	6.5
1969	382.9	328.2	349.3	144.2	60.4	30.0	103.9	5.8
1970	383.1	311.9	338.3	143.1	61.2	30.9	103.4	5.4
1971	397.8	319.3	349.4	145.3	57.7	29.2	103.8	5.4
1972	396.9	304.0	338.3	137.9	51.1	26.9	97.2	5.1
1973	403.8	313.1	346.6	139.9	59.5	28.1	100.9	4.4
1974	356.3	301.4	322.2	131.7	52.0	24.1	93.2	4.4
1975	368.7	267.9	304.3	118.2	48.3	23.9	87.3	4.4
1976	356.3	277.5	305.0	116.7	43.7	23.4	86.0	3.9
1977	351.2	278.9	305.0	117.7	43.1	23.7	85.7	3.5
1978	335.6	246.7	276.7	104.6	40.2	20.5	77.6	3.1
1979	309.2	237.0	262.6	92.8	38.5	19.2	71.3	2.5
1980	227.0	172.6	237.6	80.6	33.1	17.3	65.4	2.6
1981	288.2	179.8	217.4	80.0	30.0	16.2	60.0	2.5
1982	240.8	161.2	188.3	70.4	27.5	15.4	53.6	2.5
1983	224.9	149.6	176.2	66.9	30.6	13.1	50.9	2.2
1984	213.7	149.2	172.6	58.7	30.0	15.5	50.4	2.2
1985	213.8	126.3	157.2	65.9	28.9	14.6	48.7	2.1
1986	204.7	136.1	160.9	54.2	28.6	13.7	46.6	2.1

Deaths at under 24 hours of age per 1,000 live births

Year	1,000g and under	1,001–1,500g	1,500g and under	1,501–2,000g	2,001–2,250g	2,251–2,500g	2,500 and under	2,501 and over, estimated
1953			441.4	96.9	31.6	15.1	84.0	1.9
1954			449.1	91.0	33.9	15.6	82.0	2.1
1955	..	..	445.2	90.2	30.5	14.9	81.9	2.1
1956	..	..	442.0	93.4	32.3	14.5	81.7	2.0
1957	..	..	447.9	93.2	31.1	15.1	82.3	2.0
1958	..	..	449.2	93.4	31.4	15.6	81.3	2.1
1959	..	..	461.6	99.9	31.4	15.7	84.9	2.0
1960	..	..	468.7	95.3	36.0	15.6	85.5	1.9
1961	..	..	447.5	96.0	34.2	15.8	84.4	2.1
1962	..	..	475.1	92.4	30.2	14.6	82.8	2.0
1963	666.7	314.3	443.0	89.8	30.1	14.0	79.8	2.1
1964	653.1	310.4	436.7	88.3	31.2	15.0	79.7	2.2

59

Stillbirth and neonatal mortality rates by birthweight, England and Wales, 1953–86

Year	1,000g and under	1,001– 1,500g	1,500g and under	1,501– 2,000g	2,001– 2,250g	2,251– 2,500g	2,500 and under	2,501 and over, estimated
	Deaths at under 24 hours of age per 1,000 live births							
1965	628.5	296.2	418.4	88.3	26.9	11.9	73.2	2.1
1966	674.4	317.5	451.4	82.6	28.6	12.6	75.4	1.7
1967	677.6	297.9	430.3	79.9	28.1	11.7	72.0	1.7
1968	595.7	285.0	399.7	81.8	24.5	10.7	69.5	1.8
1969	627.8	274.5	403.7	72.8	24.7	10.0	66.0	1.7
1970	603.1	282.6	393.2	78.8	26.9	11.6	73.4	1.7
1971	592.4	290.7	397.7	84.9	25.7	11.5	68.9	1.7
1972	609.5	272.8	386.1	75.1	26.0	10.2	64.0	1.7
1973	614.2	255.7	376.5	74.6	26.9	10.2	62.9	1.5
1974	572.1	238.4	358.7	69.6	22.4	11.2	61.4	1.2
1975	591.1	223.3	343.7	63.8	23.8	12.1	60.4	1.2
1976	545.2	193.3	307.1	51.9	16.9	7.4	50.6	1.6
1977	540.5	197.9	313.4	46.3	15.8	8.1	49.7	1.0
1978	495.6	165.7	267.9	46.4	14.6	6.0	45.8	0.8
1979	517.7	138.3	264.5	36.9	10.5	6.3	42.6	1.0
1980	462.6	115.9	225.3	36.6	11.6	5.6	38.3	0.9
1981	393.5	90.5	186.1	27.4	10.6	4.5	32.0	0.9
1982	407.0	76.4	181.6	23.1	9.3	3.3	31.1	0.7
1983	344.8	67.2	159.4	23.4	7.9	4.4	29.1	0.7
1984	310.6	60.9	147.1	18.9	8.4	3.6	26.0	0.8
1985	329.1	59.7	148.4	18.6	8.0	3.5	26.5	0.7
1986	289.1	48.4	130.9	17.5	7.5	2.8	23.3	0.9
	Deaths at 1-6 days of age per 1,000 live births							
1963	163.4	155.0	158.1	62.9	23.8	11.8	40.2	2.6
1964	162.4	148.4	153.6	60.8	25.0	11.8	39.5	2.5
1965	193.5	145.3	159.7	56.5	22.2	11.2	38.2	2.4
1966	161.9	149.4	154.1	51.6	19.7	9.1	34.4	2.5
1967	196.6	142.9	152.9	51.5	18.1	9.9	34.3	2.3
1968	189.5	142.2	159.7	47.4	22.3	9.4	35.6	2.1
1969	173.5	147.3	156.9	58.7	16.7	8.4	34.9	2.1
1970	167.9	133.6	145.4	47.7	18.5	8.5	34.9	2.2
1971	181.0	118.1	140.4	44.6	16.8	8.8	31.0	2.1
1972	139.2	130.3	133.3	50.4	16.2	8.2	30.4	2.2
1973	173.1	128.8	143.8	45.9	16.7	7.5	30.2	2.2
1974	155.4	131.9	140.4	39.6	15.1	8.1	29.0	2.5
1975	157.8	124.6	135.4	40.1	15.7	8.1	29.9	2.3
1976	175.7	108.2	130.0	37.9	13.1	6.4	27.3	1.9
1977	172.7	107.2	129.2	34.8	13.8	5.9	26.3	1.9
1978	197.7	88.8	122.5	29.9	9.8	5.5	24.5	1.9
1979	163.1	97.7	119.4	27.9	8.8	5.1	23.2	1.6
1980	173.9	77.9	108.2	25.6	6.7	4.3	21.3	1.5
1981	165.8	58.8	92.5	17.6	6.8	4.1	17.9	1.2
1982	133.6	68.1	88.9	16.2	6.9	3.6	17.8	1.1
1983	134.1	54.1	80.6	14.6	5.7	3.1	16.4	1.1
1984	150.5	44.3	81.0	11.8	5.1	1.9	15.0	0.9
1985	143.1	46.6	78.4	10.4	5.7	3.0	15.0	0.9
1986	138.7	52.3	82.0	12.2	4.4	2.5	15.6	0.8
	Deaths at 7-27 days of age per 1,000 live births							
1963	21.1	26.5	24.6	9.6	6.4	5.0	8.4	1.6
1964	24.2	28.0	26.6	10.4	6.9	3.9	8.3	1.4

Stillbirth and neonatal mortality rates by birthweight, England and Wales, 1953–86

Year	1,000g and under	1,001– 1,500g	1,500g and under	1,501– 2,000g	2,001– 2,250g	2,251– 2,500g	2,500 and under	2,501 and over, estimated
	Deaths at 7-27 days of age per 1,000 live births							
1965	23.2	26.2	25.1	12.9	9.5	7.9	11.0	1.1
1966	19.4	25.5	23.2	10.1	7.2	4.3	8.0	1.3
1967	29.4	22.2	24.7	12.1	6.0	4.7	8.4	1.3
1968	24.0	23.3	23.6	10.8	6.5	4.6	8.2	1.3
1969	29.2	25.2	26.7	11.8	7.5	4.1	8.6	1.2
1970	37.8	22.5	27.8	9.4	6.2	4.2	8.7	1.2
1971	26.5	26.2	26.3	9.9	5.9	3.8	7.7	1.3
1972	25.2	34.1	31.1	12.5	5.1	5.8	9.4	1.2
1973	21.1	23.8	22.9	11.4	6.2	4.0	7.7	1.2
1974	21.7	25.8	24.3	10.5	5.5	4.1	7.7	1.3
1975	37.3	25.8	29.6	8.8	4.5	3.1	7.4	1.3
1976	36.2	26.3	29.5	11.1	5.6	4.2	8.6	1.0
1977	47.3	31.3	36.7	9.9	5.8	3.3	8.7	1.1
1978	60.7	36.8	44.2	9.6	5.3	3.6	9.8	1.0
1979	58.2	38.4	45.0	9.2	4.1	2.5	8.9	1.0
1980	63.6	31.9	41.9	7.9	3.8	2.7	8.6	1.0
1981	65.1	28.2	39.8	8.0	3.9	1.8	8.0	0.9
1982	64.0	28.7	40.0	7.7	2.9	1.7	7.9	0.8
1983	54.1	24.6	34.4	6.1	2.8	2.4	7.4	0.7
1984	53.2	25.3	34.9	6.6	2.9	1.6	7.2	0.7
1985	51.9	15.1	27.2	5.3	3.7	2.3	6.5	0.6
1986	53.0	22.1	32.7	6.4	1.8	1.7	6.7	0.6
	Neonatal deaths per 1,000 live births							
1953	..	..	686.8	201.1	78.8	40.4	154.4	8.0
1954	..	..	684.8	198.6	81.1	44.0	152.0	7.9
1955	..	..	681.8	188.5	77.8	39.3	149.2	7.5
1956	..	..	666.2	184.1	80.3	38.8	145.9	7.4
1957	..	..	665.3	177.3	71.4	41.1	143.8	7.0
1958	..	..	686.6	182.7	69.3	40.8	142.4	6.9
1959	..	..	662.6	183.7	71.4	38.0	142.1	6.8
1960	..	..	665.2	173.3	72.6	33.8	138.4	6.7
1961	..	..	651.3	169.9	69.9	36.9	138.8	6.4
1962	..	..	655.6	163.4	64.2	36.1	133.3	6.6
1963	851.2	495.9	625.7	162.3	60.3	30.8	128.3	6.3
1964	839.7	486.8	616.9	159.5	63.1	30.7	127.5	6.1
1965	845.1	467.7	606.5	157.6	58.6	31.0	122.4	5.6
1966	855.7	492.4	628.7	144.4	55.5	26.0	117.7	5.6
1967	903.7	463.0	608.0	143.5	52.3	26.2	114.7	5.4
1968	809.1	450.5	582.9	140.0	53.3	24.7	113.3	5.2
1969	830.4	447.1	587.2	143.3	48.9	22.6	109.5	5.0
1970	808.7	438.7	566.5	135.8	51.5	24.4	117.1	5.2
1971	799.9	435.0	564.4	139.4	48.3	24.0	107.6	5.1
1972	773.8	435.6	550.5	138.0	47.3	24.2	103.8	5.0
1973	808.4	408.3	543.2	131.8	49.9	21.7	100.9	4.9
1974	749.2	396.2	523.4	119.7	42.9	23.3	98.1	4.9
1975	786.2	373.7	508.7	112.7	44.0	23.3	97.8	4.8
1976	757.2	327.8	466.7	100.9	35.6	18.0	86.5	4.5
1977	760.5	336.4	479.3	91.0	35.4	17.3	84.6	4.1
1978	754.0	291.3	434.7	85.8	29.7	15.2	80.2	3.8
1979	738.9	274.4	428.9	74.0	23.5	13.9	74.6	3.5

A3.5.1 *continued*

Stillbirth and neonatal mortality rates by birthweight, England and Wales, 1953–86

Year	1,000g and under	1,001– 1,500g	1,500g and under	1,501– 2,000g	2,001– 2,250g	2,251– 2,500g	2,500 and under	2,501 and over, estimated
	Neonatal deaths per 1,000 live births							
1980	700.1	225.7	375.4	70.1	22.1	12.6	68.3	3.4
1981	624.4	177.5	318.4	53.0	21.2	10.3	57.9	3.0
1982	604.7	173.2	310.5	47.0	19.1	47.9	56.8	2.6
1983	533.1	145.9	274.4	44.1	16.4	9.9	52.9	2.4
1984	514.4	130.5	263.0	37.3	16.3	7.1	48.3	2.4
1985	524.1	121.4	254.1	34.3	17.4	8.8	47.9	2.3
1986	480.8	122.8	245.5	36.1	13.7	7.0	45.5	2.3

∗ Rate per 1,000 live and still births
+ Rate per 1,000 live births
Data for more recent years are in table A3.5.2

Source: Derived from DHSS LHS 27/1 low birthweight returns

Rates for babies weighing over 2,500g were imputed using OPCS' birth and death registration data.

This was Table A 3.7 in the first edition of *Birth counts*

A3.5.2

Stillbirth, neonatal and postneonatal mortality deaths by birthweight, England and Wales, 1982–96

Year of birth	All weights	Total stated	Under 1,000g	1,000–1,499	Under 1,500g	1,500–1,999	2,000–2,499	Under 2,500g	2,500–2,999	3,000–3,499	3,500–3,999	4,000 and over	2,500 and over	Not stated
Numbers														
Stillbirths at 28 or more completed weeks of gestational age														
1982	3,943	3,501	440	618	1,058	568	558	2,184	558	455	198	106	1,317	442
1983	3,632	3,580	472	642	1,114	587	565	2,266	577	425	217	95	1,314	52
1984	3,650	3,581	490	612	1,102	533	615	2,250	563	427	237	104	1,331	69
1985	3,650	3,589	499	580	1,079	584	575	2,238	576	472	189	114	1,351	61
1986	3,548	3,521	497	621	1,118	500	589	2,207	530	466	213	105	1,314	27
1987	3,421	3,388	461	566	1,027	579	495	2,101	553	407	218	109	1,287	33
1988	3,385	3,365	413	545	958	541	525	2,024	525	460	241	115	1,341	20
1989	3,231	3,110	391	449	840	502	521	1,863	506	423	217	101	1,247	121
1990	3,259	3,107	386	511	897	544	465	1,906	455	442	215	89	1,201	152
1991	3,255	3,091	367	492	859	509	476	1,844	500	420	219	108	1,247	164
1992	3,156	2,992	522	417	939	426	435	1,800	438	429	221	104	1,192	164
1993	2,960	2,744	384	398	782	413	426	1,621	438	387	204	94	1,123	216
1994	2,925	2,796	413	402	815	386	414	1,615	443	403	213	122	1,181	129
1995	2,704	2,654	353	419	772	391	400	1,563	426	375	198	92	1,091	50
1996	2,598	2,555	370	367	737	370	373	1,480	441	365	185	84	1,075	43
Stillbirths at 24 or more completed weeks of gestational age														
1993	3,866	3,586	1,136	472	1,608	420	430	2,458	440	388	204	96	1,128	280
1994	3,816	3,666	1,195	473	1,668	396	416	2,480	444	403	214	125	1,186	150
1995	3,597	3,522	1,119	506	1,625	399	402	2,426	429	376	198	93	1,096	75
1996	3,539	3,477	1,214	435	1,649	376	374	2,399	443	365	185	85	1,078	62
Early neonatal														
1982	3,120	2,573	738	459	1,197	314	268	1,779	288	299	142	65	794	547
1983	2,936	2,779	870	490	1,360	324	309	1,993	300	261	167	58	786	157
1984	2,795	2,650	904	431	1,335	287	283	1,905	293	271	130	51	745	145
1985	2,817	2,696	902	461	1,363	275	298	1,936	293	267	132	68	760	121
1986	2,783	2,688	939	425	1,364	296	265	1,925	269	283	153	58	763	95
1987	2,657	2,559	927	480	1,407	253	210	1,870	230	252	143	64	689	98
1988	2,675	2,593	968	456	1,424	248	214	1,886	260	244	145	58	707	82
1989	2,501	2,149	863	336	1,199	202	154	1,555	208	186	146	54	594	352
1990	2,439	2,014	881	284	1,165	174	139	1,478	178	196	110	52	536	425
1991	2,371	1,937	885	257	1,142	154	158	1,454	187	157	92	47	483	434
1992	2,231	1,839	861	231	1,092	136	139	1,367	154	167	100	51	472	392
1993	2,160	1,795	852	215	1,067	144	114	1,325	149	171	97	53	470	365

A3.5.2 continued

Stillbirth, neonatal and postneonatal mortality deaths by birthweight, England and Wales, 1982–96

Year of birth	All weights	Total stated	Under 1,000g	1,000–1,499	Under 1,500g	1,500–1,999	2,000–2,499	Under 2,500g	2,500–2,999	3,000–3,499	3,500–3,999	4,000 and over	2,500 and over	Not stated
1994	2,144	1,846	880	242	1,122	129	115	1,366	149	156	106	69	480	298
1995	2,073	2,015	937	211	1,148	135	135	1,418	149	188	129	131	597	58
1996	2,039	1,970	1,077	211	1,288	111	123	1,522	146	151	94	57	448	69
Neonatal														
1982	3,903	3,276	825	577	1,402	373	349	2,124	394	465	215	78	1,152	627
1983	3,643	3,466	972	603	1,575	374	383	2,332	434	392	231	77	1,134	177
1984	3,518	3,352	1,014	537	1,551	357	344	2,252	422	409	200	69	1,100	166
1985	3,483	3,347	1,010	536	1,546	324	377	2,247	407	395	210	88	1,100	136
1986	3,447	3,345	1,054	537	1,591	358	327	2,276	373	400	218	78	1,069	102
1987	3,420	3,309	1,080	600	1,680	322	278	2,280	349	380	217	83	1,029	111
1988	3,379	3,285	1,118	576	1,694	314	290	2,298	346	360	207	74	987	94
1989	3,251	2,853	1,018	454	1,472	255	220	1,947	315	297	218	76	906	398
1990	3,134	2,653	1,028	370	1,398	224	196	1,818	281	314	168	72	835	481
1991	3,016	2,519	1,038	337	1,375	204	209	1,788	259	246	154	72	731	497
1992	2,869	2,420	1,020	320	1,340	181	186	1,707	236	259	149	69	713	449
1993	2,774	2,371	1,034	309	1,343	186	162	1,691	218	257	140	65	680	403
1994	2,729	2,396	1,054	319	1,373	168	166	1,707	213	245	142	89	689	333
1995	2,667	2,604	1,123	300	1,423	169	194	1,786	219	262	183	154	818	63
1996	2,607	2,530	1,283	285	1,568	140	174	1,882	208	226	138	76	648	77
Postneonatal														
1982	2,701	2,555	74	117	191	150	243	584	587	825	426	133	1,971	146
1983	2,656	2,644	95	116	211	141	279	631	613	846	449	105	2,013	12
1984	2,327	2,315	95	113	208	128	231	567	547	669	429	103	1,748	12
1985	2,688	2,679	102	132	234	169	299	702	563	812	465	137	1,977	9
1986	2,710	2,695	119	126	245	172	289	706	618	759	451	161	1,989	15
1987	2,773	2,765	111	133	244	159	268	671	633	831	482	148	2,094	8
1988	2,650	2,644	126	146	272	175	292	739	572	759	430	144	1,905	6
1989	2,434	2,351	142	118	260	147	267	674	487	674	400	116	1,677	83
1990	2,216	2,110	138	133	271	153	215	639	442	579	328	122	1,471	106
1991	1,750	1,656	126	85	211	106	226	543	309	438	276	90	1,113	94
1992	1,511	1,443	163	102	265	91	165	521	299	376	180	67	922	68
1993	1,366	1,321	151	86	237	98	161	496	249	319	190	67	825	45
1994	1,254	1,220	148	86	234	84	125	443	255	310	154	58	777	34
1995	1,291	1,277	179	96	275	89	152	516	262	294	151	54	761	14
1996	1,246	1,241	154	92	246	86	175	507	233	301	144	56	734	5

A3.5.2 continued

Stillbirth, neonatal and postneonatal mortality rates by birthweight, England and Wales, 1982–96

Year of birth	All weights	Total stated	Under 1,000g	1,000–1,499	Under 1,500g	1,500–1,999	2,000–2,499	Under 2,500g	2,500–2,999	3,000–3,499	3,500–3,999	4,000 and over	2,500 and over	Not stated
1982	6.3	5.8	233.8	156.5	181.5	70.1	19.8	51.9	4.9	2.0	1.2	2.1	2.4	15.9
1983	5.7	5.7	215.7	151.7	173.5	69.0	19.2	51.1	4.9	1.7	1.3	1.7	2.2	56.7
1984	5.7	5.6	207.3	142.6	165.6	61.4	20.8	50.1	4.8	1.7	1.3	1.9	2.2	78.3
1985	5.5	5.4	206.1	127.2	154.6	63.9	18.7	47.7	4.8	1.9	1.0	2.0	2.2	65.7
1986	5.3	5.3	194.0	133.9	155.3	53.2	18.8	46.0	4.4	1.8	1.2	1.8	2.1	41.5
1987	5.0	5.0	177.0	114.9	136.4	60.0	15.7	43.2	4.6	1.6	1.1	1.7	2.0	61.7
1988	4.9	4.8	157.5	112.4	128.3	56.8	17.1	42.4	4.4	1.8	1.2	1.7	2.1	23.5
1989	4.7	4.6	138.2	98.5	113.7	54.1	17.3	39.8	4.4	1.7	1.1	1.5	2.0	5.7
1990	4.6	4.6	143.0	108.8	121.3	57.5	15.0	39.7	3.9	1.7	1.1	1.3	1.9	5.4
1991	4.6	4.6	137.5	105.5	117.1	52.8	15.2	38.2	4.4	1.7	1.1	1.5	2.0	6.3
1992	4.6	4.5	178.0	89.7	123.9	46.7	14.5	38.6	3.9	1.8	1.1	1.4	1.9	6.3
1993	4.4	4.2	131.5	87.0	104.3	43.7	14.6	35.2	4.1	1.6	1.1	1.3	1.9	9.8
1994	4.4	4.3	126.4	83.2	100.6	40.5	14.2	34.5	4.1	1.7	1.1	1.7	2.0	7.6
1995	4.2	4.1	109.2	81.8	92.4	38.8	13.1	32.0	3.9	1.6	1.1	1.3	1.8	22.1
1996	4.0	3.9	105.1	71.4	85.1	37.9	12.3	30.4	4.0	1.6	1.0	1.2	1.8	27.2
Stillbirth rates at 24 or more weeks gestation per 1,000 total births														
1993	5.7	5.5	309.3	101.5	193.2	44.4	14.8	52.4	4.1	1.6	1.1	1.3	1.9	12.6
1994	5.7	5.6	295.1	96.5	186.3	41.5	14.3	52.0	4.1	1.7	1.1	1.7	2.0	8.8
1995	5.5	5.4	279.9	97.1	176.5	39.6	13.2	48.8	3.9	1.6	1.1	1.3	1.8	32.7
1996	5.4	5.3	278.2	83.6	172.3	38.4	12.4	48.4	4.0	1.6	1.0	1.2	1.8	38.8
Perinatal mortality rates per 1,000 total births														
1982	11.2	10.1	625.9	272.8	386.8	108.9	29.3	94.1	7.5	3.2	2.1	3.3	3.8	35.6
1983	10.4	10.1	613.3	267.5	385.4	107.1	29.7	96.0	7.5	2.8	2.2	2.8	3.6	227.9
1984	10.1	9.7	589.7	243.0	366.1	94.5	30.4	92.6	7.3	2.8	2.1	2.8	3.5	242.9
1985	9.8	9.5	578.7	228.4	349.9	94.0	28.4	89.0	7.2	2.9	1.8	3.1	3.4	195.9
1986	9.5	9.4	560.5	225.6	344.8	84.7	27.2	86.2	6.6	3.0	2.0	2.7	3.4	187.4
1987	8.9	8.7	533.0	212.3	323.2	86.3	22.4	81.7	6.5	2.5	1.9	2.7	3.1	244.9
1988	8.7	8.6	526.7	206.5	318.9	82.8	24.1	82.0	6.6	2.7	1.9	2.5	3.2	119.9
1989	8.3	7.9	443.3	172.2	276.0	75.8	22.4	73.0	6.2	2.4	1.7	2.3	3.0	20.7
1990	8.0	7.5	469.3	169.3	278.8	75.8	19.4	70.6	5.4	2.5	1.9	2.0	2.7	22.3
1991	8.0	7.4	468.9	160.6	272.9	68.8	20.3	68.4	6.0	2.3	1.7	2.2	2.8	22.9
1992	7.8	7.2	471.7	139.4	267.9	61.6	19.2	67.9	5.3	2.5	1.6	2.1	2.7	21.3
1993	7.6	7.0	423.1	134.0	246.7	58.9	18.5	63.9	5.5	2.4	1.7	2.0	2.6	26.3
1994	7.6	7.1	395.7	133.3	239.2	54.0	18.1	63.7	5.5	2.4	1.6	2.7	2.8	25.1
1995	7.3	7.2	399.1	123.0	229.8	52.2	17.6	61.0	5.2	2.4	1.8	3.2	2.8	47.6
1996	7.1	7.0	411.1	112.5	233.9	49.2	16.4	61.7	5.4	2.2	1.5	2.0	2.5	70.8

A3.5.2 continued

Stillbirth, neonatal and postneonatal mortality rates by birthweight, England and Wales, 1982–96

Year of birth	All weights Total	Total stated	Under 1,000g	1,000–1,499	Under 1,500g	1,500–1,999	2,000–2,499	Under 2,500g	2,500–2,999	3,000–3,499	3,500–3,999	4,000 and over	2,500 and over	Not stated
Perinatal mortality, including stillbirths at 24-27 weeks of gestational age per 1,000 total births														
1993	8.9	8.2	541.2	147.8	321.5	59.6	18.7	80.6	5.5	2.4	1.6	2.1	2.6	29.1
1994	8.9	8.5	512.3	145.9	311.7	55.0	18.2	80.7	5.5	2.4	1.7	2.7	2.8	26.3
1995	8.7	8.5	514.3	137.6	301.2	53.0	17.6	77.3	5.3	2.4	1.8	3.2	2.8	58.0
1996	8.5	8.4	525.2	124.1	306.9	49.8	16.4	79.1	5.4	2.2	1.5	2.0	2.5	81.9
Neonatal mortality rates per 1,000 live births														
1982	6.2	5.5	572.1	173.3	293.8	49.5	12.6	53.2	3.5	2.0	1.3	1.5	2.1	22.9
1983	5.8	5.5	566.4	168.0	296.8	47.2	13.3	55.4	3.7	1.6	1.3	1.4	1.9	204.6
1984	5.5	5.3	541.1	145.9	279.3	43.8	11.9	52.8	3.6	1.7	1.1	1.2	1.9	204.4
1985	5.3	5.1	525.5	134.7	262.0	37.9	12.5	50.3	3.4	1.6	1.2	1.5	1.8	156.7
1986	5.2	5.1	510.4	133.7	261.6	40.3	10.6	49.8	3.1	1.6	1.2	1.3	1.7	163.5
1987	5.0	4.9	504.0	137.6	258.3	35.5	9.0	49.0	2.9	1.5	1.1	1.3	1.6	221.1
1988	4.9	4.7	506.1	133.9	260.2	34.9	9.6	50.3	2.9	1.4	1.0	1.1	1.5	113.1
1989	4.7	4.3	417.6	110.5	224.8	29.0	7.4	43.3	2.7	1.2	1.1	1.1	1.5	18.9
1990	4.4	3.9	444.3	88.4	215.1	25.1	6.4	39.5	2.4	1.2	0.9	1.0	1.3	17.3
1991	4.3	3.7	450.7	80.8	212.4	22.3	6.8	38.6	2.3	1.0	0.8	1.0	1.2	19.2
1992	4.2	3.6	423.2	75.6	201.7	20.8	6.3	38.1	2.1	1.1	0.8	1.0	1.2	17.3
1993	4.1	3.7	407.6	74.0	200.1	20.6	5.6	38.0	2.0	1.1	0.7	0.9	1.1	18.4
1994	4.1	3.7	369.2	72.0	188.5	18.4	5.8	37.8	2.0	1.0	0.8	1.2	1.1	19.7
1995	4.1	4.0	390.1	63.8	187.7	17.5	6.5	37.7	2.0	1.1	1.0	2.2	1.4	28.4
1996	4.0	3.9	407.3	59.7	198.0	14.9	5.8	39.9	1.9	1.0	0.7	1.1	1.1	50.1
Postneonatal mortality rates per 1,000 live births														
1982	4.3	4.3	51.3	35.1	40.0	19.9	8.8	14.6	5.2	3.6	2.6	2.6	3.5	5.3
1983	4.2	4.2	55.4	32.3	39.8	17.8	9.7	15.0	5.2	3.5	2.6	1.9	3.4	13.9
1984	3.7	3.6	50.7	30.7	37.5	15.7	8.0	13.3	4.7	2.7	2.4	1.9	2.9	14.8
1985	4.1	4.1	53.1	33.2	39.7	19.8	9.9	15.7	4.7	3.2	2.6	2.4	3.2	10.4
1986	4.1	4.1	57.6	31.4	40.3	19.3	9.4	15.4	5.2	3.0	2.5	2.7	3.2	24.0
1987	4.1	4.1	51.8	30.5	37.5	17.5	8.7	14.4	5.2	3.2	2.5	2.3	3.3	15.9
1988	3.8	3.8	57.0	33.9	41.8	19.5	9.7	16.2	4.8	2.9	2.2	2.1	2.9	7.2
1989	3.5	3.5	58.2	28.7	39.7	16.7	9.0	15.0	4.2	2.7	2.1	1.7	2.7	3.9
1990	3.1	3.1	59.6	31.8	41.7	17.1	7.0	13.9	3.8	2.3	1.7	1.8	2.3	3.8
1991	2.5	2.5	54.7	20.4	32.6	11.6	7.3	11.7	2.7	1.8	1.4	1.3	1.8	3.6
1992	2.2	2.2	67.6	24.1	39.9	10.5	5.6	11.6	2.7	1.6	0.9	0.9	1.5	2.6

A3.5.2 continued

Stillbirth, neonatal and postneonatal mortality rates by birthweight, England and Wales, 1982–96

Year of birth	All weights	Total stated	Under 1,000g	1,000–1,499	Under 1,500g	1,500–1,999	2,000–2,499	Under 2,500g	2,500–2,999	3,000–3,499	3,500–3,999	4,000 and over	2,500 and over	Not stated
Postneonatal mortality rates per 1,000 live births														
1993	2.0	2.0	59.5	20.6	35.3	10.8	5.6	11.2	2.3	1.4	1.0	0.9	1.4	2.1
1994	1.9	1.9	51.8	19.4	32.1	9.2	4.3	9.8	2.4	1.3	0.8	0.8	1.3	2.0
1995	2.0	2.0	62.2	20.4	36.3	9.2	5.1	10.9	2.4	1.3	0.8	0.8	1.3	6.3
1996	1.9	1.9	48.9	19.3	31.1	9.1	5.9	10.7	2.1	1.3	0.8	0.8	1.2	3.3
Infant mortality rates per 1,000 live births														
1982	10.6	9.7	623.4	208.4	333.8	69.5	21.4	67.8	8.7	5.6	3.9	4.1	5.6	28.3
1983	10.0	9.7	621.8	200.3	336.6	65.0	22.9	70.4	9.0	5.1	4.0	3.4	5.4	218.5
1984	9.2	8.9	591.8	176.6	316.7	59.5	19.9	66.1	8.3	4.4	3.6	3.1	4.8	219.2
1985	9.4	9.2	578.6	167.9	301.7	57.6	22.4	66.0	8.1	4.8	3.7	3.9	5.0	167.1
1986	9.3	9.1	568.0	165.1	301.9	59.6	20.0	65.2	8.3	4.6	3.7	4.0	5.0	187.5
1987	9.1	8.9	555.8	168.0	295.8	53.1	17.6	63.4	8.1	4.7	3.7	3.6	4.9	237.1
1988	8.7	8.6	563.2	167.8	302.0	54.4	19.3	66.5	7.7	4.3	3.2	3.2	4.5	120.3
1989	8.3	7.8	475.8	139.2	264.5	45.8	16.4	58.3	7.0	3.9	3.2	2.9	4.2	22.8
1990	7.6	7.0	503.9	120.2	256.8	42.2	13.4	53.3	6.2	3.5	2.6	2.8	3.6	21.1
1991	6.8	6.2	505.4	101.2	245.0	34.0	14.1	50.3	5.0	2.7	2.2	2.3	2.9	22.8
1992	6.4	5.8	490.9	99.7	241.6	31.3	11.9	49.7	4.8	2.6	1.7	1.9	2.6	19.9
1993	6.2	5.7	467.1	94.6	235.4	31.4	11.2	49.2	4.4	2.4	1.7	1.8	2.5	20.5
1994	6.0	5.6	421.0	91.4	220.6	27.6	10.1	47.6	4.4	2.4	1.6	2.0	2.4	21.7
1995	6.1	6.0	452.2	84.2	223.9	26.7	11.5	48.6	4.4	2.4	1.8	3.0	2.6	34.7
1996	5.9	5.8	456.2	79.0	229.0	24.0	11.7	50.6	4.0	2.2	1.5	1.9	2.3	53.3

Source: Authors' analysis of ONS data up to 1996

Data for earlier years are in Table A3.5.1

Data extract: live births 1993 (7/94), 1994 (7/95), 1995 (3/7/96), 1996 (8/4/97)
linked 1993 (3/4/96), 1994 (18/9/96), 1995 (3/11/97)
Data about 1996 birth cohort from *Mortality statistics, Series DH3, no 30*

This is similar to Table A3.7 in the first edition of *Birth counts*

A3.5.3

Neonatal mortality rates by birthweight, Scotland, 1984–98

	Birthweight, g									Total
	Under 1,000	1,000– 1,499	1,500– 1,999	2,000– 2,499	2,500– 2,999	3,000– 3,499	3,500– 3,999	4,000 and over	Not known	
	Neonatal deaths per 1,000 live births									
1984	553.3	168.7	55.6	14.0	3.7	1.6	1.0	1.6	42.5	6.4
1985	585.6	163.5	48.1	10.0	3.2	1.4	1.0	1.6	19.4	5.5
1986	567.8	134.7	39.9	8.5	3.8	1.4	0.6	1.2	27.4	5.2
1987	578.3	145.0	25.8	10.1	2.7	1.2	0.7	1.4	14.7	4.7
1988	533.7	97.1	28.5	8.9	4.3	1.1	1.2	0.8	31.8	4.5
1989	505.0	139.9	34.3	12.0	2.4	1.2	0.6	0.9	71.8	4.7
1990	526.6	78.7	26.8	10.8	2.3	1.2	0.7	1.2	17.7	4.4
1991	469.8	101.6	21.4	10.0	2.5	1.2	1.1	2.0	8.6	4.4
1992	509.3	81.9	33.1	11.8	2.7	1.4	0.9	1.7	6.0	4.6
1993	386.7	92.8	31.0	7.7	2.9	1.5	0.7	1.1	8.8	4.0
1994	478.3	58.1	18.3	5.6	2.5	1.0	0.6	1.3	5.5	4.0
1995	555.6	80.2	13.9	10.8	1.9	1.4	0.7	0.9	2.7	4.0
1996	556.1	63.1	26.6	7.3	2.0	1.1	0.9	1.2	–	3.9
1997	404.9	43.5	14.0	4.6	1.8	1.2	0.8	1.0	285.7	3.2
1998*	436.9	42.4	21.3	4.7	2.8	1.0	0.5	0.4	800.0	3.6

* Provisional

Source: ISD Scottish stillbirth and infant death reports and SMR2 returns

This is a new table for this edition of *Birth counts*

A3.5.4

Neonatal mortality rates by gestational age, Scotland 1984–98

	Gestational age, weeks							Total
	Less than 26	26–31	28–31	32–36	37–41	42 or more	Not known	
	Neonatal deaths per 1,000 live births							
1984	793.1	472.4	165.6	20.0	2.0	2.2	16.0	6.4
1985	897.1	471.1	133.3	19.0	1.8	1.5	9.3	5.5
1986	763.2	454.5	128.9	15.5	1.7	2.3	9.9	5.2
1987	852.9	392.9	144.7	16.3	1.3	1.3	6.1	4.7
1988	700.0	384.6	89.6	13.9	1.6	1.0	13.4	4.5
1989	910.3	360.4	119.9	12.0	1.4	1.4	19.9	4.7
1990	802.3	283.2	102.3	11.7	1.5	0.8	7.5	4.4
1991	756.1	298.0	92.0	11.4	1.5	0.8	12.3	4.4
1992	666.7	382.8	60.2	14.4	1.7	0.9	4.5	4.6
1993	666.7	243.0	74.9	15.2	1.5	0.3	5.9	4.0
1994	710.5	292.0	59.7	9.1	1.1	3.1	2.7	4.0
1995	823.5	355.6	63.8	10.5	1.3	0.7	0.0	3.9
1996	..	..	..	..	..	..	..	..
1997	818.2	178.9	41.6	6.7	1.2	1.3	142.9	3.2
1998*	729.0	273.7	40.5	8.2	1.1	0.0	111.1	3.6

* Provisional

Source: ISD Scottish stillbirth and infant death reports and SMR2 returns

This is a new table for this edition of *Birth counts*

A3.5.5

Stillbirth and neonatal mortality rates for normally-formed babies by gestational age, singleton births, Scotland, 1985–98

Year	Gestational age, weeks					Total
	Under 24	24–27	28–31	32–36	37 and over	
	Stillbirths+ per 1,000 total births					
1985	..	..	163.9	37.1	1.9	4.7
1986	..	..	181.4	32.2	2.4	5.0
1987	..	..	152.7	28.8	2.2	4.4
1988	..	..	169.1	31.6	2.0	4.8
1989	..	..	176.3	31.2	2.0	4.5
1990	..	..	154.0	32.0	2.0	4.7
1991	..	..	136.7	29.8	2.2	4.5
1992	142.9	116.0	139.0	29.3	2.1	4.8
1993	71.4	405.7	137.2	29.6	2.0	5.5
1994	157.9	362.0	106.4	26.8	2.0	5.3
1995	222.2	457.4	120.1	28.7	1.9	5.5
1996	45.5	374.3	161.1	26.5	1.9	5.5
1997	–	322.4	100.7	27.0	1.3	4.3
1998*	76.9	314.0	127.4	23.1	2.0	4.9
	Early neonatal deaths+ per 1,000 live births					
1985	..	547.4	83.6	5.3	0.5	2.6
1986	..	438.6	80.5	7.4	0.6	2.3
1987	..	409.1	90.2	5.7	0.5	2.2
1988	..	398.3	27.2	5.3	0.4	1.8
1989	..	360.0	69.9	2.8	0.5	2.0
1990	..	339.9	62.8	4.7	0.4	2.1
1991	..	341.3	49.9	4.4	0.4	1.8
1992	..	362.5	31.4	5.1	0.5	2.1
1993	..	271.3	43.2	4.4	0.5	1.7
1994	..	285.7	26.5	3.2	0.2	1.5
1995	..	336.4	44.8	2.9	0.5	1.6
1996	..	362.1	29.1	2.6	0.3	1.7
1997	–	254.1	25.0	1.1	0.4	1.4
1998*	–	248.8	21.7	2.9	0.5	1.6
	Late neonatal deaths+ per 1,000 live births					
1985	..	73.0	30.7	1.4	0.1	0.5
1986	..	52.6	14.4	0.4	0.1	0.3
1987	..	68.2	27.4	1.4	0.2	0.6
1988	..	67.8	22.4	2.3	0.1	0.5
1989	..	88.0	24.4	1.4	0.1	0.5
1990	..	52.3	21.1	1.7	0.2	0.6
1991	..	113.8	23.7	1.4	0.2	0.7
1992	..	62.5	13.2	0.3	0.3	0.5
1993	..	78.1	27.2	0.0	0.1	0.4
1994	..	121.4	13.3	0.4	0.3	0.7
1995	..	84.1	11.2	0.0	0.1	0.4
1996	..	86.2	20.3	1.8	0.2	0.6
1997	–	82.0	5.6	1.1	0.2	0.5
1998*	–	67.8	6.2	0.7	0.2	0.4

* Provisional

+ Excluding stillbirths and deaths with major malformations

Source: ISD Scottish stillbirth and infant death reports and SMR2 returns

This is a new table for this edition of *Birth counts*

A3.6.1

Mortality in the first year of life by year of birth, England and Wales, 1970–96

Year of birth	Number of live births	Stillbirths per 1,000 total births		Deaths per 1,000 live births								
		24+ weeks	28+ weeks	Early neonatal	Late neonatal	Neonatal	1–2 months	3–5 months	1–5 months	6–11 months	Post-neonatal	Infant
(a) All causes												
1970	785,163	..	..	10.6	1.7	..	2.7	2.0	4.7	1.4	6.1	18.3
1971	782,602	..	..	9.9	1.7	..	2.4	1.8	4.2	1.3	5.5	17.1
1972	725,114	..	..	9.9	1.7	..	2.5	1.9	4.4	1.3	5.6	17.2
1973	673,766	..	..	9.5	1.6	..	2.4	1.9	4.3	1.1	5.4	16.5
1974	639,699	..	..	9.4	1.7	..	2.2	1.7	4.0	1.0	5.0	16.0
1975	603,493	..	..	9.1	1.6	..	2.1	1.8	3.9	1.1	4.9	15.6
1976	584,390	..	..	8.1	1.5	..	1.8	1.5	3.3	1.1	4.4	14.1
1977	569,068	..	..	7.7	1.6	..	1.8	1.7	3.5	1.0	4.6	13.9
1978	596,650	..	..	7.1	1.6	..	2.0	1.6	3.7	1.0	4.7	13.4
1979	637,797	..	..	6.7	1.5	..	1.9	1.6	3.5	1.1	4.6	12.8
1979	638,028	..	8.0	6.7	1.5	8.2	1.9	1.6	3.5	1.0	4.5	12.6
1980	656,234	..	7.2	6.1	1.4	7.6	1.8	1.5	3.2	0.9	4.1	11.7
1981	634,492	..	6.6	5.2	1.4	6.6	1.8	1.5	3.4	1.0	4.3	10.9
1982	625,931	..	6.3	5.0	1.3	6.2	1.8	1.6	3.3	1.0	4.3	10.6
1983	629,134	..	5.7	4.7	1.1	5.8	1.9	1.4	3.3	0.9	4.2	10.0
1984	636,818	..	5.7	4.4	1.1	5.5	1.6	1.3	2.8	0.8	3.7	9.2
1985	656,417	..	5.5	4.3	1.0	5.3	1.7	1.4	3.2	0.9	4.1	9.4
1986	661,018	..	5.3	4.2	1.0	5.2	1.8	1.4	3.2	0.9	4.1	9.3
1987	681,511	..	5.0	3.9	1.1	5.0	1.7	1.5	3.2	0.9	4.1	9.1
1988	693,577	..	4.9	3.9	1.0	4.9	1.6	1.4	3.0	0.8	3.8	8.7
1989	687,725	..	4.7	3.6	1.1	4.7	1.5	1.3	2.8	0.7	3.5	8.3
1990	706,140	..	4.6	3.5	1.0	4.4	1.3	1.1	2.4	0.7	3.1	7.6
1991	699,217	..	4.6	3.4	0.9	4.3	1.1	0.8	2.0	0.5	2.5	6.8
1992	689,656	..	4.6	3.2	0.9	4.2	0.9	0.7	1.6	0.6	2.2	6.4
1993	671,224	5.7	4.4	3.2	0.9	4.1	0.8	0.7	1.5	0.6	2.0	6.2
1994	664,256	5.7	4.4	3.2	0.9	4.1	0.8	0.6	1.4	0.5	1.9	6.0
1995	648,001	5.5	4.2	3.2	0.9	4.1	0.9	0.7	1.5	0.5	2.0	6.1
1996	649,489	5.4	4.0	3.1	0.9	4.0	..	..	..	..	1.9	6.0

A3.6.1 *continued*

Mortality in the first year of life by year of birth, England and Wales, 1970–96

Year of birth	Number of live births	Stillbirths per 1,000 total births		Deaths per 1,000 live births								
		24+ weeks	28+ weeks	Early neonatal	Late neonatal	Neonatal	1–2 months	3–5 months	1–5 months	6–11 months	Post-neonatal	Infant

(b) Congenital anomalies

ICD 740-759

Year of birth	Number of live births	24+ weeks	28+ weeks	Early neonatal	Late neonatal	Neonatal	1–2 months	3–5 months	1–5 months	6–11 months	Post-neonatal	Infant
1970	785,163	:	:	1.7	0.7	:	0.6	0.4	1.0	0.3	1.3	3.7
1971	782,602	:	:	1.8	0.8	:	0.6	0.3	0.9	0.3	1.2	3.7
1972	725,114	:	:	1.8	0.9	:	0.6	0.4	0.9	0.3	1.2	3.8
1973	673,766	:	:	1.7	0.8	:	0.5	0.3	0.9	0.3	1.2	3.7
1974	639,699	:	:	1.9	0.9	:	0.5	0.4	0.8	0.3	1.1	3.9
1975	603,493	:	:	1.8	0.9	:	0.5	0.3	0.8	0.2	1.0	3.7
1976	584,390	:	:	1.7	0.8	:	0.4	0.3	0.7	0.2	0.9	3.4
1977	569,068	:	:	1.7	0.8	:	0.5	0.3	0.7	0.2	1.0	3.5
1978	596,650	:	:	1.8	0.7	:	0.5	0.3	0.7	0.2	0.9	3.4
1979	637,797	:	:	1.7	0.7	:	0.4	0.3	0.6	0.2	0.9	3.3

ONS cause group 1

Year of birth	Number of live births	24+ weeks	28+ weeks	Early neonatal	Late neonatal	Neonatal	1–2 months	3–5 months	1–5 months	6–11 months	Post-neonatal	Infant
1979	638,028	:	1.5	1.7	0.7	2.4	0.4	0.3	0.7	0.3	1.0	3.4
1980	656,234	:	1.2	1.7	0.6	2.3	0.4	0.3	0.6	0.3	0.9	3.2
1981	634,492	:	1.0	1.5	0.6	2.1	0.4	0.2	0.7	0.3	0.9	3.0
1982	625,931	:	0.8	1.6	0.5	2.0	0.4	0.3	0.7	0.3	1.0	3.0
1983	629,134	:	0.7	1.4	0.5	1.9	0.4	0.3	0.7	0.3	1.0	2.8
1984	636,818	:	0.5	1.3	0.4	1.8	0.4	0.2	0.6	0.3	0.9	2.6
1985	656,417	:	0.5	1.3	0.4	1.7	0.3	0.3	0.6	0.2	0.8	2.5
1986	661,018	:	0.5	1.5	0.4	1.9	0.4	0.2	0.6	0.2	0.8	2.7
1987	681,511	:	0.5	1.3	0.4	1.8	0.3	0.2	0.6	0.2	0.8	2.5
1988	693,577	:	0.4	1.3	0.4	1.8	0.3	0.2	0.5	0.2	0.7	2.3
1989	687,725	:	0.5	1.2	0.4	1.6	0.3	0.2	0.5	0.2	0.7	2.2
1990	706,140	:	0.4	1.0	0.4	1.6	0.2	0.2	0.4	0.2	0.6	2.0
1991	699,217	:	0.4	1.0	0.3	1.4	0.3	0.2	0.4	0.2	0.6	2.0
1992	689,656	:	0.4	1.0	0.3	1.4	0.2	0.2	0.4	0.2	0.6	1.9
1993	671,224	0.5	0.3	0.8	0.3	1.3	0.2	0.2	0.3	0.2	0.5	1.6
1994	664,256	0.5	0.3	0.8	0.3	1.1	0.2	0.2	0.3	0.2	0.5	1.6
1995	648,001	0.5	0.3	0.8	0.3	1.1	0.2	0.1	0.3	0.1	0.5	1.6
1996	649,489	0.5	0.3	0.8	0.3	1.0	0.2	0.1	:	:	0.5	1.5

(c) Causes other than congenital anomalies

ICD codes other than 740-759

Year of birth	Number of live births	24+ weeks	28+ weeks	Early neonatal	Late neonatal	Neonatal	1–2 months	3–5 months	1–5 months	6–11 months	Post-neonatal	Infant
1970	785,163	:	:	8.8	1.0	:	2.1	1.6	3.7	1.1	4.8	14.6
1971	782,602	:	:	8.1	1.0	:	1.8	1.5	3.3	1.0	4.3	13.4
1972	725,114	:	:	8.1	0.8	:	1.9	1.5	3.5	1.0	4.4	13.4

A3.6.1 continued

Mortality in the first year of life by year of birth, England and Wales, 1970–96

Year of birth	Number of live births	Stillbirths per 1,000 total births		Deaths per 1,000 live births								
		24+ weeks	28+ weeks	Early neonatal	Late neonatal	Neonatal	1–2 months	3–5 months	1–5 months	6–11 months	Post-neonatal	Infant
1973	673,766	..	..	7.8	0.8	..	1.9	1.5	3.4	0.9	4.2	12.8
1974	639,699	..	..	7.5	0.8	..	1.7	1.4	3.1	0.8	3.9	12.2
1975	603,493	..	..	7.2	0.8	..	1.6	1.5	3.1	0.8	3.9	11.9
1976	584,390	..	..	6.4	0.8	..	1.4	1.3	2.6	0.8	3.5	10.6
1977	569,068	..	..	5.9	0.8	..	1.4	1.4	2.8	0.8	3.6	10.4
1978	596,650	..	..	5.4	0.9	..	1.6	1.4	3.0	0.8	3.8	10.0
1979	637,797	..	..	5.0	0.8	..	1.5	1.4	2.9	0.8	3.7	9.5
ONS cause groups other than 1												
1979	638,028	..	6.5	4.9	0.8	5.7	1.5	1.3	2.8	0.7	3.5	9.2
1980	656,234	..	6.0	4.4	0.8	5.2	1.4	1.2	2.6	0.7	3.2	8.5
1981	634,492	..	5.6	3.7	0.8	4.4	1.4	1.3	2.7	0.7	3.4	7.9
1982	625,931	..	5.5	3.4	0.8	4.2	1.4	1.3	2.6	0.7	3.4	7.5
1983	629,134	..	5.1	3.3	0.7	3.9	1.4	1.2	2.6	0.7	3.3	7.2
1984	636,818	..	5.2	3.1	0.7	3.8	1.2	1.0	2.2	0.6	2.8	6.5
1985	656,417	..	5.1	3.0	0.6	3.6	1.4	1.2	2.6	0.7	3.3	6.9
1986	661,018	..	4.8	2.7	0.6	3.3	1.4	1.2	2.6	0.7	3.3	6.6
1987	681,511	..	4.5	2.6	0.7	3.3	1.4	1.2	2.6	0.7	3.3	6.6
1988	693,577	..	4.4	2.6	0.6	3.2	1.4	1.2	2.6	0.6	3.1	6.4
1989	687,725	..	4.2	2.5	0.7	3.1	1.3	1.1	2.5	0.6	2.9	6.0
1990	706,140	..	4.2	2.4	0.6	3.1	1.1	1.0	2.3	0.5	2.5	5.6
1991	699,217	..	4.3	2.4	0.6	2.9	0.9	0.7	2.0	0.4	1.9	4.9
1992	689,656	..	4.2	2.3	0.6	2.9	0.7	0.5	1.5	0.4	1.6	4.4
1993	671,224	5.3	4.1	2.4	0.6	3.0	0.6	0.5	1.2	0.4	1.5	4.5
1994	664,256	5.2	4.0	2.4	0.6	3.0	0.6	0.5	1.1	0.3	1.4	4.4
1995	648,001	5.0	3.8	2.4	0.6	3.0	0.7	0.5	1.1	0.3	1.5	4.5
1996	649,489	4.9	3.7	2.4	0.6	3.0	:	:	1.2	:	1.5	4.4

Source: Authors' analysis of OPCS and ONS data. The first series, covering 1973 to 1979 was derived from unlinked data.

Data extract: live births 1993 (7/94), 1994 (7/95), 1995 (3/7/96), 1996 (8/4/97)
linked 1993 (3/4/96), 1994 (18/9/96), 1995 (3/11/97)

1996 data from ONS, *Mortality statistics*, Series DH3

This was Table A3.8 in the first edition of *Birth counts*

A3.6.2

Age distribution of infant deaths, England and Wales, 1888–1998

Year	Percentage of infant deaths				Total infant deaths	
	0–2 months	3–5 months	6–11 months		Number	Rate*
1888-1890	48.1	20.4	31.5		378,232	143.5
1891-1895	48.9	20.7	30.5		683,217	150.5
1896-1900	47.7	21.5	30.8		720,502	156.1
1901-1905	50.5	20.2	29.3		646,845	137.8
1906-1910	53.8	18.8	27.4		539,136	117.1
	Early neonatal	Late neonatal	Neonatal	Postneonatal		
1905	19.7	13.0	32.6	67.4	119,091	128.1
1906	18.9	12.8	31.6	68.4	123,895	132.5
1907	20.7	13.9	34.6	65.4	107,978	117.6
1908	20.2	13.3	33.5	66.5	113,254	120.4
1909	22.7	13.9	36.6	63.4	99,430	108.7
1910	22.9	13.7	36.5	63.5	94,579	105.4
1911	18.8	12.6	31.4	68.6	114,600	129.2
1912	25.6	15.0	40.5	59.5	82,779	94.7
1913	22.5	13.8	36.3	63.7	95,608	108.9
1914	23.1	13.8	36.9	63.1	91,971	104.4
1915	22.1	13.5	35.6	64.4	89,380	105.8
1916	25.5	15.0	40.5	59.5	71,646	91.1
1917	25.7	15.0	40.7	59.3	64,483	91.1
1918	23.7	13.7	37.4	62.6	64,386	97.9
1919	27.8	15.6	43.3	56.7	61,715	93.2
1920	25.9	15.5	41.4	58.6	76,552	84.5
1921	27.6	15.8	43.3	56.7	70,250	81.2
1922	29.5	15.9	45.4	54.6	60,121	74.7
1923	30.5	15.6	46.1	53.9	52,582	69.2
1924	29.4	15.1	44.5	55.5	54,813	74.2
1925	28.5	14.9	43.4	56.6	53,316	74.5
1926	30.3	15.1	45.4	54.6	48,757	70.2
1927	31.9	14.5	46.3	53.7	45,610	69.7
1928	33.2	14.6	47.7	52.3	42,960	65.1
1929	29.9	14.2	44.2	55.8	47,868	74.4
1930	36.7	14.9	51.6	48.4	38,908	60.0
1931	33.3	14.3	47.6	52.4	41,939	66.4
1932	34.5	14.1	48.6	51.4	39,933	65.0
1933	36.0	14.6	50.6	49.4	36,960	63.7
1934	38.6	14.8	53.4	46.6	35,017	58.6
1935	38.7	14.7	53.4	46.6	34,092	56.9
1936	37.4	14.1	51.5	48.5	35,425	58.5
1937	38.2	13.4	51.7	48.3	35,175	57.6
1938	40.1	13.6	53.7	46.3	32,724	52.7
1939	41.9	13.9	55.8	44.2	31,190	50.8
1940	37.2	14.4	51.6	48.4	33,892	57.4
1941	34.6	13.9	48.5	51.5	34,550	59.7
1942	39.4	15.4	54.8	45.2	32,258	49.5
1943	37.5	14.1	51.6	48.4	33,431	48.9
1944	39.2	15.3	54.5	45.5	33,455	44.5
1945	38.5	14.4	52.9	47.1	31,959	47.0
1946	43.1	16.1	59.2	40.8	33,541	40.9
1947	39.7	14.8	54.6	45.4	36,849	41.8
1948	45.4	11.9	57.3	42.7	26,766	34.5
1949	47.8	11.2	59.1	40.9	23,882	32.7

A3.6.2 continued

Age distribution of infant deaths, England and Wales, 1888–1998

	Early neonatal	Late neonatal	Neonatal	Postneonatal		
1950	50.9	11.1	62.1	37.9	20,817	29.9
1951	51.9	11.3	63.2	36.8	20,223	29.8
1952	55.0	11.5	66.5	33.5	18,555	27.5
1953	55.3	10.7	66.0	34.0	18,324	26.8
1954	58.6	11.1	69.6	30.4	17,160	25.5
1955	58.7	10.6	69.3	30.7	16,613	24.9
1956	60.0	11.2	71.2	28.8	16,554	23.6
1957	60.9	10.3	71.2	28.8	16,720	23.1
1958	61.2	10.5	71.7	28.3	16,685	22.5
1959	61.2	10.3	71.4	28.6	16,629	22.2
1960	61.2	10.0	71.2	28.8	17,118	21.8
1961	61.9	9.6	71.5	28.5	17,393	21.4
1962	59.9	9.7	69.6	30.4	18,187	21.7
1963	58.2	9.3	67.5	32.5	18,042	21.1
1964	60.4	9.0	69.4	30.6	17,445	19.9
1965	59.4	9.0	68.3	31.7	16,395	19.0
1966	58.5	9.2	67.7	32.3	16,147	19.0
1967	58.6	9.8	68.3	31.7	15,266	18.3
1968	57.9	9.6	67.6	32.4	14,982	18.3
1969	57.2	9.5	66.7	33.3	14,391	18.0
1970	58.4	9.4	67.7	32.3	14,267	18.2
1971	56.5	9.9	66.4	33.6	13,720	17.5
1972	57.2	9.8	67.0	33.0	12,498	17.2
1973	56.4	9.6	66.0	34.0	11,407	16.9
1974	57.3	10.3	67.6	32.4	10,459	16.3
1975	57.7	10.5	68.2	31.8	9,488	15.7
1976	57.2	10.8	68.0	32.0	8,334	14.3
1977	55.5	11.8	67.3	32.7	7,841	13.8
1978	53.8	12.0	65.8	34.2	7,881	13.2
1979	52.7	11.6	64.3	35.7	8,178	12.8
1980	51.2	12.4	63.6	36.4	7,899	12.0
1981	47.8	12.4	60.2	39.8	7,021	11.1
1982	46.5	11.5	57.9	42.1	6,775	10.8
1983	46.2	11.5	57.7	42.3	6,381	10.1
1984	46.7	12.0	58.7	41.3	6,037	9.5
1985	46.5	11.0	57.5	42.5	6,141	9.4
1986	44.7	10.5	55.3	44.7	6,313	9.6
1987	42.8	12.2	55.0	45.0	6,272	9.2
1988	43.1	11.5	54.6	45.4	6,270	9.0
1989	43.3	13.0	56.3	43.7	5,808	8.4
1990	44.9	13.0	57.9	42.1	5,564	7.9
1991	46.5	12.7	59.2	40.8	5,158	7.4
1992	50.5	14.6	65.1	34.9	4,539	6.6
1993	51.3	14.6	65.9	34.1	4,242	6.3
1994	52.0	14.7	66.7	33.3	4,120	6.2
1995	52.8	14.9	67.8	32.2	3,982	6.1
1996	52.2	14.6	66.8	33.2	3,959	6.1
1997	51.1	15.2	66.3	33.7	3,799	5.9
1998	50.9	16.0	66.8	33.1	3,605	5.7

∗ Rate per 1,000 live births

Source: *Annual reports of the Registrar General*, *Registrar General's statistical reviews*, OPCS and ONS *Birth statistics*, Series FM1 and *Mortality statistics*, Series DH1 and DH3

This was Table A3.9 in the first edition of *Birth counts*

A3.7.1

Stillbirths by underlying cause, England and Wales, 1968–78

ICD Number	Cause	1968	1969	1970	1971	1972	1973	1974	1975	1976	1977	1978
		Numbers										
000-999	**All causes**	**11,848**	**10,654**	**10,345**	**9,899**	**8,799**	**7,936**	**7,175**	**6,295**	**5,709**	**5,405**	**5,108**
740-759	**Congenital anomalies**	**2,153**	**2,058**	**2,010**	**2,123**	**1,976**	**1,735**	**1,605**	**1,422**	**1,246**	**1,143**	**1,050**
740	Anencephalus	1,225	1,208	1,201	1,259	1,118	973	927	835	691	624	553
741	Spina bifida	270	240	207	252	209	200	166	161	129	146	130
742	Congenital hydrocephalus	319	270	259	268	251	241	185	164	160	129	137
743-744	Other congenital anomalies of central nervous system and eye	46	33	34	45	27	35	37	34	41	36	27
746-747	Congenital anomalies of circulatory system	38	41	33	40	34	23	39	27	29	25	22
760-779	**Certain causes of perinatal morbidity and mortality**	**9,695**	**8,596**	**8,335**	**7,776**	**6,823**	**6,201**	**5,570**	**4,873**	**4,463**	**4,262**	**4,058**
760-761	Maternal conditions	428	424	420	435	378	362	283	267	228	250	272
762	Toxaemias of pregnancy	1,290	1,110	955	946	793	668	651	562	501	491	438
763	Maternal ante and post partum infection*	30	24	21	16	16	11	14	15	18	26	16
764-768	Difficult labour	537	516	485	415	380	298	272	212	186	151	139
769	Other complications of pregnancy and childbirth	711	545	606	593	541	455	417	408	370	354	341
769.4	Multiple pregnancy	126	110	108	130	102	98	96	97	124	139	136
770	Conditions of the placenta	3,012	2,700	2,668	2,428	2,173	2,114	1,816	1,675	1,490	1,447	1,405
771	Conditions of the cord	1,014	883	867	850	755	706	624	505	492	445	400
772	Birth injury without mention of cause	121	117	87	86	76	49	45	31	36	40	33
774-775	Haemolytic disease of newborn	496	439	418	338	272	207	171	124	108	92	85
776	Anoxic and hypoxic conditions not elsewhere classified	619	530	581	569	460	451	410	373	373	343	337
777	Immaturity	134	111	122	112	81	70	74	55	58	43	31
778-779	Other conditions of fetus and newborn	1,303	1,197	1,105	988	898	810	793	645	602	580	561
		Rates per 1,000 total births										
000-999	**All causes**	**14.26**	**13.18**	**13.02**	**12.48**	**11.98**	**11.60**	**11.09**	**10.32**	**9.68**	**9.41**	**8.49**
740-759	**Congenital anomalies**	**2.59**	**2.55**	**2.53**	**2.68**	**2.69**	**2.54**	**2.48**	**2.33**	**2.11**	**1.99**	**1.75**
740	Anencephalus	1.47	1.49	1.51	1.59	1.62	1.42	1.43	1.37	1.17	1.09	0.92
741	Spina bifida	0.32	0.30	0.26	0.32	0.28	0.29	0.26	0.26	0.22	0.25	0.22
742	Congenital hydrocephalus	0.38	0.33	0.33	0.34	0.34	0.35	0.29	0.27	0.27	0.22	0.23
743-744	Other congenital anomalies of central nervous system and eye	0.06	0.04	0.04	0.06	0.04	0.05	0.06	0.06	0.07	0.06	0.04

A3.7.1 continued

Stillbirths by underlying cause, England and Wales, 1968–78

ICD Number	Cause	1968	1969	1970	1971	1972	1973	1974	1975	1976	1977	1978
		Rates per 1,000 total births										
746-747	Congenital anomalies of circulatory system	0.05	0.05	0.04	0.05	0.05	0.03	0.06	0.04	0.05	0.04	0.04
760-779	**Certain causes of perinatal morbidity and mortality**	**11.66**	**10.64**	**10.49**	**9.81**	**9.29**	**9.07**	**8.61**	**7.99**	**7.56**	**7.42**	**6.75**
760-761	Maternal conditions	0.51	0.52	0.53	0.55	0.51	0.53	0.44	0.44	0.39	0.44	0.45
762	Toxaemias of pregnancy	1.55	1.37	1.20	1.19	1.08	0.98	1.01	0.92	0.85	0.85	0.73
763	Maternal ante and post partum infection*	0.04	0.03	0.03	0.02	0.02	0.02	0.02	0.02	0.03	0.05	0.03
764-768	Difficult labour	0.65	0.64	0.61	0.52	0.52	0.44	0.42	0.35	0.32	0.26	0.23
769	Other complications of pregnancy and childbirth	0.86	0.67	0.76	0.75	0.74	0.67	0.64	0.67	0.63	0.62	0.57
769.4	Multiple pregnancy	0.15	0.14	0.14	0.16	0.14	0.14	0.15	0.16	0.21	0.24	0.23
770	Conditions of the placenta	3.62	3.34	3.36	3.06	2.96	3.09	2.81	2.75	2.53	2.52	2.34
771	Conditions of the cord	1.22	1.09	1.09	1.07	1.03	1.03	0.96	0.83	0.83	0.77	0.66
772	Birth injury without mention of cause	0.15	0.14	0.11	0.11	0.10	0.07	0.07	0.05	0.06	0.07	0.05
774-775	Haemolytic disease of newborn	0.60	0.54	0.53	0.43	0.37	0.30	0.26	0.20	0.18	0.16	0.14
776	Anoxic and hypoxic conditions not elsewhere classified	0.74	0.66	0.73	0.72	0.63	0.66	0.63	0.61	0.63	0.60	0.56
777	Immaturity	0.16	0.14	0.15	0.14	0.11	0.11	0.11	0.09	0.10	0.07	0.05
778-779	Other conditions of fetus and newborn	1.57	1.48	1.39	1.25	1.22	1.18	1.23	1.06	1.02	1.01	0.93

* For the years 1968-73, ICD 763 is described as 'maternal ante and intra partum infection'

Source: Derived from data in OPCS *Mortality statistics, childhood, Series DH3*

This was Table A3.10 in the first edition of *Birth counts*

A3.7.2

Perinatal deaths by underlying cause, England and Wales, 1968–78

ICD Number	Cause	1968	1969	1970	1971	1972	1973	1974	1975	1976	1977	1978
		Numbers										
000-999	All causes	20,530	18,886	18,633	17,631	15,980	14,374	13,157	11,716	10,416	9,717	9,313
000-136	Infective and parasitic diseases	32	32	32	45	41	46	45	45	48	52	62
460-519	Diseases of the respiratory system	235	201	213	163	170	127	130	109	103	74	74
480-486	Pneumonia	220	188	195	150	159	117	121	107	99	71	71
740-759	Congenital anomalies	3,612	3,431	3,372	3,524	3,263	2,893	2,800	2,529	2,236	2,115	2,078
740	Anencephalus	1,408	1,366	1,372	1,419	1,335	1,084	1,041	914	781	696	620
741	Spina bifida	441	389	377	455	412	384	389	373	292	329	278
742	Congenital hydrocephalus	378	320	299	313	288	291	229	203	191	160	165
743-744	Other congenital anomalies of central nervous system and eye	107	97	97	108	79	77	91	85	97	93	77
746-747	Congenital anomalies of circulatory system	504	492	465	477	432	391	353	361	309	281	323
760-779	Certain causes of perinatal morbidity and mortality	16,336	14,957	14,704	13,623	12,234	11,060	9,950	8,818	7,870	7,345	6,923
760-761	Maternal conditions	472	457	468	473	418	393	306	290	243	269	289
762	Toxaemias of pregnancy	1,380	1,226	1,030	1,024	870	734	711	602	540	517	467
763	Maternal ante and post partum infection*	37	30	28	20	20	19	17	25	21	31	26
764-768	Difficult labour	724	677	606	532	505	403	350	296	252	211	194
769	Other complications of pregnancy and childbirth	1,418	1,255	1,260	1,204	1,119	957	907	868	739	668	652
769.4	Multiple pregnancy	660	664	644	626	550	489	516	479	426	390	389
770	Conditions of the placenta	3,140	2,819	2,787	2,551	2,270	2,206	1,889	1,731	1,558	1,499	1,461
771	Conditions of the cord	1,078	937	929	906	810	756	664	537	526	478	439
772	Birth injury without mention of cause	1,024	828	825	750	724	561	490	382	360	351	351
774-775	Haemolytic disease of newborn	734	672	615	525	391	309	242	181	149	139	117
776	Anoxic and hypoxic conditions not elsewhere classified	2,966	3,127	3,190	2,982	2,886	2,694	2,457	2,271	1,994	1,805	1,684

A3.7.2 continued

Perinatal deaths by underlying cause, England and Wales, 1968–78

ICD Number	Cause	1968	1969	1970	1971	1972	1973	1974	1975	1976	1977	1978
		Numbers										
777	Immaturity	1,849	1,548	1,625	1,492	1,179	1,050	960	822	732	646	535
778-779	Other conditions of fetus and newborn	1,514	1,381	1,341	1,164	1,042	978	957	813	756	731	708
780-796	**Symptoms and ill-defined conditions**	**8**	**6**	**8**	**6**	**14**	**14**	**11**	**11**	**12**	**18**	**12**
795	Sudden death cause unknown	0	0	0	3	9	9	8	10	7	15	12
E800-E999	**Accidents, poisoning and violence**	**75**	**47**	**42**	**44**	**53**	**34**	**35**	**34**	**17**	**13**	**24**
		Rates per 1,000 total births										
000-999	**All causes**	**24.70**	**23.37**	**23.44**	**22.23**	**21.76**	**21.02**	**20.33**	**19.21**	**17.65**	**16.91**	**15.48**
000-136	**Infective and parasitic diseases**	**0.04**	**0.04**	**0.04**	**0.06**	**0.06**	**0.07**	**0.07**	**0.07**	**0.08**	**0.09**	**0.10**
460-519	**Diseases of the respiratory system**	**0.28**	**0.25**	**0.27**	**0.21**	**0.23**	**0.19**	**0.20**	**0.18**	**0.17**	**0.13**	**0.12**
480-486	Pneumonia	0.26	0.23	0.25	0.19	0.22	0.17	0.19	0.18	0.17	0.12	0.12
740-759	**Congenital anomalies**	**4.35**	**4.25**	**4.24**	**4.44**	**4.44**	**4.23**	**4.33**	**4.15**	**3.79**	**3.68**	**3.45**
740	Anencephalus	1.69	1.69	1.73	1.79	1.82	1.59	1.61	1.50	1.32	1.21	1.03
741	Spina bifida	0.53	0.48	0.47	0.57	0.56	0.56	0.60	0.61	0.49	0.57	0.46
742	Congenital hydrocephalus	0.45	0.40	0.38	0.39	0.39	0.43	0.35	0.33	0.32	0.28	0.27
743-744	Other congenital anomalies of central nervous system and eye	0.13	0.12	0.12	0.14	0.11	0.11	0.14	0.14	0.16	0.16	0.13
746-747	Congenital anomalies of circulatory system	0.61	0.61	0.59	0.60	0.59	0.57	0.55	0.59	0.52	0.49	0.54
760-779	**Certain causes of perinatal morbidity and mortality**	**19.66**	**18.51**	**18.50**	**17.18**	**16.66**	**16.17**	**15.38**	**14.46**	**13.34**	**12.78**	**11.51**
760-761	Maternal conditions	0.57	0.57	0.59	0.60	0.57	0.57	0.47	0.48	0.41	0.47	0.48
762	Toxaemias of pregnancy	1.66	1.52	1.30	1.29	1.18	1.07	1.10	0.99	0.92	0.90	0.78
763	Maternal ante and post partum infection*	0.04	0.04	0.04	0.03	0.03	0.03	0.03	0.04	0.04	0.05	0.04
764-768	Difficult labour	0.87	0.84	0.76	0.67	0.69	0.59	0.54	0.49	0.43	0.37	0.32

A3.7.2 continued

Perinatal deaths by underlying cause, England and Wales, 1968–78

ICD Number	Cause	1968	1969	1970	1971	1972	1973	1974	1975	1976	1977	1978
		Rates per 1,000 total births										
769	Other complications of pregnancy and childbirth	1.71	1.55	1.59	1.52	1.52	1.40	1.40	1.42	1.25	1.16	1.08
769.4	Multiple pregnancy	0.79	0.82	0.81	0.79	0.75	0.72	0.80	0.79	0.72	0.68	0.65
770	Conditions of the placenta	3.78	3.49	3.51	3.22	3.09	3.23	2.92	2.84	2.64	2.61	2.43
771	Conditions of the cord	1.30	1.16	1.17	1.14	1.10	1.11	1.03	0.88	0.89	0.83	0.73
772	Birth injury without mention of cause	1.23	1.02	1.04	0.95	0.99	0.82	0.76	0.63	0.61	0.61	0.58
774-775	Haemolytic disease of newborn	0.88	0.83	0.77	0.66	0.53	0.45	0.37	0.30	0.25	0.24	0.19
776	Anoxic and hypoxic conditions not elsewhere classified	3.57	3.87	4.01	3.76	3.93	3.94	3.80	3.72	3.38	3.14	2.80
777	Immaturity	2.22	1.92	2.04	1.88	1.61	1.54	1.48	1.35	1.24	1.12	0.89
778-779	Other conditions of fetus and newborn	1.82	1.71	1.69	1.47	1.42	1.43	1.48	1.33	1.28	1.27	1.18
780-796	**Symptoms and ill-defined conditions**	**0.01**	**0.01**	**0.01**	**0.01**	**0.02**	**0.02**	**0.02**	**0.02**	**0.02**	**0.03**	**0.02**
795	Sudden death cause unknown	–	–	–	0.00	0.01	0.01	0.01	0.02	0.01	0.03	0.02
E800-E999	**Accidents, poisoning and violence**	**0.09**	**0.06**	**0.05**	**0.06**	**0.07**	**0.05**	**0.05**	**0.06**	**0.03**	**0.02**	**0.04**

* For the years 1968–73, ICD 763 is described as 'maternal ante and intra partum infection'

Source: Derived from data in OPCS *Mortality statistics, childhood, Series DH3*

This was Table A3.11 in the first edition of *Birth counts*

A3.7.3

Neonatal deaths by underlying cause, England and Wales, 1968–78

ICD Number	Cause	1968	1969	1970	1971	1972	1973	1974	1975	1976	1977	1978
		Numbers										
000-999	**All causes**	**10,125**	**9,599**	**9,661**	**9,113**	**8,375**	**7,528**	**7,067**	**6,408**	**5,598**	**5,231**	**5,140**
000-136	**Infective and parasitic diseases**	**127**	**117**	**113**	**126**	**124**	**103**	**106**	**94**	**111**	**114**	**140**
460-519	**Diseases of the respiratory system**	**517**	**472**	**435**	**411**	**322**	**275**	**261**	**212**	**208**	**158**	**164**
480-486	Pneumonia	454	403	377	343	280	231	221	182	187	136	141
740-759	**Congenital anomalies**	**2,086**	**1,942**	**1,940**	**1,997**	**1,894**	**1,724**	**1,782**	**1,643**	**1,441**	**1,435**	**1,464**
740	Anencephalus	186	160	171	163	154	112	118	80	90	72	69
741	Spina bifida	298	266	286	371	403	383	466	455	350	367	320
742	Congenital hydrocephalus	63	58	44	50	44	60	52	49	42	41	36
743-744	Other congenital anomalies of central nervous system and eye	91	83	81	76	73	58	70	66	71	72	60
746-747	Congenital anomalies of circulatory system	758	732	727	719	649	511	532	521	437	435	469
760-779	**Certain causes of perinatal morbidity and mortality**	**6,887**	**6,592**	**6,651**	**6,105**	**5,584**	**5,029**	**4,553**	**4,138**	**3,567**	**3,290**	**3,085**
760-761	Maternal conditions	45	36	52	41	40	35	26	25	17	20	20
762	Toxaemias of pregnancy	93	117	77	79	77	66	61	41	40	27	32
763	Maternal ante and post partum infection	7	7	8	5	7	8	4	10	3	5	12
764-768	Difficult labour	191	157	128	120	125	105	81	85	66	62	56
769	Other complications of pregnancy and childbirth	713	713	664	620	575	503	495	468	376	319	317
769.4	Multiple pregnancy	537	554	545	473	444	392	423	388	305	255	258
770	Conditions of placenta	128	119	122	122	99	92	75	58	69	54	57
771	Conditions of the cord	65	53	66	59	55	51	40	32	35	34	39
772	Birth injury without mention of cause	966	768	782	711	692	564	485	376	355	344	363
774-775	Haemolytic disease of newborn	249	238	208	195	124	106	75	60	43	48	38
776	Anoxic and hypoxic conditions not elsewhere classified	2,407	2,675	2,702	2,511	2,487	2,316	2,108	1,990	1,691	1,581	1,446
777	Immaturity	1,776	1,476	1,570	1,428	1,136	1,000	914	797	695	628	522
778-779	Other conditions of fetus and newborn	247	233	272	214	167	183	189	196	177	168	183
780-796	**Symptoms and ill-defined conditions**	**9**	**7**	**14**	**25**	**33**	**44**	**38**	**40**	**49**	**59**	**47**
795	Sudden death cause unknown	0	0	2	17	26	38	33	39	44	55	46
E800-E999	**Accidents, poisoning and violence**	**105**	**90**	**83**	**78**	**78**	**48**	**50**	**41**	**31**	**23**	**34**

Neonatal deaths by underlying cause, England and Wales, 1968–78

ICD Number	Cause	1968	1969	1970	1971	1972	1973	1974	1975	1976	1977	1978
		Rates per 1,000 live births										
000-999	All causes	12.36	12.04	12.32	11.64	11.54	11.14	11.04	10.62	9.58	9.19	8.62
000-136	Infective and parasitic diseases	0.16	0.15	0.14	0.16	0.17	0.15	0.17	0.16	0.19	0.20	0.23
460-519	Diseases of the respiratory system	0.63	0.59	0.55	0.52	0.44	0.41	0.41	0.35	0.36	0.28	0.27
480-486	Pneumonia	0.55	0.51	0.48	0.44	0.39	0.34	0.35	0.30	0.32	0.24	0.24
740-759	Congenital anomalies	2.55	2.43	2.47	2.55	2.61	2.55	2.78	2.72	2.47	2.52	2.45
740	Anencephalus	0.23	0.20	0.22	0.21	0.21	0.17	0.18	0.13	0.15	0.13	0.12
741	Spina bifida	0.36	0.33	0.36	0.47	0.56	0.57	0.73	0.75	0.60	0.64	0.54
742	Congenital hydrocephalus	0.08	0.07	0.06	0.06	0.06	0.09	0.08	0.08	0.07	0.07	0.06
743-744	Other congenital anomalies of central nervous system and eye	0.11	0.10	0.10	0.10	0.10	0.09	0.11	0.11	0.12	0.13	0.10
746-747	Congenital anomalies of circulatory system	0.93	0.92	0.93	0.92	0.89	0.76	0.83	0.86	0.75	0.76	0.79
760-779	Certain causes of perinatal morbidity and mortality	8.41	8.27	8.48	7.80	7.70	7.44	7.12	6.86	6.11	5.78	5.17
760-761	Maternal conditions	0.05	0.05	0.07	0.05	0.06	0.05	0.04	0.04	0.03	0.04	0.03
762	Toxaemias of pregnancy	0.11	0.15	0.10	0.10	0.11	0.10	0.10	0.07	0.07	0.05	0.05
763	Maternal ante and post partum infection	0.01	0.01	0.01	0.01	0.01	0.01	0.01	0.02	0.01	0.01	0.02
764-768	Difficult labour	0.23	0.20	0.16	0.15	0.17	0.16	0.13	0.14	0.11	0.11	0.09
769	Other complications of pregnancy and childbirth	0.87	0.89	0.85	0.79	0.79	0.74	0.77	0.78	0.64	0.56	0.53
769.4	Multiple pregnancy	0.66	0.69	0.69	0.60	0.61	0.58	0.66	0.64	0.52	0.45	0.43
770	Conditions of placenta	0.16	0.15	0.16	0.16	0.14	0.14	0.12	0.10	0.12	0.09	0.10
771	Conditions of the cord	0.08	0.07	0.08	0.08	0.08	0.08	0.06	0.05	0.06	0.06	0.07
772	Birth injury without mention of cause	1.18	0.96	1.00	0.91	0.95	0.83	0.76	0.62	0.61	0.60	0.61
774-775	Haemolytic disease of newborn	0.30	0.30	0.27	0.25	0.17	0.16	0.12	0.10	0.07	0.08	0.06
776	Anoxic and hypoxic conditions not elsewhere classified	2.94	3.35	3.44	3.21	3.43	3.43	3.29	3.30	2.89	2.78	2.42
777	Immaturity	2.17	1.85	2.00	1.82	1.57	1.48	1.43	1.32	1.19	1.10	0.88
778-779	Other conditions of fetus and newborn	0.30	0.29	0.35	0.27	0.23	0.27	0.30	0.32	0.30	0.30	0.31
780-796	Symptoms and ill-defined conditions	0.01	0.01	0.02	0.03	0.05	0.07	0.06	0.07	0.08	0.10	0.08
795	Sudden death cause unknown		.	0.00	0.02	0.04	0.06	0.05	0.06	0.08	0.10	0.08
E800-E999	Accidents, poisoning and violence	0.13	0.11	0.11	0.10	0.11	0.07	0.08	0.07	0.05	0.04	0.06

Source: Derived from data in OPCS *Mortality statistics, childhood, Series DH3*

This was Table A3.12 in the first edition of *Birth counts*

A3.7.4

Postneonatal deaths by underlying cause, England and Wales, 1968–78

ICD Number	Cause	1968	1969	1970	1971	1972	1973	1974	1975	1976	1977	1978
		Numbers										
000-999	**All causes**	**4,857**	**4,792**	**4,606**	**4,607**	**4,123**	**3,879**	**3,392**	**2,915**	**2,582**	**2,480**	**2,590**
000-136	**Infective and parasitic diseases**	**444**	**473**	**416**	**437**	**345**	**346**	**258**	**219**	**136**	**121**	**149**
460-519	**Diseases of the respiratory system**	**2,212**	**2,208**	**2,095**	**2,017**	**1,583**	**1,345**	**1,143**	**949**	**824**	**724**	**758**
460-466	Acute respiratory infections	695	744	683	710	575	460	414	345	308	252	258
480-486	Pneumonia	1,350	1,292	1,220	1,078	814	719	594	490	404	351	394
740-759	**Congenital anomalies**	**1,051**	**959**	**976**	**953**	**863**	**828**	**728**	**610**	**535**	**522**	**514**
740	Anencephalus	1	4	1	2	1	1	0	0	1	2	1
741	Spina bifida	185	148	165	154	183	171	130	121	91	77	90
743-744	Other congenital anomalies of central nervous system and eye	37	39	30	36	26	21	19	24	28	22	23
746-747	Congenital anomalies of heart and circulatory system	571	550	566	541	477	454	398	332	270	274	280
760-779	Certain conditions originating in the perinatal period	49	45	41	54	47	55	54	35	60	46	43
769.4	Multiple pregnancies	0	0	0	0	0	1	0	0	4	0	1
780-796	**Symptoms and ill-defined conditions**	**15**	**16**	**87**	**271**	**491**	**559**	**591**	**613**	**590**	**637**	**715**
795	Sudden death (cause unknown)	1	2	48	225	434	529	545	565	551	610	652
E800-E999	**Accidents, poisoning and violence**	**501**	**532**	**432**	**373**	**313**	**291**	**241**	**189**	**191**	**163**	**161**
E911	Inhalation and ingestion of food causing obstruction of respiratory tract or suffocation	205	231	202	165	128	129	106	81	88	71	76
E913	Accidental mechanical suffocation	151	139	112	89	64	41	47	38	33	33	23
		Rates per 1,000 live births										
000-999	**All causes**	**5.93**	**6.01**	**5.87**	**5.88**	**5.68**	**5.74**	**5.30**	**4.83**	**4.42**	**4.36**	**4.34**
000-136	**Infective and parasitic diseases**	**0.54**	**0.59**	**0.53**	**0.56**	**0.48**	**0.51**	**0.40**	**0.36**	**0.23**	**0.21**	**0.25**
460-519	**Diseases of the respiratory system**	**2.70**	**2.77**	**2.67**	**2.58**	**2.18**	**1.99**	**1.79**	**1.57**	**1.41**	**1.27**	**1.27**
460-466	Acute respiratory infections	0.85	0.93	0.87	0.91	0.79	0.68	0.65	0.57	0.53	0.44	0.43
480-486	Pneumonia	1.65	1.62	1.56	1.38	1.12	1.06	0.93	0.81	0.69	0.62	0.66
740-759	**Congenital anomalies**	**1.28**	**1.20**	**1.24**	**1.22**	**1.19**	**1.22**	**1.14**	**1.01**	**0.92**	**0.92**	**0.86**
740	Anencephalus	0.00	0.01	0.00	0.00	0.00	0.00	–	0.00	0.00	0.00	0.00
741	Spina bifida	0.23	0.19	0.21	0.20	0.25	0.25	0.20	0.20	0.16	0.14	0.15

A3.7.4 continued

Postneonatal deaths by underlying cause, England and Wales, 1968–78

ICD Number	Cause	1968	1969	1970	1971	1972	1973	1974	1975	1976	1977	1978
		Rates per 1,000 live births										
743-744	Other congenital anomalies of central nervous system and eye	0.05	0.05	0.04	0.05	0.04	0.03	0.03	0.04	0.05	0.04	0.04
746-747	Congenital anomalies of heart and circulatory system	0.70	0.69	0.72	0.69	0.66	0.67	0.62	0.55	0.46	0.48	0.47
760-779	**Certain conditions originating in the perinatal period**	**0.06**	**0.06**	**0.05**	**0.07**	**0.06**	**0.08**	**0.08**	**0.06**	**0.10**	**0.08**	**0.07**
769.4	Multiple pregnancies	–	–	–	–	–	0.00	–	–	0.01	–	–
780-796	Symptoms and ill-defined conditions	0.02	0.02	0.11	0.35	0.68	0.83	0.92	1.02	1.01	1.12	1.20
795	Sudden death (cause unknown)	0.00	0.00	0.06	0.29	0.60	0.78	0.85	0.94	0.94	1.07	1.09
E800-E999	**Accidents, poisoning and violence**	**0.61**	**0.67**	**0.55**	**0.48**	**0.43**	**0.43**	**0.38**	**0.31**	**0.33**	**0.29**	**0.27**
E911	Inhalation and ingestion of food causing obstruction of respiratory tract or suffocation	0.25	0.29	0.26	0.21	0.18	0.19	0.17	0.13	0.15	0.12	0.13
E913	Accidental mechanical suffocation	0.18	0.17	0.14	0.11	0.09	0.06	0.07	0.06	0.06	0.06	0.04

Source: Derived from data in OPCS *Mortality statistics, childhood, Series DH3*

This was Table A3.13 in the first edition of *Birth counts*

A3.8.1

Stillbirths by underlying cause, England and Wales, 1979–85

ICD Number	Cause	1979	1980	1981	1982	1983	1984	1985
		Numbers						
000-999	**All causes**	**5125**	**4773**	**4207**	**3939**	**3631**	**3643**	**3645**
740-759	**Congenital anomalies**	**939**	**809**	**615**	**494**	**421**	**329**	**298**
740	Anencephalus and similar anomalies	461	342	251	151	104	65	59
741	Spina bifida	125	114	88	66	44	51	36
742	Other congenital anomalies of central nervous system	141	149	114	93	101	57	50
745-747	Congenital anomalies of the heart and circulatory system	34	27	15	25	24	32	35
760-779	**Certain conditions originating in the perinatal period**	**4175**	**3952**	**3581**	**3438**	**3198**	**3302**	**3335**
760-761	Maternal conditions	720	629	577	496	482	416	358
761.5	Multiple pregnancy	99	80	86	70	84	60	43
762	Conditions of placenta, cord or membrane	2081	1955	1746	1632	1483	1595	1460
763	Other complications of labour and delivery	122	100	87	75	68	82	50
764-765	Slow fetal growth, fetal malnutrition and immaturity	74	76	63	73	65	68	64
767	Birth trauma	23	16	16	12	9	5	6
768-770	Hypoxia, birth asphyxia and other respiratory conditions	392	412	390	422	363	357	400
771	Infections specific to perinatal period	8	12	6	13	9	11	8
773	Haemolytic diseases of fetus or newborn	61	58	33	33	18	16	10
		Rates per 1,000 total births						
000-999	**All causes**	**7.97**	**7.22**	**6.59**	**6.25**	**5.74**	**5.69**	**5.52**
740-759	**Congenital anomalies**	**1.46**	**1.22**	**0.96**	**0.78**	**0.67**	**0.51**	**0.45**
740	Anencephalus and similar anomalies	0.72	0.52	0.39	0.24	0.16	0.10	0.09
741	Spina bifida	0.19	0.17	0.14	0.10	0.07	0.08	0.05
742	Other congenital anomalies of central nervous system	0.22	0.23	0.18	0.15	0.16	0.09	0.08
745-747	Congenital anomalies of the heart and circulatory system	0.05	0.04	0.02	0.04	0.04	0.05	0.05
760-779	**Certain conditions originating in the perinatal period**	**6.49**	**5.98**	**5.61**	**5.46**	**5.05**	**5.16**	**5.05**
760-761	Maternal conditions	1.12	0.95	0.90	0.79	0.76	0.65	0.54
761.5	Multiple pregnancies	0.15	0.12	0.13	0.11	0.13	0.09	0.07
762	Conditions of placenta, cord or membrane	3.24	2.96	2.73	2.59	2.34	2.49	2.21
763	Other complications of labour and delivery	0.19	0.15	0.14	0.12	0.11	0.13	0.08
764-765	Slow fetal growth, fetal malnutrition and immaturity	0.12	0.11	0.10	0.12	0.10	0.11	0.10
767	Birth trauma	0.04	0.02	0.03	0.02	0.01	0.01	0.01
768-770	Hypoxia, birth asphyxia and other respiratory conditions	0.61	0.62	0.61	0.67	0.57	0.56	0.61
771	Infections specific to perinatal period	0.01	0.02	0.01	0.02	0.01	0.02	0.01
773	Haemolytic diseases of fetus or newborn	0.09	0.09	0.05	0.05	0.03	0.02	0.02

Source: OPCS. *Mortality statistics, perinatal and infant, Series DH3.*

This was Table A3.14 in the first edition of *Birth counts*

A3.8.2

Perinatal deaths by underlying cause, England and Wales, 1979–85

ICD Number	Cause	1979	1980	1981	1982	1983	1984	1985
		Numbers						
000-999	**All causes**	**9,402**	**8,796**	**7,521**	**7,060**	**6,561**	**6,440**	**6,463**
480-486	**Pneumonia**	**45**	**39**	**29**	**32**	**21**	**23**	**16**
740-759	**Congenital anomalies**	**2,038**	**1,940**	**1,579**	**1,468**	**1,291**	**1,162**	**1,156**
740	Anencephalus	529	410	303	181	129	97	83
741	Spina bifida	272	256	171	129	99	99	80
742	Other congenital anomalies of central nervous system	204	220	162	156	164	98	92
745-747	Congenital anomalies of heart and circulatory system	314	298	248	290	265	252	283
760-779	**Certain conditions originating in the perinatal period**	**7,164**	**6,634**	**5,796**	**5,465**	**5,144**	**5,144**	**5,176**
760-761	Maternal conditions	894	792	680	618	617	522	457
761.5	Multiple pregnancy	227	191	160	155	184	132	112
762	Conditions of placenta, cord or membrane	2,185	2,062	1,836	1,705	1,578	1,692	1,554
763	Other complications of labour and delivery	172	143	120	104	92	107	69
764-765	Slow fetal growth, fetal malnutrition and immaturity	663	562	517	487	467	423	396
767	Birth trauma	180	150	129	81	83	77	50
768-770	Hypoxia, birth asphyxia and other respiratory conditions	1,930	1,774	1,499	1,443	1,307	1,276	1,402
771	Infections to specific perinatal periods	56	73	56	67	49	56	58
773	Haemolytic diseases of fetus or newborn	93	84	52	53	30	28	23
780-799	**Symptoms, signs and ill-defined conditions**	**12**	**15**	**21**	**10**	**18**	**19**	**15**
798	Sudden death, cause unknown	12	13	19	10	15	16	12
E800-E999	**External causes of injury and poisoning**	**21**	**26**	**14**	**17**	**16**	**9**	**14**
		Rates per 1,000 total births						
000-999	**All causes**	**14.62**	**13.31**	**11.78**	**11.21**	**10.37**	**10.06**	**9.79**
480-486	**Pneumonia**	**0.07**	**0.06**	**0.05**	**0.05**	**0.03**	**0.04**	**0.02**
740-759	**Congenital anomalies**	**3.17**	**2.93**	**2.47**	**2.33**	**2.04**	**1.81**	**1.75**
740	Anencephalus	0.82	0.62	0.47	0.29	0.20	0.15	0.13
741	Spina bifida	0.42	0.39	0.27	0.20	0.16	0.15	0.12
742	Other congenital anomalies of central nervous system	0.32	0.33	0.25	0.25	0.26	0.15	0.14
745-747	Congenital anomalies of heart and circulatory system	0.49	0.45	0.39	0.46	0.42	0.39	0.43
760-779	**Certain conditions originating in the perinatal period**	**11.14**	**10.04**	**9.07**	**8.68**	**8.13**	**8.03**	**7.84**
760-761	Maternal conditions	1.39	1.20	1.06	0.98	0.98	0.82	0.69
761.5	Multiple pregnancy	0.35	0.29	0.25	0.25	0.29	0.21	0.17
762	Conditions of placenta, cord or membrane	3.40	3.12	2.87	2.71	2.49	2.64	2.35

A3.8.2 continued

Perinatal deaths by underlying cause, England and Wales, 1979–85

ICD Number	Cause	1979	1980	1981	1982	1983	1984	1985
		Rates per 1,000 total births						
763	Other complications of labour and delivery	0.27	0.22	0.19	0.17	0.15	0.17	0.10
764-765	Slow fetal growth, fetal malnutrition and immaturity	1.03	0.85	0.81	0.77	0.74	0.66	0.60
767	Birth trauma	0.28	0.23	0.20	0.13	0.13	0.12	0.08
768-770	Hypoxia, birth asphyxia and other respiratory conditions	3.00	2.68	2.35	2.29	2.07	1.99	2.12
771	Infections to specific perinatal periods	0.09	0.11	0.09	0.11	0.08	0.09	0.09
773	Haemolytic diseases of fetus or newborn	0.14	0.13	0.08	0.08	0.05	0.04	0.03
780-799	**Symptoms, signs and ill-defined conditions**	**0.02**	**0.02**	**0.03**	**0.02**	**0.03**	**0.03**	**0.02**
798	Sudden death, cause unknown	0.02	0.02	0.03	0.02	0.02	0.02	0.02
E800-E999	**External causes of injury and poisoning**	**0.03**	**0.04**	**0.02**	**0.03**	**0.03**	**0.01**	**0.02**

Source: OPCS. *Mortality statistics, perinatal and infant, Series DH3*.

This was Table A3.15 in the first edition of *Birth counts*

A3.8.3

Neonatal deaths by underlying cause, England and Wales, 1979–85

ICD Number	Cause	1979	1980	1981	1982	1983	1984	1985
		Numbers						
000-999	**All causes**	**5,216**	**4,987**	**4,176**	**3,890**	**3,653**	**3,515**	**3,489**
000-139	**Infectious and parasitic diseases**	**21**	**20**	**26**	**19**	**12**	**15**	**30**
460-519	**Diseases of the respiratory system**	**134**	**118**	**105**	**86**	**57**	**63**	**48**
480-486	Pneumonia	107	94	78	68	40	49	34
740-759	**Congenital anomalies**	**1,530**	**1,551**	**1,332**	**1,272**	**1,147**	**1,113**	**1,115**
740	Anencephalus and similar anomalies	69	68	57	30	26	33	24
741	Spina bifida	312	270	191	131	111	102	100
742	Other congenital anomalies of central nervous system	97	102	73	82	84	56	55
745-747	Congenital anomalies of heart and circulatory system	444	452	392	410	391	348	380
760-779	**Certain conditions originating in the perinatal period**	**3,299**	**3,011**	**2,506**	**2,327**	**2,244**	**2,123**	**2,106**
760-761	Maternal conditions	176	170	107	126	138	106	100
762	Conditions of placenta, cord or membrane	105	109	92	76	98	98	97
763	Other complications of labour and delivery	52	44	41	30	25	25	21
764-765	Slow fetal growth, fetal malnutrition and immaturity	609	513	470	433	424	371	343
767	Birth trauma	182	152	128	89	89	82	57
768-770	Hypoxia, birth asphyxia and other respiratory conditions	1,676	1,506	1,230	1,165	1,080	1,052	1,124
771	Infections specific perinatal periods	80	86	76	73	72	90	79
773	Haemolytic diseases of fetus or newborn	33	28	19	21	15	12	14
798	Sudden death, cause unknown	48	78	69	50	63	64	57
E800-E999	**External causes of injury and poisoning**	**33**	**39**	**21**	**26**	**26**	**15**	**22**
		Rates per 1,000 live births						
000-999	**All causes**	**8.18**	**7.60**	**6.58**	**6.21**	**5.81**	**5.52**	**5.32**
000-139	**Infectious and parasitic diseases**	**0.03**	**0.03**	**0.04**	**0.03**	**0.02**	**0.02**	**0.05**
460-519	**Diseases of the respiratory system**	**0.21**	**0.18**	**0.17**	**0.14**	**0.09**	**0.10**	**0.07**
480-486	Pneumonia	0.17	0.14	0.12	0.11	0.06	0.08	0.05
740-759	**Congenital anomalies**	**2.40**	**2.36**	**2.10**	**2.03**	**1.82**	**1.75**	**1.70**
740	Anencephalus and similar anomalies	0.11	0.10	0.09	0.05	0.04	0.05	0.04
741	Spina bifida	0.49	0.41	0.30	0.21	0.18	0.16	0.15
742	Other congenital anomalies of central nervous system	0.15	0.16	0.12	0.13	0.13	0.09	0.08
745-747	Congenital anomalies of heart and circulatory system	0.70	0.69	0.62	0.66	0.62	0.55	0.58

A3.8.3 *continued*

Neonatal deaths by underlying cause, England and Wales, 1979–85

ICD Number	Cause	1979	1980	1981	1982	1983	1984	1985
		Rates per 1,000 live births						
760-779	**Certain conditions originating in the perinatal period**	**5.17**	**4.59**	**3.95**	**3.72**	**3.57**	**3.33**	**3.21**
760-761	Maternal conditions	0.28	0.26	0.17	0.20	0.22	0.17	0.15
762	Conditions of placenta, cord or membrane	0.16	0.17	0.14	0.12	0.16	0.15	0.15
763	Other complications of labour and delivery	0.08	0.07	0.06	0.05	0.04	0.04	0.03
764-765	Slow fetal growth, fetal malnutrition and immaturity	0.95	0.78	0.74	0.69	0.67	0.58	0.52
767	Birth trauma	0.29	0.23	0.20	0.14	0.14	0.13	0.09
768-770	Hypoxia, birth asphyxia and other respiratory conditions	2.63	2.29	1.94	1.86	1.72	1.65	1.71
771	Infections specific perinatal periods	0.13	0.13	0.12	0.12	0.11	0.14	0.12
773	Haemolytic diseases of fetus or newborn	0.05	0.04	0.03	0.03	0.02	0.02	0.02
798	Sudden death, cause unknown	0.08	0.12	0.11	0.08	0.10	0.10	0.09
E800-E999	**External causes of injury and poisoning**	**0.05**	**0.06**	**0.03**	**0.04**	**0.04**	**0.02**	**0.03**

Source: OPCS. *Mortality statistics, perinatal and infant, Series DH3.*

This was Table A3.16 in the first edition of *Birth counts*

A3.8.4

Postneonatal deaths by underlying cause, England and Wales, 1979–92

ICD Number/Cause		1979	1980	1981	1982	1983	1984	1985	1986	1987	1988	1989	1990	1991	1992
		Numbers													
000-999	**All causes**	**2,848**	**2,803**	**2,709**	**2,773**	**2,631**	**2,430**	**2,538**	**2,760**	**2,742**	**2,793**	**2,478**	**2,270**	**2,049**	**1,524**
001-139	**Infectious and parasitic diseases**	**128**	**103**	**94**	**81**	**84**	**74**	**76**	**98**	**112**	**82**	**116**	**100**	**90**	**73**
460-519	**Diseases of the respiratory system**	**784**	**677**	**549**	**543**	**444**	**347**	**378**	**306**	**292**	**318**	**238**	**204**	**200**	**119**
460-466	Acute respiratory infections	271	212	155	196	150	127	111	114	99	95	75	58	68	25
480-486	Pneumonia	383	353	286	264	218	160	177	129	120	136	99	94	73	55
740-759	**Congenital anomalies**	**508**	**507**	**531**	**542**	**505**	**494**	**439**	**465**	**449**	**380**	**399**	**335**	**325**	**341**
740	Anencephalus and similar anomalies	0	1	1	0	1	1	0	1	1	0	1	1	0	2
741	Spina bifida	91	87	96	61	73	39	42	42	16	20	10	10	4	4
742-743	Other congenital anomalies of central nervous system and eye	40	37	44	33	46	46	50	45	42	27	33	28	33	44
745-747	Congenital anomalies of heart and circulatory system	248	267	265	303	259	242	225	263	270	219	223	204	196	183
760-779	**Certain conditions originating in the perinatal period**	**96**	**110**	**121**	**111**	**154**	**143**	**156**	**202**	**172**	**222**	**208**	**226**	**220**	**218**
798	Sudden death, cause unknown	806	929	975	1,066	1,029	1,002	1,094	1,284	1,326	1,382	1,151	1,034	862	428
E800-E999	**External causes of injury and poisoning**	**197**	**145**	**139**	**110**	**89**	**96**	**94**	**94**	**86**	**103**	**85**	**85**	**82**	**75**
E911	Inhalation and ingestion of food causing obstruction of respiratory tract or suffocation	96	64	60	39	27	29	38	30	27	25	21	7	21	9
E913	Accidental mechanical suffocation	25	28	18	17	14	17	7	11	5	7	6	8	9	7
		Rates per 1,000 live births													
000-999	**All causes**	**4.46**	**4.27**	**4.27**	**4.43**	**4.18**	**3.82**	**3.87**	**4.18**	**4.02**	**4.03**	**3.60**	**3.21**	**2.93**	**2.21**
001-139	**Infective and parasitic diseases**	**0.20**	**0.16**	**0.15**	**0.13**	**0.13**	**0.12**	**0.12**	**0.15**	**0.16**	**0.12**	**0.17**	**0.14**	**0.13**	**0.11**
460-519	**Diseases of the respiratory system**	**1.23**	**1.03**	**0.87**	**0.87**	**0.71**	**0.54**	**0.58**	**0.46**	**0.43**	**0.46**	**0.35**	**0.29**	**0.29**	**0.17**
460-465	Acute respiratory infections	0.42	0.32	0.24	0.31	0.24	0.20	0.17	0.17	0.15	0.14	0.11	0.08	0.10	0.08
480-486	Pneumonia	0.60	0.54	0.45	0.42	0.35	0.25	0.27	0.20	0.18	0.20	0.14	0.13	0.10	0.08
740-759	**Congenital anomalies**	**0.80**	**0.77**	**0.84**	**0.87**	**0.80**	**0.78**	**0.67**	**0.70**	**0.66**	**0.55**	**0.58**	**0.47**	**0.46**	**0.49**
740	Anencephalus and similar anomalies	–	0.00	0.00	–	0.00	0.00	0.00	0.00	0.00	0.00	0.00	0.00	–	0.00
741	Spina bifida	0.14	0.13	0.15	0.10	0.12	0.06	0.06	0.06	0.02	0.03	0.01	0.01	0.01	0.01

A3.8.4 continued

Postneonatal deaths by underlying cause, England and Wales, 1979–92

ICD Number	Cause	1979	1980	1981	1982	1983	1984	1985	1986	1987	1988	1989	1990	1991	1992
		Rates per 1,000 live births													
742	Other congenital anomalies of central nervous system and eye	0.06	0.06	0.07	0.05	0.07	0.07	0.08	0.07	0.06	0.04	0.05	0.04	0.05	0.06
745-747	Congenital anomalies of heart and circulatory system	0.39	0.41	0.42	0.48	0.41	0.38	0.34	0.40	0.40	0.32	0.32	0.29	0.28	0.27
760-779	**Certain conditions originating in the perinatal period**	**0.15**	**0.17**	**0.19**	**0.18**	**0.24**	**0.22**	**0.24**	**0.31**	**0.25**	**0.32**	**0.30**	**0.32**	**0.31**	**0.32**
798	Sudden death, cause unknown	1.26	1.42	1.54	1.70	1.64	1.57	1.67	1.94	1.95	1.99	1.67	1.46	1.23	0.62
E800-E999	**External causes of injury and poisoning**	**0.31**	**0.22**	**0.22**	**0.18**	**0.14**	**0.15**	**0.14**	**0.14**	**0.13**	**0.15**	**0.12**	**0.12**	**0.12**	**0.11**
E911	Inhalation and ingestion of food causing obstruction of respiratory tract or suffocation	0.15	0.10	0.09	0.06	0.04	0.05	0.06	0.05	0.04	0.04	0.03	0.01	0.03	0.01
E913	Accidental mechanical suffocation	0.04	0.04	0.03	0.03	0.02	0.03	0.01	0.02	0.01	0.01	0.01	0.01	0.01	0.01

Source: *OPCS. Mortality statistics, perinatal and infant, Series* DH3.

These data come from tabulations of OPCS' linked files. Data were not tabulated in this way after 1992.

This was Table A3.17 in the first edition of *Birth counts*

A3.9.1

Stillbirths by ONS cause group, England and Wales, 1979–96

Numbers

Stillbirths at 28 or more completed weeks of gestation

Year of birth	ONS cause group										All causes
	1	2	3	4	5	6	7	8a	8b	0	
1979	940	2	105	3,105	0	8	189			783	5,132
1980	812	9	81	2,932	0	8	167			773	4,782
1981	615	4	48	2,666	0	5	151			718	4,207
1982	493	6	74	2,504	0	11	135			720	3,943
1983	422	10	45	2,261	0	9	138			747	3,632
1984	327	6	34	2,372	0	10	109			792	3,650
1985	298	7	30	2,201	5	6	128			975	3,650
1981–85	2,155	33	231	12,004	5	41	661			3,952	19,082
1986	332	14	35	262	0	10	114	1,834	908	39	3,548
1987	321	11	45	238	0	12	126	1,742	906	20	3,421
1988	311	12	50	244	0	12	119	1,678	927	32	3,385
1989	313	16	51	205	0	21	116	1,600	883	26	3,231
1990	272	10	38	182	0	17	118	1,469	1,109	44	3,259
1986–90	1,549	63	219	1,131	0	72	593	8,323	4,733	161	16,844
1991	267	7	27	172	0	13	104	1,410	1,205	50	3,255
1992	276	15	53	184	0	21	110	1,275	1,172	50	3,156
1993	208	6	26	131	1	6	115	1,095	1,321	51	2,960
1994	226	3	20	132	0	7	104	998	1,387	48	2,925
1995	212	4	26	128	0	3	85	843	1,338	65	2,704
1991–95	1,189	35	152	747	1	50	518	5,621	6,423	264	15,000
1996	209	3	17	84	2	7	99	863	1,257	57	2,598
1993–96	855	16	89	475	3	23	403	3,799	5,303	221	11,187

Stillbirths by ONS cause group, England and Wales, 1979–96

Year of birth	ONS cause group										All causes
	1	2	3	4	5	6	7	8a	8b	0	
Stillbirths at 24 or more completed weeks of gestation											
1993*	308	14	129	183	1	11	146	1,341	1,667	66	3,866
1994*	361	13	108	191	0	16	126	1,204	1,737	60	3,816
1995*	320	12	116	173	0	11	118	1,068	1,696	83	3,597
1996*	359	8	116	126	2	14	131	1,093	1,613	77	3,539
1993–96*	1,348	47	469	673	3	52	521	4,706	6,713	286	14,818
Rates per 1,000 total births											
Stillbirths at 28 or more completed weeks of gestation											
1979	1.46	0.00	0.16	4.83	0.00	0.01	0.29			1.22	7.98
1980	1.23	0.01	0.12	4.44	0.00	0.01	0.25			1.17	7.23
1981	0.96	0.01	0.08	4.17	0.00	0.01	0.24			1.12	6.59
1982	0.78	0.01	0.12	3.98	0.00	0.02	0.21			1.14	6.26
1983	0.67	0.02	0.07	3.57	0.00	0.01	0.22			1.18	5.74
1984	0.51	0.01	0.05	3.70	0.00	0.02	0.17			1.24	5.70
1985	0.45	0.01	0.05	3.33	0.01	0.01	0.19			1.48	5.53
1981–85	0.67	0.01	0.07	3.75	0.00	0.01	0.21			1.23	5.96
1986	0.50	0.02	0.05	0.39	0.00	0.02	0.17	2.76	1.37	0.06	5.34
1987	0.47	0.02	0.07	0.35	0.00	0.02	0.18	2.54	1.32	0.03	4.99
1988	0.45	0.02	0.07	0.35	0.00	0.02	0.17	2.41	1.33	0.05	4.86
1989	0.45	0.02	0.07	0.30	0.00	0.03	0.17	2.32	1.28	0.04	4.68
1990	0.38	0.01	0.05	0.26	0.00	0.02	0.17	2.07	1.56	0.06	4.59
1986–90	0.45	0.02	0.06	0.33	0.00	0.02	0.17	2.41	1.37	0.05	4.89
1991	0.38	0.01	0.04	0.24	0.00	0.02	0.15	2.01	1.72	0.07	4.63
1992	0.40	0.02	0.08	0.27	0.00	0.03	0.16	1.84	1.69	0.07	4.56
1993	0.31	0.01	0.04	0.19	0.00	0.01	0.17	1.62	1.96	0.08	4.39
1994	0.34	0.00	0.03	0.20	0.00	0.01	0.16	1.50	2.08	0.07	4.38
1995	0.33	0.01	0.04	0.20	0.00	0.00	0.13	1.30	2.06	0.10	4.16

A3.9.1 continued

Stillbirths by ONS cause group, England and Wales, 1979–96

Year of birth	ONS cause group										All causes
	1	2	3	4	5	6	7	8a	8b	0	
Rates per 1,000 total births											
Stillbirths at 28 or more completed weeks of gestation											
1991–95	0.35	0.01	0.04	0.22	0.00	0.01	0.15	1.66	1.90	0.08	4.43
1996	0.32	0.00	0.03	0.13	0.00	0.01	0.15	1.32	1.93	0.09	3.98
1993–96	0.32	0.01	0.03	0.18	0.00	0.01	0.15	1.44	2.01	0.08	4.23
Stillbirths at 24 or more completed weeks of gestation											
1993*	0.46	0.02	0.19	0.27	0.00	0.02	0.22	1.99	2.47	0.10	5.73
1994*	0.54	0.02	0.16	0.29	0.00	0.02	0.19	1.80	2.60	0.09	5.71
1995*	0.49	0.02	0.18	0.27	0.00	0.02	0.18	1.64	2.60	0.13	5.52
1996*	0.55	0.01	0.18	0.19	0.00	0.02	0.20	1.67	2.47	0.12	5.42
1993–96*	0.51	0.02	0.18	0.25	0.00	0.02	0.20	1.78	2.54	0.11	5.60

* Including stillbirths at 24–27 weeks of gestational age

ONS cause groups:
1 = Congenital defects
2 = Antepartum infections
3 = Conditions relating to immaturity
4 = Intrapartum deaths with mentions of causes likely to lead to asphyxia, anoxia or trauma
5 = External conditions
6 = Infections
7 = Other specific conditions
8a = Antepartum deaths with mentions of causes likely to lead to asphyxia, anoxia or trauma
8b = Remaining antepartum deaths
0 = Other conditions

Source: Authors' analysis of ONS data

Data extracts: live births 1993 (7/94), 1994 (7/95), 1995 (3/7/96), 1996 (8/4/97)
    linked 1993 (3/4/96),1994 (18/9/96),1995 (3/11/97)

This is similar to Table A3.14 in the first edition of *Birth counts*

A3.9.2

Neonatal deaths by ONS cause group, England and Wales, 1979–96

Year of birth	ONS cause group									All causes
	1	2	3	4	5	6	7	9	0	
Numbers										
1979	1,554	15	2,023	767	45	257	123	48	369	5,201
1980	1,541	26	1,879	703	46	240	119	80	329	4,963
1981	1,342	11	1,520	610	25	240	108	65	244	4,165
1982	1,280	18	1,459	539	31	201	90	59	226	3,903
1983	1,171	20	1,325	556	27	153	91	56	244	3,643
1984	1,129	16	1,290	512	20	196	76	66	213	3,518
1985	1,119	31	1,271	493	21	148	100	52	248	3,483
1981–85	6,041	96	6,865	2,710	124	938	465	298	1,175	18,712
1986	1,258	22	1,476	418	16	108	39	66	44	3,447
1987	1,193	24	1,505	386	13	126	44	74	55	3,420
1988	1,137	32	1,499	405	20	128	35	71	52	3,379
1989	1,093	32	1,425	399	9	123	32	65	73	3,251
1990	972	25	1,466	369	12	118	45	70	57	3,134
1986–90	5,653	135	7,371	1,977	70	603	195	346	281	16,631
1991	964	28	1,373	374	13	107	40	60	57	3,016
1992	902	41	1,334	337	5	96	40	54	60	2,869
1993	758	19	1,373	344	12	112	35	39	82	2,774
1994	733	15	1,388	345	7	95	25	41	80	2,729
1995	705	21	1,296	345	9	102	32	45	112	2,667
1991–95	4,062	124	6,764	1,745	46	512	172	239	391	14,055
1996	676	16	1,329	297	6	111	31	47	94	2,607
Rates per 1,000 live births										
1979	2.44	0.02	3.17	1.20	0.07	0.40	0.19	0.08	0.58	8.15
1980	2.35	0.04	2.86	1.07	0.07	0.37	0.18	0.12	0.50	7.56
1981	2.12	0.02	2.40	0.96	0.04	0.38	0.17	0.10	0.38	6.56
1982	2.04	0.03	2.33	0.86	0.05	0.32	0.14	0.09	0.36	6.24
1983	1.86	0.03	2.11	0.88	0.04	0.24	0.14	0.09	0.39	5.79
1984	1.77	0.03	2.03	0.80	0.03	0.31	0.12	0.10	0.33	5.52
1985	1.70	0.05	1.94	0.75	0.03	0.23	0.15	0.08	0.38	5.31
1981–85	1.90	0.03	2.16	0.85	0.04	0.29	0.15	0.09	0.37	5.88

Neonatal deaths by ONS cause group, England and Wales, 1979–96

Year of birth	ONS cause group									All causes
	1	2	3	4	5	6	7	9	0	
	Rates per 1,000 live births									
1986	1.90	0.03	2.23	0.63	0.02	0.16	0.06	0.10	0.07	5.21
1987	1.75	0.04	2.21	0.57	0.02	0.18	0.06	0.11	0.08	5.02
1988	1.64	0.05	2.16	0.58	0.03	0.18	0.05	0.10	0.07	4.87
1989	1.59	0.05	2.07	0.58	0.01	0.18	0.05	0.09	0.11	4.73
1990	1.38	0.04	2.08	0.52	0.02	0.17	0.06	0.10	0.08	4.44
1986–90	1.65	0.04	2.15	0.58	0.02	0.18	0.06	0.10	0.08	4.85
1991	1.38	0.04	1.96	0.53	0.02	0.15	0.06	0.09	0.08	4.31
1992	1.31	0.06	1.93	0.49	0.01	0.14	0.06	0.08	0.09	4.16
1993	1.13	0.03	2.05	0.51	0.02	0.17	0.05	0.06	0.12	4.13
1994	1.10	0.02	2.09	0.52	0.01	0.14	0.04	0.06	0.12	4.11
1995	1.09	0.03	2.00	0.53	0.01	0.16	0.05	0.07	0.17	4.12
1991–95	1.20	0.04	2.01	0.52	0.01	0.15	0.05	0.07	0.12	4.17
1996	1.04	0.02	2.05	0.46	0.01	0.17	0.05	0.07	0.14	4.01

ONS cause groups
1 = Congenital defects
2 = Antepartum infections
3 = Conditions relating to immaturity
4 = Asphyxia, anoxia or trauma
5 = External conditions
6 = Infections
7 = Other specific conditions
9 = Sudden infant deaths
0 = Other conditions

Source: Authors' analysis of ONS data up to 1995 birth cohort
1996 birth cohort from *Mortality statistics, Series DH3, no 30*

Data extract: live births 1993 (7/94), 1994 (7/95), 1995 (3/7/96), 1996 (8/4/97)
linked   1993 (3/4/96), 1994 (18/9/96), 1995 (3/11/97)

A3.9.3

Postneonatal deaths by ONS cause group, England and Wales, 1979–96

Year of birth	ONS cause group									All causes
	1	2	3	4	5	6	7	9	0	
Numbers										
1979	625	5	58	19	186	814	56	859	234	2,856
1980	589	1	63	21	144	707	61	944	190	2,720
1981	584	3	85	16	131	623	66	1,052	187	2,747
1982	604	3	91	19	111	591	62	1,053	167	2,701
1983	602	5	105	30	110	488	52	1,110	154	2,656
1984	551	4	107	23	84	398	60	948	152	2,327
1985	548	4	104	28	99	475	52	1,216	162	2,688
1981–85	2,889	19	492	116	535	2,575	292	5,379	822	13,119
1986	539	4	167	25	90	375	55	1,297	158	2,710
1987	523	8	157	23	103	367	50	1,386	156	2,773
1988	476	3	173	26	101	375	48	1,281	167	2,650
1989	448	6	175	20	95	356	57	1,128	149	2,434
1990	421	5	190	32	89	303	37	990	149	2,216
1986–90	2,407	26	862	126	478	1,776	247	6,082	779	12,783
1991	409	4	171	23	80	232	42	655	134	1,750
1992	417	8	186	21	71	210	47	417	134	1,511
1993	337	2	115	9	68	224	42	400	169	1,366
1994	307	5	108	9	68	195	42	336	184	1,254
1995	312	3	132	11	64	205	42	341	181	1,291
1991–95	1,782	22	712	73	351	1,066	215	2,149	802	7,172
1996	302	2	105	9	60	207	43	333	185	1,246
Rates per 1,000 live births										
1979	0.98	0.01	0.09	0.03	0.29	1.28	0.09	1.35	0.37	4.48
1980	0.90	0.00	0.10	0.03	0.22	1.08	0.09	1.44	0.29	4.14
1981	0.92	0.00	0.13	0.03	0.21	0.98	0.10	1.66	0.29	4.33
1982	0.96	0.00	0.15	0.03	0.18	0.94	0.10	1.68	0.27	4.32
1983	0.96	0.01	0.17	0.05	0.17	0.78	0.08	1.76	0.24	4.22
1984	0.87	0.01	0.17	0.04	0.13	0.62	0.09	1.49	0.24	3.65
1985	0.83	0.01	0.16	0.04	0.15	0.72	0.08	1.85	0.25	4.09

A3.9.3 continued

Postneonatal deaths by ONS cause group, England and Wales, 1979–96

Year of birth	ONS cause group										All causes
	1	2	3	4	5	6	7	9	0	
	Rates per 1,000 live births										
1981–85	0.91	0.01	0.15	0.04	0.17	0.81	0.09	1.69	0.26		4.12
1986	0.82	0.01	0.25	0.04	0.14	0.57	0.08	1.96	0.24		4.10
1987	0.77	0.01	0.23	0.03	0.15	0.54	0.07	2.03	0.23		4.07
1988	0.69	0.00	0.25	0.04	0.15	0.54	0.07	1.85	0.24		3.82
1989	0.65	0.01	0.25	0.03	0.14	0.52	0.08	1.64	0.22		3.54
1990	0.60	0.01	0.27	0.05	0.13	0.43	0.05	1.40	0.21		3.14
1986–90	0.70	0.01	0.25	0.04	0.14	0.52	0.07	1.77	0.23		3.73
1991	0.58	0.01	0.24	0.03	0.11	0.33	0.06	0.94	0.19		2.50
1992	0.60	0.01	0.27	0.03	0.10	0.30	0.07	0.60	0.19		2.19
1993	0.50	0.00	0.17	0.01	0.10	0.33	0.06	0.60	0.25		2.04
1994	0.46	0.01	0.16	0.01	0.10	0.29	0.06	0.51	0.28		1.89
1995	0.48	0.00	0.20	0.02	0.10	0.32	0.06	0.53	0.28		1.99
1991–95	0.53	0.01	0.21	0.02	0.10	0.32	0.06	0.64	0.24		2.13
1996	0.46	0.00	0.16	0.01	0.09	0.32	0.07	0.51	0.28		1.92

ONS cause groups
1 = Congenital defects
2 = Antepartum infections
3 = Conditions relating to immaturity
4 = Asphyxia, anoxia or trauma
5 = External conditions
6 = Infections
7 = Other specific conditions
9 = Sudden infant deaths
0 = Other conditions

Source: Authors' analysis of ONS data up to 1995 birth cohort
1996 birth cohort from *Mortality statistics, Series DH3, no 30*, Table 33

Data extract: live births 1993 (7/94), 1994 (7/95), 1995 (3/7/96), 1996 (8/4/97)
linked   1993 (3/4/96), 1994 (18/9/96), 1995 (3/11/97)

A3.9.4

Infant deaths by ONS cause group, England and Wales, 1979-96

Year of birth	ONS cause group									All causes
	1	2	3	4	5	6	7	9	0	
Numbers										
1979	2,179	20	2,081	786	231	1,071	179	907	603	8,057
1980	2,130	27	1,942	724	190	947	180	1,024	519	7,683
1981	1,926	14	1,605	626	156	863	174	1,117	431	6,912
1982	1,884	21	1,550	558	142	792	152	1,112	393	6,604
1983	1,773	25	1,430	586	137	641	143	1,166	398	6,299
1984	1,680	20	1,397	535	104	594	136	1,014	365	5,845
1985	1,667	35	1,375	521	120	623	152	1,268	410	6,171
1981-85	8,930	115	7,357	2,826	659	3,513	757	5,677	1,997	31,831
1986	1,797	26	1,643	443	106	483	94	1,363	202	6,157
1987	1,716	32	1,662	409	116	493	94	1,460	211	6,193
1988	1,613	35	1,672	431	121	503	83	1,352	219	6,029
1989	1,541	38	1,600	419	104	479	89	1,193	222	5,685
1990	1,393	30	1,656	401	101	421	82	1,060	206	5,350
1986-90	8,060	161	8,233	2,103	548	2,379	442	6,428	1,060	29,414
1991	1,373	32	1,544	397	93	339	82	715	191	4,766
1992	1,319	49	1,520	358	76	306	87	471	194	4,380
1993	1,095	21	1,488	353	80	336	77	439	251	4,140
1994	1,040	20	1,496	354	75	290	67	377	264	3,983
1995	1,017	24	1,428	356	73	307	74	386	293	3,958
1991-95	5,844	146	7,476	1,818	397	1,578	387	2,388	1,193	21,227
1996	978	18	1,434	306	66	318	74	380	279	3,853
Rates per 1,000 live births										
1979	3.42	0.03	3.26	1.23	0.36	1.68	0.28	1.42	0.95	12.63
1980	3.25	0.04	2.96	1.10	0.29	1.44	0.27	1.56	0.79	11.71
1981	3.04	0.02	2.53	0.99	0.25	1.36	0.27	1.76	0.68	10.89
1982	3.01	0.03	2.48	0.89	0.23	1.27	0.24	1.78	0.63	10.55
1983	2.82	0.04	2.27	0.93	0.22	1.02	0.23	1.85	0.63	10.01
1984	2.64	0.03	2.19	0.84	0.16	0.93	0.21	1.59	0.57	9.18
1985	2.54	0.05	2.09	0.79	0.18	0.95	0.23	1.93	0.62	9.40

A3.9.4 continued

Infant deaths by ONS cause group, England and Wales, 1979–96

Year of birth	ONS cause group									All causes
	1	2	3	4	5	6	7	9	0	
	Rates per 1,000 live births									
1981–85	2.81	0.04	2.31	0.89	0.21	1.10	0.24	1.78	0.63	10.00
1986	2.72	0.04	2.49	0.67	0.16	0.73	0.14	2.06	0.31	9.31
1987	2.52	0.05	2.44	0.60	0.17	0.72	0.14	2.14	0.31	9.09
1988	2.33	0.05	2.41	0.62	0.17	0.73	0.12	1.95	0.32	8.69
1989	2.24	0.06	2.33	0.61	0.15	0.70	0.13	1.73	0.32	8.27
1990	1.97	0.04	2.35	0.57	0.14	0.60	0.12	1.50	0.29	7.58
1986–90	2.35	0.05	2.40	0.61	0.16	0.69	0.13	1.87	0.31	8.58
1991	1.96	0.05	2.21	0.57	0.13	0.48	0.12	1.02	0.27	6.82
1992	1.91	0.07	2.20	0.52	0.11	0.44	0.13	0.68	0.28	6.35
1993	1.63	0.03	2.22	0.53	0.12	0.50	0.11	0.65	0.37	6.17
1994	1.57	0.03	2.25	0.53	0.11	0.44	0.10	0.57	0.40	6.00
1995	1.57	0.04	2.20	0.55	0.11	0.47	0.11	0.60	0.45	6.11
1991–95	1.73	0.04	2.22	0.54	0.12	0.47	0.11	0.71	0.35	6.29
1996	1.51	0.03	2.21	0.47	0.10	0.49	0.11	0.59	0.43	5.93

ONS cause groups
1 = Congenital defects
2 = Antepartum infections
3 = Conditions relating to immaturity
4 = Asphyxia, anoxia or trauma
5 = External conditions
6 = Infections
7 = Other specific conditions
9 = Sudden infant deaths
0 = Other conditions

Source: Authors' analysis of ONS data up to 1995 birth cohort
1996 birth cohort from *Mortality statistics, Series DH3, no 30*, Table 33

Data extract: live births 1993 (7/94), 1994 (7/95), 1995 (3/7/96), 1996 (8/4/97)
 linked   1993 (3/4/96), 1994 (18/9/96), 1995 (3/11/97)

A3.10.1

Bridge coding of 25 per cent sample of infant deaths in England and Wales in 1978: tabulation by ICD chapter

8th Revision	Numbers of deaths 9th Revision																	
	I	II	III	IV	V	VI	VII	VIII	IX	X	XI	XII	XIII	XIV	XV	XVI	XVII	Total
I	39														23			62
II		8																8
III		1	14												1			16
IV				3											1			4
V																		
VI						44								1				45
VII						1	6											7
VIII	2						1	227						1	3			234
IX									12					15	2			29
X										5								5
XI																		
XII												1						1
XIII													1					1
XIV						1	1		1					462	5			470
XV							1	1						2	683			687
XVI			1	1			1									180		183
XVII																	45	45
Total	41	9	15	4		46	10	228	13	5		1	1	481	718	180	45	1797

A3.10.1 continued

Bridge coding of 25 per cent sample of infant deaths in England and Wales in 1978: tabulation by ICD chapter

ICD 8th and 9th Revision chapters by title

	8th Revision		9th Revision
I	Infective and parasitic diseases (000-136)	I	Infective and parasitic diseases (001-139)
II	Neoplasms (140-239)	II	Neoplasms (140-239)
III	Endocrine, nutritional and metabolic diseases (240-279)	III	Endocrine, nutritional and metabolic diseases and immunity disorders (240-279)
IV	Diseases of blood and blood forming organs (280-289)	IV	Diseases of blood and blood forming organs (280-289)
V	Mental disorders (290-315)	V	Mental disorders (290-319)
VI	Diseases of the nervous system and sense organs (320-389)	VI	Diseases of the nervous system and sense organs (320-389)
VII	Diseases of the circulatory system (390-458)	VII	Diseases of the circulatory system (390-459)
VIII	Diseases of the respiratory system (460-519)	VIII	Diseases of the respiratory system (460-519)
IX	Diseases of the digestive system (520-577)	IX	Diseases of the digestive system (520-579)
X	Diseases of the genito-urinary system (580-629)	X	Diseases of the genito-urinary system (580-629)
XI	Complications of pregnancy, childbirth and the puerperium (630-678)	XI	Complications of pregnancy, childbirth and the puerperium (630-676)
XII	Diseases of the skin and subcutaneous tissue (680-709)	XII	Diseases of the skin and subcutaneous tissue (680-709)
XIII	Diseases of the musculoskeletal system and connective tissue (710-738)	XIII	Diseases of the musculoskeletal system and connective tissue (710-739)
XIV	Congenital anomalies (740-759)	XIV	Congenital anomalies (740-759)
XV	Certain causes of perinatal morbidity and mortality (760-779)	XV	Certain conditions originating in the perinatal period (760-779)
XVI	Symptoms and ill-defined conditions (780-796)	XVI	Symptoms, signs and ill-defined conditions (780-799)
XVII	Accidents, poisonings and violence (external cause) (E800-E999)	XVII	Injury and poisoning (external cause) (800-900)
			Supplementary classification of external causes of injury and poisoning (E800-E999)

Source: OPCS unpublished data

This was Table A3.18 in the first edition of *Birth counts*

A3.10.2

Bridge coding of 25 per cent sample of infant deaths in England and Wales in 1978: tabulation by 3 digit code within ICD chapters – Diseases of the respiratory system

8th Revision	Numbers of deaths 9th Revision																Total in chapter	Total outside chapter	Total
	464	465	466	478	480	481	482	485	486	487	490	494	507	516	518	519			
465		5															5		5
466			56														56		56
471										1							1		1
480					13												13		13
481						4		1									5		5
482							5		1								6		6
484														2			2	2	4
485								74					1				75	1	76
486									32				1				33	3	36
490											6						6		6
508	1			3													4		4
517														1			1		1
518												1					1		1
519															1	18	19	1	20
Total in chapter	1	5	56	3	13	4	5	75	33	1	6	1	2	3	1	18	227	7	234
Total outside chapter										1							1		1
Total	1	5	56	3	13	4	5	76	33	1	6	1	2	3	1	18	228	7	235

A3.10.2 continued

Bridge coding of 25 per cent sample of infant deaths in England and Wales in 1978: tabulation by 3 digit code within ICD chapters – Diseases of the respiratory system

8th Revision	9th Revision	Description
–	464	Acute laryngitis and tracheitis
465	465	Acute upper respiratory infections of multiple or unspecified sites
466	466	Acute bronchitis and bronchiolitis
471	–	Influenza with pneumonia
–	478	Other diseases of upper respiratory tract
480	480	Viral pneumonia
481	481	Pneumococcal pneumonia
482	482	Other bacterial pneumonia
484	–	Acute interstitial pneumonia
485	485	Bronchopneumonia, organism unspecified
486	486	Pneumonia, organism unspecified
–	487	Influenza
490	490	Bronchitis, not specified as acute or chronic
–	507	Pneumonitis due to solids and liquids
508	–	Other diseases of other respiratory tract
–	516	Other alveolar and parietoalveolar pneumopathy
517	–	Other chronic interstitial pneumonia
518	494	Bronchiectasis
–	518	Other diseases of lung
519	519	Other diseases of respiratory system

Source: OPCS unpublished data

This was Table A3.19a in the first edition of *Birth counts*

A3.10.3

Bridge coding of 25 per cent sample of infant deaths in England and Wales in 1978: tabulation by 3 digit code within ICD chapters – Congenital anomalies (740–759)

8th Revision	Numbers of deaths 9th Revision																	Total in chapter	Total outside chapter	Total
	740	741	742	744	745	746	747	748	749	750	751	753	755	756	757	758	759			
740	13																	13		13
741		92																92		92
742			6															6		6
743			12															12	1	13
745				1														1		1
746					63	73		1										137	1	138
747							39											39		39
748								25										25	5	30
749									2									2		2
750										8								8	1	9
751											17			1				18		18
753												23						23		23
755													4					4		4
756														11				11		11
757															1			1		1
758														2			6	8		8
759	1													2		22	37	62		62
Total in chapter	14	92	18	1	63	73	39	26	2	8	17	23	4	16	1	22	43	462	8	470
Total outside chapter			1			1								17				19		19
Total	14	92	19	1	63	74	39	26	2	8	17	23	4	33	1	22	43	481	8	489

105

A3.10.3 continued

Bridge coding of 25 per cent sample of infant deaths in England and Wales in 1978: tabulation by 3 digit code within ICD chapters – Congenital anomalies (740–759)

8th Revision	9th Revision	Description
740	740	Anencephalus and similar anomalies
741	741	Spina bifida
742	–	Congenital hydrocephalus
743	742	Other congenital anomalies of nervous system
745	744	Congenital anomalies of ear, face and neck"
–	745	Bulbus cordis anomalies and anomalies of cardiac septal closure
746	746	Other congenital anomalies of heart
747	747	Other congenital anomalies of circulatory system
748	748	Congenital anomalies of respiratory system
749	749	Cleft palate and cleft lip
750	750	Other congenital anomalies of upper alimentary tract
751	751	Other congenital anomalies of digestive system
753	753	Congenital anomalies of urinary system
755	755	Other congenital anomalies of limbs
756	756	Other congenital musculoskeletal anomalies
757	–	Congenital anomalies of skin, hair and nails
–	757	Congenital anomalies of the integument
–	758	Chromosomal anomalies
758	759	Other and unspecified congenital anomalies
759	–	Congenital syndromes affecting multiple systems

Source: OPCS unpublished data

This was Table A3.19b in the first edition of *Birth counts*

A3.10.4

Bridge coding of 25 per cent sample of infant deaths in England and Wales in 1978: tabulation by 3 digit code within ICD chapters – Certain conditions originating in the perinatal period (760–779)

8th Revision	760	761	762	763	765	767	768	769	770	771	772	773	775	776	777	778	779	Total in chapter	Total outside chapter	Total
	Numbers of deaths — 9th Revision																			
761	1							1		1			1					4		4
762	5						1		1	1								8		8
763	1		1															2		2
766				8	1				1									10		10
767				1		1												2		2
768				2	1	1												4		4
769		31	9			1	2	9	9									61		61
770			13					2	2									17		17
771			4															4		4
772			1		1	37	1	1			27							68	1	69
775												5		1				6		6
776							56	179	104					2				341		341
777					122													122	2	124
778									11		3			3	1	3	13	34	1	35
Total in chapter	7	31	28	11	125	40	60	192	128	2	30	5	1	6	1	3	13	683	4	687
Total outside chapter								3	6	10					15	1			35	35
Total	7	31	28	11	125	40	60	195	134	12	30	5	1	6	16	4	13	718	4	722

A3.10.4 *continued*

Bridge coding of 25 per cent sample of infant deaths in England and Wales in 1978: tabulation by 3 digit code within ICD chapters – Certain conditions originating in the perinatal period (760–779)

	Description for 8th revision		Description for 9th revision
761	Other maternal conditions unrelated to pregnancy	760	Fetus or newborn affected by maternal conditions which may be unrelated to present pregnancy
762	Toxaemia of pregnancy	761	Fetus or newborn affected by maternal complications of pregnancy
763	Maternal ante and intrapartum infection	762	Fetus or newborn affected by complications of placenta, cord and membranes
766	Difficult labour with malposition of fetus	763	Fetus or newborn affected by other complications of labour and delivery
767	Difficult labour with abnormality of forces of labour	765	Disorders relating to short gestation and unspecified low birthweight
768	Difficult labour with other and unspecified complications	767	Birth trauma
769	Other complications of pregnancy and childbirth	768	Intrauterine hypoxia and birth asphyxia
770	Conditions of placenta	769	Respiratory distress syndrome
771	Conditions of umbilical cord	770	Other respiratory conditions of fetus and newborn
772	Birth injury without mention of cause	771	Infections specific to the perinatal period
775	Haemolytic disease of newborn without mention of kernicterus	772	Fetal and neonatal haemorrhage
776	Anoxic and hypoxic conditions not elsewhere classified	773	Haemolytic disease of fetus or newborn, due to isoimmunisation
777	Immaturity, unqualified	775	Endocrine and metabolic disturbances specific to the fetus and newborn
778	Other conditions of fetus or newborn	776	Haematological disorders of fetus and newborn
		777	Perinatal disorders of digestive system
		778	Conditions involving the integument and temperature regulation of fetus and newborn
		779	Other and ill-defined conditions originating in the perinatal period

Source: OPCS unpublished data

This was Table A3.19c in the first edition of *Birth counts*

A3.10.5

Bridge coding of 25 per cent sample of infant deaths in England and Wales in 1978: tabulation by 3 digit code within ICD chapters – Sudden death, cause unknown

8th Revision	Numbers of deaths 9th Revision		Total in chapter	Total outside chapter	Total
	798	799			
782	3	3	6	1	7
795	173	1	174	0	174
Total in chapter	176	4	180	1	181
Total outside chapter	0	0	0	0	0
Total	176	4	180	1	181

	8th Revision	9th Revision	Description
	782	-	Symptoms referable to cardiovascular and lymphatic system
	795	798	Sudden death, cause unknown
	-	799	Other ill-defined and unknown causes of morbidity and mortality

Source: OPCS unpublished data

This was Table A3.19d in the first edition of *Birth counts*

A3.11.1

Births by day of the week, England and Wales, 1966 and 1970–96

Year of birth	Ratio of the average number of births on each day of the week to the annual overall daily average							Total number of births
	Day of birth							
	Sunday	Monday	Tuesday	Wednesday	Thursday	Friday	Saturday	
1966	0.92	0.94	1.02	1.03	1.04	1.05	1.02	178,735*
1970	0.88	0.92	1.03	1.06	1.06	1.05	1.00	795,503
1971	0.87	0.92	1.04	1.06	1.06	1.07	0.99	792,493
1972	0.84	0.93	1.04	1.07	1.06	1.08	0.98	733,916
1973	0.81	0.94	1.04	1.07	1.08	1.08	0.98	683,650
1974	0.79	0.96	1.06	1.08	1.08	1.09	0.95	646,842
1975	0.78	0.96	1.07	1.09	1.08	1.09	0.93	609,787
1976	0.77	0.97	1.07	1.08	1.09	1.08	0.93	590,098
1977	0.77	0.97	1.06	1.09	1.08	1.10	0.92	574,467
1978	0.78	0.97	1.05	1.08	1.09	1.11	0.93	601,765
1979	0.79	0.97	1.05	1.09	1.09	1.09	0.93	642,917
1980	0.79	0.97	1.05	1.08	1.08	1.08	0.93	661,076
1979	0.79	0.97	1.05	1.09	1.09	1.09	0.93	643,160
1980	0.79	0.97	1.06	1.08	1.08	1.08	0.93	661,016
1981	0.79	0.97	1.07	1.09	1.08	1.08	0.92	638,699
1982	0.79	0.97	1.06	1.08	1.09	1.08	0.93	629,874
1983	0.81	0.96	1.05	1.08	1.08	1.09	0.94	632,766
1984	0.82	0.97	1.05	1.07	1.07	1.08	0.93	640,468
1985	0.82	0.98	1.05	1.06	1.07	1.08	0.94	660,067
1986	0.83	0.98	1.06	1.06	1.06	1.07	0.93	664,566
1987	0.84	0.98	1.06	1.07	1.06	1.07	0.93	684,932
1988	0.84	0.98	1.05	1.06	1.07	1.07	0.93	696,962
1989	0.85	0.98	1.05	1.06	1.06	1.07	0.93	690,956
1990	0.85	0.99	1.04	1.06	1.06	1.07	0.93	709,399
1991	0.85	0.99	1.04	1.05	1.06	1.07	0.93	702,472
1992	0.84	0.99	1.05	1.06	1.06	1.07	0.92	692,812
1993	0.84	0.98	1.06	1.07	1.08	1.07	0.91	674,184
1994	0.84	0.99	1.05	1.07	1.07	1.08	0.91	667,181
1995	0.83	0.98	1.05	1.07	1.08	1.07	0.91	650,705
1996	0.83	0.99	1.06	1.06	1.07	1.07	0.92	652,087

* Sample of births in year.

Source: Authors' analysis of OPCS and ONS data

The numbers of births each year differ from those in Tables A3.1.1. In Table A3.11.1, births after the 'cut off date' have been reclassified into the year in which they actually occurred. Up to 1993, the 'cut off date' was January 31 of the following year. It is now February 11. The first series of data for 1970–80 appeared in the first edition of *Birth Counts* and were derived on a slightly different basis from those used in the more recent set of analyses for 1979–96.

Data extract: live births 1993 (7/94), 1994 (7/95), 1995 (3/7/96), 1996 (8/4/97)

This was Table A3.20 in the first edition of *Birth counts*

A3.11.2

Perinatal mortality by day of the week of birth, England and Wales, 1970–95

Year of birth	Perinatal deaths per 1,000 total births							
	Day of birth							All days
	Sunday	Monday	Tuesday	Wednesday	Thursday	Friday	Saturday	
1970	25.5	23.7	22.8	22.8	23.1	22.4	24.0	23.4
1971	23.6	22.6	21.3	22.3	21.8	21.6	22.8	22.2
1972	23.6	22.0	20.6	21.7	21.3	20.7	22.9	21.8
1973	22.9	20.5	20.9	19.9	20.5	21.3	21.3	21.0
1974	21.9	19.9	19.5	19.0	19.6	20.8	22.3	20.4
1975	21.6	18.3	18.0	18.8	19.0	18.4	21.7	19.3
1976	20.0	15.9	17.5	17.1	17.4	17.2	19.2	17.6
1977	19.6	16.5	15.3	16.2	16.5	17.0	18.8	17.0
1978	18.0	15.1	14.2	15.0	14.6	15.3	17.7	15.6
1979	16.8	13.5	14.7	13.6	14.0	14.3	16.2	14.6
1979	16.3	13.7	14.7	13.7	14.2	14.5	15.5	14.6
1980	14.4	13.0	12.6	13.4	13.4	12.9	13.9	13.3
1981	12.5	11.2	11.4	11.7	11.4	11.3	13.1	11.8
1982	11.9	10.8	10.7	11.2	11.1	11.2	11.8	11.2
1983	11.1	9.6	10.1	10.3	10.1	10.6	11.0	10.4
1984	10.3	9.3	9.9	10.3	9.7	9.8	11.3	10.1
1985	10.2	9.0	9.6	10.0	9.6	9.8	10.5	9.8
1986	9.6	9.0	8.9	9.9	9.4	9.8	10.1	9.5
1987	9.3	7.8	8.8	9.0	9.3	9.1	8.8	8.9
1988	8.3	8.0	8.8	8.8	8.5	8.9	9.4	8.7
1989	8.0	7.7	7.8	8.8	8.7	8.5	8.4	8.3
1990	8.4	7.5	7.8	8.2	8.3	7.8	8.3	8.0
1991	8.1	7.5	7.8	8.4	8.0	7.7	8.6	8.0
1992	7.7	7.1	7.7	7.7	8.1	7.9	8.2	7.8
1993	7.2	6.7	7.8	7.4	8.2	7.9	7.7	7.6
1994	8.1	6.8	7.3	7.7	7.9	7.7	7.8	7.6
1995	7.5	6.9	6.7	7.6	7.7	7.1	8.0	7.3

Stillbirths at 24–27 weeks of gestation are excluded from these analyses

Source: Authors' analysis of OPCS and ONS data

The first set of rates, for 1970–79, were derived from unlinked data. The second set for 1979–95 were derived from birth cohort infant mortality linkage.

Data extract: live births 1993 (7/94), 1994 (7/95), 1995 (3/7/96), 1996 (8/4/97)
            linked   1993 (3/4/96), 1994 (18/9/96), 1995 (3/11/97)

This was Table A3.21 in the first edition of *Birth counts*

A3.11.3

Percentage of low weight births by day of the week, England and Wales, 1982–96

Year of birth	Percentage of live births with birthweights under 2,500g							
	Day of birth							All days
	Sunday	Monday	Tuesday	Wednesday	Thursday	Friday	Saturday	
1982	7.18	6.63	6.48	6.56	6.68	6.64	6.65	6.67
1983	6.94	6.52	6.67	6.73	6.51	6.65	6.94	6.70
1984	6.86	6.74	6.46	6.54	6.76	6.68	6.95	6.70
1985	6.91	6.91	6.61	6.75	6.78	6.92	6.85	6.81
1986	7.04	6.73	6.87	6.82	6.88	7.08	7.09	6.92
1987	6.80	6.76	6.66	6.82	6.91	7.08	6.77	6.83
1988	6.47	6.53	6.56	6.53	6.68	6.79	6.56	6.59
1989	6.51	6.54	6.83	6.74	6.88	7.04	6.61	6.75
1990	6.49	6.66	6.85	6.78	7.00	6.79	6.89	6.79
1991	6.61	6.76	6.94	6.83	7.04	7.24	6.71	6.89
1992	6.46	6.67	6.82	6.70	6.99	6.93	6.62	6.75
1993	6.43	6.69	6.79	6.82	7.00	7.31	6.78	6.85
1994	6.64	6.62	6.90	7.30	7.13	7.36	6.78	6.98
1995	6.83	7.10	7.37	7.50	7.65	7.66	7.00	7.33
1996	6.79	7.17	7.24	7.36	7.52	7.53	7.26	7.28

Source: Authors' analysis of OPCS and ONS data

Data extract: live births 1993 (7/94), 1994 (7/95), 1995 (3/7/96), 1996 (8/4/97)

This was Table A3.22 in the first edition of *Birth counts*

A3.12.1

Live births, stillbirths and infant deaths by regional health authority and country of residence, 1995

Region/country of residence	Numbers						Rates				
	Births		Deaths								
	Live births	Stillbirths	Early neonatal	Neonatal	Postneonatal	Infant	Stillbirths*	Perinatal*	Neonatal+	Postneonatal+	Infant+
England and Wales**	648,001	3,597	2,104	2,698	1,284	3,982	5.5	8.7	4.2	2.0	6.1
England	613,064	3,403	2,000	2,553	1,186	3,739	5.5	8.8	4.2	1.9	6.1
Standard regions											
North	35,932	239	130	162	77	239	6.6	10.2	4.5	2.1	6.7
Yorkshire and Humberside	62,764	339	243	303	132	435	5.4	9.2	4.8	2.1	6.9
East Midlands	49,556	275	149	186	97	283	5.5	8.5	3.8	2.0	5.7
East Anglia	24,809	113	59	85	51	136	4.5	6.9	3.4	2.1	5.5
South East	239,588	1,357	725	931	426	1,357	5.6	8.6	3.9	1.8	5.7
Greater London	104,128	662	352	445	217	662	6.3	9.7	4.3	2.1	6.4
South West	54,355	249	157	201	88	289	4.6	7.4	3.7	1.6	5.3
West Midlands	67,091	400	285	353	122	475	5.9	10.1	5.3	1.8	7.1
North West	79,014	431	252	332	193	525	5.4	8.6	4.2	2.4	6.6
Regional health authorities											
Northern	34,096	230	122	154	73	227	6.7	10.3	4.5	2.1	6.7
Yorkshire	46,742	241	168	208	96	304	5.1	8.7	4.4	2.1	6.5
Trent	57,712	342	211	264	110	374	5.9	9.5	4.6	1.9	6.5
East Anglian	32,630	164	87	121	74	195	5.0	7.7	3.7	2.3	6.0
North West Thames	41,209	240	130	158	76	234	5.8	8.9	3.8	1.8	5.7
North East Thames	55,261	341	165	214	97	311	6.1	9.1	3.9	1.8	5.6
South East Thames	48,880	281	148	186	96	282	5.7	8.7	3.8	2.0	5.8
South West Thames	38,780	202	126	153	70	223	5.2	8.4	3.9	1.8	5.8
Wessex	37,490	176	114	150	68	218	4.7	7.7	4.0	1.8	5.8
Oxford	33,994	159	74	104	47	151	4.7	6.8	3.1	1.4	4.4
South Western	37,951	184	110	148	58	206	4.8	7.7	3.9	1.5	5.4

A3.12.1 continued

Live births, stillbirths and infant deaths by regional health authority and country of residence, 1995

Region/country of residence	Numbers						Rates				
	Births		Deaths								
	Live births	Stillbirths	Early neonatal	Neonatal	Postneonatal	Infant	Stillbirths*	Perinatal*	Neonatal+	Postneonatal+	Infant+
West Midlands	67,090	400	285	353	122	475	5.9	10.1	5.3	1.8	7.1
Mersey	28,643	141	80	113	62	175	4.9	7.7	3.9	2.2	6.1
North Western	52,586	302	180	227	137	364	5.7	9.1	4.3	2.6	6.9
Wales	34,486	175	98	133	70	203	5.0	7.9	3.9	2.0	5.9
Scotland	60,051	397	185	241	132	375	6.6	9.6	10.6	2.2	6.2
Northern Ireland	23,693	145	103	131	38	169	6.1	10.4	5.5	1.6	7.1
Irish Republic	48,787	::	190	232	79	311	::	::	4.8	1.6	6.4
Jersey	1,112	6	6	7	0	7	5.4	10.7	6.3	·	6.3
Guernsey	624	4	1	1	1	2	6.4	7.9	1.6	1.6	3.2
Isle of Man	847	4	0	1	0	1	4.7	4.7	1.2	·	1.2

** Including births and deaths to persons normally resident outside England and Wales.

* Rate per 1,000 total births

+ Rate per 1,000 live births

Source: ONS Mortality statistics, Series DH3, 1995

Annual report of the Registrar General Scotland, 1995

Annual report of the Registrar General, Northern Ireland, 1995

Central Statistics Office, Republic of Ireland

States of Jersey. Report of the Medical Officer of Health, 1995

States of Guernsey. Report of the Medical Officer of Health, 1995.

Isle of Man. Chief Registrar's annual report and statistical review of births, deaths and marriages in the Isle of Man.

This is similar to Table A3.23 and A3.24 in the first edition of Birth counts

A3.12.2

Live births, stillbirths and infant deaths by regional office and country of residence, 1996

Region/country of residence	Numbers						Rates				
	Births		Deaths								
	Live births	Stillbirths	Early neonatal	Neonatal	Postneonatal	Infant	Stillbirths*	Perinatal*	Neonatal+	Postneonatal+	Infant+
England and Wales**	649,489	3,539	2,066	2,645	1,314	3,959	5.4	8.6	4.1	2.0	6.1
England	614,188	3,345	1,966	2,503	1,207	3,710	5.4	8.6	4.1	2.0	6.0
Standard regions											
North	35,535	202	112	140	70	210	5.7	8.8	3.9	2.0	5.9
Yorkshire and Humberside	62,018	318	198	260	144	404	5.1	8.3	4.2	2.3	6.5
East Midlands	49,401	263	167	208	101	309	5.3	8.7	4.2	2.0	6.3
East Anglia	24,478	100	74	88	48	136	4.1	7.1	3.6	2.0	5.6
South East	240,846	1,351	722	937	441	1,378	5.6	8.6	3.9	1.8	5.7
Greater London	105,411	664	354	463	205	668	6.3	9.6	4.4	1.9	6.3
South West	54,836	257	158	209	90	299	4.7	7.5	3.8	1.6	5.5
West Midlands	67,508	412	279	334	125	459	6.1	10.2	4.9	1.9	6.8
North West	79,566	442	256	327	188	515	5.5	8.7	4.1	2.4	6.5
NHSE Regional offices											
Northern and Yorkshire	76,198	411	242	310	168	478	5.4	8.5	4.1	2.2	6.3
Trent	60,975	330	203	258	126	384	5.4	8.7	4.2	2.1	6.3
Anglia and Oxford	66,581	327	190	247	139	386	4.9	7.7	3.7	2.1	5.8
North Thames	97,785	597	291	381	162	543	6.1	9.0	3.9	1.7	5.6
South Thames	87,595	468	285	355	174	529	5.3	8.6	4.1	2.0	6.0
South and West	75,709	348	215	285	120	405	4.6	7.4	3.8	1.6	5.3
West Midlands	67,508	412	279	334	125	459	6.1	10.2	4.9	1.9	6.8
North West	81,837	452	261	333	193	526	5.5	8.7	4.1	2.4	6.4
Wales	34,894	172	89	123	67	190	4.9	7.4	3.5	1.9	5.4
Scotland	59,296	381	171	233	132	365	6.4	9.2	3.9	2.2	6.2

A3.12.2 continued

Live births, stillbirths and infant deaths by regional office and country of residence, 1996

Region/country of residence	Numbers							Rates				
	Births		Deaths									
	Live births	Stillbirths	Early neonatal	Neonatal	Postneonatal	Infant	Stillbirths*	Perinatal*	Neonatal+	Postneonatal+	Infant+
Northern Ireland	24,382	153	77	92	50	142	6.2	9.4	3.7	2.0	5.8
Irish Republic	50,390	..	..	..	..	..	..	..	..	..	..
Jersey	1,108	3	2	3	3	6	2.7	4.5	2.7	2.7	5.4
Guernsey	660	3	2	4	1	5	4.5	7.5	6.1	1.5	7.6
Isle of Man	835	3	0	2	0	2	3.6	3.6	2.4	–	2.4

.. Including births and deaths to persons normally resident outside England and Wales.

* Rate per 1,000 total births

+ Rate per 1,000 live births

Source: ONS Mortality statistics, Series DH3, 1996

Annual report of the Registrar General Scotland, 1996

Annual report of the Registrar General, Northern Ireland, 1996

Central Statistics Office, Republic of Ireland

States of Jersey. Report of the Medical Officer of Health, 1996

States of Guernsey. Report of the Medical Officer of Health, 1996.

Isle of Man. Chief Registrar's annual report and statistical review of births, deaths and marriages in the Isle of Man.

This is similar to Table A3.23 and A3.24 in the first edition of Birth counts

A3.12.3

Live births, stillbirths and infant deaths by region and country of residence, 1997

Region/country of residence	Numbers						Rates				
	Births		Deaths								
	Live births	Stillbirths	Early neonatal	Neonatal	Postneonatal	Infant	Stillbirths*	Perinatal*	Neonatal+	Postneonatal+	Infant+
England and Wales**	643,095	3,439	1,959	2,534	1,291	3,825	5.3	8.3	3.9	2.0	5.9
England	608,202	3,250	1,856	2,388	1,203	3,591	5.3	8.4	3.9	2.0	5.9
NHSE regional offices											
Northern and Yorkshire	74,331	399	215	306	159	465	5.3	8.2	4.1	2.1	6.3
Trent	59,561	296	177	239	116	355	4.9	7.9	4.0	1.9	6.0
Anglia and Oxford	66,891	326	177	222	115	337	4.8	7.5	3.3	1.7	5.0
North Thames	97,740	568	261	337	183	520	5.8	8.4	3.4	1.9	5.3
South Thames	88,329	449	250	320	146	466	5.1	7.9	3.6	1.7	5.3
South and West	74,836	407	228	290	146	436	5.4	8.4	3.9	2.0	5.8
West Midlands	66,695	361	285	333	139	472	5.4	9.6	5.0	2.1	7.1
North West	79,819	444	263	341	199	540	5.5	8.8	4.3	2.5	6.8
Wales	34,520	176	99	135	69	204	5.1	7.9	3.9	2.0	5.9
Government office regions											
North East	29,404	162	75	108	62	170	5.5	8.0	3.7	2.1	5.8
North West and Merseyside	82,934	463	273	356	198	554	5.6	8.8	4.3	2.4	6.7
North West	66,420	373	224	292	158	450	5.6	8.9	4.4	2.4	6.8
Merseyside	16,514	90	49	64	40	104	5.4	8.4	3.9	2.4	6.3
Yorkshire and The Humber	60,400	313	188	264	127	391	5.2	8.3	4.4	2.1	6.5
East Midlands	48,518	235	138	179	95	274	4.8	7.7	3.7	2.0	5.6
West Midlands	66,695	361	283	332	131	463	5.4	9.6	5.0	2.0	6.9
Eastern	64,788	312	165	211	99	310	4.8	7.3	3.3	1.5	4.8

117

A3.12.3 continued

Live births, stillbirths and infant deaths by region and country of residence, 1997

Region/country of residence	Numbers						Rates				
	Births		Deaths								
	Live births	Stillbirths	Early neonatal	Neonatal	Postneonatal	Infant	Stillbirths*	Perinatal*	Neonatal+	Postneonatal+	Infant+
London	105,587	652	298	385	229	614	6.1	8.9	3.6	2.2	5.8
South East	95,399	440	256	327	149	476	4.6	7.3	3.4	1.6	5.0
South West	54,477	312	163	210	105	315	5.7	8.7	3.9	1.9	5.8
Scotland	59,440	319	147	189	127	316	5.3	7.8	3.2	2.1	5.3
Northern Ireland	24,087	131	79	102	35	137	5.4	8.7	4.2	1.4	5.6
Jersey	1,100	2	3	3	2	5	1.8	4.5	2.7	1.8	4.5
Guernsey	672	3	3	3	0	3	4.4	8.9	4.5	-	4.5
Isle of Man	870	5	2	3	0	3	5.7	8.0	3.4	-	3.4

** Including births and deaths to persons normally resident outside England and Wales.

* Stillbirths and perinatal mortality rates per 1,000 live and stillbirths

+ Neonatal, postneonatal and infant mortality rates per 1,000 live births

Source: ONS Mortality statistics, Series DH3, 1997

Annual report of the Registrar General for Scotland, 1997

Annual report of the Registrar General, Northern Ireland, 1997

States of Jersey, Report of the Medical Officer of Health, 1997

States of Guernsey, Report of the Medical Officer of Health, 1997

Isle of Man, Chief Registrar's Annual Report and Statistical review of births, deaths and marriages in the Isle of Man, 1997

A3.12.4

Live births, stillbirths and infant deaths by region and country of residence, 1998

Region/country of residence	Numbers						Rates*				
	Births		Deaths								
	Live births	Stillbirths	Early neonatal	Neonatal	Postneonatal	Infant	Stillbirths	Perinatal	Neonatal	Postneonatal	Infant
England and Wales**	635,901	3,417	1,835	2,410	1,195	3,605	5.3	8.2	3.8	1.9	5.7
England	602,111	3,219	1,743	2,277	1,094	3,371	5.3	8.2	3.8	1.8	5.6
NHSE regional offices											
Northern and Yorkshire	72,941	416	212	276	170	446	4.7	7.2	3.4	1.8	5.1
Trent	59,186	323	194	243	109	352	5.6	8.3	3.7	1.7	5.5
Anglia and Oxford	66,265	315	164	222	119	341	5.3	8.0	3.6	1.4	5.0
North Thames	97,777	550	269	366	170	536	4.6	6.9	3.1	1.6	4.7
South Thames	88,304	472	242	318	127	445	5.6	9.3	4.7	1.7	6.4
South and West	74,328	340	172	228	122	350	5.6	8.7	4.1	2.1	6.2
West Midlands	65,035	365	241	305	113	418	5.4	8.0	3.6	2.0	5.7
North West	78,275	438	249	319	164	483	5.5	8.8	4.3	2.5	6.8
Wales	33,438	182	87	122	67	189	6.1	8.7	3.6	2.0	5.6
Scotland	57,319	351	153	206	114	320	6.1	8.7	3.6	2.0	5.6
Northern Ireland	23,668	122	72	93	41	134	3.7	6.8	3.9	1.7	5.7
Jersey	1,126	1	5	5	1	6	0.9	5.3	4.4	0.9	5.3
Guernsey	678	7	2	2	0	2	10.2	13.1	2.9	-	2.9
Isle of Man	936	4	1	1	0	1	4.3	5.3	1.1	-	1.1

** Including births and deaths to persons normally resident outside England and Wales.

* Stillbirths and perinatal mortality rates per 1,000 live and stillbirths

+ Neonatal, postneonatal and infant mortality rates per 1,000 live births

Source: ONS *Mortality statistics, Series DH3, 1998, Health statistics quarterly 2*

Annual report of the Registrar General for Scotland, 1998

Annual report of the Registrar General, Northern Ireland, 1998

States of Jersey, Report of the Medical Officer of Health, 1998

States of Guernsey, Report of the Medical Officer of Health, 1998.

Isle of Man, Chief Registrar's annual report and statistical review of births, deaths and marriages in the Isle of Man, 1998.

A3.12.5

Live births, stillbirths and infant deaths by area of residence, Scotland and Northern Ireland, 1994–96, Irish Republic, 1992–94

Region/country of residence	Numbers						Rates				
	Births		Deaths								
	Live births	Stillbirths	Early neonatal	Neonatal	Postneonatal	Infant	Stillbirths*	Perinatal*	Neonatal+	Postneonatal+	Infant+
Scotland 1994-96	181,015	1,159	533	720	402	1,122	6.4	9.3	4.0	2.2	6.2
Argyle & Clyde	15,251	97	53	73	37	110	6.3	9.8	4.8	2.4	7.2
Ayrshire & Arran	12,609	91	31	36	23	59	7.2	9.6	2.9	1.8	4.7
Borders	3,452	17	5	7	5	12	4.9	6.3	2.0	1.4	3.5
Dumfries & Galloway	4,996	34	20	26	17	43	6.8	10.7	5.2	3.4	8.6
Fife	11,973	67	39	52	30	82	5.6	8.8	4.3	2.5	6.8
Forth Valley *	9,582	64	28	34	20	54	6.6	9.5	3.5	2.1	5.6
Grampian	18,813	119	46	65	35	100	6.3	8.7	3.5	1.9	5.3
Greater Glasgow	33,426	228	116	160	86	246	6.8	10.2	4.8	2.6	7.4
Highland	7,274	42	17	23	15	38	5.7	8.1	3.2	2.1	5.2
Lanarkshire	20,460	140	61	78	39	117	6.8	9.8	3.8	1.9	5.7
Lothian	27,583	158	87	120	59	179	5.7	8.8	4.4	2.1	6.5
Orkney	695	6	0	2	1	3	8.6	8.6	2.9	1.4	4.3
Shetland	875	3	1	1	0	1	3.4	4.6	1.1	0.0	1.1
Tayside	13,143	82	28	41	31	72	6.2	8.3	3.1	2.4	5.5
Western Isles	883	9	1	2	3	5	10.1	11.2	2.3	3.4	5.7
Northern Ireland 1994-96	72,731	456	262	346	112	458	6.2	9.8	4.8	1.5	6.3
Eastern	27,412	178	119	154	44	198	6.5	10.8	5.6	1.6	7.2
Northern	17,521	99	53	78	25	103	5.6	8.6	4.5	1.4	5.9
Southern	14,409	88	52	60	22	82	6.1	9.7	4.2	1.5	5.7
Western	13,389	91	38	54	21	75	6.8	9.6	4.0	1.6	5.6

A3.12.5 continued

Live births, stillbirths and infant deaths by area of residence, Scotland and Northern Ireland, 1994–96, Irish Republic, 1992–94

Region/country of residence	Numbers							Rates					
	Births		Deaths										
	Live births	Stillbirths	Early neonatal	Neonatal	Postneonatal	Infant	Stillbirths*	Perinatal*	Neonatal+	Postneonatal+	Infant+
Irish Republic 1992–94	148,648	654	504	610	300	910	4.4	7.8	4.1	2.0	6.1
Eastern	55,525	243	213	255	114	369	4.4	8.2	4.6	2.1	6.6
South Eastern	15,949	71	46	59	33	92	4.4	7.3	3.7	2.1	5.8
Midland	8,445	41	20	25	22	47	4.8	7.2	3.0	2.6	5.6
North Eastern	12,157	47	41	49	27	76	3.9	7.2	4.0	2.2	6.3
Mid-Western	13,206	51	37	47	27	74	3.8	6.6	3.6	2.0	5.6
Southern	21,631	109	96	113	39	152	5.0	9.4	5.2	1.8	7.0
West	13,377	61	23	29	25	54	4.5	6.3	2.2	1.9	4.0
North-Western	8,358	31	28	33	13	46	3.7	7.0	3.9	1.6	5.5

* Rate per 1,000 total births
+ Rate per 1,000 live births

Source: ISD *Scottish Stillbirth and Infant Death Report*, 1994, 1995, 1996
       Annual report of the Registrar General, Northern Ireland, 1994, 1995, 1996
       Central Statistics Office, Republic of Ireland

This is similar to Table A3.23 and A3.24 in the first edition of *Birth counts*

A3.13.1

Perinatal mortality by regional health authority and country of residence, 1970–85

Region/country of residence	1970*	1971*	1972*	1973*	1974	1975	1976	1977	1978	1979	1980	1981	1982	1983	1984	1985
Numbers, all causes																
England and Wales**	18,671	17,649	15,943	14,374	13,169	11,769	10,472	9,757	9,350	9,432	8,815	7,563	7,087	6,582	6,464	6,498
England	17,572	16,583	15,004	13,534	12,366	11,072	9,807	9,157	8,766	8,839	8,316	7,044	6,670	6,158	6,065	6,100
Regional health authorities																
Northern	1,203	1,147	1,060	906	910	765	710	695	679	687	622	531	468	424	434	403
Yorkshire	1,344	1,201	1,192	1,039	1,059	973	797	754	718	775	717	653	577	550	545	513
Trent	1,849	1,790	1,618	1,405	1,257	1,044	1,047	882	837	856	792	660	636	618	568	563
East Anglian	574	565	534	464	399	360	310	282	296	311	282	243	240	215	213	241
North West Thames	1,511	1,324	1,163	1,092	799	791	714	623	622	624	524	499	443	395	420	435
North East Thames	1,142	1,174	1,042	955	970	857	768	728	708	675	719	556	577	496	499	488
South East Thames	1,080	1,025	895	871	869	816	717	675	636	629	592	539	441	451	473	450
South West Thames	1,097	982	895	787	619	580	462	454	444	467	382	372	367	327	302	340
Wessex	657	681	573	585	616	553	471	462	411	425	402	331	331	312	293	323
Oxford	679	685	585	536	483	455	399	427	400	371	417	299	311	278	277	284
South Western	1,000	957	896	822	739	611	564	560	543	505	495	429	322	335	340	343
West Midlands	2,318	2,123	1,956	1,793	1,597	1,446	1,341	1,193	1,109	1,155	1,085	875	941	848	852	825
Mersey	1,045	997	844	775	778	699	586	539	459	506	446	397	344	298	286	338
North Western	2,073	1,932	1,751	1,504	1,271	1,122	921	883	904	853	841	672	611	563	563	554
Wales	1,099	1,066	904	817	778	678	642	575	566	569	483	508	400	405	380	378
Scotland	2,200	2,151	1,888	1,690	1,617	1,448	1,199	1,150	999	973	909	808	766	696	718	656
Northern Ireland	900	877	790	757	696	677	593	544	480	472	450	422	363	359	301	308
Irish Republic	1,584	1,558	1,608	1,590	1,532	1,463	1,352	1,334	451	1,186	1,107	978	967	926	879	776
Numbers, congenital malformations ICD 740-759																
England and Wales**	3,376	3,522	3,263	2,893	2,806	2,538	2,245	2,121	2,085	2,041	1,944	1,590	1,474	1,296	1,164	1,164
England	3,153	3,261	3,046	2,714	2,616	2,374	2,112	1,986	1,962	1,918	1,859	1,468	1,386	1,213	1,110	1,102

A3.13.1 continued

Perinatal mortality by regional health authority and country of residence, 1970–85

Region/country of residence	1970*	1971*	1972*	1973*	1974	1975	1976	1977	1978	1979	1980	1981	1982	1983	1984	1985
Numbers, congenital malformations ICD 740-759																
Regional health authorities																
Northern	218	249	220	174	181	158	155	151	157	168	109	96	99	85	79	72
Yorkshire	207	205	208	186	215	219	173	141	144	158	170	147	106	115	105	94
Trent	345	352	354	334	302	252	236	208	192	170	173	136	121	127	111	104
East Anglian	101	120	118	86	83	85	85	69	84	91	74	73	62	44	43	54
North West Thames	272	234	242	222	151	151	150	120	135	104	115	97	96	82	82	84
North East Thames	182	216	189	172	199	189	139	148	135	127	121	93	107	86	94	72
South East Thames	192	196	176	187	175	150	137	147	132	125	141	107	92	79	74	70
South West Thames	153	181	168	152	125	93	102	101	103	108	90	85	73	51	60	58
Wessex	118	157	126	139	144	134	127	127	344	104	109	72	76	67	61	67
Oxford	126	143	141	122	128	110	93	109	105	85	87	66	63	49	57	45
South Western	202	221	215	196	184	144	141	151	145	127	138	100	84	71	62	76
West Midlands	421	427	369	324	314	311	269	238	249	298	266	187	212	162	155	169
Mersey	203	214	188	161	176	150	127	119	99	99	106	89	64	74	40	48
North Western	413	346	332	259	239	228	178	157	194	154	160	120	131	121	87	89
Wales	217	261	212	173	182	159	124	128	122	122	81	117	84	79	53	55
Scotland	481	544	428	416	401	350	292	269	238	223	192	163	144	138	137	129
Northern Ireland	230	232	220	167	175	153	130	129	115	126	126	92	93	79	77	79
Irish Republic	..	..	..	..	..	..	..	..	..	..	278	255	225	219	208	185
Numbers, all other causes																
England and Wales**	15,295	14,127	12,680	11,481	10,363	9,231	8,227	7,636	7,265	7,391	6,871	5,973	5,613	5,286	5,300	5,334
England	14,419	13,322	11,958	10,830	9,750	8,698	7,695	7,171	6,804	6,921	6,457	5,576	5,284	4,945	4,955	4,998
Regional health authorities																
Northern	985	898	840	732	729	607	555	544	522	519	513	435	369	339	355	331
Yorkshire	1,137	996	984	853	844	754	624	613	574	617	547	506	471	435	440	419
Trent	1,504	1,438	1,264	1,071	955	792	811	674	645	686	619	524	515	491	457	459

A3.13.1 continued

Perinatal mortality by regional health authority and country of residence, 1970–85

Region/country of residence	1970*	1971*	1972*	1973*	1974	1975	1976	1977	1978	1979	1980	1981	1982	1983	1984	1985
Regional health authorities																
Numbers, all other causes																
East Anglian	473	445	416	378	316	275	225	213	212	220	208	170	178	171	170	187
North West Thames	1,239	1,090	921	870	648	640	564	503	487	520	409	402	347	313	338	351
North East Thames	960	958	853	783	771	668	629	580	573	548	598	463	470	410	405	416
South East Thames	888	829	719	684	694	666	580	528	504	504	451	432	349	372	399	380
South West Thames	944	801	727	635	494	487	360	353	341	359	292	287	294	276	242	282
Wessex	539	524	447	446	472	419	344	335	323	321	293	259	255	245	232	256
Oxford	553	542	444	414	355	345	306	318	295	286	330	233	248	229	220	239
South Western	798	736	681	626	555	467	423	409	398	378	357	329	238	275	278	267
West Midlands	1,897	1,696	1,587	1,469	1,283	1,135	1,072	955	860	857	819	688	729	686	697	656
Mersey	842	783	656	614	602	549	459	420	360	407	340	308	280	224	246	290
North Western	1,660	1,586	1,419	1,245	1,032	894	743	726	710	699	681	540	541	490	476	465
Wales	882	805	692	644	596	519	518	447	444	447	402	391	316	326	327	323
Scotland	1,719	1,607	1,460	1,274	1,216	1,098	907	881	761	750	717	645	622	558	581	527
Northern Ireland	670	645	570	590	521	524	463	415	365	346	324	330	270	280	224	229
Irish Republic	:	:	:	:	:	:	:	:	:	:	829	723	742	707	671	591
Rates per 1,000 total births, all causes																
England and Wales**	23.5	22.3	21.7	21.0	20.4	19.3	17.7	17.0	15.5	14.7	13.3	11.8	11.3	10.4	10.1	9.8
England	23.4	22.1	21.6	21.0	20.3	19.3	17.6	16.9	15.4	14.6	13.4	11.7	11.2	10.3	10.0	9.8
Regional health authorities																
Northern	24.3	23.0	23.5	21.8	22.5	19.9	19.1	19.1	17.6	16.4	15.0	13.2	11.8	10.8	11.0	9.8
Yorkshire	24.7	22.4	24.2	22.9	22.2	21.6	18.4	18.1	16.3	16.6	14.9	13.9	12.5	11.8	11.6	10.6
Trent	23.5	22.8	22.5	21.0	21.0	18.6	19.3	16.7	15.3	14.6	13.0	11.4	11.2	10.8	9.8	9.5
East Anglian	20.8	19.9	19.5	17.4	16.6	15.8	14.0	13.0	13.3	13.0	11.3	10.2	10.4	9.3	8.9	9.8
North West Thames	22.2	19.8	18.7	19.2	17.5	18.4	17.0	14.8	14.1	13.2	11.0	10.6	9.7	8.6	9.0	9.1
North East Thames	21.5	21.9	20.9	20.4	19.2	18.0	16.6	16.1	15.1	13.5	13.8	10.9	11.6	9.9	9.7	9.3
South East Thames	21.0	20.1	19.0	19.6	19.5	19.2	17.4	16.8	15.0	14.1	12.9	12.0	10.0	10.2	10.5	9.5

A3.13.1 continued

Perinatal mortality by regional health authority and country of residence, 1970–85

Region/country of residence	1970*	1971*	1972*	1973*	1974	1975	1976	1977	1978	1979	1980	1981	1982	1983	1984	1985
Rates per 1,000 total births, all causes																
South West Thames	22.3	20.1	19.7	18.8	18.1	18.0	14.9	14.6	13.5	13.3	10.8	10.4	10.6	9.4	8.6	9.3
Wessex	20.8	21.4	19.3	20.6	17.8	17.1	15.1	15.5	13.2	12.8	11.7	10.0	10.0	9.4	8.6	9.2
Oxford	19.6	19.7	17.7	17.0	15.7	15.6	13.8	15.0	13.4	11.6	12.6	9.4	9.9	8.9	8.7	8.5
South Western	21.0	19.9	19.9	19.0	19.0	16.9	16.1	16.2	15.1	13.3	12.6	12.0	9.1	9.7	9.3	9.1
West Midlands	25.6	23.7	23.9	23.6	22.5	21.8	21.1	19.4	17.2	16.8	15.1	12.9	13.8	12.3	12.3	11.7
Mersey	26.8	26.2	24.2	24.6	23.6	22.1	19.5	18.8	15.2	15.6	13.7	12.4	10.9	9.3	9.0	10.2
North Western	27.1	25.3	25.0	23.4	23.1	21.9	18.7	18.5	18.1	15.9	15.3	12.3	12.5	11.3	10.3	9.9
Wales	25.5	24.4	22.3	21.4	21.2	19.7	19.0	17.9	16.8	15.6	12.8	14.1	11.1	11.3	10.5	10.2
Scotland	24.8	24.5	23.7	22.5	22.8	21.1	18.3	18.3	15.4	14.1	13.1	11.6	11.5	10.6	11.0	9.8
Northern Ireland	27.6	27.2	26.0	25.6	25.3	25.5	22.3	21.1	18.1	16.6	15.6	15.3	13.3	13.1	10.8	11.1
Irish Republic	24.3	22.8	23.2	22.9	22.0	21.5	19.9	19.2	17.6	16.2	14.8	13.4	13.5	13.7	13.6	12.3
Rates, congenital malformations, ICD 740-759																
England and Wales**	4.2	4.4	4.4	4.2	4.3	4.2	3.8	3.7	3.5	3.2	2.9	2.5	2.3	2.0	1.8	1.8
England	4.2	4.4	4.4	4.2	4.3	4.1	3.8	3.7	3.5	3.2	3.0	2.4	2.3	2.0	1.8	1.8
Regional health authorities																
Northern	4.4	5.0	4.9	4.2	4.5	4.1	4.2	4.2	4.1	4.0	2.6	2.4	2.5	2.2	2.0	1.8
Yorkshire	3.8	3.8	4.2	4.1	4.5	4.9	4.0	3.4	3.3	3.4	3.5	3.1	2.3	2.5	2.2	1.9
Trent	4.4	4.5	4.9	5.0	5.1	4.5	4.3	3.9	3.5	2.9	2.8	2.3	2.1	2.2	1.9	1.8
East Anglian	3.7	4.2	4.3	3.2	3.5	3.7	3.8	3.2	3.8	3.8	3.0	3.1	2.7	1.9	1.8	2.2
North West Thames	4.0	3.5	3.9	3.9	3.3	3.5	3.6	2.8	3.0	2.2	2.4	2.1	2.1	1.8	1.8	1.8
North East Thames	3.4	4.0	3.8	3.7	3.9	4.0	3.0	3.3	2.9	2.5	2.3	1.8	2.1	1.7	1.8	1.4
South East Thames	3.7	3.8	3.7	4.2	3.9	3.5	3.3	3.6	3.1	2.8	3.1	2.4	2.1	1.8	1.6	1.5
South West Thames	3.1	3.7	3.7	3.6	3.7	2.9	3.3	3.3	3.1	3.1	2.5	2.4	2.1	1.5	1.7	1.6
Wessex	3.7	4.9	4.2	4.9	4.2	4.1	4.1	4.2	2.8	3.1	3.2	2.2	2.3	2.0	1.8	1.9
Oxford	3.6	4.1	4.3	3.9	4.2	3.8	3.2	3.8	3.5	2.7	2.6	2.1	2.0	1.6	1.8	1.4

A3.13.1 continued

Perinatal mortality by regional health authority and country of residence, 1970–85

Region/country of residence	1970*	1971*	1972*	1973*	1974	1975	1976	1977	1978	1979	1980	1981	1982	1983	1984	1985
Regional health authorities																
South Western	4.2	4.6	4.8	4.5	4.7	4.0	4.0	4.4	4.0	3.3	3.5	2.8	2.4	2.0	1.7	2.0
West Midlands	4.6	4.8	4.5	4.3	4.4	4.7	4.2	3.9	3.9	4.3	3.7	2.8	3.1	2.4	2.2	2.4
Mersey	5.2	5.6	5.4	5.1	5.3	4.7	4.2	4.1	3.3	3.0	3.3	2.8	2.0	2.3	1.3	1.5
North Western	5.4	4.5	4.7	4.0	4.3	4.4	3.6	3.3	3.9	2.9	2.9	2.2	2.4	2.2	1.6	1.6
Wales	5.0	6.0	5.2	4.5	5.0	4.6	3.7	4.0	3.6	3.3	2.2	3.2	2.3	2.2	1.5	1.5
Scotland	5.4	6.2	5.4	5.5	5.7	5.1	4.5	4.3	3.7	3.2	2.8	2.3	2.2	2.1	2.1	1.9
Northern Ireland	7.1	7.2	7.2	5.6	6.4	5.8	4.9	5.0	4.3	4.4	4.4	3.3	3.4	2.9	2.8	2.8
Irish Republic	:	:	:	:	:	:	:	:	:	:	3.8	3.5	3.2	3.3	3.2	3.0
Rates, all other causes																
England and Wales**	19.2	17.8	17.3	16.8	16.0	15.1	13.9	13.3	12.1	11.5	10.4	9.4	8.9	8.4	8.3	8.1
England	19.2	17.8	17.3	16.8	16.0	15.1	13.8	13.2	12.0	11.4	10.4	9.3	8.9	8.3	8.2	8.0
Regional health authorities																
Northern	19.9	18.0	18.6	17.6	18.1	15.8	14.9	15.0	13.5	12.4	12.4	10.8	9.3	8.6	9.0	8.1
Yorkshire	20.9	18.5	20.0	18.8	17.7	16.7	14.4	14.7	13.0	13.2	11.4	10.8	10.2	9.3	9.4	8.7
Trent	19.1	18.3	17.6	16.0	16.0	14.1	14.9	12.8	11.8	11.7	10.2	9.0	9.1	8.6	7.9	7.8
East Anglian	17.1	15.7	15.2	14.1	13.1	12.1	10.1	9.8	9.5	9.2	8.3	7.1	7.7	7.4	7.1	7.6
North West Thames	18.2	16.3	14.8	15.3	14.2	14.9	13.4	11.9	11.0	11.0	8.6	8.5	7.6	6.8	7.3	7.4
North East Thames	18.1	17.9	17.1	16.7	15.3	14.0	13.6	12.8	12.2	11.0	11.5	9.1	9.4	8.2	7.9	8.0
South East Thames	17.3	16.2	15.2	15.4	15.6	15.7	14.1	13.1	11.9	11.3	9.8	9.6	7.9	8.4	8.9	8.1
South West Thames	19.2	16.4	16.0	15.2	14.5	15.1	11.6	11.4	10.4	10.2	8.2	8.0	8.5	7.3	6.9	7.7
Wessex	17.0	16.5	15.1	15.7	13.7	12.9	11.1	11.2	10.4	9.7	8.5	7.8	7.7	7.3	6.8	7.3
Oxford	16.0	15.6	13.4	13.2	11.5	11.8	10.6	11.2	9.9	8.9	9.9	7.3	7.9	7.7	6.9	7.2
South Western	16.8	15.3	15.1	14.5	14.3	12.9	12.1	11.8	11.1	9.9	9.1	9.2	6.7	7.7	7.6	7.1

A3.13.1 continued

Perinatal mortality by regional health authority and country of residence, 1970–85

Region/country of residence	1970*	1971*	1972*	1973*	1974	1975	1976	1977	1978	1979	1980	1981	1982	1983	1984	1985
Rates, all other causes																
Regional health authorities																
West Midlands	20.9	19.0	19.4	19.4	18.1	17.1	16.9	15.5	13.3	12.5	11.4	10.1	10.7	10.0	10.1	9.3
Mersey	21.6	20.5	18.8	19.5	18.3	17.4	15.3	14.6	11.9	12.5	10.5	9.6	8.8	7.0	7.7	8.8
North Western	21.7	20.8	20.2	19.4	18.7	17.4	15.1	15.2	14.2	13.1	12.4	10.1	10.1	9.1	8.7	8.3
Wales	20.5	18.4	17.1	16.9	16.3	15.1	15.4	13.9	13.2	12.3	10.7	10.8	8.8	9.1	9.1	8.7
Scotland	19.4	18.3	18.3	16.9	17.1	16.0	13.8	14.0	11.7	10.9	10.3	9.3	9.3	8.5	8.9	7.9
Northern Ireland	20.6	20.0	18.7	19.9	18.9	19.8	17.4	16.1	13.8	12.2	11.2	12.0	9.9	10.2	8.0	8.2
Irish Republic	:	:	:	:	:	:	:	:	:	:	11.2	10.0	10.5	10.5	10.5	9.5

* Regions before 1974 were those of the Regional Hospital Boards, which differed from those of Regional health authorities

** Including births and deaths to persons normally resident outside England and Wales.

Data for Northern Ireland have not been adjusted to exclude births to non-residents from 1981 onwards.

Source: ONS and OPCS. *Mortality statistics, Series DH3.*

GRO for Northern Ireland. *Annual report of the Registrar General, Northern Ireland*

GRO Scotland. *Annual report of the Registrar General for Scotland*

Central Statistics Office, Republic of Ireland.

This is similar to Table A3.27 in the first edition of *Birth counts*

A3.13.1 continued

Perinatal mortality by regional health authority and country of residence, 1986–95

Region/country of residence	1986	1987	1988	1989	1990	1991	1992	1993*	1994*	1995*
Numbers, all causes										
England and Wales**	6,372	6,107	6,083	5,751	5,754	5,650	5,238	6,044	5,958	5,701
England	5,977	5,742	5,749	5,433	5,464	5,332	4,951	5,705	5,597	5,403
Regional health authorities										
Northern	408	344	362	362	322	388	304	357	318	352
Yorkshire	499	469	460	423	410	412	358	464	437	409
Trent	606	572	567	524	538	548	533	526	546	553
East Anglian	191	206	180	174	157	176	162	183	275	251
North West Thames	416	430	410	414	380	395	364	441	366	370
North East Thames	513	525	516	468	503	470	435	555	539	506
South East Thames	407	428	468	433	430	384	407	473	447	429
South West Thames	302	288	310	274	282	293	255	310	277	328
Wessex	317	331	331	317	271	261	246	297	299	290
Oxford	297	279	247	258	299	273	229	318	274	233
South Western	363	302	324	273	292	281	272	320	308	294
West Midlands	776	725	752	712	771	735	664	694	733	685
Mersey	302	296	249	270	268	238	209	240	246	221
North Western	580	547	555	522	527	478	513	527	532	482
Wales	384	351	334	318	290	301	263	306	329	273
Scotland	673	594	594	553	574	582	597	611	558	582
Northern Ireland	268	276	259	214	202	222	212	220	236	250
Irish Republic	732	610	624	542	543	502	476	450	451	:
Numbers, congenital malformations ICD 740-759										
England and Wales**	:	:	:	:	:	:	:	:	:	:
Scotland	116	108	114	83	96	99	95	107	87	84

A3.13.1 *continued*

Perinatal mortality by regional health authority and country of residence, 1986–95

Region/country of residence	1986	1987	1988	1989	1990	1991	1992	1993*	1994*	1995*
Numbers, congenital malformations ICD 740-759										
Northern Ireland	73	65	53	51	36	44	47	55	40	43
Irish Republic	160	141	153	119	121	140	132	113	107	::
Numbers, all other causes										
England and Wales**	:	:	:	:	:	:	:	:	:	:
Scotland	557	486	480	470	478	483	502	504	471	479
Northern Ireland	195	211	206	163	166	178	165	165	196	207
Irish Republic	572	469	471	423	422	362	344	337	344	
Rates per 1,000 total births, all causes										
England and Wales**	9.6	8.9	8.7	8.3	8.1	8.0	7.5	8.9	8.9	8.7
England	9.5	8.9	8.7	8.3	8.2	8.0	7.6	8.9	8.8	8.8
Regional health authorities										
Northern	10.1	8.5	9.0	9.2	7.9	9.4	7.6	9.2	9.0	10.3
Yorkshire	10.3	9.5	9.2	8.5	8.0	8.1	7.2	9.6	9.2	8.7
Trent	10.2	9.3	9.2	8.5	8.4	8.6	8.5	8.6	9.1	9.5
East Anglian	7.7	7.9	6.7	6.7	5.9	6.7	6.2	7.1	8.1	7.7
North West Thames	8.6	8.6	8.1	8.3	7.4	7.6	7.0	8.8	8.6	8.9
North East Thames	9.6	9.4	9.1	8.3	8.6	8.2	7.6	9.8	9.6	9.1
South East Thames	8.5	8.5	9.1	8.4	8.2	7.4	7.9	9.3	8.9	8.7
South West Thames	8.2	7.5	7.9	7.0	7.0	7.3	6.3	8.1	7.1	8.4
Wessex	8.8	8.9	8.7	8.3	7.0	7.0	6.6	7.6	7.7	7.7
Oxford	8.9	8.0	6.9	7.2	8.2	7.5	6.3	9.1	7.7	6.8

A3.13.1 continued

Perinatal mortality by regional health authority and country of residence, 1986–95

Region/country of residence	1986	1987	1988	1989	1990	1991	1992	1993*	1994*	1995*
Rates per 1,000 total births, all causes										
Regional health authorities										
South Western	9.5	7.5	7.9	6.7	7.1	6.9	6.8	8.1	7.9	7.7
West Midlands	11.0	9.9	10.3	9.7	10.2	9.9	9.2	9.9	10.6	10.1
Mersey	9.2	9.0	7.4	8.2	7.9	7.1	6.6	7.8	8.2	7.7
North Western	10.4	9.6	9.6	9.2	8.9	8.2	9.1	9.6	9.7	9.1
Wales	10.3	9.2	8.6	8.3	7.4	7.9	7.0	8.3	9.2	7.9
Scotland	10.2	8.9	8.9	8.7	8.7	8.6	8.5	9.6	9.0	9.6
Northern Ireland	9.5	9.8	9.3	8.2	7.6	8.4	8.3	8.8	9.7	10.4
Irish Republic	11.8	10.4	11.3	10.4	10.2	9.5	9.3	9.1	9.3	..

* From 1993 onwards, stillbirths at 24–27 weeks of gestation are included except in the Republic of Ireland

+ In 1994, Bedfordshire was transferred from North West Thames to East Anglian Region in preparation for the major reconfiguration which took place in 1996

** Including births and deaths to persons normally resident outside England and Wales.

Source: ONS/OPCS. *Mortality statistics, Series DH3.*

GRO Northern Ireland. *Annual report of the Registrar General, Northern Ireland*

GRO Scotland. *Annual report of the Registrar General for Scotland*

Central Statistics Office, Republic of Ireland.

This is similar to Table A3.27 in the first edition of *Birth counts*

A3.13.2

Infant mortality by regional health authority and country of residence, 1970–85

Region/country of residence	1970*	1971*	1972*	1973*	1974	1975	1976	1977	1978	1979	1980	1981	1982	1983	1984	1985
Numbers, all causes																
England and Wales**	14,267	13,720	12,498	11,407	10,459	9,488	8,334	7,841	7,881	8,178	7,899	7,021	6,775	6,381	6,037	6,141
England	13,473**	12,926**	11,807	10,752	9,802	8,950	7,834	7,345	7,370	7,671	7,410	6,502	6,342	5,931	5,672	5,716
Regional health authorities																
Northern	919	928	867	729	690	568	558	536	532	553	509	426	407	398	370	343
Yorkshire	1,093	1,049	932	895	920	800	646	638	597	660	614	586	526	524	499	513
Trent	1,464	1,460	1,296	1,058	927	867	796	729	720	726	657	632	591	591	524	505
East Anglian	431	421	412	356	335	332	258	241	238	301	258	232	215	208	195	231
North West Thames	1,147	1,115	913	862	640	647	581	493	534	548	520	476	464	400	397	429
North East Thames	857	875	800	767	785	701	616	626	625	592	617	519	545	481	474	441
South East Thames	853	732	723	662	672	664	602	524	556	580	561	506	430	413	442	445
South West Thames	838	763	713	670	476	467	394	356	421	385	388	358	370	301	298	332
Wessex	478	515	465	408	511	496	392	388	380	423	410	378	337	335	329	316
Oxford	518	534	491	428	420	367	370	358	365	358	376	259	306	288	270	271
South Western	797	742	725	644	564	518	448	427	441	452	451	392	357	349	309	320
West Midlands	1,689	1,565	1,487	1,434	1,185	1,109	986	917	871	942	934	788	818	740	771	741
Mersey	811	794	622	624	600	513	422	409	364	420	412	361	329	296	252	293
North Western	1,578	1,433	1,361	1,215	1,077	901	765	703	726	731	703	589	647	607	542	536
Wales	794	794	639	615	617	493	457	430	440	447	426	452	378	379	314	362
Scotland	1,714	1,722	1,477	1,412	1,326	1,168	959	1,004	830	878	831	780	753	646	672	624
Northern Ireland	734	722	616	610	567	534	483	438	417	417	382	360	369	329	291	265
Irish Republic	547	1,214	1,236	1,234	1,227	1,176	1,052	1,069	1,046	311	821	746	745	677	617	552
Numbers, congenital malformations ICD 740-759																
England and Wales**	2,916	2,950	2,757	2,552	2,510	2,303	2,014	2,009	2,033	2,083	2,113	1,914	1,864	1,699	1,638	1,600
England	2,756	2,753	2,601	2,404	2,333	2,147	1,876	1,856	1,884	1,927	1,958	1,752	1,719	1,551	1,539	1,480

Infant mortality by regional health authority and country of residence, 1970–85

Region/country of residence	1970*	1971*	1972*	1973*	1974	1975	1976	1977	1978	1979	1980	1981	1982	1983	1984	1985
Numbers, congenital malformations ICD 740-759																
Regional health authorities																
Northern	194	185	218	163	160	123	143	135	145	145	140	125	109	111	112	98
Yorkshire	198	176	183	181	214	195	156	149	137	139	149	161	132	130	130	129
Trent	299	316	302	271	243	229	204	208	210	200	203	197	163	170	144	129
East Anglian	102	95	105	81	89	96	78	67	58	81	79	65	77	47	52	65
North West Thames	244	256	195	172	160	150	138	125	142	128	152	139	119	108	123	124
North East Thames	180	203	168	167	200	172	140	154	147	153	132	119	144	114	124	110
South East Thames	182	133	138	134	148	128	135	134	124	142	146	119	113	102	107	99
South West Thames	164	163	166	153	115	103	90	91	112	93	105	92	109	75	90	85
Wessex	87	140	109	93	140	130	99	105	92	99	119	92	86	76	92	77
Oxford	96	127	125	124	111	99	104	102	109	92	95	76	89	67	81	78
South Western	188	187	180	177	140	146	121	117	121	128	140	122	97	95	93	89
West Midlands	356	350	303	310	277	249	213	231	226	280	254	208	217	227	206	199
Mersey	164	149	124	129	116	110	86	82	77	94	98	90	83	84	58	59
North Western	302	273	285	249	220	217	169	156	184	153	146	147	181	145	127	139
Wales	160	197	138	128	156	127	115	114	109	126	114	121	108	108	73	85
Scotland	391	459	334	360	349	287	242	287	239	241	225	200	193	186	177	165
Northern Ireland	177	183	146	133	131	138	108	126	115	133	125	92	107	103	101	89
Irish Republic	..	..	..	..	..	..	..	..	..	..	270	272	239	234	186	202
England and Wales**	11,351	10,170	9,741	8,855	7,949	7,185	6,320	5,832	5,848	6,095	5,786	5,107	4,911	4,682	4,399	4,541
England	10,717	10,173	9,206	8,348	7,469	6,803	5,958	5,489	5,486	5,744	5,452	4,750	4,623	4,380	4,133	4,236
Numbers, all other causes																
Regional health authorities																
Northern	725	743	649	566	530	445	415	401	387	408	369	301	298	287	258	245
Yorkshire	895	873	749	714	706	605	490	489	460	521	465	425	394	394	369	384

Infant mortality by regional health authority and country of residence, 1970–85

Region/country of residence	1970*	1971*	1972*	1973*	1974	1975	1976	1977	1978	1979	1980	1981	1982	1983	1984	1985
Numbers, all other causes																
Regional health authorities																
Trent	1,165	1,144	994	787	684	638	592	521	510	526	454	435	428	421	380	376
East Anglian	329	326	307	275	246	236	180	174	180	220	179	167	138	161	143	166
North West Thames	903	859	718	690	480	497	443	368	392	420	368	337	345	292	274	305
North East Thames	677	672	632	600	585	529	476	472	478	439	485	387	401	367	350	331
South East Thames	671	599	585	528	524	536	467	390	432	438	415	387	317	311	335	346
South West Thames	674	600	547	517	361	364	304	265	309	292	283	266	261	226	208	247
Wessex	391	375	9	315	371	366	293	283	6	324	291	286	251	259	237	239
Oxford	422	407	366	304	309	268	266	256	256	266	281	183	217	221	189	193
South Western	609	555	545	467	424	372	327	310	320	324	311	270	260	254	216	231
West Midlands	1,333	1,215	1,184	1,124	908	860	773	686	645	662	680	580	601	513	565	542
Mersey	647	645	498	495	484	403	336	327	287	326	314	271	246	212	194	234
North Western	1,276	1,160	1,076	966	857	684	596	547	542	578	557	442	466	462	415	397
Wales	634	597	501	487	461	366	342	316	331	321	312	331	270	271	241	277
Scotland	1,323	1,263	1,143	1,052	977	881	717	717	591	637	606	580	560	460	495	459
Northern Ireland	557	539	470	477	436	396	375	312	302	284	257	268	262	226	190	176
Irish Republic	..	..	..	..	..	..	..	..	..	..	551	474	506	443	431	350
Rates per 1,000 live births, all causes																
England and Wales **	18.2	17.5	17.2	16.9	16.3	15.7	14.3	13.8	13.2	12.8	12.0	11.1	10.8	10.1	9.5	9.4
England	18.2	17.5	17.3	16.9	16.3	15.7	14.2	13.7	13.1	12.8	12.0	10.9	10.8	10.0	9.4	9.2
Regional health authorities																
Northern	18.8	18.9	19.5	17.7	17.3	14.9	15.1	14.9	13.9	13.3	12.4	10.7	10.4	10.2	9.4	8.4
Yorkshire	20.4	19.8	19.2	19.9	19.5	17.9	15.1	15.5	13.7	14.3	12.9	12.6	11.5	11.3	10.7	10.7
Trent	18.9	18.8	18.3	16.0	15.7	15.6	14.8	13.9	13.2	12.5	10.9	10.9	10.5	10.3	9.1	8.6
East Anglian	15.8	15.0	15.2	13.5	14.1	14.7	11.7	11.2	10.8	12.6	10.4	9.8	9.4	9.0	8.2	9.4

Infant mortality by regional health authority and country of residence, 1970–85

Region/country of residence	1970*	1971*	1972*	1973*	1974	1975	1976	1977	1978	1979	1980	1981	1982	1983	1984	1985
Rates per 1,000 live births, all causes																
Regional health authorities																
North West Thames	17.0	16.9	14.9	15.3	14.2	15.2	13.9	11.8	12.2	11.7	10.9	10.2	10.2	8.8	8.6	9.0
North East Thames	16.3	16.5	16.2	16.6	15.7	14.9	13.4	14.0	13.4	11.9	12.0	10.2	11.0	9.6	9.3	8.5
South East Thames	16.8	14.5	15.5	15.0	15.2	15.8	14.8	13.1	13.3	13.1	12.3	11.4	9.8	9.4	9.9	9.5
South West Thames	17.3	15.8	15.9	16.2	14.1	14.6	12.8	11.6	12.9	11.1	11.0	10.0	10.7	8.7	8.5	9.1
Wessex	15.3	16.4	15.8	14.6	14.9	15.4	12.7	13.1	12.3	12.8	12.0	11.4	10.3	10.1	9.7	9.0
Oxford	15.1	15.5	15.0	13.7	13.8	12.7	12.9	12.7	12.3	11.3	11.4	8.2	9.8	9.3	8.5	8.2
South Western	17.0	15.6	16.3	15.0	14.7	14.5	12.9	12.5	12.4	12.0	11.5	11.0	10.1	9.8	8.5	8.5
West Midlands	18.9	17.7	18.4	19.1	16.9	16.9	15.7	15.0	13.7	13.8	13.1	11.7	12.0	10.8	11.2	10.5
Mersey	21.1	21.1	18.1	20.1	18.5	16.4	14.2	14.4	12.2	13.0	12.8	11.3	10.5	9.3	8.0	8.9
North Western	20.9	19.1	19.7	19.2	19.8	17.8	15.7	14.8	14.7	13.8	12.9	11.1	12.1	11.3	10.0	9.6
Wales	18.7	18.4	16.0	16.4	17.0	14.5	13.7	13.5	13.2	12.4	11.4	12.6	10.6	10.7	8.8	9.8
Scotland	19.6	19.9	18.8	19.0	18.9	17.2	14.8	16.1	12.9	12.8	12.1	11.3	11.4	9.9	10.3	9.4
Northern Ireland	22.9	22.7	20.5	20.9	20.9	20.4	18.3	17.2	15.9	14.8	13.4	13.2	13.7	12.1	10.5	9.6
Irish Republic	18.4	18.0	18.0	18.0	17.8	17.5	15.7	15.5	14.9	12.8	11.1	10.3	10.5	10.1	9.6	8.8
Congenital malformations ICD 740-759																
England and Wales **	3.7	3.8	3.8	3.8	3.9	3.8	3.4	3.5	3.4	3.3	3.2	3.0	3.0	2.7	2.6	2.4
England	3.7	3.7	3.8	3.8	3.9	3.8	3.4	3.5	3.3	3.2	3.2	2.9	2.9	2.6	2.6	2.4
Regional health authorities																
Northern	4.0	3.8	4.9	4.0	4.0	3.2	3.9	3.8	3.8	3.5	3.4	3.1	2.8	2.8	2.9	2.4
Yorkshire	3.7	3.3	3.8	4.0	4.5	4.4	3.6	3.6	3.1	3.0	3.1	3.5	2.9	2.8	2.8	2.7
Trent	3.9	4.1	4.3	4.1	4.1	4.1	3.8	4.0	3.9	3.4	3.4	3.4	2.9	3.0	2.5	2.2
East Anglian	3.7	3.4	3.9	3.1	3.7	4.2	3.5	3.1	2.6	3.4	3.2	2.7	3.4	2.0	2.2	2.7

A3.13.2 continued

Infant mortality by regional health authority and country of residence, 1970–85

Region/country of residence	1970*	1971*	1972*	1973*	1974	1975	1976	1977	1978	1979	1980	1981	1982	1983	1984	1985
Congenital malformations ICD 740-759																
Regional health authorities																
North West Thames	3.6	3.9	3.2	3.1	3.5	3.5	3.3	3.0	3.2	2.7	3.2	3.0	2.6	2.4	2.7	2.6
North East Thames	3.4	3.8	3.4	3.6	4.0	3.6	3.0	3.4	3.2	3.1	2.6	2.3	2.9	2.3	2.4	2.1
South East Thames	3.6	2.6	3.0	3.0	3.4	3.0	3.3	3.4	3.0	3.2	3.2	2.7	2.6	2.3	2.4	2.1
South West Thames	3.4	3.4	3.7	3.7	3.4	3.2	2.9	3.0	3.4	2.7	3.0	2.6	3.2	2.2	2.6	2.3
Wessex	2.8	4.5	3.7	3.3	4.1	4.0	3.2	3.5	3.0	3.0	3.5	2.8	2.6	2.3	2.7	2.2
Oxford	2.8	3.7	3.8	4.0	3.6	3.4	3.6	3.6	3.7	2.9	2.9	2.4	2.9	2.2	2.5	2.4
South Western	4.0	3.9	4.0	4.1	3.6	4.1	3.5	3.4	3.4	3.4	3.6	3.4	2.7	2.7	2.6	2.4
West Midlands	4.0	4.0	3.7	4.1	4.0	3.8	3.4	3.8	3.5	4.1	3.6	3.1	3.2	3.3	3.0	2.8
Mersey	4.3	4.0	3.6	4.1	3.6	3.5	2.9	2.9	2.6	2.9	3.0	2.8	2.6	2.6	1.8	1.8
North Western	4.0	3.6	4.1	3.9	4.0	4.3	3.5	3.3	3.7	2.9	2.7	2.8	3.4	2.7	2.3	2.5
Wales	3.8	4.6	3.5	3.4	4.3	3.7	3.4	3.6	3.3	3.5	3.1	3.4	3.0	3.0	2.0	2.3
Scotland	4.5	5.3	4.3	4.8	5.0	4.2	3.7	4.6	3.7	3.5	3.3	2.9	2.9	2.9	2.7	2.5
Northern Ireland	5.5	5.8	4.9	4.6	4.8	5.3	4.1	5.0	4.4	4.7	4.4	3.4	4.0	3.8	3.6	3.2
Irish Republic	:	:	:	:	:	:	:	:	:	:	3.6	3.8	3.4	3.5	2.9	3.2
All other causes																
England and Wales**	14.5	13.0	13.4	13.1	12.4	11.9	10.8	10.2	9.8	9.6	8.8	8.0	7.8	7.4	6.9	6.9
England	14.4	13.7	13.4	13.1	12.4	12.0	10.8	10.2	9.8	9.6	8.8	7.9	7.8	7.4	6.9	6.8
Regional health authorities																
Northern	14.8	15.1	14.6	13.8	13.3	11.7	11.3	11.2	10.1	9.8	9.0	7.6	7.6	7.3	6.6	6.0
Yorkshire	16.7	16.5	15.4	15.9	14.9	13.6	11.4	11.9	10.5	11.3	9.7	9.2	8.6	8.5	7.9	8.0
Trent	15.0	14.7	14.0	11.9	11.6	11.5	11.0	10.0	9.4	9.1	7.5	7.5	7.6	7.4	6.6	6.4
East Anglian	12.0	11.6	11.3	10.4	10.3	10.4	8.2	8.1	8.2	9.2	7.2	7.1	6.0	7.0	6.0	6.8
North West Thames	13.4	13.0	11.7	12.3	10.6	11.7	10.6	8.8	8.9	9.0	7.7	7.2	7.6	6.4	5.9	6.4
North East Thames	12.9	12.7	12.8	13.0	11.7	11.2	10.4	10.5	10.3	8.9	9.4	7.9	8.1	7.4	6.8	6.4

A3.13.2 continued

Infant mortality by regional health authority and country of residence, 1970–85

Region/country of residence	1970*	1971*	1972*	1973*	1974	1975	1976	1977	1978	1979	1980	1981	1982	1983	1984	1985
All other causes																
Regional health authorities																
South East Thames	13.2	11.9	12.5	12.0	11.9	12.8	11.4	9.8	10.3	9.9	9.1	8.7	7.2	7.1	7.5	7.4
South West Thames	13.9	12.4	12.2	12.5	10.7	11.4	9.9	8.6	9.5	8.4	8.0	7.5	7.6	6.5	6.0	6.8
Wessex	12.5	11.9	12.1	11.3	10.8	11.4	9.5	9.5	9.3	9.8	8.5	8.6	7.6	7.8	7.0	6.8
Oxford	12.3	11.8	11.2	9.8	10.1	9.3	9.3	9.1	8.7	8.4	8.5	5.8	7.0	7.1	5.9	5.8
South Western	13.0	11.7	12.2	10.9	11.0	10.4	9.4	9.1	9.0	8.6	7.9	7.6	7.4	7.2	6.0	6.2
West Midlands	14.9	13.8	14.6	15.0	13.0	13.1	12.3	11.3	10.1	9.7	9.6	8.6	8.9	7.5	8.2	7.7
Mersey	16.8	17.2	14.5	15.9	14.9	12.9	11.3	11.5	9.6	10.1	9.7	8.5	7.8	6.7	6.1	7.1
North Western	16.9	15.4	15.6	15.2	15.7	13.5	12.2	11.6	11.0	10.9	10.2	8.3	8.7	8.6	7.7	7.1
Wales	14.9	13.9	12.5	13.0	12.7	10.8	10.2	9.9	9.9	8.9	8.4	9.2	7.6	7.6	6.7	7.5
Scotland	15.1	14.6	14.6	14.1	13.9	13.0	11.0	11.5	9.2	9.3	8.8	8.4	8.5	7.1	7.6	6.9
Northern Ireland	17.4	17.0	15.7	16.3	16.1	15.2	14.2	12.3	11.5	10.1	9.0	9.8	9.7	8.3	6.9	6.4
Irish Republic	..	..	..	..	..	..	..	..	..	..	7.4	6.6	7.1	6.6	6.7	5.6

* Regions before 1974 were those of the Regional Hospital Boards, which differed from those of Regional health authorities

**Including births and deaths to persons normally resident outside England and Wales

Data for Northern Ireland have not been adjusted to exclude births to non-residents from 1981 onwards.

Source: ONS/OPCS. *Mortality statistics, Series DH3.*

GRO Northern Ireland. *Annual report of the Registrar General, Northern Ireland*

GRO Scotland. *Annual report of the Registrar General for Scotland*

Central Statistics Office, Republic of Ireland.

This is similar to Table A3.28 in the first edition of *Birth counts*

A3.13.2 continued

Infant mortality by regional health authority and country of residence, 1986–95

Region/country of residence	1986	1987	1988	1989	1990	1991	1992	1993*	1994*	1995*
Numbers, all causes										
England and Wales**	6,313	6,272	6,270	5,808	5,564	5,158	4,539	4,242	4,120	3,982
England	5,917	5,845	5,923	5,452	5,238	4,855	4,259	3,994	3,845	3,739
Regional health authorities										
Northern	394	353	337	330	322	351	286	259	220	227
Yorkshire	513	498	481	450	467	433	329	339	342	304
Trent	585	553	586	499	496	508	426	424	429	374
East Anglian	198	201	183	166	183	159	121	122	187	195
North West Thames	412	411	416	406	349	324	286	286	236	234
North East Thames	491	549	471	470	403	384	403	364	359	311
South East Thames	408	463	487	431	423	378	327	312	292	282
South West Thames	323	323	339	297	275	222	231	210	175	223
Wessex	326	352	340	332	272	234	206	197	181	218
Oxford	299	299	301	282	264	265	218	199	200	151
South Western	361	342	395	298	281	263	222	239	208	206
West Midlands	706	687	745	724	744	647	587	492	498	475
Mersey	307	279	257	251	256	222	182	178	162	175
North Western	594	535	585	516	503	465	435	373	356	364
Wales	352	359	294	304	268	250	225	203	220	203
Scotland	581	563	543	554	510	473	449	412	382	375
Northern Ireland	286	242	248	180	198	194	153	176	147	169
Irish Republic	547	464	484	423	434	401	331	302	277	311
Numbers, congenital malformations ICD 740-759										
England and Wales**	:	:	:	:	:	:	:	:	:	:
Scotland	131	130	146	138	123	121	137	133	104	:

A3.13.2 continued

Infant mortality by regional health authority and country of residence, 1986–95

Region/country of residence	1986	1987	1988	1989	1990	1991	1992	1993*	1994*	1995*
Northern Ireland	83	67	72	58	54	55	52	72	54	62
Irish Republic	160	144	147	134	148	177	131	134	115	107
Numbers, all other causes										
England and Wales**	:	:	:	:	:	:	:	:	:	:
Scotland	450	433	397	416	387	352	312	279	278	:
Northern Ireland	203	175	176	122	144	139	101	104	93	107
Irish Republic	387	320	337	289	286	224	200	168	162	202
Rates per 1,000 live births, all causes										
England and Wales**	9.6	9.2	9.0	8.4	7.9	7.4	6.6	6.3	6.2	6.1
England	9.5	9.1	9.1	8.4	7.9	7.3	6.5	6.3	6.1	6.1
Regional health authorities										
Northern	9.8	8.7	8.4	8.4	7.9	8.5	7.1	6.7	6.3	6.7
Yorkshire	10.6	10.1	9.6	9.1	9.1	8.5	6.6	7.0	7.2	6.5
Trent	9.9	9.1	9.5	8.1	7.8	8.0	6.9	7.0	7.2	6.5
East Anglian	8.1	7.8	6.9	6.4	6.9	6.0	4.6	4.8	5.5	6.0
North West Thames	8.6	8.3	8.2	8.2	6.9	6.3	5.5	5.7	5.6	5.7
North East Thames	9.3	9.9	8.3	8.4	6.9	6.7	7.1	6.5	6.4	5.6
South East Thames	8.6	9.3	9.5	8.4	8.1	7.4	6.4	6.2	5.8	5.8
South West Thames	8.8	8.4	8.6	7.7	6.9	5.6	5.7	5.5	4.5	5.8
Wessex	9.1	9.5	9.0	8.8	7.1	6.3	5.5	5.0	4.7	5.8
Oxford	9.0	8.6	8.4	7.9	7.2	7.3	6.0	5.7	5.6	4.4

A3.13.2 continued

Infant mortality by regional health authority and country of residence, 1986–95

Region/country of residence	1986	1987	1988	1989	1990	1991	1992	1993*	1994*	1995*
Rates per 1,000 live births, all causes										
Regional health authorities										
South Western	9.5	8.6	9.6	7.3	6.8	6.5	5.5	6.1	5.3	5.4
West Midlands	10.0	9.5	10.2	9.9	9.9	8.7	8.2	7.0	7.2	7.1
Mersey	9.4	8.5	7.7	7.6	7.6	6.7	5.7	5.8	5.4	6.1
North Western	10.7	9.4	10.2	9.1	8.5	8.0	7.7	6.9	6.5	6.9
Wales	9.5	9.5	7.6	8.0	6.9	6.6	6.0	5.5	6.2	5.9
Scotland	8.8	8.5	8.2	8.7	7.7	7.1	6.8	6.5	6.2	6.2
Northern Ireland	10.2	8.7	8.9	6.9	7.5	7.4	6.0	7.1	6.1	7.1
Irish Republic	8.9	7.9	8.9	8.1	8.2	7.6	6.5	6.1	5.7	6.4

+ In 1994, Bedfordshire was transferred from North West Thames to East Anglian Region in preparation for the major reconfiguration which took place in 1996
**Including births and deaths to persons normally resident outside England and Wales.

Data for Northern Ireland have not been adjusted to exclude births to non-residents from 1981 onwards. Revised data can be found in Table A3.3.3.

Source: ONS/OPCS. *Mortality statistics, Series DH3.*

GRO Northern Ireland. *Annual report of the Registrar General, Northern Ireland*

GRO Scotland. *Annual report of the Registrar General for Scotland*

Central Statistics Office, Republic of Ireland.

This is similar to Table A3.28 in the first edition of *Birth counts*

A3.13.3

Perinatal and infant mortality rate by standard region of residence of mother, England, 1970–97

Perinatal deaths per 1,000 total births

Year	England	North	Yorkshire and Humberside	Northwest	East Midlands	West Midlands	East Anglia	South East	Greater London	South West
1970	23.4	24.4	25.0	27.0	22.0	25.6	20.8	21.4	22.6	21.4
1971	22.1	23.0	22.7	25.6	22.0	23.7	20.1	20.5	21.3	20.1
1972	21.7	23.4	23.7	24.7	21.5	23.9	19.7	19.2	20.9	20.2
1973	21.0	21.7	22.3	23.8	20.4	23.6	17.7	19.3	20.1	19.1
1974	20.3	22.5	21.8	23.3	20.5	22.5	16.6	18.2	19.4	18.5
1975	19.3	19.9	20.9	22.0	18.1	21.8	15.8	18.0	19.2	16.9
1976	17.6	19.1	18.7	19.0	18.6	21.1	14.0	16.0	17.0	16.0
1977	16.9	19.1	17.5	18.6	17.0	19.4	13.0	15.5	16.2	16.2
1978	15.4	17.6	15.7	17.0	15.6	17.2	13.3	14.2	15.2	14.6
1979	14.6	16.4	16.1	15.8	14.5	16.8	13.0	13.1	13.9	13.5
1980	13.4	15.0	14.7	14.7	12.8	15.1	11.3	12.2	12.4	12.3
1981	11.7	13.2	13.5	12.4	11.4	12.9	10.2	10.7	10.3	10.8
1982	11.2	11.8	12.3	11.9	11.3	13.8	10.4	10.3	10.6	9.3
1983	10.3	10.8	11.5	10.6	10.8	12.3	9.3	9.4	9.5	9.2
1984	10.0	11.0	11.2	9.8	9.6	12.3	8.9	9.3	9.9	9.3
1985	9.8	9.8	10.6	10.0	8.9	11.7	9.8	8.9	9.9	9.1
1986	9.5	10.1	10.5	10.0	10.1	11.0	7.7	8.7	9.5	9.4
1987	8.9	8.5	9.6	9.4	9.5	9.9	7.9	8.5	9.0	7.5
1988	8.7	9.0	9.3	8.8	8.6	10.3	6.7	8.4	8.8	8.2
1989	8.3	9.2	8.7	8.8	8.2	9.7	6.7	7.9	8.6	7.3
1990	8.1	7.9	8.2	8.5	8.3	10.2	5.9	7.9	8.5	6.9
1991	8.0	9.4	8.4	7.8	8.2	9.9	6.7	7.6	8.1	6.7
1992	7.6	7.6	7.4	8.2	8.4	9.2	6.1	7.1	8.0	6.5
1993*	8.9	9.2	9.4	9.0	8.7	9.9	7.1	8.9	9.5	7.9
1994*	8.9	9.0	9.4	9.2	9.2	9.9	7.6	8.4	9.5	7.9
1995*	8.8	10.2	9.2	8.6	8.5	10.6	6.9	8.6	9.7	7.4
1996*	8.6	8.8	8.3	8.7	8.7	10.1	7.1	8.6	9.6	7.5
1997*	8.3	8.0	8.3	8.9	7.7	9.6	7.4	8.0	9.0	8.7

Infant deaths per 1,000 live births

Year	England	North	Yorkshire and Humberside	Northwest	East Midlands	West Midlands	East Anglia	South East	Greater London	South West
1970	18.2	18.7	20.6	21.0	17.6	18.9	16.0	15.4	17.8	16.9
1971	17.5	18.7	19.8	19.8	18.0	17.7	15.2	15.9	17.4	15.9
1972	17.3	19.3	18.9	19.2	17.7	18.4	15.6	15.3	17.1	16.9

A3.13.3 continued

Perinatal and infant mortality rate by standard region of residence of mother, England, 1970–97

Year	England	North	Yorkshire and Humberside	Northwest	East Midlands	West Midlands	East Anglia	South East	Greater London	South West
Infant deaths per 1,000 live births										
1973	16.9	17.7	18.7	19.5	15.9	19.1	13.8	15.3	16.8	14.9
1974	16.3	17.3	18.7	19.3	15.4	16.9	14.1	14.8	15.9	14.5
1975	15.7	14.9	17.3	17.3	15.1	16.9	14.7	15.0	16.0	14.4
1976	14.2	15.1	14.8	15.1	14.7	15.7	11.7	13.6	14.4	12.9
1977	13.7	14.9	15.3	14.7	13.8	15.0	11.2	12.6	13.6	13.0
1978	13.1	13.9	13.3	13.7	13.4	13.7	10.8	12.8	14.0	12.4
1979	12.8	13.3	13.9	13.5	12.4	13.8	12.6	11.9	12.7	12.5
1980	12.0	12.4	12.7	12.9	10.5	13.1	10.4	11.6	11.9	11.6
1981	10.9	10.7	12.1	11.2	11.0	11.7	9.8	10.4	10.7	10.4
1982	10.8	10.4	11.1	11.5	10.8	12.0	9.4	10.3	10.5	10.2
1983	10.0	10.2	10.9	10.6	10.6	10.8	9.0	9.2	9.4	10.1
1984	9.4	9.4	10.3	9.3	8.9	11.2	8.2	9.0	9.5	9.1
1985	9.2	8.4	10.3	9.4	8.3	10.5	9.4	9.0	9.3	8.5
1986	9.5	9.8	10.5	10.2	10.1	10.0	8.1	8.8	9.1	9.3
1987	9.1	8.7	9.9	9.1	9.3	9.5	7.8	9.0	9.5	8.5
1988	9.1	8.4	9.3	9.3	10.0	10.2	6.9	8.6	8.9	9.5
1989	8.4	8.4	8.8	8.6	8.3	9.9	6.4	8.1	8.7	7.9
1990	7.9	7.9	8.9	8.2	7.8	9.9	6.9	7.2	7.9	6.8
1991	7.3	8.5	8.6	7.5	7.8	8.7	6.1	6.6	7.0	6.4
1992	6.5	7.1	6.7	7.0	6.9	8.2	4.6	6.1	7.1	5.7
1993	6.3	6.7	7.3	6.5	6.6	7.1	4.8	5.9	6.5	5.8
1994	6.1	6.3	7.7	6.2	6.9	7.3	5.2	5.5	6.3	5.3
1995	6.1	6.7	6.9	6.6	5.7	7.1	5.5	5.7	6.4	5.3
1996	6.0	5.9	6.5	6.5	6.3	6.8	5.6	5.7	6.3	5.5
1997	5.9	5.8	6.5	6.7	5.7	7.0	5.4	5.3	5.8	5.8

* Includes stillbirths at 24-27 weeks of gestational age

Source: ONS, OPCS *Local authority vital statistics, Series VS 1-20*
ONS, OPCS *Mortality statistics, Series DH3 11-29*

This was Table A3.29 in the first edition of *Birth counts*

A3.13.4

Live and stillbirths by regional health authority and country of residence of mother, 1970–95

Region/country of residence	1970*	1971*	1972*	1973*	1974	1975	1976	1977	1978	1979	1980	1981	1982	1983	1984
Live births															
England and Wales**	784,486	783,155	725,440	675,953	639,885	603,445	584,270	569,259	596,418	638,028	656,234	634,492	625,931	629,134	636,818
Outside England and Wales	..	..	613	559	526	573	509	541	521	538	506	487	500	385	384
England	741,999	740,099	684,872	637,797	603,153	568,900	550,383	536,953	562,589	601,316	618,371	598,163	589,711	593,255	600,573
Regional health authorities															
Northern	48,827	49,163	44,570	41,129	39,850	38,030	36,883	35,915	38,264	41,645	41,191	39,832	39,292	39,117	39,248
Yorkshire	53,652	53,053	48,604	44,867	47,227	44,617	42,832	41,237	43,628	46,306	47,739	46,443	45,809	46,507	46,672
Trent	77,499	77,663	70,928	65,931	59,032	55,624	53,800	52,292	54,373	58,018	60,356	58,110	56,393	57,165	57,652
East Anglian	27,328	28,013	27,080	26,452	23,816	22,629	21,987	21,480	22,071	23,799	24,782	23,687	22,834	23,075	23,685
North West Thames	67,308	66,095	61,396	56,285	45,145	42,535	41,732	41,798	43,932	46,816	47,524	46,383	45,636	45,596	46,207
North East Thames	52,425	52,940	49,384	46,300	49,880	47,127	45,921	44,787	46,599	49,571	51,598	50,034	49,458	49,894	51,228
South East Thames	50,750	50,495	46,750	44,060	44,142	42,000	40,805	39,891	41,955	44,401	45,681	44,505	43,837	44,007	44,644
South West Thames	48,572	48,295	44,955	41,447	33,803	31,999	30,861	30,756	32,581	34,781	35,288	34,517	34,511	34,688	34,908
Wessex	31,253	31,427	29,374	27,984	34,208	32,143	30,850	29,652	30,873	32,954	34,194	33,222	32,828	33,044	33,810
Oxford	34,248	34,443	32,776	31,149	30,498	28,952	28,689	28,208	29,555	31,798	33,016	31,645	31,178	30,948	31,811
South Western	46,992	47,495	44,593	42,817	38,496	35,817	34,695	34,203	35,528	37,748	39,159	37,596	35,294	35,523	36,193
West Midlands	89,340	88,280	80,878	74,913	70,115	65,473	62,692	60,950	63,809	68,185	71,186	67,457	67,892	68,224	68,726
Mersey	38,418	37,569	34,421	31,116	32,515	31,246	29,760	28,430	29,928	32,191	32,265	31,841	31,441	31,850	31,601
North Western	75,387	75,168	69,163	63,347	54,426	50,708	48,876	47,354	49,493	53,103	54,392	52,891	53,308	53,617	54,188
Wales	42,487	43,056	39,955	37,597	36,206	33,972	33,378	31,765	33,308	36,174	37,357	35,842	35,720	35,494	35,861
Scotland	87,335	86,728	78,550	74,392	70,092	67,943	64,895	62,342	64,294	68,366	68,890	69,054	66,196	65,078	65,106
Northern Ireland	32,086	31,765	29,994	29,200	27,160	26,130	26,361	25,437	26,239	28,178	28,582	27,302	27,028	27,255	27,693
Irish Republic	64,284	67,551	68,527	68,713	68,907	67,178	67,178	68,892	70,299	72,539	74,064	72,158	70,843	67,117	64,062

A3.13.4 continued

Live and stillbirths by regional health authority and country of residence of mother, 1970–95

Region/country of residence	1985	1986	1987	1988	1989	1990	1991	1992	1993	1994	1995
	Live births										
England and Wales**	656,417	661,018	681,511	693,577	687,725	706,140	699,217	689,656	673,467	664,726	648,001
Outside England and Wales	345	371	365	390	349	354	332	349	416	404	451
England	619,301	623,609	643,330	654,363	649,357	666,920	660,806	651,784	636,473	628,956	613,064
Regional health authorities											
Northern	40,878	40,239	40,404	40,105	39,097	40,656	41,128	40,003	38,598	35,028	34,096
Yorkshire	48,022	48,340	49,344	49,972	49,637	51,187	50,769	49,703	48,275	47,276	46,742
Trent	58,751	59,284	61,050	61,618	61,666	63,571	63,129	62,142	60,809	59,582	57,712
East Anglian	24,487	24,592	25,799	26,600	25,979	26,590	26,288	26,095	25,586	33,697	32,630
North West Thames	47,468	48,124	49,633	50,639	49,666	50,793	51,459	51,992	50,039	42,397	41,209
North East Thames	52,006	52,959	55,314	56,466	56,094	57,999	57,059	56,968	56,351	55,878	55,261
South East Thames	46,902	47,558	49,956	51,402	51,073	52,086	51,412	51,313	50,481	50,155	48,880
South West Thames	36,367	36,734	38,236	39,258	38,822	40,101	39,975	40,229	38,264	38,931	38,780
Wessex	34,957	35,772	37,175	37,942	37,810	38,571	37,122	37,205	39,125	38,744	37,490
Oxford	33,070	33,201	34,661	35,698	35,809	36,424	36,187	36,076	34,805	35,425	33,994
South Western	37,560	38,119	39,840	40,981	40,772	41,090	40,342	40,125	39,384	38,914	37,951
West Midlands	70,351	70,408	72,469	72,809	73,346	75,092	74,210	71,992	69,846	68,727	67,090
Mersey	32,889	32,712	32,788	33,515	32,934	33,771	33,361	31,675	30,539	29,758	28,643
North Western	55,593	55,567	56,661	57,358	56,652	58,989	58,365	56,266	54,371	54,444	52,586
Wales	36,771	37,038	37,816	38,824	38,019	38,866	38,079	37,523	36,578	35,366	34,486
Scotland	66,676	65,812	66,241	66,212	63,480	65,973	67,024	65,789	63,337	61,656	60,051
Northern Ireland	27,635	28,152	27,865	27,767	26,080	26,499	26,265	25,572	24,909	24,289	23,860
Irish Republic	62,388	61,620	58,433	54,600	52,018	53,044	52,718	51,089	49,304	48,255	48,787

A3.13.4 continued

Live and stillbirths by regional health authority and country of residence of mother, 1970–95

Region/country of residence	1970*	1971*	1972*	1973*	1974	1975	1976	1977	1978	1979	1980	1981	1982	1983	1984
Stillbirths															
England and Wales **	10,345	9,899	8,799	7,936	7,175	6,295	5,709	5,405	5,108	5,125	4,773	4,207	3,939	3,631	3,643
Outside England and Wales	..	..	12	7	9	5	10	10	4	7	5	4	3	6	9
England	9,708	9,280	8,255	7,437	6,741	5,918	5,339	5,087	4,791	4,811	4,523	3,939	3,731	3,412	3,425
Regional health authorites															
Northern	691	655	549	496	509	436	382	399	381	357	345	323	269	233	250
Yorkshire	746	665	668	532	571	492	443	393	382	421	401	380	333	300	315
Trent	1,062	956	905	819	721	567	561	475	445	469	427	360	349	248	315
East Anglian	313	312	315	262	217	192	183	170	168	170	151	132	139	133	134
North West Thames	804	727	644	598	437	416	386	351	332	347	293	284	261	224	227
North East Thames	623	643	582	524	533	480	426	409	381	385	411	305	310	277	299
South East Thames	584	583	461	491	479	441	391	387	353	356	331	300	259	259	260
South West Thames	564	537	487	411	321	296	247	265	235	254	199	201	193	190	182
Wessex	366	387	317	348	352	274	265	243	214	215	214	175	190	172	157
Oxford	382	381	326	300	241	254	203	234	195	191	209	176	165	150	150
South Western	548	558	502	475	404	331	314	330	319	271	264	252	189	179	200
West Midlands	1,295	1,218	1,072	953	878	756	719	642	640	639	592	477	505	463	431
Mersey	590	543	473	420	421	380	337	301	272	278	238	207	214	156	181
North Western	1,140	1,115	954	808	657	603	482	488	474	458	448	367	355	328	324
Wales	637	619	532	492	425	372	360	308	313	307	245	264	205	213	209
Scotland	1,234	1,155	1,053	873	850	765	629	553	524	475	463	436	386	379	379
Northern Ireland	465	462	434	389	374	375	278	310	243	246	266	241	187	204	164
Irish Republic	904	881	901	829	867	774	765	757	659	684	681	600	571	581	542

A3.13.4 continued

Live and stillbirths by regional health authority and country of residence of mother, 1970-95

Region/country of residence	1985	1986	1987	1988	1989	1990	1991	1992	1993+	1994+	1995+
	Stillbirths										
England and Wales**	3,645	3,549	3,423	3,382	3,236	3,256	3,254	2,944	3,855	3,813	3,597
Outside England and Wales	5	3	3	8	4	8	5	14	19	21	19
England	3,426	3,337	3,224	3,188	3,056	3,068	3,072	2,777	3,621	3,583	3,403
Regional health authorites											
Northern	223	223	199	219	200	185	220	157	229	217	230
Yorkshire	270	261	255	262	256	218	235	220	304	264	241
Trent	323	324	318	303	294	288	318	297	322	307	342
East Anglian	127	111	124	102	97	95	112	105	115	172	164
North West Thames	241	230	254	237	245	217	238	220	298	259	240
North East Thames	297	283	275	318	266	315	271	229	343	357	341
South East Thames	262	261	236	280	246	258	226	246	295	296	281
South West Thames	178	171	169	166	158	152	174	140	197	189	202
Wessex	190	187	182	181	168	162	160	155	187	215	176
Oxford	169	147	149	130	144	181	153	116	211	166	159
South Western	192	212	162	170	161	161	166	164	205	205	184
West Midlands	442	425	396	370	358	390	376	319	419	418	400
Mersey	179	180	175	135	167	154	141	116	158	169	141
North Western	333	322	330	315	296	292	282	293	338	349	302
Wales	214	209	196	186	176	180	177	153	215	209	175
Scotland	366	385	339	357	319	349	369	321	409	381	397
Northern Ireland	178	125	171	139	133	116	124	120	130	154	147
Irish Republic	516	479	416	386	330	327	301	285	291	297	..

+ Including stillbirths at 24-27 weeks of gestational age

* Regions before 1974 were those of the Regional Hospital Boards, which differed from those of regional health authorities

** Including births and deaths to persons normally resident outside England and Wales. These were not identified separately before 1972.

Data for Northern Ireland have not been adjusted to exclude births to non-residents from 1981 onwards. Revised data can be found in Table A3.3.3.

Source: ONS and OPCS. *Mortality statistics, Series DH3.*
   GRO for Northern Ireland. *Annual report of the Registrar General, Northern Ireland*
   GRO for Scotland. *Annual report of the Registrar General for Scotland*
   Central Statistics Office, Republic of Ireland.

This is a new table for this edition of *Birth counts*

A3.13.5

Maturities by regional health authority or NHS regional office and country of residence of mother, 1974–98

Region/country of residence	1974	1975	1976	1977	1978	1979	1980	1981~	1982	1983
England and Wales**	640,777	603,666	584,263	569,073	595,515	636,884	654,501	..	623,511	626,277
Outside England and Wales	533	573	516	539	522	542	505	..	496	388
England	603,947	569,051	550,332	536,764	561,681	600,229	616,734	..	587,438	590,545
Regional health authorities										
Northern	39,978	38,105	36,907	36,004	38,270	41,647	41,151	..	39,173	38,941
Yorkshire	47,356	44,660	42,847	41,224	43,575	46,261	47,671	..	45,701	46,332
Trent	59,222	55,666	53,839	52,272	54,306	57,903	60,204	..	56,198	56,904
East Anglian	23,808	22,618	21,977	21,427	22,022	23,735	24,675	..	22,732	22,995
North West Thames	45,111	42,487	41,661	41,778	43,827	46,681	47,362	..	45,420	45,341
North East Thames	49,881	47,152	45,908	44,733	46,515	49,509	51,420	..	49,287	49,667
South East Thames	44,193	41,998	40,795	39,860	41,851	44,314	45,547	..	43,620	43,806
South West Thames	33,787	31,925	30,818	30,679	32,473	34,657	35,144	..	34,293	34,502
Wessex	34,199	32,068	30,836	29,621	30,733	32,847	34,068	..	32,635	32,882
Oxford	30,429	28,912	28,595	28,147	29,432	31,639	32,871	..	31,037	30,767
South Western	38,535	35,767	34,687	34,186	35,478	37,650	39,026	..	35,141	35,312
West Midlands	70,306	65,546	62,773	61,008	63,823	68,141	71,099	..	67,682	67,983
Mersey	32,583	31,304	29,817	28,451	29,912	32,150	32,180	..	31,351	31,693
North Western	54,559	50,843	48,872	47,374	49,464	53,095	54,316	..	53,168	53,420
Wales	36,297	34,042	33,415	31,770	33,312	36,113	37,262	..	35,577	35,344
Scotland	70,256	68,077	64,911	62,300	64,216	68,188	68,689	68,865	65,963	64,776
Northern Ireland	27,237	25,846	26,106	25,475	26,229	28,138	28,542	27,229	26,905	27,188

A3.13.5 continued

Maternities by regional health authority or NHS regional office and country of residence of mother, 1974–98

Region/country of residence	1984	1985	1986	1987	1988	1989	1990	1991	1992	1993+	1994+
England and Wales**	633,965	653,142	657,308	677,467	689,153	682,979	701,030	693,857	683,854	668,511	659,545
Outside England and Wales	385	345	364	366	381	347	358	330	351	426	419
England	597,879	616,192	620,043	639,456	650,161	644,837	662,048	655,703	646,266	631,710	624,004
Regional health authorities											
Northern	39,137	40,658	40,020	40,166	39,880	38,888	40,435	40,877	39,691	38,359	34,795
Yorkshire	46,500	47,780	48,059	49,094	49,660	49,373	50,816	50,442	49,300	47,950	46,879
Trent	57,380	58,470	58,936	60,681	61,289	61,288	63,166	62,728	61,711	60,406	59,120
East Anglian	23,567	24,357	24,425	25,629	26,360	25,756	26,384	26,086	25,870	25,354	33,385
North West Thames	45,987	47,216	47,830	49,341	50,243	49,245	50,373	50,984	51,483	49,604	42,016
North East Thames	51,004	51,755	52,616	54,930	56,150	55,694	57,576	56,577	56,450	55,933	55,477
South East Thames	44,447	46,655	47,300	49,638	51,101	50,726	51,669	50,980	50,902	50,088	49,756
South West Thames	34,742	36,121	36,454	37,940	38,934	38,491	39,739	39,590	39,800	37,894	38,556
Wessex	33,631	34,770	35,582	36,945	37,691	37,493	38,251	36,830	36,884	38,774	38,449
Oxford	31,619	32,893	32,978	34,442	35,413	35,530	36,126	35,822	35,721	34,549	35,090
South Western	35,994	37,377	37,917	39,555	40,707	40,480	40,781	39,989	39,785	39,083	38,591
West Midlands	68,452	70,072	70,084	72,126	72,359	72,875	74,608	73,677	71,409	69,349	68,194
Mersey	31,461	32,718	32,522	32,613	33,301	32,699	33,523	33,124	31,366	30,317	29,544
North Western	53,958	55,350	55,320	56,356	57,073	56,299	58,601	57,997	55,894	54,050	54,152
Wales	35,701	36,605	36,901	37,645	38,611	37,795	38,624	37,824	37,237	36,375	35,122
Scotland	64,800	66,342	65,456	65,839	65,842	63,090	65,556	66,630	65,307	62,946	61,224
Northern Ireland	27,547	27,529	27,989	27,694	27,614	25,928	25,338	26,058	25,425	24,741	24,142

147

A3.13.5 continued

Maternities by regional health authority or NHS regional office and country of residence of mother, 1974–96

Region/country of residence	1995+	1996+	1997+	1998+
England and Wales~~	642,404	643,862	637,001	629,926
Outside England and Wales	407	414	375	354
England	607,793	608,845	602,454	596,429
NHSE regional offices				
Northern and Yorkshire	76,380	75,528	73,655	72,323
Trent	61,050	60,454	59,020	58,603
Anglia and Oxford	65,978	65,937	66,199	65,558
North Thames	95,629	97,026	96,811	96,823
South Thames	86,815	86,797	87,378	87,407
South and West	74,763	74,951	74,082	73,619
West Midlands	66,561	66,921	66,044	64,455
North West	80,617	81,231	79,263	77,625
Wales	34,204	34,603	34,174	33,159
Scotland	59,571	58,831	58,925	56,819
Northern Ireland	23,663	24,398	24,064	..

+ Includes maternities associated with stillbirths at 24–27 weeks of gestational age

* Regions before 1974 were those of the Regional Hospital Boards, which differed from those of regional health authorities

** Including maternities to persons normally resident outside England and Wales.

~ Following industrial action by local registrars in England and Wales, numbers of maternities are not available for 1981.

Data for Northern Ireland have not been adjusted to exclude births to non-residents from 1981 onwards.

Source: ONS and OPCS. *Mortality statistics, Series DH3.*

GRO Northern Ireland. *Annual report of the Registrar General, Northern Ireland*

GRO Scotland. *Annual report of the Registrar General for Scotland*

This is a new table for this edition of *Birth counts*

A3.14.1

Age-specific fertility rates and total period fertility rates by region and country of residence, 1996

Region/country of residence	All ages	Age of mother at birth						Total period fertility rate (TPFR)
		Under 20	20–24	25–29	30–34	35–39	40 and over	
Rates per 1,000 women in age-group*								
England and Wales**	60.5	29.8	77.5	106.9	88.6	37.2	7.2	1.73
England	60.4	29.3	76.7	106.4	88.9	37.5	7.3	1.73
Standard Statistical regions								
North	56.4	39.0	82.9	106.5	74.0	27.0	4.5	1.67
North West	60.8	36.7	85.5	108.3	83.0	32.9	6.0	1.76
Yorkshire and Humberside	60.3	35.8	87.7	113.1	78.7	29.9	6.0	1.76
East Midlands	58.3	30.6	77.8	110.3	82.3	31.3	5.8	1.69
West Midlands	62.7	33.1	90.2	113.4	85.4	34.5	6.6	1.82
East Anglia	57.2	24.6	73.9	103.8	85.0	34.2	6.2	1.64
South East	61.6	23.5	67.2	100.8	97.9	45.7	9.3	1.72
South West	58.3	24.2	71.1	110.4	91.0	36.1	6.7	1.70
Government Office regions								
North East	56.1	40.6	83.2	106.1	72.6	26.4	4.5	1.67
North West and Merseyside	60.5	36.3	85.3	108.3	83.0	32.7	5.9	
North West	61.0	36.3	87.1	109.0	83.2	32.4	5.9	1.77
Merseyside	58.6	36.1	78.5	105.7	82.0	33.6	5.9	1.71
Yorkshire and the Humber	60.3	35.8	87.7	113.1	78.7	29.9	6.0	1.76
East Midlands	58.3	30.6	77.8	110.3	82.3	31.3	5.8	1.69
West Midlands	62.7	33.1	90.2	113.4	85.4	34.5	6.6	1.82
Eastern	59.9	23.7	71.6	105.8	95.0	38.1	7.0	1.71
London	63.9	25.3	69.1	96.6	95.8	51.4	12.1	1.75
South East	59.2	22.2	64.0	103.0	98.9	42.1	7.6	1.69
South West	58.3	24.2	71.1	110.4	91.0	36.1	6.7	1.70
NHSE regional offices								
Northern and Yorkshire	58.7	36.3	84.9	111.3	77.7	29.2	5.4	1.72
Trent	58.5	34.0	81.8	109.3	79.1	29.4	5.7	1.69
Anglia and Oxford	59.2	23.3	70.3	104.3	93.3	39.3	7.1	1.69
North Thames	63.4	23.8	71.5	101.9	96.7	47.4	10.8	1.76
South Thames	60.8	23.9	62.8	97.3	99.1	46.9	9.3	1.69
South and West	58.4	24.5	70.2	109.7	91.5	36.2	6.5	1.69
West Midlands	62.7	33.1	90.2	113.4	85.4	34.5	6.6	1.81
North West	60.7	36.5	85.3	108.2	83.1	32.9	6.0	1.76
Wales	61.1	37.7	91.5	115.6	81.6	30.5	6.0	1.82
Scotland	54.0	29.6	64.6	97.9	81.6	31.4	5.4	1.55
Northern Ireland	67.6	25.6	73.5	128.3	108.2	45.4	8.8	1.95
Irish Republic	61.3	16.3	51.7	104.9	126.3	64.0	12.3	1.88

* The rates for women of all ages, under 20 and 40 and over, are derived by dividing the relevant numbers of births by the estimated numbers of women aged 15–44, 15–19 and 40–44 respectively.

** Including births to persons normally resident outside England and Wales.

Source: ONS *Birth statistics, Series FM1*

GRO Scotland. *Annual report of the Registrar General*

GRO Northern Ireland. *Annual report of the Registrar General, Northern Ireland*

Central Statistics Office, Republic of Ireland

This was Table A3.25 in the first edition of *Birth counts*

A3.14.2

Conception rates by region and country of residence, 1996

Region/country of residence	Number, thousands	Rates per 1,000 women						
		All ages	Under 20*	20–24	25–29	30–34	35–39	40 and over
England and Wales**	816.9	76.1	63.3	110.9	127.9	95.1	40.4	8.4
England	774.5	76.2	62.9	110.3	127.8	95.6	40.8	8.5
NHSE regional office areas**								
Northern and Yorkshire	91.0	70.2	68.4	109.5	123.5	80.2	30.8	6.1
Trent	73.1	70.2	66.3	107.8	121.3	81.4	31.7	6.3
Anglia and Oxford	81.3	72.4	50.9	98.0	121.3	100.0	41.6	8.4
North Thames	134.9	87.5	61.0	122.2	137.3	111.5	55.0	12.7
South Thames	116.8	81.0	59.2	104.9	128.0	111.2	52.4	11.1
South and West	91.9	70.8	53.5	98.0	126.3	94.8	38.4	7.8
West Midlands	84.3	78.3	70.5	122.1	132.4	90.9	37.8	8.0
North West	100.3	74.3	70.3	114.5	125.0	86.9	35.1	7.3
Wales	42.4	74.2	70.7	120.1	130.5	85.6	32.8	6.5

*   Rates for women aged under 20, 40 and over and all ages are per 1,000 women aged 15-19, 40-44 and 15-44 respectively.

**   Including births to persons normally resident outside England and Wales.

*** In 1999, ONS amended the way it estimates age at conception. Revised figures are very similar to those previously published. Full details are given in an article in Population Trends 97. The figures for England, Wales and England & Wales were calculated on the revised basis but revised figures for the NHSE regional office areas were not available in time for publication.

The published figures for 1996 are also affected by an error in the processing of birth registrations. There are now 1,002 more births on the database for 1997 than when the original conceptions data for 1997 were assembled. Some of these births would have been conceived in 1996.

Source: *ONS Monitor FM1 98/1* (NHSE regional offices), ONS (revised figures for England, Wales and England and Wales)

This is a new table for this edition of *Birth counts*

A3.14.3

Underage conception rates by area of usual residence and outcome, 1992–94 and 1995–97

Region/country of	Conceptions at ages under 16	Rates per 1,000 women aged 13–15			Conceptions at ages under 16	Rates per 1,000 women aged 13–15		
	Number	Total	Maternities	Abortions	Number	Total	Maternities	Abortions
	1992–94				**1995–97**			
England and Wales**	22,279	8.3	4.2	4.1	25,179	9.0	4.6	4.4
NHSE regional offices								
Northern and Yorkshire	3,406	10.1	5.4	4.6	3,784	10.8	6.0	4.8
Trent	2,672	10.1	5.2	4.9	2,878	10.5	5.8	4.7
Anglia & Oxford	1,709	6.0	2.7	3.3	2,074	7.0	3.4	3.6
North Thames	2,364	6.9	3.1	3.9	2,767	7.8	3.4	4.3
South Thames	2,404	7.2	3.4	3.9	2,904	8.4	3.9	4.5
South and West	2,131	6.4	2.9	3.5	2,479	7.1	3.5	3.7
West Midlands	2,871	10.1	5.3	4.8	3,113	10.5	5.4	5.1
North West	3,282	9.2	5.1	4.1	3,405	9.1	4.9	4.2
Wales	1,440	9.2	5.1	4.1	1,775	10.7	6.1	4.6
	1993				**1996**			
Scotland*	772	8.4	4.0	4.4	903	9.5	4.6	4.5

* Conceptions at ages 13–15
** Including births to persons normally resident outside England and Wales.

Source: ONS revised conception statistics, ISD *Health briefing* 99/04

This is a new table fopr this edition of *Birth counts*

A3.15.1

Incidence of low birthweight by regional health authority and country of residence, 1995

Region/country of residence	All births registered	All with stated birthweight	Number of births with birthweight, g								
			Under 1,000	1,000– 1,499	1,500– 1,999	2,000– 2,499	2,500– 2,999	3,000– 3,499	3,500– 3,999	4,000 and over	Not stated
Live births											
England and Wales**	648,001	645,784	2,879	4,704	9,679	30,062	109,436	234,752	185,122	69,150	2,217
Outside England and Wales	451	431	9	10	15	27	73	153	104	40	20
England	613,064	611,035	2,736	4,441	9,136	28,547	103,812	222,246	174,887	65,230	2,029
Regional health authorities											
Northern	34,096	34,069	132	257	519	1,653	5,701	12,238	9,933	3,636	27
Yorkshire	46,742	46,646	235	343	729	2,345	8,390	16,981	13,013	4,610	96
Trent	57,712	57,514	246	401	856	2,726	9,762	20,882	16,309	6,332	198
East Anglian	32,630	32,614	137	205	498	1,407	5,246	11,728	9,678	3,715	16
North West Thames	41,209	41,081	209	311	607	1,989	7,459	15,390	11,156	3,960	128
North East Thames	55,261	55,137	261	399	719	2,682	10,045	20,711	15,083	5,237	124
South East Thames	48,880	48,446	242	373	772	2,124	7,958	17,688	13,947	5,342	434
South West Thames	38,780	38,529	177	270	559	1,602	6,176	13,850	11,558	4,337	251
Wessex	37,490	37,448	127	255	529	1,592	5,822	13,471	11,215	4,437	42
Oxford	33,994	33,816	135	209	452	1,447	5,571	12,244	10,025	3,733	178
South Western	37,951	37,891	167	265	531	1,586	5,960	13,759	11,358	4,265	60
West Midlands	67,090	66,975	333	541	1,115	3,387	11,877	24,229	18,632	6,861	115
Mersey	28,643	28,545	115	235	409	1,237	4,507	10,029	8,476	3,537	98
North Western	52,586	52,324	220	377	841	2,770	9,338	19,046	14,504	5,228	262
Wales	34,486	34,318	134	253	528	1,488	5,551	12,353	10,131	3,880	168
Scotland+	60,016	60,010	248	395	844	2,690	9,461	21,174	17,948	7,250	6
Northern Ireland	24,354	23,818	93	142	287	854	3,295	8,453	7,887	3,343	0
Irish Republic	48,530	48,235	151	250	1,867–		1,020*	::	::	::	295
Jersey	1,112	1,112	16	19	19	38	::	::	::	::	::

A3.15.1 continued

Incidence of low birthweight by regional health authority and country of residence, 1995

Region/country of residence	All births registered	All with stated birthweight	Number of births with birthweight, g								
			Under 1,000	1,000–1,499	1,500–1,999	2,000–2,499	2,500–2,999	3,000–3,499	3,500–3,999	4,000 and over	Not stated
Stillbirths											
England and Wales**	3,597	3,522	1,119	506	399	402	429	376	198	93	75
Outside England and Wales	19	18	5	5	5	2	1	0	0	0	1
England	3,463	3,330	1,052	480	370	380	410	362	188	88	73
Regional health authorities											
Northern	230	228	61	36	21	34	23	34	13	6	2
Yorkshire	241	237	74	33	24	28	37	22	10	9	4
Trent	342	338	107	40	31	50	45	33	26	6	4
East Anglian	164	158	56	23	13	19	18	17	10	2	6
North West Thames	240	235	68	43	20	27	26	25	20	6	5
North East Thames	341	333	92	44	44	32	44	46	20	11	8
South East Thames	281	270	87	40	25	27	38	29	16	8	11
South West Thames	202	190	64	24	24	21	27	17	11	2	12
Wessex	176	173	54	24	19	14	15	31	11	5	3
Oxford	159	156	46	30	17	18	26	8	9	2	3
South Western	184	182	62	22	25	19	22	16	9	7	2
West Midlands	400	396	128	66	55	50	37	36	15	9	4
Mersey	141	137	42	16	18	13	18	18	5	7	4
North Western	302	297	111	39	34	28	34	30	13	8	5
Wales	175	174	62	21	24	20	18	14	10	5	1
Scotland+	358	355	108	52	41	48	43	31	22	10	3

A3.15.1 *continued*

Incidence of low birthweight by regional health authority and country of residence, 1995

Percentage of births with stated birthweight, g

	Under 1,000	1,000– 1,499	Under 1,500	1,500– 1,999	2,000– 2,499	Under 2,500	2,500– 2,999	3,000– 3,499	3,500– 3,999	4,000 and over
Live births										
England and Wales**	0.45	0.73	1.17	1.50	4.66	7.33	16.95	36.35	28.67	10.71
Outside England and Wales	2.09	2.32	4.41	3.48	6.26	14.15	16.94	35.50	24.13	9.28
England	0.45	0.73	1.17	1.50	4.67	7.34	16.99	36.37	28.62	10.68
Regional health authorities										
Northern	0.39	0.75	1.14	1.52	4.85	7.52	16.73	35.92	29.16	10.67
Yorkshire	0.50	0.74	1.24	1.56	5.03	7.83	17.99	36.40	27.90	9.88
Trent	0.43	0.70	1.12	1.49	4.74	7.35	16.97	36.31	28.36	11.01
East Anglian	0.42	0.63	1.05	1.53	4.31	6.89	16.09	35.96	29.67	11.39
North West Thames	0.51	0.76	1.27	1.48	4.84	7.59	18.16	37.46	27.16	9.64
North East Thames	0.47	0.72	1.20	1.30	4.86	7.37	18.22	37.56	27.36	9.50
South East Thames	0.50	0.77	1.27	1.59	4.38	7.25	16.43	36.51	28.79	11.03
South West Thames	0.46	0.70	1.16	1.45	4.16	6.77	16.03	35.95	30.00	11.26
Wessex	0.34	0.68	1.02	1.41	4.25	6.68	15.55	35.97	29.95	11.85
Oxford	0.40	0.62	1.02	1.34	4.28	6.63	16.47	36.21	29.65	11.04
South Western	0.44	0.70	1.14	1.40	4.19	6.73	15.73	36.31	29.98	11.26
West Midlands	0.50	0.81	1.30	1.66	5.06	8.03	17.73	36.18	27.82	10.24
Mersey	0.40	0.82	1.23	1.43	4.33	6.99	15.79	35.13	29.69	12.39
North Western	0.42	0.72	1.14	1.61	5.29	8.04	17.85	36.40	27.72	9.99
Wales	0.39	0.74	1.13	1.54	4.34	7.00	16.18	36.00	29.52	11.31
Scotland+	0.41	0.66	1.07	1.41	4.48	6.96	15.77	35.28	29.91	12.08
Northern Ireland	0.39	0.60	0.99	1.20	3.59	5.78	13.83	35.49	33.11	14.04
Irish Republic	0.31	0.52	0.83	3.87–		4.70	..	..	..	..
Jersey	1.44	1.71	3.15	1.71	3.42	8.27	..	..	..	..

A3.15.1 continued

Incidence of low birthweight by regional health authority and country of residence, 1995

Region/country of residence	Percentage of births with stated birthweight, g									
	Under 1,000	1,000–1,499	Under 1,500	1,500–1,999	2,000–2,499	Under 2,500	2,500–2,999	3,000–3,499	3,500–3,999	4,000 and over
Total births										
England and Wales**	0.62	0.80	1.42	1.55	4.69	7.66	16.92	36.21	28.54	10.66
Outside England and Wales	3.12	3.34	6.46	4.45	6.46	17.37	16.48	34.08	23.16	8.91
England	0.62	0.80	1.42	1.55	4.71	7.67	16.96	36.23	28.50	10.63
Regional health authorities										
Northern	0.56	0.85	1.42	1.57	4.92	7.91	16.69	35.78	29.00	10.62
Yorkshire	0.66	0.80	1.46	1.61	5.06	8.13	17.97	36.27	27.78	9.85
Trent	0.61	0.76	1.37	1.53	4.80	7.70	16.95	36.15	28.24	10.96
East Anglian	0.59	0.70	1.28	1.56	4.35	7.20	16.06	35.84	29.56	11.34
North West Thames	0.67	0.86	1.53	1.52	4.88	7.92	18.12	37.31	27.05	9.60
North East Thames	0.64	0.80	1.44	1.38	4.89	7.70	18.19	37.42	27.23	9.46
South East Thames	0.68	0.85	1.52	1.64	4.42	7.57	16.41	36.37	28.66	10.98
South West Thames	0.62	0.76	1.38	1.51	4.19	7.08	16.02	35.81	29.88	11.21
Wessex	0.48	0.74	1.22	1.46	4.27	6.95	15.52	35.89	29.84	11.81
Oxford	0.53	0.70	1.24	1.38	4.31	6.93	16.48	36.06	29.54	10.99
South Western	0.60	0.75	1.36	1.46	4.22	7.03	15.71	36.18	29.86	11.22
West Midlands	0.68	0.90	1.59	1.74	5.10	8.42	17.68	36.02	27.68	10.20
Mersey	0.55	0.88	1.42	1.49	4.36	7.27	15.78	35.03	29.57	12.36
North Western	0.63	0.79	1.42	1.66	5.32	8.40	17.81	36.25	27.59	9.95
Wales	0.57	0.79	1.36	1.60	4.37	7.34	16.15	35.85	29.40	11.26
Scotland+	0.59	0.74	1.33	1.47	4.54	7.33	15.74	35.13	29.77	12.03

* Births weighing 2.500g or over
** Includes births to women resident outside England and Wales
+ Financial year 1994/95. Some home births missing
~ 1.500–2.499g

Source: England and Wales, ONS mortality statistics, Series DH3, unpublished data
Scotland: Information and Statistics Division, SMR2
Northern Ireland: Department of Health and Social Services
Irish Republic: Central Statistics Office
States of Jersey: *Report of the Medical Officer of Health*

This is similar to Table A3.26 in the first edition of *Birth counts*

A3.15.2

Incidence of low birthweight by regional office and country of residence, 1996

Region/country of residence	All births registered	All with stated birthweight	Number of births with birthweight, g								
			Under 1,000	1,000– 1,499	1,500– 1,999	2,000– 2,499	2,500– 2,999	3,000– 3,499	3,500– 3,999	4,000 and over	Not stated
Live births											
England and Wales**	649,489	647,951	3,150	4,770	9,405	29,862	109,053	234,310	187,009	70,392	1,538
Outside England and Wales	407	406	11	18	11	32	62	143	87	42	1
England	614,188	612,715	3,010	4,492	8,879	28,316	103,395	221,712	176,509	66,402	1,473
NHSE Regional offices											
Northern and Yorkshire	76,198	76,091	373	519	1,135	3,603	13,376	27,607	21,530	7,948	107
Trent	60,975	60,924	258	456	909	2,800	10,140	21,927	17,682	6,752	51
Anglia and Oxford	66,581	66,520	315	466	864	2,923	10,799	23,883	19,654	7,616	61
North Thames	97,785	97,297	522	684	1,409	4,611	17,490	36,134	26,889	9,558	488
South Thames	87,595	87,246	423	665	1,205	3,720	14,012	31,513	25,914	9,794	349
South and West	75,709	75,590	325	534	1,003	3,273	11,825	27,089	22,818	8,723	119
West Midlands	67,508	67,403	391	561	1,075	3,428	12,023	24,070	18,795	7,060	105
North West	81,837	81,644	403	607	1,279	3,958	13,730	29,489	23,227	8,951	193
Wales	34,894	34,830	129	260	515	1,514	5,596	12,455	10,413	3,948	64
Scotland+	55,909	55,906	174	371	812	2,471	8,981	19,975	16,606	6,516	3
Northern Ireland	23,819	23,818	112	145	267	844	3,321	8,315	7,617	3,197	1
Irish Republic	50,390	50,113	149	220		2,015-	:	:	:	:	277
Jersey	1,108	1,108	3	11	17	44	1033*	:	:	:	:

A3.15.2 *continued*

Incidence of low birthweight by regional office and country of residence, 1996

Area	All births registered	All with stated birthweight	Number of births with birthweight, g Under 1,000	1,000– 1,499	1,500– 1,999	2,000– 2,499	2,500– 2,999	3,000– 3,499	3,500– 3,999	4,000 and over	Not stated
Stillbirths											
England and Wales**	3,539	3,477	1,216	435	376	374	443	365	185	83	62
Outside England and Wales	22	22	11	5	3	2	0	1	0	0	0
England	3,345	3,288	1,156	408	352	349	417	350	175	81	57
NHSE Regional offices											
Northern and Yorkshire	411	407	125	72	46	42	54	40	17	11	4
Trent	330	329	118	49	31	37	34	45	12	3	1
Anglia and Oxford	327	322	110	37	30	49	36	34	19	7	5
North Thames	597	580	213	70	57	57	75	56	37	15	17
South Thames	468	458	158	52	43	38	71	57	29	10	10
South and West	348	343	116	41	33	29	46	42	26	10	5
West Midlands	412	405	150	45	56	44	48	32	17	13	7
North West	452	444	166	42	56	53	53	44	18	12	8
Wales	172	167	49	22	21	23	26	14	10	2	5
Scotland+	351	350	105	50	40	49	42	37	17	10	1

A3.15.2 continued

Incidence of low birthweight by regional office and country of residence, 1996

Region/country of residence	Percentage of births with stated birthweight, g									
	Under 1,000	1,000– 1,499	Under 1,500	1,500– 1,999	2,000– 2,499	Under 2,500	2,500– 2,999	3,000– 3,499	3,500– 3,999	4,000 and over
Live births										
England and Wales**	0.49	0.74	1.22	1.45	4.61	7.28	16.8	36.2	28.9	10.9
Outside England and Wales	2.71	4.43	7.14	2.71	7.88	17.73	15.3	35.2	21.4	10.3
England	0.49	0.73	1.22	1.45	4.62	7.29	16.9	36.2	28.8	10.8
NHSE regional offices										
Northern and Yorkshire	0.49	0.68	1.17	1.49	4.74	7.40	17.6	36.3	28.3	10.4
Trent	0.42	0.75	1.17	1.49	4.60	7.26	16.6	36.0	29.0	11.1
Anglia and Oxford	0.47	0.70	1.17	1.30	4.39	6.87	16.2	35.9	29.5	11.4
North Thames	0.54	0.70	1.24	1.45	4.74	7.43	18.0	37.1	27.6	9.8
South Thames	0.48	0.76	1.25	1.38	4.26	6.89	16.1	36.1	29.7	11.2
South and West	0.43	0.71	1.14	1.33	4.33	6.79	15.6	35.8	30.2	11.5
West Midlands	0.58	0.83	1.41	1.59	5.09	8.09	17.8	35.7	27.9	10.5
North West	0.49	0.74	1.24	1.57	4.85	7.65	16.8	36.1	28.4	11.0
Wales	0.37	0.75	1.12	1.48	4.35	6.94	16.1	35.8	29.9	11.3
Scotland+	0.31	0.66	0.97	1.45	4.42	6.85	16.1	35.7	29.7	11.7
Northern Ireland	0.47	0.61	1.08	1.12	3.54	5.74	13.9	34.9	32.0	13.4
Irish Republic	0.30	0.44	0.74	4.02–		4.76	..	..	..	..
Jersey	0.27	0.99	1.26	1.53	3.97	6.77	..	..	..	..

Incidence of low birthweight by regional office and country of residence, 1996

	Percentage of births with stated birthweight, g									
	Under 1,000	1,000–1,499	Under 1,500	1,500–1,999	2,000–2,499	Under 2,500	2,500–2,999	3,000–3,499	3,500–3,999	4,000 and over
Total births										
England and Wales**	0.67	0.80	1.47	1.50	4.64	7.61	16.8	36.0	28.7	10.8
Outside England and Wales	5.14	5.37	10.51	3.27	7.94	21.73	14.5	33.6	20.3	9.8
England	0.68	0.80	1.47	1.50	4.65	7.62	16.9	36.0	28.7	10.8
NHSE regional offices										
Northern and Yorkshire	0.65	0.77	1.42	1.54	4.76	7.73	17.6	36.1	28.2	10.4
Trent	0.61	0.82	1.44	1.53	4.63	7.60	16.6	35.9	28.9	11.0
Anglia and Oxford	0.64	0.75	1.39	1.34	4.45	7.17	16.2	35.8	29.4	11.4
North Thames	0.75	0.77	1.52	1.50	4.77	7.79	17.9	37.0	27.5	9.8
South Thames	0.66	0.82	1.48	1.42	4.28	7.19	16.1	36.0	29.6	11.2
South and West	0.58	0.76	1.34	1.36	4.35	7.05	15.6	35.7	30.1	11.5
West Midlands	0.80	0.89	1.69	1.67	5.12	8.48	17.8	35.5	27.7	10.4
North West	0.69	0.79	1.48	1.63	4.89	8.00	16.8	36.0	28.3	10.9
Wales	0.51	0.81	1.31	1.53	4.39	7.24	16.1	35.6	29.8	11.3
Scotland+	0.50	0.75	1.24	1.51	4.48	7.24	16.0	35.6	29.5	11.6

* Births weighing 2,500g or over
** Includes births to women resident outside England and Wales
+ Financial year 1995/96. Some home births missing
~ 1,500–2,499g

Source: ONS Mortality statistics, England and Wales., Series DH3, unpublished data

Information and Statistics Division, Scotland, SMR2

Department of Health and Social Services, Northern Ireland

Irish Republic: Central Statistics Office

States of Jersey, *Report of the Medical Officer of Health*

This is similar to Table A3.26 in the first edition of *Birth counts*

A3.16.1

Stillbirth and infant mortality rates by birthweight and regional health authority or country of residence, England and Wales, 1995

Area	All weights	Total stated	Under 1,000g	1,000–1,499	Under 1,500g	1,500–1,999	2,000–2,499	Under 2,500g	2,500–2,999	3,000–3,499	3,500–3,999	4,000 and over	2,500 and over	Not stated
Numbers														
Early neonatal deaths														
England and Wales**	2,084	2,025	941	213	1,154	134	137	1,425	150	191	128	131	600	59
Outside England and Wales	3	3	0	0	0	2	1	3	0	0	0	0	0	0
England	1,984	1,928	903	200	1,103	122	131	1,356	141	184	123	124	572	56
Regional health authorities														
Northern	122	121	52	12	64	9	6	79	7	17	9	9	42	1
Yorkshire	167	162	77	15	92	10	11	113	13	16	9	11	49	5
Trent	209	203	104	19	123	9	18	150	11	21	10	11	53	6
East Anglian	87	86	43	12	55	1	3	59	9	11	3	4	27	1
North West Thames	128	122	55	10	65	9	8	82	11	8	12	9	40	6
North East Thames	164	159	81	14	95	11	10	116	11	11	12	9	43	5
South East Thames	146	139	63	14	77	4	7	88	15	19	6	11	51	7
South West Thames	126	119	61	9	70	3	8	81	12	7	9	10	38	7
Wessex	114	112	47	18	65	9	10	84	7	7	6	8	28	2
Oxford	71	70	27	13	40	4	7	51	7	4	6	3	19	1
South Western	110	110	44	14	58	9	8	75	6	12	5	10	35	0
West Midlands	285	279	136	20	156	25	16	197	8	25	20	16	82	6
Mersey	79	74	37	12	49	7	6	62	1	4	7	0	12	5
North Western	176	172	76	18	94	12	13	119	9	22	9	13	53	4
Wales	97	94	38	13	51	10	5	66	9	7	5	7	28	3
Neonatal deaths														
England and Wales**	2,669	2,605	1,124	301	1,425	167	197	1,789	217	267	179	153	816	64
Outside England and Wales	5	5	2	0	2	2	1	5	0	0	0	0	0	0
England	2,532	2,471	1,069	280	1,349	155	188	1,692	207	257	169	146	779	61
Regional health authorities														
Northern	153	152	61	15	76	10	9	95	14	24	10	9	57	1
Yorkshire	207	202	94	20	114	10	12	136	15	21	16	14	66	5
Trent	262	255	120	25	145	14	22	181	18	31	14	11	74	7

A3.16.1 continued

Stillbirth and infant mortality rates by birthweight and regional health authority or country of residence, England and Wales, 1995

Numbers

Neonatal deaths

Region/country of residence	All weights	Total stated	Under 1,000g	1,000– 1,499	Under 1,500g	1,500– 1,999	2,000– 2,499	Under 2,500g	2,500– 2,999	3,000– 3,499	3,500– 3,999	4,000 and over	2,500 and over	Not stated
East Anglian	121	120	55	15	70	2	9	81	14	16	4	5	39	1
North West Thames	155	148	61	16	77	10	10	97	13	14	14	10	51	7
North East Thames	213	208	96	28	124	13	14	151	18	16	14	9	57	5
South East Thames	183	176	80	21	101	6	9	116	18	22	9	11	60	7
South West Thames	153	146	69	12	81	5	9	95	16	13	9	13	51	7
Wessex	150	148	52	25	77	12	16	105	14	11	8	10	43	2
Oxford	100	98	37	14	51	6	10	67	8	7	11	5	31	2
South Western	148	148	55	16	71	11	14	96	12	16	12	12	52	0
West Midlands	352	345	152	32	184	30	23	237	34	30	25	19	108	7
Mersey	112	106	46	15	61	8	11	80	3	10	10	3	26	6
North Western	223	219	91	26	117	18	20	155	10	26	13	15	64	4
Wales	132	129	53	21	74	10	8	92	10	10	10	7	37	3

Postneonatal deaths

	All weights	Total stated	Under 1,000g	1,000– 1,499	Under 1,500g	1,500– 1,999	2,000– 2,499	Under 2,500g	2,500– 2,999	3,000– 3,499	3,500– 3,999	4,000 and over	2,500 and over	Not stated
England and Wales**	1,244	1,225	168	87	255	91	142	488	238	298	147	54	737	19
Outside England and Wales	2	2	2	0	2	0	0	2	0	0	0	0	0	0
England	1,173	1,155	158	81	239	86	135	460	222	281	140	52	695	18

Regional health authorities

	All weights	Total stated	Under 1,000g	1,000– 1,499	Under 1,500g	1,500– 1,999	2,000– 2,499	Under 2,500g	2,500– 2,999	3,000– 3,499	3,500– 3,999	4,000 and over	2,500 and over	Not stated
Northern	73	73	6	9	15	6	8	29	12	24	5	3	44	0
Yorkshire	95	93	8	5	13	8	9	30	15	29	14	5	63	2
Trent	109	108	13	3	16	8	15	39	20	34	10	5	69	1
East Anglian	74	73	10	5	15	8	11	34	11	19	7	2	39	1
North West Thames	74	73	21	8	29	4	5	38	7	19	7	2	35	1
North East Thames	97	95	15	7	22	6	10	38	18	22	12	5	57	2
South East Thames	94	89	16	5	21	6	9	36	14	25	11	3	53	5
South West Thames	70	70	9	2	11	4	10	25	17	18	7	3	45	0
Wessex	65	65	8	7	15	3	13	31	18	8	6	3	34	0
Oxford	47	47	8	3	11	3	5	19	10	10	7	1	28	0
South Western	58	57	13	4	17	8	3	28	5	12	5	7	29	1

A3.16.1 continued

Stillbirth and infant mortality rates by birthweight and regional health authority or country of residence, England and Wales, 1995

Region/country of residence	All weights	Total stated	Under 1,000g	1,000–1,499	Under 1,500g	1,500–1,999	2,000–2,499	Under 2,500g	2,500–2,999	3,000–3,499	3,500–3,999	4,000 and over	2,500 and over	Not stated
Numbers														
Postneonatal deaths														
West Midlands	121	119	11	4	15	11	16	42	33	18	21	5	77	2
Mersey	62	60	9	6	15	5	5	25	12	14	7	2	35	2
North Western	134	133	11	13	24	6	16	46	30	29	21	7	87	1
Wales	69	68	8	6	14	5	7	26	16	17	7	2	42	1
Rates														
Stillbirths per 1,000 total births														
England and Wales**	5.5	5.4	279.9	97.1	176.5	39.6	13.2	48.8	3.9	1.6	1.1	1.3	1.8	32.7
England	5.5	5.4	277.7	97.5	175.9	39.9	13.1	48.4	3.9	1.6	1.1	1.3	1.8	34.7
Regional health authorities														
Northern	6.7	6.6	316.1	122.9	199.6	38.9	20.2	56.0	4.0	2.8	1.3	1.6	2.4	69.0
Yorkshire	5.1	5.1	239.5	87.8	156.2	31.9	11.8	41.7	4.4	1.3	0.8	1.9	1.8	40.0
Trent	5.9	5.8	303.1	90.7	185.1	34.9	18.0	51.2	4.6	1.6	1.6	0.9	2.1	19.8
East Anglian	5.0	4.8	290.2	100.9	187.6	25.4	13.3	47.1	3.4	1.4	1.0	0.5	1.5	272.7
North West Thames	5.8	5.7	245.5	121.5	175.9	31.9	13.4	48.3	3.5	1.6	1.8	1.5	2.0	37.6
North East Thames	6.1	6.0	260.6	99.3	170.9	57.7	11.8	49.6	4.4	2.2	1.3	2.1	2.4	60.6
South East Thames	5.7	5.5	264.4	96.9	171.2	31.4	12.6	48.5	4.8	1.6	1.1	1.5	2.0	24.7
South West Thames	5.2	4.9	265.6	81.6	164.5	41.2	12.9	48.5	4.4	1.2	1.0	0.5	1.6	45.6
Wessex	4.7	4.6	298.3	86.0	169.6	34.7	8.7	42.5	2.6	2.3	1.0	1.1	1.8	66.7
Oxford	4.7	4.6	254.1	125.5	181.0	36.2	12.3	47.2	4.6	0.7	0.9	0.5	1.4	16.6
South Western	4.8	4.8	270.7	76.7	162.8	45.0	11.8	47.8	3.7	1.2	0.8	1.6	1.5	32.3
West Midlands	5.9	5.9	277.7	108.7	181.6	47.0	14.5	52.7	3.1	1.5	0.8	1.3	1.6	33.6
Mersey	4.9	4.8	267.5	63.7	142.2	42.2	10.4	42.7	4.0	1.8	0.6	2.0	1.8	39.2
North Western	5.7	5.6	335.3	93.8	200.8	38.9	10.0	48.0	3.6	1.6	0.9	1.5	1.8	18.7
Wales	5.0	5.0	316.3	76.6	176.6	43.5	13.3	50.2	3.2	1.1	1.0	1.3	1.5	5.9

A3.16.1 continued

Stillbirth and infant mortality rates by birthweight and regional health authority or country of residence, England and Wales, 1995

Region/country of residence	All weights	Total stated	Under 1,000g	1,000– 1,499	Under 1,500g	1,500– 1,999	2,000– 2,499	Under 2,500g	2,500– 2,999	3,000– 3,499	3,500– 3,999	4,000 and over	2,500 and over	Not stated
Rates														
Perinatal deaths per 1,000 total births														
England and Wales**	8.7	8.5	515.3	138.0	301.8	52.9	17.7	77.4	5.3	2.4	1.8	3.2	2.2	58.5
England	8.7	8.6	516.1	138.2	302.6	51.8	17.7	77.2	5.3	2.5	1.8	3.2	2.3	61.4
Regional health authorities														
Northern	10.3	10.2	585.5	163.8	331.3	55.6	23.7	85.1	5.2	4.2	2.2	4.1	3.1	103.4
Yorkshire	8.7	8.5	488.7	127.7	290.5	45.2	16.4	71.4	5.9	2.2	1.5	4.3	2.2	90.0
Trent	9.5	9.4	597.7	133.8	340.1	45.1	24.5	84.8	5.7	2.6	2.2	2.7	2.3	49.5
East Anglian	7.7	7.4	513.0	153.5	318.3	27.4	15.4	72.1	5.1	2.4	1.3	1.6	2.0	318.2
North West Thames	8.9	8.6	444.0	149.7	278.9	46.3	17.4	73.3	4.9	2.1	2.9	3.8	2.5	82.7
North East Thames	9.1	8.9	490.1	130.9	290.2	72.1	15.5	76.8	5.5	2.7	2.1	3.8	2.5	98.5
South East Thames	8.7	8.4	455.9	130.8	274.9	36.4	15.8	72.4	6.6	2.7	1.6	3.6	2.6	40.4
South West Thames	8.4	8.0	518.7	112.2	295.3	46.3	17.9	78.1	6.3	1.7	1.7	2.8	2.2	72.2
Wessex	7.7	7.6	558.0	150.5	310.9	51.1	14.9	74.6	3.8	2.8	1.5	2.9	2.2	111.1
Oxford	6.7	6.7	403.3	179.9	276.2	44.8	17.1	68.8	5.7	1.0	1.5	1.3	1.3	22.1
South Western	7.7	7.7	462.9	125.4	275.2	61.2	16.8	75.8	5.0	2.0	1.2	4.0	1.9	32.3
West Midlands	10.1	10.0	572.7	141.7	327.7	68.4	19.2	87.4	4.9	2.5	1.9	3.6	2.4	84.0
Mersey	7.6	7.4	503.2	111.6	262.3	58.5	15.2	72.4	4.2	2.2	1.4	2.0	1.7	88.2
North Western	9.0	8.9	565.0	137.0	326.6	52.6	14.7	74.9	4.6	2.7	1.5	4.0	2.3	33.7
Wales	7.8	7.8	510.2	124.1	285.1	61.6	16.6	76.3	4.8	1.7	1.5	3.1	1.8	23.7
Neonatal deaths per 1,000 live births														
England and Wales**	4.1	4.0	390.4	64.0	187.9	17.3	6.6	37.8	2.0	1.1	1.0	2.2	1.4	28.9
England	4.1	4.0	390.7	63.0	188.0	17.0	6.6	37.7	2.0	1.2	1.0	2.2	1.4	30.1
Regional health authorities														
Northern	4.5	4.5	462.1	58.4	195.4	19.3	5.4	37.1	2.5	2.0	1.0	2.5	1.8	37.0
Yorkshire	4.4	4.3	400.0	58.3	197.2	13.7	5.1	37.2	1.8	1.2	1.2	3.0	1.5	52.1
Trent	4.5	4.4	487.8	62.3	224.1	16.4	8.1	42.8	1.8	1.5	0.9	1.7	1.4	35.4
East Anglian	3.7	3.7	401.5	73.2	204.7	4.0	6.4	36.0	2.7	1.4	0.4	1.3	1.3	62.5
North West Thames	3.8	3.6	291.9	51.4	148.1	16.5	5.0	31.1	1.7	0.9	1.3	2.5	1.3	54.7

A3.16.1 continued

Stillbirth and infant mortality rates by birthweight and regional health authority or country of residence, England and Wales, 1995

Region/country of residence	All weights	Total stated	Under 1,000g	1,000–1,499	Under 1,500g	1,500–1,999	2,000–2,499	Under 2,500g	2,500–2,999	3,000–3,499	3,500–3,999	4,000 and over	2,500 and over	Not stated
Rates														
Neonatal deaths per 1,000 live births														
North East Thames	3.9	3.8	367.8	70.2	187.9	18.1	5.2	37.2	1.8	0.8	0.9	1.7	1.1	40.3
South East Thames	3.7	3.6	330.6	56.3	164.2	7.8	4.2	33.0	2.3	1.2	0.6	2.1	1.3	16.1
South West Thames	3.9	3.8	389.8	44.4	181.2	8.9	5.6	36.4	2.6	0.9	0.8	3.0	1.4	27.9
Wessex	4.0	4.0	409.4	98.0	201.6	22.7	10.1	41.9	2.4	0.8	0.7	2.3	1.2	47.6
Oxford	2.9	2.9	274.1	67.0	148.3	13.3	6.9	29.9	1.4	0.6	1.1	1.3	1.0	11.2
South Western	3.9	3.9	329.3	60.4	164.4	20.7	8.8	37.7	2.0	1.2	1.1	2.8	1.5	0.0
West Midlands	5.2	5.2	456.5	59.1	210.5	26.9	6.8	44.1	2.9	1.2	1.3	2.8	1.8	60.9
Mersey	3.9	3.7	400.0	63.8	174.3	19.6	8.9	40.1	0.7	1.0	1.2	0.8	1.0	61.2
North Western	4.2	4.2	413.6	69.0	196.0	21.4	7.2	36.8	1.1	1.4	0.9	2.9	1.3	15.3
Wales	3.8	3.8	395.5	83.0	157.4	18.9	5.4	38.3	1.8	0.8	1.0	1.8	1.2	17.9
Postneonatal deaths per 1,000 live births														
England and Wales**	1.9	1.9	58.4	18.5	33.6	9.4	4.7	10.3	2.2	1.3	0.8	0.8	1.2	8.6
England	1.9	1.9	57.7	18.2	33.3	9.4	4.7	10.3	2.1	1.3	0.8	0.8	1.2	8.9
Regional health authorities														
Northern	2.1	2.1	45.5	35.0	38.6	11.6	4.8	11.3	2.1	2.0	0.5	0.8	1.4	0.0
Yorkshire	2.0	2.0	34.0	14.6	22.5	11.0	3.8	8.2	1.8	1.7	1.1	1.1	1.5	20.8
Trent	1.9	1.9	52.8	7.5	24.7	9.3	5.5	9.2	2.0	1.6	0.6	0.8	1.3	5.1
East Anglian	2.3	2.2	73.0	24.4	43.9	16.1	7.8	15.1	2.1	1.6	0.7	0.5	1.3	62.5
North West Thames	1.8	1.8	100.5	25.7	55.8	6.6	2.5	12.2	0.9	1.2	0.6	0.5	0.9	7.8
North East Thames	1.8	1.7	57.5	17.5	33.3	8.3	3.7	9.4	1.8	1.1	0.8	1.0	1.1	16.1
South East Thames	1.9	1.8	66.1	13.4	34.1	7.8	4.2	10.3	1.8	1.4	0.8	0.6	1.2	11.5
South West Thames	1.8	1.8	50.8	7.4	24.6	7.2	6.2	9.6	2.8	1.3	0.6	0.7	1.3	0.0
Wessex	1.7	1.7	63.0	27.5	39.3	5.7	8.2	12.4	3.1	0.6	0.5	0.7	1.0	0.0
Oxford	1.4	1.4	59.3	14.4	32.0	6.6	3.5	8.5	1.8	0.8	0.7	0.3	0.9	0.0
South Western	1.5	1.5	77.8	15.1	39.4	15.1	1.9	11.0	0.8	0.9	0.4	1.6	0.8	16.7
West Midlands	1.8	1.8	33.0	7.4	17.2	9.9	4.7	7.8	2.8	0.7	1.1	0.7	1.3	17.4
Mersey	2.2	2.1	78.3	25.5	42.9	12.2	4.0	12.5	2.7	1.4	0.8	0.6	1.3	20.4
North Western	2.5	2.5	50.0	34.5	40.2	7.1	5.8	10.9	3.2	1.5	1.4	1.3	1.8	3.8
Wales	2.0	2.0	59.7	23.7	36.2	9.5	4.7	10.8	2.9	1.4	0.7	0.5	1.3	6.0

A3.16.1 continued

Stillbirth and infant mortality rates by birthweight and regional health authority or country of residence, England and Wales, 1995

Region/country of residence	All weights	Total stated	Under 1,000g	1,000–1,499	Under 1,500g	1,500–1,999	2,000–2,499	Under 2,500g	2,500–2,999	3,000–3,499	3,500–3,999	4,000 and over	2,500 and over	Not stated
Rates														
Infant deaths per 1,000 live births														
England and Wales**	6.0	5.9	448.8	82.5	221.5	26.7	11.3	48.1	4.2	2.4	1.8	3.0	2.6	37.4
England	6.0	5.9	448.5	81.3	221.3	26.4	11.3	48.0	4.1	2.4	1.8	3.0	2.6	38.9
Regional health authorities														
Northern	6.6	6.6	507.6	93.4	233.9	30.8	10.3	48.4	4.6	3.9	1.5	3.3	3.2	37.0
Yorkshire	6.5	6.3	434.0	72.9	219.7	24.7	9.0	45.5	3.6	2.9	2.3	4.1	3.0	72.9
Trent	6.4	6.3	540.7	69.8	248.8	25.7	13.6	52.0	3.9	3.1	1.5	2.5	2.7	40.4
East Anglian	6.0	5.9	474.5	97.6	248.5	20.1	14.2	51.2	4.8	3.0	1.1	1.9	2.6	125.0
North West Thames	5.6	5.4	392.3	77.2	203.8	23.1	7.5	43.3	2.7	2.1	1.9	3.0	2.3	62.5
North East Thames	5.6	5.5	425.3	87.7	221.2	26.4	8.9	46.5	3.6	1.8	1.7	2.7	2.2	56.5
South East Thames	5.7	5.5	396.7	69.7	198.4	15.5	8.5	43.3	4.0	2.7	1.4	2.6	2.5	27.6
South West Thames	5.8	5.6	440.7	51.9	205.8	16.1	11.9	46.0	5.3	2.2	1.4	3.7	2.7	27.9
Wessex	5.7	5.7	472.4	125.5	240.8	28.4	18.2	54.3	5.5	1.4	1.2	2.7	2.2	47.6
Oxford	4.3	4.3	333.3	81.3	180.2	19.9	10.4	38.3	3.2	1.4	1.8	1.6	1.9	11.2
South Western	5.4	5.4	407.2	75.5	203.7	35.8	10.7	48.6	2.9	2.0	1.5	4.5	2.3	16.7
West Midlands	7.1	6.9	489.5	66.5	227.7	36.8	11.5	51.9	5.6	2.0	2.5	3.5	3.0	78.3
Mersey	6.1	5.8	478.3	89.4	217.1	31.8	12.9	52.6	3.3	2.4	2.0	1.4	2.3	81.6
North Western	6.8	6.7	463.6	103.4	236.2	28.5	13.0	47.8	4.3	2.9	2.3	4.2	3.1	19.1
Wales	5.8	5.7	455.2	106.7	227.4	28.4	10.1	49.1	4.7	2.2	1.7	2.3	2.5	23.8

** Includes births to women resident outside England and Wales

Source: ONS, Mortality statistics, Series DH3. Unpublished data

This table is similar to Table A3.30 in the first edition of *Birth counts*

Stillbirth and infant mortality rates by birthweight and regional office or country of residence, 1996

Region/country of residence	All weights	Total stated	Under 1,000g	1,000–1,499	Under 1,500g	1,500–1,999	2,000–2,499	Under 2,500g	2,500–2,999	3,000–3,499	3,500–3,999	4,000 and over	2,500 and over	Not stated
Numbers														
Early neonatal deaths														
England and Wales**	2,038	1,969	1,076	211	1,287	111	123	1,521	146	149	96	57	448	69
Outside England and Wales	8	8	5	3	8	0	0	8	0	0	0	0	0	0
England	1,943	1,885	1,030	196	1,226	107	116	1,449	140	141	90	55	426	68
NHSE regional offices														
Northern and Yorkshire	241	231	125	13	138	11	21	170	18	19	20	4	61	10
Trent	203	203	112	26	138	15	11	164	12	7	11	7	37	2
Anglia and Oxford	189	189	94	26	120	7	15	142	9	23	9	3	44	3
North Thames	281	281	147	32	179	13	12	204	22	23	12	12	69	8
South Thames	281	281	135	26	161	18	12	191	28	20	15	12	75	15
South and West	215	215	117	15	132	12	19	163	18	13	6	5	42	10
West Midlands	275	34	166	31	197	15	12	224	16	13	7	7	43	8
North West	258	133	134	99	233	16	14	263	17	23	10	5	55	12
Wales	87	76	41	12	53	4	7	64	6	8	6	2	22	1
Neonatal deaths														
England and Wales**	2,604	2,526	1,278	282	1,560	142	173	1,875	209	224.	140	78	651	78
Outside England and Wales	9	9	6	3	9	0	0	9	0	0	0	0	0	0
England	2,475	2,399	1,221	261	1,482	134	164	1,780	199	211	134	75	619	76
NHSE regional offices														
Northern and Yorkshire	307	297	145	27	172	13	27	212	24	31	22	8	85	10
Trent	258	256	138	29	167	17	16	200	14	15	19	8	56	2
Anglia and Oxford	246	242	110	33	143	13	18	174	15	33	15	5	68	4
North Thames	369	360	178	39	217	17	20	254	34	36	22	14	106	9
South Thames	351	332	163	31	194	21	20	235	38	27	20	12	97	19
South and West	284	273	141	28	169	12	23	204	27	21	12	9	69	11
West Midlands	330	322	185	38	223	21	18	262	22	18	9	11	60	8
North West	330	317	161	36	197	20	22	239	25	30	15	8	78	13
Wales	120	118	51	18	69	8	9	86	10	13	6	3	32	2

A3.16.2 continued

Stillbirth and infant mortality rates by birthweight and regional office or country of residence, 1996

Region/country of residence	All weights	Total stated	Under 1,000g	1,000–1,499	Under 1,500g	1,500–1,999	2,000–2,499	Under 2,500g	2,500–2,999	3,000–3,499	3,500–3,999	4,000 and over	2,500 and over	Not stated
Numbers														
Postneonatal deaths														
England and Wales**	1,263	1,259	147	93	240	88	177	505	248	292	154	60	754	4
Outside England and Wales	2	2	0	0	0	1	0	1	0	1	0	0	1	0
England	1,195	1,191	142	89	231	86	169	486	233	270	147	55	706	4
NHSE regional offices														
Northern and Yorkshire	168	168	13	12	25	15	22	62	33	47	21	5	106	0
Trent	126	126	10	10	20	12	20	52	25	29	14	6	74	0
Anglia and Oxford	137	137	14	11	25	10	26	61	31	27	13	5	76	0
North Thames	158	157	29	9	38	4	28	70	23	32	22	10	87	1
South Thames	173	171	31	15	46	13	22	81	33	32	19	6	90	2
South and West	120	120	12	13	25	6	14	45	26	29	14	6	75	0
West Midlands	124	124	11	3	14	13	17	44	23	31	19	7	80	0
North West	189	188	22	16	38	13	20	71	39	43	25	10	117	1
Wales	66	66	5	4	9	1	8	18	15	21	7	5	48	0
Stillbirths per 1,000 total births														
England and Wales**	5.4	5.3	278.5	83.6	172.5	38.4	12.4	48.4	4.0	1.6	1.0	1.2	1.8	38.8
England	5.4	5.3	277.5	83.3	172.5	37.8	14.5	48.2	4.0	1.6	1.0	1.2	1.8	37.2
NHSE regional offices														
Northern and Yorkshire	5.4	5.3	251.0	121.8	180.9	39.0	11.5	48.2	4.0	1.4	0.8	1.4	1.7	36.0
Trent	5.4	5.4	313.8	97.0	189.6	33.0	13.0	50.5	3.3	2.0	0.7	0.4	1.7	19.2
Anglia and Oxford	4.9	4.8	258.8	73.6	158.4	33.6	16.5	47.1	3.3	1.4	1.0	0.9	1.5	75.8
North Thames	6.1	5.9	289.8	92.8	190.1	38.9	12.2	52.1	4.3	1.5	1.4	1.6	2.0	33.7
South Thames	5.3	5.2	271.9	72.5	161.8	34.5	10.1	46.2	5.0	1.8	1.1	1.0	2.1	27.9
South and West	4.6	4.5	263.0	71.3	154.5	31.9	8.8	40.9	3.9	1.5	1.1	1.1	1.8	40.3
West Midlands	6.1	6.0	277.3	74.3	170.0	49.5	12.7	51.3	4.0	1.3	0.9	1.8	1.8	62.5
North West	5.5	5.4	291.7	64.7	170.8	41.9	13.2	48.3	3.8	1.5	0.8	1.3	1.7	39.8
Wales	4.9	4.8	275.3	78.0	154.3	39.2	15.0	45.4	4.6	1.1	1.0	0.5	1.6	72.5

A3.16.2 continued

Stillbirth and infant mortality rates by birthweight and regional office or country of residence, 1996

Region/country of residence	All weights	Total stated	Under 1,000g	1,000–1,499	Under 1,500g	1,500–1,999	2,000–2,499	Under 2,500g	2,500–2,999	3,000–3,499	3,500–3,999	4,000 and over	2,500 and over	Not stated
Perinatal deaths per 1,000 total births														
England and Wales**	8.5	8.4	525.0	124.1	314.2	49.8	16.4	79.1	5.4	2.2	1.5	2.0	2.0	81.9
England	8.6	8.4	524.7	123.3	315.0	49.4	18.6	79.1	5.4	2.2	1.5	2.0	2.0	81.7
NHSE regional offices														
Northern and Yorkshire	8.51	8.3	502.0	143.8	378.0	48.3	17.3	118.7	5.4	2.1	1.7	1.9	3.7	126.1
Trent	8.69	8.7	611.7	148.5	384.3	48.9	16.9	84.8	4.5	2.4	1.3	1.5	1.9	57.7
Anglia and Oxford	7.71	7.6	480.0	125.2	311.8	41.4	21.5	83.0	4.2	2.4	1.4	1.3	2.1	121.2
North Thames	8.92	8.8	489.8	135.3	430.9	47.7	14.8	133.6	5.5	2.2	1.8	2.8	3.4	49.5
South Thames	8.51	8.4	504.3	108.8	387.2	48.9	13.3	106.6	7.0	2.4	1.7	2.2	3.4	69.6
South and West	7.40	7.3	528.3	97.4	330.3	43.4	14.5	87.8	5.4	2.0	1.4	1.7	2.5	121.0
West Midlands	10.11	6.5	584.1	125.4	405.7	62.8	16.1	109.2	5.3	1.9	1.3	2.8	2.4	133.9
North West	8.63	7.0	527.2	106.3	490.2	53.9	16.7	144.5	5.1	2.3	1.2	1.9	2.7	99.5
Wales	7.39	6.9	505.6	120.6	316.5	46.6	19.5	74.3	5.7	1.8	1.5	1.0	1.4	87.0
Neonatal deaths per 1,000 live births														
England and Wales**	4.0	3.9	405.7	59.1	197.0	15.1	5.8	39.7	1.9	1.0	0.7	1.1	1.1	50.7
England	4.0	3.9	405.6	58.1	197.5	15.1	5.8	39.8	1.9	1.0	0.8	1.1	1.1	51.6
NHSE regional offices														
Northern and Yorkshire	4.0	3.9	388.7	52.0	192.8	11.5	7.5	37.7	1.8	1.1	1.0	1.0	1.2	93.5
Trent	4.2	4.2	534.9	63.6	233.9	18.7	5.7	45.2	1.4	0.7	1.1	1.2	1.0	39.2
Anglia and Oxford	3.7	3.6	349.2	70.8	183.1	15.0	6.2	38.1	1.4	1.4	0.8	0.7	1.1	65.6
North Thames	3.8	3.7	341.0	57.0	179.9	12.1	4.3	35.2	1.9	1.0	0.8	1.5	1.2	18.4
South Thames	4.0	3.8	385.3	46.6	178.3	17.4	5.4	39.1	2.7	0.9	0.8	1.2	1.2	54.4
South and West	3.8	3.6	433.8	52.4	196.7	12.0	7.0	39.7	2.3	0.8	0.5	1.0	1.0	92.4
West Midlands	4.9	4.8	473.1	67.7	234.2	19.5	5.3	48.0	1.8	0.7	0.5	1.6	1.0	76.2
North West	4.0	3.9	399.5	59.3	195.0	15.6	5.6	38.3	1.8	1.0	0.6	0.9	1.0	67.4
Wales	3.4	3.4	395.3	69.2	177.4	15.5	5.9	35.6	1.8	1.0	0.6	0.8	1.0	31.3

Stillbirth and infant mortality rates by birthweight and regional office or country of residence, 1996

Region/country of residence	All weights	Total stated	Under 1,000g	1,000–1,499	Under 1,500g	1,500–1,999	2,000–2,499	Under 2,500g	2,500–2,999	3,000–3,499	3,500–3,999	4,000 and over	2,500 and over	Not stated
Postneonatal deaths per 1,000 live births														
England and Wales**	1.9	1.9	46.7	19.5	30.3	9.4	5.9	10.7	2.3	1.2	0.8	0.9	1.3	2.6
England	1.9	1.9	47.2	19.8	30.8	9.7	6.0	10.9	2.3	1.2	0.8	0.8	1.2	2.7
NHSE regional offices														
Northern and Yorkshire	2.2	2.2	34.9	23.1	28.0	13.2	6.1	11.0	2.5	1.7	1.0	0.6	1.5	0.0
Trent	2.1	2.1	38.8	21.9	28.0	13.2	7.1	11.8	2.5	1.3	0.8	0.9	1.3	0.0
Anglia and Oxford	2.1	2.1	44.4	23.6	32.0	11.6	8.9	13.4	2.9	1.1	0.7	0.7	1.2	0.0
North Thames	1.6	1.6	55.6	13.2	31.5	2.8	6.1	9.7	1.3	0.9	0.8	1.0	1.0	2.0
South Thames	2.0	2.0	73.3	22.6	42.3	10.8	5.9	13.5	2.4	1.0	0.7	0.6	1.1	5.7
South and West	1.6	1.6	36.9	24.3	29.1	6.0	4.3	8.8	2.2	1.1	0.6	0.7	1.1	0.0
West Midlands	1.8	1.8	28.1	5.3	14.7	12.1	5.0	8.1	1.9	1.3	1.0	1.0	1.3	0.0
North West	2.3	2.3	54.6	26.4	37.6	10.2	5.1	11.4	2.8	1.5	1.1	1.1	1.6	5.2
Wales	1.9	1.9	38.8	15.4	23.1	1.9	5.3	7.4	2.7	1.7	0.7	1.3	1.5	0.0
Infant deaths per 1,000 live births														
England and Wales**	6.0	5.8	452.4	78.6	227.3	24.5	11.7	50.4	4.2	2.2	1.6	2.0	2.3	53.3
England	6.0	5.9	452.8	77.9	228.3	24.8	11.8	50.7	4.2	2.2	1.6	2.0	2.3	54.3
NHSE regional offices														
Northern and Yorkshire	6.2	6.1	423.6	75.1	220.9	24.7	13.6	48.7	4.3	2.8	2.0	1.6	2.7	93.5
Trent	6.3	6.3	573.6	85.5	261.9	31.9	12.9	57.0	3.8	2.0	1.9	2.1	2.3	39.2
Anglia and Oxford	5.8	5.7	393.7	94.4	215.1	26.6	15.1	51.4	4.3	2.5	1.4	1.3	2.3	65.6
North Thames	5.4	5.3	396.6	70.2	211.4	14.9	10.4	44.8	3.3	1.9	1.6	2.5	2.1	20.5

A3.16.2 continued

Stillbirth and infant mortality rates by birthweight and regional office or country of residence, 1996

Infant deaths per 1,000 live births

Region/country of residence	All weights	Total stated	Under 1,000g	1,000–1,499	Under 1,500g	1,500–1,999	2,000–2,499	Under 2,500g	2,500–2,999	3,000–3,499	3,500–3,999	4,000 and over	2,500 and over	Not stated
South Thames	6.0	5.8	458.6	69.2	220.6	28.2	11.3	52.6	5.1	1.9	1.5	1.8	2.3	60.2
South and West	5.3	5.2	470.8	76.8	225.8	17.9	11.3	48.5	4.5	1.8	1.1	1.7	2.0	92.4
West Midlands	6.7	6.6	501.3	73.1	248.9	31.6	10.2	56.1	3.7	2.0	1.5	2.5	2.3	76.2
North West	6.3	6.2	454.1	85.7	232.7	25.8	10.6	49.6	4.7	2.5	1.7	2.0	2.6	72.5
Wales	5.3	5.3	434.1	84.6	200.5	17.5	11.2	43.0	4.5	2.7	1.2	2.0	2.5	31.3

* * Includes births to women resident outside England and Wales

Source: ONS, Mortality statistics, Series DH3. Unpublished data

This table is similar to Table A3.30 in the first edition of *Birth counts*

Use of birth control services, England, 1975–1998/99

Year	Women using family planning clinics and domiciliary services		Women registered with general practitioners		Numbers of men using clinics	Numbers of attendances at family planning clinics	Numbers of domiciliary visits	Prescriptions for emergency contraception	
	Numbers	Percentage of women aged 15–44	Numbers	Percentage of women aged 15–44				At clinics	General practitioners*
1975	1,426,700	16	1,157,000	13	17,100	3,658,000	66,600	–	–
1976	1,460,500	16	1,898,000	21	16,500	3,672,000	66,800	–	–
1977	1,537,500	17	2,038,000	22	17,800	3,734,300	69,200	–	–
1978	1,516,700	16	1,959,000	21	21,200	3,554,600	64,600	–	–
1979	1,488,900	16	1,921,800	20	21,400	3,367,400	60,900	–	–
1980	1,490,500	15	2,023,900	21	19,200	3,329,400	60,000	–	–
1981	1,470,400	15	2,091,500	21	18,500	3,210,300	59,400	–	–
1982	1,457,300	15	2,190,600	22	20,200	3,159,600	60,300	–	–
1983	1,465,000	15	2,358,200	24	20,300	3,162,500	56,900	–	–
1984	1,501,100	15	2,374,400	24	22,900	3,255,100	52,200	–	–
1985	1,468,000	14	2,455,800	24	25,900	3,157,100	51,600	–	–
1986	1,419,300	14	2,571,000	25	27,000	3,034,200	45,400	–	–
1987/88	1,331,500	13	2,554,900	25	33,600	2,861,700	46,700	–	–
1988/89	1,198,800	12	2,658,900	26	32,500	2,657,800	35,200	–	75,200
1989/90	1,172,100	11	2,755,700	26	32,300	2,587,000	34,500	37,900	122,700
1990/91	1,082,700	10	2,864,000	28	32,500	2,401,400	30,300	46,800	189,600
1991/92	1,069,800	10	2,950,300	28	39,400	2,357,700	32,300	64,700	232,800
1992/93	1,080,500	11	3,081,200	30	47,300	2,370,300	29,000	78,500	272,200
1993/94	1,094,700	11	2,948,900	29	55,900	2,405,500	29,300	94,400	313,300
1994/95	1,129,000	11	3,521,700	35	63,300	2,474,200	37,300	114,600	363,800
1995/96	1,159,700	11	..	..	71,800	2,624,300	26,800	161,600	475,400
1996/97	1,182,200	12	..	..	78,600	2,602,200	26,700	198,700	565,600
1997/98	1,190,700	12	..	..	79,300	2,580,300	23,200	210,200	552,800
1998/99	1,178,700	12	..	..	81,300	2,569,000	18,800	217,500	559,000

Some women use both clinic and family practitioner services

* Excluding IUDs prescribed for emergency contraception. These are included in clinic figures.

Source: Department of Health, *Health and personal services statistics for England* and statistical return KT31

This was part of Table A4.1 in the first edition of *Birth counts*

A4.1.2

Use of birth control services, Wales, 1975–1997/98

Year	Numbers of women using services+			Total		Numbers of men using clinics#	Numbers of attendances	Numbers of visits
	Family planning clinics	Domiciliary services	General practitioners	Number	Percentage of women aged 15–44		Family planning clinics	Domiciliary services
1975	78,006	..	..	..	..	..	..	..
1976	82,964	745	103,302	187,011	35	..	..	..
1977	90,770	554	104,546	195,870	36	299	204,841	2864
1978	85,287	591	101,181	187,059	34	609	195,259	2983
1979	81,067	540	96,802	178,409	32	640	183,009	2713
1980	80,256	521	103,026	183,803	33	462	181,196	2829
1981	79,283	481	103,664	183,428	32	353	176,641	2647
1982	76,471	259	109,816	186,546	33	485	173,453	1711
1983	79,306	245	118,929	198,480	34	288	177,188	1987
1984	83,204	168	116,726	200,098	34	210	182,882	1564
1985	80,905	134	119,394	200,433	34	253	176,651	1460
1986	76,932	122	126,021	203,075	34	976	166,265	1582
1987	72,723	67	125,538	198,328	33	507	159,312	1460
1988	68,208	74	134,949	203,231	34	481	151,438	1639
1989/90	62,494	*	137,286	201,026	34	267	137,606	1,246
1990/91	49,850	*	145,052	195,892	33	775	134,746	990
1991/92	50,167	*	156,442	207,510	35	1,080	133,916	901
1992/93	49,592	*	161,640	211,995	36	2,029	128,955	763
1993/94	48,506	*	162,176	211,200	37	2,808	133,257	518
1994/95	48,759	*	168,237	218,236	38	3,635	136,687	1,240
1995/96	50,953	*	172,871	224,830	39	4,534	147,337	1,006
1996/97	39,461~	+	176,887	216,348~	..	3,392~	109,132~	1,375~
1997/98	39,586~	+	..	..	..	3,447~	137,402~	1,168~

+ Women attending family planning clinics and women registered with GPs for contraceptive services

* From 1989 figures for attendances at family planning clinics include domiciliary services

Vasectomies only up to 1989/90

~ Excluding Gwent Community Health NHS Trust, which has not provided these data since 1995/6.

Source: Welsh Office, *Health and personal social services statistics for Wales*, up to 1994
  Welsh Office, *Health statistics Wales*, 1995–98

This was part of Table A4.1 in the first edition of *Birth counts*

A4.1.3

Use of birth control services, Scotland, 1975–97

| Year | Numbers of women using services | | | | Percentage of women aged 15–44 | Numbers of men using clinics | Numbers of attendances | Numbers of visits |
	Family planning clinics	Domiciliary services	General practitioners	Total Number			Family planning clinics	Domiciliary services
1975	126,562	601	171,396	298,559	29	::	318,618	7,201
1976	125,601	1,073	224,464	351,138	34	::	292,785	11,254
1977	133,284	1,324	238,800	373,408	35	::	325,101	15,564
1978	130,491	1,233	227,475	359,199	34	::	317,468	19,998
1979	133,966	3,353	222,065	359,384	33	3,353	295,221	22,118
1980	137,947	3,347	217,227	358,521	33	3,533	298,923	24,388
1981	133,781	3,873	221,586	359,240	33	3,047	284,045	26,422
1982	134,437	3,422	233,276	371,135	34	2,808	283,729	23,414
1983	135,310	3,179	248,303	386,792	35	3,067	289,094	23,100
1984	132,484	3,018	254,277	389,779	35	3,188	288,957	21,147
1985	131,938	2,787	260,425	395,150	35	3,371	284,613	22,421
1986	127,404	2,735	270,797	400,936	36	3,611	270,487	22,011
1987	122,755	2,994	272,598	398,347	35	4,200	260,111	21,486
1988	113,249	2,651	276,232	392,132	35	3,869	238,888	20,572
1989	111,337	2,545	283,421	397,303	35	4,023	232,478	20,731
1990	105,270	2,309	299,178	406,757	36	4,232	213,696	17,210
1991	99,953	2,236	308,650	410,839	37	3,783	215,937	14,127
1992	101,531	2,086	317,126	420,743	38	4,461	202,397	12,837
1993	106,529	2,028	318,753	427,310	39	4,784	217,644	13,275
1994	111,526	2,124	323,684	437,334	40	6,111	226,974	12,769
1995	119,591	1,825	325,410	446,826	41	8,026	260,969	11,267
1996	116,613	902	326,161	443,676	40	8,610	234,976	9,632
1997*	132,468+	721	327,847	461,036	40	8,115+	235,514+	9,490

* Provisional

+ Includes, for the first time, figures from the Highland Brook Advisory Centre.

Source: ISD, *Scottish health statistics*

This was part of Table A4.1 in the first edition of *Birth counts*

A4.1.4

Use of birth control services, Northern Ireland, 1975–81

Year	Numbers of women using services				Percentage of women aged 15–44*	Numbers of men using clinics
	Family planning clinics	Domiciliary services	General practitioners	Total		
1975	..	..	30,800	..	38	..
1976	..	..	44,400	..	39	..
1977	..	..	37,700	..	39	..
1978	..	..	38,800	..	40	..
1979	..	..	30,300	..	40	..
1980	..	..	32,300	..	40	..
1981	..	..	31,700	..	41	..

Data are not available for years from 1982 onwards.

* Percentage of women aged 15–44 registered with general practitioners for contraceptive services

Source: DHSS, Northern Ireland

This was part of Table A4.2 in the first edition of *Birth counts*

Primary method of birth control chosen by people attending family planning clinics, England, 1975–1998/99

Year	Main method										Total men and women using a method	Attending but not using a method
	Oral contraceptives	Sheath	IUD	Cap/ diaphragm	Injectables	Vasectomy	Female sterilisation	Chemicals including sponge	Rhythm	Other		
Numbers												
1975	978,900	79,400	210,200	90,400	–	14,000	600	13,800	200	9,500	1,397,100	36,900
1976	965,400	94,100	236,000	99,800	–	16,700	900	13,100	200	6,900	1,433,100	47,800
1977	982,700	110,600	266,700	102,100	–	16,500	1,400	13,300	200	7,600	1,501,000	56,800
1978	880,800	132,500	302,500	115,400	–	17,000	1,500	14,100	200	8,900	1,472,900	65,700
1979	809,000	143,300	320,900	117,700	–	16,000	2,000	12,500	200	10,600	1,432,100	73,800
1980	806,700	145,000	311,900	122,200	–	15,900	1,400	10,200	200	10,100	1,423,700	81,200
1981	826,600	146,400	270,200	120,100	–	15,000	1,600	9,300	600	11,500	1,401,300	81,500
1982	839,900	148,800	248,600	114,300	–	14,300	2,400	8,500	300	10,300	1,387,400	87,100
1983	848,700	155,900	237,400	112,300	–	12,700	2,400	7,600	300	11,000	1,388,300	94,200
1984	831,100	182,800	235,100	128,200	–	14,900	3,100	8,200	300	13,000	1,416,700	106,000
1985	787,600	187,200	224,000	133,100	–	14,300	1,700	8,300	600	15,900	1,372,700	121,700
1986	756,800	187,000	203,800	132,300	–	12,700	1,700	9,500	400	23,500	1,327,800	115,100
1987/88	681,200	211,200	170,600	114,200	–	12,400	2,300	9,800	400	24,100	1,226,100	126,800
1988/89	623,100	189,700	134,900	88,000	3,400	12,900	2,400	8,400	600	18,800	1,082,200	149,100
1989/90	596,600	184,800	123,300	85,500	15,600	13,500	2,800	5,900	800	13,100	1,041,800	162,600
1990/91	559,400	178,200	104,800	71,500	15,700	12,700	2,100	5,600	600	12,400	963,000	152,200
1991/92	539,100	198,700	93,900	59,300	17,800	13,200	2,200	5,100	500	13,700	943,600	165,600
1992/93	528,300	238,300	82,500	51,300	21,500	12,700	2,300	5,200	600	14,300	956,900	170,900
1993/94	515,300	258,400	73,700	42,800	27,500	11,500	1,600	4,900	500	15,800	951,900	198,600
1994/95	505,900	278,300	64,600	36,500	36,500	11,100	900	5,700	900	25,100	965,500	226,800
1995/96	479,900	325,000	60,000	32,900	42,400	11,500	1,300	5,400	800	31,100	990,100	241,300
1996/97	442,900	353,400	63,300	28,800	48,200	10,600	1,300	5,400	900	33,800	988,600	272,200
1997/98	436,000	361,600	62,100	22,700	52,100	10,700	1,400	4,800	600	39,500	991,400	278,600
1998/99	421,400	363,400	63,400	18,300	56,700	10,800	1,200	4,400	600	51,900	992,100	267,900
Percentages												
1975	70.1	5.7	15.0	6.5	–	1.0	0.0	1.0	0.0	0.7	100.0	
1976	67.4	6.6	16.5	7.0	–	1.2	0.1	0.9	0.0	0.5	100.0	

175

A4.2.1 continued

Primary method of birth control chosen by people attending family planning clinics, England, 1975–1998/99

Year	Main method Oral contraceptives	Sheath	IUD	Cap/ diaphragm	Injectables	Vasectomy	Chemicals including sponge	Female steri-li-sation	Rhythm	Other	Total men and women using a method
Percentages											
1977	65.5	7.4	17.8	6.8	–	1.1	0.1	0.9	0.0	0.5	100.0
1978	59.8	9.0	20.5	7.8	–	1.2	0.1	1.0	0.0	0.6	100.0
1979	56.5	10.0	22.4	8.2	–	1.1	0.1	0.9	0.0	0.7	100.0
1980	56.7	10.2	21.9	8.6	–	1.1	0.1	0.7	0.0	0.7	100.0
1981	59.0	10.4	19.3	8.6	–	1.1	0.1	0.7	0.0	0.8	100.0
1982	60.5	10.7	17.9	8.2	–	1.0	0.2	0.6	0.0	0.7	100.0
1983	61.1	11.2	17.1	8.1	–	0.9	0.2	0.5	0.0	0.8	100.0
1984	58.7	12.9	16.6	9.1	–	1.1	0.2	0.6	0.0	0.9	100.0
1985	57.4	13.6	16.3	9.7	–	1.0	0.1	0.6	0.0	1.2	100.0
1986	57.0	14.1	15.3	10.0	–	1.0	0.1	0.7	0.0	1.8	100.0
1987/88	55.6	17.2	13.9	9.3	–	1.0	0.2	0.8	0.0	2.0	100.0
1988/89	57.6	17.5	12.5	8.1	0.3	1.2	0.2	0.8	0.1	1.7	100.0
1989/90	57.3	17.7	11.8	8.2	1.5	1.3	0.3	0.6	0.1	1.3	100.0
1990/91	58.1	18.5	10.9	7.4	1.6	1.3	0.2	0.6	0.1	1.3	100.0
1991/92	57.1	21.1	10.0	6.3	1.9	1.4	0.2	0.5	0.0	1.4	100.0
1992/93	55.2	24.9	8.6	5.4	2.3	1.3	0.2	0.5	0.1	1.5	100.0
1993/94	54.1	27.1	7.7	4.5	2.9	1.2	0.2	0.5	0.1	1.7	100.0
1994/95	52.4	28.8	6.7	3.8	3.8	1.2	0.1	0.6	0.1	2.6	100.0
1995/96	48.5	32.8	6.1	3.3	4.3	1.1	0.1	0.5	0.1	3.2	100.0
1996/97	44.8	35.7	6.4	2.9	4.9	1.1	0.1	0.5	0.1	3.4	100.0
1997/98	44.0	36.5	6.3	2.3	5.2	1.1	0.1	0.5	0.1	4.0	100.0
1998/99	42.5	36.6	6.4	1.8	5.7	1.1	0.1	0.4	0.1	5.2	100.0

Source: Department of Health, statistical return KT31

This was part of Table A4.2 in the first edition of *Birth counts*

A4.2.2

Primary method of birth control chosen by people attending family planning clinics, Wales, 1975–1997/98

Year ending 31 March	Main method used at first contact							
	Oral contraceptives	Sheath	IUD	Cap/ diaphragm	Other	Total men and women using a method	Attending but not using a method	Not known
	Numbers							
1975	54,940	7,020	7,303	3,228	4,457	76,948	2,312	0
1976	57,026	7,277	9,436	4,109	3,667	81,515	2,194	90
1977	61,182	7,987	11,019	4,219	3,732	88,139	2,973	0
1978	50,254	9,508	12,553	4,652	4,886	81,853	3,831	0
1979	42,893	10,582	14,346	4,726	3,802	76,349	4,395	323
1980	42,325	10,876	14,028	5,127	3,637	75,993	4,259	4
1981	43,591	10,801	12,240	5,015	3,383	75,030	4,017	236
1982	43,055	10,435	11,469	4,538	2,995	72,492	3,724	255
1983	45,854	11,356	10,726	4,392	3,177	75,505	3,690	111
1984	45,507	13,321	11,141	5,309	3,644	78,922	4,147	225
1985	42,095	12,736	11,332	5,295	4,629	76,087	4,607	211
1986	39,723	12,419	10,275	5,005	4,818	72,240	4,565	127
1987	36,324	14,075	9,138	4,459	3,670	67,666	4,753	304
1988	34,545	12,589	7,936	3,835	3,588	62,493	5,019	696
1989/90	31,081	11,351	6,707	3,331	2,322	54,792	7,774	..
1990/91	29,713	10,177	5,660	2,774	2,301	50,614	6,338	..
1991/92	29,557	11,217	5,528	2,432	2,513	51,247	7,293	..
1992/93	28,821	13,173	4,617	2,032	2,978	51,621	7,743	..
1993/94	28,056	13,745	4,087	1,601	3,825	51,314	8,648	..
1994/95	27,700	15,323	3,641	1,629	4,101	52,394	9,204	..
1995/96	27,609	19,162	3,375	1,439	3,902	55,487	12,311	..
1996/97~	20,543	15,354	2,611	1,152	3,193	42,853	..	..
1997/98~	20,304	15,947	2,501	956	3,325	43,033	..	..
	Percentages							
1975	71.4	9.1	9.5	4.2	5.8	100.0		
1976	70.0	8.9	11.6	5.0	4.5	100.0		
1977	69.4	9.1	12.5	4.8	4.2	100.0		
1978	61.4	11.6	15.3	5.7	6.0	100.0		
1979	56.2	13.9	18.8	6.2	5.0	100.0		
1980	55.7	14.3	18.5	6.7	4.8	100.0		
1981	58.1	14.4	16.3	6.7	4.5	100.0		
1982	59.4	14.4	15.8	6.3	4.1	100.0		
1983	60.7	15.0	14.2	5.8	4.2	100.0		
1984	57.7	16.9	14.1	6.7	4.6	100.0		
1985	55.3	16.7	14.9	7.0	6.1	100.0		
1986	55.0	17.2	14.2	6.9	6.7	100.0		
1987	53.7	20.8	13.5	6.6	5.4	100.0		
1988	55.3	20.1	12.7	6.1	5.7	100.0		
1989/90	56.7	20.7	12.2	6.1	4.2	100.0		
1990/91	58.7	20.1	11.2	5.5	4.5	100.0		
1991/92	57.7	21.9	10.8	4.7	4.9	100.0		
1992/93	55.8	25.5	8.9	3.9	5.8	100.0		
1993/94	54.7	26.8	8.0	3.1	7.5	100.0		
1994/95	52.9	29.2	6.9	3.1	7.8	100.0		
1995/96	49.8	34.5	6.1	2.6	7.0	100.0		
1996/97~	47.9	35.8	6.1	2.7	7.5	100.0		
1997/98~	47.2	37.1	5.8	2.2	7.7	100.0		

~ Data for 1996/97 onwards exclude Gwent Community trust

Source: Welsh Office, unpublished data and *Health statistics Wales*

A4.2.3

Primary method of birth control chosen by people attending family planning clinics, Scotland, 1975–98

Year	Method Oral contraceptives pill	Combined pill	Progestogen pill	Sheath/ condom	IUD	Cap/ diaphragm	Injectables	Vasectomy	Female sterilisation	Other	Total men and women using a method	Attending but not using a method	Not known
	Numbers												
1975	96,329	::	::	5,904	12,424	5,755	::	1,229	79	1,787	123,507	4,644	0
1976	87,354	::	::	7,346	13,909	6,543	::	1,965	187	1,042	118,346	5,472	4,177
1977	94,072	::	::	6,983	17,057	6,564	::	1,420	211	1,942	128,249	6,057	0
1978	83,002	::	::	10,658	20,481	7,731	::	4,759	282	1,534	128,447	6,872	6
1979	78,700	::	::	11,572	22,928	7,994	::	3,722	328	1,674	126,918	10,401	0
1980	77,183	::	::	13,737	24,333	9,030	295	3,931	399	1,947	130,855	10,625	0
1981	75,872	68,804	7,068	13,208	22,474	8,831	566	3,042	573	1,258	125,824	9,715	0
1982	78,162	71,211	6,951	11,771	21,981	7,991	758	1,755	391	1,832	124,641	11,330	0
1983	83,026	75,076	7,950	11,718	22,158	8,255	909	1,926	237	1,420	129,649	8,738	0
1984	78,649	70,731	7,918	12,302	21,574	9,129	1,055	2,264	227	1,810	127,010	5,468	0
1985	76,163	68,424	7,739	12,992	20,676	9,794	1,288	2,831	281	1,656	125,681	6,286	3,342
1986	72,132	64,477	7,655	13,981	18,625	9,618	1,606	3,006	269	1,802	121,039	5,962	4,019
1987	68,222	60,776	7,446	15,622	16,099	8,911	1,806	3,184	255	2,420	116,519	6,346	4,090
1988	64,342	57,415	6,927	13,077	14,268	7,597	2,013	3,052	199	2,374	106,922	6,376	3,820
1989	63,226	56,540	6,686	13,050	13,394	7,257	2,489	3,442	208	2,579	105,645	6,808	2,907
1990	58,332	51,889	6,443	14,143	11,665	6,402	2,676	3,033	257	3,301	99,809	7,677	2,016
1991	55,785	49,399	6,386	14,714	10,321	5,129	2,799	2,667	329	2,992	94,736	7,411	1,589
1992	56,359	49,815	6,544	16,855	9,357	4,951	3,148	2,787	343	2,107	95,907	8,291	1,794
1993	55,262	49,280	5,982	22,246	9,290	4,239	3,612	2,836	320	2,383	100,188	9,147	2,349
1994	54,318	47,871	6,447	21,199	8,323	3,536	4,625	2,530	367	3,709	98,607	9,466	3,363
1995	61,646	54,944	6,702	26,944	6,808	3,350	4,369	2,369	302	3,162	108,950	10,561	6,990
1996	57,928	50,187	7,741	27,652	6,849	2,986	5,661	2,649	431	2,915	107,071	11,575	7,579
1997+	63,087	54,810	8,277	33,297	8,340	2,948	7,379	2,239	517	3,373	121,180	15,441	4,000
1998*	58,956	51,047	7,909	31,495	8,565	2,220	8,049	2,092	581	3,022	114,980	18,095	3,410
	Percentages												
1975	78.0	::	::	4.8	10.1	4.7	::	1.0	0.1	1.4	100.0		
1976	73.8	::	::	6.2	11.8	5.5	::	1.7	0.2	0.9	100.0		

Primary method of birth control chosen by people attending family planning clinics, Scotland, 1975–98

Year	Method Oral contraceptives pill	Combined pill	Progestogen pill	Sheath/ condom	IUD	Cap/ diaphragm	Injectables	Vasectomy	Female sterilisation	Other	Total men and women using a method
Percentages											
1977	73.4	..	..	5.4	13.3	5.1	..	1.1	0.2	1.5	100.0
1978	64.6	..	..	8.3	15.9	6.0	..	3.7	0.2	1.2	100.0
1979	62.0	..	..	9.1	18.1	6.3	..	2.9	0.3	1.3	100.0
1980	59.0	..	..	10.5	18.6	6.9	0.2	3.0	0.3	1.5	100.0
1981	60.3	54.7	5.6	10.5	17.9	7.0	0.4	2.4	0.5	1.0	100.0
1982	62.7	57.1	5.6	9.4	17.6	6.4	0.6	1.4	0.3	1.5	100.0
1983	64.0	57.9	6.1	9.0	17.1	6.4	0.7	1.5	0.2	1.1	100.0
1984	61.9	55.7	6.2	9.7	17.0	7.2	0.8	1.8	0.2	1.4	100.0
1985	60.6	54.4	6.2	10.3	16.5	7.8	1.0	2.3	0.2	1.3	100.0
1986	59.6	53.3	6.3	11.6	15.4	7.9	1.3	2.5	0.2	1.5	100.0
1987	58.6	52.2	6.4	13.4	13.8	7.6	1.5	2.7	0.2	2.1	100.0
1988	60.2	53.7	6.5	12.2	13.3	7.1	1.9	2.9	0.2	2.2	100.0
1989	59.8	53.5	6.3	12.4	12.7	6.9	2.4	3.3	0.2	2.4	100.0
1990	58.4	52.0	6.5	14.2	11.7	6.4	2.7	3.0	0.3	3.3	100.0
1991	58.9	52.1	6.7	15.5	10.9	5.4	3.0	2.8	0.3	3.2	100.0
1992	58.8	51.9	6.8	17.6	9.8	5.2	3.3	2.9	0.4	2.2	100.0
1993	55.2	49.2	6.0	22.2	9.3	4.2	3.6	2.8	0.3	2.4	100.0
1994	55.1	48.5	6.5	21.5	8.4	3.6	4.7	2.6	0.4	3.8	100.0
1995	56.6	50.4	6.2	24.7	6.2	3.1	4.0	2.2	0.3	2.9	100.0
1996	54.1	46.9	7.2	25.8	6.4	2.8	5.3	2.5	0.4	2.7	100.0
1997+	52.1	45.2	6.8	27.5	6.9	2.4	6.1	1.8	0.4	2.8	100.0
1998*	51.3	44.4	6.9	27.4	7.4	1.9	7.0	1.8	0.5	2.6	100.0

From 1980 to 1985, condom includes condom plus spermicide.

From 1975 to 1985, other includes spermicides, rhythm method and coitus interruptus, which were shown as separate categories

Data collection methods changed in 1986, so data for subsequent years may be incompatible with those for previous years.

+ Data for 1997 onwards include those from the Highland Brook Advisory Centre

* Provisional

Source: Information and Statistics Division, Scotland

This was Table A4.2 in the first edition of *Birth counts*

A4.3.1

General practitioners providing contraceptive services, England, 1975–98

	Number of general practitioners registered	Number of women registered with general practitioners		
		IUD fitting	Other services	Total
1975	18,809	13,577	1,143,677	1,157,254
1975	18,809	13,600	1,143,700	1,157,300
1976	19,515	53,800	1,844,500	1,898,300
1977	19,900	67,700	1,970,300	2,038,000
1978	20,100	97,500	1,861,500	1,959,000
1979	20,500	110,000	1,811,800	1,921,800
1980	20,500	106,900	1,917,000	2,023,900
1981	21,500	102,900	1,988,600	2,091,500
1982	22,100	..	..	2,190,600
1983	22,600	..	..	2,358,200
1984	23,200	..	..	2,374,400
1985	23,400	..	..	2,455,800
1986	23,900	120,400	2,450,600	2,571,000
1987	24,200	100,200	2,467,800	2,568,000
1988	25,549	92,900	2,566,100	2,658,900
1989	25,938	78,500	2,657,300	2,735,700
1990	25,968	69,400	2,794,600	2,864,000
1991	25,732	49,000	2,949,000	2,998,000
1992	25,113	41,900	3,034,700	3,076,600
1993	26,142	31,500	2,785,100	2,816,600
1994	25,648	60,900	3,013,100	3,074,100
1995	26,368	71,200	3,224,400	3,295,600

Unrestricted principals and equivalents providing contraceptive services as at October 1

	Services to list patients only	Services to any patient	Total
1996	3,935	22,850	26,785
1997	3,843	23,183	27,026
1998	3,783	23,517	27,300

Data for 1987 onwards differ from those in Table A4.1.1, which relate to financial years.

Data for 1986 to 1995 should be used with caution as the Department of Health is unsure how they were derived.

Personal Medical Services were introduced in April 1998. For comparison with earlier years, data for 1998 relate to unrestricted principals and equivalents, who include PMS contracted GPs and PMS salaried GPs.

Source: GMP Census, National Health Service Executive, Leeds

A4.3.2

General practitioners providing contraceptive services, Wales, 1975–98

	Number of general practitioners registered	Number of women registered with general practitioners		
		IUD fitting	Other services	Total
1975	1,219	435	66,963	67,398
1976	1,235	1,576	101,726	103,302
1977	1,256	2,201	102,345	104,546
1978	1,274	3,730	97,451	101,181
1979	1,299	3,932	92,870	96,802
1980	1,342	3,913	99,113	103,026
1981	1,376	4,145	99,519	103,664
1982	1,403	..	..	109,816
1983	1,437	..	..	118,929
1984	1,490	..	..	116,726
1985	1,505	..	..	119,394
1986	1,530	..	..	126,021
1987	1,558	..	..	125,538
1988	1,574	..	..	134,949
1989	1,674	..	..	137,286
1990	1,485	..	..	135,605
1991	1,656	..	..	156,442
1992	1,678	..	..	161,640
1993	1,704	..	..	162,176
1994	1,709	..	..	168,237
1995	1,721	..	..	172,871

Unrestricted principals and equivalents providing contraceptive services as at October 1

	Services to list patients only	Services to any patient	Total
1996	256	1,471	1,727
1997	255	1,492	1,747
1998	246	1,498	1,744

Personal Medical Services were introduced in April 1998. For comparison with earlier years, data for 1998 relate to unrestricted principals and equivalents, who include PMS contracted GPs and PMS salaried GPs.

Source: Welsh Office, *Health statistics Wales*, from NHS Executive GMP census

A4.3.3

General practitioners' claims for providing contraceptive services, Scotland, 1975–97

	Number of general practitioners registered	Number of women registered with general practitioners			Temporary residents
		Ordinary contraceptive services	IUD fitting	Total	
1975	2,689	170,477	919	171,396	659
1976	2,732	221,524	2,940	224,464	558
1977	2,767	234,608	4,192	238,800	580
1978	2,800	221,447	6,028	227,475	493
1979	2,858	214,401	7,664	222,065	511
1980	2,899	208,168	9,059	217,227	487
1981	2,948	212,739	8,847	221,586	507
1982	3,009	224,010	9,266	233,276	593
1983	3,071	238,032	10,271	248,303	652
1984	3,122	242,205	12,072	254,277	687
1985	3,184	248,517	11,908	260,425	637
1986	3,232	260,111	10,686	270,797	640
1987	3,273	262,966	9,632	272,598	582
1988	3,328	267,305	8,927	276,232	662
1989	3,345	274,606	8,815	283,421	695
1990	3,332	290,364	8,814	299,178	841
1991	3,364	300,630	8,020	308,650	842
1992	3,368	309,429	7,697	317,126	992
1993	3,456	311,796	6,957	318,753	1,014
1994	3,494	317,635	6,049	323,684	1,145
1995	3,528	319,768	5,642	325,410	1,261
1996	3,589	320,423	5,738	326,161	1,395
1997*	3,634	322,713	5,134	327,847	1,151

* Provisional

Source: ISD, *Scottish health statistics*

This was part of Table A4.3 in the first edition of *Birth counts*

A4.3.4

General practitioners' claims for providing contraceptive services, Northern Ireland, 1975–81

	Number of general practitioners registered	Number of women registered with general practitioners		
		IUD fitting	Other services	Total
1975	587	179	30,834	31,013
1976	614	397	44,415	44,812
1977	616	324	37,727	38,051
1978	645	702	38,787	39,489
1979	648	1,160	30,297	31,457
1980	698	1,277	32,292	33,569
1981	723	1,226	31,725	32,951

Data are not available for years from 1982 onwards.

Source: DHSS, Northern Ireland

This was part of Table A4.3 in the first edition of *Birth counts*

A4.4.1

Estimated numbers of prescriptions for contraceptives by general practitioners, England and Wales, 1967–81

Year	Oestrogen-progestogen combinations*	Oral contraceptives*	Contraceptive appliances*
	Numbers of prescriptions, thousands		
1967	715		
1968	820		
1969	803		
1970	771		
1971	876		
1972	923		
1973	986		
1974	1,340		
1975	3,713	3,757	36
1976		5,939	85
1977		5,786	95
1978		5,188	121
1979		5,116	158
1980		5,042	133
1981		5,288	120

* Estimates based on a 1 in 200 sample in England and Wales

Source: Department of Health and Social Security

A4.4.2

Estimated numbers of prescriptions for contraceptives by general practitioners, England, 1980–98

	Combined oral contraceptives	Oral progestogen only contraceptives	Parenteral progestogen-only contraceptives	IUD progestogen-only contraceptives	Spermicidal contraceptives	Contraceptive devices
	BNF 7.3.1	BNF 7.3.2.1	BNF 7.3.2.2	BNF 7.3.2.3	BNF 7.3.3	
Numbers of prescriptions, thousands						
1980	4,363.7	347.1	..	..	100.4	118.3
1981	4,562.5	370.8	..	..	116.8	110.2
1982	4,873.6	407.9	..	..	118.3	126.5
1983	5,237.8	453.5	..	..	115.8	120.4
1984	5,120.8	455.4	..	..	141.2	157.5
1985	5,177.4	465.4	0.4	..	164.9	157.2
1986	5,692.1	498.0	1.5	..	181.6	175.0
1987	5,351.9	513.2	0.2	..	173.6	151.5
1988	5,760.1	555.1	12.0	..	178.6	136.6
1989	6,008.6	581.6	25.9	..	172.8	136.4
1990	6,241.9	617.2	51.5	..	177.5	127.7
1991	6,817.1	699.2	111.8	..	176.9	191.5
1992	7,078.9	725.0	156.8	..	164.0	184.1
1993	7,216.4	733.7	223.3	..	141.0	163.6
1994	7,278.7	759.1	360.1	..	125.5	147.1
1995	7,514.8	773.8	462.6	9.2	117.6	143.6
1996	7,261.9	788.4	549.0	18.9	106.9	138.8
1997	6,854.3	792.6	600.0	22.9	84.1	115.7
1998	6,735.2	819.5	684.3	32.4	69.5	108.4

Data up to 1990 are not consistent with data from 1991 onwards.

Figures for 1980–90 are based on fees and on a sample of 1 in 200 prescriptions dispensed by community pharmacists and appliance contractors only.

Figures for 1991 onwards are based on items and cover all prescriptions dispensed by community pharmacists, applicance contractors, dispensing doctors and prescriptions submitted by prescribing doctors for items personally administered.

The data in this table are based on BNF Number 30, September 1995.

Source: Department of Health, Statistics Division 1E, Prescription Cost Analysis system

This was similar to Table A4.4 in the first edition of *Birth counts*

A4.4.3

Estimated numbers of prescriptions for contraceptives by general practitioners, Wales, 1996–97

	Combined oral contraceptives	Oral progestogen-contraceptives	Parenteral progestogen-contraceptives	IUD progestogen-contraceptives	Spermicidal contraceptives	Contraceptive devices
	BNF 7.3.1	BNF 7.3.2.1	BNF 7.3.2.2	BNF 7.3.2.3	BNF 7.3.3	BNF 21.04
	Numbers of prescriptions					
1996	434,010	40,954	32,905	1,290	3,528	12,822
1997	409,956	40,673	35,518	1,522	2,809	13,457

Source: Prescribing Information and Pricing Services, Welsh Health Common Services Authority

This was similar to Table A4.4 in the first edition of *Birth counts*

A4.4.4

Estimated numbers of prescriptions for contraceptives by general practitioners, Scotland, 1975–1998/99

	Oral contraceptives	Contraceptive devices
	BNF 7.3	BNF 21.04
	Numbers of prescriptions	
1975	393,000	0
1976	647,000	0
1977	627,000	0
1978	549,000	0
1979	528,000	1,000
1980	550,000	4,000
1981	580,000	4,000
1982	587,000	3,000
1983	600,000	5,000
1984	683,000	13,000
1985	682,000	24,000
1986	713,000	20,000
1987	643,000	13,000
1987/88	697,000	8,000
1988/89	649,000	8,000
1989/90	768,000	11,000
1990/91	772,000	10,000
1991/92	800,000	11,000
1992/93	799,000	11,000
1993/94	805,000	10,000
1994/95	845,000	9,000
1995/96	902,000	8,000
1996/97	837,000	7,000
1997/98	817,000	7,000
1998/99	817,000	6,000

* Data from 1991 onwards are derived from computer priced prescriptions and are not directly comparable to those published earlier.

Source: Common Services Agency, Pharmacy Practice Division

This was part of Table A4.4 in the first edition of *Birth counts*

A4.4.5

Estimated numbers of prescriptions for contraceptives by general practitioners, Northern Ireland, 1971–81

Year	Oestrogen-progestogen combinations	Oral contraceptives	Contraceptive appliances
	Numbers of prescriptions, thousands		
1971	31		..
1972	36		..
1973	44		..
1974	48		..
1975	82		..
1976	138	136	..
1977		135	..
1978		132	..
1979		114	..
1980		108	..
1981		113	..

Data are not available for 1982 onwards.

Source: Department of Health and Social Services, Northern Ireland

This was part of Table A4.4 in the first edition of *Birth counts*

A4.5.1

Estimates of sales and imports of contraceptive sheaths, United Kingdom, 1974–95

Sales and imports of contraceptive sheaths, United Kingdom, 1974–82

Years ending 31 March	Sales by London Rubber Company Products Ltd in UK		Imported into UK	
	Number of sheaths, thousand gross	£, thousands	Weight of sheaths and packing, thousand kg	£, thousands
1974	840	3,845	na	336
1975	737	3,649	97.3	521
1976	823	4,003	78.7	461
1977	790	4,004	73.3	625
1978	752	4,537	25.2	250
1979	779	5,425	25.0	208
1980	785	6,036	50.8	401
1981	757	7,033	51.6	425
1982	712	7,241	43.2	361

London Rubber Company sales figures were obtained from the company. Import data were obtained from Customs and Excise. Data for 1974 include an unknown proportion of rubber items which were not sheaths. As imported sheaths were in packages of different sizes, there is no way of converting the weight, which includes packaging, into numbers of sheaths.

Source: Monopolies and Mergers Commission. *Contraceptive sheaths*. London: HMSO, 1982.

Estimated size of the United Kingdom market, millions of condoms, 1983–95

Year	Estimated sales, millions
1983	109
1984	111
1985	109
1986	112
1987	136
1988	138
1989	138
1990	144
1991	148
1992	151
1993	154
1994	157
1995	160

Source: Estimates by Nielsen's and the London Rubber Company

Cited in: Goodrich J, Wellings K, McVey D. *Using condom data to assess the impact of HIV/AIDS prevention interventions.*

Health Education Research 1998;13: 13(2): 267–74.

This is similar to Table A4.5 in the first edition of *Birth counts*

A4.6.1

Estimated percentages of women using contraception, 1910–75

Percentage of women interviewed in 1946 who had no pre-nuptial conceptions and first used contraception at marriage

Year of marriage	
Before 1910	6
1910–19	11
1920–24	16
1925–29	21
1930–34	26
1935–39	33
1940–42	40

Women who had been married for less than five years at the time of interview in 1946 were excluded from the analysis.

The survey covered married women in selected hospitals in England and Scotland.

Source: Lewis Faning E, *Family limitation*, Table 68

Percentage of women interviewed in 1975 who had ever used contraception in their first interpregnancy interval, England and Wales

Year in which interval began	
1946–50	47
1951–55	50
1956–60	52
1961–65	61
1966–70	72
1971–75	83

Source: Bone M, *The family planning services, changes and effects*, Table 7.1

This was Table A4.6 in the first edition of *Birth counts*

A4.6.2

Current use of contraception among women aged 16–49, Great Britain, 1976, 1983, 1986, 1989, 1991, 1993, 1995, 1997 and 1998

Current usual method of contraception	1976	1983*	1986	1989	1991	1993	1995	1997	1998
	Percentage of women aged 16–49*								
Using one or more methods									
Non-surgical **									
Pill	29	28	23	22	23	25	25	26	24
IUD	6	6	7	5	5	5	4	4	5
Condom	14	13	13	15	16	17	18	21	18
Cap	2	1	2	1	1	1	1	2	1
Withdrawal	5	4	4	4	3	3	3	4	3
Safe period	1	1	1	1	1	1	1	2	1
Other	1	1	1	1	1	1	2	2	2
At least one	55	53	49	46	46	48	49	..	49
Surgical									
Female sterilisation	7	11	12	11	12	12	12	11	11
Male sterilisation	6	10	11	12	13	12	11	10	12
All using at least one method	68	75	71	69	70	72	73	74	72
Not using a method									
Sterile after another operation	2	2	3	5	3	2	3	4	2
Pregnant/wanting to get pregnant	7	7	7	7	9	8	8	4	6
Abstinence/no partner	..	..	15	16	16	15	14	15	14
Other#	23	16	5	5	5	5	6	4	4
All not using a method	32	25	29	31	30	29	28	26	28
Base=100%##	5,231	4,444	5,866	5,802	5,571	5,303	5,067	3,357	4,251

* Figures for 1976 and 1983 refer to women aged 18–44

** Abstinence is not included here as a method of contraception. Those who said 'going without sex to avoid getting pregnant' was their only method of contraception are shown with 'others' as not using a method.

Includes 'abstinence'/no partner for 1976 and 1983

Percentages add to more than 100 because some women used more than one non-surgical method or had more than one reason for not using a method

Source: ONS/OPCS, *General Household Survey*
OPCS *Family Formation Survey 1976*, ONS *Omnibus Survey*, 1997

This was Table A4.4 in the first edition of *Birth counts*

A4.6.3

Current use of contraception by age, Great Britain, 1995

Current usual method of contraception	Age, years								
	16–17	18–19	20–24	25–29	30–34	35–39	40–44	45–49	Total
Percentage of women in each age group									
Using one or more methods									
Non-surgical*									
Pill+	25	37	49	41	29	20	9	3	25
Mini pill	7	6	8	8	7	7	4	2	6
Combined pill	17	30	39	32	21	12	4	1	18
IUD	0	0	1	4	5	5	4	5	4
Condom	13	26	21	20	20	16	16	14	18
Cap	0	0	1	1	2	2	2	1	1
Withdrawal	1	2	3	4	3	3	3	2	3
Safe period	0	0	1	1	2	1	2	1	1
Spermicides	0	0	1	1	0	1	1	0	0
Injection	0	2	2	2	2	0	1	0	1
At least one method	33	52	70	67	58	45	35	25	49
Surgical									
Female sterilisation	0	0	0	4	9	15	24	26	12
Male sterilisation	0	0	1	4	9	17	20	20	11
All using at least one method	33	52	70	74	76	78	79	71	73
Not using a method									
Sterile after another operation	0	1	0	0	1	3	4	8	3
Pregnant now	1	3	4	8	5	2	0	0	3
Going without sex to avoid pregnancy	0	1	1	1	0	0	1	0	0
No sexual relationship	64	37	20	9	9	10	9	10	14
Wants to get pregnant	0	1	4	9	9	4	1	0	5
Unlikely to conceive because of menopause	0	0	0	0	0	0	1	6	1
Possibly infertile	0	1	1	2	1	2	3	2	2
Doesn't like contraception	0	2	1	1	1	1	2	1	1
Just doesn't use contraception	0	1	0	0	0	0	0	0	0
Others	1	3	2	2	2	1	1	2	2
All not using a method	67	48	30	26	24	22	21	29	28
Base=100 per cent#	219	155	565	773	1,008	822	692	833	5,067

* Abstinence is not included here as a method of contraception. Those who said 'going without sex to avoid getting pregnant' was their only method of contraception are shown with 'others' as not using a method

+ The overall percentage using the pill includes those who did not know which type of pill

Percentages add to more than 100 because some women used more than one non-surgical method or had more than one reason for not using a method

Source: ONS/OPCS, *General Household Survey*

This is a new table for this editiion of *Birth counts*

A4.6.4

Use of the pill as a method of contraception by age, Great Britain, 1976, 1983, 1986, 1989, 1991, 1993, 1995 and 1997

Age, years	1976	1983	1986	1989	1991	1993	1995	1997
Percentage of women who currently used the pill								
16–17	..	..	20	19	16	20	25	24
18–19	36	43	42	39	46	42	37	51
20–24	48	51	55	48	48	50	49	51
25–29	37	45	38	36	42	44	41	46
30–34	26	23	21	22	25	29	29	27
35–39	16	10	8	12	11	16	20	20
40–44	11	4	4	4	4	7	9	10
45–49	..	..	1	3	2	4	3	3
All aged 16–49*	29	28	23	22	23	25	25	26
Numbers of women in sample								
16–17	..	..	352	307	267	233	219	178
18–19	..	328	317	318	260	212	155	155
20–24	..	822	877	835	758	710	565	364
25–29	..	842	953	948	931	852	773	532
30–34	..	874	893	862	956	912	1,008	588
35–39	..	859	1,023	845	753	785	822	545
40–44	..	719	816	968	857	782	692	505
45–49	..	..	635	719	789	817	822	490
All aged 16–49	..	4,444	5,866	5,802	5,571	5,303	5,067	3,357

Bases for 1976 are not available

* Figures for 1976 and 1983 refer to women aged 18-44

Source: ONS/OPCS, *General Household Survey*
OPCS *Family Formation Survey* 1976
ONS *Omnibus Survey* 1997

This is a new table for this edition of *Birth counts*

A4.6.5

Use of condoms as a usual method of contraception by age, Great Britain, 1976, 1983, 1986, 1989, 1991, 1993, 1995 and 1997

Age of woman, years	1976	1983	1986	1989	1991	1993	1995	1997
Percentage whose partners+ currently used the condom								
16–17	..	..	6	6	10	17	13	22
18–19	6	5	6	12	15	22	26	34
20–24	7	7	9	14	14	18	21	26
25–29	15	14	13	17	19	21	20	27
30–34	19	15	15	19	17	18	20	27
35–39	21	15	15	16	20	17	16	19
40–44	21	18	14	16	13	14	16	14
45–49	..	..	16	15	12	12	14	10
All aged 16–49*	14	13	13	15	16	17	18	21
Numbers of women in sample								
16–17	..	..	352	307	267	233	219	178
18–19	..	328	317	318	260	212	155	155
20–24	..	822	877	835	758	710	565	364
25–29	..	842	953	948	931	852	773	532
30–34	..	874	893	862	956	912	1,008	588
35–39	..	859	1,023	845	753	785	882	545
40–44	..	719	816	968	857	782	692	505
45–49	..	..	635	719	789	817	822	490
All aged 16–49	..	4,444	5,866	5,802	5,571	5,303	5,067	3,357

Bases for 1976 are not available

* Figures for 1976 and 1983 refer to women aged 18–44

+ Refers to the woman's partner whether in household or not

Source: ONS/OPCS, *General Household Survey*
      OPCS *Family Formation Survey* 1976
      ONS *Omnibus Survey* 1997

This is a new table for this edition of *Birth counts*

A4.6.6

Use of emergency contraception during the two years prior to interview by women's marital status and age, Great Britain, 1995

Women aged 16–49 excluding those where the woman or her partner* were sterilised at least two years ago

Age, years	Single women		Married/cohabiting women		All marital statuses of women**		Single women	Married/cohabiting women	All marital statuses of women**
	Used once	Used more than once	Used once	Used more than once	Used once	Used more than once			
	Percentage						**Base**		
16-17	9	3	#	#	10	3	216	4	220
18-19	10	3	#	#	9	4	138	16	155
20-24	14	5	9	0	12	3	343	210	567
25-29	10	4	5	1	7	2	202	486	746
30-34	5	3	3	0	5	1	151	632	871
35-39	5	0	2	0	3	1	73	419	584
40-44	{ 1~	{ 0~	1	0	1	0	{ 68~	264	379
45-49			0	0	0	0		309	412
Total	10	3	3	1	6	2	1191	2340	3934

* Refers to the woman's partner whether in the household or not

\# Bases are too small to enable reliable estimates to be made

** All marital statuses includes widowed/divorced/separated

~ Single women aged 40–49.

Source: ONS *General Household Survey*, 1995

This is a new table for this edition of *Birth counts*

A4.6.7

Contraceptive status by ethnic group, Great Britain, 1991, 1993 and 1995 combined

	Women aged 16–29 years				Women aged 30–49 years			
	White	African-Caribbean	Indian	Pakistani/ Bangladeshi	White	African-Caribbean	Indian	Pakistani/ Bangladeshi
Percentage of women in age group								
No sex	22.6	30.5	42.3	42.9	8.8	19.7	8.5	11.6
Pregnant	5.6	4.8	5.8	11.0	2.1	4.4	3.0	4.3
Contraception users	65.9	57.1	41.3	31.9	80.8	65.0	72.7	55.1
Contraception non-users	5.9	7.6	10.6	14.3	8.2	10.9	15.8	29.0
All women in age group	100.0	100.0	100.0	100.0	100.0	100.0	100.0	100.0
Percentage of contraception users								
Condom	24.7	23.2	43.5	37.5	18.6	18.0	29.6	26.8
Pill	59.1	49.3	30.4	34.4	16.5	25.0	17.6	14.6
IUD	3.1	2.9	15.2	12.5	6.7	11.0	12.0	9.8
Male sterilisation	..	..	..	..	22.6	2.0	3.2	2.4
Female sterilisation	..	..	..	..	21.9	19.0	24.0	26.8
Other	13.1	24.6	10.9	15.6	13.7	25.0	13.6	19.5
All contraceptive users	100.0	100.0	100.0	100.0	100.0	100.0	100.0	100.0

Percentages may not add up to 100.0, due to rounding.

Source: Special analysis of data from ONS/OPCS General Household Survey, 1991, 1993, 1995

Raleigh VS, Almond C, Kiri V. *Health Trends* 1997/98;29:104–113

This is a new table for this edition of *Birth counts*

A4.7.1

Estimated numbers of sterilisations by method, England and Wales, 1971–81, England 1979–1995/96, Wales 1979–1997/98

Year	Division and ligation of oviducts 684		Endoscopic sterilisation 687		Method not stated/other	All methods		
	In-patients	Day cases	In-patients	Day cases	In-patients	In-patients	Day cases	Total
England and Wales	**Interval sterilisations**							
1971	14,170	–	1,310	–	5,400	20,880	–	
1972	12,890	–	6,150	–	5,380	24,420	–	
1973	12,780	–	8,950	–	7,180	28,910	–	
1974	10,617	–	8,936	–	10,223	29,776	–	
1975	7,505	60	8,670	960	7,505	23,680	1,120	
1976	10,057	120	15,002	1,120	10,057	35,116	1,240	
1977	12,850	90	23,530	1,910	5,800	42,180	2,000	
1978	14,290	30	32,660	2,530	6,310	53,260	2,560	
	Number of operations							
1979	11,240	::	33,650	::	::	44,890	::	::
1980	10,420	::	36,660	::	::	47,080	::	::
1981	8,370	::	31,690	::	::	40,060	::	::
England								
1979	10,300	::	::	::	::	::	::	::
1980	9,710	::	::	::	::	::	::	::
1981	7,740	::	::	::	::	::	::	::
1982	5,670	::	21,040	::	::	26,710	::	::
1983	6,900	::	24,050	::	::	30,950	::	::
1984	5,950	::	24,850	::	::	30,800	::	::
1985	5,530	::	24,010	::	::	29,540	::	::
Wales								
1979	948	3	924	5		1,872	8	1,880
1980	781	3	1,030	4		1,811	7	1,818
1981	613	2	990	4		1,603	6	1,609
1982	534	3	865	1		1,399	4	1,403
1983	696	4	1,475	7		2,171	11	2,182
1984	712	3	1,446	19		2,158	22	2,180
1985	602	1	1,506	3		2,108	4	2,112

A4.7.1 continued

Estimated numbers of sterilisations by method, England and Wales, 1971–81, England 1979–1995/96, Wales 1979–1997/98

	Open occlusion of fallopian tube, Q27–28		Endoscopic occlusion of fallopian tube, Q35–36		All methods		
	In-patients	Day cases	In-patients	Day cases	In-patients	Day cases	Total
England	**Completed episodes by main operation**						
1988/89	5,412	432	31,804	7,886	37,216	8,318	45,534
1989/90	5,007	173	32,476	9,547	37,483	9,720	47,203
1990/91	3,913	97	28,551	11,659	32,464	11,756	44,220
1991/92	3,203	155	28,683	17,856	31,886	18,011	49,897
1992/93	2,831	125	25,900	24,034	28,731	24,159	52,890
1993/94	1,789	203	19,563	31,732	21,352	31,935	53,287
1994/95	1,376	184	14,403	37,061	15,779	37,245	53,024
1995/96	1,048	235	12,216	38,785	13,264	39,020	52,284
Wales							
1985/86	591	1	1,487	6	2,078	7	2,085
1986/87	500	3	1,625	26	2,125	29	2,154
1987/88	507	1	1,586	11	2,093	12	2,105
1988/89	771	10	1,876	23	2,647	33	2,680
1989/90	759	33	1,764	41	2,523	74	2,597
1990/91	634	3	1,449	51	2,083	54	2,137
1991/92	770	9	1,978	156	2,748	165	2,913
1992/93	381	30	1,876	670	2,257	700	2,957
1993/94	306	41	1,640	1,043	1,946	1,084	3,030
1994/95	297	48	1,278	1,273	1,575	1,321	2,896
1995/96	224	38	1,251	1,877	1,475	1,915	3,390
1996/97	220	62	1,107	2,240	1,327	2,302	3,629
1997/98	139	15	930	1,920	1,069	1,935	3,004

Source: 1971–78: OPCS, DHSS and the Welsh Office, Hospital In-patient Enquiry, reference tables.
England 1979–85: Hospital In-patient Enquiry main tables
Wales 1979–1990/91: Hospital Activity Analysis
England 1988/89 onwards: Department of Health: Hospital Episode Statistics
Wales 1991/92 onwards: Patient Episode Database Wales

This is similar to Table A4.8 in the first edition of *Birth counts*

A4.7.2

Estimated numbers of sterilisations by method, Scotland, 1980–96

Years ending 31 December	Operations associated with sterilisation								
	Open occlusion of fallopian tube*		Endoscopic occlusion of fallopian tube~		Other^		All		
	In-patient	Day case	In-patient	Day case	In-patient	Day case	In-patient	Day case	All
1980	1,249	44	9,186	920	701	18	11,136	982	12,118
1981	840	45	8,336	979	376	29	9,552	1,053	10,605
1982+	414	22	4,301	468	201	27	4,916	517	5,433
1983	561	26	7,999	1,096	389	26	8,949	1,148	10,097
1984	456	56	7,165	1,093	288	23	7,909	1,172	9,081
1985	410	56	6,922	1,170	291	19	7,623	1,245	8,868
1986	409	78	6,845	1,156	316	30	7,570	1,264	8,834
1987	286	66	6,313	1,188	197	27	6,796	1,281	8,077
1988	245	142	5,762	1,151	185	29	6,192	1,322	7,514
1989	394	52	5,302	1,383	202	49	5,898	1,484	7,382
1990	274	78	5,006	1,338	148	36	5,428	1,452	6,880
1991	198	86	5,235	1,722	196	91	5,629	1,899	7,528
1992	122	1	5,188	2,345	186	170	5,496	2,516	8,012
1993	115	1	4,484	2,949	149	78	4,748	3,028	7,776
1994	70	21	3,288	3,764	322	76	3,680	3,861	7,541
1995	39	21	2,354	4,628	395	82	2,788	4,731	7,519
1996	23	9	2,037	5,719	109	21	2,169	5,749	7,918

Notes:

All information relates to in-patient/day case operations associated with sterilisation for contraceptive management. In terms of ICD coding, this means that all operations must be associated with a main diagnosis of ICD9 V25.2 or ICD10 Z30.2. Diagnostic information was recorded in the NHSiS using ICD9 until 31 March 1996 and using ICD10 thereafter. Both principal and secondary operations are included.

* OPCS3 684 until 31 December 1988, then OPCS4 Q27-Q28.

~ OPCS3 687 until 31 December 1988 then OPCS4 Q35-Q36.

^ Other operations not included in the two preceding categories, where the main diagnosis was ICD9 V25.2 or ICD10 Z30.2.

+ Under-recorded due to industrial action.

Source: ISD, Inpatient & Day Case Record Summary Sheet, form SMR1 Date: 9 June 1998. Ref: ISD/HCIU/U2980583.

This is similar to Table A4.8 in the first edition of *Birth counts*

A4.7.3

Estimated numbers of sterilisations by method, Northern Ireland, 1979–1996/97

Year	Division and ligation of oviducts* 684		Endoscopic sterilisation 687		Method not stated/other	Total		
	In-patients	Day cases	In-patients	Day cases	In-patients	In-patients	Day cases	All
1979	274	0	462	0	0	736	0	736
1980	302	0	413	0	0	715	0	715
1981	248	0	427	0	0	675	0	675
1982	462	0	478	0	0	940	0	940
1983	371	0	907	0	1	1,279	0	1,279
1984	315	0	834	0	1	1,150	0	1,150
1985	376	0	796	0	0	1,172	0	1,172
1986	319	0	873	1	3	1,195	1	1,196
1987	313	1	1,068	3	1	1,382	4	1,386
1988	442	1	1,098	40	4	1,544	41	1,585
1988/89	135		316	9	–	451	9	460
1989/90	220	8	1,024	21	–	1,244	29	1,273
1990/91	243	47	1,228	41	–	1,471	88	1,559
1991/92	290	51	1,487	119	–	1,777	170	1,947
1992/93	161	25	1,575	270	–	1,736	295	2,031
1993/94	165	3	1,489	753	–	1,654	756	2,410
1994/95	158	6	1,205	1,112	–	1,363	1,118	2,481
1995/96	88	3	955	1,551	–	1,043	1,554	2,597
1996/97	98	1	786	1,603	–	884	1,604	2,488

* Division and ligation of oviducts is described as 'open occlusion' from 1988 onwards

Source: DHSS, Northern Ireland

This is similar to Table A4.8 in the first edition of *Birth counts*

A4.8.1

Sterilisation, England and Wales, 1971–80, England 1979–1995/96

	Interval* In-patient	Interval* Day case	Interval* Total	With delivery*	With legal abortion*	Total	Rate#
Estimated numbers							
Principal diagnosis V43, prophylactic sterilisation							
England and Wales							
1971	20,880	-	20,880	26,650	14,462	61,992	664.9
1972	24,420	-	24,420	22,600	13,891	60,911	651.2
1973	28,910	-	28,910	21,860	11,918	62,688	667.1
1974	29,776	-	29,776	19,219	10,733	59,728	630.8
1975	23,680	1,020	24,700	17,444	9,172	51,316	539.4
1976	35,116	1,240	36,356	16,333	8,909	61,598	641.8
1977	42,180	2,000	44,180	14,641	8,872	67,693	698.0
1978	53,260	2,560	55,820	14,447	9,145	79,412	808.3
Principal diagnosis, sterilisation, V25.2							
1979	51,870	4,110	55,980	::	9,371	::	::
1980	53,590	5,190	58,780	13,660^	9,426	81,866	800.9
England only							
1979	::	4,180	::	::^	::	::	::
1980	::	5,090	::	12,630^	::	::	::
1981	::	5,670	::	::	8,194	::	::
1982	37,190	3,210	40,400	9,480^	7,673	::	::
1983	44,580	4,920	49,500	9,200^	7,121	65,821	660.4
1984	44,940	5,180	50,120	9,110	7,228	66,458	659.9
1985	42,700	6,550	49,250	::	6,718	::	::

199

A4.8.1 continued

Sterilisation in England and Wales, England and Wales, 1971–80, England 1979–1995/96

	Interval*			With delivery*	With legal abortion*	Total
	In-patient	Day case	Total			
Principal diagnosis, sterilisation, VO32					Calendar years*	
1988/89	::	::	49,073	::	5,297	::
1989/90	::	::	48,944	::	5,129	::
1990/91	::	::	45,623	::	4,701	::
1991/92	::	::	51,371	::	4,520	::
1992/93	::	::	53,115	::	3,878	::
1993/94	::	::	53,620	::	4,022	::
1994/95	::	::	53,620	::	3,600	::
Principal diagnosis, sterilisation, Z30.2						
1995/96	39,236	13,076	52,312	::	3,263	::

Numbers of day cases for England and Wales for 1979 and 1980 derived from OPCS monitor MB4 83/1
Numbers of day cases for England for 1979–85 derived from DHSS and OPCS Series MB4 no 29

From 1988/89 onwards, data about sterilisation with legal abortion are for the corresponding calendar year, in other words for 1988 onwards.

\# Rate per 100,000 women aged 15–44.

* NHS hospitals only.

\+ NHS and private hospitals.

^ Includes a small number of cases where a delivery did not take place.

Data about sterilisations done at the time of the legal abortion are derived from abortion notifications.

Routine tabulations do not distinguish between in-patients and day cases.

Source: OPCS, DHSS and the Welsh Office, *Hospital In-Patient Enquiry*
Department of Health, *Hospital Episode Statistics*
ONS/OPCS, *Abortion statistics, Series AB*

This is similar to Table A4.7 in the first edition of *Birth counts*

A4.8.2

Sterilisation with legal abortion, residents of England and Wales 1968–98

Year	In NHS hospitals		In 'other approved places'				Total	
	Number	Percentage of all abortions in NHS hospitals	NHS agency	Non-NHS	All	Percentage of all abortions in 'other approved places'	Number	Percentage of all abortions
1968	:	:	:	:	:	:	5,128	23.0
1969	:	:	:	:	:	:	11,126	22.3
1970	13,732	29.0	:	:	214	0.7	13,946	18.4
1971	14,193	26.6	:	:	269	0.7	14,462	15.3
1972	13,512	23.8	:	:	379	0.7	13,891	12.8
1973	11,434	20.6	:	:	484	0.9	11,918	10.8
1974	10,250	18.3	:	:	483	0.9	10,733	9.8
1975	8,515	16.7	:	:	657	1.2	9,172	8.6
1976	8,145	16.1	:	:	764	1.5	8,909	8.7
1977	7,889	15.0	:	:	983	2.0	8,872	8.6
1978	7,971	14.5	:	:	1,174	2.1	9,145	8.2
1979	7,972	14.3	:	:	1,399	2.2	9,371	7.8
1980	8,077	13.3	:	:	1,349	2.0	9,426	7.3
1981	7,351	12.0	:	:	1,306	1.9	8,657	6.7
1982	6,687	10.7	:	:	1,386	2.1	8,073	6.3
1983	5,999	9.6	:	:	1,450	2.2	7,449	5.8
1984	5,775	8.9	:	:	1,754	2.5	7,529	5.5
1985	5,304	8.1	:	:	1,702	2.2	7,006	5.0
1986	5,243	7.8	:	:	1,502	1.9	6,745	4.6
1987	4,969	7.2	:	:	1,215	1.4	6,184	4.0
1988	4,219	6.1	:	:	1,348	1.4	5,567	3.3
1989	4,146	5.9	:	:	1,259	1.3	5,405	3.2
1990	3,858	5.2	:	:	1,131	1.1	4,989	2.9
1991	3,794	5.0	:	:	995	1.1	4,789	2.9
1992	3,352	4.2	95	637	732	0.9	4,084	2.5
1993	3,560	4.2	113	569	682	0.9	4,242	2.7
1994	3,168	3.7	145	498	643	0.9	3,811	2.4
1995	2,855	3.4	208	360	568	0.8	3,423	2.2
1996	2,575	2.9	257	383	640	0.8	3,215	1.9
1997	2,366	2.7	267	339	606	0.7	2,972	1.7
1998	2,268	2.6	271	271	542	0.6	2,810	1.6

Source: ONS/OPCS *Abortion Statistics*, *Series AB*, Tables 1 and 18.

This was Table A4.11 in the first edition of *Birth counts*

A4.8.3

Sterilisation in Scotland, 1975–97

Year	With delivery		With legal abortion		Other in-patient sterilisations		Total	
	Number	Rate*	Number	Rate*	Number	Rate*	Number	Rate*
1975	2,610	253.9	1,200	116.7	8,213	798.9	12,023	1169.5
1976	2,339	225.1	1,002	96.4	9,442	908.7	12,783	1230.3
1977	1,805	172.0	1,087	103.6	9,464	902.0	12,356	1177.6
1978	1,679	158.7	1,111	105.0	12,308	1163.0	15,098	1426.7
1979	1,833	169.6	1,004	92.9	11,351	1050.5	14,188	1313.0
1980	1,600	148.1	970	89.8	12,122	1121.8	14,692	1359.6
1981	1,544	141.1	1,000	91.4	10,788	986.0	13,332	1218.6
1982	1,284	116.6	819	74.4	5,778	524.6	7,881	715.6
1983	1,230	111.0	820	74.0	10,383	937.1	12,433	1122.1
1984	1,670	149.7	760	68.1	9,472	848.9	11,902	1066.7
1985	1,115	99.5	598	53.3	9,034	805.9	10,747	958.7
1986	1,044	92.7	577	51.3	8,970	796.8	10,591	940.7
1987	799	70.9	506	44.9	8,427	747.5	9,732	863.2
1988	830	74.0	462	41.2	8,139	726.1	9,431	841.3
1989	732	65.4	109	9.7	8,661	773.8	9,502	848.9
1990	690	61.5	106	9.4	8,173	728.2	8,969	799.1
1991	672	59.9	56	5.0	8,553	762.6	9,281	827.5
1992	718	64.8	55	5.0	8,794	793.1	9,567	862.9
1993	681	61.8	43	3.9	8,576	777.6	9,300	843.3
1994	663	60.2	16	1.5	8,365	759.2	9,044	820.8
1995	553	50.2	5	0.5	8,250	749.0	8,808	799.7
1996	616	55.5	..	..	8,447	769.1	9,063	825.1
1997+	592	54.1	..	..	7,279	664.8	7,871	718.9

+ Provisional

* Rate per 100,000 women aged 15–44

Source: ISD, *Scottish health statistics*

This was Table A4.10 in the first edition of *Birth counts*

A4.9.1

Estimated numbers of vasectomies in NHS hospitals and family planning clinics, England and Wales, 1975–81, England 1979–1998/99, Wales 1980–1997/98

Year	NHS hospitals In-patients	Day cases	Total	Family planning clinics*
England and Wales				
Discharges and deaths				
1975	2,380	15,080	17,460	17,604
1976	2,960	19,280	22,240	17,528
1977	3,220	27,130	30,350	17,182
1978	4,340	35,880	40,220	18,097
1979	3,470	38,760	42,230	16,336
1980	3,340	36,810	40,150	14,432
1981	2,810	34,790	37,600	14,189
England				
1979	3,240	36,140	39,380	15,600
1980	3,130	34,940	38,070	15,700
1981	2,580	32,590	35,170	14,800
1982	2,400	25,780	28,180	14,100
1983	2,970	36,840	39,810	12,500
1984	3,770	37,860	41,630	14,700
1985	3,640	42,060	45,700	14,100
1986	..	..	..	12,400
1987	..	..	..	12,300
Finished consultant episodes				
1989/90	4,200	32,900	37,100	11,000
1990/91	3,300	33,400	36,700	9,500
1991/92	4,100	35,100	39,200	11,700
1992/93	2,600	34,800	37,300	11,000
1993/94	2,000	34,800	36,800	10,500
1994/95	1,900	36,500	38,400	9,200
1995/96	1,800	37,200	39,000	9,900
1996/97	1,300*	34,700*	36,000*	10,200
1997/98	1,600*	29,500*	31,200*	9,700
1998/99	..	..	..	10,400
Wales				
Discharges and deaths				
1979	248	1,367	1,615	..
1980	284	1,170	1,454	..
1981	262	1,234	1,496	..
1982	186	1,087	1,273	..
1983	347	1,540	1,887	..
1984	416	2,194	2,610	..
1985	442	2,267	2,709	..
1985/86	440	2,245	2,685	..
1986/87	448	2,762	3,210	..
1987/88	333	2,232	2,565	..
1988/89	387	2,127	2,514	..
1989/90	328	2,445	2,773	..
1990/91	294	2,053	2,347	..

A4.9.1 *continued*

Estimated numbers of vasectomies in NHS hospitals and family planning clinics, England and Wales, 1975–81, England, 1979–1998/99, Wales, 1980–1997/98

Year	NHS hospitals			Family planning clinics
	In-patients	Day cases	Total	
	Finished consultant episodes			
1991/92	259	1,968	2,227	..
1992/93	294	2,623	2,917	..
1993/94	199	2,568	2,767	..
1994/95	200	2,784	2,984	..
1995/96	176	2,733	2,909	..
1996/97	174	3,947	4,121	..
1997/98	100	3,198	3,298	..

* Ungrossed, so probably about three per cent underestimated and provisional.

Source: Hospital In-patient Enquiry, Hospital Episode Statistics, Statistical return KT31

Hospital Activity Analysis, Patient Episode Database Wales

This is similar to Table A4.12 in the first edition of *Birth counts*

A4.9.2

Estimated numbers of vasectomies in NHS hospitals and family planning clinics, Scotland, 1975–97

	NHS hospitals			Family planning clinics
	In-patients	Day cases	Total	
1975	..	..	485	982
1976	..	..	884	1,497
1977	..	..	1,152	1,737
1978	..	..	2,776	2,585
1979	..	..	3,615	2,802
1980	502	4,010	4,512	2,706
1981	403	4,012	4,415	2,303
1982	193	2,570	2,763	1,614
1983	429	4,799	5,228	2,068
1984	409	5,042	5,451	2,243
1985	311	5,553	5,864	2,086
1986	343	5,511	5,854	2,188
1987	266	5,650	5,916	2,419
1988	285	5,493	5,778	2,256
1989	279	5,970	6,249	2,395
1990	238	5,896	6,134	2,026
1991	203	5,401	5,604	1,905
1992	219	5,495	5,714	1,977
1993	289	5,644	5,933	1,954
1994	281	5,859	6,140	1,923
1995	444	5,951	6,395	1,977
1996	246	6,598	6,844	2,006
1997*	..	..	6,373	1,984

All information relates to in-patient/day case operations associated with sterilisation for contraceptive management. In terms of ICD coding, this means that all operations must be associated with a main diagnosis of ICD9 V25.2 or ICD10 Z30.2. Diagnostic information was recorded in the NHSiS using ICD9 until 31 March 1996 and using ICD10 thereafter. Both principal and secondary operations are included.

Operations coded as OPCS3 651 until 31 December 1988 or OPCS4 N17 thereafter

* provisional

Source: ISD, Inpatient & Day Case Record Summary Sheet (form SMR1) and ISD, *Scottish health statistics*

This was part of Table A4.12 in the first edition of *Birth counts*

A4.9.3

Estimated numbers of vasectomies in NHS hospitals and family planning clinics, Northern Ireland, 1975–1994/95

Year	NHS hospitals			Family planning clinics
	In-patients	Day cases	Total	
1975	..	..	111	..
1976	..	..	136	..
1977	..	..	155	..
1978	..	..	248	..
1979	..	..	235	..
1980	..	..	271	..
1981	..	..	293	..
1982	569	..	569	..
1983	506	84	590	..
1984	428	278	706	..
1985	482	294	776	..
1986	260	421	681	..
1987	212	602	814	..
1988	314	630	944	..
1988/89	34	132	166	..
1989/90	66	731	797	..
1990/91	65	986	1,051	..
1991/92	71	1,511	1,582	..
1992/93	66	1,481	1,547	..
1993/94	70	1,596	1,666	..
1994/95	89	2,046	2,135	..

Source: Department of Health and Social Services, Northern Ireland

This was part of Table A4.12 in the first edition of *Birth counts*

A4.10.1

Selected gynaecological operations associated with sterility, England and Wales, 1970-81, England, 1982-1995/96, Wales, 1979-1997/98

Year	Rates per 100,000 women			Numbers				
	15–44	45–64	65 and over	15–44	45–64	65 and over	Not stated	All
England and Wales								
Hysterectomy 078=690-696								
1970	302.3	451.5	128.5	:	:	:	:	:
1971	321.4	442.1	148.6	:	:	:	:	:
1972	339.0	445.5	129.2	:	:	:	:	:
1973	332.9	433.0	129.3	:	:	:	:	:
1974	341.5	403.9	137.0	32,362	24,165	5,761	-	62,310
1975	295.9	401.3	127.7	28,185	23,819	5,436	-	57,461
1976	324.5	406.9	146.6	31,146	23,947	6,323	-	61,416
1977	333.2	394.6	113.3	32,220	23,040	4,940	-	60,200
1978	315.3	370.1	114.7	30,980	21,370	5,060	-	57,410
1979	322.7	393.5	135.3	32,510	22,510	6,090	-	61,120
1980	340.3	418.6	141.8	34,790	23,720	6,460	-	64,980
1981	333.3	405.7	136.7	34,500	22,860	6,260	-	63,620
England								
1982	312.0	383.7	133.5	30,800	20,330	5,760	-	56,910
1983	321.1	417.1	154.8	32,000	22,210	6,650	-	60,860
1984	342.4	457.2	161.9	34,480	24,440	6,940	-	65,860
1985	349.4	449.3	165.1	35,570	23,660	7,220	-	66,470
Hysterectomy Q07-Q08								
1988/89	408.1	529.7	182.1	42,519	27,189	8,218	57	77,983
1989/90	365.1	526.0	176.8	38,025	27,091	8,033	101	73,250
1990/91	351.4	506.1	172.4	36,560	26,175	7,852	79	70,666
1991/92	345.8	525.6	181.0	35,948	27,349	8,276	48	71,621
1992/93	350.0	542.4	181.0	35,945	28,895	8,289	19	73,148
1993/94	351.4	542.5	179.4	35,775	29,420	8,225	85	73,505
1994/95	349.9	536.4	161.5	35,553	29,485	7,398	26	72,462
1995/96	334.2	532.3	173.4	33,947	29,578	7,955	69	71,559

A4.10.1 *continued*

Selected gynaecological operations associated with sterility, England and Wales, 1970–81, England, 1982–1995/96, Wales, 1979–1997/98

Year	Rates per 100,000 women			Numbers				
	15–44	45–64	65 and over	15–44	45–64	65 and over	Not stated	All
Colpectomy and colpoleisis P17-P18								
England								
1988/89	2.1	1.0	1.4	220	53	64	3	346
1989/90	1.1	1.0	0.3	118	50	13	0	181
1990/91	1.1	1.0	0.9	118	54	40	0	212
1991/92	1.4	0.9	1.9	143	47	85	0	275
1992/93	1.4	0.8	2.7	146	44	124	4	318
1993/94	0.8	1.2	1.4	78	65	63	9	219
1994/95	1.2	0.9	1.8	121	51	83	0	255
1995/96	1.2	1.2	1.8	118	66	83	0	270
Oophorectomy 074=671,672								
England and Wales								
1971	57.3	19.3	17.1	..	..	..	..	..
1972	46.6	21.2	13.9	..	..	..	..	..
1973	47.6	22.1	16.9	..	..	..	..	..
1974	45.0	23.1	15.1	4,269	1,383	636	–	6,409
1975	47.2	21.1	12.7	4,496	1,254	540	–	6,376
1976	49.0	18.3	13.6	4,700	1,079	587	–	6,526
1977	39.6	14.6	13.1	3,840	850	570	–	5,370
1978	41.5	17.1	12.2	4,080	990	540	–	5,670
1979	46.3	17.1	17.5	4,660	980	790	–	6,590
1980	47.8	18.2	15.4	4,890	1,030	700	–	6,720
1981	50.9	19.0	22.7	5,270	1,070	1,040	–	7,200
England								
1982	46.1	14.3	13.9	4,550	760	600	–	5,980
1983	46.0	17.7	12.6	4,580	940	540	–	6,100
1984	44.0	15.5	17.3	4,430	830	740	–	6,090
1985	42.7	13.7	14.2	4,350	720	620	–	5,780

A4.10.1 continued

Selected gynaecological operations associated with sterility, England and Wales, 1970–81, England, 1982–1995/96, Wales, 1979–1997/98

Year	Rates per 100,000 women			Numbers				
	15–44	45–64	65 and over	15–44	45–64	65 and over	Not stated	All
Oophorectomy and salpingectomy O74=671,672 and 681,682								
England and Wales								
1979	112.1	27.6	21.8	11,290	1,580	980	–	14,070
1980	110.2	28.4	15.4	11,270	1,610	700	–	13,980
1981	109.6	28.6	15.7	11,350	1,610	720	–	14,140
England								
1982	94.6	23.6	19.7	9,340	1,250	850	–	11,550
1983	95.1	29.7	17.5	9,480	1,580	750	–	11,890
1984	97.1	26.6	20.8	9,780	1,420	890	–	12,190
1985	91.8	25.6	20.4	9,350	1,350	890	–	11,730
Oophorectomy and salpingectomy Q22–Q24				**Oophorectomy and salpingectomy 671,672 and 681,682**				
1988/89	89.9	29.2	18.3	9,369	1,498	826	2	11,766
1989/90	90.3	28.9	17.1	9,409	1,488	775	4	11,763
1990/91	89.5	27.4	15.3	9,313	1,419	698	15	11,480
1991/92	89.4	30.0	16.1	9,292	1,563	735	14	11,638
1992/93	93.6	34.8	18.7	9,610	1,853	858	7	12,407
1993/94	99.1	33.4	18.2	10,092	1,813	835	0	12,798
1994/95	99.7	39.4	18.4	10,130	2,165	842	7	13,209
1995/96	99.0	43.2	21.4	10,057	2,398	982	12	13,521

Numbers

Wales	Hysterectomy 691–696	Oophorectomy and salpingectomy 671,672 and 681,682
1979	3,147	542
1980	3,239	542
1981	3,395	566
1982	2,921	482
1983	3,413	487
1984	3,629	515
1985	3,638	583
1985/86	3,595	589
1986/87	3,789	533

A4.10.1 continued

Selected gynaecological operations associated with sterility, England and Wales, 1970–81, England, 1982–1995/96, Wales, 1979–1997/98

Numbers

Wales	Hysterectomy 691–696	Oophorectomy and salpingectomy 671,672 and 681,682
1987/88	3,833	587
1988/89	3,945	501
1989/90	3,827	517
1990/91	3,090	482
1991/92	3,724	588
1992/93	3,880	626
1993/94	3,884	686
1994/95	3,842	945
1995/96	3,870	742
1996/97	3,659	811
1997/98	3,226	593

Source: 1970–78: OPCS, DHSS and the Welsh Office, Hospital In-patient Enquiry, reference tables.

England 1979–85: Hospital In-patient Enquiry main tables

Wales 1979–1990/91: Hospital Activity Analysis

England 1988/89 onwards: Department of Health: Hospital Episode Statistics

Wales 1991/92 onwards: Patient Episode Database Wales

This is similar to Table A4.13 in the first edition of *Birth counts*

A4.11.1

Operations associated with sterilisation and gynaecological operations resulting in sterility, in private hospitals, England and Wales, 1997/98

OPCS4 operation code	Operation	Age, years				All ages	Under contract to the NHS
		15–44	45–64	65 and over	Not known		
		Estimated number of operations on men resident in England and Wales					
N17	Vasectomy	3,603	706	0	0	4,309	1,873
		Estimated number of operations on women resident in England and Wales					
Q27-Q28	Open occlusion and ligation of oviducts	60	0	0	0	60	60
Q35-Q36	Endoscopic occlusion	821	37	0	0	858	389
P17-20	Colpectomy, colpoleisis and other operations on vagina	180	184	44	0	408	0
P22-25	Colporraphy	641	2,834	1,831	0	5,306	108
Q07-08	Hysterectomy	4,383	6,033	601	0	11,017	562
Q22	Salpingectomy	158	283	104	0	545	23
Q23	Oophorectomy	212	83	17	0	312	16

Source: Brian Williams, *Survey of independent hospitals*, unpublished data

This is a new table for this edition of *Birth counts*

A4.12.1

Percentage of women sterilised or with partners sterilised for contraceptive reasons, Great Britain, 1976, 1986, 1989, 1991, 1993, 1995 and 1997

Age of woman	1976	1986	1989	1991	1993	1995	1997
Percentages of women in age group							
16–24*	3	1	1	1	0	0	..
25–29	8	6	7	8	5	7	6
30–34	20	25	23	21	21	18	16
35–39	25	42	40	38	34	32	26
40–44	19	48	47	50	47	45	42
45–49	..	35	37	47	47	46	43
All aged 16–49*	13	23	23	25	24	24	21
Bases = 100%							
16–24	..	1,546	1,460	1,285	1,155	939	697
25–29	..	953	948	931	852	773	532
30–34	..	893	862	956	912	1,008	588
35–39	..	1,023	845	753	785	822	545
40–44	..	816	968	857	782	692	505
45–49	..	635	719	789	817	833	490
All aged 16–49	..	5,866	5,802	5,571	5,303	5,067	3,357

* Figures for 1976 refer to women aged 18–44

Source: OPCS *Family Formation Survey 1976*, OPCS and ONS *General Household Survey* 1986, 1989, 1991, 1993 and 1995,

ONS *Omnibus Survey* 1997

This is similar to Table A4.14 in the first edition of Birth counts

A4.12.2

Percentage of women aged 40–49 sterilised, sterile for other reason or menopausal, Great Britain, 1983, 1986, 1989, 1991, 1993, 1995 and 1997

	1983	1986	1989	1991	1993	1995	1997
Women aged 40–44							
Sterilised	24	28	24	23	25	24	22
Sterile after other operation	7	6	10	5	4	4	7
Unlikely to conceive because of menopause	3	1	0	1	2	1	0
Possibly infertile	..	2	3	4	3	3	1
All	34	37	42	33	34	32	30
Women aged 45–49							
Sterilised	..	21	17	26	25	25	23
Sterile after other operation	..	11	15	10	8	7	14
Unlikely to conceive because of menopause	..	9	8	7	6	6	4
Possibly infertile	..	2	3	3	2	3	1
All	..	43	43	46	41	41	42

Source: ONS/OPCS *General Household Survey*, ONS *Omnibus Survey* 1997

This is similar to Table A4.15 in the first edition of *Birth counts*

A4.12.3

Menopausal status by age, England and Wales, 1975

Age, years	Percentage of women who were:			Number of women 'at risk'* in sample
	Pre-menopausal	Menopausal	Post-menopausal	
40	97	1	1	75
41	98	1	1	81
42	98	2	0	80
43	97	0	3	75
44	93	0	7	87
45	91	0	9	87
46	93	3	4	70
47	84	1	15	73
48	76	3	21	95
49	57	6	37	63
50	55	4	41	104
51	37	6	57	79
52	23	7	69	94
53	19	4	78	80
54	6	0	94	84
55	3	0	97	39

* 'At risk' here means at risk of being menopausal and excludes those who were otherwise sterile.

Source: Bone M, *Family Planning services: changes and effects*

This was table A4.15 in the first edition of Birth counts

A4.13.1

Legal abortions in England and Wales to residents and non-residents by category of premises, 1968–98

Year	All abortions	Residents					Non-residents		
		NHS	NHS agency	Non-NHS	Total	Rate per 1,000 women aged 14 to 49**	NHS	Non-NHS	Total
1968*	23,641	14,492	..	7,840	22,332	2.0	68	1,241	1,309
1969	54,819	33,562	..	16,267	49,829	4.4	166	4,824	4,990
1970	86,565	47,370	..	28,592	75,962	6.7	308	10,295	10,603
1971	126,777	53,455	..	41,115	94,570	8.4	251	31,956	32,207
1972	159,884	56,861	..	51,704	108,565	9.6	225	51,094	51,319
1973	167,149	55,456	..	55,112	110,568	9.8	181	56,400	56,581
1974	162,940	56,076	..	53,369	109,445	9.6	244	53,251	53,495
1975	139,702	50,941	..	55,283	106,224	9.3	206	33,272	33,478
1976	129,673	50,569	..	51,343	101,912	8.9	205	27,556	27,761
1977	133,004	52,530	..	50,147	102,677	8.8	202	30,125	30,327
1978	141,558	55,040	..	56,811	111,851	9.5	207	29,500	29,707
1979	149,746	55,558	..	65,053	120,611	10.2	209	28,926	29,135
1980	160,903	60,594	..	68,333	128,927	10.8	224	31,752	31,976
1981	162,480	61,103	2,343	65,135	128,581	10.6	173	33,726	33,899
1982	163,045	62,409	4,425	61,719	128,553	10.6	123	34,369	34,492
1983	162,161	62,609	4,614	60,152	127,375	10.4	208	34,578	34,786
1984	169,993	64,823	4,912	66,653	136,388	11.0	103	33,502	33,605
1985	171,873	65,176	5,929	69,996	141,101	11.3	78	30,694	30,772
1986	172,286	67,451	6,819	73,349	147,619	11.7	78	24,589	24,667
1987	174,276	69,442	8,041	78,708	156,191	12.3	63	18,022	18,085
1988	183,798	69,103	9,357	89,838	168,298	13.2	74	15,426	15,500
1989	183,974	70,722	9,200	90,541	170,463	13.4	64	13,447	13,511
1990	186,912	73,517	9,582	90,801	173,900	13.6	65	12,947	13,012
1991	179,522	75,172	9,197	83,007	167,376	13.1	73	12,073	12,146
1992	172,069	79,543	11,982	68,976	160,501	12.5	97	11,471	11,568
1993	168,714	84,071	14,835	58,940	157,846	12.3	117	10,751	10,868
1994	166,876	85,243	19,551	51,745	156,539	12.2	87	10,250	10,337
1995	163,638	84,478	24,363	45,474	154,315	12.0	101	9,222	9,323
1996	177,495	88,410	33,255	46,251	167,916	13.0	110	9,469	9,579
1997	179,746	86,414	37,472	46,259	170,145	13.3	91	9,510	9,601
1998	187,402	87,568	44,332	45,971	177,871	13.9	125	9,406	9,531

** Rate is abortions at all ages per thousand resident women aged 14–49.

* Data for 1968 relate to only 8 months as the legislation came into effect on 27 April 1968.

Source: ONS/OPCS Abortion statistics, Series AB

This was Table A4.16 in the first edition of Birth counts

A4.13.2

Legal abortions to residents of Scotland, 1968–98

Year	Numbers						All abortions	Rate per 1000 women aged 15–44	
	Performed in Scotland			Performed in England and Wales				Performed in Scotland	All abortions
	NHS	Other	All	NHS	Other	All			
1968	1,495	49	1,544	:	:	:	:	1.5	:
1969	3,489	67	3,556	:	:	:	:	3.5	3.5
1970	5,177	77	5,254	:	:	309	5,563	5.2	5.5
1971	6,249	84	6,333	:	:	524	6,857	6.3	6.8
1972	7,510	99	7,609	:	:	835	8,444	7.5	8.4
1973	7,454	88	7,542	:	:	1,068	8,610	7.4	8.5
1974	7,436	132	7,568	:	:	1,026	8,594	7.4	8.4
1975	7,172	155	7,327	9	1,045	1,054	8,381	7.1	8.1
1976	7,041	178	7,219	:	:	950	8,169	6.9	7.8
1977	7,139	195	7,334	:	:	840	8,174	6.9	7.7
1978	7,251	200	7,451	:	:	976	8,427	7.0	7.9
1979	7,592	192	7,784	:	:	1,028	8,812	7.2	8.2
1980	7,722	183	7,905	23	1,156	1,179	9,084	7.3	8.4
1981	8,811	196	9,007	:	:	998	10,005	8.2	9.1
1982	8,187	238	8,425	:	:	898	9,323	7.6	8.5
1983	8,257	202	8,459	:	:	814	9,273	7.6	8.4
1984	8,934	221	9,155	29	752	781	9,936	8.2	8.9
1985	8,976	213	9,189	15	713	728	9,917	8.2	8.8
1986	9,432	196	9,628	17	734	751	10,379	8.6	9.2
1987	9,239	221	9,460	17	725	742	10,202	8.4	9.0
1988	9,882	246	10,128	23	828	851	10,979	9.0	9.8
1989	9,989	220	10,209	20	768	788	10,997	9.1	9.8
1990	10,010	209	10,219	20	764	784	11,003	9.1	9.8
1991	10,874	194	11,068	20	692	712	11,780	9.9	10.5
1992	10,675	143	10,818	25	548	573	11,391	9.8	10.3
1993	10,945	131	11,076	34	407	441	11,517	10.0	10.4
1994	11,280	112	11,392	13	350	363	11,755	10.3	10.7
1995	11,026	117	11,143	20	271	291	11,434	10.1	10.4
1996	11,861	117	11,978	33	296	329	12,307	10.9	11.2
1997	11,922	187	12,109	:	:	322	12,431	11.1	11.4
1998	12,255	169	12,424	:	:	377	12,801	11.4	11.7

Source: ISD, Scotland, *Scottish health statistics*, *Health briefings* and unpublished data
ONS/OPCS. *Abortion statistics*, *Series AB*

This was Table A4.17 in the first edition of *Birth counts*

A4.13.3

Legal abortions to non-residents carried out in England and Wales, 1970–98

Stated country of usual residence

	All non-residents	British Isles and Ireland							Other European					Rest of the World
		All	Scotland	Northern Ireland	Irish Republic	Channel Islands	Isle of Man	Channel Islands and Isle of Man	All	France	Germany	Italy	Spain	All
1970	10,603	934	309	199	261	..	..	165	..	2,267	3,621	..	..	..
1971	32,207	1,965	524	648	578	..	..	215	29,064	11,986	13,560	..	..	1,178
1972	51,319	2,879	835	775	974	..	..	295	47,912	25,189	17,531	480	730	528
1973	56,581	3,574	1,068	1,007	1,193	..	..	306	52,413	35,293	11,326	1,171	1,763	594
1974	53,495	3,910	1,026	1,092	1,421	..	..	371	49,060	36,443	5,991	1,751	2,978	525
1975	33,478	4,115	1,054	1,115	1,573	..	..	373	28,766	14,056	3,404	5,647	4,393	597
1976	27,761	4,249	950	1,142	1,821	..	..	336	22,796	4,568	2,384	8,211	6,397	716
1977	30,327	4,657	840	1,244	2,184	..	..	389	24,869	4,143	1,705	7,549	10,187	801
1978	29,707	5,248	976	1,311	2,548	..	..	413	23,579	3,187	1,171	3,911	14,015	880
1979	29,135	5,714	1,028	1,425	2,804	..	..	457	22,495	3,047	722	959	17,061	926
1980	31,976	6,548	1,179	1,565	3,320	..	..	484	24,426	4,117	584	774	18,342	1,002
1981	33,899	6,497	998	1,441	3,603	..	..	455	26,260	4,100	514	642	20,454	1,142
1982	34,492	6,528	898	1,510	3,653	..	..	467	26,699	3,825	365	626	21,415	1,265
1983	34,786	6,413	814	1,460	3,677	..	..	462	27,143	3,796	298	617	22,002	1,230
1984	33,605	6,711	781	1,530	3,946	..	..	454	25,425	3,931	258	715	20,060	1,469
1985	30,772	6,768	728	1,637	3,888	..	..	515	22,683	3,782	184	630	17,688	1,321
1986	24,667	6,959	751	1,724	3,918	418	148	566	16,483	3,369	142	664	11,935	1,225
1987	18,085	6,735	742	1,746	3,673	416	158	574	10,230	3,262	133	584	5,878	1,120
1988	15,500	7,132	851	1,815	3,839	445	182	627	7,357	3,047	146	631	3,188	1,011
1989	13,511	7,034	788	1,816	3,721	488	221	709	5,423	2,973	114	674	1,332	1,054
1990	13,012	7,400	784	1,855	4,064	465	232	697	4,712	2,787	144	620	886	900
1991	12,146	7,294	712	1,775	4,154	462	191	653	4,165	2,486	109	658	604	687
1992	11,568	7,130	573	1,794	4,254	370	139	509	3,654	2,154	108	650	464	784
1993	10,868	7,012	441	1,629	4,402	401	139	540	3,060	1,706	99	648	317	796
1994	10,337	7,123	363	1,678	4,590	349	143	492	2,467	1,390	75	598	127	747
1995	9,323	6,768	291	1,548	4,532	273	124	397	2,054	1,113	62	517	86	501
1996	9,579	7,246	329	1,573	4,894	290	160	450	1,926	1,073	56	427	66	407
1997	9,601	7,540	311	1,572	5,340	132	174	306	1,708	887	74	433	52	351
1998	9,531	8,046	377	1,581	5,891	64	133	197	1,180	435	71	395	39	296

Note: For the period 1971-90, figures for East Germany, West Germany and Germany (not otherwise stated) have been combined to produce totals for unified Germany.

Source: ONS, *Abortion statistics, Series AB*

This was Table A4.18 in the first edition of *Birth counts*

A4.14.1

Legal abortions to residents of England and Wales by gestational age, 1970–98

	Gestational age, weeks					
	Under 9	9–12	13–19	20 and over	Not stated	Total
	Numbers					
1970	10,029	42,466	20,204	953	2,310	75,962
1975	25,028	59,615	16,814	971	3,796	106,224
1980	30,851	71,516	20,106	2,234	4,220	128,927
1985	48,080	74,172	16,709	2,116	24	141,101
1990	62,235	90,431	18,967	2,262	5	173,900
1991	58,873	88,621	17,811	2,071	0	167,376
1992	57,536	83,077	16,470	1,851	2	158,936
1993	61,916	78,489	15,602	1,836	3	157,846
1994	63,456	75,751	15,468	1,863	1	156,539
1995	64,696	73,000	14,785	1,834	0	154,315
1996	67,091	81,728	16,904	2,192	1	167,916
1997	70,178	81,489	16,369	2,109	0	170,145
1998	73,625	84,702	17,229	2,315	0	177,871
	Percentage of abortions with stated gestational age					
1970	13.6	57.7	27.4	1.3		
1975	24.4	58.2	16.4	0.9		
1980	24.7	57.3	16.1	1.8		
1985	34.1	52.6	11.8	1.5		
1990	35.8	52.0	10.9	1.3		
1991	35.2	52.9	10.6	1.2		
1992	36.2	52.3	10.4	1.2		
1993	39.2	49.7	9.9	1.2		
1994	40.5	48.4	9.9	1.2		
1995	41.9	47.3	9.6	1.2		
1996	40.0	48.7	10.1	1.3		
1997	41.2	47.9	9.6	1.2		
1998	41.4	47.6	9.7	1.3		

Source: ONS *Abortion Statistics, Series AB*, Table 2

This is a new table for this edition of *Birth counts*

A4.14.2

Legal abortions to residents of Scotland by gestational age, 1968–98

| | Gestational age, weeks | | | | | | | |
	Under 10	10–13	14–17	18–19	20–24	25 and over	Not stated	Total
	Numbers							
1968	404	572	383	78	53	2	52	1,544
1969	948	1,462	791	168	98	7	82	3,556
1970	1,506	2,397	965	202	97	4	83	5,254
1971	1,861	2,929	1,079	219	89	4	152	6,333
1972	2,537	3,547	1,105	207	88	0	125	7,609
1973	2,729	3,468	1,002	183	91	2	67	7,542
1974	2,855	3,598	888	159	67	1	0	7,568
1975	2,747	3,470	845	170	89	6	0	7,327
1976	2,844	3,310	830	147	82	4	2	7,219
1977	3,003	3,320	773	133	96	5	4	7,334
1978	3,093	3,439	702	131	75	3	8	7,451
1979	3,282	3,454	804	154	84	2	4	7,784
1980	3,336	3,528	785	154	98	4	0	7,905
1981	3,876	4,124	790	126	85	6	0	9,007
1982	3,804	3,683	710	153	71	4	0	8,425
1983	3,964	3,562	691	170	71	1	0	8,459
1984	4,219	3,858	857	163	54	4	0	9,155
1985	4,305	3,867	835	136	44	2	0	9,189
1986	4,506	4,191	770	104	55	2	0	9,628
1987	4,427	4,019	807	147	58	2	0	9,460
1988	4,875	4,106	941	157	48	1	0	10,128
1989	5,281	4,081	709	109	28	1	0	10,209
1990	5,203	4,129	711	121	50	5	0	10,219
1991	5,884	4,339	652	126	64	3	0	11,068
1992	6,041	3,965	639	115	55	3	0	10,818
1993	6,610	3,682	604	122	44	4	10	11,076
1994	6,898	3,687	620	124	49	8	6	11,392
1995	7,068	3,399	533	94	44	5	0	11,143
1996	7,482	3,711	594	125	42	7	0	11,961
1997*	7,435	3,960	558	104	50	2	0	12,109
1998*	7,678	3,956	598	133	57	2	0	12,424

A4.14.2 *continued*

Legal abortions to residents of Scotland by gestational age, 1968–98

Gestational age, weeks

Percentage of abortions with stated gestational age

	Under 10	10–13	14–17	18–19	20–24	25 and over
1968	27.1	38.3	25.7	5.2	3.6	0.1
1969	27.3	42.1	22.8	4.8	2.8	0.2
1970	29.1	46.4	18.7	3.9	1.9	0.1
1971	30.1	47.4	17.5	3.5	1.4	0.1
1972	33.9	47.4	14.8	2.8	1.2	0.0
1973	36.5	46.4	13.4	2.4	1.2	0.0
1974	37.7	47.5	11.7	2.1	0.9	0.1
1975	37.5	47.4	11.5	2.3	1.2	0.1
1976	39.4	45.9	11.5	2.0	1.1	0.1
1977	41.0	45.3	10.5	1.8	1.3	0.0
1978	41.6	46.2	9.4	1.8	1.0	0.0
1979	42.2	44.4	10.3	2.0	1.1	0.1
1980	42.2	44.6	9.9	1.9	1.2	0.1
1981	43.0	45.8	8.8	1.4	0.9	0.0
1982	45.2	43.7	8.4	1.8	0.8	0.0
1983	46.9	42.1	8.2	2.0	0.8	0.0
1984	46.1	42.1	9.4	1.8	0.6	0.0
1985	46.8	42.1	9.1	1.5	0.5	0.0
1986	46.8	43.5	8.0	1.1	0.6	0.0
1987	46.8	42.5	8.5	1.6	0.6	0.0
1988	48.1	40.5	9.3	1.6	0.5	0.0
1989	51.7	40.0	6.9	1.1	0.3	0.0
1990	50.9	40.4	7.0	1.2	0.5	0.0
1991	53.2	39.2	5.9	1.1	0.6	0.0
1992	55.8	36.7	5.9	1.1	0.5	0.0
1993	59.7	33.3	5.5	1.1	0.4	0.0
1994	60.6	32.4	5.4	1.1	0.4	0.1
1995	63.4	30.5	4.8	0.8	0.4	0.0
1996	62.6	31.0	5.0	1.0	0.4	0.1
1997*	61.4	32.7	4.6	0.9	0.4	0.0
1998*	61.8	31.8	4.8	1.1	0.5	0.0

* Excluding abortions performed in England and Wales

Source: Information and Statistics Division, Scotland, *Scottish health statistics* and *Health briefings*

This is a new table for this edition of *Birth counts*

A4.15.1

Legal abortions in England, Wales and Scotland by country and regional health authority of usual residence, 1970–93

	1975	1980	1985	1990	1991	1992	1993
	Numbers						
England and Wales	106,224	128,927	141,101	173,900	167,376	160,501	157,846
England	101,392	122,636	134,504	166,460	160,189	153,645	150,922
Wales	4,832	6,291	6,597	7,440	7,187	6,856	6,924
Scotland	8,381	9,084	9,917	11,003	11,780	11,391	11,517
Northern Ireland	1,115	1,565	1,637	1,855	1,775	1,794	1,629
Irish Republic	1,573	3,320	3,888	4,064	4,154	4,254	4,402
Regional health authorities							
Northern	5,174	5,619	5,939	7,289	6,873	6,827	6,865
Yorkshire	6,311	7,574	8,087	10,221	10,136	9,675	9,491
Trent	7,810	9,927	10,183	12,509	12,641	12,222	12,349
East Anglian	2,985	3,861	4,384	5,112	4,776	4,785	4,589
North West Thames	13,175	14,845	15,211	18,465	17,929	16,668	16,402
North East Thames	11,690	14,653	16,835	22,015	20,797	19,840	19,211
South East Thames	9,091	10,906	12,356	16,748	15,675	15,399	14,880
South West Thames	7,197	8,505	9,581	11,778	11,594	10,601	10,068
Wessex	4,464	5,546	6,589	8,002	7,557	7,401	7,496
Oxford	4,438	5,703	6,348	8,074	7,693	7,495	7,233
South Western	5,685	6,497	6,765	7,903	7,575	7,368	7,391
West Midlands	11,543	14,050	15,478	18,380	17,692	16,692	16,306
Mersey	4,690	5,692	6,307	7,520	7,163	7,028	7,040
North Western	7,139	9,258	10,441	12,444	12,088	11,644	11,601
	*Rates per 1,000 women aged 14–49						
England and Wales	9.61	11.14	11.26	13.62	13.07	12.51	12.30
England	9.71	11.21	11.36	13.81	13.23	12.66	12.43
Wales	7.93	9.85	9.59	10.47	10.32	9.86	9.97
Scotland+	7.04	7.34	7.81	8.66	9.25	8.96	9.06
Northern Ireland#	2.17	3.03	4.90	5.41	5.12	5.14	4.63
Irish Republic	..	4.82	5.16	5.29	5.35	5.42	5.57

221

A4.15.1 continued

Legal abortions in England, Wales and Scotland by country and regional health authority of usual residence, 1970–93

	1975	1980	1985	1990	1991	1992	1993
Regional health authorities							
Northern	7.31	7.75	7.80	9.51	9.03	8.95	8.98
Yorkshire	7.94	9.13	9.03	11.14	11.12	10.55	10.34
Trent	7.61	9.22	8.76	10.56	10.80	10.38	10.47
East Anglian	7.54	8.78	8.99	10.03	9.28	9.34	8.97
North West Thames	15.82	17.52	16.56	20.01	18.75	17.38	17.48
North East Thames	13.70	16.71	17.48	22.31	21.14	20.05	19.41
South East Thames	11.49	13.43	13.83	18.41	16.74	16.39	15.86
South West Thames	11.13	12.88	12.94	15.77	14.91	13.59	13.15
Wessex	7.58	8.92	9.40	11.08	10.40	10.17	9.76
Oxford	8.59	10.18	9.86	11.91	11.41	11.06	10.67
South Western	8.39	8.88	8.83	9.91	9.54	9.27	9.30
West Midlands	9.78	11.59	11.89	14.08	13.55	12.80	12.53
Mersey	8.29	9.79	10.32	12.45	11.94	11.74	11.78
North Western	7.98	10.01	10.56	12.39	12.17	11.73	11.67

Northern Ireland rates are calculated for women aged 15–44. In 1999, populations for years for 1981 onwards were revised.

Source: ONS *Abortion Statistics, Series AB*
ISD, *Scottish health statistics*

This was Table A4.19 in the first edition of *Birth counts*

A4.15.2

Legal abortions in England, Wales and Scotland by country and regional office of usual residence, 1994–98

	1994	1995	1996	1997	1998
Numbers					
England and Wales	156,539	154,315	167,916	170,145	177,871
England	149,764	147,875	160,629	162,757	170,042
Wales	6,775	6,440	7,287	7,388	7,829
Scotland	11,755	11,143	12,307	12,431	12,801
Northern Ireland	1,678	1,548	1,573	1,572	1,581
Irish Republic	4,590	4,532	4,894	5,340	5,891
Regional office areas					
Northern and Yorkshire	16,260	14,998	16,170	16,304	17,115
Trent	11,822	11,264	12,917	12,980	13,964
Anglia and Oxford	12,872	13,125	14,148	14,530	15,119
North Thames	34,234	35,018	37,139	37,855	39,575
South Thames	25,434	25,355	28,313	28,601	29,960
South and West	14,706	14,540	15,990	16,254	17,033
West Midlands	16,000	15,882	17,027	16,854	17,274
North West	18,436	17,693	18,925	19,379	19,997

	1994	1995	1996	1997	1998
Rates per 1,000 women aged 14–49*					
England and Wales	12.18	11.99	13.03	13.28	13.92
England	12.62	12.44	13.49	13.42	14.06
Wales	9.76	9.30	10.52	10.75	11.47
Scotland	10.67	10.12	11.21	11.35	11.74
Northern Ireland	4.73	4.34	4.36	4.33	4.34
Irish Republic	5.76	5.63	5.95	..	..
Regional office areas					
Northern and Yorkshire	9.89	9.14	10.36	10.56	11.16
Trent	10.03	9.57	10.32	10.46	11.33
Anglia and Oxford	9.64	9.76	10.46	10.76	11.20
North Thames	19.06	19.40	20.44	20.84	21.70
South Thames	14.88	14.78	16.45	16.65	17.44
South and West	9.36	9.24	10.16	10.36	10.89
West Midlands	12.33	12.26	13.16	13.14	13.53
North West	11.31	10.88	11.67	12.07	12.51

* Rates for Scotland, Northern Ireland and Irish Republic are based on women aged 15–44

The denominators are the mid-year estimated resident populations

Source: ONS/OPCS *Abortion statistics, Series AB*

    ISD, *Scottish health statistics*

This is similar to Table A4.19 in the first edition of *Birth counts*

A4.16.1

Legal abortions to residents of England and Wales by procedure, 1985–98

Procedure

	Vacuum aspiration (only)	Vacuum aspiration with D and E	Dilation and evacuation	Prosta-glandins only	Prostaglandins with other agents	Antiprogesterone *	Other methods	All operations
Percentage of all abortions in each year								
1985	76.3	14.5	1.5	2.6	3.6	–	1.5	100.0
1986	76.9	14.5	1.6	2.4	3.2	–	1.3	100.0
1987	75.9	15.5	1.8	2.4	3.0	–	1.7	100.0
1988	74.4	16.8	1.8	2.4	2.8	–	1.7	100.0
1989	75.3	16.6	1.6	2.5	2.3	–	1.7	100.0
1990	74.8	17.4	2.1	2.5	1.6	–	1.0	100.0
1991	79.4	13.2	2.7	2.3	1.4	*	1.0	100.0
1992	83.4	8.4	3.1	2.4	1.3	1.0	0.1	100.0
1993	84.8	6.1	3.3	2.1	1.0	2.5	0.2	100.0
1994	83.7	6.8	2.9	1.8	0.9	3.6	0.2	100.0
1995	83.8	6.2	2.7	1.4	0.7	5.0	0.2	100.0
1996	84.1	6.0	2.3	1.1	0.5	5.8	0.1	100.0
1997	83.6	5.8	2.6	0.8	0.5	6.6	0.1	100.0
1998	82.2	5.9	2.8	0.6	0.4	7.8	0.2	100.0

* This method was introduced in July 1991. From July to December 1991, terminations by this method were grouped with 'Prostaglandins with other agents'. From 1992 onwards, they have been shown as a separate category, 'antiprogesterone with or without prostaglandins'.

Source: OPCS/ONS *Abortion statistics, Series AB*

This was Table A4.20 in the first edition of *Birth counts*

A4.16.2

Legal abortions to residents of England and Wales by age, 1970-98

Age, years

	Under 15	15	16–19	20–24	25–29	30–34	35–39	40–44	45 and over	Not stated	All
	Numbers										
1970	499	1,233	13,518	19,838	13,751	11,901	9,141	4,107	394	1,580	75,962
1975	879	2,691	24,122	25,065	20,259	15,047	10,933	4,905	471	1,852	106,224
1980	933	2,717	31,878	33,014	22,042	19,419	12,730	5,307	547	340	128,927
1985	1,024	2,978	34,208	41,880	26,009	17,202	12,979	4,372	425	24	141,101
1990	873	2,549	35,520	55,281	38,770	22,431	12,956	5,104	404	12	173,900
1991	886	2,272	31,130	52,678	38,611	23,445	13,035	4,901	408	10	167,376
1992	905	2,095	27,589	49,052	38,430	23,870	13,252	4,844	452	12	160,501
1993	964	2,119	25,806	46,846	38,139	24,690	13,885	4,889	494	14	157,846
1994	1,080	2,166	25,223	44,871	38,081	25,507	14,156	5,008	440	7	156,539
1995	946	2,324	24,945	43,394	37,254	25,759	14,352	4,868	457	16	154,315
1996	1,098	2,547	28,790	46,356	39,311	28,228	16,118	5,027	428	13	167,916
1997	1,020	2,414	29,947	44,960	40,159	28,892	16,858	5,413	482	0	170,145
1998	1,103	2,656	33,236	45,766	40,366	30,449	18,174	5,576	511	0	177,871

Source: ONS/OPCS *Abortion statistics, Series AB*

This is a new table for this edition of *Birth counts*

A4.16.3

Legal abortions to residents of England and Wales by marital status, 1970–98

Year	Marital status					
	Single	Married	Divorced/ Separated	Widowed	Not stated	All
	Numbers					
1970	34,492	34,314	6,409	634	113	75,962
1975	52,335	43,066	10,123	601	99	106,224
1980	68,756	44,253	14,008	667	1,243	128,927
1985	87,213	37,698	14,047	602	1,541	141,101
1990	116,150	38,151	15,631	509	3,459	173,900
1991	110,879	37,809	14,732	515	3,441	167,376
1992	105,636	36,394	14,645	512	3,314	160,501
1993	103,784	35,408	14,539	479	3,636	157,846
1994	102,532	34,632	13,272	449	5,654	156,539
1995	102,274	33,018	12,381	425	6,217	154,315
1996	114,086	34,262	11,308	511	7,749	167,916
1997	116,425	34,181	11,590	430	7,519	170,145
1998	122,661	34,466	11,030	534	9,180	177,871

Source: ONS/OPCS *Abortion statistics, Series AB*

This was Table A4.22 in the first edition of *Birth counts*

A4.16.4

Legal abortions to residents of England and Wales by marital status and number of previous liveborn children, 1996

	Number of previous live born children								
	0	1	2	3	4	5 and over	Not known	Not stated	Total
All	90,206	29,142	29,447	12,619	4,244	2,009	4	245	167,916
Single	80,404	18,397	10,026	3,562	1,105	468	3	121	114,086
Married	4,480	6,431	13,669	6,353	2,171	1,118	0	40	34,262
Divorced	741	1,361	2,071	1,014	354	154	1	6	5,702
Widowed	91	101	193	79	29	18	0	0	511
Separated	1,089	1,348	1,873	883	287	120	0	6	5,606
Not known	2,359	987	1,039	477	197	80	0	7	5,146
Not stated	1,042	517	576	251	101	51	0	65	2,603

Source: ONS unpublished data

This was Table A4.23 in the first edition of *Birth counts*

A4.16.5

Legal abortions to residents of England and Wales by gestational age and category of premises, 1996

Gestational age, weeks	NHS hospitals		NHS agency		Non-NHS		All	
	Number	Percentage	Number	Percentage	Number	Percentage	Number	Percentage
Under 9	26,439	29.9	12,485	37.5	28,167	60.9	67,091	40.0
9–12	54,590	61.7	14,022	42.2	13,116	28.4	81,728	48.7
13–14	3,927	4.4	2,585	7.8	1,832	4.0	8,344	5.0
15–16	1,558	1.8	1,996	6.0	1,394	3.0	4,948	2.9
17–18	841	1.0	1,117	3.4	814	1.8	2,772	1.7
19–20	578	0.7	517	1.6	436	0.9	1,531	0.9
21–22	294	0.3	393	1.2	332	0.7	1,019	0.6
23–24	98	0.1	140	0.4	159	0.3	397	0.2
25 and over	85	0.1	0	–	0	–	85	0.1
Not stated	0	–	0	–	1	0.0	1	0.0
All	88,410	100.0	33,255	100.0	46,251	100.0	167,916	100.0

Source: ONS *Abortion statistics, Series AB*

This was Table A4.24 in the first edition of *Birth counts*

A4.17.1

Legal abortions on grounds of known or suspected abnormality, England and Wales, 1979–98

Year	Principal medical condition							
	Central nervous system malformation in fetus	Chromosomal abnormality in fetus	Hereditary disease in family possibly affecting fetus	Suspected damage to fetus from viral disease in mother	Suspected damage to fetus from drugs	Suspected damage to fetus from radiation	Other known or suspected fetal abnormality	Suspected damage to fetus from other disease in the mother and unspecified fetal abnormality
ICD ninth revision	**655.0**	**655.1**	**655.2**	**655.3**	**655.5**	**655.6**	**655.8**	**655.4-655.9**
1979	285	173	89	757	254	113	655	402
1980	418	173	66	328	298	128	603	412
1981	441	262	85	218	277	141	456	353
1982	467	282	81	255	310	115	317	306
1983	502	250	93	331	289	112	261	320
1984	521	263	96	256	289	106	282	303
1985	506	276	97	124	261	93	277	344
1986	549	296	108	177	209	72	258	330
1987	524	280	69	135	218	74	305	306
1988	459	308	74	84	171	51	364	242
1989	473	306	79	84	176	37	334	203
1990	450	273	83	56	193	33	363	200
1991	490	341	79	55	173	36	422	146
1992	519	402	93	58	126	21	453	80
1993	521	453	101	36	96	14	535	69
1994	465	443	95	18	42	10	533	68
ICD tenth revision	**Q00-Q07**	**Q90-Q99**	**Z80-Z84**	**Z20-Z22**				
1995	494	468	91	19	..	..	..	..
1996	520	561	107	17	..	..	..	..
1997	426	580	80	11	..	..	..	..
1998	448	568	68	24	..	..	..	..

Data for the years 1982–91 specify conditions relating to the current pregnancy.

Source: ONS/OPCS *Abortion statistics, Series AB*

This is a new table for this edition of *Birth counts*

A4.18.1

Conceptions by age of women and outcome, England and Wales, 1969–97

Year of conception	Number of conceptions, thousands			Conception rates per 1,000 women in age group		
	Total conceptions	Conceptions leading to maternities	Conception terminated by abortion*	Total conceptions	Conceptions leading to maternities	Conceptions terminated by abortion*
	All ages**					
1969	832,713	778,602	54,111	89.1	83.3	5.8
1970	876,916	796,218	80,698	93.8	85.1	8.6
1971	835,467	736,704	98,763	89.1	78.5	10.5
1972	801,002	689,605	111,397	85.0	73.2	11.8
1973	762,084	650,512	111,572	80.4	68.6	11.8
1974	724,273	614,407	109,866	76.1	64.5	11.5
1975	693,338	586,951	106,387	72.4	61.3	11.1
1976	671,558	567,497	104,061	69.4	58.6	10.8
1977	686,377	581,833	104,544	70.1	59.4	10.7
1978	747,939	631,959	115,980	75.3	63.6	11.7
1979	774,091	648,505	125,586	76.8	64.4	12.5
1980	764,961	638,441	126,520	74.8	62.5	12.4
1981	752,252	623,822	128,430	72.7	60.3	12.4
1982	755,257	626,764	128,493	72.3	60.0	12.3
1983	753,383	625,038	128,345	71.4	59.3	12.2
1984	790,116	653,804	136,312	74.2	61.4	12.8
1985	797,209	654,349	142,860	74.1	60.8	13.3
1986	818,917	671,259	147,658	75.1	61.6	13.5
1987	850,400	689,452	160,948	77.4	62.7	14.6
1988	849,549	681,831	167,718	77.1	61.9	15.2
1989	864,720	693,541	171,179	78.5	63.0	15.5
1990	871,495	697,680	173,815	79.2	63.4	15.8
1991	853,675	688,443	165,232	77.7	62.7	15.0
1992	828,049	667,902	160,147	76.3	61.5	14.8
1993	819,038	662,038	157,000	76.1	61.5	14.6
1994	801,576	645,548	156,028	74.7	60.1	14.5
1995	790,265	634,440	155,825	73.7	59.1	14.5
1996	816,893	647,175	169,718	76.1	60.3	15.8
1997	800,361	629,860	170,501	74.4	58.6	15.9
	Under 16#					
1969	6,576	4,905	1,671	6.9	5.1	1.7
1970	7,713	5,258	2,455	7.9	5.4	2.5
1971	8,825	5,575	3,250	8.8	5.5	3.2
1972	9,608	5,679	3,929	9.3	5.5	3.8
1973	9,792	5,392	4,400	9.2	5.1	4.1
1974	9,371	4,843	4,528	8.5	4.4	4.1
1975	9,181	4,394	4,787	8.1	3.9	4.2
1976	9,191	4,298	4,893	7.9	3.7	4.2
1977	9,003	4,226	4,777	7.6	3.6	4.0
1978	9,103	4,412	4,691	7.6	3.7	3.9
1979	9,108	4,079	5,029	7.5	3.4	4.2
1980	8,580	3,935	4,645	7.2	3.3	3.9
1981	8,561	3,694	4,867	7.3	3.1	4.1
1982	8,999	3,875	5,124	7.8	3.4	4.4

Conceptions by age of women and outcome, England and Wales, 1969–97

Year of conception	Number of conceptions, thousands			Conception rates per 1,000 women in age group		
	Total conceptions	Conceptions leading to maternities	Conception terminated by abortion*	Total conceptions	Conceptions leading to maternities	Conceptions terminated by abortion*
1983	9,369	4,046	5,323	8.3	3.6	4.7
1984	9,649	4,278	5,371	8.7	3.8	4.8
1985	9,406	4,169	5,237	8.7	3.8	4.8
1986	9,194	4,222	4,972	8.8	4.0	4.7
1987	9,135	4,185	4,950	9.3	4.2	5.0
1988	8,258	3,845	4,413	8.8	4.1	4.7
1989	7,950	3,814	4,136	8.9	4.3	4.6
1990	8,139	4,006	4,133	9.5	4.7	4.8
1991	7,480	3,655	3,825	8.9	4.3	4.6
1992	7,217	3,707	3,510	8.4	4.3	4.1
1993	7,267	3,643	3,624	8.1	4.1	4.0
1994	7,795	3,875	3,920	8.3	4.1	4.2
1995	8,051	4,218	3,833	8.6	4.5	4.1
1996	8,857	4,498	4,359	9.5	4.8	4.7
1997	8,271	4,164	4,107	8.9	4.5	4.4
	Under 20–					
1969	123,880	112,658	11,222	75.3	68.5	6.8
1970	134,809	116,979	17,830	82.7	71.7	10.9
1971	133,130	109,847	23,283	81.5	67.3	14.3
1972	130,599	102,868	27,731	79.3	62.5	16.8
1973	125,687	96,780	28,907	75.3	58.0	17.3
1974	118,191	88,573	29,618	69.6	52.2	17.4
1975	111,976	82,320	29,656	64.1	47.2	17.0
1976	105,654	75,955	29,699	58.7	42.2	16.5
1977	107,394	77,100	30,294	58.0	41.6	16.3
1978	114,607	81,885	32,722	60.2	43.0	17.2
1979	120,944	84,301	36,643	61.9	43.2	18.8
1980	117,244	80,883	36,361	58.7	40.5	18.2
1981	115,161	78,436	36,725	57.1	38.9	18.2
1982	113,932	76,985	36,947	56.4	38.1	18.3
1983	112,351	74,997	37,354	55.9	37.3	18.6
1984	118,228	78,755	39,473	59.8	39.8	20.0
1985	119,267	78,922	40,345	61.7	40.8	20.9
1986	118,777	79,131	39,646	62.3	41.5	20.8
1987	123,152	80,540	42,612	66.2	43.3	22.9
1988	118,898	76,167	42,731	65.8	42.2	23.7
1989	115,727	74,502	41,225	66.8	43.0	23.8
1990	113,330	72,825	40,505	68.0	43.7	24.3
1991	101,625	66,576	35,049	64.1	42.0	22.1
1992	93,418	61,770	31,648	61.9	41.0	21.0
1993	87,173	57,303	29,870	59.9	39.4	20.5
1994	85,352	55,723	29,629	58.9	38.4	20.4
1995	86,587	56,639	29,948	58.9	38.6	20.4
1996	94,873	60,485	34,388	63.3	40.4	23.0
1997	96,007	60,708	35,299	62.6	39.6	23.0

A4.18.1 *continued*

Conceptions by age of women and outcome, England and Wales, 1969–97

Year of conception	Number of conceptions, thousands			Conception rates per 1,000 women in age group		
	Total conceptions	Conceptions leading to maternities	Conception terminated by abortion*	Total conceptions	Conceptions leading to maternities	Conceptions terminated by abortion*
	20–24					
1969	311,147	297,205	13,942	168.2	160.6	7.5
1970	329,013	307,700	21,313	176.3	164.9	11.4
1971	305,739	280,128	25,611	163.6	149.9	13.7
1972	278,413	250,917	27,496	156.9	141.4	15.5
1973	255,254	228,130	27,124	148.6	132.8	15.8
1974	236,408	209,941	26,467	140.0	124.3	15.7
1975	221,782	196,649	25,133	133.0	118.0	15.1
1976	210,032	185,778	24,254	126.0	111.4	14.5
1977	215,295	191,113	24,182	127.9	113.5	14.4
1978	233,339	205,507	27,832	136.6	120.3	16.3
1979	241,574	210,912	30,662	139.2	121.5	17.7
1980	242,002	209,931	32,071	135.3	117.4	17.9
1981	238,095	204,292	33,803	128.9	110.6	18.3
1982	240,671	206,254	34,417	127.1	108.9	18.2
1983	237,889	202,965	34,924	122.2	104.3	17.9
1984	249,075	210,599	38,476	124.4	105.2	19.2
1985	249,165	207,156	42,009	121.6	101.1	20.5
1986	253,131	208,356	44,775	122.2	100.6	21.6
1987	261,876	211,444	50,432	126.4	102.1	24.3
1988	255,368	201,991	53,377	124.6	98.6	26.1
1989	250,771	196,087	54,684	124.2	97.1	27.1
1990	244,451	189,990	54,461	124.0	96.4	27.6
1991	233,336	181,496	51,840	120.2	93.5	26.7
1992	215,949	167,798	48,151	114.0	88.6	25.4
1993	203,608	157,200	46,408	110.8	85.5	25.2
1994	190,359	145,786	44,573	107.8	82.5	25.2
1995	181,145	137,362	43,783	106.3	80.6	25.7
1996	179,811	133,516	46,295	110.9	82.3	28.5
1997	167,261	122,628	44,633	108.0	79.2	28.8
	25–29					
1969	224,121	214,078	10,043	148.1	141.4	6.6
1970	238,556	223,809	14,747	153.9	144.4	9.5
1971	234,371	216,081	18,290	145.2	133.9	11.3
1972	240,651	219,264	21,387	137.8	125.5	12.2
1973	240,198	218,493	21,705	132.0	120.1	11.9
1974	234,196	213,124	21,072	127.2	115.8	11.4
1975	227,876	207,467	20,409	122.9	111.9	11.0
1976	223,746	203,860	19,886	120.4	109.7	10.7
1977	218,914	200,063	18,851	123.7	113.1	10.7
1978	232,940	212,358	20,582	135.6	123.6	12.0
1979	234,813	213,268	21,545	138.7	126.0	12.7
1980	229,115	207,665	21,450	137.0	124.1	12.8
1981	221,849	200,257	21,592	132.7	119.8	12.9
1982	224,984	202,998	21,986	134.1	121.0	13.1

A4.18.1 *continued*

Conceptions by age of women and outcome, England and Wales, 1969–97

Year of conception	Number of conceptions, thousands			Conception rates per 1,000 women in age group		
	Total conceptions	Conceptions leading to maternities	Conception terminated by abortion*	Total conceptions	Conceptions leading to maternities	Conceptions terminated by abortion*
1983	226,341	204,322	22,019	133.6	120.6	13.0
1984	238,642	214,716	23,926	137.9	124.1	13.8
1985	242,643	216,475	26,168	135.9	121.2	14.7
1986	253,799	225,557	28,242	137.2	121.9	15.3
1987	264,646	233,178	31,468	138.6	122.1	16.5
1988	267,685	233,437	34,248	136.4	118.9	17.4
1989	278,565	242,057	36,508	138.1	120.0	18.1
1990	284,240	245,868	38,372	138.0	119.4	18.6
1991	281,532	243,767	37,765	135.1	117.0	18.1
1992	274,875	236,616	38,259	131.7	113.4	18.3
1993	271,719	234,033	37,686	131.4	113.1	18.2
1994	261,849	224,335	37,514	128.1	109.8	18.4
1995	250,285	213,203	37,082	125.0	106.5	18.5
1996	252,612	213,085	39,527	127.9	107.9	20.0
1997	242,572	202,769	39,803	125.4	104.8	20.6
30–34						
1969	110,562	101,747	8,815	77.7	71.5	6.2
1970	111,454	98,695	12,759	77.9	69.0	8.9
1971	102,574	87,613	14,961	72.1	61.6	10.5
1972	95,614	79,039	16,575	67.1	55.4	11.6
1973	90,654	74,521	16,133	62.3	51.2	11.1
1974	89,197	73,545	15,652	59.9	49.4	10.5
1975	88,292	73,182	15,110	57.9	48.0	9.9
1976	91,346	76,482	14,864	57.5	48.2	9.4
1977	103,319	87,525	15,794	60.0	50.8	9.2
1978	121,416	103,499	17,917	67.8	57.8	10.0
1979	128,076	109,026	19,050	70.3	59.8	10.5
1980	126,889	107,966	18,923	68.9	58.6	10.3
1981	126,239	107,649	18,590	68.4	58.3	10.1
1982	121,922	104,472	17,450	69.7	59.8	10.0
1983	120,919	104,195	16,724	71.4	61.6	9.9
1984	126,011	109,030	16,981	75.6	65.4	10.2
1985	127,766	110,600	17,166	77.4	67.0	10.4
1986	133,024	115,352	17,672	80.2	69.5	10.6
1987	139,041	120,131	18,910	82.6	71.4	11.2
1988	144,231	124,401	19,830	84.3	72.7	11.6
1989	153,704	132,650	21,054	88.0	75.9	12.1
1990	161,421	139,102	22,319	89.7	77.3	12.4
1991	167,479	144,595	22,884	90.1	77.8	12.3
1992	172,039	148,207	23,832	89.9	77.4	12.5
1993	180,962	156,552	24,410	92.0	79.6	12.4
1994	184,998	159,903	25,095	91.3	79.0	12.4
1995	190,332	164,540	25,792	91.7	79.3	12.4
1996	199,983	171,800	28,183	95.1	81.7	13.4
1997	200,906	172,342	28,564	95.2	81.6	13.5

A4.18.1 *continued*

Conceptions by age of women and outcome, England and Wales, 1969–97

Year of conception	Number of conceptions, thousands			Conception rates per 1,000 women in age group		
	Total conceptions	Conceptions leading to maternities	Conception terminated by abortion*	Total conceptions	Conceptions leading to maternities	Conceptions terminated by abortion*
35–39						
1969	49,570	42,631	6,939	35.0	30.1	4.9
1970	49,266	39,625	9,641	35.4	28.5	6.9
1971	46,069	34,632	11,437	33.4	25.1	8.3
1972	42,623	30,231	12,392	30.9	21.9	9.0
1973	38,567	26,438	12,129	27.7	19.0	8.7
1974	35,570	23,926	11,644	25.3	17.0	8.3
1975	33,451	22,461	10,990	23.6	15.9	7.8
1976	31,507	21,038	10,469	22.5	15.0	7.5
1977	31,849	21,506	10,343	22.7	15.3	7.4
1978	35,773	24,110	11,663	25.0	16.8	8.1
1979	38,595	26,291	12,304	26.2	17.8	8.3
1980	39,336	27,010	12,326	25.9	17.8	8.1
1981	40,944	28,331	12,613	25.9	17.9	8.0
1982	44,190	31,295	12,895	25.8	18.3	7.5
1983	46,396	33,564	12,832	26.0	18.8	7.2
1984	48,504	35,586	12,918	26.7	19.6	7.1
1985	48,776	36,098	12,678	26.5	19.6	6.9
1986	50,266	37,503	12,763	27.2	20.3	6.9
1987	50,787	38,186	12,601	28.9	21.7	7.2
1988	51,819	39,469	12,350	30.3	23.1	7.2
1989	54,126	41,549	12,577	32.2	24.7	7.5
1990	56,021	43,056	12,965	33.6	25.8	7.8
1991	57,574	44,920	12,654	34.4	26.9	7.6
1992	59,598	46,387	13,211	35.1	27.4	7.8
1993	63,026	49,444	13,582	36.5	28.7	7.9
1994	66,161	52,199	13,962	37.5	29.6	7.9
1995	68,672	54,479	14,193	37.9	30.1	7.8
1996	75,500	59,487	16,013	40.4	31.8	8.6
1997	78,876	62,275	16,601	41.0	32.3	8.6
40 and over* **						
1969	13,433	10,283	3,150	8.9	6.9	2.1
1970	13,818	9,410	4,408	9.3	6.3	3.0
1971	13,584	8,403	5,181	9.3	5.7	3.5
1972	13,102	7,286	5,816	9.1	5.0	4.0
1973	11,724	6,150	5,574	8.2	4.3	3.9
1974	10,711	5,298	5,413	7.7	3.8	3.9
1975	9,961	4,872	5,089	7.2	3.5	3.7
1976	9,273	4,384	4,889	6.8	3.2	3.6
1977	9,606	4,526	5,080	7.1	3.3	3.7
1978	9,864	4,600	5,264	7.2	3.3	3.8
1979	10,089	4,707	5,382	7.2	3.4	3.9
1980	10,375	4,986	5,389	7.4	3.5	3.8
1981	9,964	4,857	5,107	7.2	3.5	3.7
1982	9,558	4,760	4,798	6.9	3.4	3.4

A4.18.1 *continued*

Conceptions by age of women and outcome, England and Wales, 1969–97

| Year of conception | Number of conceptions, thousands | | | Conception rates per 1,000 women in age group | | |
	Total conceptions	Conceptions leading to maternities	Conception terminated by abortion*	Total conceptions	Conceptions leading to maternities	Conceptions terminated by abortion*
1983	9,487	4,995	4,492	6.7	3.5	3.2
1984	9,656	5,118	4,538	6.6	3.5	3.1
1985	9,592	5,098	4,494	6.4	3.4	3.0
1986	9,920	5,360	4,560	6.3	3.4	2.9
1987	10,898	5,973	4,925	6.4	3.5	2.9
1988	11,548	6,366	5,182	6.5	3.6	2.9
1989	11,827	6,696	5,131	6.5	3.7	2.8
1990	12,032	6,839	5,193	6.6	3.7	2.8
1991	12,129	7,089	5,040	6.6	3.8	2.7
1992	12,170	7,124	5,046	6.9	4.1	2.9
1993	12,550	7,506	5,044	7.4	4.4	3.0
1994	12,857	7,602	5,255	7.6	4.5	3.1
1995	13,244	8,217	5,027	7.9	4.9	3.0
1996	14,114	8,802	5,312	8.4	5.3	3.2
1997	14,739	9,138	5,601	8.7	5.4	3.3

*   Abortions under the 1967 Act
**   Rates per thousand women aged 15–44
\#   Rates per thousand women aged 13–15
\~   Rates per thousand women aged 15–19
*** Rates per thousand women aged 40–44

Revised data: In 1999, ONS amended the way it estimates age at conception. Revised figures are very similar to those previously published. Full details are given in an article in Population Trends 97. Statistics for 1988–97 have been calculated on the revised basis. Revised figures for earlier years were not available at the time of publication.

The published figures for 1996 are also affected by an error in the processing of birth registrations. In late 1999, there were 1,002 more births on the database for 1997 than when the original conceptions data for 1997 were assembled. Some of these births would have been conceived in 1996.

Source: ONS Birth statistics, Series FM1, Table 12.2

This is a new table for this edition of *Birth counts*

A4.19.1

Offences recorded by the police and persons sent for trial and found guilty or cautioned for procuring illegal abortion, England and Wales, 1900–97

Year	Offences recorded by the police	Persons sent for trial	Persons found guilty or cautioned
	Average number per year		
1900–1904	12	11	0
1905–1909	33	20	0
1910–1914	40	30	0
1915–1919	65	43	0
1920–1924	48	32	0
1925–1929	82	53	0
1930–1934	80	48	0
1935–1939	156	72	0
1940–1944	347	119	0
1945–1949	271	100	0
1950–1954	244	60	0
1955–1959	164	47	0
1960–1964	276	65	0
1965–1969	242	62	76
1970–1974	82	24	37
1975–1979	9	2	3
1980–1984	3	1	3
1985–1989	4	3	3
1990–1994	3	2	9
	Number per year		
1965	184	67	70
1966	208	61	65
1967	314	56	78
1968	247	72	93
1969	257	55	72
1970	212	50	55
1971	80	31	54
1972	62	25	48
1973	36	8	11
1974	21	7	17
1975	14	1	1
1976	9	3	5
1977	11	3	3
1978	7	3	4
1979	3	1	0
1980*	2	3	5
1981	3	0	3
1982	3	0	1
1983	4	1	4
1984	1	3	2
1985	4	2	1
1986	3	1	2
1987	3	2	6
1988	3	4	5
1989	5	5	3

A4.19.1 *continued*

Offences recorded by the police and persons sent for trial and found guilty or cautioned for procuring illegal abortion, England and Wales, 1900–97

Year	Offences recorded by the police	Persons sent for trial	Persons found guilty or cautioned
1990	5	1	31
1991	3	1	2
1992	1	0	1
1993	2	0	2
1994	3	6	0
1995	5	1	0
1996	7	0	3
1997	0	0	6

* New counting procedure introduced in 1980

Source: Home Office, *Criminal Statistics*

This was Table A4.26 in the first edition of *Birth counts*

A4.19.2

Offences against children recorded in criminal statistics, England and Wales, 1900–97

Year	Infanticide, offences recorded by the police*	Initially recorded as homicide#	Child destruction	Concealment of birth	Abandoning child under the age of two years	Offences currently recorded as homicide of children aged under one year+	Murder known to the police of children aged under one year
Five year averages							
1900–1904	..	..	..	79	53	..	65
1905–1909	..	..	..	96	39	..	48
1910–1914	..	..	..	85	22	..	55
1915–1919	..	..	..	100	36	..	52
1920–1924	14-	..	..	113	26	..	49
1925–1929	20	..	..	105	20	32	37
1930–1934	21	..	0.4	89	17	30	31
1935–1939	20-	..	0.4	67	25	22	24
1940–1944	35	..	0.8	89	32	19	25
1945–1949	45	..	0.4	85	27	26	29
1950–1954	25	0	0.2	46	17	11	11
1955–1959	20	0	0.8	40	12	11	11
1960–1964	19	0	1.2	44	12	12	12
1965–1969	22	17	1.8	34	20	12	12
1970–1974	22	15	0.8	22	13	19	4
1975–1979	–	6	1.0	14	8	27	–
1980–1984	–	7	0.6	16	14	25	–
1985–1989	–	4	2.6	13	26	26	–
1990–1994	–	4	2.4	14	41	26	–
Number per year							
1980	–	10	2	9	8	29	–
1981	–	7	1	23	11	25	–
1982	–	6	–	15	15	24	–
1983	–	11	–	9	22	28	–
1984	–	2	1	24	15	19	–
1985	–	8	1	15	26	29	–
1986	–	3	–	13	22	20	–
1987	–	1	2	17	25	30	–

A4.19.2 continued

Offences against children recorded in criminal statistics, England and Wales, 1900–97

Year	Infanticide, offences recorded by the police*	Initially recorded as homicide#	Child destruction	Concealment of birth	Abandoning child under the age of two years	Offences currently recorded as homicide of children aged under one year+	Murder known to the police of children aged under one year
Number per year							
1988	–	7	8	9	23	36	–
1989	–	1	2	12	34	16	–
1990	–	4	–	9	23	24	–
1991	–	5	2	19	47	28	–
1992	–	6	–	14	40	27	–
1993	–	5	3	16	45	27	–
1994	–	2	7	11	51	24	–
1995	–	2	8	15	46	17	–
1996	–	3	2	5	65	27	–
1997	–	:	:	:	:	37	–

* From 1973 onwards infanticide included in recorded homicide figure only

\# Decided by court to be homicide. Recorded in the Homicide Index which started in 1967.

~ Average figures for the years 1920–24 and 1935–39

\+ A combination of murder, manslaughter and infanticide, compiled from ad-hoc data found in various criminal statistics, command papers and on the Homicide Index which started in 1967.

Source: Home Office

This is a new table for this edition of *Birth counts*

239

Live births inside marriage by social class of father, England and Wales, 1950, 1964 and 1970–98

Year	Inside marriage						Outside marriage	All live births
	Social class of father					All		
	I and II	IIIn	IIIm	IV and V	Other			
	Number of live births, thousands							
1950	108.7	:	:	178.0	0.1	658.4	38.7	697,097
1964	:	:	371.6	:	:	:	:	875,972
1970	148.2	76.2	300.8	167.7	26.8	719.7	64.7	784,486
1971	154.7	75.3	297.9	160.1	29.5	717.5	65.7	783,155
1972	151.6	71.3	272.1	140.4	27.1	662.5	62.5	725,440
1973	148.1	64.5	245.8	130.7	28.8	617.9	58.1	675,953
1974	146.1	59.0	232.5	120.4	25.4	583.4	56.5	639,885
1975	141.6	57.0	214.1	111.8	24.1	548.6	54.9	603,445
1976	140.8	55.5	204.6	110.2	19.4	530.5	53.8	584,270
1977	142.3	53.2	193.4	106.6	18.4	513.9	55.4	569,259
1978	150.5	54.6	202.1	111.5	17.1	535.8	60.6	596,418
1979	157.0	56.7	217.1	119.9	17.9	568.6	69.5	638,028
1979*	160.1	60.2	209.3	121.2	17.8	568.6	69.5	638,028
1980	164.5	61.9	212.2	120.4	19.9	578.9	77.4	656,234
1981	163.3	60.4	198.2	111.4	20.1	553.5	81.0	634,492
1982	158.7	58.0	190.0	109.2	20.2	536.1	89.9	625,931
1983	156.0	57.1	188.3	107.7	20.8	529.9	99.2	629,134
1984	154.8	57.6	185.5	106.3	22.2	526.4	110.5	636,818
1985	158.4	56.2	184.3	105.9	25.3	530.2	126.3	656,417
1986	160.1	55.2	179.5	101.1	23.8	519.7	141.3	661,018
1987	164.6	53.9	180.9	99.3	24.4	523.1	158.4	681,511
1988	167.7	54.8	175.0	94.1	24.7	516.2	177.4	693,577
1989	172.1	49.9	169.7	87.8	22.4	501.9	185.8	687,725
1990	177.4	53.2	168.8	85.3	21.4	506.1	200.0	706,140
1991	173.3	50.7	162.0	79.1	22.8	487.9	211.3	699,217

A5.1.1 continued

Live births inside marriage by social class of father, England and Wales, 1950, 1964 and 1970–98

Year	Inside marriage						Outside marriage	All live births
	Social class of father							
	I and II	IIIn	IIIm	IV and V	Other	All		
1992	170.5	49.4	153.6	77.1	23.9	474.4	215.2	689,656
1993	165.8	50.6	139.0	77.7	23.9	456.9	216.5	673,467
1994	166.1	50.5	134.9	75.6	22.1	449.2	215.5	664,726
1995	161.6	48.2	124.7	72.5	21.2	428.2	219.9	648,138
1996	161.5	47.6	117.8	70.1	19.7	416.8	232.7	649,485
1997	162.5	44.0	112.0	67.0	19.3	404.2	238.2	643,095
1998	162.8	42.5	105.5	65.7	18.8	395.3	240.6	635,901
Percentage of all live births								
1950	15.6	53.3		25.5	0.5	94.9	5.1	697,097
1964	15.3	47.1		27.1	3.3	92.8	7.2	875,972
1970	18.9	9.7	38.3	21.4	3.4	91.7	8.3	784,486
1971	19.8	9.6	38.0	20.4	3.8	91.6	8.4	783,155
1972	20.9	9.8	37.5	19.4	3.7	91.3	8.6	725,440
1973	21.9	9.5	36.4	19.3	4.3	91.4	8.6	675,953
1974	22.8	9.2	36.3	18.8	4.0	91.2	8.8	639,885
1975	23.5	9.4	35.5	18.5	4.0	90.9	9.1	603,445
1976	24.1	9.5	35.0	18.9	3.3	90.8	9.2	584,270
1977	25.0	9.3	34.0	18.7	3.2	90.3	9.7	569,259
1978	25.2	9.2	33.9	18.7	2.9	89.8	10.2	596,418
1979	24.6	8.9	34.0	18.8	2.8	89.1	10.9	638,028
1980	25.1	9.4	32.3	18.3	3.0	88.2	11.8	656,234
1981	25.7	9.5	31.2	17.6	3.2	87.2	12.8	634,492
1982	25.4	9.3	30.4	17.4	3.2	85.6	14.4	625,931
1983	24.8	9.1	29.9	17.1	3.3	84.2	15.8	629,134
1984	24.3	9.0	29.1	16.7	3.5	82.7	17.3	636,818
1985	24.1	8.6	28.1	16.1	3.9	80.8	19.2	656,417
1986	24.2	8.4	27.2	15.3	3.6	78.6	21.4	661,018
1987	24.2	7.9	26.5	14.6	3.6	76.8	23.2	681,511
1988	24.2	7.9	25.2	13.6	3.6	74.4	25.6	693,577

A5.1.1 continued

Live births inside marriage by social class of father, England and Wales, 1950, 1964 and 1970–98

Year	Inside marriage						Outside marriage	All live births
	Social class of father							
	I and II	IIIn	IIIm	IV and V	Other	All		
1989	25.0	7.3	24.7	12.8	3.3	73.0	27.0	687,725
1990	25.1	7.5	23.9	12.1	3.0	71.7	28.3	706,140
1991	24.8	7.3	23.2	11.3	3.3	69.8	30.2	699,217
1992	24.7	7.2	22.3	11.2	3.5	68.8	31.2	689,656
1993	24.6	7.5	20.6	11.5	3.5	67.8	32.2	673,467
1994	25.0	7.6	20.3	11.4	3.3	67.6	32.4	664,726
1995	24.9	7.4	19.2	11.2	3.3	66.1	33.9	648,138
1996	24.9	7.3	18.1	10.8	3.0	64.2	35.8	649,485
1997	25.3	6.8	17.4	10.4	3.0	62.8	37.0	643,095
1998	25.6	6.7	16.6	10.3	3.0	62.2	37.9	635,091

Data for 1970 onwards are based on a 10 per cent sample of all live births

* Revised 1979 figures based on 1980 classification of occupations

Source: *Studies on Medical and Population Subjects, Nos. 15 and 19. ONS/OPCS Birth statistics, Series FM1.*

This was Table A5.1 in the first edition of *Birth counts*

A5.1.2

Jointly registered live births outside marriage by social class of father, England and Wales, 1970–98

Year	Jointly registered live births outside marriage								Sole registration by mother	All live births outside marriage
	Social class of father									
	I and II	IIIn	IIIm	IV and V	Other	Non-manual classes	Manual classes	All		
	Numbers of live births, thousands									
1970	3.6	1.7	13.5	8.6	0.9	5.3	22.1	28.3	36.4	64.7
1971	4.0	2.3	13.6	9.1	0.9	6.3	22.7	29.9	35.8	65.7
1972	4.1	2.1	12.6	9.3	0.7	6.2	21.9	28.8	33.7	62.5
1973	3.8	1.6	12.1	8.6	0.9	5.4	20.6	26.9	31.2	58.1
1974	3.8	1.6	11.9	8.8	1.0	5.4	20.7	27.1	29.4	56.5
1975	3.6	1.6	11.8	8.7	1.2	5.2	20.5	26.9	28.0	54.9
1976	3.6	1.6	12.7	8.6	0.9	5.2	21.3	27.4	26.4	53.8
1977	4.3	1.4	12.9	9.9	0.8	5.7	22.8	29.3	26.1	55.4
1978	4.8	1.9	14.8	10.2	1.1	6.8	24.9	32.8	27.8	60.6
1979	5.5	2.3	17.0	12.5	1.0	7.8	29.5	38.3	31.2	69.5
1980	5.9	2.7	19.6	14.7	1.3	8.6	34.3	44.2	33.2	77.4
1981	6.2	3.0	20.6	15.6	1.7	9.2	36.2	47.1	33.9	81.0
1982	7.2	3.5	22.6	18.1	2.0	10.7	40.7	53.4	36.5	89.9
1983	8.2	3.7	25.4	21.0	2.5	11.9	46.4	60.8	38.4	99.2
1984	9.2	4.6	29.3	23.5	3.3	13.8	52.8	69.9	40.6	110.5
1985	10.7	5.0	34.6	27.4	4.1	15.7	62.0	81.8	44.5	126.3
1986	13.3	5.8	38.3	31.8	4.4	19.1	70.0	93.5	47.8	141.3
1987	15.4	6.8	44.3	36.1	5.4	22.3	80.3	108.0	50.5	158.4
1988	18.8	8.1	51.4	39.7	5.4	26.9	91.1	123.4	53.9	177.4
1989	22.1	7.7	56.3	40.6	5.6	29.8	96.9	132.3	53.5	185.8
1990	23.1	9.5	62.7	44.6	5.6	32.6	107.3	145.2	54.8	200.0
1991	26.4	10.9	66.8	46.4	6.8	37.2	113.2	157.2	54.1	211.3
1992	28.5	11.6	69.7	46.7	8.7	40.1	116.4	165.2	50.0	215.2
1993	28.9	12.0	66.3	49.2	9.9	40.9	115.5	166.3	50.2	216.5

A5.1.2 continued

Jointly registered live births outside marriage by social class of father, England and Wales, 1970–98

Year	Jointly registered live births outside marriage								Sole registration by mother	All live births outside marriage
	Social class of father									
	I and II	IIIn	IIIm	IV and V	Other	Non-manual classes	Manual classes	All		
1994	29.5	12.3	65.7	48.0	11.0	41.8	113.7	166.5	49.0	215.5
1995	31.6	13.0	67.9	49.3	10.1	44.6	117.3	172.0	47.9	219.9
1996	33.9	13.8	70.7	52.4	10.6	47.8	123.2	181.6	51.1	232.7
1997	37.7	14.2	69.8	55.0	10.8	52.0	124.8	187.6	50.6	238.2
1998	40.2	14.6	70.2	55.2	10.6	54.8	125.3	190.7	49.0	240.6
Percentage of all live births outside marriage										
1970	5.6	2.6	20.9	13.3	1.4	8.2	34.1	43.7	56.3	
1971	6.1	3.5	20.7	13.9	1.4	9.6	34.6	45.5	54.5	
1972	6.6	3.4	20.2	14.9	1.1	9.9	35.0	46.1	53.9	
1973	6.5	2.8	20.8	14.8	1.5	9.3	35.5	46.3	53.7	
1974	6.7	2.8	21.1	15.6	1.8	9.6	36.6	48.0	52.0	
1975	6.6	2.9	21.5	15.8	2.2	9.5	37.3	49.0	51.0	
1976	6.7	3.0	23.6	16.0	1.7	9.7	39.6	51.0	49.0	
1977	7.8	2.5	23.3	17.9	1.4	10.3	41.2	52.9	47.1	
1978	7.9	3.1	24.4	16.8	1.8	11.2	41.1	54.1	45.9	
1979	7.9	3.3	24.5	18.0	1.4	11.2	42.5	55.1	44.9	
1980	7.6	3.5	25.3	19.0	1.7	11.1	44.3	57.1	42.9	
1981	7.7	3.7	25.4	19.3	2.1	11.4	44.7	58.2	41.8	
1982	8.0	3.9	25.2	20.1	2.2	11.9	45.3	59.4	40.6	
1983	8.3	3.7	25.6	21.2	2.5	12.0	46.8	61.3	38.7	
1984	8.3	4.2	26.5	21.3	3.0	12.5	47.8	63.3	36.7	
1985	8.5	4.0	27.4	21.7	3.2	12.4	49.1	64.8	35.2	
1986	9.4	4.1	27.1	22.5	3.1	13.5	49.5	66.2	33.8	
1987	9.7	4.3	28.0	22.8	3.4	14.1	50.7	68.2	31.9	

A5.1.2 *continued*

Jointly registered live births outside marriage by social class of father, England and Wales, 1970–98

Year	Jointly registered live births outside marriage								Sole registration by mother	All live births outside marriage
	Social class of father					Non-manual classes	Manual classes	All		
	I and II	IIIn	IIIm	IV and V	Other					
1988	10.6	4.6	29.0	22.4	3.0	15.2	51.4	69.6	30.4	
1989	11.9	4.1	30.3	21.9	3.0	16.0	52.2	71.2	28.8	
1990	11.6	4.8	31.4	22.3	2.8	16.3	53.7	72.6	27.4	
1991	12.5	5.2	31.6	22.0	3.2	17.6	53.6	74.4	25.6	
1992	13.2	5.4	32.4	21.7	4.0	18.6	54.1	76.1	23.9	
1993	13.3	5.5	30.6	22.7	4.6	18.9	53.3	76.8	23.2	
1994	13.7	5.7	30.5	22.3	5.1	19.4	52.8	77.2	22.8	
1995	14.4	5.9	30.9	22.4	4.6	20.3	53.3	78.2	21.8	
1996	14.6	5.9	30.4	22.5	4.6	20.5	53.0	78.1	21.9	
1997	15.8	6.0	29.3	23.1	4.5	21.8	52.4	78.8	21.2	
1998	16.7	6.1	29.2	22.9	4.4	22.8	52.1	79.3	20.4	

Data are based on a 10 per cent sample of all live births

Source: ONS/OPCS *Birth statistics, Series FM1*

This is a new table for this edition of *Birth counts*

A5.2.1

Birthweight distribution of live births by marital status of parents and social class of father, England and Wales, 1982–96

Social class of father	Birthweight, g										Number with birthweight stated	Percentage without birthweight stated	Number of live births
	Under 1,000	1,000– 1,499	1,500– 1,999	2,000– 2,499	Under 2,500	2,500– 2,999	3,000– 3,499	3,500– 3,999	4,000 and over	All			
	Percentage of live births in each class 1982–85												
Inside marriage													
I Professional	0.2	0.4	1.0	3.6	5.3	15.9	38.2	30.3	10.3	100.0	157,460	1.3	159,460
II Managerial and technical	0.2	0.5	1.0	3.8	5.5	15.6	38.2	30.3	10.4	100.0	462,580	1.2	468,220
IIn Skilled non manual	0.2	0.5	1.1	3.8	5.6	16.7	38.7	29.3	9.7	100.0	225,910	1.3	228,820
IIm Skilled manual	0.3	0.6	1.3	4.4	6.5	18.3	38.4	27.8	8.9	100.0	738,110	1.2	747,230
IV Partly skilled	0.3	0.6	1.3	5.3	7.5	20.1	38.4	26.0	8.0	100.0	302,120	1.3	306,140
V Unskilled	0.3	0.6	1.5	5.5	7.9	21.3	38.4	24.9	7.5	100.0	120,720	1.2	122,220
Other	0.3	0.6	1.2	4.4	6.4	18.1	38.7	27.8	8.9	100.0	87,370	1.1	88,370
All	0.2	0.5	1.2	4.3	6.3	17.8	38.4	28.3	9.2	100.0	2,094,270	1.2	2,120,460
Jointly registered outside marriage													
I Professional	0.4	1.0	1.2	3.7	6.4	21.7	37.7	26.1	8.1	100.0	4,830	0.8	4,870
II Managerial and technical	0.5	0.8	1.6	5.3	8.3	18.3	38.4	27.0	8.1	100.0	30,390	0.8	30,650
IIn Skilled non manual	0.5	0.6	1.8	5.5	8.5	22.5	39.4	23.1	6.5	100.0	16,960	0.2	17,000
IIm Skilled manual	0.4	1.0	1.7	5.7	8.8	21.6	39.3	24.2	6.2	100.0	112,350	0.8	113,200
IV Partly skilled	0.4	0.9	1.7	6.1	9.1	22.6	38.8	23.9	5.5	100.0	50,340	0.8	50,750
V Unskilled	0.5	0.9	1.8	6.0	9.2	23.7	40.0	21.1	5.9	100.0	40,010	0.6	40,260
Other	0.4	0.5	1.7	5.4	7.9	23.9	37.5	23.7	7.0	100.0	11,960	0.7	12,040
All	0.4	0.9	1.7	5.7	8.8	21.9	39.1	24.0	6.3	100.0	266,840	0.7	268,770
All with fathers													
I Professional	0.2	0.4	1.0	3.6	5.3	16.1	38.2	30.2	10.2	100.0	162,290	1.2	164,330
II Managerial and technical	0.2	0.5	1.1	3.9	5.7	15.8	38.2	30.1	10.2	100.0	492,970	1.2	498,870
IIn Skilled non manual	0.2	0.5	1.1	3.9	5.8	17.1	38.8	28.9	9.5	100.0	242,870	1.2	245,820
IIm Skilled manual	0.3	0.6	1.4	4.6	6.8	18.7	38.5	27.4	8.6	100.0	850,460	1.2	860,430
IV Partly skilled	0.3	0.6	1.3	5.4	7.7	20.5	38.5	25.7	7.7	100.0	352,460	1.2	356,890
V Unskilled	0.3	0.7	1.6	5.6	8.3	21.9	38.8	24.0	7.1	100.0	160,730	1.1	162,480
Other	0.3	0.6	1.3	4.5	6.6	18.8	38.6	27.3	8.7	100.0	99,330	1.1	100,410
All	0.3	0.6	1.3	4.5	6.6	18.3	38.5	27.8	8.9	100.0	2,361,110	1.2	2,389,230

A5.2.1 continued

Birthweight distribution of live births by marital status of parents and social class of father, England and Wales, 1982–96

Social class of father	Birthweight, g										Number with birthweight stated	Percentage without birthweight stated	Number of live births
	Under 1,000	1,000–1,499	1,500–1,999	2,000–2,499	Under 2,500	2,500–2,999	3,000–3,499	3,500–3,999	4,000 and over	All			
Sole registration by mother													
All	0.4	0.9	1.9	6.5	9.7	23.1	38.9	22.7	5.6	100.0	158,407	0.9	159,921
All live births	0.3	0.6	1.3	4.6	6.7	18.6	38.6	27.5	8.7	100.0	2,518,403	1.2	2,548,300
Percentage of live births in each class 1986–90													
Inside marriage													
I Professional	0.2	0.5	0.9	3.3	5.0	14.5	37.8	31.0	11.7	100.0	206,300	1.9	210,210
II Managerial and technical	0.3	0.5	1.0	3.5	5.3	15.0	37.0	31.4	11.3	100.0	620,230	1.6	630,310
IIIn Skilled non manual	0.3	0.5	1.2	3.8	5.8	15.5	37.2	30.5	11.0	100.0	262,700	1.5	266,680
IIIm Skilled manual	0.3	0.6	1.2	4.4	6.5	17.2	37.2	28.9	10.2	100.0	861,500	1.4	873,640
IV Partly skilled	0.3	0.7	1.4	4.7	7.1	18.5	37.6	27.2	9.5	100.0	338,110	1.3	342,560
V Unskilled	0.3	0.5	1.4	5.5	7.7	19.4	37.4	26.3	9.2	100.0	123,240	1.3	124,910
Other	0.3	0.6	1.4	4.0	6.2	16.8	36.8	29.1	11.1	100.0	114,260	2.1	116,690
All	0.3	0.6	1.2	4.1	6.1	16.5	37.3	29.5	10.6	100.0	2,526,340	1.5	2,565,000
Jointly registered outside marriage													
I Professional	0.6	0.6	1.6	4.6	7.4	15.9	39.4	28.8	8.4	100.0	13,980	1.5	14,190
II Managerial and technical	0.4	0.7	1.5	4.5	7.1	18.0	38.5	27.5	8.9	100.0	77,500	1.4	78,620
IIIn Skilled non manual	0.6	0.8	1.7	4.4	7.6	19.3	38.7	26.2	8.2	100.0	37,460	1.4	38,010
IIIm Skilled manual	0.4	0.8	1.6	5.5	8.2	19.6	38.7	25.6	7.9	100.0	249,730	1.4	253,330
IV Partly skilled	0.4	0.9	1.7	5.5	8.6	19.6	38.7	25.6	7.5	100.0	115,440	1.2	116,850
V Unskilled	0.5	0.9	1.8	5.9	9.1	22.5	38.1	23.1	7.2	100.0	75,330	1.1	76,130
Other	0.7	1.3	1.4	5.9	9.2	21.2	39.0	24.0	6.6	100.0	25,770	1.6	26,200
All	0.5	0.8	1.6	5.3	8.2	19.7	38.6	25.6	7.8	100.0	595,210	1.3	603,330

A5.2.1 *continued*

Birthweight distribution of live births by marital status of parents and social class of father, England and Wales, 1982–96

Social class of father	Birthweight, g										Number with birthweight stated	Percentage without birthweight stated	Number of live births
	Under 1,000	1,000–1,499	1,500–1,999	2,000–2,499	Under 2,500	2,500–2,999	3,000–3,499	3,500–3,999	4,000 and over	All			
All with fathers													
I Professional	0.3	0.5	0.9	3.4	5.1	14.6	37.9	30.9	11.5	100.0	220,280	1.8	224,400
II Managerial and technical	0.3	0.5	1.0	3.6	5.5	15.3	37.2	30.9	11.0	100.0	697,730	1.6	708,930
IIIn Skilled non manual	0.4	0.5	1.3	3.8	6.0	16.0	37.4	30.0	10.7	100.0	300,160	1.5	304,690
IIIm Skilled manual	0.3	0.6	1.3	4.7	6.9	17.7	37.6	28.1	9.7	100.0	1,111,230	1.4	1,126,970
IV Partly skilled	0.3	0.7	1.5	4.9	7.5	18.8	37.9	26.8	9.0	100.0	453,550	1.3	459,410
V Unskilled	0.4	0.7	1.5	5.6	8.2	20.6	37.7	25.1	8.5	100.0	198,570	1.2	201,040
Other	0.4	0.7	1.4	4.3	6.7	17.6	37.2	28.2	10.3	100.0	140,030	2.0	142,890
All	0.3	0.6	1.3	4.3	6.5	17.1	37.5	28.7	10.1	100.0	3,121,550	1.5	3,168,330
Sole registration by mother													
All	0.5	0.9	1.9	6.1	9.3	21.7	38.7	23.8	6.5	100.0	257,200	1.3	260,608
All live births	0.3	0.6	1.3	4.5	6.8	17.5	37.7	28.3	9.7	100.0	3,379,135	1.5	3,429,971

Percentage of live births in each class 1991–95

Social class of father	Under 1,000	1,000–1,499	1,500–1,999	2,000–2,499	Under 2,500	2,500–2,999	3,000–3,499	3,500–3,999	4,000 and over	All	Number with birthweight stated	Percentage without birthweight stated	Number of live births
Inside marriage													
I Professional	0.3	0.5	1.1	3.4	5.3	13.9	36.1	31.6	13.1	100.0	199,520	3.2	206,110
II Managerial and technical	0.3	0.5	1.2	3.7	5.7	14.3	35.7	31.7	12.6	100.0	614,370	2.7	631,550
IIIn Skilled non manual	0.3	0.6	1.3	3.7	5.9	15.3	35.8	31.0	12.1	100.0	242,830	2.7	249,550
IIIm Skilled manual	0.4	0.6	1.4	4.4	6.8	16.1	36.1	29.6	11.5	100.0	694,870	2.7	713,950
IV Partly skilled	0.4	0.7	1.4	4.9	7.3	17.7	35.8	28.4	10.9	100.0	276,070	2.9	284,180
V Unskilled	0.4	0.6	1.7	5.1	7.7	18.5	37.0	26.9	9.9	100.0	94,630	3.1	97,640
Other	0.5	0.6	1.3	4.8	7.2	17.4	36.3	28.4	10.8	100.0	109,230	3.9	113,680
All	0.4	0.6	1.3	4.1	6.4	15.7	36.0	30.2	11.8	100.0	2,231,520	2.8	2,296,660

A5.2.1 continued

Birthweight distribution of live births by marital status of parents and social class of father, England and Wales, 1982–96

Social class of father	Birthweight, g										Number with birthweight stated	Percentage without birthweight stated	Number of live births
	Under 1,000	1,000–1,499	1,500–1,999	2,000–2,499	Under 2,500	2,500–2,999	3,000–3,499	3,500–3,999	4,000 and over	All			
Jointly registered outside marriage													
I Professional	0.6	0.6	1.4	3.5	6.0	15.9	36.6	30.5	11.0	100.0	21,370	2.6	21,940
II Managerial and technical	0.4	0.6	1.3	4.4	6.7	16.8	37.4	28.6	10.6	100.0	119,720	2.5	122,780
IIIn Skilled non manual	0.7	0.9	1.5	4.8	7.9	17.8	36.6	27.7	10.0	100.0	57,460	3.2	59,350
IIIm Skilled manual	0.5	0.8	1.5	5.1	8.0	18.5	37.5	27.0	8.9	100.0	327,870	2.3	335,480
IV Partly skilled	0.5	0.8	1.7	5.3	8.4	18.9	37.5	26.4	8.8	100.0	150,240	2.1	153,500
V Unskilled	0.4	0.7	1.8	5.8	8.7	19.9	38.0	25.4	8.1	100.0	83,050	2.2	84,900
Other	0.7	0.8	2.1	5.3	9.0	20.7	38.7	24.5	7.1	100.0	43,220	4.1	45,070
All	0.5	0.8	1.6	5.1	7.9	18.5	37.5	27.0	9.1	100.0	802,930	2.4	823,020
All with fathers													
I Professional	0.3	0.5	1.1	3.4	5.4	14.1	36.1	31.5	12.9	100.0	220,890	3.1	228,050
II Managerial and technical	0.3	0.5	1.2	3.8	5.9	14.7	36.0	31.2	12.3	100.0	734,090	2.7	754,330
IIIn Skilled non manual	0.4	0.6	1.3	3.9	6.2	15.8	36.0	30.3	11.7	100.0	300,290	2.8	308,900
IIIm Skilled manual	0.4	0.7	1.4	4.6	7.2	16.8	36.6	28.8	10.7	100.0	1,022,740	2.5	1,049,430
IV Partly skilled	0.4	0.7	1.5	5.0	7.7	18.1	36.4	27.7	10.1	100.0	426,310	2.6	437,680
V Unskilled	0.4	0.6	1.7	5.4	8.2	19.2	37.4	26.2	9.0	100.0	177,680	2.7	182,540
Other	0.5	0.7	1.6	4.9	7.7	18.4	36.9	27.3	9.7	100.0	152,450	4.0	158,750
All	0.4	0.6	1.4	4.4	6.8	16.4	36.4	29.3	11.1	100.0	3,034,450	2.7	3,119,680
Sole registration by mother													
All	0.5	0.9	1.9	6.0	9.3	20.9	37.9	24.4	7.6	100.0	245,533	2.8	252,562
All live births	0.4	0.7	1.4	4.5	7.0	16.7	36.5	29.0	10.8	100.0	3,279,510	2.8	3,372,354

Data for live births are estimated from a ten per cent sample

Data for 1981 have not been included in this table because of anomalies arising following industrial action by local registrars of births and deaths

Source: Authors' analysis of ONS data

Data extract: live births 1993 (7/94), 1994 (7/95), 1995 (3/7/96), 1996 (8/4/97)

This is similar to Table A5.2 in the first edition of Birth counts

A5.2.2

Birthweight distribution of stillbirths by social class of father, England and Wales, 1982-96

Percentage of stillbirths at 28 or more weeks of gestational age in class

Social class of father	Birthweight, g										Number with birthweight stated	Percentage without birthweight stated	Number of live births
	Under 1,000	1,000– 1,499	1,500– 1,999	2,000– 2,499	Under 2,500	2,500– 2,999	3,000– 3,499	3,500– 3,999	4,000 and over	All			
1982–85													
All with fathers													
I Professional	11.4	17.2	11.5	16.6	56.8	18.0	15.8	6.6	2.8	100.0	650	3.8	676
II Managerial and technical	13.1	16.6	15.0	17.2	61.9	15.5	12.7	7.4	2.6	100.0	2,155	4.5	2,256
IIIn Skilled non manual	13.9	15.2	15.2	15.7	59.9	16.9	14.5	5.9	2.8	100.0	1,201	4.0	1,251
IIIm Skilled manual	13.4	17.2	16.7	15.9	63.2	15.7	12.2	5.4	3.5	100.0	4,575	4.3	4,780
IV Partly skilled	13.5	16.9	15.5	16.0	62.0	15.7	13.3	6.3	2.7	100.0	2,281	3.7	2,368
V Unskilled	12.8	17.7	17.0	16.4	63.9	15.5	10.9	6.1	3.6	100.0	1,113	3.6	1,155
Other	13.2	20.1	13.8	15.9	63.0	14.3	12.9	6.3	3.4	100.0	552	4.8	580
All	13.3	17.0	15.7	16.2	62.1	15.8	12.8	6.1	3.1	100.0	12,528	4.1	13,067
Sole registration by mother													
All	14.0	18.6	17.9	16.3	66.9	16.9	10.0	4.2	1.9	100.0	1,723	4.7	1,808
All stillbirths	13.3	17.2	15.9	16.2	62.7	16.0	12.5	5.9	2.9	100.0	14,251	4.2	14,875
1986–90													
All with fathers													
I Professional	14.5	14.1	14.8	16.1	59.5	14.1	14.4	8.6	3.4	100.0	765	2.4	784
II Managerial and technical	11.1	14.6	16.1	15.6	57.4	15.6	15.7	7.6	3.8	100.0	2,633	1.9	2,683
IIIn Skilled non manual	12.6	14.5	17.2	14.5	58.7	16.4	14.2	6.8	3.9	100.0	1,321	1.5	1,341
IIIm Skilled manual	13.1	17.0	15.6	15.6	61.4	15.9	12.6	6.9	3.2	100.0	5,135	2.3	5,258
IV Partly skilled	12.9	15.9	15.2	15.9	59.9	16.6	14.1	6.6	2.8	100.0	2,467	1.8	2,513
V Unskilled	13.6	17.2	17.2	15.3	63.3	15.1	11.7	7.0	2.9	100.0	1,211	1.2	1,226
Other	14.6	17.2	16.6	17.2	65.6	12.6	12.1	6.6	3.0	100.0	767	2.9	790
All	12.9	16.0	15.9	15.6	60.4	15.7	13.6	7.1	3.3	100.0	14,299	2.0	14,595
Sole registration by mother													
All	14.0	18.3	17.9	16.3	66.6	15.1	11.7	4.3	2.3	100.0	2,192	2.5	2,249
All stillbirths	13.0	16.3	16.2	15.7	61.3	15.6	13.3	6.7	3.1	100.0	16,491	2.1	16,844

251

A5.2.2 continued

Birthweight distribution of stillbirths by social class of father, England and Wales, 1982–96

Social class of father	Birthweight, g										Number with birthweight stated	Percentage without birthweight stated	Number of live births
	Under 1,000	1,000–1,499	1,500–1,999	2,000–2,499	Under 2,500	2,500–2,999	3,000–3,499	3,500–3,999	4,000 and over	All			
1991–95, excluding stillbirths at 24–27 weeks of gestational age													
All with fathers													
I Professional	15.5	14.1	14.5	12.8	56.8	15.1	14.7	9.1	4.2	100.0	760	5.6	805
II Managerial and technical	13.1	15.0	13.9	14.3	56.2	15.4	16.4	7.8	4.1	100.0	2,537	5.3	2,678
IIIn Skilled non manual	14.3	12.4	15.8	15.3	57.9	15.4	14.7	8.7	3.3	100.0	1,182	4.2	1,234
IIIm Skilled manual	14.6	15.1	13.9	15.0	58.6	16.5	14.1	7.0	3.8	100.0	4,291	4.6	4,498
IV Partly skilled	13.9	14.7	14.5	16.2	59.3	16.7	12.5	7.6	3.9	100.0	2,082	3.4	2,155
V Unskilled	13.9	13.5	16.8	15.2	59.4	17.4	14.1	6.8	2.4	100.0	1,066	3.2	1,101
Other	14.6	16.5	15.4	16.0	62.5	11.6	13.1	8.6	4.2	100.0	881	7.6	953
All	14.1	14.7	14.5	15.0	58.4	15.9	14.3	7.6	3.8	100.0	12,799	4.7	13,424
Sole registration by mother													
All	15.4	16.8	17.9	15.4	65.4	14.5	12.2	5.3	2.6	100.0	1,478	6.2	1,576
All stillbirths	14.3	14.9	14.9	15.1	59.1	15.7	14.1	7.4	3.6	100.0	14,277	4.8	15,000
1993–96, excluding stillbirths at 24–27 weeks of gestational age													
All with fathers													
I Professional	15.2	14.0	13.4	12.5	55.1	17.0	15.0	8.0	4.8	100.0	599	4.2	625
II Managerial and technical	13.5	14.0	13.7	14.5	55.8	14.6	17.0	8.5	4.2	100.0	1,987	4.7	2,084
IIIn Skilled non manual	14.6	10.7	16.5	14.3	56.1	17.5	15.2	8.9	2.4	100.0	936	3.7	972
IIIm Skilled manual	15.3	15.3	13.3	14.4	58.4	16.8	14.0	6.8	4.0	100.0	3,088	3.6	3,204
IV Partly skilled	13.3	14.6	14.2	17.1	59.3	16.6	13.6	7.0	3.7	100.0	1,637	2.6	1,681
V Unskilled	13.9	14.3	17.0	15.0	60.2	16.8	13.1	7.4	2.5	100.0	769	3.0	793
Other	12.7	16.5	15.5	16.2	60.8	15.2	10.8	9.1	4.0	100.0	692	4.4	724
All	14.2	14.4	14.3	14.9	57.9	16.3	14.4	7.6	3.8	100.0	9,708	3.7	10,083
Sole registration by mother													
All	13.2	17.9	16.6	15.7	63.3	16.2	12.5	5.6	2.4	100.0	1,041	5.7	1,104
All stillbirths	14.1	14.8	14.5	15.0	58.4	16.3	14.2	7.4	3.6	100.0	10,749	3.9	11,187

A5.2.2 continued

Birthweight distribution of stillbirths by social class of father, England and Wales, 1982–96

Percentage of stillbirths at 24 or more weeks of gestational age in each class 1993–96, including stillbirths at 24–27 weeks of gestational age

Social class of father	Birthweight, g										Number with birthweight stated	Percentage without birthweight stated	Number of live births
	Under 1,000	1,000–1,499	1,500–1,999	2,000–2,499	Under 2,500	2,500–2,999	3,000–3,499	3,500–3,999	4,000 and over	All			
All with fathers													
I Professional	33.2	12.7	10.5	9.5	65.8	13.0	11.4	6.1	3.7	100.0	790	4.1	824
II Managerial and technical	32.0	12.8	10.6	11.1	66.5	11.0	12.8	6.4	3.2	100.0	2,628	4.2	2,744
IIn Skilled non manual	33.4	10.3	12.5	10.8	67.0	13.2	11.3	6.6	1.8	100.0	1,254	3.5	1,300
IIm Skilled manual	33.8	13.5	10.2	10.9	68.4	12.7	10.6	5.1	3.1	100.0	4,087	3.5	4,234
IV Partly skilled	31.3	13.2	11.2	13.1	68.9	12.6	10.3	5.3	2.8	100.0	2,145	2.9	2,208
V Unskilled	31.3	13.6	13.1	11.5	69.4	12.9	10.1	5.7	2.0	100.0	1,003	2.9	1,033
Other	32.3	14.5	12.0	12.0	70.8	11.3	8.0	6.7	3.1	100.0	934	4.4	977
All	32.6	13.0	11.0	11.4	68.0	12.4	10.9	5.8	2.9	100.0	12,841	3.6	13,320
Sole registration by mother													
All	33.5	15.4	12.3	11.6	72.8	12.1	9.2	4.1	1.8	100.0	1,410	5.9	1,498
All stillbirths	32.7	13.2	11.2	11.4	68.5	12.3	10.8	5.6	2.8	100.0	14,251	3.8	14,818

Data for 1981 have not been included in this table because of anomalies arising following industrial action by local registrars of births and deaths

Source: Authors' analysis of OPCS data

Data extract: live births 1993 (7/94), 1994 (7/95), 1995 (3/7/96), 1996 (8/4/97)

linked   1993 (3/4/96), 1994 (18/9/96), 1995 (3/11/97)

This is similar to Table A5.2 in the first edition of *Birth counts*

A5.3.1

Singleton and multiple live births by birthweight and social class of father, England and Wales, 1982–85, 1986–90 and 1991–95

Social class of father and marital status	Percentage of live births with stated birthweight					Number with birthweight stated	Percentage without birthweight stated	All live births
	Birthweight, g							
	Under 1,000	1,000–1,499	1,500–1,999	2,000–2,499	Under 2,500			
Singletons born 1982–85								
Births within marriage and jointly registered births outside marriage								
I Professional	0.2	0.3	0.8	3.0	4.3	158,510	1.2	160,480
II Managerial and technical	0.2	0.4	0.8	3.4	4.7	482,130	1.2	487,880
IIIn Skilled non manual	0.2	0.4	0.9	3.4	4.9	237,640	1.2	240,450
IIIm Skilled manual	0.3	0.5	1.1	4.1	6.0	834,740	1.1	844,370
IV Partly skilled	0.2	0.5	1.2	4.9	6.8	345,790	1.2	350,100
V Unskilled	0.3	0.6	1.3	5.2	7.4	157,590	1.1	159,310
Other	0.2	0.5	1.0	3.9	5.7	97,320	1.0	98,340
All	0.2	0.5	1.0	4.0	5.7	2,313,720	1.2	2,340,930
Sole registration	0.4	0.8	1.6	6.1	8.8	155,788	0.9	157,271
All	0.2	0.5	1.0	4.1	5.8	2,468,001	1.2	2,497,149
Singletons born 1986–90								
Births within marriage and jointly registered births outside marriage								
I Professional	0.2	0.4	0.7	2.7	4.0	214,640	1.8	218,650
II Managerial and technical	0.2	0.4	0.8	3.0	4.4	680,900	1.6	691,890
IIIn Skilled non manual	0.3	0.4	1.0	3.3	5.0	293,250	1.5	297,690
IIIm Skilled manual	0.3	0.5	1.0	4.1	5.9	1,087,380	1.4	1,102,810
IV Partly skilled	0.3	0.6	1.2	4.4	6.5	444,350	1.3	450,070
V Unskilled	0.3	0.5	1.3	5.1	7.3	194,670	1.2	197,070
Other	0.3	0.6	1.0	3.9	5.8	136,970	2.0	139,790
All	0.3	0.5	1.0	3.8	5.5	3,052,160	1.5	3,097,970
Sole registration	0.4	0.8	1.6	5.6	8.4	252,686	1.3	256,015
All	0.3	0.5	1.0	3.9	5.7	3,304,689	1.5	3,354,355

A5.3.1 *continued*

Singleton and multiple live births by birthweight and social class of father, England and Wales, 1982–85, 1986–90 and 1991–95

Social class of father and marital status	Percentage of live births with stated birthweight — Birthweight, g					Number with birthweight stated	Percentage without birthweight stated	All live births
	Under 1,000	1,000–1,499	1,500–1,999	2,000–2,499	Under 2,500			
Singletons born 1991–95								
Births within marriage and jointly registered births outside marriage								
I Professional	0.2	0.4	0.8	2.7	4.0	214,150	3.1	221,040
II Managerial and technical	0.2	0.4	0.8	3.1	4.5	712,780	2.7	732,250
IIIn Skilled non manual	0.3	0.5	1.0	3.3	5.0	292,580	2.8	300,970
IIIm Skilled manual	0.3	0.6	1.1	4.0	5.9	996,900	2.5	1,022,890
IV Partly skilled	0.4	0.6	1.2	4.4	6.5	416,030	2.6	427,160
V Unskilled	0.4	0.5	1.4	4.8	7.1	173,400	2.7	178,140
Other	0.5	0.5	1.2	4.4	6.6	148,870	4.0	155,020
All	0.3	0.5	1.0	3.7	5.5	2,954,710	2.7	3,037,470
Sole registration	0.4	0.8	1.6	5.5	8.2	240,416	2.8	247,275
All	0.3	0.5	1.1	3.9	5.7	3,195,965	2.7	3,286,125
Multiples born 1982–85								
Births within marriage and jointly registered births outside marriage								
I Professional	2.4	4.2	11.4	31.5	49.5	3,780	1.8	3,850
II Managerial and technical	2.1	4.9	12.3	28.7	48.0	10,840	1.4	10,990
IIIn Skilled non manual	1.7	5.5	13.8	26.8	47.8	5,230	2.6	5,370
IIIm Skilled manual	2.9	6.0	14.6	30.2	53.8	15,720	2.1	16,060
IV Partly skilled	3.0	5.7	10.8	33.6	53.1	6,670	1.8	6,790
V Unskilled	2.5	6.1	16.2	27.4	52.2	3,140	0.9	3,170
Other	2.5	2.5	16.4	30.3	51.7	2,010	2.9	2,070
All	2.5	5.4	13.4	29.9	51.2	47,390	1.9	48,300
Sole registration	3.7	7.5	17.0	32.4	60.6	2,619	1.2	2,650
All	2.5	5.4	13.6	30.0	51.5	50,402	1.5	51,151

A5.3.1 continued

Singleton and multiple live births by birthweight and social class of father, England and Wales, 1982–85, 1986–90 and 1991–95

Social class of father and marital status	Percentage of live births with stated birthweight					Number with birthweight stated	Percentage without birthweight stated	All live births
	Birthweight, g							
	Under 1,000	1,000–1,499	1,500–1,999	2,000–2,499	Under 2,500			
Multiples born 1986–90								
Births within marriage and jointly registered births outside marriage								
I Professional	2.5	5.5	10.1	29.8	47.9	5,640	1.9	5,750
II Managerial and technical	2.9	5.9	12.2	28.3	49.3	16,830	1.2	17,040
IIIn Skilled non manual	2.2	5.6	13.2	27.9	48.9	6,910	1.3	7,000
IIIm Skilled manual	3.6	5.6	14.0	31.1	54.3	23,850	1.3	24,160
IV Partly skilled	3.9	6.4	16.1	29.6	56.0	9,200	1.5	9,340
V Unskilled	3.6	6.7	14.4	30.5	55.1	3,900	1.8	3,970
Other	2.6	6.2	17.0	25.2	51.0	3,060	1.3	3,100
All	3.2	5.9	13.6	29.5	52.2	69,390	1.4	70,360
Sole registration	3.9	7.5	16.5	33.0	60.8	4,514	1.7	4,593
All	3.0	5.9	14.1	29.8	52.8	74,446	1.5	75,616
Multiples born 1991–95								
Births within marriage and jointly registered births outside marriage								
I Professional	3.4	5.0	13.1	27.6	49.1	6,740	3.9	7,010
II Managerial and technical	2.8	5.3	13.6	29.8	51.5	21,310	3.5	22,080
IIn Skilled non manual	4.0	5.3	13.9	28.5	51.8	7,710	2.8	7,930
IIIm Skilled manual	4.2	6.3	15.2	29.7	55.4	25,840	2.6	26,540
IV Partly skilled	2.3	5.5	14.9	32.5	55.3	10,280	2.3	10,520
V Unskilled	1.6	4.4	17.3	29.7	53.0	4,280	2.7	4,400
Other	3.6	7.5	14.8	28.2	54.2	3,580	4.0	3,730
All	3.3	5.7	14.5	29.7	53.3	79,740	3.0	82,210
Sole registration	3.9	7.1	17.0	31.9	59.8	5,117	3.2	5,287
All	3.3	6.1	14.3	29.6	53.3	83,545	3.1	86,229

Data for live births are estimated from a ten per cent sample

Data for 1981 have not been included in this table because of anomalies arising following industrial action by local registrars of births and deaths

Source: Authors' analysis of ONS/OPCS data

Data extract: live births 1993 (7/94), 1994 (7/95), 1995 (3/7/96), 1996 (8/4/97)

This is similar to Table A5.6 in the first edition of Birth counts

A5.3.2

Singleton and multiple stillbirths by birthweight and social class of father, England and Wales, 1982–85, 1986–90, 1991–95 and 1993–96

Social class of father and marital status	Percentage of live births with stated birthweight					Number with birthweight stated	Percentage without birthweight stated	All stillbirths
	Birthweight, g							
	Under 1,000	1,000–1,499	1,500–1,999	2,000–2,499	Under 2,500			
Singletons born 1982–85								
Births within marriage and jointly registered births outside marriage								
I Professional	11.2	15.1	10.9	16.4	53.6	578	3.5	599
II Managerial and technical	12.4	16.1	13.7	17.5	59.7	1,978	4.3	2,067
IIIn Skilled non manual	12.7	14.7	14.6	15.2	57.2	1,108	3.9	1,153
IIIm Skilled manual	12.3	16.6	16.4	16.0	61.4	4,265	3.9	4,439
IV Partly skilled	13.2	16.5	14.9	16.1	60.7	2,165	3.5	2,243
V Unskilled	11.7	17.6	17.0	16.6	62.9	1,056	3.4	1,093
Other	12.9	19.4	12.9	15.9	61.0	521	5.1	549
All	12.4	16.5	15.1	16.2	60.3	11,671	3.9	12,143
Sole registration	13.5	18.8	17.8	16.5	66.6	1,662	4.8	1,745
All	12.6	16.8	15.5	16.3	61.1	13,334	4.0	13,889
Singletons born 1986–90								
Births within marriage and jointly registered births outside marriage								
I Professional	13.5	13.0	13.7	16.0	56.2	694	2.0	708
II Managerial and technical	9.8	13.8	15.2	15.6	54.4	2,403	1.7	2,445
IIIn Skilled non manual	11.1	14.1	17.0	14.5	56.7	1,206	1.4	1,223
IIIm Skilled manual	12.3	15.9	15.2	15.7	59.0	4,766	2.0	4,862
IV Partly skilled	12.2	14.6	14.8	15.9	57.6	2,302	1.6	2,339
V Unskilled	13.1	16.9	16.0	15.7	61.8	1,141	1.0	1,153
Other	13.2	16.8	15.9	17.5	63.4	710	2.9	731
All	11.9	15.1	15.3	15.7	58.0	13,222	1.8	13,461
Sole registration	13.1	18.1	18.0	16.5	65.6	2,098	2.6	2,153
All	12.0	15.5	15.7	15.8	59.1	15,320	1.9	15,614

A5.3.2 continued

Singleton and multiple stillbirths by birthweight and social class of father, England and Wales, 1982-85, 1986-90, 1991-95 and 1993-96

Social class of father and marital status	Percentage of live births with stated birthweight Birthweight, g					Number with birthweight stated	Percentage without birthweight stated	All stillbirths
	Under 1,000	1,000–1,499	1,500–1,999	2,000–2,499	Under 2,500			
Singletons born 1991-95								
Births within marriage and jointly registered births outside marriage								
I Professional	11.7	13.5	15.0	13.1	53.3	673	4.5	705
II Managerial and technical	11.0	14.2	13.4	14.1	52.7	2,299	4.9	2,418
IIIn Skilled non manual	12.6	12.0	15.4	15.1	55.0	1,087	4.5	1,138
IIIm Skilled manual	13.0	14.6	13.3	15.1	55.9	3,954	4.3	4,130
IV Partly skilled	12.6	14.0	14.2	16.3	57.0	1,946	3.1	2,009
V Unskilled	12.8	12.4	16.8	15.1	57.1	986	3.2	1,019
Other	12.6	16.5	15.4	15.8	60.3	824	6.9	885
All	12.4	14.1	14.2	15.0	55.7	11,769	4.3	12,304
Sole registration	14.0	16.8	17.8	15.6	64.2	1,419	6.3	1,514
All	12.6	14.4	14.6	15.1	56.6	13,188	4.6	13,818
Singletons born 1993-96 at 24 or more weeks of gestation								
Births within marriage and jointly registered births outside marriage								
I Professional	30.2	12.6	11.1	9.5	63.4	696	2.9	717
II Managerial and technical	28.9	12.5	10.8	11.0	63.2	2,342	3.9	2,436
IIIn Skilled non manual	31.3	10.0	12.2	10.7	64.3	1,147	3.4	1,187
IIIm Skilled manual	31.6	13.1	10.0	11.2	66.0	3,736	3.1	3,854
IV Partly skilled	29.9	12.7	10.9	13.2	66.7	1,983	2.7	2,039
V Unskilled	29.8	12.8	13.2	11.6	67.3	924	2.8	951
Other	31.2	14.2	12.0	12.1	69.4	876	3.8	911
All	30.5	12.6	11.0	11.4	65.6	11,704	3.2	12,095
Sole registration	32.1	15.6	12.4	11.8	71.9	1,344	5.9	1,428
All	30.7	12.9	11.2	11.5	66.2	13,048	3.5	13,523

A5.3.2 continued

Singleton and multiple stillbirths by birthweight and social class of father, England and Wales, 1982–85, 1986–90, 1991–95 and 1993–96

Social class of father and marital status	Percentage of live births with stated birthweight					Number with birthweight stated	Percentage without birthweight stated	All stillbirths
	Birthweight, g							
	Under 1,000	1,000–1,499	1,500–1,999	2,000–2,499	Under 2,500			
Multiples born 1982–85								
Births within marriage and jointly registered births outside marriage								
I Professional	12.5	34.7	16.7	18.1	81.9	72	6.5	77
II Managerial and technical	21.5	22.0	29.4	14.1	87.0	177	6.3	189
IIIn Skilled non manual	28.0	20.4	21.5	21.5	91.4	93	5.1	98
IIIm Skilled manual	27.4	24.8	20.6	15.5	88.4	310	9.1	341
IV Partly skilled	20.7	24.1	25.9	15.5	86.2	116	7.2	125
V Unskilled	33.3	19.3	17.5	12.3	82.5	57	8.1	62
Other	19.4	32.3	29.0	16.1	96.8	31	0.0	31
All	24.2	24.4	23.0	15.9	87.5	856	7.3	923
Sole registration	27.9	14.8	21.3	9.8	73.8	61	3.2	63
All	24.4	23.8	22.9	15.5	86.6	917	7.0	986
Multiples born 1986–90								
Births within marriage and jointly registered births outside marriage								
I Professional	23.9	25.4	25.4	16.9	91.5	71	6.6	76
II Managerial and technical	25.2	23.0	24.8	15.7	88.7	230	3.4	238
IIIn Skilled non manual	28.7	18.3	19.1	13.9	80.0	115	2.5	118
IIIm Skilled manual	24.7	31.2	21.4	15.4	92.7	369	6.8	396
IV Partly skilled	22.4	33.3	20.0	15.8	91.5	165	5.2	174
V Unskilled	21.4	21.4	35.7	8.6	87.1	70	4.1	73
Other	31.6	22.8	24.6	14.0	93.0	57	3.4	59
All	25.0	26.9	23.0	14.9	89.9	1,077	5.0	1,134
Sole registration	35.1	24.5	16.0	11.7	87.2	94	2.1	96
All	25.8	26.7	22.5	14.7	89.7	1,171	4.8	1,230

A5.3.2 continued

Singleton and multiple stillbirths by birthweight and social class of father, England and Wales, 1982–85, 1986–90, 1991–95 and 1993–96

Social class of father and marital status	Percentage of live births with stated birthweight Birthweight, g					Number with birthweight stated	Percentage without birthweight stated	All stillbirths
	Under 1,000	1,000–1,499	1,500–1,999	2,000–2,499	Under 2,500			
Multiples born 1991–95								
Births within marriage and jointly registered births outside marriage								
I Professional	44.8	18.4	10.3	10.3	83.9	87	13.0	100
II Managerial and technical	32.8	22.7	18.5	16.4	90.3	238	8.5	260
IIn Skilled non manual	33.7	17.9	21.1	17.9	90.5	95	1.0	96
IIm Skilled manual	33.2	21.4	21.1	13.9	89.6	337	8.4	368
IV Partly skilled	33.1	25.7	18.4	14.7	91.9	136	6.8	146
V Unskilled	27.5	27.5	16.3	16.3	87.5	80	2.4	82
Other	43.9	15.8	15.8	19.3	94.7	57	16.2	68
All	34.3	21.8	18.5	15.1	89.8	1,030	8.0	1,120
Sole registration	50.8	15.3	18.6	10.2	94.9	59	4.8	62
All	35.2	21.5	18.5	14.9	90.1	1,089	7.9	1,182
Multiples born 1993–96 at 24 or more weeks of gestation								
Births within marriage and jointly registered births outside marriage								
I Professional	55.3	12.8	6.4	9.6	84.0	94	12.1	107
II Managerial and technical	57.0	15.0	8.7	12.2	93.0	286	7.1	308
IIn Skilled non manual	56.1	13.1	15.9	11.2	96.3	107	5.3	113
IIm Skilled manual	56.7	17.4	12.0	8.0	94.0	351	7.6	380
IV Partly skilled	49.4	19.1	14.2	13.0	95.7	162	4.1	169
V Unskilled	49.4	22.8	11.4	10.1	93.7	79	3.7	82
Other	50.0	19.0	12.1	10.3	91.4	58	12.1	66
All	54.7	16.7	11.3	10.5	93.2	1,137	7.2	1,225
Sole registration	62.1	12.1	10.6	7.6	92.4	66	5.7	70
All	55.1	16.5	11.3	10.3	93.2	1,203	7.1	1,295

Data for 1981 have not been included in this table because of anomalies arising following industrial action by local registrars of births and deaths

Source: Authors' analysis of ONS/OPCS data

Data extract: live births 1993 (7/94), 1994 (7/95), 1995 (3/7/96), 1996 (8/4/97)

linked   1993 (3/4/96), 1994 (18/9/96), 1995 (3/11/97)

This is similar to Table A5.6 in the first edition of Birth counts

A5.3.3

Singleton and multiple births by birthweight and social class, Scotland, 1995

| | Birthweight, g | | | | | | | | | | | | |
	Under 500	500–999	1,000–1,499	1,500–1,999	2,000–2,499	2,500–2,999	3,000–3,499	3,500–3,999	4,000–4,499	4,500 and over	Total	Under 1,500	Under 2,500
	Numbers of live and stillbirths											Percentages of births	
	Singleton												
All singleton births	40	190	339	656	2,232	9,188	20,987	17,584	5,877	1,053	58,146	0.98	5.95
Births within marriage by social class of father*													
Professional	0	5	20	27	86	435	1,366	1,403	536	103	3,981	0.63	3.47
Executive	0	21	43	100	305	1,411	3,898	3,763	1,340	245	11,126	0.58	4.22
Skilled manual	4	34	60	124	450	1,897	4,611	3,831	1,355	258	12,624	0.78	5.32
Skilled non-manual	0	12	27	80	280	1,216	2,777	2,354	750	110	7,606	0.51	5.25
Semi-skilled	2	19	47	108	373	1,451	2,967	2,356	738	144	8,205	0.83	6.69
Unskilled	0	6	18	34	136	611	1,204	974	316	55	3,354	0.72	5.78
Inadequate description	0	5	7	7	18	97	223	167	45	7	576	2.08	6.42
Not stated	1	11	30	48	212	774	1,460	1,059	289	49	3,933	1.07	7.68
All inside marriage	7	113	252	528	1,860	7,892	18,506	15,907	5,369	971	51,405	0.72	5.37
Births outside marriage by social class of mother*													
Professional	0	0	0	0	0	0	3	6	0	0	9	–	–
Executive	0	0	1	2	10	57	94	73	21	3	261	0.38	4.98
Skilled manual	0	0	3	6	22	92	157	89	27	5	401	0.75	7.73
Skilled non-manual	0	0	5	11	42	155	289	200	45	15	762	0.66	7.61
Semi-skilled	0	0	9	10	51	189	329	184	52	7	831	1.08	8.42
Unskilled	0	0	0	2	13	37	65	45	18	0	180	–	8.33
Inadequate description	0	0	0	0	4	11	12	13	1	1	42	–	9.52
Not stated	33	77	69	97	230	755	1,532	1,067	344	51	4,255	4.21	11.89
All outside marriage	33	77	87	128	372	1,296	2,481	1,677	508	82	6,741	2.92	10.34

A5.3.3 continued

Singleton and multiple births by birthweight and social class, Scotland, 1995

	Birthweight, g										Total	Under 1,500	Under 2,500
	Under 500	500–999	1,000–1,499	1,500–1,999	2,000–2,499	2,500–2,999	3,000–3,499	3,500–3,999	4,000–4,499	4,500 and over			
All multiple births	7	61	115	245	499	519	233	16	3	1	1,699	10.77	54.56
Births within marriage by social class of father*													
Professional	0	5	13	11	31	50	27	1	0	0	138	13.04	43.48
Executive	2	6	22	51	112	128	65	3	0	0	389	7.71	49.61
Skilled manual	3	13	21	61	121	125	47	4	1	0	396	9.34	55.30
Skilled non-manual	1	14	13	25	47	56	19	3	0	0	178	15.73	56.18
Semi-skilled	0	9	20	37	65	65	35	4	2	1	238	12.18	55.04
Unskilled	1	4	12	13	37	35	13	0	0	0	115	14.78	58.26
Inadequate description	0	0	1	3	8	7	0	1	0	0	20	5.00	60.00
Not stated	0	4	4	16	35	26	16	0	0	0	101	7.92	58.42
All inside marriage	7	55	106	217	456	492	222	16	3	1	1,575	10.67	53.40
Births outside marriage by social class of mother*													
Professional	0	0	0	0	0	0	0	0	0	0	0	–	–
Executive	0	0	0	3	1	1	1	0	0	0	6	–	66.67
Skilled manual	0	0	0	3	1	0	0	0	0	0	4	–	100.00
Skilled non-manual	0	0	0	1	8	1	2	0	0	0	12	–	75.00
Semi-skilled	0	2	0	2	6	2	0	0	0	0	12	16.67	83.33
Unskilled	0	1	1	1	1	0	0	0	0	0	4	50.00	100.00
Inadequate description	0	0	0	0	2	1	1	0	0	0	4	–	50.00
Not stated	0	3	8	18	24	22	7	0	0	0	82	13.41	64.63
All outside marriage	0	6	9	28	43	27	11	0	0	0	124	12.10	69.35

Singleton and multiple births by birthweight and social class, Scotland, 1995

	Birthweight, g										Total	Under 1,500	Under 2,500
	Under 500	500–999	1,000–1,499	1,500–1,999	2,000–2,499	2,500–2,999	3,000–3,499	3,500–3,999	4,000–4,499	4,500 and over			
All births	47	251	454	901	2,731	9,707	21,220	17,600	5,880	1,054	59,845	1.26	7.33
Births within marriage by social class of father*													
Professional	0	10	33	38	117	485	1,393	1,404	536	103	4,119	1.04	4.81
Executive	2	27	65	151	417	1,539	3,963	3,766	1,340	245	11,515	0.82	5.75
Skilled manual	7	47	81	185	571	2,022	4,658	3,835	1,356	258	13,020	1.04	6.84
Skilled non-manual	1	26	40	105	327	1,272	2,796	2,357	750	110	7,784	0.86	6.41
Semi-skilled	2	28	67	145	438	1,516	3,002	2,360	740	145	8,443	1.15	8.05
Unskilled	1	10	30	47	173	646	1,217	974	316	55	3,469	1.18	7.52
Inadequate description	0	5	8	10	26	104	223	168	45	7	596	2.18	8.22
Not stated	1	15	34	64	247	800	1,476	1,059	289	49	4,034	1.24	8.95
All inside marriage	14	168	358	745	2,316	8,384	18,728	15,923	5,372	972	52,980	1.02	6.80
Births outside marriage by social class of mother*													
Professional	0	0	0	0	0	0	3	6	0	0	9	–	–
Executive	0	0	1	5	11	58	95	73	21	3	267	0.37	6.37
Skilled manual	0	0	3	9	23	92	157	89	27	5	405	0.74	8.64
Skilled non-manual	0	0	5	12	50	156	291	200	45	15	774	0.65	8.66
Semi-skilled	0	2	9	12	57	191	329	184	52	7	843	1.30	9.49
Unskilled	0	1	1	3	14	37	65	45	18	0	184	1.09	10.33
Inadequate description	0	0	0	0	6	12	13	13	1	1	46	0.00	13.04
Not stated	33	80	77	115	254	777	1,539	1,067	344	51	4,337	4.38	12.89
All outside marriage	33	83	96	156	415	1,323	2,492	1,677	508	82	6,865	3.09	11.41

* The social class information provided is based on information supplied by the General Register Office for Scotland and is based on employment status, occupation and marital status. For married women, the social class of the father is used; for unmarried women, the social class of the mother is used. For those who are currently unemployed, their previous occupation (if any) is used.

~ Data are available only for the first baby of a multiple.

Source: ISD, Scottish Morbidity Record SMR 2.

This was Table A5.6 in the first edition of *Birth counts*

A5.3.4

Singleton and multiple births by gestational age and social class, Scotland, 1990–95

	Estimated gestational age, weeks						Percentages of births	
	20–27	28–31	32–36	37 and over	Not stated	Total	Before 32 weeks	Before 37 weeks
Numbers of live and stillbirths								
Singleton								
All singletons	1,253	2,665	17,773	348,651	1,300	371,642	1.06	5.86
Births within marriage by social class of father*								
Professional	33	107	891	24,112	44	25,187	0.56	4.10
Executive	135	333	2,715	65,696	164	69,043	0.68	4.62
Skilled manual	196	525	3,733	76,864	285	81,603	0.89	5.48
Skilled non-manual	115	259	2,149	42,793	159	45,475	0.83	5.57
Semi-skilled	183	393	2,908	56,864	266	60,614	0.95	5.77
Unskilled	64	204	1,361	26,568	118	28,315	0.95	5.78
Inadequate description	10	23	181	3,313	6	3,533	0.94	6.07
Not stated	78	164	1,207	19,882	82	21,413	1.13	6.79
All inside marriage	814	2,008	15,145	316,092	1,124	335,183	0.84	5.38
Births outside marriage by social class of mother*								
Professional	0	0	1	65	1	67	-	1.52
Executive	6	11	86	1,564	11	1,678	1.02	6.18
Skilled manual	11	21	182	3,040	23	3,277	0.98	6.58
Skilled non-manual	10	39	299	4,601	30	4,979	0.99	7.03
Semi-skilled	21	37	329	5,011	32	5,430	1.07	7.17
Unskilled	9	13	120	2,010	15	2,167	1.02	6.60
Inadequate description	2	5	16	271	1	295	2.38	7.82
Not stated	380	531	1,595	15,997	63	18,566	4.92	13.54
All outside marriage	439	657	2,628	32,559	176	36,459	3.02	10.26

A5.3.4 continued

Singleton and multiple births by gestational age and social class, Scotland, 1990–95

	Estimated gestational age, weeks						Before 32 weeks	Before 37 weeks
	20–27	28–31	32–36	37 and over	Not stated	Total		
Multiple								
All multiples	726	1,222	7,522	9,562	10	19,042	10.24	49.76
Births within marriage by social class of father*								
Professional	16	58	566	916	4	1,560	4.76	41.13
Executive	96	256	1,558	2,132	0	4,042	8.71	47.25
Skilled manual	174	300	1,672	2,212	0	4,358	10.88	49.24
Skilled non-manual	112	140	908	1,068	2	2,230	11.31	52.06
Semi-skilled	122	188	1,094	1,484	0	2,888	10.73	48.61
Unskilled	48	82	640	670	0	1,440	9.03	53.47
Inadequate description	4	14	92	64	0	174	10.34	63.22
Not stated	68	56	414	480	0	1,018	12.18	52.85
All inside marriage	640	1,094	6,944	9,026	6	17,710	9.79	49.02
Births outside marriage by social class of mother*								
Professional	0	0	0	8	0	8	-	56.52
Executive	0	0	52	40	0	92	10.26	46.15
Skilled manual	8	8	56	84	0	156	17.70	59.29
Skilled non-manual	16	24	94	92	0	226	16.33	61.22
Semi-skilled	12	20	88	76	0	196	19.23	46.15
Unskilled	4	16	28	56	4	108	0.00	60.00
Inadequate description	0	0	12	8	0	20	20.15	67.30
Not stated	46	60	248	172	0	526	16.11	59.64
All outside marriage	86	128	578	536	4	1,332		
All singletons and multiples								
Inside marriage	1,454	3,102	22,089	325,118	1,130	352,893	1.30	7.57
Outside marriage	525	785	3,206	33,095	180	37,791	3.48	12.01

* The social class information provided is based on information supplied by the General Register Office for Scotland and is based on employment status, occupation and marital status. For married women, the social class of the father is used; for unmarried women, the social class of the mother is used. For those who are currently unemployed, their previous occupation, if any, is used.

Source: ISD, Scottish Morbidity Record SMR 2.

This is a new table for this edition of *Birth counts*

A5.4.1

Stillbirths by social class of father, England and Wales, 1979–96

Year of birth	All births within marriage and jointly registered births outside marriage								Sole registrations by mother
	Social class of father							All#	All#
	I	II	IIIn	IIIm	IV	V	Others		

Numbers

Stillbirths at 28 or more weeks of gestation, all causes

Year of birth	I	II	IIIn	IIIm	IV	V	Others	All#	Sole All#
1979	204	785	424	1,800	885	350	171	4,619	513	5,132
1980	209	769	397	1,686	760	354	151	4,326	456	4,782
1981	195	702	345	1,393	622	316	151	3,724	483	4,207
1982	182	618	349	1,310	635	271	144	3,510	433	3,943
1983	169	581	300	1,192	586	271	108	3,207	425	3,632
1984	161	541	288	1,144	580	320	145	3,179	471	3,650
1985	164	516	314	1,134	567	293	183	3,171	479	3,650
1986	155	518	300	1,124	504	270	194	3,065	483	3,548
1987	156	537	267	1,065	559	244	143	2,971	450	3,421
1988	163	525	279	1,028	486	261	159	2,901	484	3,385
1989	135	563	241	993	455	244	157	2,788	443	3,231
1990	175	540	254	1,048	509	207	137	2,870	389	3,259
1991	156	533	248	1,039	452	247	200	2,875	380	3,255
1992	173	574	227	987	435	206	201	2,803	353	3,156
1993	169	526	268	840	424	240	201	2,668	292	2,960
1994	157	567	267	839	412	213	172	2,627	298	2,925
1995	150	478	224	793	432	195	179	2,451	253	2,704
1996	149	513	213	732	413	145	172	2,337	261	2,598

Stillbirths at 24 or more weeks of gestation, all causes

Year of birth	I	II	IIIn	IIIm	IV	V	Others	All#	Sole All#
1993	222	683	351	1,117	558	292	249	3,472	394	3,866
1994	207	715	346	1,107	536	270	238	3,419	397	3,816
1995	198	626	311	1,019	572	272	252	3,250	347	3,597
1996	197	720	292	991	542	199	238	3,179	360	3,539

A5.4.1 continued

Stillbirths by social class of father, England and Wales, 1979–96

Year of birth	All births within marriage and jointly registered births outside marriage								Sole registrations by mother	
	Social class of father							All#		All#
	I	II	IIIn	IIIm	IV	V	Others			
Rates per thousand total births										
Stillbirths at 28 or more weeks of gestation, all causes										
1979	5.2	6.2	6.7	7.9	9.2	9.1	9.0	7.6	16.2	8.0
1980	5.0	6.0	6.1	7.2	7.8	9.1	7.1	6.9	13.5	7.2
1981	:	:	:	:	:	:	:	:	:	:
1982	4.3	4.9	5.6	6.1	7.1	6.9	6.5	5.9	11.7	6.3
1983	4.2	4.7	4.9	5.5	6.6	6.6	4.6	5.4	10.9	5.7
1984	3.9	4.4	4.6	5.3	6.4	7.9	5.6	5.3	11.5	5.7
1985	3.9	4.0	5.1	5.1	6.2	6.8	6.2	5.2	10.7	5.5
1986	3.6	3.9	4.9	5.1	5.5	6.4	6.8	5.0	10.0	5.3
1987	3.6	3.9	4.4	4.7	6.0	5.8	4.8	4.7	8.8	5.0
1988	3.7	3.7	4.4	4.5	5.2	6.3	5.2	4.5	8.9	4.9
1989	2.9	3.8	4.2	4.4	5.0	6.4	5.6	4.4	8.2	4.7
1990	3.7	3.5	4.0	4.5	5.5	5.4	5.1	4.4	7.0	4.6
1991	3.4	3.4	4.0	4.5	5.2	6.4	6.7	4.4	7.0	4.6
1992	3.8	3.7	3.7	4.4	5.0	5.5	6.2	4.4	6.8	4.6
1993	3.7	3.5	4.3	4.1	4.7	6.6	5.9	4.3	5.8	4.4
1994	3.4	3.8	4.2	4.2	4.7	5.9	5.4	4.2	6.0	4.4
1995	3.3	3.2	3.7	4.1	4.9	5.7	5.7	4.1	5.3	4.2
1996	3.3	3.4	3.4	3.9	4.5	4.6	5.6	3.9	5.1	4.0
Stillbirths at 24 or more weeks of gestation, all causes										
1993	4.8	4.6	5.6	5.4	6.2	8.0	7.3	5.6	7.8	5.7
1994	4.4	4.8	5.5	5.5	6.1	7.4	7.5	5.5	8.0	5.7
1995	4.3	4.2	5.1	5.3	6.5	7.9	8.0	5.4	7.2	5.5
1996	4.4	4.7	4.7	5.2	5.9	6.4	7.7	5.3	7.0	5.4
Stillbirths at 28 or more weeks of gestation, all causes except congenital anomalies, ONS cause group 1										
1979	4.0	5.0	5.5	6.5	7.3	7.5	7.3	6.1	13.8	6.5
1980	4.2	5.0	5.0	6.0	6.3	7.3	6.0	5.7	12.0	6.0

A5.4.1 *continued*

Stillbirths by social class of father, England and Wales, 1979–96

Year of birth	All births within marriage and jointly registered births outside marriage								Sole registrations by mother	All#
	Social class of father									
	I	II	IIIn	IIIm	IV	V	Others	All#		
1981	::	::	::	::	::	::	::	::	::	::
1982	3.8	4.3	4.8	5.3	6.3	5.9	5.6	5.2	10.7	5.5
1983	3.8	4.2	4.4	4.9	5.6	5.8	4.2	4.8	9.8	5.1
1984	3.6	4.1	4.3	4.8	5.8	7.1	5.3	4.8	10.4	5.2
1985	3.6	3.7	4.6	4.8	5.7	6.2	5.6	4.7	9.8	5.1
1986	3.3	3.6	4.4	4.7	4.9	5.8	6.0	4.5	8.9	4.8
1987	3.1	3.6	4.0	4.3	5.4	5.2	4.4	4.2	8.0	4.5
1988	3.2	3.4	4.0	4.2	4.7	5.6	4.8	4.1	8.0	4.4
1989	2.5	3.4	3.7	4.0	4.7	5.8	5.1	4.0	7.5	4.2
1990	3.2	3.1	3.7	4.2	5.0	5.0	4.6	4.0	6.5	4.2
1991	3.1	3.1	3.7	4.1	4.9	6.0	6.0	4.1	6.4	4.3
1992	3.5	3.4	3.6	4.0	4.5	4.9	5.4	4.0	6.2	4.2
1993	3.5	3.2	3.9	3.8	4.4	6.2	5.3	4.0	5.4	4.1
1994	3.0	3.4	3.8	3.9	4.3	5.4	5.1	3.9	5.6	4.0
1995	2.9	3.0	3.5	3.8	4.6	5.2	5.0	3.8	4.8	3.8
1996	3.6	3.6	3.7	4.2	4.8	5.2	6.1	4.2	5.5	4.3
Stillbirths at 24 or more weeks of gestation, all causes except congenital anomalies, ONS cause group 1										
1993	4.5	4.2	5.1	5.0	5.7	7.5	6.6	5.1	7.2	5.3
1994	4.0	4.2	4.8	5.0	5.5	6.8	7.0	5.0	7.1	5.2
1995	3.8	3.8	4.7	4.8	6.0	7.2	7.1	4.9	6.6	5.0
1996	4.8	5.2	5.2	5.8	6.4	7.1	8.7	5.8	7.6	6.0

Includes cases where the father's social class was not stated

Rates for 1981 have not been included in this table because of anomalies arising following industrial action by local registrars of births and deaths

Source: Authors' analysis of ONS/OPCS data

Data extract: live births 1993 (7/94), 1994 (7/95), 1995 (3/7/96), 1996 (8/4/97)

linked   1993 (3/4/96), 1994 (18/9/96), 1995 (3/11/97)

This is similar to Table A5.3 in the first edition of *Birth counts*

A5.4.2

Perinatal mortality by social class of father, England and Wales, 1979–95

Year of birth	Social class of father							All#	Sole registrations by mother	All#
	I	II	IIIn	IIIm	IV	V	Others			

All births within marriage and jointly registered births outside marriage

Numbers
Perinatal deaths, all causes
Early neonatal deaths plus stillbirths at 28 or more weeks of gestation

Year	I	II	IIIn	IIIm	IV	V	Others	All#	Sole reg.	All#
1979	406	1,474	800	3,192	1,596	687	362	8,517	870	9,387
1980	405	1,429	767	3,012	1,418	638	354	8,023	776	8,799
1981	347	1,228	621	2,509	1,147	570	328	6,750	760	7,510
1982	339	1,121	640	2,294	1,151	513	301	6,360	703	7,063
1983	302	1,055	561	2,132	1,078	495	259	5,882	686	6,568
1984	293	981	512	2,093	1,040	544	278	5,741	704	6,445
1985	317	973	542	2,028	1,006	516	358	5,740	727	6,467
1986	302	950	526	2,001	909	489	375	5,562	769	6,331
1987	302	976	473	1,922	947	444	295	5,369	709	6,078
1988	299	976	495	1,863	888	452	316	5,299	761	6,060
1989	270	1,037	451	1,756	840	403	289	5,048	684	5,732
1990*	321	953	444	1,849	889	375	268	5,102	596	5,698
1991	273	990	477	1,725	773	404	369	5,023	603	5,626
1992	304	977	438	1,703	732	344	367	4,868	519	5,387
1993	285	931	465	1,513	724	364	347	4,655	465	5,120
1994	269	990	466	1,472	731	340	319	4,601	468	5,069
1995	263	894	404	1,375	785	343	300	4,378	399	4,777

Perinatal deaths, all causes
Early neonatal deaths plus stillbirths at 24 or more weeks of gestation

Year	I	II	IIIn	IIIm	IV	V	Others	All#	Sole reg.	All#
1993	338	1,088	548	1,790	858	416	395	5,459	567	6,026
1994	319	1,138	545	1,740	855	397	385	5,393	567	5,960
1995	311	1,042	491	1,601	925	420	373	5,177	493	5,670

A5.4.2 continued

Perinatal mortality by social class of father, England and Wales, 1979–95

Year of birth	All births within marriage and jointly registered births outside marriage								Sole registrations by mother
	Social class of father							All#	All#
	I	II	IIIn	IIIm	IV	V	Others		

Rates per thousand total births
Perinatal deaths, all causes
Early neonatal deaths plus stillbirths at 28 or more weeks of gestation

Year of birth	I	II	IIIn	IIIm	IV	V	Others	All#	Sole All#
1979	10.3	11.6	12.7	14.0	16.5	18.0	19.1	13.9	27.5	14.6
1980	9.7	11.1	11.8	12.9	14.6	16.3	16.6	12.8	23.1	13.3
1981	..	..	..	..	..	..	..	..	..	..
1982	8.1	9.0	10.3	10.7	12.9	13.1	13.5	10.7	19.1	11.2
1983	7.5	8.5	9.2	9.9	12.2	12.1	11.1	9.9	17.7	10.4
1984	7.1	7.9	8.2	9.7	11.5	13.4	10.8	9.6	17.1	10.1
1985	7.6	7.6	8.8	9.2	11.0	12.0	12.1	9.3	16.2	9.8
1986	7.0	7.2	8.6	9.1	9.9	11.6	13.2	9.0	15.9	9.5
1987	6.9	7.1	7.8	8.5	10.1	10.5	9.9	8.5	13.9	8.9
1988	6.7	6.9	7.8	8.2	9.5	10.9	10.4	8.2	14.0	8.7
1989	5.8	7.0	7.8	7.7	9.2	10.5	10.3	7.9	12.7	8.3
1990*	6.8	6.2	7.1	7.9	9.6	9.8	9.9	7.8	10.8	8.0
1991	6.0	6.4	7.7	7.5	8.9	10.4	12.3	7.8	11.1	8.0
1992	6.7	6.3	7.2	7.6	8.5	9.1	11.2	7.6	10.0	7.8
1993	6.2	6.2	7.4	7.4	8.0	10.0	10.3	7.5	9.2	7.6
1994	5.8	6.6	7.4	7.3	8.3	9.4	10.1	7.4	9.5	7.6
1995	5.8	6.0	6.6	7.1	8.9	10.0	9.5	7.3	8.3	7.3

Early neonatal deaths plus stillbirths at 24 or more weeks of gestation

Year of birth	I	II	IIIn	IIIm	IV	V	Others	All#	Sole All#
1993	7.4	7.3	8.8	8.8	9.5	11.5	11.7	8.8	11.3	9.0
1994	6.9	7.6	8.7	8.7	9.7	11.0	12.2	8.8	11.6	9.0
1995	6.8	7.1	8.0	8.3	10.6	12.3	11.9	8.6	10.3	8.7

Perinatal deaths, all causes except congenital anomalies, ONS cause group 1
Early neonatal deaths plus stillbirths at 28 or more weeks of gestation

Year of birth	I	II	IIIn	IIIm	IV	V	Others	All#	Sole All#
1979	7.4	8.9	10.0	11.0	12.7	14.2	14.4	10.8	23.1	11.4
1980	7.4	8.5	9.1	10.1	11.2	12.2	12.9	9.9	19.6	10.4
1981	..	..	..	..	..	..	..	..	..	..

A5.4.2 continued

Perinatal mortality by social class of father, England and Wales, 1979–95

Year of birth	All births within marriage and jointly registered births outside marriage								Sole registrations by mother	All#
	Social class of father							All#		
	I	II	IIIn	IIIm	IV	V	Others			
Perinatal deaths, all causes except congenital anomalies, ONS cause group 1										
Early neonatal deaths plus stillbirths at 28 or more weeks of gestation										
1982	6.3	7.1	8.0	8.4	10.4	10.2	10.0	8.4	16.3	8.9
1983	6.0	6.7	7.2	8.0	9.4	9.9	8.2	7.9	15.0	8.3
1984	5.8	6.5	6.7	7.9	9.4	10.8	9.0	7.8	14.7	8.2
1985	5.9	6.3	7.1	7.5	8.9	9.5	10.1	7.6	14.3	8.0
1986	5.2	5.7	6.6	7.3	7.6	9.4	9.9	7.1	13.3	7.5
1987	5.3	5.7	6.3	6.8	7.9	7.9	8.1	6.7	11.6	7.1
1988	5.2	5.4	6.2	6.7	7.6	8.6	8.2	6.6	11.8	7.0
1989	4.2	5.5	6.2	6.3	7.6	8.6	8.3	6.3	10.8	6.7
1990*	5.3	4.9	6.0	6.7	7.8	8.1	7.9	6.4	9.4	6.6
1991	5.0	5.1	6.3	6.1	7.6	9.0	9.9	6.4	9.6	6.6
1992	5.1	5.3	6.0	6.3	7.0	7.6	8.7	6.2	8.7	6.4
1993	5.5	5.2	6.3	6.2	6.7	8.8	8.5	6.3	8.2	6.5
1994	4.9	5.5	6.2	6.3	6.8	8.1	8.4	6.3	8.4	6.4
1995	4.8	5.0	5.6	6.1	7.6	8.5	7.9	6.2	7.1	6.2
Early neonatal deaths plus stillbirths at 24 or more weeks of gestation										
1993	6.5	6.2	7.6	7.5	8.1	10.2	9.8	7.5	10.1	7.7
1994	5.8	6.3	7.2	7.5	8.1	9.6	10.3	7.4	10.0	7.6
1995	5.7	5.9	6.9	7.2	9.0	10.6	10.0	7.3	8.9	7.5

\# Includes cases where the father's social class was not stated

Rates for 1981 have not been included in this table because of anomalies arising following industrial action by local registrars of births and deaths

* The 1990 *Classification of Occupations* was used for births and deaths occurring from 1991 onwards including deaths of babies born in 1990 and dying in 1991. This led to a discontinuity in data. See text for details

Source: Authors' analysis of ONS/OPCS data

Data extract: live births 1993 (7/94), 1994 (7/95), 1995 (3/7/96), 1996 (8/4/97) linked 1993 (3/4/96), 1994 (18/9/96), 1995 (3/11/97)

This is similar to Table A5.3 in the first edition of *Birth counts*

A5.4.3

Neonatal mortality by social class of father, England and Wales, 1979–95

Year of birth	All births within marriage and jointly registered births outside marriage								Sole registrations by mother
	Social class of father								
	I	II	IIIn	IIIm	IV	V	Others	All#	All#
Numbers									
Neonatal deaths, all causes									
1979	255	860	453	1,675	886	401	232	4,762	439	5,201
1980	234	818	447	1,644	814	365	261	4,583	380	4,963
1981	197	660	356	1,395	682	326	216	3,832	333	4,165
1982	185	645	357	1,220	651	302	203	3,563	340	3,903
1983	167	584	324	1,188	604	273	189	3,329	314	3,643
1984	171	549	285	1,181	591	277	170	3,224	294	3,518
1985	192	561	287	1,107	547	267	221	3,182	301	3,483
1986	173	547	269	1,088	517	272	218	3,098	349	3,447
1987	176	556	272	1,091	528	268	194	3,095	325	3,420
1988	175	565	274	1,052	510	247	199	3,037	342	3,379
1989	184	605	263	1,023	482	210	177	2,949	302	3,251
1990*	172	524	259	995	496	229	175	2,855	279	3,134
1991	144	575	287	914	402	197	214	2,749	267	3,016
1992	160	517	261	923	377	193	219	2,655	214	2,869
1993	140	534	251	847	390	159	198	2,554	219	2,773
1994	146	518	255	831	395	164	191	2,519	210	2,729
1995	146	528	225	773	429	197	152	2,470	197	2,667
Rates per thousand live births									
Neonatal deaths, all causes									
1979	6.5	6.8	7.3	7.4	9.3	10.6	12.4	7.9	14.1	8.2
1980	5.6	6.4	6.9	7.1	8.5	9.4	12.3	7.4	11.4	7.6
1981	..	..	..	..	..	..	..	..	..	..
1982	4.4	5.2	5.8	5.7	7.4	7.8	9.2	6.0	9.3	6.2
1983	4.2	4.7	5.3	5.6	6.9	6.7	8.1	5.6	8.2	5.8
1984	4.2	4.5	4.6	5.5	6.6	6.9	6.7	5.4	7.2	5.5
1985	4.6	4.4	4.7	5.0	6.0	6.2	7.5	5.2	6.8	5.3
1986	4.0	4.2	4.4	5.0	5.7	6.5	7.7	5.0	7.3	5.2
1987	4.0	4.1	4.5	4.8	5.7	6.4	6.5	4.9	6.4	5.0
1988	4.0	4.0	4.4	4.6	5.5	6.0	6.6	4.7	6.3	4.9
1989	3.9	4.1	4.6	4.5	5.3	5.5	6.3	4.7	5.6	4.7
1990*	3.6	3.4	4.1	4.3	5.4	6.0	6.5	4.4	5.1	4.4
1991	3.2	3.7	4.7	4.0	4.7	5.1	7.2	4.3	4.9	4.3

A5.4.3 continued

Neonatal mortality by social class of father, England and Wales, 1979–95

Year of birth	All births within marriage and jointly registered births outside marriage								Sole registrations by mother	All#
	Social class of father							All#		
	I	II	IIIn	IIIm	IV	V	Others			
1992	3.5	3.4	4.3	4.1	4.4	5.2	6.7	4.2	4.2	4.2
1993	3.1	3.6	4.0	4.1	4.3	4.4	5.9	4.1	4.4	4.1
1994	3.1	3.5	4.0	4.1	4.5	4.6	6.1	4.1	4.3	4.1
1995	3.2	3.6	3.7	4.0	4.9	5.8	4.8	4.1	4.1	4.1
Neonatal deaths, all causes except congenital anomalies, ONS cause group 1										
1979	3.9	4.7	5.2	5.1	6.5	7.6	8.6	5.4	11.2	5.7
1980	3.7	4.3	4.9	4.9	5.8	6.3	8.5	5.0	8.9	5.2
1981	..	..	..	..	..	..	..	..	..	..
1982	2.8	3.5	3.9	3.8	4.9	5.5	6.0	4.0	7.1	4.2
1983	2.7	3.1	3.4	3.8	4.6	4.9	5.1	3.8	6.2	3.9
1984	2.7	2.9	3.0	3.7	4.7	4.4	4.7	3.6	5.3	3.8
1985	2.9	3.1	3.2	3.4	3.9	4.0	5.6	3.5	5.3	3.6
1986	2.2	2.6	2.5	3.2	3.5	4.4	4.9	3.2	5.1	3.3
1987	2.7	2.6	3.0	3.2	3.4	3.7	4.6	3.2	4.5	3.3
1988	2.5	2.5	2.7	3.2	3.6	3.8	4.2	3.1	4.7	3.2
1989	2.3	2.7	3.0	3.0	3.6	3.7	3.8	3.1	4.2	3.1
1990*	2.5	2.2	2.9	3.0	3.7	4.1	4.5	3.0	3.7	3.1
1991	2.2	2.4	3.1	2.6	3.3	3.8	4.9	2.9	3.7	2.9
1992	2.0	2.3	3.0	2.8	3.1	3.7	4.3	2.8	3.1	2.9
1993	2.3	2.5	3.0	3.0	3.0	3.3	4.1	3.0	3.5	3.0
1994	2.3	2.4	3.0	3.2	3.1	3.4	4.1	3.0	3.5	3.0
1995	2.3	2.5	2.7	3.0	3.6	4.3	3.5	3.0	3.1	3.0

Includes cases where the father's social class was not stated

Rates for 1981 have not been included in this table because of anomalies arising following industrial action by local registrars of births and deaths

* The 1990 Classification of Occupations was used for births and deaths occurring from 1991 onwards including deaths of babies born in 1990 and dying in 1991. This led to a discontinuity in data. See text for details

Source: Authors' analysis of ONS/OPCS data

Data extract: live births 1993 (7/94), 1994 (7/95), 1995 (3/7/96), 1996 (8/4/97)

        linked   1993 (3/4/96), 1994 (18/9/96), 1995 (3/11/97)

This is similar to Table A5.3 in the first edition of Birth counts

A5.4.4

Postneonatal mortality by social class of father, England and Wales, 1979–95

Year of birth	All births within marriage and jointly registered births outside marriage								Sole registrations by mother
	Social class of father							All#	All#
	I	II	IIIn	IIIm	IV	V	Others		
Numbers									
Postneonatal deaths, all causes									
1979	137	411	202	883	490	275	207	2,605	251	2,856
1980	138	359	219	840	462	258	191	2,467	253	2,720
1981	119	401	211	900	395	268	208	2,502	245	2,747
1982	109	400	204	804	456	259	177	2,409	292	2,701
1983	98	375	200	777	437	255	198	2,340	316	2,656
1984	94	335	160	715	352	211	186	2,053	274	2,327
1985	114	385	176	798	403	268	185	2,339	349	2,688
1986	111	362	184	795	437	219	191	2,326	384	2,710
1987	133	359	187	810	401	271	193	2,372	401	2,773
1988	132	392	185	747	393	216	177	2,265	385	2,650
1989	97	322	137	653	404	212	176	2,017	417	2,434
1990*	54	223	211	430	469	249	229	1,873	343	2,216
1991	59	234	105	510	247	141	164	1,476	274	1,750
1992	71	204	100	434	207	114	141	1,324	187	1,511
1993	68	203	100	395	162	104	102	1,159	207	1,366
1994	57	166	89	336	173	97	117	1,056	198	1,254
1995	56	198	115	339	193	95	93	1,114	177	1,291
Rates per thousand live births									
Postneonatal deaths, all causes									
1979	3.5	3.3	3.2	3.9	5.1	7.3	11.0	4.3	8.1	4.5
1980	3.3	2.8	3.4	3.6	4.8	6.7	9.0	4.0	7.6	4.1
1981	..	..	..	..	..	..	..	..	..	..
1982	2.6	3.2	3.3	3.8	5.2	6.7	8.0	4.1	8.0	4.3
1983	2.4	3.0	3.3	3.6	5.0	6.3	8.5	4.0	8.2	4.2
1984	2.3	2.7	2.6	3.3	3.9	6.3	7.3	3.4	6.7	3.7
1985	2.8	3.0	2.9	3.6	4.4	6.3	6.3	3.8	7.9	4.1
1986	2.6	2.8	3.0	3.6	4.8	5.2	6.8	3.8	8.0	4.1
1987	3.1	2.6	3.1	3.6	4.3	6.4	6.5	3.8	7.9	4.1
1988	3.0	2.8	2.9	3.3	4.2	5.2	5.9	3.5	7.1	3.8
1989	2.1	2.2	2.4	2.9	4.5	5.6	6.3	3.2	7.8	3.5
1990*	1.1	1.5	3.4	1.9	5.1	6.6	8.5	2.9	6.3	3.1
1991	1.3	1.5	1.7	2.2	2.9	3.7	5.5	2.3	5.1	2.5
1992	1.6	1.3	1.6	1.9	2.4	3.0	4.3	2.1	3.6	2.2

A5.4.4 continued

Postneonatal mortality by social class of father, England and Wales, 1979–95

Year of birth	All births within marriage and jointly registered births outside marriage								Sole registrations by mother	
	Social class of father						Others	All#		All#
	I	II	IIIn	IIIm	IV	V				
1993	1.5	1.4	1.6	1.9	1.8	2.9	3.0	1.9	4.1	2.0
1994	1.2	1.1	1.4	1.7	2.0	2.7	3.7	1.7	4.0	1.9
1995	1.2	1.3	1.9	1.8	2.2	2.8	3.0	1.9	3.7	2.0

Rates per thousand live births
Postneonatal deaths, all causes except congenital anomalies, ONS cause group 1

Year of birth	I	II	IIIn	IIIm	IV	V	Others	All#	Sole reg. by mother	All#
1979	2.5	2.4	2.4	2.9	4.2	6.1	9.5	3.3	6.7	3.5
1980	2.4	2.1	2.4	2.8	3.8	5.3	7.3	3.1	6.7	3.2
1981	..	..	..	..	..	..	..	..	..	..
1982	2.0	2.4	2.6	2.9	3.8	5.3	6.9	3.1	6.7	3.4
1983	1.8	2.2	2.3	2.7	3.8	5.4	7.0	3.0	7.1	3.3
1984	1.6	2.0	1.8	2.5	2.9	4.2	5.8	2.6	5.7	2.8
1985	2.3	2.3	2.1	2.9	3.5	5.3	5.1	3.0	6.7	3.3
1986	2.0	2.0	2.2	2.9	3.8	4.1	5.6	3.0	7.1	3.3
1987	2.2	2.1	2.5	2.9	3.4	5.4	5.6	3.0	7.0	3.3
1988	2.2	2.1	2.2	2.6	3.5	4.6	4.9	2.8	6.5	3.1
1989	1.6	1.7	1.8	2.3	3.5	4.5	5.3	2.5	7.2	2.9
1990*	0.8	1.1	2.6	1.5	4.0	5.4	7.1	2.3	5.6	2.5
1991	0.8	1.0	1.2	1.7	2.2	2.9	3.9	1.7	4.4	1.9
1992	1.0	0.9	1.2	1.3	1.8	2.4	3.0	1.5	3.1	1.6
1993	1.1	0.9	1.2	1.5	1.3	2.1	2.3	1.4	3.5	1.5
1994	0.8	0.7	1.1	1.3	1.4	2.1	2.7	1.3	3.4	1.4
1995	0.7	1.0	1.3	1.4	1.6	2.2	2.1	1.4	3.2	1.5

Includes cases where the father's social class was not stated

Rates for 1981 have not been included in this table because of anomalies arising following industrial action by local registrars of births and deaths

* The 1990 *Classification of Occupations* was used for births and deaths occurring from 1991 onwards including deaths of babies born in 1990 and dying in 1991. This led to a discontinuity in data. See text for details

Source: Authors' analysis of ONS/OPCS data

Data extract: live births 1993 (7/94), 1994 (7/95), 1995 (3/7/96), 1996 (8/4/97)

linked 1993 (3/4/96), 1994 (18/9/96), 1995 (3/11/97)

This similar to Table A5.3 in the first edition of *Birth counts*

A5.4.5

Infant mortality by social class of father, England and Wales, 1979–95

Year of birth	All births within marriage and jointly registered births outside marriage								Sole registrations by mother
	Social class of father							All#	All#
	I	II	IIIn	IIIm	IV	V	Others		

Numbers

Infant deaths, all causes

Year of birth	I	II	IIIn	IIIm	IV	V	Others	All#	All#
1979	392	1,271	655	2,558	1,376	676	439	7,367	8,057
1980	372	1,177	666	2,484	1,276	623	452	7,050	7,683
1981	316	1,061	567	2,295	1,077	594	424	6,334	6,912
1982	294	1,045	561	2,024	1,107	561	380	5,972	6,604
1983	265	959	524	1,965	1,041	528	387	5,669	6,299
1984	265	884	445	1,896	943	488	356	5,277	5,845
1985	306	946	463	1,905	950	535	406	5,521	6,171
1986	284	909	453	1,883	954	491	409	5,424	6,157
1987	309	915	459	1,901	929	539	387	5,467	6,193
1988	307	957	459	1,799	903	463	376	5,302	6,029
1989	281	927	400	1,676	886	422	353	4,966	5,685
1990*	226	747	470	1,425	965	478	404	4,728	5,350
1991	203	809	392	1,424	649	338	378	4,225	4,766
1992	231	721	361	1,357	584	307	360	3,979	4,380
1993	208	737	351	1,242	552	263	300	3,713	4,139
1994	203	684	344	1,167	568	261	308	3,575	3,983
1995	202	726	340	1,112	622	292	245	3,584	3,958

Rates per thousand live births

Infant deaths, all causes

Year of birth	I	II	IIIn	IIIm	IV	V	Others	All#	All#
1979	10.0	10.1	10.5	11.3	14.4	17.8	23.4	12.1	22.2	12.6
1980	8.9	9.2	10.3	10.7	13.3	16.1	21.4	11.3	19.1	11.7
1981	..	..	..	..	..	..	..	..	..	..
1982	7.0	8.4	9.1	9.5	12.5	14.5	17.2	10.1	17.3	10.6
1983	6.6	7.7	8.6	9.2	11.8	13.0	16.6	9.6	16.4	10.0
1984	6.5	7.2	7.2	8.8	10.5	12.1	13.9	8.8	14.0	9.2
1985	7.4	7.4	7.6	8.7	10.5	12.5	13.8	9.0	14.6	9.4
1986	6.6	6.9	7.4	8.6	10.5	11.8	14.5	8.8	15.3	9.3
1987	7.1	6.7	7.6	8.4	10.0	12.8	13.1	8.7	14.4	9.1
1988	6.9	6.8	7.3	7.9	9.7	11.2	12.5	8.3	13.5	8.7
1989	6.1	6.3	7.0	7.4	9.8	11.1	12.7	7.8	13.4	8.3
1990*	4.8	4.9	7.5	6.2	10.5	12.6	15.0	7.3	11.3	7.6

A5.4.5 continued

Infant mortality by social class of father, England and Wales, 1979–95

Year of birth	All births within marriage and jointly registered births outside marriage								Sole registrations by mother
	Social class of father							All#	All#
	I	II	IIIn	IIIm	IV	V	Others		
1991	4.5	5.2	6.4	6.2	7.5	8.8	12.7	6.6	10.0	6.8
1992	5.1	4.7	5.9	6.1	6.8	8.2	11.1	6.2	7.8	6.4
1993	4.6	4.9	5.6	6.1	6.1	7.2	8.9	6.0	8.5	6.2
1994	4.4	4.6	5.5	5.8	6.5	7.3	9.8	5.8	8.3	6.0
1995	4.4	4.9	5.6	5.8	7.1	8.5	7.8	6.0	7.8	6.1

Rates per thousand live births
Infant deaths, all causes except congenital anomalies, ONS cause group 1

Year of birth	I	II	IIIn	IIIm	IV	V	Others	All#	Sole All#	All#
1979	6.5	7.0	7.6	8.1	10.6	13.7	18.1	8.8	18.0	9.2
1980	6.1	6.4	7.2	7.7	9.6	11.6	15.8	8.1	15.5	8.5
1981	..	..	..	..	..	..	..	..	..	..
1982	4.9	5.9	6.5	6.6	8.8	10.8	12.9	7.2	13.7	7.5
1983	4.5	5.3	5.7	6.5	8.4	10.3	12.1	6.8	13.4	7.2
1984	4.3	4.9	4.8	6.3	7.6	8.6	10.5	6.2	11.0	6.5
1985	5.1	5.3	5.3	6.2	7.3	9.3	10.7	6.5	12.0	6.9
1986	4.2	4.7	4.7	6.1	7.3	8.6	10.6	6.1	12.2	6.6
1987	4.9	4.7	5.5	6.1	6.8	9.2	10.2	6.2	11.5	6.6
1988	4.7	4.6	5.0	5.8	7.1	8.4	9.2	6.0	11.3	6.4
1989	3.9	4.5	4.8	5.3	7.1	8.2	9.1	5.6	11.4	6.0
1990*	3.4	3.3	5.6	4.4	7.7	9.5	11.6	5.3	9.4	5.6
1991	3.1	3.4	4.3	4.4	5.5	6.7	8.8	4.6	8.2	4.9
1992	3.1	3.2	4.2	4.1	4.9	6.1	7.3	4.3	6.2	4.4
1993	3.4	3.4	4.2	4.5	4.3	5.4	6.4	4.3	7.0	4.5
1994	3.1	3.2	4.1	4.4	4.5	5.6	6.8	4.2	6.8	4.4
1995	3.0	3.5	4.0	4.4	5.2	6.5	5.6	4.4	6.4	4.5

Includes cases where the father's social class was not stated

Rates for 1981 have not been included in this table because of anomalies arising following industrial action by local registrars of births and deaths

* The 1990 Classification of Occupations was used for births and deaths occurring from 1991 onwards including deaths of babies born in 1990 and dying in 1991. This led to a discontinuity in data. See text for details

Source: Authors' analysis of ONS/OPCS data

Data extract: live births 1993 (7/94), 1994 (7/95), 1995 (3/7/96), 1996 (8/4/97)

            linked   1993 (3/4/96), 1994 (18/9/96), 1995 (3/11/97)

This is similar to Table A5.3 in the first edition of Birth counts

A 5.4.6

Live births by social class of father, England and Wales, 1979–96

Year of birth	All births within marriage and jointly registered births outside marriage								Sole registrations by mother	All#
	Social class of father									
	I	II	IIIn	IIIm	IV	V	Others	All#		
1979	39,280	126,130	62,430	226,240	95,740	37,910	18,760	606,490	31,118	638,028
1980	41,700	128,420	64,500	231,560	96,140	38,700	21,150	622,170	33,204	656,234
1981	..	..	..	..	..	..	..	..	..	..
1982	41,890	124,490	61,520	212,180	88,300	38,760	22,110	589,250	36,453	625,931
1983	40,220	124,160	60,840	213,800	88,120	40,640	23,290	591,070	38,417	629,134
1984	40,820	122,960	62,200	215,040	89,670	40,230	25,530	596,450	40,593	636,818
1985	41,400	127,260	61,260	219,410	90,800	42,850	29,480	612,460	44,458	656,417
1986	42,900	130,910	61,150	218,020	91,190	41,760	28,220	614,150	47,822	661,018
1987	43,600	136,300	60,680	224,980	93,060	42,060	29,650	630,330	50,474	681,511
1988	44,470	141,540	62,870	226,570	92,910	41,230	30,170	639,760	53,944	693,577
1989	46,230	147,310	57,400	225,850	90,380	37,990	27,890	633,050	53,537	687,725
1990	47,200	152,870	62,590	231,550	91,870	38,000	26,960	651,040	54,831	706,140
1991	45,180	154,590	61,320	228,560	86,180	38,550	29,790	644,170	54,131	699,217
1992	45,400	153,480	60,900	223,040	86,150	37,450	32,460	638,880	51,472	689,656
1993	45,600	148,910	62,580	204,400	90,060	36,300	33,640	621,490	50,009	671,224
1994	46,430	149,700	62,970	201,120	87,850	35,990	31,460	615,520	49,023	664,256
1995	45,440	147,650	61,130	192,310	87,440	34,250	31,400	599,620	47,927	648,001
1996	44,640	151,090	61,580	189,000	91,880	31,050	30,560	599,800	51,017	649,489

Includes cases where the father's social class was not stated

Estimates for 1981 have not been included in this table because of anomalies arising following industrial action by local registrars of births and deaths

Numbers of live births in each social class are estimated from a ten per cent sample

Source: Authors' analysis of ONS/OPCS data

Data extract: live births 1993 (7/94), 1994 (7/95), 1995 (3/7/96), 1996 (8/4/97)

linked   1993 (3/4/96), 1994 (18/9/96), 1995 (3/11/97)

This is similar to Table A5.3 in the first edition of *Birth counts*

A5.5.1

Stillbirths inside marriage by social class of father, England and Wales, 1970–96

Stillbirths at 28 or more weeks of gestation
Numbers

Year of birth	Inside marriage							All inside marriage#	All outside marriage	All#
	Social class of father									
	I	II	IIIn	IIIm	IV	V	Other			
1970–72*	4,650	11,085	8,402	30,585	12,995	4,338	17,333	76,436	..	..
1975	304	832	505	2,268	1,023	405	242	5,579	716	6,295
1976	298	795	499	2,009	925	335	161	5,022	687	5,709
1977	281	696	432	1,940	872	313	172	4,706	699	5,405
1978	287	717	411	1,737	801	310	146	4,409	699	5,108
1979	200	772	413	1,715	837	317	161	4,415	717	5,132
1980	205	747	387	1,577	708	315	144	4,083	699	4,782
1981	191	683	335	1,304	577	281	146	3,517	690	4,207
1982	178	600	334	1,200	590	249	132	3,284	659	3,943
1983	166	560	279	1,059	535	221	94	2,914	718	3,632
1984	157	507	267	998	515	257	126	2,827	823	3,650
1985	162	485	292	983	477	221	157	2,777	873	3,650
1986	150	478	266	939	419	187	159	2,598	950	3,548
1987	147	475	239	838	419	172	112	2,402	1,019	3,421
1988	146	469	248	796	363	172	131	2,325	1,060	3,385
1989	129	486	208	749	324	141	129	2,166	1,065	3,231
1990	160	459	220	746	365	123	105	2,178	1,081	3,259
1991	138	450	203	715	284	150	159	2,099	1,156	3,255
1992	151	487	181	681	289	111	133	2,033	1,123	3,156
1993	152	434	224	522	267	137	130	1,866	1,094	2,960
1994	134	460	209	530	274	117	97	1,821	1,104	2,925
1995	128	399	173	483	281	113	120	1,697	1,007	2,704
1996	124	400	165	467	242	69	106	1,573	1,025	2,598

A5.5.1 continued

Stillbirths inside marriage by social class of father, England and Wales, 1970–96

Year of birth	Inside marriage							All inside marriage#	All outside marriage	All#
	Social class of father									
	I	II	IIIn	IIIm	IV	V	Other			
Stillbirths at 24 or more completed weeks of gestation										
1993	202	561	284	706	352	169	162	2,436	1,430	3,866
1994	178	585	268	710	343	144	133	2,361	1,455	3,816
1995	171	517	240	606	369	154	167	2,224	1,373	3,597
1996	165	562	218	619	310	99	141	2,114	1,425	3,539
Stillbirths at 28 or more weeks of gestation per thousand total births										
1970–72*	8.9	10.2	11.6	12.7	13.2	17.8	18.1	12.7	..	..
1975	7.2	8.3	8.8	10.5	11.9	14.7	10.1	10.1	12.9	10.3
1976	7.2	7.9	8.9	9.7	10.8	13.1	8.3	9.4	12.6	9.7
1977	6.7	6.9	8.1	9.9	10.6	12.3	9.3	9.1	12.5	9.7
1978	6.3	6.8	7.5	8.5	9.2	12	8.5	8.2	11.4	8.5
1979	5.2	6.3	6.8	8.1	9.4	9.6	9.0	7.7	10.1	8.0
1980	5.0	6.0	6.2	7.4	8.0	9.6	7.2	7.0	8.9	7.2
1981	..	..	..	..	..	..	..	6.3	8.5	6.6
1982	4.3	5.0	5.7	6.3	7.5	8.0	6.5	6.1	7.3	6.3
1983	4.2	4.8	4.9	5.6	7.0	7.0	4.5	5.5	7.1	5.7
1984	4.0	4.4	4.6	5.3	6.7	8.5	5.6	5.3	7.4	5.7
1985	4.1	4.1	5.2	5.3	6.3	7.2	6.2	5.2	6.8	5.5
1986	3.7	4.0	4.8	5.2	5.7	6.6	6.6	5.0	6.7	5.3
1987	3.5	3.8	4.4	4.6	5.8	6.6	4.6	4.6	6.4	5.0
1988	3.5	3.7	4.5	4.5	5.2	6.3	5.3	4.5	6.0	4.9
1989	3.0	3.8	4.2	4.4	5.0	6.7	5.7	4.3	5.7	4.7
1990	3.6	3.4	4.1	4.4	5.7	6.2	4.9	4.3	5.4	4.6
1991	3.3	3.4	4.0	4.4	4.9	5.6	6.9	4.3	5.4	4.6
1992	3.6	3.8	3.7	4.4	5.1	6.9	5.6	4.3	5.2	4.6
1993	3.7	3.5	4.4	3.8	4.6	5.5	5.4	4.1	5.1	4.4
1994	3.2	3.7	4.1	3.9	4.8	6.3	4.4	4.0	5.1	4.4

Stillbirths inside marriage by social class of father, England and Wales, 1970–96

Year of birth	Inside marriage							All inside marriage#	All outside marriage	All#
	Social class of father									
	I	II	IIIn	IIIm	IV	V	Other			
1995	3.1	3.3	3.6	3.8	5.1	6.2	5.6	3.9	4.6	4.2
1996	3.2	3.2	3.4	3.9	4.3	4.5	5.3	3.7	4.4	4.0
Stillbirths at 24 or more weeks of gestation per thousand total births										
1993	4.9	4.5	5.6	5.1	6.0	8.6	6.8	5.3	6.6	5.7
1994	4.2	4.7	5.3	5.2	6.0	7.7	6.0	5.2	6.8	5.7
1995	4.2	4.2	4.9	4.8	6.7	8.5	7.8	5.2	6.2	5.5
1996	4.2	4.6	4.5	5.2	5.6	6.4	7.0	5.0	6.1	5.4

* Year of registration

Includes cases where father's social class was not stated

Live births and rates for 1981 have not been included in this table because of anomalies arising following industrial action by local registrars of births and deaths

Data for live births are estimated from a ten per cent sample

Source: Authors' analysis of ONS/OPCS data

Data extract: live births 1993 (7/94), 1994 (7/95), 1995 (3/7/96), 1996 (8/4/97)
    linked 1993 (3/4/96), 1994 (18/9/96), 1995 (3/11/97)

This is similar to Table A5.7 in the first edition of *Birth counts*

A5.5.2

Perinatal mortality inside marriage by social class of father, England and Wales, 1970–95

Perinatal deaths including stillbirths at 28 or more weeks of gestation

Numbers

Year of birth	Inside marriage							All inside marriage#	All outside marriage	All#
	Social class of father									
	I	II	IIIn	IIIm	IV	V	Other			
1970–72*	:	:	:	:	:	:	:	:	:	:
1975	585	1,563	922	4,093	1,837	746	502	10,248	1,468	11,716
1976	525	1,441	871	3,542	1,661	636	427	9,093	1,323	10,416
1977	490	1,319	754	3,338	1,544	562	404	8,411	1,306	9,717
1978	543	1,301	765	3,087	1,450	523	351	8,020	1,293	9,313
1979	398	1,440	768	3,016	1,485	614	300	8,021	1,366	9,387
1980	398	1,382	732	2,788	1,322	562	303	7,487	1,312	8,799
1981	341	1,189	590	2,324	1,056	498	273	6,271	1,239	7,510
1982	330	1,072	603	2,079	1,046	448	261	5,840	1,223	7,063
1983	289	996	520	1,877	955	401	218	5,256	1,312	6,568
1984	283	919	473	1,832	890	427	218	5,042	1,403	6,445
1985	308	893	495	1,710	837	380	299	4,922	1,545	6,467
1986	292	867	463	1,606	733	323	302	4,589	1,742	6,331
1987	285	873	421	1,480	713	295	238	4,311	1,767	6,078
1988	268	857	433	1,401	659	285	244	4,150	1,910	6,060
1989	244	892	372	1,322	579	232	231	3,872	1,860	5,732
1990+	289	806	382	1,272	610	209	197	3,765	1,933	5,698
1991	246	822	378	1,188	480	232	270	3,618	2,008	5,626
1992	274	824	343	1,117	444	181	252	3,436	1,951	5,387
1993	258	763	378	939	449	194	221	3,215	1,905	5,120
1994	237	801	356	934	484	175	185	3,180	1,889	5,069
1995	224	728	309	827	492	177	184	2,948	1,829	4,777

Rates per thousand total births

Year of birth	I	II	IIIn	IIIm	IV	V	Other	All inside marriage#	All outside marriage	All#
1970–72*	16.3	18.6	20.6	22.1	23.9	32.1	31.7	..	29.6	23.0
1975	13.8	15.6	16.0	18.9	21.4	27.0	20.9	18.5	26.4	19.2
1976	12.7	14.3	15.6	17.1	19.2	24.9	21.9	17.0	24.3	17.7
1977	11.6	13.0	14.1	17.1	18.8	22.0	21.8	16.2	23.3	16.9
1978	11.9	12.3	13.9	15.1	16.7	20.3	20.4	14.8	21.1	15.5

A5.5.2 continued

Perinatal mortality inside marriage by social class of father, England and Wales, 1970–95

| Year of birth | Inside marriage | | | | | | | All inside marriage# | All outside marriage | All# |
| | Social class of father | | | | | | | | | |
	I	II	IIIn	IIIm	IV	V	Other			
1979	10.3	11.8	12.7	14.3	16.6	18.7	16.8	14.0	19.3	14.6
1980	9.7	11.1	11.8	13.1	15.0	17.1	15.1	12.9	16.8	13.3
1981	..	..	..	..	..	..	..	11.2	15.2	11.8
1982	8.0	9.0	10.3	10.9	13.3	14.5	12.9	10.8	13.5	11.2
1983	7.3	8.5	9.1	9.9	12.4	12.8	10.4	9.9	13.0	10.4
1984	7.1	8.0	8.2	9.8	11.6	14.1	9.8	9.5	12.6	10.1
1985	7.7	7.5	8.8	9.2	11.1	12.4	11.7	9.3	12.0	9.8
1986	7.1	7.2	8.3	8.9	10.0	11.4	12.6	8.8	12.2	9.5
1987	6.9	7.1	7.8	8.2	9.9	10.8	9.7	8.2	11.1	8.9
1988	6.4	6.8	7.9	8.0	9.5	11.1	9.8	8.0	10.7	8.7
1989	5.7	6.9	7.5	7.8	8.9	10.3	10.3	7.7	9.9	8.3
1990+	6.6	6.0	7.2	7.5	9.5	9.6	9.2	7.4	9.6	8.0
1991	6.0	6.2	7.4	7.3	8.3	10.7	11.8	7.4	9.4	8.0
1992	6.6	6.4	6.9	7.3	7.8	9.0	10.5	7.2	9.0	7.8
1993	6.2	6.1	7.4	6.7	7.7	9.9	9.2	7.0	8.8	7.6
1994	5.7	6.4	7.0	6.9	8.4	9.3	8.3	7.0	8.8	7.6
1995	5.5	6.0	6.4	6.6	9.0	9.8	8.6	6.8	8.3	7.3

* Year of registration

Includes cases where father's social class was not stated

+ See footnote to Table A4.4.2 and text.

Live births and rates for 1981 have not been included in this table because of anomalies arising following industrial action by local registrars of births and deaths

Data for live births are estimated from a ten per cent sample

Source: *Authors' analysis of ONS/OPCS data*

Data extract: live births 1993 (7/94), 1994 (7/95), 1995 (3/7/96), 1996 (8/4/97)

linked   1993 (3/4/96), 1994 (18/9/96), 1995 (3/11/97)

This is similar to Table A5.7 in the first edition of *Birth counts*

A5.5.3

Neonatal mortality inside marriage by social class of father, England and Wales, 1970–95

Year of birth	Inside marriage							All inside marriage#	All outside marriage	All#
	Social class of father									
	I	II	IIn	IIIm	IV	V	Other			
Numbers										
1970–72*	:	:	:	:	:	:	:	:	:	:
1975	338	848	502	2,150	978	402	307	5,525	883	6,408
1976	279	771	449	1,817	868	352	312	4,848	750	5,598
1977	254	751	405	1,703	828	291	286	4,518	713	5,231
1978	309	738	431	1,644	800	257	245	4,424	716	5,140
1979	250	832	427	1,563	810	345	171	4,398	803	5,201
1980	229	785	422	1,505	758	319	201	4,219	744	4,963
1981	192	630	325	1,273	618	276	157	3,471	694	4,165
1982	178	606	333	1,078	572	242	163	3,172	731	3,903
1983	152	537	301	1,028	520	218	156	2,912	731	3,643
1984	163	512	260	1,033	484	216	121	2,789	729	3,518
1985	184	501	258	898	451	188	180	2,660	823	3,483
1986	167	489	236	839	399	167	169	2,472	975	3,447
1987	163	511	241	808	397	164	161	2,451	969	3,420
1988	160	486	234	758	370	145	145	2,303	1,076	3,379
1989	163	516	206	766	325	119	137	2,233	1,018	3,251
1990+	154	439	221	664	313	123	123	2,038	1,096	3,134
1991	134	468	225	638	248	99	142	1,958	1,058	3,016
1992	149	434	201	563	196	101	151	1,796	1,073	2,869
1993	125	430	196	528	240	77	124	1,740	1,034	2,774
1994	133	412	186	526	262	76	117	1,721	1,008	2,729
1995	123	405	170	462	249	90	81	1,590	1,077	2,667
Rates per thousand live births										
1970–72*	:	:	:	:	:	:	:	:	:	:
1975	8.0	8.5	8.8	10.0	11.5	14.8	12.9	10.1	16.1	10.6
1976	6.8	7.7	8.1	8.9	10.2	14.0	16.1	9.1	13.9	9.6
1977	6.1	7.5	7.6	8.8	10.2	11.6	15.6	8.8	12.9	9.2
1978	6.8	7.0	7.9	8.1	9.3	10.1	14.4	8.3	11.8	8.6

A5.5.3 continued

Neonatal mortality inside marriage by social class of father, England and Wales, 1970–95

Year of birth	Inside marriage							All inside marriage#	All outside marriage	All#
	Social class of father									
	I	II	IIIn	IIIm	IV	V	Other			
1979	6.5	6.9	7.1	7.5	9.2	10.6	9.7	7.8	11.4	8.2
1980	5.6	6.4	6.8	7.1	8.7	9.8	10.1	7.3	9.6	7.6
1981	..	..	..	..	..	..	..	6.3	8.6	6.6
1982	4.4	5.1	5.7	5.7	7.3	7.9	8.1	5.9	8.1	6.2
1983	3.9	4.6	5.3	5.5	6.8	7.0	7.5	5.5	7.3	5.8
1984	4.1	4.5	4.5	5.6	6.3	7.2	5.5	5.3	6.6	5.5
1985	4.6	4.2	4.6	4.9	6.0	6.2	7.1	5.0	6.4	5.3
1986	4.1	4.1	4.3	4.7	5.5	5.9	7.1	4.7	6.9	5.2
1987	3.9	4.2	4.5	4.5	5.5	6.0	6.6	4.7	6.1	5.0
1988	3.8	3.9	4.3	4.3	5.4	5.7	5.9	4.5	6.1	4.9
1989	3.8	4.0	4.1	4.5	5.0	5.3	6.1	4.5	5.5	4.7
1990+	3.5	3.3	4.2	3.9	4.9	5.7	5.7	4.0	5.5	4.4
1991	3.3	3.6	4.4	3.9	4.3	4.6	6.2	4.0	5.0	4.3
1992	3.6	3.4	4.1	3.7	3.4	5.0	6.3	3.8	5.0	4.2
1993	3.0	3.5	3.9	3.8	4.1	4.0	5.2	3.8	4.8	4.1
1994	3.2	3.3	3.7	3.9	4.6	4.1	5.3	3.8	4.7	4.1
1995	3.0	3.3	3.5	3.7	4.6	5.0	3.8	3.7	4.9	4.1

* Year of registration

Includes cases where father's social class was not stated

+ See footnote to Table A4.4.3 and text.

Live births and rates for 1981 have not been included in this table because of anomalies arising following industrial action by local registrars of births and deaths

Data for live births are estimated from a ten per cent sample

Source: Authors' analysis of ONS/OPCS data

Data extract: live births 1993 (7/94), 1994 (7/95), 1995 (3/7/96), 1996 (8/4/97)

linked   1993 (3/4/96), 1994 (18/9/96), 1995 (3/11/97)

This is similar to Table A5.7 in the first edition of Birth counts

A5.5.4

Postneonatal mortality inside marriage by social class of father, England and Wales, 1970–95

Year of birth	Inside marriage							All inside marriage#	All outside marriage	All#
	Social class of father									
	I	II	IIIn	IIIm	IV	V	Other			
Numbers										
1970–72*	..	..	..	..	..	..	..	..	..	..
1975	127	324	200	949	485	237	178	2,500	415	2,915
1976	107	280	171	827	431	211	171	2,198	384	2,582
1977	120	305	172	712	408	202	160	2,079	401	2,480
1978	135	326	177	855	374	181	152	2,200	390	2,590
1979	135	382	186	786	445	233	168	2,335	521	2,856
1980	133	342	198	735	411	212	146	2,177	543	2,720
1981	116	372	195	783	336	214	153	2,169	578	2,747
1982	105	372	190	702	395	188	149	2,101	600	2,701
1983	92	342	180	654	365	189	162	1,984	672	2,656
1984	89	308	148	563	297	148	143	1,696	631	2,327
1985	108	348	148	640	326	171	145	1,892	796	2,688
1986	105	320	158	576	334	138	145	1,785	925	2,710
1987	129	307	153	586	290	161	134	1,765	1,008	2,773
1988	127	334	158	519	274	122	101	1,644	1,006	2,650
1989	86	268	111	427	254	117	125	1,392	1,042	2,434
1990+	51	192	176	280	303	144	129	1,277	939	2,216
1991	52	190	84	308	151	67	107	964	786	1,750
1992	63	159	73	276	123	48	88	840	671	1,511
1993	61	156	72	233	84	51	60	732	634	1,366
1994	50	135	64	187	108	49	58	658	596	1,254
1995	43	162	84	203	106	41	44	692	599	1,291
Rates per 1,000 live births										
1970–72*	2.9	3.7	3.9	5.6	6.7	13.1	9.7	..	8.5	6.0
1975	3.0	3.3	3.5	4.4	5.7	8.7	7.5	4.6	7.6	4.8
1976	2.6	2.8	3.1	4.0	5.1	8.4	8.8	4.1	7.1	4.4
1977	2.9	3.0	3.2	3.7	5.0	8.0	8.7	4.0	7.2	4.4
1978	3.0	3.1	3.2	4.2	4.3	7.1	8.9	4.1	6.4	4.3

A5.5.4 continued

Postneonatal mortality inside marriage by social class of father, England and Wales, 1970–95

Year of birth	Inside marriage							All inside marriage#	All outside marriage	All#
	Social class of father									
	I	II	IIIn	IIIm	IV	V	Other			
1979	3.5	3.1	3.1	3.8	5.0	7.2	9.5	4.1	7.4	4.5
1980	3.3	2.8	3.2	3.5	4.7	6.5	7.3	3.8	7.0	4.2
1981	..	..	..	..	..	..	..	3.9	7.2	4.3
1982	2.6	3.1	3.3	3.7	5.1	6.1	7.4	3.9	6.7	4.3
1983	2.3	2.9	3.2	3.5	4.8	6.1	7.8	3.7	6.7	4.2
1984	2.3	2.7	2.6	3.0	3.9	4.9	6.4	3.2	5.7	3.7
1985	2.7	2.9	2.6	3.5	4.3	5.6	5.7	3.6	6.2	4.1
1986	2.6	2.7	2.9	3.2	4.6	4.9	6.1	3.4	6.5	4.1
1987	3.1	2.5	2.8	3.2	4.0	5.9	5.5	3.4	6.4	4.1
1988	3.0	2.7	2.9	3.0	4.0	4.8	4.1	3.2	5.7	3.8
1989	2.0	2.1	2.2	2.5	3.9	5.2	5.6	2.8	5.6	3.5
1990+	1.2	1.4	3.3	1.7	4.8	6.7	6.0	2.5	4.7	3.1
1991	1.3	1.4	1.7	1.9	2.6	3.1	4.7	2.0	3.7	2.5
1992	1.5	1.2	1.5	1.8	2.2	2.4	3.7	1.8	3.1	2.2
1993	1.5	1.3	1.4	1.7	1.4	2.6	2.5	1.6	2.9	2.0
1994	1.2	1.1	1.3	1.4	1.9	2.6	2.6	1.5	2.8	1.9
1995	1.1	1.3	1.7	1.6	1.9	2.3	2.1	1.6	2.7	2.0

* Year of registration

Includes cases where father's social class was not stated

+ See footnote to Table A5.4.4 and text.

Live births and rates for 1981 have not been included in this table because of anomalies arising following industrial action by local registrars of births and deaths

Data for live births are estimated from a ten per cent sample

Source: Authors' analysis of ONS/OPCS data

Data extract: live births 1993 (7/94), 1994 (7/95), 1995 (3/7/96), 1996 (8/4/97)

      linked   1993 (3/4/96), 1994 (18/9/96), 1995 (3/11/97)

This is similar to Table A5.7 in the first edition of *Birth counts*

A5.5.5

Infant mortality inside marriage by social class of father, England and Wales, 1970–95

Year of birth	Inside marriage							All inside marriage#	All outside marriage	All#
	Social class of father									
	I	II	IIn	IIIm	IV	V	Other			
Numbers										
1970–72*	1,622	4,529	3,659	15,591	7,627	4,001	3,456	40,485		
1975	465	1,172	702	3,099	1,463	639	485	8,025	1,298	9,323
1976	386	1,051	620	2,644	1,299	563	483	7,046	1,134	8,180
1977	374	1,056	577	2,415	1,236	493	446	6,597	1,114	7,711
1978	444	1,064	608	2,499	1,174	438	397	6,624	1,106	7,730
1979	385	1,214	613	2,349	1,255	578	339	6,733	1,324	8,057
1980	362	1,127	620	2,240	1,169	531	347	6,396	1,287	7,683
1981	308	1,002	520	2,056	954	490	310	5,640	1,272	6,912
1982	283	978	523	1,780	967	430	312	5,273	1,331	6,604
1983	244	879	481	1,682	885	407	318	4,896	1,403	6,299
1984	252	820	408	1,596	781	364	264	4,485	1,360	5,845
1985	292	849	406	1,538	777	359	325	4,552	1,619	6,171
1986	272	809	394	1,415	733	305	314	4,257	1,900	6,157
1987	292	818	394	1,394	687	325	295	4,216	1,977	6,193
1988	287	820	392	1,277	644	267	246	3,947	2,082	6,029
1989	249	784	317	1,193	579	236	262	3,625	2,060	5,685
1990+	205	631	397	944	616	267	252	3,315	2,035	5,350
1991	186	658	309	946	399	166	249	2,922	1,844	4,766
1992	212	593	274	839	319	149	239	2,636	1,744	4,380
1993	186	586	268	761	324	128	184	2,472	1,668	4,140
1994	183	547	250	713	370	125	175	2,379	1,604	3,983
1995	166	567	254	665	355	131	125	2,282	1,676	3,958
Rates per thousand live births										
1970–72*	11.6	13.6	14.5	17.0	19.6	30.7	26.3	17.7		
1975	11.1	11.8	12.3	14.5	17.3	23.5	20.4	14.0	23.6	15.4
1976	9.4	10.5	11.2	12.9	15.3	22.3	25.0	13.3	21.1	14.0
1977	9.0	10.5	10.8	12.5	15.2	19.6	24.3	12.8	20.1	13.5
1978	9.8	10.1	11.1	12.4	13.6	17.2	23.3	12.4	18.2	13.0

Infant mortality inside marriage by social class of father, England and Wales, 1970–95

Year of birth	Inside marriage							All inside marriage#	All outside marriage	All#
	Social class of father									
	I	II	IIIn	IIIm	IV	V	Other			
1979	10.0	10.0	10.2	11.2	14.2	17.7	19.2	11.9	18.9	12.6
1980	8.9	9.1	10.0	10.6	13.4	16.3	17.4	11.1	16.6	11.7
1981	..	..	..	..	..	..	..	10.2	15.8	10.9
1982	6.9	8.3	9.0	9.4	12.4	14.0	15.5	9.8	14.8	10.6
1983	6.2	7.5	8.4	8.9	11.6	13.0	15.3	9.2	14.1	10.0
1984	6.4	7.1	7.1	8.6	10.2	12.2	11.9	8.5	12.3	9.2
1985	7.3	7.2	7.2	8.4	10.3	11.8	12.9	8.6	12.6	9.4
1986	6.7	6.8	7.1	7.9	10.0	10.8	13.2	8.2	13.4	9.3
1987	7.0	6.6	7.3	7.7	9.6	12.0	12.1	8.1	12.5	9.1
1988	6.9	6.5	7.2	7.3	9.3	10.5	9.9	7.6	11.8	8.7
1989	5.9	6.1	6.4	7.0	8.9	10.5	11.7	7.3	11.0	8.3
1990+	4.7	4.7	7.5	5.6	9.7	12.3	11.8	6.6	10.2	7.6
1991	4.5	5.0	6.1	5.9	7.0	7.7	11.0	6.0	8.7	6.8
1992	5.1	4.6	5.6	5.5	5.6	7.4	10.0	5.6	8.1	6.3
1993	4.5	4.7	5.3	5.5	5.6	6.6	7.7	5.4	7.8	6.2
1994	4.4	4.4	4.9	5.3	6.5	6.7	7.9	5.3	7.5	6.0
1995	4.1	4.7	5.3	5.3	6.5	7.3	5.9	5.3	7.7	6.1

* Year of registration

Includes cases where father's social class was not stated

+ See footnote to Table A5.4.5 and text.

Live births and rates for 1981 have not been included in this table because of anomalies arising following industrial action by local registrars of births and deaths

Data for live births are estimated from a ten per cent sample

Source: Authors' analysis of ONS/OPCS data

Data extract: live births 1993 (7/94), 1994 (7/95), 1995 (3/7/96), 1996 (8/4/97)

    linked   1993 (3/4/96), 1994 (18/9/96), 1995 (3/11/97)

This is similar to Table A5.7 in the first edition of *Birth counts*

A5.5.6

Live and total births inside marriage by social class of father, England and Wales, 1970–96

Year of birth	Inside marriage							All inside marriage#	All outside marriage	All#
	Social class of father									
	I	II	IIIn	IIIm	IV	V	Other			
Live births										
1970–72*	139,500	332,550	252,060	917,550	389,850	130,140	131,430	2,293,080	::	::
1975	42,000	99,700	57,000	214,200	84,700	27,200	23,800	548,554	54,891	603,445
1976	40,900	99,900	55,500	204,600	85,000	25,200	19,400	530,504	53,766	584,270
1977	41,800	100,500	53,200	193,500	81,400	25,200	18,400	513,880	55,379	569,259
1978	45,400	105,100	54,600	202,100	86,100	25,400	17,100	535,781	60,637	596,418
1979	38,500	121,310	60,070	208,890	88,380	32,570	17,670	567,390	70,218	637,608
1980	40,730	123,360	61,790	211,890	87,540	32,610	19,890	577,810	77,564	655,374
1981	::	::	::	::	::	::	::	554,060	80,698	634,758
1982	40,860	118,280	57,970	189,490	78,210	30,690	20,110	535,610	90,093	625,703
1983	39,230	116,920	57,110	188,090	76,330	31,200	20,780	529,660	99,827	629,487
1984	39,540	115,030	57,610	185,620	76,420	29,920	22,190	526,330	110,713	637,043
1985	39,830	117,990	56,130	184,030	75,180	30,410	25,290	528,860	128,058	656,918
1986	40,900	119,580	55,330	179,700	72,950	28,170	23,860	520,490	141,482	661,972
1987	41,450	123,080	53,820	180,550	71,880	27,110	24,360	522,250	158,554	680,804
1988	41,640	125,650	54,780	175,320	69,090	25,500	24,730	516,710	176,994	693,704
1989	42,410	128,850	49,650	169,220	65,010	22,480	22,340	499,960	186,627	686,587
1990	43,810	133,150	53,100	168,850	63,630	21,650	21,400	505,590	200,281	705,871
1991	41,140	131,740	50,600	161,590	57,410	21,530	22,730	486,740	211,561	698,301
1992	41,310	129,030	49,310	153,310	56,900	20,030	23,820	473,710	216,642	690,352
1993	41,400	124,430	50,680	138,590	57,940	19,490	23,810	456,340	215,159	671,499
1994	41,750	124,850	50,680	135,420	57,260	18,600	22,100	450,660	213,883	664,543
1995	40,510	121,500	48,280	125,040	54,670	17,990	21,220	429,210	218,337	647,547
1996	39,130	122,880	47,850	118,920	55,530	15,410	19,920	419,640	231,177	650,817
Total births at 28 or more weeks of gestation										
1970–72*	144,150	343,635	260,462	948,135	402,845	134,478	148,763	2,369,516	::	::
1975	42,304	100,532	57,505	216,468	85,723	27,605	24,042	548,554	54,891	603,445
1976	41,198	100,695	55,999	206,609	85,925	25,535	19,561	530,504	53,766	584,270
1977	42,081	101,196	53,632	195,440	82,272	25,513	18,572	513,880	55,379	569,259
1978	45,687	105,817	55,011	203,837	86,901	25,710	17,246	535,781	60,637	601,526

A5.5.6

Live and total births inside marriage by social class of father, England and Wales, 1970–96

Year of birth	Inside marriage — Social class of father							All inside marriage#	All outside marriage	All#
	I	II	IIIn	IIIm	IV	V	Other			
1979	38,700	122,082	60,483	210,605	89,217	32,887	17,831	571,805	70,935	642,740
1980	40,935	124,107	62,177	213,467	88,248	32,925	20,034	581,893	78,263	660,156
1981	:	:	:	:	:	:	:	557,577	81,388	638,965
1982	41,038	118,880	58,304	190,690	78,800	30,939	20,242	538,894	90,752	629,646
1983	39,396	117,480	57,389	189,149	76,865	31,421	20,874	532,574	100,545	633,119
1984	39,697	115,537	57,877	186,618	76,935	30,177	22,316	529,157	111,536	640,693
1985	39,992	118,475	56,422	185,013	75,657	30,631	25,447	531,637	128,931	660,568
1986	41,050	120,058	55,596	180,639	73,369	28,357	24,019	523,088	142,432	665,520
1987	41,597	123,555	54,059	181,388	72,299	27,282	24,472	524,652	159,573	684,225
1988	41,786	126,119	55,028	176,116	69,453	25,672	24,861	519,035	178,054	697,089
1989	42,539	129,336	49,858	169,969	65,334	22,621	22,469	502,126	187,692	689,818
1990	43,970	133,609	53,320	169,596	63,995	21,773	21,505	507,768	201,362	709,130
1991	41,278	132,190	50,803	162,305	57,694	21,680	22,889	488,839	212,717	701,556
1992	41,461	129,517	49,491	153,991	57,189	20,141	23,953	475,743	217,765	693,508
1993	41,552	124,864	50,904	139,112	58,207	19,627	23,940	458,206	216,253	674,459
1994	41,884	125,310	50,889	135,950	57,534	18,717	22,197	452,481	214,987	667,468
1995	40,638	121,899	48,453	125,523	54,951	18,103	21,340	430,907	219,344	650,251
1996	39,254	123,280	48,015	119,387	55,772	15,479	20,026	421,213	232,202	653,415
Total births at 24 or more weeks of gestation										
1993	41,602	124,991	50,964	139,296	58,292	19,659	23,972	458,776	216,589	675,365
1994	41,928	125,435	50,948	136,130	57,603	18,744	22,233	453,021	215,338	668,359
1995	40,681	122,017	48,520	125,646	55,039	18,144	21,387	431,434	219,710	651,144
1996	39,295	123,442	48,068	119,539	55,840	15,509	20,061	421,754	232,602	654,356

* Year of registration

Includes cases where father's social class was not stated

Live births and rates for 1981 have not been included in this table because of anomalies arising following industrial action by local registrars of births and deaths

Data for live births are estimated from a ten per cent sample

Source: Authors' analysis of ONS/OPCS data

Data extract: live births 1993 (7/94), 1994 (7/95), 1995 (3/7/96), 1996 (8/4/97)

            linked   1993 (3/4/96), 1994 (18/9/96), 1995 (3/11/97)

This is similar to Table A5.7 in the first edition of Birth counts

A5.6.1

Stillbirths and infant deaths within marriage by 1970 and 1980 social class classifications, England and Wales, 1979

		All within marriage	I	II	III	IV	V
Numbers							
Stillbirths	1970 classification	4,410	252	704	2,161	850	282
	1980 classification	4,410	200	771	2,128	835	316
Perinatal	1970 classification	8,034	487	1,324	3,858	1,511	551
	1980 classification	8,034	400	1,442	3,798	1,479	615
Neonatal	1970 classification	4,411	293	768	2,035	826	313
	1980 classification	4,411	251	835	2,000	806	348
Postneonatal	1970 classification	2,326	144	219	991	454	261
	1980 classification	2,326	129	341	970	464	263
Infant	1970 classification	6,737	437	1,087	3,026	1,280	574
	1980 classification	6,737	380	1,176	2,970	1,270	611
Live births	1970 classification	568,561	45,094	111,935	273,834	91,101	28,790
	1980 classification	568,561	38,579	121,560	269,515	88,562	32,637
Rates							
Stillbirths *	1970 classification	7.7	5.6	6.3	7.8	9.2	9.7
	1980 classification	7.7	5.2	6.3	7.8	9.2	9.6
Perinatal *	1970 classification	14.0	10.7	11.8	14.0	16.4	19.0
	1980 classification	14.0	10.3	11.8	14.0	16.5	18.7
Neonatal#	1970 classification	7.8	6.5	6.9	7.4	9.1	10.9
	1980 classification	7.8	6.5	6.9	7.4	9.1	10.7
Postneonatal#	1970 classification	4.1	3.2	2.8	3.6	5.0	9.1
	1980 classification	4.1	3.3	2.8	3.6	5.2	8.1
Infant#	1970 classification	11.8	9.7	9.7	11.1	14.1	19.9
	1980 classification	11.8	9.8	9.7	11.0	14.3	18.7

* Rates per 1,000 total births

Rates per 1,000 live births

Source: *OPCS Monitor DH3 82/5*

This was Table A5.9 in the first edition of *Birth counts*

A5.7.1

Aggregated stillbirth and mortality rates in the first year of life by social class of father, England and Wales, 1982–85, 1986–90, and 1991–95

Marital status and social class of father	Numbers					Rates				
	Stillbirths	Early neonatal deaths	Neonatal deaths	Post-neonatal deaths	Live births	Stillbirth*	Perinatal*	Neonatal*	Post-neonatal*	Infant*
Stillbirths and infant deaths among babies born 1982–85										
All causes										
Inside marriage										
I	663	547	677	394	159,460	4.1	7.6	4.2	2.5	6.7
II	2,152	1,728	2,156	1,370	468,220	4.6	8.2	4.6	2.9	7.5
IIIn	1,172	919	1,152	666	228,820	5.1	9.1	5.0	2.9	7.9
IIIm	4,240	3,258	4,037	2,559	747,230	5.6	10.0	5.4	3.4	8.8
IV	2,117	1,611	2,027	1,383	306,140	6.9	12.1	6.6	4.5	11.1
V	948	708	864	696	122,220	7.7	13.4	7.1	5.7	12.8
Other	509	487	620	599	88,370	5.7	11.2	7.0	6.8	13.8
All#	11,802	9,258	11,533	7,673	2,120,460	5.5	9.9	5.4	3.6	9.1
Jointly registered outside marriage										
I	13	28	38	21	4,870	2.7	8.4	7.8	4.3	12.1
II	104	146	183	125	30,650	3.4	8.1	6.0	4.1	10.0
IIIn	79	85	101	74	17,000	4.6	9.6	5.9	4.4	10.3
IIIm	540	509	659	535	113,200	4.7	9.2	5.8	4.7	10.5
IV	251	296	366	265	50,750	4.9	10.7	7.2	5.2	12.4
V	207	205	255	297	40,260	5.1	10.2	6.3	7.4	13.7
Other	71	129	163	147	12,040	5.9	16.5	13.5	12.2	25.7
All#	1,265	1,398	1,765	1,468	268,770	4.7	9.9	6.6	5.5	12.0
All with fathers										
I	676	575	715	415	164,330	4.1	7.6	4.4	2.5	6.9
II	2,256	1,874	2,339	1,495	498,870	4.5	8.2	4.7	3.0	7.7
IIIn	1,251	1,004	1,253	740	245,820	5.1	9.1	5.1	3.0	8.1
IIIm	4,780	3,767	4,696	3,094	860,430	5.5	9.9	5.5	3.6	9.1
IV	2,368	1,907	2,393	1,648	356,890	6.6	11.9	6.7	4.6	11.3
V	1,155	913	1,119	993	162,480	7.1	12.6	6.9	6.1	13.0
Other	580	616	783	746	100,410	5.7	11.8	7.8	7.4	15.2
All#	13,067	10,656	13,298	9,141	2,389,230	5.4	9.9	5.6	3.8	9.4

A5.7.1 continued

Aggregated stillbirth and mortality rates in the first year of life by social class of father, England and Wales, 1982–85, 1986–90, and 1991–95

Marital status and social class of father	Numbers					Rates				
	Stillbirths	Early neonatal deaths	Neonatal deaths	Post-neonatal deaths	Live births	Stillbirth*	Perinatal*	Neonatal*	Post-neonatal*	Infant*
Sole registration	1,808	1,012	1,249	1,231	159,921	11.2	17.4	7.8	7.7	15.5
All	14,875	11,668	14,547	10,372	2,548,300	5.8	10.4	5.7	4.1	9.8
Congenital anomalies, ONS cause group 1										
Inside marriage										
I	63	183	242	93	159,460	0.4	1.5	1.5	0.6	2.1
II	211	550	728	360	468,220	0.4	1.6	1.6	0.8	2.3
IIIn	125	322	418	177	228,820	0.5	1.9	1.8	0.8	2.6
IIIm	462	1,050	1,393	633	747,230	0.6	2.0	1.9	0.8	2.7
IV	253	511	681	351	306,140	0.8	2.5	2.2	1.1	3.4
V	110	228	294	132	122,220	0.9	2.7	2.4	1.1	3.5
Other	48	176	214	108	88,370	0.5	2.5	2.4	1.2	3.6
All#	1,272	3,020	3,970	1,854	2,120,460	0.6	2.0	1.9	0.9	2.7
Jointly registered outside marriage										
I	3	10	16	7	4,870	0.6	2.7	3.3	1.4	4.7
II	9	34	47	29	30,650	0.3	1.4	1.5	0.9	2.5
IIIn	7	15	16	16	17,000	0.4	1.3	0.9	0.9	1.9
IIIm	39	107	151	103	113,200	0.3	1.3	1.3	0.9	2.2
IV	17	77	99	47	50,750	0.3	1.8	2.0	0.9	2.9
V	22	54	65	41	40,260	0.5	1.9	1.6	1.0	2.6
Other	8	19	34	23	12,040	0.7	2.2	2.8	1.9	4.7
All#	105	316	428	266	268,770	0.4	1.6	1.6	1.0	2.6
All with fathers										
I	66	193	258	100	164,330	0.4	1.6	1.6	0.6	2.2
II	220	584	775	389	498,870	0.4	1.6	1.6	0.8	2.3
IIIn	132	337	434	193	245,820	0.5	1.9	1.8	0.8	2.6
IIIm	501	1,157	1,544	736	860,430	0.6	1.9	1.8	0.9	2.6

A5.7.1 *continued*

Aggregated stillbirth and mortality rates in the first year of life by social class of father, England and Wales, 1982–85, 1986–90, and 1991–95

Marital status and social class of father	Numbers					Rates				
	Stillbirths	Early neonatal deaths	Neonatal deaths	Post-neonatal deaths	Live births	Stillbirth*	Perinatal*	Neonatal*	Post-neonatal*	Infant*
IV	270	588	780	398	356,890	0.8	2.4	2.2	1.1	3.3
V	132	282	359	173	162,480	0.8	2.5	2.2	1.1	3.3
Other	56	195	248	131	100,410	0.6	2.5	2.5	1.3	3.8
All#	1,377	3,336	4,398	2,120	2,389,230	0.6	2.0	1.8	0.9	2.7
Sole registration	163	228	301	185	159,921	1.0	2.4	1.9	1.2	3.0
All#	1,540	3,564	4,699	2,305	2,548,300	0.6	2.0	1.8	0.9	2.7
All causes except congenital anomalies, ONS cause group 1										
Inside marriage										
I	600	364	435	301	159,460	3.7	6.0	2.7	1.9	4.6
II	1,941	1,178	1,428	1,010	468,220	4.1	6.6	3.0	2.2	5.2
IIIn	1,047	597	734	489	228,820	4.6	7.1	3.2	2.1	5.3
IIIm	3,778	2,208	2,644	1,926	747,230	5.0	8.0	3.5	2.6	6.1
IV	1,864	1,100	1,346	1,032	306,140	6.0	9.6	4.4	3.4	7.8
V	838	480	570	564	122,220	6.8	10.7	4.7	4.6	9.3
Other	461	311	406	491	88,370	5.2	8.7	4.6	5.6	10.2
All#	10,530	6,238	7,563	5,819	2,120,460	4.9	7.9	3.6	2.7	6.3
Jointly registered outside marriage										
I	10	18	22	14	4,870	2.0	5.7	4.5	2.9	7.4
II	95	112	136	96	30,650	3.1	6.7	4.4	3.1	7.6
IIIn	72	70	85	58	17,000	4.2	8.3	5.0	3.4	8.4
IIIm	501	402	508	432	113,200	4.4	7.9	4.5	3.8	8.3
IV	234	219	267	218	50,750	4.6	8.9	5.3	4.3	9.6
V	185	151	190	256	40,260	4.6	8.3	4.7	6.4	11.1
Other	63	110	129	124	12,040	5.2	14.3	10.7	10.3	21.0
All#	1,160	1,082	1,337	1,202	268,770	4.3	8.3	5.0	4.5	9.4

Aggregated stillbirth and mortality rates in the first year of life by social class of father, England and Wales, 1982–85, 1986–90, and 1991–95

Marital status and social class of father	Numbers					Rates				
	Stillbirths	Early neonatal deaths	Neonatal deaths	Post-neonatal deaths	Live births	Stillbirth*	Perinatal*	Neonatal*	Post-neonatal*	Infant*
All with fathers										
I	610	382	457	315	164,330	3.7	6.0	2.8	1.9	4.7
II	2,036	1,290	1,564	1,106	498,870	4.1	6.6	3.1	2.2	5.4
IIIn	1,119	667	819	547	245,820	4.5	7.2	3.3	2.2	5.6
IIIm	4,279	2,610	3,152	2,358	860,430	4.9	8.0	3.7	2.7	6.4
IV	2,098	1,319	1,613	1,250	356,890	5.8	9.5	4.5	3.5	8.0
V	1,023	631	760	820	162,480	6.3	10.1	4.7	5.0	9.7
Other	524	421	535	615	100,410	5.2	9.4	5.3	6.1	11.5
All#	11,690	7,320	8,900	7,021	2,389,230	4.9	7.9	3.7	2.9	6.7
Sole registration	1,645	784	948	1,046	159,921	10.2	15.0	5.9	6.5	12.5
All	13,335	8,104	9,848	8,067	2,548,300	5.2	8.4	3.9	3.2	7.0

Stillbirths and infant deaths among babies born 1986–90
All causes

	Stillbirths	Early neonatal deaths	Neonatal deaths	Post-neonatal deaths	Live births	Stillbirth*	Perinatal*	Neonatal*	Post-neonatal*	Infant*
Inside marriage										
I	732	646	807	498	210,210	3.5	6.5	3.8	2.4	6.2
II	2,367	1,928	2,441	1,421	630,310	3.7	6.8	3.9	2.3	6.1
IIIn	1,181	890	1,138	756	266,680	4.4	7.7	4.3	2.8	7.1
IIIm	4,068	3,013	3,835	2,388	873,640	4.6	8.1	4.4	2.7	7.1
IV	1,890	1,404	1,804	1,455	342,560	5.5	9.6	5.3	4.2	9.5
V	795	549	718	682	124,910	6.3	10.7	5.7	5.5	11.2
Other	636	576	735	634	116,690	5.4	10.3	6.3	5.4	11.7
All#	11,669	9,018	11,497	7,863	2,565,000	4.5	8.0	4.5	3.1	7.5
Jointly registered outside marriage										
I	52	64	73	29	14,190	3.7	8.1	5.1	2.0	7.2
II	316	281	356	237	78,620	4.0	7.6	4.5	3.0	7.5
IIIn	160	158	199	148	38,010	4.2	8.3	5.2	3.9	9.1
IIIm	1,190	1,120	1,414	1,047	253,330	4.7	9.1	5.6	4.1	9.7

A5.7.1 continued

Aggregated stillbirth and mortality rates in the first year of life by social class of father, England and Wales, 1982-85, 1986-90, and 1991-95

Marital status and social class of father	Numbers					Rates				
	Stillbirths	Early neonatal deaths	Neonatal deaths	Post-neonatal deaths	Live births	Stillbirth*	Perinatal*	Neonatal*	Post-neonatal*	Infant*
IV	623	556	729	649	116,850	5.3	10.0	6.2	5.6	11.8
V	431	388	508	485	76,130	5.6	10.7	6.7	6.4	13.0
Other	154	177	228	332	26,200	5.8	12.6	8.7	12.7	21.4
All#	2,926	2,767	3,537	2,990	603,330	4.8	9.4	5.9	5.0	10.8
All with fathers										
I	784	710	880	527	224,400	3.5	6.6	3.9	2.3	6.3
II	2,683	2,209	2,797	1,658	708,930	3.8	6.9	3.9	2.3	6.3
IIIn	1,341	1,048	1,337	904	304,690	4.4	7.8	4.4	3.0	7.4
IIIm	5,258	4,133	5,249	3,435	1,126,970	4.6	8.3	4.7	3.0	7.7
IV	2,513	1,960	2,533	2,104	459,410	5.4	9.7	5.5	4.6	10.1
V	1,226	937	1,226	1,167	201,040	6.1	10.7	6.1	5.8	11.9
Other	790	753	963	966	142,890	5.5	10.7	6.7	6.8	13.5
All#	14,595	11,785	15,034	10,853	3,168,330	4.6	8.3	4.7	3.4	8.2
Sole registration	2,249	1,270	1,597	1,930	260,608	8.6	13.4	6.1	7.4	13.5
All	16,844	13,055	16,631	12,783	3,429,971	4.9	8.7	4.8	3.7	8.6
Inside marriage										
Congenital anomalies, ONS cause group 1										
I	89	249	314	129	210,210	0.4	1.6	1.5	0.6	2.1
II	236	686	904	347	630,310	0.4	1.5	1.4	0.6	2.0
IIIn	111	305	413	196	266,680	0.4	1.6	1.5	0.7	2.3
IIIm	356	1,003	1,336	550	873,640	0.4	1.5	1.5	0.6	2.2
IV	178	524	672	342	342,560	0.5	2.0	2.0	1.0	3.0
V	77	198	266	145	124,910	0.6	2.2	2.1	1.2	3.3
Other	62	206	275	117	116,690	0.5	2.3	2.4	1.0	3.4
All#	1,109	3,173	4,185	1,830	2,565,000	0.4	1.7	1.6	0.7	2.3

Aggregated stillbirth and mortality rates in the first year of life by social class of father, England and Wales, 1982–85, 1986–90, and 1991–95

Marital status and social class of father	Numbers					Rates				
	Stillbirths	Early neonatal deaths	Neonatal deaths	Post-neonatal deaths	Live births	Stillbirth*	Perinatal*	Neonatal*	Post-neonatal*	Infant*
Jointly registered outside marriage										
I	7	13	16	5	14,190	0.5	1.4	1.1	0.4	1.5
II	29	74	98	38	78,620	0.4	1.3	1.2	0.5	1.7
IIIn	12	45	58	18	38,010	0.3	1.5	1.5	0.5	2.0
IIIm	78	314	409	141	253,330	0.3	1.5	1.6	0.6	2.2
IV	50	163	220	89	116,850	0.4	1.8	1.9	0.8	2.6
V	42	122	164	54	76,130	0.5	2.1	2.2	0.7	2.9
Other	13	42	55	37	26,200	0.5	2.1	2.1	1.4	3.5
All#	231	779	1,030	384	603,330	0.4	1.7	1.7	0.6	2.3
All with fathers										
I	96	262	330	134	224,400	0.4	1.6	1.5	0.6	2.1
II	265	760	1,002	385	708,930	0.4	1.4	1.4	0.5	2.0
IIIn	123	350	471	214	304,690	0.4	1.5	1.5	0.7	2.2
IIIm	434	1,317	1,745	691	1,126,970	0.4	1.5	1.5	0.6	2.2
IV	228	687	892	431	459,410	0.5	2.0	1.9	0.9	2.9
V	119	320	430	199	201,040	0.6	2.2	2.1	1.0	3.1
Other	75	248	330	154	142,890	0.5	2.2	2.3	1.1	3.4
All#	1,340	3,952	5,215	2,214	3,168,330	0.4	1.7	1.6	0.7	2.3
Sole registration	209	333	438	193	260,608	0.8	2.1	1.7	0.7	2.4
All	1,549	4,285	5,653	2,407	3,429,971	0.4	1.7	1.6	0.7	2.3
All causes except congenital anomalies, ONS cause group 1										
Inside marriage										
I	643	397	493	369	210,210	3.0	4.9	2.3	1.8	4.1
II	2,131	1,242	1,537	1,074	630,310	3.4	5.3	2.4	1.7	4.1

A5.7.1 continued

Aggregated stillbirth and mortality rates in the first year of life by social class of father, England and Wales, 1982–85, 1986–90, and 1991–95

Marital status and social class of father	Numbers					Rates				
	Stillbirths	Early neonatal deaths	Neonatal deaths	Post-neonatal deaths	Live births	Stillbirth*	Perinatal*	Neonatal*	Post-neonatal*	Infant*
IIIn	1,070	585	725	560	266,680	4.0	6.2	2.7	2.1	4.8
IIIm	3,712	2,010	2,499	1,838	873,640	4.2	6.5	2.9	2.1	5.0
IV	1,712	880	1,132	1,113	342,560	5.0	7.5	3.3	3.2	6.6
V	718	351	452	537	124,910	5.7	8.5	3.6	4.3	7.9
Other	574	370	460	517	116,690	4.9	8.0	3.9	4.4	8.4
All#	10,560	5,845	7,312	6,033	2,565,000	4.1	6.4	2.9	2.4	5.2
Jointly registered outside marriage										
I	45	51	57	24	14,190	3.2	6.7	4.0	1.7	5.7
II	287	207	258	199	78,620	3.6	6.3	3.3	2.5	5.8
IIIn	148	113	141	130	38,010	3.9	6.8	3.7	3.4	7.1
IIIm	1,112	806	1,005	906	253,330	4.4	7.5	4.0	3.6	7.5
IV	573	393	509	560	116,850	4.9	8.2	4.4	4.8	9.1
V	389	266	344	431	76,130	5.1	8.6	4.5	5.7	10.2
Other	141	135	173	295	26,200	5.4	10.5	6.6	11.3	17.9
All#	2,695	1,988	2,507	2,606	603,330	4.4	7.7	4.2	4.3	8.5
All with fathers										
I	688	448	550	393	224,400	3.1	5.0	2.5	1.8	4.2
II	2,418	1,449	1,795	1,273	708,930	3.4	5.4	2.5	1.8	4.3
IIIn	1,218	698	866	690	304,690	4.0	6.3	2.8	2.3	5.1
IIIm	4,824	2,816	3,504	2,744	1,126,970	4.3	6.7	3.1	2.4	5.5
IV	2,285	1,273	1,641	1,673	459,410	4.9	7.7	3.6	3.6	7.2
V	1,107	617	796	968	201,040	5.5	8.5	4.0	4.8	8.8
Other	715	505	633	812	142,890	5.0	8.5	4.4	5.7	10.1
All#	13,255	7,833	9,819	8,639	3,168,330	4.2	6.6	3.1	2.7	5.8
Sole registration	2,040	937	1,159	1,737	260,608	7.8	11.3	4.4	6.7	11.1
All	15,295	8,770	10,978	10,376	3,429,971	4.4	7.0	3.2	3.0	6.2

A5.7.1 continued

Aggregated stillbirth and mortality rates in the first year of life by social class of father, England and Wales, 1982–85, 1986–90, and 1991–95

Stillbirths at 28 or more weeks of gestational age and infant deaths among babies born 1991–95

Marital status and social class of father	Numbers					Rates				
	Stillbirths	Early neonatal deaths	Neonatal deaths	Post-neonatal deaths	Live births	Stillbirth*	Perinatal*	Neonatal*	Post-neonatal*	Infant*
Inside marriage										
All causes										
I	703	536	664	269	206,110	2.6	6.0	3.2	1.3	4.5
II	2,230	1,708	2,149	802	631,550	2.7	6.2	3.4	1.3	4.7
IIIn	990	774	978	377	249,550	3.1	7.0	3.9	1.5	5.4
IIIm	2,931	2,074	2,717	1,207	713,950	2.9	7.0	3.8	1.7	5.5
IV	1,395	954	1,195	572	284,180	3.3	8.2	4.2	2.0	6.2
V	628	331	443	256	97,640	3.4	9.8	4.5	2.6	7.2
Other	639	473	615	357	113,680	4.1	9.7	5.4	3.1	8.6
All#	9,516	6,881	8,805	3,886	2,296,660	3.0	7.1	3.8	1.7	5.5
Jointly registered outside marriage										
I	102	53	72	42	21,940	2.4	7.0	3.3	1.9	5.2
II	448	396	523	203	122,780	3.2	6.8	4.3	1.7	5.9
IIIn	244	242	301	132	59,350	4.1	8.2	5.1	2.2	7.3
IIIm	1,567	1,216	1,571	807	335,480	3.6	8.3	4.7	2.4	7.1
IV	760	636	798	410	153,500	4.1	9.0	5.2	2.7	7.9
V	473	363	467	295	84,900	4.3	9.8	5.5	3.5	9.0
Other	314	276	359	260	45,070	6.1	13.0	8.0	5.8	13.7
All#	3,908	3,220	4,142	2,243	823,020	3.9	8.6	5.0	2.7	7.8
All with fathers										
I	805	589	736	311	228,050	2.6	6.1	3.2	1.4	4.6
II	2,678	2,104	2,672	1,005	754,330	2.8	6.3	3.5	1.3	4.9
IIIn	1,234	1,016	1,279	509	308,900	3.3	7.3	4.1	1.6	5.8
IIIm	4,498	3,290	4,288	2,014	1,049,430	3.1	7.4	4.1	1.9	6.0
IV	2,155	1,590	1,993	982	437,680	3.6	8.5	4.6	2.2	6.8
V	1,101	694	910	551	182,540	3.8	9.8	5.0	3.0	8.0
Other	953	749	974	617	158,750	4.7	10.7	6.1	3.9	10.0
All#	13,424	10,101	12,947	6,129	3,119,680	3.2	7.5	4.2	2.0	6.1

A5.7.1 continued

Aggregated stillbirth and mortality rates in the first year of life by social class of father, England and Wales, 1982–85, 1986–90, and 1991–95

Marital status and social class of father	Numbers					Rates				
	Stillbirths	Early neonatal deaths	Neonatal deaths	Post-neonatal deaths	Live births	Stillbirth*	Perinatal*	Neonatal*	Post-neonatal*	Infant*
Sole registration	1,576	878	1,107	1,043	252,562	3.5	9.7	4.4	4.1	8.5
All	15,000	10,979	14,054	7,172	3,372,354	3.2	7.7	4.2	2.1	6.3
Congenital anomalies, ONS cause group 1										
Inside marriage										
I	62	156	210	93	206,110	0.8	1.1	1.0	0.5	1.5
II	198	531	712	262	631,550	0.8	1.2	1.1	0.4	1.5
IIIn	77	218	291	120	249,550	0.9	1.2	1.2	0.5	1.6
IIIm	234	624	839	380	713,950	0.9	1.2	1.2	0.5	1.7
IV	109	291	383	175	284,180	1.0	1.4	1.3	0.6	2.0
V	53	95	134	71	97,640	1.0	1.5	1.4	0.7	2.1
Other	71	164	222	117	113,680	1.4	2.1	2.0	1.0	3.0
All#	804	2,092	2,809	1,222	2,296,660	0.9	1.3	1.2	0.5	1.8
Jointly registered outside marriage										
I	8	15	19	14	21,940	0.7	1.0	0.9	0.6	1.5
II	31	84	129	51	122,780	0.7	0.9	1.1	0.4	1.5
IIIn	10	58	74	21	59,350	1.0	1.1	1.2	0.4	1.6
IIIm	106	277	383	135	335,480	0.8	1.1	1.1	0.4	1.5
IV	48	154	200	80	153,500	1.0	1.3	1.3	0.5	1.8
V	29	74	103	49	84,900	0.9	1.2	1.2	0.6	1.8
Other	27	58	90	55	45,070	1.3	1.9	2.0	1.2	3.2
All#	259	726	1,005	408	823,020	0.9	1.2	1.2	0.5	1.7
All with fathers										
I	70	171	229	107	228,050	0.7	1.1	1.0	0.5	1.5
II	229	615	841	313	754,330	0.8	1.1	1.1	0.4	1.5
IIIn	87	276	365	141	308,900	0.9	1.2	1.2	0.5	1.6

A5.7.1 continued

Aggregated stillbirth and mortality rates in the first year of life by social class of father, England and Wales, 1982-85, 1986-90, and 1991-95

Marital status and social class of father	Numbers					Rates				
	Stillbirths	Early neonatal deaths	Neonatal deaths	Post-neonatal deaths	Live births	Stillbirth*	Perinatal*	Neonatal*	Post-neonatal*	Infant*
IIIm	340	901	1,222	515	1,049,430	0.9	1.2	1.2	0.5	1.7
IV	157	445	583	255	437,680	1.0	1.4	1.3	0.6	1.9
V	82	169	237	120	182,540	0.9	1.4	1.3	0.7	2.0
Other	98	222	312	172	158,750	1.4	2.0	2.0	1.1	3.0
All#	1,063	2,818	3,814	1,630	3,119,680	0.9	1.2	1.2	0.5	1.7
Sole registration	126	184	248	152	252,562	0.7	1.2	1.0	0.6	1.6
All	1,189	3,002	4,062	1,782	3,372,354	0.9	1.2	1.2	0.5	1.7
All causes except congenital anomalies, ONS cause group 1										
Inside marriage										
I	641	380	454	176	206,110	1.8	4.9	2.2	0.9	3.1
II	2,032	1,177	1,437	540	631,550	1.9	5.1	2.3	0.9	3.1
IIIn	913	556	687	257	249,550	2.2	5.9	2.8	1.0	3.8
IIIm	2,697	1,450	1,878	827	713,950	2.0	5.8	2.6	1.2	3.8
IV	1,286	663	812	397	284,180	2.3	6.8	2.9	1.4	4.3
V	575	236	309	185	97,640	2.4	8.3	3.2	1.9	5.1
Other	568	309	393	240	113,680	2.7	7.7	3.5	2.1	5.6
All#	8,712	4,789	5,996	2,664	2,296,660	2.1	5.9	2.6	1.2	3.8
Jointly registered outside marriage										
I	94	38	53	28	21,940	1.7	6.0	2.4	1.3	3.7
II	417	312	394	152	122,780	2.5	5.9	3.2	1.2	4.4
IIIn	234	184	227	111	59,350	3.1	7.0	3.8	1.9	5.7
IIIm	1,461	939	1,188	672	335,480	2.8	7.1	3.5	2.0	5.5
IV	712	482	598	330	153,500	3.1	7.7	3.9	2.1	6.0
V	444	289	364	246	84,900	3.4	8.6	4.3	2.9	7.2
Other	287	218	269	205	45,070	4.8	11.1	6.0	4.5	10.5
All#	3,649	2,494	3,137	1,835	823,020	3.0	7.4	3.8	2.2	6.0

Aggregated stillbirth and mortality rates in the first year of life by social class of father, England and Wales, 1982–85, 1986–90, and 1991–95

Marital status and social class of father	Numbers					Rates				
	Stillbirths	Early neonatal deaths	Neonatal deaths	Post-neonatal deaths	Live births	Stillbirth*	Perinatal*	Neonatal*	Post-neonatal*	Infant*
All with fathers										
I	735	418	507	204	228,050	1.8	5.0	2.2	0.9	3.1
II	2,449	1,489	1,831	692	754,330	2.0	5.2	2.4	0.9	3.3
IIn	1,147	740	914	368	308,900	2.4	6.1	3.0	1.2	4.2
IIIm	4,158	2,389	3,066	1,499	1,049,430	2.3	6.2	2.9	1.4	4.3
IV	1,998	1,145	1,410	727	437,680	2.6	7.1	3.2	1.7	4.9
V	1,019	525	673	431	182,540	2.9	8.4	3.7	2.4	6.0
Other	855	527	662	445	158,750	3.3	8.7	4.2	2.8	7.0
All#	12,361	7,283	9,133	4,499	3,119,680	2.3	6.3	2.9	1.4	4.4
Sole registration	1,450	694	859	891	252,562	2.7	8.4	3.4	3.5	6.9
All	13,811	7,977	9,992	5,390	3,372,354	2.4	6.4	3.0	1.6	4.6

\# Includes cases where the father's social class was not stated

* Rate per thousand total births

+ Rate per thousand live births

Data for live births are estimated from a ten per cent sample

Data for 1981 have not been included in this table because of anomalies arising following industrial action by local registrars of births and deaths

Source: Authors' analysis of ONS/OPCS data

Data extract: live births 1993 (7/94), 1994 (7/95), 1995 (3/7/96), 1996 (8/4/97)

     linked   1993 (3/4/96), 1994 (18/9/96), 1995 (3/11/97)

This is similar to Table A5.3 in the first edition of Birth counts

A5.8.1

Deaths of one, two and three year olds by year of birth and social class of father, England and Wales, 1993–95

Year of birth	Age at death	All	Social class of father					
			I	II	IIIn	IIIm	IV	V
Numbers								
1993	Under 1	3,714	210	717	341	1,153	499	242
	1	261	10	37	28	70	43	23
	2	174	13	32	8	48	23	13
	3	113	4	26	8	26	18	3
1994	Under 1	3,574	201	676	328	1,088	537	239
	1	266	13	41	25	63	44	22
	2	161	7	24	17	54	32	14
1995	Under 1	3,578	192	703	323	1,031	576	243
	1	251	6	45	32	81	30	12
Rates per 100,000 live births								
1993	Under 1	598	458	480	544	562	553	664
	1	42	22	25	45	34	48	64
	2	28	28	22	13	24	26	36
	3	18	9	18	13	13	20	8
1994	Under 1	581	433	451	520	541	611	663
	1	43	28	27	40	31	50	61
	2	26	15	16	27	27	37	39
1995	Under 1	596	422	476	528	536	659	710
	1	42	13	31	53	42	35	35

Source: ONS, *Health Statistics quarterly* 2, page 44

This is a new table for this edition of *Birth counts*

A5.8.2

Deaths of one, two and three year olds born inside and outside marriage, England and Wales, 1993–95

Year of birth	Age at death, years	All	Inside marriage	Outside marriage, joint registration, same address	Outside marriage, joint registration, different address	Outside marriage, sole registration
Numbers						
1993	Under 1	4,141	2,472	863	379	427
	1	299	168	67	26	38
	2	192	128	25	21	18
	3	122	73	30	9	10
1994	Under 1	3,982	2,378	820	376	408
	1	301	173	57	36	35
	2	179	104	40	17	18
1995	Under 1	3,948	2,278	906	394	370
	1	293	161	64	26	42
Rates per 100,000 live births						
1993	Under 1	617	543	730	800	854
	1	45	37	57	55	77
	2	29	28	21	45	36
	3	18	16	26	19	20
1994	Under 1	599	530	662	884	832
	1	46	39	46	85	72
	2	27	23	33	40	37
1995	Under 1	609	532	709	892	772
	1	46	38	50	59	88

Source: ONS, *Health statistics quarterly 2*, page 46

This is a new table for this edition of *Birth counts*

A5.9.1

Aggregated stillbirth and mortality rates in the first year of life by social class of mother, England and Wales, 1986–90, 1991–95, and stillbirths, 1993–96

Social class of mother and marital status	Stillbirths	Neonatal deaths	Postneonatal deaths	Live births	Stillbirth*	Neonatal*	Postneonatal*	Infant*
	Numbers				Rates			

Stillbirths and infant deaths among babies born 1986–90

Social class of mother and marital status	Stillbirths	Neonatal deaths	Postneonatal deaths	Live births	Stillbirth*	Neonatal*	Postneonatal*	Infant*
Inside marriage								
I	107	152	85	39,460	2.7	3.9	2.2	6.0
II	1,117	1,383	612	372,650	3.0	3.7	1.6	5.4
IIIn	1,554	1,680	588	451,780	3.4	3.7	1.3	5.0
IIIm	316	372	159	87,740	3.6	4.2	1.8	6.1
IV	500	473	225	118,510	4.2	4.0	1.9	5.9
V	55	52	45	10,970	5.0	4.7	4.1	8.8
Unclassified-	54	69	27	14,190	3.8	4.9	1.9	6.8
No occupation stated	7,966	7,287	6,072	1,469,700	5.4	5.0	4.1	9.1
All	11,669	11,497	7,863	2,565,000	4.5	4.5	3.1	7.5
Jointly registered outside marriage								
I	12	14	10	2,980	4.0	4.7	3.4	8.1
II	168	233	115	48,050	3.5	4.8	2.4	7.2
IIIn	351	493	193	92,160	3.8	5.3	2.1	7.4
IIIm	112	154	78	28,090	4.0	5.5	2.8	8.3
IV	250	322	119	51,440	4.8	6.3	2.3	8.6
V	24	48	28	5,250	4.6	9.1	5.3	14.5
Unclassified-	19	13	13	3,930	4.8	3.3	3.3	6.6
No occupation stated	1,990	2,259	2,420	371,430	5.3	6.1	6.5	12.6
All	2,926	3,537	2,990	603,330	4.8	5.9	5.0	10.8
Sole registration by mother								
I	5	1	2	560	8.8	1.8	3.6	5.4
II	99	71	46	12,150	8.1	5.8	3.8	9.6
IIIn	217	215	125	30,580	7.0	7.0	4.1	11.1
IIIm	65	76	46	11,100	5.8	6.8	4.1	11.0
IV	182	141	99	26,100	6.9	5.4	3.8	9.2
V	24	22	14	2,130	11.1	10.3	6.6	16.9

A5.9.1 *continued*

Aggregated stillbirth and mortality rates in the first year of life by social class of mother, England and Wales, 1986–90, 1991–95, and stillbirths, 1993–96

Social class of mother and marital status	Stillbirths	Neonatal deaths	Postneonatal deaths	Live births	Stillbirth*	Neonatal*	Postneonatal*	Infant*
Unclassified-	18	10	7	1,370	13.0	7.3	5.1	12.4
No occupation stated	1,639	1,059	1,588	177,160	9.2	6.0	9.0	14.9
All	2,249	1,597	1,930	261,150	8.5	6.1	7.4	13.5
All births								
I	124	167	97	43,000	2.9	3.9	2.3	6.1
II	1,384	1,687	773	432,850	3.2	3.9	1.8	5.7
IIIn	2,122	2,388	906	574,520	3.7	4.2	1.6	5.7
IIIm	493	602	283	126,930	3.9	4.7	2.2	7.0
IV	932	936	443	196,050	4.7	4.8	2.3	7.0
V	103	122	87	18,350	5.6	6.6	4.7	11.4
Unclassified-	91	92	47	19,490	4.6	4.7	2.4	7.1
No occupation stated	11,595	10,605	10,080	2,018,290	5.7	5.3	5.0	10.2
All	16,844	16,631	12,783	3,429,971	4.9	4.8	3.7	8.6

Stillbirths at 28 or more weeks of gestational age and infant deaths among babies born 1991–95

	Stillbirths	Neonatal deaths	Postneonatal deaths	Live births	Stillbirth*	Neonatal*	Postneonatal*	Infant*
Inside marriage								
I	190	152	76	63,270	3.0	3.2	1.2	4.4
II	1,440	1,383	534	473,450	3.0	3.3	1.1	4.4
IIIn	1,588	1,680	506	530,660	3.0	3.3	1.0	4.3
IIIm	305	372	100	97,020	3.1	3.6	1.0	4.6
IV	518	473	157	129,050	4.0	3.7	1.2	4.9
V	92	52	34	20,990	4.4	5.3	1.6	6.9
Unclassified-	98	69	41	22,960	4.3	5.5	1.8	7.3
No occupation stated	5,285	7,287	2,420	959,260	5.5	4.4	2.5	6.9
All	9,516	11,497	3,886	2,296,660	4.1	3.8	1.7	5.5
Jointly registered outside marriage								
I	25	14	12	6,340	3.9	3.8	1.9	5.7
II	318	233	146	90,680	3.5	4.5	1.6	6.1
IIIn	516	493	195	149,720	3.4	4.2	1.3	5.5

A5.9.1 continued

Aggregated stillbirth and mortality rates in the first year of life by social class of mother, England and Wales, 1986-90, 1991-95, and stillbirths, 1993-96

Social class of mother and marital status	Stillbirths	Neonatal deaths	Postneonatal deaths	Live births	Stillbirth*	Neonatal*	Postneonatal*	Infant*
IIIm	176	154	97	48,180	3.6	4.3	2.0	6.3
IV	367	322	133	78,460	4.7	5.1	1.7	6.8
V	50	48	34	11,540	4.3	5.9	2.9	8.8
Unclassified-	53	13	60	9,350	5.6	6.6	6.4	13.0
No occupation stated	2,403	2,259	1,559	428,750	5.6	5.4	3.6	9.1
All	3,908	3,537	2,243	823,020	4.7	5.0	2.7	7.8
Sole registration by mother								
I	5	1	0	750	6.6	8.0	0.0	8.0
II	65	71	34	14,730	4.4	5.0	2.3	7.3
IIIn	153	215	60	29,830	5.1	3.8	2.0	5.8
IIIm	61	76	26	11,340	5.4	3.6	2.3	5.9
IV	112	141	69	21,810	5.1	4.8	3.2	7.9
V	13	22	10	3,550	3.6	5.1	2.8	7.9
Unclassified~	10	10	8	2,300	4.3	5.2	3.5	8.7
No occupation stated	1,157	1,059	830	168,100	6.8	4.4	4.9	9.3
All	1,576	1,597	1,043	252,410	6.2	4.4	4.1	8.5
All births								
I	220	167	88	70,360	3.1	2.4	1.3	3.6
II	1,823	1,687	714	578,860	3.1	2.9	1.2	4.1
IIIn	2,257	2,388	761	710,210	3.2	3.4	1.1	4.4
IIIm	542	602	223	156,540	3.5	3.8	1.4	5.3
IV	997	936	359	229,320	4.3	4.1	1.6	5.6
V	155	122	78	36,080	4.3	3.4	2.2	5.5
Unclassified~	161	92	109	34,610	4.6	2.7	3.1	5.8
No occupation stated	8,845	10,605	4,809	1,556,110	5.7	6.8	3.1	9.9
All	15,000	16,631	7,172	3,372,090	4.4	4.9	2.1	7.1

Stillbirths at 24 or more weeks of gestational age among babies born 1993-96

All births	Numbers				Rates*			
I	230	14	6	250	4.2	2.5	9.0	4.1
II	1,605	407	106	2,118	4.1	5.0	8.9	4.4
IIIn	1,749	632	143	2,524	4.1	4.9	6.1	4.4
IIIm	349	221	53	623	4.6	5.4	5.9	5.0

A5.9.1 continued

Aggregated stillbirth and mortality rates in the first year of life by social class of mother, England and Wales, 1986–90, 1991–95, and stillbirths, 1993–96

Stillbirths at 24 or more weeks of gestational age among babies born 1993-96

Social class of mother	Inside marriage	Outside marriage	Sole registration	All	Inside marriage	Outside marriage	Sole registration	All
	Numbers				**Rates***			
IV	578	418	111	1,107	5.3	6.0	6.3	5.7
V	113	69	18	200	6.6	6.6	6.3	6.6
Unclassified~	95	49	17	161	6.0	7.7	10.7	6.7
No occupation stated	4,416	2,375	1,044	7,835	6.5	7.0	7.9	6.8
All	9,135	4,185	1,498	14,818	5.2	6.1	7.5	5.6

~ Includes armed forces

* Rate per thousand total births

+ Rate per thousand live births

Source: Authors' analysis of ONS data

Data extract: live births 1993 (7/94), 1994 (7/95), 1995 (3/7/96), 1996 (8/4/97)

linked 1993 (3/4/96), 1994 (18/9/96), 1995 (3/11/97)

This is a new table for this edition of *Birth counts*

A5.10.1

Births outside marriage and premarital conceptions, England and Wales, 1938–98

Year	All births outside marriage			Jointly registered by both parents					Sole registration by the mother alone			Conceived outside marriage†
	Live births	Stillbirths	Total	Same address	Different address	Live births	Stillbirths	Total	Live births	Stillbirths	Total	Live births
	Numbers											
1938	26,379	1,376	27,755	:	:	:	:	:	:	:	:	64,530
1939	25,570	1,272	26,842	:	:	:	:	:	:	:	:	60,346
1940	25,633	1,282	26,915	:	:	:	:	:	:	:	:	
1941	31,058	1,492	32,550	:	:	:	:	:	:	:	:	
1942	36,467	1,549	38,016	:	:	:	:	:	:	:	:	
1943	43,709	1,702	45,411	:	:	:	:	:	:	:	:	43,146**
1944	55,173	1,957	57,130	:	:	:	:	:	:	:	:	
1945	63,420	2,063	65,483	:	:	:	:	:	:	:	:	
1946	53,919	1,849	55,768	:	:	:	:	:	:	:	:	
1947	46,603	1,472	48,075	:	:	:	:	:	:	:	:	52,557**
1948	41,574	1,358	42,932	:	:	:	:	:	:	:	:	
1949	36,907	1,123	38,030	:	:	:	:	:	:	:	:	
1950	35,250	1,056	36,306	:	:	:	:	:	:	:	:	54,188
1951	32,771	1,068	33,839	:	:	:	:	:	:	:	:	50,477
1952	32,549	996	33,545	:	:	:	:	:	:	:	:	44,239
1953	32,503	1,000	33,503	:	:	:	:	:	:	:	:	43,988
1954	31,609	951	32,560	:	:	:	:	:	:	:	:	44,319
1955	31,145	922	32,067	:	:	:	:	:	:	:	:	43,601
1956	33,534	1,002	34,536	:	:	:	:	:	:	:	:	47,377
1957	34,562	1,023	35,585	:	:	:	:	:	:	:	:	48,611
1958	36,174	1,058	37,232	:	:	:	:	:	:	:	:	49,775
1959	38,161	1,074	39,235	:	:	:	:	:	:	:	:	50,871
1960	42,707	1,092	43,799	:	:	:	:	:	:	:	:	54,576
1961	48,490	1,201	49,691	:	:	18,456	:	:	31,235	:	:	59,115
1962	55,376	1,289	56,665	:	:	21,748	:	:	34,917	:	:	62,455
1963	59,104	1,236	60,340	:	:	23,944	:	:	36,396	:	:	64,427
1964	63,340	1,309	64,649	:	:	25,746	:	:	38,903	:	:	67,933
1965	66,249	1,284	67,533	:	:	25,884	:	:	41,649	:	:	70,457
1966	67,056	1,268	68,324	:	:	25,842	:	:	43,382	:	:	71,648
1967	69,928	1,332	71,260	:	:	26,562	:	:	44,698	:	:	73,667

A5.10.1 continued

Births outside marriage and premarital conceptions, England and Wales, 1938–98

Year	All births outside marriage			Jointly registered by both parents					Sole registration by the mother alone			Conceived outside marriage
	Live births	Stillbirths	Total	Same address	Different address	Live births	Stillbirths	Total	Live births	Stillbirths	Total	Live births
1968	69,806	1,232	71,038	::	::	27,432	::	::	43,606	::	::	74,531
1969	67,041	1,107	68,148	::	::	27,601	::	::	40,547	::	::	72,595
1970	64,744	1,045	65,789	::	::	28,425	::	::	37,364	::	::	70,623
1971	65,678	1,072	66,750	::	::	30,093	::	::	36,657	::	::	67,294
1972	62,511	951	63,462	::	::	29,028	::	::	34,434	::	::	59,836
1973	58,097	879	58,976	::	::	27,113	::	::	31,863	::	::	52,293
1974	56,486	834	57,320	::	::	27,088	169	27,257	29,398	665	30,063	45,981
1975	54,891	716	55,607	::	::	26,905	161	27,066	27,986	555	28,541	40,293
1976	53,766	687	54,453	::	::	27,407	161	27,568	26,359	526	26,885	35,383
1977	55,379	699	56,078	::	::	29,315	168	29,483	26,064	531	26,595	32,913
1978	60,637	699	61,336	::	::	32,802	184	32,986	27,835	515	28,350	34,533
1979	69,467	715	70,182	::	::	38,349	204	38,553	31,118	511	31,629	37,448
1980	77,372	696	78,068	::	::	44,168	242	44,410	33,204	454	33,658	39,798
1981	80,983	697	81,680	::	::	46,883	217	47,100	33,850	480	34,330	36,170
1982	89,857	657	90,514	::	::	53,404	225	53,629	36,453	432	36,885	33,994
1983	99,211	718	99,929	7427*	2730*	60,794	293	61,087	38,417	425	38,842	33,347
1984	110,465	818	111,283	8843*	3373*	69,872	352	70,224	40,593	466	41,059	33,231
1985	126,250	872	127,122	10274*	3960*	81,792	394	82,186	44,458	478	44,936	34,328
1986	141,345	949	142,294	65,844	27,679	93,523	465	93,988	47,822	484	48,306	33,838
1987	158,431	1,019	159,450	75,572	32,385	107,957	571	108,528	50,474	448	50,922	33,269
1988	177,352	1,060	178,412	87,601	35,807	123,408	575	123,983	53,944	485	54,429	32,779
1989	185,804	1,067	186,871	95,858	36,409	132,267	623	132,890	53,537	485	54,022	31,233
1990	199,999	1,080	201,079	106,001	39,167	145,168	691	145,859	54,831	389	55,220	29,114
1991	211,294	1,154	212,448	115,298	41,865	157,163	776	157,939	54,131	378	54,509	25,765
1992	215,225	1,046	216,271	119,239	44,514	163,753	670	164,423	51,472	296	51,768	24,634
1993	216,548	1,424	217,972	118,758	47,548	166,306	1,029	167,335	50,242	395	50,637	22,673
1994	215,536	1,452	216,988	123,874	42,632	166,506	1,056	167,562	49,030	396	49,426	21,683
1995	219,949	1,376	221,325	127,789	44,244	172,033	1,028	173,061	47,916	348	48,264	20,250
1996	232,663	1,425	234,088	135,282	46,365	181,647	1,065	182,712	51,106	360	51,466	20,175
1997	238,222	1,429	239,651	141,740	45,900	187,640	1,065	188,705	50,582	364	50,946	19,596
1998	240,611	1,451	242,062	146,521	44,130	190,651	1,086	191,737	49,960	365	50,325	19,438

A5.10.1 continued

Births outside marriage and premarital conceptions, England and Wales, 1938–98

	All outside marriage	Jointly registered by both parents		Sole registration by the mother alone	Sole registration by the mother alone	Conceived outside marriage+	All outside marriage	Jointly registered by both parents	Sole registration by the mother alone
		Same address	Different address	All					
1938	4.2	..	..	..	..	10.4	4.3	..	..
1939	4.2	..	..	..	..	9.8	4.2	..	..
1940	4.3	..	..	..	..	..	4.4	..	..
1941	5.4	..	..	..	..	..	5.4	..	..
1942	5.6	..	..	..	..	..	5.6	..	..
1943	6.4	..	..	..	..	..	6.4	..	..
1944	7.3	..	..	..	..	..	7.4	..	..
1945	9.3	..	..	..	..	..	9.4	..	..
1946	6.6	..	..	..	..	..	6.6	..	..
1947	5.3	..	..	..	..	..	5.3	..	..
1948	5.4	..	..	..	..	..	5.4	..	..
1949	5.1	..	..	..	..	..	5.1	..	..
1950	5.1	..	..	..	..	7.8	5.1	..	..
1951	4.8	..	..	..	..	7.5	4.9	..	..
1952	4.8	..	..	..	..	6.6	4.9	..	..
1953	4.7	..	..	..	..	6.4	4.8	..	..
1954	4.7	..	..	..	..	6.6	4.7	..	..
1955	4.7	..	..	..	..	6.5	4.7	..	..
1956	4.8	..	..	..	..	6.8	4.8	..	..
1957	4.8	..	..	..	..	6.7	4.8	..	..
1958	4.9	..	..	..	..	6.7	4.9	..	..
1959	5.1	..	..	..	..	6.8	5.1	..	..
1960	5.4	..	..	..	..	7.0	5.5	..	..
1961	6.0	..	..	2.3	3.9	7.3	6.0	..	..
1962	6.6	..	..	2.6	4.2	7.4	6.6	..	..
1963	6.9	..	..	2.8	4.3	7.5	6.9	..	..

A5.10.1 continued

Births outside marriage and premarital conceptions, England and Wales, 1938–98

	All outside marriage	Jointly registered by both parents			Sole registration by the mother alone	Conceived outside marriage+	All outside marriage	Jointly registered by both parents	Sole registration by the mother alone
		Same address	Different address	All					
1964	7.2	..	..	2.9	4.4	7.8	7.3	..	..
1965	7.7	..	..	3.0	4.8	8.2	7.7	..	..
1966	7.9	..	..	3.0	5.1	8.4	7.9	..	..
1967	8.4	..	..	3.2	5.4	8.9	8.4	..	..
1968	8.5	..	..	3.3	5.3	9.1	8.5	..	..
1969	8.4	..	..	3.5	5.1	9.1	8.4	..	..
1970	8.3	..	..	3.6	4.8	9.0	8.3	..	..
1971	8.4	..	..	3.8	4.7	8.6	8.4	..	..
1972	8.6	..	..	4.0	4.7	8.2	8.4	..	..
1973	8.6	..	..	4.0	4.7	7.7	8.6	..	..
1974	8.8	..	..	4.2	4.6	7.2	8.9	4.2	4.6
1975	9.1	..	..	4.5	4.6	6.7	9.1	4.4	4.7
1976	9.2	..	..	4.7	4.5	6.1	9.2	4.7	4.6
1977	9.7	..	..	5.1	4.6	5.8	9.8	5.1	4.6
1978	10.2	..	..	5.5	4.7	5.8	10.2	5.5	4.7
1979	10.9	..	..	6.0	4.9	5.9	10.9	6.0	4.9
1980	11.8	..	..	6.7	5.1	6.1	11.8	6.7	5.1
1981	12.8	..	..	7.4	5.3	5.7	12.8	7.4	5.4
1982	14.4	..	..	8.5	5.8	5.4	14.4	8.5	5.9
1983	15.8	..	..	9.7	6.1	5.3	15.8	9.7	6.1
1984	17.3	..	..	11.0	6.4	5.2	17.4	11.0	6.4
1985	19.2	..	..	12.5	6.8	5.2	19.3	12.5	6.8
1986	21.4	10.0	4.2	14.1	7.2	5.1	21.4	14.1	7.3
1987	23.2	11.1	4.8	15.8	7.4	4.9	23.3	15.8	7.4
1988	25.6	12.6	5.2	17.8	7.8	4.7	25.6	17.8	7.8
1989	27.0	13.9	5.3	19.2	7.8	4.5	27.0	19.2	7.8

A5.10.1 continued

Births outside marriage and premarital conceptions, England and Wales, 1938–98

	All outside marriage	Jointly registered by both parents			Sole registration by the mother alone	Conceived outside marriage+	All outside marriage	Jointly registered by both parents	Sole registration by the mother alone
		Same address	Different address	All					
1989	27.0	13.9	5.3	19.2	7.8	4.5	27.0	19.2	7.8
1990	28.3	15.0	5.5	20.6	7.8	4.1	28.3	20.6	7.8
1991	30.2	16.5	6.0	22.5	7.7	3.7	30.2	22.5	7.8
1992	31.2	17.3	6.5	23.7	7.5	3.6	31.2	23.7	7.5
1993	32.3	17.7	7.1	24.8	7.5	3.4	32.3	24.8	7.5
1994	32.4	18.6	6.4	25.1	7.4	3.3	32.5	25.1	7.4
1995	33.9	19.7	6.8	26.5	7.4	3.1	34.0	26.6	7.4
1996	35.8	20.8	7.1	28.0	7.9	3.1	35.8	28.0	7.9
1997	37.0	22.0	7.1	29.2	7.9	..	37.1	29.2	7.9
1998	37.8	23.0	6.9	30.0	7.9	..	37.9	30.0	7.9

+   From 1952 onwards the figures relate to women married only once. Until 1951 the figures are for births occurring within 8 1/2 months of marriage, thereafter within 8 months.

*   Births registered in July and November only.

** Annual averages for 1940-44 and 1945-49

Source: ONS/OPCS *Birth statistics*, *Series FM1*, Tables 1.1, 1.2, 3.4, 3.9, 3.10, 5.2

This was Table A5.10 in the first edition of *Birth counts*

A5.11.1

Adoptions, England and Wales 1927–98

Year	All ages	Age, years					
		Under 1	1–4	5–9	10–14	15–17*	Not stated
	Numbers of children adopted						
1927	2,943	..	..	..	..	..	..
1928	3,278	..	..	..	..	..	..
1929	3,294	..	..	..	..	..	..
1930	4,511	..	..	..	..	..	..
1931	4,119	..	..	..	..	..	..
1932	4,465	..	..	..	..	..	..
1933	4,524	..	..	..	..	..	..
1934	4,756	..	..	..	..	..	..
1935	4,844	..	..	..	..	..	..
1936	5,180	..	..	..	..	..	..
1937	5,547	..	..	..	..	..	..
1938	6,193	..	..	..	..	..	..
1939	6,826	..	..	..	..	..	..
1940	7,775	..	..	..	..	..	..
1941	7,429	..	..	..	..	..	..
1942	10,409	..	..	..	..	..	..
1943	11,548	..	..	..	..	..	..
1944	13,027	..	..	..	..	..	..
1945	16,319	..	..	..	..	..	..
1946	21,272	..	..	..	..	..	..
1947	18,255	..	..	..	..	..	..
1948	18,540	..	..	..	..	..	..
1949	17,317	..	..	..	..	..	..
1950	12,739	..	..	..	..	..	..
1951	13,850	..	..	..	..	..	..
1952	13,894	..	..	..	..	..	..
1953	12,995	..	..	..	..	..	..
1954	13,003	..	..	..	..	..	..
1955	13,001	..	..	..	..	..	..
1956	13,198	..	..	..	..	..	..
1957	13,401	..	..	..	..	..	..
1958	13,303	..	..	..	..	..	..
1959	14,105	..	..	..	..	..	..
1960	15,099	7,253	3,840	1,808	1,307	891	0
1961	16,000	8,239	3,867	1,765	1,197	932	0
1962	16,894	9,214	3,872	1,863	1,096	849	0
1963	17,782	9,896	4,129	1,974	1,037	746	0
1964	20,412	11,506	4,719	2,337	1,107	763	0
1965	21,032	11,650	5,049	2,431	1,146	756	0
1966	22,792	12,308	5,611	2,918	1,220	735	0
1967	22,802	12,170	5,688	3,116	1,245	583	0
1968	24,831	12,641	6,313	3,717	1,517	643	0
1969	23,708	11,096	6,344	4,043	1,638	587	0
1970	22,373	8,833	6,776	4,522	1,755	487	0
1971	21,495	7,780	6,499	4,973	1,815	425	0
1972	21,599	6,502	6,421	5,918	2,220	447	0
1973	22,247	6,026	6,298	6,657	2,780	486	0
1974	22,502	5,172	6,148	7,462	3,132	588	0

Adoptions, England and Wales 1927–98

Year	All ages	Age, years					
		Under 1	1–4	5–9	10–14	15–17*	Not stated
	Numbers of children adopted						
1974	22,502	5,172	6,148	7,462	3,132	588	0
1975	21,299	4,548	5,523	7,278	3,316	634	0
1976	17,621	3,608	4,216	6,161	3,125	511	0
1977	12,748	2,945	3,002	4,185	2,192	424	0
1978	12,121	2,816	2,593	3,996	2,225	491	0
1979	10,870	2,649	2,183	3,572	2,013	453	0
1980	10,609	2,599	2,090	3,414	2,041	465	0
1981	9,284	2,365	1,910	2,784	1,823	402	0
1982	10,240	2,177	2,162	3,197	2,151	553	0
1983	9,029	1,962	2,094	2,651	1,832	490	0
1984	8,648	1,836	1,935	2,605	1,728	526	18
1985	7,615	1,605	1,645	2,261	1,625	454	25
1986	7,892	1,572	1,748	2,349	1,652	495	76
1987	7,201	1,333	1,694	2,164	1,462	495	53
1988	7,390	1,235	1,975	2,231	1,415	453	81
1989	7,044	1,115	1,875	2,244	1,331	458	21
1990	6,533	969	1,871	2,099	1,197	392	5+
1991	7,171	895	2,071	2,409	1,381	415	0
1992	7,342	661	2,270	2,592	1,418	399	2+
1993	6,859	465	1,894	2,543	1,570	387	0
1994	6,239	359	1,623	2,450	1,432	375	0
1995	5,797	322	1,494	2,216	1,433	332	0
1996	5,962	253	1,598	2,311	1,434	366	0
1997	5,306	225	1,606	1,914	1,265	296	0
1998	4,387	195	1,489	1,545	938	220	0
	Percentages of children adopted						
1960	100.0	48.0	25.4	12.0	8.7	5.9	
1961	100.0	51.5	24.2	11.0	7.5	5.8	
1962	100.0	54.5	22.9	11.0	6.5	5.0	
1963	100.0	55.7	23.2	11.1	5.8	4.2	
1964	100.0	56.4	23.1	11.4	5.4	3.7	
1965	100.0	55.4	24.0	11.6	5.4	3.6	
1966	100.0	54.0	24.6	12.8	5.4	3.2	
1967	100.0	53.4	24.9	13.7	5.5	2.6	
1968	100.0	50.9	25.4	15.0	6.1	2.6	
1969	100.0	46.8	26.8	17.1	6.9	2.5	
1970	100.0	39.5	30.3	20.2	7.8	2.2	
1971	100.0	36.2	30.2	23.1	8.4	2.0	
1972	100.0	30.1	29.7	27.4	10.3	2.1	
1973	100.0	27.1	28.3	29.9	12.5	2.2	
1974	100.0	23.0	27.3	33.2	13.9	2.6	
1975	100.0	21.4	25.9	34.2	15.6	3.0	
1976	100.0	20.5	23.9	35.0	17.7	2.9	
1977	100.0	23.1	23.5	32.8	17.2	3.3	
1978	100.0	23.2	21.4	33.0	18.4	4.1	
1979	100.0	24.4	20.1	32.9	18.5	4.2	

A5.11.1 *continued*

Adoptions, England and Wales 1927–98

Year	All ages	Age, years				
		Under 1	1–4	5–9	10–14	15–17*
	Percentages of children adopted					
1980	100.0	24.5	19.7	32.2	19.2	4.4
1981	100.0	25.5	20.6	30.0	19.6	4.3
1982	100.0	21.3	21.1	31.2	21.0	5.4
1983	100.0	21.7	23.2	29.4	20.3	5.4
1984	100.0	21.2	22.4	30.1	20.0	6.1
1985	100.0	21.1	21.6	29.7	21.3	6.0
1986	100.0	19.9	22.1	29.8	20.9	6.3
1987	100.0	18.5	23.5	30.1	20.3	6.9
1988	100.0	16.7	26.7	30.2	19.1	6.1
1989	100.0	15.8	26.6	31.9	18.9	6.5
1990	100.0	14.8	28.6	32.1	18.3	6.0
1991	100.0	12.5	28.9	33.6	19.3	5.8
1992	100.0	9.0	30.9	35.3	19.3	5.4
1993	100.0	6.8	27.6	37.1	22.9	5.6
1994	100.0	5.8	26.0	39.3	23.0	6.0
1995	100.0	5.6	25.8	38.2	24.7	5.7
1996	100.0	4.2	26.8	38.8	24.1	6.1
1997	100.0	4.2	30.3	36.1	27.0	6.9
1998	100.0	4.4	33.9	35.2	21.4	5.0

* before 1974, data relate to 'children' aged 15–20

+ aged over 17

Source: *Registrar General's Statistical Reviews, Population, Table T5.*
ONS/OPCS *Marriage and divorce statistics, Series FM2*

This was Table A5.11 in the first edition of *Birth counts*

A5.12.1

Marriages and remarriages, England and Wales, 1845–1997

Year	Total	First marriage of both parties	First marriage of one party only	Remarriage of both parties
1845	143,743	119,539	17,863	6,341
1846	145,664	121,324	18,209	6,131
1847	135,845	112,576	17,372	5,897
1848	138,230	113,284	18,622	6,324
1849	141,883	116,134	19,257	6,492
1850	152,744	124,031	21,133	7,580
1851	154,206	126,018	20,938	7,250
1852	158,782	130,672	20,740	7,370
1853	164,520	135,023	21,878	7,619
1854	159,727	131,141	21,015	7,571
1855	152,113	123,398	21,055	7,660
1856	159,337	129,960	21,625	7,572
1857	159,097	130,317	21,201	7,579
1858	156,070	127,165	21,261	7,644
1859	167,723	137,005	22,555	8,163
1860	170,156	139,435	22,459	8,262
1861	163,706	133,703	22,108	7,895
1862	164,030	134,702	21,432	7,896
1863	173,510	142,918	22,363	8,229
1864	180,387	147,898	23,638	8,851
1865	185,474	151,701	24,510	9,263
1866	187,776	153,641	24,468	9,667
1867	179,154	145,543	24,242	9,369
1868	176,962	144,544	23,310	9,108
1869	176,970	144,482	23,465	9,023
1870	181,655	148,819	23,524	9,312
1871	190,112	155,304	24,828	9,980
1872	201,267	164,544	26,027	10,696
1873	205,615	167,938	26,510	11,167
1874	202,010	164,971	25,785	11,254
1875	201,212	163,674	26,168	11,370
1876	201,874	164,202	25,941	11,731
1877	194,352	158,741	24,914	10,697
1878	190,054	155,960	23,710	10,384
1879	182,082	149,679	22,805	9,598
1880	191,965	158,474	23,427	10,064
1881	197,290	163,796	23,527	9,967
1882	204,405	170,624	23,813	9,968
1883	206,384	172,333	23,980	10,071
1884	204,301	170,298	23,855	10,148
1885	197,745	164,684	23,465	9,596
1886	196,071	164,038	22,726	9,307
1887	200,518	168,500	22,616	9,402
1888	203,821	171,710	22,802	9,309
1889	213,865	181,225	23,149	9,491
1890	223,028	189,150	23,934	9,944
1891	226,526	192,240	24,277	10,009
1892	227,135	192,209	24,793	10,133
1893	218,689	185,666	23,560	9,463
1894	226,449	192,990	23,922	9,537

A5.12.1 *continued*

Marriages and remarriages, England and Wales, 1845–1997

Year	Total	First marriage of both parties	First marriage of one party only	Remarriage of both parties
1895	228,204	195,214	23,684	9,306
1896	242,764	209,284	23,937	9,543
1897	249,145	216,435	23,561	9,149
1898	255,379	222,407	23,990	8,982
1899	262,334	229,343	23,688	9,303
1900	257,480	224,484	23,807	9,189
1901	259,400	224,792	24,985	9,623
1902	261,750	228,558	24,234	8,958
1903	261,103	228,991	23,590	8,522
1904	257,856	227,205	22,678	7,973
1905	260,742	229,712	22,891	8,139
1906	270,038	238,427	23,289	8,322
1907	276,421	243,914	24,043	8,464
1908	264,940	232,987	23,646	8,307
1909	260,544	229,629	22,887	8,028
1910	267,721	236,227	23,291	8,203
1911	274,943	242,902	23,547	8,494
1912	283,834	251,096	24,195	8,543
1913	286,583	252,823	25,080	8,680
1914	294,401	259,349	25,961	9,091
1915	360,885	320,463	30,224	10,198
1916	279,846	240,141	29,200	10,505
1917	258,855	217,064	30,744	11,047
1918	287,163	239,759	35,030	12,374
1919	369,411	300,643	52,333	16,435
1920	379,982	317,044	47,979	14,959
1921	320,852	272,056	36,946	11,850
1922	299,524	257,049	31,966	10,509
1923	292,408	253,552	29,004	9,852
1924	296,416	258,400	28,114	9,902
1925	295,689	259,010	26,898	9,781
1926	279,860	245,631	25,207	9,022
1927	308,370	271,721	26,729	9,920
1928	303,228	267,525	26,023	9,680
1929	313,316	276,848	26,556	9,912
1930	315,109	279,548	26,256	9,305
1931	311,847	276,990	25,743	9,114
1932	307,184	273,387	25,102	8,695
1933	318,191	283,698	25,872	8,621
1934	342,307	306,827	26,357	9,123
1935	349,536	313,519	26,926	9,091
1936	354,644	318,411	26,972	9,261
1937	359,160	320,875	28,449	9,836
1938	361,768	321,754	29,689	10,325
1939	439,694	396,538	32,568	10,588
1940	470,549	426,101	33,156	11,292
1941	388,921	345,044	32,143	11,734
1942	369,744	325,183	32,654	11,907
1943	296,432	252,884	31,478	12,070
1944	302,714	256,116	33,981	12,617

A5.12.1 *continued*

Marriages and remarriages, England and Wales, 1845–1997

Year	Total	First marriage of both parties	First marriage of one party only	Remarriage of both parties
1945	397,626	339,734	43,388	14,504
1946	385,606	313,580	54,370	17,656
1947	401,210	310,827	67,560	22,823
1948	396,891	308,662	64,625	23,604
1949	375,041	297,872	54,894	22,275
1950	358,490	286,808	50,479	21,203
1951	360,624	293,000	46,781	20,843
1952	349,308	281,738	45,910	21,660
1953	344,998	280,765	43,211	21,022
1954	341,731	280,622	40,779	20,330
1955	357,918	296,092	40,902	20,924
1956	352,944	294,776	38,281	19,887
1957	346,903	291,544	36,017	19,342
1958	339,913	288,166	33,326	18,421
1959	340,126	287,598	33,561	18,967
1960	343,614	290,887	33,474	19,253
1961	346,678	294,018	33,064	19,596
1962	347,732	294,120	33,523	20,089
1963	351,329	295,460	35,153	20,716
1964	359,307	300,897	36,492	21,918
1965	371,127	311,205	37,787	22,135
1966	384,497	321,157	39,427	23,913
1967	386,052	320,561	40,180	25,311
1968	407,822	338,801	42,357	26,664
1969	396,746	326,950	42,174	27,622
1970	415,487	339,873	45,761	29,853
1971	404,737	320,347	50,264	34,126
1972	426,241	312,957	65,428	47,856
1973	400,435	288,003	63,680	48,752
1974	384,389	271,672	63,553	49,164
1975	380,620	264,945	64,344	51,331
1976	358,567	243,770	63,435	51,362
1977	356,954	237,961	65,339	53,654
1978	368,258	240,512	69,080	58,666
1979	368,853	240,744	69,664	58,445
1980	370,022	241,001	69,964	59,057
1981	351,973	227,713	67,048	57,212
1982	342,166	220,427	65,316	56,423
1983	344,334	220,949	66,161	57,224
1984	349,186	224,015	67,798	57,373
1985	346,389	221,927	67,531	56,931
1986	347,924	220,372	68,976	58,576
1987	351,761	226,308	69,092	56,361
1988	348,492	219,791	69,419	59,282
1989	346,697	218,904	69,185	58,608
1990	331,150	209,043	67,013	55,094
1991	306,756	192,238	63,159	51,359
1992	311,564	191,732	66,296	53,536
1993	299,197	181,956	64,551	52,690
1994	291,069	174,200	64,009	52,860
1995	283,012	166,418	63,975	52,619
1996	278,975	160,680	64,653	53,642
1997	272,536	156,907	62,911	52,718

Source: ONS *Marriage and divorce statistics, Series FM2*

This is a new table for this edition of *Birth counts*

Divorce decrees made absolute and number of children aged under 16, England and Wales, 1957–97

Year	Number of couples divorcing			Number of children of divorcing couples by age, years*					
	Total	Couples with no child stated	Couples with one or more children under 16	0–4	5–10	11–15	All under 16	16 or over	All children
1957	23,785	7,995	..	..	..	..	..	..	30,765
1958	22,654	7,703	..	..	..	..	..	..	29,148
1959	24,286	8,145	..	..	..	..	..	..	31,677
1960	23,868	7,591	..	..	..	..	..	..	32,534
1961	25,394	8,061	..	..	..	..	..	..	34,820
1962	28,935	8,955	..	..	..	..	..	..	40,281
1963	32,052	9,818	..	..	..	..	..	..	45,115
1964	34,868	10,507	..	..	..	..	..	..	50,342
1965	37,785	10,965	..	..	..	..	..	..	55,982
1966	39,067	11,028	..	..	..	..	..	..	59,591
1967	43,093	11,791	..	..	..	..	..	..	67,539
1968	45,794	12,300	..	..	..	..	..	..	72,790
1969	51,310	13,906	..	..	..	..	..	..	81,106
1970	58,239	15,183	35,876	18,837	34,996	17,503	71,336	22,406	88,839
1971	74,437	20,457	42,039	20,734	40,700	20,870	82,304	34,422	103,174
1972	119,025	30,824	66,816	30,359	64,180	36,364	130,903	64,776	167,267
1973	106,003	26,318	63,792	29,802	61,584	35,542	126,928	53,156	162,470
1974	113,500	28,870	68,594	31,772	64,830	38,732	135,334	55,004	174,066
1975	120,522	30,962	73,881	33,372	68,678	43,046	145,096	57,379	188,142
1976	126,694	33,729	78,095	34,014	71,084	47,072	152,170	57,237	199,242
1977	129,053	37,818	77,489	33,567	68,680	46,545	148,792	52,557	195,337
1978	143,667	43,065	85,815	37,269	73,736	51,650	162,655	57,787	214,305
1979	138,706	41,805	83,176	37,055	69,308	49,062	155,425	54,850	204,487
1980	148,301	45,334	88,202	39,499	71,446	52,276	163,221	58,628	215,497
1981	145,713	42,292	86,838	40,281	67,582	51,540	159,403	66,572	210,943
1982	146,698	42,174	87,253	42,216	65,111	50,941	158,268	68,455	209,209
1983	147,479	42,458	86,695	44,374	61,240	49,948	155,562	70,987	205,510
1984	144,501	41,831	83,530	43,909	56,810	47,881	148,600	71,620	196,481
1985	160,300	51,912	88,955	50,265	57,664	47,811	155,740	71,152	203,551

A5.13.1 continued

Divorce decrees made absolute and number of children aged under 16, England and Wales, 1957–97

Year	Number of couples divorcing			Number of children of divorcing couples by age, years*					
	Total	Couples with no child stated	Couples with one or more children under 16	0–4	5–10	11–15	All under 16	16 or over	All children
1986	153,903	47,330	86,286	49,396	57,296	45,272	151,964	71,394	197,236
1987	151,007	46,770	84,254	48,195	58,149	42,567	148,911	68,394	191,478
1988	152,633	47,049	84,268	48,940	60,258	40,978	150,176	70,120	191,154
1989	150,872	46,910	82,795	49,037	60,946	38,179	148,162	68,405	186,341
1990	153,386	47,119	84,751	50,495	64,069	38,313	152,877	68,181	191,190
1991	158,745	48,115	88,346	52,738	68,074	39,872	160,684	69,695	200,556
1992	160,385	46,979	91,425	54,510	70,954	42,784	168,248	69,886	211,032
1993	165,018	47,652	94,915	55,451	75,189	45,321	175,961	70,204	221,282
1994	158,175	48,286	88,491	50,210	70,935	43,689	164,834	66,840	208,523
1995	155,499	48,560	85,867	46,953	69,631	43,979	160,563	65,802	204,541
1996	157,107	48,800	86,933	46,029	71,620	44,849	162,498	66,004	228,502
1997	146,689	45,556	80,670	41,524	67,085	41,700	150,309	62,408	212,717

* Children of divorcing couples are defined as children of the family according to the Matrimonial Causes Act, 1973.

They are either children of both the parties or those treated by both parties as children of their family.

Source: ONS/OPCS *Marriage and divorce statistics, Series FM2* Tables 4.10 and 4.11

This was Table A5.13 in the first edition of *Birth counts*

A5.14.1

Families with dependent children by type, Great Britain, 1971–96

Year	Married couples	Lone mothers					Lone fathers	All lone parents	Base=100%
		All	Single	Widowed	Divorced	Separated			
	Percentage of families in sample with dependent children								
1971	92	7	1	2	2	2	1	8	4,864
1972	:	:	:	:	:	:	:	:	:
1973	90	8	:	:	:	:	1	:	4,567
1974	90	9	1	2	2	2	1	10	4,309
1975	90	9	1	2	3	2	1	10	4,776
1976	:	:	:	:	:	:	:	:	:
1977	90	9	2	2	3	2	1	10	4,481
1978	:	:	:	:	:	:	:	:	:
1979	88	10	2	2	4	3	2	12	4,203
1980	:	:	:	:	:	:	:	:	:
1981	87	11	2	2	4	2	2	13	4,445
1982	:	:	:	:	:	:	:	:	:
1983	86	12	3	2	5	2	1	14	3,538
1984	87	12	3	1	6	2	1	13	3,365
1985	86	12	3	1	5	3	2	14	3,348
1986	86	13	3	1	6	3	1	14	3,337
1987	85	12	4	1	5	2	1	14	3,361
1988	84	15	5	1	6	3	1	16	3,195
1989	83	15	5	1	6	3	2	17	3,223
1990	80	18	6	1	7	4	2	20	3,023
1991	81	18	6	1	6	4	1	19	3,143
1992	79	19	7	1	6	5	2	21	3,121
1993	78	20	8	1	7	4	2	22	3,145
1994	77	21	8	1	7	5	2	23	3,168
1995	78	20	8	1	7	5	2	22	3,022
1996	79	20	7	1	6	5	2	21	2,975

Dependent children are persons aged under 16, or aged 16-18 and in full-time education, in the family unit and living in the household.

Source: ONS/OPCS, *General Household Survey*, various years

This is similar to Table A5.13 in the first edition of *Birth counts*

A5.14.2

Family type and number of dependent children, Great Britain, 1971–96

Year	Married		Lone mother		Lone father		Base = 100%
	Dependent children						
	1	2 or more	1	2 or more	1	2 or more	
	Percentage of families in sample with dependent children						
1971	:	:	:	:	:	:	:
1972	16	76	2	5	0	1	9,474
1973	:	:	:	:	:	:	:
1974	:	:	:	:	:	:	:
1975	17	74	3	6	0	1	9,293
1976	:	:	:	:	:	:	:
1977	17	73	3	6	0	1	8,566
1978	:	:	:	:	:	:	:
1979	18	70	3	7	1	1	7,803
1980	:	:	:	:	:	:	:
1981	18	70	3	7	1	1	8,216
1982	18	71	4	6	0	1	6,523
1983	18	69	3	8	0	1	6,522
1984	18	70	4	7	0	1	6,127
1985	19	69	4	7	1	1	5,966
1986	18	69	4	8	1	1	6,054
1987	19	69	4	7	0	1	6,016
1988	19	67	5	9	0	1	5,739
1989	18	67	4	9	1	1	5,827
1990	18	64	6	11	1	1	5,424
1991	17	66	5	12	0	1	5,799
1992	17	64	5	12	1	1	5,688
1993	15	65	6	12	1	1	5,794
1994	16	64	6	14	1	0	5,762
1995	16	64	5	14	1	1	5,559
1996	17	63	5	13	0	1	5,431

Dependent children are persons aged under 16, or aged 16–18 and in full-time education, in the family unit and living in the household.

Source: ONS/OPCS *General Household Survey*, various years

This is similar to Table A5.13 in the first edition of *Birth counts*

A5.14.3

Stepfamilies with dependent children* and family head aged 16-59, Great Britain, 1995 and 1996

Type of stepfamily	1995			1996	
	Percentage of all stepfamilies with dependent children	Percentage of all families with dependent children		Percentage of all stepfamilies with dependent children	Percentage of all families with dependent children
Couple with child or children from mother's previous marriage**	86	7		84	
Couple with child or children from father's previous marriage**	10	1		12	
Couple with child or children from both partners' previous marriage**	4	0		4	
All step families	100	8		100	
All families with dependent children+		100			
Base	193	2,305		170	

The 1995 sample contained 2,305 families with heads aged 15–59 and dependent children, of which 193 were stepfamilies

* Dependent children are persons under 16, or aged 16–18, and in full-time education, in the family unit, and living in the household.

** Includes previous cohabitations.

+ Families whose head is aged 16–59

Source: ONS *General Household Survey, 1995, 1996*

This is a new table for this edition of *Birth counts*

A5.15.1

Family status of children aged 0–4 in the 1991 census, Great Britain and constituent countries

	Great Britain	England and Wales	England	Wales	Scotland
Total children aged 0-4	356,357	325,295	306,596	18,699	31,062
Dependent child in family	354,287	323,377	304,796	18,581	30,910
In married couple family	260,485	237,773	224,343	13,430	22,712
In cohabiting couple family	29,965	28,041	26,614	1,427	1,924
In lone parent family	63,837	57,563	53,839	3,724	6,274
Not in family	2,070	1,918	1,800	118	152
Total males	182,272	166,409	156,857	9,552	15,863
Dependent child in family	181,227	165,440	155,947	9,493	15,787
In married couple family	133,044	121,523	114,676	6,847	11,521
In cohabiting couple family	15,482	14,462	13,758	704	1,020
In lone parent family	32,701	29,455	27,513	1,942	3,246
Not in family	1,045	969	910	59	76
Total females	174,085	158,886	149,739	9,147	15,199
Dependent child in family	173,060	157,937	148,849	9,088	15,123
In married couple family	127,441	116,250	109,667	6,583	11,191
In cohabiting couple family	14,483	13,579	12,856	723	904
In lone parent family	31,136	28,108	26,326	1,782	3,028
Not in family	1,025	949	890	59	76

Source: OPCS and GRO Scotland, *1991 Census, children and young adults, Great Britain*

This is a new table for this edition of *Birth counts*

A5.16.1

Percentage distribution of live births by mother's country of birth, England and Wales, 1973–80

Birthplace of mother		1973	1974	1975	1976	1977	1978	1979	1980
All countries of birth	Number	675,953	639,885	603,445	584,270	569,259	596,418	638,028	656,234
	Percentage	100.0	100.0	100.0	100.0	100.0	100.0	100.0	100.0
United Kingdom*		88.3	88.2	87.9	87.5	86.9	86.8	86.9	86.7
All outside United Kingdom		11.5	11.6	11.9	12.4	13.0	13.1	13.1	13.2
Irish Republic+		2.4	2.3	2.1	1.9	1.8	1.6	1.5	1.4
Australia, Canada, New Zealand		0.4	0.4	0.4	0.4	0.4	0.4	0.4	0.4
New Commonwealth and Pakistan		6.1	6.2	6.6	7.2	7.8	8.0	8.2	8.5
Bangladesh		0.1	0.1	0.2	0.2	0.3	0.3	0.3	0.4
India		1.9	1.9	2.0	2.1	2.2	2.1	2.1	2.0
Sri Lanka**		0.1	0.1	0.1	0.1	0.1	0.1	0.1	0.1
Hong Kong		0.2	0.2	0.2	0.2	0.2	0.2	0.2	0.2
South East Asia***		0.1	0.1	0.1	0.2	0.2	0.2	0.3	0.3
East African Commonwealth++		0.4	0.5	0.6	0.7	0.9	0.9	1.0	1.0
Other African Commonwealth+++		0.4	0.4	0.4	0.4	0.5	0.5	0.5	0.5
Caribbean~		1.3	1.3	1.3	1.2	1.2	1.2	1.1	1.1
Malta, Gibraltar, Cyprus		0.4	0.4	0.5	0.5	0.5	0.5	0.5	0.5
Remainder of New Commonwealth		0.1	0.1	0.1	0.1	0.1	0.1	0.2	0.2
Pakistan		1.0	1.1	1.2	1.4	1.7	1.9	2.0	2.1
European Community~~		0.9	1.0	0.9	0.9	0.9	0.9	0.9	0.9
Other Europe		0.7	0.7	0.7	0.6	0.6	0.6	0.6	0.6
United States of America		0.3	0.4	0.4	0.4	0.4	0.4	0.4	0.4
South Africa		0.1	0.1	0.1	0.1	0.1	0.1	0.1	0.1
South East Asia (excluding Commonwealth)~~~		0.0	0.1	0.1	0.1	0.1	0.1	0.1	0.2
Other foreign (including USSR)		0.5	0.6	0.7	0.7	0.8	0.9	0.9	0.8
Not stated		0.2	0.2	0.2	0.1	0.1	0.1	0.1	0.0

*   Including Isle of Man and Channel Islands
\+   Including Ireland, part not stated
**   Including Laccadive and Maldive Islands
***   Including Malaysia, Brunei, Singapore and other Asian Commonwealth not listed
\+\+   Including Kenya, Malawi, Tanzania, Uganda, Zambia and other East African Commonwealth not listed
\+\+\+ Including Botswana, Ghana, Gambia, Lesotho, Nigeria, Sierra Leone, Swaziland and Zimbabwe
~   Including Guyana and Belize
~~   Excluding UK and Irish Republic
~~~   Including Vietnam, Indonesia, Phillipines and Thailand

Source: OPCS *Birth statistics, Series FM1*
This was Table A5.14 in the first edition of *Birth counts*

A5.16.2

Numbers and percentage distribution of live births by mother's country of birth, England and Wales, 1981-98

Country of birth of mother	1981	1982	1983	1984	1985	1986	1987	1988	1989	1990	1991	1992	1993	1994	1995	1996	1997	1998
Numbers																		
All	634,492	625,931	629,134	636,818	656,417	661,018	681,511	693,577	687,725	706,140	699,217	689,656	673,467	664,726	648,138	649,485	643,095	635,901
United Kingdom*	551,432	544,407	549,435	556,518	575,220	579,322	600,734	612,530	607,228	624,160	617,343	607,709	592,056	582,613	566,452	566,352	558,591	549,432
All outside United Kingdom	82,829	81,303	79,536	80,175	81,063	81,591	80,688	80,987	80,434	81,946	81,839	81,902	81,367	82,101	81,677	83,123	84,497	86,456
Irish Republic	8,262	7,302	6,711	6,428	6,311	6,188	6,000	6,483	6,561	6,424	6,035	5,675	5,149	5,174	5,011	4,844	4,781	4,673
Australia, Canada and New Zealand	2,313	2,187	2,246	2,321	2,361	2,470	2,498	2,653	2,772	2,998	3,099	3,066	3,161	3,249	3,051	3,182	3,319	3,393
New Commonwealth	53,165	53,186	52,010	52,445	52,733	52,705	51,574	50,570	49,532	49,790	49,297	48,816	47,793	47,386	46,370	46,049	45,841	46,023
India	12,402	12,152	11,502	11,102	11,110	10,650	9,991	9,542	8,830	8,570	8,070	7,694	7,316	7,032	6,684	6,608	6,553	6,513
Pakistan	13,349	13,416	13,423	13,399	13,643	13,559	12,919	12,500	12,249	12,359	12,638	12,815	13,023	12,779	12,324	12,319	12,571	13,069
Bangladesh	3,079	3,437	3,896	4,067	4,238	4,717	4,845	4,799	5,085	5,618	5,544	5,532	5,854	6,253	6,783	6,930	7,307	7,424
East Africa	6,610	6,638	6,589	6,959	7,110	7,142	7,181	6,995	6,742	6,590	6,445	6,237	5,698	5,641	5,127	5,114	4,739	4,498
Southern Africa	:	:	:	:	:	:	:	:	:	:	:	:	:	:	:	:	:	1,437
Rest of Africa	3,519	3,533	3,481	3,472	3,593	3,700	3,965	4,175	4,721	4,954	5,366	5,639	5,511	5,603	5,773	5,845	5,698	6,135
Caribbean	6,247	5,876	5,307	5,255	4,851	4,674	4,565	4,219	4,032	3,809	3,459	3,378	3,124	3,074	2,912	2,754	2,627	2,564
Far East+	3,324	3,525	3,482	3,736	3,795	3,934	3,805	4,139	3,847	3,963	3,834	3,855	3,710	3,489	3,311	3,122	2,947	1,682
Mediterranean⁻	2,966	2,993	2,737	2,886	2,802	2,795	2,715	2,621	2,511	2,345	2,302	2,086	1,994	1,890	1,782	1,580	1,557	1,369
Remainder of New Commonwealth	1,669	1,616	1,593	1,569	1,591	1,534	1,588	1,580	1,515	1,582	1,639	1,580	1,563	1,625	1,674	1,777	1,842	1,332
Other European countries	8,774	8,379	8,193	8,266	8,725	8,749	8,915	9,150	9,488	9,988	10,155	10,339	10,713	11,354	11,941	12,837	13,742	14,936
United States of America	2,504	2,585	2,688	2,882	3,109	3,136	3,206	3,272	3,301	3,338	3,231	3,269	2,932	2,725	2,630	2,578	2,779	2,857
Rest of the world	7,811	7,664	7,688	7,833	7,824	8,343	8,495	8,859	8,780	9,408	10,022	10,737	11,619	12,213	12,674	13,633	14,035	14,574
Not stated	231	221	163	125	134	105	89	60	63	34	35	45	44	12	9	10	7	13

A5.16.2 continued

Numbers and percentage distribution of live births by mother's country of birth, England and Wales, 1981-98

Country of birth of mother	1981	1982	1983	1984	1985	1986	1987	1988	1989	1990	1991	1992	1993	1994	1995	1996	1997	1998
	Percentages																	
All	100.0	100.0	100.0	100.0	100.0	100.0	100.0	100.0	100.0	100.0	100.0	100.0	100.0	100.0	100.0	100.0	100.0	100.0
United Kingdom*	86.9	87.0	87.3	87.4	87.6	87.6	88.1	88.3	88.3	88.4	88.3	88.1	87.9	87.6	87.4	87.2	86.9	86.4
All outside United Kingdom	13.1	13.0	12.6	12.6	12.3	12.3	11.8	11.7	11.7	11.6	11.7	11.9	12.1	12.4	12.6	12.8	13.1	13.6
Irish Republic	1.3	1.2	1.1	1.0	1.0	0.9	0.9	0.9	1.0	0.9	0.9	0.8	0.8	0.8	0.8	0.7	0.7	0.7
Australia, Canada and New Zealand	0.4	0.3	0.4	0.4	0.4	0.4	0.4	0.4	0.4	0.4	0.4	0.4	0.5	0.5	0.5	0.5	0.5	0.5
New Commonwealth	8.4	8.5	8.3	8.2	8.0	8.0	7.6	7.3	7.2	7.1	7.1	7.1	7.1	7.1	7.2	7.1	7.1	7.2
India	2.0	1.9	1.8	1.7	1.7	1.6	1.5	1.4	1.3	1.2	1.2	1.1	1.1	1.1	1.0	1.0	1.0	1.0
Pakistan	2.1	2.1	2.1	2.1	2.1	2.1	1.9	1.8	1.8	1.8	1.8	1.9	1.9	1.9	1.9	1.9	2.0	2.1
Bangladesh	0.5	0.5	0.6	0.6	0.6	0.7	0.7	0.7	0.7	0.8	0.8	0.8	0.9	0.9	1.0	1.1	1.1	1.2
East Africa	1.0	1.1	1.0	1.1	1.1	1.1	1.1	1.0	1.0	0.9	0.9	0.9	0.8	0.8	0.8	0.8	0.7	0.7
Southern Africa	:	:	:	:	:	:	:	:	:	:	:	:	:	:	:	:	:	0.2
Rest of Africa	0.6	0.6	0.6	0.5	0.5	0.6	0.6	0.6	0.7	0.7	0.8	0.8	0.8	0.8	0.9	0.9	0.9	1.0
Caribbean	1.0	0.9	0.8	0.8	0.7	0.7	0.7	0.6	0.6	0.5	0.5	0.6	0.5	0.5	0.4	0.4	0.4	0.4
Far East+	0.5	0.6	0.6	0.6	0.6	0.6	0.6	0.6	0.6	0.6	0.5	0.6	0.6	0.5	0.5	0.5	0.5	0.4
Mediterranean~	0.5	0.5	0.4	0.5	0.4	0.4	0.4	0.4	0.4	0.3	0.3	0.3	0.3	0.3	0.3	0.2	0.2	0.3
Remainder of New Commonwealth	0.3	0.3	0.3	0.2	0.2	0.2	0.2	0.2	0.2	0.2	0.2	0.2	0.2	0.2	0.3	0.3	0.3	0.2
Other European countries	1.4	1.3	1.3	1.3	1.3	1.3	1.3	1.3	1.4	1.4	1.5	1.5	1.6	1.7	1.8	2.0	2.1	2.3
United States of America	0.4	0.4	0.4	0.5	0.5	0.5	0.5	0.5	0.5	0.5	0.5	0.5	0.4	0.4	0.4	0.4	0.4	0.4
Rest of the world	1.2	1.2	1.2	1.2	1.2	1.3	1.2	1.3	1.3	1.3	1.4	1.6	1.7	1.8	2.0	2.1	2.2	2.3
Not stated	0.0	0.0	0.0	0.0	0.0	0.0	0.0	0.0	0.0	0.0	0.0	0.0	0.0	0.0	0.0	0.0	0.0	0.0

* Including Isle of Man and Channel Islands

+ Hong Kong, Malaysia, Singapore and Brunei

~ Cyprus, Gibraltar and Malta

Source: ONS/OPCS *Birth statistics, Series FM1*

This is similar to Table 5.14 in the first edition of Birth counts

A5.17.1

Live births to women born outside the United Kingdom by region and country of residence, England and Wales, 1996

Country and region of usual residence	All live births	Live births to women born outside United Kingdom					
		Number			Percentage of all live births		
		All outside United Kingdom	New Commonwealth	Other	All outside United Kingdom	New Commonwealth	Other
England and Wales	649,078	82,977	46,013	36,964	13	7	6
England	614,184	81,511	45,388	36,123	13	7	6
Wales	34,894	1,466	625	841	4	2	2
Standard statistical regions							
North	35,535	1,492	724	768	4	2	2
North West	79,566	6,572	4,236	2,336	8	5	3
Yorkshire and Humberside	62,018	5,792	4,149	1,643	9	7	3
East Midlands	49,400	3,935	2,542	1,393	8	5	3
West Midlands	67,508	7,531	5,894	1,637	11	9	3
East Anglia	24,478	2,195	720	1,475	9	3	6
South East	240,843	50,678	25,934	24,744	21	11	10
South West	54,836	3,316	1,189	2,127	6	2	4
Government Office Regions							
North East	30,101	1,329	677	652	4	2	2
North West Merseyside	85,000	6,735	4,283	2,452	8	5	3
North West	67,789	6,131	4,081	2,050	9	6	3
Merseyside	17,211	604	202	402	4	1	2
Yorkshire and the Humber	62,018	5,792	4,149	1,643	9	7	3
East Midlands	49,400	3,935	2,542	1,393	8	5	3
West Midlands	67,508	7,531	5,894	1,637	11	9	2
Eastern	64,564	5,923	2,660	3,263	9	4	5
London	105,411	37,628	20,023	17,605	36	19	17
South East	95,346	9,322	3,971	5,351	10	4	6
South West	54,836	3,316	1,189	2,127	6	2	4

Source: ONS *Birth statistics 1996, Series FM1, Table 9.2*

This is similar to Table A5.15 in the first edition of *Birth counts*

A5.18.1

Percentage distribution of birthweights of live births by mother's country of birth, England and Wales, 1995

Mother's country of birth	Birthweight, g									Not stated	All with stated birthweight	All live births
	Under 1,000	1,000–1,499	1,500–1,999	2,000–2,499	Under 2,500	2,500–2,999	3,000–3,499	3,500–3,999	4,000 and over			
Numbers												
All countries	2,879	4,704	9,679	30,062	47,324	109,436	234,752	185,122	69,150	2,217	645,784	648,001
United Kingdom	2,412	4,072	8,430	25,498	40,412	92,255	203,992	165,231	62,620	1,821	564,510	566,331
Irish Republic	24	39	80	220	363	736	1,804	1,557	685	21	5,145	5,166
Rest of the European Union	26	42	86	337	491	1,284	2,972	2,404	842	33	7,993	8,026
Australia, Canada, New Zealand	11	18	30	93	152	403	1,079	978	425	15	3,037	3,052
New Commonwealth	321	426	881	3,200	4,828	11,821	18,020	9,660	2,788	220	47,117	47,337
Bangladesh	19	45	121	561	746	2,146	2,642	1,005	217	27	6,756	6,783
India	38	59	136	515	748	1,971	2,633	1,076	233	18	6,661	6,679
Pakistan	81	93	238	867	1,279	3,231	4,732	2,420	632	38	12,294	12,332
East Africa	34	49	116	424	623	1,432	1,876	908	263	20	5,102	5,122
Caribbean	41	47	66	183	337	566	1,080	679	228	20	2,890	2,910
Other	85	107	172	714	1,078	2,937	6,885	5,292	1,790	107	17,982	18,089

Mother's country of birth	Under 1,000	1,000–1,499	1,500–1,999	2,000–2,499	Under 2,500	2,500–2,999	3,000–3,499	3,500–3,999	4,000 and over	Percentage unstated
Percentages of births with stated birthweight										
All countries	0.45	0.73	1.50	4.66	7.33	16.9	36.4	28.7	10.7	0.3
United Kingdom	0.43	0.72	1.49	4.52	7.16	16.3	36.1	29.3	11.1	0.3
Irish Republic	0.47	0.76	1.55	4.28	7.06	14.3	35.1	30.3	13.3	0.4
Rest of the European Union	0.33	0.53	1.08	4.22	6.14	16.1	37.2	30.1	10.5	0.4
Australia, Canada, New Zealand	0.36	0.59	0.99	3.06	5.00	13.3	35.5	32.2	14.0	0.5
New Commonwealth	0.68	0.90	1.87	6.79	10.25	25.1	38.2	20.5	5.9	0.5
Bangladesh	0.28	0.67	1.79	8.30	11.04	31.8	39.1	14.9	3.2	0.4
India	0.57	0.89	2.04	7.73	11.23	29.6	39.5	16.2	3.5	0.3
Pakistan	0.66	0.76	1.94	7.05	10.40	26.3	38.5	19.7	5.1	0.3
East Africa	0.67	0.96	2.27	8.31	12.21	28.1	36.8	17.8	5.2	0.4
Caribbean	1.42	1.63	2.28	6.33	11.66	19.6	37.4	23.5	7.9	0.7
Other	0.47	0.60	0.96	3.97	5.99	16.3	38.3	29.4	10.0	0.6

Source: ONS *Mortality statistics DH3*

This is similar to A5.16 in the first edition of *Birth counts*

A5.18.2

Stillbirths and infant mortality by mother's country of birth, England and Wales, 1996

Mother's country of birth	Numbers						Rates				
	Live births	Stillbirths	Early neonatal	Neonatal	Post-neonatal	Infant	Stillbirth+	Perinatal+	Neonatal~	Post-neonatal~	Infant~
All	649,489	3,539	2,037	2,601	1,255	3,856	5.4	8.5	4.0	1.9	5.9
United Kingdom	566,356	2,901	1,745	2,225	1,066	3,291	5.1	8.2	3.9	1.9	5.8
Irish Republic	4,968	31	18	25	15	40	6.2	9.8	5.0	3.0	8.1
Rest of the European Union	8,604	43	22	31	19	50	5.0	7.5	3.6	2.2	5.8
Australia, Canada, New Zealand	3,182	17	9	12	2	14	5.3	8.1	3.8	0.6	4.4
New Commonwealth	47,104	416	183	238	123	361	8.8	12.6	5.1	2.6	7.7
Bangladesh	6,930	44	22	29	15	44	6.3	9.5	4.2	2.2	6.3
India	6,608	54	21	26	10	36	8.1	11.3	3.9	1.5	5.4
Pakistan	12,319	138	59	80	44	124	11.1	15.8	6.5	3.6	10.1
East Africa	5,114	46	18	21	10	31	8.9	12.4	4.1	2.0	6.1
Caribbean	2,754	22	10	13	10	23	7.9	11.5	4.7	3.6	8.4
Other*	19,275	131	60	70	30	100	6.8	9.8	3.6	1.6	5.2

+ Stillbirths and perinatal deaths per 1,000 live and stillbirths

~ Neonatal, postneonatal and infant deaths per 1,000 live births

* Includes country of birth not stated

Source: ONS *monitor DH3 97/3*, compiled from data on deaths database on 9 June 1997

This was Table A5.17 in the first edition of *Birth counts*

A5.19.1

Reported ethnic group of women of childbearing age and whether born in the UK, Great Britain and constituent countries, 1991

Ethnic group	Number of women by age			Number born outside UK by age			Percentage of each age group born outside UK		
	16–19	20–29	30–44	16–19	20–29	30–44	16–19	20–29	30–44
Great Britain									
Total	1,416,129	4,292,335	5,864,672	67,222	344,691	583,876	4.7	8.0	10.0
White	1,317,532	3,984,799	5,513,173	37,649	190,471	275,858	2.9	4.8	5.0
Black Caribbean	12,926	61,798	57,410	841	6,468	41,686	6.5	10.5	72.6
Black African	5,867	29,936	27,649	2,998	19,209	24,298	51.1	64.2	87.9
Black other	7,193	22,265	11,376	593	2,746	4,550	8.2	12.3	40.0
Indian	27,276	76,077	108,878	5,720	46,844	103,916	21.0	61.6	95.4
Pakistani	18,169	40,421	45,662	5,931	25,814	43,569	32.6	63.9	95.4
Bangladeshi	7,315	11,947	13,191	5,431	10,444	12,706	74.2	87.4	96.3
Chinese	5,175	17,523	24,993	2,473	14,495	24,050	47.8	82.7	96.2
Other groups									
Asian	5,231	20,697	36,484	3,286	17,765	35,395	62.8	85.8	97.0
Other	9,445	26,872	25,856	2,300	10,435	17,848	24.4	38.8	69.0
England and Wales									
Total	1,283,608	3,899,944	5,864,672	63,906	330,350	564,050	5.0	8.5	9.6
White	1,187,049	3,598,575	5,513,173	34,900	179,915	262,618	2.9	5.0	4.8
Black Caribbean	12,901	61,698	57,410	834	6,438	41,605	6.5	10.4	72.5
Black African	5,807	29,657	27,649	2,967	18,985	23,979	51.1	64.0	86.7
Black other	7,103	21,992	11,376	579	2,632	4,462	8.2	12.0	39.2
Indian	26,974	75,151	108,878	5,672	46,366	102,802	21.0	61.7	94.4
Pakistani	17,336	38,385	45,662	5,762	24,772	41,541	33.2	64.5	91.0
Bangladeshi	7,296	11,834	13,191	5,421	10,357	12,608	74.3	87.5	95.6
Chinese	4,810	16,470	24,993	2,319	13,613	22,586	48.2	82.7	90.4
Other groups									
Asian	5,132	20,138	36,484	3,230	17,270	34,518	62.9	85.8	94.6
Other	9,200	26,044	25,856	2,222	10,002	17,331	24.2	38.4	67.0

A5.19.1 continued

Reported ethnic group of women of childbearing age and whether born in the UK, Great Britain and constituent countries, 1991

Ethnic group	Number of women by age			Number born outside UK by age			Percentage of each age group born outside UK		
	16-19	20-29	30-44	16-19	20-29	30-44	16-19	20-29	30-44
England									
Total	1,209,719	3,697,734	5,031,547	62,245	324,150	554,039	5.1	8.8	11.0
White	1,114,586	3,400,114	4,692,099	33,744	175,853	256,259	3.0	5.2	5.5
Black Caribbean	12,804	61,360	56,989	825	6,409	41,442	6.4	10.4	72.7
Black African	5,735	29,428	26,989	2,926	18,848	23,767	51.0	64.0	88.1
Black other	6,952	21,667	10,875	568	2,595	4,410	8.2	12.0	40.6
Indian	26,750	74,598	106,755	5,599	46,001	102,008	20.9	61.7	95.6
Pakistani	17,128	37,866	42,892	5,708	24,459	41,025	33.3	64.6	95.6
Bangladeshi	7,136	11,542	12,785	5,306	10,100	12,322	74.4	87.5	96.4
Chinese	4,658	15,922	22,790	2,251	13,172	21,948	48.3	82.7	96.3
Other groups									
Asian	5,020	19,784	34,910	3,148	16,947	33,874	62.7	85.7	97.0
Other	8,950	25,453	24,463	2,170	9,766	16,984	24.2	38.4	69.4
Wales									
Total	73,889	202,210	291,019	1,661	6,200	10,011	2.2	3.1	3.4
White	72,463	198,461	286,458	1,156	4,062	6,359	1.6	2.0	2.2
Black Caribbean	97	338	306	9	29	163	9.3	8.6	53.3
Black African	72	229	279	41	137	212	56.9	59.8	76.0
Black other	151	325	295	11	37	52	7.3	11.4	17.6
Indian	224	653	859	73	365	794	32.6	55.9	92.4
Pakistani	208	519	564	54	313	516	26.0	60.3	91.5
Bangladeshi	160	292	300	115	257	286	71.9	88.0	95.3
Chinese	152	548	672	68	441	638	44.7	80.5	94.9
Other groups									
Asian	112	354	663	82	323	644	73.2	91.2	97.1
Other	250	591	623	52	236	347	20.8	39.9	55.7

Reported ethnic group of women of childbearing age and whether born in the UK, Great Britain and constituent countries, 1991

Ethnic group	Number of women by age			Number born outside UK by age			Percentage of each age group born outside UK		
	16-19	20-29	30-44	16-19	20-29	30-44	16-19	20-29	30-44
Scotland									
Total	132,521	392,391	542,106	3,316	14,341	19,826	2.5	3.7	3.7
White	130,483	386,224	534,616	2,749	10,556	13,240	2.1	2.7	2.5
Black Caribbean	25	100	115	7	30	81	28.0	30.0	70.4
Black African	60	279	381	31	224	319	51.7	80.3	83.7
Black other	90	273	206	14	114	88	15.6	41.8	42.7
Indian	302	926	1,264	48	478	1,114	15.9	51.6	88.1
Pakistani	833	2,036	2,206	169	1,042	2,028	20.3	51.2	91.9
Bangladeshi	19	113	106	10	87	98	52.6	77.0	92.5
Chinese	365	1,053	1,531	154	882	1,464	42.2	83.8	95.6
Other groups									
Asian	99	559	911	56	495	877	56.6	88.6	96.3
Other	245	828	770	78	433	517	31.8	52.3	67.1

Source: OPCS and GRO Scotland, *1991 census, Ethnic group and country of birth, Great Britain*

This is a new table for this edition of *Birth counts*

A5.19.2

Families by type and ethnic group of head of family, Great Britain, 1991

Type of family	Ethnic group of head of family*											
	Black-Caribbean	Black-African	Black-other	Indian	Pakistani	Bangladeshi	Chinese	Other-Asian	Other-other	All ethnic minority groups	White	All ethnic groups
Percentage of families of each type in each ethnic group												
All married couples	48.0	55.0	45.0	90.0	87.0	88.0	85.0	83.0	71.0	74.0	81.0	81.0
no children	14.0	14.0	11.0	17.0	10.0	6.0	20.0	18.0	20.0	15.0	36.0	35.0
dependent children	22.0	37.0	29.0	63.0	71.0	78.0	56.0	58.0	44.0	51.0	32.0	32.0
non dependent children only	12.0	4.0	5.0	10.0	6.0	4.0	9.0	7.0	7.0	9.0	13.0	13.0
All cohabiting couples	9.0	6.0	9.0	1.0	1.0	2.0	3.0	2.0	4.0	4.0	6.0	5.0
no children	4.0	3.0	6.0	1.0	0.5	1.0	2.0	0.5	2.0	2.0	4.0	4.0
dependent children	4.0	2.0	2.0	0.3	0.6	0.9	0.4	1.0	2.0	2.0	2.0	2.0
non dependent children only	0.2	0.0	0.0	0.2	0.1	0.0	0.0	0.3	0.2	0.2	0.2	0.2
All lone fathers	4.0	7.0	3.0	2.0	3.0	2.0	1.0	3.0	3.0	3.0	2.0	2.0
dependent children	2.0	5.0	1.0	0.9	2.0	1.0	0.4	2.0	1.0	2.0	0.7	0.7
non dependent children only	2.0	2.0	1.0	0.9	1.0	0.9	0.7	2.0	1.0	1.0	1.0	1.0
All lone mothers	40.0	32.0	44.0	7.0	9.0	7.0	11.0	12.0	22.0	19.0	11.0	12.0
dependent children	29.0	29.0	41.0	5.0	8.0	7.0	8.0	8.0	17.0	15.0	7.0	7.0
non dependent children only	10.0	4.0	3.0	2.0	1.0	0.9	3.0	4.0	5.0	4.0	4.0	4.0
All families, percentage	100.0	100.0	100.0	100.0	100.0	100.0	100.0	100.0	100.0	100.0	100.0	100.0
All families, number in sample	1,253	394	218	1,847	810	228	271	396	491	5,908	134,375	140,283
All families with dependent children												
Married couples	38.0	51.0	40.0	92.0	88.0	90.0	87.0	85.0	68.0	74.0	77.0	77.0
Cohabiting couples	7.0	3.0	3.0	0.4	0.8	1.0	0.6	1.0	3.0	2.0	4.0	4.0
Lone fathers	4.0	6.0	2.0	1.0	2.0	2.0	0.6	2.0	2.0	2.0	2.0	2.0
Lone mothers	51.0	40.0	55.0	7.0	9.0	8.0	12.0	12.0	27.0	22.0	17.0	18.0
All families with dependent children	100.0	100.0	100.0	100.0	100.0	100.0	100.0	100.0	100.0	100.0	100.0	100.0
Numbers in sample	717	285	161	1,270	655	198	174	273	317	4,050	55,149	59,199

* Conventionally the husband/male partner of a couple family was taken as the head

Source: Census one per cent samples of anonymised records (SARs) Analysis published in *Population Trends 88*, page 27.

This is a new table for this edition of *Birth counts*

A5.20.1

Stillbirths by age of mother, England and Wales, 1979–96

Year of birth	Age of mother, years					
	All ages	Under 20	20–24	25–29	30–34	35 and over
	Numbers					
	Stillbirths at 28 or more weeks of gestation					
1979	5,132	579	1,522	1,598	958	475
1980	4,782	508	1,389	1,463	954	468
1981	4,207	456	1,231	1,277	826	417
1982	3,943	398	1,187	1,149	766	443
1983	3,632	397	1,041	1,106	689	399
1984	3,650	397	1,100	1,116	632	405
1985	3,650	362	1,040	1,111	745	392
1986	3,548	367	1,016	1,095	681	389
1987	3,421	319	958	1,079	661	404
1988	3,385	337	896	1,047	706	399
1989	3,231	324	834	1,010	681	382
1990	3,259	332	805	1,042	672	408
1991	3,255	279	823	1,036	702	415
1992	3,156	226	798	961	729	442
1993	2,960	249	671	926	713	401
1994	2,925	222	646	922	698	437
1995	2,704	225	542	796	716	425
1996	2,598	212	495	768	690	433
	Stillbirths at 24 or more weeks of gestation					
1993	3,866	327	872	1,203	939	525
1994	3,816	292	843	1,196	928	557
1995	3,597	292	728	1,076	932	569
1996	3,539	293	692	1,054	913	587
	Rates per thousand total births					
	Stillbirths at 28 or more weeks of gestation					
1979	8.0	9.7	7.8	7.1	7.6	12.4
1980	7.2	8.3	6.8	6.5	7.3	11.4
1981	6.6	8.0	6.3	5.9	6.5	10.1
1982	6.3	7.1	6.1	5.4	6.3	9.6
1983	5.7	7.3	5.4	5.1	5.7	8.2
1984	5.7	7.2	5.7	5.1	5.1	8.0
1985	5.5	6.3	5.3	4.9	5.9	7.5
1986	5.3	6.4	5.3	4.8	5.2	7.3
1987	5.0	5.5	4.9	4.5	4.8	7.3
1988	4.9	5.7	4.6	4.3	5.0	7.0
1989	4.7	5.8	4.5	4.1	4.7	6.5
1990	4.6	5.9	4.4	4.1	4.3	6.6
1991	4.6	5.3	4.7	4.1	4.3	6.5
1992	4.6	4.7	4.9	3.9	4.4	6.6
1993	4.4	5.5	4.4	3.9	4.2	5.8
1994	4.4	5.3	4.6	4.0	3.9	5.9
1995	4.2	5.3	4.1	3.6	3.9	5.5
1996	4.0	4.7	3.9	3.6	3.7	5.3

A5.20.1 *continued*

Stillbirths by age of mother, England and Wales, 1979–96

Year of birth	Age of mother, years					
	All ages	Under 20	20–24	25–29	30–34	35 and over
	Stillbirths at 24 or more weeks of gestation, all causes					
1993	5.7	7.2	5.7	5.1	5.5	7.5
1994	5.7	6.9	6.0	5.2	5.1	7.5
1995	5.5	6.9	5.5	4.9	5.1	7.3
1996	5.4	6.5	5.5	5.0	4.9	7.1

Live births for 1981 have been taken from published estimates based on a 10 per cent sample because of gaps in coding following industrial action by registrars of births and deaths

Source: Authors' analysis of ONS/OPCS data

Data extract: live births 1993 (7/94), 1994 (7/95), 1995 (3/7/96), 1996 (8/4/97)

            linked   1993 (3/4/96), 1994 (18/9/96), 1995 (3/11/97)

This is similar to Table A5.4 in the first edition of *Birth counts*

A5.20.2

Perinatal mortality by age of mother, England and Wales, 1979–96

Year of birth	Age of mother, years					
	All ages	Under 20	20–24	25–29	30–34	35 and over
Numbers						
Early neonatal deaths plus stillbirths at 28 or more weeks of gestation						
1979	9,387	1,173	2,863	2,831	1,722	798
1980	8,799	1,012	2,698	2,699	1,659	731
1981	7,510	849	2,312	2,245	1,378	726
1982	7,063	768	2,187	2,075	1,318	715
1983	6,568	746	1,956	2,005	1,191	670
1984	6,445	747	1,926	1,991	1,109	672
1985	6,467	701	1,882	1,974	1,263	647
1986	6,331	723	1,829	1,940	1,172	667
1987	6,078	592	1,746	1,909	1,189	642
1988	6,060	640	1,677	1,887	1,189	667
1989	5,732	597	1,490	1,847	1,157	641
1990	5,698	588	1,496	1,779	1,167	668
1991	5,626	526	1,421	1,819	1,193	667
1992	5,387	413	1,403	1,642	1,222	707
1993	5,120	424	1,187	1,596	1,245	668
1994	5,069	415	1,124	1,558	1,264	708
1995	4,777	407	1,025	1,440	1,211	694
1996	4,636	383	901	1,393	1,252	707
Early neonatal deaths plus stillbirths at 24 or more weeks of gestation						
1993	6,026	502	1,388	1,873	1,471	792
1994	5,960	485	1,321	1,832	1,494	828
1995	5,670	474	1,211	1,720	1,427	838
1996	5,577	464	1,098	1,679	1,475	861
Rates per thousand total births						
Early neonatal deaths plus stillbirths at 28 or more weeks of gestation						
1979	14.6	19.6	14.7	12.7	13.6	20.8
1980	13.3	16.5	13.3	12.0	12.7	17.8
1981	11.8	14.9	11.8	10.3	10.8	17.5
1982	11.2	13.8	11.3	9.7	10.8	15.6
1983	10.4	13.7	10.1	9.3	9.8	13.8
1984	10.1	13.6	10.0	9.1	9.0	13.3
1985	9.8	12.2	9.7	8.6	10.0	12.4
1986	9.5	12.5	9.5	8.4	9.0	12.5
1987	8.9	10.2	9.0	8.0	8.7	11.5
1988	8.7	10.8	8.6	7.7	8.4	11.7
1989	8.3	10.7	8.0	7.6	7.9	10.8
1990	8.0	10.5	8.3	7.0	7.4	10.8
1991	8.0	10.0	8.2	7.3	7.4	10.4
1992	7.8	8.6	8.5	6.7	7.3	10.5
1993	7.6	9.4	7.8	6.8	7.3	9.6
1994	7.6	9.8	8.0	6.8	7.0	9.5
1995	7.3	9.7	7.8	6.6	6.7	9.0
1996	7.1	8.5	7.1	6.6	6.7	8.6

A5.20.2 *continued*

Perinatal mortality by age of mother, England and Wales, 1979–96

Year of birth	Age of mother, years					
	All ages	Under 20	20–24	25–29	30–34	35 and over
	Early neonatal deaths plus stillbirths at 24 or more weeks of gestation					
1993	8.9	11.1	9.1	7.9	8.6	11.4
1994	8.9	11.5	9.4	8.0	8.3	11.1
1995	8.7	11.2	9.2	7.9	7.8	10.8
1996	8.5	10.3	8.7	7.9	7.9	10.5

Live births for 1981 have been taken from published estimates based on a 10 per cent sample because of gaps in coding following industrial action by registrars of births and deaths

Source: Authors' analysis of ONS/OPCS data

Data extract: live births 1993 (7/94), 1994 (7/95), 1995 (3/7/96), 1996 (8/4/97)

    linked 1993 (3/4/96), 1994 (18/9/96), 1995 (3/11/97)

    1996 DH3 no 29, *Mortality statistics, childhood, infant and perinatal*

This is similar to Table A5.4 in the first edition of *Birth counts*

A5.20.3

Neonatal mortality by age of mother, England and Wales, 1979–96

Year of birth	Age of mother, years					
	All ages	Under 20	20–24	25–29	30–34	35 and over
	Numbers					
1979	5,201	705	1,629	1,544	936	387
1980	4,963	615	1,611	1,538	875	324
1981	4,165	496	1,328	1,254	711	376
1982	3,903	467	1,260	1,169	676	331
1983	3,643	422	1,125	1,118	634	344
1984	3,518	426	1,058	1,118	595	321
1985	3,483	406	1,050	1,071	626	330
1986	3,447	428	1,019	1,065	603	332
1987	3,420	373	1,013	1,044	676	314
1988	3,379	393	971	1,066	617	332
1989	3,251	351	866	1,062	647	325
1990	3,134	326	878	960	643	327
1991	3,016	303	763	991	627	332
1992	2,869	253	787	879	626	324
1993	2,774	230	674	847	675	348
1994	2,729	243	617	827	696	346
1995	2,667	231	615	833	638	350
1996	2,604	230	509	791	725	349
	Rates per thousand live births					
1979	8.2	11.9	8.4	7.0	7.4	10.2
1980	7.6	10.1	8.0	6.9	6.7	8.0
1981	6.6	8.8	6.8	5.8	5.6	9.2
1982	6.2	8.4	6.6	5.5	5.6	7.3
1983	5.8	7.8	5.9	5.2	5.2	7.1
1984	5.5	7.8	5.5	5.1	4.8	6.4
1985	5.3	7.1	5.4	4.7	5.0	6.4
1986	5.2	7.5	5.3	4.6	4.7	6.3
1987	5.0	6.5	5.2	4.4	5.0	5.7
1988	4.9	6.7	5.0	4.4	4.4	5.9
1989	4.7	6.3	4.7	4.4	4.5	5.5
1990	4.4	5.9	4.9	3.8	4.1	5.3
1991	4.3	5.8	4.4	4.0	3.9	5.2
1992	4.2	5.3	4.8	3.6	3.8	4.8
1993	4.1	5.1	4.4	3.6	4.0	5.0
1994	4.1	5.8	4.4	3.6	3.9	4.7
1995	4.1	5.5	4.7	3.8	3.5	4.6
1996	4.0	5.1	4.0	3.7	3.9	4.3

Live births for 1981 have been taken from published estimates based on a 10 per cent sample because of gaps in coding following industrial action by registrars of births and deaths

Source: Authors' analysis of ONS/OPCS data

Data extract: live births 1993 (7/94), 1994 (7/95), 1995 (3/7/96), 1996 (8/4/97)

        linked   1993 (3/4/96), 1994 (18/9/96), 1995 (3/11/97)

        1996   DH3 No 29, *Mortality statistics, childhood, infant and perinatal*

This is similar to Table A5.4 in the first edition of *Birth counts*

A5.20.4

Postneonatal mortality by age of mother, England and Wales, 1979–96

Year of birth	Age of mother, years					
	All ages	Under 20	20–24	25–29	30–34	35 and over
	Numbers					
1979	2,856	461	985	853	420	137
1980	2,720	447	996	759	387	131
1981	2,747	399	1,040	758	387	163
1982	2,701	424	956	771	389	161
1983	2,656	396	976	727	407	150
1984	2,327	352	879	617	350	129
1985	2,688	401	949	748	405	185
1986	2,710	424	984	761	365	176
1987	2,773	444	983	802	371	173
1988	2,650	437	901	728	413	171
1989	2,434	374	837	680	385	158
1990	2,216	324	762	639	344	147
1991	1,750	255	570	516	278	131
1992	1,511	212	465	420	276	138
1993	1,366	180	378	402	276	130
1994	1,254	180	377	365	222	110
1995	1,291	167	342	354	273	155
1996	1,263	178	341	341	261	142
	Rates per thousand live births					
1979	4.5	7.8	5.1	3.8	3.3	3.6
1980	4.1	7.4	4.9	3.4	3.0	3.2
1981	4.3	7.1	5.3	3.5	3.1	4.0
1982	4.3	7.6	5.0	3.6	3.2	3.5
1983	4.2	7.3	5.1	3.4	3.4	3.1
1984	3.7	6.5	4.6	2.8	2.9	2.6
1985	4.1	7.0	4.9	3.3	3.2	3.6
1986	4.1	7.4	5.1	3.3	2.8	3.3
1987	4.1	7.7	5.1	3.4	2.7	3.1
1988	3.8	7.4	4.7	3.0	2.9	3.0
1989	3.5	6.7	4.5	2.8	2.6	2.7
1990	3.1	5.8	4.2	2.5	2.2	2.4
1991	2.5	4.9	3.3	2.1	1.7	2.1
1992	2.2	4.4	2.8	1.7	1.7	2.1
1993	2.0	4.0	2.5	1.7	1.6	1.9
1994	1.9	4.3	2.7	1.6	1.2	1.5
1995	2.0	4.0	2.6	1.6	1.5	2.0
1996	1.9	4.0	2.7	1.6	1.4	1.7

Live births for 1981 have been taken from published estimates based on a 10 per cent sample because of gaps in coding following industrial action by registrars of births and deaths

Source: Authors' analysis of ONS/OPCS data

Data extract: live births 1993 (7/94), 1994 (7/95), 1995 (3/7/96), 1996 (8/4/97)

        linked   1993 (3/4/96), 1994 (18/9/96), 1995 (3/11/97)

        1996   DH3 No 29, *Mortality statistics, childhood, infant and perinatal*

This is similar to Table A5.4 in the first edition of *Birth counts*

A5.20.5

Infant mortality by age of mother, England and Wales, 1979–96

Year of birth	Age of mother, years					
	All ages	Under 20	20–24	25–29	30–34	35 and over
	Numbers					
1979	8,057	1,166	2,614	2,397	1,356	524
1980	7,683	1,062	2,607	2,297	1,262	455
1981	6,912	895	2,368	2,012	1,098	539
1982	6,604	891	2,216	1,940	1,065	492
1983	6,299	818	2,101	1,845	1,041	494
1984	5,845	778	1,937	1,735	945	450
1985	6,171	807	1,999	1,819	1,031	515
1986	6,157	852	2,003	1,826	968	508
1987	6,193	817	1,996	1,846	1,047	487
1988	6,029	830	1,872	1,794	1,030	503
1989	5,685	725	1,703	1,742	1,032	483
1990	5,350	650	1,640	1,599	987	474
1991	4,766	558	1,333	1,507	905	463
1992	4,380	465	1,252	1,299	902	462
1993	4,140	410	1,052	1,249	951	478
1994	3,983	423	994	1,192	918	456
1995	3,958	398	957	1,187	911	505
1996	3,867	408	850	1,132	986	491
	Rates per thousand live births					
1979	12.6	19.7	13.5	10.8	10.8	13.8
1980	11.7	17.5	12.9	10.3	9.7	11.2
1981	10.9	15.8	12.2	9.3	8.7	13.1
1982	10.6	16.1	11.5	9.2	8.8	10.8
1983	10.0	15.1	11.0	8.6	8.6	10.3
1984	9.2	14.3	10.1	8.0	7.7	9.0
1985	9.4	14.2	10.3	8.0	8.2	9.9
1986	9.3	14.8	10.4	8.0	7.5	9.6
1987	9.1	14.2	10.3	7.7	7.7	8.8
1988	8.7	14.1	9.7	7.4	7.3	8.9
1989	8.3	13.1	9.2	7.2	7.1	8.2
1990	7.6	11.7	9.1	6.3	6.3	7.7
1991	6.8	10.6	7.7	6.1	5.6	7.3
1992	6.4	9.7	7.7	5.3	5.4	6.9
1993	6.2	9.1	6.9	5.3	5.6	6.9
1994	6.0	10.1	7.1	5.2	5.1	6.2
1995	6.1	9.5	7.3	5.5	5.0	6.6
1996	6.0	9.1	6.8	5.4	5.3	6.0

Live births for 1981 have been taken from published estimates based on a 10 per cent sample because of gaps in coding following industrial action by registrars of births and deaths

Source: Authors' analysis of ONS/OPCS data

Data extract: live births 1993 (7/94), 1994 (7/95), 1995 (3/7/96), 1996 (8/4/97)

        linked   1993 (3/4/96), 1994 (18/9/96), 1995 (3/11/97)

        1996   DH3 No 29 *Mortality statistics, childhood, infant and perinatal*

This is similar to Table A5.4 in the first edition of *Birth counts*

A5.20.6

Live and total births by age of mother, England and Wales, 1979–96

Year of birth	Age of mother, years					
	All ages	Under 20	20–24	25–29	30–34	35 and over
	Live births					
1979	638,028	59,143	193,209	222,102	125,664	37,910
1980	656,234	60,754	201,541	223,438	129,908	40,593
1981	634,492	56,570	194,500	215,760	126,590	41,070
1982	625,931	55,435	192,322	211,905	120,758	45,511
1983	629,134	54,059	191,852	214,078	120,996	48,149
1984	636,818	54,508	191,455	218,031	122,774	50,050
1985	656,417	56,929	193,958	227,486	126,185	51,859
1986	661,018	57,406	192,064	229,035	129,487	53,026
1987	681,511	57,545	193,232	238,929	136,558	55,247
1988	693,577	58,741	193,726	243,460	140,974	56,676
1989	687,725	55,543	185,239	242,822	145,320	58,801
1990	706,140	55,541	180,136	252,577	156,264	61,622
1991	699,217	52,396	173,356	248,727	161,259	63,479
1992	689,656	47,861	163,311	244,798	166,839	66,847
1993	671,224	44,999	151,512	235,184	170,499	69,030
1994	664,256	42,006	140,087	228,903	179,505	73,755
1995	648,001	41,926	130,729	217,356	181,140	76,850
1996	649,489	44,668	125,733	211,105	186,377	81,606
	Total births					
	Live births plus stillbirths at 28 or more weeks of gestation					
1979	643,160	59,722	194,731	223,700	126,622	38,385
1980	661,016	61,262	202,930	224,901	130,862	41,061
1981	638,699	57,026	195,731	217,037	127,416	41,487
1982	629,874	55,833	193,509	213,054	121,524	45,954
1983	632,766	54,456	192,893	215,184	121,685	48,548
1984	640,468	54,905	192,555	219,147	123,406	50,455
1985	660,067	57,291	194,998	228,597	126,930	52,251
1986	664,566	57,773	193,080	230,130	130,168	53,415
1987	684,932	57,864	194,190	240,008	137,219	55,651
1988	696,962	59,078	194,622	244,507	141,680	57,075
1989	690,956	55,867	186,073	243,832	146,001	59,183
1990	709,399	55,873	180,941	253,619	156,936	62,030
1991	702,472	52,675	174,179	249,763	161,961	63,894
1992	692,812	48,087	164,109	245,759	167,568	67,289
1993	674,184	45,248	152,183	236,110	171,212	69,431
1994	667,181	42,228	140,733	229,825	180,203	74,192
1995	650,705	42,151	131,271	218,152	181,856	77,275
1996	652,087	44,880	126,228	211,873	187,067	82,039
	Live births plus stillbirths at 24 or more weeks of gestation					
1993	675,090	45,326	152,384	236,387	171,438	69,555
1994	668,072	42,298	140,930	230,099	180,433	74,312
1995	651,598	42,218	131,457	218,432	182,072	77,419
1996	653,028	44,961	126,425	212,159	187,290	82,193

Live births for 1981 have been taken from published estimates based on a 10 per cent sample because of gaps in coding following industrial action by registrars of births and deaths

Source: Authors' analysis of ONS/OPCS data

Data extract: live births 1993 (7/94), 1994 (7/95), 1995 (3/7/96), 1996 (8/4/97)
         linked   1993 (3/4/96), 1994 (18/9/96), 1995 (3/11/97)
This is similar to Table A5.4 in the first edition of *Birth counts*

A5.21.1

Deaths of one, two and three year olds by age of mother, England and Wales, 1993–95

Year of birth	Age at death, years	All	Age of mother					
			Under 20	20–24	25–29	30–34	35–39	40 and over
		Numbers						
1993	Under 1	4,141	410	1,051	1,250	952	386	92
	1	299	27	96	87	60	23	6
	2	192	29	42	58	42	16	5
	3	122	13	38	40	16	13	2
1994	Under 1	3,982	423	994	1,192	917	392	64
	1	301	33	91	90	52	30	5
	2	179	16	48	56	36	21	2
1995	Under 1	3,948	397	954	1,183	910	411	93
	1	293	34	82	85	63	24	5
		Rates per 100,000 live births						
1993	Under 1	617	909	692	530	557	656	874
	1	45	60	64	37	35	39	58
	2	29	65	28	25	25	27	48
	3	18	29	25	17	9	22	19
1994	Under 1	599	1,007	709	520	511	622	597
	1	46	79	65	40	29	48	47
	2	29	39	35	25	20	34	19
1995	Under 1	609	947	730	544	502	627	822
	1	46	82	63	39	35	37	45

Source: ONS, *Health Statistics quarterly 2*, page 45

This is a new table for this edition of *Birth counts*

A5.22.1

Stillbirths at 28 or more weeks of gestation by social class of father and age of mother, England and Wales, 1991–95

Social class of father	Age of mother											
	Stillbirths at 28 or more weeks of gestation, born 1991–95						Rates per thousand total births					
	All ages	Under 20	20–24	25–29	30–34	35 and over	All ages	Under 20	20–24	25–29	30–34	35 and over
Inside marriage												
I	703	1	29	214	291	168	3.40	1.88	2.31	3.24	3.33	4.17
II	2,230	24	234	707	790	475	3.52	5.56	3.65	3.09	3.34	4.75
IIIn	990	20	159	342	300	169	3.95	6.06	4.17	3.42	3.73	5.89
IIIm	2,931	57	593	1,085	774	422	4.09	4.86	4.10	3.58	4.03	6.50
IV	1,395	37	340	494	332	192	4.88	5.15	4.74	4.25	5.02	7.89
V	628	16	146	248	135	83	6.39	4.74	5.23	6.43	6.62	10.33
Other	639	36	158	241	117	87	5.59	7.75	4.93	5.60	4.54	9.89
All#	9,516	191	1,659	3,331	2,739	1,596	4.13	5.45	4.24	3.72	3.87	5.80
Outside marriage												
I	102	4	22	30	16	30	4.63	3.80	5.27	4.42	2.81	6.93
II	448	26	119	146	85	72	3.64	3.31	3.90	3.81	2.91	4.16
IIIn	244	34	84	67	37	22	4.09	4.21	4.27	4.04	3.62	4.38
IIIm	1,567	241	524	408	250	144	4.65	4.78	4.32	4.30	5.03	6.88
IV	760	149	285	157	111	58	4.93	5.00	4.83	3.93	5.89	8.67
V	473	100	178	104	52	39	5.54	5.54	5.22	4.99	5.86	11.05
Other	314	81	106	64	40	23	6.92	5.88	6.81	6.86	8.23	12.35
All#	3,908	635	1,318	976	591	388	4.73	4.92	4.64	4.31	4.64	6.50
All with fathers												
I	805	5	51	244	307	198	3.52	3.15	3.04	3.35	3.30	4.44
II	2,678	50	353	853	875	547	3.54	4.11	3.73	3.19	3.30	4.66
IIIn	1,234	54	243	409	337	191	3.98	4.74	4.21	3.51	3.72	5.67
IIIm	4,498	298	1,117	1,493	1,024	566	4.27	4.79	4.20	3.75	4.24	6.59
IV	2,155	186	625	651	443	250	4.90	5.03	4.78	4.17	5.22	8.06
V	1,101	116	324	352	187	122	6.00	5.42	5.23	5.92	6.39	10.55
Other	953	117	264	305	157	110	5.97	6.35	5.54	5.82	5.13	10.32
All#	13,424	826	2,977	4,307	3,330	1,984	4.28	5.03	4.41	3.83	3.98	5.93
Sole registration by mother	1,576	375	503	334	228	136	6.20	5.73	5.72	5.89	7.63	9.68
All#	15,000	1,201	3,480	4,641	3,558	2,120	4.43	5.21	4.56	3.93	4.12	6.02

Includes cases where father's social class was not stated

Source: Authors' analysis of ONS/OPCS data

Data extract: live births 1993 (7/94), 1994 (7/95), 1995 (3/7/96), 1996 (8/4/97) linked 1993 (3/4/96), 1994 (18/9/96), 1995 (3/11/97)

This is similar to Table A5.4 in the first edition of Birth counts

A5.22.2

Stillbirths at 24 or more weeks of gestation by social class of father and age of mother, England and Wales, 1993–96

Social class of father	Age of mother												
	Stillbirths at 24 or more weeks of gestation, born 1993–96						Rates per thousand total births						
	All ages	Under 20	20–24	25–29	30–34	35 and over	All ages	Under 20	20–24	25–29	30–34	35 and over	
Inside marriage													
I	716	0	33	212	291	180	4.38	0.00	3.95	4.35	4.03	5.30	
II	2,225	20	220	674	803	508	4.49	6.19	5.03	3.97	4.14	5.96	
IIIn	1,010	15	147	340	335	173	5.09	6.32	5.36	4.42	5.02	6.91	
IIIm	2,641	50	454	932	787	418	5.07	6.63	4.88	4.36	5.17	7.73	
IV	1,374	30	300	500	354	190	6.06	6.17	5.90	5.47	6.05	8.98	
V	566	14	122	216	135	79	7.86	7.16	6.67	7.53	8.06	12.37	
Other	603	28	145	217	124	89	6.88	7.43	6.18	6.63	6.06	12.36	
All#	9,135	157	1,421	3,091	2,829	1,637	5.18	6.51	5.36	4.67	4.87	7.02	
Outside marriage													
I	108	4	16	33	18	37	5.56	5.24	4.98	5.56	3.27	9.21	
II	519	35	127	169	114	74	4.98	5.60	5.42	5.30	4.25	4.66	
IIIn	290	46	86	83	49	26	5.68	6.97	5.33	5.93	5.04	5.64	
IIIm	1,593	244	484	451	246	168	5.89	6.49	5.29	5.74	5.55	9.10	
IV	834	142	316	193	113	70	6.29	5.90	6.72	5.35	6.12	10.01	
V	467	100	149	106	63	49	7.02	7.28	5.91	6.34	8.13	15.61	
Other	374	103	118	72	56	25	9.26	8.18	8.99	8.46	12.92	13.77	
All#	4,185	674	1,296	1,107	659	449	6.11	6.63	5.90	5.77	5.64	8.18	
All with fathers													
I	824	4	49	245	309	217	4.50	3.50	4.23	4.49	3.98	5.72	
II	2,744	55	347	843	917	582	4.57	5.80	5.17	4.18	4.15	5.75	
IIIn	1,300	61	233	423	384	199	5.21	6.80	5.35	4.65	5.02	6.72	
IIIm	4,234	294	938	1,383	1,033	586	5.35	6.51	5.08	4.73	5.26	8.08	
IV	2,208	172	616	693	467	260	6.14	5.95	6.29	5.43	6.07	9.24	
V	1,033	114	271	322	198	128	7.45	7.26	6.23	7.00	8.08	13.43	
Other	977	131	263	289	180	114	7.63	8.01	7.19	7.00	7.26	12.65	
All#	13,320	831	2,717	4,198	3,488	2,086	5.44	6.61	5.60	4.92	5.00	7.24	
Sole registration by mother	1,498	373	418	331	224	152	7.51	7.50	6.32	7.31	8.67	12.10	
All#	1,4818	1,204	3135	4529	3,712	2,238	5.60	6.89	5.69	5.05	5.15	7.37	

Includes cases where father's social class was not stated

Source: Authors' analysis of ONS/OPCS data

Data extract: live births 1993 (7/94), 1994 (7/95), 1995 (3/7/95), 1996 (8/4/97) linked 1993 (3/4/96), 1994 (18/9/96), 1995 (3/11/97)

This is similar to Table A5.4 in the first edition of *Birth counts*

Neonatal mortality by social class of father and age of mother, England and Wales, 1991–95

Social class of father	Age of mother											
	Neonatal deaths among babies born 1991–95						Rates per thousand live births					
	All ages	Under 20	20–24	25–29	30–34	35 and over	All ages	Under 20	20–24	25–29	30–34	35 and over
Inside marriage												
I	664	1	45	204	250	164	3.22	1.89	3.59	3.10	2.87	4.09
II	2,149	18	293	696	737	405	3.40	4.20	4.59	3.05	3.13	4.07
IIIn	978	7	160	389	296	126	3.92	2.13	4.22	3.90	3.70	4.42
IIIm	2,717	61	566	1,014	748	328	3.81	5.23	3.93	3.35	3.91	5.08
IV	1,195	41	327	443	248	136	4.21	5.73	4.58	3.83	3.77	5.63
V	443	18	144	148	82	51	4.54	5.36	5.19	3.86	4.05	6.42
Other	615	32	184	184	156	59	5.41	6.94	5.77	4.30	6.08	6.77
All#	8,805	178	1,725	3,093	2,533	1,276	3.83	5.10	4.43	3.46	3.59	4.67
Outside marriage												
I	72	4	8	21	18	21	3.28	3.81	1.93	3.11	3.17	4.88
II	523	41	141	155	106	80	4.26	5.24	4.64	4.06	3.64	4.64
IIIn	301	50	91	87	48	25	5.07	6.21	4.65	5.27	4.71	5.00
IIIm	1,571	287	557	393	224	110	4.68	5.72	4.62	4.16	4.53	5.29
IV	798	175	294	175	102	52	5.20	5.90	5.01	4.40	5.44	7.84
V	467	101	182	121	44	19	5.50	5.63	5.37	5.83	4.99	5.44
Other	359	124	110	70	34	21	7.97	9.05	7.12	7.56	7.05	11.41
All#	4,142	804	1,400	1,028	579	331	5.03	6.26	4.95	4.55	4.57	5.58
All with fathers												
I	736	5	53	225	268	185	3.23	3.16	3.17	3.10	2.89	4.16
II	2,672	59	434	851	843	485	3.54	4.87	4.60	3.19	3.19	4.15
IIIn	1,279	57	251	476	344	151	4.14	5.03	4.36	4.09	3.81	4.51
IIIm	4,288	348	1,123	1,407	972	438	4.09	5.62	4.24	3.55	4.04	5.13
IV	1,993	216	621	618	350	188	4.55	5.87	4.77	3.97	4.14	6.11
V	910	119	326	269	126	70	4.99	5.59	5.29	4.55	4.33	6.12
Other	974	156	294	254	190	80	6.14	8.52	6.21	4.88	6.24	7.58
All#	12,947	982	3,125	4,121	3,112	1,607	4.15	6.01	4.65	3.68	3.74	4.83
Sole registration by mother	1,108	278	331	256	150	93	4.39	4.27	3.78	4.54	5.06	6.68
All#	14,055	1,260	3,456	4,377	3,262	1,700	4.17	5.50	4.55	3.73	3.80	4.86

Source: Authors' analysis of ONS/OPCS data

Data extract: live births 1993 (7/94), 1994 (7/95), 1995 (3/7/95), 1996 (8/4/97) linked 1993 (3/4/96), 1994 (18/9/96), 1995 (3/11/97)

This is similar to Table A5.4 in the first edition of *Birth counts*

A5.22.4

Postneonatal mortality by social class of father and age of mother, England and Wales, 1991–95

Social class of father	Age of mother											
	Postneonatal deaths among babies born 1991–95						Rates per thousand live births					
	All ages	Under 20	20–24	25–29	30–34	35 and over	All ages	Under 20	20–24	25–29	30–34	35 and over
Inside marriage												
I	269	2	25	78	93	71	1.31	3.77	1.99	1.19	1.07	1.77
II	802	8	113	290	262	129	1.27	1.86	1.77	1.27	1.11	1.30
IIIn	377	10	85	131	104	47	1.51	3.05	2.24	1.31	1.30	1.65
IIIm	1,207	49	303	447	283	125	1.69	4.20	2.10	1.48	1.48	1.94
IV	572	34	184	186	112	56	2.01	4.76	2.58	1.61	1.70	2.32
V	256	18	89	87	42	20	2.62	5.36	3.21	2.27	2.07	2.52
Other	357	28	134	112	48	35	3.14	6.07	4.20	2.62	1.87	4.02
All#	3,886	154	946	1,345	953	488	1.69	4.42	2.43	1.51	1.35	1.78
Outside marriage												
I	42	2	8	16	8	8	1.91	1.90	1.93	2.37	1.41	1.86
II	203	20	51	56	47	29	1.65	2.55	1.68	1.47	1.61	1.68
IIIn	132	33	37	33	21	8	2.22	4.10	1.89	2.00	2.06	1.60
IIIm	807	185	308	190	87	37	2.41	3.68	2.55	2.01	1.76	1.78
IV	410	93	171	90	41	15	2.67	3.14	2.91	2.26	2.19	2.26
V	295	76	122	64	25	8	3.47	4.24	3.60	3.08	2.83	2.29
Other	260	73	98	55	25	9	5.77	5.33	6.34	5.94	5.19	4.89
All#	2,243	521	830	512	263	117	2.73	4.06	2.93	2.27	2.07	1.97
All with fathers												
I	311	4	33	94	101	79	1.36	2.53	1.98	1.30	1.09	1.78
II	1,005	28	164	346	309	158	1.33	2.31	1.74	1.30	1.17	1.35
IIIn	509	43	122	164	125	55	1.65	3.80	2.12	1.41	1.38	1.64
IIIm	2,014	234	611	637	370	162	1.92	3.78	2.31	1.61	1.54	1.90
IV	982	127	355	276	153	71	2.24	3.45	2.73	1.77	1.81	2.31
V	551	94	211	151	67	28	3.02	4.41	3.42	2.56	2.30	2.45
Other	617	101	232	167	73	44	3.89	5.52	4.90	3.21	2.40	4.17
All#	6,129	675	1,776	1,857	1,216	605	1.96	4.13	2.64	1.66	1.46	1.82
Sole registration by mother	1,043	319	356	200	109	59	4.13	4.90	4.07	3.55	3.67	4.24
All#	7,172	994	2,132	2,057	1,325	664	2.13	4.34	2.81	1.75	1.54	1.90

Includes cases where father's social class was not stated

Source: Authors' analysis of ONS/OPCS data

Data extract: live births 1993 (7/94), 1994 (7/95), 1995 (7/95), 1996 (8/4/97) linked 1993 (3/4/96), 1994 (18/9/96), 1995 (3/11/97)

This is similar to Table A5.4 in the first edition of *Birth counts*

A5.22.5

Infant mortality by social class of father and age of mother, England and Wales, 1991-95

Social class of father	Age of mother											
	Infant deaths among babies born 1991-95						Rates per thousand live births					
	All ages	Under 20	20–24	25–29	30–34	35 and over	All ages	Under 20	20–24	25–29	30–34	35 and over
Inside marriage												
I	933	3	70	282	343	235	4.53	5.66	5.58	4.28	3.94	5.86
II	2,951	26	406	986	999	534	4.67	6.06	6.36	4.32	4.24	5.36
IIIn	1,355	17	245	520	400	173	5.43	5.18	6.46	5.21	4.99	6.07
IIIm	3,924	110	869	1,461	1,031	453	5.50	9.43	6.03	4.83	5.39	7.02
IV	1,767	75	511	629	360	192	6.22	10.49	7.15	5.44	5.48	7.95
V	699	36	233	235	124	71	7.16	10.71	8.40	6.13	6.12	8.93
Other	972	60	318	296	204	94	8.55	13.02	9.97	6.91	7.95	10.79
All#	12,691	332	2,671	4,438	3,486	1,764	5.53	9.52	6.86	4.97	4.94	6.45
Outside marriage												
I	114	6	16	37	26	29	5.20	5.71	3.86	5.47	4.58	6.74
II	726	61	192	211	153	109	5.91	7.79	6.32	5.53	5.25	6.33
IIIn	433	83	128	120	69	33	7.30	10.31	6.53	7.26	6.77	6.60
IIIm	2,378	472	865	583	311	147	7.09	9.40	7.17	6.18	6.29	7.07
IV	1,208	268	465	265	143	67	7.87	9.04	7.93	6.66	7.63	10.11
V	762	177	304	185	69	27	8.98	9.87	8.97	8.92	7.82	7.74
Other	619	197	208	125	59	30	13.73	14.38	13.46	13.50	12.24	16.30
All#	6,385	1,325	2,230	1,540	842	448	7.76	10.32	7.89	6.82	6.64	7.56
All with fathers												
I	1,047	9	86	319	369	264	4.59	5.70	5.15	4.40	3.98	5.94
II	3,677	87	598	1,197	1,152	643	4.87	7.18	6.34	4.49	4.35	5.51
IIIn	1,788	100	373	640	469	206	5.79	8.83	6.48	5.51	5.19	6.15
IIIm	6,302	582	1,734	2,044	1,342	600	6.01	9.41	6.55	5.15	5.58	7.03
IV	2,975	343	976	894	503	259	6.80	9.32	7.50	5.75	5.95	8.42
V	1,461	213	537	420	193	98	8.00	10.00	8.71	7.11	6.63	8.57
Other	1,591	257	526	421	263	124	10.02	14.04	11.11	8.09	8.63	11.75
All#	19,076	1,657	4,901	5,978	4,328	2,212	6.11	10.15	7.29	5.34	5.20	6.65
Sole registration by mother	2,151	597	687	456	259	152	8.52	9.17	7.85	8.08	8.73	10.92
All#	21,227	2,254	5,588	6,434	4,587	2,364	6.29	9.83	7.36	5.48	5.34	6.76

Includes cases where father's social class was not stated

Source: Authors' analysis of ONS/OPCS data

Data extract: live births 1993 (7/94), 1994 (7/95), 1995 (3/7/96), 1996 (8/4/97) linked 1993 (3/4/96), 1994 (18/9/96), 1995 (3/11/97)

This is similar to Table A5.4 in the first edition of *Birth counts*

A5.22.6

Live births by social class of father and age of mother, England and Wales, 1991–95

Social class of father	Age of mother					
	Numbers					
	All ages	Under 20	20–24	25–29	30–34	35 and over
Inside marriage						
I	206,110	530	12,550	65,820	87,090	40,120
II	631,550	4,290	63,850	228,460	235,400	99,550
IIIn	249,550	3,280	37,950	99,720	80,090	28,510
IIIm	713,950	11,660	144,130	302,350	191,280	64,530
IV	284,180	7,150	71,420	115,720	65,750	24,140
V	97,640	3,360	27,750	38,310	20,270	7,950
Other	113,680	4,610	31,900	42,810	25,650	8,710
All	2,296,660	34,880	389,550	893,190	705,530	273,510
Outside marriage						
I	21,940	1,050	4,150	6,760	5,680	4,300
II	122,780	7,830	30,400	38,180	29,140	17,230
IIIn	59,350	8,050	19,590	16,520	10,190	5,000
IIIm	335,480	50,210	120,640	94,410	49,420	20,800
IV	153,500	29,640	58,670	39,810	18,750	6,630
V	84,900	17,940	33,900	20,750	8,820	3,490
Other	45,070	13,700	15,450	9,260	4,820	1,840
All	823,020	128,420	282,800	225,690	126,820	59,290
All with fathers						
I	228,050	1,580	16,700	72,580	92,770	44,420
II	754,330	12,120	94,250	266,640	264,540	116,780
IIIn	308,900	11,330	57,540	116,240	90,280	33,510
IIIm	1,049,430	61,870	264,770	396,760	240,700	85,330
IV	437,680	36,790	130,090	155,530	84,500	30,770
V	182,540	21,300	61,650	59,060	29,090	11,440
Other	158,750	18,310	47,350	52,070	30,470	10,550
All	3,119,680	163,300	672,350	1,118,880	832,350	332,800
Sole registration by mother	252,562	65,095	87,488	56,405	29,660	13,914
All	3,372,354	229,188	758,995	1,174,968	859,242	349,961

Estimated numbers of live births are based on a 10 per cent sample coded for occupation

Source: Authors' analysis of ONS/OPCS data

Data extract: live births 1993 (7/94), 1994 (7/95), 1995 (3/7/96), 1996 (8/4/97)

This is similar to Table A5.5 in the first edition of *Birth counts*

A5.23.1

Stillbirths and mortality in the first year of life by social class of mother and age of mother, England and Wales, 1991-95, 1993-96

Numbers

Stillbirths at 28 or more weeks of gestational age, 1991-95

Social class of mother	All ages	Under 20	20-24	25-29	30-34	35 and over
I	220	1	4	55	90	70
II	1,823	13	179	579	644	408
IIIn	2,257	96	474	846	548	293
IIIm	542	35	156	181	125	45
IV	997	101	335	287	185	89
V	155	5	54	43	34	19
Unclassified-	161	5	48	41	42	25
No occupation stated	8,845	945	2,230	2,609	1,890	1,171
All	15,000	1,201	3,480	4,641	3,558	2,120

Stillbirths at 24 or more weeks of gestational age, 1993-96

Social class of mother	All ages	Under 20	20-24	25-29	30-34	35 and over
I	250	1	4	64	97	84
II	2,118	13	193	621	807	484
IIIn	2,524	89	478	930	679	348
IIIm	623	40	174	196	146	67
IV	1,107	102	327	347	220	111
V	200	8	57	69	40	26
Unclassified-	161	8	41	41	45	26
No occupation stated	7,835	943	1,861	2,261	1,678	1,092
All	14,818	1,204	3,135	4,529	3,712	2,238

Neonatal deaths, 1991-95

Social class of mother	All ages	Under 20	20-24	25-29	30-34	35 and over
I	235	0	5	66	97	67
II	2,054	22	211	658	739	424
IIIn	2,519	112	562	925	643	277
IIIm	591	49	173	190	129	50
IV	984	86	325	324	176	73

Rates per thousand total births

Stillbirths at 28 or more weeks of gestational age, 1991-95

Social class of mother	All ages	Under 20	20-24	25-29	30-34	35 and over
I	3.1	9.0	1.9	2.9	2.7	4.4
II	3.1	3.0	3.4	2.8	3.0	4.1
IIIn	3.2	4.2	3.2	3.0	2.9	4.6
IIIm	3.5	3.2	3.5	3.1	3.9	4.4
IV	4.3	5.0	4.4	3.6	4.6	6.0
V	4.3	1.9	5.4	3.3	4.7	5.9
Unclassified-	4.6	2.6	5.5	3.5	5.0	6.4
No occupation stated	5.7	5.7	5.3	5.2	5.6	8.6
All	4.4	5.2	4.6	3.9	4.1	6.1

Stillbirths at 24 or more weeks of gestational age, 1993-96

Social class of mother	All ages	Under 20	20-24	25-29	30-34	35 and over
I	4.1	19.6	2.6	4.4	3.2	5.8
II	4.4	4.2	5.0	3.9	4.2	5.4
IIIn	4.4	5.5	4.4	4.1	4.0	6.0
IIIm	5.0	5.0	5.4	4.1	5.2	7.2
IV	5.7	6.6	5.7	5.1	5.6	7.4
V	6.6	4.0	7.0	6.3	6.3	9.0
Unclassified-	6.7	6.9	7.0	5.2	7.2	9.3
No occupation stated	6.8	7.3	6.2	6.2	6.6	10.1
All	5.6	6.9	5.7	5.0	5.1	7.4

Rates per thousand live births

Neonatal deaths, 1991-95

Social class of mother	All ages	Under 20	20-24	25-29	30-34	35 and over
I	3.3	–	2.4	3.5	2.9	4.3
II	3.5	5.1	4.0	3.2	3.4	4.2
IIIn	3.5	4.9	3.8	3.2	3.4	4.4
IIIm	3.8	4.5	3.9	3.2	4.0	4.9
IV	4.3	4.3	4.3	4.1	4.4	5.0

A5.23.1 *continued*

Stillbirths and mortality in the first year of life by social class of mother and age of mother, England and Wales, 1991–95, 1993–96

Social class of mother	Age of mother											
	All ages	Under 20	20–24	25–29	30–34	35 and over	All ages	Under 20	20–24	25–29	30–34	35 and over
V	197	16	54	71	37	19	5.5	6.2	5.4	5.4	5.2	6.0
Unclassified-	201	8	57	69	45	22	5.8	4.1	6.6	5.9	5.4	5.7
No occupation stated	7,242	966	2,058	2,067	1,386	765	4.7	5.8	4.9	4.1	4.1	5.6
All	14,055	1,260	3,456	4,377	3,262	1,700	4.2	5.5	4.6	3.7	3.8	4.9
Postneonatal deaths, 1991–95												
I	88	1	5	32	32	18	1.25	9.09	2.43	1.71	0.95	1.15
II	714	8	85	226	255	140	1.23	1.87	1.60	1.10	1.18	1.40
IIIn	761	49	194	227	200	91	1.07	2.16	1.30	0.79	1.05	1.44
IIIm	223	26	79	58	37	23	1.42	2.40	1.77	0.99	1.15	2.24
IV	359	63	116	115	45	20	1.57	3.16	1.54	1.45	1.13	1.36
V	78	8	19	29	10	12	2.16	3.08	1.90	2.21	1.40	3.76
Unclassified-	109	11	60	26	6	6	3.15	5.67	6.94	2.21	0.72	1.55
No occupation stated	4,809	824	1,565	1,336	735	349	3.09	4.96	3.75	2.65	2.20	2.58
All	7,172	994	2,132	2,057	1,325	664	2.13	4.35	2.81	1.75	1.54	1.92
Infant deaths, 1991–95												
I	323	1	10	98	129	85	4.6	9.1	4.9	5.3	3.8	5.4
II	2,768	30	296	884	994	564	4.8	7.0	5.6	4.3	4.6	5.6
IIIn	3,280	161	756	1,152	843	368	4.6	7.1	5.1	4.0	4.4	5.8
IIIm	814	75	252	248	166	73	5.2	6.9	5.7	4.2	5.2	7.1
IV	1,343	149	441	439	221	93	5.9	7.5	5.9	5.5	5.5	6.3
V	275	24	73	100	47	31	7.6	9.2	7.3	7.6	6.6	9.7
Unclassified-	310	19	117	95	51	28	9.0	9.8	13.5	8.1	6.1	7.2
No occupation stated	12,051	1,790	3,623	3,403	2,121	1,114	7.7	10.8	8.7	6.8	6.4	8.2
All	21,227	2,254	5,588	6,434	4,587	2,364	6.3	9.9	7.4	5.5	5.3	6.8
Live births, 1991–95												
I	70,360	110	2,060	18,660	33,860	15,670						
II	578,860	4,280	53,190	204,540	216,530	100,320						
IIIn	710,210	22,700	148,690	285,650	190,130	63,040						
IIIm	156,540	10,830	44,520	58,810	32,130	10,250						

A5.23.1 *continued*

Stillbirths and mortality in the first year of life by social class of mother and age of mother, England and Wales, 1991–95, 1993–96

Social class of mother	Age of mother					
	All ages	Under 20	20–24	25–29	30–34	35 and over
IV	229,320	19,920	75,230	79,490	39,940	14,740
V	36,080	2,600	10,020	13,120	7,150	3,190
Unclassified~	34,610	1,940	8,650	11,770	8,380	3,870
No occupation stated	1,556,110	165,980	417,000	503,610	334,010	135,510
All	3,372,090	228,360	759,360	1,175,650	862,130	346,590
Live births 1993–96						
I	60,670	50	1,510	14,400	30,190	14,520
II	480,220	3,050	38,280	159,830	189,800	89,260
IIIn	574,410	16,100	106,990	226,660	167,250	57,410
IIIm	124,490	8,020	32,260	47,210	27,730	9,270
IV	194,440	15,270	57,450	67,980	38,900	14,840
V	30,160	1,990	8,060	10,920	6,320	2,870
Unclassified~	23,790	1,150	5,840	7,790	6,230	2,780
No occupation stated	1,145,840	128,870	296,250	359,950	253,310	107,460
All	2,634,020	174,500	546,640	894,740	719,730	298,410

~ Includes Armed Forces

Source: Authors' analysis of ONS data

Data extract: live births 1993 (7/94), 1994 (7/95), 1995 (3/7/96), 1996 (8/4/97)

     linked   1993 (3/4/96), 1994 (18/9/96), 1995 (3/11/97)

This is a new table for this edition of *Birth counts*

A5.24.1

Teenage pregnancies, maternities by age of mother, England and Wales, 1939–98

| Year | Age of mother, years | | | | | | | | | All aged 11–15 | All aged 16–19 | Rate per 1,000 women aged 11–15 | Rate per 1,000 women aged 16–19 |
	11	12	13	14	15	16	17	18	19				
1939	0	0	4	34	161	833	3,282	8,802	16,045	199	28,962	..	..
1940	0	1	6	30	153	777	2,964	8,010	15,737	190	27,488	..	..
1941	0	0	7	43	168	799	2,786	6,996	14,080	218	24,661	..	..
1942	0	1	3	39	197	884	2,821	6,958	13,534	240	24,197	..	..
1943	0	0	5	36	219	852	2,891	6,971	13,623	260	24,337	..	..
1944	0	0	7	29	214	1,001	2,936	7,166	13,704	250	24,807	..	..
1945	0	0	12	34	246	1,089	3,321	7,355	13,659	292	25,424	..	..
1946	0	0	4	38	239	969	3,070	7,063	13,776	281	24,878	..	..
1947	0	0	9	37	158	871	3,135	8,012	15,829	204	27,847	..	..
1948	0	2	1	37	176	954	3,466	8,795	17,322	216	30,537	..	..
1949	0	3	3	31	169	960	3,926	9,354	17,694	206	31,934	..	..
1950	0	0	6	39	176	890	3,686	9,039	17,312	221	39,927	..	..
1951	0	0	4	25	167	821	3,359	8,674	16,397	196	29,251	..	..
1952	0	0	5	36	176	959	3,562	8,767	16,090	217	29,378	..	..
1953	0	0	10	46	170	961	3,738	9,144	16,740	226	30,583	..	..
1954	0	0	5	33	155	981	3,926	9,786	17,289	193	31,982	..	..
1955	0	0	8	40	185	1,027	4,414	9,836	17,945	233	33,222	..	..
1956	0	0	5	56	208	1,313	5,164	11,632	20,115	269	38,224	..	..
1957	0	2	9	45	243	1,441	5,606	12,635	21,776	299	41,458	..	..
1958	1	1	10	62	309	1,666	5,936	13,442	23,021	383	44,065	..	..
1959	0	4	10	78	393	2,099	6,729	13,808	23,516	485	46,152	..	..
1960	0	0	15	98	601	2,784	8,505	15,491	24,744	714	51,524	..	..
1961	0	0	23	133	731	3,789	10,390	18,470	26,929	887	59,578	0.5	47.0
1962	0	1	19	192	929	3,892	11,482	20,876	30,595	1,141	66,845	0.6	51.0
1963	0	3	22	174	984	4,854	11,871	21,764	32,578	1,183	71,067	0.7	50.7
1964	0	5	15	172	901	4,952	14,902	22,434	34,037	1,093	76,325	0.7	52.6
1965	0	1	23	170	970	4,722	14,399	27,521	34,478	1,164	81,120	0.7	55.2
1966	1	7	27	193	1,068	4,744	13,673	25,970	41,733	1,296	86,120	0.8	57.7
1967	1	6	30	194	1,009	4,932	13,929	25,697	39,423	1,240	83,981	0.8	59.6
1968	0	4	25	194	1,100	5,206	14,263	25,216	36,738	1,323	81,423	0.8	60.3
1969	4	11	32	207	1,253	5,506	14,569	25,296	35,382	1,507	80,753	0.9	61.1
1970	4	9	25	219	1,184	5,652	14,980	24,876	34,634	1,441	80,142	0.9	61.1
1971	2	4	35	233	1,267	5,894	15,614	25,871	34,298	1,541	81,677	0.9	62.6
1972	1	4	28	241	1,336	6,290	16,160	24,282	32,184	1,610	77,916	1.1	59.4
1973	1	7	39	272	1,377	6,102	14,135	21,941	29,869	1,696	72,047	0.9	54.4
1974	0	6	26	264	1,299	5,587	14,008	20,842	27,132	1,595	67,569	0.8	50.4

A5.24.1 continued

Teenage pregnancies, maternities by age of mother, England and Wales, 1939–98

Year	Age of mother, years									All aged 11–15	All aged 16–19	Rate per 1,000 women aged 11–15	Rate per 1,000 women aged 16–19
	11	12	13	14	15	16	17	18	19				
1975	1	3	37	230	1,272	4,755	12,345	19,587	25,575	1,543	62,262	0.8	45.1
1976	1	3	35	215	1,174	4,389	10,752	17,684	23,966	1,428	56,791	0.7	40.0
1977	1	3	23	212	1,088	4,415	10,222	16,465	22,381	1,327	53,483	0.7	36.6
1978	2	1	22	197	1,175	4,458	10,549	16,796	23,072	1,397	54,875	0.7	36.4
1979	2	2	27	212	1,143	4,327	11,062	18,087	24,510	1,386	57,986	0.7	37.5
1980	9	8	18	191	1,057	4,321	10,938	18,661	25,711	1,283	59,631	0.7	37.5
1981	10	9	20	190	970	4,160	9,900	17,020	24,420	1,190	55,500	0.6	34.3
1982	0	0	15	192	956	3,994	10,035	16,639	23,651	1,174	54,319	0.6	33.4
1983	0	11	22	174	1,064	4,038	9,695	16,165	22,982	1,263	52,880	0.7	32.5
1984	1	3	20	214	1,088	4,113	10,025	16,192	22,962	1,328	53,292	0.7	33.4
1985	0	5	21	217	1,163	4,441	10,492	17,121	23,513	1,403	55,567	0.8	35.4
1986	0	2	31	194	1,151	4,323	10,700	17,429	23,565	1,377	56,017	0.8	36.5
1987	2	1	19	178	1,107	4,401	10,488	17,535	23,790	1,309	56,214	0.8	37.2
1988	1	3	19	196	1,049	4,513	11,172	17,555	24,230	1,268	57,470	0.9	38.9
1989	0	3	22	181	1,110	4,238	10,316	17,025	22,624	1,319	54,203	0.9	38.0
1990	0	6	16	188	1,103	4,165	10,337	16,539	23,187	1,307	54,228	0.9	39.6
1991	0	0	27	217	1,184	4,150	9,473	15,527	21,793	1,430	50,943	1.0	39.2
1992	0	2	23	202	1,091	3,810	8,882	14,097	19,693	1,318	46,482	0.9	37.7
1993	0	2	26	226	1,153	3,909	8,511	13,332	18,001	1,407	43,753	0.9	37.2
1994	1	1	29	244	1,079	3,666	7,839	12,516	16,662	1,358	40,683	0.9	35.5
1995	0	6	33	251	1,221	4,052	7,960	12,074	16,343	1,508	40,429	1.0	35.1
1996	1	2	32	262	1,334	4,509	9,406	12,772	16,368	1,630	43,055	1.0	36.4
1997+	0	2	26	258	1,314	4,515	9,794	14,023	16,435	1,602	44,767	1.0	36.6
1998*	1	3	41	247	1,258	4,280	9,984	14,569	17,893	1,548	46,726	1.0	37.3

+ Not revised to include the 1,002 live births omitted from published data for 1997

Source: *Registrar General's Statistical Review*, 1939–73
OPCS/ONS *Birth statistics, Series FM1*, 1974–1998

This was Table A5.18 in the first edition of *Birth counts*

A5.24.2

Teenage pregnancies, abortions by age of mother, England and Wales, 1968-98

Year	Age of mother, years									All aged 11-15	All aged 16-19	Rate per 1,000 women aged 11-15	Rate per 1,000 women aged 16-19
	11	12	13	14	15	16	17	18	19				
1968	3	6	21	150	363	559	693	945	1,088	543	3,285	0.3	2.4
1969	2	7	38	279	848	1,445	1,816	2,255	2,543	1,174	8,059	0.7	6.1
1970	3	20	85	391	1,233	2,530	3,188	3,864	3,936	1,732	13,518	1.0	10.3
1971	3	16	77	529	1,671	3,465	4,426	5,193	5,092	2,296	18,176	1.3	13.9
1972	0	7	98	586	2,113	4,318	5,395	6,038	6,035	2,804	21,786	1.9	16.6
1973	5	14	108	693	2,270	5,082	5,775	6,374	6,249	3,090	23,480	1.7	17.7
1974	1	9	117	718	2,490	5,348	6,225	6,564	6,060	3,335	24,197	1.8	18.0
1975	0	12	120	747	2,691	5,411	6,394	6,389	5,928	3,570	24,122	1.9	17.5
1976	6	14	122	738	2,545	5,429	6,285	6,282	5,967	3,425	23,963	1.7	16.9
1977	1	13	105	804	2,701	5,510	6,367	6,576	6,139	3,624	24,592	1.8	16.8
1978	3	20	113	708	2,454	5,675	6,733	7,276	6,679	3,298	26,363	1.7	17.5
1979	9	18	116	698	2,693	6,030	7,412	8,028	7,722	3,534	29,192	1.8	18.9
1980	5	17	141	770	2,717	6,370	8,108	8,756	8,644	3,650	31,878	1.9	20.1
1981	9	13	98	710	2,701	6,190	7,949	8,719	8,535	3,531	31,393	1.9	19.4
1982	9	15	138	778	2,921	6,334	7,791	8,561	8,663	3,852	31,349	2.0	19.3
1983	0	9	127	893	3,058	6,468	7,744	8,585	8,434	4,087	31,231	2.2	19.2
1984	1	9	111	898	3,139	6,802	8,406	9,072	9,134	4,158	33,414	2.3	20.9
1985	0	7	118	899	2,978	6,648	8,432	9,536	9,592	4,002	34,208	2.3	21.8
1986	0	5	77	842	2,970	6,175	8,309	9,570	9,765	3,894	33,819	2.4	22.0
1987	2	10	114	781	2,858	6,251	8,252	10,023	10,641	3,765	35,167	2.4	23.3
1988	0	7	88	764	2,709	6,513	9,212	10,598	11,605	3,568	37,928	2.4	25.7
1989	0	9	72	722	2,580	5,961	8,560	10,625	11,036	3,383	36,182	2.3	25.4
1990	2	7	100	764	2,549	5,555	8,156	10,407	11,402	3,422	35,520	2.4	26.0
1991	2	8	119	757	2,272	4,940	7,053	8,860	10,277	3,158	31,130	2.2	24.0
1992	0	8	135	762	2,095	4,436	6,251	7,826	9,076	3,000	27,589	2.0	22.4
1993	0	8	133	823	2,119	4,109	5,844	7,407	8,446	3,083	25,806	2.0	22.0
1994	1	13	148	918	2,166	4,270	5,699	7,162	8,092	3,246	25,223	2.1	22.0
1995	1	12	129	804	2,324	4,345	5,791	6,989	7,820	3,270	24,945	2.1	21.7
1996	0	7	173	917	2,547	5,209	6,994	8,070	8,517	3,644	28,790	2.3	24.3
1997	1	17	140	862	2,414	5,231	7,427	8,601	8,688	3,434	29,947	2.2	24.5
1998	2	11	162	928	2,656	5,372	8,055	9,813	9,996	3,759	33,236	2.4	26.5

Figures for 1973, 1981 and 1987 each include one 10 year old in the 11 year old column.

Source: ONS *Abortion Statistics, Series AB*, Table 4

This was Table A5.18 in the first edition of *Birth counts*

A5.24.3

Teenage conceptions by single year of age and outcome, England and Wales, 1969–97

Year	Number of conceptions			Conception rates per 1,000 women in age-group/age		
	Total conceptions	Conceptions leading to maternities	Conceptions terminated by abortion	Total conceptions	Conceptions leading to maternities	Conceptions terminated by abortion
	Under 16 years					
1969	6,576	4,905	1,671	6.9	5.1	1.7
1970	7,713	5,258	2,455	7.9	5.4	2.5
1971	8,825	5,575	3,250	8.6	5.5	3.2
1972	9,608	5,679	3,929	9.3	5.5	3.8
1973	9,792	5,392	4,400	9.2	5.1	4.1
1974	9,371	4,843	4,528	8.5	4.4	4.1
1975	9,181	4,394	4,787	8.1	3.9	4.2
1976	9,191	4,298	4,893	7.9	3.7	4.2
1977	9,003	4,226	4,777	7.6	3.6	4.0
1978	9,103	4,412	4,691	7.6	3.7	3.9
1979	9,108	4,079	5,029	7.5	3.4	4.2
1980	8,580	3,935	4,645	7.2	3.3	3.9
1981	8,561	3,694	4,867	7.3	3.1	4.1
1982	8,999	3,875	5,124	7.8	3.4	4.4
1983	9,369	4,046	5,323	8.3	3.6	4.7
1984	9,649	4,278	5,371	8.7	3.8	4.8
1985	9,406	4,169	5,237	8.7	3.8	4.8
1986	9,194	4,222	4,972	8.8	4.0	4.7
1987	9,135	4,185	4,950	9.3	4.2	5.0
1988	8,258	3,845	4,413	8.8	4.1	4.7
1989	7,950	3,814	4,136	8.9	4.3	4.6
1990	8,139	4,006	4,133	9.5	4.7	4.8
1991	7,480	3,655	3,825	8.9	4.3	4.6
1992	7,217	3,707	3,510	8.4	4.3	4.1
1993	7,267	3,643	3,624	8.1	4.1	4.0
1994	7,795	3,875	3,920	8.3	4.1	4.2
1995	8,051	4,218	3,833	8.6	4.5	4.1
1996	8,857	4,498	4,359	9.5	4.8	4.7
1997	8,271	4,164	4,107	8.9	4.5	4.4
	Under 14 years					
1969	247	149	98	0.8	0.5	0.3
1970	379	193	186	1.1	0.6	0.6
1971	351	179	172	1.0	0.5	0.5
1972	392	194	198	1.1	0.5	0.6
1973	396	180	216	1.1	0.5	0.6
1974	393	185	208	1.0	0.5	0.5
1975	401	159	242	1.1	0.4	0.7
1976	377	153	224	1.0	0.4	0.6
1977	376	138	238	0.9	0.3	0.6
1978	395	163	232	1.0	0.4	0.6
1979	381	144	237	1.0	0.4	0.6
1980	352	125	227	0.9	0.3	0.6
1981	435	171	264	1.1	0.4	0.7
1982	428	138	290	1.1	0.4	0.8
1983	367	148	219	1.0	0.4	0.6
1984	378	151	227	1.0	0.4	0.6

Teenage conceptions by single year of age and outcome, England and Wales, 1969–97

Year	Number of conceptions			Conception rates per 1,000 women in age-group/age		
	Total conceptions	Conceptions leading to maternities	Conceptions terminated by abortion	Total conceptions	Conceptions leading to maternities	Conceptions terminated by abortion
1985	325	139	186	0.9	0.4	0.5
1986	292	120	172	0.9	0.4	0.5
1987	346	145	201	1.1	0.5	0.7
1988	270	126	144	0.9	0.4	0.5
1989	223	110	113	0.8	0.4	0.4
1990	316	133	183	1.2	0.5	0.7
1991	318	126	192	1.1	0.5	0.7
1992	363	147	216	1.2	0.5	0.7
1993	368	165	203	1.2	0.5	0.6
1994	397	167	230	1.3	0.5	0.7
1995	382	150	232	1.2	0.5	0.8
1996	451	192	259	1.5	0.6	0.8
1997	365	149	216	1.2	0.5	0.7
14 years						
1969	1,225	814	411	3.9	2.6	1.3
1970	1,446	842	604	4.5	2.6	1.9
1971	1,763	952	811	5.3	2.8	2.4
1972	1,874	950	924	5.4	2.8	2.7
1973	1,987	963	1,024	5.6	2.7	2.9
1974	1,922	878	1,044	5.3	2.4	2.9
1975	1,919	837	1,082	5.1	2.2	2.8
1976	1,898	782	1,116	4.9	2.0	2.9
1977	1,916	792	1,124	4.9	2.0	2.9
1978	1,822	810	1,012	4.5	2.0	2.5
1979	1,904	760	1,144	4.7	1.9	2.8
1980	1,714	669	1,045	4.3	1.7	2.6
1981	1,817	684	1,133	4.6	1.7	2.9
1982	1,868	702	1,166	4.9	1.8	3.1
1983	2,034	790	1,244	5.4	2.1	3.3
1984	2,018	794	1,224	5.5	2.2	3.4
1985	2,063	836	1,227	5.6	2.3	3.3
1986	1,980	809	1,171	5.7	2.3	3.4
1987	1,899	736	1,163	5.8	2.2	3.5
1988	1,652	663	989	5.4	2.2	3.2
1989	1,650	722	928	5.5	2.4	3.1
1990	1,754	760	994	6.1	2.7	3.5
1991	1,686	717	969	6.1	2.6	3.5
1992	1,632	730	902	5.8	2.6	3.2
1993	1,774	761	1,013	5.8	2.5	3.3
1994	1,938	804	1,134	6.1	2.5	3.6
1995	1,834	878	956	5.8	2.8	3.0
1996	1,961	838	1,123	6.3	2.7	3.6
1997	1,964	866	1,098	6.3	2.8	3.5
15 years						
1969	5,104	3,942	1,162	15.8	12.2	3.6
1970	5,888	4,223	1,665	18.4	13.2	5.2
1971	6,711	4,444	2,267	20.5	13.5	6.9

Teenage conceptions by single year of age and outcome, England and Wales, 1969–97

Year	Number of conceptions			Conception rates per 1,000 women in age-group/age		
	Total conceptions	Conceptions leading to maternities	Conceptions terminated by abortion	Total conceptions	Conceptions leading to maternities	Conceptions terminated by abortion
1972	7,342	4,535	2,807	21.9	13.5	8.4
1973	7,409	4,249	3,160	21.4	12.3	9.1
1974	7,056	3,780	3,276	19.8	10.6	9.2
1975	6,861	3,398	3,463	18.8	9.3	9.5
1976	6,916	3,363	3,553	18.2	8.8	9.3
1977	6,711	3,296	3,415	17.2	8.5	8.8
1978	6,886	3,439	3,447	17.5	8.7	8.7
1979	6,823	3,175	3,648	16.8	7.8	9.0
1980	6,513	3,140	3,373	16.0	7.7	8.3
1981	6,309	2,839	3,470	15.8	7.1	8.7
1982	6,703	3,035	3,668	17.1	7.7	9.3
1983	6,968	3,108	3,860	18.3	8.1	10.1
1984	7,253	3,333	3,920	19.1	8.8	10.3
1985	7,018	3,194	3,824	19.2	8.7	10.5
1986	6,922	3,293	3,629	18.6	8.9	9.8
1987	6,890	3,304	3,586	19.7	9.4	10.3
1988	6,336	3,056	3,280	19.3	9.3	10.0
1989	6,077	2,982	3,095	19.7	9.7	10.0
1990	6,069	3,113	2,956	20.3	10.4	9.9
1991	5,476	2,812	2,664	19.1	9.8	9.3
1992	5,222	2,830	2,392	19.0	10.3	8.7
1993	5,125	2,717	2,408	18.3	9.7	8.6
1994	5,460	2,904	2,556	17.9	9.5	8.4
1995	5,835	3,190	2,645	18.4	10.1	8.3
1996	6,445	3,468	2,977	20.4	11.0	9.4
1997	5,942	3,149	2,793	19.2	10.2	9.0
	16 years					
1969	14,341	12,516	1,825	44.3	38.7	5.6
1970	16,234	13,250	2,984	49.5	40.5	9.1
1971	17,292	13,122	4,170	54.1	41.0	13.0
1972	17,612	12,607	5,005	53.5	38.3	15.2
1973	18,034	12,419	5,615	53.4	36.8	16.6
1974	16,553	10,722	5,831	47.6	30.8	16.8
1975	15,278	9,447	5,831	42.8	26.5	16.3
1976	14,567	8,761	5,806	39.7	23.9	15.8
1977	14,940	8,895	6,045	39.1	23.3	15.8
1978	15,770	9,422	6,348	40.3	24.1	16.2
1979	16,106	9,307	6,799	40.6	23.5	17.2
1980	15,210	8,600	6,610	37.4	21.1	16.3
1981	15,410	8,782	6,628	37.7	21.5	16.2
1982	15,030	8,331	6,699	37.6	20.8	16.8
1983	15,229	8,431	6,798	38.7	21.4	17.3
1984	15,995	8,842	7,153	41.8	23.1	18.7
1985	16,146	9,107	7,039	42.4	23.9	18.5
1986	15,425	8,933	6,492	42.1	24.4	17.7
1987	16,512	9,415	7,097	44.4	25.3	19.1

Teenage conceptions by single year of age and outcome, England and Wales, 1969–97

Year	Number of conceptions			Conception rates per 1,000 women in age-group/age		
	Total conceptions	Conceptions leading to maternities	Conceptions terminated by abortion	Total conceptions	Conceptions leading to maternities	Conceptions terminated by abortion
1988	15,395	8,590	6,805	43.9	24.5	19.4
1989	14,703	8,396	6,307	44.6	25.5	19.1
1990	13,923	8,051	5,872	45.1	26.1	19.0
1991	12,623	7,505	5,118	42.1	25.0	17.1
1992	11,932	7,202	4,730	41.5	25.1	16.5
1993	11,031	6,708	4,323	40.1	24.4	15.7
1994	11,336	6,833	4,503	40.5	24.4	16.1
1995	12,382	7,668	4,714	40.6	25.2	15.5
1996	14,284	8,606	5,678	45.0	27.1	17.9
1997	14,058	8,364	5,694	44.5	26.5	18.0
17 years						
1969	24,578	22,382	2,196	77.2	70.3	6.9
1970	27,385	23,673	3,712	84.0	72.6	11.4
1971	27,587	22,577	5,010	83.6	68.5	15.2
1972	26,574	20,597	5,977	82.8	64.2	18.6
1973	25,896	19,759	6,137	78.4	59.8	18.6
1974	24,994	18,435	6,559	73.8	54.4	19.4
1975	23,349	16,747	6,602	66.9	48.0	18.9
1976	21,681	15,165	6,516	60.5	42.3	18.2
1977	21,757	15,154	6,603	59.1	41.2	17.9
1978	23,518	16,256	7,262	61.2	42.3	18.9
1979	24,868	16,694	8,174	63.3	42.5	20.8
1980	23,894	15,791	8,103	60.0	39.6	20.3
1981	23,179	14,990	8,189	56.8	36.7	20.1
1982	22,964	15,049	7,915	55.8	36.6	19.2
1983	22,575	14,452	8,123	55.9	35.8	20.1
1984	24,209	15,642	8,567	61.2	39.6	21.7
1985	24,619	15,922	8,697	64.0	41.4	22.6
1986	24,776	16,101	8,675	64.8	42.1	22.7
1987	24,809	15,915	8,894	67.4	43.2	24.2
1988	25,088	15,623	9,465	67.2	41.9	25.4
1989	23,817	14,941	8,876	67.6	42.4	25.2
1990	22,694	14,316	8,378	68.4	43.2	25.3
1991	19,985	12,913	7,072	64.2	41.5	22.7
1992	18,403	11,965	6,438	61.4	39.9	21.5
1993	17,504	11,426	6,078	60.9	39.8	21.1
1994	16,960	11,036	5,924	61.6	40.1	21.5
1995	17,447	11,321	6,126	62.1	40.3	21.8
1996	20,349	12,975	7,374	66.6	42.5	24.1
1997	21,029	13,242	7,787	66.1	41.6	24.5
18 years						
1969	34,722	32,044	2,678	104.2	96.2	8.0
1970	37,624	33,309	4,315	116.9	103.5	13.4
1971	36,656	31,165	5,491	111.7	95.0	16.7
1972	35,399	28,943	6,456	106.9	87.4	19.5
1973	32,885	26,444	6,441	102.0	82.0	20.0
1974	31,439	24,938	6,501	94.8	75.2	19.6

A5.24.3 *continued*

Teenage conceptions by single year of age and outcome, England and Wales, 1969–97

Year	Number of conceptions			Conception rates per 1,000 women in age-group/age		
	Total conceptions	Conceptions leading to maternities	Conceptions terminated by abortion	Total conceptions	Conceptions leading to maternities	Conceptions terminated by abortion
1975	29,952	23,555	6,397	88.0	69.2	18.8
1976	27,563	21,114	6,449	78.5	60.1	18.4
1977	28,270	21,522	6,748	78.6	59.8	18.8
1978	30,344	22,842	7,502	81.9	61.7	20.3
1979	32,752	24,206	8,546	84.8	62.7	22.1
1980	32,093	23,378	8,715	81.2	59.2	22.1
1981	30,564	21,894	8,670	76.2	54.6	21.6
1982	30,325	21,769	8,556	74.0	53.1	20.9
1983	29,860	21,196	8,664	72.1	51.2	20.9
1984	31,382	22,302	9,080	77.6	55.2	22.5
1985	31,939	22,235	9,704	80.4	56.0	24.4
1986	32,177	22,456	9,721	83.3	58.1	25.2
1987	33,648	23,114	10,534	87.7	60.2	27.5
1988	31,957	21,466	10,491	86.7	58.3	28.5
1989	32,414	21,641	10,773	86.8	57.9	28.8
1990	31,183	20,676	10,507	88.4	58.6	29.8
1991	27,851	18,984	8,867	83.6	57.0	26.6
1992	25,218	17,373	7,845	80.9	55.7	25.2
1993	23,422	15,910	7,512	78.0	53.0	25.0
1994	22,614	15,389	7,225	78.5	53.4	25.1
1995	22,402	15,073	7,329	81.0	54.5	26.5
1996	24,150	15,912	8,238	85.7	56.5	29.2
1997	25,618	16,828	8,790	83.6	54.9	28.7
19 years						
1969	43,663	40,811	2,852	125.8	117.6	8.2
1970	45,853	41,489	4,364	136.6	123.6	13.0
1971	42,770	37,408	5,362	130.9	114.5	16.4
1972	41,406	35,042	6,364	125.7	106.4	19.3
1973	39,080	32,766	6,314	117.4	98.4	19.0
1974	35,834	29,635	6,199	110.7	91.6	19.2
1975	34,216	28,177	6,039	102.5	84.4	18.1
1976	32,652	26,617	6,035	95.3	77.7	17.6
1977	33,424	27,303	6,121	94.7	77.4	17.3
1978	35,872	28,953	6,919	99.1	80.0	19.1
1979	38,110	30,015	8,095	102.4	80.6	21.7
1980	37,475	29,187	8,288	96.4	75.1	21.3
1981	37,458	29,087	8,371	94.0	73.0	21.0
1982	36,614	27,961	8,653	90.1	68.8	21.3
1983	35,318	26,872	8,446	84.9	64.6	20.3
1984	36,993	27,691	9,302	89.2	66.8	22.4
1985	37,157	27,489	9,668	91.4	67.6	23.8
1986	37,205	27,419	9,786	93.2	68.7	24.5
1987	39.048	27,419	11,137	100.6	71.9	28.7
1988	38,200	26,643	11,557	99.3	69.2	30.0
1989	36,843	25,710	11,133	99.6	69.5	30.1
1990	37,391	25,776	11,615	99.9	68.9	31.0

A5.24.3 *continued*

Teenage conceptions by single year of age and outcome, England and Wales, 1969–97

Year	Number of conceptions			Conception rates per 1,000 women in age-group/age		
	Total conceptions	Conceptions leading to maternities	Conceptions terminated by abortion	Total conceptions	Conceptions leading to maternities	Conceptions terminated by abortion
1991	33,686	23,519	10,167	94.9	66.2	28.6
1992	30,648	21,523	9,125	91.7	64.4	27.3
1993	27,949	19,616	8,333	89.4	62.8	26.7
1994	26,647	18,590	8,057	88.4	61.7	26.7
1995	26,305	18,359	7,946	90.8	63.4	27.4
1996	27,233	18,494	8,739	97.9	66.5	31.4
1997	27,031	18,110	8,921	95.4	63.9	31.5

Revised data: In 1999, ONS amended the way it estimates age at conception. Revised figures are very similar to those previously published. Full details are given in an article in *Population Trends* 97. Statistics for 1988-1997 have been calculated on the revised basis. Revised figures for earlier years were not available at the time of publication

The published figures for 1996 are also affected by an error in the processing of birth registrations. In late 1999, there were 1,002 more births on the database for 1997 than there were when the original conceptions data for 1997 were assembled. Some of these births would have been conceived in 1996.

Source: ONS/OPCS, *Birth statistics, Series FM1*.

This is a new table for this edition of *Birth counts*

A5.24.4

Teenage pregnancies by year and age of mother at conception, Scotland, 1987–98

Year	Age of mother at conception						
	13	14	15	16	17	18	19
	Numbers						
1987	16	161	626	1,691	2,621	3,297	3,788
1988	20	161	647	1,750	2,551	3,178	3,922
1989	22	130	642	1,555	2,536	3,180	3,536
1990	22	156	572	1,588	2,393	3,195	3,551
1991	21	148	604	1,546	2,405	3,052	3,502
1992	34	146	581	1,400	2,210	2,879	3,224
1993	34	175	563	1,377	2,151	2,633	2,907
1994	35	169	597	1,290	1,907	2,429	2,759
1995	32	195	601	1,363	1,814	2,382	2,644
1996	34	215	654	1,460	2,065	2,364	2,586
1997	40	184	631	1,576	2,156	2,527	2,547
1998*	27	142	613	1,453	2,055	2,428	2,500
	Rates per 1,000 women						
1987	0.5	4.6	16.6	42.2	65.0	79.4	88.8
1988	0.6	5.0	18.7	46.5	64.1	79.5	95.3
1989	0.7	4.1	19.9	44.9	67.6	80.4	88.9
1990	0.8	5.0	18.1	49.2	69.3	85.7	89.3
1991	0.7	5.2	19.5	48.9	74.8	89.6	94.1
1992	1.1	5.0	20.5	45.4	70.2	90.6	92.4
1993	1.1	5.7	19.4	48.6	69.9	84.1	88.3
1994	1.1	5.3	19.5	44.4	67.3	78.9	84.6
1995	1.0	6.0	18.8	44.6	62.6	84.0	81.9
1996	1.1	6.8	20.1	45.7	67.7	81.8	87.3
1997	1.3	5.9	19.9	48.7	67.7	83.4	84.2
1998*	0.9	4.6	19.3	44.9	64.5	80.1	82.6

Year	13–15	16–19	13–19		13–15	16–19	13–19
	Numbers				**Rates per 1,000 women**		
1987	803	11,397	12,200		7.7	69.3	45.3
1988	828	11,401	12,229		8.4	71.9	47.6
1989	794	10,807	11,601		8.4	71.3	47.1
1990	750	10 727	11,477		8.3	74.6	48.9
1991	773	10 505	11,278		8.8	77.8	50.5
1992	761	9,713	10,474		8.6	75.3	48.3
1993	772	9,068	9,840		8.4	73.5	45.8
1994	801	8,385	9,186		8.4	73.5	42.5
1995	828	8,203	9,031		8.6	68.2	41.7
1996	903	8,475	9,378		9.5	70.1	43.4
1997	855	8,306	9,661		9.2	70.6	44.3
1998*	782	8,436	9,218		8.4	67.6	42.3

*1998 data are provisional

Source: ISD health briefings. *Teenage pregnancy in Scotland, 1987–96, Teenage pregnancy in Scotland, 1989–1998*

This is a new table for this edition of *Birth counts*

A5.24.5

Teenage pregnancies by year, age of mother at conception and outcome, Scotland, 1987–98

Year	Age of mother at conception					
	13–15		16–19		13–19	
	Aborted	Delivered	Aborted	Delivered	Aborted	Delivered
	Numbers					
1987	401	402	3,553	7,844	3,954	8,246
1988	419	409	3,655	7,746	4,074	8,155
1989	405	389	3,678	7,129	4,083	7,518
1990	383	367	3,816	6,911	4,199	7,278
1991	405	368	3,696	6,809	4,101	7,177
1992	386	375	3,462	6,251	3,848	6,626
1993	407	365	3,306	5,762	3,713	6,127
1994	433	368	3,219	5,166	3,652	5,534
1995	435	393	3,105	5,098	3,540	5,491
1996	461	442	3,324	5,151	3,785	5,593
1997	399	456	3,321	5,485	3,720	5,941
1998*	416	366	3,617	4,819	4,033	5,185
	Rates per 1,000 women					
1987	3.8	3.8	21.6	47.7	14.7	30.6
1988	4.3	4.2	23.1	48.9	15.9	31.7
1989	4.3	4.1	24.3	47.1	16.6	30.5
1990	4.2	4.0	26.5	48.1	17.9	31.0
1991	4.6	4.2	27.4	50.4	18.4	32.1
1992	4.4	4.3	26.8	48.5	17.7	30.5
1993	4.4	4.0	26.8	46.7	17.3	28.5
1994	4.5	3.9	26.6	42.8	16.9	25.6
1995	4.5	4.1	25.8	42.4	16.3	25.3
1996	4.8	4.6	27.5	42.6	17.5	25.9
1997	4.3	4.9	26.6	44.0	17.1	27.3
1998*	4.5	3.9	29.0	38.6	18.5	23.8

* 1998 data are provisional. Rates are based on 1997 population statistics.

Source: ISD health briefings. *Teenage pregnancy in Scotland, 1987–96, Teenage pregnancy in Scotland 1989–1998*

This is a new table for this edition of *Birth counts*

A5.25.1

Singleton births by mother's height, marital status and social class, Scotland, 1995

	Mother's height, cm								Total
	Under 150	150–154	155–159	160–164	165–169	170–174	175 and over	Not stated	
All singleton births	**Numbers of live and stillbirths**								
All singleton births	938	4,907	11,211	16,675	12,259	5,750	1,854	4,552	58,146
Births within marriage by social class of father*									
Professional	24	234	594	1,079	1,027	499	191	333	3,981
Executive	141	768	1,893	3,198	2,570	1,306	418	832	11,126
Skilled manual	209	1,105	2,651	3,672	2,568	1,214	387	818	12,624
Skilled non-manual	98	631	1,486	2,183	1,645	809	218	536	7,606
Semi-skilled	164	797	1,696	2,350	1,683	686	241	588	8,205
Unskilled	78	329	697	913	641	310	90	296	3,354
Inadequate description	7	48	119	186	108	53	21	34	576
Not stated	92	377	792	1,189	702	310	99	372	3,933
All inside marriage	813	4,289	9,928	14,770	10,944	5,187	1,665	3,809	51,405
Births outside marriage by social class of mother*									
Professional	0	1	1	1	2	1	1	2	9
Executive	3	23	42	61	61	34	15	22	261
Skilled manual	3	37	80	116	71	36	11	47	401
Skilled non-manual	7	78	142	227	141	62	25	80	762
Semi-skilled	18	75	177	239	146	75	26	75	831
Unskilled	7	24	34	51	34	8	4	18	180
Inadequate description	0	2	13	12	9	3	1	2	42
Not stated	87	378	794	1,198	851	344	106	497	4,255
All outside marriage	125	618	1,283	1,905	1,315	563	189	743	6,741

Singleton births by mother's height, marital status and social class, Scotland, 1995

	Mother's height, cm							Not stated	Percentage missing
	Under 150	150–154	155–159	160–164	165–169	170–174	175 and over		
All singleton births	**Percentage of stated heights**								
	1.8	9.2	20.9	31.1	22.9	10.7	3.5		7.8
Births within marriage by social class of father*									
Professional	0.7	6.4	16.3	29.6	28.2	13.7	5.2		8.4
Executive	1.4	7.5	18.4	31.1	25.0	12.7	4.1		7.5
Skilled manual	1.8	9.4	22.5	31.1	21.8	10.3	3.3		6.5
Skilled non-manual	1.4	8.9	21.0	30.9	23.3	11.4	3.1		7.0
Semi-skilled	2.2	10.5	22.3	30.9	22.1	9.0	3.2		7.2
Unskilled	2.6	10.8	22.8	29.9	21.0	10.1	2.9		8.8
Inadequate description	1.3	8.9	22.0	34.3	19.9	9.8	3.9		5.9
Not stated	2.6	10.6	22.2	33.4	19.7	8.7	2.8		9.5
All inside marriage	1.7	9.0	20.9	31.0	23.0	10.9	3.5		7.4
Births outside marriage by social class of mother*									
Professional	0.0	14.3	14.3	14.3	28.6	14.3	14.3		22.2
Executive	1.3	9.6	17.6	25.5	25.5	14.2	6.3		8.4
Skilled manual	0.8	10.5	22.6	32.8	20.1	10.2	3.1		11.7
Skilled non-manual	1.0	11.4	20.8	33.3	20.7	9.1	3.7		10.5
Semi-skilled	2.4	9.9	23.4	31.6	19.3	9.9	3.4		9.0
Unskilled	4.3	14.8	21.0	31.5	21.0	4.9	2.5		10.0
Inadequate description	0.0	5.0	32.5	30.0	22.5	7.5	2.5		4.8
Not stated	2.3	10.1	21.1	31.9	22.6	9.2	2.8		11.7
All outside marriage	2.1	10.3	21.4	31.8	21.9	9.4	3.2		11.0

* The social class information provided is based on information supplied by the General Register Office for Scotland and is based on employment status, occupation and marital status. For married women, the social class of the father is used; for unmarried women, the social class of the mother is used. For those who are currently unemployed, their previous occupation, if any, is used.

Source: ISD, *Scottish Morbidity Record, SMR 2.*

This is similar to Table A5.19 in the first edition of *Birth counts*

A5.25.2

Singleton births to primaparae by mother's height and birthweight, Scotland, 1994–95

Birthweight, g	Height, cm								
	Less than 150	150–154	155–159	160–164	165–169	170–174	175 and over	Not known	All
Numbers of live and stillbirths									
Under 500	1	5	8	9	9	2	2	10	46
500–999	4	24	47	68	34	26	5	63	271
1,000–1,499	14	45	74	73	70	24	4	98	402
1,500–1,999	16	86	152	210	111	51	21	115	762
2,000–2,499	68	314	526	624	360	159	56	245	2,352
2,500–2,999	233	999	2,087	2,645	1,553	633	162	837	9,149
3,000–3,499	287	1,484	3,842	5,808	4,163	1,859	575	1,660	19,678
3,500–3,999	106	783	2,190	4,091	3,656	1,974	660	1,214	14,674
4,000–4,499	11	158	529	1,105	1,111	648	297	325	4,184
4,500 and over	2	15	64	146	162	132	60	47	628
Total stated	742	3,913	9,519	14,779	11,229	5,508	1,842	4,614	52,146
Not stated	1	0	0	0	0	0	. 0	1	2
Total	743	3,913	9,519	14,779	11,229	5,508	1,42	4,615	52,148
Percentage of stated birthweights									
Under 1,000	0.67	0.74	0.58	0.52	0.38	0.51	0.38	1.58	0.61
Under 1,500	2.56	1.89	1.36	1.01	1.01	0.94	0.60	3.71	1.38
Under 2,500	13.88	12.11	8.48	6.66	5.20	4.76	4.78	11.51	7.35
Mean birthweight									
1994	3,002.73	3,105.92	3,210.26	3,298.28	3,390.16	3,447.92	3,535.94	3,217.35	3,298.80
1995	2,989.42	3,098.91	3,200.39	3,289.74	3,381.56	3,459.33	3,515.68	3,168.29	3,291.69

Source: ISD, Scottish Morbidity Record SMR 2.

This is similar to Table A5.19 in the first edition of *Birth counts*

A5.26.1

Infant mortality by mother's housing tenure at 1981 census and birthweight, England and Wales, 1981–94

Year of birth		Hazard ratio	95% confidence interval	p	Number of infant deaths
	Mother's housing tenure, 1981				
1981–87					
	Owner occupied	1.00			211
	Private rented	1.19	0.89–1.60	0.24	55
	Local authority	1.11	0.89–1.39	0.35	134
1988–94					
	Owner occupied	1.00			133
	Private rented	1.04	0.70–1.56	0.82	29
	Local authority	1.24	0.96–1.60	0.10	112
1981–94					
	Owner occupied	1.00			344
	Private rented	1.16	0.91–1.47	0.23	84
	Local authority	1.13	0.96–1.34	0.15	246
	Birthweight				
1981–87					
	2,500g and over	1.00			220
	Under 2,500g	11.00*	9.11–13.68	0.00	161
	Missing	12.37*	9.36–16.36	0.00	64
1988-94					
	2,500g and over	1.00			133
	Under 2,500g	15.72	12.44–19.88	0.00	148
	Missing	9.16	6.51–12.89	0.00	44
1981-94					
	2,500g and over	1.00			353
	Under 2,500g	12.81*	11.00–14.93	0.00	309
	Missing	10.22*	8.24–12.69	0.00	108
	Birthweight and mother's housing tenure				
1981–94					
	Under 2,500g				
	Owner occupied	1.00			158
	Private rented	0.56*	0.33–0.96	0.03	45
	Local authority	0.73*	0.51–1.04	0.08	115
	2,500g and over				
	Owner occupied	1.00			139
	Private rented	1.36	0.98–1.90	0.06	25
	Local authority	1.17	0.92–1.49	0.21	98
	Missing				
	Owner occupied	1.00			47
	Private rented	0.95	0.48–1.88	0.89	14
	Local authority	0.98	0.59–1.63	0.94	33

* p<0.05

Source: Unpublished analysis of data from the ONS Longitudinal Study

This is a new table replacing Table A5.21 in the first edition of *Birth counts*

A5.27.1

Housing profile of families with dependent children, Great Britain, 1975–96

Years	Tenure		Central heating	Persons per room			
	Owner occupied	Rented		Under 0.5	0.5–0.99	1.0–1.49	1.5 or more
	Percentage of families of each type with dependent children*						
	Families headed by lone parents						
1975–76	33	66	42	..	..	..	..
1977–78	32	67	42	13	69	17	0
1979–80	29	71	50	14	69	15	1
1980–81	28	72	53	17	68	13	1
1981–82	27	73	56	17	68	14	1
1982–83	29	71	58	17	69	14	1
1987–88	36	66	70	20	71	8	1
1988–89	35	65	71	20	71	9	1
1989–90	36	65	73	19	70	10	1
1990–91	36	64	76	17	72	10	1
1991–92	36	64	77	16	75	9	0
1992–93	35	65	78	19	72	9	0
1993–94	34	66	80	21	71	8	1
1994–95	35	65	81	19	73	7	0
1995–96	35	65	85	19	73	8	0
	Other families						
1975–76	58	43	58	..	..	..	..
1977–78	60	39	58	3	73	23	1
1979–80	62	38	66	3	73	22	1
1980–81	63	36	67	4	73	24	1
1981–82	64	34	69	4	72	24	1
1982–83	67	32	72	4	73	22	1
1987–88	75	26	83	5	76	18	1
1988–89	76	24	85	6	76	18	1
1989–90	76	24	86	6	75	18	1
1990–91	76	24	87	5	75	19	1
1991–92	77	23	88	6	76	18	1
1992–93	76	24	88	5	76	17	1
1993–94	76	25	89	5	74	20	1
1994–95	77	24	91	6	74	20	1
1995–96	77	23	92	6	75	18	1

* Dependent children are persons aged under 16, or aged 16–18 and in full-time education, in the family unit and living in the household.

Source: ONS/OPCS *General Household Survey*

This is similar to Table A5.22 in the first edition of *Birth counts*

A5.28.1

Incidence of breastfeeding by age at which mother completed full-time education and birth order, Great Britain, 1980–95

	Age at which mother completed full time education, years			All mothers
	16 or under	17 or 18	Over 18	
	Percentage who breastfed initially			
First birth				
1980	65	81	94	74
1985	58	80	94	69
1990	57	75	93	69
1995	59	78	89	73
Later births				
1980	48	70	85	58
1985	49	70	86	59
1990	46	68	88	58
1995	47	67	88	61
All babies				
1980	55	76	89	65
1985	53	75	89	64
1990	50	71	91	63
1995	52	72	89	66
	Percentage breastfeeding at 6 weeks			
All babies				
1980	30	49	75	41
1985	26	48	73	38
1990	26	45	71	39
1995	27	45	74	43

Source: ONS/OPCS *Infant Feeding Survey*, 1990, 1995

This is a new table for this edition of *Birth counts*

A5.29.1

Economic activity of women aged 16–59 with dependent children aged under 5, Great Britain, 1973–96

Year	Working			Unemployed	All economically active	Base=100%
	Full time	Part time	All			
	Percentage of women aged 16–59 with dependent children aged under 5					
1973	7	18	25	2	27	1,936
1974	..	..	..	..	..	..
1975	6	22	28	2	30	1,847
1976	..	..	..	..	..	..
1977	5	22	27	3	31	1,669
1978	6	21	28	3	31	1,540
1979	6	22	28	3	31	1,527
1980	7	23	30	4	34	1,485
1981	6	18	25	5	30	1,604
1982	6	19	25	6	31	1,271
1983	5	18	24	5	29	1,386
1984	6	22	28	4	32	1,337
1985	8	22	30	6	36	1,339
1986	9	24	33	6	39	1,238
1987	11	24	35	7	42	1,408
1988	11	25	36	5	41	1,281
1989	12	29	41	5	46	1,325
1990	13	28	41	4	45	1,276
1991	13	29	43	6	50	1,352
1992	11	31	43	7	49	1,298
1993	14	32	46	7	54	1,372
1994	16	30	47	5	52	1,320
1995	16	32	49	6	55	1,210
1996	16	33	49	4	53	1,189

Source: ONS/OPCS *General Household Survey.*

This is similar to Table A5.23 in the first edition of *Birth counts*

Economic activity of women aged 16–59 with dependent children aged under 5 by marital status, Great Britain, 1977–96

Time period	Married				Lone mothers			
	Working full time	Working part time	All	Base = 100%	Working full time	Working part time	All	Base = 100%
	Percentage of women aged 16–59 with dependent children aged under 5							
1977–79	5	22	27	4,374	13	13	26	382
1979–81	6	22	28	4,244	12	12	24	397
1981–83	6	19	25	3,838	7	11	18	434
1983–85	6	22	28	3,626	7	9	16	441
1985–87	9	25	34	3,560	9	11	20	472
1987–89	12	28	40	3,448	8	13	21	566
1989–91	14	32	46	3,263	8	14	23	703
1991–93	14	34	49	3,268	7	15	23	802
1993–95	17	36	53	3,111	9	16	25	778
1994–96	18	36	54	2,975	9	17	27	728

Source: ONS/OPCS *General Household Survey*, 1995, 1996

This is similar to Table A5.23 in the first edition of *Birth counts*

Percentage of parents of disabled children in employment and gross weekly earnings, Great Britain, 1985

	Men			Women			Numbers of earners in family unit		
	Full-time	Part-time	All	Full-time	Part-time	All	0	1	2
	Percentage of parents in employment								
General population*	88	1	89	15	33	48	18	43	20
Parents of disabled children	73	2	75	9	31	40	32	36	32
	Gross weekly earnings, £								
General population*	214.26			108.19	31.55				
Parents of disabled children	196.60			111.11	37.05				

* 1985 FES population adjusted to include only those with one or more dependent children under 16

Source: OPCS *surveys of disability in Great Britain, Report 5*

This is a new table for this edition of *Birth counts*

A5.31.1

Smoking and drinking prevalence before and during pregnancy and whether women gave up smoking during pregnancy by social class of husband or partner, 1995

	Social class								
	I	II	IIIn	IIIm	IV	V	Unclassified	No partner	All
Smoked before pregnancy	14	22	27	35	40	52	32	62	35
Smoked during pregnancy	7	12	14	23	28	37	23	47	24
Base: all mothers	344	1,259	397	1,244	541	182	323	827	5,118
Gave up smoking during pregnancy	50	44	47	33	31	29	29	24	33
Base: smoked before pregnancy	49	276	107	428	217	93	103	511	1,784
Drank alcohol during pregnancy*	73	72	66	66	64	59	49	62	66
Base: all mothers	346	1,271	402	1,252	544	185	327	835	5,165

Source: OPCS/ONS *Infant Feeding Survey, 1995*, unpublished

This is a new table for this edition of *Birth counts*

A5.32.1

Selected social and economic indicators, constituent countries of the UK and Government Office Regions in England

Area	Household income and employment			Government expenditure on benefits[2] Percentage of households receiving			Housing	Households with selected durable goods, 1995/96[4]			Occupation density[2]	Household expenditure and consumption			
												Average weekly household expenditure 1996-97[1]		Consumption of selected foods 1994-95[6]	
	Weekly disposable income 1996-97[1]	Households with less than £275 gross weekly income 1995/96[2]	Unemployment 1996[3]	Family credit or income support 1995/96	Housing benefit 1995/96	Child benefit or one parent benefit 1995/96	Owner occupation 1995	Washing machine	Refrigerator	Telephone	Houses at or below bedroom standard[5]	Alcoholic drink	Tobacco	Fresh and other fruit	Vegetables and vegetable products
	£	Percentage	Percentage	Percentage	Percentage	Percentage	Percentage	Percentage	Percentage	Percentage	Percentage	£	£	Kg per person per week	Kg per person per week
United Kingdom	324.7	45.7	8.2	:	:	:	:	:	:	:	:	12.41	6.07	:	:
Great Britain	:	:	:	21	20	32	67	89	99	92	30	:	:	0.98	2.07
North East	267.0	53.7	10.8	27	26	29	59	88	98	87	30	13.54	6.69	0.75	2.20
North West and Merseyside	309.5	48.7	8.4	25	23	34	68	89	99	90	30	14.81	7.08	0.87	2.01
Yorkshire and the Humber	300.2	51.1	8.1	22	20	31	65	92	98	91	29	14.02	5.99	0.94	2.15
East Midlands	306.6	43.1	7.4	21	18	33	71	93	99	91	26	11.49	6.34	0.99	2.21
West Midlands	299.9	45.4	9.2	22	20	34	68	89	99	91	30	12.79	6.21	0.98	2.22
Eastern	345.9	43.4	6.2	16	15	32	71	90	99	94	28	11.12	5.16	1.09	2.01
London	363.6	42.2	11.3	25	26	31	57	82	99	93	46	10.81	5.78	1.21	2.00
South East	386.1	39.0	6.0	14	13	31	74	90	99	96	29	12.49	4.74	:	:
South West	328.6	42.0	6.3	18	17	31	72	89	99	94	29	11.40	4.78	1.14	2.14
England	329.7	44.7	8.1	21	19	32	68	89	99	92	32	12.54	5.79	1.00	2.09
Wales	299.5	47.4	8.3	25	20	32	71	90	99	89	28	11.63	6.68	0.93	2.29
Scotland	305.6	50.3	8.7	24	28	32	58	91	99	88	41	12.28	7.84	0.83	1.71
Northern Ireland	266.4	53.6	9.7	:	:	:	69	90	99	89	29	9.89	8.30	:	:

Sources and notes:
1. ONS, *Family Spending 1996-7*
2. Derived from *Regional Trends 32, 1997 Table 8.2*
3. Unemployment for spring quarter, ILO definition from Labour Force Survey, Source: *Regional Trends 1997 Table 5.21*
4. Based on Family Resources Survey, Source *Regional Trends 1997, Table 8.12*
5. See text for details of this measure of housing density
6. From National Food Survey, Source: *Regional Trends 1997*, Table 8.11. Data are presented by Standard Statistical Region for these variables.
This was Table A5.24 in the first edition of *Birth counts*

A6.1.1

Singleton and multiple live births by birthweight, England and Wales, 1982–96

Year of birth	Birthweight, g											All stated	Not stated	All birthweights
	Under 1,000	1,000–1,499	Under 1,500	1,500–1,999	2,000–2,499	Under 2,500	2,500–2,999	3,000–3,499	3,500–3,999	4,000–4,499	4,500 and over			
Numbers														
Singleton														
1982	1,218	2,709	3,927	5,941	24,084	33,952	108,685	230,024	163,083	44,542	6,537	586,823	26,724	613,547
1983	1,401	2,885	4,286	6,262	25,089	35,637	112,714	241,379	171,724	47,407	6,849	615,710	810	616,520
1984	1,524	3,024	4,548	6,430	25,177	36,155	112,927	243,370	175,693	47,981	7,253	623,379	769	624,148
1985	1,558	3,254	4,812	6,664	26,153	37,629	115,999	249,954	180,399	50,513	7,595	642,089	845	642,934
1986	1,653	3,173	4,826	6,894	26,546	38,266	115,216	250,307	182,850	51,828	7,860	646,327	597	646,924
1987	1,704	3,497	5,201	7,040	26,581	38,822	116,003	256,844	190,787	55,464	8,583	666,503	474	666,977
1988	1,744	3,407	5,151	6,884	25,771	37,806	113,903	258,855	198,315	59,285	9,430	677,594	792	678,386
1989	1,985	3,252	5,237	6,680	25,117	37,034	110,125	247,532	190,295	57,206	9,391	651,583	20,619	672,202
1990	1,859	3,244	5,103	6,684	25,977	37,764	111,700	250,666	193,434	59,425	9,693	662,682	27,184	689,866
1991	1,804	3,248	5,052	6,792	25,873	37,717	108,663	247,755	193,222	59,854	9,993	657,204	25,263	682,467
1992	1,925	3,338	5,263	6,530	24,483	36,276	105,229	240,316	193,065	61,928	10,550	647,364	25,234	672,598
1993	1,986	3,191	5,177	6,621	24,056	35,854	101,632	233,482	189,786	61,514	10,775	633,043	21,181	654,224
1994	2,289	3,370	5,659	6,753	23,850	36,262	101,605	232,156	188,650	61,179	10,717	630,569	16,319	646,888
1995	2,228	3,510	5,738	7,018	24,786	37,542	103,607	232,675	184,856	59,063	10,042	627,785	2,163	629,948
1996	2,461	3,519	5,980	6,839	24,634	37,453	103,503	232,239	186,709	59,840	10,537	630,281	1,479	631,760
Multiple														
1982	224	621	845	1,588	3,548	5,981	3,943	1,566	252	11	3	11,756	628	12,384
1983	315	705	1,020	1,655	3,777	6,452	4,222	1,619	248	17	1	12,559	55	12,614
1984	350	656	1,006	1,715	3,755	6,476	4,274	1,648	216	11	2	12,627	43	12,670
1985	364	724	1,088	1,892	4,055	7,035	4,464	1,699	247	14	1	13,460	23	13,483
1986	412	843	1,255	2,000	4,207	7,462	4,594	1,728	264	14	5	14,067	27	14,094
1987	439	865	1,304	2,026	4,377	7,707	4,693	1,814	270	18	4	14,506	28	14,534
1988	465	895	1,360	2,105	4,410	7,875	4,905	2,077	278	14	3	15,152	39	15,191
1989	453	857	1,310	2,105	4,529	7,944	4,940	1,846	277	20	2	15,029	494	15,523
1990	455	942	1,397	2,240	4,654	8,291	5,054	2,022	308	14	3	15,692	582	16,274
1991	499	923	1,422	2,339	4,891	8,652	5,150	1,974	308	10	1	16,095	655	16,750
1992	485	894	1,379	2,163	5,013	8,555	5,365	2,084	328	23	0	16,355	703	17,058
1993	551	985	1,536	2,415	4,656	8,607	5,309	2,080	268	18	3	16,285	715	17,000

A6.1.1 continued

Singleton and multiple live births by birthweight, England and Wales, 1982–96

Year of birth	Birthweight, g											All stated	Not stated	All birthweights
	Under 1,000	1,000–1,499	Under 1,500	1,500–1,999	2,000–2,499	Under 2,500	2,500–2,999	3,000–3,499	3,500–3,999	4,000–4,499	4,500 and over			
1994	566	1,059	1,625	2,392	4,902	8,919	5,504	2,094	270	20	4	16,811	557	17,368
1995	651	1,194	1,845	2,661	5,276	9,782	5,829	2,077	266	32	13	17,999	54	18,053
1996	689	1,251	1,940	2,566	5,228	9,734	5,550	2,071	300	12	3	17,670	59	17,729
Percentages														
Singleton														
1982	0.2	0.5	0.7	1.0	4.1	5.8	18.5	39.2	27.8	7.6	1.1	100.0	4.4	
1983	0.2	0.5	0.7	1.0	4.1	5.8	18.3	39.2	27.9	7.7	1.1	100.0	0.1	
1984	0.2	0.5	0.7	1.0	4.0	5.8	18.1	39.0	28.2	7.7	1.2	100.0	0.1	
1985	0.2	0.5	0.7	1.0	4.1	5.9	18.1	38.9	28.1	7.9	1.2	100.0	0.1	
1986	0.3	0.5	0.7	1.1	4.1	5.9	17.8	38.7	28.3	8.0	1.2	100.0	0.1	
1987	0.3	0.5	0.8	1.1	4.0	5.8	17.4	38.5	28.6	8.3	1.3	100.0	0.1	
1988	0.3	0.5	0.8	1.0	3.8	5.6	16.8	38.2	29.3	8.7	1.4	100.0	0.1	
1989	0.3	0.5	0.8	1.0	3.9	5.7	16.9	38.0	29.2	8.8	1.4	100.0	3.1	
1990	0.3	0.5	0.8	1.0	3.9	5.7	16.9	37.8	29.2	9.0	1.5	100.0	3.9	
1991	0.3	0.5	0.8	1.0	3.9	5.7	16.5	37.7	29.4	9.1	1.5	100.0	3.7	
1992	0.3	0.5	0.8	1.0	3.8	5.6	16.3	37.1	29.8	9.6	1.6	100.0	3.8	
1993	0.3	0.5	0.8	1.0	3.8	5.7	16.1	36.9	30.0	9.7	1.7	100.0	3.2	
1994	0.4	0.5	0.9	1.1	3.8	5.8	16.1	36.8	29.9	9.7	1.7	100.0	2.5	
1995	0.4	0.6	0.9	1.1	3.9	6.0	16.5	37.1	29.4	9.4	1.6	100.0	0.3	
1996	0.4	0.6	0.9	1.1	3.9	5.9	16.4	36.8	29.6	9.5	1.7	100.0	0.2	
Multiple														
1982	1.9	5.3	7.2	13.5	30.2	50.9	33.5	13.3	2.1	0.1	0.0	100.0	5.1	
1983	2.5	5.6	8.1	13.2	30.1	51.4	33.6	12.9	2.0	0.1	0.0	100.0	0.4	
1984	2.8	5.2	8.0	13.6	29.7	51.3	33.8	13.1	1.7	0.1	0.0	100.0	0.3	
1985	2.7	5.4	8.1	14.1	30.1	52.3	33.2	12.6	1.8	0.1	0.0	100.0	0.2	
1986	2.9	6.0	8.9	14.2	29.9	53.0	32.7	12.3	1.9	0.1	0.0	100.0	0.2	
1987	3.0	6.0	9.0	14.0	30.2	53.1	32.4	12.5	1.9	0.1	0.0	100.0	0.2	
1988	3.1	5.9	9.0	13.9	29.1	52.0	32.4	13.7	1.8	0.1	0.0	100.0	0.3	
1989	3.0	5.7	8.7	14.0	30.1	52.9	32.9	12.3	1.8	0.1	0.0	100.0	3.2	

A6.1.1 *continued*

Singleton and multiple live births by birthweight, England and Wales, 1982–96

Year of birth	Birthweight, g													All birthweights
	Under 1,000	1,000–1,499	Under 1,500	1,500–1,999	2,000–2,499	Under 2,500	2,500–2,999	3,000–3,499	3,500–3,999	4,000–4,499	4,500 and over	All stated	Not stated	
1990	2.9	6.0	8.9	14.3	29.7	52.8	32.2	12.9	2.0	0.1	0.0	100.0	3.6	
1991	3.1	5.7	8.8	14.5	30.4	53.8	32.0	12.3	1.9	0.1	0.0	100.0	3.9	
1992	3.0	5.5	8.4	13.2	30.7	52.3	32.8	12.7	2.0	0.1	0.0	100.0	4.1	
1993	3.4	6.0	9.4	14.8	28.6	52.9	32.6	12.8	1.6	0.1	0.0	100.0	4.2	
1994	3.4	6.3	9.7	14.2	29.2	53.1	32.7	12.5	1.6	0.1	0.0	100.0	3.2	
1995	3.6	6.6	10.3	14.8	29.3	54.3	32.4	11.5	1.5	0.2	0.1	100.0	0.3	
1996	3.9	7.1	11.0	14.5	29.6	55.1	31.4	11.7	1.7	0.1	0.0	100.0	0.3	

Data for all births are in Table A3.4.2

Source: Authors' analysis of ONS/OPCS data

Data extract: live births 1993 (7/94), 1994 (7/95), 1995 (3/7/96), 1996 (8/4/97)

This is similar to Table A6.2 in the first edition of *Birth counts*

A6.1.2

Singleton and multiple stillbirths by birthweight, England and Wales, 1982–96

Year of birth	Birthweight, g											All stated	Not stated	All birthweights
	Under 1,000	1,000– 1,499	Under 1,500	1,500– 1,999	2,000– 2,499	Under 2,500	2,500– 2,999	3,000– 3,499	3,500– 3,999	4,000– 4,499	4,500 and over			

Singleton

Numbers of stillbirths at 28 or more weeks of gestation

Year of birth	Under 1,000	1,000–1,499	Under 1,500	1,500–1,999	2,000–2,499	Under 2,500	2,500–2,999	3,000–3,499	3,500–3,999	4,000–4,499	4,500 and over	All stated	Not stated	All birthweights
1982	392	574	966	515	519	2,000	530	449	197	67	39	3,282	408	3,690
1983	404	579	983	524	537	2,044	561	422	214	74	21	3,336	35	3,371
1984	435	554	989	491	575	2,055	547	421	232	72	32	3,359	59	3,418
1985	446	527	973	532	540	2,045	546	464	188	84	30	3,357	53	3,410
1986	429	554	983	431	555	1,969	516	460	211	69	36	3,261	17	3,278
1987	404	499	903	523	462	1,888	528	404	218	70	39	3,147	22	3,169
1988	356	480	836	498	482	1,816	506	456	239	84	31	3,132	15	3,147
1989	332	396	728	455	491	1,674	483	420	217	65	35	2,894	105	2,999
1990	325	450	775	496	433	1,704	441	438	214	61	28	2,886	135	3,021
1991	301	442	743	459	438	1,640	482	415	218	68	39	2,862	150	3,012
1992	440	376	816	386	402	1,604	423	426	220	69	35	2,777	139	2,916
1993	313	359	672	377	395	1,444	427	381	204	64	30	2,550	193	2,743
1994	327	344	671	346	377	1,394	426	395	213	88	34	2,550	113	2,663
1995	275	373	648	355	377	1,380	412	367	198	65	27	2,449	35	2,484
1996	288	328	616	347	341	1,304	426	362	185	60	24	2,361	28	2,389

Numbers of stillbirths at 24 or more weeks of gestation

Year of birth	Under 1,000	1,000–1,499	Under 1,500	1,500–1,999	2,000–2,499	Under 2,500	2,500–2,999	3,000–3,499	3,500–3,999	4,000–4,499	4,500 and over	All stated	Not stated	All birthweights
1993	985	430	1,415	384	399	2,198	429	382	204	64	32	3,309	249	3,558
1994	1,028	412	1,440	356	379	2,175	427	395	214	90	35	3,336	132	3,468
1995	950	454	1,404	363	378	2,145	415	368	198	65	28	3,219	55	3,274
1996	1,038	392	1,430	352	342	2,124	428	362	185	60	25	3,184	39	3,223

Multiple

Numbers of stillbirths at 28 or more weeks of gestation

Year of birth	Under 1,000	1,000–1,499	Under 1,500	1,500–1,999	2,000–2,499	Under 2,500	2,500–2,999	3,000–3,499	3,500–3,999	4,000–4,499	4,500 and over	All stated	Not stated	All birthweights
1982	48	44	92	53	39	184	28	6	1	0	0	219	34	253
1983	68	63	131	63	28	222	16	3	3	0	0	244	17	261
1984	55	58	113	42	40	195	16	6	5	0	0	222	10	232
1985	53	53	106	52	35	193	30	8	1	1	0	232	8	240
1986	68	67	135	69	34	238	14	6	2	0	0	260	10	270
1987	57	67	124	56	33	213	25	3	0	0	0	241	11	252

A6.1.2 continued

Singleton and multiple stillbirths by birthweight, England and Wales, 1982–96

Year of birth	Birthweight, g													All birthweights
	Under 1,000	1,000– 1,499	Under 1,500	1,500– 1,999	2,000– 2,499	Under 2,500	2,500– 2,999	3,000– 3,499	3,500– 3,999	4,000– 4,499	4,500 and over	All stated	Not stated	
1988	57	65	122	43	43	208	19	4	2	0	0	233	5	238
1989	59	53	112	47	30	189	23	3	0	1	0	216	16	232
1990	61	61	122	48	32	202	14	4	1	0	0	221	17	238
1991	66	50	116	50	38	204	18	5	1	0	1	229	14	243
1992	82	41	123	40	33	196	15	3	1	0	0	215	25	240
1993	71	39	110	36	31	177	11	6	0	0	0	194	23	217
1994	86	58	144	40	37	221	17	8	0	0	0	246	16	262
1995	78	46	124	36	23	183	14	8	0	0	0	205	15	220
1996	82	39	121	23	32	176	15	3	0	0	0	194	15	209
Numbers of stillbirths at 24 or more weeks of gestation														
1993	151	42	193	36	31	260	11	6	0	0	0	277	31	308
1994	167	61	228	40	37	305	17	8	0	0	0	330	18	348
1995	169	52	221	36	24	281	14	8	0	0	0	303	20	323
1996	176	43	219	24	32	275	15	3	0	0	0	293	23	316
Percentages of stillbirths at 28 or more weeks of gestation														
Singleton														
1982	11.9	17.5	29.4	15.7	15.8	60.9	16.1	13.7	6.0	2.0	1.2	100.0	11.1	
1983	12.1	17.4	29.5	15.7	16.1	61.3	16.8	12.6	6.4	2.2	0.6	100.0	1.0	
1984	13.0	16.5	29.4	14.6	17.1	61.2	16.3	12.5	6.9	2.1	1.0	100.0	1.7	
1985	13.3	15.7	29.0	15.8	16.1	60.9	16.3	13.8	5.6	2.5	0.9	100.0	1.6	
1986	13.2	17.0	30.1	13.2	17.0	60.4	15.8	14.1	6.5	2.1	1.1	100.0	0.5	
1987	12.8	15.9	28.7	16.6	14.7	60.0	16.8	12.8	6.9	2.2	1.2	100.0	0.7	
1988	11.4	15.3	26.7	15.9	15.4	58.0	16.2	14.6	7.6	2.7	1.0	100.0	0.5	
1989	11.5	13.7	25.2	15.7	17.0	57.8	16.7	14.5	7.5	2.2	1.2	100.0	3.5	
1990	11.3	15.6	26.9	17.2	15.0	59.0	15.3	15.2	7.4	2.1	1.0	100.0	4.5	
1991	10.5	15.4	26.0	16.0	15.3	57.3	16.8	14.5	7.6	2.4	1.4	100.0	5.0	
1992	15.8	13.5	28.0	13.9	14.5	57.8	15.2	15.3	7.9	2.5	1.3	100.0	4.8	
1993	12.3	14.1	26.4	14.8	15.5	56.6	16.7	14.9	8.0	2.5	1.2	100.0	7.0	
1994	12.8	13.5	26.3	13.6	14.8	54.7	16.7	15.5	8.4	3.5	1.3	100.0	4.2	

381

A6.1.2 continued

Singleton and multiple stillbirths by birthweight, England and Wales, 1982–96

Year of birth	Birthweight, g												All birthweights
	Under 1,000	1,000– 1,499	Under 1,500	1,500– 1,999	2,000– 2,499	Under 2,500	2,500– 2,999	3,000– 3,499	3,500– 3,999	4,000– 4,499	4,500 and over	All stated	Not stated
1995	11.2	15.2	26.5	14.5	15.4	56.3	16.8	15.0	8.1	2.7	1.1	100.0	1.4
1996	12.2	13.9	25.8	14.7	14.4	55.2	18.0	15.3	7.8	2.5	1.0	100.0	1.2
Percentages of stillbirths at 24 or more weeks of gestation													
1993	29.8	13.0	42.8	11.6	12.1	66.4	13.0	11.5	6.2	1.9	1.0	100.0	7.0
1994	30.8	12.4	43.2	10.7	11.4	65.2	12.8	11.8	6.4	2.7	1.0	100.0	3.8
1995	29.5	14.1	43.6	11.3	11.7	66.6	12.9	11.4	6.2	2.0	0.9	100.0	1.7
1996	32.6	12.3	44.9	11.1	10.7	66.7	13.4	11.4	5.8	1.9	0.8	100.0	1.2
Percentages of stillbirths at 28 or more weeks of gestation													
1982	21.9	20.1	42.0	24.2	17.8	84.0	12.8	2.7	0.5	–	–	100.0	13.4
1983	27.9	25.8	53.7	25.8	11.5	91.0	6.6	1.2	1.2	–	–	100.0	6.5
1984	24.8	26.1	50.9	18.9	18.0	87.8	7.2	2.7	2.3	–	–	100.0	4.3
1985	22.8	22.8	45.7	22.4	15.1	83.2	12.9	3.4	0.4	–	–	100.0	3.3
1986	26.2	25.8	51.9	26.5	13.1	91.5	5.4	2.3	0.8	–	–	100.0	3.7
1987	23.7	27.8	51.5	23.2	13.7	88.4	10.4	1.2	–	–	–	100.0	4.4
1988	24.5	27.9	52.4	18.5	18.5	89.3	8.2	1.7	0.9	–	–	100.0	2.1
1989	27.3	24.5	51.9	21.8	13.9	87.5	10.6	1.4	–	–	–	100.0	6.9
1990	27.6	27.6	55.2	21.7	14.5	91.4	6.3	1.8	–	0.5	–	100.0	7.1
1991	28.8	21.8	50.7	21.8	16.6	89.1	7.9	2.2	0.5	–	–	100.0	5.8
1992	38.1	19.1	51.3	18.6	15.3	91.2	7.0	1.4	0.4	–	0.4	100.0	10.4
1993	36.6	20.1	56.7	18.6	16.0	91.2	5.7	3.1	0.5	–	–	100.0	10.6
1994	35.0	23.6	58.5	16.3	15.0	89.8	6.9	3.3	–	–	–	100.0	6.1
1995	38.0	22.4	60.5	17.6	11.2	89.3	6.8	3.9	–	–	–	100.0	6.8
1996	42.3	20.1	57.9	11.9	16.5	90.7	7.7	1.5	–	–	–	100.0	7.2
Percentages of stillbirths at 24 or more weeks of gestation													
1993	54.5	15.2	69.7	13.0	11.2	93.9	4.0	2.2	–	–	–	100.0	–
1994	50.6	18.5	69.1	12.1	11.2	92.4	5.2	2.4	–	–	–	100.0	–
1995	55.8	17.2	72.9	11.9	7.9	92.7	4.6	2.6	–	–	–	100.0	–
1996	60.1	14.7	74.7	8.2	10.9	93.9	5.1	1.0	–	–	–	100.0	–

Multiple

A6.1.2 *continued*

Singleton and multiple stillbirths by birthweight, England and Wales, 1982–96

Year of birth	Birthweight, g													All birthweights
	Under 1,000	1,000–1,499	Under 1,500	1,500–1,999	2,000–2,499	Under 2,500	2,500–2,999	3,000–3,499	3,500–3,999	4,000–4,499	4,500 and over	All stated	Not stated	

Singleton

Rates
Stillbirths at 28 or more weeks of gestation per thousand live and still births

1982	243.5	174.8	197.4	79.8	21.1	55.6	4.9	1.9	1.2	1.5	5.9	5.6	15.0	6.0
1983	223.8	167.1	186.6	77.2	21.0	54.2	5.0	1.7	1.2	1.6	3.1	5.4	41.4	5.4
1984	222.1	154.8	178.6	70.9	22.3	53.8	4.8	1.7	1.3	1.5	4.4	5.4	71.3	5.4
1985	222.6	139.4	168.2	73.9	20.2	51.5	4.7	1.9	1.0	1.7	3.9	5.2	59.0	5.3
1986	206.1	148.6	169.2	58.8	20.5	48.9	4.5	1.8	1.2	1.3	4.6	5.0	27.7	5.0
1987	191.7	124.9	147.9	69.2	17.1	46.4	4.5	1.6	1.1	1.3	4.5	4.7	44.4	4.7
1988	169.5	123.5	139.6	67.5	18.4	45.8	4.4	1.8	1.2	1.4	3.3	4.6	18.6	4.6
1989	143.3	108.6	122.0	63.8	19.2	43.2	4.4	1.7	1.1	1.1	3.7	4.4	5.1	4.4
1990	148.8	121.8	131.8	69.1	16.4	43.2	3.9	1.7	1.0	1.0	2.9	4.3	4.9	4.4
1991	143.0	119.8	128.2	63.3	16.6	41.7	4.4	1.7	1.1	1.1	3.9	4.3	5.9	4.4
1992	186.0	101.2	134.2	55.8	16.2	42.3	4.0	1.8	1.1	1.1	3.3	4.3	5.5	4.3
1993	136.1	101.1	114.9	53.9	16.2	38.7	4.2	1.6	1.1	1.0	2.8	4.0	9.0	4.2
1994	125.0	92.6	106.0	48.7	15.6	37.0	4.2	1.7	1.1	1.4	3.2	4.0	6.9	4.1
1995	109.9	96.1	101.5	48.1	15.0	35.5	4.0	1.6	1.1	1.1	2.7	3.9	15.9	3.9
1996	104.8	85.3	93.4	48.3	13.7	33.6	4.1	1.6	1.0	1.0	2.3	3.7	18.6	3.8

Stillbirths at 24 or more weeks of gestation per thousand live and still births

1993	331.5	118.8	214.7	54.8	16.3	57.8	4.2	1.6	1.1	1.0	3.0	5.2	11.6	5.7
1994	309.9	108.9	202.8	50.1	15.6	56.6	4.2	1.7	1.1	1.5	3.3	5.3	8.0	5.4
1995	298.9	114.5	196.6	49.2	15.0	54.0	4.0	1.6	1.1	1.1	2.8	5.1	24.8	5.2
1996	296.7	100.2	193.0	49.0	13.7	53.7	4.1	1.6	1.0	1.0	2.4	5.0	25.7	5.1

Multiple

Stillbirths at 28 or more weeks of gestation per thousand live and still births

1982	176.5	66.2	98.2	32.3	10.9	29.8	7.1	3.8	4.0	–	–	18.3	51.4	20.0
1983	177.5	82.0	113.8	36.7	7.4	33.3	3.8	1.8	12.0	–	–	19.1	236.1	20.3
1984	135.8	81.2	101.0	23.9	10.5	29.2	3.7	3.6	22.6	–	–	17.3	188.7	18.0
1985	127.1	68.2	88.8	26.7	8.6	26.7	6.7	4.7	4.0	–	–	16.9	258.1	17.5

A6.1.2 continued

Singleton and multiple stillbirths by birthweight, England and Wales, 1982–96

Year	Birthweight, g											All stated	Not stated	All birthweights
	Under 1,000	1,000– 1,499	Under 1,500	1,500– 1,999	2,000– 2,499	Under 2,500	2,500– 2,999	3,000– 3,499	3,500– 3,999	4,000– 4,499	4,500 and over			
1986	141.7	73.6	97.1	33.3	8.0	30.9	3.0	3.5	7.5	–	–	18.1	270.3	18.8
1987	114.9	71.9	86.8	26.9	7.5	26.9	5.3	1.7	–	–	–	16.3	282.1	17.0
1988	109.2	67.7	82.3	20.0	9.7	25.7	3.9	1.9	7.1	–	–	15.1	113.6	15.4
1989	115.2	58.2	78.8	21.8	6.6	23.2	4.6	1.6	–	47.6	–	14.2	31.4	14.7
1990	118.2	60.8	80.3	21.0	6.8	23.8	2.8	2.0	3.2	–	–	13.9	28.4	14.4
1991	116.8	51.4	75.4	20.9	7.7	23.0	3.5	2.5	3.2	–	500.0	14.0	20.9	14.3
1992	144.6	43.9	81.9	18.2	6.5	22.4	2.8	1.4	3.0	–	–	13.0	34.3	13.9
1993	114.1	38.1	66.8	14.7	6.6	20.2	2.1	2.9	–	–	–	11.8	31.2	12.6
1994	131.9	51.9	81.4	16.4	7.5	24.2	3.1	3.8	–	–	–	14.4	27.9	14.9
1995	107.0	37.1	63.0	13.3	4.3	18.4	2.4	3.8	–	–	–	11.3	217.4	12.0
1996	106.4	30.2	58.7	8.9	6.1	17.8	2.7	1.4	–	–	–	10.9	202.7	11.7
Stillbirths at 24 or more weeks of gestation per thousand live and still births														
1993	215.1	40.9	111.6	14.7	6.6	29.3	2.1	2.9	–	–	–	16.7	41.6	24.8
1994	227.8	54.5	123.0	16.4	7.5	33.1	3.1	3.8	–	–	–	19.3	31.3	26.9
1995	206.1	41.7	107.0	13.3	4.5	27.9	2.4	3.8	–	–	–	16.6	270.3	55.7
1996	203.5	33.2	101.4	9.3	6.1	27.5	2.7	1.4	–	–	–	16.3	280.5	17.5

Data for all births are in Tables A3.4.2 and A3.5.2

Source: Authors' analysis of ONS/OPCS data

Data extract: live births 1993 (7/94), 1994 (7/95), 1995 (3/7/96), 1996 (8/4/97)

linked 1993(3/4/96), 1994 (18/9/96), 1995 (3/11/97)

This is similar to Table A6.2 in the first edition of *Birth counts*

A6.1.3

Singleton and multiple neonatal deaths by birthweight, England and Wales, 1982–96

Year of birth	Birthweight, g											All stated	Not stated	All birthweights
	Under 1,000	1,000– 1,499	Under 1,500	1,500– 1,999	2,000– 2,499	Under 2,500	2,500– 2,999	3,000– 3,499	3,500– 3,999	4,000– 4,499	4,500 and over			
Singleton	**Numbers**													
1982	672	488	1,160	341	332	1,833	384	460	211	54	24	2,966	554	3,520
1983	772	514	1,286	336	364	1,986	417	389	229	57	19	3,097	153	3,250
1984	789	449	1,238	318	320	1,876	405	405	199	53	14	2,952	149	3,101
1985	800	463	1,263	280	358	1,901	389	390	210	75	13	2,978	124	3,102
1986	805	429	1,234	311	300	1,845	359	395	209	62	15	2,885	91	2,976
1987	815	496	1,311	292	259	1,862	335	374	216	65	18	2,870	98	2,968
1988	846	474	1,320	276	258	1,854	331	354	205	55	19	2,818	78	2,896
1989	756	370	1,126	220	199	1,545	306	309	216	60	15	2,437	346	2,783
1990	768	281	1,049	203	183	1,435	270	295	166	54	18	2,252	423	2,675
1991	766	273	1,039	181	187	1,407	241	241	154	54	17	2,114	415	2,529
1992	769	269	1,038	155	165	1,358	225	254	148	49	19	2,053	401	2,454
1993	758	245	1,003	160	153	1,316	205	252	139	46	19	1,977	353	2,330
1994	790	251	1,041	146	143	1,330	199	239	138	51	31	1,988	278	2,266
1995	848	228	1,076	145	177	1,398	204	253	174	86	49	2,164	55	2,219
1996	951	222	1,173	121	161	1,455	200	225	137		75	2,092	69	2,161
Multiple														
1982	153	89	242	32	17	291	10	4	5	0	0	310	73	383
1983	200	89	289	38	19	346	17	2	3	1	0	369	24	393
1984	225	88	313	39	24	376	17	1	4	0	2	400	17	417
1985	210	73	283	44	19	346	18	0	5	0	0	369	12	381
1986	249	108	357	47	27	431	14	9	5	1	0	460	11	471
1987	265	104	369	30	19	418	14	1	6	0	0	439	13	452
1988	272	102	374	38	32	444	15	2	6	0	0	467	16	483
1989	262	84	346	35	21	402	9	2	2	1	0	416	52	468
1990	260	89	349	21	13	383	11	2	5	0	0	401	58	459
1991	272	64	336	23	22	381	18	0	5	0	1	405	82	487
1992	251	51	302	26	21	349	11	1	5	1	0	367	48	415
1993	276	64	340	21	9	375	13	1	6	0	0	394	50	444
1994	264	68	332	22	23	377	14	1	9	4	3	408	55	463
1995	275	72	347	24	17	388	15	9	9	11	8	440	8	448
1996	332	63	395	19	13	427	8	1	1		1	438	8	446
Singleton	**Rates per thousand live births**													
1982	551.7	180.1	295.4	57.4	13.8	54.0	3.5	2.0	1.3	1.2	3.7	5.1	20.7	5.7
1983	551.0	178.2	300.0	53.7	14.5	55.7	3.7	1.6	1.3	1.2	2.8	5.0	188.9	5.3
1984	517.7	148.5	272.2	49.5	12.7	51.9	3.6	1.7	1.1	1.1	1.9	4.7	193.8	5.0

A6.1.3 continued

Singleton and multiple neonatal deaths by birthweight, England and Wales, 1982–96

Year of birth	Birthweight, g													All birthweights
	Under 1,000	1,000–1,499	Under 1,500	1,500–1,999	2,000–2,499	Under 2,500	2,500–2,999	3,000–3,499	3,500–3,999	4,000–4,499	4,500 and over	All stated	Not stated	
1987	478.3	141.8	252.1	41.5	9.7	48.0	2.9	1.5	1.1	1.2	2.1	4.3	206.8	4.4
1988	485.1	139.1	256.3	40.1	10.0	49.0	2.9	1.4	1.0	0.9	2.0	4.2	98.5	4.3
1989	380.9	113.8	215.0	32.9	7.9	41.7	2.8	1.2	1.1	1.0	1.6	3.7	16.8	4.1
1990	413.1	86.6	205.6	30.4	7.0	38.0	2.4	1.2	0.9	0.9	1.9	3.4	15.6	3.9
1991	424.6	84.1	205.7	26.6	7.2	37.3	2.2	1.0	0.8	0.9	1.7	3.2	16.4	3.7
1992	399.5	80.6	197.2	23.7	6.7	37.4	2.1	1.1	0.8	0.8	1.8	3.2	15.9	3.6
1993	381.7	76.8	193.7	24.2	6.4	36.7	2.0	1.1	0.7	0.7	1.8	3.1	16.7	3.6
1994	345.1	74.5	184.0	21.6	6.0	36.7	2.0	1.0	0.7	0.8	2.9	3.2	17.0	3.5
1995	380.6	65.0	187.5	20.7	7.1	37.2	2.0	1.1	0.9	1.5	4.9	3.4	25.4	3.5
1996	386.4	63.1	196.2	17.7	6.5	38.8	1.9	1.0	0.7	..	..	3.3	46.7	3.4
Multiple														
1982	683.0	143.3	286.4	20.2	4.8	48.7	2.5	3.2	15.9	–	–	26.4	116.2	30.9
1983	634.9	126.2	283.3	23.0	5.0	53.6	4.0	1.9	8.1	58.8	–	29.4	436.4	31.2
1984	642.9	134.1	311.1	22.7	6.4	58.1	4.0	2.4	4.6	–	1000.0	31.7	395.3	32.9
1985	576.9	100.8	260.1	23.3	4.7	49.2	4.0	2.9	–	–	–	27.4	521.7	28.3
1986	604.4	128.1	284.5	23.5	6.4	57.8	3.0	2.9	34.1	71.4	–	32.7	407.4	33.4
1987	603.6	120.2	283.0	14.8	4.3	54.2	3.0	3.3	3.7	–	–	30.3	464.3	31.1
1988	584.9	114.0	275.0	18.1	7.3	56.4	3.1	2.9	7.2	–	–	30.8	410.3	31.8
1989	578.4	98.0	264.1	16.6	4.6	50.6	1.8	1.1	7.2	50.0	–	27.7	105.3	30.1
1990	571.4	94.5	249.8	9.4	2.8	46.2	2.2	2.5	6.5	–	–	25.6	99.7	28.2
1991	545.1	69.3	236.3	9.8	4.5	44.0	3.5	2.5	–	–	1000.0	25.2	125.2	29.1
1992	517.5	57.0	219.0	12.0	4.2	40.8	2.1	2.4	3.0	43.5	–	22.4	68.3	24.3
1993	500.9	65.0	221.4	10.8	1.9	43.6	2.4	2.4	3.7	–	–	24.2	69.9	26.1
1994	466.4	64.2	204.3	9.2	4.7	42.3	2.5	2.9	14.8	200.0	750.0	24.3	98.7	26.7
1995	422.4	60.3	188.1	9.0	3.2	39.7	2.6	4.3	33.8	343.8	615.4	24.4	148.1	24.8
1996	481.9	50.4	203.6	7.4	2.5	43.9	1.4	0.5	3.3	..	..	24.8	135.6	25.2

Data for all births are in Table A3.5.2

Source: Authors' analysis of ONS/OPCS data

Data extract: live births 1993 (7/94), 1994 (7/95), 1995 (3/7/96), 1996 (8/4/97)
 linked 1993 (3/4/96), 1994 (18/9/96), 1995 (3/11/97), 1996 Mortality statistics, DH3, no 30, Table 28

This is similar to Table A6.3 in the first edition of Birth counts

A6.1.4

Singleton and multiple postneonatal deaths by birthweight, England and Wales, 1982–96

Year of birth	Birthweight, g											All stated	Not stated	All birthweights
	Under 1,000	1,000– 1,499	Under 1,500	1,500– 1,999	2,000– 2,499	Under 2,500	2,500– 2,999	3,000– 3,499	3,500– 3,999	4,000– 4,499	4,500 and over			

Singleton

Numbers

1982	66	94	160	122	209	491	565	818	424	112	21	2,431	138	2,569
1983	80	93	173	124	247	544	592	836	447	86	19	2,524	12	2,536
1984	83	95	178	106	203	487	522	666	429	87	16	2,207	10	2,217
1985	82	110	192	140	252	584	543	804	464	115	22	2,532	8	2,540
1986	97	98	195	139	248	582	577	751	446	139	22	2,517	15	2,532
1987	87	105	192	130	234	556	591	823	480	122	26	2,598	7	2,605
1988	97	117	214	145	252	611	545	753	429	122	22	2,482	6	2,488
1989	116	96	212	118	231	561	468	665	397	95	21	2,207	75	2,282
1990	106	110	216	129	188	533	419	571	327	106	16	1,972	93	2,065
1991	102	71	173	90	202	465	294	431	274	74	16	1,554	85	1,639
1992	138	78	216	78	149	443	285	369	178	56	11	1,342	62	1,404
1993	117	72	189	82	148	419	244	315	190	50	16	1,234	40	1,274
1994	115	78	193	73	116	382	245	303	154	50	8	1,142	31	1,173
1995	131	78	209	76	135	420	254	292	150	50	8	1,168	12	1,180
1996	126	79	205	78	152	435	226	297	144	48	4	1,158	5	1,163

56

Multiple

1982	8	23	31	28	34	93	22	7	2	0	0	124	8	132
1983	15	23	38	17	32	87	21	10	2	0	0	120	0	120
1984	12	18	30	22	28	80	25	3	0	0	0	108	2	110
1985	20	22	42	29	47	118	20	8	1	0	0	147	1	148
1986	22	28	50	33	41	124	41	8	5	0	0	178	0	178
1987	24	28	52	29	34	115	42	8	2	0	0	167	1	168
1988	29	29	58	30	40	128	27	6	1	0	0	162	0	162
1989	26	22	48	29	36	113	19	9	3	0	0	144	8	152
1990	32	23	55	29	27	106	23	8	1	0	0	138	13	151
1991	24	14	38	24	16	78	15	7	2	0	0	102	9	111
1992	25	24	49	16	13	78	14	7	2	0	0	101	6	107
1993	34	14	48	16	13	77	5	4	0	1	0	87	5	92
1994	33	8	41	11	9	61	10	7	0	0	0	78	3	81
1995	48	18	66	13	17	96	8	2	1	0	2	109	2	111
1996	28	13	41	8	23	72	7	4	0	0	0	83	0	83

Rates per thousand live births

Singleton

1982	54.2	34.7	40.7	20.5	8.7	14.5	5.2	3.6	2.6	2.5	3.2	4.1	5.2	4.2
1983	57.1	32.2	40.4	19.8	9.8	15.3	5.3	3.5	2.6	1.8	2.8	4.1	14.8	4.1
1984	54.5	31.4	39.1	16.5	8.1	13.5	4.6	2.7	2.4	1.8	2.2	3.5	13.0	3.6

A6.1.4 continued

Singleton and multiple postneonatal deaths by birthweight, England and Wales, 1982–96

Year of birth	Birthweight, g												Not stated	All birthweights
	Under 1,000	1,000–1,499	Under 1,500	1,500–1,999	2,000–2,499	Under 2,500	2,500–2,999	3,000–3,499	3,500–3,999	4,000–4,499	4,500 and over	All stated		
1985	52.6	33.8	39.9	21.0	9.6	15.5	4.7	3.2	2.6	2.3	2.9	3.9	9.5	4.0
1986	58.7	30.9	40.4	20.2	9.3	15.2	5.0	3.0	2.4	2.7	2.8	3.9	25.1	3.9
1987	51.1	30.0	36.9	18.5	8.8	14.3	5.1	3.2	2.5	2.2	3.0	3.9	14.8	3.9
1988	55.6	34.3	41.5	21.1	9.8	16.2	4.8	2.9	2.2	2.1	2.3	3.7	7.6	3.7
1989	58.4	29.5	40.5	17.7	9.2	15.1	4.2	2.7	2.1	1.7	2.2	3.4	3.6	3.4
1990	57.0	33.9	42.3	19.3	7.2	14.1	3.8	2.3	1.7	1.8	1.7	3.0	3.4	3.0
1991	56.5	21.9	34.2	13.3	7.8	12.3	2.7	1.7	1.4	1.2	1.6	2.4	3.4	2.4
1992	71.7	23.4	41.0	11.9	6.1	12.2	2.7	1.5	0.9	0.9	1.0	2.1	2.5	2.1
1993	58.9	22.6	36.5	12.4	6.2	11.7	2.4	1.3	1.0	0.8	1.5	1.9	1.9	1.9
1994	50.2	23.1	34.1	10.8	4.9	10.5	2.4	1.3	0.8	0.8	0.7	1.8	1.9	1.8
1995	58.8	22.2	36.4	10.8	5.4	11.2	2.5	1.3	0.8	0.8	0.4	1.9	5.5	1.9
1996	51.2	22.4	34.3	11.4	6.2	11.6	2.2	1.3	0.8	..	..	1.8	3.4	1.8
Multiple														
1982	35.7	37.0	36.7	17.6	9.6	15.5	5.6	4.5	7.9	–	–	10.5	12.7	10.7
1983	47.6	32.6	37.3	10.3	8.5	13.5	5.0	6.2	8.1	–	–	9.6	–	9.5
1984	34.3	27.4	29.8	12.8	7.5	12.4	5.8	1.8	–	–	–	8.6	46.5	8.7
1985	54.9	30.4	38.6	15.3	11.6	16.8	4.5	4.7	4.0	–	–	10.9	43.5	11.0
1986	53.4	33.2	39.8	16.5	9.7	16.6	8.9	4.6	18.9	–	–	12.7	–	12.6
1987	54.7	32.4	39.9	14.3	7.8	14.9	8.9	4.4	7.4	–	–	11.5	35.7	11.6
1988	62.4	32.4	42.6	14.3	9.1	16.3	5.5	2.9	3.6	–	–	10.7	–	10.7
1989	57.4	25.7	36.6	13.8	7.9	14.2	3.8	4.9	10.8	–	–	9.6	16.2	9.8
1990	70.3	24.4	39.4	10.7	5.8	12.8	4.6	4.0	3.2	–	–	8.8	22.3	9.3
1991	48.1	15.2	26.7	6.8	4.9	9.0	2.9	3.5	6.5	–	–	6.3	13.7	6.6
1992	51.5	26.8	35.5	6.0	3.2	9.1	2.6	3.4	6.1	–	–	6.2	8.5	6.3
1993	61.7	14.2	31.3	6.6	2.8	8.9	0.9	1.9	–	55.6	–	5.3	7.0	5.4
1994	58.3	7.6	25.2	4.6	1.8	6.8	1.8	3.3	–	–	–	4.6	5.4	4.7
1995	73.7	15.1	35.8	4.9	3.2	9.8	1.4	1.0	3.8	–	153.8	6.1	37.0	6.1
1996	40.6	10.4	21.1	3.1	4.4	7.4	1.3	1.9	–	–	–	4.7	–	4.7

Data for all births are in Table A3.5.2

Source: Authors' analysis of ONS/OPCS data

Data extract: live births 1993 (3/7/94), 1994 (7/95), 1995 (3/7/96), 1996 (8/4/97)

linked 1993 (3/4/96), 1994 (18/9/96), 1995 (3/11/97), 1996 Mortality statistics, DH3, no 30, Table 28

This is similar to Table A6.3 in the first edition of Birth counts

A6.1.5

Singleton and multiple infant deaths by birthweight, England and Wales, 1982–96

Year	Birthweight, g													All birthweights
	Under 1,000	1,000– 1,499	Under 1,500	1,500– 1,999	2,000– 2,499	Under 2,500	2,500– 2,999	3,000– 3,499	3,500– 3,999	4,000– 4,499	4,500 and over	All stated	Not stated	
Singleton														
1982	738	582	1,320	463	541	2,324	949	1,278	635	166	45	5,397	692	6,089
1983	852	607	1,459	460	611	2,530	1,009	1,225	676	143	38	5,621	165	5,786
1984	872	544	1,416	424	523	2,363	927	1,071	628	140	30	5,159	159	5,318
1985	882	573	1,455	420	610	2,485	932	1,194	674	190	35	5,510	132	5,642
1986	902	527	1,429	450	548	2,427	936	1,146	655	201	37	5,402	106	5,508
1987	902	601	1,503	422	493	2,418	926	1,197	696	187	44	5,468	105	5,573
1988	943	591	1,534	421	510	2,465	876	1,107	634	177	41	5,300	84	5,384
1989	872	466	1,338	338	430	2,106	774	960	613	155	36	4,644	421	5,065
1990	874	391	1,265	332	371	1,968	689	880	493	160	34	4,224	516	4,740
1991	868	344	1,212	271	389	1,872	535	672	428	128	33	3,668	500	4,168
1992	907	347	1,254	233	314	1,801	510	623	326	105	30	3,395	463	3,858
1993	875	317	1,192	242	301	1,735	449	567	329	96	35	3,211	393	3,604
1994	905	329	1,234	219	259	1,712	444	542	292	101	39	3,130	309	3,439
1995	979	306	1,285	221	312	1,818	458	545	324	134	53	3,332	67	3,399
1996	1,077	301	1,378	199	313	1,890	426	522	281	134	131	3,250	74	3,324
Multiple														
1982	161	112	273	60	51	384	32	12	6	0	0	434	81	515
1983	215	112	327	55	51	433	38	13	4	1	0	489	24	513
1984	237	106	343	61	52	456	42	7	1	0	2	508	19	527
1985	230	95	325	73	66	464	38	13	1	0	0	516	13	529
1986	271	136	407	80	68	555	55	13	14	1	0	638	11	649
1987	289	132	421	59	53	533	56	14	3	0	0	606	14	620
1988	301	131	432	68	72	572	42	12	3	0	0	629	16	645
1989	288	106	394	64	57	515	28	11	5	1	0	560	60	620
1990	292	112	404	45	40	489	34	13	3	0	0	539	71	610
1991	296	78	374	39	46	459	33	12	2	0	1	507	91	598
1992	276	75	351	39	37	427	25	12	3	1	0	468	54	522
1993	310	78	388	42	22	452	18	9	1	1	0	481	55	536
1994	297	76	373	33	32	438	24	13	4	4	3	486	58	544
1995	323	90	413	37	34	484	23	11	10	11	10	549	10	559
1996	360	76	436	27	36	499	15	5	1	1	1	521	8	529
Rates per thousand live births														
Singleton														
1982	605.9	214.8	336.1	77.9	22.5	68.4	8.7	5.6	3.9	3.7	6.9	9.2	25.9	9.9
1983	608.1	210.4	340.4	73.5	24.4	71.0	9.0	5.1	3.9	3.0	5.5	9.1	203.7	9.4

A6.1.5 continued

Singleton and multiple infant deaths by birthweight, England and Wales, 1982–96

Year	Birthweight, g											All stated	Not stated	All birthweights
	Under 1,000	1,000– 1,499	Under 1,500	1,500– 1,999	2,000– 2,499	Under 2,500	2,500– 2,999	3,000– 3,499	3,500– 3,999	4,000– 4,499	4,500 and over			
1984	572.2	179.9	311.3	65.9	20.8	65.4	8.2	4.4	3.6	2.9	4.1	8.3	206.8	8.5
1985	566.1	176.1	302.4	63.0	23.3	66.0	8.0	4.8	3.7	3.8	4.6	8.6	156.2	8.8
1986	545.7	166.1	296.1	65.3	20.6	63.4	8.1	4.6	3.6	3.9	4.7	8.4	177.6	8.5
1987	529.3	171.9	289.0	59.9	18.5	62.3	8.0	4.7	3.6	3.4	5.1	8.2	221.5	8.4
1988	540.7	173.5	297.8	61.2	19.8	65.2	7.7	4.3	3.2	3.0	4.3	7.8	106.1	7.9
1989	439.3	143.3	255.5	50.6	17.1	56.9	7.0	3.9	3.2	2.7	3.8	7.1	20.4	7.5
1990	470.1	120.5	247.9	49.7	14.3	52.1	6.2	3.5	2.5	2.7	3.5	6.4	19.0	6.9
1991	481.2	105.9	239.9	39.9	15.0	49.6	4.9	2.7	2.2	2.1	3.3	5.6	19.8	6.1
1992	471.2	104.0	238.3	35.7	12.8	49.6	4.8	2.6	2.2	1.7	2.8	5.2	18.3	5.7
1993	440.6	99.3	230.2	36.6	12.5	48.4	4.4	2.4	1.7	1.7	3.2	5.1	18.6	5.5
1994	395.4	97.6	218.1	32.4	10.9	47.2	4.4	2.3	1.5	1.6	3.6	5.0	18.9	5.3
1995	439.4	87.2	223.9	31.5	12.6	48.4	4.4	2.3	1.8	1.7	3.6	5.3	31.0	5.4
1996	437.6	85.5	230.4	29.1	12.7	50.5	4.1	2.2	1.5	2.3	::	5.2	50.0	5.3
Multiple														
1982	718.8	180.4	323.1	37.8	14.4	64.2	8.1	7.7	23.8	–	–	36.9	129.0	41.6
1983	682.5	158.9	320.6	33.2	13.5	67.1	9.0	8.0	16.1	58.8	–	38.9	436.4	40.7
1984	677.1	161.6	341.0	35.6	13.8	70.4	9.8	4.2	4.6	–	1000.0	40.2	441.9	41.6
1985	631.9	131.2	298.7	38.6	16.3	66.0	8.5	7.7	4.0	–	–	38.3	565.2	39.2
1986	657.8	161.3	324.3	40.0	16.2	74.4	12.0	7.5	53.0	71.4	–	45.4	407.4	46.0
1987	658.3	152.6	322.9	29.1	12.1	69.2	11.9	7.7	11.1	–	–	41.8	500.0	42.7
1988	647.3	146.4	317.6	32.3	16.3	72.6	8.6	5.8	10.8	–	–	41.5	410.3	42.5
1989	635.8	123.7	300.8	30.4	12.6	64.8	5.7	6.0	18.1	50.0	–	37.3	121.5	39.9
1990	641.8	118.9	289.2	20.1	8.6	59.0	6.7	6.4	9.7	–	–	34.3	122.0	37.5
1991	593.2	84.5	263.0	16.7	9.4	53.1	6.4	6.1	6.5	–	1000.0	31.5	138.9	35.7
1992	569.1	83.9	254.5	18.0	7.4	49.9	4.7	5.8	9.1	–	–	28.6	76.8	30.6
1993	562.6	79.2	252.6	17.4	4.7	52.5	3.4	4.3	3.7	43.5	–	29.5	76.9	31.5
1994	524.7	71.8	229.5	13.8	6.5	49.1	4.4	6.2	14.8	55.6	750.0	28.9	104.1	31.3
1995	496.2	75.4	223.8	13.9	6.4	49.5	3.9	5.3	37.6	200.0	769.2	30.5	185.2	31.0
1996	522.5	60.8	224.7	10.5	6.9	51.3	2.7	2.4	3.3	343.8	::	29.5	66.7	29.8

Data for all births are in Table A3.5.2

Source: Authors' analysis of ONS/OPCS data

Data extract: live births 1993 (7/94), 1994 (7/95), 1995 (3/7/96), 1996 (8/4/97)

linked   1993 (3/4/96), 1994 (18/9/96), 1995 (3/11/97), 1996 Mortality statistics, DH3, no 30, Table 28

This is similar to Table A6.3 in the first edition of Birth counts

Mortality of one, two and three year olds by multiplicity and birthweight, England and Wales, 1993–95

Year of birth and age at death, years	Birthweight, g													All birthweights
	Under 1,000	1,000–1,499	Under 1,500	1,500–1,999	2,000–2,499	Under 2,500	2,500–2,999	3,000–3,499	3,500–3,999	4,000–4,499	4,500 and over	All stated	Not stated	
1993														
Numbers														
Singleton														
Under 1	875	317	1,192	242	301	1,735	449	567	329	96	35	3,211	393	3,604
1	6	6	12	13	18	43	66	92	53	18	2	274	13	287
2	0	3	3	3	13	19	35	67	52	8	1	182	5	187
3	1	0	1	3	4	8	10	19	13	3	0	53	0	53
Multiple														
Under 1	310	78	388	42	22	452	18	9	1	1	0	481	55	536
1	1	2	3	3	3	9	2	0	0	0	0	11	1	12
2	0	1	1	1	2	4	1	0	0	0	0	5	0	5
3	0	0	0	0	1	1	0	0	0	0	0	1	0	1
All														
Under 1	1,034	309	1,343	186	162	1,691	218	257	140	46	19	2,371	403	2,774
1	7	8	15	16	21	52	68	92	53	18	2	285	14	299
2	0	4	4	4	15	23	36	67	52	8	1	187	5	192
3	1	0	1	3	4	8	10	19	13	3	0	53	0	53
Rates per thousand live births														
Singleton														
Under 1	381.7	76.8	193.7	24.2	6.4	36.7	2.0	1.1	0.7	0.7	1.8	3.1	16.7	3.6
1	3.0	1.9	2.3	2.0	0.7	1.2	0.6	0.4	0.3	0.3	0.2	0.4	0.6	0.4
2	–	0.9	0.6	0.5	0.5	0.5	0.3	0.3	0.3	0.1	0.1	0.3	0.2	0.3
3	0.5	–	0.2	0.5	0.2	0.2	0.1	0.1	0.1	–	–	0.1	–	0.1
Multiple														
Under 1	500.9	65.0	221.4	10.8	1.9	43.6	2.4	2.4	3.7	–	–	24.2	69.9	26.1
1	1.8	2.0	2.0	1.2	0.6	1.0	0.4	–	–	–	–	0.7	1.4	0.7
2	–	1.0	0.7	0.4	0.4	0.5	0.2	–	–	–	–	0.3	–	0.3
3	–	–	–	–	0.2	0.1	–	–	–	–	–	0.1	–	0.1
All														
Under 1	407.6	74.0	200.1	20.6	5.6	38.0	2.0	1.1	0.7	0.7	1.8	3.7	18.4	4.1
1	2.8	1.9	2.2	1.8	0.7	1.2	0.6	0.4	0.3	0.3	0.2	0.4	0.6	0.4
2	–	1.0	0.6	0.4	0.5	0.5	0.3	0.3	0.3	0.1	0.1	0.3	0.2	0.3
3	0.4	–	0.1	0.3	0.1	0.2	0.1	0.1	0.1	–	–	0.1	–	0.1

A6.1.6 continued

Mortality of one, two and three year olds by multiplicity and birthweight, England and Wales, 1993–95

Year of birth and age at death, years	Birthweight, g													All birthweights
	Under 1,000	1,000–1,499	Under 1,500	1,500–1,999	2,000–2,499	Under 2,500	2,500–2,999	3,000–3,499	3,500–3,999	4,000–4,499	4,500 and over	All stated	Not stated	
1994														
Numbers														
Singleton														
Under 1	905	329	1,234	219	259	1,712	444	542	292	101	39	3,130	309	3,439
1	5	7	12	14	25	51	59	93	58	19	3	283	6	289
2	0	1	1	2	5	8	21	29	24	6	1	89	1	90
Multiple														
Under 1	297	76	373	33	32	438	24	13	4	4	3	486	58	544
1	2	4	6	0	2	8	3	0	2	0	0	13	0	13
2	1	0	1	0	0	1	1	0	0	0	0	2	0	2
All														
Under 1	1,054	319	1,373	168	166	1,707	213	245	142	55	34	2,396	333	2,729
1	7	11	18	14	27	59	62	93	60	19	3	296	6	302
2	1	1	2	2	5	9	22	29	24	6	1	91	1	92
Rates per thousand live births														
Singleton														
Under 1	345.1	74.5	184.0	21.6	6.0	36.7	2.0	1.0	0.7	0.8	2.9	3.2	17.0	3.5
1	2.2	2.1	2.1	2.1	1.0	1.4	0.6	0.4	0.3	0.3	0.3	0.4	0.4	0.4
2	–	0.3	0.2	0.3	0.2	0.2	0.2	0.1	0.1	0.1	0.1	0.1	0.1	0.1
Multiple														
Under 1	466.4	64.2	204.3	9.2	4.7	42.3	2.5	2.9	14.8	200.0	750.0	24.3	98.7	26.7
1	3.5	3.8	3.7	–	0.4	0.9	0.5	–	7.4	–	–	0.8	–	0.7
2	1.8	–	0.6	–	–	0.1	0.2	–	–	–	–	0.1	–	0.1
All														
Under 1	369.2	72.0	188.5	18.4	5.8	37.8	2.0	1.0	0.8	0.9	3.2	3.7	19.7	4.1
1	2.5	2.5	2.5	1.5	0.9	1.3	0.6	0.4	0.3	0.3	0.3	0.5	0.4	0.5
2	0.4	0.2	0.3	0.2	0.2	0.2	0.2	0.1	0.1	0.1	0.1	0.1	0.1	0.1
1995														
Numbers														
Singleton														
Under 1	979	306	1,285	221	312	1,818	458	545	324	134	53	3,332	67	3,399
1	5	2	7	3	18	28	35	54	26	4	1	148	3	151

Mortality of one, two and three year olds by multiplicity and birthweight, England and Wales, 1993–95

Year of birth and age at death, years	Birthweight, g													All birthweights
	Under 1,000	1,000– 1,499	Under 1,500	1,500– 1,999	2,000– 2,499	Under 2,500	2,500– 2,999	3,000– 3,499	3,500– 3,999	4,000– 4,499	4,500 and over	All stated	Not stated	
Multiple														
Under 1	323	90	413	37	34	484	23	11	10	11	10	549	10	559
1	1	2	3	4	0	7	0	0	0	0	0	7	0	7
All														
Under 1	1,123	300	1,423	169	194	1,786	219	262	183	97	57	2,604	63	2,667
1	6	4	10	7	18	35	35	54	26	4	1	155	3	158
Rates per thousand live births														
Singleton														
Under 1	380.6	65.0	187.5	20.7	7.1	37.2	2.0	1.1	0.9	1.5	4.9	3.4	25.4	3.5
1	2.2	0.6	1.2	0.4	0.7	0.7	0.3	0.2	0.1	0.1	0.1	0.2	1.4	0.2
Multiple														
Under 1	422.4	60.3	188.1	9.0	3.2	39.7	2.6	4.3	33.8	343.8	615.4	24.4	148.1	24.8
1	1.5	1.7	1.6	1.5	–	0.7	–	–	–	–	–	0.4	–	0.4
All														
Under 1	390.1	63.8	187.7	17.5	6.5	37.7	2.0	1.1	1.0	1.6	5.7	4.0	28.4	4.1
1	2.1	0.9	1.3	0.7	0.6	0.7	0.3	0.2	0.1	0.1	0.1	0.2	1.4	0.2

Source: Authors' analysis of ONS/OPCS data

Data extract: live births 1993 (7/94), 1994 (7/95), 1995 (3/7/96), 1996 (8/4/97)

linked   1993 (3/4/96), 1994 (18/9/96), 1995 (3/11/97)

The data in this table differ from those published in *Health statistics quarterly 2*, as different extracts were used.

This is a new table for this edition of *Birth counts*

A6.2.1

Stillbirths by ONS cause group and birthweight, England and Wales, 1981-85, 1986-90, 1991-95

Year of birth	Birthweight, g	ONS cause group										All
		1	2	3	4	5	6	7	8A	8B	0	
1981-85		**Numbers of stillbirths at 28 or more weeks of gestation**										
	Under 1,000	350	2	32	1,370	1	2	58	–	–	568	2,383
	1,000–1,499	425	6	70	1,864	0	8	73	–	–	623	3,069
	1,500–1,999	368	5	37	1,775	1	11	81	–	–	556	2,834
	2,000–2,499	294	6	26	1,844	0	6	105	–	–	553	2,834
	Under 2,500	1,437	19	165	6,853	2	27	317	–	–	2,300	11,120
	2,500 and over	491	14	38	4,213	2	12	287	–	–	1,347	6,404
		Rates per thousand total births										
	Under 1,000	35.0	0.2	3.2	137.0	0.1	0.2	5.8	–	–	56.8	238.3
	1,000–1,499	22.3	0.3	3.7	97.8	–	0.4	3.8	–	–	32.7	161.0
	1,500–1,999	9.6	0.1	1.0	46.4	0.0	0.3	2.1	–	–	14.5	74.1
	2,000–2,499	2.2	0.0	0.2	14.1	–	0.0	0.8	–	–	4.2	21.6
	Under 2,500	7.2	0.1	0.8	34.5	0.0	0.1	1.6	–	–	11.6	56.1
	2,500 and over	0.2	0.0	0.0	1.6	0.0	0.0	0.1	–	–	0.5	2.4
1986-90		**Numbers of stillbirths at 28 or more weeks of gestation**										
	Under 1,000	266	8	54	32	0	6	41	1,072	666	3	2,148
	1,000–1,499	337	14	76	74	0	16	79	1,335	751	10	2,692
	1,500–1,999	319	13	33	94	0	16	79	1,420	678	14	2,666
	2,000–2,499	217	6	24	146	0	14	94	1,391	683	20	2,595
	Under 2,500	1,139	41	187	346	0	52	293	5,218	2,778	47	10,101
	2,500 and over	377	22	20	768	0	18	289	2,965	1,822	109	6,390
		Rates per thousand total births										
	Under 1,000	20.0	0.6	4.1	2.4	–	0.5	3.1	80.5	50.0	0.2	161.3
	1,000–1,499	14.2	0.6	3.2	3.1	–	0.7	3.3	56.4	31.7	0.4	113.7
	1,500–1,999	6.7	0.3	0.7	2.0	–	0.3	1.7	30.0	14.3	0.3	56.3
	2,000–2,499	1.4	0.0	0.2	0.9	–	0.1	0.6	9.0	4.4	0.1	16.8
	Under 2,500	4.8	0.2	0.8	1.4	–	0.2	1.2	21.8	11.6	0.2	42.3
	2,500 and over	0.1	0.0	0.0	0.2	–	0.0	0.1	0.9	0.6	0.0	2.0

A6.2.1 *continued*

Stillbirths by ONS cause group and birthweight, England and Wales, 1981–85, 1986–90, 1991–95

Year of birth	Birthweight, g	ONS cause group										All
		1	2	3	4	5	6	7	8A	8B	0	
1991–95		**Numbers of stillbirths at 28 or more weeks of gestation**										
	Under 1,000	229	8	59	32	0	2	49	735	912	13	2,039
	1,000–1,499	243	5	36	46	0	10	73	837	863	15	2,128
	1,500–1,999	222	7	23	60	0	8	65	911	815	14	2,125
	2,000–2,499	171	6	10	86	0	8	73	877	890	30	2,151
	Under 2,500	865	26	128	224	0	28	260	3,360	3,480	72	8,443
	2,500 and over	230	6	9	498	0	22	226	2,023	2,632	188	5,834
		Rates per thousand total births										
	Under 1,000	15.2	0.5	3.9	2.1	–	0.1	3.3	48.9	60.7	0.9	135.7
	1,000–1,499	10.2	0.2	1.5	1.9	–	0.4	3.1	35.1	36.2	0.6	89.3
	1,500–1,999	4.6	0.1	0.5	1.3	–	0.2	1.4	19.1	17.0	0.3	44.4
	2,000–2,499	1.1	0.0	0.1	0.6	–	0.1	0.5	5.8	5.9	0.2	14.3
	Under 2,500	3.7	0.1	0.5	0.9	–	0.1	1.1	14.2	14.7	0.3	35.7
	2,500 and over	0.1	0.0	0.0	0.2	–	0.0	0.1	0.7	0.9	0.1	1.9

For descriptions of ONS cause groups, see Table A3.9.1

Source: Authors' analysis of ONS/OPCS data

Data extract: live births 1993 (7/94), 1994 (7/95), 1995 (3/7/96), 1996 (8/4/97)

linked   1993 (3/4/96), 1994 (18/9/96), 1995 (3/11/97)

This is a new table for this edition of *Birth counts*

A6.2.2

Neonatal deaths by ONS cause group and birthweight, England and Wales, 1981–85, 1986–90, 1991–95

Year of birth	Birthweight, g	ONS cause group									All
		1	2	3	4	5	6	7	9	0	
1981–85		**Numbers**									
	Under 1,000	207	19	3,321	359	6	113	47	0	613	4,685
	1,000–1,499	580	9	1,646	302	6	136	51	0	127	2,857
	1,500–1,999	761	10	565	225	6	119	69	9	76	1,840
	2,000–2,499	998	17	268	287	14	116	69	18	64	1,851
	Under 2,500	2,546	55	5,800	1,173	32	484	236	27	880	11,233
	2,500 and over	2,995	38	378	1,252	63	405	187	269	199	5,786
		Rates per thousand live births									
	Under 1,000	27.2	2.5	436.1	47.1	0.8	14.8	6.2	–	80.5	615.2
	1,000–1,499	36.3	0.6	102.9	18.9	0.4	8.5	3.2	–	7.9	178.6
	1,500–1,999	21.5	0.3	16.0	6.4	0.2	3.4	1.9	0.3	2.1	52.0
	2,000–2,499	7.8	0.1	2.1	2.2	0.1	0.9	0.5	0.1	0.5	14.4
	Under 2,500	13.6	0.3	31.0	6.3	0.2	2.6	1.3	0.1	4.7	60.0
	2,500 and over	1.1	0.0	0.1	0.5	0.0	0.2	0.1	0.1	0.1	2.2
1986–90		**Numbers**									
	Under 1,000	438	42	4,478	196	3	53	19	1	68	5,298
	1,000–1,499	689	22	1,475	169	2	105	29	3	43	2,537
	1,500–1,999	794	13	406	139	3	71	24	3	20	1,473
	2,000–2,499	817	11	143	181	9	76	26	27	21	1,311
	Under 2,500	2,738	88	6,502	685	17	305	98	34	152	10,619
	2,500 and over	2,548	39	327	1,113	42	275	78	302	102	4,826
		Rates per thousand live births									
	Under 1,000	39.2	3.8	400.9	17.5	0.3	4.7	1.7	0.1	6.1	474.3
	1,000–1,499	32.8	1.0	70.3	8.1	0.1	5.0	1.4	0.1	2.1	121.0
	1,500–1,999	17.8	0.3	9.1	3.1	0.1	1.6	0.5	0.1	0.4	33.0
	2,000–2,499	5.4	0.1	0.9	1.2	0.1	0.5	0.2	0.2	0.1	8.6
	Under 2,500	12.0	0.4	28.4	3.0	0.1	1.3	0.4	0.1	0.7	46.4
	2,500 and over	0.8	0.0	0.1	0.4	0.0	0.1	0.0	0.1	0.0	1.5

A6.2.2 *continued*

Neonatal deaths by ONS cause group and birthweight, England and Wales, 1981–85, 1986–90, 1991–95

Year of birth	Birthweight, g	ONS cause group									All
		1	2	3	4	5	6	7	9	0	
1991–95		**Numbers**									
	Under 1,000	430	39	4,377	185	0	90	31	0	117	5,269
	1,000–1,499	441	17	844	130	1	74	20	1	57	1,585
	1,500–1,999	484	8	204	120	2	43	15	7	25	908
	2,000–2,499	507	11	86	157	4	64	18	31	39	917
	Under 2,500	1,862	75	5,511	592	7	271	84	39	238	8,679
	2,500 and over	1,674	33	386	921	28	203	77	189	120	3,631
		Rates per thousand live births									
	Under 1,000	33.1	3.0	337.1	14.2	–	6.9	2.4	–	9.0	405.8
	1,000–1,499	20.3	0.8	38.9	6.0	0.0	3.4	0.9	0.0	2.6	73.0
	1,500–1,999	10.6	0.2	4.5	2.6	0.0	0.9	0.3	0.2	0.5	19.9
	2,000–2,499	3.4	0.1	0.6	1.1	0.0	0.4	0.1	0.2	0.3	6.2
	Under 2,500	8.2	0.3	24.2	2.6	0.0	1.2	0.4	0.2	1.0	38.0
	2,500 and over	0.5	0.0	0.1	0.3	0.0	0.1	0.0	0.1	0.0	1.2

For descriptions of ONS cause groups, see Table A3.9.2

Source: Authors' analysis of ONS/OPCS data

Data extract: live births 1993 (7/94), 1994 (7/95), 1995 (3/7/96), 1996 (8/4/97)
linked 1993 (3/4/96), 1994 (18/9/96), 1995 (3/11/97)

This is similar to Table A6.5 in the first edition of *Birth counts*

A6.2.3

Postneonatal deaths by ONS cause group and birthweight, England and Wales, 1981–85, 1986–90, 1991–95

Year of birth	Birthweight, g	ONS cause group									All
		1	2	3	4	5	6	7	9	0	
1981–85		**Numbers**									
	Under 1,000	29	2	235	14	3	63	8	31	42	427
	1,000–1,499	100	3	151	13	8	107	10	136	49	577
	1,500–1,999	220	3	37	10	14	144	14	218	56	716
	2,000–2,499	437	7	17	8	50	241	26	445	81	1,312
	Under 2,500	786	15	440	45	75	555	58	830	228	3,032
	2,500 and over	2,016	4	28	67	449	1,956	227	4,454	577	9,778
		Rates per thousand live births									
	Under 1,000	3.8	0.3	30.9	1.8	0.4	8.3	1.1	4.1	5.5	56.1
	1,000–1,499	6.3	0.2	9.4	0.8	0.5	6.7	0.6	8.5	3.1	36.1
	1,500–1,999	6.2	0.1	1.0	0.3	0.4	4.1	0.4	6.2	1.6	20.2
	2,000–2,499	3.4	0.1	0.1	0.1	0.4	1.9	0.2	3.5	0.6	10.2
	Under 2,500	4.2	0.1	2.3	0.2	0.4	3.0	0.3	4.4	1.2	16.2
	2,500 and over	0.8	0.0	0.0	0.0	0.2	0.7	0.1	1.7	0.2	3.7
1986–90		**Numbers**									
	Under 1,000	32	1	467	6	7	31	4	34	54	636
	1,000–1,499	93	4	261	4	16	57	9	153	59	656
	1,500–1,999	221	2	69	8	11	105	11	318	61	806
	2,000–2,499	389	4	17	8	41	207	26	564	75	1,331
	Under 2,500	735	11	814	26	75	400	50	1,069	249	3,429
	2,500 and over	1,627	15	27	94	395	1,349	189	4,923	517	9,136
		Rates per thousand live births									
	Under 1,000	2.9	0.1	41.8	0.5	0.6	2.8	0.4	3.0	4.8	56.9
	1,000–1,499	4.4	0.2	12.4	0.2	0.8	2.7	0.4	7.3	2.8	31.3
	1,500–1,999	4.9	0.0	1.5	0.2	0.2	2.4	0.2	7.1	1.4	18.0
	2,000–2,499	2.6	0.0	0.1	0.1	0.3	1.4	0.2	3.7	0.5	8.7
	Under 2,500	3.2	0.0	3.6	0.1	0.3	1.7	0.2	4.7	1.1	15.0
	2,500 and over	0.5	0.0	0.0	0.0	0.1	0.4	0.1	1.6	0.2	2.9

A6.2.3 continued

Postneonatal deaths by ONS cause group and birthweight, England and Wales, 1981–85, 1986–90, 1991–95

Year of birth / Birthweight, g	ONS cause group									All
	1	2	3	4	5	6	7	9	0	
1991–95	**Numbers**									
Under 1,000	53	0	456	8	5	110	11	13	111	767
1,000–1,499	89	1	148	4	9	79	6	64	55	455
1,500–1,999	156	2	26	4	17	71	10	124	58	468
2,000–2,499	289	7	13	6	30	113	19	261	91	829
Under 2,500	587	10	643	22	61	373	46	462	315	2,519
2,500 and over	1,139	12	24	46	277	649	158	1,620	473	4,398
	Rates per thousand live births									
Under 1,000	4.1	–	35.1	0.6	0.4	8.5	0.8	1.0	8.5	59.1
1,000–1,499	4.1	0.0	6.8	0.2	0.4	3.6	0.3	2.9	2.5	21.0
1,500–1,999	3.4	0.0	0.6	0.1	0.4	1.6	0.2	2.7	1.3	10.2
2,000–2,499	2.0	0.0	0.1	0.0	0.2	0.8	0.1	1.8	0.6	5.6
Under 2,500	2.6	0.0	2.8	0.1	0.3	1.6	0.2	2.0	1.4	11.0
2,500 and over	0.4	0.0	0.0	0.0	0.1	0.2	0.1	0.5	0.2	1.4

For descriptions of ONS cause groups, see Table A3.9.3

Source: Authors' analysis of ONS/OPCS data

Data extract: live births 1993 (7/94), 1994 (7/95), 1995 (3/7/96), 1996 (8/4/97)
linked 1993 (3/4/96), 1994 (18/9/96), 1995 (3/11/97)

This is a new table for this edition of *Birth counts*

A6.2.4

Infant deaths by ONS cause group and birthweight, England and Wales, 1981–85, 1986–90, 1991–95

Year of birth	Birthweight, g	ONS cause group									All
		1	2	3	4	5	6	7	9	0	
1981–85		**Numbers**									
	Under 1,000	236	21	3,556	373	9	176	55	31	655	5,112
	1,000–1,499	680	12	1,797	315	14	243	61	136	176	3,434
	1,500–1,999	981	13	602	235	20	263	83	227	132	2,556
	2,000–2,499	1,435	24	285	295	64	357	95	463	145	3,163
	Under 2,500	3,332	70	6,240	1,218	107	1,039	294	857	1,108	14,265
	2,500 and over	5,011	42	406	1,319	512	2,361	414	4,723	776	15,564
		Rates per thousand live births									
	Under 1,000	31.0	2.8	467.0	49.0	1.2	23.1	7.2	4.1	86.0	671.3
	1,000–1,499	42.5	0.8	112.3	19.7	0.9	15.2	3.8	8.5	11.0	214.7
	1,500–1,999	27.7	0.4	17.0	6.6	0.6	7.4	2.3	6.4	3.7	72.2
	2,000–2,499	11.2	0.2	2.2	2.3	0.5	2.8	0.7	3.6	1.1	24.7
	Under 2,500	17.8	0.4	33.3	6.5	0.6	5.5	1.6	4.6	5.9	76.2
	2,500 and over	1.9	0.0	0.2	0.5	0.2	0.9	0.2	1.8	0.3	6.0
1986–90		**Numbers**									
	Under 1,000	470	43	4,945	202	10	84	23	35	122	5,934
	1,000–1,499	782	26	1,736	173	18	162	38	156	102	3,193
	1,500–1,999	1,015	15	475	147	14	176	35	321	81	2,279
	2,000–2,499	1,206	15	160	189	50	283	52	591	96	2,642
	Under 2,500	3,473	99	7,316	711	92	705	148	1,103	401	14,048
	2,500 and over	4,175	54	354	1,207	437	1,624	267	5,225	619	13,962
		Rates per thousand live births									
	Under 1,000	42.1	3.8	442.7	18.1	0.9	7.5	2.1	3.1	10.9	531.3
	1,000–1,499	37.3	1.2	82.8	8.2	0.9	7.7	1.8	7.4	4.9	152.2
	1,500–1,999	22.7	0.3	10.6	3.3	0.3	3.9	0.8	7.2	1.8	51.0
	2,000–2,499	7.9	0.1	1.1	1.2	0.3	1.9	0.3	3.9	0.6	17.4
	Under 2,500	15.2	0.4	32.0	3.1	0.4	3.1	0.6	4.8	1.8	61.4
	2,500 and over	1.3	0.0	0.1	0.4	0.1	0.5	0.1	1.7	0.2	4.4

A6.2.4 *continued*

Infant deaths by ONS cause group and birthweight, England and Wales, 1981-85, 1986-90, 1991-95

Year of birth	Birthweight, g	ONS cause group									All
		1	2	3	4	5	6	7	9	0	
1991-95		**Numbers**									
	Under 1,000	483	39	4,833	193	5	200	42	13	228	6,036
	1,000-1,499	530	18	992	134	10	153	26	65	112	2,040
	1,500-1,999	640	10	230	124	19	114	25	131	83	1,376
	2,000-2,499	796	18	99	163	34	177	37	292	130	1,746
	Under 2,500	2,449	85	6,154	614	68	644	130	501	553	11,198
	2,500 and over	2,813	45	410	967	305	852	235	1,809	593	8,029
		Rates per thousand live births									
	Under 1,000	37.2	3.0	372.2	14.9	0.4	15.4	3.2	1.0	17.6	464.9
	1,000-1,499	24.4	0.8	45.7	6.2	0.5	7.0	1.2	3.0	5.2	94.0
	1,500-1,999	14.0	0.2	5.0	2.7	0.4	2.5	0.5	2.9	1.8	30.1
	2,000-2,499	5.4	0.1	0.7	1.1	0.2	1.2	0.3	2.0	0.9	11.8
	Under 2,500	10.7	0.4	27.0	2.7	0.3	2.8	0.6	2.2	2.4	49.1
	2,500 and over	0.9	0.0	0.1	0.3	0.1	0.3	0.1	0.6	0.2	2.6

For descriptions of ONS cause groups, see Table A3.9.4

Source: Authors' analysis of ONS/OPCS data

Data extract: live births 1993 (7/94), 1994 (7/95), 1995 (3/7/96), 1996 (8/4/97)

linked 1993 (3/4/96), 1994 (18/9/96), 1995 (3/11/97)

This is similar to Table A6.6 in the first edition of *Birth counts*

A6.3.1

Deliveries in NHS hospitals by multiplicity and gestational age, England, 1994/95

Gestational age, weeks	Estimated numbers				Percentage of maternities			
	All	Singleton	Twin	Triplet and higher order	All	Singleton	Twin	Triplet and higher order
All	604,300	596,100	7,900	260	100.0	100.0	100.0	100
Under 20	50	50	0	0	0.0	0.0	0.0	0
20–23	400	400	30	10	0.1	0.1	0.4	4
24–27	2,300	2,000	220	20	0.4	0.3	2.8	8
28–31	4,900	4,300	500	40	0.8	0.7	6.3	15
32–36	33,200	30,200	2,900	140	5.5	5.1	36.7	54
All under 37	40,850	36,950	3,650	210	6.8	6.2	46.2	81
37–41	530,300	525,800	4,200	50	87.8	88.2	53.2	19
42 or over	33,300	33,300	30	0	5.5	5.6	0.4	0

Source: Maternity Hospital Episode Statistics, Department of Health *Statistical bulletin 1997/28, Table 22*

This is a new table for this edition of *Birth counts*

A6.4.1

Median birthweight of singleton, twin and higher order multiple NHS hospital deliveries by gestational age, England, 1994/95

Gestational age, weeks	Singleton deliveries			Multiple deliveries	
	Median birthweight, g	Birthweight range, g		Median birthweight of first baby, g	
		5th percentile	95th percentile	Twins	Triplets
All	3,380	2,390	4,230	2,500	1,930
Under 20	3,200	260	3,950	–	–
20	540	270	3,920	–	–
21	400	210	1,550	–	–
22	510	300	1,470	–	–
23	600	430	3,060	–	–
24	670	300	1,500	650	–
25	750	350	2,090	800	–
26	850	410	2,010	860	–
27	970	500	1,700	980	–
28	1,100	540	2,210	1,110	–
29	1,280	720	2,390	1,250	–
30	1,450	890	2,920	1,420	–
31	1,620	1,010	2,760	1,590	–
32	1,820	1,160	2,890	1,750	–
33	2,050	1,340	2,850	1,900	–
34	2,280	1,550	3,060	2,140	1,790
35	2,500	1,770	3,320	2,260	2,200
36	2,720	1,960	3,550	2,430	–
37	2,960	2,230	3,770	2,620	–
38	3,170	2,450	3,940	2,780	–
39	3,320	2,620	4,080	2,920	–
40	3,480	2,780	4,250	2,960	–
41	3,600	2,900	4,390	3,140	–
42	3,670	2,920	4,470	–	–
43	3,570	2,740	4,400	–	–
44 or over	3,530	2,720	4,390	–	–

Source: Maternity Hospital Episode Statistics, Department of Health *Statistical bulletin 1997/28, Table 24*

This is a new table for this edition of *Birth counts*

A6.5.1

Live births by birthweight, gestational age and multiplicity, Scotland, 1996/7

Birthweight, g	Gestational age, weeks							
	All	Less than 24	24–27	28–31	32–36	37–41	42 and over	Not known
All live births **Numbers**								
All	57,143	23	159	500	3,372	50,833	2,240	16
Under 500	14	8	5	0	0	1	0	0
500–999	189	13	119	53	4	0	0	0
1,000–1,499	398	1	32	263	99	3	0	0
1,500–1,999	846	0	1	154	584	107	0	0
2,000–2,499	2,450	0	0	21	1,163	1,255	8	3
2,500–2,999	9,029	0	0	3	1,081	7,837	107	1
3,000–3,499	20,026	1	0	3	346	19,067	600	9
3,500–3,999	17,274	0	0	1	83	16,244	944	2
4,000–4,499	5,866	0	0	1	9	5,381	474	1
4,500 and over	1,046	0	0	0	2	937	107	0
Not known	5	0	2	1	1	1	0	0
Percentage of live births with stated birthweight								
Under 1,500	1.1	95.7	99.4	63.3	3.1	0.0	0.0	0.0
Under 2,500	6.8	95.7	100.0	98.4	54.9	2.7	0.4	18.8
Singleton live births **Numbers**								
All	55,632	17	125	356	2,723	50,155	2,240	16
Under 500	8	4	3	0	0	1	0	0
500–999	148	11	93	41	3	0	0	0
1,000–1,499	272	1	26	175	68	2	0	0
1,500–1,999	593	0	1	116	391	85	0	0
2,000–2,499	2,024	0	0	17	891	1,105	8	3
2,500–2,999	8,570	0	0	3	957	7,502	107	1
3,000–3,499	19,845	1	0	1	318	18,916	600	9
3,500–3,999	17,255	0	0	1	83	16,225	944	2

A6.5.1 continued

Live births by birthweight, gestational age and multiplicity, Scotland, 1996/7

Birthweight, g	Gestational age, weeks							
	All	Less than 24	24–27	28–31	32–36	37–41	42 and over	Not known
4,000–4,499	5,866	0	0	1	9	5,381	474	1
4,500 and over	1,046	0	0	0	2	937	107	0
Not known	5	0	2	1	1	1	0	0
Percentage of live births with stated birthweight								
Under 1,500	0.8	94.1	99.2	60.8	2.6	0.0	0.0	0.0
Under 2,500	5.5	94.1	100.0	98.3	49.7	2.4	0.4	18.8
Multiple live births								
Numbers								
All	1,511	6	34	144	649	678	0	0
Under 500	6	4	2	0	0	0	0	0
500–999	41	2	26	12	1	0	0	0
1,000–1,499	126	0	6	88	31	1	0	0
1,500–1,999	253	0	0	38	193	22	0	0
2,000–2,499	426	0	0	4	272	150	0	0
2,500–2,999	459	0	0	0	124	335	0	0
3,000–3,499	181	0	0	2	28	151	0	0
3,500–3,999	19	0	0	0	0	19	0	0
4,000–4,499	0	0	0	0	0	0	0	0
4,500 and over	0	0	0	0	0	0	0	0
Not known	0	0	0	0	0	0	0	0
Percentage of live births with stated birthweight								
Under 1,500	11.4	100.0	100.0	69.4	4.9	0.1	–	–
Under 2,500	56.4	100.0	100.0	98.6	76.6	25.5	–	–

The data in this table are for the year ending 31 March 1997

Source: ISD, *Scottish health statistics 1997, Table 1.8*

This is similar to Table A6.9 in the first edition of *Birth counts*

A6.6.1

Live births, stillbirths and infant deaths by sex, England and Wales, 1928–98

Year	Live births Numbers		Stillbirths Numbers		Infant deaths Numbers		Stillbirths Rate*		Infant deaths Rate#	
	Males	Females	Males	Females	Male	Female	Males	Females	Male	Female
1928	337,182	323,085	15,099	12,481	22,422	16,490	42.9	37.2	66.5	51.0
1929	328,642	315,031	14,961	11,886	24,685	18,625	43.5	36.4	75.1	59.1
1930	331,380	317,431	15,241	12,336	20,478	14,923	44.0	37.4	61.8	47.0
1931	323,565	308,516	14,951	11,982	24,332	17,607	44.2	37.4	75.2	57.1
1932	314,407	299,565	14,523	11,948	23,075	16,858	44.2	38.4	73.4	56.3
1933	296,729	283,684	13,576	11,508	21,311	15,649	43.8	39.0	71.8	55.2
1934	306,874	290,768	13,690	11,519	20,061	14,956	42.7	38.1	65.4	51.4
1935	307,552	291,204	13,790	11,645	19,654	14,438	42.9	38.5	63.9	49.6
1936	310,605	294,687	13,639	11,406	20,562	14,863	42.1	37.3	66.2	50.4
1937	313,618	296,939	13,479	11,327	20,281	14,894	41.2	36.7	64.7	50.2
1938	318,387	302,817	13,349	11,380	18,945	13,779	40.2	36.2	59.5	45.5
1939	315,606	298,873	13,088	11,232	17,870	13,320	39.8	36.2	56.6	44.6
1940	302,615	287,505	12,296	10,483	19,700	14,199	39.1	35.2	65.1	49.4
1941	297,054	282,037	11,268	9,608	19,912	14,638	36.6	32.9	67.0	51.9
1942	335,760	315,743	11,868	10,515	18,573	13,685	34.1	32.2	55.3	43.3
1943	352,798	331,536	11,469	9,793	19,192	14,239	31.5	28.7	54.4	42.9
1944	387,638	363,840	11,493	9,813	19,162	14,293	28.8	26.3	49.4	39.3
1945	350,072	329,865	10,367	8,966	18,387	13,572	28.8	26.5	52.5	41.1
1946	422,299	398,420	12,357	10,558	19,458	14,083	28.4	25.8	46.1	35.3
1947	453,590	427,436	11,792	10,003	21,225	15,624	25.3	22.9	46.8	36.6
1948	399,112	376,194	9,937	8,462	15,447	11,319	24.3	22.0	38.7	30.1
1949	376,064	354,454	9,129	7,818	13,854	10,028	23.7	21.6	36.8	28.3
1950	358,715	338,382	8,693	7,391	12,058	8,759	23.7	21.4	33.6	25.9
1951	348,604	328,925	8,669	7,316	11,773	8,450	24.3	21.8	33.8	25.7
1952	345,878	327,857	8,368	7,268	10,663	7,892	23.6	21.7	30.8	24.1
1953	352,037	332,335	8,311	7,370	10,487	7,837	23.1	21.7	29.8	23.6
1954	346,455	327,196	8,467	7,733	9,955	7,205	23.9	23.1	28.7	22.0
1955	343,673	324,138	8,303	7,526	9,653	6,960	23.6	22.7	28.1	21.5
1956	359,881	340,454	8,609	7,796	9,629	6,925	23.4	22.4	26.8	20.3
1957	372,298	351,083	8,613	8,002	9,591	7,129	22.6	22.3	25.8	20.3
1958	380,944	359,771	8,486	7,802	9,634	7,051	21.8	21.2	25.3	19.6
1959	385,689	362,812	8,242	7,659	9,454	7,175	20.9	20.7	24.5	19.8
1960	404,150	380,855	8,098	7,721	9,911	7,207	19.6	19.9	24.5	18.9
1961	417,768	393,513	8,076	7,651	9,987	7,406	19.0	19.1	23.9	18.8
1962	431,633	407,103	7,957	7,507	10,575	7,614	18.1	18.1	24.5	18.7
1963	438,476	415,579	7,884	7,105	10,401	7,641	17.7	16.8	23.7	18.4
1964	451,072	424,900	7,566	6,980	10,011	7,434	16.5	16.2	22.2	17.5

Live births, stillbirths and infant deaths by sex, England and Wales, 1928–98

Year	Live births Numbers		Stillbirths Numbers		Infant deaths Numbers		Stillbirths Rate*		Infant deaths Rate#	
	Males	Females	Males	Females	Male	Female	Males	Females	Male	Female
1965	443,190	419,535	7,200	6,641	9,518	6,877	16.0	15.6	21.5	16.4
1966	437,262	412,561	6,857	6,386	9,357	6,790	15.4	15.2	21.4	16.5
1967	427,901	404,263	6,520	6,008	8,673	6,593	15.0	14.6	20.3	16.3
1968	421,130	398,142	6,109	5,739	8,705	6,277	14.3	14.2	20.7	15.8
1969	410,052	387,486	5,620	5,034	8,331	6,060	13.5	12.8	20.3	15.6
1970	403,371	381,115	5,288	5,057	8,269	5,998	12.9	13.1	20.5	15.7
1971	403,223	379,932	5,036	4,863	7,974	5,746	12.3	12.6	19.8	15.1
1972	373,982	351,458	4,413	4,386	7,210	5,288	11.7	12.3	19.3	15.0
1973	348,678	327,275	4,036	3,900	6,599	4,808	11.4	11.8	18.9	14.7
1974	329,459	310,426	3,579	3,596	6,137	4,322	10.8	11.5	18.6	13.9
1975	310,751	292,694	3,115	3,180	5,430	4,058	9.9	10.8	17.5	13.9
1976	300,313	283,957	2,950	2,759	4,879	3,455	9.7	9.6	16.2	12.2
1977	292,957	276,302	2,813	2,592	4,519	3,322	9.5	9.3	15.4	12.0
1978	307,088	289,330	2,634	2,474	4,513	3,368	8.5	8.5	14.7	11.6
1979	328,308	309,720	2,656	2,469	4,731	3,447	8.0	7.9	14.4	11.1
1980	335,954	320,280	2,483	2,290	4,471	3,428	7.3	7.1	13.3	10.7
1981	325,711	308,781	2,186	2,021	4,119	2,902	6.7	6.5	12.6	9.4
1982	321,352	304,579	2,092	1,847	3,914	2,861	6.5	6.0	12.2	9.4
1983	323,192	305,942	1,960	1,671	3,654	2,727	6.0	5.4	11.3	8.9
1984	326,039	310,779	1,967	1,676	3,443	2,594	6.0	5.4	10.6	8.3
1985	336,835	319,582	1,983	1,662	3,510	2,631	5.9	5.2	10.4	8.2
1986	338,852	322,166	1,904	1,645	3,724	2,589	5.6	5.1	11.0	8.0
1987	349,624	331,887	1,869	1,554	3,637	2,635	5.3	4.7	10.4	7.9
1988	354,954	338,623	1,811	1,571	3,649	2,621	5.1	4.6	10.3	7.7
1989	352,381	335,344	1,762	1,474	3,368	2,440	5.0	4.4	9.6	7.3
1990	361,412	344,728	1,753	1,503	3,207	2,357	4.8	4.3	8.9	6.8
1991	358,407	340,810	1,725	1,529	2,966	2,192	4.8	4.5	8.3	6.4
1992	353,694	335,962	1,592	1,352	2,606	1,933	4.5	4.0	7.4	5.8
1993	345,835	327,632	2,076	1,779	2,407	1,835	6.0	5.4	7.0	5.6
1994	341,321	323,405	2,034	1,779	2,367	1,753	5.9	5.5	6.9	5.4
1995	332,188	315,950	1,912	1,688	2,305	1,677	5.7	5.3	6.9	5.3
1996	333,490	315,995	1,808	1,731	2,287	1,672	5.4	5.4	6.9	5.3
1997	329,577	313,518	1,801	1,638	2,160	1,665	5.4	5.2	6.6	5.3
1998	325,903	309,998	1,822	1,547	2,058	1,547	5.6	5.1	6.3	5.0

* Stillbirths per thousand total births. From 1993 onwards, stillbirths include those at 24–27 weeks of gestation.

Deaths per thousand live births

Source: ONS/OPCS *Birth statistics, Series FM1* and *Registrar General's Statistical Reviews*

A6.6.2

Stillbirth and infant death rates by sex, Scotland, 1946–98

Year	Stillbirth rate* 28 or more weeks of gestation		Stillbirth rate* 24 or more weeks of gestation		Neonatal mortality**		Postneonatal mortality**	
	Males	Females	Males	Females	Males	Females	Males	Females
1946–50	29.9	28.5	:	:	29.3	22.8	23.9	18.3
1951–55	25.8	25.1	:	:	23.5	17.8	13.3	11.0
1956–60	22.4	23.3	:	:	21.9	15.9	9.7	8.2
1961–65	18.6	19.6	:	:	19.6	14.3	8.7	7.3
1966–70	14.7	15.3	:	:	15.5	11.9	8.3	6.5
1971–75	12.0	12.5	:	:	14.4	10.8	6.6	5.6
1976–80	7.9	8.1	:	:	10.7	7.8	4.6	4.1
1981–85	6.3	5.3	:	:	6.8	5.9	4.9	3.3
1986–90	5.4	5.2	:	:	5.3	4.1	4.3	3.0
1991–95	5.3	4.5	6.4	5.5	4.8	3.6	2.6	2.1
1976	9.6	9.6	:	:	11.8	8.6	5.1	3.9
1977	7.6	10.0	:	:	13.0	9.5	5.3	4.3
1978	8.2	7.9	:	:	10.3	7.2	4.2	4.0
1979	7.2	6.6	:	:	9.7	7.6	4.5	4.1
1980	6.7	6.7	:	:	9.1	6.4	5.3	4.1
1981	6.5	6.0	:	:	7.1	6.7	4.7	3.6
1982	6.4	5.1	:	:	8.1	6.1	5.2	3.7
1983	6.3	5.2	:	:	6.1	5.5	4.7	3.0
1984	6.7	4.8	:	:	7.1	5.7	4.6	3.2
1985	5.7	5.2	:	:	5.5	5.5	4.3	3.2
1986	6.1	5.5	:	:	5.6	4.8	4.4	2.9
1987	4.6	5.6	:	:	5.3	4.1	4.2	3.1
1988	5.4	5.3	:	:	5.3	3.7	4.9	3.1
1989	5.7	4.3	:	:	4.7	4.1	4.1	2.6
1990	5.4	5.1	:	:	5.5	4.1	3.2	2.1
1991	5.9	5.1	:	:	5.5	3.2	2.4	2.0
1992	5.3	4.4	5.9	4.9	4.5	3.7	2.9	2.1
1993	5.3	4.2	7.1	5.7	4.4	3.5	2.4	2.0
1994	4.7	4.4	6.4	5.8	4.1	3.6	2.2	2.2
1995	5.3	4.4	7.0	6.2	4.3	3.9	2.5	2.2
1996	5.5	4.5	7.0	5.7	3.4	3.5	2.7	2.0
1997	4.0	4.2	5.3	5.3	4.0	2.9	2.2	1.6
1998	4.8	4.2	6.5	5.6		3.2		1.7

*   Stillbirths per thousand total births

** Deaths per thousand live births

Source: Data from Registrar General Scotland, cited in ISD, *Births in Scotland 1976–1995*, GRO Scotland, *Annual report*

This is a new table for this edition of *Birth counts*

A6.7.1

Infant mortality by sex and underlying cause of death, England and Wales, 1901–85

Year	All causes	Underlying causes grouped according to successive revisions of the International Classification of Diseases				
		Infections	Respiratory causes	Congenital anomalies	Perinatal causes	Other causes
	Deaths per thousand live births					
1901–10 Codes		**First revision of ICD** 1-8,13-29, 40-57,83	12,36-39,114-122	78	76,79-82	
Male	140.3	40.4	25.4	4.9	27.5	42.1
Female	114.3	35.2	20.0	4.0	22.0	33.1
All	127.5	37.8	22.7	4.5	24.8	37.7
1911–20 Codes		**Second revision of ICD** 1-9,11-12,14-25, 28-35,37-38,61A-B, 62,67,106-7,112, 121,164	10,86,87,89-95, 97-98,100A	150	151-152	
Male	111.7	27.8	22.9	4.3	38.9	17.9
Female	88.7	23.4	17.6	3.6	30.5	13.6
All	100.4	25.6	20.3	3.9	34.7	15.8
1921–30 Codes		**Third revision of ICD** 1-10,12-14,16-42, 72,76,115-6,121, 130,175	11, 97-104, 106-7,109(1)	159.0	160-62	
Male	73.0	7.5	18.6	5.0	31.3	10.7
Female	56.6	6.7	14.0	4.1	24.1	7.7
All	65.0	7.1	16.4	4.6	27.8	9.2
1931–39 Codes		**Fourth revision of ICD** 1-10,12-44,80, 83,177	11,104-111(1), 113-4,115(2-3)	157.0	158-61	
Male	66.3	10.4	13.5	6.4	28.6	7.4
Female	51.1	8.4	10.3	5.4	21.8	5.2
All	58.9	9.4	11.9	5.9	25.3	6.3
1940–49 Codes		**Fifth revision of ICD** 1-32,34-43,44c-d, 177	33,104-110, 111b-c,113-4, 115b-c	157.0	158-61	
Male	50.3	7.3	10.4	5.9	21.7	5.0
Female	39.1	5.7	8.2	5.1	16.3	3.7
All	44.9	6.5	9.3	5.5	19.1	4.4

A6.7.1 *continued*

Infant mortality by sex and underlying cause of death, England and Wales, 1901–85

Year	All causes	Underlying causes grouped according to successive revisions of the International Classification of Diseases				
		Infections	Respiratory causes	Congenital anomalies	Perinatal causes	Other causes
1950–57		**Sixth revision of ICD**				
Codes		1-138	470-527	750-759	760-776	
Male	29.6	1.6	3.9	4.6	16.6	2.9
Female	22.9	1.3	3.2	4.4	11.9	2.2
All	26.4	1.4	3.6	4.5	14.4	2.5
1958–67		**Seventh revision of ICD**				
Codes		1-138	470-527	750-759	760-776	
Male	23.1	0.7	3.1	4.3	12.8	2.2
Female	18.0	0.5	2.4	4.1	9.3	1.7
All	20.7	0.6	2.8	4.2	11.1	2.0
1968–78		**Eighth revision of ICD**				
Codes		1-7,10-136	460-519	740-759	760-776	
Male	18.6	0.7	2.9	3.8	8.6	2.5
Female	14.3	0.5	2.1	3.6	6.1	1.9
All	16.5	0.6	2.6	3.7	7.4	2.3
1979–85		**Ninth revision of ICD**				
Codes		1-7,10-136,	460-519	740-759	760-776	
Male	12.1	0.2	1.1	3.0	4.8	3.0
Female	9.4	0.2	0.8	2.7	3.5	2.2
All	10.8	0.2	1.0	2.9	4.2	2.6

In 1985, a new form of certificate was introduced for certifying neonatal deaths and a single 'underlying cause' could no longer be coded

See Volume 1 for a discussion of the extent to which the cause groups in this table can be compared over time.

Source: ONS *Twentieth century mortality files on CD-ROM*, ONS *Birth statistics, Series FM1*

This is a new table for this edition of *Birth counts*

A6.8.1

Stillbirths by sex and ONS cause group, England and Wales, 1981–85, 1986–90, 1991–95, 1993–96

Year of birth		ONS cause group										
		1	2	3	4	5	6	7	8A	8B	0	All
1981–85		**Numbers of stillbirths at 28 or more weeks of gestation**										
	Males	961	13	136	6,603	2	23	387	–	–	2,073	10,198
	Females	1,194	20	95	5,401	3	18	274	–	–	1,879	8,884
		Rates per thousand total births										
	Males	0.58	0.01	0.08	4.02	0.00	0.01	0.24	–	–	1.26	6.21
	Females	0.77	0.01	0.06	3.47	0.00	0.01	0.18	–	–	1.21	5.70
1986–90		**Numbers of stillbirths at 28 or more weeks of gestation**										
	Males	813	37	128	594	0	40	338	4,570	2,501	76	9,097
	Females	736	26	91	537	0	32	255	3,753	2,232	85	7,747
		Rates per thousand total births										
	Males	0.46	0.02	0.07	0.34	–	0.02	0.19	2.59	1.42	0.04	5.15
	Females	0.44	0.02	0.05	0.32	–	0.02	0.15	2.23	1.33	0.05	4.61
1991–95		**Numbers of stillbirths at 28 or more weeks of gestation**										
	Males	631	20	90	413	0	30	281	3,096	3,360	135	8,056
	Females	558	15	62	334	1	20	237	2,525	3,063	129	6,944
		Rates per thousand total births										
	Males	0.36	0.01	0.05	0.24	–	0.02	0.16	1.78	1.93	0.08	4.63
	Females	0.34	0.01	0.04	0.20	0.00	0.01	0.14	1.53	1.86	0.08	4.21
1993–96		**Numbers of stillbirths at 24 or more weeks of gestation**										
	Males	704	28	253	357	1	27	293	2,517	3,500	152	7,832
	Females	644	19	216	316	2	25	228	2,189	3,213	134	6,986
		Rates per thousand total births										
	Males	0.52	0.02	0.19	0.26	0.00	0.02	0.22	1.85	2.57	1.76	1.98
	Females	0.50	0.01	0.17	0.25	0.00	0.02	0.18	1.70	2.49	1.66	1.87

For description of ONS cause groups and data for all births and deaths see Table A3.9.1

Source: Authors' analysis of ONS/OPCS data

Data extract: live births 1993 (7/94), 1994 (7/95), 1995 (3/7/96), 1996 (8/4/97)
linked   1993 (3/4/96), 1994 (18/9/96), 1995 (3/11/97)

This was part of Table A6.10 in the first edition of *Birth counts*

411

A6.8.2

Neonatal deaths by sex and ONS cause group, England and Wales, 1981–85, 1986–90, 1991–95

Year of birth	ONS cause group									
	1	2	3	4	5	6	7	9	0	All
1981–85	**Numbers**									
Males	3,410	58	4,083	1,563	70	543	258	177	666	10,828
Females	2,631	38	2,782	1,147	54	395	207	121	509	7,884
	Rates per thousand live births									
Males	2.09	0.04	2.50	0.96	0.04	0.33	0.16	0.11	0.41	6.63
Females	1.70	0.02	1.80	0.74	0.03	0.25	0.13	0.08	0.33	5.09
1986–90	**Numbers**									
Males	3,190	81	4,417	1,098	38	342	106	214	146	9,632
Females	2,463	54	2,954	879	32	261	89	132	135	6,999
	Rates per thousand live births									
Males	1.82	0.05	2.51	0.62	0.02	0.19	0.06	0.12	0.08	5.48
Females	1.47	0.03	1.77	0.53	0.02	0.16	0.05	0.08	0.08	4.18
1991–95	**Numbers**									
Males	2,244	65	3,999	967	24	284	95	129	228	8,035
Females	1,818	59	2,765	778	22	228	77	110	163	6,020
	Rates per thousand live births									
Males	1.30	0.04	0.39	0.35	0.30	0.25	0.21	0.16	0.13	0.11
Females	1.11	0.04	0.35	0.32	0.29	0.26	0.22	0.19	0.10	0.16

For description of ONS cause groups and data for all deaths, see Table A3.9.2
Source: Authors' analysis of ONS/OPCS data

Data extract: live births 1993 (7/94), 1994 (7/95), 1995 (3/7/96), 1996 (8/4/97)
linked 1993 (3/4/96), 1994 (18/9/96), 1995 (3/11/97)

This is similar to Table A6.10 in the first edition of *Birth counts*

A6.8.3

Postneonatal deaths by sex and ONS cause group, England and Wales, 1981–85, 1986–90, 1991–95

Year of birth		ONS cause group									
		1	2	3	4	5	6	7	9	0	All
1981–85		**Numbers**									
	Males	1,490	11	306	69	318	1,513	147	3,260	464	7,578
	Females	1,399	8	186	47	217	1,062	145	2,119	358	5,541
		Rates per thousand live births									
	Males	0.91	0.01	0.19	0.04	0.19	0.93	0.09	2.00	0.28	4.64
	Females	0.90	0.01	0.12	0.03	0.14	0.69	0.09	1.37	0.23	3.58
1986–90		**Numbers**									
	Males	1,244	17	511	75	282	1,057	130	3,727	457	7,500
	Females	1,163	9	351	51	196	719	117	2,355	322	5,283
		Rates per thousand live births									
	Males	0.71	0.01	0.29	0.04	0.16	0.60	0.07	2.12	0.26	4.27
	Females	0.70	0.01	0.21	0.03	0.12	0.43	0.07	1.41	0.19	3.16
1991–95		**Numbers**									
	Males	946	14	426	37	189	625	114	1,349	453	4,153
	Females	836	8	286	36	162	441	101	800	349	3,019
		Rates per thousand live births									
	Males	0.55	0.01	0.25	0.02	0.11	0.36	0.07	0.78	0.26	2.40
	Females	0.51	0.00	0.17	0.02	0.10	0.27	0.06	0.49	0.21	1.84

For description of ONS cause groups and data for all deaths, see Table A3.9.3

Source: Authors' analysis of ONS/OPCS data

Data extract: live births 1993 (7/94), 1994 (7/95), 1995 (3/7/96), 1996 (8/4/97)
linked 1993 (3/4/96), 1994 (18/9/96), 1995 (3/11/97)

This is similar to Table A6.10 in the first edition of *Birth counts*

A6.8.4

Infant deaths by sex and ONS cause group, England and Wales, 1981–85, 1986–90, 1991–95

Year of birth		ONS cause group										
		1	2	3	4	5	6	7	9	0	All
1981–85		**Numbers**										
	Males	4,900	69	4,389	1,632	388	2,056	405	3,437	1,130	18,406
	Females	4,030	46	2,968	1,194	271	1,457	352	2,240	867	13,425
		Rates per thousand live births										
	Males	3.00	0.04	2.69	1.00	0.24	1.26	0.25	2.10	0.69	11.27
	Females	2.60	0.03	1.92	0.77	0.17	0.94	0.23	1.45	0.56	8.66
1986–90		**Numbers**										
	Males	4,434	98	4,928	1,173	320	1,399	236	3,941	603	17,132
	Females	3,626	63	3,305	930	228	980	206	2,487	457	12,282
		Rates per thousand live births										
	Males	2.52	0.06	2.80	0.67	0.18	0.80	0.13	2.24	0.34	9.75
	Females	2.17	0.04	1.98	0.56	0.14	0.59	0.12	1.49	0.27	7.34
1991–95		**Numbers**										
	Males	3,190	79	4,425	1,004	213	909	209	1,478	681	12,188
	Females	2,654	67	3,051	814	184	669	178	910	512	9,039
		Rates per thousand live births										
	Males	1.84	0.05	2.56	0.58	0.12	0.53	0.12	0.85	0.39	7.04
	Females	1.62	0.04	1.86	0.50	0.11	0.41	0.11	0.55	0.31	5.50

For description of ONS cause groups and data for all deaths, see Table A3.9.4

Source: Authors' analysis of ONS/OPCS data

Data extract: live births 1993 (7/94), 1994 (7/95), 1995 (3/7/96), 1996 (8/4/97)

linked 1993 (3/4/96), 1994 (18/9/96), 1995 (3/11/97)

This was part of Table A6.10 in the first edition of *Birth counts*

A6.9.1

Live births by sex and birthweight, England and Wales, 1982–98

Year of birth	Birthweight, g													All birthweights
	Under 1,000	1,000–1,499	Under 1,500	1,500–1,999	2,000–2,499	Under 2,500	2,500–2,999	3,000–3,499	3,500–3,999	4,000–4,499	4,500 and over	All stated	Not stated	
Numbers														
Males														
1982	748	1,695	2,443	3,779	12,589	18,811	49,509	113,235	92,433	28,646	4,600	307,234	14,118	321,352
1983	834	1,878	2,712	3,884	13,189	19,785	51,706	118,867	97,090	30,420	4,855	322,723	469	323,192
1984	936	1,934	2,870	4,087	13,233	20,190	51,097	119,367	99,116	30,756	5,072	325,598	441	326,039
1985	947	2,006	2,953	4,177	13,779	20,909	52,957	122,911	101,991	32,280	5,312	336,360	475	336,835
1986	1,098	2,084	3,182	4,406	14,008	21,596	52,944	122,696	102,735	33,120	5,434	338,525	327	338,852
1987	1,066	2,285	3,351	4,540	14,215	22,106	53,199	125,578	107,092	35,422	5,957	349,354	270	349,624
1988	1,092	2,277	3,369	4,529	13,974	21,872	52,054	125,944	110,579	37,541	6,518	354,508	446	354,954
1989	1,234	2,120	3,354	4,392	13,714	21,460	50,588	120,604	106,078	36,339	6,493	341,562	10,819	352,381
1990	1,149	2,104	3,253	4,450	14,092	21,795	51,794	121,511	107,794	37,611	6,685	347,190	14,222	361,412
1991	1,172	2,151	3,323	4,520	14,051	21,894	50,213	120,591	107,908	37,716	6,832	345,154	13,253	358,407
1992	1,225	2,209	3,434	4,187	13,578	21,199	49,006	116,460	107,275	39,116	7,255	340,311	13,383	353,694
1993	1,283	2,200	3,483	4,427	13,430	21,340	47,071	114,012	105,034	38,603	7,369	333,429	11,259	344,688
1994	1,467	2,299	3,766	4,594	13,308	21,668	47,409	112,870	104,604	38,475	7,370	332,396	8,692	341,088
1995	1,469	2,376	3,845	4,782	14,029	22,656	48,393	113,513	102,412	37,225	6,844	331,043	1,105	332,148
1996	1,570	2,429	3,999	4,631	13,728	22,358	48,146	113,206	104,081	37,628	7,259	332,678	813	333,491
1997	1,482	2,514	3,996	4,850	13,779	22,625	48,065	111,918		145,919*		328,527	545	329,072
1998	1,503	2,376	3,879	4,691	14,021	22,591	47,473	110,190		145,247*		325,501	402	325,903
Females														
1982	694	1,635	2,329	3,750	15,043	21,122	63,119	118,355	70,902	15,907	1,940	291,345	13,234	304,579
1983	882	1,712	2,594	4,033	15,677	22,304	65,230	124,131	74,882	17,004	1,995	305,546	396	305,942
1984	938	1,746	2,684	4,058	15,699	22,441	66,104	125,651	76,793	17,236	2,183	310,408	371	310,779
1985	975	1,972	2,947	4,379	16,429	23,755	67,506	128,742	78,655	18,247	2,284	319,189	393	319,582
1986	967	1,932	2,899	4,488	16,745	24,132	66,866	129,339	80,379	18,722	2,431	321,869	297	322,166
1987	1,077	2,077	3,154	4,526	16,743	24,423	67,497	133,080	83,965	20,060	2,630	331,655	232	331,887
1988	1,117	2,025	3,142	4,460	16,207	23,809	66,754	134,988	88,014	21,758	2,915	338,238	385	338,623
1989	1,204	1,989	3,193	4,393	15,932	23,518	64,477	128,774	84,494	20,887	2,900	325,050	10,294	335,344
1990	1,165	2,082	3,247	4,474	16,539	24,260	64,960	131,177	85,948	21,828	3,011	331,184	13,544	344,728
1991	1,131	2,020	3,151	4,611	16,713	24,475	63,600	129,138	85,622	22,148	3,162	328,145	12,665	340,810
1992	1,185	2,023	3,208	4,506	15,918	23,632	61,588	125,940	86,118	22,835	3,295	323,408	12,554	335,962
1993	1,254	1,976	3,230	4,609	15,282	23,121	59,870	121,550	85,020	22,929	3,409	315,899	10,637	326,536
1994	1,388	2,130	3,518	4,551	15,444	23,513	59,700	121,380	84,316	22,724	3,351	314,984	8,184	323,168

415

A6.9.1 continued

Live births by sex and birthweight, England and Wales, 1982–98

Year of birth	Birthweight, g											All stated	Not stated	All birthweights
	Under 1,000	1,000–1,499	Under 1,500	1,500–1,999	2,000–2,499	Under 2,500	2,500–2,999	3,000–3,499	3,500–3,999	4,000–4,499	4,500 and over			
1995	1,410	2,328	3,738	4,897	16,033	24,668	61,043	121,239	82,710	21,870	3,211	314,741	1,112	315,853
1996	1,580	2,341	3,921	4,774	16,134	24,829	60,907	121,104	82,928	22,224	3,281	315,273	725	315,998
1997	1,544	2,333	3,877	4,983	16,257	25,117	60,354	119,512		107,482*		312,465	556	313,021
1998	1,545	2,316	3,861	4,814	16,244	24,919	59,414	117,788		107,494*		309,615	383	309,998

Percentages of all live births with stated birthweight

Males

Year of birth	Under 1,000	1,000–1,499	Under 1,500	1,500–1,999	2,000–2,499	Under 2,500	2,500–2,999	3,000–3,499	3,500–3,999	4,000–4,499	4,500 and over	All stated	Not stated
1982	0.2	0.6	0.8	1.2	4.1	6.1	16.1	36.9	30.1	9.3	1.5	100.0	4.4
1983	0.3	0.6	0.8	1.2	4.1	6.1	16.0	36.8	30.1	9.4	1.5	100.0	0.1
1984	0.3	0.6	0.9	1.3	4.1	6.2	15.7	36.7	30.4	9.4	1.6	100.0	0.1
1985	0.3	0.6	0.9	1.2	4.1	6.2	15.7	36.5	30.3	9.6	1.6	100.0	0.1
1986	0.3	0.6	0.9	1.3	4.1	6.4	15.6	36.2	30.3	9.8	1.6	100.0	0.1
1987	0.3	0.7	1.0	1.3	4.1	6.3	15.2	35.9	30.7	10.1	1.7	100.0	0.1
1988	0.3	0.6	1.0	1.3	3.9	6.2	14.7	35.5	31.2	10.6	1.8	100.0	0.1
1989	0.4	0.6	1.0	1.3	4.0	6.3	14.8	35.3	31.1	10.6	1.9	100.0	3.1
1990	0.3	0.6	0.9	1.3	4.1	6.3	14.9	35.0	31.0	10.8	1.9	100.0	3.9
1991	0.3	0.6	1.0	1.3	4.1	6.3	14.5	34.9	31.3	10.9	2.0	100.0	3.7
1992	0.4	0.6	1.0	1.2	4.0	6.2	14.4	34.2	31.5	11.5	2.1	100.0	3.8
1993	0.4	0.7	1.0	1.3	4.0	6.4	14.1	34.2	31.5	11.6	2.2	100.0	3.3
1994	0.4	0.7	1.1	1.4	4.0	6.5	14.3	34.0	31.5	11.6	2.2	100.0	2.5
1995	0.4	0.7	1.2	1.4	4.2	6.8	14.6	34.3	30.9	11.2	2.1	100.0	0.3
1996	0.5	0.7	1.2	1.4	4.1	6.7	14.5	34.0	31.3	11.3	2.2	100.0	0.2
1997	0.4	0.8	1.2	1.5	4.2	6.9	14.6	34.1		44.3*		100.0	0.2
1998	0.5	0.7	1.2	1.4	4.3	6.9	14.6	33.9		44.6*		100.0	0.1

Females

Year of birth	Under 1,000	1,000–1,499	Under 1,500	1,500–1,999	2,000–2,499	Under 2,500	2,500–2,999	3,000–3,499	3,500–3,999	4,000–4,499	4,500 and over	All stated	Not stated
1982	0.2	0.6	0.8	1.3	5.2	7.2	21.7	40.6	24.3	5.5	0.7	100.0	4.3
1983	0.3	0.6	0.8	1.3	5.1	7.3	21.3	40.6	24.5	5.6	0.7	100.0	0.1
1984	0.3	0.6	0.9	1.3	5.1	7.2	21.3	40.5	24.7	5.6	0.7	100.0	0.1
1985	0.3	0.6	0.9	1.4	5.1	7.4	21.1	40.3	24.6	5.7	0.7	100.0	0.1

Live births by sex and birthweight, England and Wales, 1982–98

Year of birth	Birthweight, g											All stated	All birthweights Not stated
	Under 1,000	1,000–1,499	Under 1,500	1,500–1,999	2,000–2,499	Under 2,500	2,500–2,999	3,000–3,499	3,500–3,999	4,000–4,499	4,500 and over		
1986	0.3	0.6	0.9	1.4	5.2	7.5	20.8	40.2	25.0	5.8	0.8	100.0	0.1
1987	0.3	0.6	1.0	1.4	5.0	7.4	20.4	40.1	25.3	6.0	0.8	100.0	0.1
1988	0.3	0.6	0.9	1.3	4.8	7.0	19.7	39.9	26.0	6.4	0.9	100.0	0.1
1989	0.4	0.6	1.0	1.4	4.9	7.2	19.8	39.6	26.0	6.4	0.9	100.0	3.1
1990	0.4	0.6	1.0	1.4	5.0	7.3	19.6	39.6	26.0	6.6	0.9	100.0	3.9
1991	0.3	0.6	1.0	1.4	5.1	7.5	19.4	39.4	26.1	6.7	1.0	100.0	3.7
1992	0.4	0.6	1.0	1.4	4.9	7.3	19.0	38.9	26.6	7.1	1.0	100.0	3.7
1993	0.4	0.6	1.0	1.5	4.8	7.3	19.0	38.5	26.9	7.3	1.1	100.0	3.3
1994	0.4	0.7	1.1	1.4	4.9	7.5	19.0	38.5	26.8	7.2	1.1	100.0	2.5
1995	0.4	0.7	1.2	1.6	5.1	7.8	19.4	38.5	26.3	6.9	1.0	100.0	0.4
1996	0.5	0.7	1.2	1.5	5.1	7.9	19.3	38.4	26.3	7.0	1.0	100.0	0.2
1997	0.5	0.7	1.2	1.6	5.2	8.0	19.3	38.2		34.3*		100.0	0.2
1998	0.5	0.7	1.2	1.6	5.2	8.0	19.2	38.0		34.7*		100.0	0.1

* 3,500g and over

Data for all live births are in Table A3.4.2

Source: Authors' analysis of ONS/OPCS data

Data extract: live births 1993 (7/94), 1994 (7/95), 1995 (3/7/96), 1996 (8/4/97)

1997 and 1998 from VS5 tabulations. Data for 1997 have not been revised to include the 1,002 live births initially omitted from published data.

This is a new table for this edition of *Birth counts*

A6.9.2

Stillbirths by sex and birthweight, England and Wales, 1982–98

Numbers of stillbirths at 28 or more weeks of gestation

Year of birth	Birthweight, g											All stated	Not stated	All birthweights
	Under 1,000	1,000–1,499	Under 1,500	1,500–1,999	2,000–2,499	Under 2,500	2,500–2,999	3,000–3,499	3,500–3,999	4,000–4,499	4,500 and over			
Males														
1982	220	334	554	328	288	1,170	270	251	100	47	28	1,866	229	2,095
1983	230	354	584	327	316	1,227	289	221	121	57	15	1,930	31	1,961
1984	248	318	566	318	340	1,224	281	231	138	43	18	1,935	36	1,971
1985	249	320	569	328	317	1,214	298	258	102	65	14	1,951	34	1,985
1986	249	335	584	262	329	1,175	286	242	120	43	22	1,888	16	1,904
1987	249	311	560	326	272	1,158	299	205	121	36	28	1,847	22	1,869
1988	201	306	507	309	275	1,091	268	233	131	54	22	1,799	12	1,811
1989	199	251	450	302	296	1,048	267	200	115	41	21	1,692	68	1,760
1990	205	278	483	284	256	1,023	248	232	115	37	19	1,674	79	1,753
1991	186	267	453	269	263	985	268	194	123	36	27	1,633	92	1,725
1992	244	229	473	276	231	980	233	222	134	34	27	1,630	82	1,712
1993	195	230	425	223	232	880	232	181	111	48	24	1,476	114	1,590
1994	221	224	445	191	224	860	223	219	114	56	15	1,487	78	1,565
1995	175	210	385	216	219	820	232	213	109	38	20	1,432	32	1,464
1996	182	195	377	191	206	774	221	177	103	28	15	1,318	20	1,338
Females														
1982	220	284	504	240	270	1,014	288	204	98	20	11	1,635	213	1,848
1983	242	288	530	260	249	1,039	288	204	96	17	6	1,650	21	1,671
1984	242	294	536	215	275	1,026	282	196	99	29	14	1,646	33	1,679
1985	250	260	510	256	258	1,024	278	214	87	19	16	1,638	27	1,665
1986	248	286	534	238	260	1,032	244	224	93	26	14	1,633	11	1,644
1987	212	255	467	253	223	943	254	202	97	34	11	1,541	11	1,552
1988	212	239	451	232	250	933	257	227	110	30	9	1,566	8	1,574
1989	192	198	390	200	225	815	239	223	102	25	14	1,418	53	1,471
1990	181	233	414	260	209	883	207	210	100	24	9	1,433	73	1,506
1991	181	225	406	240	213	859	232	226	96	32	13	1,458	72	1,530
1992	278	188	466	150	204	820	205	207	87	35	8	1,362	82	1,444
1993	189	168	357	190	194	741	206	206	93	16	6	1,268	102	1,370

A6.9.2 continued

Stillbirths by sex and birthweight, England and Wales, 1982–98

Year of birth	Birthweight, g												All stated	Not stated	All birthweights
	Under 1,000	1,000–1,499	Under 1,500	1,500–1,999	2,000–2,499	Under 2,500	2,500–2,999	3,000–3,499	3,500–3,999	4,000–4,499	4,500 and over			
1994	192	178	370	195	190	755	220	184	99	32	19	1,309	51	1,360
1995	178	209	387	175	181	743	194	162	89	27	7	1,222	18	1,240
1996	188	172	360	179	167	706	220	188	82	32	9	1,237	23	1,260

Numbers of stillbirths at 24 or more weeks of gestation

Males

Year of birth	Under 1,000	1,000–1,499	Under 1,500	1,500–1,999	2,000–2,499	Under 2,500	2,500–2,999	3,000–3,499	3,500–3,999	4,000–4,499	4,500 and over	All stated	Not stated	All birthweights
1993	597	273	870	227	235	1,332	234	181	111	48	24	1,930	148	2,078
1994	628	272	900	196	225	1,321	223	219	114	58	15	1,950	85	2,035
1995	539	268	807	220	220	1,247	233	213	109	38	21	1,861	50	1,911
1996	595	237	832	194	206	1,232	222	177	103	28	16	1,778	30	1,808
1997	555	230	785	191	217	1,193	225	178		162*		1,758	43	1,801
1998	579	246	825	209	209	1,243	196	183		158*		1,780	42	1,822

Females

Year of birth	Under 1,000	1,000–1,499	Under 1,500	1,500–1,999	2,000–2,499	Under 2,500	2,500–2,999	3,000–3,499	3,500–3,999	4,000–4,499	4,500 and over	All stated	Not stated	All birthweights
1993	539	199	738	193	195	1,126	206	207	93	16	8	1,656	132	1,788
1994	567	201	768	200	191	1,159	221	184	100	32	20	1,716	65	1,781
1995	580	238	818	179	182	1,179	196	163	89	27	7	1,661	25	1,686
1996	619	198	817	182	168	1,167	221	188	82	32	9	1,699	32	1,731
1997	565	180	745	189	183	1,117	192	173		122*		1,604	34	1,638
1998	549	212	761	165	182	1,108	197	160		113*		1,578	17	1,595

Percentages of stillbirths at 28 or more weeks of gestation

Males

Year of birth	Under 1,000	1,000–1,499	Under 1,500	1,500–1,999	2,000–2,499	Under 2,500	2,500–2,999	3,000–3,499	3,500–3,999	4,000–4,499	4,500 and over	All stated	Not stated
1982	11.8	17.9	29.7	17.6	15.4	62.7	14.5	13.5	5.4	2.5	1.5	100.0	10.9
1983	11.9	18.3	30.3	16.9	16.4	63.6	15.0	11.5	6.3	3.0	0.8	100.0	1.6
1984	12.8	16.4	29.3	16.4	17.6	63.3	14.5	11.9	7.1	2.2	0.9	100.0	1.8
1985	12.8	16.4	29.2	16.8	16.2	62.2	15.3	13.2	5.2	3.3	0.7	100.0	1.7
1986	13.2	17.7	30.9	13.9	17.4	62.2	15.1	12.8	6.4	2.3	1.2	100.0	0.8
1987	13.5	16.8	30.3	17.7	14.7	62.7	16.2	11.1	6.6	1.9	1.5	100.0	1.2
1988	11.2	17.0	28.2	17.2	15.3	60.6	14.9	13.0	7.3	3.0	1.2	100.0	0.7

Stillbirths by sex and birthweight, England and Wales, 1982–98

Year of birth	Birthweight, g												All birthweights	
	Under 1,000	1,000–1,499	Under 1,500	1,500–1,999	2,000–2,499	Under 2,500	2,500–2,999	3,000–3,499	3,500–3,999	4,000–4,499	4,500 and over	All stated	Not stated
1989	11.8	14.8	26.6	17.8	17.5	61.9	15.8	11.8	6.8	2.4	1.2	100.0	3.9
1990	12.2	16.6	28.9	17.0	15.3	61.1	14.8	13.9	6.9	2.2	1.1	100.0	4.5
1991	11.4	16.4	27.7	16.5	16.1	60.3	16.4	11.9	7.5	2.2	1.7	100.0	5.3
1992	15.0	14.0	29.0	16.9	14.2	60.1	14.3	13.6	8.2	2.1	1.7	100.0	4.8
1993	13.2	15.6	28.8	15.1	15.7	59.6	15.7	12.3	7.5	3.3	1.6	100.0	7.2
1994	14.9	15.1	29.9	12.8	15.1	57.8	15.0	14.7	7.7	3.8	1.0	100.0	5.0
1995	12.2	14.7	26.9	15.1	15.3	57.3	16.2	14.9	7.6	2.7	1.4	100.0	2.2
1996	13.8	14.8	28.6	14.5	15.6	58.7	16.8	13.4	7.8	2.1	1.1	100.0	1.5
Females													
1982	13.5	17.4	30.8	14.7	16.5	62.0	17.6	12.5	6.0	1.2	0.7	100.0	11.5
1983	14.7	17.5	32.1	15.8	15.1	63.0	17.5	12.4	5.8	1.0	0.4	100.0	1.3
1984	14.7	17.9	32.6	13.1	16.7	62.3	17.1	11.9	6.0	1.8	0.9	100.0	2.0
1985	15.3	15.9	31.1	15.6	15.8	62.5	17.0	13.1	5.3	1.2	1.0	100.0	1.6
1986	15.2	17.5	32.7	14.6	15.9	63.2	14.9	13.7	5.7	1.6	0.9	100.0	0.7
1987	13.8	16.5	30.3	16.4	14.5	61.2	16.5	13.1	6.3	2.2	0.7	100.0	0.7
1988	13.5	15.3	28.8	14.8	16.0	59.6	16.4	14.5	7.0	1.9	0.6	100.0	0.5
1989	13.5	14.0	27.5	14.1	15.9	57.5	16.9	15.7	7.2	1.8	1.0	100.0	3.6
1990	12.6	16.3	28.9	18.1	14.6	61.6	14.4	14.7	7.0	1.7	0.6	100.0	4.8
1991	12.4	15.4	27.8	16.5	14.6	58.9	15.9	15.5	6.6	2.2	0.9	100.0	4.7
1992	20.4	13.8	34.2	11.0	15.0	60.2	15.1	15.2	6.4	2.6	0.6	100.0	5.7
1993	14.9	13.2	28.2	15.0	15.3	58.4	16.2	16.2	7.3	1.3	0.5	100.0	7.4
1994	14.7	13.6	28.3	14.9	14.5	57.7	16.8	14.1	7.6	2.4	1.5	100.0	3.8
1995	14.6	17.1	31.7	14.3	14.8	60.8	15.9	13.3	7.3	2.2	0.6	100.0	1.5
1996	15.2	13.9	29.1	14.5	13.5	57.1	17.8	15.2	6.6	2.6	0.7	100.0	1.8

Percentages of stillbirths at 24 or more weeks of gestation

Year of birth	Under 1,000	1,000–1,499	Under 1,500	1,500–1,999	2,000–2,499	Under 2,500	2,500–2,999	3,000–3,499	3,500–3,999	4,000–4,499	4,500 and over	All stated	Not stated
Males													
1993	30.9	14.1	45.1	11.8	12.2	69.0	12.1	9.4	5.8	2.5	1.2	100.0	7.1
1994	32.2	13.9	46.2	10.1	11.5	67.7	11.4	11.2	5.8	3.0	0.8	100.0	4.2

A6.9.2 *continued*

Stillbirths by sex and birthweight, England and Wales, 1982–98

Year of birth	Birthweight, g Under 1,000	1,000– 1,499	Under 1,500	1,500– 1,999	2,000– 2,499	Under 2,500	2,500– 2,999	3,000– 3,499	3,500– 3,999	4,000– 4,499	4,500 and over	All stated	Not stated	All birthweights
1995	29.0	14.4	43.4	11.8	11.8	67.0	12.5	11.4	5.9	2.0	1.1	100.0	2.6	
1996	33.5	13.3	46.8	10.9	11.6	69.3	12.5	10.0	5.8	1.6	0.9	100.0	1.7	
1997	30.8	13.1	44.7	10.9	12.3	67.9	12.8	10.1		9.0*		100.0	2.4	
1998	31.8	13.8	46.3	11.7	11.7	69.8	11.0	10.3		8.7*		100.0	2.3	
Females														
1993	32.5	12.0	44.6	11.7	11.8	68.0	12.4	12.5	5.6	1.0	0.5	100.0	7.4	
1994	33.0	11.7	44.8	11.7	11.1	67.5	12.9	10.7	5.8	1.9	1.2	100.0	3.6	
1995	34.9	14.3	49.2	10.8	11.0	71.0	11.8	9.8	5.4	1.6	0.4	100.0	1.5	
1996	36.4	11.7	48.1	10.7	9.9	68.7	13.0	11.1	4.8	1.9	0.5	100.0	1.8	
1997	34.5	11.2	46.4	11.8	11.4	69.6	12.0	10.8		7.4*		100.0	2.1	
1998	34.4	13.4	48.2	10.4	11.5	70.2	12.4	10.1		7.1*		100.0	1.1	

Stillbirths at 28 or more weeks of gestation per thousand total births

Year of birth	Under 1,000	1,000– 1,499	Under 1,500	1,500– 1,999	2,000– 2,499	Under 2,500	2,500– 2,999	3,000– 3,499	3,500– 3,999	4,000– 4,499	4,500 and over	All stated	Not stated	All birthweights
Males														
1982	227.3	164.6	184.9	79.9	22.4	58.6	5.4	2.2	1.1	1.6	6.1	6.0	16.0	6.5
1983	216.2	158.6	177.2	77.7	23.4	58.4	5.6	1.9	1.2	1.9	3.1	5.9	62.0	6.0
1984	209.5	141.2	164.7	72.2	25.0	57.2	5.5	1.9	1.4	1.4	3.5	5.9	75.5	6.0
1985	208.2	137.6	161.6	72.8	22.5	54.9	5.6	2.1	1.0	2.0	2.6	5.8	66.8	5.9
1986	184.9	138.5	155.1	56.1	22.9	51.6	5.4	2.0	1.2	1.3	4.0	5.5	46.6	5.6
1987	189.4	119.8	143.2	67.0	18.8	49.8	5.6	1.6	1.1	1.0	4.7	5.3	75.3	5.3
1988	155.5	118.5	130.8	63.9	19.3	47.5	5.1	1.8	1.2	1.4	3.4	5.0	26.2	5.1
1989	138.9	105.9	118.3	64.3	21.1	46.6	5.3	1.7	1.1	1.1	3.2	4.9	6.2	5.0
1990	151.4	116.7	129.3	60.0	17.8	44.8	4.8	1.9	1.1	1.0	2.8	4.8	5.5	4.8
1991	137.0	110.4	120.0	56.2	18.4	43.1	5.3	1.6	1.1	1.0	3.9	4.7	6.9	4.8
1992	166.1	93.9	121.1	61.8	16.7	44.2	4.7	1.9	1.2	0.9	3.7	4.8	6.1	4.8
1993	131.9	94.7	108.8	48.0	17.0	39.6	4.9	1.6	1.1	1.2	3.2	4.4	10.0	4.6
1994	130.9	88.8	105.7	39.9	16.6	38.2	4.7	1.9	1.1	1.5	2.0	4.5	8.9	4.6

A6.9.2 continued

Stillbirths by sex and birthweight, England and Wales, 1982–98

Year of birth	Birthweight, g											All stated	Not stated	All birthweights
	Under 1,000	1,000–1,499	Under 1,500	1,500–1,999	2,000–2,499	Under 2,500	2,500–2,999	3,000–3,499	3,500–3,999	4,000–4,499	4,500 and over			
1995	106.4	81.2	91.0	43.2	15.4	34.9	4.8	1.9	1.1	1.0	2.9	4.3	28.1	4.4
1996	103.9	74.3	86.2	39.6	14.8	33.5	4.6	1.6	1.0	0.7	2.1	3.9	24.0	4.0
Females														
1982	240.7	148.0	177.9	60.2	17.6	45.8	4.5	1.7	1.4	1.3	5.6	5.6	15.8	6.0
1983	215.3	144.0	169.7	60.6	15.6	44.5	4.4	1.6	1.3	1.0	3.0	5.4	50.4	5.4
1984	205.1	144.1	166.5	50.3	17.2	43.7	4.2	1.6	1.3	1.7	6.4	5.3	81.7	5.4
1985	204.1	116.5	147.5	55.2	15.5	41.3	4.1	1.7	1.1	1.0	7.0	5.1	64.3	5.2
1986	204.1	128.9	155.5	50.4	15.3	41.0	3.6	1.7	1.2	1.4	5.7	5.0	35.7	5.1
1987	164.5	109.3	129.0	52.9	13.1	37.2	3.7	1.5	1.2	1.7	4.2	4.6	45.3	4.7
1988	159.5	105.6	125.5	49.4	15.2	37.7	3.8	1.7	1.2	1.4	3.1	4.6	20.4	4.6
1989	137.5	90.5	108.8	43.5	13.9	33.5	3.7	1.7	1.2	1.2	4.8	4.3	5.1	4.4
1990	134.5	100.6	113.1	54.9	12.5	35.1	3.2	1.6	1.2	1.1	3.0	4.3	5.4	4.3
1991	138.0	100.2	114.1	49.5	12.6	33.9	3.6	1.7	1.1	1.4	4.1	4.4	5.7	4.5
1992	190.0	85.0	126.8	32.2	12.7	33.5	3.3	1.6	1.0	1.5	2.4	4.2	6.5	4.3
1993	131.0	78.4	99.5	39.6	12.5	31.1	3.4	1.7	1.1	0.7	1.8	4.0	9.5	4.2
1994	121.5	77.1	95.2	41.1	12.2	31.1	3.7	1.5	1.2	1.4	5.6	4.1	6.2	4.2
1995	112.1	82.4	93.8	34.5	11.2	29.2	3.2	1.3	1.1	1.2	2.2	3.9	15.9	3.9
1996	106.3	68.4	84.1	36.1	10.2	27.6	3.6	1.5	1.0	1.4	2.7	3.9	30.7	4.0

Stillbirths at 24 or more weeks of gestation per thousand total births

Year of birth	Under 1,000	1,000–1,499	Under 1,500	1,500–1,999	2,000–2,499	Under 2,500	2,500–2,999	3,000–3,499	3,500–3,999	4,000–4,499	4,500 and over	All stated	Not stated	All birthweights
Males														
1993	326.1	114.1	206.0	49.1	16.8	58.4	4.6	1.5	1.0	1.3	3.7	5.6	13.5	5.9
1994	353.4	114.5	216.7	42.2	15.7	57.1	4.3	1.8	1.1	1.5	2.2	5.6	5.9	5.6
1995	315.0	110.8	195.4	46.4	15.4	53.9	4.6	1.8	1.0	1.0	3.1	5.4	3.8	5.3
1996	326.9	96.9	195.0	44.3	14.9	54.9	4.5	1.5	1.0	0.7	2.2	5.2	2.2	5.1
1997	272.5	83.8	164.2	37.9	15.5	50.1	4.7	1.6		1.1*		5.3	73.1	5.4
1998	278.1	93.8	175.4	42.7	14.7	52.2	4.1	1.7		1.1*		5.4	94.6	5.6

Stillbirths by sex and birthweight, England and Wales, 1982–98

Year of birth	Birthweight, g													All birthweights
	Under 1,000	1,000– 1,499	Under 1,500	1,500– 1,999	2,000– 2,499	Under 2,500	2,500– 2,999	3,000– 3,499	3,500– 3,999	4,000– 4,499	4,500 and over	All stated	Not stated	
Females														
1993	300.6	91.5	186.0	40.2	12.6	46.4	3.4	1.7	1.1	0.7	2.3	5.2	12.3	5.4
1994	290.0	86.2	179.2	42.1	12.2	47.0	3.7	1.5	1.2	1.4	5.9	5.4	7.9	5.5
1995	291.5	92.8	179.5	35.3	11.2	45.6	3.2	1.3	1.1	1.2	2.2	5.2	22.0	5.3
1996	281.5	78.0	172.4	36.7	10.3	44.9	3.6	1.5	1.0	1.4	2.7	5.4	42.3	5.4
1997	267.9	71.6	161.2	36.5	11.1	42.6	3.2	1.4		1.1*		5.1	57.6	5.2
1998	262.2	83.9	164.6	33.1	11.1	42.6	3.3	1.4		1.1*		5.1	42.5	5.1

* 3,500g and over

Data for all stillbirths are in Tables A3.4.2 and A3.5.2

Source: Authors' analysis of ONS/OPCS data

Data extract: live births 1993 (7/94), 1994 (7/95), 1995 (3/7/96), 1996 (8/4/97)
linked 1993 (3/4/96), 1994 (18/9/96), 1995 (3/11/97), 1997 and 1998 from VS5 tabulations

This is a new table for this edition of *Birth counts*

A6.9.3

Neonatal mortality by sex and birthweight, England and Wales, 1982–95

Year of birth	Birthweight, g Under 1,000	1,000– 1,499	Under 1,500	1,500– 1,999	2,000– 2,499	Under 2,500	2,500– 2,999	3,000– 3,499	3,500– 3,999	4,000– 4,499	4,500 and over	All stated	Not stated	All birthweights
Males	**Numbers**													
1982	472	343	815	212	200	1,227	191	276	139	36	14	1,883	370	2,253
1983	517	353	870	227	216	1,313	238	217	152	37	7	1,964	116	2,080
1984	551	346	897	224	180	1,301	229	228	130	42	11	1,941	100	2,041
1985	561	332	893	175	203	1,271	220	223	135	41	7	1,897	75	1,972
1986	622	323	945	215	188	1,348	193	234	136	35	9	1,955	60	2,015
1987	597	389	986	188	150	1,324	183	213	141	48	10	1,919	64	1,983
1988	621	371	992	168	164	1,324	200	194	123	44	9	1,894	54	1,948
1989	592	292	884	154	124	1,162	169	170	138	41	9	1,689	224	1,913
1990	571	215	786	131	105	1,022	161	178	107	34	10	1,512	261	1,773
1991	586	210	796	127	102	1,025	133	138	80	36	12	1,424	271	1,695
1992	539	195	734	98	102	934	136	159	94	31	18	1,372	251	1,623
1993	579	212	791	102	85	978	116	143	88	26	13	1,364	225	1,589
1994	611	214	825	97	82	1,004	115	140	94	36	20	1,409	184	1,593
1995	652	189	841	92	96	1,029	113	154	114	61	27	1,498	37	1,535
Females														
1982	353	234	587	161	149	897	203	189	76	18	10	1,393	257	1,650
1983	455	250	705	147	167	1,019	196	175	79	21	12	1,502	61	1,563
1984	463	191	654	133	164	951	193	181	70	11	5	1,411	66	1,477
1985	449	204	653	149	174	976	187	172	75	34	6	1,450	61	1,511
1986	432	214	646	143	139	928	180	166	82	28	6	1,390	42	1,432
1987	483	211	694	134	128	956	166	167	76	17	8	1,390	47	1,437
1988	497	205	702	146	126	974	146	166	84	11	10	1,391	40	1,431
1989	426	162	588	101	96	785	146	127	80	20	6	1,164	174	1,338
1990	457	155	612	93	91	796	120	136	61	20	8	1,141	220	1,361
1991	452	127	579	77	107	763	126	108	74	18	6	1,095	226	1,321
1992	481	125	606	83	84	773	100	100	55	19	1	1,048	198	1,246
1993	455	97	552	84	77	713	102	114	52	20	6	1,007	178	1,185
1994	443	105	548	71	84	703	98	105	48	19	14	987	149	1,136
1995	471	111	582	77	98	757	106	108	69	36	30	1,106	26	1,132
Males	**Rates per thousand live births**													
1982	631.0	202.4	333.6	56.1	15.9	65.2	3.9	2.4	1.5	1.3	3.0	6.1	26.2	7.0
1983	619.9	188.0	320.8	58.4	16.4	66.4	4.6	1.8	1.6	1.2	1.4	6.1	247.3	6.4
1984	588.7	178.9	312.5	54.8	13.6	64.4	4.5	1.9	1.3	1.4	2.2	6.0	226.8	6.3

A6.9.3 continued

Neonatal mortality by sex and birthweight, England and Wales, 1982–95

Year of birth	Birthweight, g											All stated	Not stated	All birthweights
	Under 1,000	1,000– 1,499	Under 1,500	1,500– 1,999	2,000– 2,499	Under 2,500	2,500– 2,999	3,000– 3,499	3,500– 3,999	4,000– 4,499	4,500 and over			
1985	592.4	165.5	302.4	41.9	14.7	60.8	4.2	1.8	1.3	1.3	1.3	5.6	157.9	5.9
1986	566.5	155.0	297.0	48.8	13.4	62.4	3.6	1.9	1.3	1.1	1.7	5.8	183.5	5.9
1987	560.0	170.2	294.2	41.4	10.6	59.9	3.4	1.7	1.3	1.4	1.7	5.5	237.0	5.7
1988	568.7	162.9	294.4	37.1	11.7	60.5	3.8	1.5	1.1	1.2	1.4	5.3	121.1	5.5
1989	479.7	137.7	263.6	35.1	9.0	54.1	3.3	1.4	1.3	1.1	1.4	4.9	20.7	5.4
1990	497.0	102.2	241.6	29.4	7.5	46.9	3.1	1.5	1.0	0.9	1.5	4.4	18.4	4.9
1991	500.0	97.6	239.5	28.1	7.3	46.8	2.6	1.1	0.7	1.0	1.8	4.1	20.4	4.7
1992	440.0	88.3	213.7	23.4	7.5	44.1	2.8	1.4	0.9	0.8	2.5	4.0	18.8	4.6
1993	451.3	96.4	227.1	23.0	6.3	45.8	2.5	1.3	0.8	0.7	1.8	4.1	20.0	4.6
1994	416.5	93.1	219.1	21.1	6.2	46.3	2.4	1.2	0.9	0.9	2.7	4.2	21.2	4.7
1995	443.8	79.5	218.7	19.2	6.8	45.4	2.3	1.4	1.1	1.6	3.9	4.5	33.5	4.6
Females														
1982	508.6	143.1	252.0	42.9	9.9	42.5	3.2	1.6	1.1	1.1	5.2	4.8	19.4	5.4
1983	515.9	146.0	271.8	36.4	10.7	45.7	3.0	1.4	1.1	1.2	6.0	4.9	154.0	5.1
1984	493.6	109.4	243.7	32.8	10.4	42.4	2.9	1.4	0.9	0.6	2.3	4.5	177.9	4.8
1985	460.5	103.4	221.6	34.0	10.6	41.1	2.8	1.3	1.0	1.9	2.6	4.5	155.2	4.7
1986	446.7	110.8	222.8	31.9	8.3	38.5	2.7	1.3	1.0	1.5	2.5	4.3	141.4	4.4
1987	448.5	101.6	220.0	29.6	7.6	39.1	2.5	1.3	0.9	0.8	3.0	4.2	202.6	4.3
1988	444.9	101.2	223.4	32.7	7.8	40.9	2.2	1.2	1.0	0.5	3.4	4.1	103.9	4.2
1989	353.8	81.4	184.2	23.0	6.0	33.4	2.3	1.0	0.9	1.0	2.1	3.6	16.9	4.0
1990	392.3	74.4	188.5	20.8	5.5	32.8	1.8	1.0	0.7	0.9	2.7	3.4	16.2	3.9
1991	399.6	62.9	183.8	16.7	6.4	31.2	2.0	0.8	0.9	0.8	1.9	3.3	17.8	3.9
1992	405.9	61.8	188.9	18.4	5.3	32.7	1.6	0.8	0.6	0.8	0.3	3.2	15.8	3.7
1993	362.8	49.1	170.9	18.2	5.0	30.8	1.7	0.9	0.6	0.9	1.8	3.2	16.7	3.6
1994	319.2	49.3	155.8	15.6	5.4	29.9	1.6	0.9	0.6	0.8	4.2	3.1	18.2	3.5
1995	334.0	47.7	155.7	15.7	6.1	30.7	1.7	0.9	0.8	1.6	9.3	3.5	23.4	3.6

Data for all births are in Table A3.5.2

Source: Authors' analysis of ONS/OPCS data

Data extract: live births 1993 (7/94), 1994 (7/95), 1995 (3/7/96), 1996 (8/4/97)
linked 1993 (3/4/96), 1994 (18/9/96), 1995 (3/11/97)

This is a new table for this edition of *Birth counts*

A6.9.4

Postneonatal mortality by sex and birthweight, England and Wales, 1982–95

Year of birth	Birthweight, g													All birthweights
	Under 1,000	1,000– 1,499	Under 1,500	1,500– 1,999	2,000– 2,499	Under 2,500	2,500– 2,999	3,000– 3,499	3,500– 3,999	4,000– 4,499	4,500 and over	All stated	Not stated	

Numbers

Males

1982	40	68	108	78	136	322	324	471	276	87	16	1,496	85	1,581
1983	47	63	110	79	157	346	314	500	282	63	13	1,518	8	1,526
1984	48	66	114	66	117	297	282	401	256	59	13	1,308	6	1,314
1985	54	72	126	99	162	387	300	480	305	82	19	1,573	5	1,578
1986	66	80	146	95	146	387	356	448	296	94	17	1,598	10	1,608
1987	60	83	143	90	136	369	349	483	313	89	19	1,622	2	1,624
1988	52	86	138	95	153	386	300	452	290	89	13	1,530	5	1,535
1989	70	64	134	76	153	363	270	422	261	69	16	1,401	48	1,449
1990	73	84	157	90	112	359	242	331	206	70	13	1,221	63	1,284
1991	67	52	119	53	124	296	169	276	178	56	13	988	56	1,044
1992	97	67	164	55	79	298	160	227	110	38	8	841	39	880
1993	83	49	132	38	92	262	127	179	112	37	11	728	24	752
1994	74	57	131	51	62	244	141	189	103	31	7	715	23	738
1995	96	57	153	51	81	285	132	174	100	36	4	731	8	739

Females

1982	34	49	83	72	107	262	263	354	150	25	5	1,059	61	1,120
1983	48	53	101	62	122	285	299	346	167	23	6	1,126	4	1,130
1984	47	47	94	62	114	270	265	268	173	28	3	1,007	6	1,013
1985	48	60	108	70	137	315	263	332	160	33	3	1,106	4	1,110
1986	53	46	99	77	143	319	262	311	155	45	5	1,097	5	1,102
1987	51	50	101	69	132	302	284	348	169	33	7	1,143	6	1,149
1988	74	60	134	80	139	353	272	307	140	33	9	1,114	1	1,115
1989	72	54	126	71	114	311	217	252	139	26	5	950	35	985
1990	65	49	114	63	103	280	200	248	122	36	3	889	43	932
1991	59	33	92	53	102	247	140	162	98	18	3	668	38	706
1992	66	35	101	36	86	223	139	149	70	18	3	602	29	631
1993	68	37	105	60	69	234	122	140	78	14	5	593	21	614
1994	74	29	103	33	63	199	114	121	51	19	1	505	11	516
1995	83	39	122	38	71	231	130	120	51	12	2	546	6	552

Rates per thousand live births

Males

1982	53.5	40.1	44.2	20.6	10.8	17.1	6.5	4.2	3.0	3.0	3.5	4.9	6.0	4.9
1983	56.4	33.5	40.6	20.3	11.9	17.5	6.1	4.2	2.9	2.1	2.7	4.7	17.1	4.7

A6.9.4 continued

Postneonatal mortality by sex and birthweight, England and Wales, 1982–95

Year of birth	Birthweight, g Under 1,000	1,000– 1,499	Under 1,500	1,500– 1,999	2,000– 2,499	Under 2,500	2,500– 2,999	3,000– 3,499	3,500– 3,999	4,000– 4,499	4,500 and over	All stated	Not stated	All birthweights
1984	51.3	34.1	39.7	16.1	8.8	14.7	5.5	3.4	2.6	1.9	2.6	4.0	13.6	4.0
1985	57.0	35.9	42.7	23.7	11.8	18.5	5.7	3.9	3.0	2.5	3.6	4.7	10.5	4.7
1986	60.1	38.4	45.9	21.6	10.4	17.9	6.7	3.7	2.9	2.8	3.1	4.7	30.6	4.7
1987	56.3	36.3	42.7	19.8	9.6	16.7	6.6	3.8	2.9	2.5	3.2	4.6	7.4	4.6
1988	47.6	37.8	41.0	21.0	10.9	17.6	5.8	3.6	2.6	2.4	2.0	4.3	11.2	4.3
1989	56.7	30.2	40.0	17.3	11.2	16.9	5.3	3.5	2.5	1.9	2.5	4.1	4.4	4.1
1990	63.5	39.9	48.3	20.2	7.9	16.5	4.7	2.7	1.9	1.9	1.9	3.5	4.4	3.6
1991	57.2	24.2	35.8	11.7	8.8	13.5	3.4	2.3	1.6	1.5	1.9	2.9	4.2	2.9
1992	79.2	30.3	47.8	13.1	5.8	14.1	3.3	1.9	1.0	1.0	1.1	2.5	2.9	2.5
1993	64.7	22.3	37.9	8.6	6.9	12.3	2.7	1.6	1.1	1.0	1.5	2.2	2.1	2.2
1994	50.4	24.8	34.8	11.1	4.7	11.3	3.0	1.7	1.0	0.8	0.9	2.2	2.6	2.2
1995	65.4	24.0	39.8	10.7	5.8	12.6	2.7	1.5	1.0	1.0	0.6	2.2	7.2	2.2
Females														
1982	49.0	30.0	35.6	19.2	7.1	12.4	4.2	3.0	2.1	1.6	2.6	3.6	4.6	3.7
1983	54.4	31.0	38.9	15.4	7.8	12.8	4.6	2.8	2.2	1.4	3.0	3.7	10.1	3.7
1984	50.1	26.9	35.0	15.3	7.3	12.0	4.0	2.1	2.3	1.6	1.4	3.2	16.2	3.3
1985	49.2	30.4	36.6	16.0	8.3	13.3	3.9	2.6	2.0	1.8	1.3	3.5	10.2	3.5
1986	54.8	23.8	34.1	17.2	8.5	13.2	3.9	2.4	1.9	2.4	2.1	3.4	16.8	3.4
1987	47.4	24.1	32.0	15.2	7.9	12.4	4.2	2.6	2.0	1.6	2.7	3.4	25.9	3.5
1988	66.2	29.6	42.6	17.9	8.6	14.8	4.1	2.3	1.6	1.5	3.1	3.3	2.6	3.3
1989	59.8	27.1	39.5	16.2	7.2	13.2	3.4	2.0	1.6	1.2	1.7	2.9	3.4	2.9
1990	55.8	23.5	35.1	14.1	6.2	11.5	3.1	1.9	1.4	1.6	1.0	2.7	3.2	2.7
1991	52.2	16.3	29.2	11.5	6.1	10.1	2.2	1.3	1.1	0.8	0.9	2.0	3.0	2.1
1992	55.7	17.3	31.5	8.0	5.4	9.4	2.3	1.2	0.8	0.8	0.9	1.9	2.3	1.9
1993	54.2	18.7	32.5	13.0	4.5	10.1	2.0	1.2	0.9	0.6	1.5	1.9	2.0	1.9
1994	53.3	13.6	29.3	7.3	4.1	8.5	1.9	1.0	0.6	0.8	0.3	1.6	1.3	1.6
1995	58.9	16.8	32.6	7.8	4.4	9.4	2.1	1.0	0.6	0.5	0.6	1.7	5.4	1.7

Data for all births are in Table A3.5.2

Source: Authors' analysis of ONS/OPCS data

Data extract: live births 1993 (7/94), 1994 (7/95), 1995 (3/7/96), 1996 (8/4/97)

linked 1993 (3/4/96), 1994 (18/9/96), 1995 (3/11/97)

This is a new table for this edition of *Birth counts*

A6.9.5

Infant mortality by sex and birthweight, England and Wales, 1982–95

Year of birth	Birthweight, g											All stated	Not stated	All birthweights
	Under 1,000	1,000– 1,499	Under 1,500	1,500– 1,999	2,000– 2,499	Under 2,500	2,500– 2,999	3,000– 3,499	3,500– 3,999	4,000– 4,499	4,500 and over			
Males														
1982	512	411	923	290	336	1,549	515	747	415	123	30	3,379	455	3,834
1983	564	416	980	306	373	1,659	552	717	434	100	20	3,482	124	3,606
1984	599	412	1,011	290	297	1,598	511	629	386	101	24	3,249	106	3,355
1985	615	404	1,019	274	365	1,658	520	703	440	123	26	3,470	80	3,550
1986	688	403	1,091	310	334	1,735	549	682	432	129	26	3,553	70	3,623
1987	657	472	1,129	278	286	1,693	532	696	454	137	29	3,541	66	3,607
1988	673	457	1,130	263	317	1,710	500	646	413	133	22	3,424	59	3,483
1989	662	356	1,018	230	277	1,525	439	592	399	110	25	3,090	272	3,362
1990	644	299	943	221	217	1,381	403	509	313	104	23	2,733	324	3,057
1991	653	262	915	180	226	1,321	302	414	258	92	25	2,412	327	2,739
1992	636	262	898	153	181	1,232	296	386	204	69	26	2,213	290	2,503
1993	662	261	923	140	177	1,240	243	322	200	63	24	2,092	249	2,341
1994	685	271	956	148	144	1,248	256	329	197	67	27	2,124	207	2,331
1995	748	246	994	143	177	1,314	245	328	214	97	31	2,229	45	2,274
Females														
1982	387	283	670	233	256	1,159	466	543	226	43	15	2,452	318	2,770
1983	503	303	806	209	289	1,304	495	521	246	44	18	2,628	65	2,693
1984	510	238	748	195	278	1,221	458	449	243	39	8	2,418	72	2,490
1985	497	264	761	219	311	1,291	450	504	235	67	9	2,556	65	2,621
1986	485	260	745	220	282	1,247	442	477	237	73	11	2,487	47	2,534
1987	534	261	795	203	260	1,258	450	515	245	50	15	2,533	53	2,586
1988	571	265	836	226	265	1,327	418	473	224	44	19	2,505	41	2,546
1989	498	216	714	172	210	1,096	363	379	219	46	11	2,114	209	2,323
1990	522	204	726	156	194	1,076	320	384	183	56	11	2,030	263	2,293
1991	511	160	671	130	209	1,010	266	270	172	36	9	1,763	264	2,027
1992	547	160	707	119	170	996	239	249	125	37	4	1,650	227	1,877
1993	523	134	657	144	146	947	224	254	130	34	11	1,600	199	1,799
1994	517	134	651	104	147	902	212	226	99	38	15	1,492	160	1,652
1995	554	150	704	115	169	988	236	228	120	48	32	1,652	32	1,684
Rates per thousand live births														
Males														
1982	684.5	242.5	377.8	76.7	26.7	82.3	10.4	6.6	4.5	4.3	6.5	11.0	32.2	11.9
1983	676.3	221.5	361.4	78.8	28.3	83.9	10.7	6.0	4.5	3.3	4.1	10.8	264.4	11.2
1984	640.0	213.0	352.3	71.0	22.4	79.1	10.0	5.3	3.9	3.3	4.7	10.0	240.4	10.3

Infant mortality by sex and birthweight, England and Wales, 1982–95

Year of birth	Birthweight, g												All stated	Not stated	All birthweights
	Under 1,000	1,000– 1,499	Under 1,500	1,500– 1,999	2,000– 2,499	Under 2,500	2,500– 2,999	3,000– 3,499	3,500– 3,999	4,000– 4,499	4,500 and over				
1985	649.4	201.4	345.1	65.6	26.5	79.3	9.8	5.7	4.3	3.8	4.9	10.3	168.4	10.5
1986	626.6	193.4	342.9	70.4	23.8	80.3	10.4	5.6	4.2	3.9	4.8	10.5	214.1	10.7
1987	616.6	206.6	336.9	61.2	20.1	76.6	10.0	5.5	4.2	3.9	4.9	10.1	244.4	10.3
1988	616.3	200.7	335.4	58.1	22.7	78.2	9.6	5.1	3.7	3.5	3.4	9.7	132.3	9.8
1989	536.5	167.9	303.5	52.4	20.2	71.1	8.7	4.9	3.8	3.0	3.9	9.0	25.1	9.5
1990	560.5	142.1	289.9	49.7	15.4	63.4	7.8	4.2	2.9	2.8	3.4	7.9	22.8	8.5
1991	557.2	121.8	275.4	39.8	16.1	60.3	6.0	3.4	2.4	2.4	3.7	7.0	24.7	7.6
1992	519.2	118.6	261.5	36.5	13.3	58.1	6.0	3.3	1.9	1.8	3.6	6.5	21.7	7.1
1993	516.0	118.6	265.0	31.6	13.2	58.1	5.2	2.8	1.9	1.6	3.3	6.3	22.1	6.8
1994	466.9	117.9	253.9	32.2	10.8	57.6	5.4	2.9	1.9	1.7	3.7	6.4	23.8	6.8
1995	509.2	103.5	258.5	29.9	12.6	58.0	5.1	2.9	2.1	2.6	4.5	6.7	40.7	6.8
Females														
1982	557.6	173.1	287.7	62.1	17.0	54.9	7.4	4.6	3.2	2.7	7.7	8.4	24.0	9.1
1983	570.3	177.0	310.7	51.8	18.4	58.5	7.6	4.2	3.3	2.6	9.0	8.6	164.1	8.8
1984	543.7	136.3	278.7	48.1	17.7	54.4	6.9	3.6	3.2	2.3	3.7	7.8	194.1	8.0
1985	509.7	133.9	258.2	50.0	18.9	54.3	6.7	3.9	3.0	3.7	3.9	8.0	165.4	8.2
1986	501.6	134.6	257.0	49.0	16.8	51.7	6.6	3.7	2.9	3.9	4.5	7.7	158.2	7.9
1987	495.8	125.7	252.1	44.9	15.5	51.5	6.7	3.9	2.9	2.5	5.7	7.6	228.4	7.8
1988	511.2	130.9	266.1	50.7	16.4	55.7	6.3	3.5	2.5	2.0	6.5	7.4	106.5	7.5
1989	413.6	108.6	223.6	39.2	13.2	46.6	5.6	2.9	2.6	2.2	3.8	6.5	20.3	6.9
1990	448.1	98.0	223.6	34.9	11.7	44.4	4.9	2.9	2.1	2.6	3.7	6.1	19.4	6.7
1991	451.8	79.2	212.9	28.2	12.5	41.3	4.2	2.1	2.0	1.6	2.8	5.4	20.8	5.9
1992	461.6	79.1	220.4	26.4	10.7	42.1	3.9	2.0	1.5	1.6	1.2	5.1	18.1	5.6
1993	417.1	67.8	203.4	31.2	9.6	41.0	3.7	2.1	1.5	1.5	3.2	5.1	18.7	5.5
1994	372.5	62.9	185.0	22.9	9.5	38.4	3.6	1.9	1.2	1.7	4.5	4.7	19.6	5.1
1995	392.9	64.4	188.3	23.5	10.5	40.1	3.9	1.9	1.5	2.2	10.0	5.2	28.8	5.3

Data for all births are in Table A3.5.2

Source: Authors' analysis of ONS/OPCS data

Data extract: live births 1993 (7/94), 1994 (7/95), 1995 (3/7/96), 1996 (8/4/97)
linked 1993 (3/4/96), 1994 (18/9/96), 1995 (3/11/97)

This is a new table for this edition of *Birth counts*

A6.9.6

Mortality of one, two and three year olds by sex and birthweight, England and Wales, 1993-95

Year of birth and age at death, years	Birthweight, g													All birthweights
	Under 1,000	1,000–1,499	Under 1,500	1,500–1,999	2,000–2,499	Under 2,500	2,500–2,999	3,000–3,499	3,500–3,999	4,000–4,499	4,500 and over	All stated	Not stated	
1993														
Numbers														
Males														
Under 1	662	261	923	140	177	1,240	243	322	200	63	24	2,092	249	2,341
1	5	4	9	13	9	31	28	45	32	13	2	151	7	158
2	0	3	3	1	10	14	17	34	30	6	1	102	4	106
3	1	0	1	2	3	6	4	10	9	2	0	31	0	31
Females														
Under 1	523	134	657	144	146	947	224	254	130	34	11	1,600	199	1,799
1	2	4	6	3	12	21	40	47	21	5	0	134	7	141
2	0	1	1	3	5	9	19	33	22	2	0	85	5	90
3	0	0	0	1	2	3	6	9	4	1	0	23	0	23
Rates per thousand live births														
Males														
Under 1	516.0	118.6	265.0	31.6	13.2	58.1	5.2	2.8	1.9	1.6	3.3	6.3	22.1	6.8
1	3.9	1.8	2.6	2.9	0.7	1.5	0.6	0.4	0.3	0.3	0.3	0.5	0.6	0.5
2	–	1.4	0.9	0.2	0.7	0.7	0.4	0.3	0.3	0.2	0.1	0.3	0.4	0.3
3	0.8	–	0.3	0.5	0.2	0.3	0.1	0.1	0.1	0.1	–	0.1	–	0.1
Females														
Under 1	417.1	67.8	203.4	31.2	9.6	41.0	3.7	2.1	1.5	1.5	3.2	5.1	18.7	5.5
1	1.6	2.0	1.9	0.7	0.8	0.9	0.7	0.4	0.2	0.2	–	0.4	0.7	0.4
2	–	0.5	0.3	0.7	0.3	0.4	0.3	0.3	0.1	0.1	–	0.3	0.5	0.3
3	–	–	–	0.2	0.1	0.1	0.1	0.1	0.0	0.0	–	0.1	–	0.1
1994														
Numbers														
Males														
Under 1	685	271	956	148	144	1,248	256	329	197	67	27	2,124	207	2,331
1	3	5	8	6	19	33	32	47	33	11	1	157	2	159
2	0	1	1	1	2	4	15	15	13	4	0	51	0	51
Females														
Under 1	517	134	651	104	147	902	212	226	99	38	15	1,492	160	1,652
1	4	6	10	8	8	26	30	46	27	8	2	139	4	143
2	1	0	1	1	3	5	7	14	11	2	1	40	1	41

A6.9.6 *continued*

Mortality of one, two and three year olds by sex and birthweight, England and Wales, 1993–95

Year of birth and age at death, years	Birthweight, g													All birthweights
	Under 1,000	1,000–1,499	Under 1,500	1,500–1,999	2,000–2,499	Under 2,500	2,500–2,999	3,000–3,499	3,500–3,999	4,000–4,499	4,500 and over	All stated	Not stated	
Rates per thousand live births														
Males														
Under 1	466.9	117.9	253.9	32.2	10.8	57.6	5.4	2.9	1.9	1.7	3.7	6.4	23.8	6.8
1	2.0	2.2	2.1	1.3	1.4	1.5	0.7	0.4	0.3	0.3	0.1	0.5	0.2	0.5
2	–	0.4	0.3	0.2	0.2	0.2	0.3	0.1	0.1	0.1	–	0.2	–	0.1
Females														
Under 1	372.5	62.9	185.0	22.9	9.5	38.4	3.6	1.9	1.2	1.7	4.5	4.7	19.6	5.1
1	2.9	2.8	2.8	1.8	0.5	1.1	0.5	0.4	0.3	0.4	0.6	0.4	0.5	0.4
2	0.7	–	0.3	0.2	0.2	0.2	0.1	0.1	0.1	0.1	0.3	0.1	0.1	0.1
1995														
Numbers														
Males														
Under 1	748	246	994	143	177	1,314	245	328	214	97	31	2,229	45	2,274
1	4	2	6	4	12	22	21	32	17	2	1	95	0	95
Females														
Under 1	554	150	704	115	169	988	236	228	120	48	32	1,652	32	1,684
1	2	2	4	3	6	13	14	22	9	2	0	60	3	63
Rates per thousand live births														
Males														
Under 1	509.2	103.5	258.5	29.9	12.6	58.0	5.1	2.9	2.1	2.6	4.5	6.7	40.7	6.8
1	2.7	0.8	1.6	0.8	0.9	1.0	0.4	0.3	0.2	0.1	0.1	0.3	–	0.3
Females														
Under 1	392.9	64.4	188.3	23.5	10.5	40.1	3.9	1.9	1.5	2.2	10.0	5.2	28.8	5.3
1	1.4	0.9	1.1	0.6	0.4	0.5	0.2	0.2	0.1	0.1	0.0	0.2	2.7	0.2

Data for all births are in Table Table A6.1.6

Source: Authors' analysis of ONS/OPCS data

Data extract: live births 1993 (7/94), 1994 (7/95), 1995 (3/7/96), 1996 (8/4/97)
linked 1993 (3/4/96), 1994 (18/9/96), 1995 (3/11/97)

This is a new table for this edition of *Birth counts*

A6.10.1

Sex ratio of live and stillbirths by month of occurrence of birth, England and Wales, 1996

Quarter/month of occurrence	Live births			Stillbirths			Total births		
	Male	Female	Sex ratio m/f	Male	Female	Sex ratio m/f	Male	Female	Sex ratio m/f
Annual total	333,490	315,995	1.06	1,808	1,731	1.04	335,298	317,726	1.06
March quarter	81,016	76,265	1.06	452	423	1.07	81,468	76,688	1.06
June quarter	81,026	77,057	1.05	455	431	1.06	81,481	77,488	1.05
September quarter	87,205	82,744	1.05	458	459	1.00	87,663	83,203	1.05
December quarter	84,243	79,929	1.05	443	418	1.06	84,686	80,347	1.05
January	27,564	25,959	1.06	144	142	1.01	27,708	26,101	1.06
February	25,882	24,506	1.06	150	137	1.09	26,032	24,643	1.06
March	27,570	25,800	1.07	158	144	1.10	27,728	25,944	1.07
April	25,910	24,585	1.05	152	125	1.22	26,062	24,710	1.05
May	27,520	26,323	1.05	147	145	1.01	27,667	26,468	1.05
June	27,596	26,149	1.06	156	161	0.97	27,752	26,310	1.05
July	29,508	28,098	1.05	155	155	1.00	29,663	28,253	1.05
August	28,778	27,178	1.06	146	146	1.00	28,924	27,324	1.06
September	28,919	27,468	1.05	157	158	0.99	29,076	27,626	1.05
October	28,837	27,384	1.05	153	155	0.99	28,990	27,539	1.05
November	27,608	26,144	1.06	143	144	0.99	27,751	26,288	1.06
December	27,798	26,401	1.05	147	119	1.24	27,945	26,520	1.05

Source: ONS *Birth statistics, Series FM1*, Table 2.4

This was Table A6.12 in the first edition of *Birth counts*

A6.11.1

Maternities with multiple births, England and Wales, 1938–98

Year	Numbers of maternities							Rates per thousand maternities		
	All maternities	Multiple maternities	Twin	Triplet	Quadruplet	Quintuplet	Sextuplet	All multiple maternities	Twin	Triplet and higher order maternities
1938	614,874	7,494	7,440	54	0	0	0	12.2	12.1	0.09
1939	636,060	7,539	7,477	61	1	0	0	11.9	11.8	0.10
1940	622,376	7,319	7,254	65	0	0	0	11.8	11.7	0.10
1941	592,813	7,087	7,020	67	0	0	0	12.0	11.8	0.11
1942	665,838	7,976	7,904	72	0	0	0	12.0	11.9	0.11
1943	697,267	8,259	8,193	62	4	0	0	11.8	11.8	0.09
1944	763,092	9,604	9,520	80	4	0	0	12.6	12.5	0.11
1945	690,934	8,274	8,212	62	0	0	0	12.0	11.9	0.09
1946	832,761	10,788	10,703	85	0	0	0	13.0	12.9	0.10
1947	891,504	11,221	11,130	86	5	0	0	12.6	12.5	0.10
1948	783,926	9,687	9,597	88	2	0	0	12.4	12.2	0.11
1949	738,050	9,328	9,241	87	0	0	0	12.6	12.5	0.12
1950	704,102	8,979	8,880	98	1	0	0	12.8	12.6	0.14
1951	684,407	9,005	8,905	98	2	0	0	13.2	13.0	0.15
1952	680,715	8,590	8,525	64	1	0	0	12.6	12.5	0.10
1953	691,180	8,787	8,703	83	0	1	0	12.7	12.6	0.12
1954	681,058	8,724	8,655	69	0	0	0	12.8	12.7	0.10
1955	675,026	8,525	8,437	87	1	0	0	12.6	12.5	0.13
1956	707,921	8,739	8,660	78	1	0	0	12.3	12.2	0.11
1957	730,524	9,371	9,273	95	3	0	0	12.8	12.7	0.13
1958	747,536	9,377	9,287	90	0	0	0	12.5	12.4	0.12
1959	755,294	9,021	8,934	87	0	0	0	11.9	11.8	0.12
1960	791,584	9,163	9,086	77	0	0	0	11.6	11.5	0.10
1961	817,271	9,653	9,570	82	1	0	0	11.8	11.7	0.10
1962	844,265	9,845	9,756	88	1	0	0	11.7	11.6	0.11
1963	858,884	10,060	9,960	100	0	0	0	11.7	11.6	0.12
1964	880,173	10,238	10,135	99	4	0	0	11.6	11.5	0.12
1965	866,713	9,774	9,695	79	0	0	0	11.3	11.2	0.09
1966	853,481	9,501	9,418	82	1	0	0	11.1	11.0	0.10
1967	835,433	9,187	9,117	68	2	0	1	11.0	10.9	0.08
1968	822,247	8,783	8,697	84	1	1	1	10.7	10.6	0.10
1969	799,763	8,341	8,259	79	1	1	0	10.4	10.3	0.10
1970	786,587	8,143	8,042	100	1	0	0	10.4	10.2	0.13
1971	784,899	8,074	8,000	69	3	2	0	10.3	10.2	0.09
1972	726,715	7,431	7,345	81	3	2	0	10.2	10.1	0.12

A6.11.1 continued

Maternities with multiple births, England and Wales, 1938–98

Year	All maternities	Multiple maternities	Twin	Triplet	Quadruplet	Quintuplet	Sextuplet	All multiple maternities	Twin	Triplet and higher order maternities
1973	677,125	6,688	6,615	71	2	0	0	9.9	9.8	0.11
1974	640,777	6,215	6,151	60	4	0	0	9.7	9.6	0.10
1975	603,666	5,988	5,909	72	7	0	0	9.9	9.8	0.13
1976	584,263	5,621	5,538	76	4	2	1	9.6	9.5	0.14
1977	569,073	5,519	5,449	68	2	0	0	9.7	9.6	0.12
1978	595,515	5,930	5,859	62	8	1	0	10.0	9.8	0.12
1979	636,884	6,181	6,099	76	6	0	0	9.7	9.6	0.13
1980	654,501	6,404	6,308	91	4	1	0	9.8	9.6	0.15
1981	632,350	::	::	::	::	::	::	::	::	::
1982	623,511	6,277	6,201	70	6	0	0	10.1	9.9	0.12
1983	626,277	6,387	6,293	89	4	0	1	10.2	10.0	0.15
1984	633,965	6,406	6,321	80	5	0	0	10.1	10.0	0.13
1985	653,142	6,803	6,700	93	7	2	1	10.4	10.3	0.16
1986	657,308	7,105	6,969	123	10	2	1	10.8	10.6	0.21
1987	677,467	7,320	7,186	125	7	1	1*	10.8	10.6	0.20
1988	689,153	7,622	7,452	157	12	1	0	11.1	10.8	0.25
1989	682,979	7,774	7,579	183	11	1	0	11.4	11.1	0.29
1990	701,030	8,145	7,934	201	10	0	0	11.6	11.3	0.30
1991	693,857	8,380	8,160	208	10	2	0	12.1	11.8	0.32
1992	683,854	8,525	8,314	202	8	1	0	12.5	12.2	0.31
1993	668,511	8,549	8,302	234	12	0	1	12.8	12.4	0.37
1994	659,545	8,719	8,451	260	8	0	0	13.2	12.8	0.41
1995	642,404	9,038	8,749	282	7	0	0	14.1	13.6	0.45
1996	643,862	8,883	8,615	259	8	0	1*	13.8	13.4	0.42
1997	637,001	9,217	8,915	295	7	0	0	14.5	14.0	0.47
1998	629,296	9,080	8,776	297	7	0	0	14.4	13.9	0.48

* 1 set of septuplets in 1987 and 1996

+ Data for 1997 have not been revised to include the 1,002 live births initially omitted from published data, so the numbers of maternities differ from those in revised data shown in Table A6.12.1

Source: ONS/OPCS, *Birth statistics, Series FM1*

This was Table A6.13 in the first edition of *Birth counts*

A6.11.2

Maternities with multiple births, Scotland, 1960–98

Year	All maternities	Multiple maternities	Twin	Triplet	Quadruplet	Quintuplet	Sextuplet	All multiple maternities	Twin	Triplet and higher order maternities
	Numbers of maternities							**Rates per thousand maternities**		
1960	102,395	1,133	1,117	16	0	0	0	11.1	10.9	0.16
1961	102,071	1,238	1,231	7	1	0	0	12.1	12.1	0.07
1962	105,152	1,292	1,281	10	1	0	0	12.3	12.2	0.10
1963	103,464	1,213	1,203	9	1	0	0	11.7	11.6	0.10
1964	104,959	1,279	1,262	17	0	0	0	12.2	12.0	0.16
1965	101,351	1,130	1,117	12	1	0	0	11.1	11.0	0.13
1966	97,042	1,071	1,060	10	1	0	0	11.0	10.9	0.11
1967	96,706	1,048	1,037	11	0	0	0	10.8	10.7	0.11
1968	95,191	1,013	1,006	7	0	0	0	10.6	10.6	0.07
1969	90,653	909	898	11	0	0	0	10.0	9.9	0.12
1970	87,636	924	915	9	0	0	0	10.5	10.4	0.10
1971	86,972	907	903	4	0	0	0	10.4	10.4	0.05
1972	78,782	810	801	8	0	1	0	10.3	10.2	0.11
1973	74,500	756	747	9	0	0	0	10.1	10.0	0.12
1974	70,256	682	677	5	0	0	0	9.7	9.6	0.07
1975	68,077	628	625	3	0	0	0	9.2	9.2	0.04
1976	64,911	603	595	7	0	1	0	9.3	9.2	0.12
1977	62,300	592	589	3	0	0	0	9.5	9.5	0.05
1978	64,216	596	589	7	0	0	0	9.3	9.2	0.11
1979	68,188	645	638	6	1	0	0	9.5	9.4	0.10
1980	68,689	662	658	4	0	0	0	9.6	9.6	0.06
1981	68,865	618	611	7	0	0	0	9.0	8.9	0.10
1982	65,963	613	607	6	0	0	0	9.3	9.2	0.09
1983	64,776	679	677	2	0	0	0	10.5	10.5	0.03
1984	64,800	675	665	10	0	0	0	10.4	10.3	0.15
1985	66,342	691	682	9	0	0	0	10.4	10.3	0.14
1986	65,456	731	721	10	0	0	0	11.2	11.0	0.15
1987	65,839	731	721	10	0	0	0	11.1	11.0	0.15
1988	65,842	716	706	9	1	0	0	10.9	10.7	0.15
1989	63,090	692	677	13	2	0	0	11.0	10.7	0.24
1990	65,556	748	731	16	1	0	0	11.4	11.2	0.26
1991	66,630	735	709	24	2	0	0	11.0	10.6	0.39
1992	65,308	822	807	15	0	0	0	12.6	12.4	0.23
1993	62,946	790	780	10	0	0	0	12.6	12.4	0.16
1994	61,227	794	778	16	0	0	0	13.0	12.7	0.26
1995	59,571	846	816	29	1	0	0	14.2	13.7	0.50
1996	58,831	829	800	29	0	0	0	14.1	13.6	0.49
1997	58,925	812	791	20	1	0	0	13.8	13.4	0.36
1998	56,819	830	810	19	1	0	0	14.6	14.3	0.35

Source: GRO for Scotland. *Annual report of the Registrar General for Scotland*
This is similar to Table A6.13 in the first edition of *Birth counts*

A6.11.3

Maternities with multiple births, Northern Ireland, 1961–98

Year	All maternities	Multiple maternities	Twin	Triplet	Quadruplet	Quintuplet	Sextuplet	All multiple maternities	Twin	Triplet and higher order maternities
	Numbers of maternities							**Rates per thousand maternities**		
1961	32,195	446	445	1	0	0	0	13.9	13.8	0.03
1962	32,889	419	417	2	0	0	0	12.7	12.7	0.06
1963	33,609	463	458	5	0	0	0	13.8	13.6	0.15
1964	34,611	409	404	5	0	0	0	11.8	11.7	0.14
1965	34,161	386	383	3	0	0	0	11.3	11.2	0.09
1966	33,409	366	363	3	0	0	0	11.0	10.9	0.09
1967	33,638	367	363	4	0	0	0	10.9	10.8	0.12
1968	33,353	356	351	5	0	0	0	10.7	10.5	0.15
1969	32,535	392	389	3	0	0	0	12.0	12.0	0.09
1970	32,192	356	354	1	1	0	0	11.1	11.0	0.03
1971	31,877	346	342	4	0	0	0	10.9	10.7	0.13
1972	30,096	328	325	2	1	0	0	10.9	10.8	0.07
1973	29,297	291	290	1	0	0	0	9.9	9.9	0.03
1974	27,237	294	291	3	0	0	0	10.8	10.7	0.11
1975	25,846	294	294	0	0	0	0	11.4	11.4	0.00
1976	26,106	269	264	5	0	0	0	10.3	10.1	0.19
1977	25,475	269	266	3	0	0	0	10.6	10.4	0.12
1978	26,229	251	249	2	0	0	0	9.6	9.5	0.08
1979	28,138	281	276	5	0	0	0	10.0	9.8	0.18
1980	28,542	302	298	4	0	0	0	10.6	10.4	0.14
1981	27,093	308	304	3	1	0	0	11.4	11.2	0.11
1982	26,752	305	303	2	0	0	0	11.4	11.3	0.07
1983	26,956	270	266	4	0	0	0	10.0	9.9	0.15
1984	27,328	307	304	3	0	0	0	11.2	11.1	0.11
1985	27,330	272	269	3	0	0	0	10.0	9.8	0.11
1986	27,813	283	280	2	1	0	0	10.2	10.1	0.07
1987	27,486	330	323	7	0	0	0	12.0	11.8	0.25
1988	27,364	284	282	1	1	0	0	10.4	10.3	0.04
1989	25,679	283	281	2	0	0	0	11.0	10.9	0.08
1990	26,090	272	266	5	0	1	0	10.4	10.2	0.19
1991	25,828	313	307	6	0	0	0	12.1	11.9	0.23
1992	25,207	263	255	8	0	0	0	10.4	10.1	0.32
1993	24,551	291	283	8	0	0	0	11.9	11.5	0.33
1994	23,949	296	290	6	0	0	0	12.4	12.1	0.25
1995	23,492	335	326	7	2	0	0	14.3	13.9	0.30
1996	24,193	327	314	11	2	0	0	13.5	13.0	0.45
1997	23,880	330	323	6	1	0	0	13.8	13.5	0.25
1998	23,471	312	305	7	0	0	0	13.3	13.0	0.30

The data in this table have been revised to exclude births to non-residents from 1981 onwards
Source: GRO for Northern Ireland. *Annual report of the Registrar General, Northern Ireland*
This is similar to Table 6.13 in the first edition of Birth counts

A6.11.4

Maternities with multiple live births, Irish Republic, 1960–96

Year of occurrence	All maternities	Multiple maternities	Twin	Triplet	Quadruplet	Quintuplet	All multiple maternities	Twin	Triplet and higher order maternities
	Numbers of maternities						**Rates per thousand maternities**		
1960	59,817	907	896	11	0	0	15.2	15.0	0.2
1961	58,902	917	911	6	0	0	15.6	15.5	0.1
1962	60,826	940	926	12	2	0	15.5	15.2	0.2
1963	62,264	971	960	11	0	0	15.6	15.4	0.2
1964	63,177	884	873	11	0	0	14.0	13.8	0.2
1965	62,648	863	850	12	1	0	13.8	13.6	0.2
1966	61,339	867	858	9	0	0	14.1	14.0	0.1
1967	60,457	843	836	7	0	0	13.9	13.8	0.1
1968	60,165	830	821	9	0	0	13.8	13.6	0.1
1969	62,033	864	849	15	0	0	13.9	13.7	0.2
1970	63,528	844	834	10	0	0	13.3	13.1	0.2
1971	66,688	851	839	12	0	0	12.8	12.6	0.2
1972	67,657	862	854	8	0	0	12.7	12.6	0.1
1973	67,861	845	838	7	0	0	12.5	12.4	0.1
1974	68,081	820	814	6	0	0	12.0	12.0	0.1
1975	66,379	792	785	7	0	0	11.9	11.8	0.1
1976	66,933	781	777	4	0	0	11.7	11.6	0.1
1977	68,072	810	800	10	0	0	11.9	11.8	0.1
1978	69,450	832	816	15	1	0	12.0	11.7	0.2
1979	71,793	740	734	6	0	0	10.3	10.2	0.1
1980	73,271	781	769	12	0	0	10.7	10.5	0.2
1981	71,425	726	719	7	0	0	10.2	10.1	0.1
1982	70,055	779	770	9	0	0	11.1	11.0	0.1
1983	66,352	753	741	12	0	0	11.3	11.2	0.2
1984	63,368	692	690	2	0	0	10.9	10.9	0.0
1985	61,730	651	644	7	0	0	10.5	10.4	0.1
1986	60,974	635	628	7	0	0	10.4	10.3	0.1
1987	57,801	620	608	12	0	0	10.7	10.5	0.2
1988	53,966	629	624	5	0	0	11.7	11.6	0.1
1989	51,388	623	616	7	0	1	12.1	12.0	0.1
1990	52,400	633	624	8	0	0	12.1	11.9	0.2
1991	52,116	592	584	6	2	0	11.4	11.2	0.1
1992	50,484	592	581	8	3	0	11.7	11.5	0.2
1993	48,726	565	552	13	0	0	11.6	11.3	0.3
1994	47,647	594	579	14	1	0	12.5	12.2	0.3
1995	48,110	662	646	16	0	0	13.8	13.4	0.3
1996	49,967	668	647	21	0	0	13.4	13.0	0.4

Source: Central Statistics Office, Republic of Ireland.

This is similar to Table A6.13 in the first edition of *Birth counts*

437

A6.12.1

Multiple maternities and all maternities by age of mother, England and Wales, 1938–98

Year	Age of mother, years							All
	Under 20	20–24	25–29	30–34	35–39	40–44	45 and over	
	Numbers of multiple maternities							
1938	142	1,320	2,172	2,178	1,348	322	12	7,494
1939	181	1,177	2,265	2,053	1,417	344	18	7,455
1940	170	1,270	2,132	2,008	1,285	295	14	7,174
1941	166	1,260	2,113	1,883	1,291	364	10	7,087
1942	159	1,380	2,328	2,309	1,424	361	15	7,976
1943	143	1,530	2,210	2,348	1,628	384	16	8,259
1944	157	1,776	2,470	2,816	1,924	440	21	9,604
1945	149	1,466	2,141	2,438	1,653	408	19	8,274
1946	160	1,844	3,162	3,112	2,078	410	22	10,788
1947	181	2,036	3,548	2,985	2,000	452	19	11,221
1948	186	1,874	3,063	2,404	1,734	420	6	9,687
1949	201	1,843	3,213	2,121	1,574	364	12	9,328
1950	214	1,703	3,012	2,133	1,572	334	11	8,979
1951	166	1,817	2,933	2,337	1,450	289	13	9,005
1952	172	1,727	2,702	2,347	1,339	291	12	8,590
1953	199	1,741	2,711	2,535	1,282	310	9	8,787
1954	202	1,826	2,699	2,467	1,233	285	12	8,724
1955	220	1,804	2,677	2,280	1,293	241	10	8,525
1956	238	1,850	2,696	2,329	1,336	281	9	8,739
1957	312	2,010	2,969	2,340	1,476	253	11	9,371
1958	282	2,125	2,935	2,400	1,398	223	14	9,377
1959	290	2,038	2,801	2,220	1,429	228	15	9,021
1960	323	2,142	2,832	2,183	1,379	299	5	9,163
1961	368	2,217	3,039	2,306	1,413	298	12	9,653
1962	429	2,343	3,066	2,301	1,378	320	8	9,845
1963	477	2,448	3,078	2,352	1,396	300	9	10,060
1964	490	2,541	3,198	2,384	1,319	296	10	10,238
1965	518	2,442	3,110	2,216	1,214	263	11	9,774
1966	557	2,591	3,036	1,967	1,120	222	8	9,501
1967	519	2,629	2,831	1,954	1,011	234	9	9,187
1968	518	2,590	2,682	1,811	991	183	8	8,783

Multiple maternities and all maternities by age of mother, England and Wales, 1938–98

Year	Age of mother, years							All
	Under 20	20–24	25–29	30–34	35–39	40–44	45 and over	
1969	458	2,461	2,637	1,771	843	166	5	8,341
1970	469	2,570	2,618	1,571	773	140	2	8,143
1971	491	2,430	2,726	1,505	761	154	7	8,074
1972	486	2,136	2,746	1,312	617	125	9	7,431
1973	423	1,817	2,608	1,207	511	117	5	6,688
1974	410	1,670	2,418	1,170	453	90	4	6,215
1975	390	1,572	2,339	1,171	409	101	6	5,988
1976	360	1,403	2,314	1,121	350	68	5	5,621
1977	301	1,379	2,139	1,278	347	72	3	5,519
1978	327	1,494	2,231	1,393	417	60	8	5,930
1979	348	1,499	2,284	1,551	426	66	7	6,181
1980	345	1,572	2,315	1,609	487	72	4	6,404
1981	:	:	:	:	:	:	:	:
1982	336	1,512	2,246	1,532	575	69	7	6,277
1983	312	1,616	2,243	1,559	592	61	4	6,387
1984	282	1,583	2,270	1,518	655	94	4	6,406
1985	320	1,677	2,375	1,628	707	85	11	6,803
1986	372	1,633	2,503	1,754	754	85	4	7,105
1987	339	1,589	2,671	1,847	766	102	6	7,320
1988	337	1,689	2,714	1,966	790	122	4	7,622
1989	344	1,641	2,754	2,118	796	118	3	7,774
1990	333	1,600	2,892	2,287	920	108	5	8,145
1991	298	1,561	2,833	2,558	994	125	11	8,380
1992	271	1,447	2,962	2,627	1,068	145	5	8,525
1993	286	1,407	2,800	2,794	1,096	154	12	8,549
1994	277	1,269	2,836	2,914	1,263	150	10	8,719
1995	291	1,306	2,906	2,993	1,348	175	19	9,038
1996	273	1,152	2,643	3,192	1,408	194	21	8,883
1997	263	1,124	2,615	3,360	1,599	233	23	9,217
1998	303	1,078	2,457	3,332	1,627	252	31	9,080
Multiple maternities per thousand maternities								
1938	5.7	9.2	11.0	15.2	17.4	12.8	5.4	12.2
1939	6.2	8.2	11.0	13.8	17.6	13.7	7.6	11.7
1940	6.1	8.6	10.6	14.3	16.6	11.8	6.3	11.5

A6.12.1 continued

Multiple maternities and all maternities by age of mother, England and Wales, 1938–98

Year	Age of mother, years							All
	Under 20	20–24	25–29	30–34	35–39	40–44	45 and over	
1941	6.6	8.4	11.5	14.5	17.1	14.2	4.7	12.0
1942	6.5	8.2	11.4	15.1	16.6	13.0	6.8	12.0
1943	5.8	8.6	11.1	14.1	17.0	12.9	6.9	11.8
1944	6.2	9.1	12.1	14.8	17.1	13.3	9.4	12.6
1945	5.8	8.3	11.6	14.7	16.0	12.8	8.2	12.0
1946	6.3	9.3	12.6	15.2	17.6	12.4	9.6	13.0
1947	6.4	8.9	12.5	15.1	17.2	13.5	8.0	12.6
1948	6.0	8.8	12.2	15.2	17.5	13.9	2.7	12.4
1949	6.2	9.1	13.0	15.3	17.7	13.6	6.1	12.6
1950	6.8	8.9	13.1	15.4	18.6	13.3	6.0	12.8
1951	5.6	9.6	13.3	16.5	18.5	12.2	7.6	13.2
1952	5.8	9.0	12.5	16.1	18.2	12.6	7.0	12.6
1953	6.5	8.9	12.4	16.7	18.4	13.7	5.7	12.7
1954	6.3	9.3	12.7	16.4	18.9	12.6	7.9	12.8
1955	6.6	9.3	12.5	16.0	19.2	11.2	6.9	12.6
1956	6.2	9.0	12.0	16.1	18.5	13.2	6.4	12.3
1957	7.5	9.4	12.8	16.1	19.4	12.4	7.6	12.8
1958	6.3	9.5	12.5	16.5	17.9	11.7	9.9	12.5
1959	6.2	8.8	11.9	15.4	18.2	12.4	10.7	11.9
1960	6.2	8.9	11.6	14.4	17.5	14.1	3.4	11.6
1961	6.1	8.8	12.2	15.1	18.0	13.2	8.2	11.8
1962	6.3	8.9	11.9	14.9	17.9	13.8	5.8	11.7
1963	6.6	9.1	11.7	15.2	18.6	13.1	7.2	11.7
1964	6.3	9.2	11.8	15.5	17.3	13.0	7.8	11.6
1965	6.3	8.7	11.8	15.3	16.7	12.3	7.7	11.3
1966	6.4	9.0	11.9	14.4	16.6	11.6	5.7	11.1
1967	6.1	9.0	11.6	15.0	15.9	13.1	6.8	11.0
1968	6.3	8.7	11.1	14.4	17.0	11.3	6.7	10.7
1969	5.6	8.5	11.1	14.7	15.9	11.4	4.7	10.4
1970	5.7	8.9	11.0	13.8	15.9	10.8	2.1	10.4
1971	5.9	8.5	11.0	13.7	16.8	12.7	8.3	10.3
1972	6.1	8.6	11.1	13.3	15.4	11.9	12.6	10.2
1973	5.7	8.1	10.7	13.2	14.9	13.3	7.7	9.9

Multiple maternities and all maternities by age of mother, England and Wales, 1938–98

Year	Age of mother, years							
	Under 20	20–24	25–29	30–34	35–39	40–44	45 and over	All
1974	5.9	8.0	10.3	13.1	14.9	11.8	7.1	9.7
1975	6.1	8.3	10.4	13.3	14.5	15.0	10.1	9.9
1976	6.2	7.7	10.5	12.4	13.4	11.2	9.8	9.6
1977	5.5	7.9	10.3	12.7	13.6	12.9	6.5	9.7
1978	5.8	8.2	10.6	12.4	15.0	10.4	15.2	10.0
1979	5.9	7.8	10.3	12.4	13.6	10.9	13.0	9.7
1980	5.7	7.8	10.4	12.5	14.4	11.8	6.3	9.8
1981	..	..	..	..	..	..	..	..
1982	6.1	7.9	10.7	12.8	14.8	11.7	10.9	10.1
1983	5.8	8.4	10.5	13.0	14.4	9.8	6.0	10.2
1984	5.2	8.3	10.5	12.5	15.4	14.4	7.1	10.1
1985	5.6	8.7	10.5	13.0	16.1	12.4	18.9	10.4
1986	6.5	8.5	11.0	13.7	16.8	12.1	7.5	10.8
1987	5.9	8.3	11.3	13.6	16.6	12.6	11.3	10.8
1988	5.7	8.8	11.2	14.1	16.8	14.4	7.8	11.1
1989	6.2	8.9	11.4	14.7	16.3	13.4	6.1	11.4
1990	6.0	8.9	11.5	14.8	17.9	11.7	9.9	11.6
1991	5.7	9.0	11.5	16.1	18.8	13.5	21.5	12.1
1992	5.7	8.9	12.2	15.9	19.1	15.1	10.0	12.5
1993	6.3	9.3	12.0	16.5	18.9	15.5	22.3	12.8
1994	6.6	9.1	12.5	16.4	20.3	14.7	20.7	13.2
1995	6.9	10.0	13.5	16.7	20.9	16.3	36.5	14.1
1996	6.1	9.2	12.6	17.4	20.6	17.0	36.9	13.8
1997	5.7	9.5	13.0	18.2	21.7	19.1	40.6	14.5
1998	6.3	9.5	12.8	17.9	21.0	19.7	56.7	14.4
Numbers of all maternities								
1938	24,943	144,146	197,342	143,750	77,403	25,062	2,228	614,874
1939	29,405	143,939	205,708	148,806	80,682	25,141	2,379	636,060
1940	27,909	148,281	200,926	140,820	77,263	24,943	2,234	622,376
1941	25,081	150,377	183,927	130,268	75,413	25,607	2,140	592,813
1942	24,605	168,336	204,211	152,940	85,690	27,857	2,199	665,838
1943	24,751	178,873	198,912	166,960	95,657	29,806	2,308	697,267
1944	25,192	195,890	204,224	189,790	112,749	33,024	2,223	763,092

441

A6.12.1 continued

Multiple maternities and all maternities by age of mother, England and Wales, 1938–98

Year	Age of mother, years							All
	Under 20	20–24	25–29	30–34	35–39	40–44	45 and over	
1945	25,849	177,190	184,352	165,820	103,426	31,974	2,323	690,934
1946	25,279	197,693	250,830	205,306	118,386	32,982	2,285	832,761
1947	28,182	229,851	283,787	197,410	116,321	33,579	2,374	891,504
1948	30,868	212,039	251,855	157,724	99,003	30,237	2,200	783,926
1949	32,260	202,649	246,817	138,500	89,026	26,833	1,965	738,050
1950	31,256	192,282	230,484	138,823	84,291	25,125	1,841	704,102
1951	29,540	189,170	220,614	141,243	78,419	23,710	1,711	684,407
1952	29,595	191,175	215,924	145,721	73,568	23,022	1,710	680,715
1953	30,809	196,634	218,204	151,705	69,569	22,670	1,589	691,180
1954	32,175	195,587	213,218	150,561	65,393	22,612	1,512	681,058
1955	33,455	194,487	213,785	142,864	67,392	21,584	1,459	675,026
1956	38,493	205,838	224,553	144,258	72,167	21,212	1,400	707,921
1957	41,757	213,635	232,135	144,920	76,250	20,386	1,441	730,524
1958	44,448	223,749	235,598	145,304	78,045	18,982	1,410	747,536
1959	46,637	230,933	235,104	144,539	78,346	18,336	1,399	755,294
1960	52,238	241,950	244,293	151,832	78,579	21,213	1,479	791,584
1961	60,465	251,573	249,661	153,132	78,458	22,513	1,469	817,271
1962	67,986	262,521	257,364	154,809	77,039	23,160	1,386	844,265
1963	72,250	268,847	264,193	154,397	75,052	22,896	1,249	858,884
1964	77,418	277,168	271,497	153,949	76,037	22,815	1,289	880,173
1965	82,284	279,999	264,001	145,022	72,626	21,349	1,432	866,713
1966	87,416	286,743	254,249	136,785	67,664	19,209	1,415	853,481
1967	85,221	292,766	244,225	130,422	63,584	17,883	1,332	835,433
1968	82,746	296,951	241,142	125,562	58,414	16,240	1,192	822,247
1969	82,260	289,875	238,550	120,347	53,150	14,517	1,064	799,763
1970	81,583	289,959	238,340	114,166	48,584	13,014	941	786,587
1971	83,218	286,413	247,294	109,581	45,410	12,142	841	784,899
1972	79,526	249,664	247,570	98,705	40,031	10,503	716	726,715
1973	73,743	224,179	243,696	91,746	34,322	8,793	646	677,125
1974	69,164	208,572	235,392	88,991	30,477	7,616	565	640,777
1975	63,805	190,438	225,773	88,119	28,221	6,718	592	603,666
1976	58,219	182,415	220,283	90,575	26,175	6,085	511	584,263

A6.12.1 continued

Multiple maternities and all maternities by age of mother, England and Wales, 1938–98

Year	Age of mother, years							All
	Under 20	20–24	25–29	30–34	35–39	40–44	45 and over	
1977	54,810	174,762	207,473	100,432	25,564	5,568	464	569,073
1978	56,272	182,560	209,927	112,568	27,885	5,778	525	595,515
1979	59,372	193,215	221,368	125,050	31,301	6,039	539	636,884
1980	60,914	201,342	222,547	129,211	33,741	6,108	638	654,501
1981	::						::	632,350
1982	55,493	191,975	210,775	119,973	38,743	5,910	642	623,511
1983	54,143	191,257	212,904	120,089	40,996	6,218	670	626,277
1984	54,620	190,948	216,845	121,861	42,579	6,547	565	633,965
1985	56,970	193,302	226,180	125,259	43,975	6,875	581	653,142
1986	57,394	191,425	227,579	128,357	45,011	7,009	533	657,308
1987	57,523	192,585	237,277	135,319	46,138	8,092	533	677,467
1988	58,738	192,910	241,723	139,652	47,144	8,470	516	689,153
1989	55,522	184,414	241,018	143,794	48,944	8,792	495	682,979
1990	55,535	179,317	250,670	154,553	51,259	9,193	503	701,030
1991	52,373	172,592	246,854	159,312	52,940	9,274	512	693,857
1992	47,800	162,572	242,651	164,802	55,900	9,630	499	683,854
1993	45,160	151,426	234,267	169,097	58,088	9,935	538	668,511
1994	42,041	139,801	227,399	177,450	62,170	10,201	483	659,545
1995	41,937	130,150	215,499	179,017	64,557	10,724	520	642,404
1996	44,865	125,258	209,441	183,976	68,495	11,438	569	643,862
1997	46,424	118,088	201,062	189,942	73,702	12,217	566	637,001
1998	48,274	113,078	191,588	185,969	77,646	12,824	547	629,926

Source: ONS/OPCS *Birth statistics, Series FM1*

This is a new table for this edition of *Birth counts*

443

A6.13.1

Mortality among singleton and multiple births in the first year of life, England and Wales, 1949/50 and 1975–96

Year of birth	Live births	Stillbirths~	Perinatal deaths~	Neonatal deaths	Postneonatal deaths	Infant deaths	Stillbirths*	Perinatal*	Neonatal+	Postneonatal+	Infant+
	Numbers						**Rates**				
Singleton births											
1949/50	1,392,505	31,023	..	23,291	15,588	38,879	21.8	..	16.7	11.2	27.9
1975	591,736	5,942	10,640	5,612	2,776	8,388	9.9	17.8	9.5	4.7	14.2
1976	573,254	5,388	9,532	4,970	2,404	7,374	9.3	16.5	8.7	4.2	12.9
1977	558,473	5,081	8,942	4,722	2,435	7,157	9.0	15.9	8.5	4.4	12.8
1978	584,818	4,767	8,452	4,572	2,600	7,172	8.1	14.3	7.8	4.4	12.3
1979	625,903	4,800	8,581	4,651	2,744	7,395	7.6	13.6	7.4	4.4	11.8
1980	643,660	4,446	8,024	4,445	2,612	7,575	6.9	12.4	6.9	4.1	11.8
1981	..	..	..	..	..	..	..	..	..	..	..
1982	613,547	3,690	6,484	3,520	2,569	6,089	6.0	10.5	5.7	4.2	9.9
1983	616,520	3,371	5,978	3,250	2,536	5,786	5.4	9.6	5.3	4.1	9.4
1984	624,148	3,418	5,871	3,101	2,217	5,318	5.4	9.4	5.0	3.6	8.5
1985	642,934	3,405	5,891	3,102	2,540	5,642	5.3	9.1	4.8	4.0	8.8
1986	646,924	3,280	5,667	2,976	2,532	5,508	5.0	8.7	4.6	3.9	8.5
1987	666,977	3,170	5,448	2,968	2,605	5,573	4.7	8.1	4.4	3.9	8.4
1988	678,386	3,145	5,414	2,896	2,488	5,384	4.6	7.9	4.3	3.7	7.9
1989	672,202	3,003	5,115	2,783	2,282	5,065	4.4	7.6	4.1	3.4	7.5
1990	689,866	3,019	5,063	2,675	2,065	4,740	4.4	7.3	3.9	3.0	6.9
1991	682,467	3,010	4,964	2,529	1,639	4,168	4.4	7.2	3.7	2.4	6.1
1992	672,598	2,725	4,598	2,454	1,404	3,858	4.0	6.8	3.6	2.1	5.7
1993	654,224	3,558	5,357	2,330	1,274	3,604	5.4	8.1	3.6	1.9	5.5
1994	646,887	3,468	5,216	2,267	1,177	3,444	5.3	8.0	3.5	1.8	5.3
1995	629,948	3,274	4,981	2,219	1,180	3,399	5.2	7.9	3.5	1.9	5.4
1996	631,760	3,223	4,895	2,161	1,163	3,324	5.1	7.7	3.4	1.8	5.3
Multiple births											
1949/50	34,879	2,008	..	3,423	874	4,297	54.4	..	98.1	25.1	123.2
1975	11,709	353	1,067	774	106	880	29.3	88.5	66.1	9.1	75.2
1976	11,015	321	880	616	91	707	28.3	77.6	55.9	8.3	64.2
1977	10,786	324	795	528	84	612	29.2	71.6	49	7.8	56.7

A6.13.1 continued

Mortality among singleton and multiple births in the first year of life, England and Wales, 1949/50 and 1975–96

Year of birth	Live births	Stillbirths~	Perinatal deaths~	Neonatal deaths	Postneonatal deaths	Infant deaths	Stillbirths*	Perinatal*	Neonatal+	Postneonatal+	Infant+
1978	11,600	341	878	588	112	700	28.6	73.5	50.7	9.7	60.3
1979	12,125	325	799	550	112	662	26.1	64.2	45.4	9.2	54.6
1980	12,574	336	775	518	108	108	26.0	60.0	41.2	8.6	8.6
1981	::	::	::	::	::	::	::	::	::	::	::
1982	12,384	253	579	383	132	515	20.0	45.8	30.9	10.7	41.6
1983	12,614	261	590	393	120	513	20.3	45.8	31.2	9.5	40.7
1984	12,670	232	574	417	110	527	18.0	44.5	32.9	8.7	41.6
1985	13,483	240	571	381	148	529	17.5	41.6	28.3	11.0	39.2
1986	14,094	269	665	471	178	649	18.7	46.3	33.4	12.6	46.0
1987	14,534	253	632	452	168	620	17.1	42.7	31.1	11.6	42.7
1988	15,191	237	643	483	162	645	15.4	41.7	31.8	10.7	42.5
1989	15,523	233	622	468	152	620	14.8	39.5	30.1	9.8	39.9
1990	16,274	237	632	459	151	610	14.4	38.3	28.2	9.3	37.5
1991	16,750	244	661	487	111	598	14.4	38.9	29.1	6.6	35.7
1992	17,058	219	577	415	107	522	12.7	33.4	24.3	6.3	30.6
1993	17,000	308	669	444	92	536	17.8	38.7	26.1	5.4	31.5
1994	17,369	348	744	463	82	545	19.6	42.0	26.7	4.7	31.4
1995	18,053	323	689	448	111	559	17.6	37.5	24.8	6.1	31.0
1996	17,729	316	683	446	83	529	17.5	37.8	25.2	4.7	29.8

~ Stillbirths at 28 or more weeks of gestation up to 1992. Stillbirths at 24 or more weeks of gestation from 1993 onwards.

* Stillbirths and perinatal deaths per thousand total births

+ Neonatal, postneonatal and infant deaths per thousand live births

Source: OPCS unpublished data, ONS/OPCS *Mortality statistics, Series DH3*.

This was Table A6.14 in the first edition of *Birth counts*

A6.13.2

Mortality among twins and other multiple births, England and Wales, 1975–96

Year of birth	All twins	Two males	One male and one female	Two females	Other multiple births	All twins	Two males	One male and one female	Two females	Other multiple births
	Numbers					**Rates per thousand live and stillbirths**				
	Stillbirths at 28 or more completed weeks of gestation									
1975	343	157	44	142	10	29.0	38.8	11.8	35.2	:
1976	309	128	59	122	12	27.9	32.8	17.9	31.5	:
1977	307	154	40	113	17	28.2	37.8	12.7	30.6	:
1978	327	140	63	124	14	27.9	32.2	19.0	30.5	:
1979	318	140	54	124	7	26.1	31.0	15.8	29.0	27.8
1980	320	131	52	137	16	25.4	29.6	13.9	30.8	54.4
1981	:	:	:	:	:	:	:	:	:	:
1982	249	102	48	99	4	20.1	22.6	13.6	22.7	17.1
1983	249	102	48	99	12	19.8	23.1	12.8	22.3	41.5
1984	224	91	51	82	8	17.7	20.1	14.0	18.4	30.8
1985	232	113	34	85	8	17.3	23.8	8.8	17.7	24.8
1986	255	119	51	85	14	18.3	24.3	12.2	17.5	32.9
1987	245	118	45	82	8	17.0	23.3	10.3	16.5	19.3
1988	227	104	31	92	8	15.2	20.0	7.0	17.5	19.1
1989	223	108	33	82	10	14.7	21.1	7.1	15.2	16.7
1990	220	97	31	92	10	13.9	17.3	6.5	16.6	26.4
1991	231	108	54	69	17	14.2	19.8	10.4	12.2	19.3
1992	208	:	:	:	13	12.5	:	:	:	17.1
					11					
	Stillbirths at 24 or more completed weeks of gestation									
1993	284	:	:	:	24	17.2	:	:	:	31.7
1994	325	:	:	:	23	19.2	:	:	:	28.2
1995	309	:	:	:	14	17.7	:	:	:	16.1
1996	300	:	:	:	16	17.4	:	:	:	19.7

Mortality among twins and other multiple births, England and Wales, 1975–96

Year of birth	All twins	Two males	One male and one female	Two females	Other multiple births	All twins	Two males	One male and one female	Two females	Other multiple births
Perinatal deaths, including stillbirths at 28 or more completed weeks of gestation										
1975	1,005	406	244	355	62	85.0	100.4	65.2	88.0	:
1976	835	383	175	277	45	75.4	98.0	53.1	71.5	:
1977	753	341	143	269	42	69.1	83.8	45.6	72.9	:
1978	819	343	179	297	59	69.9	79.0	54.0	73.2	:
1979	756	344	147	265	43	62.0	76.2	43.1	62.0	170.6
1980	725	321	131	273	50	57.5	72.7	34.9	61.4	170.1
1981	:	:	:	:	:	:	:	:	:	:
1982	563	268	100	195	16	45.4	59.4	28.4	44.7	68.4
1983	563	232	126	205	27	44.7	52.6	33.6	46.3	93.4
1984	541	226	123	192	33	42.8	49.9	33.8	43.0	126.9
1985	550	231	108	211	21	41.0	48.6	28.1	44.0	65.0
1986	618	281	146	191	47	44.3	57.3	34.8	39.4	110.6
1987	591	265	127	199	41	41.1	52.3	29.2	40.2	98.8
1988	605	269	117	219	38	40.6	51.7	26.3	41.7	72.5
1989	576	269	122	185	46	38.0	52.5	26.2	34.4	76.9
1990	586	245	126	215	46	36.9	43.8	26.6	38.9	71.5
1991	598	281	139	178	63	36.6	51.4	26.8	31.4	93.5
1992	531	:	:	:	46	31.9	:	:	:	71.3
Perinatal deaths, including stillbirths at 24 or more completed weeks of gestation										
1993	607	:	:	:	62	36.7	:	:	:	82.0
1994	682	:	:	:	62	40.4	:	:	:	76.1
1995	631	:	:	:	58	36.0	:	:	:	66.6
1996	634	:	:	:	49	36.8	:	:	:	60.2

A6.13.2 continued

Mortality among twins and other multiple births, England and Wales, 1975–96

Year of birth	Numbers					Rates per thousand live births				
	All twins	Two males	One male and one female	Two females	Other multiple births	All twins	Two males	One male and one female	Two females	Other multiple births
Neonatal deaths										
1975	720	266	217	237	54	62.7	68.5	58.6	60.9	..
1976	578	275	127	176	38	53.7	72.8	39.2	46.9	..
1977	502	217	111	174	26	47.4	55.4	35.8	48.6	..
1978	539	228	131	180	49	47.3	54.3	40.3	45.7	..
1979	512	238	109	165	38	43.1	54.4	32.5	39.7	155.1
1980	481	216	100	165	37	39.1	50.4	27.0	38.3	133.1
1981	..	..	..	..	..	..	..	..	..	..
1982	366	189	63	114	17	30.1	42.9	18.1	26.7	73.9
1983	376	159	96	121	17	30.5	36.9	26.0	27.9	61.4
1984	389	169	89	131	28	31.3	38.1	24.8	29.9	111.1
1985	363	134	90	139	18	26.5	28.2	23.4	29.0	57.1
1986	435	197	111	127	36	30.4	40.2	26.5	26.2	87.6
1987	414	180	99	135	38	28.1	35.5	22.8	27.2	93.4
1988	448	200	100	148	35	29.3	38.4	22.5	28.2	68.1
1989	418	185	107	126	50	26.9	36.1	23.0	23.4	85.0
1990	421	168	107	146	38	25.9	30.0	22.6	26.4	60.7
1991	430	203	92	135	57	25.8	37.1	17.8	23.8	86.2
1992	373	..	..	..	42	22.7	..	..	..	66.2
1993	397	..	..	..	47	24.4	..	..	..	64.2
1994	420	..	..	..	43	25.3	..	..	..	54.3
1995	396	..	..	..	52	23.0	..	..	..	60.7
1996	406	..	..	..	40	23.9	..	..	..	50.1
Postneonatal deaths										
1975	104	32	41	31	2	9.1	8.2	11.1	8.0	..
1976	87	35	27	25	4	8.1	9.3	8.3	6.7	..
1977	84	38	26	20	0	7.9	9.7	8.4	5.6	..
1978	109	47	32	30	3	9.6	11.2	9.8	7.6	..
1979	109	41	29	39	3	9.2	9.4	8.6	9.4	12.2
1980	102	42	23	37	6	8.3	9.8	6.2	8.6	21.6

A6.13.2 continued

Mortality among twins and other multiple births, England and Wales, 1975–96

Year of birth	All twins	Two males	One male and one female	Two females	Other multiple births	All twins	Two males	One male and one female	Two females	Other multiple births
1981	:	:	:	:	:	:	:	:	:	:
1982	130	54	31	45	2	10.7	12.2	8.9	10.5	8.7
1983	116	38	36	42	4	9.4	8.8	9.7	9.7	14.4
1984	103	40	32	31	7	8.3	9.0	8.9	7.1	27.8
1985	141	59	45	37	7	10.7	12.7	11.8	7.8	22.2
1986	176	74	52	50	2	12.9	15.5	12.6	10.5	4.9
1987	160	53	50	57	8	11.3	10.7	11.6	11.7	19.7
1988	145	57	30	58	17	9.9	11.2	6.8	11.3	33.1
1989	144	62	34	48	8	9.6	12.4	7.4	9.1	13.6
1990	144	59	41	44	7	9.2	10.7	8.7	8.1	11.2
1991	101	44	34	23	10	6.3	8.2	6.6	4.1	15.1
1992	100	:	:	:	7	6.1	:	:	:	11.0
1993	84	:	:	:	8	5.2	:	:	:	10.9
1994	74	:	:	:	8	4.5	:	:	:	10.1
1995	97	:	:	:	14	5.6	:	:	:	16.3
1996	79	:	:	:	4	4.7	:	:	:	5.0
Infant deaths										
1975	824	298	258	268	56	71.8	76.7	69.7	68.9	:
1976	665	310	154	201	42	61.8	82.0	47.6	53.6	:
1977	586	255	137	194	26	55.3	65.1	44.2	54.2	:
1978	648	275	163	210	52	56.9	65.4	50.1	53.4	:
1979	621	279	138	204	41	52.3	63.8	41.1	49.1	167.3
1980	583	258	123	202	43	47.4	60.2	33.2	46.9	154.7
1981	:	:	:	:	:	:	:	:	:	:
1982	496	243	94	159	19	40.8	55.1	27.0	37.3	82.6
1983	492	197	132	163	21	39.9	45.8	35.7	37.6	75.8
1984	492	209	121	162	35	39.6	47.1	33.7	36.9	138.9
1985	504	193	135	176	25	38.3	41.6	35.4	37.3	79.4
1986	611	271	163	177	38	44.7	56.7	39.4	37.2	92.5
1987	574	233	149	192	46	40.6	47.1	34.6	39.4	113
1988	593	257	130	206	52	40.4	50.4	29.4	40.0	101.2

Mortality among twins and other multiple births, England and Wales, 1975–96

Year of birth	All twins	Two males	One male and one female	Two females	Other multiple births	All twins	Two males	One male and one female	Two females	Other multiple births
1989	562	247	141	174	58	37.6	49.2	30.5	32.8	98.6
1990	565	227	148	190	45	36.1	41.3	31.4	34.9	71.9
1991	531	247	126	158	67	33.0	46.1	24.6	28.2	101.4
1992	473	:	:	:	49	28.8	:	:	:	77.3
1993	481	:	:	:	55	29.6	:	:	:	75.1
1994	494	:	:	:	51	29.8	:	:	:	64.4
1995	493	:	:	:	66	28.7	:	:	:	77.0
1996	485	:	:	:	44	28.6	:	:	:	55.1
Live births										
1975	11475	3885	3700	3890						
1976	10,767	3,780	3,237	3,750	:					
1977	10,591	3,916	3,098	3,577	:					
1978	11,391	4,202	3,253	3,936	:					
1979	11,880	4,374	3,354	4,152	245					
1980	12,296	4,283	3,702	4,311	278					
1981										
1982	12,154	4,410	3,476	4,268	230					
1983	12,337	4,306	3,698	4,333	277					
1984	12,418	4,439	3,593	4,386	252					
1985	13,168	4,637	3,816	4,715	315					
1986	13,683	4,781	4,139	4,763	411					
1987	14,127	4,950	4,303	4,874	407					
1988	14,677	5,104	4,419	5,154	514					
1989	14,935	5,016	4,619	5,300	588					
1990	15,648	5,495	4,713	5,440	626					
1991	16,089	5,358	5,128	5,603	661					
1992	16,424	:	:	:	634					
1993	16,268	:	:	:	732					
1994	16,577	:	:	:	792					
1995	17,196	:	:	:	857					
1996	16,931	:	:	:	798					

Source: OPCS unpublished data and ONS/OPCS *Mortality statistics, Series DH3*

This was Table A6.15 in the first edition of *Birth counts*

A6.13.3

Mortality among triplets and other higher order multiple births, England and Wales, 1975–95

Year of birth	Numbers					Rates				
	Stillbirths	Early neonatal deaths	Neonatal deaths	Postneonatal deaths	Live births	Stillbirths[~]	Perinatal[−]	Neonatal[+]	Postneonatal[+]	Infant[+]
Triplets										
1975	8	44	45	1	208	37.0	240.7	216.3	4.8	221.2
1976	11	28	31	3	217	48.2	171.1	142.9	13.8	156.7
1977	16	22	23	0	188	78.4	186.3	122.3	0.0	122.3
1978	13	29	33	3	173	69.9	225.8	190.8	17.3	208.1
1979	7	28	30	3	221	30.7	153.5	135.7	13.6	149.3
1980	16	34	37	6	257	58.6	183.2	144.0	23.3	167.3
1975–80	71	185	199	16	1,264	53.2	191.8	157.4	12.7	170.1
1981	10	3	4	1						
1982	4	12	17	2	206	19.0	76.2	82.5	9.7	92.2
1983	11	15	17	4	256	41.2	97.4	66.4	15.6	82.0
1984	8	16	19	7	232	33.3	100.0	81.9	30.2	112.1
1985	8	7	11	3	271	28.7	53.8	40.6	11.1	51.7
1982-85	31	50	64	16	965	31.1	81.3	66.3	16.6	82.9
1986	13	24	26	2	356	35.2	100.3	73.0	5.6	78.7
1987	8	27	30	7	367	21.3	93.3	81.7	19.1	100.8
1988	7	23	29	10	464	14.9	63.7	62.5	21.6	84.1
1989	10	31	42	5	539	18.2	74.7	77.9	9.3	87.2
1990	16	25	33	7	587	26.5	68.0	56.2	11.9	68.1
1986–90	54	130	160	31	2,313	22.8	77.7	69.2	13.4	82.6
1991	12	42	47	5	612	19.2	86.5	76.8	8.2	85.0
1992	11	30	37	7	595	18.2	49.5	62.2	11.8	73.9
1993	19	29	37	8	683	27.1	68.4	54.2	11.7	65.9
1994	20	31	34	8	760	25.6	65.4	44.7	10.5	55.3

451

Mortality among triplets and other higher order multiple births, England and Wales, 1975–95

Year of birth	Stillbirths	Early neonatal deaths	Neonatal deaths	Postneonatal deaths	Live births	Stillbirths~	Perinatal~	Neonatal+	Postneonatal+	Infant+
1995	11	37	44	14	835	13.0	43.7	52.7	16.8	69.5
1991–95	73	169	199	42	3,485	20.5	47.5	57.1	12.1	69.2
1993–95*	56	97	115	30	2,272	24.1	41.7	50.6	13.2	63.8
Quadruplets										
1975–80#	4	32	33	2	120	32.3	219.2	275.0	16.7	291.7
1982–85	1	15	16	4	87	11.4	181.8	183.9	46.0	229.9
1986–90	5	29	37	11	203	24.0	163.5	182.3	54.2	236.5
1991–95	7	37	42	5	173	38.9	205.6	242.8	28.9	271.7
1993–95*	5	24	27	0	103	46.3	222.2	262.1	0.0	262.1

* Including stillbirths at 24 to 27 weeks of gestation. These are excluded from other totals

~ Per thousand total births

+ Per thousand live births

Data for 1975 to 1979 are from Botting B, Macdonald Davies I and Macfarlane AJ *Recent trends in the incidence of multiple births and their mortality. Archives of Diseases in Childhood* 1987:62:941–50

Source: Authors' analysis of ONS/OPCS data

Data extract: live births 1993 (7/94), 1994 (7/95), 1995 (3/7/96), 1996 (8/4/97)
linked 1993 (3/4/96), 1994 (18/9/96), 1995 (3/11/97)

This was Table A6.16 in the first edition of *Birth counts*

A6.14.1

Reported ethnic group and limiting long-term illness in children aged under five by sex, Great Britain, 1991

Reported ethnic group of child	Children aged 0–4			Children aged 0–4 with long-term illness			Percentage with long-term illness		
	Male	Female	Total	Male	Female	Total	Male	Female	Total
All ethnic groups	1,853,994	1,770,794	3,624,788	39,672	30,094	69,766	2.1	1.7	1.9
White	1,685,048	1,606,884	3,291,932	35,117	26,367	61,484	2.1	1.6	1.9
Black – Caribbean	18,850	18,743	37,593	704	574	1,278	3.7	3.1	3.4
Black – African	12,320	12,221	24,541	510	477	987	4.1	3.9	4.0
Black – other	18,228	17,768	35,996	672	476	1,148	3.7	2.7	3.2
Indian	37,702	36,169	73,871	643	527	1,170	1.7	1.5	1.6
Pakistani	31,829	30,583	62,412	847	751	1,598	2.7	2.5	2.6
Bangladeshi	12,254	12,058	24,312	346	259	605	2.8	2.1	2.5
Chinese	5,689	5,410	11,099	73	55	128	1.3	1.0	1.2
Other groups – Asian	7,843	7,879	15,722	159	123	282	2.0	1.6	1.8
Other groups – other	24,231	23,079	47,310	601	485	1,086	2.5	2.1	2.3
Children born in Ireland	2,936	2,778	5,714	103	102	205	3.5	3.7	3.6

Source: OPCS and GRO Scotland, *1991 Census, Limiting long-term illness, Table 3*

This is a new table for this edition of *Birth counts*

A7.1.1

Sizes of maternity units and numbers of births, England, 1973–96

Year	All	Size of unit, number of births						
		Less than 10	10–199	200–999	1,000–1,999	2,000–2,999	3,000–3,999	4,000 and over
Number of units								
All units								
1973	527	..	85	225	121	58	25	13
1978	423	..	93	119	104	63	28	16
1980	400	..	91	89	82	81	32	25
1981	380	..	90	80	80	79	30	21
1986	333	..	88	38	57	72	49	29
1990	417	115	56	35	40	72	56	43
1996	341	75	45	22	43	63	62	31
Units with GP beds only *								
1973	221	..	76	144	1	0	0	0
1978	148	..	82	66	0	0	0	0
1980	132	..	78	53	1	0	0	0
1981	118	2	72	44	0	0	0	0
1986	92	4	69	19	0	0	0	0
Units with GP and consultant beds *								
1973	87	..	2	20	27	21	9	8
1978	106	..	3	10	39	33	11	10
1980	115	..	5	13	29	41	14	13
1981	108	..	1	12	29	40	15	11
1986	103	..	2	6	15	41	26	13
Units with consultant beds only *								
1973	219	..	7	61	93	37	16	5
1978	169	..	8	43	65	30	17	6
1980	153	..	8	23	52	40	18	12
1981	149	1	4	24	53	41	14	12
1986	129	0	3	13	39	35	23	16
Total numbers of births occurring in maternity units								
All units								
1973	591,669	..	9,785	111,080	180,477	140,365	84,618	65,344
1978	551,294	..	9,373	56,992	158,907	154,105	95,856	76,061
1980	607,879	..	8,438	41,684	127,191	198,984	108,696	122,886
1981	589,862	28	8,055	37,939	130,118	200,018	102,574	111,130
1986	610,682	18	6,662	17,255	92,051	185,669	168,442	140,585
1990	664,097	223	5,007	14,723	63,565	179,636	191,858	209,085
1996	604,705	162	4,438	10,341	66,489	157,470	215,855	149,950

A7.1.1 *continued*

Sizes of maternity units and numbers of births, England, 1973–96

Year	All	Size of unit, number of births						
		Less than 10	10–199	200–999	1,000–1,999	2,000–2,999	3,000–3,999	4,000 and over

Total numbers of births occurring in maternity units								
Units with GP beds only *								
1973	69,763	..	9,503	58,908	1,352	0	0	0
1978	30,640	..	8,067	22,573	0	0	0	0
1980	26,711	..	7,549	18,074	1,088	0	0	0
1981	22,019	14	7,504	14,501	0	0	0	0
1986	11,995	18	6,210	5,767	0	0	0	0
Units with GP and consultant beds *								
1973	176,036	..	77	11,661	41,754	52,573	30,366	39,605
1978	230,353	..	463	6,028	61,750	78,340	36,844	46,928
1980	271,083	..	283	7,923	46,921	101,374	47,738	66,844
1981	263,706	0	162	7,219	47,713	100,415	51,625	56,572
1986	281,114	0	361	2,977	23,249	99,396	88,329	66,802
Units with consultant beds only *								
1973	345,870	..	205	40,511	137,371	87,789	54,255	25,739
1978	290,301	..	843	28,391	97,157	75,765	59,012	29,133
1980	310,085	..	606	15,687	79,182	97,610	60,958	56,042
1981	300,519	2	401	16,219	82,405	99,603	47,331	54,558
1986	317,573	0	91	8,511	68,802	86,273	80,113	73,783

* Statistical breakdown by type of bed not available after 1986

Source: Department of Health and Social Security, SH3 tabulations, 1980, 1981 and 1986. Authors' analysis of ONS registration data for births occurring in 1990 and 1996

This was Table A7.1 in the first edition of *Birth counts*

A7.1.2

Sizes of maternity units and numbers of births, Wales, 1980–96

Year	All	Size of unit, number of births						
		Less than 10	10–199	200–999	1,000–1,999	2,000–2,999	3,000–3,999	4,000 and over
	Number of units							
1980	40	–	19	5	9	6	1	0
1981	19	–	1	2	10	3	1	2
1986	21	–	4	2	7	4	2	1
1990	45	11	16	3	7	5	2	1
1996	31	3	12	1	7	6	2	0
	Total numbers of births occurring in maternity units							
1980	35,741	–	1,256	3,056	13,755	14,230	3,444	0
1981	33,968	–	160	1,119	15,669	6,946	3,509	9,762
1986	35,319	–	407	949	11,106	11,683	6,776	4,401
1990	37,365	15	1,049	2,094	10,864	11,928	6,971	4,444
1996	33,300	4	727	515	9,948	14,587	7,519	0

Source: Welsh Office

This is similar to Table A7.2 in the first edition of *Birth counts*

A7.1.3

Sizes of maternity units and numbers of births, Scotland, 1980–96

Year	All	Size of unit, number of births						
		Less than 10	10–199	200–999	1,000–1,999	2,000–2,999	3,000–3,999	4,000 and over
	Number of units							
1980	82	–	45	12	12	6	3	4
1981	79	–	42	12	12	6	3	4
1986	74	–	43	6	12	6	3	4
1990	62	–	31	6	13	4	5	3
1996	54	–	30	2	9	5	5	3
	Total numbers of births occurring in maternity units							
1980	67,700	–	2,992	4,054	17,583	15,243	10,605	7,223
1981	68,484	–	2,659	3,875	18,556	15,909	10,785	16,700
1986	65,430	–	2,797	1,881	17,507	15,101	11,128	17,016
1990	65,316	–	1,787	1,921	20,122	9,348	17,404	14,734
1996	57,717	–	1,553	1,015	12,204	11,370	17,140	14,435

Source: ISD, Scotland

This is similar to Table A7.2 in the first edition of *Birth counts*

A7.1.4

Sizes of maternity units and numbers of births, Northern Ireland, 1980–95/96

Year	All	Size of unit, number of births						
		Less than 10	10–199	200–999	1,000–1,999	2,000–2,999	3,000–3,999	4,000 and over
	Number of units							
1980	33	–	8	14	7	2	2	0
1981	34	–	11	11	8	3	1	0
1986	29	–	8	10	5	2	3	0
1989/90	18	1	1	8	5	3	1	0
1994/95	17	–	1	5	6	5	0	0
1995/96	16	–	1	3	7	4	1	0
	Total numbers of births occurring in maternity units							
1980	28,682	–	815	7,043	9,428	4,795	6,601	0
1981	27,437	–	1,088	5,379	10,127	7,260	3,583	0
1986	28,060	7	707	6,797	6,379	4,342	9,828	0
1989/90	25,240	–	80	6,244	7,580	8,151	3,185	0
1994/95	24,370	–	134	3,529	7,949	12,758	0	0
1995/96	24,163	–	40	2,102	9,254	9,727	3,040	0

Source: Department of Health and Social Services, Northern Ireland

This is similar to Table A7.2 in the first edition of *Birth counts*

A7.1.5

Sizes of maternity units and numbers of births by NHS region, England, 1980–96

	Year	All	Size of unit, number of births						
			Less than 10	10-199	200-999	1,000-1,999	2,000-2,999	3,000-3,999	4000 and over
Regional office areas									
Number of units									
Northern and Yorkshire	1996	49	12	5	4	13	7	4	4
Trent	1996	32	6	6	1	4	7	5	3
Anglia and Oxford	1996	32	5	5	2	3	5	7	5
North Thames	1996	54	16	4	3	3	9	15	4
South Thames	1996	41	7	2	1	7	13	11	0
South and West	1996	59	12	17	8	6	6	5	5
West Midlands	1996	37	10	5	3	1	7	5	6
North West	1996	37	7	1	0	6	9	10	4
Number of births occuring in maternity units									
Northern and Yorkshire	1996	73,917	22	625	2,500	21,272	16,105	14,028	19,365
Trent	1996	59,686	22	461	267	6,452	18,466	17,818	16,200
Anglia and Oxford	1996	65,954	6	506	1,231	3,814	11,903	23,712	24,782
North Thames	1996	97,390	33	380	671	4,664	23,027	51,593	17,022
South Thames	1996	83,561	17	183	806	11,378	31,986	39,191	0
South and West	1996	72,054	41	1,702	3,176	8,704	15,176	17,921	25,334
West Midlands	1996	67,851	11	417	1,690	1,800	17,590	17,520	28,823
North West	1996	84,292	10	164	0	8,405	23,217	34,072	18,424
Regional health authorities									
Number of units									
Northern	1980	31	–	4	8	12	6	1	0
	1981	28	–	4	6	11	6	3	0
	1986	27	–	5	5	9	6	1	1
	1990	29	5	3	4	9	6	0	2
Yorkshire	1980	33	–	8	8	5	7	4	1
	1981	30	–	6	7	7	6	3	1
	1986	26	–	6	3	4	9	1	3
	1990	33	11	2	2	4	8	3	3
Trent	1980	40	–	11	13	3	8	2	3
	1981	38	–	10	13	1	9	1	4
	1986	34	–	13	6	1	6	3	5
	1990	37	10	9	1	4	4	4	5

A7.1.5 continued

Sizes of maternity units and numbers of births by NHS region, England, 1980–96

	Year	All	Size of unit, number of births						
			Less than 10	10–199	200–999	1,000–1,999	2,000–2,999	3,000–3,999	4,000 and over
East Anglia	1980	19	–	7	5	1	2	2	2
	1981	18	–	6	5	3	0	2	2
	1986	15	–	4	3	1	3	3	1
	1990	17	4	1	4	0	4	2	2
Oxford	1980	23	–	8	6	1	5	0	3
	1981	22	–	9	5	0	5	0	3
	1986	19	–	8	1	2	4	2	2
	1990	19	1	5	3	1	3	3	3
North West Thames	1980	23	–	1	4	9	6	2	1
	1981	23	–	2	4	8	7	1	1
	1986	18	–	0	0	9	7	1	1
	1990	34	11	4	2	2	9	4	2
North East Thames	1980	28	–	1	5	9	10	3	0
	1981	28	–	2	4	7	12	3	0
	1986	26	–	2	3	7	7	7	0
	1990	37	11	3	4	2	5	9	3
South East Thames	1980	29	–	3	5	13	5	3	0
	1981	27	–	1	5	14	5	2	0
	1986	23	–	2	2	6	7	6	0
	1990	31	10	2	1	4	7	6	1
South West Thames	1980	19	–	2	1	8	8	0	0
	1981	19	–	2	1	10	6	0	0
	1986	14	–	0	0	6	5	3	0
	1990	22	6	1	0	3	9	2	1
Wessex	1980	33	–	16	6	5	3	1	2
	1981	31	–	14	6	4	5	1	1
	1986	28	–	14	4	2	4	2	1
	1990	37	11	9	6	2	4	3	2
South Western	1980	39	–	18	10	5	1	2	3
	1981	36	–	16	9	4	2	2	3
	1986	30	–	16	3	2	4	2	3
	1990	33	9	10	3	2	3	2	4

A7.1.5 continued

Sizes of maternity units and numbers of births by NHS region, England, 1980–96

	Year	All	Size of unit, number of births						
			Less than 10	10–199	200–999	1,000–1,999	2,000–2,999	3,000–3,999	4,000 and over
West Midlands	1980	37	–	5	11	4	8	4	5
	1981	35	–	6	9	4	9	3	4
	1986	32	–	5	6	4	6	6	5
	1990	42	13	4	4	1	6	7	7
Mersey	1980	17	–	4	2	3	3	4	1
	1981	15	–	2	2	3	3	4	1
	1986	10	–	0	0	2	2	4	2
	1990	16	5	1	0	2	1	3	4
North Western	1980	28	–	3	5	4	9	4	3
	1981	25	–	0	5	5	10	3	2
	1986	25	–	3	3	4	5	8	2
	1990	30	8	2	1	4	3	8	4
Number of births occuring in maternity units									
Northern	1980	41,403	–	306	3,555	18,247	15,653	3,642	0
	1981	39,843	–	384	3,281	17,247	15,349	3,582	0
	1986	39,651	–	365	2,397	14,332	14,536	3,858	4,163
	1990	40,733	7	406	1,931	15,522	14,067	0	8,800
Yorkshire	1980	47,112	–	823	3,700	7,586	16,350	14,071	4,582
	1981	45,632	–	815	3,219	11,209	15,031	10,819	4,539
	1986	47,308	–	676	1,357	6,243	21,631	3,708	13,693
	1990	51,317	23	321	501	6,108	19,847	10,448	14,069
Trent	1980	55,922	–	1,036	6,965	4,593	20,113	7,340	15,875
	1981	53,859	–	1,014	6,684	1,541	21,773	3,399	19,448
	1986	55,265	–	1,068	2,849	1,779	15,336	9,824	24,409
	1990	59,682	25	697	461	6,234	11,061	13,961	27,243
East Anglia	1980	24,372	–	671	2,481	1,526	4,010	7,049	8,635
	1981	23,250	–	539	2,254	5,407	0	6,771	8,279
	1986	24,246	–	319	1,142	1,798	6,184	10,401	4,402
	1990	28,310	12	72	2,225	0	9,367	7,320	9,314

A7.1.5 continued

Sizes of maternity units and numbers of births by NHS region, England, 1980–96

	Year	All	Size of unit, number of births						
			Less than 10	10–199	200–999	1,000–1,999	2,000–2,999	3,000–3,999	4,000 and over
Oxford	1980	32,551	—	553	2,015	1,161	13,000	0	15,822
	1981	30,988	—	827	2,367	0	12,426	0	15,368
	1986	32,034	—	549	201	2,964	10,436	6,837	11,047
	1990	36,401	1	267	1,219	1,244	7,177	10,026	16,467
North West Thames	1980	40,443	—	81	1,937	13,162	14,755	6,263	4,245
	1981	39,193	—	199	2,659	12,051	16,884	3,145	4,255
	1986	39,574	—	0	0	14,192	17,768	3,315	4,299
	1990	47,550	22	221	693	3,061	22,006	12,961	8,586
North East Thames	1980	52,874	—	187	2,682	14,489	25,344	10,172	0
	1981	51,363	—	210	1,854	10,643	28,837	9,819	0
	1986	54,210	—	352	1,323	11,142	17,891	23,502	0
	1990	60,898	21	316	1,360	3,342	13,086	30,223	12,550
South East Thames	1980	45,342	—	203	3,222	20,825	11,462	9,630	0
	1981	44,102	—	89	3,101	22,262	12,284	6,366	0
	1986	46,682	—	160	1,505	9,040	16,206	19,771	0
	1990	51,451	13	215	823	6,309	18,457	20,942	4,692
South West Thames	1980	33,197	—	255	652	13,392	18,898	0	0
	1981	33,164	—	209	707	17,187	15,061	0	0
	1986	31,736	—	0	0	10,809	11,112	9,815	0
	1990	38,354	11	144	0	5,390	21,704	6,847	4,258
Wessex	1980	33,385	—	1,848	3,068	7,362	6,872	3,089	11,139
	1981	32,070	—	1,485	2,883	5,759	12,284	3,650	6,009
	1986	35,036	—	1,451	2,503	2,955	9,210	6,973	11,944
	1990	38,317	20	1,100	2,239	2,415	9,482	10,589	12,472
South Western	1980	36,488	—	1,501	3,440	8,225	2,268	6,503	14,551
	1981	34,955	—	1,326	2,691	6,037	4,381	6,314	14,206
	1986	35,019	—	1,093	1,145	3,105	7,585	6,816	15,275
	1990	40,647	28	704	1,357	3,534	8,006	6,910	20,108
West Midlands	1980	72,510	—	648	4,762	6,510	20,657	13,483	26,450
	1981	68,166	—	783	4,411	6,975	23,479	11,019	21,499
	1986	71,305	—	502	2,843	6,088	15,220	21,405	25,247
	1990	76,508	22	224	1,671	1,097	14,643	23,550	35,301

A7.1.5 continued

Sizes of maternity units and numbers of births by NHS region, England, 1980–96

	Year	All	Size of unit, number of births						
			Less than 10	10–199	200–999	1,000–1,999	2,000–2,999	3,000–3,999	4,000 and over
Mersey	1980	31,644	–	284	1,120	4,182	7,168	14,411	4,479
	1981	31,163	–	195	917	4,178	7,123	14,471	4,279
	1986	31,887	–	0	0	2,480	5,614	15,247	8,546
	1990	33,169	7	63	0	2,793	2,996	10,234	17,076
North Western	1980	56,162	–	42	2,085	5,931	22,427	13,043	12,634
	1981	54,242	–	0	1,784	7,723	25,730	10,560	8,445
	1986	55,672	–	239	932	6,316	12,606	27,034	8,545
	1990	60,760	11	257	243	6,516	7,737	27,847	18,149

Source: Department of Health and Social Security, SH3 tabulations, 1980, 1981 and 1986. Authors' analysis of ONS registration data for births occurring in 1990 and 1996

This is similar to Table A7.2 in the first edition of *Birth counts*

A7.2.1

Available maternity beds, England, 1949, 1963, 1968, 1975–1998/99

Year	Obstetrics	Mixed beds	GP maternity	All maternity beds	Revised totals+	
	Average number available daily					**Beds per thousand total births**
1949	..	–	..	15,975	–	52.4
1963	..	–	..	19,681	–	37.2
1968	..	–	..	21,618	–	34.7
						Beds per thousand maternities
1975	16,984	–	4,273	21,257	–	37.4
1976	16,662	–	3,997	20,659	–	37.5
1977	16,098	–	3,637	19,735	–	36.8
1978	15,810	–	3,265	19,075	–	34.0
1979	15,541	–	3,099	18,640	–	31.1
1980	15,490	–	2,916	18,406	–	29.8
1981	15,239	–	2,917	18,156	–	..
1982	15,394	–	2,675	18,068	–	30.8
1983	15,246	–	2,553	17,800	–	30.1
1984	14,902	–	2,278	17,180	–	28.7
1985	14,183	–	2,275	16,458	–	26.7
1986	14,320	–	1,841	16,161	16,166	26.1
1987/88	14,496	–	1,437	15,933	15,932	24.9
1988/89	11,192	2,998	1,177	15,367	15,367	23.6
1989/90	10,803	2,898	1,008	14,709	14,706	22.8
1990/91	10,263	3,005	902	14,170	14,170	21.4
1991/92	9,925	2,957	887	13,769	13,770	21.0
1992/93	9,568	2,984	759	13,311	13,167	20.4
1993/94	8,902	3,413	720	13,035	12,521	19.8
1994/95	8,527	3,190	654	12,371	11,971	19.2
1995/96	8,064	2,680	614	11,358	11,358	18.7
1996/97	–	–	–	–	11,000	18.1
1997/98	–	–	–	–	10,781	17.9
1998/99	–	–	–	–	10,398	17.4

+ Data were revised in 1999.

Source: Department of Health, KH03, 1987–1998/99. DHSS, SH3 1981–86. Charles Webster, *Health services since the war*, Volume 2

This is similar to Table A7.3 in the first edition of *Birth counts*

A7.2.2

Available maternity beds, Wales, 1949, 1963, 1968, 1975–1997/98

Year	Obstetrics	GP maternity	All maternity beds	
	Average number available daily			**Beds per thousand total births**
1949	..	..	1,097	52.0
1963	..	..	1,343	38.0
1968	..	..	1,417	35.8
				Beds per thousand maternities
1975	998	271	1,269	37.3
1976	976	258	1,234	37.5
1977	984	240	1,224	36.7
1978	977	216	1,193	33.9
1979	982	187	1,169	31.0
1980	952	197	1,149	29.8
1981	972	171	1,143	..
1982	977	168	1,145	32.2
1983/84	943	156	1,099	31.1
1984/85	943	146	1,089	30.5
1985/86	913	132	1,046	28.6
1986/87	916	115	1,030	27.9
1987/88	898	109	1,006	26.7
1988/89	843	104	947	24.5
1989/90	823	104	927	25.6
1990/91	821	95	916	24.8
1991/92	822	94	916	24.2
1992/93	787	82	869	23.3
1993/94	729	77	806	22.2
1994/95	715	72	788	22.4
1995/96	652	58	710	20.8
1996/97	638	57	696	20.1
1997/98	614	51	665	19.5

Source: Welsh Office. Charles Webster, *Health services since the war*, Volume 2

This is similar to Table A7.3 in the first edition of *Birth counts*

A7.2.3

Available maternity beds, Scotland, 1949, 1963, 1968, 1975–1998/99

Year	Obstetrics	GP maternity	All maternity beds	
	Average number available daily			**Beds per thousand total**
births				
1949	..	..	2,698	52.2
1963	..	..	3,044	36.7
1968	..	..	3,235	36.7
Years ending September 30				**Beds per thousands maternities**
1975	2,361	674	3,035	44.6
1976	2,348	631	2,979	45.9
1977	2,272	602	2,874	46.1
1978	2,201	575	2,776	43.2
1979	2,226	524	2,750	40.3
1980	2,218	471	2,689	39.1
1981	2,246	433	2,679	38.9
1982	2,210	434	2,644	40.1
1983	2,213	450	2,663	41.1
1984	2,212	421	2,633	40.6
1985	2,192	371	2,563	38.6
Financial years				
1985/86	2,121	368	2,489	37.5
1986/87	2,039	349	2,388	36.5
1987/88	2,047	327	2,374	36.1
1988/89	1,954	301	2,255	34.2
1989/90	1,865	233	2,099	33.3
1990/91	1,801	205	2,006	30.6
1991/92	1,746	178	1,925	28.9
1992/93	1,677	157	1,834	28.1
1993/94	1,521	137	1,658	26.3
1994/95	1,445	118	1,563	25.5
1995/96	1,381	106	1,487	25.0
1996/97	1,311	89	1,400	23.8
1997/98	1,252	102	1,354	23.0
1998/99*	1,165	98	1,263	22.2

* Provisional
Subtotals may not add up to totals because of rounding

Source: ISD Scotland, *Scottish health statistics.* Charles Webster, *Health services since the war*, Volume 2

This is similar to Table A7.3 in the first edition of *Birth counts*

A7.2.4

Available maternity beds, Northern Ireland, 1949, 1963, 1968, 1975–1998/99

Year	Obstetrics	GP maternity	All maternity beds	
	Average number available daily			**Beds per thousand maternities**
1975	733	253	986	38.1
1976	700	245	945	36.2
1977	709	240	949	37.3
1978	770	199	969	36.9
1979	728	185	913	32.4
1980	744	185	929	32.5
1981	741	190	931	34.4
1982	733	176	910	34.0
1983	735	157	892	33.1
1984	740	142	882	32.3
1985	737	156	893	32.3
1986	727	127	854	30.7
1987	710	113	823	29.9
1988/89	702	65	767	28.0
1989/90	702	30	732	28.5
1990/91	688	30	718	27.5
1991/92	657	30	687	26.6
1992/93	614	30	644	25.5
1993/94	565	28	593	24.2
1994/95	531	9	540	22.5
1995/96	518	4	522	22.2
1996/97	491	0	491	20.3
1997/98	474	0	474	19.8
1998/99	472	0	472	20.1

Source: DHSS, *Health and Personal Social Services Statistics for Northern Ireland,* central return KH03A

This is similar to Table A7.3 in the first edition of *Birth counts*

A7.2.5

Available maternity beds, regional hospital boards, England, Wales and Scotland, 1949, 1963, 1968

Regional hospital board and country	1949	1963	1968	1949*	1963	1968
	Numbers of maternity beds			**Maternity beds per thousand total births**		
England	15,975	19,681	21,618	23.6	24.0	27.5
Newcastle	852	1,439	1,524	16.3	25.0	29.8
Leeds	1,136	1,460	1,541	22.4	25.5	27.7
Sheffield	1,615	1,825	1,919	23.4	21.7	23.3
East Anglian	413	575	644	15.8	21.0	22.9
NW Metropolitan	1,468	1,940	2,046	24.9	24.2	28.4
NE Metropolitan	1,456	1,724	1,800	27.5	28.7	31.6
SE Metropolitan	1,417	1,458	1,595	32.6	24.6	29.2
SW Metropolitan and Wessex	1,615	1,885	2,512	22.9	21.4	25.2
Oxford	457	753	915	20.1	22.0	25.7
South Western	1,089	1,368	1,505	25.2	27.0	30.6
Birmingham	1,516	1,999	2,193	20.8	21.1	23.2
Manchester	1,956	2,134	2,280	25.5	26.0	28.7
Liverpool	985	1,121	1,144	27.2	24.8	27.9
Wales	1,097	1,343	1,417	25.1	28.0	31.5
Scotland	2,698	3,044	3,235	26.1	29.1	33.6

Data for maternity beds in 1949 relate to 31 December 1949. They exclude 891 beds in provincial teaching hospitals and 823 beds in London teaching hospitals. Bed data for 1949 relate to available beds, which equate with staffed beds or available staffed beds for later years. Data for live and still births are calculated from the information supplied about local health authorities for 1950, included in the Cranbrook Report, Appendix III, pp106–9.

Wessex was split off from the South West Metropolitan RHB in 1959. To facilitate comparisons with 1949, Wessex and S. W. Metropolitan RHB are included together in data for 1963 and 1968.

Source: Charles Webster, *Health services since the war*, Volume 2. Derived from Ministry of Health, Annual Report 1949, Appendix II, *Maternity Services in Hospitals and Homes. Report of the Maternity Services Committee*, 1959, known as the Cranbrook report. *Registrar General, Statistical Review* 1963. *Digest of Health Statistics for England and Wales* 1969, 1970, 1972. Department of Health for Scotland, *Annual Report* 1949, *Scottish health statistics* 1963, 1972. *Domiciliary Midwifery and Maternity Bed Needs*, 1970

This is similar to Table A7.4 in the first edition of *Birth counts*

A7.2.6

Available maternity beds, regional health authorities, England, 1980–86

	1980	1981	1982	1983	1984	1985	1986
Average number available daily							
All maternity beds							
England	18,406	18,295	18,121	17,800	17,180	16,849	16,161
Regional health authorities							
Northern	1,284	1,253	1,280	1,276	1,252	1,410	1,176
Yorkshire	1,532	1,727	1,514	1,497	1,474	1,374	1,354
Trent	1,747	1,744	1,764	1,735	1,680	1,617	1,536
East Anglian	732	726	718	704	698	670	636
NW Thames	1,287	1,277	1,168	1,181	1,110	1,092	1,067
NE Thames	1,582	1,544	1,565	1,589	1,510	1,446	1,434
SE Thames	1,342	1,304	1,283	1,260	1,226	1,224	1,170
SW Thames	1,034	1,013	950	932	860	785	718
Wessex	1,058	1,021	1,024	1,005	999	980	953
Oxford	879	874	863	813	778	793	765
South Western	1,122	1,113	1,117	1,087	1,031	1,019	1,030
West Midlands	2,008	1,980	2,002	1,955	1,897	1,825	1,746
Mersey	979	944	924	923	859	840	834
North Western	1,682	1,635	1,703	1,650	1,624	1,589	1,572
SHAs	137	139	244	192	183	187	171
Consultant beds							
England	15,490	15,378	15,446	15,246	14,902	14,574	14,320
Regional health authorities							
Northern	1,124	1,109	1,129	1,123	1,104	1,069	1,043
Yorkshire	1,285	1,281	1,266	1,256	1,246	1,184	1,185
Trent	1,385	1,403	1,437	1,425	1,385	1,330	1,275
East Anglian	601	606	597	601	625	600	568
NW Thames	1,255	1,244	1,136	1,149	1,078	1,069	1,049
NE Thames	1,448	1,425	1,451	1,433	1,400	1,343	1,339
SE Thames	1,249	1,220	1,206	1,196	1,175	1,179	1,130
SW Thames	921	926	869	851	793	756	698
Wessex	752	741	743	740	748	740	734
Oxford	648	650	646	619	598	621	622
South Western	758	763	758	734	722	736	806
West Midlands	1,553	1,564	1,592	1,554	1,548	1,490	1,433
Mersey	898	875	872	887	833	823	818
North Western	1,476	1,431	1,501	1,485	1,466	1,447	1,449
SHAs	137	139	244	192	183	187	171
General practitioner beds							
England	2,916	2,917	2,675	2,553	2,278	2,275	1,841
Regional health authorities							
Northern	160	143	152	153	148	341	133
Yorkshire	247	446	248	241	227	189	168
Trent	362	341	327	310	295	287	260
East Anglian	131	120	121	104	74	69	67
NW Thames	32	33	33	32	32	23	18

A7.2.6 *continued*

Available maternity beds, regional health authorities, England, 1980–86

	1980	1981	1982	1983	1984	1985	1986
NE Thames	134	119	114	156	110	103	96
SE Thames	93	84	77	63	51	45	40
SW Thames	113	87	81	81	67	29	20
Wessex	306	280	281	265	252	240	220
Oxford	231	224	216	194	180	172	144
South Western	364	350	359	353	309	282	224
West Midlands	455	417	410	400	349	335	312
Mersey	81	69	52	35	27	17	16
North Western	206	204	203	165	158	143	123
SHAs	0	0	0	0	0	0	0

Source: DHSS SH3 returns

This is similar to Table A7.4 in the first edition of *Birth counts*

A7.2.7

Available maternity beds, regional health authorities, England, 1988/89–1994/95

	1988/89	1989/90	1990/91	1991/92	1992/93	1993/94	1994/95
Average number available daily							
All maternity beds							
England	15,367	14,709	14,170	13,770	13,311	13,035	12,371
Regional health authorities							
Northern	1,109	1,058	1,033	1,043	1,003	1,438	1,234
Yorkshire	1,300	1,253	1,210	1,170	1,173	1,024	1,039
Trent	1,429	1,344	1,258	1,178	1,159	1,132	1,086
East Anglian	632	613	586	560	553	544	553
NW Thames	938	845	837	819	893	857	827
NE Thames	1,346	1,240	1,163	1,120	1,014	1,015	963
SE Thames	1,104	1,070	1,010	1,000	934	852	868
SW Thames	736	704	685	735	735	637	675
Wessex	1,054	1,032	1,001	891	843	792	768
Oxford	715	691	678	673	633	585	538
South Western	903	902	892	873	830	736	722
West Midlands	1,684	1,626	1,556	1,531	1,479	1,414	1,287
Mersey	761	711	689	638	615	620	583
North Western	1,480	1,454	1,418	1,386	1,305	1,277	1,228
SHAs	175	165	152	152	142	112	–
Consultant beds							
England	11,192	10,803	10,263	9,925	9,568	8,902	8,527
Regional health authorities							
Northern	846	830	821	835	814	793	679
Yorkshire	787	756	707	686	594	510	528
Trent	1,009	1,092	971	921	913	896	856
East Anglian	523	515	503	473	453	440	461
NW Thames	835	668	602	575	667	653	637
NE Thames	1,126	1,019	965	888	808	772	799
SE Thames	810	833	732	671	670	580	526
SW Thames	528	512	518	577	572	458	501
Wessex	707	695	616	456	463	395	448
Oxford	403	374	360	420	353	351	329
South Western	348	383	418	404	381	365	356
West Midlands	1,109	1,081	1,044	1,073	1,119	995	898
Mersey	727	679	662	614	594	594	557
North Western	1,258	1,199	1,193	1,180	1,025	988	952
SHAs	175	165	152	152	142	112	–
Mixed beds							
England	2,998	2,898	3,005	2,957	2,984	3,413	3,190
Regional health authorities							
Northern	179	154	152	162	153	610	528
Yorkshire	411	418	438	421	514	457	455
Trent	304	175	229	202	192	183	171
East Anglian	68	67	55	60	71	71	63
NW Thames	97	176	235	244	226	204	190
NE Thames	133	139	125	159	138	180	108
SE Thames	276	221	260	315	254	271	342

A7.2.7 continued

Available maternity beds, regional health authorities, England, 1988/89–1994/95

	1988/89	1989/90	1990/91	1991/92	1992/93	1993/94	1994/95
SW Thames	208	192	167	158	163	179	174
Wessex	156	155	198	173	223	255	181
Oxford	245	264	271	206	240	195	178
South Western	448	434	392	391	371	298	286
West Midlands	327	307	307	292	189	241	254
Mersey	28	27	22	19	16	21	21
North Western	117	170	152	155	234	248	239
SHAs	0	0	0	0	0	0	–
General practitioner beds							
England	1,177	1,008	902	887	759	720	654
Regional health authorities							
Northern	84	74	60	46	36	35	27
Yorkshire	102	79	65	63	65	57	56
Trent	116	77	58	55	54	53	59
East Anglian	41	31	28	27	29	33	29
NW Thames	6	1	0	0	0	0	0
NE Thames	87	82	73	73	68	63	56
SE Thames	18	16	18	14	10	1	0
SW Thames	0	0	0	0	0	0	0
Wessex	191	182	187	262	157	142	139
Oxford	67	53	47	47	40	39	31
South Western	107	85	82	78	78	73	80
West Midlands	248	238	205	166	171	178	135
Mersey	6	5	5	5	5	5	5
North Western	105	85	73	51	46	41	37
SHAs	0	0	0	0	0	0	–

Source: Department of Health KH03, Special tabulation

This is similar to Table A7.4 in the first edition of *Birth counts*

A7.2.8

Available maternity beds, regional office areas, England, 1994/95–1998/99

	1994/95	1995/96	1996/97	1997/98	1997/98
	Average number available daily				**Rate per thousand maternities**
England	11,971	11,358	11,010	10,781	17.9
Regional office areas					
Northern and Yorkshire	1,746	1,592	1,522	1,476	20.1
Trent	1,194	1,126	1,006	1,007	17.1
Anglia and Oxford	1,190	1,160	1,069	1,023	15.4
North Thames	1,691	1,691	1,745	1,774	18.4
South Thames	1,543	1,511	1,416	1,404	16.1
South and West	1,489	1,412	1,368	1,387	18.7
West Midlands	1,287	1,131	1,207	1,093	16.6
North West	1,830	1,736	1,667	1,616	20.4

	1998/99
	Average number available daily
England	10,398
Regional office areas	
Northern and Yorkshire	1,438
Trent	951
West Midlands	1,054
North West	1,496
Eastern	1,034
London	1,786
South East	1,636
South West	1,004

Source: Department of Health KH03, special tabulation

This is similar to Table A7.4 in the first edition of *Birth counts*

A7.3.1

Cots for neonatal care, England, Wales, Scotland, Northern Ireland, 1974–1997/98

Year	Available cots		Year	Available cots	
	Number	Cots per 1,000 live births		Number	Cots per 1,000 live births
England			**Wales**		
1974	3,922	6.5	1974	234	6.5
1975	3,978	7.0	1975	232	6.8
1976	4,018	7.3	1976	235	7.0
1977	4,007	7.5	1977	239	7.5
1978	3,972	7.1	1978	237	7.1
1979	3,945	6.6	1979	237	6.6
1980	3,959	6.4	1980	237	6.3
1981	3,940	6.6	1981	238	6.6
1982	3,902	6.6	1982	236	6.6
1983	3,898	6.6	1983	231	6.5
1984	3,872	6.4			
1985	3,756	6.1	1983/84	230	6.5
1986	3,651	5.9	1984/85	229	6.4
1987	3,572	5.6	1985/86	223	6.1
	Neonatal cots*		1986/87	219	5.9
1987/88	3,625	5.6	1987/88	217	5.7
1988/89	3,581	5.5	1988/89	219	5.6
1989/90	3,496	5.4	1989/90	217	5.7
1990/91	3,375	5.1	1990/91	194	5.0
1991/92	3,412	5.2	1991/92	218	5.7
1992/93	3,395	5.2	1992/93	215	5.7
1993/94	3,287	5.2	1993/94	214	5.8
1994/95	3,341	5.3	1994/95	226	6.4
1995/96	3,219	5.2	1995/96	208	6.0
			1996/97	182	5.2
	Neonatal intensive care beds~		1997/98	..	..
1996/97	1,537	2.4			
1997/98	1,530	2.5			

A7.3.1 continued

Cots for neonatal care, England, Wales, Scotland, Northern Ireland, 1974–1997/98

| Year ending 30 September | Available staffed beds Northern Ireland | | Cots | | |
	Number	Cots per 1,000 live births	Year	Number	Cots per 1,000 live births
Scotland			**Northern Ireland**		
1974	..	..	1974	194	7.1
1975	..	..	1975	191	7.3
1976	634	9.8	1976	191	7.2
1977	625	9.0	1977	195	7.6
1978	635	9.9	1978	193	7.4
1979	628	9.2	1979	195	6.9
1980	626	9.1	1980	195	6.8
1981	621	9.0	1981	198	7.3
1982	619	9.4	1982	..	..
1983	608	9.3	1983	208	7.6
1984	597	9.2	1984	218	7.9
1985	580	8.7	1985	218	7.9
			1986	208	7.4
			1987	..	..
1986/87	563	8.5			
1987/88	552	8.3	1987/88	..	..
1988/89	543	7.9	1988/89	176	6.3
1989/90	520	7.8	1989/90	171	6.5
1990/91	497	7.2	1990/91	171	6.5
1991/92	477	6.9	1991/92	170	6.5
1992/93	465	6.8	1992/93	169	6.6
1993/94	448	6.7	1993/94	168	6.7
1994/95	426	6.9	1994/95	166	6.8
1995/96	421	7.0	1995/96+	..	..
1996/97	404	6,8	1996/97+	..	..
1997/98	430	7.2			

+ Average daily number of available neonatal cots in non-maternity wards, lines 10 and 11 on KH03
~ Average daily number of available and occupied neonatal intensive care beds, line 1 on KH03
* From 1995/96 onwards in Northern Ireland, 'sick babies', specialty 422, was incorporated within paediatrics, specialty 420
Sources:
DHSS, Form SH3, 'special care baby unit' cots, 1974–85
DH/DHSS, Form KH03, lines 10 and 1, 1987/88–1995/96
Department of Health, Form KH03, Line 1, 1996/97 onwards

Welsh Office
ISD, Scotland, Form ISD(S)1
Department of Health and Social Services, Northern Ireland

This is similar to Table A7.5 in the first edition of *Birth counts*

A7.3.2

Cots for neonatal care, England, regional health authorities, 1974–1994/95

Area	1974	1975	1976	1977	1978	1979	1980
Average numbers of cots available daily in special care baby units							
England	3,932	3,978	4,018	4,007	3,972	3,945	3,959
Regional health authorities							
Northern	344	333	335	336	332	324	323
Yorkshire	330	336	339	339	341	344	337
Trent	347	349	360	358	349	345	334
East Anglian	155	154	140	140	140	140	141
NW Thames	288	287	300	309	323	319	324
NE Thames	348	362	369	365	342	331	349
SE Thames	268	294	303	286	289	291	286
SW Thames	209	214	213	225	212	211	216
Wessex	194	199	197	195	191	190	191
Oxford	211	210	216	202	194	194	194
South Western	190	190	207	207	207	207	207
West Midlands	405	406	407	405	431	438	446
Mersey	246	247	245	236	234	207	203
North Western	377	377	367	364	367	385	388

Area	1981	1982	1983	1984	1985	1986	
Average numbers of cots available daily in special care baby units							
England	3,920	3,885	4,058	3,832	3,716	3,611	
Regional health authorities							
Northern	316	312	307	296	289	273	
Yorkshire	334	333	333	333	304	293	
Trent	335	344	348	342	341	331	
East Anglian	142	137	139	145	145	135	
NW Thames	307	294	299	294	293	297	
NE Thames	353	328	333	332	318	300	
SE Thames	292	293	292	302	281	277	
SW Thames	216	204	405	192	187	188	
Wessex	195	195	195	195	193	180	
Oxford	191	191	190	197	196	192	
South Western	207	201	201	201	208	200	
West Midlands	446	472	449	451	434	428	
Mersey	197	192	190	189	188	188	
North Western	389	390	377	363	341	328	

A7.3.2 continued

Cots for neonatal care, England, regional health authorities, 1974–1994/95

Area	1987/88	1988/89	1989/90	1990/91	1991/92	1992/93	1993/94	1994/95
	Average daily number of neonatal cots*							
England	3,625	3,581	3,496	3,375	3,412	3,395	3,287	3,341
Regional health authorities								
Northern	258	260	262	260	258	258	252	253
Yorkshire	324	316	314	282	302	297	301	301
Trent	321	310	302	295	287	291	290	302
East Anglian	134	135	132	121	122	118	120	122
NW Thames	278	269	238	248	260	250	244	278
NE Thames	291	298	291	275	284	297	299	297
SE Thames	290	304	278	271	266	256	260	264
SW Thames	185	181	189	189	186	192	177	195
Wessex	278	186	191	183	182	178	185	185
Oxford	193	190	186	180	181	180	184	185
South Western	197	166	169	148	154	155	113	119
West Midlands	396	402	384	371	380	388	335	331
Mersey	190	187	185	172	171	169	170	170
North Western	333	332	334	340	340	338	333	338
SHAs	47	46	41	41	39	27	24	0

* Average daily number of available neonatal cots in non-maternity wards, lines 10 and 11 on KH03

Source: DHSS SH3 returns, Department of Health, Form KH03

This is similar to Table A7.5 in the first edition of *Birth counts*

A7.3.3

Cots for neonatal care, England, regional office areas, 1995/96–1997/98

	Neonatal cots*	Neonatal intensive care beds~				
	1995/96	1996/97	1997/98	1996/97	1997/98	1997/98
	Average available daily			**Average occupied daily**		**Beds / 1,000 live births**
England	3,219	1,537	1,530	1,077	1,052	2.5
Regional office area						
Northern and Yorkshire	476	223	198	143	123	2.7
Trent	303	182	171	124	111	2.9
Anglia and Oxford	332	135	150	107	111	2.2
North Thames	555	278	315	196	216	3.2
South Thames	464	245	228	163	139	2.6
South and West	293	167	183	123	139	2.4
West Midlands	293	107	110	82	84	1.6
North West	503	201	174	139	128	2.2

* Average daily number of available neonatal cots in non-maternity wards, lines 10 and 11 on KH03

~ Average daily number of available and occupied neonatal intensive care beds, line 1 on KH03

Source: Department of Health Form KH03

This is similar to Table A7.5 in the first edition of *Birth counts*

A7.4.1

Day nurseries, playgroups, childminders and nursery education, England, 1984–98

	Day nurseries provided by local authorities[1,2]			Playgroups run by local authorities[1,2]			Registered day nurseries[1,3]		Registered playgroups[1,2,3]		Registered childminders[1,2,3,4]		Pupils in nursery schools, at January	
	Premises	Places	Children on register	Premises	Places	Children on register	Premises	Places	Premises	Places	Persons	Places	Full-time	Part-time
1984	654	28,872	33,775	109	2,692	2,968	829	23,124	16,100	384,523	53,041	116,331	12,367	37,260
1985	664	28,904	32,911	115	2,811	3,196	908	25,242	16,558	399,930	58,390	126,847	12,046	37,796
1988	688	28,951	34,398	109	2,572	3,205	1,355	36,252	17,026	401,173	74,588	163,700	11,407	38,596
1989	694	28,789	32,585	95	2,051	2,717	1,696	45,026	16,983	399,460	83,904	186,356	11,135	39,305
1990	695	27,978	32,413	94	2,045	2,525	2,165	57,669	17,460	409,563	93,074	205,567	10,622	41,196
1991	672	27,039	30,302	92	1,918	2,319	2,861	77,092	17,617	420,526	106,004	233,258	10,275	42,101
1992	580	23,800	28,400	80	1,400	1,600	3,400	91,600	17,200	409,800	109,200	254,300	9,935	42,158
1993	530	21,400	27,100	80	1,500	1,600	3,900	111,000	17,000	394,400	87,200	300,700	9,672	43,635
1994	560	22,300	29,000	90	1,600	2,300	4,400	124,000	17,100	407,600	96,000	357,500	9,140	43,474
1995	540	20,900	27,500	80	1,700	2,300	4,800	139,300	16,700	406,200	97,100	373,600	8,871	43,897
1996	510	19,900	23,500	70	1,200	1,400	5,200	156,600	16,400	394,000	102,600	376,200	8,846	43,563
1997	530	20,200	24,200	70	1,300	1,300	5,500	172,000	15,600	380,900	98,500	365,200	8,614	42,224
1998	500	18,670	21,700	50	1,200	1,600	6,100	203,000	15,600	381,200	94,700	370,700	8,247	40,389

* Prior to 1992 data were collected for children aged under 5 only; after that date the numbers relate to children aged under 8. Data for 1992 onwards have been rounded.

1 Prior to 1992, where a local authority had not submitted a return, the latest available data for that authority were substituted. Figures since 1992 are estimates which have been rounded.

2 Including facilities provided by voluntary organisations under agency arrangement under Section 22 of the National Health Service Act 1946.

3 From October 1991, registered under the Children Act 1989 and prior to that date registered under the Nurseries and Child Minders Regulation Act 1948, as amended by Section 60 of the Health Services and Public Health Act 1968.

4 From 1992 figures for childminders relate to registration from children aged under 8. In 1995 20,400 places were with childminders registered.

Sources: **DH/DHSS** *Health and personal social services statistics for England 1984–95;* DH *Children's Day Care Facilities at 31st March 1996 (England),* and Department for Education and Employment.

This is similar to Table A7.7 in the first edition of *Birth counts*

A7.5.1

NHS hospital and community health services midwifery staff, England, 1975–98

Year*	All midwifery staff	Students+	Qualified midwives	
	Whole-time equivalent~			**Rate per 1,000 maternities**
1975	18,579	4,244	14,335	25.2
1976	19,422	4,482	14,940	27.1
1977	19,921	4,738	15,183	28.3
1978	19,890	5,116	14,774	26.3
1979	20,022	4,640	15,382	25.6
1980	19,936	4,231	15,705	25.5
1981	21,031	4,758	16,272	..
1982	20,250	3,764	16,486	28.1
1983	22,070	4,750	17,320	29.3
1984	22,570	4,740	17,830	29.8
1985	22,810	4,380	18,430	29.9
1986	23,030	4,180	18,850	30.4
1987	23,300	3,980	19,320	30.2
1988	23,310	4,020	19,290	29.7
1989	23,170	3,750	19,420	30.1
1990	23,980	3,810	20,170	30.5
1991	22,830	3,220	19,610	29.9
1992	22,800	2,560	20,240	31.3
1993	21,530	2,020	19,510	30.9
1994	20,740	1,500	19,240	30.8
1995	19,542	1,250	18,292	30.1
1996	19,548	1,000	18,548	30.5
1997	19,300	990	18,310	30.4
1998	19,419	940	18,479	31.0

* Data for years prior to 1982 relate to December, while those for subsequent years are staff in post on September 30

~ Whole time equivalent is calculated by dividing each person's working hours by the number of full time hours.

The number of full time hours was reduced from 40 to 37.5 during 1980 and the 37.5 hour week became mandatory on 31 March 1981

This means that figures for whole time equivalents before 1980 are not directly comparable with those for subsequent years

+ Excluding Project 2000 students

Source: DHSS, SH3 returns. Department of Health, Non-Medical Workforce Census.

Data for 1975–80 were published in the first edition of *Birth counts*

Data for 1981 were derived from an existing tabulation of SH3 data

Data for 1982–1994 were tabulated specially and do not necessarily agree with published data.

Up to 1994, staff were classified according to their pay scale. From 1995 onwards, their occupations were coded directly.

This means that figures for 1995 onwards are not directly comparable with those for previous years.

From 1995 onwards, qualified midwives include staff teaching midwifery and managers in maternity services with midwifery qualifications.

This is similar to Table A7.8 in the first edition of *Birth counts*

A7.5.2

Midwives in training and education, England, 1991–99

	1991	1992	1993	1994	1995+
All pre- and post-registration midwives in training at 31 March~					
England	2,976	3,124	3,305	3,275	3,226
Northern	140	149*	201*	177	129
Yorkshire	225	181	173	210	224
Trent	273	275	349	370	379
East Anglian	99	119	145	104	88
NW Thames	283	291*	310	265	274
NE Thames	250	266	267	281	225
SE Thames	293	302	341	348	379
SW Thames	172	134	154	133	109
Wessex	228	244*	223*	239	262
Oxford	149	186*	196*	202	207
South Western	171	168	176	158	129
West Midlands	320	412	370	372	411
Mersey	146	137	144*	170	181
North Western	227	260	256*	246	229

	1996+	1997+	1998+	1999	
England	3,331	3,521	3,263	3,559	
Northern and Yorkshire	404	380	391	395	
Trent	386	394	345	350	
Anglia and Oxford	240	210	207	205	
North Thames	523	578	483	624	
South Thames	547	619	570	592	
South and West	406	420	374	437	
West Midlands	343	402	441	455	
North West	482	518	452	501	

* Includes integrated degree students

~ Registration refers to whether or not midwives in training were registered nurses.

+ Revised national totals for England for the years 1995 to 1998 were published in 1999, but no regional breakdown was given. The revised totals were 3,259 in 1995, 3,259 in 1996, 3,395 in 1997 and 3,518 in 1998.

Source: English National Board of Nursing, Midwifery and Health Visiting, *Annual report* 1991–98

This is a new table for this edition of *Birth counts*

A7.5.3

NHS hospital and community health services midwifery staff by region, England, 1975–98

Year*	1975	1976	1977	1978	1979	1980	1981
Whole-time equivalent staff, including learners[1]							
England	18,579	19,422	19,921	19,890	20,022	19,936	21,031
Regional health authorities							
Northern	1,243	1,256	1,248	1,206	1,350	1,289	1,315
Yorkshire	1,323	1,347	1,429	1,445	1,464	1,484	1,691
Trent	1,781	1,662	1,712	1,652	1,815	1,873	2,080
East Anglian	737	769	782	875	918	795	882
NW Thames	1,480	1,393	1,456	1,436	1,461	1,432	1,515
NE Thames	1,602	1,763	1,826	1,908	1,736	1,612	1,744
SE Thames[3]	1,583	1,565	1,635	1,587	1,515	1,580	1,706
SW Thames	1,005	1,104	1,004	1,033	1,052	1,118	1,201
Wessex	995	911	1,150	1,076	1,103	1,083	1,184
Oxford	903	932	885	982	991	1,004	1,040
South Western	1,096	1,184	1,250	1,330	1,348	1,170	1,071
West Midlands	1,933	2,301	2,217	2,162	2,038	2,033	2,098
Mersey	886	1,140	1,155	1,061	1,122	1,093	1,189
North Western	1,891	1,943	2,013	1,994	1,953	2,202	2,167
SHAs+	..	..	..	..	..	..	148

Year*	1982	1983	1984	1985	1986	1987	1988
Whole-time equivalent staff, including learners[1]							
England	20,250	22,070	22,570	22,810	23,030	23,300	23,310
Regional health authorities							
Northern	1,250	1,390	1,480	1,500	1,530	1,550	1,610
Yorkshire	1,580	1,750	1,800	1,810	1,850	1,900	1,950
Trent	2,060	2,120	2,120	2,160	2,140	2,170	2,160
East Anglian	880	930	970	950	950	970	980
NW Thames	1,370	1,420	1,450	1,470	1,490	1,480	1,500
NE Thames	1,670	1,860	1,870	1,830	1,820	1,850	1,960
SE Thames[3]	1,570	1,730	1,750	1,700	1,760	1,560	1,240
SW Thames	1,070	1,160	1,190	1,200	1,190	1,260	1,280
Wessex	1,220	1,290	1,320	1,330	1,320	1,360	1,440
Oxford	980	1,110	1,150	1,200	1,220	1,230	1,190
South Western	1,070	1,220	1,220	1,290	1,340	1,400	1,260
West Midlands	2,170	2,370	2,530	2,570	2,580	2,680	2,700
Mersey	1,120	1,170	1,180	1,200	1,230	1,220	1,210
North Western	2,050	2,330	2,310	2,390	2,410	2,430	2,610
SHAs+	200	220	220	210	210	220	210

A7.5.3 *continued*

NHS hospital and community health services midwifery staff by region, England, 1975–98

Year*	1989	1990	1991	1992	1993	1994
	Whole-time equivalent staff, including learners[1]					
England	23,170	23,980	22,830	22,800	21,530	20,740
Regional health authorities						
Northern	1,570	1,490	1,470	1,490	1,480	1,440
Yorkshire	1,950	1,990	1,840	1,730	1,760	1,790
Trent	2,150	2,210	2,120	2,090	1,840	1,680
East Anglian	950	960	900	840	790	820
NW Thames	1,500	1,510	1,400	1,270	1,200	1,260
NE Thames	1,900	1,920	1,870	1,920	1,820	1,700
SE Thames[3]	950	1,730	1,570	1,610	1,530	1,400
SW Thames	1,330	1,240	1,180	1,430	1,220	1,200
Wessex	1,410	1,420	1,400	1,350	1,260	1,250
Oxford	1,200	1,230	1,170	1,060	1,030	940
South Western	1,510	1,510	1,350	1,390	1,360	1,250
West Midlands	2,770	2,820	2,670	2,790	2,640	2,580
Mersey	1,260	1,320	1,260	1,230	1,150	1,060
North Western	2,490	2,480	2,470	2,430	2,360	2,260
SHAs+	220	140	170	150	100	100

Year*	1995	1996	1997	1998
	Whole-time equivalent qualified midwives~			
England	18,292	18,548	18,310	18,479
NHSE regional office areas				
Northern and Yorkshire	2,620	2,699	2,445	2,375
Trent	1,598	1,694	1,794	1,845
Anglia and Oxford	1,925	1,731	1,669	1,820
North Thames	2,437	2,535	2,545	2,524
South Thames	2,232	2,256	2,192	2,249
South and West	2,399	2,455	2,436	2,416
West Midlands	1,867	2,056	2,138	2,266
North and West	3,212	3,130	3,078	2,975

Totals may not equal sums of components, due to rounding.

* Data for years prior to 1982 relate to December, while those for subsequent years are staff in post on 30 September
~ Whole time equivalent is calculated by dividing each person's working hours by the number of full time hours.
+ SHAs were special health authorities in London providing postgraduate medical education and research and also clinical care. They included Queen Charlotte's, the Hammersmith and Great Ormond Street hospitals.

The number of full time hours was reduced from 40 to 37.5 during 1980 and the 37.5 hour week became mandatory on 31 March 1981 This means that figures for whole time equivalents before 1980 are not directly comparable with those for subsequent years
1 Excluding Project 2000 students
2 Comparisons between 1993 and other years at sub-national level should be treated with caution
3 Figures for South East Thames and subsequently to a lesser extent the England totals, should be treated with caution. There was evidence of considerable under recording of the occupation codes used to allocate staff to particular areas of work in the SE Thames region in 1989 and several years prior to this.

Data for 1975–80 were published in the first edition of Birth counts
Data for 1981 were derived from an existing tabulation of SH3 data
Data for 1982–1994 were tabulated specially and do not necessarily agree with published data.
Up to 1994, staff were classified according to their pay scale, From 1995 onwards, their occupations were coded directly.
This means that figures for 1995 onwards are not directly comparable with those for previous years. See footnote to A7.5.1.

Source: DHSS 'Manpower'. Department of Health, Non-Medical Workforce Census.

This is similar to Table A7.8 in the first edition of *Birth counts*

A7.5.4

NHS hospital and community health services midwifery staff per thousand maternities by region, England, 1982–98

Year*	1982	1983	1984	1985	1986	1987	1988
Whole-time equivalent staff, including learners[1], per thousand maternities							
England	34.5	37.4	37.8	37.0	37.1	36.4	35.9
Regional health authorities							
Northern	31.9	35.7	37.8	36.9	38.2	38.6	40.4
Yorkshire	34.6	37.8	38.7	37.9	38.5	38.7	39.3
Trent	36.7	37.3	36.9	36.9	36.3	35.8	35.2
East Anglian	38.7	40.4	41.2	39.0	38.9	37.8	37.2
NW Thames	30.2	31.3	31.5	31.1	31.2	30.0	29.9
NE Thames	33.9	37.4	36.7	35.4	34.6	33.7	34.9
SE Thames3	36.0	39.5	39.4	36.4	37.2	31.4	24.3
SW Thames	31.2	33.6	34.3	33.2	32.6	33.2	32.9
Wessex	37.4	39.2	39.2	38.3	37.1	36.8	38.2
Oxford	31.6	36.1	36.4	36.5	37.0	35.7	33.6
South Western	30.4	34.5	33.9	34.5	35.3	35.4	31.0
West Midlands	32.1	34.9	37.0	36.7	36.8	37.2	37.3
Mersey	35.7	36.9	37.5	36.7	37.8	37.4	36.3
North Western	38.6	43.6	42.8	43.2	43.6	43.1	45.7
SHAs+	–	–	–	–	–	–	–

Year*	1989	1990	1991	1992	1993	1994	
Whole–time equivalent staff, including learners[1], per thousand maternities							
England	36.0	36.2	34.8	35.3	34.2	33.2	
Regional health authorities							
Northern	40.4	36.8	36.0	37.3	38.6	41.4	
Yorkshire	39.5	39.2	36.5	35.1	36.7	38.2	
Trent	35.1	35.0	33.8	33.9	30.5	28.4	
East Anglian	36.9	36.4	34.5	32.5	33.8	24.6	
NW Thames	30.5	30.0	27.5	24.7	24.2	30.0	
NE Thames	34.1	33.3	33.1	34.0	32.5	30.6	
SE Thames3	18.9	33.5	30.8	31.6	30.5	28.1	
SW Thames	34.6	31.2	29.8	35.9	32.2	31.1	
Wessex	37.6	37.1	38.0	36.6	32.5	32.5	
Oxford	33.8	34.0	32.7	29.7	29.8	26.8	
South Western	37.3	37.0	33.8	34.9	34.8	32.4	
West Midlands	38.0	37.8	36.2	39.1	38.1	37.8	
Mersey	38.5	39.4	38.0	39.2	37.9	35.9	
North Western	44.2	42.3	42.6	43.5	43.7	41.7	
SHAs	–	–	–	–	–	–	

A7.5.4 continued

NHS hospital and community health services midwifery staff per thousand maternities by region, England, 1982–98

Year*	1995	1996	1997	1998
	Whole-time equivalent qualified staff per thousand maternities			
England	30.1	30.5	30.4	31.0
Regional office areas				
Northern and Yorkshire	34.3	35.7	33.2	32.8
Trent	26.2	28.0	30.4	31.5
Anglia and Oxford	29.2	26.2	25.2	27.8
North Thames	25.5	26.1	26.3	26.1
South Thames	25.7	26.0	25.1	25.7
South and West	32.1	32.7	32.9	32.8
West Midlands	28.0	30.7	32.4	35.2
North and West	39.8	38.5	38.8	38.3

*+1 See footnotes to previous table.

Because of possible inconsistencies in data, rates have not been calculated for 1975–81. See text for details

Source: DHSS, 'Manpower'. Department of Health, Non-medical Workforce Census.

This is similar to Table A7.9 in the first edition of *Birth counts*

A7.5.5

NHS midwifery and nursing staff in maternity units and health visiting, Wales, 1996–98

	1996	1997	1998
Maternity services*	**Whole time equivalent staff in post on September 30**		
Manager	19	18	25
Registered sick children's nurse	1	6	6
Registered midwife	979	1,067	1,049
Other 1st level nurse	368	361	344
Other 2nd level nurse	75	69	56
Nursery nurse	13	68	82
Nursing assistant/auxillary	192	194	201
All	1,646	1,785	1,764
Health visitors	645	643	644
Student midwives:			
Pre-registration	0	0	2
Post 1st level registration	42	31	36
Post 2nd level registration	2	3	1
Total	44	34	39

* Excludes education staff

Source: Welsh Office, *Health statistics Wales*

This is a new table for this edition of *Birth counts*

A7.5.6

Midwives employed in Scotland, 1975, 1980, 1981, 1991–98

	1975	1980	1981	1991	1992	1993	1994	1995	1996	1997	1998
All	4,160.0	3,927.0	4,066.8	3,298.4	3,299.8	3,313.5	3,284.6	3,184.9	3,125.2	3,075.6	2,994.7
Whole time equivalent midwifery staff1 by grade at 30 September											
Rate per 1,000 maternities											
All	61.1	57.2	59.1	49.5	50.5	52.6	53.6	53.5	53.1	52.2	52.7
Whole time equivalent midwifery staff1 by grade at 30 September											
Hospital midwives	1,839.0	1,930.3	2,049.9	2,488.8	2,510.4	2,532.3	2,495.2	2,462.4	2,407.4	2,404.7	2,354.5
Grade I	–	–	–	43.0	34.0	27.8	22.8	18.8	16.8	16.8	12.8
Grade H	–	–	–	59.0	50.3	41.2	34.3	31.7	31.5	32.7	33.0
Grade G	–	–	–	549.0	532.5	523.2	514.2	479.1	472.3	452.8	430.4
Grade F	–	–	–	723.4	702.3	713.9	688.1	665.3	668.1	660.7	660.4
Grade E	–	–	–	1,114.4	1,191.3	1,226.2	1,235.8	1,267.5	1,218.6	1,236.3	1,210.4
Grade D	–	–	–	–	–	–	–	–	0.0	5.4	7.5
Community	998.0	859.0	840.5	809.6	789.3	781.2	789.4	722.4	717.8	670.9	640.2
Community midwife	123.0	123.5	142.8	276.7	272.7	282.1	309.4	283.4	307.0	290.9	302.0
Triple duty	332.0	101.0	105.3	134.2	127.7	119.2	106.6	91.0	83.8	79.3	64.4
DN+/Midwife	536.0	625.5	585.4	359.8	351.7	342.5	337.1	313.1	295.8	271.2	245.4
HV*/Midwife	7.0	9.0	7.0	39.0	37.1	37.4	36.3	35.0	31.3	29.6	28.4
Teaching	45.0	49.7	48.4	:	:	:	:	:	:	:	:
In training											
Student midwives	1,278.0	1,088.0	1,128.0	656.0	515.6	301.0	171.0	128.0	106.0	41.0	–
Students on '1992' courses in midwifery2	–	–	–	–	121.0	283.0	424.0	456.0	481.0	488.0	497.0

– Not applicable. The data for 1975, 1980 and 1981 come from the first edition of *Birth counts* and were compiled on a different basis from those for 1991 onwards. See footnote to Table A7.5.1 about changes affecting definitions of whole time equivalent in the early 1980s.

+ District nurse. *Health visitor.

1 Staff identified on file as holding a midwifery qualification.

2 Headcount at 31 October.

Source: ISD, Scotland, National Workforce Statistics from payroll

Students: National Board for Nursing, Midwifery and Health Visiting for Scotland

This is similar to Table A7.10 in the first edition of *Birth counts*

A7.5.7

Midwives employed in Northern Ireland, 1980, 1990–98

	Hospital	Community	All qualified	Students	All	All qualified	All
	Whole time equivalent midwives					**Whole time equivalent midwives per thousand maternities**	
1980	839.0	373.5	1363.5	151.0	1,514.5	47.8	53.1
1990	929.9	123.1	1053.0	157.0	1,210.0	40.0	45.9
1991	939.3	118.8	1058.1	153.1	1,211.2	40.6	46.5
1992	911.9	147.4	1059.3	137.1	1,196.4	41.7	47.1
1993	907.1	130.1	1037.2	88.0	1,125.2	41.9	45.5
1994	893.1	140.7	1033.8	24.0	1,057.8	42.8	43.8
1995	899.3	156.1	1055.4	25.0	1,080.4	44.6	45.7
1996	863.9	163.7	1027.6	41.0	1,068.6	42.1	43.8
1997	..	..	..	..	..	..	..
1998	831.3	171.3	1,002.7	57.0	1,059.0	44.8	42.4

Source: Personnel Information Management System (PIMS)

This was Table A7.11 in the first edition of *Birth counts*

A7.5.8

Comparison between the number of midwives on the effective register and practising midwives in the UK, 1991–2000

Year ending March 31	Practising midwives	Registered midwives	Percentage of registered midwives practising	Practising midwives per thousand maternities
1991	34,143	102,649	33.3	43.4
1992	34,626	104,423	33.2	44.7
1993	35,013	105,495	33.2	46.3
1994	35,127	105,723	33.2	47.2
1995	35,309	98,975	35.7	48.7
1996	35,230	98,337	35.8	48.5
1997	34,408	97,283	35.4	47.8
1998	33,138	96,797	34.2	46.7
1999	32,803	93,776	35.0	..
2000	33,803	92,022	36.7	..

Source: United Kingdom Central Council for Nursing Midwifery and Health Visiting, 1998

This is similar to Table T7.1 in the first edition of *Birth counts*

A7.6.1

NHS hospital and community health services nursing staff working in the area of maternity by region, England, 1975–98

Year+	1975	1976	1977	1978	1979	1980	1981
Whole-time equivalents, ˜ excluding seniors[1]							
England	9,045	8,707	8,521	8,409	8,958	9,004	9,368
Regional health authorities							
Northern	688	646	668	642	581	607	593
Yorkshire	805	827	780	765	790	336	831
Trent	944	869	789	794	860	1,064	932
East Anglian	336	453	417	365	329	374	336
NW Thames	545	506	527	667	670	391	514
NW Thames	827	900	841	521	566	714	699
SE Thames[3]	684	755	602	589	624	672	735
SW Thames	389	470	462	419	461	443	472
Wessex	440	462	430	461	493	497	498
Oxford	538	498	431	342	479	548	452
South Western	499	465	570	567	517	553	689
West Midlands	932	476	680	973	1,057	1,157	1,186
Mersey	538	519	502	524	524	578	481
North Western	809	771	757	705	934	936	884
SHAs	–	–	–	–	–	–	67

Year+	1982	1983	1984	1985	1986	1987	1988
England	10,670	9,840	9,520	9,250	9,100	8,780	8,590
Regional health authorities							
Northern	670	650	620	620	590	600	570
Yorkshire	920	810	750	760	720	710	660
Trent	1,120	1,080	1,030	990	970	970	990
East Anglian	420	430	440	420	420	440	410
NW Thames	610	590	610	580	570	530	580
NW Thames	810	690	670	620	600	600	610
SE Thames[3]	800	770	740	730	730	570	450
SW Thames	440	440	410	380	400	400	380
Wessex	530	510	490	510	490	480	500
Oxford	540	450	490	470	460	450	450
South Western	710	620	610	580	550	530	660
West Midlands	1,400	1,260	1,140	1,130	1,140	1,130	1,080
Mersey	560	510	490	480	470	450	410
North Western	1,010	920	910	850	850	790	740
SHAs	130	110	130	120	120	140	110

A7.6.1 *continued*

NHS hospital and community health services nursing staff working in the area of maternity by region, England,1975–98

Year+	1989	1990	1991	1992	1993[2]	1994
	Whole-time equivalents,~ excluding seniors per 1,000 maternities					
England	8,100	7,930	8,240	8,160	8,630	8,030
Regional health authorities						
Northern	530	510	510	440	620	510
Yorkshire	600	600	620	550	740	750
Trent	930	900	890	870	820	780
East Anglian	400	360	440	390	370	400
NW Thames	510	510	560	510	460	550
NW Thames	640	640	640	650	640	630
SE Thames[3]	610	510	510	570	660	550
SW Thames	340	300	390	450	460	380
Wessex	470	480	490	540	690	640
Oxford	410	400	430	410	410	400
South Western	440	440	530	520	530	490
West Midlands	1,020	1,040	990	1,010	950	830
Mersey	400	400	390	380	370	360
North Western	710	690	710	720	720	590
SHAs	90	160	160	150	190	180

Year+	1995	1996	1997	1998
England	8,237	8,009	7,691	7,869
NHSE regional office areas				
Northern and Yorkshire	1,305	1,120	1,086	1,129
Trent	856	776	780	757
Anglia and Oxford	720	939	976	865
North Thames	1,228	1,089	1,027	1,062
South Thames	1,284	1,414	1,185	1,287
South and West	1,090	847	818	811
West Midlands	814	819	740	790
North West	942	1,005	1,078	1,167

Figures for 1982–94 are rounded to the nearest ten whole time equivalents.
Total may not equal sum of components due to rounding.
+ Data for years up to 1982 relate to December, while those for subsequent years are staff in post on September 30
~ Whole time equivalent is calculated by dividing each person's working hours by the number of full time hours.
The number of full time hours was reduced from 40 to 37.5 during 1980 and the 37.5 hour week became mandatory on 31 March 1981
This means that figures for whole time equivalents before 1980 are not directly comparable with those for subsequent years
Up to 1994, staff were classified according to their pay scale, From 1995 onwards, their occupations were coded directly.
This means that figures for 1995 onwards are not directly comparable with those for previous years.

1 Figures exclude senior managers and, from 1992, Project 2000 students
2 Comparisons between 1993 and other years at sub-national level should be treated with caution.
3 Figures for South East Thames and subsequently to a lesser extent the England totals, should be treated with caution. There was evidence of considerable under recording of the occupation codes used to allocate staff to particular areas of work in the South East Thames region in 1989 and several years prior to this.

Source: Department of Health, Non-Medical Workforce Census.

This is similar to Table A7.12 in the first edition of *Birth counts*

A7.6.2

NHS hospital and community health services nursing staff working in the area of maternity per thousand maternities by region, England, 1975–98

Year+	1975	1976	1977	1978	1979	1980	1981
Whole-time equivalents, excluding seniors, per thousand maternities[1]							
England	15.9	15.8	15.9	15.0	14.9	14.6	..
Regional health authorities							
Northern	18.1	17.5	18.6	16.8	14.0	14.8	..
Yorkshire	18.0	19.3	18.9	17.6	17.1	7.0	..
Trent	17.0	16.1	15.1	14.6	14.9	17.7	..
East Anglian	14.9	20.6	19.5	16.6	13.9	15.2	..
NW Thames	12.8	12.1	12.6	15.2	14.4	8.3	..
NW Thames	17.5	19.6	18.8	11.2	11.4	13.9	..
SE Thames[3]	16.3	18.5	15.1	14.1	14.1	14.8	..
SW Thames	12.2	15.3	15.1	12.9	13.3	12.6	..
Wessex	13.7	15.0	14.5	15.0	15.0	14.6	..
Oxford	18.6	17.4	15.3	11.6	15.1	16.7	..
South Western	14.0	13.4	16.7	16.0	13.7	14.2	..
West Midlands	14.2	7.6	11.1	15.2	15.5	16.3	..
Mersey	17.2	17.4	17.6	17.5	16.3	18.0	..
North Western	15.9	15.8	16.0	14.3	17.6	17.2	..
SHAs	–	–	–	–	–	–	–

Year+	1982	1983	1984	1985	1986	1987	1988
England	18.2	16.7	15.9	15.0	14.7	13.7	13.2
Regional health authorities							
Northern	17.1	16.7	15.8	15.3	14.7	14.9	14.3
Yorkshire	20.1	17.5	16.1	15.9	15.0	14.5	13.3
Trent	19.9	19.0	18.0	16.9	16.5	16.0	16.2
East Anglian	18.5	18.7	18.7	17.2	17.2	17.2	15.6
NW Thames	13.4	13.0	13.3	12.3	11.9	10.7	11.5
NW Thames	16.4	13.9	13.1	12.0	11.4	10.9	10.9
SE Thames[3]	18.3	17.6	16.7	15.7	15.4	11.5	8.8
SW Thames	12.8	12.8	11.8	10.5	11.0	10.5	9.8
Wessex	16.2	15.5	14.6	14.7	13.8	13.0	13.3
Oxford	17.4	14.6	15.5	14.3	14.0	13.1	12.7
South Western	20.2	17.6	17.0	15.5	14.5	13.4	16.2
West Midlands	20.7	18.5	16.7	16.1	16.3	15.7	14.9
Mersey	17.9	16.1	15.6	14.7	14.5	13.8	12.3
North Western	19.0	17.2	16.9	15.4	15.4	14.0	13.0
SHAs	–	–	–	–	–	–	–

A7.6.2 *continued*

NHS hospital and community health services nursing staff working in the area of maternity per thousand maternities by region, England, 1975–98

Year+	1989	1990	1991	1992	1993[2]	1994
England	12.5	12.0	12.6	12.6	13.7	12.9
Regional health authorities						
Northern	13.6	12.6	12.5	11.0	16.2	14.7
Yorkshire	12.2	11.8	12.3	11.2	15.4	16.0
Trent	15.2	14.3	14.2	14.1	13.6	13.2
East Anglian	15.5	13.6	16.9	15.1	15.8	12.0
NW Thames	10.4	10.1	11.0	9.9	9.3	13.1
NW Thames	11.5	11.1	11.3	11.5	11.4	11.4
SE Thames[3]	12.1	9.9	10.0	11.2	13.2	11.1
SW Thames	8.8	7.6	9.9	11.3	12.1	9.9
Wessex	12.5	12.6	13.3	14.6	17.8	16.7
Oxford	11.5	11.1	12.0	11.5	11.9	11.4
South Western	10.9	10.8	13.3	13.1	13.6	12.7
West Midlands	14.0	13.9	13.4	14.1	13.7	12.2
Mersey	12.2	11.9	11.8	12.1	12.2	12.2
North Western	12.6	11.8	12.2	12.9	13.3	10.9
SHAs	–	–	–	–	–	–

Year+	1995	1996	1997	1998
England	13.6	13.2	12.8	13.2
NHSE regional office areas				
Northern and Yorkshire	17.1	14.8	14.8	15.6
Trent	14.0	12.8	13.2	12.9
Anglia and Oxford	10.9	14.2	14.8	13.2
North Thames	12.8	11.2	10.6	11.0
South Thames	14.8	16.3	13.6	14.7
South and West	14.6	11.3	11.0	11.0
West Midlands	12.2	12.2	11.2	12.3
North West	11.7	12.4	13.6	15.0

See footnotes to Table A7.6.1.

Source: Department of Health Non-Medical Workforce Census.

This is similar to Table A7.13 in the first edition of *Birth counts*

A7.6.3

Nursing staff working in maternity units, Scotland, 1991–97

	1975	1980	1991	1992	1993	1994	1995	1996	1997
Whole time equivalent at 30 September									
All	1,629.0	1,522.1	1,046.8	1,093.8	1,075.9	1,080.4	1,094.4	1,080.4	1,019.8
Rate per thousand maternities									
All	23.9	22.2	15.7	16.7	17.1	17.6	18.4	18.4	17.3
Whole time equivalent at 30 September									
Qualified nurses	313	304.2	182.9	215.4	223.9	253.0	311.6	329.0	317.9
Registered	..	..	97.0	126.0	141.1	176.5	234.7	256.2	245.1
Grade I	–	–	1.0	5.0	4.0	10.0	16.5	8.5	7.5
Grade H	–	–	0.9	2.9	5.7	12.8	23.9	15.4	14.3
Grade G	–	–	8.0	14.7	15.9	27.8	32.1	32.8	24.1
Grade F	–	–	12.9	12.5	19.1	22.9	27.5	28.9	33.8
Grade E	–	–	51.6	64.4	67.7	67.7	84.4	110.2	102.5
Grade D	–	–	22.6	26.5	28.8	35.2	50.3	60.3	62.9
Enrolled	..	..	85.9	89.4	82.9	76.4	76.9	72.8	72.8
Grade E	–	–	4.0	3.2	6.4	6.0	6.5	6.8	5.1
Grade D	–	–	27.1	26.0	29.4	31.0	34.7	31.6	32.2
Grade C	–	–	54.8	60.3	47.1	39.4	35.7	34.4	35.5
Unqualified	1,316.0	1,217.9	864.0	878.5	852.0	827.4	782.8	751.5	701.9
Grade C	–	–	44.6	41.6	42.8	41.7	43.9	42.7	42.6
Grade B	–	–	77.6	75.3	59.7	62.5	56.2	55.6	52.1
Grade A	–	–	741.8	761.6	749.5	723.3	682.7	653.2	607.2

Source: ISD, Scotland, National Workforce Statistics from payroll

This was Table A7.14 in the first edition of *Birth counts*

A7.7.1

NHS hospital and community health services health visitors by region, England and Scotland, 1976–98, Wales, 1996–98 Northern Ireland, 1998

Year+	1976	1977	1978	1979	1980	1981	
Whole-time equivalents, excluding learners[1]							
England	8,059	8,477	8,674	9,010	8,797	8,997	
Northern	533	562	551	559	575	603	
Yorkshire	599	639	643	672	709	679	
Trent	688	748	765	775	748	860	
East Anglian	277	291	293	311	302	272	
NW Thames	612	659	666	685	718	711	
NE Thames	553	569	574	595	537	646	
SE Thames[3]	601	670	686	710	656	671	
SW Thames	487	625	633	673	661	656	
Wessex	522	511	497	525	477	527	
Oxford	519	505	510	526	518	460	
South Western	849	548	576	594	587	554	
West Midlands	411	883	935	981	935	979	
Mersey	755	428	470	487	484	471	
North Western	512	840	876	915	890	908	
SHAs	–	–	–	–	–	–	
Scotland	1,030	1,084	1,174	1,267	1,338	1,360	

Year+	1982	1983	1984	1985	1986	1987	1988
England	9,540	9,710	9,300	10,280	10,430	10,360	10,340
Northern	620	650	630	680	690	680	700
Yorkshire	670	740	730	790	740	800	810
Trent	900	910	910	930	960	960	950
East Anglian	350	350	280	370	370	380	380
NW Thames	750	720	680	790	810	810	790
NE Thames	660	650	580	710	740	770	720
SE Thames[3]	750	750	650	750	830	760	770
SW Thames	640	640	620	650	640	640	650
Wessex	560	580	560	600	610	590	600
Oxford	470	510	470	570	560	570	560
South Western	600	610	600	660	680	700	680
West Midlands	1,030	1,040	1,010	1,110	1,120	1,110	1,070
Mersey	490	500	490	520	500	500	520
North Western	1,010	1,050	1,090	1,150	1,170	1,100	1,120
SHAs	30	30	0	0	0	0	–
Scotland	1,369	1,329	1,255	1,437	1,295	1,475	1,516

A7.7.1 continued

NHS hospital and community health services health visitors by region, England and Scotland, 1976–98, Wales, 1996–98, Northern Ireland, 1998

Year+	1989	1990	1991	1992	1993[2]	1994	1995
England	9,290	9,690	10,370	10,240	10,180	9,670	9,987
Northern	670	660	680	680	690	550	502
Yorkshire	790	770	820	790	840	820	772
Trent	940	940	1,000	990	950	950	913
East Anglian	360	330	370	350	340	340	478
NW Thames	650	640	820	710	750	650	750
NE Thames	640	650	750	760	770	760	697
SE Thames[3]	220	710	700	770	640	570	748
SW Thames	590	590	590	560	590	630	625
Wessex	590	600	650	620	640	600	599
Oxford	540	530	580	580	660	560	563
South Western	620	680	670	670	660	650	692
West Midlands	1,060	1,020	1,110	1,120	1,050	1,040	1063
Mersey	530	500	500	490	500	450	472
North Western	1,100	1,090	1,150	1,150	1,120	1,090	1113
Scotland	1,560	1,509	1,546	1,497	1,479	1,443	1,430

Year+	1995	1996	1997	1998
England	9,987	10,132	10,025	10,068
Northern and Yorkshire	1,274	1,335	1,276	1,288
Trent	913	1,013	1,051	1,046
Anglia and Oxford	1,041	1,059	1,047	1,004
North Thames	1,447	1,359	1,347	1,311
South Thames	1,372	1,465	1,413	1,536
South and West	1,290	1,273	1,259	1,234
West Midlands	1,063	1,063	1,076	1,105
North and West	1,585	1,565	1,557	1,544
Wales	..	645	643	644
Scotland	1,430	1,426	1,443	1,459
Northern Ireland	..	..	..	434

Totals may not equal sums of components, due to rounding.
+ Data for 1982 relate to December, while those for subsequent years are staff in post on September 30
~ Whole time equivalent is calculated by dividing each person's working hours by the number of full time hours.
The number of full time hours was reduced from 40 to 37.5 during 1980 and the 37.5 hour week became mandatory on 31 March 1981
This means that figures for whole time equivalents before 1980 are not directly comparable with those for subsequent years
Up to 1994, staff were classified according to their pay scale, From 1995 onwards, their occupations were coded directly.
This means that figures for 1995 onwards are not directly comparable with those for previous years.
1 Excluding Project 2000 students
2 Comparisons between 1993 and other years at sub-national level should be treated with caution
3 Figures for South East Thames and subsequently to a lesser extent the England totals, should be treated with caution. There was
   evidence of considerable under recording of the occupation codes used to allocate staff to particular areas of work in the SE Thames
   region in 1989 and several years prior to this.
Source: Department of Health, Non-Medical Workforce Census, Welsh Office, *Health statistics Wales*, ISD Scotland, Workforce
Statistics from payroll.

This is similar to Table A7.15 in the first edition of *Birth counts*

A7.8.1

Numbers and rates of hospital medical staff in obstetric and paediatric specialties in the United Kingdom, 1975–98

Obstetrics and gynaecology

	Number in post on 30 September				Whole-time equivalents				Whole-time equivalents per 1,000 maternities			
	England	Wales	Scotland	Northern Ireland	England	Wales	Scotland	Northern Ireland	England	Wales	Scotland	Northern Ireland
1975	2,349	134	397	..	2,168.1	130.6	359.6	..	3.8	3.8	5.3	..
1976	2,348	133	427	114	2,175.9	130.1	386.3	106.5	4.0	3.9	6.0	4.1
1977	2,374	142	416	123	2,195.3	137.8	379.4	115.6	4.1	4.3	6.1	4.5
1978	2,396	148	418	136	2,216.6	144.8	379.9	127.9	4.0	4.4	5.9	4.9
1979	2,422	147	434	124	2,243.6	143.6	391.0	117.2	3.7	4.0	5.7	4.2
1980	2,460	146	443	129	2,312.9	143.0	399.4	121.5	3.8	3.8	5.8	4.3
1981	2,507	151	449	131	2,359.1	147.2	407.8	125.1	..	..	5.9	4.6
1982	3,203	163	450	..	2,547.0	157.0	406.7	..	4.3	4.4	6.2	..
1983	3,226	161	453	133	2,575.0	157.3	408.7	127.2	4.4	4.5	6.3	4.7
1984	2,566	157	450	135	2,452.0	151.3	406.0	128.8	4.1	4.2	6.3	4.7
1985	2,574	164	447	141	2,462.5	160.0	404.1	132.6	4.0	4.4	6.1	4.8
1986	3,164	162	439	141	2,590.1	157.2	391.6	133.7	4.2	4.3	6.0	4.8
1987	3,149	..	440	139	2,566.7	..	386.0	131.6	4.0	..	5.9	4.8
1988	3,306	176	457	137	2,724.3	171.5	408.9	130.2	4.2	4.4	6.2	4.7
1989	3,408	183	463	132	2,805.9	179.2	409.2	126.7	4.3	5.0	6.5	4.9
1990	3,409	185	486	135	2,814.9	180.1	428.0	130.0	4.2	4.9	6.5	4.9
1991	3,585	182	484	134	2,968.4	176.2	422.3	128.6	4.5	4.7	6.3	4.9
1992	3,553	202	490	142	3,017.2	195.8	428.4	138.1	4.7	5.3	6.6	5.4
1993	3,592	205	520	148	3,093.5	198.1	456.4	144.6	4.9	5.4	7.3	5.8
1994	3,718	202	518	155	3,232.0	198.9	455.8	150.6	5.2	5.7	7.4	6.2
1995	3,887	217	529	157	3,405.7	204.4	461.1	152.0	5.6	6.0	7.7	6.4
1996	4,010	252	552	163	3,540.9	231.5	486.5	157.6	5.8	6.7	8.3	6.5
1997	4,012	222	557	..	3,607.9	210.6	495.9	..	6.0	6.2	8.4	..
1998	4,094	259	547	..	3,684.7	231.8	488.1	..	6.2	7.0	8.6	..

Paediatrics

	Number in post on 30 September				Whole-time equivalents				Whole-time equivalents per 1,000 births			
	England	Wales	Scotland	Northern Ireland	England	Wales	Scotland	Northern Ireland	England	Wales	Scotland	Northern Ireland
1975	1,394	87	193	..	1,246.1	82.7	175.1	..	2.2	2.2	2.6	..
1976	1,464	90	207	46	1,313.6	84.3	183.0	42.6	2.4	2.5	2.8	1.6

Numbers and rates of hospital medical staff in obstetric and paediatric specialties in the United Kingdom, 1975–98

Paediatrics

	Number in post on 30 September				Whole-time equivalents				Whole-time equivalents per 1,000 maternities			
	England	Wales	Scotland	Northern Ireland	England	Wales	Scotland	Northern Ireland	England	Wales	Scotland	Northern Ireland
1977	1,506	94	208	48	1,336.4	89.1	183.3	45.0	2.5	2.8	2.9	1.8
1978	1,552	102	227	52	1,390.1	96.3	199.0	49.5	2.5	2.9	3.1	1.9
1979	1,653	103	240	50	1,484.7	98.2	213.5	47.5	2.5	2.7	3.1	1.7
1980	1,736	108	243	56	1,568.5	103.2	212.7	51.7	2.5	2.8	3.1	1.8
1981	1,872	112	232	59	1,690.0	106.3	205.9	54.2	..	..	3.0	2.0
1982	2,021	114	247	..	1,731.0	108.8	219.6	..	2.9	3.0	3.3	..
1983	2,055	120	247	66	1,787.0	116.4	220.4	61.8	3.0	3.3	3.4	2.3
1984	1,876	121	251	69	1,758.1	118.3	221.8	66.1	2.9	3.3	3.4	2.4
1985	1,950	126	260	70	1,815.9	121.6	227.6	64.5	2.9	3.3	3.4	2.3
1986	2,204	131	277	75	1,914.0	124.4	231.9	69.2	3.1	3.4	3.5	2.5
1987	2,256	..	278	76	1,975.5	..	235.8	71.7	3.1	..	3.6	2.6
1988	2,305	130	287	81	2,031.9	122.5	244.5	76.7	3.1	3.2	3.7	2.8
1989	2,479	139	295	81	2,198.7	132.9	250.8	77.2	3.4	3.5	4.0	3.0
1990	2,603	150	299	82	2,316.2	144.2	264.6	77.7	3.5	3.7	4.0	2.9
1991	2,662	161	309	85	2,388.5	157.9	276.2	79.3	3.6	4.1	4.1	3.0
1992	2,794	166	301	98	2,536.8	159.6	272.4	93.7	3.9	4.3	4.1	3.7
1993	3,075	195	315	100	2,804.3	187.1	282.5	96.2	4.4	5.1	4.5	3.9
1994	3,319	222	343	108	3,040.8	213.4	308.6	103.2	4.8	6.0	5.0	4.2
1995	3,859	235	354	133	3,519.3	226.0	320.7	126.2	5.7	6.6	5.3	5.3
1996	3,945	256	375	145	3,617.0	234.9	349.2	137.2	5.9	6.7	5.9	5.6
1997	4,275	269	392	..	3,952.9	245.9	369.1	..	6.5	7.1	6.2	..
1998	4,462	274	402	..	4,118.7	256.6	373.8	..	6.8	7.7	6.5	..

Paediatric neurology

	Number in post on 30 September				Whole-time equivalents				Whole-time equivalents per 10,000 live births			
	England	Wales	Scotland	Northern Ireland	England	Wales	Scotland	Northern Ireland	England	Wales	Scotland	Northern Ireland
1982	16	1	–	..	14.0	0.9	–	..	0.24	0.25	–	..
1983	14	1	–	..	13.0	1.0	–	..	0.22	0.28	–	..
1984	19	2	–	..	17.7	2.0	–	..	0.29	0.56	–	..
1985	22	1	–	..	19.9	1.0	–	..	0.32	0.27	–	..
1986	19	1	–	..	17.1	0.8	–	..	0.27	0.22	–	..

A7.8.1 continued

Numbers and rates of hospital medical staff in obstetric and paediatric specialties in the United Kingdom, 1975–98

Paediatric neurology

	Number in post on 30 September				Whole-time equivalents				Whole-time equivalents per 1,000 maternities			
	England	Wales	Scotland	Northern Ireland	England	Wales	Scotland	Northern Ireland	England	Wales	Scotland	Northern Ireland
1987	23	4	–	:	18.6	:	–	:	0.29	:	–	:
1988	23	2	–	:	20.0	1.8	–	:	0.31	0.46	–	:
1989	28	2	–	:	23.7	1.8	–	:	0.36	0.47	–	:
1990	27	2	–	:	22.9	0.8	–	:	0.34	0.21	–	:
1991	28	2	–	:	23.9	0.8	–	:	0.36	0.21	–	:
1992	25	1	–	:	22.3	0.8	–	:	0.34	0.21	–	:
1993	31	1	–	:	28.6	0.8	–	:	0.45	0.22	–	:
1994	31	3	–	:	28.8	2.8	–	:	0.46	0.79	–	:
1995	33	2	–	:	31.6	1.8	–	:	0.52	0.53	–	:
1996	28	3	–	:	26.1	2.8	–	:	0.42	0.80	–	:
1997	30	4	–	:	27.9	3.7	–	:	0.46	1.07	–	:
1998	25	4	–	:	23.5	3.7	–	:	0.39	1.11	–	:

Paediatric surgery

	Number in post on 30 September				Whole-time equivalents				Whole-time equivalents per 10,000 live births			
	England	Wales	Scotland	Northern Ireland	England	Wales	Scotland	Northern Ireland	England	Wales	Scotland	Northern Ireland
1975	92	4	44	:	77.9	3.1	39.7	:	1.4	0.9	5.8	:
1976	104	3	44	7	92.6	2.1	39.8	6.8	1.7	0.6	6.1	2.6
1977	129	4	37	12	117.6	3.1	36.1	12.0	2.2	1.0	5.8	4.7
1978	126	5	38	13	114.1	4.1	37.1	13.0	2.0	1.2	5.8	5.0
1979	143	6	40	11	129.1	5.1	38.7	11.0	2.2	1.4	5.7	3.9
1980	124	5	40	11	112.0	4.1	38.9	11.0	1.8	1.1	5.6	3.9
1981	114	6	40	11	100.3	5.0	37.5	11.0	:	:	5.4	4.0
1982	112	6	40	:	106.9	5.1	38.2	:	1.8	1.4	5.8	:
1983	105	6	38	11	101.0	5.1	36.2	11.0	1.7	1.4	5.6	4.0
1984	119	7	47	14	113.7	6.2	45.2	14.0	1.9	1.7	6.9	5.1
1985	104	5	45	14	99.5	4.1	43.2	14.0	1.6	1.1	6.5	5.1
1986	128	6	42	13	119.2	5.1	40.3	13.0	1.9	1.4	6.1	4.6
1987	138	:	47	12	131.4	:	45.2	12.0	2.0	:	6.8	4.3
1988	134	8	55	12	126.6	7.1	53.3	12.0	1.9	1.8	8.0	4.3
1989	151	8	56	13	141.2	7.1	54.3	13.0	2.2	1.9	8.6	5.0

497

A7.8.1 continued

Numbers and rates of hospital medical staff in obstetric and paediatric specialties in the United Kingdom, 1975–98

Paediatric surgery

	Number in post on 30 September				Whole-time equivalents				Whole-time equivalents per 10,000 live births			
	England	Wales	Scotland	Northern Ireland	England	Wales	Scotland	Northern Ireland	England	Wales	Scotland	Northern Ireland
1990	135	9	50	9	127.6	6.1	48.3	9.0	1.9	1.6	7.3	3.4
1991	160	8	35	11	154.8	4.2	33.3	11.0	2.3	1.1	5.0	4.2
1992	168	3	50	11	156.6	3.0	48.9	11.0	2.4	0.8	7.4	4.3
1993	175	3	45	10	163.1	3.0	43.9	10.0	2.6	0.8	6.9	4.0
1994	171	7	52	9	161.9	7.0	50.9	9.0	2.6	2.0	8.3	3.7
1995	205	4	57	9	195.9	4.0	55.9	9.0	3.2	1.2	9.3	3.8
1996	223	3	51	10	212.9	3.0	49.2	10.0	3.5	0.9	8.3	4.1
1997	227	7	52	..	218.8	7.0	49.8	..	3.6	2.0	8.4	..
1998	268	7	40	..	258.5	7.0	38.6	..	4.3	2.1	6.7	..

* Paediatric neurology is not a separate specialty in Scotland

Source: DH/DHSS *Health and personal social services statistics for England*

Welsh Office: *Health and personal social services statistics for Wales / Health statistics Wales*

ISD: *Scottish Health Statistics*

DHSS: *Health and personal social services statistics for Northern Ireland / Hospital statistics, Northern Ireland*

This is similar to Tables A7.16 and A7.17 in the first edition of *Birth counts*

A7.8.2

Hospital medical staff in obstetrics and gynaecology by grade, regional office areas, England, Wales, Scotland and Northern Ireland, 1996

	All Staff	Consultant	Staff grade	Associate specialist	Senior registrar*	Registrar	Senior house officer	House officer	Other staff	Hospital practitioner	Clinical assistant
	Number										
England	4,008	982	146	74	510	353	1,501	16	0	38	387
Regional office areas											
Northern and Yorkshire	652	153	26	14	125	25	228	1	0	9	71
Trent	362	93	19	3	51	10	147	14	0	3	21
Anglia and Oxford	401	107	11	12	53	35	144	0	0	5	34
North Thames	688	157	14	10	68	101	248	1	0	3	86
South Thames	540	136	24	10	61	70	212	0	0	3	24
South and West	428	101	13	8	39	50	160	0	0	5	52
West Midlands	396	101	17	7	61	26	144	0	0	6	34
North West	541	134	22	10	52	36	218	0	0	4	65
Wales	252	60	18	3	20	20	114	0	17	0	0
Scotland	552	142	27	6	87	20	220	0	0	0	47
Northern Ireland	163	51	0	3	9	26	74	0	0	0	0
	Whole-time equivalent										
England	3,540.1	909.8	142.1	65.2	487.2	339.6	1,480.0	16.0	0.0	7.0	93.4
Regional office areas											
Northern and Yorkshire	572.1	146.2	23.9	13.4	117.0	24.4	225.5	1.0	0.0	1.8	18.8
Trent	329.9	84.5	19.0	3.0	48.2	10.0	146.3	14.0	0.0	0.4	4.6
Anglia and Oxford	353.7	98.7	10.3	9.0	50.2	34.1	142.8	0.0	0.0	0.6	8.0
North Thames	595.1	137.5	13.7	9.2	66.1	99.1	245.8	1.0	0.0	0.5	22.2
South Thames	501.3	123.7	23.8	7.6	59.7	67.7	210.2	0.0	0.0	0.7	8.0
South and West	363.9	94.9	12.8	7.4	36.5	44.8	156.2	0.0	0.0	1.0	10.4
West Midlands	352.8	95.3	17.0	6.1	59.5	25.0	143.0	0.0	0.0	1.0	6.0
North West	471.3	129.0	21.6	9.5	50.0	34.5	210.2	0.0	0.0	1.0	15.4
Wales	231.5	52.6	17.7	3.0	20.0	20.0	113.5	0.0	4.7	0.0	0.0
Scotland	485.5	135.0	25.2	5.1	79.9	17.0	216.7	0.0	0.0	0.0	6.6
Northern Ireland	157.6	47.7	0.0	2.9	7.5	25.5	74.0	0.0	0.0	0.0	0.0

* For Wales and Scotland includes specialist registrar

Source: Department of Health, Medical and Dental Workforce Census

Welsh Office

ISD, Scotland, Workforce statistics from payroll

DHSS Northern Ireland

This was part of Table A7.18 in the first edition of *Birth counts*

A7.8.3

Hospital medical staff in paediatrics and paediatric neurology by grade, regional office areas England, Wales, Scotland and Northern Ireland, 1996

	All Staff	Consultant	Staff grade	Associate specialist	Senior registrar*	Registrar	Senior house officer	House officer	Other staff	Hospital practitioner	Clinical assistant
Number											
England	3,971	1,143	283	59	290	458	1,593	14	0	27	104
Regional office areas											
Northern and Yorkshire	526	156	44	8	37	71	192	3	0	2	13
Trent	374	104	20	7	28	31	163	11	0	0	10
Anglia and Oxford	421	118	35	8	28	52	150	0	0	6	24
North Thames	656	178	22	6	68	107	263	0	0	0	12
South Thames	624	184	42	10	36	60	287	0	0	1	4
South and West	450	124	43	10	40	39	172	0	0	9	13
West Midlands	353	110	29	0	17	24	153	0	0	4	16
North West	567	169	48	10	36	74	213	0	0	5	12
Wales	259	73	15	6	18	18	125	0	4	0	0
Scotland	375	97	18	3	26	43	174	2	0	4	8
Northern Ireland	145	40	8	2	12	15	68	0	0	0	0
Whole-time equivalent											
England	3,641.1	1,050.5	226.3	43.1	265.1	431.3	1,573.9	14.0	0.0	5.7	31.8
Regional office areas											
Northern and Yorkshire	482.9	147.1	31.5	7.5	33.7	66.8	188.0	3.0	0.0	0.5	5.2
Trent	347.3	94.0	18.3	6.4	24.4	29.2	161.3	11.0	0.0	0.0	2.8
Anglia and Oxford	365.6	106.2	25.4	5.9	26.0	48.5	148.1	0.0	0.0	1.1	4.5
North Thames	609.9	157.1	17.2	4.0	63.1	102.8	261.0	0.0	0.0	0.0	4.8
South Thames	580.6	166.7	34.6	4.9	32.4	56.7	284.1	0.0	0.0	0.5	0.8
South and West	403.3	116.0	32.5	7.4	34.9	34.9	169.9	0.0	0.0	1.2	6.6
West Midlands	332.2	105.5	27.5	0.0	16.1	23.6	153.0	0.0	0.0	1.5	4.5
North West	519.3	157.7	39.3	7.0	34.5	68.8	208.5	0.0	0.0	0.9	2.6
Wales	237.7	60.6	12.9	4.2	19.0	15.9	124.0	0.0	1.1	0.0	0.0
Scotland	349.2	91.1	17.0	2.3	22.7	40.5	171.6	2.0	0.0	1.5	0.6
Northern Ireland	137.2	36.1	7.4	0.7	10.5	14.5	68.0	0.0	0.0	0.0	0.0

* For Wales includes specialist registrar

Source: Department of Health, Medical and Dental Workforce Census

Welsh Office

ISD, Scotland, Workforce statistics from payroll

DHSS Northern Ireland

This was part of Table A7.18 in the first edition of *Birth counts*

A7.8.4

Hospital medical staff in paediatric surgery by grade, regional office areas England, Wales, Scotland and Northern Ireland, 1996

	All staff	Consultant	Staff grade	Associate specialist	Senior registrar*	Registrar	Senior house officer	House officer	Other staff	Hospital practitioner	Clinical assistant
Number											
England	221	68	2	2	26	20	98	3	0	0	2
Regional office areas											
Northern and Yorkshire	57	17	1	1	7	0	31	0	0	0	0
Trent	21	7	0	0	1	3	8	2	0	0	0
Anglia and Oxford	14	6	0	0	2	0	4	1	0	0	1
North Thames	16	6	0	0	4	1	5	0	0	0	0
South Thames	21	8	1	1	3	1	7	0	0	0	0
South and West	24	10	0	0	1	5	8	0	0	0	0
West Midlands	22	5	0	0	2	3	11	0	0	0	1
North West	46	9	0	0	6	7	24	0	0	0	0
Wales	3	1	0	0	0	0	1	1	0	0	0
Scotland	51	15	0	0	3	3	20	10	0	0	0
Northern Ireland	10	3	0	0	1	1	5	0	0	0	0
Whole-time equivalent											
England	212.3	63.0	2.0	2.0	25.3	20.0	96.6	3.0	0.0	0.0	0.5
Regional office areas											
Northern and Yorkshire	54.7	16.8	1.0	1.0	6.3	0.0	29.6	0.0	0.0	0.0	0.0
Trent	20.6	6.6	0.0	0.0	1.0	3.0	8.0	2.0	0.0	0.0	0.0
Anglia and Oxford	12.8	5.5	0.0	0.0	2.0	0.0	4.0	1.0	0.0	0.0	0.3
North Thames	14.1	4.1	0.0	0.0	4.0	1.0	5.0	0.0	0.0	0.0	0.0
South Thames	20.2	7.2	1.0	1.0	3.0	1.0	7.0	0.0	0.0	0.0	0.0
South and West	24.0	10.0	0.0	0.0	1.0	5.0	8.0	0.0	0.0	0.0	0.0
West Midlands	21.2	5.0	0.0	0.0	2.0	3.0	11.0	0.0	0.0	0.0	0.2
North West	44.7	7.7	0.0	0.0	6.0	7.0	24.0	0.0	0.0	0.0	0.0
Wales	3.0	1.0	0.0	0.0	0.0	0.0	1.0	1.0	0.0	0.0	0.0
Scotland	49.2	13.6	0.0	0.0	2.6	3.0	20.0	10.0	0.0	0.0	0.0
Northern Ireland	10.0	3.0	0.0	0.0	1.0	1.0	5.0	0.0	0.0	0.0	0.0

* For Wales includes specialist registrar

Source: Department of Health, Medical and Dental Workforce Census

Welsh Office

ISD, Scotland, Workforce statistics from payroll

DHSS Northern Ireland

This was part of Table A7.18 in the first edition of *Birth counts*

A7.9.1

Public health and community health services medical staff, Wales, Scotland and regions of England, 1975–98

	1975	1976	1977	1978	1979	1980	1981
	Whole-time equivalent						
England	2,565	2,681	2,735	2,782	2,795	2,821	2,880
Regional health authorities							
Northern	172	184	180	178	178	181	180
Yorkshire	196	207	210	201	205	209	220
Trent	203	215	226	237	229	226	230
East Anglia	66	68	70	80	81	84	90
North West Thames	227	231	243	236	247	243	240
North East Thames	241	249	240	243	239	238	240
South East Thames	227	246	248	269	254	248	260
South West Thames	185	205	226	223	227	219	220
Wessex	149	150	150	151	149	149	150
Oxford	104	106	111	111	118	124	120
South Western	138	142	144	157	158	163	170
West Midlands	260	273	271	276	286	302	310
Mersey	158	165	165	160	160	156	150
North Western	241	241	250	261	265	279	310
Wales	187	205	209	204	215	218	209
Scotland	448	..	..	..	..	455	..

	1982	1983	1984	1985	1986	1987	1988
England	2,860	2,910	2,880	2,930	2,920	2,760	2,800
Regional health authorities							
Northern	180	190	180	190	180	180	180
Yorkshire	220	220	180	210	200	190	180
Trent	230	230	240	240	250	240	230
East Anglia	90	100	100	110	110	110	110
North West Thames	250	240	250	250	240	220	230
North East Thames	230	230	230	230	230	230	240
South East Thames	240	260	260	260	260	230	230
South West Thames	220	220	220	220	210	190	200
Wessex	140	150	110	130	140	130	140
Oxford	120	120	120	120	120	140	130
South Western	180	170	190	170	170	150	150
West Midlands	310	320	320	330	330	320	320
Mersey	150	160	160	160	160	140	160
North Western	310	320	310	310	320	290	290
Wales	212	203	200	193	211	190	216
Scotland	..	..	..	445	..	..	..

A7.9.1 *continued*

Public health and community health services medical staff, Wales, Scotland and regions of England, 1975–98

	1989	1990	1991	1992	1993	1994
England	2,770	2,730	2,780	2,600	2,590	2,370
Regional health authorities						
Northern	190	170	190	170	140	100
Yorkshire	180	180	190	220	210	200
Trent	230	220	230	240	230	190
East Anglia	100	110	120	130	120	150
North West Thames	220	240	230	210	180	170
North East Thames	220	220	200	190	180	140
South East Thames	230	230	240	200	230	200\
South West Thames	200	190	190	130	190	180
Wessex	140	140	140	140	150	140
Oxford	120	120	120	90	90	80
South Western	150	140	150	120	130	140
West Midlands	320	300	300	300	300	300
Mersey	160	160	160	160	150	130
North Western	310	320	320	300	290	270
Wales	201	198	190	192	181	184
Scotland	..	429	426	408	396	399

	1995	1996	1997	1998
England	2,302	2,102	1,984	1,858
Regional office areas				
Northern and Yorkshire	312	284	239	240
Trent	220	215	215	185
Anglia and Oxford	218	187	157	151
North Thames	323	289	281	247
South Thames	363	329	309	291
South and West	254	206	208	202
West Midlands	280	289	283	264
North West	332	303	293	278
Wales	165	145	138	142
Scotland	408	391	368	359

* Figures for the years 1981–94 are rounded to the nearest 10.

Staff holding appointments in more than one region are counted separately in each region, but only once in the England totals

Source: Department of Health, Medical and Dental Workforce Census, *Health statistics Wales, Scottish health statistics*

This was Table A7.19 in the first edition of *Birth counts*

A7.10.1

General medical practitioners, England, regional office areas and Wales, 1997

	All practitioners	Unrestricted principals	Principals on obstetric list		Contraceptive services of principals	
			Number	Rate per 1,000 maternities in region in 1997	Number providing services to list patients only	Number providing services to any patients
England	29,389	27,099	26,618	44.3	3,843	23,183
Regional office areas						
Northern and Yorkshire	3,786	3,540	3,496	47.5	479	3,055
Trent	2,929	2,741	2,706	46.0	485	2,252
Anglia and Oxford	3,206	3,004	2,989	45.2	388	2,613
North Thames	4,343	3,793	3,657	37.9	553	3,228
South Thames	4,037	3,653	3,581	41.0	425	3,215
South and West	4,245	3,955	3,892	52.5	516	3,435
West Midlands	3,026	2,840	2,797	42.5	376	2,452
North West	3,817	3,573	3,500	44.3	621	2,933
Wales	1,874	1,753	1,731	50.7	255	1,492
England and Wales	31,263	28,852	28,349	44.6	4,098	24,675

Source: General Medical Services Statistics, England and Wales, October 1997

This was Table A7.20 in the first edition of *Birth counts*

A7.10.2

Estimates of general practitioners' claims for fees for maternity medical services, England 1975–1994/95 and Wales, 1979–88

| | Total number of claims | Services for which fees were paid* | | | | Miscarriage | Other, including delivery only |
| | | Care including delivery | | Care without delivery | | | |
		Complete care	Partial antenatal or postnatal care	Complete care	Partial antenatal or postnatal care		
England							
1975	556,860	113,900	14,500	31,402	353,890	41,328	1,840
1976	535,492	101,010	11,875	31,707	347,305	40,658	2,937
1977	526,635	88,695	16,358	35,975	339,358	42,416	3,833
1978	542,910	79,894	10,458	44,845	355,104	46,642	5,967
1979	598,743	82,122	8,656	49,530	402,526	50,678	5,231
1980	625,102	77,154	9,103	59,630	420,952	52,966	5,297
1981	613,978	69,501	18,081	60,510	410,070	50,669	5,147
1982	610,449	62,396	15,633	59,899	416,522	49,671	6,328
1983	617,918	60,500	14,274	64,904	420,849	50,721	6,670
1984	625,920	57,487	5,965	67,430	434,623	52,521	7,894
1985	651,825	53,246	7,431	64,644	465,760	52,537	8,207
1986	..	..	..	..	..	..	..
1987	..	..	..	..	..	..	..
1988	719,709	48,660	8,130	90,860	497,650	61,790	11,800
1989	..	..	..	..	..	..	..
1990	734,136	50,430	54,585	153,916	428,502	64,785	16,094
1991/92	585,849	59,380	70,249	170,575	413,381	75,994	15,253
1992/93	535,384	37,150	35,970	126,700	278,190	54,060	17,520
1993/94	699,403	42,540	35,200	181,010	342,700	67,600	30,110
1994/95	687,533	41,790	42,380	203,070	325,420	65,830	30,760
1995/96	662,663	..	..	..	..	..	..
Wales							
1979	37,359	1,932	492	3,300	28,064	3,310	261
1980	38,868	2,023	522	4,387	28,565	3,079	292
1981	37,767	1,792	371	4,076	28,371	2,575	582
1982	37,126	1,795	681	3,384	27,902	2,951	413
1983	38,342	1,664	1,431	3,709	28,518	2,700	320
1984	38,103	1,314	320	3,789	29,209	3,009	462
1985	38,898	1,277	383	3,689	30,258	2,746	545
1986	..	..	..	..	..	..	..
1987	..	..	..	..	..	..	..
1988	41,046	1,490	300	5,890	30,120	2,700	450

* Estimates based on a ten per cent sample, using the following categories on the SBE 504 summary:

Complete care with delivery	1
Partial care with delivery	3a, 4a, 5a, 6a and 7a
Complete care without delivery	2
Partial care without delivery	3b, 4b, 5b, 6 b and 7b
Miscarriage	9
Other, including delivery only	8

Warning: Data are of poor quality and should be interpreted with care. See text for details

Source: Department of Health/DHSS SBE 504 summaries

This was Table A7.21 in the first edition of *Birth counts*

A7.11.1

GP prescriptions for the medical management of sub-fertility, England, 1980–98 and Wales, 1996–8

Year	Chorionic gonadotrophin	Clomiphene citrate	Corticotrophin*	Cyclofenil	Follitropin alfa	Follitropin beta	Gonadorelin	Menoptrophin	Urofollitrophin	All in BNF 6.5.1+
	BNF 6.5.1 Hypothalamic and pituitary hormones and anti-oestrogens+									
England	**Numbers of prescriptions, thousands**									
1980	3.1	28.4	32.0	–	–	–	–	–	–	82.2
1981	4.7	30.5	35.2	–	–	–	–	0.6	–	89.0
1982	4.1	35.5	31.2	0.4	–	–	–	0.6	0.2	85.2
1983	4.7	35.6	26.0	1.0	–	–	–	0.4	–	82.8
1984	4.8	39.0	22.2	1.0	–	–	–	1.7	–	81.3
1985	6.0	42.4	23.5	1.0	–	–	–	4.6	0.8	86.7
1986	8.4	46.0	26.4	0.6	–	–	–	9.7	1.6	105.9
1987	6.4	48.1	19.0	2.4	–	–	0.2	10.5	0.8	100.7
1988	10.8	48.9	17.6	5.0	–	–	–	17.0	1.9	120.3
1989	10.3	47.4	16.9	5.2	–	–	0.2	18.6	4.0	140.8
1990	12.1	51.2	13.3	7.3	–	–	0.2	16.5	2.4	137.1
1991	16.6	56.9	11.9	7.1	–	–	0.1*	20.6	8.0	166.5
1992	19.5	59.5	5.9	6.4	–	–	0.1	24.2	9.9	173.6
1993	23.7	61.7	4.4	4.6	–	–	0.1	28.5	13.3	183.2
1994	26.3	61.2	3.8	0.7	–	–	0.1	30.7	14.5	182.4
1995	23.8	55.8	2.7	–	–	–	–	17.8	22.9	166.3
1996	23.6	48.3	2.1	–	0.7	0.4	0.1	4.1	32.9	155.2
1997	20.9	41.6	1.2	–	7.1	4.7	0.1	1.0	19.1	138.2
1998	16.4	35.6	1.0	–	7.9	4.1	–	1.7	10.3	123.7
Wales	**Numbers of prescriptions**									
1996	720	2,501	338	0	58	26	4	146	919	7,476
1997	702	2,298	305	0	262	389	3	21	548	6,936
1998	538	1,852	221	0	113	329	2	60	284	6,078

* No longer available

+ British National Formulary code 6.5.1.

This table excludes somatropin, tetracosactrin and raloxilene hydrochloride which are in BNF 6.5.1 but are not used for management of subfertility, but they are included in the overall total.

Data for years up to 1990 are not consistent with data for years from 1991 onwards.

Estimates for 1990 and earlier years are based on fees and on a sample of 1 in 200 prescriptions dispensed by community pharmacists and appliance contractors only.

Data for England for 1991 onwards are based on items and cover all prescriptions dispensed by community pharmacists, applicance contractors, dispensing doctors and prescriptions submitted by prescribing doctors for items personally administered.

Products with less than 50 prescriptions are excluded from the analysis of data for England but the prescriptions are included in the total.

The data for England in this table are based on British National Formulary Number 30, September 1995.

Source: Department of Health, Statistics Division 1E, Prescription Cost Analysis System

Welsh Health Common Services Authority, Prescribing Information and Pricing Services

This is a new table for this edition of *Birth counts*

A7.12.1

In-vitro fertilisation and donor insemination, United Kingdom 1985–1997/98

Year	In-vitro fertilisation treatment cycles, including frozen embryo replacements and micromanipulation			Donor insemination including GIFT using donor gametes and intrauterine insemination		
	Number	Percentage leading to clinical pregnancy	Percentage leading to live births	Number	Percentage leading to clinical pregnancy	Percentage leading to live births
1985	4,308	11.2	8.6	..	..	..
1986	7,043	9.9	8.6	..	..	..
1987	8,899	12.5	10.1	..	..	..
1988	10,489	12.9	9.1	..	..	..
1989	10,413	15.4	11.1	..	..	..
1990	11,583	17.3	12.5	..	..	..
1991*	6,653	17.8	13.9	9,262	6.5	4.9
1992	18,224	16.9	12.7	26,063	6.7	5.0
1993	21,823	18.0	14.2	24,035	7.9	6.5
1994	24,672	18.0	13.8	21,180	9.7	7.9
1995	29,185	18.4	14.9	17,857	10.6	8.7
1995/96	25,494	19.2	15.8	16,874	11.2	9.3
1996/97	27,288	21.5	17.9	14,333	11.6	9.6
1997/98	28,550	21.0	17.6	12,753	11.6	9.6

* Data available only for 1 August to 31 December

Source: Human Fertilisation and Embryology Authority

This is a new table for this edition of *Birth counts*

A7.13.1

Use of outpatient and community services for antenatal care, England, 1975–1998/99

Year	Women attending antenatal clinics at NHS hospitals*	Outpatient attendances at maternity departments in NHS Hospitals		Women attending community antenatal clinics+
		New outpatients	All attendances including postnatal	
1975	511,105	700,700	3,356,200	234,383
1976	503,922	681,500	3,336,900	266,948
1977	518,345	690,200	3,376,700	241,782
1978	560,917	727,300	3,622,000	277,422
1979	589,686	760,000	3,818,700	–
1980	607,674	769,800	3,897,300	–
1981	594,719	738,000	3,761,200	–
1982	597,367	726,200	3,632,400	–
1983	593,975	715,900	3,564,200	–
1984	615,538	731,200	3,532,700	–
1985	623,377	732,000	3,517,000	–
1986	633,383	728,000	3,465,000	–
1987/88	629,040	695,000	3,321,000	–
1988/89	635,473	650,000	3,057,000	–
1989/90	678,215	689,000	3,017,000	–
1990/91	–	695,000	2,982,000	–
1991/92	–	684,000	2,895,000	–
1992/93	–	612,000	2,623,000	–
1993/94	–	600,000	2,443,000	–
1994/95	–	587,000	2,307,000	–
1995/96	–	583,000	2,178,000	–
1996/97	–	588,000	2,155,000	–
1997/98	–	590,000	2,074,000	–

Antenatal face to face contacts with midwives and health visitors

	Midwife only clinics	Midwife domiciliary visits	Health visitor domiciliary visits
1988/89	1,793,000	1,068,100	190,300
1989/90	1,972,600	1,007,100	195,700
1990/91	2,100,600	964,000	181,600
1991/92	2,289,600	935,000	162,900
1992/93	2,465,800	921,400	162,400
1993/94	2,748,600	1,016,400	177,000
1994/95	2,987,400	1,066,600	162,000
1995/96	3,116,500	1,080,700	145,800
1996/97	3,375,100	1,048,400	159,400
1997/98	3,444,100	1,024,400	151,000
1998/99	3,483,300	936,100	143,800

* Including GP obstetric clinincs in hospitals
+ Excluding women attending sessions held by their own general practitioner. Data not collected after 1978.

Source: Department of Health/ Department of Health and Social Security

This is similar to Table A7.23 in the first edition of *Birth counts*

A7.13.2

Use of outpatient and community services for antenatal and postnatal care, Scotland, 1977–1998/99

| Year+ | Hospital obstetric clinics | | Year | Domiciliary care, number of visits, thousands | | | |
| | First attendances | Total attendances | | Community midwives | | Health visitors* | |
				Antenatal	Postnatal	Antenatal	Postnatal
1977	70,963	397,047	1977	..	..	..	..
1978	71,103	398,752	1978	29.2	287.4	46.6	171.2
1979	72,651	422,196	1979	34.3	249.2	45.8	153.0
1980	74,814	429,668	1980	36.2	260.3	51.4	157.0
1981	83,637	436,968	1981	43.1	346.6	57.6	194.5
1982	79,077	410,197	1982	45.5	345.4	57.7	187.8
1983	80,452	397,965	1983	50.6	350.8	57.0	189.3
1983/84	78,218	379,522	1984	52.7	370.2	58.1	193.7
1984/85	78,351	377,397	1985	58.8	385.3	55.1	203.1
1985/86	78,092	375,515	1986	64.8	380.3	53.2	198.3
1986/87	79,051	361,915	1987	71.1	407.8	50.1	202.9
1987/88	78,314	357,209	1988	80.0	416.0	53.0	215.2
1988/89	75,942	335,083	1989	75.9	386.4	47.3	192.6
1989/90	75,055	324,582	1990	97.7	395.9	45.6	191.3
1990/91	78,753	329,254	1991	85.9	413.0	46.8	208.4
1991/92	76,543	324,942	1992	80.4	403.2	43.9	204.3
1992/93	69,578	315,273					
1993/94	65,234	301,048	1993/94	71.5	356.8	38.0	176.5
1994/95	63,405	284,213	1994/95*	63.9	318.8	33.5	168.0
1995/96	62,063	280,094	1995/96*	65.9	329.1	37.0	165.3
1996/97	61,515	270,702	1996/97*	95.4	327.0	31.0	131.6
1997/98	59,822	252,048	1997/98*	64.5	315.4	26.0	127.8
1998/99	57,095	242,914	1998/99*	74.1	315.2	25.2	135.6

+ Up to 1983, years ended 30 September of the stated year.
* Data for health visitors for Greater Glasgow Health Board are unavailable for 1995 to 1999 inclusive. Data for 1994 have been used for 1995 and 1996 and figures for 1997 to 1999 exclude Greater Glasgow Health Board. Data for health visitors for Lothian Health Board are unavailable for 1995, so data for 1994 have been substituted.

Source: ISD, *Scottish health statistics*

This was Table A7.24 in the first edition of *Birth counts*

A7.14.1

In-patient maternity care, England and Wales, 1973–81, England 1980–1994/95

Year	Type of care					
	Antenatal care only~	Antenatal care with delivery and postnatal care^	Delivery and postnatal care only**	All care involving delivery	Postnatal care only	All, including abortive outcomes and other discharges
England and Wales						
	Estimated numbers of discharges and deaths					
1973	99,790	285,500	338,100	623,600	27,570	750,960
1974	98,360	293,850	308,510	602,360	22,770	723,490
1975	100,720	266,320	307,720	574,040	21,810	696,580
1976	103,430	209,120	351,590	560,710	23,160	687,300
1977	102,200	197,100	332,620	529,720	24,200	656,120
1978	106,370	199,170	354,120	553,290	26,370	686,030
1979	125,080	200,800	388,870	589,670	32,160	748,430
1980	126,400	195,230	408,870	604,100	34,520	767,040
1981*	127,780	187,320	387,350	574,670	31,190	739,240
England						
	Estimated numbers of discharges and deaths					
1980+	165,610	195,840	405,620	601,460	47,150	817,270
1981	..	..	..	..	..	..
1982	170,690	189,650	384,970	574,620	46,200	794,560
1983	177,610	190,270	388,110	578,380	45,400	804,670
1984	193,370	179,600	406,510	586,110	42,810	825,000
1985	204,080	186,610	418,510	605,120	43,500	855,450
	Estimated numbers of finished consultant episodes					
1989/90	..	..	..	633,500	..	..
1990/91	..	..	..	652,100	..	..
1991/92	..	..	..	643,800	..	..
1992/93	..	..	..	624,600	..	..
1993/94	..	..	..	620,200	..	..
1994/95	..	..	..	604,300	..	..

* figures unvalidated
+ revised figures
~ discharged undelivered
^ admitted before labour, discharged delivered
** admitted in labour, discharged delivered

Source: OPCS, DHSS and the Welsh Office, Hospital In-patient Enquiry, maternity
Department of Health, Hospital Episode Statistics, from *Statistical bulletin 1997/28*, Table 1

This was Table A7.25 in the first edition of *Birth counts*

A7.14.2

In-patient stays in maternity units, regional health authorities, England, 1981–86

	1981	1982	1983	1984	1985	1986
Discharges and deaths*						
Obstetric						
England	696,852	697,447	710,435	732,516	760,223	779,282
Regional health authorities						
Northern	48,727	48,947	48,557	50,389	52,850	53,283
Yorkshire	53,911	53,676	55,738	57,032	58,610	59,814
Trent	64,684	63,228	66,205	69,189	71,207	72,968
East Anglia	26,842	26,064	26,807	28,379	30,071	30,192
North West Thames	50,209	48,649	48,918	49,698	51,241	52,601
North East Thames	61,928	62,559	63,484	65,276	66,839	68,345
South East Thames	56,009	56,786	57,617	57,948	63,410	63,709
South West Thames	39,137	37,592	37,642	39,018	39,984	40,846
Wessex	34,480	34,858	35,992	37,701	39,665	41,036
Oxford	33,138	32,395	32,438	33,676	35,899	37,399
South Western	39,778	39,941	40,746	42,642	44,443	46,406
West Midlands	72,607	75,030	76,393	79,388	78,970	82,524
Mersey	40,315	39,427	40,933	40,439	42,286	43,044
North Western	69,480	72,749	73,138	75,806	78,490	81,061
Special health authorities	5,607	5,546	5,827	5,935	6,258	6,054
GP maternity						
England	98,612	93,648	89,977	86,932	86,384	80,875
Regional health authorities						
Northern	3,846	3,549	3,650	3,598	4,098	4,041
Yorkshire	8,862	8,757	8,908	8,719	8,723	8,391
Trent	11,318	10,193	9,620	9,663	9,421	8,833
East Anglia	4,227	3,782	3,351	2,819	2,781	2,911
North West Thames	974	802	797	744	548	308
North East Thames	5,274	4,783	5,004	4,837	5,008	4,895
South East Thames	2,385	2,232	1,943	1,798	1,664	1,539
South West Thames	2,784	2,629	2,231	2,111	1,421	1,066
Wessex	9,750	10,066	9,800	9,971	10,436	10,682
Oxford	10,120	9,302	8,788	9,006	9,202	8,114
South Western	11,312	11,785	12,439	11,768	10,919	9,125
West Midlands	17,392	16,768	15,770	14,974	15,684	15,127
Mersey	2,018	1,549	1,370	945	617	581
North Western	8,350	7,451	6,306	5,979	5,862	5,262

511

A7.14.2 *continued*

In-patient stays in maternity units, regional health authorities, England, 1981–86

	1981	1982	1983	1984	1985	1986
England	**All maternity** 795,464	791,095	800,412	819,448	846,607	860,157
Regional health authorities						
Northern	52,573	52,496	52,207	53,987	56,948	57,324
Yorkshire	62,773	62,433	64,646	65,751	67,333	68,205
Trent	76,002	73,421	75,825	78,852	80,628	81,801
East Anglia	31,069	29,846	30,158	31,198	32,852	33,103
North West Thames	51,183	49,451	49,715	50,442	51,789	52,909
North East Thames	67,202	67,342	68,488	70,113	71,847	73,240
South East Thames	58,394	59,018	59,560	59,746	65,074	65,248
South West Thames	41,921	40,221	39,873	41,129	41,405	41,912
Wessex	44,230	44,924	45,792	47,672	50,101	51,718
Oxford	43,258	41,697	41,226	42,682	45,101	45,513
South Western	51,090	51,726	53,185	54,410	55,362	55,531
West Midlands	89,999	91,798	92,163	94,362	94,654	97,651
Mersey	42,333	40,976	42,303	41,384	42,903	43,625
North Western	77,830	80,200	79,444	81,785	84,352	86,323
Special health authorities	5,607	5,546	5,827	5,935	6,258	6,054

* In-patient stays were measured as numbers of discharges and deaths

Source: DHSS Form SH3

This is a new table for this edition of *Birth counts*

A7.14.3

Finished consultant episodes for maternity and 'well babies', regional health authorities, England, 1987/88–1994/95

	1987/88	1988/89	1989/90	1990/91	1991/92	1992/93	1993/94	1994/95
Finished consultant episodes*								
Maternity								
England	950,501	950,945	968,320	989,883	1,010,049	1,003,330	1,055,593	1,058,535
Regional health authorities								
Northern	57,145	54,149	54,405	59,963	59,508	58,345	58,883	63,785
Yorkshire	93,928	95,810	90,287	92,198	90,882	88,892	87,993	88,300
Trent	83,166	82,734	84,153	87,818	87,932	87,214	87,564	91,372
East Anglia	46,117	45,277	46,953	48,250	49,612	53,687	52,088	47,859
North West Thames	54,543	51,450	56,813	57,359	57,657	53,515	57,121	58,480
North East Thames	69,317	73,369	81,039	78,809	97,844	98,605	104,505	106,471
South East Thames	70,315	69,728	68,501	72,810	73,075	74,761	76,445	75,848
South West Thames	49,426	51,763	55,208	53,450	54,799	59,757	61,864	60,159
Wessex	59,757	62,636	57,666	57,750	54,787	55,044	70,577	66,635
Oxford	47,231	44,814	47,140	48,635	49,141	50,449	57,619	57,713
South Western	75,304	72,655	70,357	67,275	58,097	55,197	66,021	66,574
West Midlands	103,950	108,350	114,049	119,134	125,811	115,897	124,049	129,027
Mersey	44,707	43,637	44,772	46,166	50,808	52,482	52,872	51,816
North Western	95,595	94,573	96,977	100,266	100,096	95,485	97,632	94,496
Well babies								
England	586,803	595,478	611,927	619,006	618,309	609,306	599,761	592,493
Regional health authorities								
Northern	36,597	34,740	34,300	37,790	37,328	34,827	34,664	34,210
Yorkshire	46,125	47,900	44,900	45,800	45,469	48,032	46,744	45,785
Trent	50,174	50,798	53,437	53,528	55,372	54,151	52,437	51,532
East Anglia	35,750	33,200	35,815	35,293	34,296	33,307	32,767	32,440
North West Thames	35,860	32,475	35,300	34,845	33,655	34,642	35,384	35,780
North East Thames	45,718	48,800	55,300	52,600	56,343	54,252	53,906	53,872
South East Thames	45,783	45,842	47,000	49,700	49,864	49,229	47,224	46,042
South West Thames	32,487	34,215	33,075	34,957	36,778	37,981	36,258	38,609
Wessex	41,243	47,300	43,874	40,647	40,706	41,287	38,784	39,256
Oxford	29,881	28,000	32,895	33,937	33,711	32,657	33,237	32,968
South Western	42,542	43,700	42,000	40,600	34,426	34,134	34,269	33,075
West Midlands	64,610	68,501	71,911	74,709	73,366	70,783	70,285	69,101
Mersey	26,290	25,200	26,000	26,600	29,006	28,465	27,762	27,501
North Western	53,743	54,807	56,100	58,000	57,989	55,559	56,040	52,322

* Finished consultant episodes include ordinary and day case admissions. An in-patient stay can include more than one episode.

Source: DH/DHSS form KP70

This is a new table for this edition of *Birth counts*

A7.14.4

Finished consultant episodes for maternity and 'well babies', regional office areas, England, 1995/96–1997/98

	1995/96	1996/97	1997/98	1995/96	1996/97	1997/98
	Finished consultant episodes*					
	Maternity			**'Well babies'**		
England	1,148,930	1,148,554	1,129,106	571,892	566,926	557,357
Regional health office areas						
Northern and Yorkshire	148,745	149,620	146,683	72,002	70,422	67,450
Trent	108,946	109,165	104,496	53,985	53,406	52,146
Anglia and Oxford	108,903	111,308	115,471	61,640	60,950	61,695
North Thames	176,931	170,245	165,293	89,602	90,354	90,740
South Thames	159,592	152,175	153,135	82,800	82,318	81,937
South and West	142,385	141,191	143,535	69,762	69,025	66,493
West Midlands	131,665	136,692	129,864	66,588	64,445	63,327
North West	171,763	178,158	170,629	75,513	76,006	73,569

* Finished consultant episodes include ordinary and day case admissions. An in-patient stay can include more than one episode.

Source: Department of Health form KP70

This is a new table for this edition of *Birth counts*

A7.14.5

In-patient maternity care, Scotland, 1981–1996/97

Year	Antenatal In-patient and day case	Delivery Specialist unit	GP Unit	Midwife-led unit	Transfers	All deliveries	Postnatal In-patient and day case	Other In-patient and day case	All
	Numbers of discharges								
1981	23,713	61,098	6,734	–	::	67,882	6,669	6,767	105,706
1982	24,605	58,834	6,096	–	::	64,965	6,677	6,751	102,998
1983	24,836	55,848	5,508	–	::	61,361	6,853	6,466	99,516
1984	28,252	58,988	5,212	–	::	64,205	6,829	7,033	106,319
1985	29,269	58,840	4,918	–	::	63,761	6,406	6,382	105,818
1986	30,841	59,383	4,512	–	::	63,900	6,537	6,188	107,466
1987	::	::	::	–	::	::	::	::	::
1988	33,741	56,136	4,044	–	::	60,184	5,893	5,419	105,237
1989	41,197	58,171	3,897	–	::	62,095	6,217	6,301	115,810
1990	49,793	60,666	3,818	–	::	64,502	5,655	6,354	126,304
1991	51,559	61,851	3,826	–	::	65,710	5,704	6,414	129,386
1992	52,508	60,309	3,804	–	::	64,150	4,600	6,110	127,368
1993/94	53,710	56,916	3,319	–	::	60,283	4,218	6,176	124,387
1994/95	58,281	56,818	2,766	–	::	59,587	4,662	6,055	128,585
1995/96	54,654	53,727	1,733	–	::	55,460	4,249	4,609	118,972
1996/97	60,920	54,943	1,304	160	243	56,650	4,045	4,980	126,595

Source: ISD, *Scottish health statistics*

This is similar to Table A7.27 in the first edition of *Birth counts*

A7.15.1

Maternities at home, regions of England, Wales and Scotland, 1975, 1980, 1985, 1990–98

	1975	1980	1985	1990	1991	1992	1993	1994
Numbers of maternities at home								
England, Wales and elsewhere	19,441	8,131	5,924	7,346	7,812	9,211	10,569	11,852
England and Wales	19,440	8,131	5,924	7,346	7,810	9,210	10,566	11,850
England	18,853	7,751	5,582	6,656	7,439	8,713	9,938	11,193
Regional health authorities								
Northern	895	311	186	184	203	233	274	284
Yorkshire	1,443	725	442	438	433	458	522	583
Trent	2,336	844	517	584	615	670	749	790
East Anglian	1,376	561	407	421	431	456	465	715
North West Thames	1,412	575	399	490	546	737	820	745
North East Thames	2,048	760	585	747	848	988	1,072	1,136
South East Thames	1,858	730	503	898	926	1,092	1,438	1,739
South West Thames	714	259	319	151	576	654	764	822
Wessex	692	332	277	412	465	567	708	777
Oxford	419	266	251	338	385	452	525	576
South Western	739	427	414	688	742	891	1,016	1,172
West Midlands	2,235	994	707	660	583	699	736	891
Mersey	960	353	202	193	255	263	291	346
North Western	1,726	614	373	452	431	553	558	617
Wales	587	380	342	393	371	497	628	657
Scotland	642	377	373	374	391	415	422	462
Percentage of maternities								
England and Wales	3.2	1.2	1.0	1.2	1.2	1.4	1.6	1.8
England	3.3	1.3	1.0	1.1	1.2	1.4	1.6	1.8
Regional health authorities								
Northern	2.3	0.8	0.5	0.5	0.5	0.6	0.7	0.8
Yorkshire	3.2	1.5	0.9	0.9	0.9	0.9	1.1	1.2
Trent	4.2	1.4	0.9	0.9	1.0	1.1	1.2	1.3
East Anglian	6.1	2.3	1.7	1.6	1.7	1.8	2.0	2.1
North West Thames	3.3	1.2	0.8	1.0	1.1	1.4	1.7	1.8
North East Thames	4.3	1.5	1.1	1.3	1.5	1.8	1.9	2.0

A7.15.1 continued

Maternities at home, regions of England, Wales and Scotland, 1975, 1980, 1985, 1990–98

	1975	1980	1985	1990	1991	1992	1993	1994
South East Thames	4.4	1.5	1.1	1.7	1.8	2.1	2.9	3.5
South West Thames	2.2	0.7	0.9	0.4	1.5	1.6	2.0	2.1
Wessex	2.2	1.0	0.8	1.1	1.3	1.5	1.8	2.0
Oxford	1.4	0.8	0.8	0.9	1.1	1.3	1.5	1.6
South Western	2.1	1.1	1.1	1.7	1.9	2.2	2.6	3.0
West Midlands	3.4	1.4	1.0	0.9	0.8	1.0	1.1	1.3
Mersey	3.1	1.1	0.6	0.6	0.8	0.8	1.0	1.2
North Western	3.4	1.1	0.7	0.8	0.7	1.0	1.0	1.1
Wales	1.7	1.0	0.9	1.0	1.0	1.3	1.7	1.9
Scotland	1.0	0.6	0.6	0.6	0.6	0.6	0.7	0.8

	Numbers				Percentage of maternities			
	1995	1996	1997	1998	1995	1996	1997	1998
England and Wales	12,487	13,460	14,412	13,815	1.9	2.1	2.3	2.2
England	11,752	12,719	13,621	13,104	1.9	2.1	2.3	2.2
Regional office areas								
Northern and Yorkshire	780	867	976	947	1.0	1.1	1.3	1.3
Trent	920	965	1,030	1,085	1.5	1.6	1.7	1.9
Anglia and Oxford	1,459	1,495	1,712	1,662	2.2	2.3	2.6	2.5
North Thames	1,822	2,036	2,127	1,987	1.9	2.1	2.2	2.1
South Thames	2,741	2,825	3,124	3,007	3.2	3.3	3.6	3.4
South and West	2,085	2,475	2,527	2,490	2.8	3.3	3.4	3.4
West Midlands	955	1,014	1,033	949	1.4	1.5	1.6	1.5
North West	990	1,042	1,092	977	1.2	1.3	1.4	1.3
Wales	735	741	791	711	2.1	2.1	2.3	2.1
Scotland	541	476	543	502	0.9	0.8	0.9	0.9

Source: ONS/OPCS *Birth statistics, Series FM1.* General Register Office, Scotland

This is a new table for this edition of *Birth counts*

A7.15.2

Maternities in isolated GP units, regions of England and Wales, 1975, 1980, 1985, 1990–92

	1975	1980	1985	1990	1991	1992
	Numbers of maternities in 'NHS A' hospitals*					
England, Wales and elsewhere	43,756	27,185	16,427	11,112	9,662	9,369
England and Wales	43,704	27,148	16,457	11,090	9,649	9,355
England	41,777	26,101	15,584	10,383	8,964	8,705
Regional health authorities						
Northern	3,101	2,071	1,551	1,212	580	588
Yorkshire	2,408	1,710	1,520	1,323	742	700
Trent	4,831	3,626	2,188	1,049	874	767
East Anglian	1,854	1,452	544	73	94	81
North West Thames	453	325	33	5	1	2
North East Thames	2,081	1,281	1,155	1,228	1,364	1,393
South East Thames	1,162	767	189	74	53	66
South West Thames	360	245	19	7	4	4
Wessex	3,220	1,733	2,210	2,274	2,311	2,243
Oxford	3,839	1,805	1,348	211	233	239
South Western	7,047	4,840	1,926	1,310	1,324	1,327
West Midlands	7,094	4,141	1,861	1,103	985	963
Mersey	1,151	522	2	0	2	4
North Western	3,176	1,583	1,038	514	397	328
Wales	1,927	1,047	873	707	685	650
	Percentage of maternities					
England, Wales and elsewhere	7.2	4.2	2.6	1.8	1.5	1.4
England and Wales	7.2	4.1	2.6	1.8	1.5	1.4
England	7.3	4.2	2.7	1.8	1.5	1.4
Regional health authorities						
Northern	8.1	5.0	4.0	3.1	1.5	1.4
Yorkshire	5.4	3.6	3.3	2.9	1.6	1.5
Trent	8.7	6.0	3.9	1.8	1.5	1.3
East Anglian	8.2	5.9	2.4	0.3	0.4	0.3
North West Thames	1.1	0.7	0.1	0.0	0.0	0.0
North East Thames	4.4	2.5	2.3	2.5	2.7	2.7
South East Thames	2.8	1.6	0.4	0.2	0.1	0.1
South West Thames	1.1	0.7	0.1	0.0	0.0	0.0
Wessex	10.0	5.1	6.8	6.9	6.9	6.5
Oxford	13.3	5.5	4.3	0.7	0.7	0.7
South Western	19.7	12.4	5.5	3.7	3.7	3.6
West Midlands	10.8	5.8	2.7	1.6	1.4	1.4
Mersey	3.7	1.6	0.0	0.0	0.0	0.0
North Western	6.2	2.9	2.0	1.0	0.7	0.6
Wales	5.7	2.8	2.5	2.0	1.9	1.8

* NHS A hospitals were those without consultant obstetric departments.

Source: ONS/OPCS *Birth statistics, Series FM1*

This is a new table for this edition of *Birth counts*

Maternities by place of delivery, England and Wales, 1964–98

Year	Place of delivery							
	'NHS A' hospitals*	'NHS B' hospitals*	All NHS hospitals	Other hospitals	All hospitals	At home	Elsewhere	Total maternities
	Numbers of maternities							
1964	:	:	588,206	25,945	614,151	252,114	13,908	880,173
1965	:	:	603,159	23,581	626,740	227,884	12,089	866,713
1966	:	:	616,187	22,117	638,304	204,403	10,774	853,481
1967	:	:	628,506	19,901	648,407	178,039	8,987	835,433
1968	:	:	644,757	16,992	661,749	153,245	7,254	822,248
1969	98,454	554,591	653,045	15,089	668,134	126,247	5,382	799,763
1970	92,934	572,759	665,693	14,100	679,793	102,698	4,095	786,586
1971	91,708	592,328	684,036	14,480	698,516	83,387	2,996	784,899
1972	79,682	571,202	650,884	13,229	664,113	60,474	2,128	726,715
1973	67,127	556,482	623,609	11,854	635,463	40,301	1,362	677,126
1974	49,970	552,357	602,327	10,909	613,236	26,558	983	640,777
1975	43,756	530,284	574,040	9,403	583,443	19,441	782	603,666
1976	45,366	515,365	560,731	8,284	569,015	14,623	625	584,263
1977	38,918	511,505	550,423	7,263	557,686	10,899	488	569,073
1978	35,562	542,954	578,516	6,862	585,378	9,586	551	595,515
1979	32,647	587,853	620,500	6,976	627,476	8,869	539	636,884
1980	27,185	611,125	638,310	7,508	645,818	8,131	552	654,501
1981	:	:	:	:	:	:	:	632,350
1982	21,029	587,631	608,660	7,372	616,032	6,944	535	623,511
1983	19,676	592,419	612,095	7,245	619,340	6,421	516	626,277
1984	18,407	601,807	620,214	7,142	627,356	6,130	479	633,965
1985	16,427	622,925	639,352	7,330	646,682	5,924	536	653,142
1986	14,897	628,595	643,492	7,232	650,724	6,042	542	657,308
1987	16,405	647,283	663,688	7,210	670,898	6,007	562	677,467
1988	14,645	659,678	674,323	7,776	682,099	6,442	612	689,153
1989	9,985	658,249	668,234	7,280	675,514	6,941	524	682,979
1990	11,112	674,793	685,905	7,210	693,115	7,346	569	701,030
1991	9,662	669,814	679,476	5,965	685,441	7,812	604	693,857
1992	9,369	659,741	669,110	4,916	674,026	9,211	617	683,854
1993	:	:	:	:	657,415	10,569	527	668,511

A7.16.1 continued

Maternities by place of delivery, England and Wales, 1964–98

Year	'NHS A' hospitals	'NHS B' hospitals	All NHS hospitals	Other hospitals	All hospitals	At home	Elsewhere	Total maternities
	Place of delivery							
1994	:	:	643,047	3,973	647,020	11,852	673	659,545
1995	:	:	626,633	2,667	629,300	12,487	617	642,404
1996	:	:	627,183	2,599	629,782	13,460	620	643,862
1997	:	:	619,112	2,836	621,948	14,412	641	637,001
1998	:	:	612,630	2,857	615,487	13,815	624	629,926
Percentages								
1964	:	:	66.8	2.9	69.8	28.6	1.6	100.0
1965	:	:	69.6	2.7	72.3	26.3	1.4	100.0
1966	:	:	72.2	2.6	74.8	23.9	1.3	100.0
1967	:	:	75.2	2.4	77.6	21.3	1.1	100.0
1968	:	:	78.4	2.1	80.5	18.6	0.9	100.0
1969	12.3	69.3	81.7	1.9	83.5	15.8	0.7	100.0
1970	11.8	72.8	84.6	1.8	86.4	13.1	0.5	100.0
1971	11.7	75.5	87.1	1.8	89.0	10.6	0.4	100.0
1972	11.0	78.6	89.6	1.8	91.4	8.3	0.3	100.0
1973	9.9	82.2	92.1	1.8	93.8	6.0	0.2	100.0
1974	7.8	86.2	94.0	1.7	95.7	4.1	0.2	100.0
1975	7.2	87.8	95.1	1.6	96.6	3.2	0.1	100.0
1976	7.8	88.2	96.0	1.4	97.4	2.5	0.1	100.0
1977	6.8	89.9	96.7	1.3	98.0	1.9	0.1	100.0
1978	6.0	91.2	97.1	1.2	98.3	1.6	0.1	100.0
1979	5.1	92.3	97.4	1.1	98.5	1.4	0.1	100.0
1980	4.2	93.4	97.5	1.1	98.7	1.2	0.1	100.0
1981	:	:	:	:	:	:	:	100.0
1982	3.4	94.2	97.6	1.2	98.8	1.1	0.1	100.0
1983	3.1	94.6	97.7	1.2	98.9	1.0	0.1	100.0
1984	2.9	94.9	97.8	1.1	99.0	1.0	0.1	100.0
1985	2.5	95.4	97.9	1.1	99.0	0.9	0.1	100.0
1986	2.3	95.6	97.9	1.1	99.0	0.9	0.1	100.0
1987	2.4	95.5	98.0	1.1	99.0	0.9	0.1	100.0
1988	2.1	95.7	97.8	1.1	99.0	0.9	0.1	100.0

A7.16.1 continued

Maternities by place of delivery, England and Wales, 1964–98

Year	Place of delivery							
	'NHS A' hospitals*	'NHS B' hospitals*	All NHS hospitals	Other hospitals	All hospitals	At home	Elsewhere	Total maternities
1989	1.5	96.4	97.8	1.1	98.9	1.0	0.1	100.0
1990	1.6	96.3	97.8	1.0	98.9	1.0	0.1	100.0
1991	1.4	96.5	97.9	0.9	98.8	1.1	0.1	100.0
1992	1.4	96.5	97.8	0.7	98.6	1.3	0.1	100.0
1993	::	::	::	::	98.3	1.6	0.1	100.0
1994	::	::	97.5	0.6	98.1	1.8	0.1	100.0
1995	::	::	97.5	0.4	98.0	1.9	0.1	100.0
1996	::	::	97.4	0.4	97.8	2.1	0.1	100.0
1997	::	::	97.2	0.4	97.6	2.3	0.1	100.0
1998	::	::	97.3	0.5	97.7	2.2	0.1	100.0

* NHS A hospitals were those without a consultant obstetric department. NHS B hospitals had a consultant obstetric department. From 1993 onwards, no distinction is made between types of NHS hospitals. In 1993, coding problems made it impossible to distinguish between any type of hospital.

Source: ONS/OPCS *Birth statistics, Series FM1*

This was Table A7.29a in the first edition of *Birth counts*

A7.16.2

Total births by place of delivery, England and Wales, 1954–98

Year	Place of delivery							Total births
	'NHS A' hospitals*	'NHS B' hospitals*	All NHS hospitals	Other hospitals	All hospitals	At home	Elsewhere	
	Numbers of births							
1954	::	::	408,205	30,817	439,022	234,438	16,391	689,851
1955	::	::	411,700	28,146	439,846	228,225	15,569	683,640
1956	::	::	433,194	28,028	461,222	238,688	16,830	716,740
1957	::	::	448,176	27,620	475,796	246,856	17,344	739,996
1958	::	::	457,206	26,765	483,971	254,943	18,089	757,003
1959	::	::	464,293	26,384	490,677	256,414	17,311	764,402
1960	::	::	490,622	27,186	517,808	265,931	17,085	800,824
1961	::	::	515,274	27,168	542,442	267,970	16,596	827,008
1962	::	::	536,495	26,653	563,148	274,390	16,662	854,200
1963	::	::	566,068	26,644	592,712	260,952	15,380	869,044
1964	::	::	597,438	26,163	623,601	252,959	13,958	890,518
1965	::	::	612,127	23,773	635,900	228,538	12,128	876,566
1966	::	::	624,967	22,277	647,244	205,018	10,804	863,066
1967	::	::	637,078	20,058	657,136	178,547	9,009	844,692
1968	::	::	653,107	17,114	670,221	153,626	7,273	831,120
1969	97,091	563,955	661,046	15,208	676,254	126,535	5,403	808,192
1970	93,192	580,305	673,497	14,251	687,748	102,970	4,113	794,831
1971	91,924	599,871	691,795	14,614	706,409	83,637	3,008	793,054
1972	79,801	577,806	657,607	13,268	670,875	60,636	2,103	733,614
1973	67,257	562,863	630,120	11,975	642,095	40,412	1,382	683,889
1974	50,089	558,333	608,422	11,010	619,432	26,635	993	647,060
1975	43,862	536,088	579,950	9,500	589,450	19,504	786	609,740
1976	45,458	520,865	566,323	8,360	574,683	14,667	629	589,979
1977	39,019	516,894	555,913	7,318	563,231	10,940	493	574,664
1978	35,645	548,796	584,441	6,921	591,362	9,608	556	601,526
1979	32,700	593,964	626,664	7,041	633,705	8,904	544	643,153
1980	27,225	617,485	644,710	7,576	652,286	8,162	559	661,007
1981	22,440	601,436	623,876	7,479	631,355	6,790	514	638,659
1982	21,056	593,868	614,924	7,441	622,365	6,969	536	629,870
1983	19,694	598,799	618,493	7,307	625,800	6,443	522	632,765
1984	18,435	608,178	626,613	7,217	633,830	6,149	482	640,461

A7.16.2 continued

Total births by place of delivery, England and Wales, 1954–98

Year	Place of delivery							Total births
	'NHS A' hospitals*	'NHS B' hospitals*	All NHS hospitals	Other hospitals	All hospitals	At home	Elsewhere	
1985	16,436	629,714	646,150	7,419	653,569	5,955	538	660,062
1986	14,907	635,741	650,648	7,311	657,959	6,064	544	664,567
1987	16,440	654,614	671,054	7,296	678,350	6,018	566	684,934
1988	14,681	667,314	681,995	7,883	689,878	6,468	613	696,959
1989	9,988	666,127	676,115	7,354	683,469	6,963	529	690,961
1990	11,120	683,032	694,152	7,307	701,459	7,363	574	709,396
1991	9,664	678,307	687,971	6,058	694,029	7,832	610	702,471
1992	9,374	668,398	677,772	4,976	682,748	9,234	618	692,600
1993	..	..	..	..	664,027	10,523	540	675,090
1994	..	..	651,943	4,054	655,997	11,867	675	668,539
1995	..	..	635,908	2,703	638,611	12,505	622	651,738
1996	..	..	636,259	2,666	638,925	13,476	623	653,024
1997	..	..	628,570	2,891	631,461	14,430	643	646,534
1998	..	..	621,935	2,919	624,854	13,837	627	639,318
Percentages								
1954	..	..	59.2	4.5	63.6	34.0	2.4	100.0
1955	..	..	60.2	4.1	64.3	33.4	2.3	100.0
1956	..	..	60.4	3.9	64.3	33.3	2.3	100.0
1957	..	..	60.6	3.7	64.3	33.4	2.3	100.0
1958	..	..	60.4	3.5	63.9	33.7	2.4	100.0
1959	..	..	60.7	3.5	64.2	33.5	2.3	100.0
1960	..	..	61.3	3.4	64.7	33.2	2.1	100.0
1961	..	..	62.3	3.3	65.6	32.4	2.0	100.0
1962	..	..	62.8	3.1	65.9	32.1	2.0	100.0
1963	..	..	65.1	3.1	68.2	30.0	1.8	100.0
1964	..	..	67.1	2.9	70.0	28.4	1.6	100.0
1965	..	..	69.8	2.7	72.5	26.1	1.4	100.0
1966	..	..	72.4	2.6	75.0	23.8	1.3	100.0
1967	..	..	75.4	2.4	77.8	21.1	1.1	100.0
1968	..	..	78.6	2.1	80.6	18.5	0.9	100.0
1969	12.0	69.8	81.8	1.9	83.7	15.7	0.7	100.0
1970	11.7	73.0	84.7	1.8	86.5	13.0	0.5	100.0

A7.16.2 continued

Total births by place of delivery, England and Wales, 1954–98

Year	Place of delivery							Total births
	'NHS A' hospitals*	'NHS B' hospitals*	All NHS hospitals	Other hospitals	All hospitals	At home	Elsewhere	
1971	11.6	75.6	87.2	1.8	89.1	10.5	0.4	100.0
1972	10.9	78.8	89.6	1.8	91.4	8.3	0.3	100.0
1973	9.8	82.3	92.1	1.8	93.9	5.9	0.2	100.0
1974	7.7	86.3	94.0	1.7	95.7	4.1	0.2	100.0
1975	7.2	87.9	95.1	1.6	96.7	3.2	0.1	100.0
1976	7.7	88.3	96.0	1.4	97.4	2.5	0.1	100.0
1977	6.8	89.9	96.7	1.3	98.0	1.9	0.1	100.0
1978	5.9	91.2	97.2	1.2	98.3	1.6	0.1	100.0
1979	5.1	92.4	97.4	1.1	98.5	1.4	0.1	100.0
1980	4.1	93.4	97.5	1.1	98.7	1.2	0.1	100.0
1981	3.5	94.2	97.7	1.2	98.9	1.1	0.1	100.0
1982	3.3	94.3	97.6	1.2	98.8	1.1	0.1	100.0
1983	3.1	94.6	97.7	1.2	98.9	1.0	0.1	100.0
1984	2.9	95.0	97.8	1.1	99.0	1.0	0.1	100.0
1985	2.5	95.4	97.9	1.1	99.0	0.9	0.1	100.0
1986	2.2	95.7	97.9	1.1	99.0	0.9	0.1	100.0
1987	2.4	95.6	98.0	1.1	99.0	0.9	0.1	100.0
1988	2.1	95.7	97.9	1.1	99.0	0.9	0.1	100.0
1989	1.4	96.4	97.9	1.1	98.9	1.0	0.1	100.0
1990	1.6	96.3	97.9	1.0	98.9	1.0	0.1	100.0
1991	1.4	96.6	97.9	0.9	98.8	1.1	0.1	100.0
1992	1.4	96.5	97.9	0.7	98.6	1.3	0.1	100.0
1993	:	:	:	:	98.4	1.6	0.1	100.0
1994	:	:	97.5	0.6	98.1	1.8	0.1	100.0
1995	:	:	97.6	0.4	98.0	1.9	0.1	100.0
1996	:	:	97.4	0.4	97.8	2.1	0.1	100.0
1997	:	:	97.2	0.4	97.7	2.2	0.1	100.0
1998	:	:	97.3	0.5	97.7	2.2	0.1	100.0

* See footnote to Table A7.16.1

From 1993 onwards, no distinction is made between types of NHS hospitals. In 1993, coding problems made it impossible to distinguish between any type of hospital.

Source: ONS/OPCS *Birth statistics, Series FM1*

This was Table A7.29b in the first edition of *Birth counts*

A7.17.1

Stillbirths and infant mortality by birthweight and place of delivery, England and Wales, 1996

Birthweight, g and place of birth	Numbers						Rates				
	Births		Deaths				Stillbirth*	Perinatal*	Neonatal~	Post-neonatal~	Infant~
	Live births	Stillbirths	Early neonatal	Neonatal	Post-neonatal	Infant					
All places of birth											
All	649,489	3,539	2,038	2,604	1,263	3,867	5.4	8.5	4.0	1.9	6.0
Under 1,000	3,150	1,216	1,076	1,278	147	1,425	278.5	525.0	405.7	46.7	452.4
1,000–1,499	4,770	435	211	282	93	375	83.6	124.1	59.1	19.5	78.6
Under 1,500	7,920	1,651	1,287	1,560	240	1,800	172.5	307.0	197.0	30.3	227.3
1,500–1,999	9,405	376	111	142	88	230	38.4	49.8	15.1	9.4	24.5
2,000–2,499	29,862	374	123	173	177	350	12.4	16.4	5.8	5.9	11.7
Under 2,500	47,187	2,401	1,521	1,875	505	2,380	48.4	79.1	39.7	10.7	50.4
2,500 and over	600,764	1,076	448	651	754	1,405	1.8	2.5	1.1	1.3	2.3
Not stated	1,538	62	69	78	4	82	38.8	81.9	50.7	2.6	53.3
In hospital											
All	635,448	3,480	1,986	2,545	1,248	3,793	5.4	8.6	4.0	2.0	6.0
Under 1,000	3,113	1,194	1,051	1,250	147	1,397	277.2	521.2	401.5	47.2	448.8
1,000–1,499	4,727	428	210	281	92	373	83.0	123.8	59.4	19.5	78.9
Under 1,500	7,840	1,622	1,261	1,531	239	1,770	171.4	304.7	195.3	30.5	225.8
1,500–1,999	9,342	373	109	140	87	227	38.4	49.6	15.0	9.3	24.3
2,000–2,499	29,584	371	121	171	175	346	12.4	16.4	5.8	5.9	11.7
Under 2,500	46,766	2,366	1,491	1,842	501	2,343	48.2	78.5	39.4	10.7	50.1
2,500 and over	587,310	1,061	434	633	743	1,376	1.8	2.5	1.1	1.3	2.3
Not stated	1,372	53	61	70	4	74	37.2	80.0	51.0	2.9	53.9
At home											
All	13,430	47	45	49	15	64	3.5	6.8	3.6	1.1	4.8
Under 1,000	27	16	19	19	0	19	372.1	814.0	703.7	0.0	703.7
1,000–1,499	29	7	1	1	1	2	194.4	222.2	34.5	34.5	69.0
Under 1,500	56	23	20	20	1	21	291.1	544.3	357.1	17.9	375.0
1,500–1,999	48	3	2	2	1	3	40.0	80.0	41.7	20.8	62.5
2,000–2,499	256	3	2	2	2	4	11.6	19.3	7.8	7.8	15.6

Stillbirths and infant mortality by birthweight and place of delivery, England and Wales, 1996

Birthweight, g and place of birth	Numbers		Deaths				Rates				
	Births										
	Live births	Stillbirths	Early neonatal	Neonatal	Post-neonatal	Infant	Stillbirth*	Perinatal*	Neonatal~	Post-neonatal~	Infant~
Under 2,500	360	28	24	24	4	28	72.2	134.0	66.7	11.1	77.8
2,500 and over	12,913	14	13	17	11	28	1.1	2.1	1.3	0.9	2.2
Not stated	157	5	8	8	0	8	30.9	80.2	51.0	0.0	51.0
Elsewhere											
All	611	12	7	10	0	10	19.3	30.5	16.4	0.0	16.4
Under 1,000	10	6	6	9	0	9	375.0	750.0	900.0	0.0	900.0
1,000–1,499	14	0	0	0	0	0	0.0	0.0	0.0	0.0	0.0
Under 1,500	24	6	6	9	0	9	200.0	400.0	375.0	0.0	375.0
Under 2,500	61	7	6	9	0	9	102.9	191.2	147.5	0.0	147.5
2,500 and over	541	1	1	1	0	1	1.8	3.7	1.8	0.0	1.8
Not stated	9	4	0	0	0	0	307.7	307.7	0.0	0.0	0.0

* Stillbirths and perinatal deaths per thousand live and stillbirths
~ Neonatal, postneonatal and infant deaths per thousand live births

Source: ONS *Mortality Statistics, Series DH3, no 29*

This is similar to Table A7.31 in the first edition of *Birth counts*

A7.18.1

Department of delivery in NHS hospitals, England and Wales, 1964–80, England, 1980–1994/95

	Place of delivery			All deliveries in NHS hospitals	
	Obstetric units	GP maternity unit	Other departments		
	Estimated percentage of deliveries in England and Wales*				**Number**
1964	52.2	14.3	0.3	66.8	588,206
1965	54.3	14.5	0.8	69.6	603,159
1966	56.0	15.7	0.4	72.2	616,187
1967	58.9	16.0	0.3	75.2	628,506
1968	61.9	16.3	0.2	78.4	644,757
1969	62.8	18.4	0.4	81.7	653,045
1970	66.7	17.8	0.1	84.6	665,693
1971	69.2	17.3	0.6	87.1	684,036
1972	71.6	17.6	0.3	89.6	650,883
1973	75.1	16.8	0.1	92.1	623,609
1974	77.8	16.1	0.1	94.0	602,327
1975	78.8	16.4	0.4	95.6	574,040
1976	80.2	15.6	0.2	96.0	560,731
1977	81.2	14.8	0.0	96.7	550,423
1978	83.9	13.5	0.0	97.1	578,516
1979	..	..	..	97.4	620,500
1980	84.5	9.8	3.2	97.5	638,310
	Estimated percentage of deliveries in England*				**Number**
1980	84.1	10.0	3.4	97.5	601,094
1981	..	..	..	97.6	582,010
1982	87.9	8.4	1.3	97.6	573,119
1983	88.2	8.2	1.3	97.7	576,790
1984	89.3	7.3	1.1	97.8	584,576
1985	..	..	..	97.8	602,807

	Department of delivery				All deliveries in NHS hospitals
	Consultant ward	GP ward	Consultant/ GP ward	Other	
	Estimated percentage of deliveries in NHS hospitals in England				**Number**
1989/90	64	5	30	1	100.0	633,500
1990/91	62	3	35	0	100.0	652,100
1991/92	63	3	33	0	100.0	643,800
1992/93	60	3	37	0	100.0	624,600
1993/94	58	3	38	0	100.0	620,200
1994/95	58	3	39	0	100.0	604,300

* Derived from product of percentage of deliveries in hospitals and percentage of all deliveries taking place in hospitals

Source: Maternity Hospital In-patient Enquiry and OPCS *Birth statistics, Series FM1*

Department of Health, Maternity Hospital Episode Statistics, *Statistical bulletin 1997/28*

This was Table A7.30 in the first edition of *Birth counts*

A7.18.2

Person conducting delivery, NHS hospital deliveries, England, 1989/90–1994/95

	Person conducting delivery				All deliveries	
	Hospital doctor	GP	Midwife	Other		
	Estimated percentages					**Numbers**
1989/90	23.7	0.3	75.6	0.5	100.0	633,500
1990/91	24.5	0.2	74.8	0.4	100.0	652,100
1991/92	25.1	0.2	74.3	0.5	100.0	643,800
1992/93	25.3	0.2	74.0	0.5	100.0	624,600
1993/94	26.1	0.2	73.3	0.4	100.0	620,200
1994/95	27.2	0.1	72.3	0.4	100.0	604,300
	Estimated numbers					**Numbers**
1994/95	164,500	800	436,600	2,300		604,300

Source: Department of Health, Maternity Hospital Episode Statistics, *Statistical bulletin 1997/28*

This is a new table for this edition of *Birth counts*

A7.19.1

Onset of labour, England and Wales, 1962–81, England, 1980–1994/95

	Use of ARM or oxytocics*+	Admitted before labour, discharged delivered	Induction of labour+	Elective caesarean section+
Estimated percentage of deliveries in England and Wales#				
1962	8.3	15.4	..	..
1963	8.9	16.1	..	..
1964	8.9	16.3	..	..
1965	10.2	18.2	..	..
1966	12.7	19.4	..	..
1967	16.8	23.4	..	..
1968	18.0	25.5	..	..
1969	20.3	28.9	..	..
1970	23.2	31.5	..	..
1971	26.3	34.4	..	..
1972	29.2	36.6	..	..
1973	34.9	42.2	..	..
1974	38.9	45.9	..	..
1975	35.0	44.1	..	..
1976	35.5	35.8	..	..
1977	36.8	36.0	..	..
1978	36.3	35.0	..	..
1979	32.0	33.6	21.4	4.5
1980	30.9	31.5	19.7	4.1
1981	..	32.2	..	5.0
Estimated percentage of deliveries in England				
1980	30.6	31.7	20.0	3.9
1981	..	..	..	..
1982	29.1	32.2	18.3	4.6
1983	29.9	32.0	18.5	4.6
1984	28.4	29.9	17.0	4.6
1985	28.9	30.2	17.0	4.9

	Induction				Elective caesarean section
	All	Surgical	Oxytocic drugs	Surgical and drugs	
Estimated percentage of deliveries in NHS hospitals in England					
1980	20.6	..	..	..	4.0
1985	17.5	..	..	..	4.9
1989/90	18.3	4.3	8.1	5.9	5.0
1990/91	17.7	3.6	8.4	5.7	5.3
1991/92	17.6	3.0	9.7	5.0	5.6
1992/93	16.8	2.9	9.4	4.4	5.7
1993/94	17.7	2.8	10.3	4.7	6.2
1994/95	19.5	2.9	11.7	4.9	6.8

\# Includes women resident outside England and Wales
* Including augmentation of labour. A separate breakdown was not available before 1979
+ See text for discussion of definitions of ARM, oxytocics, induction and mode of delivery

Source: Maternity Hospital In-patient Enquiry and OPCS *Birth statistics, Series FM1*
Department of Health, Maternity Hospital Episode Statistics, *Statistical bulletin 1997/28, Table 1*

This is similar to Table A7.32a in the first edition of *Birth counts*

A7.20.1

Method of delivery, England and Wales, 1953–85, England, 1980–1994/95

Year	Spontaneous*	Caesarean section	Instrumental delivery			Other and unspecified~
	All	All	All	Forceps	Ventouse	
Estimated percentage of deliveries in England and Wales						
1953	..	2.2	3.7	..	..	..
1954	..	..	..	..	..	..
1955	..	2.2	4.4	..	..	..
1956	..	2.3	4.1	..	..	..
1957	..	2.2	4.1	..	..	..
1958	..	2.3	4.4	..	..	..
1959	..	2.6	4.4	..	..	..
1960	..	2.8	4.5	..	..	..
1961	..	2.8	4.9	..	..	..
1962	..	3.0	5.1	..	..	..
1963	..	3.1	5.3	..	..	..
1964	..	3.3	5.6	..	..	..
1965	..	3.5	5.8	..	..	..
1966	..	3.4	6.0	..	..	..
1967	..	3.8	7.5	..	..	..
1968	..	4.0	7.9	..	..	..
1969	..	4.3	8.2	..	..	..
1970	..	4.3	8.8	..	..	..
1971	..	4.6	9.4	..	..	..
1972	..	4.9	10.5	..	..	..
1973	72.5	4.9	11.2	10.5	0.7	5.2
1974	69.2	5.4	12.2	11.5	0.7	8.8
1975	68.3	5.8	12.6	11.9	0.7	9.9
1976	66.6	6.4	13.2	12.6	0.6	11.2
1977	64.8	7.1	13.4	12.9	0.7	12.4
1978	69.3	7.3	13.3	12.8	0.6	8.1
1979	75.5	8.2	13.1	11.5	0.6	0.2
1980	75.7	8.8	11.7	11.2	0.6	0.1
1981	76.1	9.1	12.5	11.0	0.7	0.1
1982	..	10.1	11.8	..	..	..
1983	..	10.1	11.4	..	..	..
1984	..	10.2	11.0	..	..	..
1985	..	10.6	10.6	..	..	..
Estimated percentage of deliveries in England						
1980	75.7	8.9	13.1	11.2	0.6	0.1
1981	..	..	..	..	..	..
1982	75.9	10.0	11.8	10.2	0.6	0.0
1983	75.4	10.0	11.3	9.7	0.6	0.1
1984	75.2	10.0	11.0	9.6	0.6	0.1
1985	75.6	10.4	10.6	9.0	0.7	0.1
Estimated percentage of deliveries in NHS hospitals in England						
1989/90	78.1	11.3	9.7	7.8	1.6	0.2
1990/91	76.7	12.4	9.9	7.5	2.1	0.1
1991/92	76.3	12.9	9.8	6.9	2.7	0.2
1992/93	75.5	13.8	9.9	6.6	3.1	0.2
1993/94	73.8	15.0	10.4	6.5	3.7	0.2
1994/95	72.8	15.5	10.8	5.8	4.8	0.2

* Before 1979, 'spontaneous' includes 'breech spontaneous'
~ Before 1979 'other and unspecified' includes 'breech extraction' and 'abnormal'

Source: Maternity Hospital In-patient Enquiry and OPCS *Birth statistics, Series FM1*

Department of Health, Maternity Hospital Episode Statistics, *Statistical bulletin 1997/28, Table 3*

This is similar to Table A7.32a in the first edition of *Birth counts*

A7.20.2

Method of delivery, England and Wales, 1979–81, England, 1980–1994/95

Year	Spontaneous				Caesarean section			Instrumental delivery*	Forceps			Ventouse	Breech extraction	Other
	All	Vertex	Breech	Abnormal presentation of head*	All	Elective	Emergency	All	Low	Other	All			
Estimated percentage of deliveries in England and Wales														
1979	75.5	74.4	1.1	1.1	8.2	4.5	3.7	13.1	6.2	5.2	11.5	0.6	1.2	0.2
1980	75.7	74.5	1.1	1.0	8.8	4.0	4.9	11.7	6.0	5.2	11.2	0.6	1.2	0.1
1981	76.1	75.4	0.7	0.7	9.1	5.0	4.0	12.5	6.1	4.9	11.0	0.7	0.9	0.1
Estimated percentage of deliveries in England														
1980	75.7	74.6	1.1	1.1	8.9	3.9	5.0	13.1	6.2	5.1	11.2	0.6	1.2	0.1
1981	..	..	..	..	..	..	..	..	..	..	..	..	..	..
1982	75.9	74.9	1.0	1.0	10.0	4.6	5.4	11.8	5.6	4.6	10.2	0.6	1.0	0.0
1983	75.4	74.5	0.9	0.9	10.0	4.6	5.4	11.3	5.5	4.2	9.7	0.6	1.0	0.1
1984	75.2	74.3	0.9	0.9	10.0	4.6	5.4	11.0	5.4	4.2	9.6	0.6	0.9	0.1
1985	75.6	74.7	0.9	0.9	10.4	4.9	5.5	10.6	5.2	3.8	9.0	0.7	0.9	0.1
Estimated percentage of deliveries in NHS hospitals in England														
1989–90	78.1	76.7	1.4	0.8	11.3	4.9	6.3	9.7	3.9	3.9	7.8	1.6	0.3	0.2
1990–91	76.7	75.6	1.1	0.8	12.4	5.3	7.1	9.9	4.0	3.5	7.5	2.1	0.3	0.1
1991–92	76.3	75.1	1.2	0.8	12.9	5.5	7.4	9.8	3.9	3.0	6.9	2.7	0.2	0.2
1992–93	75.5	74.4	1.1	0.7	13.8	5.6	8.1	9.9	3.6	3.0	6.6	3.1	0.2	0.2
1993–94	73.8	72.5	1.3	0.7	15.0	6.1	8.9	10.4	3.5	3.0	6.5	3.7	0.2	0.2
1994–95	72.8	71.5	1.3	0.7	15.5	6.5	9.0	10.8	3.3	2.5	5.8	4.8	0.2	0.2

* Delivered without instruments

Source: Maternity Hospital In-patient Enquiry and OPCS *Birth statistics, Series FM1*

Department of Health, Maternity Hospital Episode Statistics, *Statistical bulletin 1997/28, Table 3*

This is similar to Table A7.32a in the first edition of *Birth counts*

A7.20.3

Deliveries with episiotomy, England and Wales 1967, 1973–80, England, 1975, 1980 1989/90–1994/95

| | All deliveries | Method of delivery | | | | | | | | |
| | | Spontaneous | | Forceps | | Ventouse | Breech | Breech extraction | Caesarean | |
		Vertex	Other	Low	Other				Elective	Emergency
Percentage of deliveries in England and Wales										
1967	25.0^	::	::	::	::	::	::	::	::	::
1973	44.0	::	::	::	::	::	::	::	::	::
1974	47.4	::	::	::	::	::	::	::	::	::
1975	48.6	::	::	::	::	::	::	::	::	::
1976	50.6	::	::	::	::	::	::	::	::	::
1977	52.0	::	::	::	::	::	::	::	::	::
1978	53.4	::	::	::	::	::	::	::	::	::
1979	::	::	::	::	::	::	::	::	::	::
1980	50.9	::	::	::	::	::	::	::	::	::
Percentage of deliveries in NHS hospitals in England with mention of episiotomy										
1975	51	::	::	::	::	::	::	::	::	::
1980	52	::	::	::	::	::	::	::	::	::
1985	37	::	::	::	::	::	::	::	::	::
1989/90	23	21	20	69	73	60	55	59	0	1
1990/91	24	21	20	77	79	68	60	60	0	1
1991/92	23	20	25	77	82	68	58	60	0	0
1992/93	21	17	19	78	81	69	54	59	0	0
1993/94	19	15	21	74	78	63	51	47	0	1
1994/95	19	15	17	77	82	65	52	52	0	0
Estimated numbers										
1994/95	115,700	62,500	2,600	15,300	12,700	19,000	2,300	600	100	200

^ Not recorded in the Birmingham Region

Source: Maternity Hospital In-patient Enquiry and OPCS *Birth statistics*, *Series FM1*
Department of Health, Maternity Hospital Episode Statistics, *Statistical bulletin 1997/28*
This is similar to Table A7.32a in the first edition of *Birth counts*

A7.20.4

Induction of labour, method of delivery and episiotomy, England and regional health authorities, 1975, 1980, 1985 and 1994/95, Wales, 1975, 1980

Area		Use of ARM or oxytocics*+	Induction of labour+	Caesarean section	Instrumental delivery	Episiotomy	All deliveries in NHS hospitals
Percentage of maternities to resident population, 1975, 1980, 1985, percentages of deliveries in area, 1994/95							
England and Wales							
	1975	35.2	..	5.7	12.4	48.5	94.9
	1980	30.6	19.7	8.8	11.7	50.9	97.5
England							
	1980	30.6	20.0	8.8	11.7	50.7	97.5
	1985	28.9	17.1	10.2	10.3	35.8	97.8
	1994/95	–	20	15	11	19	–
Regional health authorities							
Northern	1975	36.2		5.0	10.0	47.9	95.5
	1980	26.1	17.2	8.1	8.7	56.8	98.8
	1985	26.7	17.7	10.8	8.9	43.5	99.4
	1994/95	–	19	15	8	14	–
Yorkshire	1975	38.9		5.0	10.0	47.9	95.5
	1980	41.5	19.6	7.7	10.4	50.2	97.5
	1985	41.2	16.7	10.4	9.0	35.6	98.2
	1994/95	–	15	16	7	16	–
Trent	1975	32.9	..	5.1	12.4	45.6	94.8
	1980	31.0	22.9	8.9	14.0	52.2	97.6
	1985	24.5	17.9	8.7	12.5	36.4	99.0
	1994/95	–	20	15	12	21	–
East Anglian	1975	25.2	..	5.2	10.3	39.7	87.6
	1980	29.1	18.0	7.5	10.5	46.5	91.8
	1985	26.4	14.1	8.9	11.4	34.1	92.6
	1994/95	–	26	16	10	22	–
NW Thames	1975	37.6		6.2	14.4	49.6	94.6
	1980	36.6	22.5	9.9	13.7	47.7	97.1
	1985	41.4	23.5	11.0	11.6	34.8	96.9
	1994/95	–	13	16	12	19	–
NE Thames	1975	35.7		7.0	12.2	49.7	94.4
	1980	24.8	18.3	9.5	10.4	51.9	98.1
	1985	23.1	15.6	10.4	8.9	39.3	98.0
	1994/95	–	21	15	11	22	–
SE Thames	1975	36.6		6.3	12.6	50.6	94.6
	1980	31.5	18.9	8.3	12.2	50.1	98.2
	1985	23.5	14.4	9.9	10.2	31.9	98.7
	1994/95	–	22	15	10	19	–

A7.20.4 *continued*

Induction of labour, method of delivery and episiotomy, England and regional health authorities, 1975, 1980, 1985 and 1994/95, Wales, 1975, 1980

Area		Use of ARM or oxytocics*+	Induction of labour+	Caesarean section	Instrumental delivery	Episiotomy	All deliveries in NHS hospitals
		Percentage of maternities to resident population, 1975, 1980, 1985, percentages of deliveries in area, 1994/95					
SW Thames	1975	38.7	..	6.2	15.3	53.8	92.8
	1980	30.8	24.6	9.0	13.6	53.7	94.6
	1985	23.5	17.0	11.1	12.2	35.0	92.6
	1994/95	–	16	16	13	20	–
Wessex	1975	34.4	..	5.6	12.5	47.3	91.7
	1980	30.0	19.2	8.9	12.9	44.0	94.1
	1985	25.1	18.6	10.6	12.2	32.8	97.2
	1994/95	–	26	18	14	23	–
Oxford	1975	28.3	..	5.2	16.2	51.5	96.4
	1980	23.2	18.0	8.1	13.2	50.2	97.4
	1985	27.1	18.2	9.6	11.2	29.9	96.2
	1994/95	–	22	13	12	18	–
South Western	1975	40.7	..	6.5	13.3	51.0	97.7
	1980	30.5	18.7	9.0	12.4	53.5	98.8
	1985	27.2	14.6	9.3	10.4	35.0	98.7
	1994/95	–	22	14	11	18	–
West Midlands	1975	24.9	..	4.9	12.8	46.7	95.6
	1980	19.7	19.1	8.8	9.7	48.3	98.5
	1985	16.8	16.3	10.8	10.2	36.4	98.9
	1994/95	–	21	16	8	19	–
Mersey	1975	41.5	..	6.8	10.9	49.2	96.5
	1980	39.6	22.0	10.1	12.2	50.5	98.8
	1985	46.5	15.3	10.6	10.1	37.1	99.3
	1994/95	–	21	18	10	15	–
North Western	1975	34.0		5.0	10.0	43.9	96.4
	1980	34.6	20.2	8.5	10.9	50.8	98.8
	1985	33.0	17.6	10.6	8.6	35.0	99.3
	1994/95	–	20	15	9	19	–
Wales~	1975	42.4	..	5.8	11.9	48.6	97.8
	1980	30.7	14.1	9.6	11.3	54.7	98.8

* Including augmentation of labour. A separate breakdown was not available in 1975

+ See text for discussion and definitions of ARM, oxytocics, induction and mode of delivery

Source: DHSS, OPCS, Welsh Office, Maternity Hospital In-patient Enquiry

Department of Health, Maternity Hospital Episode Statistics, *Statistical bulletin 1997/28, Tables 2, 4 and 17*

This was Table A7.34 in the first edition of *Birth counts*

A7.21.1

Obstetric intervention rates by mother's age and parity, NHS hospital births, England and Wales, 1967, 1975, 1980, England, 1980, 1985, 1994/95

Mother's age		Parity				All parities
		0	1–3	4 or more	Not known	
Percentage of women delivered by instruments*						
Under 25	1967	15.9	3.3	1.6	–	10.3
	1975	17.2	4.1	2.7	22.2	12.5
	1980	18.3	3.5	1.5	18.0	12.6
	1980	18.3	3.5	1.6	16.9	12.6
	1985	15.4	2.9	2.6	16.6	10.6
	1994/95	16	3	2	18	11
25–34	1967	26.8	5.0	2.5	–	10.0
	1975	26.4	5.7	3.0	23.3	12.5
	1980	27.0	4.6	2.7	14.5	11.7
	1980	27.1	4.6	2.8	13.2	11.7
	1985	24.1	4.2	2.3	17.9	10.9
	1994/95	23	5	2	19	13
35 and over	1967	31.5	7.8	4.5	–	8.4
	1975	31.8	7.1	4.0	21.4	10.1
	1980	31.7	6.7	2.8	12.5	10.0
	1980	31.8	6.6	2.8	12.5	10.0
	1985	29.4	5.4	3.1	13.3	9.3
	1994/95	26	6	3	18	11
All ages	1967	19.3	4.8	3.3	–	10.0
	1975	21.0	5.3	3.4	22.7	12.3
	1980	22.1	4.4	2.7	16.2	12.0
	1980	22.1	4.4	2.8	15.0	12.0
	1985	19.5	3.9	2.6	17.3	10.7
	1994/95	26	6	3	18	11
Percentage of women delivered by caesarean section						
Under 25	1975	5.2	3.9	3.6	5.2	4.7
	1980	8.3	5.9	9.2	10.1	7.4
	1980	8.4	5.8	9.8	11.1	7.4
	1985	9.3	7.1	3.9	8.6	8.4
	1994/95	13	10	14	16	12
25–34	1975	7.9	5.3	5.1	8.3	6.2
	1980	12.4	8.0	7.0	13.3	9.4
	1980	12.4	7.8	6.8	13.8	9.3
	1985	13.7	9.6	8.7	13.4	10.9
	1994/95	19	14	14	22	16

A7.21.1 *continued*

Obstetric intervention rates by mother's age and parity, NHS hospital births, England and Wales, 1967, 1975, 1980, England, 1980, 1985, 1994/95

Mother's age	Parity					All parities
		0	1–3	4 or more	Not known	
Percentage of women delivered by caesarean section*						
35 and over	1975	29.4	11.6	10.0	28.6	14.1
	1980	29.6	15.0	13.8	15.6	17.1
	1980	29.8	15.0	13.9	15.6	17.2
	1985	27.7	15.4	14.5	23.3	17.4
	1994/95	30	21	18	31	24
All ages	1975	6.7	5.3	7.0	7.3	6.0
	1980	10.4	7.9	9.5	11.7	9.0
	1980	10.4	7.8	9.4	12.6	9.0
	1985	11.7	9.4	10.5	12.6	10.5
	1994/95	17	15	15	22	16
Percentage of women having an episiotomy						
Under 25	1967	48.3	18.9	6.5		34.1
	1975	65.8	37.3	10.0	81.7	55.6
	1980	69.9	37.6	6.2	63.9	57.3
	1980	69.6	37.4	6.6	62.3	57.0
	1985	52.2	20.7	8.6	38.7	39.9
	1994/95+	29	8	4	–	21
25–34	1967	55.9	22.3	6.8		27.3
	1975	72.5	39.9	9.4	67.6	49.6
	1980	71.9	41.0	12.1	56.0	50.0
	1980	71.7	40.9	11.5	54.7	49.8
	1985	58.0	25.0	6.6	41.5	35.5
	1994/95+	34	11	2	–	20
35 and over	1967	49.1	22.3	5.6		17.5
	1975	52.2	33.4	10.7	39.3	30.6
	1980	59.8	37.2	13.3	53.1	36.7
	1980	59.4	37.5	13.2	53.1	36.8
	1985	52.7	24.3	8.6	32.1	27.0
	1994/95+	31	12	3		16
All ages	1967	50.4	21.1	6.2		29.5
	1975	52.2	33.4	10.7	39.3	30.6
	1980	70.5	39.7	12.3	60.0	52.2
	1980	70.2	39.7	12.0	58.4	52.0
	1985	54.6	23.7	7.3	39.9	36.6
	1994/95+	32	10	3		20

* Forceps in 1967 and 1975, forceps or vacuum extraction from 1980 onwards
~ Numbers obtained using grossing-up factors given in MB4 no. 28 Appendix B table ii.
+ Deliveries of unknown parity excluded from overall rate for episiotomy

Source: DHSS, OPCS and Welsh Office, Maternity Hospital In-patient Enquiry
Department of Health, Hospital Episode Statistics

This is similar to Table A7.35 in the first edition of *Birth counts*

A7.22.1

Induction of labour and method of delivery, all maternities, Scotland, 1975–97

Year	Number of maternities	Inductions[+]	Mode of delivery[*]						
			Spontaneous	Forceps	Vacuum extraction	Breech	Caesarean section	Other
	Number		**Percentage of all maternities**					
1975	65,173	31,049	47.6	75.7	13.2	0.5	2.0	8.5	0.2
1976	64,039	28,128	43.9	74.7	13.7	0.5	1.7	9.4	0.0
1977	61,722	26,695	43.3	74.8	13.2	0.4	1.6	10.0	0.0
1978	63,802	25,202	39.5	72.6	12.7	0.5	1.4	10.7	2.1
1979	66,783	24,427	36.6	73.4	13.6	0.5	1.3	11.2	0.1
1980	67,062	18,456	27.5	73.6	12.9	0.4	1.3	11.6	0.0
1981	67,890	19,022	28.0	74.1	12.5	0.4	1.0	11.9	0.0
1982	64,966	17,164	26.4	73.9	11.9	0.3	1.1	12.6	0.0
1983	63,953	16,447	25.7	74.6	11.4	0.3	1.1	12.6	0.0
1984	64,214	15,197	23.7	74.1	11.7	0.3	0.9	12.9	0.0
1985	64,968	15,218	23.4	74.5	11.1	0.3	0.9	13.2	0.0
1986	64,703	14,489	22.4	74.5	10.9	0.5	0.9	13.2	0.0
1987	64,932	14,189	21.9	74.4	10.3	0.6	0.8	13.7	0.1
1988	65,440	13,388	20.5	73.2	11.2	0.6	0.8	14.2	0.0
1989	62,985	13,298	21.1	72.8	10.9	1.1	0.8	14.2	0.1
1990	64,573	13,781	21.3	72.4	10.8	1.2	0.8	14.8	0.1
1991	66,011	13,815	20.9	72.7	10.4	1.4	0.7	14.8	0.0
1992	64,240	13,561	21.1	72.2	10.3	1.7	0.7	15.1	0.0
1993	62,511	14,120	22.6	72.3	9.0	2.4	0.7	15.6	0.1
1994	60,719	14,016	23.1	72.0	8.3	3.2	0.5	16.0	0.0
1995	59,232	16,180	27.3	71.8	7.7	3.6	0.5	16.3	0.0
1996r	57,019	14,005	24.6	71.3	7.2	4.0	0.6	16.9	0.0
1997p	56,704	14,216	25.1	70.6	7.2	4.2	0.5	17.5	0.0

* In multiple deliveries mode of delivery is based on baby 1.
+ See text for definitions.
r Revised data.
p Provisional data.

Source: Information and Statistics Division (Scotland) special tabulation

This was Table A7.33 in the first edition of *Birth counts*

A7.23.1

NHS hospital deliveries deliveries with and without antenatal, delivery or postnatal complications, England, 1989/90–1994/95

ICD 9 code*	Condition	Percentage of deliveries with mention of complication/indication for care						1994/95 estimated Estimated number of deliveries
		1989/90	1990/91	1991/92	1992/93	1993/94	1994/95	
650	Delivery in a completely normal case	46.7	44.7	43.4	42.1	44.6	46.2	279,500
6500	Normal deliveries with no antenatal or postnatal complications	30.8	25.0	21.3	19.7	18.8	18.5	111,900
6501	Normal deliveries with antenatal or postnatal complications recorded	15.9	19.7	22.3	22.6	25.9	27.7	167,500
	Other deliveries, with delivery complications	53.3	55.3	56.6	57.9	55.4	53.8	324,900
	Total deliveries with complications or indications for care	69.2	75.0	78.7	80.3	81.2	81.5	492,400
Complications mainly related to pregnancy								
640	Haemorrhage in early pregnancy	0.1	0.2	0.2	0.1	0.1	0.1	700
641	Antepartum haemorrhage, abruptio placentae, placenta previa	1.8	2.0	2.3	2.4	2.5	2.5	14,800
642	Hypertension complicating pregnancy, childbirth and the puerperium	5.3	5.9	6.7	6.7	6.9	6.9	41,900
643	Excessive vomiting in pregnancy	0.2	0.2	0.2	0.2	0.1	0.1	600
644	Early or threatened labour	3.0	3.6	4.4	4.7	4.9	4.7	28,200
645	Prolonged pregnancy	5.1	5.4	6.8	7.0	7.5	7.2	43,500
646	Other complications of pregnancy	2.1	3.1	3.6	3.8	4.4	3.5	21,200
647	Infective and parasitic conditions in mother, complicating pregnancy	0.2	0.2	0.3	0.2	0.4	0.3	1,900
648	Other current conditions in mother, complicating pregnancy	4.0	5.1	6.8	7.7	9.0	9.0	54,300
Indications for care in pregnancy, labour and delivery								
651	Multiple gestation	0.7	0.7	0.9	0.9	0.9	0.9	5,500
652	Malposition and malpresentation of fetus	4.5	5.1	5.8	6.0	6.5	6.7	40,400
653	Disproportion	1.1	1.2	1.3	1.2	1.1	0.9	5,500
654	Abnormality of organs and soft tissues of pelvis	4.6	5.3	5.6	5.9	6.3	6.4	38,400
655	Known or suspected fetal abnormality affecting management of mother	0.1	0.2	0.2	0.2	0.2	0.3	1,500
656	Other fetal and placental problems affecting management of mother	17.4	20.4	22.2	23.5	25.5	25.2	152,300

A7.23.1 continued

NHS hospital deliveries deliveries with and without antenatal, delivery or postnatal complications, England, 1989/90–1994/95

| ICD 9 code* | Condition | Percentage of deliveries with mention of complication/indication for care | | | | | | | Estimated number of deliveries |
		1989/90	1990/91	1991/92	1992/93	1993/94	1994/95	1994/95 estimated
657	Polyhydramnios	0.2	0.2	0.2	0.3	0.3	0.3	1,800
658	Other problems associated with amniotic cavity and membranes	2.8	3.7	4.5	5.0	5.8	5.8	34,900
659	Other indications for care or intervention related to labour and delivery	1.1	1.5	1.9	2.1	2.4	2.6	15,600

Complications occurring mainly in the course of labour and delivery

660	Obstructed labour	2.6	2.7	3.0	3.4	3.4	3.2	19,500
661	Abnormality of forces of labour	1.2	1.5	2.4	2.4	2.4	2.4	14,400
662	Long labour	6.8	7.4	7.6	7.9	8.7	9.1	55,200
663	Umbilical cord complications	4.4	5.3	6.3	6.8	6.9	7.2	43,300
664	Trauma to perineum and vulva during delivery	25.8	28.6	32.5	33.2	33.5	33.0	199,400
665	Other obstetrical trauma	0.6	0.8	0.9	0.9	1.0	1.0	5,900
666	Postpartum haemorrhage	2.8	3.5	4.3	4.7	5.0	5.2	31,500
667	Retained placenta or membranes, without haemorrhage	0.9	1.0	1.1	1.2	1.2	1.1	6,900
668	Complications of the administration of anaesthetic or other sedation	0.1	0.1	0.1	0.1	0.1	0.1	800
669	Other complications of labour and delivery	6.0	6.0	6.0	5.0	4.2	4.3	26,100

Complications of the puerperium

670	Major puerperal infection	0.0	0.1	0.0	0.0	0.0	0.0	200
671	Venous complications in pregnancy and the puerperium	0.5	0.7	0.8	0.9	0.9	0.7	4,500
672	Pyrexia of unknown origin during the puerperium	0.3	0.4	0.5	0.6	0.6	0.4	2,700
673	Obstetrical pulmonary embolism	0.0	0.0	0.0	0.0	0.0	0.0	100
674	Other and unspecified complications of the puerperium	0.5	0.7	1.0	1.0	1.0	0.8	5,100
675	Infections of the breast and nipple associated with childbirth	0.0	0.0	0.0	0.0	0.1	0.0	300
676	Other disorders of the breast associated with child birth, and disorders of location	0.2	0.5	0.6	0.6	0.5	0.4	2,300

* ICD9, International Classification of Diseases, ninth revision

Source: Hospital Episode Statistics, from Department of Health *Statistical bulletin 1997/28, Table 20*

This is similar to Table A7.26 in the first edition of *Birth counts*

A7.24.1

Postnatal in-patient care in NHS hospitals, England and Wales, 1975–85

| | Estimated number of women | | | | | |
| | Delivery in hospital | Admitted after birth of baby | | | | |
Year	All	All	Transferred from other hospital	Admitted from elsewhere	All postnatal cases	Total maternities
England and Wales						
1975	574,050	21,810	12,930	8,880	595,860	603,666
1976	560,710	23,160	14,350	8,810	583,870	584,263
1977	529,720	24,200	16,390	7,810	553,920	569,073
1978	553,290	26,370	17,840	8,530	579,660	595,515
1979	588,920	32,160	24,770	7,390	621,080	636,884
1980	604,100	34,520	27,270	7,250	638,620	654,501
England						
1980	601,460	47,150	36,530*	10,620	648,610	616,734
1981	..	..	..	..	..	596,110~
1982	574,620	46,200	36,520	9,680	620,820	587,438
1983	578,380	45,400	35,370	10,030	623,780	590,545
1984	586,110	42,810	32,920	9,890	628,920	587,879
1985	605,120	43,500	33,100	10,400	648,620	616,192

* revised figure

~ estimated figure

Source: OPCS and DHSS Hospital In-patient Enquiry, Series MB4 and OPCS/ONS *Birth statistics, Series FM1*

This was Table A7.38 in the first edition of *Birth counts*

A7.25.1

Length of postnatal stay in NHS hospitals, England and Wales, 1958, 1962, 1967–78, England, 1970–85, 1989/90–1994/95

Year	Length of stay, days — Mean length of stay	Estimated percentage of women delivered in hospital — Under 1	1–2	All under 3	3–4	5–6	7–8	9–10	11 or more
England and Wales									
1958	9.6	:	:	5	3	4	57 (7–8 & 9–10)		31
1962	8.1	:	:	9	6	8	65 (7–8 & 9–10)		13
1967	6.8	:	:	15	12	14	27	23	8
1968	6.7	:	:	16	13	15	27	22	8
1969	6.4	:	:	17	14	16	26	20	7
1970	6.3	:	:	18	16	17	25	18	6
1971	6.1	:	:	19	17	17	24	17	6
1972	5.9	:	:	19	18	18	24	16	5
1973	5.9	:	:	19	:	:	:	:	:
1974	5.8	:	:	19	20	19	23	15	5
1975	5.8	:	:	19	20	20	22	15	4
1976	5.8	:	:	19	20	21	22	14	4
1977	5.7	:	:	19	20	22	22	13	4
1978	5.5	:	:	21	22	23	21	11	3
England									
1970	6.4	:	:	18	15	16	26	19	7
1971	6.2	:	:	19	16	17	25	18	6
1972	6.0	:	:	19	17	17	24	17	6
1973	5.9	:	:	19	20	18	23	15	5
1974	5.9	:	:	19	19	19	23	15	5
1975	5.8	:	:	19	19	20	22	15	4
1976	5.8	:	:	19	20	21	22	14	4
1977	5.7	:	:	19	20	22	21	13	4
1978	5.5	:	:	21	21	23	19	11	3
1979	5.1	:	:	23	24	23	17	9	3
1980	5.0	:	:	25	24	24	17	8	2
1981	:	:	:	:	:	:	:	:	:
1982	4.6	:	:	28	25	24	15	6	2
1983	4.5	:	:	29	26	25	13	5	2
1984	4.3	:	:	31	28	24	11	4	2
1985	4.1	:	:	33	29	23	10	3	2

A7.25.1 continued

Length of postnatal stay in NHS hospitals, England and Wales, 1958, 1962, 1967–78, England, 1970–85, 1989/90–1994/95

Year	Mean length of stay	Length of stay, days							
		Under 1	1–2	All under 3	3–4	5–6	7–8	9–10	11 or more
England		Estimated percentage of women delivered in hospital							
1989/90	::	4	40	45	30	17	6	2	1
1990/91	::	5	44	49	29	16	5	1	1
1991/92	::	7	45	51	29	15	4	1	1
1992/93	::	8	47	55	27	14	3	1	1
1993/94	::	9	49	57	26	12	3	1	1
1994/95	::	10	50	60	25	11	2	1	1

Source: OPCS and DHSS Maternity Hospital In-patient Enquiry
Tables published in *Health and personal social services statistics for England*
Department of Health, Hospital Episode Statistics, special tabulation
Data in this table are derived from ungrossed HES data.
This was Table A7.36 in the first edition of *Birth counts*

A7.25.2

Length of postnatal stay in NHS hospitals by type of unit, Scotland, 1980/81–1998/99

Year	Mean length of stay, days	Length of stay, days Under 1	1–2	Under 3	3–7	8–14	15–28	29 and over
Estimated percentage of women delivered in hospital units of each type								
Specialist units								
1980/81	5.2	0.8	14.0	14.8	70.6	14.1	0.5	0.1
1981/82	5.1	0.4	13.9	14.3	72.1	13.1	0.4	0.0
1982/83	4.9	0.5	15.2	15.7	72.1	11.9	0.3	0.0
1983/84	4.8	0.5	16.2	16.7	72.1	10.8	0.4	0.0
1984/85	4.7	0.9	16.4	17.3	72.4	9.9	0.4	0.0
1985/86	4.5	1.2	18.0	19.1	71.5	8.9	0.3	0.0
1986/87	4.3	1.3	19.5	20.8	71.3	7.6	0.3	0.0
1987/88	4.2	1.6	20.6	22.1	70.9	6.7	0.2	0.0
1988/89	4.1	1.5	22.0	23.5	70.1	6.1	0.3	0.0
1989/90	4.0	2.0	23.3	25.3	68.9	5.5	0.3	0.0
1990/91	3.9	1.8	25.8	27.6	67.8	4.3	0.3	0.0
1991/92	3.7	2.0	28.7	30.7	65.4	3.6	0.2	0.0
1992/93	3.6	2.1	30.8	32.8	63.7	3.2	0.3	0.0
1993/94	3.4	2.6	33.4	35.9	61.0	2.8	0.2	0.0
1994/95	3.3	3.1	35.6	38.8	58.1	2.8	0.2	0.0
1995/96	3.2	3.6	38.1	41.7	55.5	2.5	0.2	0.0
1996/97	3.1	4.2	40.1	44.3	52.8	2.6	0.3	0.0
1997/98	3.1	4.2	41.9	46.1	51.1	2.5	0.3	0.0
1998/99*+	2.9	5.0	44.1	49.1	48.3	2.3	0.3	0.0
GP units								
1980/81	5.6	1.2	10.0	11.2	73.2	15.3	0.2	0.0
1981/82	5.4	1.0	10.9	11.9	73.0	14.8	0.2	0.0
1982/83	5.3	1.1	11.9	12.9	70.6	16.3	0.1	0.1
1983/84	5.3	1.4	9.0	10.4	72.9	16.7	0.0	0.0
1984/85	5.2	1.5	10.3	11.8	72.5	15.5	0.2	–
1985/86	4.9	1.8	10.7	12.5	79.0	8.4	0.0	0.1
1986/87	4.7	1.5	11.6	13.1	80.7	6.1	0.1	–
1987/88	4.6	1.9	13.0	14.8	79.9	5.1	0.1	0.1
1988/89	4.4	2.3	16.0	18.2	76.8	4.9	0.0	–
1989/90	4.3	2.4	16.4	18.7	76.2	4.9	0.0	0.1
1990/91	3.9	2.3	21.8	24.1	73.2	2.6	0.0	–
1991/92	3.7	2.7	27.4	30.1	67.8	2.0	0.1	–
1992/93	3.5	3.9	28.0	31.9	66.1	2.0	0.0	0.0
1993/94	3.4	2.8	31.4	34.2	63.7	2.1	0.1	–
1994/95	3.2	4.7	33.9	38.6	59.6	1.7	0.1	–
1995/96	3.2	5.5	30.5	36.0	62.7	1.3	–	–
1996/97	3.1	6.6	32.6	39.2	58.6	2.1	0.1	0.1
1997/98	2.9	6.9	35.9	42.8	56.1	1.2	–	–
1998/99*+	3.2	8.7	36.7	45.4	51.6	2.8	–	0.2

+ The data shown for 1998/99 are based on lower than expected numbers of births due to delays in reporting the information. This under-reporting principally affects the Greater Glasgow Health Board area.

* Provisional data.

Source: ISD, Scotland, SMR2 maternity discharge sheet

This is similar to Table A7.36 in the first edition of *Birth counts*

A7.26.1

Stays in neonatal units, England, 1980–85, 1989/90–1995/96

Year	Activity			Activity rate			Mean length of stay		
	Special care+	Intensive care+	All	Special care+	Intensive care+	All	Special care+	Intensive care+	All
	Discharges and deaths			**Rate per 100 live births**			**Days**		
1980	:	:	89,277	:	:	14.4	:	:	8.6
1981	:	:	84,061	:	:	14.1	:	:	8.9
1982	:	:	76,279	:	:	12.9	:	:	9.5
1983	:	:	71,184	:	:	12.0	:	:	10.0
1984	:	:	68,777	:	:	11.5	:	:	10.5
1985	:	:	68,634	:	:	11.1	:	:	10.8
1986	:	:	66,725	:	:	10.7	:	:	11.0
	Finished consultant episodes			**Rate per 100 live births**					
1989/90	53,592	7,151	60,743	8.3	1.1	9.4	8.6	17.5	9.6
1990/91	67,443	8,102	75,545	10.1	1.2	11.3	7.7	16.7	8.7
1991/92	67,278	10,023	77,301	10.2	1.5	11.7	8.2	17.2	9.4
1992/93	64,257	10,761	75,018	9.9	1.7	11.5	8.6	18.3	10.0
1993/94	70,224	13,083	83,307	11.0	2.1	13.1	8.3	18.4	9.9
1994/95	65,695	14,534	80,229	10.4	2.3	12.8	8.8	19.0	10.6
1995/96	58,683	17,053	75,736	9.6	2.8	12.3	9.0	18.4	11.1

+ Special care: observation and treatment falling short of intensive care but exceeding routine care

Intensive care: continuous skilled supervision by nursing and medical staff for at least one hour or until death

Source: DHSS/OPCS, Hospital In-patient Enquiry
Department of Health, Hospital Episode Statistics

This is a new table for this edition of *Birth counts*

A7.26.2

Stays in neonatal units, Wales, 1980–1995/96

Year	Discharges and deaths	Rate per 100 live births	Mean length of stay, days
1980	5,359	14.3	8.1
1981	4,886	13.6	8.4
1982	4,951	13.9	8.4
1983	4,386	12.4	8.7
1983/84	4,330	12.1	8.6
1984/85	4,327	11.8	9.4
1985/86	4,097	11.1	10.0
1986/87	4,037	10.7	10.4
1987/88	3,927	10.1	10.6
1988/89	4,042	10.7	7.8
1989/90	3,892	10.0	7.4
1990/91	4,356	11.5	7.6
1991/92	3,512	9.0	7.8
1992/93	3,796	10.0	7.5
1993/94	3,546	9.5	7.5
1994/95	3,320	9.1	7.8
1995/96	3,215	9.1	..

Data for 1996/97 and 1997/98 are incomplete, so this table could not be updated.

Source: Welsh Office

This is a new table for this edition of *Birth counts*

A7.26.3

Stays in neonatal units, Scotland, 1980–1997/98

Year	Discharges and deaths	Rate per 100 live births	Mean length of stay, days
1980	20,202	29.3	6.2
1981	19,763	28.6	5.9
1982	17,824	26.9	6.1
1983	16,952	26.0	5.9
1984	15,869	24.4	6.5
1985	15,021	22.5	6.6
1986/87	14,189	21.4	6.8
1987/88	14,500	21.9	6.9
1988/89	12,925	18.5	7.4
1989/90	12,257	18.3	7.8
1990/91	11,597	15.2	8.3
1991/92	10,013	14.9	9.2
1992/93	10,020	14.2	8.8
1993/94	9,339	14.4	9.1
1994/95	9,144	14.8	9.4
1995/96	8,619	14.4	9.6
1996/97	8,758	14.8	..
1997/98	8,220	13.8	..

Source: ISD, Scotland, form ISD(S)1

This is a new table for this edition of *Birth counts*

A7.26.4

Stays in neonatal units, Northern Ireland, 1981–1994/95

Year	Babies admitted		Average length of stay or episode
	Number	Rate per 100 live births	Days
1981	3,764	13.8	9.3
1982	..	..	..
1983	3,657	13.4	9.0
1984	3,856	13.9	9.1
1985	3,667	13.3	9.6
1986	3,570	12.7	10.0
1987	3,729	..	9.9
1987/88	..	..	..
1988/89	3,420	12.3	10.3
1989/90	3,495	13.4	9.6
1990/91	3,608	13.6	9.6
1991/92	3,481	13.3	9.7
1992/93	3,103	12.1	10.2
1993/94	2,870	11.5	10.4
1994/95	2,698	11.1	11.1

From 1995/96 onwards, 'sick babies', specialty 422, was incorporated within paediatrics, specialty 420, so data are no longer available

Source: Department of Health and Social Services, Northern Ireland

This is a new table for this edition of *Birth counts*

A7.27.1

Number of finished episodes and mean duration in paediatric specialties, children aged under one year, NHS hospitals, England, 1989/90–1994/95

Age at start of episode	Finished consultant episodes				Mean duration of episode			
	Under 28 days	28 days to under 3 months	Three months to under one year	All under one year	Under 28 days	28 days to under 3 months	Three months to under one year	All under one year
Paediatrics								
1989/90	182,889	36,257	79,112	298,258	5.9	4.4	3.6	5.1
1990/91	162,436	36,059	80,146	278,641	6.2	4.4	3.3	5.2
1991/92	143,518	37,985	86,777	268,280	6.6	4.1	3.1	5.1
1992/93	144,422	35,520	84,262	264,203	6.5	4.1	3.0	5.1
1993/94	156,319	37,810	89,132	283,262	6.3	3.9	2.8	4.9
1994/95	143,518	37,985	86,777	268,280	6.6	4.1	3.1	5.1
Paediatric neurology								
1989/90	46	106	451	603	7.4	7.7	4.8	5.5
1990/91	37	85	413	535	6.8	8.1	5.2	5.8
1991/92	95	202	769	1,065	7.4	6.3	4.2	4.9
1992/93	96	183	725	1,004	5.6	6.0	3.7	4.3
1993/94	73	189	732	994	4.8	6.7	8.0	7.5
1994/95	95	202	769	1,065	7.4	6.3	4.2	4.9
Paediatric surgery								
1989/90	2,435	2,666	5,260	10,361	13.0	5.2	4.1	6.5
1990/91	1,837	2,407	4,455	8,698	12.8	4.0	3.5	5.6
1991/92	2,776	2,630	5,103	10,509	12.3	4.6	3.8	6.3
1992/93	2,228	2,776	5,102	10,106	11.7	4.6	3.5	5.6
1993/94	2,168	2,730	4,881	9,779	11.7	4.6	3.5	5.6
1994/95	2,776	2,630	5,103	10,509	11.4	4.0	3.3	5.2

Source: Department of Health, Hospital Episode Statistics

This is a new table for this edition of *Birth counts*

A7.28.1

Prevalence of breast feeding up to nine months after birth, England and Wales, Scotland, Northern Ireland, 1975–95

	Birth	1 week	2 weeks	6 weeks	4 months	6 months	9 months	Base
England and Wales	**Percentage breastfeeding at each age**							
1975	51	42	35	24	13	9	..	1,544
1980	67	58	54	42	27	23	12	3,755
1985	65	56	53	40	26	21	11	4,671
1990	64	54	51	39	25	21	12	4,942
1995	68	58	54	44	28	22	14	4,598
Scotland								
1980	50	44	41	32	21	18	9	1,718
1985	48	41	38	29	22	18	9	1,895
1990	50	41	39	30	20	16	9	1,981
1995	55	46	44	36	24	19	13	1,863
Northern Ireland								
1990	36	29	27	17	8	5	3	1,497
1995	45	35	32	25	12	8	5	1,476

The data are weighted for Scotland to give a national estimate

Source: OPCS, *Infant feeding 1990*, ONS, *Infant feeding 1995*

This is a new table for this edition of *Birth counts*

A7.28.2

Estimated association between events at birth and breastfeeding, Great Britain, 1980, 1985, 1990 and 1995

Events at or after birth	1995	1980	1985	1990	1995
	Percentage who breastfed initially	Percentage who stopped breastfeeding within two weeks			
Had general anaesthetic	55	..	27	31	..
Had other or no general anaesthetic	..	..	31	31	..
Caesarean delivery	..	..	25	27	..
Other delivery	..	..	19	19	..
Length of time until the baby was first put to the breast					
immediately	66	13	14	12	14
within an hour	69	13	15	18	16
more than 1 hr, up to 4 hrs	61	18	21	25	26
more than 4 hrs, up to 12 hr		21	24	24	26
more than 12 hrs later	51	32	31	32	30
Special care received	51	23	23	20	21
Put under a lamp	68	..	..	..	..
No special care received	66	18	18	19	19
Birthweight, g					
Under 2,500	63	27	24	24	16
2,500–2,999	61	22	20	22	23
3,000–3,499	66	18	19	18	19
3,500 or more	68	18	18	21	19

Source: OPCS *Infant feeding 1990*, ONS *Infant feeding 1995*, reports and unpublished data

This is similar to Table 7.6 in the text volume of *Birth counts*

A7.28.3

Reasons given by mothers who stopped breastfeeding within two weeks of birth, Great Britain, 1980, 1985, 1990 and 1995

Reasons given by mothers	1980	1985	1990	1995
	Percentage of mothers who gave up within two weeks who gave each reason*			
Insufficient milk	44	35	39	35
Painful breasts or nipples	24	27	30	30
Baby would not suck	24	22	24	27
Breastfeeding took too long/tiring	9	6	7	12
Mother was ill	5	11	8	12

* Mothers may have given more than one reason, so percentages do not add up to 100.

Source: OPCS *Infant feeding 1990*, ONS *Infant feeding 1995*, reports and unpublished data

This is a new table for this edition of *Birth counts*

A7.28.4

Incidence of breast feeding by social class of partner, Great Britain, 1980–95

	Social class of partner									No partner	All
	I	II	III non-manual	All non-manual	III manual	IV	V	All manual	Unclassified		
Percentage who breastfed initially											
First birth											
1980	94	88	89	90	70	64		68	51		74
1985	93	87	85	88	69	68	50	67	59	41	69
1990	89	86	76	85	68	63	50	66	51	47	69
1995	91	88	79	87	73	67	64	71	72	51	73
Later births											
1980	83	71	65	73	52	43		50	54		58
1985	83	76	68	75	55	51	38	52	53	37	59
1990	84	74	70	74	53	47	36	50	57	38	58
1995	89	77	66	77	57	51	40	54	55	42	61
All babies											
1980	87	78	77	80	59	52		57	52		65
1985	87	81	76	81	61	58	43	58	55	39	64
1990	86	79	73	79	59	53	41	57	61	43	63
1995	90	82	72	81	64	57	50	61	62	47	66
Percentage breastfeeding at 6 weeks											
All babies											
1980	74	58	46	..	33	..	..	..	..	..	41
1985	71	58	46	..	34	29	20	..	16	30	38
1990	68	56	47	..	33	27	20	..	19	40	39
1995	73	59	48	..	36	33	23	..	38	25	43

Source: OPCS *Infant feeding 1990*, ONS *Infant feeding 1995*

This is a new table for this edition of *Birth counts*

A7.28.5

Incidence of breastfeeding by birth order and ethnic group, England, 1994

Birth order	Ethnic group			
	Bangladeshi	Pakistani	Indian	White
	Percentage of all mothers in each group who breastfed initially			
First birth	94	80	89	72
Second birth	91	77	80	53
Third birth	85	80	75	50
Fourth or later birth	87	.66	68	23
Second and subsequent birth	88	74	77	54
All	90	76	82	62
Base=100%	**Numbers in sample**			
First birth	209	251	391	295
Second birth	140	206	301	194
Third birth	93	115	160	93
Fourth or later birth	165	155	78	35
Second and subsequent birth	401	480	543	324
All	610	731	934	619

Source: ONS, *Infant feeding in asian families, Table 1.1*

This is a new table for this edition of *Birth counts*

A7.29.1

Use of services for postnatal care, England, 1975–1987/88, Wales 1976–88

Year	Women attending postnatal clinics in NHS hospitals	Women attending community postnatal clinics*	Women visited at home by midwife^
England			
1975	129,518	58,209	447,024
1976	123,890	63,751	446,295
1977	120,004	67,682	452,233
1978	117,188	..	503,934
1979	118,881	..	546,836
1980	112,490	..	586,352
1981	100,657	..	571,120
1982	88,632	..	573,786
1983	86,720	..	569,061
1984	80,668	..	578,525
1985	74,138	..	603,678
1986	62,613	..	607,091
1987/88	..	..	636,384
Wales			
1976	5,772	2,458	33,123
1977	6,197	3,128	31,399
1978	5,556	3,190	33,657
1979	5,924	..	36,976
1980	5,861	..	37,671
1981	6,352	..	36,902
1982	5,023	..	36,211
1983	5,432	..	35,927
1984	5,542	..	35,945
1985	5,577	..	37,164
1986	4,817	..	35,877
1987	3,855	..	36,999
1988	4,708	..	..

* Excluding sessions held by women's own general practitioners. Data not collected after 1978.
^ After hospital delivery

Source: DHSS, *Health and personal social services statistics for England*
Welsh Office, *Health and personal social services statistics for Wales*

This is similar to Table 7.37 in the first edition of *Birth counts*

A7.29.2

Use of services for postnatal care, England, 1988/89–1998/99

Year	Midwife-only clinics	Midwife domiciliary visits	Health visitor domiciliary visits
	Community face to face contacts		
1988/89	45,900	5,128,800	763,200
1989/90	50,200	5,170,800	769,500
1990/91	40,600	5,167,300	798,000
1991/92	37,400	5,000,300	763,000
1992/93	30,600	4,787,200	764,600
1993/94	34,700	4,608,000	804,200
1994/95	28,300	4,513,700	866,600
1995/96	32,700	4,251,400	855,300
1996/97	27,500	4,158,000	922,900
1997/98	26,700	3,959,800	890,100
1998/99	39,200	3,676,500	883,400

Source: DH, Form KC54 *Community maternity services, Summary information for 1996–97, England*, Table 1

This is similar to Table 7.37 in the first edition of *Birth counts*

A7.30.1

Clinic attendances and home visits by health visitors, England, 1975–1998/99

Year	Children attending child health clinics		Children visited by health visitors[*]		Domiciliary face to face contacts by health visitors	
	Born in year	Others aged under five	Born in year	Others aged under five	Antenatal	Postnatal
	Numbers of children, thousands				**Thousands**	
1975	500.9	1,006.1	618.4	1,760.4	–	–
1976	495.9	1,005.0	609.1	1,723.7	–	–
1977	486.1	986.0	578.2	1,670.7	–	–
1978	470.2	972.0	605.4	1,654.3	–	–
1979	525.9	980.7	650.9	1,635.8	–	–
1980	550.9	1,017.0	678.5	1,650.9	–	–
1981	517.0	1,075.1	646.5	1,638.1	–	–
1982	508.1	1,098.0	632.7	1,667.8	–	–
1983	498.7	1,066.9	638.0	1,677.2	–	–
1984	497.7	1,082.5	645.3	1,672.6	–	–
1985	509.1	1,064.6	658.8	1,672.1	–	–
1986	507.8	1,069.4	671.4	1,677.2	–	–
1987/88	602.1	978.6	730.6	1,573.2	–	–
1988/89	..	..	1,020.4	1,360.6	190.3	763.2
1989/90	..	..	982.7	1,332.0	195.7	769.5
1990/91	..	..	951.6	1,225.6	181.6	798.0
1991/92	..	..	980.1	1,241.8	162.9	763.0
1992/93	..	..	991.3	1,247.7	162.4	764.6
1993/94	..	..	979.2	1,282.9	177.0	804.2
1994/95	..	..	965.0	1,287.0	162.0	866.6
1995/96	..	..	945.9	1,283.1	145.8	855.3
1996/97	..	..	954.9	1,280.1	159.4	922.9
1997/98	..	..	902.8	1,274.3	151.1	890.1
1998/99	..	..	876.3	1,273.1	143.8	883.4

* From 1988/89 onwards these are first contacts with health visitors either at home or at a clinic

Source: DH/DHSS *Health and personal social services statistics for England*, KC54 Community maternity services return, KC55 Professional advice and support return

This was part of Table A7.40 in the first edition of *Birth counts*

A7.30.2

Clinic attendances and home visits by health visitors, Wales, 1975–1997/98

Year	Children attending child health clinics		Children visited by health visitors		
	Born in year	Other children attending clinic	Born in year	Others aged under 5 years	All aged under 5 years
	Numbers of children, thousands				
1975	30.2	71.4	34.7	113.4	148.1
1976	30.7	69.2	35.7	117.2	152.9
1977	28.2	69.0	33.2	111.5	144.7
1978	29.6	63.5	34.8	108.6	143.4
1979	31.5	63.3	37.7	104.9	142.6
1980	32.6	67.5	38.7	108.2	146.9
1981	30.9	66.5	37.8	108.2	146.0
1982	38.2	69.5	38.2	104.9	143.1
1983	32.0	67.3	38.4	102.5	140.9
1984	31.1	67.5	37.3	102.0	139.3
1985	30.4	70.3	38.7	98.0	136.7
1986	30.3	69.8	39.6	96.8	136.4
1987	29.9	69.3	40.2	94.2	134.4
1988*	31.9	69.8	41.5	94.3	135.8
1989*	33.9	79.5	54.8	84.3	139.1
			Under 1	**1–4 years**	**0–4 years**
1990/91	..	..	69.1	94.6	163.7
1991/92	..	..	68.8	90.1	158.9
1992/93	..	..	65.4	84.8	150.2
1993/94	..	..	61.9	84.3	146.2
1994/95	..	..	..	..	127.1+
1995/96	..	..	..	..	124.8+
1996/97	..	..	47.9	76.0	123.9+
1997/98	..	..	..	..	126.9+

+ Excludes Gwent Community Health NHS trust, which has not been able to provide data on health visitors in this format since 1993/94.
* Estimates

Source: Welsh Office, *Health and personal social services statistics for Wales, Health statistics, Wales*

This was part of Table A7.40 in the first edition of *Birth counts*

A7.30.3

Clinic attendances and home visits by health visitors, Scotland, 1975–98

Year	Children attending child health clinics		Children visited by health visitors
	Born in year	Others aged under five	Aged under five
	Numbers of children, thousands		
1975	..	..	309.0
1976	..	..	303.1
1977	..	..	328.9
1978	..	..	290.8
1979	58.5	91.2	280.8
1980	61.4	96.9	281.0
1981	59.9	100.8	288.5
1982	53.7	..	276.7
1983	58.8	..	278.0
1984	..	..	273.9
1985	..	..	278.2
1986	..	..	268.6
1987	..	..	265.5
1988	..	..	270.4
1989	..	..	265.3
1990	..	..	258.8
1991	..	..	252.5
1992	..	..	243.0
1993	..	..	223.4
1994	..	..	223.3
1995	..	..	198.5
1996	..	..	197.8
1997	..	..	183.6
1998*	..	..	175.1

* provisional

Source: Information and Statistics Division, Scotland

This was part of Table A7.40 in the first edition of *Birth counts*

A7.31.1

Percentage of children immunised by their second birthday, England, 1967–1998/99

Year	Measles*	Measles, mumps and rubella	Diphtheria	Tetanus	Whooping cough	Polio	Haemophilus Influenzae b+
1967	–	–	78	78	76	–	–
1968	–	–	79	79	78	–	–
1969	26	–	83	83	81	–	–
1970	34	–	80	81	79	–	–
1971	47	–	80	80	78	–	–
1972	52	–	81	81	79	–	–
1973	54	–	81	81	79	–	–
1974	53	–	80	80	77	–	–
1975	47	–	74	74	60	–	–
1976	47	–	75	75	39	–	–
1977	50	–	78	78	41	78	–
1978	48	–	78	78	31	78	–
1979	51	–	80	80	35	80	–
1980	53	–	81	81	41	81	–
1981	55	–	83	83	46	82	–
1982	58	–	84	84	53	84	–
1983	60	–	84	84	59	84	–
1984	63	–	84	84	65	84	–
1985	68	–	85	85	65	85	–
1986	71	–	85	85	67	85	–
1987/88	76	–	87	87	73	87	–
1988/89	80	7	87	87	75	87	–
1989/90	84	68	89	89	78	89	–
1990/91	87	86	92	92	84	92	–
1991/92	90	90	93	93	88	93	–
1992/93	92	92	95	95	92	95	–
1993/94	91	91	95	95	93	95	75
1994/95	91	91	95	95	93	95	91
1995/96	92	92	96	96	94	96	94
1996/97	92	92	96	96	94	96	95
1997/98	91	91	96	96	94	96	95
1998/99	88	88	95	95	94	95	95

* Figures from 1988/89 onwards include children having MMR vaccine
+ Introduced in 1993

Source: DH, Statistics Division SD2B Forms SBL 607, KC51 and COVER,
DH/DHSS *Health and personal social services statistics for England,*

This is a new table for this edition of *Birth counts*

A7.31.2

Percentage of children immunised by their second birthday, Wales, 1976–1997/98

Year	Measles	Measles, mumps and rubella*	Diphtheria	Tetanus	Whooping cough	Polio	Haemophilus influenzae b+
1976	21	–	64	64	23	67	–
1977	23	–	64	64	24	63	–
1978	27	–	69	69	16	69	–
1979	30	–	72	72	19	72	–
1980	33	–	76	76	23	76	–
1981	35	–	78	78	26	78	–
1982	40	–	81	81	33	81	–
1983	44	–	82	82	42	82	–
1984	48	–	81	81	50	81	–
1985	57	–	83	83	50	83	–
1986	61	–	84	84	53	85	–
1987	67	–	85	85	61	86	–
1988	78	–	88	88	66	88	–
1989/90	81	–	90	90	71	91	–
1990/91	86	–	93	93	78	93	–
1991/92	89	–	94	94	84	94	–
1992/93	91	–	96	96	88	96	4
1993/94	92	–	97	97	91	97	76
1994/95	–	92	97	97	92	97	94
1995/96	–	92	97	97	92	97	96
1996/97	–	91	96	96	93	96	96
1997/98	–	90	96	96	93	96	96

* Figures before 1994/95 include measles only vaccine.
+ Introduced in October 1992.

Source: Welsh Office, *Health and personal social services statistics for Wales, Health statistics, Wales*

This is a new table for this edition of *Birth counts*

A7.31.3

Percentage of children immunised by their second birthday, Scotland, 1974–1997/98

Year	Measles	Measles, mumps and rubella*	Diphtheria	Tetanus	Whooping cough	Polio	Haemophilus influenzae b+
1974	55.8	–	78.2	..	77.2	78.8	–
1975	52.9	–	72.1	..	66.8	70.8	–
1976	48.6	–	72.7	..	55.2	69.6	–
1977	50.8	–	77.8	..	55.4	76.6	–
1978	54.5	–	79.1	79.0	49.1	79.0	–
1979	56.0	–	75.8	75.8	47.7	75.2	–
1980	51.8	–	79.3	79.4	51.8	79.5	–
1981	54.4	–	79.8	79.9	53.7	81.9	–
1982	57.0	–	83.0	83.0	58.1	82.4	–
1983	60.3	–	82.7	82.7	60.0	81.9	–
1984	64.3	–	85.2	85.1	68.6	84.2	–
1985	72.7	–	86.6	86.6	69.2	85.1	–
1986	76.0	–	85.6	85.7	70.7	85.3	–
1987	77.2	–	87.2	87.2	74.2	86.9	–
1988	84.0	–	88.4	88.4	76.2	87.8	–
1989	–	70.1	90.4	90.4	80.0	90.4	–
1990	–	91.5	94.0	94.0	85.9	94.0	–
1991	–	93.5	94.9	94.9	89.4	94.6	–
1992	–	94.2	96.3	96.3	92.4	96.1	–
1993	–	93.5	95.9	95.9	93.0	95.9	–
1994	–	93.5	95.9	95.9	93.8	96.0	–
1995	–	94.1	97.4	97.4	95.5	97.4	96.9
1996	–	94.6	97.9	97.9	96.2	97.9	97.5
1996/97	–	94.4	97.7	97.7	96.1	97.7	97.4
1997/98	–	94.0	97.6	97.7	96.3	97.7	97.5

* Introduced nationally on 1 October 1998
+ Data not collected before 1995

Source: ISD, Scotland, ISD(S) 11 part 1 and ISD(S) 13 part 2

This is a new table for this edition of *Birth counts*

A7.31.4

Percentage of children immunised by their second birthday, Northern Ireland, 1976–1998/99

	Measles	Measles, mumps and rubella	Diphtheria	Tetanus	Whooping cough	Polio	Haemophilus influenzae b
1976	4.9	–	62.3	62.4	37.8	62.2	–
1977	5.3	–	68.9	69.0	38.1	68.9	–
1978	5.1	–	68.8	68.4	30.4	69.7	–
1979	5.4	–	67.8	67.5	31.4	68.0	–
1980	5.9	–	66.2	65.6	35.5	66.0	–
1981	8.7	–	72.5	72.5	39.4	72.5	–
1982	11.7	–	75.2	74.7	43.6	75.6	–
1983	17.2	–	76.5	75.8	47.2	76.1	–
1984	25.3	–	78.7	78.3	54.6	78.5	–
1985	46.0	–	78.7	78.4	55.1	78.1	–
1986	51.0	–	81.3	82.1	61.7	81.7	–
1987	55.6	–	81.0	80.7	65.1	80.4	–
1988	79.0	–	83.9	84.3	68.9	84.3	–
1989/90	87.4	–	90.4	90.4	78.4	90.4	–
1990/91	–	85.4	92.7	92.7	83.2	92.6	–
1991/92	–	90.5	95.2	95.2	88.1	95.2	–
1992/93	–	92.2	96.8	96.8	91.8	96.8	–
1993/94	–	89.4	97.0	97.0	93.3	97.0	..
1994/95	–	92.0	97.0	97.0	94.3	97.0	..
1995/96	–	92.5	97.0	97.0	94.4	97.0	..
1996/97	–	92.8	97.2	97.2	95.4	97.2	97.0
1997/98	–	92.4	97.2	97.2	95.6	97.2	97.1
1998/99	–	90.1	96.8	96.8	95.6	96.8	96.8

Source: DHSS, Northern Ireland, central return KC51

This is a new table for this edition of *Birth counts*

A7.32.1

Children under one year of age on the Child Protection Register, England, Wales and Northern Ireland, 1988–99

	England	Wales	Northern Ireland
	Numbers of children on registers on March 31		
	Aged under 1		**Aged 0–4+**
1988	..	93	..
1989	2,700	147	..
1990	2,700	155	..
1991	2,800	235	502
1992	2,500	138	426
1993	2,300	138	476
1994	2,700	126	507
1995	2,900	168	532
1996	2,600	148	580
1997	2,800	170	467
1998	2,800	213	490
1999	3,000	..	..
	Rates		**Per 1,000**
	Per 1,000 live births		**children aged 0–4**
1988	..	2.4	..
1989	4.2	3.9	..
1990	4.0	4.0	..
1991	4.2	6.2	3.8
1992	3.8	3.7	3.3
1993	3.6	3.8	3.7
1994	4.3	3.6	4.0
1995	4.7	4.9	4.2
1996	4.2	4.2	4.6
1997	4.6	4.9	3.8
1998	4.7	6.4	4.0

Data for Scotland are not subdivided by age. On March 31 1998, 2,303 children aged 0–15 were on child protection registers, a rate of 2.3 per thousand children aged 0–15.

+ Data for Northern Ireland for children aged 0–4 are not subdivided further

Source: Department of Health, SD3A, *Children and young people on Child Protection Registers*

Welsh Office, Special tabulation

DHSS Northern Ireland, Special tabulation

This is a new table for this edition of *Birth counts*

A7.33.1

Children under one year of age in local authority care, England, Wales, Scotland and Northern Ireland, 1982–99

	England	Wales	Scotland	Northern Ireland
	Numbers of children on March 31			
	Aged under 1			**Aged 0–4**
1982	1,424	100	140#	..
1983	1,206	117	96#	..
1984	1,191	86	223	..
1985	1,164	85	208	..
1986	1,515	80	236	..
1987	1,607	76	226	..
1988	1,561	89	241	..
1989	1,711	84	245	512
1990	1,652	84	228	516
1991	1,654	73	..	514
1992	1,420	110	219	455
1993	1,310	55	181	512
1994	1,430	44	..	508
1995	1,600	50	..	489
1996	1,640	64	..	484
1997	1,710	82~	136*	376
1998	1,750	91	123*	373
1999	2,200+	..	..	368
	Rates			**Per 1,000 children aged 0–4**
	Per 1,000 live births			
1982	2.4	2.8	..	
1983	2.0	3.3	..	
1984	2.0	2.4	3.4	..
1985	1.9	2.3	3.1	..
1986	2.4	2.2	3.6	..
1987	2.5	2.0	3.4	..
1988	2.4	2.3	3.6	..
1989	2.6	2.2	3.9	3.8
1990	2.5	2.2	3.5	3.8
1991	2.5	1.9	..	4.0
1992	2.2	2.9	3.3	3.5
1993	2.1	1.5	2.9	3.9
1994	2.3	1.2	..	4.0
1995	2.6	1.4	..	3.9
1996	2.6	1.8	..	3.9
1997	2.8	2.4	2.3	3.1
1998	2.9	2.7	2.2	3.0

\# Excluding Glasgow, Ayr and Lanark in 1982 and Strathclyde in 1983
\+ Provisional data from form CLA100
~ Includes children in agreed series of short term placements
* In Scotland, 1997 shows children 'in care or under supervision', 1998 shows children 'looked after' both at and away from home.
Data for Northern Ireland for children aged 0–4 are not subdivided further
Source: Department of Health, SD3A *Children looked after by local authorities*
Welsh Office, Special tabulation
Scottish Office, Social Work Services Group, *Statistical bulletins, Children in care or under supervision*
DHSS Northern Ireland, Special tabulation

This is a new table for this edition of *Birth counts*

A8.1.1

Young people on registers of people with disabilities, England, 1981–98

Registers of people with physical disabilities

	Total	Very severely handicapped	Severely or appreciably handicapped	Other classified persons
Numbers of people aged 0–15 years				
1981	19,900	5,800	6,900	7,300
1984	20,700	5,800	7,400	7,400
1987	23,400	5,600	8,400	9,400
1990	21,900	4,900	8,100	8,800
Numbers of people aged 0–17 years				
1993*	27,700	5,700	10,900	11,200

Registers of blind and partially sighted people

	Blind	Partially sighted	Blind	Partially sighted
Numbers aged 0–4 years			**Numbers aged 5–15 years**	
1982	280	170	1,710	2,060
1986	380	180	1,520	1,770
1988	450	220	1,600	1,680
1991	670	370	1,890	1,780
			Numbers aged 5–17 years	
1994	580	500	2,260	2,360
1997	1,081	762	3,082	3,182

Registers of deaf or hard of hearing people

	Deaf	Hard of hearing
Numbers of people aged 0–15 years		
1983	3,326	1,648
1986	3,125	1,269
1989	3,000	1,161
1992	3,767	2,095
Numbers of people aged 0–17 years		
1995	4,421	3,536
1998	4,220	2,789

* Data were not collected in 1996 and 1999.

Source: Department of Health/ DHSS, returns SSDA 902, SSDA 910 and SSDA 911

This is similar to Table A8.1 in the first edition of *Birth counts*

A8.2.1

Educational provision for pupils with special needs, United Kingdom, 1970/71–1996/97

a) Pupils in public sector and assisted special schools

	Hospital schools England and Wales	Other special schools England**	Wales	Scotland	Northern Ireland~	United Kingdom
	Full-time pupils, thousands					
1970/71	3.6	84.3	2.5	10.6	2.1	99.5
1975/76	9.5	119.8	4.3	13.1	2.3	139.5
1980/81	7.1	120.3	4.6	11.8	2.5	139.2
1985/86	4.4	107.7	4.1	11.7*	2.6	126.0
1990/91	0.9	94.5	3.6	8.7	4.0	110.8
1991/92	0.7	94.7	3.6	8.6	4.1	111.0
1992/93	0.5	95.1	3.6	8.8	4.2	111.7
1993/94	0.6	95.7	3.5	9.0	4.4	112.6
1994/95	0.2	95.3	3.5	9.1	4.6	112.5
1995/96^	0.2	93.5	..	8.2	4.6	109.9
1996/97$	..	95.2	3.6	9.2	4.7	112.6

** From 1994/5 England figures exclude pupils who are also registered elsewhere and are not comparable with earlier years

~ From 1987/88 onwards figures include schools and pupils which were previously the responsibility of the Northern Ireland Department of Health and Social Security

* Data for Scotland relate to 1984/85

^ Data are provisional and include 1994/95 data for Wales

$ Data for Wales relate to 1995/96

(b) Pupils with statements of special needs in other public sector schools#

	England	Wales	Scotland	Northern Ireland	United Kingdom
	Pupils in public sector primary, middle and secondary schools, thousands				
1986/87	33.3	6.0	0.7	1.3	41.3
1987/88	40.9	7.5	0.8	1.1	50.2
1988/89	47.3	7.5	1.1	1.6	57.4
1989/90	54.3	7.1	1.3	1.7	64.4
1990/91	62.0	8.9	2.3	2.0	75.2
1991/92	71.2	10.5	3.0	2.2	86.9
1992/93	85.0	11.5	3.6	2.5	102.5
1993/94	100.3	12.7	4.6	2.7	120.2
1994/95	112.8	10.9	5.7	3.2	132.5
1995/96^	126.8	..	7.7	3.3	148.8
1996/97$	133.7	12.2	8.1	3.8	157.7

For Scotland, pupils with a Record of Needs

^ Data are provisional and include 1994/95 data for Wales

$ Data for Wales relate to 1995/96

Source: Department for Education and Employment, *Education Statistics for the United Kingdom*, 1994 and 1996, and unpublished data

This was Table A8.2 in the first edition of *Birth counts*

A8.3.1

Rates of cerebral palsy, sensorineural deafness and severe vision loss at the age of five by birthweight, among children born to residents of the former Oxford NHS region, 1984–92 combined

Birthweight, g	Live births	Deaths in 1st 28 days	Survivors	Numbers of children with		
				Cerebral palsy*	Sensorineural deafness	Severe vision loss
Under 1,000	881	409	472	38	9	31
1,000–1,499	1,828	193	1,635	119	21	36
1,500–1,999	3,869	125	3,744	86	13	37
2,000–2,499	13,318	110	13,208	102	35	47
2,500–2,999	52,766	174	52,592	119	63	79
3,000–3,499	115,770	146	115,624	183	98	112
3,500–3,999	88,880	93	88,787	116	62	79
4,000 and over	29,576	46	29,530	34	17	25
Not stated	6,049	93	5,956	0	0	0
All	312,937	1,389	311,548	797	318	446

Birthweight	Rates per 1,000 live births			Rates per 1,000 survivors		
	Cerebral palsy+	Sensorineural deafness	Severe vision loss	Cerebral palsy*	Sensorineural deafness	Severe vision loss
Under 1,000	43.1	10.2	35.2	80.5	19.1	65.7
1,000–1,499	65.1	11.5	19.7	72.8	12.8	22.0
1,500–1,999	22.2	3.4	9.6	23.0	3.5	9.9
2,000–2,499	7.7	2.6	3.5	7.7	2.6	3.6
2,500–2,999	2.3	1.2	1.5	2.3	1.2	1.5
3,000–3,499	1.6	0.8	1.0	1.6	0.8	1.0
3,500–3,999	1.3	0.7	0.9	1.3	0.7	0.9
4,000 and over	1.1	0.6	0.8	1.2	0.6	0.8
All	2.5	1.0	1.4	2.6	1.0	1.4

+ The numbers include children with recognised impairments who died between the ages of two and five years.

* Includes children who acquired cerebral palsy postnatally

Source: Derived from Oxford Register of Early Childhood Impairments *Annual report 1997, Appendix*

This is a new table for this edition of *Birth counts*

Notifications of selected congenital anomalies, England and Wales, 1964–98

Numbers

Year	All	Anencephalus and similar anomalies*	Spina bifida*	Congenital hydrocephalus*	All central nervous system	Eye including anophthalmia and microphthalmia	Cleft palate without cleft lip*	Total cleft lip with or without cleft palate*	Cardiovascular anomalies	Oesophageal atresia	Atresia of large gut, rectum and anus	Hypospadias and epispadias	Limb reductions*	Exomphalus and gastroschisis excluding umbilical hernia	Down's syndrome
1964	14,564	1,331	2,199		4,162	556^		1,236	835#	117	176	672	150	244	667
1965	13,841	1,347	2,158		4,086	465^		1,152	703#	119	182	637	149	234	577
1966	13,665	1,233	2,130		3,916	430^		1,198	706#	125	195	689	157	236	616
1967	14,062	1,248	2,121		3,949	515^		1,171	716#	127	199	700	155	243	613
1968	13,954	1,148	2,062		3,715	421^		1,175	768#	107	193	749	154	233	644
1969	13,959	1,118	1,556	456	3,302	123	337	798	632	82	173	815	324	180	538
1970	14,019	1,137	1,453	401	3,183	118	298	805	740	120	216	781	335	214	579
1971	14,407	1,166	1,552	432	3,378	107	321	742	714	133	186	934	316	230	582
1972	14,412	1,084	1,537	364	3,129	138	302	695	803	102	190	1,016	297	207	560
1973	13,353	849	1,267	336	2,553	99	333	652	725	121	182	945	286	192	523
1974	12,729	849	1,185	313	2,452	111	274	700	652	95	199	912	378	208	419
1975	12,230	775	1,101	249	2,227	88	279	583	623	87	166	875	320	198	454
1976	12,384	644	880	267	1,915	116	283	586	668	107	185	887	294	196	399
1977	12,402	568	881	259	1,869	101	277	566	649	98	147	907	257	170	425
1978	12,767	525	841	244	1,757	102	277	558	695	113	172	953	284	182	444
1979	13,529	455	845	227	1,637	118	273	585	771	104	190	1,079	264	167	463
1980	14,134	342	756	222	1,476	132	291	627	866	108	179	1,000	302	150	481
1981	13,450	247	663	188	1,229	95	259	605	844	112	157	1,016	256	169	475
1982	13,281	162	511	177	1,016	113	304	565	878	105	179	1,056	265	164	527
1983	13,972	114	422	194	917	124	286	568	995	105	152	1,160	297	176	497
1984	14,018	89	378	153	806	132	300	579	897	98	166	1,152	323	126	505
1985	13,347	59	360	133	728	120	276	556	868	123	171	1,072	326	132	442
1986	13,097	52	267	138	637	102	275	611	882	94	159	1,036	276	127	445
1987	13,581	31	209	117	511	126	251	588	922	97	161	1,123	311	134	459
1988	13,020	41	157	137	509	106	274	529	726	70	138	1,102	301	147	428
1989	12,462	34	135	109	426	130	275	543	820	77	125	1,063	247	133	487

A8.4.1 continued

Notifications of selected congenital anomalies, England and Wales, 1964–98

Year	All	Anencephalus and similar anomalies*	Spina bifida*	Congenital hydrocephalus*	All central nervous system	Eye including anophthalmia and microphthalmia	Cleft palate without cleft lip*	Total cleft lip with or without cleft palate*	Cardiovascular anomalies	Oesophageal atresia	Atresia of large gut, rectum and anus	Hypospadias and epispadias	Limb reductions*	Exomphalus and gastroschisis excluding umbilical hernia	Down's syndrome
1990	8,202	26	120	92	360	89	217	542	612	63	130	869	210	174	415
1991	7,127	22	104	102	324	87	261	526	577	58	126	740	258	165	440
1992	6,096	32	82	99	319	70	239	492	545	61	118	545	199	144	394
1993	5,750	14	81	71	255	71	220	438	507	52	112	551	229	149	311
1994	5,573	26	47	79	256	105	185	444	489	55	78	535	206	126	314
1995	5,552	35	75	66	253	56	187	385	459	66	96	491	191	138	315
1996	5,465	24	60	69	239	76	151	405	481	43	86	513	195	135	319
1997	5,505	30	48	61	206	68	197	375	515	43	79	466	135	130	282
1998	5,607	22	62	73	258	75	199	384	624	46	74	499	191	134	373
Rates per 10,000 total births															
1964	163.6	15.0	24.7		46.7	6.2^		13.9	9.4#	1.3	2.0	7.6	1.7	2.7	7.5
1965	157.9	15.4	24.6		46.6	5.3^		13.1	8.0#	1.4	2.1	7.3	1.7	2.7	6.6
1966	158.3	14.3	24.7		45.4	4.0^		13.9	8.2#	1.5	2.3	8.0	1.8	2.7	7.1
1967	166.5	14.8	25.1		46.8	6.1^		13.9	8.5#	1.5	2.4	8.3	1.8	2.9	7.3
1968	167.9	13.8	24.8		44.7	5.1^		14.1	9.2#	1.3	2.3	9.0	1.9	2.8	7.8
1969	172.7	13.8	19.3	5.6	40.9	1.5	4.2	9.9	7.8	1.0	2.1	10.1	4.0	2.2	6.7
1970	176.4	14.3	18.3	5.1	40.0	1.5	3.8	10.1	9.3	1.5	2.7	9.8	4.2	2.7	7.3
1971	181.7	14.7	19.6	5.5	42.6	1.3	4.1	9.4	9.0	1.7	2.4	11.8	4.0	2.9	7.3
1972	196.3	14.8	20.9	5.0	42.6	1.9	4.1	9.5	10.9	1.4	2.6	13.8	4.1	2.8	7.6
1973	195.3	12.4	18.5	4.9	37.3	1.4	4.9	9.5	10.6	1.8	2.7	13.8	4.2	2.8	7.7
1974	196.7	13.1	18.3	4.8	37.9	1.7	4.2	10.8	10.1	1.5	3.1	14.1	5.8	3.2	6.5
1975	200.6	12.7	18.1	4.1	36.5	1.4	4.6	9.6	10.2	1.4	2.7	14.4	5.3	3.3	7.5
1976	209.9	10.9	14.9	4.5	32.5	2.0	4.8	9.9	11.3	1.8	3.1	15.0	5.0	3.3	6.8
1977	215.8	9.9	15.3	4.5	32.5	1.8	4.8	9.9	11.3	1.7	2.6	15.8	4.5	3.0	7.4
1978	212.2	8.7	14.0	4.1	29.2	1.7	4.6	9.3	11.6	1.9	2.9	15.8	4.7	3.0	7.4
1979	210.4	7.1	13.1	3.5	25.5	1.8	4.2	9.1	12.0	1.6	3.0	16.8	4.1	2.6	7.2
1980	213.8	5.2	11.4	3.4	22.3	2.0	4.4	9.5	13.1	1.6	2.7	15.1	4.6	2.3	7.3

Notifications of selected congenital anomalies, England and Wales, 1964–98

Year	All	Anencephalus and similar anomalies*	Spina bifida*	Congenital hydrocephalus*	All central nervous system	Eye including anophthalmia and microphthalmia	Cleft palate without cleft lip*	Total cleft lip with or without cleft palate*	Cardiovascular anomalies	Oesophageal atresia	Atresia of large gut, rectum and anus	Hypospadias and epispadias	Limb reductions*	Exomphalus and gastroschisis excluding umbilical hernia*	Down's syndrome
1981	210.6	3.9	10.4	2.9	19.2	1.5	4.1	9.5	13.2	1.8	2.5	15.9	4.0	2.6	7.4
1982	210.9	2.6	8.1	2.8	16.1	1.8	4.8	9.0	13.9	1.7	2.8	16.8	4.2	2.6	8.4
1983	220.8	1.8	6.7	3.1	14.5	2.0	4.5	9.0	15.7	1.7	2.4	18.3	4.7	2.8	7.9
1984	218.9	1.4	5.9	2.4	12.6	2.1	4.7	9.0	14.0	1.5	2.6	18.0	5.0	2.0	7.9
1985	202.2	0.9	5.5	2.0	11.0	1.8	4.2	8.4	13.2	1.9	2.6	16.2	4.9	2.0	6.7
1986	197.1	0.8	4.0	2.1	9.6	1.5	4.1	9.2	13.2	1.4	2.4	15.6	4.2	2.0	6.7
1987	198.3	0.5	3.1	1.7	7.5	1.8	3.7	8.6	13.5	1.4	2.4	16.4	4.5	2.0	6.7
1988	186.8	0.6	2.3	2.0	7.3	1.5	3.9	7.6	10.4	1.0	2.0	15.8	4.3	2.1	6.1
1989	180.3	0.5	2.0	1.6	6.2	1.9	4.0	7.9	11.9	1.1	1.8	15.4	3.6	1.9	7.0
1990	115.7	0.4	1.7	1.3	5.1	1.3	3.1	7.6	8.6	0.9	1.8	12.3	3.0	2.5	5.9
1991	101.5	0.3	1.5	1.5	4.6	1.2	3.7	7.5	8.2	0.8	1.8	10.5	3.7	2.3	6.3
1992	88.1	0.5	1.2	1.4	4.6	1.0	3.4	7.1	7.9	0.9	1.7	7.9	2.9	2.1	5.7
1993	85.2	0.2	1.2	1.1	3.8	1.0	3.3	6.5	7.5	0.8	1.7	8.2	3.4	2.2	4.6
1994	83.4	0.4	0.7	1.2	3.8	1.6	2.8	6.6	7.3	0.8	1.2	8.0	3.1	1.9	4.7
1995	85.2	0.5	1.2	1.0	3.9	0.9	2.9	5.9	7.0	1.0	1.5	7.5	2.9	2.1	4.8
1996	83.7	0.4	0.9	1.1	3.7	1.2	2.3	6.2	7.4	0.7	1.3	7.9	3.0	2.1	4.9
1997	85.2	0.5	0.7	0.9	3.2	1.1	3.0	5.8	8.0	0.7	1.2	7.2	2.1	2.0	4.4
1998	87.8	0.3	1.0	1.1	4.0	1.2	3.1	6.0	9.8	0.7	1.2	7.8	3.0	2.1	5.8

* Definition changed in 1969

^ Includes numbers for ear anomalies

Including heart and great vessels anomalies

Source: *Registrar General's quarterly returns 1965–71*, ONS/OPCS *Congenital anomaly statistics, Series MB3*, formerly known as *Congenital malformation statistics*

This was Table A8.3 in the first edition of *Birth counts*

A8.5.1

Stillbirths due to anencephaly, by age of mother, England and Wales, 1961–85

Year	Age of mother							
	All ages	Under 20	20–24	25–29	30–34	35–39	40–44	45 and over
	Rates per 1,000 total births							
1961	2.0	2.6	2.1	1.9	1.9	2.1	2.4	4.1
1962	1.8	2.2	2.0	1.7	1.7	1.8	1.8	4.4
1963	1.8	2.2	1.9	1.5	1.7	2.1	1.9	2.4
1964	1.7	2.0	1.8	1.6	1.5	2.1	1.8	1.5
1965	1.7	2.0	1.7	1.5	1.6	1.7	1.9	2.8
1966	1.6	2.0	1.6	1.5	1.5	2.1	2.0	0.0
1967	1.6	2.2	1.5	1.4	1.4	1.7	1.8	1.5
1968	1.5	2.0	1.5	1.3	1.3	1.6	1.8	1.7
1969	1.5	1.9	1.7	1.3	1.3	1.5	1.0	1.9
1970	1.5	1.9	1.6	1.3	1.4	1.8	1.9	2.1
1971	1.6	1.8	1.7	1.4	1.4	1.5	2.7	1.2
1972	1.6	1.7	1.9	1.5	1.3	1.5	2.3	2.8
1973	1.4	1.7	1.5	1.3	1.3	1.5	2.1	1.6
1974	1.4	1.8	1.5	1.3	1.2	1.6	2.2	7.3
1975	1.4	1.6	1.5	1.3	1.2	0.9	2.1	5.3
1976	1.2	1.5	1.4	1.1	1.0	0.9	0.7	2.0
1977	1.1	1.4	1.2	1.0	0.9	1.2	0.2	0.0
1978	0.9	1.6	1.0	0.9	0.7	0.8	1.0	0.0
1979	0.7	1.1	0.7	0.7	0.7	0.5	0.5	3.9
1980	0.5	0.6	0.6	0.5	0.4	0.4	0.6	0.0
1981	0.4	0.4	0.4	0.4	0.4	0.2	1.0	1.4
1982	0.2	0.4	0.2	0.2	0.3	0.2	0.2	1.5
1983	0.2	0.3	0.2	0.1	0.2	0.1	0.2	1.5
1984	0.1	0.2	0.1	0.1	0.1	0.1	0.2	0.0
1985	0.1	0.1	0.1	0.1	0.1	0.1	0.4	0.0

Source: OPCS *Mortality statistics, Series DH3* and *Registrar General's Statistical Reviews*

This was Table A8.4 in the first edition of *Birth counts*

A8.6.1

Central nervous system anomalies, England and Wales, 1969–98

| Year | Notifications | | Stillbirths and neonatal deaths | | | | Abortions | |
	Number	Rate*	Stillbirths	Neonatal	All	Rate*	Number	Rate*
1969	3,302	38.5	1,718	484	2,202	25.7	::	::
1970	3,183	36.6	1,667	501	2,168	24.9	::	::
1971	3,378	38.1	1,779	584	2,363	26.6	::	::
1972	3,129	37.2	1,578	601	2,179	25.9	51	0.6
1973	2,553	32.2	1,414	555	1,969	24.8	45	0.6
1974	2,452	32.4	1,278	636	1,914	25.3	34	0.4
1975	2,227	31.1	1,160	584	1,744	24.4	73	1.0
1976	1,915	27.7	980	482	1,462	21.1	81	1.2
1977	1,869	27.6	899	480	1,379	20.4	124	1.8
1978	1,757	24.6	820	425	1,245	17.5	::	::
1979	1,637	21.4	727	478	1,205	15.8	285	3.7
1980	1,476	18.7	605	440	1,045	13.2	418	5.3
1981	1,229	16.0	453	321	774	10.1	441	5.8
1982	1,016	13.4	310	243	553	7.3	467	6.2
1983	917	12.1	249	221	470	6.2	502	6.6
1984	806	10.4	173	191	364	4.7	521	6.7
1985	728	9.1	145	179	324	4.0	506	6.3
1986	637	7.8	105	173	278	3.4	549	6.8
1987	511	6.1	107	170	277	3.3	529	6.3
1988	509	5.9	93	161	254	2.9	464	5.4
1989	426	4.9	75	137	212	2.5	475	5.5
1990	360	4.1	76	127	203	2.3	452	5.1
1991	324	3.7	61	137	198	2.3	492	5.7
1992	319	3.7	88	125	213	2.5	519	6.1
1993	255	3.1	72	85	157	1.9	521	6.2
1994	256	3.1	91	104	195	2.4	465	5.6
1995	253	3.1	78	102	180	2.2	515	6.4
1996	239	2.9	85	85	170	2.1	537	6.5
1997	206	2.5	75	95	170	2.1	442	5.4
1998	258	3.2	90	70	160	2.0	460	5.6

* Rate per 10,000 total births and abortions. From 1993 onwards, stillbirths included those at 24–27 weeks of gestation.

Source: ONS/OPCS, *Congenital anomaly statistics*, *Series MB3*, *Mortality statistics*, *Series DH3* and *Abortion statistics*, *Series AB*

This was Table A8.5 in the first edition of *Birth counts*

A8.7.1

Numbers of congenital rubella births reported to the National Congenital Rubella Surveillance Programme, Great Britain, 1971–97

Year of birth	Live births		Clinical manifestations at last follow-up			
	All	Known to have died	Multiple defects	Single defect	CRI only*	Imported cases+
Before 1971	77	6	62	12	3	–
1971	44	5	25	14	5	–
1972	51	8	36	10	5	–
1973	67	7	31	24	12	–
1974	34	5	19	10	5	–
1975	45	6	27	7	11	–
1976	31	4	16	10	5	–
1977	13	3	8	3	2	–
1978	53	4	22	21	10	–
1979	78	9	53	15	10	–
1980	31	2	16	8	7	–
1981	15	0	6	4	5	–
1982	37	3	17	11	9	–
1983	72	2	35	14	23	–
1984	53	2	19	17	17	–
1985	24	2	11	8	5	–
1986	30	3	13	10	7	–
1987	37	2	18	11	8	–
1988	21	3	14	4	3	–
1989	13	1	5	3	5	–
1990	11	2	3	4	4	1
1991	3	1	2	1	0	2
1992	6	1	4	2	0	2
1993	3	0	1	0	2	0
1994	7	2	5	2	0	2
1995	1	0	1	0	0	0
1996	12	1	9	2	1	2
1997	0	0	0	0	0	0
Total	869	84	478	227	164	

* No identified rubella associated problem so far

+ Not reported before 1990

Source: National Congenital Rubella Surveillance Programme

This is similar to Table A8.6 in the first edition of *Birth counts*

A8.8.1

Legal abortions on grounds of rubella, England and Wales, 1969–98

Year	Rubella	Rubella contact	Rubella immunisation	All
1969	..	..	..	907
1970	..	..	..	919
1971	791	229	43	1,063
1972	579	161	39	779
1973	681	136	23	840
1974	512	121	31	664
1975	406	98	27	531
1976	144	69	40	253
1977	118	66	37	221
1978	659	171	66	896
1979	431	144	156	731
1980	153	47	101	301
1981	88	46	63	197
1982	136	44	46	226
1983	188	50	72	310
1984	115	27	93	235
1985	57	8	41	106
1986	89	21	30	140
1987	65	10	31	106
1988	36	8	11	55
1989	10	15	17	42
1990	11	3	5	19
1991	10	9	8	27
1992	2	0	8	10
1993	11	2	4	17
1994	3	1	3	7
1995	3	2	4	9
1996	7	2	0	9
1997	0	2	4	6
1998	2	3	2	7

Source: ONS/OPCS, *Abortion statistics, Series AB*

This was Table A8.7 in the first edition of *Birth counts*

A8.9.1

Long-term illness in children aged under 5 years reported in the 1991 Census, Great Britain

	Age, years					All aged 0–4
	0	1	2	3	4	
Percentage with long-term illness						
All children						
Great Britain	1.17	1.80	2.03	2.26	2.44	1.93
England and Wales	1.18	1.81	2.03	2.25	2.42	1.93
England	1.18	1.79	2.02	2.23	2.41	1.92
Wales	1.26	2.03	2.25	2.52	2.69	2.15
Scotland	1.11	1.72	1.97	2.36	2.56	1.94
Males						
Great Britain	1.27	1.98	2.25	2.53	2.75	2.15
England and Wales	1.28	1.99	2.26	2.51	2.74	2.15
England	1.27	1.97	2.25	2.50	2.72	2.13
Wales	1.37	2.31	2.50	2.70	3.00	2.38
Scotland	1.14	1.94	2.14	2.67	2.91	2.16
Females						
Great Britain	1.08	1.61	1.79	1.98	2.10	1.71
England and Wales	1.08	1.62	1.79	1.98	2.09	1.71
England	1.07	1.61	1.78	1.95	2.08	1.69
Wales	1.15	1.73	1.98	2.34	2.37	1.91
Scotland	1.07	1.50	1.79	2.03	2.18	1.71
Numbers with long-term illness						
All children						
Great Britain	8,703	13,197	14,598	16,471	17,279	70,248
England and Wales	7,996	12,121	13,368	14,939	15,658	64,082
England	7,522	11,371	12,538	13,982	14,652	60,065
Wales	474	750	830	957	1,006	4,017
Scotland	707	1,076	1,230	1,532	1,621	6,166
Males						
Great Britain	4,806	7,440	8,285	9,434	9,991	39,956
England and Wales	4,432	6,821	7,601	8,542	9,045	36,441
England	4,169	6,383	7,128	8,021	8,469	34,170
Wales	263	438	473	521	576	2,271
Scotland	374	619	684	892	946	3,515
Females						
Great Britain	3,897	5,757	6,313	7,037	7,288	30,292
England and Wales	3,564	5,300	5,767	6,397	6,613	27,641
England	3,353	4,988	5,410	5,961	6,183	25,895
Wales	211	312	357	436	430	1,746
Scotland	333	457	546	640	675	2,651

Source: OPCS and GRO Scotland, *Children and young adults, Great Britain, 1991 census, Volume 1, Table1*

This is a new table for this edition of *Birth counts*

A8.10.1

Long standing illness among children aged 0–4, Great Britain 1972–96

Year	Male	Female	Total	Male	Female	Total
	Percentage reporting long standing illness			Percentage reporting limiting long standing illness		
1972	5	3	4	..	..	..
1973	5	5	5	2	2	2
1974	6	5	6	3	2	2
1975	8	6	7	3	2	2
1976	8	6	7	2	2	2
1977	..	..	..	..	..	..
1978	..	..	..	..	..	..
1979	8	6	7	2	2	2
1980	8	8	8	3	3	3
1981	12	7	10	3	3	3
1982	8	7	7	3	3	3
1983	11	9	10	3	2	3
1984	10	9	9	3	3	3
1985	11	9	10	4	3	3
1986	12	11	11	3	4	3
1987	10	10	10	4	3	3
1988	13	12	12	4	3	4
1989	14	10	12	6	2	4
1990	14	12	13	5	3	4
1991	13	10	12	4	3	4
1992	15	10	12	5	2	4
1993	15	12	13	5	3	4
1994	15	11	13	5	4	4
1995	14	11	13	5	3	4
1996	14	13	13	4	4	4

Source: ONS/OPCS *General Household Survey*

This is a new table for this edition of *Birth counts*

A8.11.1

Estimates of the prevalence of disability among children aged 0–4 by severity category, Great Britain, 1985 and 1988

Severity category	Male	Female	Total	Severity category	Male	Female	Total
	Estimated numbers, thousands			**Cumulative rate per thousand**			
10	1	1	2	10	1	0	0
9	2	1	3	9–10	1	1	1
8	3	2	5	8–10	3	2	3
7	5	2	7	7–10	6	4	5
6	7	3	11	6–10	10	6	8
5	3	4	7	5–10	12	8	10
4	7	3	11	4–10	16	10	13
3	6	4	10	3–10	19	12	16
2	3	2	5	2–10	20	14	17
1	7	8	15	1–10	24	18	21
Total	43	31	75				

This table is based on data from surveys of children in private households in 1985 and in communal establishments in 1988

Source: *OPCS Surveys of disability in Great Britain, Report 3, Tables 3.3–3.6*

This is a new table for this edition of *Birth counts*

A9.1.1

Notifications of whooping cough in children aged under one year, by sex, England and Wales, 1944–98

Year	Male	Female	All	Male	Female	All
	Number of notifications			**Rate per 100,000 population**		
1944	5,053	5,018	10,071	1,431.4	1,493.5	1,461.7
1945	3,312	3,337	6,649	935.6	999.1	966.4
1946	4,585	4,783	9,368	1,273.6	1,402.6	1,336.4
1947	5,426	5,574	11,000	1,213.9	1,311.5	1,261.5
1948	7,305	7,627	14,932	1,817.2	1,991.4	1,902.2
1949	4,809	4,915	9,724	1,282.4	1,380.6	1,330.2
1950	6,577	6,468	13,045	1,842.3	1,896.8	1,868.9
1951	7,333	7,463	14,796	2,125.5	2,282.3	2,201.8
1952	5,041	5,167	10,208	1,504.8	1,614.7	1,558.5
1953	6,928	7,050	13,978	2,025.7	2,175.9	2,098.8
1954	4,709	4,729	9,438	1,372.9	1,446.2	1,408.7
1955	3,517	3,576	7,093	1,049.9	1,124.5	1,086.2
1956	4,299	4,167	8,466	1,235.3	1,266.6	1,250.5
1957	3,753	3,851	7,604	1,051.3	1,136.0	1,092.5
1958	1,637	1,669	3,306	442.4	475.5	458.5
1959	1,683	1,636	3,319	445.2	457.0	451.0
1960	2,975	2,894	5,869	776.8	799.4	787.8
1961	1,257	1,179	2,436	312.4	309.9	311.2
1962	515	511	1,026	123.5	128.7	126.1
1963	2,013	2,104	4,117	475.5	519.1	496.9
1964	1,772	1,852	3,624	412.4	450.5	431.0
1965	710	723	1,433	164.3	174.6	169.3
1966	1,075	1,022	2,097	252.0	250.1	251.0
1967	1,456	1,568	3,024	345.8	389.3	367.0
1968	893	860	1,753	219.4	218.6	219.0
1969	335	293	628	82.7	75.0	78.9
1970	966	1,040	2,006	247.6	281.0	263.8
1971	1,082	1,073	2,155	269.5	282.3	275.7
1972	141	122	263	37.5	34.1	35.8
1973	167	163	330	47.0	48.8	47.9
1974	1,089	1,086	2,175	332.5	350.8	341.4
1975	706	688	1,394	224.4	231.1	227.7
1976	238	240	478	79.3	84.3	81.8
1977	959	985	1,944	334.1	362.4	347.9
1978	3,444	3,232	6,676	1,181.9	1,168.9	1,175.6
1979	1,611	1,587	3,198	507.9	528.8	518.1
1980	1,100	1,061	2,161	335.5	341.2	338.2
1981	962	954	1,916	296.5	308.1	302.2
1982	2,966	2,921	5,887	932.7	966.9	949.4
1983	894	881	1,775	279.8	290.2	284.9
1984	282	323	605	88.5	106.3	97.2
1985	1,110	1,126	2,236	333.8	355.8	344.5
1986	1,868	1,752	3,620	555.8	549.6	552.8
1987	885	832	1,717	260.4	256.5	258.5
1988	367	337	704	104.6	100.7	102.7
1989	678	667	1,345	194.8	200.9	197.8
1990	775	817	1,592	220.7	244.2	232.1
1991	294	323	617	81.7	94.3	87.9
1992	174	173	347	48.9	51.1	50.0
1993	268	269	537	78.1	82.4	80.2
1994	268	281	549	77.8	86.1	81.8
1995	160	175	335	48.1	55.3	51.6
1996	228	224	452	69.8	72.3	71.0
1997	334	368	702	100.0	116.0	107.7
1998	197	216	415*	60.8	69.9	65.6

* Including sex not stated

Source: CDSC/OPCS Notifications of communicable diseases

This was Table A9.1 in the first edition of *Birth counts*

A9.1.2

Notifications of measles in children aged under one year, by sex, England and Wales 1944–98

Year	Male	Female	All	Male	Female	All
	Number of notifications			**Rate per 100,000 population**		
1944	3,102	3,032	6,134	878.8	902.4	890.3
1945	9,724	9,422	19,146	2,746.9	2,821.0	2,782.8
1946	3,372	3,494	6,866	936.7	1,024.6	979.5
1947	8,405	8,481	16,886	1,880.3	1,995.5	1,936.5
1948	8,217	8,285	16,502	2,044.0	2,163.2	2,102.2
1949	7,445	7,487	14,932	1,985.3	2,103.1	2,042.7
1950	6,507	6,719	13,226	1,822.7	1,970.4	1,894.8
1951	10,545	10,445	20,990	3,056.5	3,194.2	3,123.5
1952	6,048	6,203	12,251	1,805.4	1,938.4	1,870.4
1953	8,654	8,737	17,391	2,530.4	2,696.6	2,611.3
1954	2,801	2,951	5,752	816.6	902.4	858.5
1955	9,917	10,109	20,026	2,960.3	3,178.9	3,066.8
1956	2,484	2,602	5,086	713.8	790.9	751.3
1957	9,294	9,360	18,654	2,603.4	2,761.1	2,680.2
1958	3,892	4,076	7,968	1,051.9	1,161.3	1,105.1
1959	8,185	8,323	16,508	2,165.3	2,324.9	2,242.9
1960	2,872	2,888	5,760	749.9	797.8	773.2
1961	12,540	12,618	25,158	3,116.3	3,317.0	3,213.8
1962	3,073	3,075	6,148	737.1	774.6	755.4
1963	10,467	10,604	21,071	2,472.7	2,616.3	2,543.0
1964	6,400	6,380	12,780	1,489.4	1,551.9	1,520.0
1965	10,090	9,766	19,856	2,334.6	2,357.8	2,345.9
1966	7,176	7,108	14,284	1,682.1	1,739.2	1,710.0
1967	9,378	9,154	18,532	2,227.0	2,272.6	2,249.3
1968	5,546	5,342	10,888	1,362.3	1,357.9	1,360.1
1969	3,556	3,403	6,959	877.6	871.4	874.6
1970	7,135	6,975	14,110	1,828.5	1,884.6	1,855.8
1971	3,493	3,259	6,752	870.0	857.4	863.9
1972	3,694	3,653	7,347	981.1	1,019.8	1,000.0
1973	3,432	3,354	6,786	966.8	1,004.2	984.9
1974	2,436	2,372	4,808	743.8	766.1	754.7
1975	2,875	2,829	5,704	913.9	950.3	931.6
1976	1,419	1,430	2,849	472.8	502.5	487.3
1977	3,498	3,371	6,869	1,218.8	1,240.3	1,229.2
1978	2,508	2,403	4,911	860.7	869.1	864.8
1979	2,081	2,010	4,091	656.1	669.8	662.7
1980	3,731	3,675	7,406	1,137.8	1,181.7	1,159.2
1981	2,050	1,987	4,037	631.9	641.8	636.8
1982	2,917	2,734	5,651	917.3	905.0	911.3
1983	2,970	2,773	5,743	929.6	913.4	921.7
1984	2,307	2,194	4,501	723.7	722.2	722.9
1985	3,369	3,166	6,535	1,013.2	1,000.3	1,006.9
1986	3,079	2,936	6,015	916.1	921.0	918.5
1987	1,940	1,863	3,803	570.8	574.3	572.5
1988	3,729	3,383	7,112	1,062.4	1,011.1	1,037.3
1989	2,184	2,011	4,195	627.6	605.7	616.9
1990	1,524	1,446	2,970	433.9	432.2	433.1
1991	1,442	1,324	2,766	400.9	386.7	394.0
1992	1,224	1,169	2,393	343.9	345.2	344.6
1993	955	965	1,920	278.3	295.6	286.7
1994	1,489	1,298	2,787	432.5	397.5	415.5
1995	953	897	1,850	286.4	283.4	284.9
1996	724	629	1,353	221.6	203.1	212.6
1997	555	475	1,030	166.2	149.7	158.0
1998	453	391	845*	139.7	126.6	133.5

* Includes sex not stated

Source: CDSC/OPCS Notifications of communicable diseases

This was Table A9.2 in the first edition of *Birth counts*

A9.1.3

Notifications of acute meningitis in children aged under one year, by sex, England and Wales, 1956–98

Year	Male	Female	All	Male	Female	All
	Number			**Rate per 100,000 population**		
	All types of meningitis*					
1956	168	111	279	48.3	33.7	41.2
1957	177	125	302	49.6	36.9	43.4
1958	158	108	266	42.7	30.8	36.9
1959	126	103	229	33.3	28.8	31.1
1960	101	66	167	26.4	18.2	22.4
1961	111	77	188	27.6	20.2	24.0
1962	90	65	155	21.6	16.4	19.0
1963	101	65	166	23.9	16.0	20.0
1964	79	47	126	18.4	11.4	15.0
1965	72	42	114	16.7	10.1	13.5
1966	67	43	110	15.7	10.5	13.2
1967	51	29	80	12.1	7.2	9.7
1968	72	47	119	17.7	11.9	14.9
1969	124	96	220	30.6	24.6	27.6
1970	134	111	245	34.3	30.0	32.2
1971	144	92	236	35.9	24.2	30.2
1972	120	99	219	31.9	27.6	29.8
1973	213	150	363	60.0	44.9	52.7
1974	266	169	435	81.2	54.6	68.3
1975	194	147	341	61.7	49.4	55.7
1976	138	112	250	46.0	39.4	42.8
1977	125	96	221	43.6	35.3	39.5
1978	142	118	260	48.7	42.7	45.8
1979	185	109	294	58.3	36.3	47.6
1980	170	124	294	51.8	39.9	46.0
1981	141	81	222	43.5	26.2	35.0
1982	122	99	221	38.4	32.8	35.6
1983	133	115	248	41.6	37.9	39.8
1984	157	116	273	49.2	38.2	43.8
1985	186	127	313	55.9	40.1	48.2
1986	286	204	490	85.1	64.0	74.8
1987	331	236	567	97.4	72.7	85.4
1988	372	281	653	106.0	84.0	95.2
1989	366	307	673	105.2	92.5	99.0
1990	328	277	605	93.4	82.8	88.2
1991	364	274	638	101.2	80.0	90.9
1992	350	291	641	98.3	85.9	92.3
1993	263	210	473	76.7	64.3	70.6
1994	258	181	439	74.9	55.4	65.4
1995	266	201	467	79.9	63.5	71.9
1996	298	230	528	91.2	74.2	83.0
1997	270	192	462	80.9	60.5	70.8
1998	270	196	467[+]	83.3	63.5	73.8
	Meningococcal meningitis					
1970	80	48	128	20.5	13.0	16.8
1971	80	42	122	19.9	11.0	15.6
1972	65	58	123	17.3	16.2	16.7
1973	145	95	240	40.8	28.4	34.8

Notifications of acute meningitis in children aged under one year, by sex, England and Wales, 1956–98

Year	Male	Female	All	Male	Female	All
1974	180	118	298	55.0	38.1	46.8
1975	103	77	180	32.7	25.9	29.4
1976	76	65	141	25.3	22.8	24.1
1977	52	34	86	18.1	12.5	15.4
1978	60	37	97	20.6	13.4	17.1
1979	70	34	104	22.1	11.3	16.8
1980	67	49	116	20.4	15.8	18.2
1981	63	35	98	19.4	11.3	15.5
1982	47	40	87	14.8	13.2	14.0
1983	50	47	97	15.6	15.5	15.6
1984	42	41	83	13.2	13.5	13.3
1985	56	41	97	16.8	13.0	14.9
1986	111	75	186	33.0	23.5	28.4
1987	147	112	259	43.2	34.5	39.0
1988	162	122	284	46.2	36.5	41.4
1989	165	106	271	47.4	31.9	39.9
1990	134	112	246	38.2	33.5	35.9
1991	144	120	264	40.0	35.0	37.6
1992	125	99	224	35.1	29.2	32.3
1993	123	102	225	35.8	31.2	33.6
1994	128	92	220	37.2	28.2	32.8
1995	126	94	220	37.9	29.7	33.9
1996	105	101	206	32.1	32.6	32.4
1997	136	87	223	40.7	27.4	34.2
1998	141	108	249[+]	43.5	35.0	39.3
	Other specified organisms					
1970	27	34	61	6.9	9.2	8.0
1971	36	33	69	9.0	8.7	8.8
1972	23	28	51	6.1	7.8	6.9
1973	34	27	61	9.6	8.1	8.9
1974	54	29	83	16.5	9.4	13.0
1975	52	43	95	16.5	14.4	15.5
1976	38	31	69	12.7	10.9	11.8
1977	50	41	91	17.4	15.1	16.3
1978	49	50	99	16.8	18.1	17.4
1979	77	49	126	24.3	16.3	20.4
1980	69	55	124	21.0	17.7	19.4
1981	50	37	87	15.4	12.0	13.7
1982	57	50	107	17.9	16.6	17.3
1983	73	54	127	22.8	17.8	20.4
1984	96	62	158	30.1	20.4	25.4
1985	101	70	171	30.4	22.1	26.3
1986	140	100	240	41.7	31.4	36.6
1987	151	109	260	44.4	33.6	39.1
1988	190	137	327	54.1	40.9	47.7
1989	167	176	343	48.0	53.0	50.4
1990	158	140	298	45.0	41.8	43.5
1991	182	142	324	50.6	41.5	46.1
1992	196	148	344	55.1	43.7	49.5
1993	114	86	200	33.2	26.3	29.9

A9.1.3 *continued*

Notifications of acute meningitis in children aged under one year, by sex, England and Wales, 1956–98

Year	Male	Female	All	Male	Female	All
1994	101	70	171	29.3	21.4	25.5
1995	92	81	173	27.6	25.6	26.6
1996	135	89	224	41.3	28.7	35.2
1997	96	77	173	28.8	24.3	26.5
1998	95	64	159⁺	29.3	20.7	25.1
	Unspecified organisms					
1970	27	29	56	6.9	7.8	7.4
1971	28	17	45	7.0	4.5	5.8
1972	32	13	45	8.5	3.6	6.1
1973	34	28	62	9.6	8.4	9.0
1974	32	22	54	9.8	7.1	8.5
1975	39	27	66	12.4	9.1	10.8
1976	24	16	40	8.0	5.6	6.8
1977	23	21	44	8.0	7.7	7.9
1978	33	31	64	11.3	11.2	11.3
1979	38	26	64	12.0	8.7	10.4
1980	34	20	54	10.4	6.4	8.5
1981	28	9	37	8.6	2.9	5.8
1982	18	9	27	5.7	3.0	4.4
1983	10	14	24	3.1	4.6	3.9
1984	19	13	32	6.0	4.3	5.1
1985	29	16	45	8.7	5.1	6.9
1986	35	29	64	10.4	9.1	9.8
1987	33	15	48	9.7	4.6	7.2
1988	20	22	42	5.7	6.6	6.1
1989	34	25	59	9.8	7.5	8.7
1990	36	25	61	10.3	7.5	8.9
1991	38	12	50	10.6	3.5	7.1
1992	29	44	73	8.1	13.0	10.5
1993	26	22	48	7.6	6.7	7.2
1994	29	19	48	8.4	5.8	7.2
1995	48	26	74	14.4	8.2	11.4
1996	58	40	98	17.8	12.9	15.4
1997	38	28	66	11.4	8.8	10.1
1998	34	24	59⁺	10.5	7.8	9.3

* Acute meningitis was known as meningoccal infection during 1956–67.

+ Including sex not stated

Source: CDSC/OPCS Notifications of communicable diseases

This was Table A9.3 in the first edition of *Birth counts*

A9.1.4

Notifications of dysentery in children aged under one year, by sex, England and Wales, 1956–98

Year	Male	Female	All	Male	Female	All
	Number			**Rate per 100,000 population**		
1956	932	810	1,742	267.8	246.2	257.3
1957	663	551	1,214	185.7	162.5	174.4
1958	898	793	1,691	242.7	225.9	234.5
1959	812	746	1,558	214.8	208.4	211.7
1960	859	757	1,616	224.3	209.1	216.9
1961	523	473	996	130.0	124.3	127.2
1962	859	672	1,531	206.0	169.3	188.1
1963	704	645	1,349	166.3	159.1	162.8
1964	595	507	1,102	138.5	123.3	131.1
1965	668	569	1,237	154.6	137.4	146.1
1966	538	444	982	126.1	108.6	117.6
1967	551	447	998	130.8	111.0	121.1
1968	511	423	934	125.5	107.5	116.7
1969	556	522	1,078	137.2	133.7	135.5
1970	310	293	603	79.4	79.2	79.3
1971	360	284	644	89.7	74.7	82.4
1972	295	260	555	78.4	72.6	75.5
1973	266	211	477	74.9	63.2	69.2
1974	242	219	461	73.9	70.7	72.4
1975	223	191	414	70.9	64.2	67.6
1976	187	143	330	62.3	50.2	56.4
1977	144	110	254	50.2	40.5	45.5
1978	117	95	212	40.2	34.4	37.3
1979	88	69	157	27.7	23.0	25.4
1980	87	71	158	26.5	22.8	24.7
1981	103	80	183	31.8	25.8	28.9
1982	95	72	167	29.9	23.8	26.9
1983	121	88	209	37.9	29.0	33.5
1984	142	101	243	44.5	33.2	39.0
1985	122	118	240	36.7	37.3	37.0
1986	137	106	243	40.8	33.2	37.1
1987	107	93	200	31.5	28.7	30.1
1988	102	74	176	29.1	22.1	25.7
1989	66	48	114	19.0	14.5	16.8
1990	47	37	84	13.4	11.1	12.2
1991	158	121	279	43.9	35.3	39.7
1992	219	175	394	61.5	51.7	56.7
1993	88	71	159	25.6	21.7	23.7
1994	71	62	133	20.6	19.0	19.8
1995	49	45	94	14.7	14.2	14.5
1996	23	23	46	7.0	7.4	7.2
1997	25	18	43	7.5	5.7	6.6
1998	9	3	14*	2.8	1.0	2.2

* Including sex not stated

Source: CDSC/OPCS Notifications of communicable diseases

This was Table A9.4 in the first edition of *Birth counts*

A9.1.5

Notifications of scarlet fever in children aged under one year, by sex, England and Wales, 1944–98

Year	Male	Female	All	Male	Female	All
	Number			**Rate per 100,000 population**		
1944	194	158	352	55.0	47.0	51.1
1945	174	176	350	49.2	52.7	50.9
1946	150	114	264	41.7	33.4	37.7
1947	111	103	214	24.8	24.2	24.5
1948	144	123	267	35.8	32.1	34.0
1949	122	108	230	32.5	30.3	31.5
1950	133	125	258	37.3	36.7	37.0
1951	87	102	189	25.2	31.2	28.1
1952	105	87	192	31.3	27.2	29.3
1953	94	84	178	27.5	25.9	26.7
1954	71	70	141	20.7	21.4	21.0
1955	64	49	113	19.1	15.4	17.3
1956	55	58	113	15.8	17.6	16.7
1957	50	45	95	14.0	13.3	13.6
1958	67	77	144	18.1	21.9	20.0
1959	96	83	179	25.4	23.2	24.3
1960	86	82	168	22.5	22.7	22.6
1961	57	54	111	14.2	14.2	14.2
1962	34	24	58	8.2	6.0	7.1
1963	47	57	104	11.1	14.1	12.6
1964	52	38	90	12.1	9.2	10.7
1965	75	54	129	17.4	13.0	15.2
1966	63	71	134	14.8	17.4	16.0
1967	48	45	93	11.4	11.2	11.3
1968	64	42	106	15.7	10.7	13.2
1969	44	51	95	10.9	13.1	11.9
1970	45	45	90	11.5	12.2	11.8
1971	28	32	60	7.0	8.4	7.7
1972	40	37	77	10.6	10.3	10.5
1973	35	36	71	9.9	10.8	10.3
1974	43	38	81	13.1	12.3	12.7
1975	27	27	54	8.6	9.1	8.8
1976	34	34	68	11.3	11.9	11.6
1977	40	39	79	13.9	14.3	14.1
1978	42	33	75	14.4	11.9	13.2
1979	39	22	61	12.3	7.3	9.9
1980	55	38	93	16.8	12.2	14.6
1981	32	33	65	9.9	10.7	10.3
1982	41	33	74	12.9	10.9	11.9
1983	30	18	48	9.4	5.9	7.7
1984	33	32	65	10.4	10.5	10.4
1985	34	22	56	10.2	7.0	8.6
1986	44	45	89	13.1	14.1	13.6
1987	32	39	71	9.4	12.0	10.7
1988	30	42	72	8.5	12.6	10.5
1989	57	51	108	16.4	15.4	15.9
1990	50	54	104	14.2	16.1	15.2
1991	54	47	101	15.0	13.7	14.4
1992	38	33	71	10.7	9.7	10.2
1993	53	46	99	15.4	14.1	14.8
1994	53	44	97	15.4	13.5	14.5
1995	50	59	109	15.0	18.6	16.8
1996	49	50	99	15.0	16.1	15.6
1997	36	41	77	10.8	12.9	11.8
1998	40	36	76*	12.3	11.7	12.0

* Including sex not stated

Source: CDSC/OPCS Notifications of communicable diseases

This was Table A9.5 in the first edition of *Birth counts*

A9.1.6

Notifications of ophthalmia neonatorum in children aged under one year, England and Wales, 1915–98

Year	Number	Rate per 100,000 population		Year	Number	Rate per 100,000 population
1915	6,802	847.1		1950	1,935	277.2
1916	7,611	1,045.5		1951	1,762	262.2
1917	6,712	988.5		1952	1,788	273.0
1918	6,532	1,092.3		1953	1,772	266.1
1919	8,648	1,498.8		1954	1,684	251.3
1920	10,302	1,199.3		1955	1,771	271.2
1921	8,312	988.3		1956	1,515	223.8
1922	7,106	920.5		1957	1,483	213.1
1923	6,592	914.3		1958	1,304	180.9
1924	6,267	895.3		1959	1,179	160.2
1925	5,748	842.8		1960	1,063	142.7
1926	5,896	886.6		1961	932	119.1
1927	5,891	919.0		1962	1,017	125.0
1928	5,609	900.3		1963	970	117.1
1929	5,448	884.4		1964	832	99.0
1930	5,481	895.6		1965	727	85.9
1931	5,158	842.7		1966	612	73.3
1932	4,730	795.4		1967	606	73.6
1933	4,056	712.0		1968	588	73.5
1934	4,487	809.2		1969	434	54.5
1935	4,369	771.5		1970	464	61.0
1936	4,586	800.8		1971	428	54.8
1937	5,050	870.4		1972	358	48.7
1938	5,168	871.6		1973	366	53.1
1939	4,594	770.9		1974	316	49.6
1940	4,390	755.6		1975	265	43.3
1941	4,195	765.5		1976	222	38.0
1942	4,516	765.4		1977	239	42.8
1943	4,502	690.5		1978	228	40.1
1944	3,659	531.1		1979	235	38.1
1945	3,314	481.7		1980	278	43.5
1946	3,416	487.3		1981	201	31.7
1947	3,245	372.1				
1948	2,729	347.6				
1949	2,229	304.9				

Year	Male	Female	All*	Male	Female	All*
	Number			**Rate per 100,000 population**		
1982	106	95	201	33.3	31.4	32.4
1983	99	109	208	31.0	35.9	33.4
1984	121	126	247	38.0	41.5	39.7
1985	146	112	258	43.9	35.4	39.8
1986	136	162	298	40.5	50.8	45.5
1987	145	155	300	42.7	47.8	45.2
1988	189	185	374	53.8	55.3	54.6
1989	223	204	427	64.1	61.4	62.8
1990	252	188	440	71.8	56.2	64.2
1991	245	188	433	68.1	54.9	61.7
1992	237	187	424	66.6	55.2	61.1
1993	180	160	340	52.5	49.0	50.8
1994	156	112	268	45.3	34.3	40.0
1995	123	122	245	37.0	38.5	37.7
1996	143	103	246	43.8	33.3	38.7
1997	110	114	224	32.9	35.9	34.4
1998	96	100	198+	29.6	32.4	31.3

* Including a few cases where the age was not stated
+ Including sex not stated

Source: CDSC/OPCS Notifications of communicable diseases

This was Table A9.6 in the first edition of *Birth counts*

A9.2.1

Children born to HIV infected mothers by year of birth, infection status and country of the United Kingdom, 1979–April 1999

Year of birth	Infected* England, Wales and Northern Ireland AIDS	Infected* England, Wales and Northern Ireland not AIDS	Infected* Scotland AIDS	Infected* Scotland not AIDS	Indeterminate** England, Wales and Northern Ireland	Indeterminate** Scotland	Not infected England, Wales and Northern Ireland	Not infected Scotland	Total number of children	Number of deaths#
1979–83	8	6	1	0	0	0	0	0	15	5
1984–85	16	10	6	4	2	2	4	11	55	12
1986–87	22	18	4	3	11	3	15	35	111	12
1988–89	43	24	2	1	10	4	27	26	137	23
1990–91	55	49	1	3	28	3	53	22	214	34
1992–93	66	46	1	3	40	3	74	12	245	39
1994–95	46	39	1	2	40	3	86	18	235	20
1996–97	44	33	3	0	55	5	136	11	287	16
1998–99	13	5	0	0	84	4	62	3	171	5
Total	313	230	19	16	270	27	457	138	1,470	166

Due to ascertainment bias, the rate of vertical transmission cannot be estimated from surveillance data.

* Includes all children with AIDS, or with virus detected, or with HIV antibody at age 18 months or over.

** Age less than 18 months when last tested positive for HIV antibody and without other evidence of HIV infection .

Includes 36 children who were lost to follow-up.

\# Deaths in children known not to be HIV infected are excluded.

Source: Public Health Laboratory Service and the Scottish Centre for Infection and Environmental Health, *AIDS/HIV Quarterly Surveillance Tables, Tables 17 and 18*
Data were compiled at the Institute of Child Health, London in collaboration with the Public Health Laboratory Service (PHLS) AIDS Centre at the Communicable Disease Service
Centre and the Scottish Centre for Infection and Environmental Health (SCIEH). Data sources include returns by obstetricians to the National Study of HIV in Pregnancy, returns
by paediatricians to the British Paediatric Surveillance Unit, reports by haemophilia centre directors to the Oxford Haemophilia Centre and reports by clinicians and microbiologists
to the PHLS AIDS Centre and SCIEH. All reporting is voluntary and confidential.

This is a new table for this edition of *Birth counts*

A9.3.1

Hospital stays by children aged under one year, England, 1994/95

Primary diagnosis, ICD, Ninth revision

Numbers of episodes

Primary diagnosis	Children aged under one month						Rates per thousand live births in 1994					
	Ordinary admissions			Day cases	Delivery facilities only	All*	Ordinary admissions			All*		
	Male	Female	All*	All*	All*		Male	Female	All*	Male	Female	All*
001–1399 Infectious and parasitic diseases	835	790	1,635	3	0	1,638	2.4	2.4	2.4	2.4	2.5	2.5
140–2399 Neoplasms	76	96	172	6	0	178	0.2	0.3	0.3	0.2	0.3	0.3
240–2799 Endocrine, nutritional and metabolic diseases and immunity disorders	165	160	332	33	0	365	0.5	0.5	0.5	0.5	0.5	0.5
280–2899 Diseases of blood and blood-forming organs	79	57	136	4	0	140	0.2	0.2	0.2	0.2	0.2	0.2
290–3199 Mental disorders	95	72	173	0	0	173	0.3	0.2	0.3	0.3	0.3	0.3
320–3899 Diseases of the nervous system and sense organs	270	210	482	11	2	495	0.8	0.6	0.7	0.8	0.7	0.7
390–4599 Diseases of the circulatory system	187	175	364	12	0	376	0.5	0.5	0.5	0.5	0.5	0.6
460–5199 Diseases of the respiratory system	1,550	1,225	2,827	7	0	2,834	4.5	3.8	4.3	4.5	4.3	4.3
520–5799 Diseases of the digestive system	917	640	1,577	14	0	1,591	2.7	2.0	2.4	2.7	2.4	2.4
580–6299 Diseases of the genitourinary system	367	163	535	33	0	568	1.1	0.5	0.8	1.1	0.8	0.9
630–6769 Complications of pregnancy, childbirth and the puerperium	3	17	20	2	0	22	0.0	0.1	0.0	0.0	0.0	0.0
680–7099 Diseases of the skin and subcutaneous tissue	347	234	591	12	0	603	1.0	0.7	0.9	1.0	0.9	0.9
710–7399 Diseases of the musculoskeletal system and connective tissue	41	44	88	2	0	90	0.1	0.1	0.1	0.1	0.1	0.1
740–7599 Congenital anomalies	5,059	3,547	8,666	152	27	8,845	14.8	11.0	13.0	14.8	13.0	13.3
760–7799 Certain conditions originating in the perinatal period	43,977	34,845	79,483	206	384	80,073	128.8	107.7	119.6	128.8	119.6	120.5
780–7999 Symptoms, signs and ill-defined conditions	18,192	16,372	34,781	132	126	35,039	53.3	50.6	52.3	53.3	52.3	52.7
800–9999 Injury and poisoning	252	209	464	6	1	471	0.7	0.6	0.7	0.7	0.7	0.7
All episodes	72,412	58,856	132,326	635	540	133,501	212.2	182.0	199.1	212.2	199.1	200.8

Hospital stays by children aged under one year, England, 1994/95

Primary diagnosis ICD, Ninth revision

| | | Children aged at least one month but under one year | | | | | | | All admissions | | |
| | | Ordinary admissions | | | Day cases | | | All | Rates per thousand live births in 1994 | | |
		Male	Female	All	Male	Female	All	All	Male	Female	All*
		Numbers of episodes									
001–1399	Infectious and parasitic diseases	10,046	7,949	18,206	41	31	72	18,278	29.6	24.7	27.5
140–2399	Neoplasms	486	427	923	216	227	444	1,367	2.1	2.0	2.1
240–2799	Endocrine, nutritional and metabolic diseases and immunity disorders	511	347	867	104	122	226	1,093	1.8	1.5	1.6
280–2899	Diseases of blood and blood-forming organs	354	263	619	77	42	119	738	1.3	0.9	1.1
290–3199	Mental disorders	573	448	1,029	14	10	27	1,056	1.7	1.4	1.6
320–3899	Diseases of the nervous system and sense organs	2,468	1,715	4,227	569	397	972	5,199	8.9	6.5	7.8
390–4599	Diseases of the circulatory system	398	293	695	39	23	62	757	1.3	1.0	1.1
460–5199	Diseases of the respiratory system	28,461	17,175	46,274	132	76	211	46,485	83.8	53.3	69.9
520–5799	Diseases of the digestive system	9,055	5,086	14,285	1,035	298	1,347	15,632	29.6	16.6	23.5
580–6299	Diseases of the genitourinary system	2,040	1,432	3,514	681	272	962	4,476	8.0	5.3	6.7
630–6769	Complications of pregnancy, childbirth and the puerperium	0	27	27	0	2	2	29	0.0	0.1	0.0
680–7099	Diseases of the skin and subcutaneous tissue	1,237	973	2,230	115	136	253	2,483	4.0	3.4	3.7
710–7399	Diseases of the musculoskeletal system and connective tissue	250	195	449	28	33	61	510	0.8	0.7	0.8
740–7599	Congenital anomalies	6,334	4,132	10,572	1,321	928	2,256	12,828	22.4	15.6	19.3
760–7799	Certain conditions originating in the perinatal period	2,353	1,640	4,057	159	66	232	4,289	7.4	5.3	6.5
780–7999	Symptoms, signs and ill-defined conditions	18,898	13,411	32,842	1,060	725	1,824	34,666	58.5	43.7	52.2
800–9999	Injury and poisoning	3,939	2,995	6,986	79	45	126	7,112	11.8	9.4	10.7
	All episodes	87,403	58,508	147,802	5,670	3,433	9,196	156,998	272.7	191.5	236.2

Source: Department of Health, Hospital Episode Statistics, special tabulation 26/01/98 16:35:19

Data in this table are grossed for coverage but are not grossed for unknown/invalid clinical data.

This is similar to Table A9.7 in the first edition of *Birth counts*

A9.4.1

Babies born in 1994 having one or more consultations with general practitioners for common conditions in the first year of life, United Kingdom

Condition or reason for consultation	OXMIS codes	Period after birth					
		0–90 days		91–270 days		Over 270 days	
		Males	Females	Males	Females	Males	Females
		Percentages of babies in sample consulting in each period for condition					
Respiratory							
URTI*	460, 462, 463, 465	13.8	12.3	36.9	35.2	24.0	21.8
Breathing problems	7832	1.8	1.2	7.3	4.2	3.4	1.9
Cough	7833&4	5.3	4.3	22.4	19.6	11.1	10.7
Chest infection	519	3.1	2.5	14.1	11.5	7.5	6.7
Bronchiolitis	466	1.5	1.1	5.1	3.8	1.5	1.3
Bronchitis	490	0.4	0.4	3.5	2.4	1.6	1.1
Croup	464	0.2	0.1	1.9	1.1	1.2	0.8
Lymph nodes swollen	7827	0.2	0.1	0.4	0.3	0.2	0.1
Asthma	493, Y060 JB, Y0601JB, Y100 AR&NA	0.1	0.1	2.5	1.3	2.5	1.4
Snuffles (nasal)	502, 503, 508	10.2	9.5	6.9	7.2	2.5	2.2
Ear problems~	380, 381, 383, 384, 387, 389	1.3	1.1	13.4	11.6	14.1	11.8
Eye problems							
Conjunctivitis	360, 361, 369	12.9	12.1	17.8	17.9	9.8	8.6
Minor eye problems	378 + all other 37 codes	0.6	0.6	0.8	0.9	0.4	0.4
Squint	373	0.3	0.3	0.9	0.8	0.4	0.3
Poor vision	7810, 7811, 379	0.0	0.0	0.1	0.1	0.0	0.0
Skin							
Allergy	6921–5, F6929F, 708	0.1	0.1	0.2	0.1	0.1	0.1
Nappy rash	698, 6928	5.9	7.4	8.9	14.1	5.6	8.8
Eczema	690, 691, 6929CE	5.4	4.3	15.2	11.2	7.1	5.7
Minor skin problems	684, 686, 709, 7882, 7883	10.1	10.2	14.2	12.6	7.4	7.3
Viral rash	057 excl 0570A	0.2	0.4	1.5	1.4	1.2	1.1
GI tract disorders							
Gastroenteritis, diarrhoea and vomiting	0090, 0092, 784	8.6	8.0	21.5	19.6	13.5	12.8

Babies born in 1994 having one or more consultations with general practitioners for common conditions in the first year of life, United Kingdom

Condition or reason for consultation	OXMIS codes	Period after birth					
		0–90 days		91–270 days		Over 270 days	
		Males	Females	Males	Females	Males	Females
		Percentages of babies in sample consulting in each period for condition					
Thrush	112 A/B	10.1	10.6	5.4	6.3	1.4	2.1
Colic	7855&7	8.8	8.0	2.7	2.4	0.4	0.3
Teething	520	0.2	0.3	4.5	4.1	2.7	2.8
Constipation	564	2.6	2.4	2.6	2.7	1.1	1.2
Infant feeding problem	269	1.9	1.7	1.4	1.3	0.4	0.4
Gastritis	530, 531, 535, 536	0.5	0.6	1.1	1.0	0.4	0.3
Jaundice	7851, 7852	1.7	0.8	0.0	0.0	0.0	0.0
Other infections							
Viral illness	52, 53, 55, 56	1.8	1.6	7.8	7.8	5.9	5.4
Urinary tract infection	599 A,D,FP	0.5	0.3	0.7	0.6	0.2	0.4
Pyrexia	7888	1.9	1.4	5.9	5.1	4.3	3.7
Other conditions – unclassified							
Crying	307, 308, T937 excl T9373S	2.7	2.6	3.6	2.7	1.3	0.8
Congenital anomalies	all 74 and 75	3.5	2.7	2.3	1.5	1.0	0.5
Requests medication	T3100	0.9	0.7	1.3	1.2	0.9	0.7
General visit	L349	3.1	3.0	1.5	1.4	0.8	0.8
Advice given	T330	2.4	2.2	3.9	3.7	2.0	1.8
Sleep problem	7806, 3064	0.1	0.1	1.1	0.9	1.1	0.8
Heart murmur	427	1.1	0.9	0.5	0.4	0.2	0.2
Injury and accidents							
Head injury	854	0.4	0.4	1.4	1.4	1.2	1.0
All other injuries and accidents	800–999 excl 854	1.5	1.3	2.7	2.8	2.8	2.2
Routine check	See 1 below	44.6	44.0	28.9	27.8	13.0	12.0
Vaccination/immunisation	See 2 below	86.7	86.7	93.5	93.7	3.7	3.7

A9.4.1 continued

Babies born in 1994 having one or more consultations with general practitioners for common conditions in the first year of life, United Kingdom

Condition or reason for consultation	OXMIS codes	Period after birth					
		0–90 days		91–270 days		Over 270 days	
		Males	Females	Males	Females	Males	Females
		Percentages of babies in sample consulting in each period for condition					
Hospital related	L010, L001 excl paediatric (L0010AS, L0010ES), T932, T937	4.4	3.7	4.6	3.8	2.8	2.3
		Numbers in sample					
All babies in sample		14,218	13,421	12,188	11,373	10,723	9,970
Total no. of babies consulting in each period		12,607	11,828	85.7	84.7	75.4	74.3
Percentage of babies consulting in each period		88.7	88.1				
Total no. of consultations in each period		52,237	46,135	71,255	59,820	39,372	33,011

* Upper respiratory tract infection, including common cold, throat soreness and tonsillitis
~ Ear problems including otitis media, otitis externa, earache, mastoiditis, deafness
Conditions recorded at routine examinations and postnatal checks are included.

1. Routine check/screening/surveillance
Developmental assessment   Y10
Paediatric clinic   Y060 excl immunisation (Y060 A2,LI), cardiac (Y060 JP) and asthma (Y060 JB , Y0601JB) clinics
Normal development   T250
Seen in paediatric clinic   L0010AS, L0010ES
Follow up consultation   Y349
Well baby examination   Y62, Y61
Test vision   L164A
Test hearing   Y029
Medical examination   Y1000

2. Vaccination/immunisation
Vaccination prophylactic   Y42
DTPol immunisation   DTPP
Immunisation clinic   Y060 A2, Y060 LI
Injection given   T9153
Prevention codes   2000001–2000111, 2010000–2010111, 2020000, 203000–2035000, 2040200, 2050000–2050700, 2060000, 2070000, 2080000–2080800, 2090000, 2110000, 2120000, 2130000, 2150000, 2160000–2210000, 2220000–2320000, 2340000, 2350000

Source: General Practice Research Database, babies born in 1994 to women in selected practices

This is a new table for this edition of *Birth counts*

A9.4.2

Babies born in 1994 having their first consultation with general practitioners for common conditions in the first year of life, United Kingdom

Condition or reason for consultation	OXMIS codes	Period after birth						Total	
		0–90 days		91–270 days		Over 270 days			
		Males	Females	Males	Females	Males	Females	Males	Females
		Percentages of babies in sample having first consultation for each condition							
Respiratory									
URTI*	460, 462, 463, 465	13.8	12.3	29.5	28.8	9.7	9.6	52.9	50.7
Breathing problems	7832	1.8	1.2	6.9	4.0	2.4	1.4	11.1	6.6
Cough	7833&4	5.3	4.3	20.2	17.9	6.0	6.1	31.5	28.2
Chest infection	519	3.1	2.5	13.0	10.8	4.6	4.7	20.7	18.0
Bronchiolitis	466	1.5	1.1	4.8	3.7	1.2	1.1	7.6	5.9
Bronchitis	490	0.4	0.4	3.4	2.3	1.3	0.9	5.1	3.7
Croup	464	0.2	0.1	1.9	1.1	1.1	0.8	3.2	2.0
Lymph nodes swollen	7827	0.2	0.1	0.4	0.3	0.2	0.1	0.7	0.4
Asthma	493, Y060 JB, Y0601JB, Y100 AR&NA	0.1	0.1	2.4	1.3	1.6	1.0	4.1	2.3
Snuffles (nasal)	502, 503, 508	10.2	9.5	5.3	5.7	1.6	1.4	17.1	16.6
Ear problems~	380, 381, 383, 384, 387, 389	1.3	1.1	13.0	11.2	9.6	8.4	23.9	20.7
Eye problems									
Conjunctivitis	360, 361, 369	12.9	12.1	13.8	13.7	6.1	5.1	32.8	31.0
Minor eye problems	378 + all other 37 codes	0.6	0.6	0.8	0.8	0.4	0.3	1.7	1.7
Squint	373	0.3	0.3	0.8	0.7	0.3	0.3	1.4	1.3
Poor vision	7810, 7811, 379	0.0	0.0	0.1	0.1	0.0	0.0	0.1	0.1
Skin									
Allergy	6921–5, F6929F, 708	0.1	0.1	0.2	0.1	0.1	0.1	0.4	0.2
Nappy rash	698, 6928	5.9	7.4	7.7	12.1	3.8	5.3	17.4	24.8
Eczema	690, 691, 6929, F6929CE	5.4	4.3	12.6	9.7	3.6	3.4	21.6	17.3
Minor skin problems	684, 686, 709, 7882, 7883	10.1	10.2	11.8	10.3	4.8	4.9	26.7	25.4
Viral rash	057 excl 0570A	0.2	0.4	1.5	1.4	1.1	1.1	2.8	2.9
GI tract disorders									
Gastroenteritis, diarrhoea and vomiting	0090, 0092, 784	8.6	8.0	18.2	16.7	8.5	8.5	35.3	33.3

A9.4.2 continued

Babies born in 1994 having their first consultation with general practitioners for common conditions in the first year of life, United Kingdom

Condition or reason for consultation	OXMIS codes	Period after birth						Total	
		0–90 days		91–270 days		Over 270 days			
		Males	Females	Males	Females	Males	Females	Males	Females
		Percentages of babies in sample having first consultation for each condition							
Thrush	112 A/B	10.1	10.6	4.3	5.0	1.0	1.4	15.4	17.1
Colic	785&7	8.8	8.0	1.7	1.5	0.3	0.2	10.9	9.7
Teething	520	0.2	0.3	4.4	4.0	1.9	2.1	6.5	6.4
Constipation	564	2.6	2.4	2.4	2.5	0.9	0.8	5.9	5.7
Infant feeding problem	269	1.9	1.7	1.2	1.1	0.3	0.3	3.4	3.1
Gastritis	530, 531, 535, 536	0.5	0.6	1.0	0.9	0.2	0.2	1.8	1.8
Jaundice	7851, 7852	1.7	0.8	0.0	0.0	0.0	0.0	1.8	0.9
Other infections									
Viral illness	52, 53, 55, 56	1.8	1.6	7.5	7.5	5.0	4.5	14.3	13.6
Urinary tract infection	599 A,D,FP	0.5	0.3	0.5	0.5	0.1	0.3	1.2	1.1
Pyrexia	7888	1.9	1.4	5.5	4.9	3.5	3.1	11.0	9.4
Other conditions – unclassified									
Crying	307, 308, T937 excl T9373S	2.7	2.6	3.2	2.5	1.0	0.7	6.9	5.7
Congenital anomalies	all 74 and 75	3.5	2.7	1.7	1.1	0.6	0.3	5.7	4.0
Requests medication	T3100	0.9	0.7	1.1	1.0	0.5	0.3	2.5	2.1
General visit	L349	3.1	3.0	1.3	1.2	0.5	0.5	4.9	4.7
Advice given	T330	2.4	2.2	3.3	3.1	1.3	1.2	7.0	6.5
Sleep problem	7806, 3064	0.1	0.1	1.1	0.9	1.0	0.7	2.1	1.7
Heart murmur	427	1.1	0.9	0.3	0.3	0.2	0.1	1.6	1.3
Injury and accidents									
Head injury	854	0.4	0.4	1.4	1.4	1.2	1.0	2.9	2.7
All other injuries and accidents	800–999 excl 854	1.5	1.3	2.5	2.7	2.5	2.1	6.6	6.1
Routine check	See 1 below	44.6	44.0	8.9	8.4	3.4	3.2	56.9	55.6
Vaccination/immunisation	See 2 below	86.7	86.7	9.1	9.0	0.3	0.2	96.0	95.9

A9.4.2 continued

Babies born in 1994 having their first consultation with general practitioners for common conditions in the first year of life, United Kingdom

Condition or reason for consultation	OXMIS codes	Period after birth						Total	
		0–90 days		91–270 days		Over 270 days			
		Males	Females	Males	Females	Males	Females	Males	Females

Percentages of babies in sample having first consultation for each condition

Condition or reason for consultation	OXMIS codes	Males	Females	Males	Females	Males	Females	Males	Females
Hospital related	L010, L001 excl paediatric (L0010AS, L0010ES), T932, T937	4.4	3.7	3.2	2.8	1.5	1.3	9.2	7.7

* Upper respiratory tract infection, including common cold, throat soreness and tonsillitis
~ Ear problems including otitis media, otitis externa, earache, mastoiditis, deafness
Conditions recorded at routine examinations and postnatal checks are included.

1. Routine check/screening/surveillance
Developmental assessment — Y10
Paediatric clinic — Y060 excl immunisation (Y060 A2,LI), cardiac (Y060 JP) and asthma (Y060 JB , Y0601JB) clinics

Normal development — T250
Seen in paediatric clinic — L0010AS, L0010ES
Follow up consultation — Y62, Y61
Well baby examination — L164A
Test vision — Y029
Test hearing — Y1000
Medical examination

2. Vaccination/immunisation
Vaccination prophylactic — Y42
DTPol immunisation — DTPP
Immunisation clinic — Y060 A2, Y060 LI
Injection given — T9153
Prevention codes — 2000001–2000111, 2010000–2010111, 2020000, 203000–2035000, 2040200, 2050000–2050700, 2060000, 2070000, 2080000–2080800, 2090000, 2110000, 2120000, 2130000, 2150000, 2160000–2210000, 2220000–2320000, 2340000, 2350000

Source: General Practice Research Database, babies born in 1994 to women in selected practices

This is a new table for this edition of *Birth counts*

A10.1.1

Deaths from puerperal fever and childbirth, England and Wales, 1847–1910

Year	Live births	Puerperal fever and childbirth	Puerperal fever	Accidents of childbirth	Puerperal fever and childbirth	Puerperal fever	Accidents of childbirth
		Numbers of deaths			**Death rate per thousand live births**		
1847	539,965	3,226	784	2,442	5.97	1.45	4.52
1848	563,059	3,445	1,365	2,080	6.12	2.42	3.69
1849	578,159	3,339	1,165	2,174	5.78	2.02	3.76
1850	593,422	3,252	1,113	2,139	5.48	1.88	3.60
1851	615,865	3,290	1,009	2,281	5.34	1.64	3.70
1852	624,012	3,247	972	2,275	5.20	1.56	3.65
1853	612,391	3,060	792	2,268	5.00	1.29	3.70
1854	634,405	3,009	954	2,055	4.74	1.50	3.24
1855	635,043	2,979	1,079	1,900	4.69	1.70	2.99
1856	657,453	2,888	1,067	1,821	4.39	1.62	2.77
1857	663,071	2,787	836	1,951	4.20	1.26	2.94
1858	655,481	3,131	1,068	2,063	4.78	1.63	3.15
1859	689,881	3,496	1,238	2,258	5.07	1.79	3.27
1860	684,048	3,173	987	2,186	4.64	1.44	3.20
1861	696,406	2,995	886	2,109	4.30	1.27	3.03
1862	712,684	3,077	940	2,137	4.32	1.32	3.00
1863	727,417	3,588	1,155	2,433	4.93	1.59	3.34
1864	740,275	4,016	1,484	2,532	5.43	2.00	3.42
1865	748,069	3,823	1,333	2,490	5.11	1.78	3.33
1866	753,870	3,682	1,197	2,485	4.88	1.59	3.30
1867	768,349	3,412	1,066	2,346	4.44	1.39	3.05
1868	786,858	3,503	1,196	2,307	4.45	1.52	2.93
1869	773,381	3,283	1,181	2,102	4.24	1.53	2.72
1870	792,787	3,875	1,492	2,383	4.89	1.88	3.01
1871	797,428	3,935	1,464	2,471	4.93	1.84	3.10
1872	825,907	3,803	1,400	2,403	4.60	1.70	2.91
1873	829,778	4,115	1,740	2,375	4.96	2.10	2.86
1874	854,956	5,927	3,108	2,819	6.93	3.64	3.30
1875	850,607	5,064	2,504	2,560	5.95	2.94	3.01
1876	887,968	4,142	1,746	2,396	4.66	1.97	2.70
1877	888,200	3,443	1,444	1,999	3.88	1.63	2.25
1878	891,906	3,300	1,415	1,885	3.70	1.59	2.11
1879	880,389	3,340	1,464	1,876	3.79	1.66	2.13
1880	881,643	3,492	1,659	1,833	3.96	1.88	2.08
1881	883,642	4,227	2,287	1,940	4.78	2.59	2.20
1882	889,014	4,524	2,564	1,960	5.09	2.88	2.20
1883	890,722	4,508	2,616	1,892	5.06	2.94	2.12
1884	906,750	4,347	2,468	1,879	4.79	2.72	2.07
1885	894,270	4,449	2,420	2,029	4.98	2.71	2.27
1886	903,760	3,877	2,078	1,799	4.29	2.30	1.99
1887	886,331	4,160	2,450	1,710	4.69	2.76	1.93
1888	879,868	4,160	2,386	1,774	4.73	2.71	2.02
1889	885,944	3,585	1,852	1,733	4.05	2.09	1.96
1890	869,937	4,255	1,956	2,299	4.89	2.25	2.64
1891	914,157	4,787	1,973	2,814	5.24	2.16	3.08
1892	897,957	5,194	2,356	2,838	5.78	2.62	3.16
1893	914,572	5,950	3,023	2,927	6.51	3.31	3.20
1894	890,289	4,775	2,167	2,608	5.36	2.43	2.93

A10.1.1 *continued*

Deaths from puerperal fever and childbirth, England and Wales, 1847–1910

Year	Live births	Puerperal fever and childbirth	Puerperal fever	Accidents of childbirth	Puerperal fever and childbirth	Puerperal fever	Accidents of childbirth
1895	922,291	4,219	1,849	2,370	4.57	2.00	2.57
1896	915,331	4,561	2,053	2,508	4.98	2.24	2.74
1897	921,683	4,250	1,836	2,414	4.61	1.99	2.62
1898	923,165	4,074	1,707	2,367	4.41	1.85	2.56
1899	928,646	4,326	1,908	2,418	4.66	2.05	2.60
1900	927,062	4,455	1,941	2,514	4.81	2.09	2.71
1901	929,807	4,394	2,079	2,315	4.73	2.24	2.49
1902	940,509	4,205	2,003	2,202	4.47	2.13	2.34
1903	948,271	3,857	1,668	2,189	4.07	1.76	2.31
1904	945,389	3,667	1,654	2,013	3.88	1.75	2.13
1905	929,293	3,905	1,734	2,171	4.20	1.87	2.34
1906	935,081	3,757	1,640	2,117	4.02	1.75	2.26
1907	918,042	3,520	1,465	2,055	3.83	1.60	2.24
1908	940,383	3,361	1,395	1,966	3.57	1.48	2.09
1909	914,472	3,379	1,429	1,950	3.70	1.56	2.13
1910	896,962	3,191	1,274	1,917	3.56	1.42	2.14

Source: General Register Office, *Annual reports of the Registrar General*

This is similar to Table A10.1 in the first edition of *Birth counts*

A10.1.2

Mortality of women in, or associated with, childbirth, England and Wales, 1891–1939

Rates per thousand live births

Year	Classification in use from 1911 onwards				Classification in use before 1911				Total mortality from, or associated with, pregnancy or childbirth~
	Puerperal sepsis including post-abortive	Other puerperal causes including abortion~	Total mortality from pregnancy and childbearing~	Associated causes*	Puerperal sepsis including post-abortive	Other puerperal causes including abortion~	Total mortality from pregnancy and childbearing~	Associated causes#	
1891–1895	:	:	:	:	2.60	2.89	5.49	:	:
1896–1900	:	:	:	:	2.12	2.57	4.69	:	:
1901–1905	:	:	:	:	1.95	2.32	4.27	1.29	5.56
1906–1910	:	:	:	:	1.56	2.18	3.74	1.26	5.00
1911–1915	1.42	2.61	4.03	0.99	1.50	2.31	3.81	1.21	5.02
1916–1920	1.51	2.61	4.12	1.68	1.59	2.29	3.88	1.92	5.80
1921–1925	1.40	2.50	3.90	1.14	1.48	2.21	3.69	1.35	5.04
1926–1930	1.73	2.54	4.27	1.24	1.78	2.23	4.01	1.50	5.51
1931–1935	1.76	2.54	4.30	1.29	1.83	2.29	4.12	1.48	5.60
1911	1.43	2.44	3.87	1.04	1.52	2.15	3.67	1.24	4.91
1912	1.39	2.59	3.98	0.97	1.47	2.31	3.78	1.17	4.95
1913	1.26	2.70	3.96	0.91	1.34	2.37	3.71	1.16	4.87
1914	1.55	2.62	4.17	0.95	1.63	2.32	3.95	1.17	5.12
1915	1.47	2.71	4.18	1.09	1.56	2.38	3.94	1.38	5.27
1916	1.38	2.74	4.12	0.94	1.47	2.40	3.87	1.19	5.06
1917	1.31	2.58	3.89	0.95	1.39	2.27	3.66	1.18	4.84
1918	1.28	2.51	3.79	3.81	1.35	2.20	3.55	4.05	7.60
1919	1.67	2.70	4.37	1.93	1.76	2.36	4.12	2.18	6.30
1920	1.81	2.52	4.33	1.13	1.87	2.25	4.12	1.34	5.46
1921	1.38	2.54	3.92	1.08	1.46	2.25	3.71	1.29	5.00
1922	1.39	2.42	3.81	1.35	1.46	2.12	3.58	1.58	5.16
1923	1.30	2.52	3.82	1.00	1.38	2.22	3.60	1.22	4.82
1924	1.39	2.51	3.90	1.16	1.48	2.22	3.70	1.36	5.06
1925	1.56	2.52	4.08	1.07	1.62	2.24	3.86	1.29	5.15
1926	1.60	2.52	4.12	1.02	1.64	2.23	3.87	1.27	5.14
1927	1.57	2.54	4.11	1.32	1.63	2.20	3.83	1.60	5.43
1928	1.79	2.63	4.42	1.20	1.85	2.30	4.15	1.47	5.62
1929	1.80	2.53	4.33	1.49	1.83	2.24	4.07	1.75	5.82
1930	1.92	2.48	4.40	1.19	1.96	2.19	4.16	1.43	5.59
1931	1.66	2.45	4.11	1.44	1.71	2.22	3.93	1.62	5.55
1932	1.61	2.60	4.21	1.16	1.68	2.33	4.01	1.36	5.37
1933	1.83	2.68	4.51	1.43	1.90	2.42	4.32	1.62	5.94

Mortality of women in, or associated with, childbirth, England and Wales, 1891–1939

Year	Classification in use from 1911 onwards				Classification in use before 1911				
	Puerperal sepsis including post-abortive	Other puerperal causes including abortion~	Total mortality from pregnancy and childbearing~	Associated causes*	Puerperal sepsis including post-abortive	Other puerperal causes including abortion~	Total mortality from pregnancy and childbearing~	Associated causes#	Total mortality from, or associated with, pregnancy or childbirth~
1934	2.03	2.57	4.60	1.25	2.10	2.30	4.39	1.45	5.85
1935	1.68	2.42	4.10	1.19	1.75	2.20	3.95	1.34	5.29
1936	1.39	2.41	3.80	1.10	1.47	2.18	3.65	1.25	4.90
1937	0.98	2.28	3.26	1.24	1.03	2.07	3.10	1.40	4.50
1938	0.89	2.19	3.09	1.01	0.93	2.04	2.97	1.13	4.10
1939	0.77	2.16	2.93	0.90	0.81	1.98	2.79	1.04	3.83

* 629 deaths in 1938 and 554 in 1939.

Adding in 1938 and 1939 respectively, 73 and 87 deaths from puerperal nephritis and albuminuria and 0 and 1 deaths from tetanus.

~ Excluding criminal abortion.

Source: General Register Office, *Registrar General's Statistical Review for 1938 and 1939.*

This was Table A10.1 in the first edition of *Birth counts*

A10.1.3

Maternal deaths from principal causes and associated maternal deaths, England and Wales, 1935–78

Year	Maternal deaths (complications of pregnancy, childbirth and puerperium, excluding abortion)								
	Puerperal phlebitis, thrombosis and embolism	Puerperal sepsis	Haemorrhage		Toxaemia	Prolonged labour	Trauma, shock, other complic-ations of delivery	Other causes	Total maternal causes other than abortion
			Antepartum	Postpartum					
ICD code	671, 673	630, 635, 670	632, 651	652, 653	636, 639	654 – 657	658 – 661	Rem 630 –639, 650 – 678	630 – 639, 650 – 678
Numbers									
1935	192	647	292		488	507		–	2,126
1936	183	561	302		510	455		–	2,011
1937	152	347	307		510	457		–	1,773
1938	178	277	312		472	503		–	1,742
1939	154	248	117	179	478	467		–	1,643
1940#	134	195	106	180	398	125	111	124	1,373
1941	134	141	101	210	381	155	109	122	1,353
1942	128	151	87	198	410	158	94	133	1,359
1943	136	132	86	187	375	165	106	112	1,299
1944	107	105	84	179	328	176	87	113	1,179
1945	86	82	68	158	321	148	72	92	1,027
1946	102	53	85	162	359	117	83	91	1,052
1947	110	33	56	156	312	110	63	77	917
1948	67	33	46	115	249	66	55	55	686
1949	56	32	38	90	199	69	60	65	609
1950#	62	26	44	38	185	42	54	66	517
1951	49	16	35	53	141	38	37	50	419
1952	52	10	19	39	122	32	43	56	373
1953	49	17	39	51	143	31	34	55	419
1954	51	13	32	44	104	32	41	55	370
1955	55	17	24	41	91	31	23	57	339
1956	32	13	33	24	93	34	15	58	302
1957	32	18	27	22	77	27	23	46	272
1958#	40	13	25	33	66	21	20	47	265
1959	30	17	21	23	57	18	26	51	243
1960	27	8	25	19	63	26	36	44	248
1961	24	6	20	23	55	15	32	45	220
1962	34	12	23	20	53	20	23	57	242
1963	20	8	17	21	46	9	18	55	194
1964	22	10	7	12	34	13	26	53	177
1965	17	5	13	11	48	12	23	40	169
1966	11	9	13	14	38	16	23	46	170
1967	10	3	7	5	44	12	13	44	138
1968#	28	7	11	8	33	16	5	42	150
1969	16	4	6	6	24	9	12	43	120
1970	10	9	7	5	24	8	15	36	114
1971	13	5	10	9	22	10	13	25	107
1972	13	3	7	4	21	4	8	26	86
1973	9	4	4	4	20	4	11	20	76
1974	8	2	2	4	16	6	7	25	70
1975	10	3	3	4	23	1	7	18	69
1976	11	4	1	5	16	3	15	16	71
1977	9	4	4	4	15	3	9	20	68
1978	11	1	3	1	23	2	9	13	63

Abortion				All forms of abortion	All maternal deaths*	Associated maternal deaths			All attributed to or associated with maternal causes	Year
Criminal		Other				Other than abortion	With abortion	All		
With sepsis	Without mention of sepsis	With sepsis	Without mention of sepsis							
642.0, 642.2	Rem 642	640, 641, 643.0 – 645.2	640, 641, 643.1 – 645.9	640 – 645	630 – 678					
64	30	262	108	464	2,590	638	74	712	3,302	1935
49	24	242	105	420	2,431	541	70	611	3,042	1936
56	28	176	109	369	2,142	585	104	689	2,831	1937
54	26	173	101	354	2,096	449	81	530	2,626	1938
80	28	167	79	354	1,997	429	49	478	2,475	1939
43	33	116	76	268	1,641	368	56	424	2,065	1940#
66	24	145	90	325	1,678	358	47	405	2,083	1941
64	12	175	62	313	1,672	363	49	412	2,084	1942
76	15	166	64	321	1,620	437	57	494	2,114	1943
75	7	168	63	313	1,492	383	52	435	1,927	1944
65	9	109	50	233	1,260	342	19	361	1,621	1945
41	5	69	42	157	1,209	353	37	390	1,599	1946
37	3	54	49	143	1,060	264	44	308	1,368	1947
34	4	55	32	125	811	231	16	247	1,058	1948
20	9	58	31	118	727	157	19	176	903	1949
25	21	39	18	103	620	180	21	201	821	1950#
33	26	34	14	107	526	151	9	160	686	1951
19	28	28	15	90	463	153	8	161	624	1952
17	24	22	13	76	495	121	7	128	623	1953
10	25	22	19	76	446	116	5	121	567	1954
17	15	19	15	66	405	108	7	115	520	1955
20	16	20	16	72	374	119	6	125	499	1956
15	15	18	13	61	333	122	6	128	461	1957
8	12	27	16	63	328	94	4	98	426	1958#
13	10	16	8	47	290	75	7	82	372	1959
12	18	21	11	62	310	70	5	75	385	1960
8	15	24	7	54	274	68	3	71	345	1961
11	18	17	11	57	299	75	2	77	376	1962
15	6	17	11	49	243	61	6	67	310	1963
13	11	16	10	50	227	54	1	55	282	1964
8	13	21	10	52	221	42	6	48	269	1965
12	18	17	6	53	223	53	3	56	279	1966
8	9	7	10	34	172	64	4	68	240	1967
10	12	16	12	50	200	41	3	44	244	1968#
8	7	10	10	35	155	62	4	66	221	1969
4	7	17	4	32	146	55	1	56	202	1970
1	5	8	13	27	134	33	2	35	168	1971
3	4	10	9	26	112	27	1	28	140	1972
2	2	4	4	12	88	31	0	31	119	1973
1	1	3	6	11	81	19	2	21	102	1974
0	1	1	6	8	77	24	1	25	102	1975
1	0	2	4	7	78	22	1	23	101	1976
1	0	3	2	6	74	24	0	24	98	1977
0	0	2	3	5	68	21	1	22	90	1978

A10.1.3 continued

Maternal deaths from principal causes and associated maternal deaths, England and Wales, 1935–78

Year	Maternal deaths (complications of pregnancy, childbirth and puerperium, excluding abortion)								
	Puerperal phlebitis, thrombosis and embolism	Puerperal sepsis	Haemorrhage		Toxaemia	Prolonged labour	Trauma, shock, other complications of delivery	Other causes	Total maternal causes other than abortion
			Antepartum	Postpartum					
ICD code	671, 673	630, 635, 670	632, 651	652, 653	636, 639	654 – 657	658 – 661	Rem 630 –639, 650 –678	630 – 639, 650 – 678
Rates per 100,000 total births									
1935	31	104	47		78	81		–	341
1936	29	89	48		81	72		–	319
1937	24	55	48		80	72		–	279
1938	28	43	48		73	78		–	270
1939	24	39	18	28	75	73		–	257
1940#	22	32	17	29	65	20	18	20	224
1941	22	24	17	35	64	26	18	20	226
1942	19	22	13	29	61	23	14	20	202
1943	19	19	12	27	53	23	15	16	184
1944	14	14	11	23	42	23	11	15	153
1945	12	12	10	23	46	21	10	13	147
1946	12	6	10	19	43	14	10	11	125
1947	12	4	6	17	35	12	7	9	102
1948	8	4	6	14	31	8	7	7	86
1949	7	4	5	12	27	9	8	9	81
1950#	9	4	6	5	26	6	8	9	72
1951	7	2	5	8	20	5	5	7	60
1952	8	1	3	6	18	5	6	8	54
1953	7	2	6	7	20	4	5	8	60
1954	7	2	5	6	15	5	6	8	54
1955	8	2	4	6	13	5	6	8	50
1956	4	2	5	3	13	5	3	8	42
1957	4	2	4	3	10	4	2	6	37
1958#	5	2	3	4	9	3	3	6	35
1959	4	2	3	3	7	2	3	7	32
1960	3	1	3	2	8	3	4	5	31
1961	3	1	2	3	7	2	4	5	27
1962	4	1	3	2	6	2	3	7	28
1963	2	1	2	2	5	1	2	6	22
1964	2	1	1	1	4	1	3	6	20
1965	2	1	1	1	5	1	3	5	19
1966	1	1	2	2	4	2	3	5	20
1967	1	0	1	1	5	1	2	5	16
1968#	3	1	1	1	4	2	1	5	18
1969	2	0	1	1	3	1	1	5	15
1970	1	1	1	1	3	1	2	5	14
1971	2	1	1	1	3	1	2	3	13
1972	2	0	1	1	3	1	1	4	12
1973	1	1	1	1	3	1	2	3	11
1974	1	0	0	1	2	1	1	4	11
1975	2	0	0	1	4	0	1	3	11
1976	2	1	0	1	3	1	3	3	12
1977	2	1	1	1	3	1	2	3	12
1978	2	0	0	0	4	0	1	2	10

* Excludes the following cases in which it was stated that the interval elapsing between the onset of maternal condition and death exceeded 12 months: 1951–40, 1952–35, 1953–32, 1954–34, 1955-34, 1956-25, 1957-16, 1958-22, 1959-21, 1960-26, 1961-11, 1962-20, 1963-24, 1964-25, 1965-9, 1966-17, 1967-11, 1968-12, 1969-13, 1970-5, 1971-3, 1972-3, 1973-7, 1974-1, 1975-2, 1976-1, 1977-2, 1978-2.
# Revision of the ICD was made in these years.

Source: ONS/OPCS mortality statistics, GRO, Registrar General's statistical reviews

This was Table A10.2a in the first edition of *Birth counts*

Abortion					All maternal deaths*	Associated maternal deaths			All attributed to or associated with maternal causes	Year
Criminal		Other		All forms of abortion		Other than abortion	With abortion	All		
With sepsis	Without mention of sepsis	With sepsis	Without mention of sepsis							
642.0, 642.2	Rem 642	640, 641, 643.0 – 645.2	640, 641, 643.1 – 645.9	640 – 645	630 – 678					
10	5	42	17	74	415	102	12	114	529	1935
8	4	38	17	67	386	86	11	97	483	1936
9	4	28	17	58	337	92	16	108	446	1937
8	4	27	16	55	324	70	13	82	407	1938
13	4	26	12	55	313	67	8	75	387	1939
7	5	19	12	44	268	60	9	69	337	1940#
11	4	24	15	54	280	60	8	68	347	1941
9	2	26	9	46	248	54	7	61	309	1942
11	2	24	9	45	230	62	8	70	300	1943
10	1	22	8	41	193	50	7	56	249	1944
9	1	16	7	33	180	49	3	52	232	1945
5	1	8	5	19	143	42	4	46	190	1946
4	0	6	5	16	117	29	5	34	152	1947
4	1	7	4	16	102	29	2	31	133	1948
3	1	8	4	16	97	21	3	24	121	1949
4	3	5	3	14	87	25	3	28	115	1950#
5	4	5	2	15	76	22	1	23	99	1951
3	4	4	2	13	67	22	1	23	91	1952
2	3	3	2	11	71	17	1	18	89	1953
1	4	3	3	11	65	17	1	18	82	1954
2	2	3	2	10	59	16	1	17	76	1955
3	2	3	2	10	52	17	1	17	70	1956
2	2	2	2	8	45	16	1	17	62	1957
1	2	4	2	8	43	12	1	13	56	1958#
2	1	2	1	6	38	10	1	11	49	1959
1	2	3	1	8	39	9	1	9	48	1960
1	2	3	1	7	33	8	0	9	42	1961
1	2	2	1	7	35	9	0	9	44	1962
2	1	2	1	6	28	7	1	8	36	1963
1	1	2	1	6	25	6	0	6	32	1964
1	1	2	1	6	25	5	1	5	31	1965
1	2	2	1	6	26	6	0	6	32	1966
1	1	1	1	4	20	8	0	8	28	1967
1	1	2	1	6	24	5	0	5	29	1968#
1	1	1	1	4	19	8	0	8	27	1969
1	1	2	1	4	18	7	0	7	25	1970
0	1	1	2	3	17	4	0	4	21	1971
0	1	1	1	4	15	4	0	4	19	1972
0	0	1	1	2	13	5	–	5	17	1973
0	0	0	1	2	13	3	0	3	16	1974
–	0	0	1	1	13	4	0	4	17	1975
0	–	0	1	1	13	4	0	4	17	1976
0	–	1	0	1	13	4	–	4	17	1977
–	–	0	0	1	11	3	0	4	15	1978

Maternal deaths from principal causes and associated maternal deaths, England and Wales, 1979–98

Year	Complications of pregnancy, childbirth and the puerperium**									
	All attributed to maternal causes	Abortions					Direct obstetric causes			
		All	Ectopic pregnancy	Spontaneous	Legally induced	Illegally induced	All	Haemorrhage of pregnancy and childbirth	Hypertension complicating pregnancy, childbirth and the puerperium	Infections of genito-urinary tract in pregnancy
ICD code	630 – 676	630 – 639	633	634	635	636	640 – 646, 651 – 676	640, 641, 666	642 – 643	646.6
Numbers										
1979#	74	9	3	1	2	0	58	8	13	1
1980	70	13	10	1	1	0	49	6	10	0
1981	57	10	6	1	1	0	36	4	12	0
1982	42	6	2	1	2	0	33	7	6	0
1983	54	8	6	2	0	0	40	2	8	0
1984	52	6	3	0	1	0	36	4	6	0
1985	46	9	4	1	3	0	29	4	6	0
1986	45	3	2	1	0	0	31	3	9	0
1987	46	5	4	0	1	0	37	5	4	0
1988	41	7	4	2	1	0	26	4	5	0
1989	56	6	6	0	0	0	41	7	10	0
1990	57	10	6	0	2	0	39	2	14	0
1991	45	6	5	1	0	0	36	6	10	0
1992	45	6	4	0	2	0	33	4	9	0
1993	36	3	1	1	1	0	30	7	7	0
1994	50	6	5	0	0	0	36	1	7	0
1995	45	8	6	1	0	0	33	1	7	0
1996	41	4	4	0	0	0	31	2	11	0
1997	35	2	1	0	0	0	22	4	5	0
1998	46	7	4	0	0	0	26	4	6	0
Rates per 100,000 maternities										
1979#	11.6	1.4	0.5	0.2	0.3	–	9.1	1.3	2.0	0.2
1980	10.7	2.0	1.5	0.2	0.2	–	7.5	0.9	1.5	–
1981	9.0	1.6	0.9	0.2	0.2	–	5.7	0.6	1.9	–
1982	6.7	1.0	0.3	0.2	0.3	–	5.3	1.1	1.0	–
1983	8.6	1.3	1.0	0.3	–	–	6.4	0.3	1.3	–
1984	8.2	0.9	0.5	–	0.2	–	5.7	0.6	0.9	–
1985	7.0	1.4	0.6	0.2	0.5	–	4.4	0.6	0.9	–
1986	6.8	0.5	0.3	0.2	–	–	4.7	0.5	1.4	–
1987	6.8	0.7	0.6	–	0.1	–	5.5	0.7	0.6	–
1988	5.9	1.0	0.6	0.3	0.1	–	3.8	0.6	0.7	–
1989	8.2	0.9	0.9	–	–	–	6.0	1.0	1.5	–
1990	8.1	1.4	0.9	–	0.3	–	5.6	0.3	2.0	–
1991	6.5	0.9	0.7	0.1	–	–	5.2	0.9	1.4	–
1992	6.6	0.9	0.6	–	0.3	–	4.8	0.6	1.3	–
1993	5.4	0.4	0.1	0.1	0.1	–	4.5	1.0	1.0	–
1994	7.6	0.9	0.8	–	–	–	5.5	0.2	1.1	–
1995	7.0	1.2	0.9	0.2	–	–	5.1	0.2	1.1	–
1996	6.4	0.6	0.6	–	–	–	4.8	0.3	1.7	–
1997	5.5	0.3	0.2	–	–	–	3.5	0.6	0.8	–
1998	7.3	1.1	0.6	–	–	–	4.1	0.6	1.0	–

* Excludes the following cases in which it was stated that the interval elapsing between the onset of the maternal condition and death exceeded 12 months: 1979–1.

\# Revision of the ICD was made in this year.

Source: ONS/OPCS mortality statistics.

This was Table A10.2b in the first edition of *Birth counts*

Indications for care in pregnancy, labour and delivery	Complications in labour and delivery	Complications of puerperium	Indirect obstetric causes			Associated maternal deaths				All attributed to, or associated, with maternal causes	Year
			All	Infective and parasitic conditions in mother	Other conditions in mother	Choriocarcinoma	Accidents and violence	Other	All		
651 – 659	660 – 669	670 – 676	647 – 648	647	648	181	E800 – E999				
5	10	21	7	1	6	6	1	5	12	86	1979#
3	11	18	8	1	7	3	2	3	8	78	1980
1	4	12	11	0	11	3	0	3	6	63	1981
1	10	11	3	0	3	2	5	1	8	50	1982
0	13	16	6	0	6	0	5	2	7	61	1983
3	6	16	10	0	10	..	..	..	..	..	1984
1	8	12	8	1	7	..	..	..	..	..	1985
0	4	15	11	0	11	..	..	..	..	..	1986
3	8	13	4	0	4	..	..	..	..	..	1987
0	5	12	8	1	7	..	..	..	..	..	1988
4	8	12	9	1	8	..	..	..	..	..	1989
1	5	16	8	2	6	..	..	..	..	..	1990
0	6	16	3	0	3	..	..	..	..	..	1991
4	6	7	6	0	6	..	..	..	..	..	1992
1	11	7	3	1	2	..	..	..	..	..	1993
1	2	22	8	2	6	..	..	..	..	..	1994
2	6	14	4	2	2	..	..	..	..	..	1995
1	4	14	6	0	6	..	..	..	..	..	1996
0	3	10	11	1	10	..	..	..	..	..	1997
3	3	10	10	0	10	..	..	..	..	..	1998
0.8	1.6	3.3	11.0	0.2	0.9	0.9	0.2	0.8	1.9	13.5	1979#
0.5	1.7	2.8	12.2	0.2	1.1	0.5	0.3	0.5	1.2	11.9	1980
0.2	0.6	1.9	17.4	–	1.7	0.5	–	0.5	0.9	10.0	1981
0.2	1.6	1.8	4.8	–	0.5	0.3	0.8	0.2	1.3	8.0	1982
–	2.1	2.6	9.6	–	1.0	–	0.8	0.3	1.1	9.7	1983
0.5	0.9	2.5	15.8	–	1.6	..	..	..	..	..	1984
0.2	1.2	1.8	12.2	0.2	1.1	..	..	..	..	..	1985
–	0.6	2.3	16.7	–	1.7	..	..	..	..	..	1986
0.4	1.2	1.9	5.9	–	0.6	..	..	..	..	..	1987
–	0.7	1.7	11.6	0.1	1.0	..	..	..	..	..	1988
0.6	1.2	1.8	13.2	0.1	1.2	..	..	..	..	..	1989
0.1	0.7	2.3	11.4	0.3	0.9	..	..	..	..	..	1990
–	0.9	2.3	4.3	–	0.4	..	..	..	..	..	1991
0.6	0.9	1.0	8.8	–	0.9	..	..	..	..	..	1992
0.1	1.6	1.0	4.5	0.1	0.3	..	..	..	..	..	1993
0.2	0.3	3.3	12.1	0.3	0.9	..	..	..	..	..	1994
0.3	0.9	2.2	6.2	0.3	0.3	..	..	..	..	..	1995
0.2	0.6	2.2	9.3	–	0.9	..	..	..	..	..	1996
–	0.5	1.6	1.7	0.2	1.6	..	..	..	..	..	1997
0.5	0.5	1.6	1.6	–	1.6	..	..	..	..	..	1998

A10.2.1

Maternal deaths by cause, Scotland, 1965–78

Year	Puerperal phlebitis, thrombosis and embolism	Puerperal sepsis	Haemorrhage		Toxaemia	Prolonged labour	Trauma, shock; other complications of delivery	Other causes	All causes other than abortion	Abortion, all forms	All maternal deaths	Year
			Ante-partum	Post-partum								
ICD code	671, 673	630, 635, 670	632, 651	652, 653	636, 639	654–657	658–661	Rest of 630–639, 650–678	630–639, 650–678	640–645	630–678	
	Numbers											
1965	5	0	1	3	10	4	0	8	31	7	38	1965
1966	4	1	2	2	6	2	0	3	20	4	24	1966
1967	1	1	2	2	3	2	2	9	22	0	22	1967
1968	3	0	0	1	0	3	3	3	13	1	14	1968
1969	2	3	2	0	0	0	1	4	10	3	13	1969
1970	2	1	2	0	0	1	1	10	17	0	17	1970
1971	3	1	1	1	0	3	1	2	12	2	14	1971
1972	3	0	0	1	1	2	0	3	10	3	13	1972
1973	0	1	1	0	1	1	2	9	14	2	16	1973
1974	3	2	1	1	1	0	0	5	13	2	16	1974
1975	0	1	1	1	1	0	1	1	6	0	6	1975
1976	2	0	0	0	1	1	1	5	10	0	10	1976
1977	1	1	0	0	0	2	0	8	12	1	13	1977
1978	1	0	2	0	0	0	0	3	3	1	4	1978

* Rates can be calculated using data given in Table A3.3.2

Source: *Annual reports of the Registrar General for Scotland*

This was Table A10.3 in the first edition of *Birth counts*

A10.2.2

Maternal deaths by cause, Scotland, 1979–98

Year	Complications of pregnancy, childbirth and the puerperium						Direct obstetric causes							Indirect obstetric causes
	All	Abortions					All	Haemorrhage of pregnancy and childbirth	Toxaemia of pregnancy	Other complications of pregnancy	Indications for care in pregnancy, labour and delivery	Complications in labour and delivery	Complications of puerperium	
		All	Ectopic pregnancy	Spontaneous	Legally induced	Illegally induced								
ICD code	630–676	630–639	633	634	635	636	640–646, 651–676	640, 641, 666	642–643	646	651–659	660–669	670–676	647, 648
Numbers*														
1979	7	1	0	1	0	0	6	1	2	1	0	2	1	0
1980	10	1	0	0	1	0	9	1	3	0	0	1	4	0
1981	13	1	1	0	0	0	10	1	0	1	1	6	2	2
1982	6	0	0	0	0	0	5	0	2	1	0	0	2	1
1983	8	2	1	1	0	0	4	0	1	0	0	0	3	2
1984	8	1	1	0	0	0	5	0	0	0	0	2	3	2
1985	9	1	1	0	0	0	4	0	0	0	1	0	3	4
1986	7	2	2	0	0	0	4	0	1	0	0	2	1	1
1987	2	0	0	0	0	0	2	0	1	0	0	0	1	0
1988	8	1	1	0	0	0	5	1	0	0	0	0	4	1
1989	4	0	0	0	0	0	2	0	0	0	0	1	1	1
1990	4	1	0	0	0	0	2	0	0	0	0	1	1	1
1991	9	0	0	0	0	0	6	0	0	0	0	0	5	3
1992	7	0	0	0	0	0	5	1	0	0	1	1	2	1
1993	7	1	0	0	1	0	2	0	0	0	0	0	1	4
1994	9	0	0	0	0	0	1	1	0	0	0	0	2	5
1995	6	0	0	0	0	0	4	0	0	0	0	1	4	2
1996	6	0	0	0	0	0	6	1	0	0	0	0	4	0
1997	4	0	0	0	0	0	3	1	0	1	1	0	0	1
1998	5	0	0	0	0	0	3	0	1	0	1	0	1	2

* Rates can be calculated using data given in Tables A3.3.2 and A3.13.5

Source: *Annual Reports of the Registrar General for Scotland*

This is similar to Table A10.3 in the first edition of *Birth counts*

Maternal mortality in administrative counties of England and Wales, 1880–1914

312

APPENDIX 13.

England and Wales, Administrative Counties with their Associated County Boroughs, if any, ranked according to their Mortality from All Puerperal Causes per 1,000 live births.

Period 1910–1914.

Rates 0 5·00 and over.

Merionethshire	8·53
Cardiganshire	8·12
Anglesey	7·47
Brecknockshire	6·69
Carmarthenshire	6·35
Montgomeryshire	6·14
Denbighshire	6·04
Pembrokeshire	6·00
Caernarvonshire	5·55
Westmorland	5·29
Monmouthshire	5·24
Flintshire	5·10
Glamorganshire	5·06

Rates from 4·50 to 4·99.

Herefordshire	4·87
Yorks., W.R.	4·72
Lancashire	4·51

Rates from 4·00 to 4·49.

Cumberland	4·47
Cheshire	4·45
Cornwall	4·45
Durham	4·29
Devonshire	4·24
Radnorshire	4·19
Northumberland	4·14

Rates from 3·50 to 3·99.

Gloucestershire	3·99
Yorks., N.R.	3·94
Staffordshire	3·90
Derbyshire	3·86
Leicestershire	3·77
Berkshire	3·75
Cambridgeshire	3·68
Warwickshire	3·63
Northamptonshire	3·61
Suffolk	3·57
Dorsetshire	3·55
Huntingdonshire	3·51
Nottinghamshire	3·50

Rates of 3·49 and under.

Surrey	3·48
Lincolnshire	3·45
Salop	3·44
Bedfordshire	3·33
Sussex	3·30
Yorks., E.R.	3·30
Somerset	3·28
Worcestershire	3·27
Wiltshire	3·25
Norfolk	3·18
Hertfordshire	3·11
Kent	3·07
Essex	3·04
London	2·99
Isle of Wight	2·97
Middlesex	2·95
Hampshire	2·81
Buckinghamshire	2·67
Oxfordshire	2·58
Rutlandshire	2·49
Isle of Ely	2·04

Period 1900–1904.

Rates of 5·00 and over.

Brecknockshire	8·06
Cardiganshire	7·43
Denbighshire	7·22
Carmarthenshire	6·82
Pembrokeshire	6·71
Montgomeryshire	6·56
Merionethshire	6·52
Glamorganshire	6·43
Monmouthshire	6·01
Westmorland	6·00
Cumberland	5·75
Flintshire	5·49
Anglesey	5·44
Cheshire	5·41
Yorks., W.R.	5·18
Caernarvonshire	5·05
Lancashire	5·04

Rates from 4·50 to 4·99.

Radnorshire	4·96
Derbyshire	4·91
Durham	4·81
Yorks., N.R.	4·66
Cornwall	4·65
Staffordshire	4·65
Lincolnshire	4·61
Northumberland	4·59
Nottinghamshire	4·55
Wiltshire	4·50

Rates from 4·00 to 4·49.

Devonshire	4·49
Rutlandshire	4·46
Yorks., E.R.	4·34
Warwickshire	4·22
Gloucestershire	4·13
Sussex	4·08
Dorsetshire	4·07
Northamptonshire	4·06
Worcestershire	4·06

Rates from 3·50 to 3·99.

Oxfordshire	3·98
Somerset	3·95
Herefordshire	3·88
Berkshire	3·78
Norfolk	3·76
Leicestershire	3·70
Suffolk	3·62
Cambridgeshire	3·59
Kent	3·57

Rates of 3·49 and under.

Bedfordshire	3·43
Salop	3·43
Buckinghamshire	3·41
Surrey	3·41
Hertfordshire	3·36
Essex	3·22
Hampshire	3·22
London	3·20
Middlesex	3·15
Huntingdonshire	2·62

Period 1890–1894.

Rates of 5·00 and over.

Merionethshire	9·62
Cardiganshire	9·12
Denbighshire	8·82
Caernarvonshire	7·99
Glamorganshire	7·60
Brecknockshire	7·32
Monmouthshire	6·97
Lancashire	6·89
Montgomeryshire	·76
Cheshire	6·64
Derbyshire	6·62
Anglesey	6·57
Yorks., W.R.	6·29
Carmarthenshire	6·29
Northumberland	6·28
Flintshire	6·18
Gloucestershire	6·04
Durham	5·86
Cornwall	5·84
Nottinghamshire	5·76
Herefordshire	5·75
Pembrokeshire	5·71
Staffordshire	5·63
Cumberland	5·51
Lincolnshire	5·23
Salop	5·19
Somerset	5·09
Yorks., N.R.	5·09
Yorks., E.R.	5·04
Westmorland	5·02

Rates from 4·50 to 4·99.

Worcestershire	4·99
Warwickshire	4·97
Norfolk	4·94
Rutlandshire	4·91
Northamptonshire	4·90
Dorsetshire	4·85
Devonshire	4·84
Berkshire	4·82
Leicestershire	4·71
Wiltshire	4·70
Surrey	4·67
Essex	4·56
Middlesex	4·54
Cambridgeshire	4·51

Rates from 4·00 to 4·49.

Sussex	4·45
London	4·44
Kent	4·37
Hertfordshire	4·36
Hampshire	4·35
Bedfordshire	4·34
Oxfordshire	4·33
Suffolk	4·31
Buckinghamshire	4·30

Rates from 3·50 to 3·99.

—

Rates of 3·49 and under.

Huntingdonshire	3·39

Period 1880–1884.

Rates of 5·00 and over.

Merionethshire	7·65
Cardiganshire	7·43
Montgomeryshire	6·91
Flintshire	6·80
Brecknockshire	6·71
Herefordshire	6·55
Caernarvonshire	6·37
Radnorshire	6·05
Denbighshire	5·95
Glamorganshire	5·88
Northumberland	5·67
Carmarthenshire	5·54
Salop	5·42
Pembrokeshire	5·40
Durham	5·38
Lancashire	5·31
Yorks., W.R.	5·31
Cheshire	5·21
Cumberland	5·19
Derbyshire	5·13
Yorks., N.R.	5·06
Nottinghamshire	5·03
Monmouthshire	5·01

Rates from 4·50 to 4·99.

Wiltshire	4·90
Anglesey	4·80
Worcestershire	4·68
Norfolk	4·64
Cambridgeshire	4·59
Staffordshire	4·59
Surrey	4·57
Leicestershire	4·54
Oxfordshire	4·51

Rates from 4·00 to 4·49.

Dorsetshire	4·45
Northamptonshire	4·45
Gloucestershire	4·44
Warwickshire	4·37
Sussex	4·32
Buckinghamshire	4·30
Lincolnshire	4·30
Huntingdonshire	4·27
Middlesex	4·26
Berkshire	4·21
Devonshire	4·21
Cornwall	4·16
Yorks., E.R.	4·13
Westmorland	4·12
London	4·09
Somerset	4·09
Hampshire	4·05

Rates from 3·50 to 3·99.

Kent	3·95
Suffolk	3·80
Essex	3·71
Hertfordshire	3·51

Rates of 3·49 and under.

Bedfordshire	3·35
Rutlandshire	3·28

Source: Reproduced from, Ministry of Health, *Report on an investigation into maternal mortality*, 1937

This was Table A10.4 in the first edition of *Birth counts*

310

PART II.

ADMINISTRATIVE COUNTIES WITH THEIR ASSOCIATED COUNTY BOROUGHS, if any, ranked in order of their puerperal mortality rates per 1,000 live births during the decennium, 1924–33, in comparison with the corresponding rate in England and Wales during the same period, having regard to the statistical significance of the local figures.

Area.	Rate and Standard Error.	Difference of rate from that of E. & W. (i.e. 4.21).		Area	Rate and Standard Error.	Difference of rate from that of E. & W. (i.e. 4.21).	
		Actual difference.	Multiples of S.E.			Actual difference.	Multiples of S.E.

Group I.—Areas in which the mortality rate was higher than that of England and Wales by an amount equivalent to at least twice the standard error of the local rate. (Note.—In this group the difference of the local rates from that of England and Wales may be regarded as definitely significant.)

Area.	Rate and Standard Error.	Actual difference.	Multiples of S.E.	Area	Rate and Standard Error.	Actual difference.	Multiples of S.E.
1. Anglesey ...	6.79± .92	+ 2.58	2.80	7. Glamorgan ...	5.61± .15	+ 1.40	9.33
2. Denbigh ...	6.56± .50	+ 2.35	4.70	8. West Riding ...	5.26± .10	+ 1.05	10.50
3. Cardigan ...	6.39± .92	+ 2.18	2.37	9. Cumberland ...	5.18± .33	+ 0.97	2.94
4. Carmarthen ...	6.34± .45	+ 2.13	4.73	10. Monmouth ...	4.95± .24	+ 0.74	3.08
5. Pembroke ...	5.70± .62	+ 1.49	2.40	11. Lancashire ...	4.81± .08	+ 0.60	7.50
6. Flint ...	5.63± .54	+ 1.42	2.63	12. Durham ...	4.72± .12	+ 0.51	4.25

Group II.—Areas in which the mortality rate was higher than that of England and Wales by an amount equivalent to at least 1.35 times the standard error (i.e. approximately twice the " probable error ") but less than twice the standard error. (Note.—In this group the difference of the local rates from that of England and Wales may be regarded as very probably significant.)

Area.	Rate and Standard Error.	Actual difference.	Multiples of S.E.	Area	Rate and Standard Error.	Actual difference.	Multiples of S.E.
13. Merioneth ...	5.84± .92	+ 1.63	1.77	16. North Riding ...	4.52± .23	+ 0.31	1.35
14. Westmorland...	5.36± .74	+ 1.15	1.55	17. Devon ...	4.50± .21	+ 0.29	1.38
15. Caernarvon ...	5.05± .53	+ 0.84	1.58				

Group III.—Areas in which the mortality rate differed from that of England and Wales by an amount equivalent to less than 1.35 times the standard error. (Note.—In this group the local rates do not differ significantly from that of England and Wales).

Area.	Rate and Standard Error.	Actual difference.	Multiples of S.E.	Area	Rate and Standard Error.	Actual difference.	Multiples of S.E.
18. Radnor ...	5.27±1.21	+ 1.06	0.88	31. Worcester ...	4.19± .24	− 0.02	0.08
19. Isle of Wight...	5.09± .67	+ 0.88	1.31	32. Lincs. Lindsey ...	4.17± .24	− 0.04	0.17
20. Montgomery ...	4.76± .75	+ 0.55	0.73	33. Somerset ...	4.15± .25	− 0.06	0.24
21. Cornwall ...	4.52± .31	+ 0.31	1.00	34. Derby ...	4.08± .17	− 0.13	0.76
22. Hunts. ...	4.49± .78	+ 0.28	0.36	35. Rutland ...	4.05±1.22	− 0.16	0.13
23. Brecon ...	4.48± .67	+ 0.27	0.40	36. Gloucester ...	4.00± .18	− 0.21	1.17
24. Cambridge ...	4.36± .48	+ 0.15	0.31	37. Leicester ...	4.00± .21	− 0.21	1.00
25. Hereford ...	4.28± .48	+ 0.07	0.15	38. Dorset ...	3.96± .33	− 0.25	0.76
26. Northumberland ...	4.27± .17	+ 0.06	0.35	39. Northants. ...	3.95± .30	− 0.26	0.87
27. Soke of Peterboro. ...	4.25± .74	+ 0.04	0.05	40. Bedford ...	3.86± .35	− 0.35	1.00
28. East Riding ...	4.24± .20	+ 0.03	0.15	41. Berks. ...	3.86± .29	− 0.35	1.21
29. Shropshire ...	4.22± .32	+ 0.01	0.03	42. Isle of Ely ...	3.85± .52	− 0.36	0.69
30. Cheshire ...	4.20± .16	− 0.01	0.06	43. West Sussex ...	3.84± .36	− 0.37	1.03

Group IV.—Areas in which the mortality rate was lower than that of England and Wales by an amount equivalent to at least 1.35 times the standard error (i.e. approximately twice the " probable error ") but less than twice the standard error.—In this group the difference of the local rates from that of England and Wales may be regarded as very probably significant.)

Area.	Rate and Standard Error.	Actual difference.	Multiples of S.E.	Area	Rate and Standard Error.	Actual difference.	Multiples of S.E.
44. Notts. ...	3.87± .18	− 0.34	1.89	46. Bucks. ...	3.62± .30	− 0.59	1.97
45. East Suffolk ...	3.77± .28	− 0.44	1.57	47. West Suffolk ...	3.39± .46	− 0.82	1.78

Group V.—Areas in which the mortality rate was lower than that of England and Wales by an amount equivalent to at least twice the standard error of the local rate. (Note.—In this group the difference of the local rates from that of England and Wales may be regarded as definitely significant.)

Area.	Rate and Standard Error.	Actual difference.	Multiples of S.E.	Area	Rate and Standard Error.	Actual difference.	Multiples of S.E.
48. Warwick ...	3.87± .12	− 0.34	2.83	56. East Sussex ...	3.44± .22	− 0.77	3.50
49. Staffs. ...	3.74± .12	− 0.47	3.75	57. Oxford ...	3.41± .33	− 0.80	2.42
50. Surrey ...	3.62± .15	− 0.59	3.93	58. Essex ...	3.40± .11	− 0.81	7.36
51. Herts. ...	3.61± .25	− 0.60	2.40	59. Lincs. Kesteven ...	3.34± .42	− 0.87	2.07
52. Southants. ...	3.60± .15	− 0.61	4.07	60. London ...	3.34± .07	− 0.87	12.43
53. Wilts. ...	3.52± .27	− 0.69	2.55	61. Norfolk ...	3.27± .20	− 0.94	4.70
54. Middlesex ...	3.51± .12	− 0.70	5.83	62. Lincs. Holland...	3.02± .41	− 1.19	2.90
55. Kent ...	3.47± .14	− 0.74	5.29				

Source: Reproduced from Ministry of Health, *Report on an investigation into maternal mortality*, 1937

This was Table A10.5 in the first edition of *Birth counts*

A10.4.1

Main causes of true maternal deaths reported to confidential enquiries, England and Wales, 1952–78

Cause	1952–54	1955–57	1958–60	1961–63	1964–66	1967–69	1970–72	1973–75	1976–78	Excluded under international definition 1976–78
Numbers										
Abortion	153	141	135	139	133	117	81	29	19**	1
Pulmonary embolism	138	157	132	129	91	75	61	35	45	2
Haemorrhage	220*	138	130	92	68	41	27	21	26	1
Hypertensive diseases of pregnancy	246	171	118	104	67	53	47	39	29	0
All other causes	369	254	227	228	220	169	139	111	108	5
All	1,094	861	742	692	579	455	355	235	227	9
Rates per million maternities										
Abortion	74.5	66.7	58.8	55.1	51.1	47.6	35.2	15.1	10.9	
Pulmonary embolism	67.2	74.3	57.5	51.2	35.0	30.5	26.5	18.2	25.7	
Haemorrhage	107.2*	65.3	56.7	36.5	26.2	16.7	11.7	10.9	14.9	
Hypertensive diseases of pregnancy	119.8	80.9	51.4	41.3	25.8	21.6	20.5	20.3	16.6	
All other causes	179.7	120.2	98.9	90.5	84.6	68.8	60.5	57.8	61.7	
All	532.9	407.4	323.4	274.6	222.7	185.2	154.5	122.3	129.8	
Deaths known to Registrar General	1,404	1,112	928	816	671	527	387	254	228	
Percentage reported to enquiry	77.9	77.4	80.0	84.8	86.3	86.3	91.7	92.5	99.6	

* Corrected figures

** Including 5 deaths from anaesthesia associated with operations for abortion for comparison with previous triennia

Source: *Confidential enquiries into maternal deaths in England and Wales*

This was Table A10.6 in the first edition of *Birth counts*

A10.4.2

Causes of direct maternal deaths reported to confidential enquiries, England and Wales, 1970–84

Causes of direct maternal death	1970–72	1973–75	1976–78	1979–81	1982–84
Numbers					
Pulmonary embolism	51	33	43	23	25
Hypertensive diseases of pregnancy	43	34	29	36	25
Anaesthesia	37	27	27	22	18
Amniotic fluid embolism	14	14	11	18	14
Abortion	73	27	14	14	11
Ectopic pregnancy	34	19	21	20	10
Haemorrhage	30	21	24	14	9
Sepsis, excluding abortion	30	19	15	8	2
Ruptured uterus	11	11	14	4	3
Other direct causes	20	22	19	19	21
All deaths	343	227	217	178	138
Rates per million pregnancies*					
Pulmonary embolism	17.6	12.8	18.5	9.0	10.0
Hypertensive diseases of pregnancy	14.9	13.2	12.5	14.2	10.0
Anaesthesia	12.8	10.5	11.6	8.7	7.2
Amniotic fluid embolism	4.8	5.4	4.7	7.1	5.6
Abortion	25.3	10.5	6.0	5.5	4.4
Ectopic pregnancy	11.5	7.4	9.0	7.9	4.0
Haemorrhage	10.4	8.1	10.3	5.5	3.6
Sepsis, excluding abortion	10.4	7.4	6.5	3.1	1.0
Ruptured uterus	3.8	4.3	6.0	1.6	1.2
Other direct causes	6.9	8.5	8.2	7.5	8.4
All deaths	118.7	88.0	93.4	70.0	55.0
Rates per million maternities					
	154.3	122.6	121.8	93.1	72.4
Thousands					
Estimated number of pregnancies*	2890.7	2578.4	2323.8	2543.2	2507.0
Estimated number of maternities	2222.5	1851.9	1781.3	1910.9	1905.8

* Pregnancies leading to registrable births, legal abortions or hospital stays for miscarriage or ectopic pregnancy

Source: *Confidential enquiries into maternal deaths in England and Wales, 1982–84, Tables 1.7, 18.1, and 18.2.*

This is similar to Table A10.6 in the first edition of *Birth counts*

A10.4.3

Causes of direct maternal deaths reported to confidential enquiries, United Kingdom 1985–96

Causes	Numbers				Rates per million maternities			
	1985–87	1988–90	1991–93	1994–96	1985–87	1988–90	1991–93	1994–96
Thrombosis and thromboembolism	32	33	35	48	14.1	14.0	15.1	21.8
Pulmonary embolism	29	24	30	46	12.8	10.2	13.0	20.9
Embolism other than pulmonary	3	9	5	2	1.3	3.8	2.2	0.9
Hypertensive disorders of pregnancy	27	27	20	20	11.9	11.4	8.6	9.1
Anaesthesia	6	4	8	1	2.6	1.7	3.5	0.5
Amniotic fluid embolism	9	11	10	17	4.0	4.7	4.3	7.7
Early pregnancy deaths including abortion	22	24	18	15	9.7	10.2	7.8	6.8
Ectopic pregnancy	16	15	8	12	7.1	6.4	3.5	5.5
Legal abortion	1	3	5	1	0.4	1.3	2.2	0.5
Other early pregnancy deaths	5	6	5	2	2.2	2.5	2.2	0.9
Antepartum and postpartum haemorrhage	10	22	15	12	4.4	9.3	6.5	5.5
Genital tract sepsis, excluding abortion	6	7	9	14	2.6	3.0	3.9	6.4
Genital tract trauma	6	3	4	5	2.6	1.3	1.7	2.3
Other direct deaths	21	14	10	2	9.3	5.9	4.3	0.9
All direct deaths	139	145	129	134	61.3	61.4	55.7	61.0
Maternal deaths known to enquiries					Rate per 100,000 maternities			
All direct and indirect	223	238	228	268	9.8	10.1	9.8	12.2
Direct	137	145	129	134	6.0	6.1	5.6	6.1
Indirect	86	93	100	134	3.8	3.9	4.3	6.1
Maternal deaths known to Registrars General	174	171	149	163	7.7	7.2	6.4	7.4
Maternities	2,268,766	2,360,309	2,315,204	2,197,640				

Source: *Confidential enquiries into maternal deaths, 1991–93*, Tables 1.8 and 1.14, and *1994–96*, Tables 1.2, 1.4 and topic chapters

This is similar to Table A10.6 in the first edition of *Birth counts*

Maternal deaths by diagnostic group, Scotland, 1965–85

Diagnostic group	Numbers					Rates per million maternities				
	1965–71	1972–75	1976–80	1981–85	1986–90	1965–71	1972–75	1976–80	1981–85	1986–90
Pulmonary embolism	25	3	7	8	::	38.1	10.3	21.3	24.2	::
Cardiac	18	5	2	8	::	27.5	17.1	6.1	24.2	::
Ectopic	3	5	1	5	::	4.6	17.1	3.0	15.1	::
Amniotic fluid embolism	7	5	6	3	::	10.7	17.1	18.3	9.1	::
Anaesthetic complication	5	7	6	3	::	7.6	24.0	18.3	9.1	::
Pregnancy hypertension	17	3	4	2	::	25.9	10.3	12.2	6.0	::
Sepsis	18	5	1	1	::	27.5	17.1	3.0	3.0	::
Dystocia	7	0	1	1	::	10.7	–	3.0	3.0	::
Abortion	14	11	5	1	::	21.4	37.7	15.2	3.0	::
Vesicular mole	1	1	0	0	::	1.5	3.4	–	–	::
Haemorrhage	16	9	7	0	::	24.4	30.9	21.3	–	::
Other–direct or indirect	35	15	24	12	::	53.4	51.4	73.1	36.3	::
All direct or indirect	166	69	64	44	27	25.3	23.7	19.5	13.3	8.3
Other–fortuitous	22	23	19	11	::	3.4	7.9	5.8	3.3	::
All maternal deaths	188	92	83	55	::	28.7	31.5	25.3	16.6	::
Maternities	655,551	291,615	328,304	330,746	325,783					

Source: Scottish Home and Health Department, *Reports on maternal and perinatal deaths in Scotland, 1981–85, 1986–90*. The numbers of deaths in 1986–90 were too low for analysis by diagnostic group

This was Table A10.7 in the first edition of *Birth counts*

A10.4.5

Main causes of true maternal deaths reported to confidential enquiries, Northern Ireland, 1956–84

Cause	1956–59	1960–63	1964–67	1968–77	1978–84
	Numbers				
Abortion	1	2	5	7	1
Ectopic pregnancy	1	1	1	2	2
Haemorrhage	23	9	2	9	3
Hypertensive disease	25	15	9	6	6
Pulmonary embolism	12	6	11	3	0
Sepsis	15	3	2	2	1
Associated with anaesthesia	3	3	2	5	2
Associated with, but not necessarily					
due to caesarean section	15	10	1	14	*
Rupture of the uterus	3	3	1	2	2
Cardiac disease*	13	13	11	6	3
Miscellaneous	0	0	0	1	3
Total deaths reported to the enquiry**	116	61	37	54	23
	Rates				
Deaths per 100,000 maternities	..	..	27.2	18.4	12.0
Deaths per 100,000 live births	96.1	47.0	27.4	18.4	12.0
	Numbers				
Maternities	..	..	135,819	294,014	191,778
Live births	120,707	129,883	134,878	293,734	192,277

* Not given explicitly for 1978–84

** Numbers and percentages may exceed the total as some deaths were included in more than one category

Source: *Confidential enquiries into maternal deaths in Northern Ireland*

This was Table A10.8 in the first edition of *Birth counts*

A10.5.1

New diagnoses of selected sexually transmitted diseases, England, 1971–98

	Syphilis	Uncomplicated gonorrhoea	Uncomplicated chlamydia	Non-specific genital infections including chlamydia	Trichomoniasis	Herpes simplex		Genital warts		Other conditions requiring treatment*	Other conditions not requiring treatment	Total new attendances at genitourinary clinics
						All	First attack	All	First attack			
Men												
1971	2,205	37,905	"	59,023	..	2,736	..	8,916	..	20,926	44,714	187,660
1972	2,180	35,033	..	62,498	..	3,116	..	10,250	..	22,927	47,023	195,778
1973	2,657	37,803	..	68,139	..	3,323	..	11,560	..	25,103	53,229	215,181
1974	2,784	37,337	..	69,307	..	3,516	..	12,451	..	24,732	52,422	216,693
1975	2,806	37,377	..	69,365	..	4,137	..	13,091	..	25,559	52,908	220,061
1976	2,999	37,030	..	72,871	..	4,458	..	14,389	..	25,139	55,520	229,806
1977	3,257	36,778	..	75,844	..	4,982	..	14,794	..	27,473	59,595	240,951
1978	3,444	35,512	..	78,436	..	5,236	..	15,590	..	29,056	62,392	249,159
1979	3,136	34,873	..	80,644	..	5,463	..	15,703	..	29,454	61,944	251,070
1980	3,134	33,951	..	89,193	1,906	6,149	..	17,930	..	34,749	66,911	271,614
1981	2,963	33,357	..	90,071	1,662	6,631	..	18,807	..	37,288	69,610	281,189
1982	2,739	32,934	..	93,983	1,620	7,810	..	20,639	..	40,878	73,525	296,675
1983	2,662	30,349	..	97,673	1,317	8,882	..	23,319	..	44,370	77,026	309,040
1984	2,315	29,718	..	99,497	1,211	9,663	..	26,899	..	47,817	76,789	319,483
1985	1,819	28,668	..	103,198	1,077	10,025	..	31,250	..	49,079	82,242	332,840
1986	1,387	24,376	..	106,291	923	9,983	..	40,253	..	53,354	87,281	349,190
1987	1,029	14,885	..	86,835	804	8,656	..	44,355	..	50,778	98,573	328,467
1988	846	10,262	13,433	15,969	523	8,712	5,403	44,948	28,586	36,257	81,387	289,870
1989	923	10,708	12,840	75,155	316	9,906	5,792	45,804	27,448	34,614	74,179	293,080
1990	810	8,719	10,332	55,917	300	10,260	4,519	44,623	19,944	28,330	55,917	223,469
1991	885	10,484	13,754	71,750	334	10,823	6,140	48,225	28,235	47,921	90,496	322,249
1992	848	7,965	13,140	62,394	371	11,602	6,247	49,450	27,169	57,590	94,696	326,956
1993	892	6,542	12,240	61,274	301	11,637	6,255	48,972	25,859	59,825	96,389	324,405
1994	883	6,439	12,495	66,833	323	11,906	5,823	49,694	25,467	66,154	101,873	353,660
1995	890	6,471	12,521	66,791	..	11,421	5,678	51,687	25,791	45,972	79,401	400,490
1996	763	7,784	13,772	70,721	230	11,467	5,614	53,415	26,757	45,134	84,012	414,855
1997	834	8,452	16,255	78,277	258	11,265	6,087	59,273	30,289	46,656	90,101	444,457
1998	809	8,360	19,049	85,731	292	11,670		61,876	30,914	52,751	97,656	475,741
Women												
1971	819	17,985	..	13,397	..	935	..	4,814	..	8,552	24,546	112,245
1972	785	18,341	..	14,418	..	1,264	..	5,570	..	9,353	26,211	121,031
1973	810	20,754	..	14,912	..	1,546	..	6,316	..	10,492	30,122	131,631
1974	857	20,734	..	14,906	..	1,729	..	6,282	..	10,940	31,125	133,889

A10.5.1 continued

New diagnoses of selected sexually transmitted diseases, England, 1971–98

	Syphilis	Uncomplicated gonorrhoea	Uncomplicated chlamydia	Non-specific genital infections including chlamydia	Trichomoniasis	Herpes simplex All	Herpes simplex First attack	Genital warts All	Genital warts First attack	Other conditions requiring treatment*	Other conditions not requiring treatment	Total new attendances at genitourinary clinics
1975	824	21,579	..	16,579	..	2,079	..	7,059	..	12,786	32,142	143,490
1976	879	21,059	..	19,510	..	2,483	..	7,570	..	13,590	33,702	150,885
1977	1,009	21,331	..	19,647	..	2,740	..	7,972	..	14,964	35,942	156,762
1978	931	20,543	..	19,954	..	3,170	..	8,546	..	17,375	36,876	161,552
1979	865	19,593	..	21,746	18,735	3,391	..	8,787	..	20,101	37,869	166,714
1980	925	19,832	..	27,665	18,562	3,894	..	10,246	..	25,214	40,212	187,365
1981	847	18,306	..	29,947	18,542	4,516	..	10,897	..	30,554	41,797	198,735
1982	825	18,678	..	34,214	16,957	5,843	..	12,704	..	38,133	43,628	220,993
1983	665	17,562	..	36,406	15,540	7,652	..	14,580	..	46,447	44,874	238,397
1984	618	17,450	..	39,855	14,304	8,638	..	17,151	..	52,396	44,162	250,445
1985	585	17,181	..	46,326	13,118	8,910	..	20,927	..	60,239	47,920	272,466
1986	545	15,943	..	51,501	9,854	8,817	..	26,815	..	66,106	55,811	298,169
1987	509	10,369	..	44,548	8,040	8,043	..	30,187	..	60,889	69,983	291,799
1988	396	6,800	16,712	19,899	7,437	8,003	5,870	30,930	23,477	30,418	61,443	270,289
1989	488	6,986	17,606	44,859	6,132	9,382	6,611	32,342	23,506	28,170	56,797	279,863
1990	495	4,704	12,631	32,858	5,929	9,902	5,074	32,489	17,267	24,293	32,858	213,376
1991	464	5,984	16,750	43,438	5,472	11,016	7,122	34,393	24,439	39,861	74,266	312,189
1992	464	4,404	15,414	38,460	4,947	12,749	7,877	35,150	23,955	48,559	80,939	329,946
1993	455	3,384	14,141	39,521	5,236	13,865	8,374	32,748	23,034	53,480	84,194	336,856
1994	510	3,205	15,203	44,216	..	14,899	9,092	37,031	23,585	63,374	95,554	378,756
1995	500	3,265	16,161	37,317	5,314	15,310	9,007	40,322	24,701	49,180	84,274	446,686
1996	440	3,926	18,320	40,594	5,742	16,172	9,393	44,342	27,272	53,300	91,303	489,659
1997	472	4,010	22,726	47,022	5,870	16,265	9,512	47,382	28,523	55,083	99,994	527,155
1998	510	4,033	25,147	51,830	..	16,435	9,619	48,964	29,059	56,702	107,239	555,749

* Includes urinary tract infection

Source: Genito-urinary medicine clinic returns on forms SBH 60, January 1971–March 1988. KC60, April 1988 onwards

This is similar to Table A10.9 in the first edition of *Birth counts*

A10.5.2

Reported new cases of sexually transmitted diseases, Wales, 1976–1997/98

	Syphilis	Gonorrhea	Non-specific genital infections (including chlamydia)	Chlamydia	Trichomon-iasis	Anogenital herpes simplex - first attack	Anogenital warts - first attack	Other conditions requiring treatment	Other conditions not requiring treatment	Total new cases
Men										
1976	111	927	1,789	..	..	..	..	2,133	1,411	6,372
1977	123	885	1,713	..	..	..	..	2,134	1,657	6,494
1978	94	862	1,577	..	..	..	..	2,143	1,592	6,271
1979	60	760	1,717	..	..	..	..	2,199	1,557	6,293
1980	79	766	1,784	..	..	..	..	2,485	1,752	6,868
1981	83	725	1,818	..	..	..	..	2,629	2,027	7,284
1982	78	707	1,936	..	..	..	..	2,598	1,845	7,167
1983	124	780	1,968	..	..	..	..	2,994	2,370	8,236
1984	129	797	2,243	..	..	..	..	3,211	2,197	8,577
1985	120	756	2,301	..	..	..	..	2,965	2,342	8,484
1986	98	644	2,444	..	..	..	..	3,764	2,302	9,252
1987	51	389	2,025	..	..	..	..	3,717	2,485	8,667
1988	38	276	1,626	..	2	..	..	3,679	2,164	7,786
1989/90	26	251	1,505	..	2	..	..	3,522	1,600	6,905
1990/91	54	267	1,963	633	8	183	1,084	1,221	2,241	8,950
1991/92	28	211	1,824	595	2	200	1,198	1,394	2,631	9,502
1992/93	18	118	1,644	504	4	189	1,179	1,754	2,615	9,917
1993/94	26	85	1,553	458	4	182	1,161	1,654	2,812	9,977
1994/95	28	111	..	454	..	188	1,179	..	..	..
1995/96	17	132	..	543	..	200	1,618	..	..	..
1996/97	13	136	..	538	..	212	1,449	..	..	..
1997/98	14	156	..	615	..	186	1,613	..	..	..
Women										
1976	48	474	219	..	..	..	..	1,464	756	2,961
1977	66	463	216	..	..	..	..	1,379	821	2,941
1978	44	460	92	..	..	..	..	1,264	835	2,695
1979	46	408	158	..	..	..	..	1,496	824	2,932
1980	29	398	224	..	..	..	..	1,779	863	3,293
1981	39	418	640	..	..	..	..	2,594	1,083	4,776

A10.5.2 *continued*

Reported new cases of sexually transmitted diseases, Wales, 1976-1997/98

	Syphilis	Gonorrhea	Non-specific genital infections (including chlamydia)	Chlamydia	Trichomon-iasis	Anogenital herpes simplex - first attack	Anogenital warts - first attack	Other conditions requiring treatment	Other conditions not requiring treatment	Total new cases
1982	22	350	580	:	:	:	:	1,928	874	3,754
1983	32	436	650	:	:	:	:	2,325	1,050	4,493
1984	39	418	640	:	:	:	:	2,594	1,083	4,776
1985	34	383	887	:	:	:	:	2,582	993	4,880
1986	37	363	1,137	:	:	:	:	3,179	1,046	5,762
1987	33	236	1,180	:	:	:	:	3,353	1,276	6,078
1988	21	149	1,081	:	:	:	:	3,414	1,111	5,778
1989/90	13	145	799	:	80	:	:	4,243	962	6,162
1990/91	19	157	1,114	488	107	173	848	1,512	1,456	7,664
1991/92	20	111	1,162	509	86	171	1,003	1,766	1,739	9,305
1992/93	16	80	1,058	444	97	226	934	1,546	1,843	8,234
1993/94	7	44	1,117	409	89	220	1,035	1,615	1,975	8,556
1994/95	17	57	:	518	:	234	1,177	:	:	:
1995/96	7	63	:	672	:	338	1,475	:	:	:
1996/97	7	76	:	641	:	293	1,357	:	:	:
1997/98	3	60	:	842	:	306	1,590	:	:	:

Source: Welsh Office, *Health And Personal Social Services Statistics for Wales*, *Health Statistics Wales*

This is similar to Table A10.9 in the first edition of *Birth counts*

A10.5.3

Reported new cases of selected sexually transmitted diseases, Scotland, 1960–1997/98

	Syphilis	Gonorrhea	Non-specific genital infection, including chlamydia	Chlamydia	Trichom -oniasis	Genital herpes simplex	Genital warts	Other	All
Men									
1960	201	2,390	1,358	..	14	..	..	1,101	5,064
1965	156	2,017	1,809	..	66	..	..	1,626	5,674
1970	128	2,620	2,730	..	33	..	..	3,311	8,822
1975	120	3,044	4,636	..	50	298	..	2,792	10,642
1976	150	2,964	4,850	..	44	..	..	2,792	10,800
1977	170	3,492	5,552	..	72	..	..	3,102	12,388
1978	171	3,241	5,327	..	52	..	..	3,021	11,812
1979	155	3,113	5,590	..	39	..	..	2,956	11,853
1980	150	3,077	5,517	..	21	337	..	3,085	11,850
1981	146	2,914	5,957	..	60	..	..	3,314	12,391
1982	135	3,277	6,471	..	30	..	..	3,573	13,486
1983	134	3,116	6,581	..	29	518	..	3,556	13,934
1984	136	2,866	7,366	..	26	522	..	3,847	14,763
1985	85	2,869	6,775	..	31	564	4,346	4,248	14,572
1986	77	2,378	7,059	..	28	594	..	5,169	15,305
1987	60	1,454	5,549	..	19	511	..	5,274	12,867
1988	49	888	4,364	..	28	464	..	5,019	10,812
1989	39	567	3,709	..	19	455	..	4,919	9,708
1990	38	536	2,513	1,729	21	487	6,137	5,745	9,340
1991	25	552	2,513	987	14	400	..	5,812	9,316
1992	31	392	2,143	882	14	424	..	5,501	8,505
1993	15	300	1,861	929	20	399	..	5,432	8,027
Women									
1960	142	547	..	..	690	..	..	509	1,888
1965	98	667	..	..	832	..	..	878	2,475
1970	81	1,259	..	..	1,394	..	..	1,517	4,251
1975	44	1,797	501	..	1,405	114	..	2,008	5,755
1976	62	1,900	504	..	1,352	..	..	2,197	6,015
1977	57	2,036	589	..	1,527	..	..	2,374	6,583
1978	77	1,894	787	..	1,425	..	..	2,285	6,468
1979	52	1,824	1,117	..	1,160	..	..	2,295	6,448
1980	54	1,779	1,187	..	1,098	145	..	2,552	6,670
1981	69	1,678	1,477	..	871	..	..	2,521	6,616
1982	61	1,819	1,742	..	912	..	..	2,539	7,073
1983	41	1,800	1,932	..	851	331	..	2,552	7,507
1984	41	1,641	1,987	..	762	330	..	3,101	7,862
1985	29	1,822	1,999	..	816	385	1,602	3,710	8,761
1986	33	1,543	2,234	..	676	411	..	4,508	9,405
1987	32	1,082	1,987	..	559	330	..	4,758	8,748
1988	19	684	1,506	..	472	334	..	4,921	7,936
1989	22	416	1,969	..	290	323	..	4,643	7,663
1990	24	312	911	789	200	353	2,538	5,591	7,391
1991	8	304	935	952	209	371	..	5,871	7,698
1992	10	212	913	863	142	380	..	5,663	7,320
1993	9	142	893	807	124	405	..	5,446	7,019

A10.5.3 continued

Reported new cases of selected sexually transmitted diseases, Scotland, 1960–1997/98

	Syphilis	Gonorrhea	Chlamydia	Genital herpes simplex		Genital warts			Trichomoniasis	Bacterial vaginosis	Non-specific genital infections	Other genital tract infections	Other sexually transmitted infections	All
				first presentation	subsequent presentation	First occurrence	recurrence	re-registered						
Men														
1994	10	196	1,852	295	104	2,441	1,164	–	5	–	1,902	–	881	7,850
1995/96	17	299	1,806	230	181	2,350	1,156	514	11	–	1,802	1,345	492	9,303
1996/97	15	321	1,842	351	199	2,557	1,228	507	16	–	1,710	1,168	547	9,455
1997/98	27	338	1,007	341	268	2,899	1,345	581	13	–	1,814	1,261	560	10,454
Women														
1994	11	76	880	382	101	2,259	617	–	97	..	980	..	1970	7,373
1995/96	7	118	831	528	196	2,257	630	506	91	1,104	304	1,938	178	8,688
1996/97	13	106	1,016	534	252	2,476	686	426	89	1,103	301	1,731	185	8,918
1997/98	12	86	1,274	512	288	2,502	772	543	107	1,272	307	1,720	197	9,592

A revised classification was introduced on 1 April 1995 and data after this date may not be compatible with those for previous years. In particular re-registered cases of genital warts were not recorded prior to 1995/96. Bacterial vaginosis was previously regarded as a non-sexually transmitted infection and was not separately recorded. The classification of non-specific genital infections, other genital tract infections and other sexually transmitted infections was revised and the 'other sexually transmited infections' data are not compatible with those for earlier years

Source: ISD Scotland Form ISD (D) 5

This is similar to Table A10.9 in the first edition of *Birth counts*

A10.5.4

New cases of selected sexually transmitted diseases seen at genitourinary clinics, Northern Ireland, 1979–1995/96

	Syphilis	Gonorrhea	Non-specific genital infections, including chlamydia	Other conditions requiring treatment	Other conditions not requiring treatment	All
Men						
1979	35	312	1,123	865	825	3,160
1980	37	280	1,303	898	879	3,397
1981	36	263	1,410	1,040	878	3,627
1982	35	319	1,687	1,129	949	4,119
1983	43	217	1,838	1,400	1,068	4,566
1984	14	280	2,007	1,920	896	5,117
1985	30	179	2,478	1,786	880	5,353
1986	15	137	2,382	1,823	943	5,300
1987	10	88	2,296	1,859	1,312	5,565
Women						
1979	35	136	520	588	451	1,730
1980	33	108	599	773	399	1,912
1981	32	145	770	752	505	2,204
1982	34	150	958	842	625	2,609
1983	26	117	1,106	1,115	686	3,050
1984	15	137	1,052	1,821	362	3,387
1985	21	83	1,588	1,409	321	3,422
1986	11	47	1,560	1,399	417	3,434
1987	6	54	1,683	1,495	548	3,786

A10.5.4 continued

New cases of selected sexually transmitted diseases seen at genitourinary clinics, Northern Ireland, 1979–1995/96

	Syphilis	Gonorrhea	Non-specific genital infection+	Chlamydia	Trichom-oniasis	Scabies/pediculosis	Genital herpes simplex	Warts virus infection	Other conditions requiring treatment	Other conditions not requiring treatment	All new cases
Men											
1988/89	5	77	1,874	..	17	142	57	728	818	749	4,467
1989/90	11	38	1,632	..	15	95	74	711	793	984	4,353
1990/91	7	60	1,599	..	20	161	78	865	1,243	1,105	5,138
1991/92	5	42	1,124	289	2	121	66	902	1,110	1,033	4,694
1992/93	7	32	1,108	255	5	107	66	979	1,271	1,128	4,958
1993/94	10	14	1,341	252	4	110	61	1,217	4,406*	3,280*	10,695
1994/95	5	29	1,257	278	1	126	73	997	2,936*	2,534*	8,236
1995/96	7	43	979	245	2	152	82	1,109	2,166*	2,456*	7,241
Women											
1988/89	7	36	1,380	..	62	54	61	514	984	522	3,620
1989/90	9	16	1,039	..	39	35	55	550	904	488	3,135
1990/91	7	20	937	..	35	40	63	604	1,123	554	3,383
1991/92	5	17	–	234	24	46	81	658	2,101	624	3,790
1992/93	6	16	–	191	28	49	76	761	1,963	632	3,722
1993/94	2	6	–	204	25	42	106	1,154	4,228*	2,261*	8,028
1994/95	3	10	–	218	32	36	129	829	3,328*	2,012*	6,597
1995/96	2	12	–	270	30	47	132	963	2,939*	1,879*	6,274

* Data for 1993/4 onwards are unreliable and are not comparable with those for previous years. Data supplied by the Royal Group of Hospitals, whose clinic is the main one in Northern Ireland included all attendances rather than just first contacts during 1993/94 and up to June 1994. Due to 'a severe computer malfunction' in the clinic at the Royal Group of Hospitals, data from April 1996 are inaccurate and those since January 1997 have been irretrievably lost. Totals for 1993/4 onwards are not the sum of the categories shown

+ Non-specific urethritis from 1991/2 onwards

Source: DHSS Northern Ireland

This is similar to Table A10.9 in the first edition of *Birth counts*

A10.6.1

Reports of AIDS and HIV infection, United Kingdom, 1984 to June 1999

Year of report	Numbers of laboratory reports of HIV infected persons			Numbers of AIDS cases reported		
	Male	Female	Total+	Male	Female	Total
1984 or earlier	244	51	300	99	7	106
1985	2,394	104	2,506	155	3	158
1986	2,368	229	2,599	289	8	297
1987	2,020	290	2,318	616	22	638
1988	1,417	200	1,621	729	25	754
1989	1,483	215	1,702	795	47	842
1990	1,881	292	2,178	1,176	87	1,263
1991	2,045	410	2,455	1,230	120	1,350
1992	1,922	467	2,389	1,329	142	1,471
1993	1,899	448	2,349	1,385	213	1,598
1994	1,892	465	2,357	1,565	208	1,773
1995	2,093	554	2,648	1,341	231	1,572
1996	2,225	588	2,813	1,572	282	1,854
1997	1,964	581	2,547	1,103	275	1,378
1998	2,108	698	2,807	761	203	964
1999#	1,012	410	1,422	310	102	412
Total	28,967	6,002	35,011	14,455	1,975	16,430

\# First quarter of 1999 only

+ Including sex not stated

Source: Public Health Laboratory Service, AIDS and STD Centre. Unpublished quarterly surveillance tables, No 44, 99/2 Tables 10 and 12

This is a new table for this edition of *Birth counts*

A10.7.1

Directly age standardised incidence rates of cancers of the reproductive organs, England and Wales, 1971–93

Year of registration   Site and ICD code, ninth revision

Registration rates per 100,000 population, standardised using the European standard population

Year of registration	Female							Male		
	Uterus, unspecified, 179	Cervix, 180	Placenta, 181	Uterus, body, 182	Ovary, 183	Other genital, 184	Carcinoma cervix, 233.1 or 234.0	Prostate, 185	Testis, 186	Other genital, 187
1971	..	15.9	0.1	11.8	14.5	2.9	10.1	29.0	2.8	1.3
1972	..	15.1	0.1	12.1	14.6	3.1	10.5	29.5	2.9	1.2
1973	..	15.3	0.1	12.6	14.0	3.0	11.7	31.4	3.0	1.2
1974	..	14.9	0.2	13.0	14.9	3.1	13.2	32.6	3.3	1.2
1975	..	15.0	0.2	13.0	14.6	3.2	14.1	32.5	3.3	1.2
1976	..	14.6	0.2	13.5	14.8	3.1	16.1	33.3	3.2	1.2
1977	..	15.0	0.2	13.4	15.4	3.2	17.2	33.8	3.3	1.3
1978	..	14.4	0.1	13.1	14.9	3.0	17.2	32.7	3.6	1.2
1979	1.4	14.7	0.1	11.7	15.1	2.9	18.8	35.3	3.3	1.4
1980	1.5	15.3	0.1	11.8	15.8	2.9	20.6	36.6	3.7	1.5
1981	1.4	15.4	0.1	11.9	15.8	2.7	25.0	37.4	3.9	1.4
1982	1.5	14.8	0.1	11.9	15.8	2.9	24.8	38.4	3.7	1.5
1983	1.5	14.9	0.1	11.9	16.4	2.8	25.9	39.3	3.7	1.4
1984	1.4	15.5	0.1	12.1	16.3	3.0	38.4	39.9	4.2	1.3
1985	1.2	16.5	0.1	12.4	17.0	2.9	53.1	42.4	4.4	1.5
1986	1.2	16.1	0.1	12.0	16.6	2.8	58.5	42.3	4.6	1.3
1987	1.2	15.9	0.1	11.8	17.5	2.8	66.4	43.7	4.8	1.4
1988	1.3	16.5	0.0	12.3	17.2	2.9	71.1	45.8	5.0	1.4
1989	1.2	15.1	0.1	12.2	17.1	2.8	67.6	46.0	5.1	1.4
1990	1.0	15.4	0.0	12.4	16.7	2.5	80.1	47.4	4.8	1.4
1991	1.0	13.0	0.0	12.6	17.5	2.9	73.4	50.0	5.2	1.4
1992	1.3	11.9	0.1	12.4	17.5	2.8	69.6	54.3	5.2	1.4
1993	0.9	11.6	0.0	12.7	17.1	2.8	68.0	59.1	5.3	1.4

Source: Office for National Statistics, *Cancer statistics, Series MB1*

Incidence data for years 1971–1992: Office for National Statistics. *Cancer 1971–1997.* (CD ROM). London: ONS, 1999.

Incidence data for years 1993–1996: Quinn MJ, Babb P, Jones J, Brock A. Registrations of cancer diagnosed in 1993–1996, England and Wales. *Health statistics quarterly* 1999; 4: 59–70.

This is similar to Table A10.10 in the first edition of *Birth counts*

A10.7.2

Provisional directly age standardised incidence rates of cancers of the reproductive organs, England and Wales, 1994–96

Site and ICD code, ninth revision	1994	1995	1996
	Registration rates per 100,000 population*		
Female			
Uterus, unspecified, 179	..	..	..
Cervix, 180	10.1	9.5	8.9
Placenta, 181	..	..	..
Uterus, body, 182	12.6	12.3	12.4
Ovary, 183	16.8	17.7	18.0
Other genital, 184	..	..	..
Carcinoma cervix, 233.1 or 234.0	..	..	..
Male			
Prostate, 185	65.6	62.3	56.1
Testis, 186	5.0	5.4	5.5
Other genital, 187	..	..	..

* Standardised using the European standard population

Source: Office for National Statistics, *Cancer statistics, Series MB1*

Quinn MJ, Babb P, Jones J, Brock A. Registrations of cancer diagnosed in 1993–1996, England and Wales. *Health statistics quarterly* 1999; 4: 59–70.

This is similar to Table A10.10 in the first edition of *Birth counts*

A10.8.1

Deaths attributed to cancers of the reproductive organs, adults aged 15–99, England and Wales, 1971–95

	Malignant neoplasm of uterus	Malignant neoplasm of cervix uteri	Malignant neoplasm of ovary and other uterine adnexa	Malignant neoplasm of other and unspecified female genital organs
ICD, ninth revision	179, 182	180	183	184
Females				
Numbers				
1971–75	7,629	10,993	17,909	2,755
1976–80	7,584	10,659	18,575	2,714
1981–85	7,609	9,764	18,821	2,596
1986–90	7,296	9,450	19,500	2,651
1991–95	6,764	7,506	19,308	2,377
Crude rates per million population				
1971–75	60	87	141	22
1976–80	60	84	146	21
1981–85	60	77	148	20
1986–90	56	73	151	21
1991–95	52	57	147	18

	Malignant neoplasm of prostate	Malignant neoplasm of testis	Malignant neoplasm of penis and other male genital organs	
ICD, ninth revision	185	186	187	
Males				
Numbers				
1971–75	21,178	1,261	479	
1976–80	23,821	1,185	528	
1981–85	28,937	723	607	
1986–90	37,493	653	574	
1991–95	43,459	501	527	
Crude rates per million population				
1971–75	176	10	4	
1976–80	198	10	4	
1981–85	239	6	5	
1986–90	305	5	5	
1991–95	345	4	4	

Source: ONS *Mortality statistics, Series DH2, No 23,* Tables 6a and 6b

This is similar to Table A10.11 in the first edition of *Birth counts*

A10.9.1

Standardised mortality ratios and age-standardised death rates for selected cancers of the reproductive organs, England and Wales, 1971–97

	Cervix uteri	Ovary and other uterine adnexa	Prostate	Cervix uteri	Ovary and other uterine adnexa	Prostate
ICD, ninth revision	180	183	185	180	183	185
	Standardised mortality ratios*			**Age-standardised mortality rates per million****		
	Females		**Males**	**Females**		**Males**
1971	119	104	92	83	127	198
1981	101	101	100	69	122	214
1984	94	107	115	65	127	251
1985	96	104	119	66	121	259
1986	98	104	122	69	121	263
1987	93	106	125	64	123	269
1988	94	102	128	64	119	275
1989	88	105	133	59	122	287
1990	79	107	135	58	123	289
1991	73	103	140	54	118	302
1992	71	103	141	52	118	303
1993	71	101	137	47	116	296
1994	65	102	137	42	114	295
1995	63	102	137	42	116	296
1996	62	107	133	41	122	287
1997	57	104	128	37	115	277
1998	54	105	128	35	117	274

* Based on 1980-82=100

** Based on the European Standard Population

Source: ONS *Mortality statistics, Series DH2, no 24*, Table 5

This is similar to Table A10.11 in the first edition of *Birth counts*

A10.10.1

Age standardised relative survival rates one and five years after diagnosis of cancers of the reproductive organs, England and Wales, 1971–75 to 1986–90

Women diagnosed in	Cervix		Uterus		Ovary		Vagina and vulva	
	Percentage	95% confidence interval	Percentage	95% confidence interval	Percentage	95% confidence interval	Percentage	95% confidence interval
Survival one year after diagnosis								
1971–75	75	75–76	78	77–79	42	41–43	62	60–63
1976–80	76	76–77	80	80–81	44	44–45	64	62–65
1981–85	80	79–80	82	82–83	51	50–52	67	66–69
1986–90	82	81–82	84	83–85	54	53–55	71	69–72
Survival five years after diagnosis								
1971–75	52	51–53	61	60–62	21	20–21	40	38–42
1976–80	54	54–55	65	64–66	22	22–23	45	44–47
1981–85	58	57–58	68	67–69	27	26–27	48	47–50
1986–90	61	61–62	70	69–70	28	28–29	51	49–52

Men diagnosed in	Prostate		Testis		Penis	
	Percentage	95% confidence interval	Percentage	95% confidence interval	Percentage	95% confidence interval
Survival one year after diagnosis						
1971–75	65	64–65	82	81–84	76	73–79
1976–80	69	68–69	87	86–88	79	77–82
1981–85	76	75–76	94	94–95	80	77–82
1986–90	76	76–77	95	94–95	83	81–85
Survival five years after diagnosis						
1971–75	31	30–32	69	67–71	60	56–64
1976–80	37	36–37	78	77–79	61	57–65
1981–85	41	40–41	88	87–89	63	59–67
1986–90	41	41–42	90	89–91	67	64–71

Source: Office for National Statistics, *Cancer survival trends in England and Wales, 1971–1995, deprivation and NHS region*, Table 4.4

This is similar to Table A10.12 in the first edition of Birth counts

A10.11.1

Uptake of cervical and breast cancer screening programmes, by region and country, 1991/92–1997/98

	1991/92	1992/93	1993/94	1994/95*	1995/96	1996/97	1997/98
a) Cervical cancer screening							
Percentage of target population aged 20 to 64 screened in the previous five and a half years							
England	80	83	84	86	84.7	84.6	85.3
Northern and Yorkshire	84	86	87	88	86.7	86.8	87.3
Trent	87	89	90	91	89.1	88.9	89.1
Anglia and Oxford	85	86	87	89	87.4	87.2	87.6
North Thames	65	71	75	77	77.5	77.9	79.1
South Thames	74	80	82	84	83.6	83.7	84.6
South West	87	88	88	88	86.2	85.6	86.4
West Midlands	84	87	87	88	86.4	85.9	86.3
North West	83	85	86	86	84.4	84.1	85.1
Wales	78.9	85.4	85.8	84.4	84.3	84.2	83.6
Scotland	..	..	..	81.0*	82.6*	85.3*	87.0
Northern Ireland	..	..	..	..	..	..	..
b) Breast cancer screening							
Percentage of target population aged 50–64 invited for screening who attended							
England	71.6	71.8	72.1	77.4	76.2	75.5	75.4
Northern and Yorkshire	74	73	73	80	77	77	79
Trent	78	78	78	80	81	81	81
Anglia and Oxford	79	78	76	83	82	82	79
North Thames	59	61	60	68	66	65	66
South Thames	69	69	69	72	74	71	73
South West	77	77	75	81	79	79	79
West Midlands	72	70	72	79	78	76	76
North West	71	74	74	78	77	77	75
Wales	..	76.0	73.3	79.5	76.8	77.7	76.8
Scotland	..	70.5	71.4	69.8	72.0	72.8	72.5
Northern Ireland	..	..	..	75.9	74.3	71.0	72.5

* Calendar years

Source: Department of Health, form KC53,
Welsh Office, *Health statistics Wales,*
ISD Scotland,
DHSS Northern Ireland, *Community statistics*

This is similar to Table A10.13 in the first edition of *Birth counts*

A10.12.1

Women having consultations with general practitioners in the first year after giving birth in 1994, by condition and age of woman, United Kingdom

Reason for consultation	OXMIS code	Age of mother at birth of baby						
		Under 20	20–24	25–29	30–34	35–39	40 and over	All ages
		Percentages of all mothers in age group who consulted						
Primary haemorrhage	653, 677	0.3	0.4	0.3	0.3	0.4	0.7	0.3
Secondary haemorrhage, including vaginal bleeding	458, 626, 629 excl 6299WD	27.1	25.2	22.9	19.1	19.1	18.4	21.9
Abdominal pain	7855D-DC	8.7	8.2	6.0	5.6	4.4	5.2	6.2
Vaginal infection, including thrush	112 excl 112 HM, 622	11.6	15.6	15.4	14.8	13.2	12.0	14.7
GU problems, including urinary tract infection and cystitis	599 A, AA, D, GI, 595, 786 excl 7860B 7867CD	15.3	12.7	10.7	10.9	11.6	8.8	11.4
Constipation	5640, 5649	3.9	4.5	4.1	4.0	3.9	3.6	4.1
Piles	455	3.0	4.2	5.3	6.5	6.6	4.6	5.5
Wound infection – surgical	998 excl 9989PD, PP RD	1.6	2.1	2.5	2.5	2.9	3.7	2.4
Fissure-in-ano	565	0.9	1.5	1.7	1.4	1.1	0.3	1.5
Faecal incontinence	7856	0.0	0.0	0.0	0.0	0.0	0.0	0.0
Pelvic infection, including endometritis	616 incl T6160PI, 622, 625, 670	6.5	7.5	6.7	6.4	6.3	5.6	6.7
Depression	3004A – 3009T +1	13.3	13.9	12.1	10.8	10.4	8.6	11.8
Back, neck and leg pain	728, 7871CP, GB, GR, 7872LC, TH, 7873A, AL, C	9.3	10.5	10.6	10.7	13.1	11.8	10.9
Headache	791	5.7	6.9	4.8	4.1	3.2	3.6	4.8
Tiredness	790	4.1	4.6	3.6	4.0	3.7	3.4	3.9
General aches and pains	7170A, 7179L–LN, 7179T–TN	2.4	3.0	2.7	2.4	2.9	3.2	2.7
Mastitis	611 excl 6111A	3.8	5.6	9.7	12.1	12.5	12.5	9.7
Anaemia	285	11.0	11.2	10.2	9.1	8.7	9.0	9.9
Skin rash	7881–7882	5.4	4.8	4.2	3.6	4.3	3.2	4.2
Pyrexia	7888	0.6	0.5	0.5	0.8	0.9	0.0	0.6
Weight loss	7884	1.2	1.0	0.5	0.4	0.4	0.5	0.6
Postnatal visit	L349, Y61 excl Y6100BB	78.9	80.4	81.1	80.8	80.4	77.2	80.6
Medical examination	Y10, excl Y10 AC, DA, DH, JA, JB, JE, NM, NN	14.6	14.5	15.0	13.6	11.3	8.1	13.9
Hospital discharge	T932	8.7	9.4	8.7	8.8	8.6	9.0	8.9

A10.12.1 *continued*

Women having consultations with general practitioners in the first year after giving birth in 1994, by condition and age of woman, United Kingdom

Reason for consultation	OXMIS code	Age of mother at birth of baby						
		Under 20	20–24	25–29	30–34	35–39	40 and over	All ages
Health advice	T330, Y060, excl T3301 AC & B, T3304HR	12.7	13.2	12.5	11.5	11.4	11.3	12.2
Bereavement counselling	T1400BC	0.0	0.1	0.1	0.0	0.1	0.2	0.1
Cervical smear	L323, L916, Y100 HB–WW, T323, 8050000	50.9	54.2	57.4	57.1	57.6	56.5	56.4
Ultrasound scan	K989	1.7	1.7	1.3	1.3	1.1	1.4	1.3
Contraception	T320–2, T324, Y10 BP, Y450, Y453, T9033, T9035 +[2]	81.4	84.0	79.9	73.5	64.8	57.5	76.7
Immunisation	Y42, A, AG, F, FA, H, HA, IV, L N +[3]	8.3	10.4	17.3	15.4	17.0	17.3	15.0
Consultation for any condition		97.4	98.2	99.0	98.7	98.9	98.3	98.7
Numbers in sample								
Number of women who gave birth		1,271	5,074	9,168	8,244	3,023	591	27,371
Number of women with consultations in the first year after giving birth		1,238	4,985	9,073	8,140	2,991	581	27,008
Total number of consultations in year after giving birth		12,431	50,899	85,554	73,748	27,462	5,434	255,528

1 Also includes women with therapy records with BNF codes in sections 4.3.1–4.3.4

2 Also includes women with therapy records with BNF codes in sections 7.3.1, 7.3.2.1, 7.3.2.2, 7.3.3, 7.3.4

3 Also includes women with prevention codes 2000001–2000111, 2010000–2010111, 2020000, 203000–2035000, 2040200, 2050000–2050700,2060000, 2070000, 2080000–2080800, 2090000, 2110000, 2120000, 2130000, 2150000, 2160000–2210000, 2220000–2320000, 2340000, 2350000

Source: General Practice Research Database, babies born in 1994 to women in selected practices

This is a new table for this edition of *Birth counts*

A10.12.2

Women having consultations with general practitioners in the first year after giving birth in 1994, by condition and time after birth, United Kingdom

Reason for consultation	OXMIS code	Time between giving birth and consultation for condition						
		Percentage of the women who gave birth						
		Any consultation for condition			First consultation for condition			
		0–14 days	15–42 days	43 days or more	0–14 days	15–42 days	43 days or moretime	Any time in first year
Primary haemorrhage	653, 677	0.3	0.0	0.0	0.3	0.0	0.0	0.3
Secondary haemorrhage, including vaginal bleeding	458, 626, 629 excl 6299WD	2.4	4.1	17.6	2.4	3.8	15.7	21.9
Abdominal pain	7855D–DC	0.8	0.9	4.9	0.8	0.8	4.6	6.2
Vaginal infection, including thrush	112 excl 112 HM, 622	1.9	2.7	11.4	1.9	2.5	10.3	14.7
GU problems, including urinary tract infection and cystitis	599 A, AA, D, GI, 595, 786 excl 7860B 7867CD	2.0	1.6	8.7	2.0	1.4	8.0	11.4
Constipation	5640, 5649	1.5	1.0	1.9	1.5	0.9	1.7	4.1
Piles	455	1.9	1.2	2.8	1.9	1.1	2.5	5.5
Wound infection - surgical	998 excl 9989PD, PP, RD	1.1	1.0	0.6	1.1	0.8	0.5	2.4
Fissure-in-ano	565	0.0	0.3	1.2	0.0	0.3	1.1	1.5
Faecal incontinence	7856	0.0	0.0	0.0	0.0	0.0	0.0	0.0
Pelvic infection, including endometritis	616 incl T6160PI, 622, 625, 670	2.3	1.7	3.3	2.3	1.5	2.9	6.7
Depression	3004A – 3009T +[1]	0.5	1.7	11.1	0.5	1.5	9.8	11.8
Back, neck and leg pain	728, 7871CP, GB, GR, 7872LC, TH, 7873A, AL, C	0.7	1.1	9.7	0.7	1.0	9.2	10.9
Headache	791	0.3	0.4	4.3	0.3	0.4	4.1	4.8
Tiredness	790	0.1	0.3	3.6	0.1	0.3	3.5	3.9
General aches and pains	7170A, 7179L–LN, 7179T–TN	0.8	0.3	1.6	0.8	0.3	1.6	2.7
Mastitis	611 excl 6111A	3.6	3.5	4.2	3.6	2.9	3.2	9.7
Anaemia	285	5.0	1.5	4.4	5.0	1.3	3.6	9.9
Skin rash	7881–7882	0.3	0.5	3.4	0.3	0.5	3.4	4.2
Pyrexia	7888	0.3	0.1	0.3	0.3	0.1	0.3	0.6
Weight loss	7884	0.0	0.0	0.6	0.0	0.0	0.6	0.6
Postnatal visit	L349, Y61 excl Y6100BB	56.0	15.7	53.9	56.0	6.5	18.2	80.6

A10.12.2 continued

Women having consultations with general practitioners in the first year after giving birth in 1994, by condition and time after birth, United Kingdom

Reason for consultation	OXMIS code	Time between giving birth and consultation for condition						
		Any consultation for condition			First consultation for condition			
		0–14 days	15–42 days	43 days or more	0–14 days	15–42 days	43 days or more time	Any time in first year
Medical examination	Y10, excl Y10 AC, DA, DH, JA, JB, JE, NM, NN	1.0	1.5	12.5	1.0	1.4	11.5	13.9
Hospital discharge	T932	7.8	0.2	1.2	7.8	0.2	0.9	8.9
Health advice	T330, Y060, excl T3301 AC & B, T3304HR	1.1	1.8	10.2	1.1	1.7	9.4	12.2
Bereavement counselling	T1400BC	0.0	0.0	0.0	0.0	0.0	0.0	0.1
Cervical smear	L323, L916, Y100 HB-WW, T323, 8050000	0.4	6.2	51.6	0.4	6.2	49.8	56.4
Ultrasound scan	K989	0.1	0.1	1.2	0.1	0.1	1.2	1.3
Contraception	T320–2, T324, Y10 BP, Y450, Y453, T9033, T9035 +2	15.8	19.3	68.7	15.8	16.9	43.9	76.7
Immunisation	Y42, A, AG, F, FA, H, HA, IV, L, N +3	0.4	0.5	14.3	0.4	14.3	14.1	15.0
Consultation for any condition		76.5	52.7	95.1				
Numbers in sample								
Number of women who gave birth		27,371	27,371	27,371				
Number of women with consultations in the first year after giving birth		20,952	14,421	26,033				
Total number of consultations		42,374	24,400	188,754				

1 Also includes women with therapy records with BNF codes in sections 4.3.1 – 4.3.4

2 Also includes women with therapy records with BNF codes in sections 7.3.1, 7.3.2.1, 7.3.2.2, 7.3.3, 7.3.4

3 Also includes women with prevention codes 2000001–2000111, 2010000–2010111, 2020000, 203000–2035000, 2040200, 2050000–2050700, 2060000, 2070000, 2080000–2080800, 2090000, 2110000, 2130000, 2150000, 2160000–2210000, 2220000–2320000, 2340000, 2350000

Source: General Practice Research Database, babies born in 1994 to women in selected practices

This is a new table for this edition of *Birth counts*

A11.1.1

Changes in prices, United Kingdom 1980–93 and 1987/88–1997/98

Year	HSCI prices[1]	HCHS pay[2]	HCHS pay and prices[3]	GDP deflators at market prices[4]	Capital charges[5]	Retail Price Index[6]
Calendar years, 1987=100						
1980	54.16	61.37	..	56.94	59.24	67.93
1981	66.78	65.99	..	69.69	79.94	74.74
1982	75.46	70.13	72.93	77.18	82.58	80.03
1983	82.29	73.82	78.91	83.07	83.93	83.75
1984	86.89	78.36	84.04	87.08	85.64	87.98
1985	92.25	82.40	88.33	91.66	89.40	93.18
1986	97.10	90.30	93.45	97.10	95.00	96.16
1987	100.00	100.00	100.00	100.00	100.00	100.00
1988	104.00	113.00	108.50	106.70	105.80	106.00
1989	109.51	120.46	120.60	114.17	115.53	114.28
1990	117.40	131.54	127.56	123.42	116.57	125.34
1991	125.03	146.67	138.65	131.19	117.60	131.29
1992	130.90	158.26	152.66	136.31	118.61	135.43
1993	132.74	164.90	163.19	140.67	119.77	137.75
Financial years, March 1986=100						
1987/88	105.20	109.70	108.50	105.32	105.10	104.20
1988/89	109.41	123.96	120.00	112.37	111.18	109.31
1989/90	115.21	132.14	127.56	120.22	121.45	117.83
1990/91	123.50	144.30	138.66	129.84	136.40	129.03
1991/92	131.53	160.89	152.66	138.13	136.95	136.64
1992/93	137.71	173.60	163.20	143.93	133.79	141.69
1993/94	139.64	180.90	168.75	148.11	136.24	143.96
1994/95	140.90	187.05	173.13	150.34	142.96	147.42
1995/96	145.40	195.28	180.06	154.51	149.29	152.58
1996/97	147.59	201.72	185.03	159.04	153.40	156.24
1997/98	148.74	206.76	188.18	163.33	159.50	161.71

1 Health service cost index
2 Hospital and community health services pay index
3 Combined weighted index of hospital and community health services pay and prices
4 Gross Domestic Product deflators reflect costs across the whole economy including imports
5 Index of inflation in capital costs/values in the NHS
6 Index of retail prices based on data collected in the Family Expenditure Survey

Source: NHS Executive, Leeds, FPA PES3

This was Table A11.1 in the first edition of *Birth counts*

A11.2.1

Total expenditure on the hospital and community health services, England, 1990/91 to 1997/98

	1990/91	1991/92	1992/93	1993/94	1994/95	1995/96	1996/97	1997/98
	£ millions							
All categories	14,710	19,733	21,265	22,096	22,573	23,890	24,128	25,329
Salaries & wages	11,212	12,562	13,639	13,913	14,303	14,961	15,580	16,099
Supplies & services - clinical	1,307	1,640	1,836	2,053	2,219	2,410	2,599	2,849
Supplies & services - general	386	451	439	464	482	507	523	634
Establishment expenses	461	540	599	637	670	703	700	869
Transport & moveable plant	101	94	101	115	121	132	141	..
Premises & fixed plant	895	1,211	1,329	1,455	1,576	1,600	1,592	1,560
Miscellaneous expenditure	516	1,088	1,205	1,470	1,391	1,510	1,069	1,145
Capital	..	1,859	1,748	1,558	1,107	1,157	1,069	1,065
Purchase of health care from non-NHS bodies	140	208	247	325	586	731	726	1,108
External contract staffing and consultancy	..	80	122	106	118	178	129	..

Source: Department of Health, *Health and Personal Social Services Statistics for England, Table E3*

This is similar to Table 11.2 in the first edition of Volume 1 of *Birth counts*

A11.3.1

Hospital and community health services programme budget, 1976/77 to 1997/98, at 1997/98 prices

	Obstetric in-patient	Obstetric out-patient	Community midwifery	Community maternity	Health visiting	Professional advice and support	All
	Old basis, £ million						
1976/77	810	107	124	–	221	–	1,262
1977/78	816	116	125	–	234	–	1,291
1978/79	801	118	117	–	238	–	1,274
1979/80	813	117	119	–	238	–	1,287
1980/81	818	121	130	–	243	–	1,312
1981/82	842	123	135	–	259	–	1,359
1982/83	854	132	138	–	273	–	1,397
1983/84	829	127	138	–	278	–	1,372
1984/85	813	136	144	–	286	–	1,379
1985/86	830	132	150	–	295	–	1,407
1986/87	813	153	162	–	309	–	1,437
1987/88	856	146	181	–	326	–	1,509
1988/89	840	120	179	–	347	–	1,486
	New basis, £ million						
1988/89	840	120	–	195	–	272	1,427
1989/90	805	109	–	209	–	294	1,417
1990/91	780	100	–	222	–	305	1,407
1991/92	854	161	–	165	–	351	1,531
1992/93	832	167	–	160	–	333	1,492
1993/94	777	151	–	161	–	336	1,425
1994/95	776	135	–	163	–	325	1,399
1995/96	751	129	–	176	–	329	1,385
1996/97	731	134	–	202	–	277	1,344
1997/98	730	137	–	210	–	266	1,343

Source: NHS Executive, Leeds, FPA PX-3

This is similar to Table A11.2 in the first edition of *Birth counts*

A11.3.2

Fees paid to general practitioners for maternity medical services, England, 1990/91–1998/99

	£
1990/91	63,491,107
1991/92	68,538,159
1992/93	71,243,169
1993/94	72,464,718
1994/95	74,017,384
1995/96	73,148,304
1996/97	76,448,934
1997/98	80,381,351
1998/99	79,726,677

Source: NHS Executive, FIS (FHS)4 part B non cash-limited returns of the 100 English health authorities. As such, they are not audited.

This was Table 11.1 in the first edition of Volume 1 of *Birth counts*

A11.4.1

Pay scales in the National Health Service, England and Wales, 1998/99

	Lowest point on scale	Highest point on scale
	Range of gross annual salary, £	
Nursing and midwifery staff		
Age under 18	7,645	7,645
Nurse / midwife scale A	8,170	9,995
Nurse / midwife scale B	9,675	11,015
Nurse / midwife scale C	11,015	13,060
Nurse / midwife scale D	12,630	14,450
Nurse / midwife scale E	14,450	16,735
Nurse / midwife scale F	16,030	19,635
Nurse / midwife scale G	18,905	21,875
Nurse / midwife scale H	21,125	24,155
Nurse / midwife scale I	23,385	26,495
Medical and dental staff, rates effective from 1 April 1998		
House officer	15,800	17,840
Senior house officer	19,715	26,340
Specialist registrar	22,040	32,135
Consultant	44,780	57,800
Associate specialist	26,560	46,180
Staff grade practitioner	23,940	39,620
Hospital practitioners, per session*	3,190	4,270

* Limited to a maximum of 5 half day sessions per week

Source: NHS Executive. *NHS Whitley Council Handbook and Advance Letter (MD) 1/98 on Pay and Conditions of Hospital Medical Staff,* supplied to NHS personnel departments.

This was Table A11.4a in the first edition of *Birth counts*

A11.4.2

Distinction awards to NHS consultants, amount and number of awards in England and Wales, 1997

	Number of eligible practitioners	All	Type of award			No award
			A+	A	B	
			Amount of award at April 1998, £			
			54,910	40,460	23,120	
			Numbers of award holders, September 1997			
Obstetrics and gynaecology	1,123	129	15	35	79	994
All specialties	22,688	2,853	235	812	1,806	19,835
Obstetrics and gynaecology	1,123	129	15	35	79	994
Paediatrics	1,457	175	16	42	117	1,282
Paediatric surgery	69	15	3	4	8	54
			Percentage of eligible practitioners in specialty			
All specialties		12.6	1.0	3.6	8.0	87.4
Obstetrics and gynaecology		11.5	1.3	3.1	7.0	88.5
Paediatrics		12.0	1.1	2.9	8.0	88.0
Paediatric surgery		21.7	4.3	5.8	11.6	78.3

Source: *Review Body on Doctors' and Dentists' Remuneration (1998) Twenty-seventh Report 1998.* London: The Stationery Office

This was Table A11.4b in the first edition of *Birth counts*

A11.4.3

Fees paid to general practitioners for maternity medical services, April 1997

Type of service	On the obstetric list*	Not on the obstetric list
	Fee applicable at April 1997, £	
Complete maternity medical services	186.00	108.50
Antenatal care		
women booking up to 16th week of pregnancy	100.40	58.60
women booking from 17th to 30th week of pregnancy	75.35	43.95
women booking after 30th week of pregnancy	50.20	29.30
Miscarriage	62.00	38.75
Care during confinement	42.80	24.80
Complete postnatal care	42.80	30.35
Partial postnatal care		
(i) each attendance,	5.70	4.05
subject to maximum of	28.50	20.25
(ii) full postnatal examination	14.30	10.10
Second practitioner called to give anaesthetic	39.35	39.35

* A practitioner whose experience in obstetrics is, for the time being, approved by the Local Obstetric Committee, or the Secretary of State

Source: Department of Health, Welsh Office. *NHS General Medical Services. Statement of fees and allowances payable to general medical practitioners in England and Wales (The Red Book)*. 1996 Edition, updated to June 1998.

This is a new table for this edition of *Birth counts*

A11.5.1

State maternity benefits awarded, Great Britain, 1983–1998/99

	Awards	Grants*	Maternity payments+	Maternity allowance
	Thousands of awards in year ending 31 March			
1983	653	658	–	330
1984	662	665	–	316
1985	667	670	–	324
1986	694	696	–	349
1987	620	625	–	332
1987/88†	–	–	193	32
1988/89	–	–	162	42
1989/90	–	–	174	40
1990/91	–	–	189	54
1991/92	–	–	230	44
1992/93	–	–	228	37
1993/94	–	–	230	34
1994/95	–	–	220	30
1995/96	–	–	216	44
1996/97	–	–	217	39
1997/98	–	–	197	..
1998/99	–	–	181	..

* A multiple birth gave rise to more than one grant. From April 1987 payment of Maternity Grant is based on needs and any payment is made from the Social Fund.

+ Discretionary payments from the Social Fund to mothers in receipt of Income Support or Family Credit, replaced universal Maternity Grant in April 1987.

† Maternity allowance awards from April 1988 are in respect of women not enitled to statutory maternity pay.

Source: *Social Security Statistics* Tables A5.01, G5.01, *Annual Reports by the Secretary of State for Social Security on the Social Fund Cm748, Cm1157, and Cm1992*

This was Table 11.3a in the first edition of Volume 1 of *Birth counts*

A11.6.1

Rates of maternity benefits, 1981-99

	Maternity grant[3]	Maternity payments[3]	Maternity allowance[1] Personal benefit			Increase for dependent adult			Increase for each child[2]
	£		£ per week Standard[1]	3/4	1/2	Standard[1]	3/4	1/2	
23-Nov-1981	25.00	–	22.50	16.88	11.25	13.90	10.43	6.95	0.80
22-Nov-1982	25.00	–	25.00	18.75	12.50	15.45	11.59	7.73	0.30
21-Nov-1983	25.00	–	25.95	19.46	12.98	16.00	12.00	8.00	0.15
26-Nov-1984	25.00	–	27.25	20.44	13.63	16.80	12.60	8.40	–
25-Nov-1985	25.00	–	29.15	21.86	14.58	18.00	13.50	9.00	–
28-Jul-1986	25.00	·	29.45	22.09	14.73	18.20	13.65	9.10	·
06-Apr-1987	–	80.00	30.05	–	–	18.60	–	–	–
11-Apr-1988	–	85.00	31.30	–	–	19.40	–	–	–
10-Apr-1989	–	85.00	33.20	–	–	20.55	–	–	–
09-Apr-1990	–	100.00	35.70	–	–	22.10	–	–	–
08-Apr-1991	–	100.00	40.60	–	–	24.50	–	–	–
06-Apr-1992	–	100.00	42.25	–	–	25.50	–	–	–
12-Apr-1993	–	100.00	43.75	–	–	26.40	–	–	–
			Higher rate[4]	Lower rate					
16-Oct-1994	–	100.00	52.50	44.55	–	26.90	–	–	–
10-Apr-1995	–	100.00	52.50	45.55	–	27.50	–	–	–
08-Apr-1996	–	100.00	54.55	47.35	–	28.55	–	–	–
07-Apr-1997	–	100.00	55.70	48.35	–	29.15	–	–	–
06-Apr-1998	–	100.00	57.70	47.35	–	30.20	–	–	–
06-Apr-1999	–	100.00	59.55	50.10	–	31.15	–	–	–

1 After December 1986 3/4 and 1/2 rates of maternity allowance ceased to be payable.

2 Child dependency addition was abolished from 26 November 1984

3 Before April 1987 there was also a one-off maternity grant of £25.
From April 1987 payment of maternity grant is based on needs and any payment made is from the Social Fund.

4 The woman must be an employee in the 15th week before the baby is expected the qualifying week

Source: Department of Social Security, *Social Security Statistics, Table G5.03*
This was Table 11.3b in the first edition of Volume 1 of *Birth counts*

A12.1.1

Indicators of maternal health and mortality around the world

Country	Contraceptive prevalence 1990–98	Total fertility rate 1960	Total fertility rate 1980	Total fertility rate 1990	Total fertility rate 1997	Percentage of births attended by trained personnel 1990–97	Maternal deaths per 100,000 live births 1990	Number of maternal deaths 1990	Life time risk of maternal death 1 in:	Category of estimate of maternal death
Afghanistan	2x	6.9	7.1	6.9	6.9	9x	1,700	13,000	7	E
Albania	::	5.9	3.8	3.0	2.6	99x	65	50	430	A
Algeria	57	7.3	6.8	4.6	3.9	77	160	1,200	120	E
Angola	8	6.4	6.9	7.2	6.7	15x	1,500	7,200	8	E
Antigua and Barbuda*	53x	::	::	1.8	1.7	100	::	::	::	B
Argentina	74x	3.1	3.3	2.9	2.6	97	100	690	290	A
Armenia	60	4.5	2.4	2.4	1.7	96	50	40	640	A
Australia	76x	3.3	2.0	1.9	1.9	100	9	25	4,900	A
Austria	71x	2.7	1.6	1.5	1.4	100	10	10	5,600	A
Azerbaijan	::	5.5	3.3	2.7	2.3	99	22	40	1,400	A
Bahamas	62x	3.8	2.8	2.1	2.0	100x	100	5	400	E
Bahrain	62	7.1	4.9	3.7	3.0	98	60	10	360	E
Bangladesh	49	6.7	6.4	4.1	3.2	8	850	33,000	21	E
Barbados	55x	4.5	2.1	1.7	1.7	100	43	5	1,100	E
Belarus	50	2.7	2.1	1.9	1.4	100x	37	50	1,300	A
Belgium	79	2.6	1.6	1.6	1.6	100x	10	10	5,200	A
Belize*	47	6.5	5.8	4.4	3.7	79	::	::	::	::
Benin	37	6.9	7.1	6.6	5.9	60	990	2,300	12	E
Bhutan	19	5.9	5.9	5.9	5.9	15	1,600	980	9	E
Bolivia	45	6.7	5.6	4.9	4.4	47	650	1,600	26	D
Bosnia and Herzegovina*	::	4.0	2.1	1.7	1.4	97	::	::	::	::
Botswana	48	6.8	6.1	5.0	4.5	78x	250	120	65	E
Brazil	77	6.2	4.0	2.7	2.2	92	220	8,400	130	E
Brunei Darussalam	::	6.9	4.1	3.2	2.7	98	60	5	430	B
Bulgaria	76x	2.2	2.1	1.7	1.5	100x	27	30	1,800	A
Burkina Faso	8	6.7	7.8	7.3	6.6	42	930	4,000	14	E
Burundi	9x	6.8	6.8	6.8	6.3	19x	1,300	3,400	9	E
Cambodia	13	6.3	4.6	4.9	4.5	31	900	3,600	17	E
Cameroon	16	5.8	6.4	5.9	5.3	64	550	2,600	26	E
Canada	73x	3.8	1.7	1.7	1.6	99x	6	25	7,700	A

Indicators of maternal health and mortality around the world

Country	Contraceptive prevalence 1990-98	Total fertility rate 1960	Total fertility rate 1980	Total fertility rate 1990	Total fertility rate 1997	Percentage of births attended by trained personnel 1990-97	Maternal deaths per 100,000 live births 1990	Number of maternal deaths 1990	Life time risk of maternal death 1 in:	Category of estimate of maternal death
Cape Verde*	27	7.0	6.5	4.3	3.6	54	..	..	..	..
Central African Rep.	15	5.6	5.8	5.5	5.0	46	700	850	21	E
Chad	4	6.0	5.9	5.9	5.5	15	1,500	3,700	9	E
Chile	43x	5.3	2.8	2.6	2.5	100	65	200	490	B
China	83	5.7	2.9	2.2	1.8	89	95	22,000	400	C
Colombia	72	6.8	3.8	3.0	2.7	85	100	800	300	E
Comoros	21	6.8	7.1	6.3	5.6	52	950	260	12	E
Congo	..	5.9	6.3	6.3	5.9	..	890	..	..	..
Congo, Dem. Rep.	8	6.0	6.6	6.7	6.3	..	870	..	..	..
Cook Islands*	50	..	..	..	..	99	..	..	..	..
Costa Rica	75	7.0	3.7	3.3	3.0	98	55	45	420	B
Cote d'Ivoire	11	7.2	7.4	6.3	5.2	45	810	4,900	14	E
Croatia*	..	2.3	2.0	1.7	1.6	..	..	..	..	..
Cuba	82	4.2	2.0	1.7	1.6	99	95	170	490	B
Cyprus	..	3.5	2.4	2.4	2.3	100x	5	5	6,900	E
Czech Rep.	69	2.3	2.2	1.8	1.4	..	15	20	2,900	A
Denmark	78x	2.6	1.6	1.6	1.8	100x	9	5	5,800	A
Djibouti	..	7.0	6.6	6.0	5.4	79x	570	110	24	E
Dominica*	50x	..	..	2.7	2.3	98	..	..	..	..
Dominican Rep.	64	7.4	4.3	3.3	2.8	96	110	220	230	E
Ecuador	57	6.7	5.1	3.8	3.1	64	150	460	150	E
Egypt	55	7.0	5.2	4.2	3.4	56	170	3,100	120	C
El Salvador	53	6.8	5.1	3.8	3.1	87	300	530	65	D
Equatorial Guinea	..	5.5	5.7	5.9	5.5	58x	820	130	17	E
Eritrea	8	6.6	6.1	5.9	5.4	21	1,400	1,900	10	E
Estonia	70	2.0	2.1	1.9	1.3	..	41	10	1,100	A
Ethiopia	4	6.9	6.9	7.0	7.0	14x	1,400	33,000	9	E
Fiji	32x	6.4	3.9	3.1	2.8	96x	90	15	300	E
Finland	80x	2.7	1.7	1.7	1.8	100	11	5	4,200	A
France	75	2.8	1.9	1.8	1.6	99	15	110	3,100	A

A12.1.1 continued

Indicators of maternal health and mortality around the world

Country	Contraceptive prevalence 1990-98	Total fertility rate				Percentage of births attended by trained personnel 1990-97	Maternal deaths per 100,000 live births 1990	Number of maternal deaths 1990	Life time risk of maternal death 1 in:	Category of estimate of maternal death
		1960	1980	1990	1997					
Gabon	::	4.1	4.4	5.0	5.4	80x	500	210	32	E
Gambia	12	6.4	6.5	5.9	5.2	44	1,100	460	13	E
Georgia	::	2.9	2.3	2.2	1.9	::	33	30	1,100	A
Germany	75	2.4	1.5	1.4	1.3	99	22	190	2,700	A
Ghana	20	6.9	6.5	6.0	5.3	41	740	4,800	18	E
Greece	::	2.2	2.1	1.5	1.4	97x	10	10	5,600	A
Grenada*	54	::	::	::	::	99	::	::	::	::
Guatemala	31	6.9	6.3	5.6	4.9	35	200	730	75	E
Guinea	29	7.0	7.0	7.0	6.6	31	1,600	4,700	7	D
Guinea-Bissau	1x	5.1	5.7	5.8	5.5	27x	910	380	16	C
Guyana*	::	6.5	3.6	2.6	2.3	95	::	::	::	::
Haiti	18	6.3	5.3	4.9	4.6	21	1,000	2,300	17	E
Honduras	50	7.5	6.3	5.1	4.4	61	220	410	75	C
Hong Kong	73x	::	::	1.8	1.4	::	7	5	9,200	A
Hungary	::	2.0	2.0	2.2	2.2	99x	30	35	1,500	A
Iceland	41	4.0	2.3	2.2	2.2	100x	0	0	0	A
India	41	5.9	4.7	3.7	3.1	34	570	147,000	37	E
Indonesia	55	5.5	4.4	3.1	2.7	54	650	31,000	41	E
Iran	73	7.2	6.7	5.7	4.8	86	120	2,700	130	C
Iraq	18x	7.2	6.5	5.9	5.3	54x	310	2,200	46	E
Ireland	::	3.8	3.2	2.1	1.8	::	10	5	3,800	A
Israel	::	3.9	3.3	3.0	2.8	99x	7	5	4,000	A
Italy	78x	2.5	1.7	1.3	1.2	::	12	65	5,300	A
Jamaica	65	5.4	3.8	2.6	2.5	91	120	65	280	C
Japan	59	2.0	1.8	1.6	1.5	100x	18	230	2,900	A
Jordan	53	7.7	7.1	5.8	5.2	97	150	260	95	E
Kazakhstan	59	4.5	3.0	2.8	2.3	100	80	300	370	A
Kenya	33	8.0	7.8	6.1	4.9	45	650	7,000	20	E
Kiribati*	28	::	::	4.0	4.4	72	::	::	::	::
Korea, Dem. People's Rep.	::	5.8	2.8	2.1	2.1	100x	70	370	500	E

Indicators of maternal health and mortality around the world

Country	Contraceptive prevalence 1990–98	Total fertility rate 1960	1980	1990	1997	Percentage of births attended by trained personnel 1990–97	Maternal deaths per 100,000 live births 1990	Number of maternal deaths 1990	Life time risk of maternal death 1 in:	Category of estimate of maternal death
Korea, Rep. of	79	6.0	2.7	1.7	1.7	98	130	900	380	B
Kuwait	35x	7.3	5.4	3.5	2.8	99x	29	15	820	E
Kyrgyzstan	60	5.1	4.1	3.8	3.2	98	110	150	190	A
Lao People's Dem. Rep.	19	6.2	6.7	6.7	6.7	::	650	1,200	19	C
Latvia	::	1.9	2.0	1.9	1.4	::	40	15	1,100	A
Lebanon	63	6.3	4.0	3.3	2.8	98	300	220	85	E
Lesotho	23	5.8	5.7	5.3	4.9	50	610	420	26	E
Liberia	6x	6.6	6.8	6.8	6.4	58x	560	690	22	E
Libya	::	7.1	7.3	6.6	6.0	76x	220	430	55	E
Lithuania	::	2.5	2.1	1.9	1.5	::	36	20	1,200	A
Luxembourg	::	2.3	1.5	1.6	1.8	99x	0	0	0	A
Madagascar	19	6.6	6.6	6.4	5.7	47	490	2,800	27	D
Malawi	22	6.9	7.6	7.3	6.7	55	560	2,700	20	D
Malaysia	48x	6.8	4.2	3.8	3.3	99	80	440	270	B
Maldives*	17	7.0	6.9	6.8	6.8	90				
Mali	7	7.1	7.1	7.1	6.7	25	1,200	5,700	10	E
Malta	::	3.4	2.0	2.1	2.1	::	0	0	0	A
Marshall Islands*	37									
Mauritania	4	6.5	6.3	5.6	5.1	40	930	750	16	E
Mauritius	75	5.8	2.8	2.3	2.3	97	120	25	300	B
Mexico	53x	6.9	4.8	3.4	2.8	91	110	2,700	220	B
Micronesia, Fed. States of*	::			4.8	4.1	90x				
Moldova, Rep. of	::	3.3	2.5	2.4	1.8	::	60	50	580	A
Mongolia	::	6.0	6.2	4.2	3.3	100	65	45	310	B
Morocco	59	7.2	5.5	4.1	3.2	43	610	4,500	33	D
Mozambique	6	6.3	6.5	6.5	6.1	44	1,500	9,800	9	E
Myanmar	33	6.0	5.1	3.9	3.3	56	580	8,100	33	E
Namibia	29	6.0	5.9	5.4	4.9	68	370	190	42	D
Nepal	30	5.8	6.2	5.6	5.0	9	1,500	11,000	10	E
Netherlands	80	3.1	1.5	1.6	1.6	100x	12	25	4,300	A
New Zealand	70x	3.9	2.1	2.1	2.0	99x	25	15	1,600	A

A12.1.1 *continued*

Indicators of maternal health and mortality around the world

Country	Contraceptive prevalence 1990-98	Total fertility rate				Percentage of births attended by trained personnel 1990-97	Maternal deaths per 100,000 live births 1990	Number of maternal deaths 1990	Life time risk of maternal death 1 in:	Category of estimate of maternal death
		1960	1980	1990	1997					
Nicaragua	49	7.3	6.2	4.7	3.9	61	160	250	100	C
Niger	4	7.3	8.1	7.6	7.1	15	1,200	5,100	9	D
Nigeria	6	6.5	6.5	6.5	6.0	31	1,000	44,000	13	E
Niue	..	..	..	..	..	99	..	..	..	..
Norway	76x	2.9	1.8	1.8	1.9	100x	6	5	7,300	A
Oman	40	7.2	7.2	7.2	7.2	93	190	150	60	E
Pakistan	17	6.9	6.8	5.8	5.1	18	340	18,000	38	E
Palau*	38x	..	..	..	..	99	..	..	..	..
Panama	58x	5.9	3.8	3.0	2.7	86	55	35	510	B
Papua New Guinea	26	6.3	5.6	5.1	4.7	53	930	1,200	17	E
Paraguay	51	6.5	5.2	4.7	4.2	61	160	240	120	E
Peru	64	6.9	5.0	3.7	3.0	56	280	1,700	85	E
Philippines	40	6.9	4.9	4.2	3.7	64	280	5,400	75	D
Poland	75x	3.0	2.3	2.0	1.7	99x	19	100	2,200	A
Portugal	66x	3.1	2.2	1.6	1.5	90x	15	20	3,500	A
Qatar*	32x	7.0	5.8	4.4	3.8	98	..	..	..	..
Romania	57	2.3	2.4	1.9	1.4	100x	130	410	340	A
Russian Federation	..	2.6	2.0	1.8	1.4	99	75	1,500	620	A
Rwanda	21	7.5	8.3	6.8	6.1	26	1,300	4,000	9	E
Saint Kitts and Nevis*	41x	..	..	2.7	2.4	100	..	..	..	..
Saint Lucia*	47x	..	..	3.3	2.6	100	..	..	..	..
Saint Vincent/Grenadines*	58x	..	5.9	2.6	2.2	96	..	..	..	..
Samoa	21	8.3	..	4.5	3.8	76	35	5	500	E
Sao Tome and Principe	10x	..	..	5.1	4.7	86x	..	..	..	D
Saudi Arabia	..	7.2	7.3	6.6	5.9	90	130	730	95	E
Senegal	13	7.0	6.9	6.3	5.7	47	1,200	3,900	11	D
Seychelles*	..	..	..	2.8	2.4	99x	..	..	..	..
Sierra Leone	4x	6.2	6.5	6.5	6.1	25x	1,800	3,600	7	E
Singapore	74x	5.5	1.8	1.8	1.8	100x	10	5	4,900	A
Slovakia*	74	3.1	2.4	2.0	1.5	..	..	..	..	..

A12.1.1 continued

Indicators of maternal health and mortality around the world

Country	Contraceptive prevalence 1990–98	Total fertility rate 1960	Total fertility rate 1980	Total fertility rate 1990	Total fertility rate 1997	Percentage of births attended by trained personnel 1990–97	Maternal deaths per 100,000 live births 1990	Number of maternal deaths 1990	Life time risk of maternal death 1 in:	Category of estimate of maternal death
Slovenia	..	2.4	2.1	1.5	1.3	..	13	5	4,000	A
Solomon Islands*	25	6.4	6.7	5.6	5.0	87[x]	..	..	..	..
Somalia	1[x]	7.0	7.0	7.0	7.0	2[x]	1,600	7,000	7	E
South Africa	50[x]	6.5	4.9	4.2	3.8	82	230	2,700	85	E
Spain	59[x]	2.8	2.2	1.4	1.2	96[x]	7	30	9,200	A
Sri Lanka	66	5.3	3.5	2.4	2.1	94	140	520	230	B
Sudan	8	6.7	6.5	5.2	4.6	69	660	6,600	21	E
Suriname*	..	6.6	3.8	2.8	2.4	91[x]	..	..	..	..
Swaziland	21[x]	6.5	6.3	5.1	4.5	56	560	160	29	E
Sweden	78[x]	2.3	1.6	2.0	1.8	100[x]	7	10	6,000	A
Switzerland	71[x]	2.4	1.5	1.5	1.5	99[x]	6	5	8,700	A
Syria	36	7.3	7.4	5.7	4.1	67	180	950	75	C
Tajikistan	..	6.3	5.7	4.9	4.0	79	130	270	120	A
Tanzania	18	6.8	6.8	6.1	5.5	38	..	..	..	..
TFYR Macedonia*	..	4.2	2.6	2.2	1.9	95	..	..	..	..
Thailand	74	6.4	3.6	2.3	1.8	71[x]	200	2,300	180	E
Togo	24	6.6	6.6	6.6	6.1	54[x]	640	1,000	20	E
Tonga*	39			4.2	4.0	92	..	..	..	..
Trinidad and Tobago	53[x]	5.1	3.3	2.5	2.1	98[x]	90	25	360	B
Tunisia	60	7.1	5.3	3.6	3.0	81	170	380	140	E
Turkey	63	6.3	4.3	3.2	2.5	76	180	2,900	130	C
Turkmenistan	..	6.4	5.1	4.3	3.6	96	55	70	350	A
Tuvalu*	..					100	..	..	..	..
Uganda	15	6.9	7.0	7.1	7.1	38	1,200	11,000	10	E
Ukraine	..	2.2	2.0	1.8	1.4	100	50	320	930	A
United Arab Emirates	28	6.9	5.4	4.2	3.5	96[x]	26	10	730	E
United Kingdom	82	2.7	1.8	1.8	1.7	100[x]	9	70	5,100	A
United Rep. of Tanzania	..					..	770	8,700	18	E
United States	74[x]	3.5	1.8	2.0	2.0	99[x]	12	480	3,500	A
Uruguay	84	2.9	2.7	2.4	2.3	96[x]	85	45	410	B

A12.1.1 continued

Indicators of maternal health and mortality around the world

Country	Contraceptive prevalence 1990–98	Total fertility rate				Percentage of births attended by trained personnel 1990–97	Maternal deaths per 100,000 live births 1990	Number of maternal deaths 1990	Life time risk of maternal death 1 in:	Category of estimate of maternal death
		1960	1980	1990	1997					
Uzbekistan	56	6.3	4.9	4.1	3.5	98	55	380	370	A
Vanuatu	15	7.2	5.4	4.8	4.4	87	280	15	60	E
Venezuela	49x	6.6	4.2	3.5	3.0	69x	120	680	200	B
Viet Nam	65	6.1	5.1	3.8	3.0	85	160	3,300	130	E
Yemen	21	7.6	7.6	7.6	7.6	43	1,400	8,100	8	E
Yugoslavia*	..	2.7	2.3	2.1	1.8	93	..	..	..	..
Zaire	..	..	..	..	..	..	870	16,000	14	E
Zambia	26	6.6	7.1	6.2	5.5	47	940	3,500	14	E
Zimbabwe	48	7.5	6.4	5.4	4.7	69	570	2,300	28	E

Definitions:

Contraceptive prevalence rate: Percentage of married women aged 15–49 currently using contraception

Total fertility rate: The number of children that would be born per woman if she was to live to the end of her child-bearing years and bear children at each age in accordance with prevailing age-specific fertility rates.

Births attended: percentage of births attended by physicians, midwives, nurses or primary health care workers trained in midwifery skills.

Maternal deaths: deaths from pregnancy related causes

.. Data not available.

* Only partial data available for some years, so overall estimates were not made

x Indicates data that refer to years or periods other than those specified in the column heading, differ from the standard definition, or refer to only part of a country.

Source: Maternal mortality from WHO/UNICEF *Revised 1990 estimates of maternal mortality*

Other data from UNICEF, *The state of the world's children, 1999*

This is a new table for this edition of *Birth Counts*.

A12.1.2

Childhood mortality and immunisation around the world

Country	Under 5 mortality		Infant mortality rate		Births, thousands	Percentage of one year old children fully immunised, 1995–97			
	1960	1997	1960	1997	1997	TB	DBT	polio	measles
Afghanistan	360	257	215	165	1,201	66	45	45	58
Albania	151	40	112	34	74	94	99	99	95
Algeria	255	39	152	34	869	94	79	79	74
Andorra	..	6	..	5	1	..	90	90	90
Angola	345	292	208	170	556	68	41	38	78
Antigua and Barbuda	..	21	..	17	1	..	100	100	93
Argentina	72	24	60	21	712	100	86	92	92
Armenia	48	30	38	25	48	72	89	95	92
Australia	24	6	20	5	262	..	86	..	87
Austria	43	5	37	5	84	..	90	95	90
Azerbaijan	75	45	55	34	149	94	95	98	97
Bahamas	68	21	51	18	5	..	86	86	93
Bahrain	203	22	130	18	12	..	98	98	95
Bangladesh	247	109	151	81	3,282	91	68	68	62
Barbados	90	12	74	11	3	..	96	96	92
Belarus	47	18	37	14	103	98	47	47	74
Belgium	35	7	31	6	114	..	62	72	64
Belize	104	43	74	35	7	95	86	85	98
Benin	300	167	176	102	241	89	78	78	82
Bhutan	300	121	175	87	78	92	87	87	84
Bolivia	255	96	152	69	260	93	82	82	98
Bosnia and Herzegovina	155	16	105	14	42	97	79	80	85
Botswana	170	49	117	39	53	59	76	80	79
Brazil	177	44	115	37	3,200	100	71	84	100
Brunei Darussalam	87	10	63	8	6	99	99	99	98
Bulgaria	70	19	49	16	86	97	94	96	93
Burkina Faso	315	169	181	110	511	46	28	28	33
Burundi	255	176	151	106	274	71	60	60	50
Cambodia	217	167	146	106	359	82	70	70	68
Cameroon	255	99	151	64	550	53	44	47	43
Canada	33	7	28	6	355	..	93x	89x	98x
Cape Verde	164	73	110	54	13	80	78	77	82
Central African Rep.	327	173	187	113	129	94	53	51	46
Chad	325	198	195	118	280	36	16	15	17
Chile	138	13	107	11	293	98	91	91	92
China	209	47	140	38	20,481	96	96	97	96
Colombia	130	30	82	25	873	98	84	85	76
Comoros	265	93	200	69	26	55	48	48	49
Congo	220	108	143	81	117	29	23	21	18
Congo, Dem. Rep.	302	207	175	128	2,167	91	71	73	63
Cook Islands	..	30	..	26	0*	84	91	91	86

Childhood mortality and immunisation around the world

Country	Under 5 mortality		Infant mortality rate		Births, thousands	Percentage of one year old children fully immunised, 1995–97			
	1960	1997	1960	1997	1997	TB	DBT	polio	measles
Costa Rica	112	14	80	12	86	91	91	93	99
Cote d'Ivoire	300	150	195	90	533	73	70	70	68
Croatia	98	9	70	8	48	98	92	92	91
Cuba	54	8	39	7	146	99	100	97	100
Cyprus	36	9	30	8	12	..	98	98	90
Czech Rep.	25	7	22	6	109	97	98	97	97
Denmark	25	6	22	6	68	..	89x	100x	84
Djibouti	289	156	186	111	24	58	49	49	47
Dominica	..	20	..	17	2	100	100	100	100
Dominican Rep.	149	53	102	44	197	88	80	79	80
Ecuador	180	39	115	30	309	100	76	77	75
Egypt	282	73	189	54	1,697	98	94	94	92
El Salvador	210	36	130	31	167	93	97	96	97
Equatorial Guinea	316	172	188	109	17	99	81	81	82
Eritrea	250	116	170	73	137	67	60	60	53
Estonia	52	14	40	13	13	99	85	86	88
Ethiopia	280	175	175	111	2,936	90	63	64	52
Fiji	97	24	71	20	18	95	86	88	75
Finland	28	4	22	4	61	100	100	100	98
France	34	5	29	5	684	83	96	97	97
Gabon	287	145	171	85	43	72	54	54	32
Gambia	364	87	207	66	46	99	96	98	91
Georgia	70	29	52	23	75	76	92	98	95
Germany	40	5	34	5	769	..	45	80	75
Ghana	215	107	127	68	705	72	60	61	59
Greece	64	8	53	7	104	70	85	95	90
Grenada	..	29	..	24	2	..	95	95	92
Guatemala	202	55	136	43	412	87	83	83	74
Guinea	380	201	215	126	365	69	53	53	56
Guinea-Bissau	336	220	200	130	45	82	63	60	51
Guyana	126	82	100	59	18	94	88	89	82
Haiti	253	132	169	92	253	40	35	32	30
Holy See	..	..	..	..	..	..	..	..	..
Honduras	204	45	137	36	202	98	94	93	89
Hungary	57	11	51	10	101	100	100	100	100
Iceland	22	5	17	5	4	98	98x	99	98
India	236	108	144	71	24,389	96	90	91	81
Indonesia	216	68	128	45	4,756	100	91	90	92
Iran	233	35	145	32	2,455	99	97	97	96
Iraq	171	122	117	94	781	97	92	92	98
Ireland	36	7	31	6	46	..	..	63x	..
Israel	39	6	32	6	117	..	92	93	94

Childhood mortality and immunisation around the world

Country	Under 5 mortality		Infant mortality rate		Births, thousands	Percentage of one year old children fully immunised, 1995–97			
	1960	1997	1960	1997	1997	TB	DBT	polio	measles
Italy	50	6	44	5	523	..	92	93	94
Jamaica	76	11	58	10	55	97	90	90	88
Japan	40	6	31	4	1,299	91	100x	98	94
Jordan	139	24	97	20	217	24	96	96	90
Kazakhstan	74	44	55	37	308	99	97	100	92
Kenya	205	87	122	57	1,054	42	36	36	32
Kiribati	..	75	..	55	2	100	91	93	82
Korea, Dem. People's Rep.	120	30	85	23	495	99	100	100	100
Korea, Rep. of	127	6	90	6	689	90	80	81	85
Kuwait	128	13	89	12	38	..	96	100	95
Kyrgyzstan	115	48	80	38	115	99	95	95	85
Lao People's Dem. Rep.	235	122	155	99	233	58	60	69	67
Latvia	44	20	35	16	24	100	75	76	97
Lebanon	85	37	65	30	76	..	92	92	89
Lesotho	203	137	137	95	75	46	50	48	43
Liberia	288	235	190	157	124	38	26	25	28
Libya	270	25	159	22	232	99	96	96	92
Liechtenstein	..	7	..	6	0*	..	..	..	..
Lithuania	70	15	52	13	39	98	90	95	96
Luxembourg	41	7	33	5	5	58	94	98	91
Madagascar	364	158	219	96	656	64	46	45	39
Malawi	361	215	205	135	488	100	95	94	87
Malaysia	105	11	73	10	536	100	91	90	89
Maldives	258	74	158	53	11	99	97	97	96
Mali	517	239	293	145	548	76	74	52	56
Malta	42	10	37	9	5	96	84	92	51
Marshall Islands	..	92	..	63	2	94	78	71	52
Mauritania	310	183	180	120	92	69	28	28	20
Mauritius	92	23	67	20	22	84	87	87	84
Mexico	134	35	94	29	2,345	99	95	95	91
Micronesia, Fed. States of	..	24	..	20	4	48	75	75	74
Moldova, Rep. of	88	31	64	25	59	99	97	98	99
Monaco	..	5	..	5	0*	90	99	99	98x
Mongolia	185	150	128	105	72	96	92	92	91
Morocco	220	72	135	58	707	94	95	95	92
Mozambique	280	208	163	130	777	79	59	55	57
Myanmar	252	114	169	81	1,285	94	90	90	88
Namibia	206	75	129	58	58	65	65	65	58
Nauru	..	30	..	25	0*	78	50	36	100
Nepal	297	104	199	75	826	96	78	78	85

Childhood mortality and immunisation around the world

Country	Under 5 mortality		Infant mortality rate		Births, thousands	Percentage of one year old children fully immunised, 1995–97			
	1960	1997	1960	1997	1997	TB	DBT	polio	measles
Netherlands	22	6	18	5	187	..	95	95	96
New Zealand	26	7	22	7	56	20x	86	100	100
Nicaragua	209	57	140	42	147	100	94	100	94
Niger	320	320	191	191	496	44	28	28	42
Nigeria	207	187	123	112	5,039	29	21	25	38
Niue	..	..	..	..	0*	100	100	100	100
Norway	23	4	19	4	58	..	92x	92x	93x
Oman	280	18	164	15	106	96	99	99	98
Pakistan	226	136	139	95	5,250	90	74	74	74
Palau	..	34	..	28	1	0	91	90	83
Panama	104	20	67	18	61	99	95	99	92
Papua New Guinea	204	112	137	79	146	68	45	35	41
Paraguay	90	33	66	27	160	87	82	82	61
Peru	234	56	142	44	613	98	98	97	94
Philippines	110	41	80	32	2,029	82	70	67	72
Poland	70	11	62	10	456	94	95	95	91
Portugal	112	8	81	7	110	91	95	99	94
Qatar	239	20	145	16	10	99	92	92	87
Romania	82	26	69	22	249	100	97	97	97
Russian Federation	65	25	48	20	1,416	99	96	98	91
Rwanda	210	170	124	105	267	79	77	77	66
Saint Kitts and Nevis	..	37	..	30	1	99	100	100	97
Saint Lucia	..	29	..	24	3	100	98	98	95
Saint Vincent/ Grenadines	..	21	..	18	2	98	100	100	100
Samoa	210	52	134	41	4	99	99	99	99
San Marino	..	6	..	5	0*	97x	98x	100x	96x
Sao Tome and Principe	..	78	..	61	6	70	73	73	60
Saudi Arabia	292	28	170	24	675	99	92	92	87
Senegal	300	124	173	72	362	80	65	65	65
Seychelles	..	18	..	14	3	100	98	98	100
Sierra Leone	390	316	220	182	208	38	26	28	26
Singapore	40	4	31	4	55	98	93	94	89
Slovakia	40	11	33	10	62	90	98	98	98
Slovenia	45	6	37	5	18	98	91	98x	92
Solomon Islands	185	28	120	23	14	73	72	70	68
Somalia	294	211	175	125	519	37	19	19	25
South Africa	126	65	89	49	1,295	95	73	73	76
Spain	57	5	46	5	386	..	88	90	90x
Sri Lanka	133	19	83	17	324	96	97	98	94
Sudan	210	115	125	73	944	79	75	75	71
Suriname	96	30	70	24	9	..	85	81	78

Childhood mortality and immunisation around the world

Country	Under 5 mortality		Infant mortality rate		Births, thousands	Percentage of one year old children fully immunised, 1995–97			
	1960	1997	1960	1997	1997	TB	DBT	polio	measles
Swaziland	233	94	157	66	33	85	82	81	82
Sweden	20	4	16	4	105	12	99	99	96
Switzerland	27	5	22	5	79	..	..	..	..
Syria	201	33	136	27	457	100	95	95	93
Tajikistan	140	76	95	56	185	99	95	92	95
Tanzania	240	143	142	92	1,303	82	74	73	69
TFYR Macedonia	177	23	120	20	31	97	97	97	98
Thailand	148	38	103	31	995	98	94	94	91
Togo	267	125	158	78	181	53	33	33	38
Tonga	..	23	..	19	2	100	95	95	97
Trinidad and Tobago	73	17	61	15	21	..	90	91	88
Tunisia	254	33	170	27	225	93	96	96	92
Turkey	219	45	163	40	1,390	73	79	79	76
Turkmenistan	150	78	100	57	122	97	98	99	100
Tuvalu	..	56	..	40	0*	100	77	78	100
Uganda	224	137	133	86	1,070	84	58	59	60
Ukraine	53	24	41	18	495	95	96	97	97
United Arab Emirates	223	10	149	9	43	98	94	94	35
United Kingdom	27	7	23	6	693	99	95	96	95
United States	30	8	26	7	3,757	..	94x	84x	89x
Uruguay	56	21	48	18	54	99	88	88	80
Uzbekistan	122	60	84	46	674	97	96	97	88
Vanuatu	225	50	141	39	5	60	66	62	59
Venezuela	75	25	56	21	571	89	60	76	68
Viet Nam	219	43	147	32	1,952	96	95	95	96
Yemen	340	100	230	76	784	54	40	46	43
Yugoslavia	120	21	87	18	130	87	94	95	94
Zambia	213	202	126	112	361	81	70	70	69
Zimbabwe	159	80	97	53	437	82	78	79	73

Definitions:

Under five mortality rate: Probability of dying between birth and exactly five years of age expressed per 1,000 live births

Infant mortality rate: Probability of dying between birth and exactly one year of age expressed per 1,000 live births

x Indicates data that refer to years or periods other than those specified in the column heading, differ from the standard definition, or refer to only part of a country.

* Less than 1,000 live births

Source: UNICEF, *The state of the world's children, 1999*

This is a new table for this edition of *Birth Counts*.

A12.2.1

Infant mortality in developed countries, 1951–55 to 1986–90 and 1991 to 1996

Years	1951–55	1956–60	1961–65	1966–70	1971–75	1976–80	1981–85	1986–90
All causes, deaths per 1,000 live births								
Albania								30.0
Australia	23.3	21.1	19.4	18.0	16.2	12.1	9.8	8.4
Austria	..	41.0	30.9	26.3	23.9	15.8	12.0	8.9
Belgium	41.1	33.6	26.4	22.4	18.2	13.3	10.6	8.9
Bulgaria	..	..	31.9	30.2	25.1	21.9	17.0	14.4
Canada	34.8	29.7	25.9	20.8	15.8	11.7	8.7	7.3
Croatia	..	..	..	..	..	..	..	13.1
Czechoslovakia, Former	38.9	29.0	22.9	22.8	21.1	19.2	15.6	12.2
Czechoslovakia, Republic	..	..	..	..	..	..	..	11.2
Denmark	27.4	22.9	19.6	15.7	11.7	9.0	7.9	7.8
Finland	31.6	24.6	18.8	14.4	11.3	8.2	6.3	5.9
France	39.8	27.2	20.4	16.7	13.2	10.9	9.0	7.7
Germany	..	..	..	..	..	..	..	..
Germany, former Democratic Republic	..	..	..	..	15.8	13.0	10.8	8.2
Germany, former Federal Republic	44.6	35.7	27.4	23.3	22.2	14.7	10.3	7.7
Greece	..		37.9	32.9	25.3	19.8	14.9	10.9
Hungary		56.3	42.7	36.5	33.8	25.7	20.1	16.6
Ireland	40.2	33.1	27.6	22.1	17.9	13.9	9.9	8.4
Israel	..	..	..	..	..	17.4	13.4	10.5
Italy	58.4	47.2	38.9	32.2	25.0	16.9	12.1	9.1
Japan	48.5	35.9	23.2	15.2	11.3	8.4	6.3	4.8
Macedonia	..	..	..	..	..	..	..	..
Netherlands	22.2	17.3	15.2	13.5	11.5	9.4	8.3	7.2
New Zealand	26.0	23.5	20.3	17.6	16.0	13.6	11.8	10.2
Norway	22.6	19.9	17.1	13.9	11.6	9.0	8.1	7.9
Poland	..	64.3	49.6	35.5	26.3	22.6	19.5	16.7
Portugal	..	85.1	75.0	59.9	42.7	29.9	19.2	13.3
Romania	..	76.4	56.4	51.9	38.0	30.5	26.0	26.2
Slovenia	..	..	..	..	..	..	..	10.0
Spain	53.6	42.4	32.3	25.4	16.6	14.8	10.8	8.3
Sweden	19.3	16.9	14.8	12.2	10.0	7.7	6.8	5.9
Switzerland	28.5	22.8	19.9	16.2	12.9	9.3	7.4	6.9
United Kingdom	28.0	23.4	21.3	18.9	17.1	13.3	10.3	8.8
USA	27.5	26.4	25.1	21.8	17.7	13.7	11.2	9.9
Yugoslavia, former	..	..	78.3	59.2	43.8	34.1	29.5	23.9

Year	1991	1992	1993	1994	1995	1996		
All causes, deaths per 1,000 live births								
Albania	..	33.8	32.9	..	..	..		
Australia	7.0	6.9	6.0	5.9	5.6			
Austria	7.5	7.5	6.5	6.3	5.4	5.1		
Belgium	8.3	8.2	..	..	..	..		
Bulgaria	16.9	15.9	15.5	16.3	..	..		
Canada	6.4	6.1	6.3	6.3	6.1	..		
Croatia	11.1	11.6	9.9	10.2	..	..		
Czechoslovakia, Former	11.5	..	..	..	..	..		
Czechoslovakia, Republic	10.4	9.9	8.5	..	..	..		
Denmark	7.2	6.5	5.4	..	..	..		

657

Infant mortality in developed countries, 1951–55 to 1986–90 and 1991 to 1996

Year	1991	1992	1993	1994	1995	1996
Finland	5.9	5.2	4.4	4.6	4.0	..
France	7.3	6.8	6.5	5.9	..	..
Germany	6.9	6.2	5.8	5.6	5.3	5.0
Germany, former Democratic Republic	..	..	..	..	..	..
Germany, former Federal Republic	..	..	..	..	..	..
Greece	9.0	8.4	8.5	7.9	8.1	..
Hungary	15.6	14.1	12.5	11.5	10.7	..
Ireland	7.6	6.5	6.1	5.7	..	..
Israel	9.2	9.4	7.8	7.5	6.8	..
Italy	8.2	7.9	7.1	..	..	..
Japan	4.4	4.5	4.3	4.2	..	..
Macedonia	28.3	30.6	24.1	22.5	22.7	16.4
Netherlands	6.5	6.3	6.3	5.7	5.5	..
New Zealand	8.4	7.3	7.3	5.5	..	..
Norway	6.4	5.9	5.1	5.2	..	..
Poland	15.0	14.5	13.4	15.1	13.6	12.2
Portugal	10.8	9.3	8.7	8.1	7.5	6.9
Romania	22.7	23.3	23.3	23.9	21.2	22.3
Slovenia	8.2	8.8	6.8	6.5	5.6	4.7
Spain	7.2	7.1	6.7	6.0	..	..
Sweden	6.1	5.2	4.8	4.3	4.0	..
Switzerland	6.2	6.4	5.6	5.1	..	..
United Kingdom	7.4	6.6	6.3	6.2	6.2	..
USA	8.9	8.5	8.4	8.0	7.6	..
Yugoslavia, former	..	..	..	..	..	..

Years	1951–55	1956–60	1961–65	1966–70	1971–75	1976–80	1981–85	1986–90
	Congenital malformations,* deaths per 1,000 live births							
Albania	..	..	..	..	..	..	..	1.3
Australia	3.9	3.9	3.7	3.3	3.4	3.2	2.9	2.2
Austria		4.6	4.3	4.3	3.9	3.8	2.9	3.0
Belgium	4.7	5.0	4.6	4.7	4.1	3.4	2.9	2.3
Bulgaria	..	..	2.5	2.6	2.9	3.1	3.7	3.7
Canada	5.2	4.7	4.5	4.0	3.5	3.1	3.3	2.8
Croatia	..	..	..	..	..	..	..	2.8
Czechoslovakia, Former	4.1	4.3	4.4	4.3	3.9	4.1	4.0	3.2
Czechoslovakia, Republic	..	..	..	..	..	..	..	3.1
Denmark	4.4	4.4	4.2	3.6	3.1	2.9	2.6	2.4
Finland	3.8	4.4	3.8	3.0	3.0	2.7	2.5	2.1
France	3.4	3.7	3.6	3.3	2.7	2.3	2.0	1.6
Germany		..	..	..	..	..	..	..
Germany, former Democratic Republic	..	..	..	..	3.2	2.8	2.4	2.1
Germany, former Federal Republic	5.0	4.9	4.5	4.0	4.2	3.4	2.7	2.1
Greece			3.3	4.1	4.5	4.5	4.6	3.7
Hungary		6.4	6.5	6.1	5.5	5.1	4.5	3.7
Ireland	6.2	6.7	7.0	5.8	5.1	4.5	3.4	2.6
Israel	..	..	..	..	..	4.5	3.3	2.9
Italy	4.0	3.7	3.6	3.4	3.5	3.2	2.8	2.3
Japan	2.1	1.9	2.0	2.1	2.2	2.1	1.8	1.7

A12.2.1 *continued*

Infant mortality in developed countries, 1951–55 to 1986–90 and 1991 to 1996

Years	1951–55	1956–60	1961–65	1966–70	1971–75	1976–80	1981–85	1986–90
	Congenital malformations,* deaths per thousand live births							
Macedonia	..	..	..	..	..	..	..	..
Netherlands	5.0	4.5	4.0	3.6	3.0	2.9	2.7	2.4
New Zealand	3.9	3.9	3.7	3.6	3.5	3.3	2.8	2.5
Norway	3.3	3.4	3.4	2.8	2.8	2.6	2.6	2.2
Poland	..	4.6	4.6	4.6	4.8	5.0	4.8	4.5
Portugal	..	2.2	2.5	2.8	3.5	3.9	3.6	3.1
Romania	..	3.7	3.2	3.4	3.4	4.0	4.3	4.9
Slovenia	..	..	..	..	..	..	..	2.8
Spain	1.7	1.6	1.9	2.0	2.8	3.5	2.9	2.4
Sweden	3.5	3.4	3.3	3.0	3.0	2.8	2.5	2.1
Switzerland	4.5	4.2	4.1	3.6	3.5	3.2	2.6	2.5
United Kingdom	4.6	4.7	4.4	3.9	3.9	3.4	2.8	1.9
USA	3.9	3.7	3.6	3.2	2.8	2.6	2.4	2.1
Yugoslavia, former	..	..	1.7	2.2	2.4	2.5	2.9	2.7

Year	1991	1992	1993	1994	1995	1996
	Congenital malformations,* deaths per thousand live births					
Albania	..	1.9	1.6	..	..	..
Australia	1.8	1.9	1.7	1.7	1.5	..
Austria	2.8	2.4	2.0	2.7	2.6	2.3
Belgium	2.2	1.9	..	..	..	..
Bulgaria	4.2	4.1	4.6	4.9	..	..
Canada	2.5	2.7	2.5	2.8	2.5	..
Croatia	2.5	2.6	2.6	2.4	..	..
Czechoslovakia, Former	2.9	..	..	..	..	..
Czechoslovakia, Republic	2.6	2.4	2.3	..	..	..
Denmark	2.0	2.3	2.2	..	..	..
Finland	2.1	1.9	1.6	1.7	1.5	..
France	1.4	1.2	1.4	1.3	..	..
Germany	1.9	2.0	1.9	1.7	1.5	1.5
Germany, former Democratic Republic	..	..	..	..	..	..
Germany, former Federal Republic	..	..	..	..	..	..
Greece	4.5	4.8	3.4	3.2	3.0	..
Hungary	3.6	3.2	3.0	2.9	2.6	..
Ireland	3.3	2.6	2.7	2.4	..	..
Israel	2.7	2.1	2.5	2.4	2.0	..
Italy	2.0	2.2	1.9	..	..	..
Japan	1.6	1.7	1.5	1.5	..	..
Macedonia	2.6	2.7	2.4	2.2	2.0	2.0
Netherlands	2.3	2.4	2.3	2.1	1.9	..
New Zealand	2.3	2.2	2.1	1.4	..	..
Norway	1.7	1.8	1.8	1.6	..	..
Poland	4.2	4.4	4.0	4.0	3.9	3.6
Portugal	2.7	2.6	2.6	2.6	2.2	2.0
Romania	3.7	3.9	3.9	3.9	3.8	4.1
Slovenia	2.5	3.2	2.6	2.1	1.8	1.8
Spain	2.3	2.3	2.3	2.2	..	..
Sweden	2.2	1.8	1.7	1.7	1.6	..

A12.2.1 *continued*

Infant mortality in developed countries, 1951–55 to 1986–90 and 1991 to 1996

Year	1991	1992	1993	1994	1995	1996
Congenital malformations,* deaths per 1,000 live births						
Switzerland	2.1	2.3	1.9	1.9	..	..
United Kingdom	1.5	1.6	1.3	1.2	1.2	..
USA	1.9	1.8	1.8	1.7	1.7	..
Yugoslavia, former	..	..	..	..	..	..

Years	1951–55	1956–60	1961–65	1966–70	1971–75	1976–80	1981–85	1986–90
Other causes, deaths per 1,000 live births								
Albania	..	..	..	..	..	..	..	28.7
Australia	19.5	17.2	15.7	14.7	12.8	8.9	6.9	6.2
Austria	..	36.5	26.5	22.0	20.0	12.0	9.1	5.8
Belgium	36.4	28.6	21.7	17.7	14.1	9.9	7.7	6.6
Bulgaria	..	..	29.4	27.5	22.2	18.8	13.3	10.7
Canada	29.6	25.0	21.4	16.8	12.3	8.6	5.4	4.5
Croatia	..	..	..	..	..	..	..	10.3
Czechoslovakia, Former	34.8	24.7	18.5	18.5	17.3	15.1	11.6	8.9
Czechoslovakia, Republic	..	..	..	..	..	..	..	8.1
Denmark	23.0	18.6	15.5	12.1	8.5	6.1	5.3	5.4
Finland	27.7	20.2	15.0	11.4	8.3	5.5	3.8	3.8
France	36.4	23.5	16.9	13.4	10.5	8.6	7.0	6.1
Germany	..	..	..	..	..	..	..	..
Germany, former Democratic Republic	..	..	..	..	12.6	10.2	8.5	6.2
Germany, former Federal Republic	39.7	30.8	22.9	19.3	18.1	11.3	7.6	5.7
Greece	..	..	34.6	28.8	20.8	15.2	10.3	7.2
Hungary	..	50.0	36.2	30.4	28.4	20.5	15.7	12.9
Ireland	34.0	26.4	20.6	16.2	12.8	9.4	6.6	5.7
Israel	..	..	..	..	..	13.0	10.1	7.6
Italy	54.4	43.5	35.3	28.8	21.6	13.7	9.3	6.8
Japan	46.4	34.0	21.2	13.1	9.1	6.3	4.5	3.2
Macedonia	..	..	..	..	..	..	..	..
Netherlands	17.2	12.8	11.1	9.9	8.5	6.5	5.6	4.8
New Zealand	22.1	19.6	16.6	14.0	12.5	10.3	9.0	7.7
Norway	19.3	16.5	13.8	11.1	8.8	6.4	5.5	5.7
Poland	..	59.7	45.0	30.9	21.5	17.6	14.7	12.1
Portugal	..	82.9	72.5	57.1	39.2	26.0	15.6	10.3
Romania	..	72.7	53.2	48.6	34.6	26.6	21.7	21.3
Slovenia	..	..	..	..	..	..	..	7.3
Spain	51.9	40.8	30.4	23.4	13.8	11.3	7.8	5.9
Sweden	15.8	13.5	11.5	9.2	7.0	4.9	4.3	3.8
Switzerland	24.0	18.6	15.8	12.7	9.4	6.2	4.8	4.5
United Kingdom	23.3	18.7	16.8	14.9	13.2	9.9	7.5	6.9
USA	23.6	22.7	21.5	18.6	14.8	11.2	8.8	7.8
Yugoslavia, former	..	..	..	..	..	..	..	..

Year	1991	1992	1993	1994	1995	1996
Other causes, deaths per 1,000 live births						
Albania	..	31.9	31.3	..	..	..
Australia	5.2	5.0	4.3	4.2	4.1	
Austria	4.6	5.2	4.5	3.6	2.9	2.8
Belgium	6.1	6.3	..	..	..	..
Bulgaria	12.8	11.8	11.0	11.5	..	..
Canada	3.9	3.4	3.8	3.5	3.6	..
Croatia	8.6	9.0	7.3	7.8	..	..

A12.2.1 *continued*

Infant mortality in developed countries, 1951–55 to 1986–90 and 1991 to 1996

Year	1991	1992	1993	1994	1995	1996
Other causes, deaths per 1,000 live births						
Czechoslovakia, Former	8.6	..	..	..	..	..
Czechoslovakia, Republic	7.7	7.5	6.2	..	..	..
Denmark	5.3	4.2	3.2	..	..	..
Finland	3.7	3.3	2.8	2.9	2.5	..
France	5.9	5.6	5.1	4.6	..	..
Germany	5.0	4.2	4.0	3.9	3.8	3.5
Germany, former Democratic Republic	..	..	..	..	..	..
Germany, former Federal Republic	..	..	..	..	..	..
Greece	4.6	3.6	5.1	4.8	5.1	..
Hungary	12.0	10.9	9.4	8.6	8.1	..
Ireland	4.3	3.9	3.4	3.4	..	..
Israel	6.5	7.3	5.3	5.1	4.8	..
Italy	6.2	5.7	5.1	..	..	..
Japan	2.8	2.8	2.8	2.8	..	..
Macedonia	25.7	27.9	21.7	20.3	20.7	14.4
Netherlands	4.2	3.9	4.0	3.5	3.6	..
New Zealand	6.0	5.1	5.3	4.2	..	..
Norway	4.6	4.0	3.3	3.6	..	..
Poland	10.7	10.1	9.4	11.2	9.7	8.6
Portugal	8.1	6.7	6.2	5.5	5.3	4.9
Romania	19.1	19.4	19.4	20.0	17.5	18.2
Slovenia	5.7	5.6	4.2	4.4	3.8	2.9
Spain	4.9	4.7	4.4	3.9	..	..
Sweden	3.9	3.4	3.1	2.7	2.5	..
Switzerland	4.1	4.1	3.7	3.2	..	..
United Kingdom	5.8	5.0	5.1	5.0	5.0	..
USA	7.1	6.7	6.6	6.3	5.9	..
Yugoslavia, former	..	..	..	..	..	..

* ICD 750–759, A127–129 or B41, seventh revision
 ICD 740–759, A126–130, or B42, eighth revision
 ICD 740–759, 440–447, or 44, ninth revision

Source: Derived from data from the World Health Organisation

This is similar to Table A12.1 in the first edition of *Birth Counts*.

Infant mortality in countries of the former Soviet Union, 1981–85, 1986–90 and 1991 to 1996

Year	1981–85	1986–90	1991	1992	1993	1994	1995	1996
All causes, deaths per 1,000 live births								
Armenia	24.1	22.1	18.0	18.9	..	..	..	..
Belarus	15.6	12.8	12.4	12.7	..	..	..	..
Estonia	16.1	14.3	13.4	15.8	15.8	14.5	14.8	..
Georgia	26.2	21.6	..	..	..	..	..	..
Kazakstan	31.7	28.1	27.6	26.3	28.8	27.4	27.9	..
Kyrgyzstan	40.2	35.0	29.7	31.6	32.9	29.6	27.7	..
Latvia	14.3	12.0	15.7	17.5	16.6	15.7	18.8	..
Lithuania	15.2	11.3	14.3	16.5	16.0	14.1	12.5	10.1
Republic of Moldova	32.6	23.3	19.3	18.3	21.8	22.9	21.5	..
Russian Federation	20.7	18.7	18.1	18.4	20.7	18.8	18.2	
Tajikistan	51.3	45.3	40.4	48.1	..	..	..	..
Turkmenistan	52.8	53.4	46.9	43.2	44.2	42.9	..	..
Ukraine	16.1	14.0	14.0	14.1	..	..	..	..
Uzbekistan	43.1	41.5	35.1	37.6	32.8	..	..	..
Former Soviet Union	25.6	24.1	..	..	..	..	..	..
Congenital malformations,* deaths per 1,000 live births								
Armenia	3.0	2.7	2.8	2.4	..	..	..	..
Belarus	3.8	3.9	4.0	3.8	..	..	..	..
Estonia	3.8	3.3	3.5	2.8	4.1	2.8	2.7	..
Georgia	1.7	1.4	..	..	..	..	..	..
Kazakstan	2.2	3.2	3.4	3.2	3.7	3.5	3.7	..
Kyrgyzstan	2.0	2.0	1.9	1.9	1.8	1.4	1.2	..
Latvia	4.2	3.8	4.0	4.2	4.6	3.8	5.1	..
Lithuania	5.6	4.3	4.5	4.6	5.1	4.0	4.2	3.3
Republic of Moldova	4.4	4.7	4.3	4.2	4.8	4.6	4.6	..
Russian Federation	3.5	3.8	3.9	3.9	4.2	4.1	4.2	..
Tajikistan	1.5	1.3	1.9	1.6	..	..	..	..
Turkmenistan	2.1	2.6	2.6	1.7	1.8	1.3	..	..
Ukraine	4.1	3.9	3.9	3.8	..	..	..	..
Uzbekistan	2.2	2.2	2.1	1.7	1.5	..	..	..
Former Soviet Union	3.2	3.3	..	..	..	..	..	..
Other causes, deaths per 1,000 live births								
Armenia	21.2	19.4	15.3	16.6	..	..	..	..
Belarus	11.8	8.9	8.3	8.8	..	..	..	..
Estonia	12.3	11.1	9.9	13.0	11.7	11.7	12.2	..
Georgia	24.5	20.1	..	..	..	..	..	..
Kazakstan	29.5	24.9	24.2	23.1	25.1	24.0	24.1	..
Kyrgyzstan	38.2	33.0	27.9	29.7	31.1	28.2	26.5	..
Latvia	10.1	8.2	11.8	13.3	12.1	11.9	13.8	..
Lithuania	9.6	7.0	9.9	11.9	10.9	10.1	8.3	6.7

A12.2.2 *continued*

Infant mortality in countries of the former Soviet Union, 1981–85, 1986–90 and 1991 to 1996

Year	1981–85	1986–90	1991	1992	1993	1994	1995	1996
Other causes, deaths per 1,000 live births								
Republic of Moldova	28.2	18.6	15.0	14.1	17.0	18.3	16.9	..
Russian Federation	17.2	14.9	14.2	14.5	16.5	14.7	14.0	..
Tajikistan	49.7	44.0	38.5	46.5	..	..	..	..
Turkmenistan	50.7	50.8	44.3	41.5	42.4	41.6	..	..
Ukraine	11.9	10.0	10.1	10.3	..	..	..	..
Uzbekistan	40.9	39.3	33.0	35.9	31.3	..	..	..
Former Soviet Union	22.4	20.8	..	..	..	..	..	..

* ICD 750–759, A127–129 or B41, seventh revision
ICD 740–759, A126–130, or B42, eighth revision
ICD 740–759, 440–447, or 44, ninth revision

Source: Derived from data from the World Health Organisation

This is similar to Table A12.1 in the first edition of *Birth Counts*.

A12.3.1

Stillbirth rates in Europe, 1901–90

Years	1901–05	1906–10	1911–15	1916–20	1921–25	1926–30	1931–35	1936–40	1941–45	1946–50	1951–55	1956–60	1961–65	1966–70	1971–75	1976–80	1981–85	1986–90
Stillbirths per 1,000 total births																		
Denmark	23.73	23.33	23.42	24.71	24.05	23.30	24.67	25.55	20.72	17.89	18.38	15.05	11.45	8.83	7.17	5.61	4.88	4.83
Finland	24.99	24.43	25.28	25.50	26.48	26.45	26.41	23.00	21.00	18.36	18.03	16.65	12.86	9.81	7.33	4.81	3.97	4.48
Iceland	30.87	30.10	31.09	29.02	24.62	25.55	20.95	20.84	22.70	17.64	15.71	13.19	13.75	11.32	8.84	5.56	3.70	3.16
Norway	23.92	22.51	22.25	22.03	21.28	24.73	24.89	22.57	20.17	17.53	15.25	14.26	12.39	11.14	9.04	7.23	5.70	4.42
Sweden	..	..	..	23.31	24.52	26.12	27.14	27.94	23.13	20.48	17.82	15.31	11.64	8.99	6.85	4.91	3.94	3.79
Austria	26.58	25.29	25.13	30.80	24.80	29.16	27.39	26.43	21.03	21.06	18.87	16.25	12.88	10.70	9.00	7.02	4.97	3.78
Belgium+	36.27	36.10	35.80	38.70	38.75	33.57	32.48	29.72	25.09	25.03	19.52	15.84	14.18	12.24	10.56	8.36	6.87	5.85
England and Wales	..	..	..	..	..	39.79	40.97	38.47	30.47	24.03	22.95	21.44	17.27	14.15	11.56	8.51	5.95	4.89
France+	45.19	44.81	43.82	42.90	33.02	28.86	32.58	33.58	27.37	20.44	18.01	17.06	15.80	14.21	11.99	9.49	7.72	6.44
Federal Republic of Germany*	30.67	29.58	29.54	30.68	32.18	31.42	27.80	23.82	..	21.80	21.08	16.79	13.24	10.89	8.89	6.21	4.62	3.70
Ireland Rep.	..	..	..	..	..	..	..	..	..	..	..	21.39	18.45	14.93	12.32	9.93	8.28	6.88
Luxemburg	28.94	28.68	32.64	35.01	33.45	33.75	35.44	28.16	24.26	24.77	17.27	15.72	16.82	13.49	8.87	6.66	5.82	4.46
Netherlands+	40.81	39.52	37.74	30.36	26.45	25.04	25.09	24.95	19.29	19.51	17.68	16.22	14.05	11.59	9.05	7.27	5.92	5.65
Northern Ireland	..	..	..	..	..	..	..	..	..	..	..	..	20.61	15.88	13.90	9.86	7.06	4.99
Scotland	..	..	..	..	..	..	..	42.18	35.72	29.22	25.49	22.85	19.11	14.98	12.28	7.98	5.83	5.31
Switzerland	34.91	32.90	30.82	28.80	27.60	24.35	22.47	21.04	16.76	16.40	15.12	12.63	11.33	9.61	7.83	5.92	4.81	4.16
Greece	..	..	..	..	11.93	9.41	10.37	9.64	..	10.02	11.05	13.19	14.72	14.35	12.42	10.39	8.89	..
Italy	42.87	42.95	40.76	43.42	43.10	36.41	33.76	31.44	28.66	31.50	29.79	26.00	21.67	17.20	13.00	9.32	7.23	5.93
Portugal	15.55	15.23	33.46	40.94	42.39	40.17	42.33	44.06	43.97	41.84	39.24	34.70	30.35	28.63	18.73	14.01	12.11	9.67
Spain~	24.95	24.26	24.99	26.71	27.58	30.76	32.04	30.18	26.03	25.89	28.68	28.21	24.29	19.37	14.71	9.32	6.68	4.88
Bulgaria	5.60	6.97	5.82	4.74	5.43	6.50	8.62	11.53	11.84	11.21	..	12.08	10.90	9.70	8.87	7.53	7.05	6.03
Czechoslovakia	29.04	27.97	27.53	22.57	23.63	20.86	20.75	23.97	16.33	16.46	13.83	10.95	8.90	7.58	6.74	6.25	5.25	4.52

A12.3.1 continued

Stillbirth rates in Europe, 1901–90

Stillbirths per 1,000 total births

Years	1901–05	1906–10	1911–15	1916–20	1921–25	1926–30	1931–35	1936–40	1941–45	1946–50	1951–55	1956–60	1961–65	1966–70	1971–75	1976–80	1981–85	1986–90
Democratic Republic of Germany*	30.67	29.58	29.54	30.68	32.18	31.42	27.80	23.82	..	23.72	20.02	16.49	14.05	11.35	8.85	7.08	5.80	4.74
Hungary	19.67	19.42	20.33	23.15	26.72	28.33	28.24	27.58	23.18	23.71	17.22	14.37	11.91	10.18	8.98	8.17	7.08	6.06
Poland	..	..	..	..	..	..	..	..	18.19	14.95	12.78	11.33	10.53	8.52	7.00	6.08	5.53
Romania	18.60	23.51	26.44	16.94	15.16	18.18	19.86	23.71	24.40	25.78	19.83	16.93	15.28	15.54	11.00	9.34	8.34	..
Yugoslavia	..	..	..	13.37	11.83	10.41	10.57	11.03	..	12.54	11.06	10.40	10.11	9.59	8.12	7.24	6.49	5.87

* Before 1945, the figures for the ex-Federal Republic of Germany and the ex-Democratic Republic both refer to the former Germany. See additional notes in article.

+ An undefined amount of early neonatal deaths, whose birth was registered after death, the so-called 'présentés sans vie' were counted as stillbirths in France for the years 1900–1919 and 1932–1945, in Belguim for the years 1914–1918 and in the Netherlands before 1918.

~ Before 1975, infant deaths occuring within 24 hours were counted as stillbirths and thus not included in the live birth and infant death figures.

Figures in italics do not cover the entire five-year periods.

Source: Vital registration. These data were used for Annex 2 in Masuy-Stroobant G. Santé et mortalité infantile en Europe. Victoires d'hier et enjeux de demain. In Masuy Stroobant G, Gourbin C, Buekens P, eds. *Santé et mortalité des enfants en Europe. Inégalités sociales d'hier et d'aujourdhui, Chaire Quetelet 1994.* Louvain-la-Neuve. Academia/L'Harmattan: 1996, 337–366.

This is a new table for this edition of *Birth Counts*.

A 12.3.2

Infant mortality in Europe, 1901–90

Years	1901–05	1906–10	1911–15	1916–20	1921–25	1926–30	1931–35	1936–40	1941–45	1946–50	1951–55	1956–60	1961–65	1966–70	1971–75	1976–80	1981–85	1986–90
	Deaths per 1,000 live births																	
Denmark	119.33	108.11	97.20	91.02	81.86	82.32	71.35	59.97	48.35	40.18	27.40	22.40	19.64	15.70	11.67	8.99	7.90	7.88
Finland	131.04	117.00	109.98	113.94	95.61	87.90	72.20	71.75	61.40	51.85	32.35	24.59	18.84	14.39	11.16	8.38	6.29	5.95
Iceland	101.10	118.69	74.39	68.53	52.42	53.26	51.14	36.15	37.65	24.40	21.45	16.44	17.24	13.17	11.57	8.25	6.23	6.02
Norway	79.87	69.31	66.20	61.92	51.69	49.49	44.91	39.38	37.24	31.08	22.64	19.85	17.13	13.91	11.63	9.04	8.07	7.89
Sweden	91.02	78.13	72.20	66.24	59.91	57.56	50.08	41.88	31.01	23.95	19.31	16.86	14.77	12.27	10.02	7.71	6.80	5.92
Austria	215.93	201.50	190.74	153.12	138.29	117.21	99.03	80.68	91.67	75.61	51.33	41.04	30.87	26.30	23.91	15.81	12.00	8.86
Belgium+	154.12	147.89	139.21	119.28	106.15	101.24	88.57	84.91	86.45	62.77	43.72	33.57	26.37	22.38	18.17	13.30	10.60	8.93
England and Wales	134.95	117.08	109.56	89.94	76.05	67.88	62.17	55.37	49.50	36.33	26.91	22.64	20.61	18.45	16.80	13.18	10.17	8.81
France+	138.86	126.22	124.19	119.78	100.34	94.28	74.33	70.11	81.86	62.10	45.11	31.62	24.40	20.14	15.49	10.90	8.99	7.72
Federal Republic of Germany*	199.07	174.20	155.18	129.38	119.25	92.55	73.04	66.43	..	70.82	48.53	36.21	27.48	23.25	22.06	14.74	10.30	7.93
Ireland Rep.	..	..	..	..	..	67.95	67.59	69.23	75.17	56.65	40.23	33.07	27.60	22.06	17.86	13.90	9.91	8.41
Luxembourg	158.83	156.14	146.16	127.76	110.30	107.57	85.55	71.19	87.38	57.80	43.04	35.76	27.93	21.41	16.16	12.67	11.61	8.62
Netherlands+	136.40	114.19	99.26	89.65	69.59	56.36	44.53	37.25	50.17	31.36	23.73	18.61	15.80	13.53	11.51	9.42	8.23	7.19
Northern Ireland	..	..	..	..	81.03	78.84	78.35	77.17	73.30	47.80	36.59	28.25	26.62	24.06	21.14	15.85	11.79	8.46
Scotland	119.95	112.42	112.75	99.03	91.75	85.45	80.75	75.80	67.71	47.31	32.93	27.93	25.02	21.17	18.81	13.69	10.46	8.39
Switzerland	134.24	115.06	99.32	82.41	65.11	54.01	48.37	44.97	40.44	36.03	28.53	22.82	19.85	16.25	12.89	9.34	7.37	6.94
Greece	..	..	..	..	87.79	95.97	120.76	113.45	..	38.55	42.51	40.53	37.93	32.88	25.25	19.71	14.87	10.80
Italy	167.41	152.14	139.89	149.55	122.66	119.41	104.73	103.01	110.10	76.55	58.44	47.23	38.88	32.24	25.23	17.10	12.31	9.21
Portugal	142.72	149.06	152.10	170.57	146.31	145.11	145.68	134.98	129.88	107.05	90.99	85.14	74.95	59.87	42.67	28.84	19.16	13.33
Spain~	172.39	158.94	152.45	161.44	142.67	123.97	112.20	119.27	109.25	76.96	60.33	49.33	41.40	32.42	21.88	15.13	10.75	8.32
Bulgaria	147.62	160.23	143.86	133.40	155.94	147.08	147.10	142.76	130.45	114.73	91.12	58.46	34.89	29.72	25.13	21.24	16.92	14.68
Czechoslovakia	225.34	205.30	191.27	161.45	155.65	138.56	119.07	127.02	..	83.22	49.45	28.98	22.89	22.81	21.13	19.15	15.65	12.16

Infant mortality in Europe, 1901–90

Years	1901– 05	1906– 10	1911– 15	1916– 20	1921– 25	1926– 30	1931– 35	1936– 40	1941– 45	1946– 50	1951– 55	1956– 60	1961– 65	1966– 70	1971– 75	1976– 80	1981– 85	1986– 90
Deaths per 1,000 live births																		
Democratic Republic of Germany*	199.07	174.20	155.18	129.38	119.25	92.55	73.04	66.43	..	93.90	55.25	43.08	30.02	20.72	16.69	12.99	10.83	8.43
Hungary	213.31	205.80	207.46	205.54	187.29	172.17	156.74	134.42	126.08	98.27	68.63	56.34	42.74	36.50	33.83	25.68	20.14	16.56
Poland	..	..	..	..	..	..	..	..	..	*108.03*	92.36	69.88	49.57	35.54	26.32	22.63	19.55	16.68
Romania	*202.53*	*172.66*	*193.07*	*212.92*	*232.21*	*195.82*	*182.47*	*177.78*	*156.69*	150.25	96.92	77.52	56.40	51.95	37.95	30.71	26.06	..
Yugoslavia	..	..	..	..	*144.15*	*151.18*	*153.32*	*137.40*	..	110.26	114.50	93.22	78.31	59.18	43.69	34.09	29.53	23.90

* Before 1945, the figures for the ex-Federal Republic of Germany and the ex-Democratic Republic both refer to the former Germany. See additional notes in article.

+ An undefined amount of early neonatal deaths, whose birth was registered after death, the so-called 'présentés sans vie' could not be included in the live births neither in the infant deaths. This was the case for Belgium for the years 1914–1918; for the Netherlands before 1918 and for France for the years 1900–1919 and 1932–1945.

~ Before 1975, infant deaths occuring within 24 hours were counted as stillbirths and thus not included in the live birth and infant death figures.

Figures in italics do not cover the entire five-year period.

Source: Vital registration. These data were used for Annex 1 in Masuy-Stroobant G. Santé et mortalité infantile en Europe. Victoires d'hier et enjeux de demain. In Masuy Stroobant G, Gourbin C, Buekens P, eds. *Santé et mortalité des enfants en Europe. Inégalités sociales d'hier et d'aujourdhui, Chaire Quetelet 1994*. Louvain-la-Neuve, Academia/L'Harmattan: 1996, 337–366.

This is a new table for this edition of *Birth Counts*.

Stillbirth and infant mortality rates in Europe as presented by Eurostat, 1960–98

	EUR 15	Belgium	Denmark	Germany	Greece	Spain	France	Ireland	Italy	Luxembourg	Netherlands	Austria	Portugal	Finland	Sweden	UK	Iceland	Liechtenstein	Norway	EEA	Switzerland
Numbers																					
Stillbirths																					
1960	115,249	2,380	958	19,814	2,274	18,548	14,155	1,361	22,844	82	3,618	1,916	5,822	1,259	1,418	18,800	63	4	873	116,185	1,089
1965	99,876	2,131	942	16,566	2,384	14,977	13,319	1,072	19,998	92	3,262	1,565	4,990	974	1,268	16,336	71	2	727	100,674	1,181
1970	74,410	1,616	604	10,852	1,922	11,847	11,469	904	14,109	43	2,588	1,141	3,826	519	926	12,044	40	0	697	75,147	886
1975	48,776	1,227	483	6,120	1,701	7,584	8,225	774	9,271	29	1,374	791	2,781	378	603	7,435	33	0	458	49,267	566
1980	35,023	990	253	4,954	1,368	4,460	6,942	681	5,453	23	1,205	602	1,886	268	436	5,502	21	0	363	35,407	361
1985	26,263	714	240	3,601	950	2,907	5,658	516	3,871	22	1,054	407	1,503	243	388	4,189	9	0	267	26,539	345
1990	21,312	682	298	3,202	735	1,617	4,488	321	3,103	21	1,139	325	1,008	209	443	3,721	13	0	266	21,591	390
1991	20,138	620	296	2,741	706	1,564	4,364	301	2,740	27	1,067	321	967	219	464	3,746	13	:	284	20,435	357
1992	18,935	651	339	2,660	629	1,602	4,055	285	2,425	24	1,114	339	835	196	396	3,385	16	:	259	19,210	337
1993	18,718p	584p	308	2,467	679	1,439	3,566	291	2,307	22	1,071	317	700	173	400	4,391	9	:	253	18,980p	348
1994	18,780p	465p	309	3,113	599	1,387	3,354	298	2,092	20	1,055	307	642	165	348	4,348	15	:	276	19,071p	286
1995	18,923p	553p	318	3,405	645	1,254	3,859	315	1,945	24	1,104	389	587	188	350	4,144	8	:	236	19,167p	336
1996	:	:	324	3,573	589	1,422	3,689	:	2,127p	16	961	399	594	162	:	4,075	20	:	276	:	309
1997	:	:		3,510	628	:	:	:	:	28	985	363	506	221	314	:	:	:	:	:	336
Neonatal deaths																					
1960	117,209e	3,153	1,226	29,253	3,063	13,363	14,479	1,236	21,798	96	3,220	3,094	5,978	1,183	1,367*	14,700	45	:	723	117,977*	1,515
1965	106,674e	2,494	1,265	23,225e	3,000	13,488	13,186	1,092	22,311	86	2,795	2,613	5,338	1,059	1,322*	13,400	50	:	792	107,516*	1,544
1970	87,134	2,022	777	17,979	2,845	11,548	10,741	821	18,551	74	2,258	2,142	4,393	676	1,007	11,300	41	:	612	87,787	1,077
1975	59,925	1,404	576	10,446	2,556	8,413	6,815	803	13,329	38	1,354	1,449	3,962	514	666	7,600	39	:	413	60,377	581
1980	38,398	938	318	6,976	2,052	4,854	4,603	498	5,800	22	1,025	851	2,447	323	482	5,800	27	:	259	38,684	433
1985	25,600	662	254	4,345	1,229	2,705	3,533	328	4,758	12	888	618	1,586	273	409	4,000	14	:	238	25,852	334
1990	19,896	520	289	3,377	666	1,997	2,708	255	3,598	21	953	401	815	245	435	3,616	19	0	239	20,154	318
1991	18,957	544	271	2,901	627	1,809	2,660	263	3,545	25	907	415	805	276	444	3,465	13	0	222	19,192	312
1992	18,033	523	276	2,746	589	1,830	2,464	219	3,349	21	863	444	692	248	406	3,363	17	0	228	18,278	342
1993	:	:	238	2,499	624	1,589	2,240	198	2,939	18	873	348	633	195	370	3,182	13	0	206	:	290
1994	:	:	276	2,480	581	1,431	2,251	193	:	18	786	357	526	227	335	3,094	5	:	224	:	271
1995	:	:	261	2,433	587	1,285	2,112	227	2,410	19	732	298	508	166	297	:	19	:	161	:	281
1996	:	:	266	2,388	526	1,266	2,912	197p	:	:	796	306	464	179	242	2,970	13	:	152	:	262
1997	:	:	276	2,350	503	:	:	196	:	12	705	265	462	164	214	:	:	:	:	:	272

A12.4.1 continued

Stillbirth and infant mortality rates in Europe as presented by Eurostat, 1960–98

	EUR 15	Bel-gium	Den-mark	Germany	Greece	Spain	France	Ireland	Italy	Luxem-bourg	Nether-lands	Austria	Portugal	Finland	Sweden	UK	Iceland	Liecht-enstein	Nor-way	EEA	Switz-erland
Numbers																					
Infant deaths																					
1960	199,773	4,824	1,636	44,105	6,300	28,826	22,484	1,777	39,950	158	4,286	4,727	16,576	1,725	1,699	20,700	64	8	1,167	201,004	1,993
1965	167,739	3,684	1,606	31,907	5,194	25,470	18,990	1,604	35,677	127	3,541	3,673	13,656	1,371	1,639	19,600	71	9	1,113	168,923	1,996
1970	128,623	2,999	1,005	23,547	4,290	18,595	15,437	1,255	26,639	110	3,045	2,908	10,027	854	1,212	16,700	53	5	823	129,499	1,495
1975	86,087	1,932	746	14,760	3,409	12,641	10,277	1,176	17,526	59	1,894	1,926	6,991	656	894	11,200	55	2	625	86,767	843
1980	57,642	1,510	484	10,779	2,658	7,048	8,010	821	9,320	48	1,557	1,303	3,852	481	671	9,100	35	3	411	58,088	667
1985	40,546	1,120	427	7,419	1,647	4,071	6,389	551	6,090	37	1,430	977	2,327	395	666	7,000	22	4	434	41,002	515
1990	33,373	985	473	6,385	993	3,050	5,599	434	4,654	36	1,397	709	1,279	368	739	6,272	28	0	428	33,829	574
1991	31,772	1,062	471	5,711	927	2,846	5,511	400	4,571	46	1,291	708	1,259	383	761	5,825	25	0	387	32,184	537
1992	29,401	1,194	444	4,992	871	2,798	5,075	331	4,489	44	1,235	718	1,068	344	657	5,141	22	4	353	29,776	557
1993	26,807	962p	367	4,665	864	2,581	4,604	302	3,905	32	1,227	618	996	287	571	4,826	22	2	305	27,134	465
1994	24,663p	887p	380	4,309	823	2,239	4,193	285	3,498p	29	1,104	578	881	308	499	4,649	14	0	312	24,988p	424
1995	22,596p	700p	353	4,053	827	1,987p	3,550p	309	3,243p	30	1,041	481	805	248	429	4,526	26	3	244	22,852p	415
1996	22,026p	652p	376	3,962	730	2,008	3,501	280p	3,109	28	1,086	451	683	242	377	4,466	16	..	246	22,291p	389
1997	21,354p	705p	356	3,951	657	2,038p	3,500p	324p	2,894p	23	968	398	727	232	328	4,253	23	..	247	21,624p	387
1998	..	642p	..	3,650e	688e	2,079	3,540p	330	2,820p	27	1,035	400	758	239	316	4,035	11p	..	232p	..	340p
Rates																					
Late fetal mortality rate																					
1960	19.5	15.1	12.4	15.5	14.3	27.3	17.0	21.9	24.5	16.1	14.9	15.0	26.5	15.1	13.7*	20.1	12.7	10.4	13.9	19.5*	11.4
1965	16.1	13.5	10.9	12.3	15.5	21.8	15.2	16.6	19.8	17.1	13.1	11.9	23.2	12.4	10.2	16.1	14.8	5.0	10.9	16.1*	10.4
1970	13.4	11.2	8.5	10.3	13.1	17.6	13.3	13.8	15.4	9.7	10.7	10.1	20.7	8.0	8.3	13.1	9.8	–	10.7	13.3*	8.9
1975	10.2	10.1	6.7	7.8	11.8	11.2	10.9	11.4	11.1	7.2	7.7	8.4	15.2	5.7	5.8	10.5	7.5	–	8.1	10.1	7.2
1980	7.5	7.9	4.4	5.7	9.2	7.8	8.6	9.1	8.4	5.5	6.6	6.6	11.8	4.2	4.5	7.2	4.6	–	7.1	7.5	4.9
1985	6.1	6.2	4.4	4.4	8.1	6.3	7.3	8.2	6.7	5.3	5.9	4.6	11.4	3.9	3.9	5.5	2.3	–	5.2	6.1	4.6
1990	4.8	5.5	4.7	3.5	7.1	4.0	5.9	6.0	5.4	4.2	5.7	3.6	8.6	3.2	3.6	4.6	2.7	–	4.3	4.8	4.6
1991	4.7	4.9	4.6	3.3	6.8	3.9	5.7	5.7	5.4	5.4	5.3	3.4	8.2	3.3	3.7	4.7	2.9	..	4.6	4.7	4.1
1992	4.4	5.2	5.0	3.3	6.0	4.0	5.4	5.5	4.8	4.6	5.6	3.5	7.2	2.9	3.2	4.3	3.5	..	4.3	4.4	3.9
1993	4.5p	4.8p	4.6	3.1	6.6	3.7	5.0	5.9	4.3	4.1	5.4	3.3	6.1	2.7	3.4	5.7	1.9	..	4.2	4.5p	4.1
1994	4.6p	4.0p	4.4	4.0	5.7	3.7	5.1	6.1	4.2	3.7	5.4	3.3	5.8	2.5	3.1	5.8	3.4	..	4.6	4.6p	3.4
1995	4.7p	4.8p	4.5	4.4	6.3	3.4	5.3	6.4	3.9	4.4	4.9	4.4	5.4	3.0	3.4	5.6	1.9	..	3.9	4.7p	4.1
1996	..	..	4.8	4.5	5.8	3.9	5.0	..	3.7	2.8	5.0	4.5	5.4	2.7	..	5.5	4.6	..	4.5	..	3.7
1997	..	..	..	4.3	6.1	..	..	..	4.0p	5.1	5.1	4.3	4.5	3.7	3.5	..	..	..	..	..	4.2

A12.4.1 continued

Stillbirth and infant mortality rates in Europe as presented by Eurostat, 1960–98

	EUR 15	Belgium	Denmark	Germany	Greece	Spain	France	Ireland	Italy	Luxembourg	Netherlands	Austria	Portugal	Finland	Sweden	UK	Iceland	Liechtenstein	Norway	EEA	Switzerland
Rates																					
Neonatal deaths per 1,000 live births																					
1960	20.3e	20.4	16.1	23.2	19.5	20.2	17.7	20.4	23.9	19.1	13.5	24.6	27.9	14.4	16.0	13.4*	9.2	::	11.7	20.2*	16.1
1965	17.5e	16.0	14.7	17.5e	19.8	20.0	15.3	17.2	22.5	16.3	11.4	20.1	25.4	13.6	13.4	10.8*	10.6	::	11.9	17.4*	13.8
1970	15.9	14.2	11.0	17.2	19.6	17.5	12.7	12.8	20.6	16.8	9.5	19.1	24.3	10.5	12.5	9.1	10.2	::	9.5	15.8	10.9
1975	12.6	11.7	11.7	13.4	18.0	12.6	9.1	12.0	16.1	9.5	7.6	15.5	22.1	7.8	10.9	6.4	8.9	::	7.3	12.6	7.4
1980	8.3	7.5	5.6	8.1	13.9	8.5	5.8	6.7	11.3	5.3	5.7	9.4	15.5	5.1	7.7	5.0	6.0	::	5.1	8.3	5.9
1985	6.0	5.8	4.7	5.3	10.6	5.9	4.6	5.3	8.2	2.9	5.0	7.1	12.2	4.3	5.3	4.2	3.6	::	4.7	6.0	4.5
1990	4.5	4.2	4.6	3.7	6.5	5.0	3.6	4.8	6.3	4.3	4.8	4.4	7.0	3.7	3.5	4.5	4.0	–	3.9	4.5	3.8
1991	4.4	4.3	4.2	3.5	6.1	4.6	3.5	5.0	6.3	5.0	4.6	4.4	6.9	4.2	3.6	4.4	2.9	–	3.7	4.4	3.6
1992	4.2	4.2	4.1	3.4	5.7	4.6	3.3	4.3	5.9	4.1	4.4	4.7	6.0	3.7	3.3	4.3	3.7	–	3.8	4.2	3.9
1993	::	::	3.5	3.1	6.1	4.1	3.1	4.0	5.3	3.4	4.5	3.7	5.6	3.0	3.1	4.2	2.8	::	3.5	::	3.5
1994	::	::	4.0	3.2	5.6	3.9	3.2	4.0	::	3.3	4.0	3.9	4.8	3.5	3.0	4.1	1.1	::	3.7	::	3.3
1995	::	::	3.7	3.2	5.8	3.5	::	4.7	4.6	3.5	3.8	3.4	4.7	2.6	2.9	::	4.4	::	2.7	::	3.4
1996	::	::	3.9	3.0	5.2	3.5	4.0	3.9p	::	::	4.2	3.4	4.2	2.9	2.5	4.0	3.0	::	2.5	::	3.2
1997	::	::	4.1	2.9	4.9	::	::	3.7	::	2.2	3.7	3.2	4.1	2.8	2.4	::	::	::	::	::	3.4
Infant deaths per 1,000 live births																					
1960	34.5	31.2	21.5	35.0	40.1	43.7	27.5	29.3	43.9	31.5	17.9	37.5	77.5	21.0	16.6	22.5	13.0	21.1	18.9	34.4	21.1
1965	27.5	23.7	18.7	24.1	34.3	37.8	22.0	25.2	36.0	24.0	14.4	28.3	64.9	17.6	13.3	19.7	15.0	22.8	16.8	27.4	17.8
1970	23.4	21.1	14.2	23.5	29.6	28.1	18.2	19.5	29.6	24.9	12.7	25.9	55.5	13.2	11.0	18.5	13.2	11.8	12.7	23.3	15.1
1975	18.1	16.1	10.4	18.9	24.0	18.9	13.8	17.5	21.2	14.8	10.6	20.5	38.9	10.0	8.6	16.1	12.5	6.5	11.1	18.0	10.7
1980	12.4	12.1	8.4	12.4	17.9	12.3	10.0	11.1	14.6	11.5	8.6	14.3	24.3	7.6	6.9	12.1	7.7	7.6	8.1	12.4	9.1
1985	9.5	9.8	7.9	9.1	14.1	8.9	8.3	8.8	10.5	9.0	8.0	11.2	17.8	6.3	6.8	9.3	5.7	10.7	8.5	9.5	6.9
1990	7.6	8.0	7.5	7.0	9.7	7.6	7.3	8.2	8.2	7.3	7.1	7.8	11.0	5.6	6.0	7.9	5.9	–	7.0	7.6	6.8
1991	7.4	8.4	7.3	6.9	9.0	7.2	7.3	7.6	8.1	9.2	6.5	7.5	10.8	5.9	6.2	7.4	5.5	–	6.4	7.4	6.2
1992	6.9	9.6	6.6	6.2	8.4	7.1	6.8	6.5	7.9	8.5	6.3	7.5	9.3	5.2	5.3	6.6	4.8	10.7	5.9	6.9	6.4
1993	6.5p	8.0	5.4	5.8	8.5	6.7	6.5	6.1	7.1	6.0	6.3	6.5	8.7	4.4	4.8	6.3	4.8	–	5.1	6.5p	5.6
1994	6.1p	7.7	5.5	5.6	7.9	6.0	5.9	5.9	6.6p	5.3	5.6	6.3	8.1	4.7	4.4	6.2	3.4	5.6	5.2	6.1p	5.1
1995	5.6p	6.1	5.1	5.3	8.1	5.5p	4.9p	6.4	6.2p	5.5	5.5	5.4	7.5	3.9	4.1	6.2	6.1	–	4.0	5.6p	5.0
1996	5.5p	5.6p	5.6	5.0	7.2	5.5	4.8	5.6p	5.9	4.9	5.7	5.1	6.9	4.0	4.0	6.1	3.7	7.4	4.0	5.4p	5.0
1997	5.3p	6.1p	5.3	4.9	6.4	5.6p	4.8p	6.2p	5.5p	4.2	5.0	4.7	6.4	3.9	3.6	5.9	5.5	::	4.1	5.3p	4.7
1998	5.2	5.6p	::	4.7e	6.8e	5.7	4.8p	6.2	5.5p	5.0	5.2	4.9	6.0	4.2	3.5	5.6	2.6p	::	4.0p	5.2	4.4p

p Provisional   e Estimated

Source: Eurostat, Luxembourg, 1999. Produced by r-cade, University of Durham, United Kingdom. Extraction date 1/12/99

This is a new table for this edition of *Birth Counts*.

A12.5.1

Incidence of low birthweight and early neonatal mortality in Europe, 1980, 1985 and 1990

Country	Low birthweight			Early neonatal mortality		
	1980	1985	1990	1980	1985	1990
	Percentage of live births weighing under 2,500g			Early neonatal deaths per 1,000 live births		
Denmark *	5.97	6.20	5.48	..	39	53~
Finland *	..	..	3.66	..	..	41
Norway *	3.84	4.38	4.62	66	60	51
Sweden *	4.15#	4.40	4.53>	45#	44	..
Austria	..	5.78	5.60	..	68	42
Belgium	5.46	5.87	6.12	73	52	38
England-Wales	6.23	6.80	6.54	49^	43	34~
F.R. Germany	5.50	5.72	5.74~	79	47	35~
Ireland Rep. *	..	4.01	4.16	..	74	61
Scotland *	..	..	6.65	..	40+	36
Switzerland	5.11	5.08$	5.11	..	..	..
Italy	5.14	5.25	..	..	91	..
Portugal	4.64	5.32	5.61	..	..	..
Czechoslovakia	5.93	5.69	5.59	..	92$	77
Hungary	10.35	9.94	9.27	120	105	75
Poland	7.58	7.78	8.05	99	96	80
Poland with unviables	7.97	8.12	8.37	147	137	118

^ Figure for 1981
# Figure for 1982
$ Figure for 1986
+ Figure for 1987
> Figure for 1988
~ Figure for 1989
* Data from medical birth registers.

Source: Vital registration and medical birth registers. These data come from Masuy-Stroobant G. Santé et mortalité infantile en Europe. Victoires d'hier et enjeux de demain. In Masuy Stroobant G, Gourbin C, Buekens P, eds. *Santé et mortalité des enfants en Europe. Inégalités sociales d'hier et d'aujourdhui, Chaire Quetelet 1994.* Louvain-la-Neuve, Academia/L'Harmattan: 1996

This is similar to Table A12.2 in the first edition of *Birth Counts*.

A12.5.2

Incidence of very low birthweight and early neonatal mortality in Europe, 1980, 1985 and 1990

Country	Very low birthweight			Early neonatal mortality		
	1980	1985	1990	1980	1985	1990
	Percentage of live births weighing under 1,500g			**Early neonatal deaths per 1,000 live births**		
Denmark *	0.72	0.80	0.81	..	213	261~
Finland *	..	..	0.63	..	..	175
Norway *	0.59	0.77	0.87	310	253	210
Sweden *	0.59#	0.62	0.69>	202#	190	191>
Austria	..	0.82	0.77	..	338	189
Belgium	0.54	0.71	0.68	401	245	..
England-Wales	0.74^	0.90	0.95~	269^	231	183~
Ireland Republic *	..	0.52	0.61	..	388	297
Scotland *	..	0.90+	0.92	..	217+	189
Switzerland	0.53	0.58	0.65	..	..	..
Italy	0.57	0.64	..	..	457	..
Portugal	0.46	0.57	0.63	..	..	..
Czechoslovakia	0.76	0.66	0.71	..	424$	378
Hungary	1.53	1.51	1.29	567	505	398
Poland	0.85	0.90	0.98	..	399	337
Poland with 'unviables'	1.27	1.27	1.33	..	574	510

^ Figure for 1981
# Figure for 1982
$ Figure for 1986
+ Figure for 1987
> Figure for 1988
~ Figure for 1989
* Data from medical birth registers.

Source: Vital registration and medical birth registers. These data come from Masuy-Stroobant G. Santé et mortalité infantile en Europe. Victoires d'hier et enjeux de demain. In Masuy Stroobant G, Gourbin C, Buekens P, eds. *Santé et mortalité des enfants en Europe. Inégalités sociales d'hier et d'aujourdhui, Chaire Quetelet 1994.* Louvain-la-Neuve, Academia/L'Harmattan: 1996

This is similar to Table A12.2 in the first edition of *Birth Counts*.

A12.6.1

Incidence of triplet and higher order deliveries in Europe, 1960–90

Country	1960	1965	1970	1975	1980	1985	1990
Rates per 10,000 deliveries							
Denmark	1.05	1.44	0.99	2.09	1.05	1.31	2.87
Finland	0.61	1.54	1.71	1.38	1.60	2.25	3.84
Norway	1.29	1.51	0.93	0.53	0.79	1.77	3.81
Sweden	0.39	1.28	0.64	0.77	1.04	0.82	2.71
Austria	0.95	0.61	0.71	0.85	0.88	2.49	1.89
Belgium	0.50	1.09	0.84	1.00	1.69	2.47	5.79
England and Wales	0.97	0.91	1.29	1.35	1.50	1.65	3.06
France	0.94	0.82	0.95	1.26	1.88	2.46	4.33
Federal Republic of Germany~	0.93	0.93	1.04	1.02	1.31	2.31	3.41
Ireland	..	..	..	..	1.62	1.12	1.52
Netherlands	1.04	0.81	0.75	1.58	1.38	1.78	6.01
Northern Ireland	0.95	0.88	0.62	0.00	1.40	1.09	1.90
Scotland	1.56	1.32	1.03	0.44	0.58	1.36	2.64
Switzerland*	1.31	0.98	1.01	1.49	2.32	3.55	3.72
Greece	1.46	1.18	1.24	1.47	0.81	..	..
Italy	1.21	0.98	1.04	0.71	1.33	1.53	3.78
Portugal	1.60	1.26	1.25	0.88	1.01	1.15	1.81
Spain	0.83	0.84	0.89	1.00	1.09	1.16	2.28
Bulgaria+	0.57	0.32	0.43	0.69	0.70	0.47	1.14
Czechoslovakia	0.55	0.74	1.05	0.94	0.97	1.07	1.15
Democratic Republic of Germany	0.75	0.85	0.84	0.61	0.90	1.13	..
Hungary	1.29	1.13	1.12	0.88	1.42	2.16	2.32
Poland	1.13	0.88	0.73	0.60	0.56	0.74	0.96

* 1961 instead of 1960

+ 1986 instead of 1985

~ 1989 instead of 1990.

Source: Vital registration. This was Table 3 in Masuy-Stroobant G. Santé et mortalité infantile en Europe. Victoires d'hier et enjeux de demain. In Masuy Stroobant G, Gourbin C, Buekens P, eds. *Santé et mortalité des enfants en Europe. Inégalités sociales d'hier et d'aujourdhui, Chaire Quetelet 1994*. Louvain-la-Neuve, Academia/L'Harmattan: 1996, 356

This is a new table for this edition of *Birth Counts*.